Test Booklet No. 3947101

Test Booklet Code CH1

arihant

SUCCESS AND NOTHING LESS

MEDACE

NEET (UG)

SELF ASSESSMENT KIT

Units and Measurement

Topics Covered

Units and Dimensions

Significant Figures and Errors in Measurement

Important Instructions

- This Booklet Contains – Two Topic Tests and One Test on Complete Chapter.
- Each question carries 4 Marks.
- For each correct response, the candidate will get 4 marks and for every incorrect response, 1 mark will be additionally deducted from total score.
- Use **Blue/Black** point pen only for filling the OMR.
- Rough work is to be done in the space provided for this purpose in the test booklet only.

Name of the Candidate (In Capitals) ____________________

____

Candidate's Signature __________

Invigilator's Signature __________

Facsimile signature stamp of center superintendent __________

Do not open this Booklet until you start attempting the Test

Topical Follow Thru

Test 1

Syllabus
- Units of Measurement
- System of Units
- SI Units
- Fundamental and Derived Units
- Dimensions of Physical Quantities
- Dimensional Analysis and Its Applications

For deeper insight **Scan the QR Code** 

Important Instructions
- The test is of 45 min duration and contains 25 Multiple Choice Questions (Four options with a single correct answer).
- Choose the correct option and fill the OMR given on the last page of this test accordingly.
- At some instances, you may find more than 1 option may be correct in such circumstances you have to judge the most appropriate answer as per the conditions given in the question.

1. If the unit of force is 1kN, the length is 20 km and time 200 s, the unit of mass will be
(a) 100 kg
(b) 1000 kg
(c) 2×10^3 kg
(d) 200 kg

2. The surface area of the cube in cm^2 is equal to the volume of a cube in cm^3. The volume of the cube will be
(a) 216 cm^3
(b) 16 m^3
(c) 216 m^3
(d) 16 cm^3

3. The physical quantity denoted by $\dfrac{\text{mass}\times\text{pressure}}{\text{density}}$ is
(a) force
(b) momentum
(c) angular momentum
(d) work

4. **Statement I** Work and torque have the same dimensions.

Statement II Angular momentum and Planck's constant have the same dimensions.

In the light of above statements, choose the most appropriate answer from the options given below.
(a) Both Statement I and Statement II are correct.
(b) Both Statement I and Statement II are incorrect.
(c) Statement I is correct but Statement II is incorrect.
(d) Statement I is incorrect but Statement II is correct.

5. If p is the radiation pressure, c is the speed of light and Q is the radiation energy striking a unit area per second, then the values of x, y and z such that $p^{x/2}Q^{y/3}c^{z/2}$ is dimensionless, are (x, y, z are non-zero integer)
(a) $2, -3, 2$
(b) $2, 3, -2$
(c) $-2, 3, 2$
(d) $2, 3, 2$

6. The potential energy of a particle is given by $U=\dfrac{A\sqrt{x}}{x^2+B}$, where U is the potential energy, A and B are dimensional constants and x is the distance. The dimensional formula for A/B is
(a) $[ML^{3/2}T^{-2}]$
(b) $[ML^{1/2}T^{-2}]$
(c) $[ML^{7/2}T^{-2}]$
(d) $[ML^{5/2}T^{-2}]$

7. The Bernoulli equation is given by the following expression, $p+\frac{1}{2}\rho V^2+\rho gh=K$ (constant)

The dimension of $\frac{p}{K}$ is same as

(a) pressure
(b) velocity
(c) energy
(d) angle

8. Distance travelled by a particle is given by $z=a+bt+ct^3$. Dimensional formula of c is

(a) $[LT^{-3}]$ (b) $[T^{-3}]$
(c) $[L]$ (d) $[LT^{-2}]$

9. If energy, mass, angular momentum and gravitational constant are denoted by E, m, L and G respectively, then the dimensions of $\frac{EL^3}{m^5G^2}$ are same as

(a) length
(b) angular momentum
(c) time
(d) mass

10. If the frequency f of vibration of a liquid drop depends on density ρ of liquid, radius r of the drop and surface tension S, then the expression of f is

(a) $k\sqrt{\frac{\rho r}{S}}$

(b) $k\sqrt{\frac{\rho r^3}{S}}$

(c) $k\sqrt{\frac{S}{\rho r^3}}$

(d) $k\sqrt{\frac{\sqrt{\rho}\sqrt{r}}{S^3}}$

where, k is dimensionless constant.

11. In the relation $p=\frac{\beta}{\alpha}e^{-\left(\frac{K\theta}{\alpha Z}\right)}$, p is pressure, Z is distance, K is Boltzmann constant and θ is the temperature. The dimensional formula of β is

(a) $[M^0L^0T^0]$ (b) $[M^2L^2T^{-4}]$
(c) $[MLT^{-2}]$ (d) $[ML^2T^{-1}]$

12. The relation $p=\frac{\alpha}{\beta}e^{\frac{-\alpha Z}{K\theta}}$, where p is pressure, Z is distance, K is Boltzmann constant and θ is temperature. The dimensional formula of β will be

(a) $[M^0L^2T^0]$ (b) $[ML^2T]$
(c) $[ML^0T^{-1}]$ (d) $[M^0L^2T^{-1}]$

13. Match the List-I with List-II.

	List-I		List-II
A.	m^{-1}	1.	Surface tension
B.	Pa	2.	Thermal capacity
C.	$J\ kg^{-1}$	3.	Rydberg constant
D.	$J\ m^{-2}$	4.	Energy density

The correct match is

	A	B	C	D
(a)	4	2	1	3
(b)	3	4	1	2
(c)	3	4	2	1
(d)	2	1	3	4

14. Force F and density ρ are related as $F=\frac{\alpha}{\beta+\sqrt{\rho}}$, then dimensional formulae of α and β respectively are

(a) $[M^{\frac{1}{2}}L^{\frac{1}{2}}T^{-2}]$ & $[M^{\frac{1}{2}}L^{\frac{3}{2}}]$

(b) $[M^{\frac{3}{2}}L^{-\frac{1}{2}}T^{-2}]$ & $[M^{\frac{1}{2}}L^{-\frac{3}{2}}]$

(c) $[M^{\frac{3}{2}}L^{-\frac{1}{2}}T^{-1}]$ & $[M^{\frac{1}{2}}L^{-\frac{3}{2}}]$

(d) Cannot be calculated

15. **Assertion** (A) In van der Waals' equation of state, $\left(p+\frac{a}{V^2}\right)(V-b)=a$ (constant) unit of ab is N-m^7.

Reason (R) We can add, subtract, multiply or divide physical quantities having same dimensions.

In the light of above statements, choose the most appropriate answer from the options given below.

(a) Both A and R are true and R is the correct explanation of A.

(b) Both A and R are true but R is not the correct explanation of A.

(c) A is true but R is false.

(d) A is false but R is true.

16. If P and Q are two physical quantities having different dimensional formulae, then which of the following can represent a new physical quantity?

(a) $P+Q$

(b) $e^{P/Q}$

(c) $\frac{P}{Q}$

(d) $\sin\left(\frac{P}{Q}\right)$

17. A quantity X is given by $\varepsilon_0 L \frac{\Delta V}{\Delta t}$, where ε_0 is the permittivity of free space, L is length, ΔV is the potential difference and Δt is the time interval, then dimensional formula of X is the same as that of

(a) resistance

(b) charge

(c) voltage

(d) current

18. Let speed of light (c), gravitational constant (G) and Planck's constant (h) are taken as fundamental quantities in a system of units. The dimensional formula of mass is

(a) $[c^{\frac{1}{2}} G^{-\frac{1}{2}} h^{\frac{1}{2}}]$

(b) $[c^{-\frac{5}{2}} G^{\frac{1}{2}} h^{\frac{1}{2}}]$

(c) $[c^{-\frac{3}{2}} G^{\frac{1}{2}} h^{\frac{1}{2}}]$

(d) $[c^5 G^{-2} h^{-1}]$

19. The maximum static friction on a body is $f = \mu N$. Here, N = normal reaction force on the body and μ = coefficient of static friction. The dimensions of μ are

(a) $[ML^2]$

(b) $[M^0L^0T^0\theta]$

(c) $[M^1L^1T^{-1}]$

(d) Dimensionless

20. The frequency of vibration f of a mass m suspended from a spring of spring constant k is given by a relation of this type $f = Cm^x k^y$, where C is a dimensionless constant. The value of $x+y$ is

(a) 1

(b) –1

(c) 0

(d) 2

21. A student determines a dimensionless quantity, $B = \frac{e^2}{2\varepsilon_0^n hc}$. The value of n is (Here, e = electric charge, ε_0 = electric permittivity of vacuum, h = Planck's constant and c = speed of light)

(a) 3

(b) 4

(c) 2

(d) 1

22. If force acting on object is given as $F = 4\sin\left(\frac{t}{\alpha}\right)\tan\left(\frac{x}{\beta}\right)$, then dimensions of $\frac{\beta}{\alpha}$ same as

(a) velocity

(b) acceleration

(c) time

(d) tength

23. If K represents kinetic energy, v is velocity and T is time are taken as the fundamental quantities, then dimensional formula of surface tension in terms of K, v and T is

(a) $[Kv^{-2}T^{-1}]$

(b) $[Kv^2T^{-1}]$

(c) $[Kv^{-2}T^{-2}]$

(d) $[Kv^2T^2]$

24. Unit for electromotive force is not same as

(a) $\frac{\text{N - m}}{\text{C}}$

(b) V

(c) eV

(d) J/C

25. Dimension of Kepler's constant in equation $T^2 = kR^3$, where k is Kepler constant, is

(a) $[T^2L^{-3}]$ (b) $[T^2L^3]$

(c) $[T^2L^{-2}]$ (d) $[T^2L^{-1}]$

Response Index

01 ⓐ ⓑ ⓒ ⓓ	11 ⓐ ⓑ ⓒ ⓓ	21 ⓐ ⓑ ⓒ ⓓ
02 ⓐ ⓑ ⓒ ⓓ	12 ⓐ ⓑ ⓒ ⓓ	22 ⓐ ⓑ ⓒ ⓓ
03 ⓐ ⓑ ⓒ ⓓ	13 ⓐ ⓑ ⓒ ⓓ	23 ⓐ ⓑ ⓒ ⓓ
04 ⓐ ⓑ ⓒ ⓓ	14 ⓐ ⓑ ⓒ ⓓ	24 ⓐ ⓑ ⓒ ⓓ
05 ⓐ ⓑ ⓒ ⓓ	15 ⓐ ⓑ ⓒ ⓓ	25 ⓐ ⓑ ⓒ ⓓ
06 ⓐ ⓑ ⓒ ⓓ	16 ⓐ ⓑ ⓒ ⓓ	
07 ⓐ ⓑ ⓒ ⓓ	17 ⓐ ⓑ ⓒ ⓓ	
08 ⓐ ⓑ ⓒ ⓓ	18 ⓐ ⓑ ⓒ ⓓ	
09 ⓐ ⓑ ⓒ ⓓ	19 ⓐ ⓑ ⓒ ⓓ	
10 ⓐ ⓑ ⓒ ⓓ	20 ⓐ ⓑ ⓒ ⓓ	

Performance Scanner

> 90% Excellent !	You have mastered these topics. The concepts of these topics are at your fingertips. Move on to the next test and maintain this momentum.
76-90% Very Good !	You have a good command over these topics. Revise the chapter again after a few days and enhance your performance.
60-75% Good !	You have a wide scope to learn more for these topics. Revise them again.
<60% Not Satisfactory!	You have a long way ahead of you to master these topics. Revise it thoroughly.

Test 2

Syllabus
- Accuracy and Precision
- Least Count
- Significant Figures
- Errors in Measurement

For deeper insight **Scan the QR Code**

Important Instructions
- The test is of 45 min duration and Contains 25 Multiple Choice Questions (Four options with a single correct answer).
- Choose the correct option and fill the OMR given on the last page of this test accordingly.
- At some instances, you may find more than 1 option may be correct in such circumstances you have to judge the most appropriate answer as per the conditions given in the question.

1. If the percentage of error occurred in the measurement of physical quantities P, Q, R and S are 2%, 9%, 7% and 4%, respectively. If $Y = \frac{P^3 Q^{1/3}}{R^4 S^{1/2}}$, then the maximum percentage of error in the measurement of Y will be

(a) 39% (b) 32%
(c) 36% (d) 37%

2. From the point of view of significant figures, the correct statement is

(a) $11.2 \text{ cm} + 7.0 \text{ cm} = 17.2 \text{ cm}$
(b) $2.46 \text{ m} - 0.4 \text{ m} = 2.06 \text{ m}$
(c) $4.0 \text{ m} \times 1.4 \text{ m} = 5.60 \text{ m}^2$
(d) $1.8 \text{ m} \div 0.9 \text{ s} = 2 \text{ ms}^{-1}$

3. If $R = (65 \pm 2)\,\Omega$, $l = (7 \pm 0.2)$ mm and $d = (10.5 \pm 1)$ mm, then error in the calculation of resistivity is

(a) 22.5%
(b) 13%
(c) 11.5%
(d) 16.4%

4. The mass and volume of a body are 2.436 g and 3.62 cm^3, respectively. Density of the material (in g/cm^3) in correct significant figures is

(a) 0.6729
(b) 0.67
(c) 0.7
(d) 0.673

5. **Statement I** Out of measurements $l = 0.6$ m, $l = 0.60$ m and $l = 0.600$ m, the most accurate one is the last one.

Statement II The number 1.0201 has 5 significant figures while 0.1020 has 4 significant figures.

In the light of above statements, choose the most appropriate answer from the options given below.

(a) Both Statement I and Statement II are correct.
(b) Both Statement I and Statement II are incorrect.
(c) Statement I is correct but Statement II is incorrect.
(d) Statement I is incorrect but Statement II is correct.

6. Arrange 3.23 cm, 4.312 cm, 4.0 cm and 2 cm in increasing order of precision.

(a) 2 cm, 4.0 cm, 3.23 cm, 4.312 cm
(b) 4.0 cm, 3.23 cm, 2 cm, 4.312 cm
(c) 4.312 cm, 3.23 cm, 4.0 cm, 2 cm
(d) 3.23 cm, 4.0 cm, 2 cm, 4.312 cm

7. The true value of a particular mass is 3.146 g. Three instruments A, B and C are used to measure this mass and gives reading 3.036 g, 3.1 g and 3.13 g. The most reliable instrument for measuring is

(a) A
(b) B
(c) C
(d) Either A or C

8. The radius of a hemisphere is measured to be (2.5 ± 0.6) cm. Surface area with error limits is
(a) $(39.25 \pm 18.84)\ \text{cm}^2$
(b) $(40.25 \pm 19.96)\ \text{cm}^2$
(c) $(36.15 \pm 17.86)\ \text{cm}^2$
(d) $(30.25 \pm 18.60)\ \text{cm}^2$

9. The main scale of a vernier caliper has n divisions/cm. n divisions of the vernier scale coincide with $(n-1)$ divisions of main scale. The least count of the vernier caliper will be
(a) $\frac{1}{n^2}$ cm
(b) $\frac{1}{(n+1)(n-1)}$ cm
(c) $\frac{1}{(n-1)}$
(d) $\frac{1}{n}$ cm

10. Which of the following statements regarding precision and accuracy is true?
(a) A most precise measurement will necessarily be most accurate.
(b) A most precise measurement may be most accurate.
(c) A most accurate measurement will necessarily be most precise.
(d) A most precise measurement will be less accurate.

11. If a physical quantity x depends on two other quantities a and b such that $x = \frac{a^m}{b^n}$, then relative error in the measurement of x is given as $\frac{\Delta x}{x} = m\left(\pm\frac{\Delta a}{a}\right) + n\left(\pm\frac{\Delta b}{b}\right)$. The expression is true when
(a) m and n both are positive value only
(b) both Δa and Δb are very small compared to their respective quantities
(c) Δa and Δb both have negative value
(d) there is no condition at given expression

12. Four quantities a, b, c and d are measured using an instrument with percentage errors of 2%, 3%, 1% and 0.5%, respectively.
A quantity x is defined as $x = \frac{a\sqrt{b}}{c^{3/2}d^4}$.
The maximum percentage error in the measurement of x will be
(a) 5%
(b) 6%
(c) 7%
(d) 9%

13. **Assertion (A)** A spherical body of radius (5 ± 0.1) mm having a particular density is falling through a liquid of constant density. The percentage error in the calculation of its terminal velocity is 4%.

Reason (R) The terminal velocity of the spherical body falling through the liquid is inversely proportional to its radius.

In the light of the above statements, choose the most appropriate answer from the options given below.
(a) Both A and R are true and R is the correct explanation of A.
(b) Both A and R are true but R is not the correct explanation of A.
(c) A is true but R is false.
(d) A is false but R is true.

14. The number of significant digits in 20.000 and 6.23×10^1 are respectively
(a) 2, 3
(b) 5, 3
(c) 2, 4
(d) 1, 3

15. The initial and final temperatures of water as recorded by a student are $(30.4 \pm 0.2)°\text{C}$ and $(51.5 \pm 0.4)°\text{C}$. The rise in temperature is
(a) $(21.1 \pm 0.2)°\text{C}$
(b) $(21.1 \pm 0.6)°\text{C}$
(c) $(19.9 \pm 0.6)°\text{C}$
(d) $(19.9 \pm 0.8)°\text{C}$

16. A student measures two quantities as $A = (1.0 \pm 0.2)$ m and $B = (2.0 \pm 0.2)$ m. The correct value of $(AB)^{1/2}$ is

(a) (1.4 ± 0.4) m
(b) (1.41 ± 0.15) m
(c) (1.4 ± 0.3) m
(d) (1.4 ± 0.2) m

17. In the following figure, vernier and main scales of vernier caliper has been shown. If each main scale division is of 1 mm and 4th division of vernier scale coincides with a main scale division, then the zero correction is

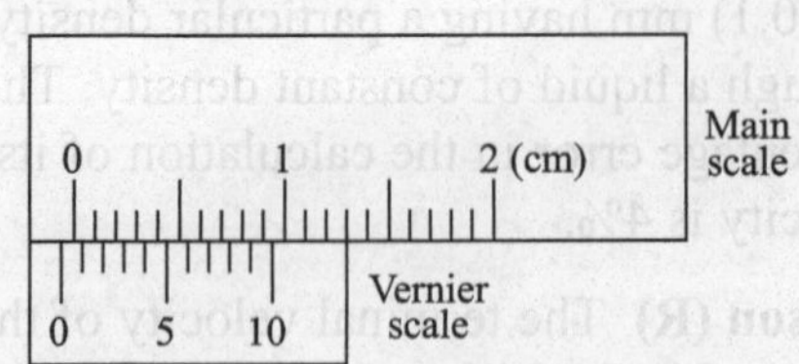

(a) 0.6 mm (b) – 0.6 mm
(c) + 0.4 mm (d) – 0.4 mm

18. The maximum error in the measurement of resistance, current and time for which current flows in an electric circuit are 1%, 2% and 3%, respectively. The maximum percentage error in the detection of the dissipated heat will be

(a) 2 (b) 4
(c) 6 (d) 8

19. A physical quantity A is related to three observable a, b and c as $A = \dfrac{a^2}{b^{1/3}\sqrt{c}}$. The percentage errors of measurement in a, b and c are 1%, 2% and 2%, respectively. The percentage error in the quantity A will be

(a) 12% (b) 7%
(c) 5% (d) 3.7%

20. The focal length f of a lens is given by $\dfrac{1}{f} = \dfrac{1}{v} - \dfrac{1}{u}$, where u and v represent object and image distances respectively. Then,

(a) $\dfrac{\Delta f}{f} = \dfrac{\Delta u}{u} + \dfrac{\Delta v}{v}$

(b) $\dfrac{\Delta f}{f} = \dfrac{\Delta u}{u} - \dfrac{\Delta v}{\Delta v}$

(c) $\dfrac{\Delta f}{f} = \dfrac{\Delta u}{u} + \dfrac{\Delta v}{v} - \dfrac{\Delta(u+v)}{u+v}$

(d) $\dfrac{\Delta f}{f} = \dfrac{\Delta u}{u} + \dfrac{\Delta v}{v} + \dfrac{\Delta u}{u+v} + \dfrac{\Delta v}{u+v}$

21. A person measures two quantities as $A = (3.0 \pm 0.1)$ m, $B = (2.0 \pm 0.2)$ m. We should report correct value for $\sqrt[4]{A/B}$ as

(a) (1.1 ± 0.037) m
(b) (1.1 ± 0.04) m
(c) (1.12 ± 0.037) m
(d) (1.12 ± 0.0367) m

22. A physical parameter a can be determined by measuring the parameters b, c, d and e, using the relation $a = \dfrac{b^{\alpha} c^{\beta}}{d^{\frac{\gamma}{2}} e^{3\delta}}$. If the maximum errors in the measurement of $b, c\ d$ and e are b_1 %, c_1 %, d_1 % and e_1 %, then the maximum percentage error in the value of a determined by the experiment is

(a) $(b_1 + c_1 + \frac{1}{2} d_1 + 3e_1)\%$
(b) $(b_1 + c_1 - d_1 - e_1)\%$
(c) $(\alpha b_1 + \beta c_1 - \gamma d_1 - \delta e_1)\%$
(d) $(\alpha b_1 + \beta c_1 + \frac{\gamma}{2} d_1 + 3\delta e_1)\%$

23. A person calculates the values of d by measuring the corresponding angles θ in the range 0 to 90° using the expression $2d \sin\theta = \lambda$. The wavelength λ is exactly known and the error in θ is constant for all the values of θ. As θ increases

(a) the absolute error in d remains constant
(b) the absolute error in d increases
(c) the fractional error in d remains constant
(d) the fractional error in d decreases

24. The kinetic energy of a particle depends on the square of speed of the particle. If error in measurement of speed is 30%, the error in the measurement of kinetic energy will be

(a) 30% (b) 60%
(c) 69% (d) 15%

25. Two resistors of resistances $R_1 = (300 \pm 3)\Omega$ and $R_2 = (500 \pm 4)\Omega$ are connected in series. The equivalent resistance of the series combination is

(a) $(800 \pm 1)\Omega$ (b) $(800 \pm 7)\Omega$
(c) $(200 \pm 7)\Omega$ (d) $(200 \pm 1)\Omega$

■ Response Index

01	a	b	c	d	**10**	a	b	c	d	**19**	a	b	c	d
02	a	b	c	d	**11**	a	b	c	d	**20**	a	b	c	d
03	a	b	c	d	**12**	a	b	c	d	**21**	a	b	c	d
04	a	b	c	d	**13**	a	b	c	d	**22**	a	b	c	d
05	a	b	c	d	**14**	a	b	c	d	**23**	a	b	c	d
06	a	b	c	d	**15**	a	b	c	d	**24**	a	b	c	d
07	a	b	c	d	**16**	a	b	c	d	**25**	a	b	c	d
08	a	b	c	d	**17**	a	b	c	d					
09	a	b	c	d	**18**	a	b	c	d					

■ Performance Scanner

> 90% Excellent !	You have mastered these topics. The concepts of these topics are at your fingertips. Move on to the next test and maintain this momentum.
76-90% Very Good !	You have a good command over these topics. Revise them again after a few days and enhance your performance.
60-75% Good !	You have a wide scope to learn more in these topics. Revise them again.
<60% Not Satisfactory!	You have a long way ahead of you to master in these topics. Revise them thoroughly.

Chapter Break Thru

Syllabus	• Units of Measurement • System of Units • SI Units	• Fundamental and Derived Units • Dimensions of Physical Quantities • Dimensional Analysis and Its Applications	• Accuracy and Precision • Least Count • Significant Figures • Errors in Measurement

Important Instructions

- The test is of 45 min duration and contains 30 multiple Choice Questions (Four options with a single correct answer).
- Choose the correct option and fill the OMR given on the last page of this test accordingly.
- At some instances, you may find more than 1 option may be correct in such circumstances you have to judge the most appropriate answer as per the conditions given in the question.

1. The dimensional formula of α in $e^{\alpha x}$ is (where, x is distance)

(a) $[M^0L^0T^0]$
(b) $[M^0LT^0]$
(c) $[M^0L^{-1}T^0]$
(d) $[M^{-1}L^0T^{-1}]$

2. An enclosed ideal gas has its pressure as a function of its volume V as $p = p_0 - \alpha V^2$, where p_0 is initial pressure and α is constant.

The physical dimensions of α are

(a) $[M^{-1}L^7T^2]$
(b) $[L^{-6}]$
(c) $[ML^{-1}T^{-2}]$
(d) $[ML^{-7}T^{-2}]$

3. An angle is required to be measured using an instrument. In the instrument, 29 divisions of the main scale exactly coincide with the 30 divisions of the vernier scale. If the smallest division of the main scale is = 0.5, then the least count of the instrument is

(a) 1 min (b) half min
(c) one degree (d) half degree

4. A massive star of mass m is in a uniform circular orbit around a supermassive black hole of mass M_b. Initially, the radius and angular frequency of the orbit are R and ω, respectively. According to the Einstein's theory of general relativity, the space around the two objects is distorted and gravitational waves are radiated. The power radiated through gravitational wave by this star is given by $P = kc^xG^yM^2R^4\omega^6$, where c = speed of light. Using dimensional analysis, the sum of values of x and y is

(a) 6 (b) – 4 (c) – 7 (d) – 6

5. The pair of physical quantities that have different dimensional formulae is

(a) Reynolds' number and coefficient of friction
(b) latent heat and gravitational potential
(c) activity and frequency of sound wave
(d) Planck's constant and torque

6. Match the List I with List II.

List I (Physical quantities)	List II (Units)
A. Pole strength (m)	1. Wb / m^2
B. Magnetic flux density (B)	2. A/m
C. Intensity of magnetisation (I)	3. A- m
D. Permeability of medium (μ)	4. T- m / A

(a) A→ 3, B→ 2, C→ 4, D→ 1
(b) A→ 1, B→ 2, C→ 3, D→ 4
(c) A→ 3, B→ 1, C→ 2, D→ 4
(d) A→ 2, B→ 1, C→ 4, D→ 3

7. **Statement I** The length of a state highway when expressed in km is 65.2. It has 3 significant figures.

Statement II The same length when expressed in metres as 65200 m, has five significant figures.

In the light of above statements, choose the most appropriate answer from the options given below.

(a) Both Statement I and Statement II are correct.
(b) Both Statement I and Statement II are incorrect.
(c) Statement I is correct but Statement II is incorrect.
(d) Statement I is incorrect but Statement II is correct.

8. The dimensional formula of time in terms of speed of light *c*, gravitational constant *G* and Planck's constant *h* is

(a) $[c^{1/2}G^{-1/2}h^{1/2}]$
(b) $[c^{-5/2}G^{1/2}h^{1/2}]$
(c) $[c^{-3/2}G^{1/2}h^{1/2}]$
(d) $[c^{5}G^{-2}h^{-1}]$

9. A physical quantity is measured and the result is expressed as *nu*, where *u* is the unit used and *n* is the numerical value. If the result is expressed in various units, then

(a) $n \propto u^2$
(b) $n \propto u$
(c) $u \propto \frac{1}{n^2}$
(d) $n \propto \frac{1}{u}$

10. In $s = a + bt + ct^2$, where *s* in measured in metres and *t* in seconds. The unit of *b* is

(a) ms^2 (b) m
(c) ms^{-1} (d) ms^{-2}

11. Drift speed of electron inside the metallic conductor is $v_d = eE^y m^z \tau$ (Here, e = electronic charge, E = electric field, m = mass of electron and τ = relaxation time). The value of $1/y$ is

(a) $\frac{3}{2}$ (b) 0
(c) $\frac{1}{2}$ (d) 1

12. If momentum *p*, area *A* and time *t* are taken to be fundamental quantities, then energy has the dimensional formula is

(a) $[p^1A^1t^{-1}]$
(b) $[p^2A^1t^1]$
(c) $[p^1A^{-1/2}t^1]$
(d) $[p^1A^{1/2}t^{-1}]$

13. **Assertion (A)** Plane angle is a dimensionless quantity.

Reason (R) All unitless quantities are dimensionless.

In the light of above statements, choose the most appropriate answer from the options given below.

(a) Both A and R are true and R is the correct explanation of A.
(b) Both A and R are true but R is not the correct explanation of A.
(c) A is true but R is false.
(d) A is false but R is true.

14. If the speed of light *c*, acceleration due to gravity *g* and pressure *p* are taken as the fundamental quantities and gravitational constant $[G] \propto c^x g^y p^z$. Then $\frac{x}{y}$ is equal to

(a) 2 (b) 0 (c) $\frac{3}{2}$ (d) −1

15. The sum of the numbers 446.26, 226.3 and 0.401 in appropriate significant figures is

(a) 672.9
(b) 673
(c) 672.96
(d) 673.0

16. Loss in kinetic energy due to direct impact is

$$\Delta K = \frac{M_1 M_2}{2(M_1 + M_2)}(V_1 - V_2)^2(1 - p^2)$$

All notations are usual except *p*. Dimensional formula of *p* is

(a) $[M^0L^0T^0]$ (b) $[M^0LT^{-1}]$
(c) $[M^1L^2T^2]$ (d) $[MLT^2]$

17. In dimension of critical velocity v_c of liquid flowing through a tube are expressed as $(\eta^x \rho^y r^z)$, where η, ρ and r are the coefficients of viscosity of liquid, density of liquid and radius of the tube respectively, then the value of $\frac{x}{y} + z$ is

(a) −2 (b) 3
(c) 2 (d) −3

18. The speed v of ripples on the surface of water depends on surface tension σ, density ρ and wavelength λ. The fourth power of speed v is proportional to

(a) $\frac{\rho}{\sigma\lambda^2}$ (b) $\frac{\sigma^2}{(\rho\lambda)^2}$
(c) $\frac{\lambda^2}{(\sigma\rho)^2}$ (d) $\rho\lambda\sigma$

19. Two numbers $a = 0.82$ and $b = 0.18$ are given. The number of significant figures present in the result after the following operation $a + b, a - b, a \times b$ and a / b respectively are

(a) 2, 2, 2, 2
(b) 3, 3, 2, 2
(c) 3, 2, 1, 1
(d) 3, 2, 2, 2

20. A physical quantity is represented by $X = M^a L^b T^{-c}$. If percentage errors in the measurement of M, L and T are α, β and γ respectively, then total percentage error is

(a) $(\alpha a + \beta b - \gamma c)$
(b) $(\alpha a + \beta b + \gamma c)$
(c) $(\alpha a - \beta b + \gamma c)$
(d) zero

21. In an experiment, the following observations were recorded $L = 2.83$ m, $M = 3.01$ kg, $l = 0.009$ cm and diameter $D = 0.141$ cm. Using the formula, $Y = \frac{4MgL}{\pi D^2 l}$, the maximum permissible error in Y is (Take, $g = 9.81 \text{ m/s}^2$)

(a) 7.96%
(b) 4.56%
(c) 13.3%
(d) 8.42%

22. From the option given below, which physical quantity has dimensional formula $[ML^2T^{-2}]$?

(a) $nA\left(\frac{\Delta V}{\Delta x}\right)$ (b) $\frac{1}{\sqrt{LC}}$
(c) CV^2 (d) $\frac{1}{\sqrt{\varepsilon_0 \mu_0}}$

23. If C and R represent capacitance and resistance respectively, then the dimensions of RC are

(a) $[M^0L^0TA^0]$
(b) $[ML^0TA^{-2}]$
(c) $[ML^0TA^2]$
(d) $[ML^0T^2A^2]$

24. Dimensional formula of which quantity is not $[ML^{-1}T^{-2}]$?

(a) Stress
(b) Modulus of elasticity
(c) Energy density
(d) Thermal capacity

25. Which quantity cannot be derived by dimensional formula?

(a) $v = \frac{d}{t}$
(b) $F = \frac{GmM}{r^2}$
(c) $I = mr^2$
(d) $b = \lambda T$

26. Find dimension of $\sqrt{\mu_0 \varepsilon_0} \times \left(\frac{F}{qB}\right)$, where F is force, q is charge and B is magnetic field.

(a) $[M^0L^0T^0]$
(b) $[MLT^{-1}]$
(c) $[M^3L^2T^7]$
(d) $[MLT^{-2}]$

27. Young's modulus of steel is 1.9×10^{11} Nm^{-2}. When expressed in CGS units of dyne cm^{-2}, it will be equal to

(a) 1.9×10^{10} (b) 1.9×10^{11}
(c) 1.9×10^{12} (d) 1.9×10^{13}

28. An experiment is performed to obtain the value of acceleration due to gravity g by using a simple pendulum of length l. In this experiment, time for 100 oscillations is measured by using a watch of 1 s least count and the value is 90.0 s. The length l is measured by using a meter scale of least count 1 mm and the value is 20.0 cm. The error in the determination of g would be

(a) 1.7% (b) 2.7%
(c) 4.4% (d) 2.27%

29. If v, A and F denote the units of fundamental quantities of velocity, acceleration and force respectively, the dimensions of Young's modulus in that system are

(a) $[FA^2v^{-4}]$
(b) $[F^2A^4v^{-1}]$
(c) $[F^4A^2v^{-1}]$
(d) $[F^{-1}A^4v^2]$

30. A gas bubble formed from an explosion under water oscillates with a period T proportional to $p^a d^b E^c$, where p is pressure, d is the density of water and E is the total energy of explosion. The values of a, b and c are

(a) $a=1, b=1, c=2$
(b) $a=1, b=2, c=1$
(c) $a=\frac{5}{6}, b=\frac{1}{2}, c=\frac{1}{3}$
(d) $a=-\frac{5}{6}, b=\frac{1}{2}, c=\frac{1}{3}$

Response Index

No.					No.					No.				
01	a	b	c	d	11	a	b	c	d	21	a	b	c	d
02	a	b	c	d	12	a	b	c	d	22	a	b	c	d
03	a	b	c	d	13	a	b	c	d	23	a	b	c	d
04	a	b	c	d	14	a	b	c	d	24	a	b	c	d
05	a	b	c	d	15	a	b	c	d	25	a	b	c	d
06	a	b	c	d	16	a	b	c	d	26	a	b	c	d
07	a	b	c	d	17	a	b	c	d	27	a	b	c	d
08	a	b	c	d	18	a	b	c	d	28	a	b	c	d
09	a	b	c	d	19	a	b	c	d	29	a	b	c	d
10	a	b	c	d	20	a	b	c	d	30	a	b	c	d

Performance Scanner

> 90% Excellent ! You have mastered this chapter. The concepts of this chapter are at your fingertips. Move on to the next chapter and maintain this momentum.

76-90% Very Good ! You have a good command over this chapter. Revise the chapter again after a few days and enhance your performance.

60-75% Good ! You have a wide scope to learn more for this chapter. Revise this chapter again.

<60% Not Satisfactory! You have a long way ahead of you to master this chapter. Revise it thoroughly.

For Online Chapter Test **Scan the QR Code**

For Online Unit Test **Scan the QR Code**

Space for Rough Work

Space for Rough Work

Space for Rough Work

Test Booklet No. 3947102

Test Booklet Code CH2

MEDACE
NEET (UG)
SELF ASSESSMENT KIT

Motion in a Straight Line

Topics Covered

Basics of Motion and Uniform Motion

Graphs of Motion and Relative Motion

Important Instructions

- This Booklet Contains – Two Topic Tests and One Test on Complete Chapter.
- Each question carries 4 Marks.
- For each correct response, the candidate, will get 4 marks and for every incorrect response, 1 mark will be additionally deducted form the total score.
- Use **Blue/Black** point pen only for filling the OMR.
- Rough work is to be done in the space provided for this purpose in the test booklet only.

Name of the Candidate (In Capitals)

____

____

Candidate's Signature __________

Invigilator's Signature __________

Facsimile signature stamp of center superintendent__________

Do not open this Booklet until you start attempting the Test

Topical Follow Thru

Test 1

Syllabus

- The Frame of Reference
- Motion in a Straight Line
- Speed and Velocity
- Uniform and Non-uniform Motion
- Average Speed and Instantaneous Velocity
- Kinematics Equations of Uniformly Accelerated Motion

For deeper insight **Scan the QR Code**

Important Instructions

- The test is of 45 minutes duration and contains 25 Multiple Choice Questions. (Four options with a single correct answer).
- Choose the correct option and fill the OMR given on the last page of this test accordingly.
- At some instances, you may find more than 1 option may be correct, in such circumstances you have to judge the most appropriate answer as per the conditions given in the questions.

1. A stone falls from a balloon that is descending at a uniform rate of 12 m/s. The displacement of the stone from the point of release after 10 s is

(a) 490 m (b) 510 m
(c) 620 m (d) 725 m

2. A particle experiences a constant acceleration for 20s after starting from rest. If it travels a distance s_1 in the first 10s and a distance s_2 in the next 10 s, then

(a) $s_1 = s_2$ (b) $s_1 = s_2 / 3$
(c) $s_1 = s_2 / 2$ (d) $s_1 = s_2 / 4$

3. A particle is moving from rest with constant acceleration 4 m/s^2 for sometime and then retards with 2 m/s^2. The total time during the motion is 12s. The maximum velocity of the particle is

(a) 16 m/s (b) 12 m/s
(c) 10 m/s (d) 20 m/s

4. A train starts from rest and for the first kilometre moves with constant acceleration, for the next 3 kilometre, it has constant velocity and for another 2 kilometre, it moves with constant retardation to come to rest after a total time of 10 min. The maximum velocity of the train is

(a) 36 kmph (b) 18 kmph
(c) 54 kmph (d) 60 kmph

5. A train accelerates from rest at a constant rate a_1 for distance s_1 and time t_1. After that it retards to rest at a constant rate a_2 for distance s_2 at time t_2. The correct relation among the following is

(a) $\frac{s_1}{s_2} = \frac{a_1}{a_2} = \frac{t_1}{t_2}$ (b) $\frac{s_1}{s_2} = \frac{a_2}{a_1} = \frac{t_1}{t_2}$

(c) $\frac{s_1}{s_2} = \frac{a_1}{a_2} = \frac{t_2}{t_1}$ (d) $\frac{s_1}{s_2} = \frac{a_2}{a_1} = \frac{t_2}{t_1}$

6. If the relation between distance x and time t is given by $t = 2x^2 + 3x$, then the retardation of particles is proportional to

(a) v^2 (b) v^3
(c) v^{-3} (d) $v^{3/2}$

7. A body moves for a time of 9s, starting from rest with uniform acceleration and then with uniform retardation, which is twice the value of uniform acceleration. The time taken during retardation is

(a) 3 s (b) 4.5 s
(c) 5 s (d) 6 s

8. A boy is falling from a high minaret travels 40 m in the last 2s of his fall to ground. Height of minaret (in m) is

(a) 60 (b) 80
(c) 68 (d) 45

9. A stone falls freely under gravity. It covers distance h_1, h_2 and h_3 in the first 5 s, the next 5 s and the next 5 s, respectively. The relation between h_1, h_2 and h_3 is

(a) $h_1 = 2h_2 = 3h_3$
(b) $h_1 = \frac{h_2}{3} = \frac{h_3}{5}$
(c) $h_2 = 3h_1$ and $h_3 = 3h_2$
(d) $h_1 = h_2 = h_3$

10. The displacement of a body along X-axis depends on time as $\sqrt{x} = t + 1$, then the velocity of body

(a) increases with time
(b) decreases with time
(c) independent of time
(d) remains same

11. A particle moves in a straight line with a constant acceleration. It changes it's velocity from 10 m/s to 20 m/s while passing through a distance 135 m in t seconds. The value of t is

(a) 12 s (b) 9 s
(c) 10 s (d) 1.8 s

12. The acceleration a of a particle starting from rest varies with time according to relation $a = \alpha t + \beta$. The velocity of the particle after a time t will be

(a) $\frac{\alpha t^2}{2} + \beta$ (b) $\frac{\alpha t^2}{2} + \beta t$
(c) $\alpha t^2 + \frac{1}{2}\beta t$ (d) $\frac{(\alpha t^2 + \beta)}{2}$

13. A body starting from rest moves with constant acceleration. The ratio of distance covered by the body during the 5th second to that covered in first 5 seconds is

(a) $\frac{9}{25}$ (b) $\frac{3}{5}$
(c) $\frac{25}{9}$ (d) $\frac{1}{25}$

14. A body starting from rest moves with uniform acceleration. The distance covered by the body in time t second is proportional to

(a) $\sqrt{t}$
(b) $t^{3/2}$
(c) t^2
(d) t^3

15. A ball starts from rest, then the ratio of the distance travelled by the ball during the 4th and 3rd second is

(a) $\frac{7}{5}$ (b) $\frac{5}{7}$
(c) $\frac{7}{3}$ (d) $\frac{3}{7}$

16. A body covers a distance of 6 m in 3rd second and 12 m in 6th second. If the motion is uniformly accelerated, how far will it travel in the next 3 s?

(a) 46 cm (b) 48 cm
(c) 84 cm (d) 132 cm

17. The velocity of a body depends on time according to the equation $v = \frac{t^2}{10} + 20$. The body is undergoing

(a) uniform acceleration
(b) uniform retardation
(c) non-uniform acceleration
(d) zero acceleration

18. The acceleration of a particle is increasing linearly with time t as bt. The particle starts from the origin with an initial velocity v_0. The distance travelled by the particle in time t will be

(a) $v_0 t + \frac{1}{3} bt^2$
(b) $v_0 t + \frac{1}{3} bt^3$
(c) $v_0 t + \frac{1}{6} bt^3$
(d) $v_0 t + \frac{1}{2} bt^2$

19. A car travels from P to Q at speed of 20 km/h and returns at a speed of 30 km/h. The average speed of the car for the whole journey is

(a) 25 km/h (b) 24 km/h
(c) 50 km/h (d) 5 km/h

20. A particle moves along X-axis in such a way that its coordinate x varies with time t according to the equation $x = (2 - 5t + 6t^2)$ m. The initial velocity of particle is

(a) –5 m/s
(b) 6 m/s
(c) –3 m/s
(d) 3 m/s

21. The relation between distance (d) and time (t) is given by $d = 4 + 9t - 5t^2$, then by match List I with List II and choose the correct combination from the options given.

	List I		List II
(A)	Initial acceleration	1.	– 21 unit
(B)	Velocity at the end of 3s	2.	2 unit
(C)	Distance travelled in 2s	3.	8 unit
(D)	Displacement at 1s	4.	–10 unit

The correct match is
(a) A-4, B-3, C- 2, D-1
(b) A-4, B-1, C-2, D-3
(c) A-2, B-3, C-4, D-1
(d) A-2, B-3, C-2, D-4

22. Two balls are dropped from different heights. One ball is dropped 2 s after the other ball. If both balls reach the ground simultaneously after 5 s of dropping the first ball, the difference of initial heights of the two balls will be ($g = 9.8$ m/s^2)

(a) 58.8 m (b) 78.4 m
(c) 98 m (d) 117.6 m

23. A car travels a distance s on a straight road in two hours and then returns to the starting point in the next three hours. Its average velocity is

(a) $\frac{s}{5}$ (b) $\frac{2s}{5}$
(c) $\frac{s}{2} + \frac{s}{3}$ (d) zero

24. When a particle moves with uniform velocity, which of the following relations are correct?
(i) Average speed = Average velocity
(ii) Instantaneous speed = Instantaneous velocity
(iii) Distance covered = Magnitude of displacement
(a) I, II, III (b) I, II
(c) II, III (d) I, III

25. The correct statement from the following is
(a) A body having zero velocity will not necessarily have zero acceleration.
(b) A body having zero velocity will necessarily have zero acceleration.
(c) A body having uniform speed can have only uniform acceleration.
(d) A body having non-uniform velocity will have zero acceleration.

Response Index

01	a	b	c	d	10	a	b	c	d	19	a	b	c	d
02	a	b	c	d	11	a	b	c	d	20	a	b	c	d
03	a	b	c	d	12	a	b	c	d	21	a	b	c	d
04	a	b	c	d	13	a	b	c	d	22	a	b	c	d
05	a	b	c	d	14	a	b	c	d	23	a	b	c	d
06	a	b	c	d	15	a	b	c	d	24	a	b	c	d
07	a	b	c	d	16	a	b	c	d	25	a	b	c	d
08	a	b	c	d	17	a	b	c	d					
09	a	b	c	d	18	a	b	c	d					

Performance Scanner

> 90% Excellent !	You have mastered these topics. The concepts of these topics are at your fingertips. Move on to the next test and maintain this momentum.
76-90% Very Good !	You have a good command over these topics. Revise them again after a few days and enhance your performance.
60-75% Good !	You have a wide scope to learn more in these topics. Revise them again.
<60% Not Satisfactory!	You have a long way ahead of you to master in these topics. Revise them thoroughly.

Test 2

Syllabus
- Velocity-Time graph
- Position-Time graph
- Acceleration-Time graph
- Relative Velocity

For deeper insight **Scan the QR Code**

Important Instructions
- The test is of 45 minutes duration and contains 25 Multiple Choice Questions (Four options with a single correct answer).
- Choose the correct option and fill the OMR given on the last page of this test accordingly.
- At some instances, you may find more than 1 option may be correct, in such circumstances you have to judge the most appropriate answer as per the conditions given in the question.

1. The displacement *versus* time graph for a body moving in a straight line as shown in figure. Which of the following regions represents the motion when no force is acting on the body?

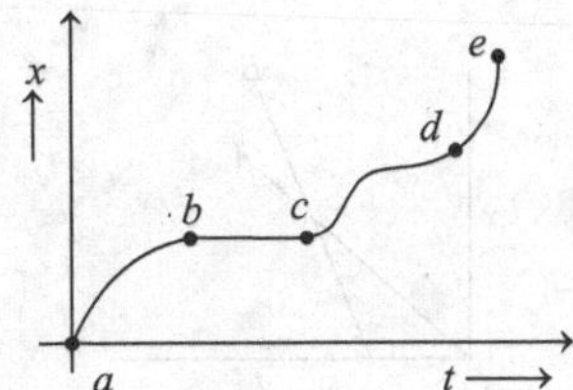

(a) *ab*
(b) *bc*
(c) *cd*
(d) *de*

2. A car decelerates at a constant rate during a period commencing at $t = 0$. Which of the following displacement-time graphs represents the displacement of the car?

(a)
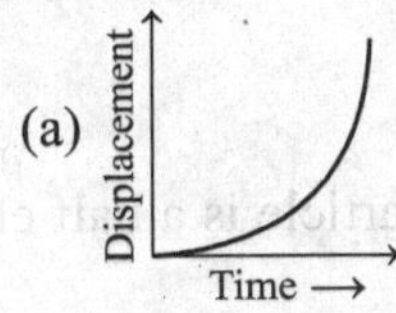

(b)
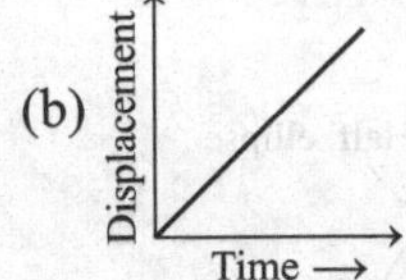

(c)
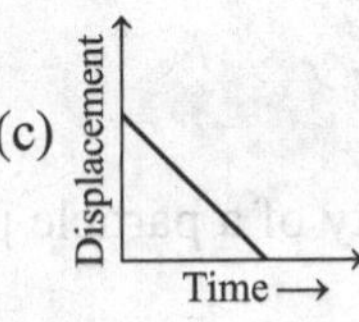

(d)
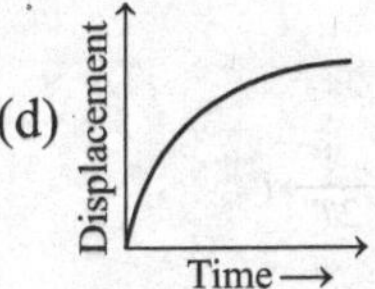

3. The *x-t* graph in figure represents

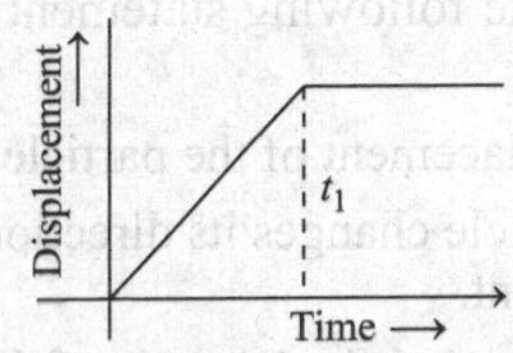

(a) constant velocity
(b) velocity of the body continuously changing
(c) instantaneous velocity
(d) the body travels with constant speed upto time t_1 and then stops

4. The variation of velocity of a particle with time moving along a straight line is illustrated in the following figure. The distance travelled by the particle in first four seconds is

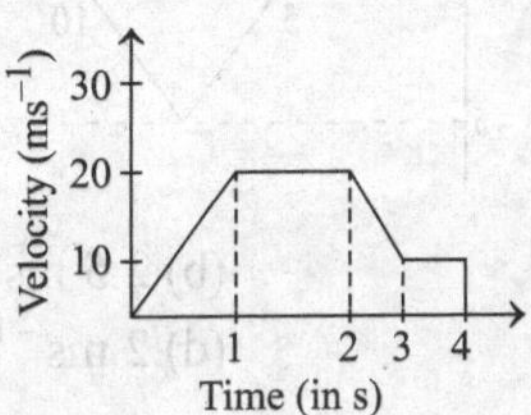

(a) 60 m (b) 55 m
(c) 25 m (d) 30 m

5. **Assertion** (A) The velocity-time graph of a body moving with uniform acceleration is a straight line.

Reason (R) In uniformly accelerated motion, the displacement is proportional to time.
In the light of above statements, choose the most appropriate answer from the options given below

(a) Both A and R are true and R is the correct explanation of A.
(b) Both A and R are true, but R is not the correct explanation of A.
(c) A is true but R is false.
(d) A is false but R is true.

6. The figure shows the velocity of a particle plotted against time *t*.

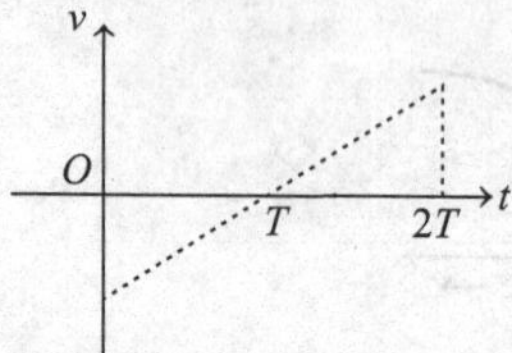

Which of the following statement (s) is/are correct?
(a) The displacement of the particle is zero.
(b) The particle changes its direction of motion at some point.
(c) The initial and final speeds of the particle are same.
(d) All of the above

7. The plot of a moving object is shown in the figure. The average velocity of the object during the first 10 s is

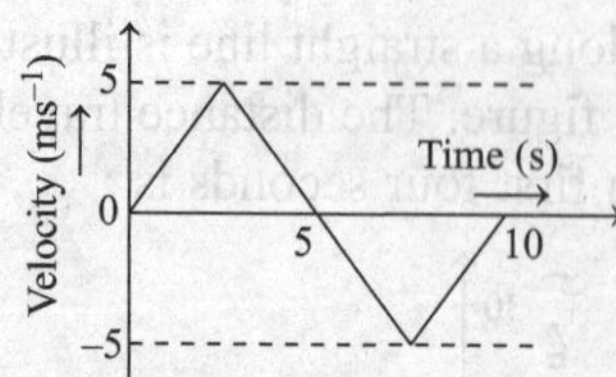

(a) 0 (b) 2.5 ms^{-1}
(c) 5 ms^{-1} (d) 2 ms^{-1}

8. Two stones are thrown up simultaneously from the edge of a cliff 240 m high with initial speed of 10 m/s and 40 m/s, respectively. Which of the following graphs best represents the time variation of relative position of the second stone with respect to the first? (Assume stones do not rebound after hitting the ground and neglect air resistance, take $g = 10\,\text{m/s}^2$)

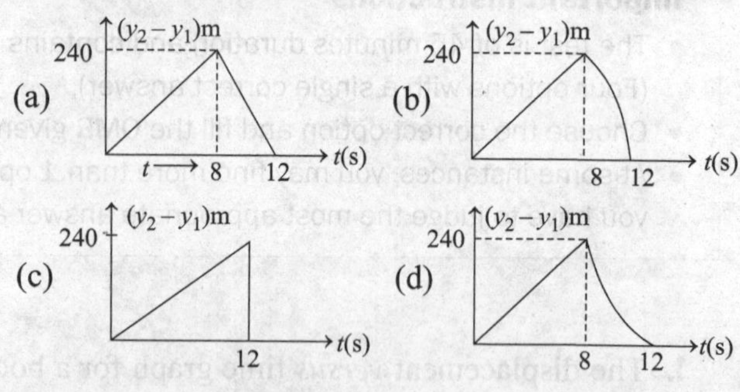

9. Two students *A* and *B* are returning to their homes from school. The position-time graph for both students is given below.

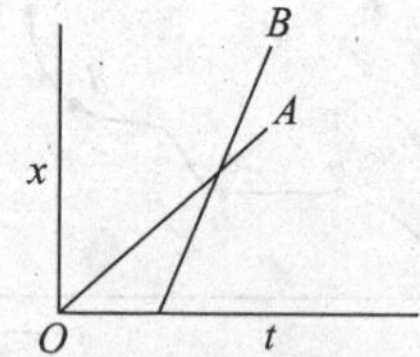

(A) *A* lives closer to the school
(B) *B* lives closer to the school
(C) *A* takes lesser time to reach home
(D) *A* travels faster than *B*
(E) *B* travels faster than *A*
Choose the correct answer from the options given below
(a) (A), (C) and (E) only
(b) (A), (C) and (D) only
(c) (A) and (E) only
(d) (B) and (E) only

10. Velocity-time graph for a particle is a half ellipse as shown,

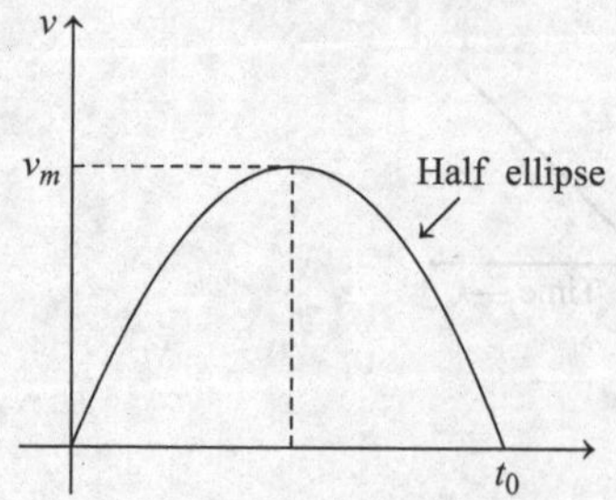

Now consider following statements,

A. Average velocity of the particle is $\frac{\pi}{4} v_m$.

B. Such motion is not possible practically.

(a) Both A and B are correct.

(b) Both A and B are incorrect.

(c) A is correct B is incorrect.

(d) B is correct A is incorrect.

11. The velocity-time (v-t) graph for a body thrown vertically upward (which eventually comes down) considering constant air friction acting on it is best shown by

(a) 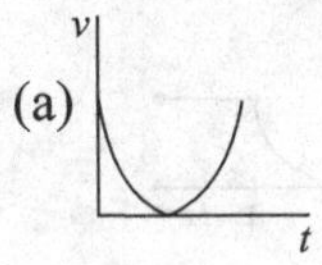

(b) 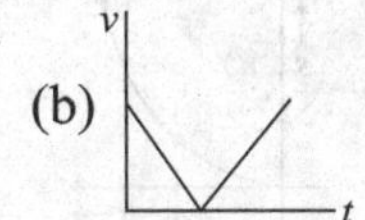

(c) 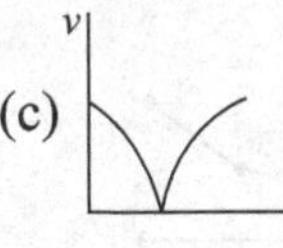

(d) 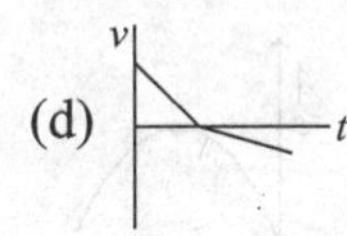

12. A plastic ball is thrown vertically upwards. Which of the following graphs represents velocity -time graph of the ball during its flight (air resistance is neglected)?

(a) 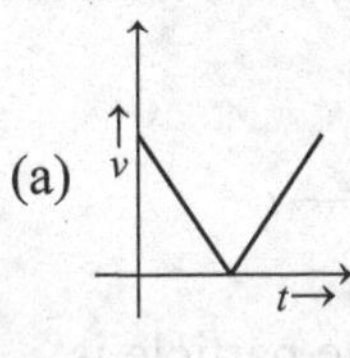

(b) 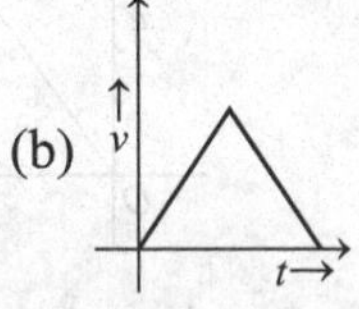

(c) 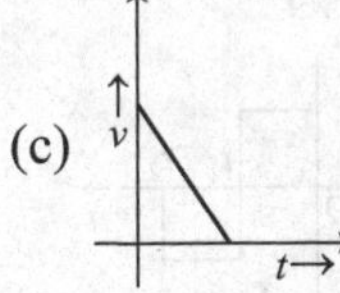

(d) 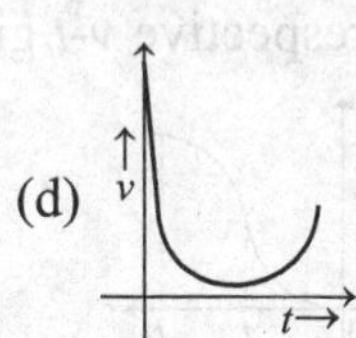

13. **Statement I** Velocity-time graph for an object in uniform motion along a straight path is a straight line parallel to the time axis.

Statement II In uniform motion of an object, velocity increases as the square of time elapsed.

In the light of above statements, choose the most appropriate answer from the options given below.

(a) Both Statement I and Statement II are correct.

(b) Both Statement I and Statement II are incorrect.

(c) Statement I is correct but Statement II is incorrect.

(d) Statement I is incorrect but Statement II is correct.

14. Two moving trains, each 80 m long are travelling in opposite directions with velocities 10 m/s and 15 m/s. The time of crossing is

(a) 2s (b) 4s

(c) $2\sqrt{3}$ s (d) 6.4 s

15. Velocity-time graph for an object in motion along a straight line with constant acceleration is given below

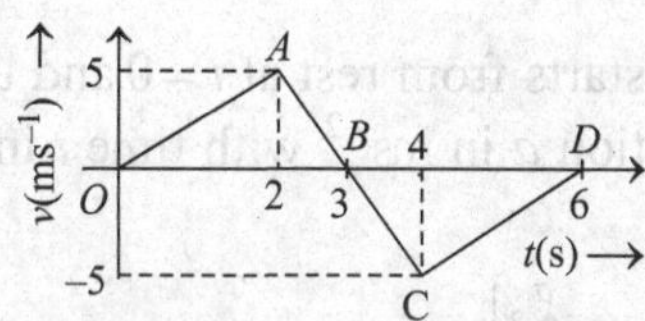

With reference to the above given v-t graph choose the incorrect pair.

(a) Motion in positive direction with positive acceleration between time interval $\rightarrow t = 0$ s to $t = 2$ s

(b) Motion in positive direction till time t_1 and then turns back with same negative acceleration between time interval $\rightarrow t = 2$ s to $t = 4$ s

(c) Motion in negative direction with positive acceleration between time interval $\rightarrow t = 3$ s to $t = 6$ s

(d) Displacement is zero between time interval $\rightarrow t = 0$ s to $t = 6$ s

16. **Statement I** The displacement-time graph of a body moving with uniform acceleration is a straight line.

Statement II The displacement is proportional to time.

In the light of the above statement, choose the most appropriate answer from the options given below

(a) Both Statement I and Statement II are correct.

(b) Both Statement I and Statement II are incorrect.

(c) Statement I is correct but Statement II is incorrect.

(d) Statement I is incorrect but Statement II is correct.

17. A particle is travelling in a straight line. If has a initial velocity of 10 m/s when it is subjected to an acceleration of -2 ms^{-2} for 8 s, the distance travelled in 8 s is

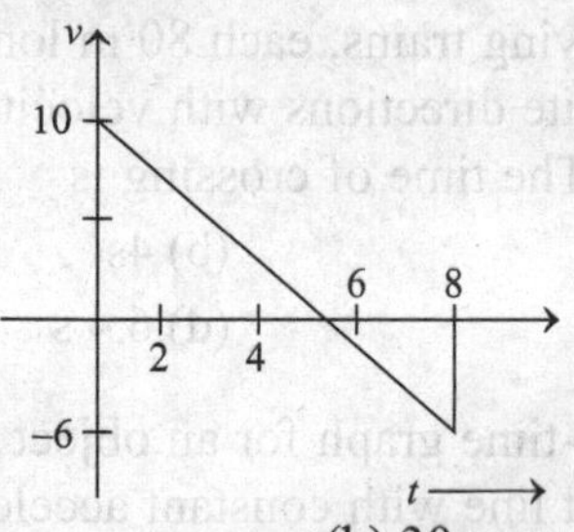

(a) 34 m (b) 30 m
(c) 24 m (d) 38 m

18. A body starts from rest at $t=0$ and undergoes an acceleration a in ms^{-2} with time t in second is as shown.

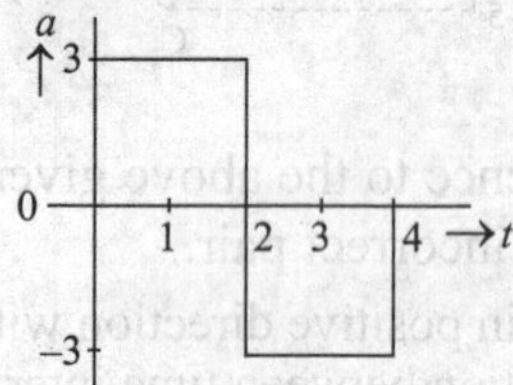

Which one of the following plots represent velocity v in ms^{-1} *versus* time t in second?

(a) 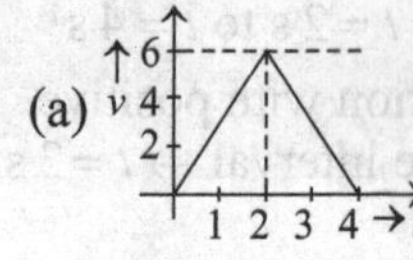
(b) 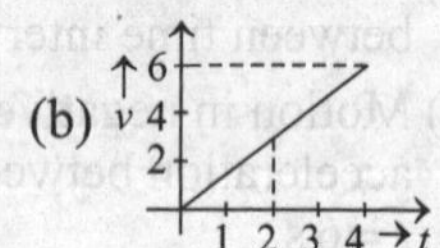
(c) 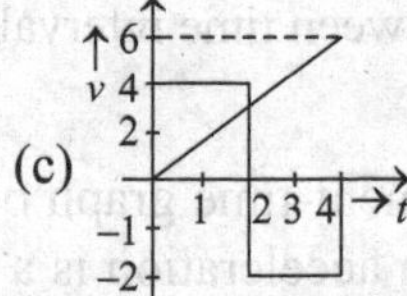
(d) 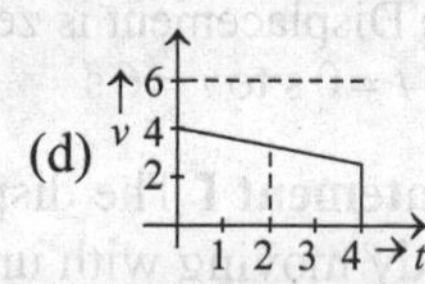

19. A particle starts moving from rest and moves with uniform acceleration, which of the following graphs represent its motion?

(a) 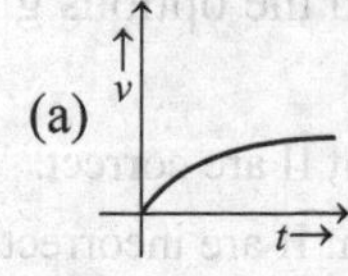
(b) 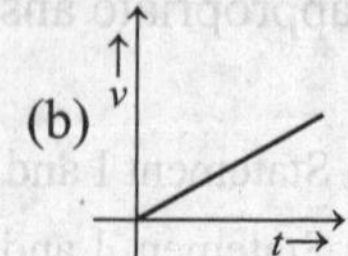
(c) 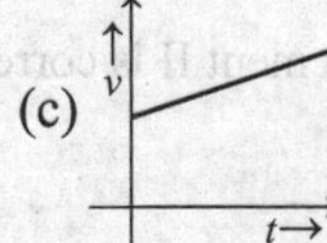
(d) 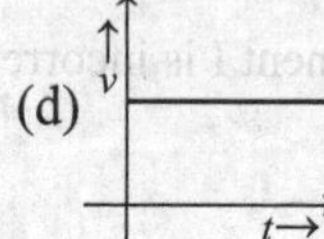

20. Two trains are moving with equal speed in opposite directions along two parallel railway tracks. If the wind is blowing with speed u along the track, so that the relative velocities of the trains with respect to the wind are in the ratio 1 : 2. The speed of each train must be

(a) $3u$ (b) $2u$
(c) $5v$ (d) $2v$

21. A car starts from rest, accelerates uniformly for 4*s* and then moves with uniform velocity. Which of the following displacement-time graphs represents the motion of the car?

(a) 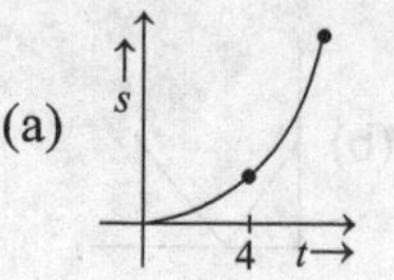
(b) 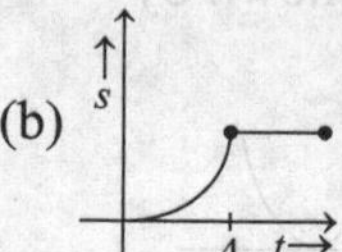
(c) 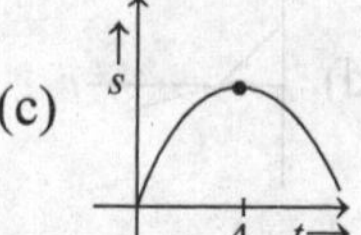
(d) 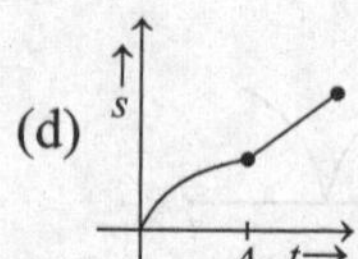

22. The acceleration *versus* time graph of a particle is shown in figure.

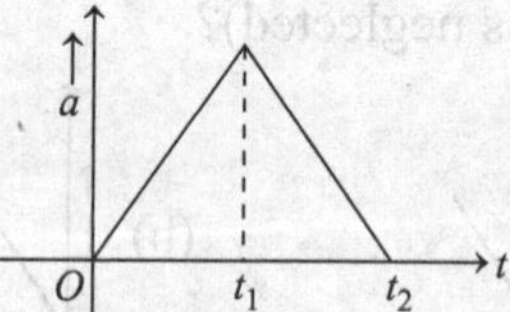

The respective *v-t* graph of the particle is

(a) 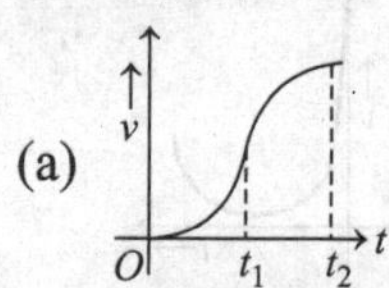
(b) 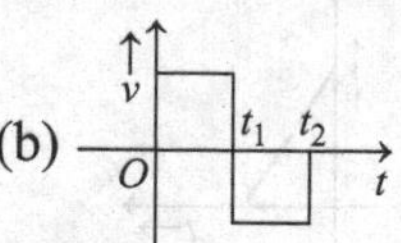
(c) 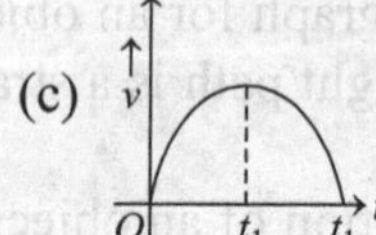
(d) 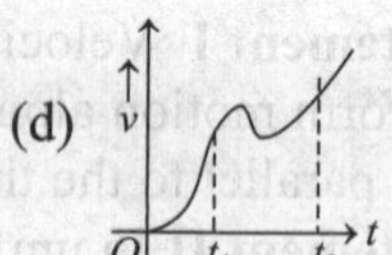

23. A ball is dropped from a high rise platform at $t=0$, starting from rest. After 6 s another ball is thrown downwards from the same platform with speed u. The two balls meet at $t=18$ s. What is the value of u? (Take, $g=10\text{ m/s}^2$)

(a) 60 m/s (b) 75 m/s
(c) 55 m/s (d) 40 m/s

24. When two persons approach uniformly towards each other,the distance between them decreases by 6m/s. If both move in the same direction with the same speeds, the distance between them increases by 4 m/s. Their speeds are

(a) 1 m/s and 5 m/s
(b) 2 m/s and 4 m/s
(c) 2 m/s and 10 m/s
(d) 2 m/s and 6 m/s

25. A particle is moving with constant acceleration *a*. Following graph shows v^2 *versus x* (displacement) plot.

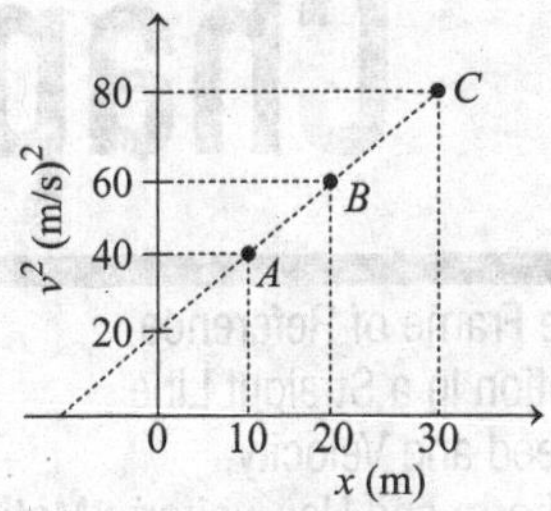

The acceleration of the particle is .... m/s^2

(a) 1
(b) 2
(c) 3
(d) 4

Response Index

01	a	b	c	d	10	a	b	c	d	19	a	b	c	d
02	a	b	c	d	11	a	b	c	d	20	a	b	c	d
03	a	b	c	d	12	a	b	c	d	21	a	b	c	d
04	a	b	c	d	13	a	b	c	d	22	a	b	c	d
05	a	b	c	d	14	a	b	c	d	23	a	b	c	d
06	a	b	c	d	15	a	b	c	d	24	a	b	c	d
07	a	b	c	d	16	a	b	c	d	25	a	b	c	d
08	a	b	c	d	17	a	b	c	d					
09	a	b	c	d	18	a	b	c	d					

Performance Scanner

> 90% Excellent !	You have mastered these topics. The concepts of these topics are at your fingertips. Move on to the next test and maintain this momentum.
76-90% Very Good !	You have a good command over these topics. Revise them again after a few days and enhance your performance.
60-75% Good !	You have a wide scope to learn more in these topics. Revise them again.
<60% Not Satisfactory!	You have a long way ahead of you to master in these topics. Revise them thoroughly.

Chapter Break Thru

Syllabus

- The Frame of Reference
- Motion in a Straight Line
- Speed and Velocity
- Uniform and Non-uniform Motion
- Average Speed and Instantaneous Velocity
- Kinematics Equations of Uniformly Accelerated
- Velocity-Time graph
- Position-Time graph
- Acceleration-Time graph
- Relative Velocity

Important Instructions

- The test is of 1 hour duration and contains 50 Multiple-Choice Questions (Four options with a single correct answer).
- Choose the correct option and fill the OMR given on the last page of this test accordingly.
- At some instances, you may find more than 1 option may be correct in such circumstances you have to judge the most appropriate answer as per the conditions given in the question.

1. A particle moves along a straight line such that its displacement at any time t is given by $s = (t^3 - 6t^2 + 3t + 4)$ m. The velocity when the acceleration is zero is

(a) $3\ \text{ms}^{-1}$
(b) $-12\ \text{ms}^{-1}$
(c) $42\ \text{ms}^{-1}$
(d) $-9\ \text{ms}^{-1}$

2. Velocity-time graph for a particle is as shown below.

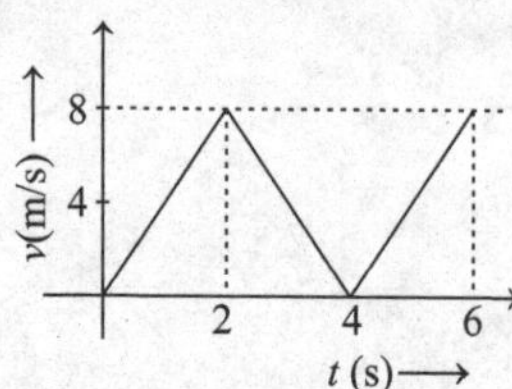

The distance travelled in the first 4 s is

(a) 16 m
(b) 18 m
(c) 17 m
(d) 26 m

3. A ball P is thrown up vertically with a speed of u and at the same instant, another ball Q is released from a height h. At time t, the speed of P relative to Q is

(a) u
(b) $2u$
(c) $u - gt$
(d) $\sqrt{(u^2 - gt)}$

4. An object is dropped from a high building from rest, then its velocity-time graph is

(a) 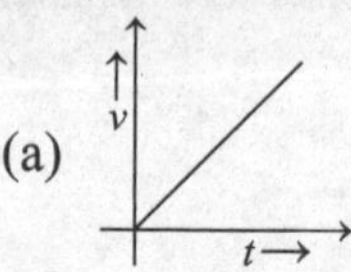

(b) 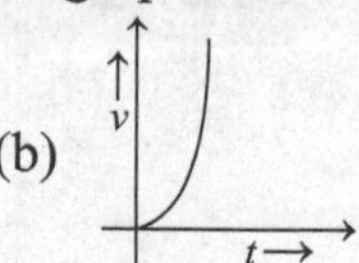

(c) 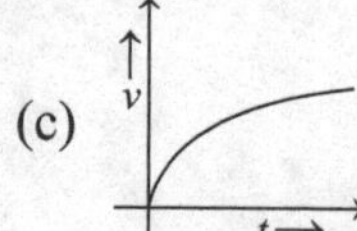

(d) 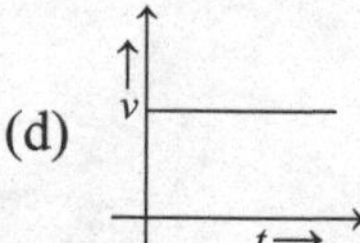

5. The displacement x of a particle along a straight line at time t is given by $x = a_0 + a_1 t + a_2 t^2$. The acceleration of the particle is

(a) a_0 (b) a_1 (c) $2a_2$ (d) a_2

6. A rocket is fired from the earth's surface such that it produces an acceleration of 19.6 m/s². If after 5 s, its engine is OFF, the rockets maximum altitude above the ground will be

(a) 245 m (b) 490 m
(c) 980 m (d) 735 m

7. An electron starting from rest has a linear increase in speed with time, i.e. $v = kt$, where $k = 2\ m/s^2$. The distance travelled by the object in the first 3 s is

(a) 9 m (b) 6 m
(c) 8 m (d) 10 m

8. **Statement I** Displacement of a body is a vector sum of the area under velocity-time graph.
Statement II Displacement is a vector quantity.
In the light of above statements, choose the most appropriate answer from the options given below.
(a) Both Statement I and Statement II are correct.
(b) Both Statement I and Statement II are incorrect.
(c) Statement I is correct but Statement II is incorrect.
(d) Statement I is incorrect but Statement II is correct.

9. If a body losses half of its velocity on penetrating 3 cm in a wooden block, then how much will it penetrate more before comming to rest?
(a) 1 cm (b) 2 cm
(c) 3 cm (d) 4 cm

10. The graph provided illustrate the relationship between velocity and displacement. Which of the following graphs accurately depicts the correspond variation of acceleration with displacement?

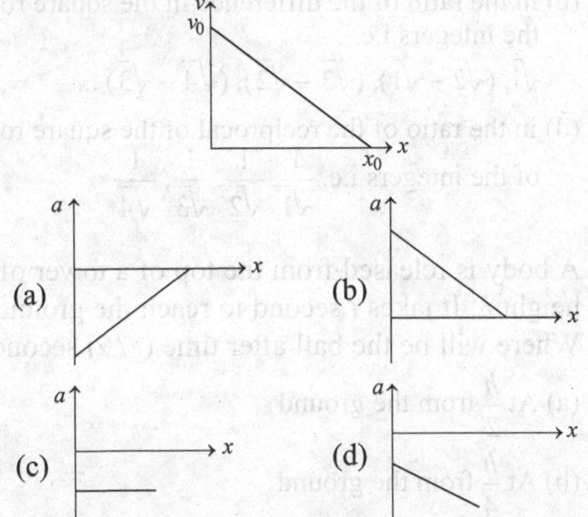

11. A car accelerates from rest at a constant rate α for sometime, after which it decelerates at a constant rate β and comes to rest. If the total time elapsed is t, then the maximum velocity acquired by the car is

(a) $\left(\frac{\alpha^2 + \beta^2}{\alpha\beta}\right)t$

(b) $\left(\frac{\alpha^2 - \beta^2}{\alpha\beta}\right)t$

(c) $\frac{(\alpha - \beta)t}{\alpha\beta}$

(d) $\frac{\alpha\beta t}{\alpha + \beta}$

12. A lift is going up. The variation in the velocity of the lift is as shown in the graph. What is the height to which the lift takes the passenger?

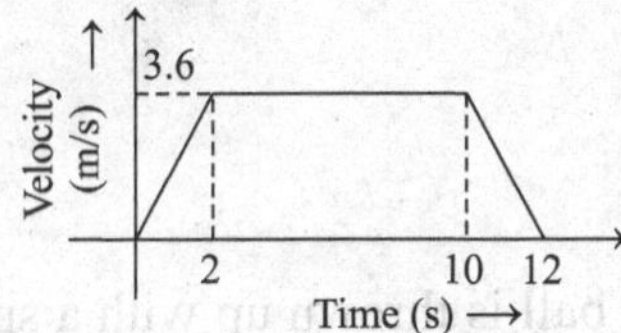

(a) 3.6 m
(b) 28.8 m
(c) 28.8 m
(d) 36.0 m

13. If a body starts from rest and travels 120 cm in the 6th second, then what is the acceleration (in m/s^2)?
(a) 0.20 (b) 0.027
(c) 0.218 (d) 0.03

14. A particle moving with a uniform acceleration travels 24 m and 64 m in the first two consecutive intervals of 4 s each. Its initial velocity is
(b) 1 m/s
(b) 10 m/s
(c) 5 m/s
(d) 2 m/s

15. A particle moves along a straight line path. After sometime, it comes to rest. The motion is with constant acceleration whose direction with respect to the direction of velocity is
(a) positive throughout motion
(b) negative throughout motion
(c) first positive, then negative
(d) first negative, then positive

16. A particle starts from rest and moving with constant acceleration covers a distance x_1 in the 3rd second and x_2 in the 5th second. The ratio $\frac{x_1}{x_2}$ =

(a) $\frac{3}{5}$ (b) $\frac{5}{9}$
(c) $\frac{9}{25}$ (d) $\frac{25}{81}$

17. The acceleration due to gravity on the planet B is 9 times the acceleration due to gravity on planet A. A man jumps to a height of 2m on the surface of A. What is the height of jump by the same person on the planet B?

(a) 18 m
(b) 6 m
(c) $\frac{2}{3}$ m
(d) $\frac{2}{9}$ m

18. A cricket ball is thrown up with a speed of 19.6 ms^{-1}. The maximum height it can reach is

(a) 9.8 m
(b) 19.6 m
(c) 29.4 m
(d) 39.2 m

19. Three different objects of masses m_1, m_2 and m_3 are allowed to fall from rest and from the same point O along three different frictionless paths. The speeds of the three objects, on reaching the ground, will be in the ratio of

(a) $m_1 : m_2 : m_3$
(b) $m_1 : 2m_2 : 3m_3$
(c) 1:1:1
(d) $\frac{1}{m_1}:\frac{1}{m_2}:\frac{1}{m_3}$

20. A body thrown vertically upwards with an initial velocity reaches maximum height in 6 s. The ratio of the distances travelled by the body in the first second and the seventh second is

(a) 1 : 1
(b) 11 : 1
(c) 1 : 2
(d) 1 : 11

21. Time taken by an object to reach the height of h_1 and h_2 is respectively t_1 and t_2, then the ratio of t_1 to t_2 is

(a) $h_1 : h_2$
(b) $\sqrt{h_1} : \sqrt{h_2}$
(c) $h_1 : 2h_2$
(d) $2h_1 : h_2$

22. A ball is dropped downwards. After 1s, another ball is dropped downwards from the same point. What is the distance between them after 3s ?

(a) 24.5 m (b) 20 m
(c) 50 m (d) 9.8 m

23. P, Q and R are three balloons ascending with velocities u, $4u$ and $8u$, respectively. If stones of the same mass be dropped from each, when they are at the same height, then

(a) they reach the ground at the same time
(b) stone from P reaches the ground first
(c) stone from R reaches the ground first
(d) stone from Q reaches the ground first

24. A particle is dropped vertically from rest from a height. The time taken by it to fall through successive distances of 1 m each will be

(a) all equal, being equal to $\sqrt{\frac{2}{g}}$ second
(b) in the ratio of square roots of the integers 1, 2, 3, ...
(c) in the ratio of the difference in the square roots of the integers i.e. $\sqrt{1}, (\sqrt{2}-\sqrt{1}), (\sqrt{3}-\sqrt{2}), (\sqrt{4}-\sqrt{3})$ ...
(d) in the ratio of the reciprocal of the square roots of the integers i.e. $\frac{1}{\sqrt{1}}, \frac{1}{\sqrt{2}}, \frac{1}{\sqrt{3}}, \frac{1}{\sqrt{4}}$

25. A body is released from the top of a tower of height h. It takes t second to reach the ground. Where will be the ball after time $(t/2)$ second?

(a) At $\frac{h}{2}$ from the ground
(b) At $\frac{h}{4}$ from the ground
(c) Depends upon mass and volume of the body
(d) At $\frac{3h}{4}$ from the ground

26. A body falls freely from rest. It covers as much distance in the last second of its motion as covered in the first three seconds. The body has fallen for a time of

(a) 3 s (b) 5s
(c) 7 s (d) 9 s

27. A stone thrown upwards with a velocity u reaches upto a height h. If the initial velocity is $2u$, the height attained would be

(a) $2h$ (b) $4h$
(c) $8h$ (d) $16h$

28. Two balls A and B are simultaneously thrown. A is thrown from ground level with a velocity of 20 ms^{-1} in the upward direction and B is thrown from a height of 40 m in the downward direction with same velocity. Where will the two balls meet?

(a) 15 m (b) 25 m
(c) 35 m (d) 45 m

29. A body is thrown vertically upwards. If air resistance is to be taken into account, then the time during which the body rises is

(a) equal to the time of fall
(b) less than the time of fall
(c) greater than the time of fall
(d) twice the time of fall

30. A passenger seated in Train A, which is moving at a speed of 90 km/h, observes another train, Train B, passing by in the opposite direction for a duration of 8 s. If Train B is travelling at a velocity of 54 km/h determine the length of Train B.

(a) 200 m (b) 320 m
(c) 120 m (d) 80 m

31. Assertion (A) A body can have acceleration even if its velocity is zero at a given instant of time.

Reason (R) A body is momentarily at rest when it reverses its direction of motion.

In the light of above statements, choose the most appropriate answer from the options given below.

(a) Both A and R are true and R is the correct explanation of A.
(b) Both A and R are true but R is not the correct explanation of A.
(c) A is true but R is false.
(d) A is false but R is true.

32. Two trains, A and B, with respective lengths l and $4l$, are simultaneously entering a tunnel of length L on parallel tracks, travelling towards each other from opposite direction. Train A has a velocity of 108 km/h, while Train B moves at 72 km/h. It is observed that Train A takes 35 s less time than Train B to completely pass through the tunnel. Given that the length L of the tunnel is 60 times the length of Train A, calculate the length of the tunnel L.

(a) 1200 m (b) 1800 m
(c) 2700 m (d) 900 m

33. A ball is moving with a uniform acceleration which is parallel to its instantaneous direction of motion. The displacement(s)-velocity (v) graph of this object is

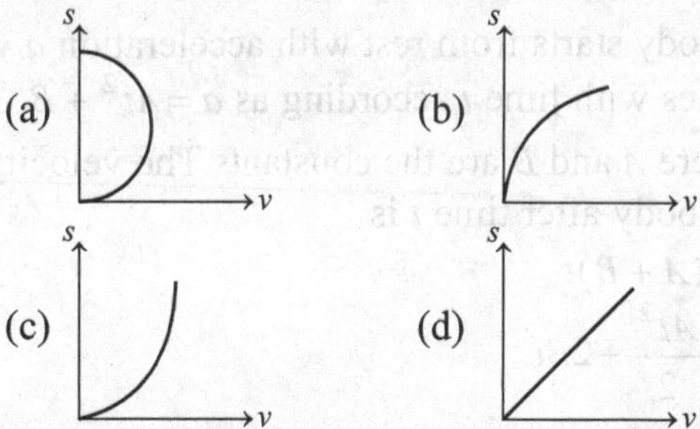

34. Two trucks, each measuring 40 m in length, are travelling in opposite direction with velocities of 20 m/s and 10 m/s respectively. What will be the time required for each other to fully cross each other?

(a) 2 s (b) 4 s
(c) $2\sqrt{3}$ s (d) 2.67 s

35. Time taken by a particle to go upto a height and come down are equal in the absence of air resistance or force. In the presence of dragging force gives a deceleration a, time to go up is

(a) 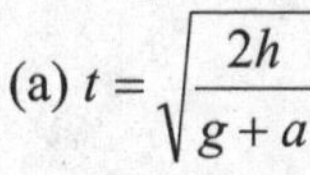 $t=\sqrt{\frac{2h}{g+a}}$ (b) 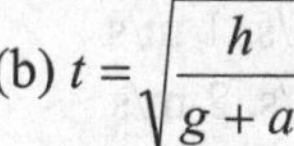 $t=\sqrt{\frac{h}{g+a}}$

(c) 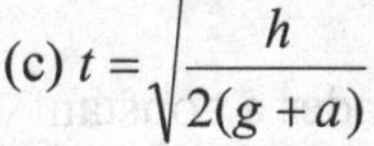 $t=\sqrt{\frac{h}{2(g+a)}}$ (d) $t=\sqrt{\frac{h}{4(g+a)}}$

36. A bullet train 160 m long is moving north at a speed of 22 m/s. An eagle flying south at a speed of 12 m/s crosses the train in time

(a) 8 s (b) 4.7 s
(c) 12 s (d) 16 s

37. **Statement I** The position-time graph of a uniform motion in one-dimension of a body can have negative slope.

Statement II When the speed of body decreases with time, the position-time graph of the moving body has negative slope.

In the light of above statements, choose the most appropriate answer from the options given below.

(a) Both Statement I and Statement II are correct.

(b) Both Statement I and Statement II are incorrect.

(c) Statement I is correct but Statement II is incorrect.

(d) Statement I is incorrect but Statement II is correct.

38. A body starts from rest with acceleration a which varies with time t according as $a = At^2 + B$, where A and B are the constants. The velocity of the body after time t is

(a) $(A+B)t$

(b) $\frac{At^2}{2} + 2Bt$

(c) $\frac{At^3}{3} + Bt$

(d) $At^2 + \frac{Bt}{2}$

39. Two particles are moving in the same direction. Due to an interaction between them, 8 m/s of velocity is lost in the gap between them and the spacing between the particles increases by 2 m/s. If these particles were initially moving at the same speed and in same direction then their initial speeds are

(a) 5 m/s, 1 m/s

(b) 4 m/s, 1 m/s

(c) 4m /s, 2 m/s

(d) 5 m/s, 3 m/s

40. An object starts from rest under a constant acceleration and let s_1 be the displacement in the first $(p-1)$ second and s_2 be the displacement in the first p second. Displacement in $(p^2 - p + 1)$th second will be

(a) $s_1 + s_2$ (b) $s_1 s_2$

(c) $s_1 - s_2$ (d) $\frac{s_1}{s_2}$

41. The engine of a motor cycle can produce a maximum acceleration of 5 ms^{-2}. Its brakes can produce a maximum retardation 10 ms^{-2}. The minimum time in which it can cover a distance of 1.5 km is

(a) 5 s (b) 10 s

(c) 15 s (d) 30 s

42. A stone dropped from the top of a tower travels 25 m in the last second of its motion. If $g = 10\ ms^{-2}$, height of the tower is

(a) 45 m

(b) 90 m

(c) 72 m

(d) 135 m

43. From the top of a building 9 m high, water drops are falling at equal intervals of time such that when the first drop reaches the ground, the fourth drop is just ready to fall. The distances between the successive drops (in m) at that instant is

(a) 1, 3, 5 (b) 5, 3, 1

(c) 1, 4, 9 (d) 9, 4, 1

44. A ball is thrown vertically upwards from the ground and a boy gazing out the window observes it moving upward past him at 5 ms^{-1}. If $g = 10\ ms^{-2}$ and the height of the window is 10 m above the ground, the ball travels through a height equal to

(a) 11.25 m

(b) 23 m

(c) 46 m

(d) 15.5 m

45. A body is allowed to fall from a height of 100 m. After 2 s, if acceleration due to gravity vanishes, the total time of its fall is (Take, $g = 10\ ms^{-2}$)

(a) 3 s

(b) 4 s

(c) 6 s

(d) 8 s

46. A body released from the top of a tower of height h. It takes time t to reach the ground. After time $\frac{2t}{3}$, its height from the ground is

(a) $\frac{h}{3}$

(b) $\frac{4h}{9}$

(c) $\frac{5h}{9}$

(d) $\frac{9h}{13}$

47. A body is to be projected vertically upwards from ground such that it passes through a point P. The product of the two times after which it passes through that point is (h is height of P above the ground)

(a) $\sqrt{2gh}$

(b) $\sqrt{gh}$

(c) $\frac{g}{2h}$

(d) $\frac{2h}{g}$

48. A stone is projected up with a velocity of $14.7\ \text{ms}^{-1}$ from the top of a tower and it reaches the ground after 5 s, then height of that tower is

(a) 9.8 m (b) 19.6 m

(c) 49 m (d) 98 m

49. Match the List I with List II

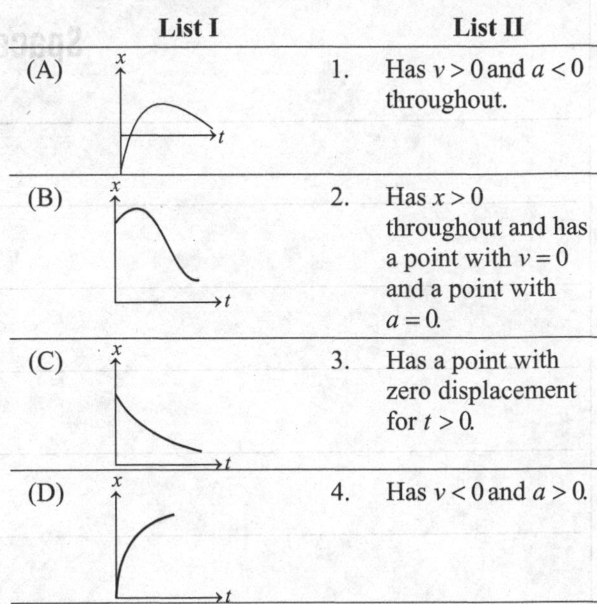

List I	List II
(A)	1. Has $v > 0$ and $a < 0$ throughout.
(B)	2. Has $x > 0$ throughout and has a point with $v = 0$ and a point with $a = 0$.
(C)	3. Has a point with zero displacement for $t > 0$.
(D)	4. Has $v < 0$ and $a > 0$.

The correct match is

(a) A- 1, B-2, C-4, D-3

(b) A- 2, B-1, C-3, D-4

(c) A- 4, B-3, C-2, D-1

(d) A-3, B-2, C- 4, D- 1

50. A body dropped from certain height travels 36% of total distance during the last second of its motion, then the height from which the body is dropped will be

(a) 78.4 m (b) 98 m

(c) 122.5 m (d) 245 m

Response Index

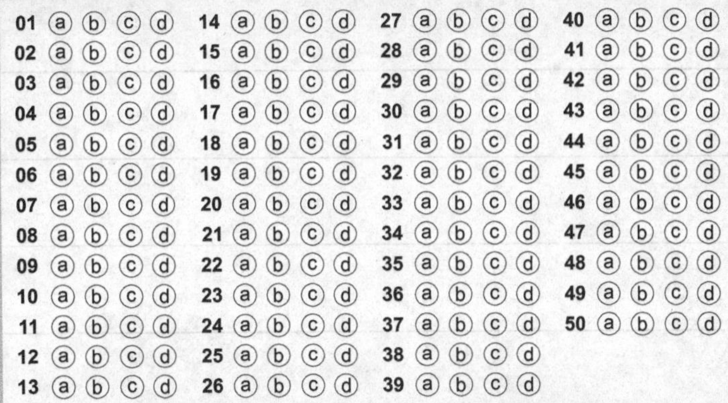

Performance Scanner

> 90% Excellent ! You have mastered this chapter. The concepts of this chapter are at your fingertips. Move on to the next chapter and maintain this momentum.

76-90% Very Good ! You have a good command over this chapter. Revise the chapter again after a few days and enhance your performance.

60-75% Good ! You have a wide scope to learn more for this chapter. Revise this chapter again.

<60% Not Satisfactory! You have a long way ahead of you to master this chapter. Revise it thoroughly.

For Online Chapter Test **Scan the QR Code**

Space for Rough Work

Test Booklet No. 3947103

Test Booklet Code CH3

MEDACE
NEET (UG)
SELF ASSESSMENT KIT

Motion in a Plane

Topics Covered

Motion in a Plane and Projectile Motion

Uniform Circular Motion

Relative Motion

Important Instructions

- This Booklet Contains – Three Topic Tests and One Test on Complete Chapter.
- Each question carries 4 Marks.
- For each correct response, the candidate will get 4 marks and for every incorrect response, 1 mark will be additionally deducted from total score.
- Use **Blue/Black** point pen only for filling the OMR.
- Rough work is to be done in the space provided for this purpose in the test booklet only.

Name of the Candidate (In Capitals)

____

Candidate's Signature ____________

Invigilator's Signature ____________

Facsimile signature stamp of center superintendent____________

Do not open this Booklet until you start attempting the Test

Topical Follow Thru

Test 1

Syllabus

- Scalars and Vectors
- Addition and Subtraction of Vectors
- Scalar and Vector Products
- Unit Vector
- Motion in a Plane
- Resolution of Vector
- Projectile Motion

For deeper insight **Scan the QR Code**

Important Instructions

- The test is of 45 min duration and contains 25 Multiple Choice Questions (Four options with a single correct answer).
- Choose the correct option and fill the OMR given on the last page of this test accordingly.
- At some instances, you may find more than 1 option may be correct in such circumstances you have to judge the most appropriate answer as per the conditions given in the question.

1. A ground to ground projectile is at point A at $t=\frac{T}{3}$, is at point B at $t=\frac{5T}{6}$ and reaches the ground at $t=T$. The difference in heights between points A and B is

(a) $\frac{gT^2}{6}$ (b) $\frac{gT^2}{12}$

(c) $\frac{gT^2}{18}$ (d) $\frac{gT^2}{24}$

2. If $\mathbf{A}=5\hat{\mathbf{i}}+7\hat{\mathbf{j}}-3\hat{\mathbf{k}}$ and $\mathbf{B}=2\hat{\mathbf{i}}+2\hat{\mathbf{j}}-c\hat{\mathbf{k}}$ are perpendicular vectors, the value of c is

(a) -2 (b) 8

(c) -7 (d) -8

3. The greatest height to which a man can throw a stone is h. The greatest distance to which he can throw will be

(a) $\frac{h}{2}$

(b) h

(c) $2h$

(d) $4h$

4. A body is projected at such angle that the horizontal range is three times the greatest height. The angle of projection is

(a) $\tan^{-1}\left(\frac{2}{3}\right)$ (b) $\tan^{-1}\left(\frac{3}{2}\right)$

(c) $\tan^{-1}\left(\frac{4}{3}\right)$ (d) $\tan^{-1}\left(\frac{3}{4}\right)$

5. Two seconds after projection, a projectile is travelling in a direction inclined at 30° with horizontal. After 1 more second, it is travelling horizontally. Then, $(g=10\,\text{m/s}^2)$

(a) the velocity of projection is $20\sqrt{3}$ m/s

(b) the angle of projection is 30° with horizontal

(c) Both (a) and (b) are correct

(d) Both (a) and (b) are wrong

6. A grasshopper assumed that it can jumps a maximum horizontal distance of 0.6 m. If it spends a negligible time on the ground, then the speed he travel along the road is

(a) 2.4 m/s (b) 2.8 m/s

(c) 104 m/s (d) 1 m/s

7. A missile is fired for maximum range with an initial velocity 45 m/s. If acceleration due to gravity is 10 m/s^2, then range of missile is

(a) 40 m

(b) 500 m

(c) 60 m

(d) 202.5 m

8. **Statement I** The direction of vector $\lambda\mathbf{A}$, $(\lambda < 0)$ is same as the direction of vector **A**.

Statement II If a vector is multiplied by zero, then the resultant is a scalar.

In the light of above statements, choose the most appropriate answer from the options given below.

(a) Both Statement I and Statement II are correct.
(b) Both Statement I and Statement II are incorrect.
(c) Statement I is correct but Statement II is incorrect.
(d) Statement I is incorrect but Statement II is correct.

9. A bomber is flying horizontally with a constant speed of 180 m/s at a height of 78.4 m. The pilot has to drop a bomb at the enemy target. The horizontal distance from the target should he release the bomb is

(a) 0 m (b) 300 m
(c) 600 m (d) 720 m

10. **Assertion** (A) When a body is projected at an angle 45°, its range is maximum.

Reason (R) For maximum of range, the value of $\sin 2\theta$ should be equal to one.

In the light of above statements, choose the most appropriate answer from the options given below.

(a) Both A and R are true and R is the correct explanation of A.
(b) Both A and R are true but R is not the correct explanation of A.
(c) A is true but R is false.
(d) A is false but R is true.

11. Vector **A** and **B** are mutually perpendicular. Component of **A** + **B** in the direction of **A** − **B** will be

(a) $\dfrac{A^2+B^2}{\sqrt{A^2-B^2}}$ (b) $\sqrt{A^2-B^2}$
(c) $\dfrac{A+B}{A-B}$ (d) $\dfrac{A^2-B^2}{\sqrt{A^2+B^2}}$

12. A bomber moving horizontally with 800 m/s drops a bomb which strikes ground in 10 s. The angle of strike with horizontal is

(a) $\sin^{-1}\left(\dfrac{1}{5}\right)$ (b) $\tan^{-1}(1)$
(c) $\tan^{-1}\left(\dfrac{1}{8}\right)$ (d) $\tan^{-1}(5)$

13. From the top of a tower of height 40 m, a ball is projected upwards with a speed of 20 ms^{-1} at an angle of elevation of 30°, then the ratio of the total time taken by the ball to hit the ground to the time taken to ball come at same level as top of tower.

(a) 2 : 1 (b) 3 : 1
(c) 3 : 2 (d) 4 : 1

14. Two tall buildings are 50 m apart. The speed with which a ball must be thrown horizontally from a window 150 m above the ground in one building, so that it enters a window 27.5 m above from the ground in the other building is

(a) 2 ms^{-1} (b) 10 ms^{-1}
(c) 4 ms^{-1} (d) 8 ms^{-1}

15. From the top of a tower 40 m high, a ball is thrown horizontally. If the line joining the point of projection to the point where it hits the ground makes an angle of 45° with the horizontal, then the initial velocity of the ball is

(a) 14 ms^{-1} (b) 4 ms^{-1}
(c) 15 ms^{-1} (d) 3 ms^{-1}

16. A particle is projected from the ground with an initial speed of v at an angle θ with horizontal. The average velocity of the particle between its point of projection and highest point of trajectory is

(a) $\dfrac{1}{2}\sqrt{1+2\cos^2\theta}$ (b) $\dfrac{v}{2}\sqrt{1+2\cos^2\theta}$
(c) $\dfrac{v}{2}\sqrt{1+3\cos^2\theta}$ (d) $v\cos\theta$

17. If $\mathbf{A} = 3\hat{\mathbf{i}} + 4\hat{\mathbf{j}}$ and $\mathbf{B} = 7\hat{\mathbf{i}} + 24\hat{\mathbf{k}}$, then the vector having the same magnitude as that of **B** and parallel to **A** is

(a) $15\hat{\mathbf{i}} + 20\hat{\mathbf{j}}$ (b) $20\hat{\mathbf{i}} + 15\hat{\mathbf{j}}$
(c) $\dfrac{7}{5}\hat{\mathbf{i}} + \dfrac{24}{5}\hat{\mathbf{k}}$ (d) $15\hat{\mathbf{i}} - 20\hat{\mathbf{j}}$

18. If a vector $2\hat{\mathbf{i}}+3\hat{\mathbf{j}}+8\hat{\mathbf{k}}$ is perpendicular to the vector $4\hat{\mathbf{i}}-4\hat{\mathbf{j}}+\alpha\hat{\mathbf{k}}$, then value of α is

(a) -1 (b) $-\frac{1}{2}$ (c) $\frac{1}{2}$ (d) 1

19. A ball is projected from the ground with velocity v such that its range is maximum. Match List I entries with the correct entries in List II.

List I	List II
A. Velocity at half at the maximum height	1. $\sqrt{3}v/2$
B. Velocity at the maximum height	2. $v/\sqrt{2}$
C. Change in its velocity when it returns to the ground	3. $v\sqrt{2}$
D. Average velocity when it reaches the maximum height	4. $v/2\cdot\sqrt{5}/\sqrt{2}$

	A	B	C	D
(a)	2	3	4	1
(b)	3	2	1	4
(c)	1	2	3	4
(d)	4	1	2	3

20. Two particles are projected from the same point with same speed u at angles of projection α and β from horizontal. The maximum heights attained by them are h_1 and h_2 respectively, R is the range for both and t_1 and t_2 their times of flight respectively, then

(a) $\alpha+\beta=\frac{\pi}{2}$ (b) $R=2\sqrt{h_1h_2}$

(c) $\frac{t_1}{t_2}=\cot\alpha$ (d) $\cot\alpha=\sqrt{h_1h_2}$

21. The range of a projectile thrown at an angle θ with the ground is R. The time of its flight is T, then $\tan\theta$ is equal to

(a) $\frac{gT^2}{2R}$ (b) $\frac{gT^2}{R}$

(c) $\frac{gR}{T^2}$ (d) $\frac{gR^2}{T}$

22. The motion of a particle is given by $y=40t-5t^2$ and $x=40\sqrt{3}t$, where x and y are in metres and t in seconds. The initial velocity of the body and angle made by it to the horizontal are

(a) 40 ms^{-1}, 60° (b) 40 ms^{-1}, 30°

(c) 80 ms^{-1}, 60° (d) 80 ms^{-1}, 30°

23. A gun throws a shell with a muzzle speed of 98 ms^{-1}. When the gun is elevated 45°, the range is observed as 900 m. Due to air resistance, its range is decreased by

(a) 40 m (b) 80 m

(c) 120 m (d) 160 m

24. The equation of a projectile is $y=px-qx^2$, then its horizontal range is

(a) p (b) q (c) pq (d) $\frac{p}{q}$

25. A body is projected horizontally with a velocity $\sqrt{29}$ ms^{-1} from a height 10 m. The velocity on reaching the ground is

(a) 10 ms^{-1} (b) 23 ms^{-1}

(c) 20 ms^{-1} (d) 15 ms^{-1}

Response Index

01	a	b	c	d	10	a	b	c	d	19	a	b	c	d
02	a	b	c	d	11	a	b	c	d	20	a	b	c	d
03	a	b	c	d	12	a	b	c	d	21	a	b	c	d
04	a	b	c	d	13	a	b	c	d	22	a	b	c	d
05	a	b	c	d	14	a	b	c	d	23	a	b	c	d
06	a	b	c	d	15	a	b	c	d	24	a	b	c	d
07	a	b	c	d	16	a	b	c	d	25	a	b	c	d
08	a	b	c	d	17	a	b	c	d					
09	a	b	c	d	18	a	b	c	d					

Performance Scanner

> 90% Excellent !	You have mastered these topics. The concepts of these topics are on your fingertips. Move on to the next test and maintain this momentum.
76-90% Very Good !	You have a good command over these topics. Revise these topics again after a few days and enhance your performance.
60-75% Good !	You have a wide scope to learn for these topics. Revise these topics again.
<60% Not Satisfactory!	You have a long way ahead of you to master these topics. Revise it thoroughly.

Test 2

Syllabus
- Uniform Circular Motion
- Centripetal Acceleration
- Acceleration of Particle in Non-Uniform Circular Motion

For deeper insight **Scan the QR Code**

Important Instructions
- The test is of 30 min duration and contains 15 Multiple Choice Questions (Four options with a single correct answer).
- Choose the correct option and fill the OMR given on the last page of this test accordingly.
- At some instances, you may find more than 1 option may be correct in such circumstances you have to judge the most appropriate answer as per the conditions given in the question.

1. A particle is moving with a uniform speed v in a circular path of radius r with the centre at O. When the particle moves from a point P to Q on the circle such that $\angle POQ = \theta$, then the magnitude of the change in velocity is

(a) $2v \cos (2\theta)$
(b) zero
(c) $2v \sin\left(\frac{\theta}{2}\right)$
(d) $\frac{v \sin \theta}{2}$

2. A particle is moves in a circle describing equal angles in equal times. Its velocity vector

(a) remains constant
(b) change in magnitude
(c) change in direction
(d) change both in magnitude and direction

3. An insect trapped in a circular groove of radius 12 cm moves along the groove steadily and completes 7 revolutions in 100 s. Which one of the following statement is correct?

(a) The angular speed of insect is 1.68 rad/s.
(b) The linear speed of the motion is 5.3 cm/s.
(c) The magnitude of acceleration is 6.78 cm/s^2.
(d) The acceleration vector is a constant vector.

4. The magnitude of the displacement of a particle moving in a circle of radius a with constant angular speed ω varies with time t as

(a) $2a \sin \omega t$
(b) $2a \sin \frac{\omega t}{2}$
(c) $2a \cos \omega t$
(d) $2a \cos \frac{\omega t}{2}$

5. A particle moves in a circle of radius 35 cm at two revolutions per second. The acceleration of the particle (in m/s^2) is

(a) π^2 (b) $2.6\pi^2$
(c) $5.6\,\pi^2$ (d) $6.2\pi^2$

6. A particle A is moving in a circle of radius a with a uniform speed v. C is the centre of the circle and PQ is a diameter. When passing through Q, the angular velocity of A about P and C are in the ratio

(a) 1 : 1
(b) 1 : 2
(c) 2 : 1
(d) 4 : 1

7. A motor car is travelling at 60 m/s on a circular road of radius 1200 m. It is increasing its speed at the rate of 4 m/s^2. The acceleration of the car is

(a) 3 m/s^2
(b) 5 m/s^2
(c) 3.16 m/s^2
(d) 7.26 m/s^2

8. A stone tied to the end of a string 400 cm long is whirled in a horizontal circle with a constant speed. If the stone makes 14 revolutions in 22 s, then the acceleration of the stone is

(a) 64 ms^{-2} (b) 4 ms^{-2}
(c) 12 ms^{-2} (d) 8 ms^{-2}

9. A particle moves in a plane with uniform acceleration having direction different from that of the instantaneous velocity. What is the nature of trajectory ?

(a) Parabola (b) Circle
(c) Straight line (d) Ellipse

10. A particle covers equal distance around a circular path in equal intervals of time. Which of the following quantities connected with the motion of the particle remains constant with time?

(a) Displacement
(b) Velocity
(c) Speed
(d) Acceleration

11. A particle is moving in XY-plane at time t and position vector is $\mathbf{r} = a(1-\cos\omega t)\,\hat{\mathbf{i}} + a\sin\omega t\,\hat{\mathbf{j}}$. The path of the particle is

(a) a circle of radius a and centre at $(a,0)$
(b) a circle of radius a and centre at (0, 0)
(c) an ellipse
(d) neither a circle nor an ellipse.

12. Statement I A body having uniform speed in circular path has a constant acceleration.
Statement II In a uniform circular motion, the direction of radial acceleration is always away towards the centre.

In the light of above statements, choose the most appropriate answer from the options given below.

(a) Both Statement I and Statement II are correct.
(b) Both Statement I and Statement II are incorrect.
(c) Statement I is correct but Statement II is incorrect.
(d) Statement I is incorrect but Statement II is correct.

13. A stone attached to a 100 cm long string, is rotated in a horizontal plane at a uniform velocity. Given that the stone completes 16 full rotations within a span of 22 seconds then the centripetal acceleration experienced by the stone is

(a) 16 m/s^2 (b) 4 m/s^2
(c) 20.79 m/s^2 (d) 0 m/s^2

14. A ball is moving along a circular path of radius 8 m and with uniform speed 8 m/s. The average acceleration when the particle complete half-revolution is

(a) zero (b) 10 m/s^2
(c) $\frac{16}{\pi}$ m/s^2 (d) 18 m/s^2

15. A truck is travelling at speed 60 m/s on a circular road of radius 700 m. It is increasing its speed at rate of 2.0 m/s^2. The total acceleration is

(a) 1.8 m/s^2 (b) 2 m/s^2
(c) 5.5 m/s^2 (d) 2.7 m/s^2

Response Index

01	a	b	c	d	10	a	b	c	d
02	a	b	c	d	11	a	b	c	d
03	a	b	c	d	12	a	b	c	d
04	a	b	c	d	13	a	b	c	d
05	a	b	c	d	14	a	b	c	d
06	a	b	c	d	15	a	b	c	d
07	a	b	c	d					
08	a	b	c	d					
09	a	b	c	d					

Performance Scanner

> 90% Excellent !	You have mastered these topics. The concepts of these topics are on your fingertips. Move on to the next test and maintain this momentum.
76-90% Very Good !	You have a good command over these topics. Revise these topics again after a few days and enhance your performance.
60-75% Good !	You have a wide scope to learn for these topics. Revise these topics again.
<60 Not Satisfactory!	You have a long way ahead of you to master these topics. Revise it thoroughly.

Test 3

Syllabus
- Relative Motion in 2D
- Rain Man Problems
- River-Boat (or Man) Problems

For deeper insight **Scan the QR Code**

Important Instructions
- The test is of 45 min duration and contains 25 Multiple Choice Questions (Four options with a single correct answer).
- Choose the correct option and fill the OMR given on the last page of this test accordingly.
- At some instances, you may find more than 1 option may be correct in such circumstances you have to judge the most appropriate answer as per the conditions given in the question.

1. To the captain of a ship P travelling with velocity $v_P = (3\hat{i} - 4\hat{j})$ km/h, a second ship Q appears to have a velocity $(5\hat{i} + 12\hat{j})$ km/h, then the true velocity of the ship Q is

(a) $2\hat{i} + 16\hat{j}$ km/h (b) $13\hat{i} + 8\hat{j}$ km/h
(c) $-2\hat{i} - 16\hat{j}$ km/h (d) $8(\hat{i} + \hat{j})$ km/h

2. A man can swim in still water with a speed of 2 m/s. If he wants to cross a river of water current speed $\sqrt{3}$ m/s along shortest possible path, then in which direction should he swim?

(a) At an angle $120°$ to the water current
(b) At an angle $150°$ to the water current
(c) At an angle $90°$ to the water current
(d) None of the above

3. Wind is blowing in the north direction at speed of 4 m/s which causes the rain to fall at some angle with the vertical, then, the velocity should a cyclist drive so that the rain appears vertical to him is

(a) 2 m/s South (b) 4 m/s North
(c) 4 m/s West (d) 4 m/s South

4. A flag is mounted on a car moving due to north with velocity of 40 km/h. Strong winds are blowing due to East with velocity of 40 km/h. The flag will point in direction

(a) east (b) north-east
(c) south-east (d) south-west

5. A man standing on a moving bus, throws a stone vertically up relative to himself. To a man, standing on the ground, the stone appears to (immediately after being thrown)

(a) rise towards the rear of the truck
(b) move along a parabolic path
(c) rise vectically up and come down
(d) rise straight and forward but inclined to the direction of motion of truck.

6. A river flows with a speed more than the maximum speed with which a person can swim in still water. He cross the river by shortest possible path, then

(a) he should start normal to the river bank
(b) he should start in such a way that he moves normal to the bank relative to the bank
(c) the man cannot cross the river in that way
(d) he should start in a particular direction making an obtuse angle with the direction of water current.

7. A river is flowing due east with a speed 5 ms^{-1}. A swimmer can swim in still water at a speed of 4 ms^{-1}. If swimmer starts swimming due to north, then the resultant velocity of the swimmer is

(a) 3.26 ms^{-1}
(b) 6.40 ms^{-1}
(c) 6.26 ms^{-1}
(d) 2.64 ms^{-1}

8. A man can swim in still water at 1 m/s. He swims across river flowing at 0.6 m/s which is 336 m wide. If he travel in shortest possible time, then time taken by man to cross the river is

(a) 250 s (b) 420 s
(c) 340 s (d) 336 s

9. A crane is going in south with a speed of 5 m/s. To a man sitting in crane a bus appears to move towards west with a speed of $2\sqrt{6}$ m/s, then the actual speed of the bus is

(a) 4 ms^{-1} (b) 3 ms^{-1}
(c) 7 ms^{-1} (d) None of these

10. A car is moving along a road with a speed of 45 km/h. In what direction must a body be projected from it with a velocity of 25 m/s, so that its resultant motion is at right angles to the direction of car?

(a) At an angle of 120° with the direction of motion of car
(b) At an angle of 60° with the direction of motion of car
(c) At an angle of 90° with the direction of motion of car
(d) At an angle of 135° with the direction of motion of car

11. A river is flowing from West to East at a speed of 8 m/min. A man on the South bank of the river, capable of swimming at 20 m/min in still water, wants to swim across the river in the shortest time. He should swim in a direction

(a) due North
(b) 30° East of North
(c) 30° West of North
(d) 60° East of North

12. A body moves due to East with velocity 20 km/h and then due to North with velocity of 15 km/h. The resultant velocity is

(a) 5 km/h (b) 15 km/h
(c) 20 km/h (d) 25 km/h

13. A train 1 moves from east to west and another train 2 moves from west to east on the equator with equal speeds relative to ground. The ratio of their centripetal acceleration of $\frac{a_1}{a_2}$ relative to centre of earth is

(a) >1 (b) $=1$
(c) <1 (d) ≥ 1

14. A boat travels from south bank to north bank of a river with a maximum speed of 8 km/h. A river current flows from west to east with a speed of 4 km/h to arrive at a point opposite to the point of start, the boat should start at an angle

(a) $\tan^{-1}(1/2)$ W of N
(b) 30° W of N
(c) $\tan^{-1}(1/2)$ N of W
(d) 30° N of W

15. Three ships P, Q and R are in motion. The motion of P as seen by Q is with speed v towoards north-east. The motion of Q as seen by R is with speed v toward the north-west, then as seen by P, R will be moving towards

(a) north (b) south
(c) east (d) west

16. Rain is falling vertically with a speed of 35 ms^{-1}. Winds starts blowing after sometime with a speed of 12 ms^{-1} in east to west direction. At what angle with the vertical should a boy waiting at a bus stop hold his umbrella to protect himself from rain?

(a) $\sin^{-1}\left(\frac{12}{35}\right)$ (b) $\cos^{-1}\left(\frac{12}{35}\right)$
(c) $\tan^{-1}\left(\frac{12}{35}\right)$ (d) $\cot^{-1}\left(\frac{12}{35}\right)$

17. A boat P is moving westwards with a speed of 10 km/h and a boat Q 100 km south of P is moving northwards with a speed of 10 km/h. The time after which the distance between them becomes shortest is

(a) $5\sqrt{2}$ h (b) $10\sqrt{2}$ h
(c) 5 h (d) 0 h

18. A man standing on a road has to hold his umbrella at 30° with the vertical to keep the rain away. He throws the umbrella and starts running at 10 km/h. He finds that raindrops are hitting his head vertically. What is the speed of rain with respect to ground?

(a) $10\sqrt{3}$ km/h (b) 20 km/h
(c) $\frac{20}{\sqrt{3}}$ km/h (d) $\frac{10}{\sqrt{3}}$ km/h

19. Ship A is sailing towards north-east with velocity $\mathbf{v} = (30\hat{\mathbf{i}} + 50\hat{\mathbf{j}})$ km/h, where $\hat{\mathbf{i}}$ points east and $\hat{\mathbf{j}}$ north. Ship B is at a distance of 80 km east and 150 km north of ship A and is sailing towards west at 10 km/h. Ship A will be at minimum distance from B in

(a) 4.2 h (b) 2.6 h
(c) 3.2 h (d) 2.2 h

20. Two boys are standing at the ends A and B of a ground, where $AB = a$. The boy at B starts running in a direction perpendicular to AB with velocity v_1. The boy at A starts running simultaneously with velocity v and catches the other boy in a time t, where t is

(a) $\dfrac{a}{\sqrt{v^2 + v_1^2}}$ (b) $\dfrac{a}{v + v_1}$

(c) $\dfrac{a}{v - v_1}$ (d) $\dfrac{a}{\sqrt{v^2 - v_1^2}}$

21. A boy is walking from west to east while rain is falling vertically with speed of 20 m/s. If boy has to hold his umbrella at an angle of 37° with vertical, then speed of boy is

(a) 5 m/s (b) 15 m/s
(c) 25 m/s (d) 35 m/s

22. A ship X moving due North with speed v observes that another ship Y is moving due West with same speed v. The actual velocity of Y is

(a) $\sqrt{2}\,v$ towards South-West
(b) $\sqrt{2}\,v$ towards North-West
(c) $\sqrt{2}\,v$ towards South-East
(d) v towards North-East

23. Two particles are separated by a horizontal distance R on the ground. Those two are projected simultaneously with velocities $\dfrac{u}{\sqrt{3}}$ and u at angles of projection 30° and 120° with the horizontal direction, so that they approach each other in the same plane. The time after which the horizontal separation between those particles becomes zero is

(a) $\dfrac{u}{2R}$ (b) $\dfrac{u}{R}$

(c) $\dfrac{R}{u}$ (d) $\dfrac{2R}{u}$

24. A swimmer crosses a river of width d flowing at velocity v. While swimming, he heads himself always at an angle of 120° with the river flow and on reaching the other end he finds a drift of $d/2$ in the direction of flow of river. The speed of the swimmer with respect to the river is

(a) $(2 - \sqrt{3})\,v$
(b) $2\,(2 - \sqrt{3})\,v$
(c) $4\,(2 - \sqrt{3})\,v$
(d) $(2 + \sqrt{3})\,v$

25. The path of one projectile as seen from another projectile is

(a) a straight line
(b) a parabola
(c) a circle
(d) hyperbola

Response Index

01	(a) (b) (c) (d)	10	(a) (b) (c) (d)	19	(a) (b) (c) (d)
02	(a) (b) (c) (d)	11	(a) (b) (c) (d)	20	(a) (b) (c) (d)
03	(a) (b) (c) (d)	12	(a) (b) (c) (d)	21	(a) (b) (c) (d)
04	(a) (b) (c) (d)	13	(a) (b) (c) (d)	22	(a) (b) (c) (d)
05	(a) (b) (c) (d)	14	(a) (b) (c) (d)	23	(a) (b) (c) (d)
06	(a) (b) (c) (d)	15	(a) (b) (c) (d)	24	(a) (b) (c) (d)
07	(a) (b) (c) (d)	16	(a) (b) (c) (d)	25	(a) (b) (c) (d)
08	(a) (b) (c) (d)	17	(a) (b) (c) (d)		
09	(a) (b) (c) (d)	18	(a) (b) (c) (d)		

Performance Scanner

> 90% Excellent !	You have mastered these topics. The concepts of these topic are on your fingertips. Move on to the next test and maintain this momentum.
76-90% Very Good !	You have a good command over these topics. Revise these topics again after a few days and enhance your performance.
60-75% Good !	You have a wide scope to learn for these topics. Revise these topics again.
<60% Not Satisfactory!	You have a long way ahead of you to master these topics. Revise it thoroughly.

Chapter Break Thru

Syllabus	
• Basic Concepts Related to Vectors • Addition and Subtraction of Vectors • Resolution of Vectors in Two & Three Dimensions • Scalar or Dot Product of Vectors • Vector or Cross Product of Vectors	• Motion in a Plane • Relative Velocity in 2D • Projectile Motion • Uniform Circular Motion

Important Instructions

- The test is of 1 hour duration and contains 50 multiple Choice Questions (Four options with a single correct answer).
- Choose the correct option and fill the OMR given on the last page of this test accordingly.
- At some instances, you may find more than 1 option may be correct in such circumstances you have to judge the most appropriate answer as per the conditions given in the question.

1. A ball of mass m thrown horizontally with velocity v from the top of house of height h touches the level ground at a distance of 250 m from the foot of the house. A ball of mass $2m$ thrown horizontally with velocity $v/2$, from the top of house of height $4h$ will touch the level ground at a distance x from the foot of house, then x will be

(a) 250 m (b) 500 m
(c) 125 m (d) $250\sqrt{2}$ m

2. A boy projects a stone vertically perpendicular to the trolley car with a speed v. If the trolley car moves with a constant velocity u, the time of flight of the stone is

(a) $\frac{u+v}{g}$ (b) $\frac{2v}{g}$
(c) $\frac{2u}{g}$ (d) $\frac{u-v}{g}$

3. A helicopter is flying horizontally at 6 m/s at an altitude 180 m when a package of emergency medical supplied is ejected horizontally backward with a speed of 12 m/s relative to the helicopter. Ignoring air resistance, then horizontal distance between the package and the helicopter when the package hits the ground and velocity of package with respect to ground are, respectively

(a) 120 m, 3 m/s
(b) 24 m, 4 m/s
(c) 36 m, 6 m/s
(d) 72 m, 12 m/s

4. A very broad lift is going up vertically with a constant acceleration of 2 m/s^2. At the instant when its velocity is 4 m/s a ball is projected from the floor of the lift with a speed of 4 m/s relative to the floor at an elevation of 30°. Time taken by the ball to return the floor is $(g = 10\,\text{m/s}^2)$.

(a) $\frac{1}{2}$s (b) $\frac{1}{3}$s
(c) $\frac{1}{4}$s (d) 1 s

5. A particle P moves in counter-clockwise direction on a circular path as shown in the figure. The movement of particle is such that it sweeps out a length $s = t^3 + 5$, where s is in metre and t is in second. The radius of the path is 16 m. The acceleration of P when $t = 2$s is

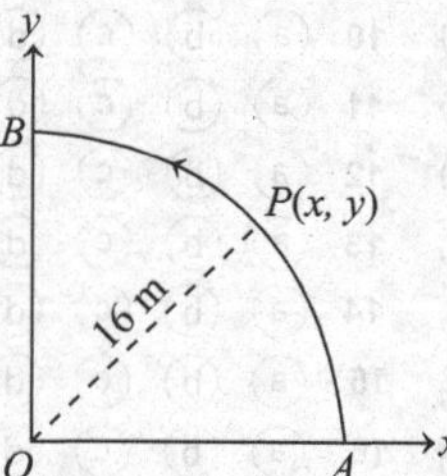

(a) 5 ms^{-2}
(b) 10 ms^{-2}
(c) 15 ms^{-2}
(d) 20 ms^{-2}

6. The speed of a boat is 5 km/h in still water. It crosses a river of width 1km along the shortest possible path in 15 min. The velocity of river water is

(a) 3 km/h (b) 4 km/h
(c) 5 km/h (d) 2 km/h

7. When two vectors **A** and **B** of magnitude a and b are added, the magnitude of the resultant vector is always

(a) equal to $(a+b)$
(b) less than $(a+b)$
(c) greater than $(a+b)$
(d) not greater than $(a+b)$

8. A cart is moving horizontally along a straight line with a constant speed of 30 m/s. A projectile is to be fired from the moving cart in such a way that it will return to the cart (at the same point on cart) after the cart has moved 80 m. At what velocity (relative to the cart) must be projectile be fired? (Take, $g = 10\ \text{m/s}^2$)

(a) 10 m/s (b) $\frac{20}{3}$ m/s
(c) $\frac{40}{3}$ m/s (d) $\frac{80}{3}$ m/s

9. A particle is projected up an inclined with initial speed $u = 20$ m/s at angle $\theta = 30°$ with the plane. The component of its velocity perpendicular to the plane when it strikes the plane is

(a) 10 m/s
(b) $5\sqrt{3}$ m/s
(c) $10\sqrt{3}$ m/s
(d) 0 m/s

10. The resultant of two vectors **P** and **Q** is **R**. If the magnitude of **Q** is doubled, the new resultant becomes perpendicular to **P**. The magnitude of **R** is

(a) $P+Q$ (b) Q
(c) P (d) $P+\frac{Q}{2}$

11. The horizontal range and the maximum height of a projectile are equal. The angle of projection of the projectile is

(a) $\theta = \tan^{-1}(2)$ (b) $\theta = \tan^{-1}\left(\frac{1}{4}\right)$
(c) $\theta = 45°$ (d) $\theta = \tan^{-1}(4)$

12. An housefly trapped in a circular groove of radius 18 cm moves along the groove steadily and completes 7 revolutions in 100 s. The linear speed of the insect is

(a) 4.3 cm s^{-1}
(b) 7.92 cm s^{-1}
(c) 6.3 cm s^{-1}
(d) 7.3 cms^{-1}

13. The position vector of points A, B, C and D are
$\mathbf{A} = 3\hat{\mathbf{i}} + 4\hat{\mathbf{j}} + 5\hat{\mathbf{k}}$, $\hat{\mathbf{B}} = 4\hat{\mathbf{i}} + 5\hat{\mathbf{j}} + 6\hat{\mathbf{k}}$
$\mathbf{C} = 7\hat{\mathbf{i}} + 9\hat{\mathbf{j}} + 3\hat{\mathbf{k}}$ and $\mathbf{D} = 4\hat{\mathbf{i}} + 6\hat{\mathbf{j}}$
Then, displacement vectors AB and CD are

(a) same
(b) parallel
(c) perpendicular
(d) anti-parallel

14. The range R of projectile is same when its maximum height are h and $4h$, then the relation between R and h is

(a) $R = 2h$ (b) $R = 6h$
(c) $R = h$ (d) $R = 8h$

15. A number of bullets are fired in all possible directions with the same initial velocity u. The maximum area of ground covered by bullets is

(a) $\pi\left(\frac{u^2}{2g}\right)^2$ (b) $\pi\left(\frac{u^2}{g}\right)^2$
(c) $\pi\left(\frac{u}{g}\right)^2$ (d) $\pi\left(\frac{u}{2g}\right)^2$

16. Balls A and B are thrown from two points lying on the same horizontal plane separated by a distance 120 m. Which of the following statement(s) is/are correct?

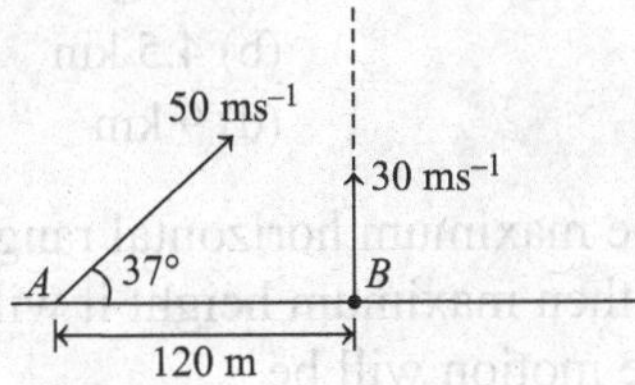

(a) The two balls can never meet
(b) The balls can meet if the ball B is thrown 1 s later
(c) The two balls meet at a height of 45 m
(d) None of the above

17. **Statement I** The projectile hits the ground with the same speed with which it was thrown.
Statement II The projectile hits the ground with the same velocity with which it was thrown.
In the light of above statements, choose the most approprite answer from options given below.
(a) Both Statement I and Statement II are correct.
(b) Both Statement I and Statement II are incorrect.
(c) Statement I is correct but Statement II is incorrect.
(d) Statement I is incorrect but Statement II is correct.

18. A stone is just released from the window of a train moving along a horizontal straight track. As seen from ground, the stone will follow
(a) straight path
(b) circular path
(c) parabolic path
(d) hyperbolic path

19. Figure shows four paths for a kicked football. Ignoring the effects of air on the flight, rank the paths according to initial horizontal velocity component highest first.

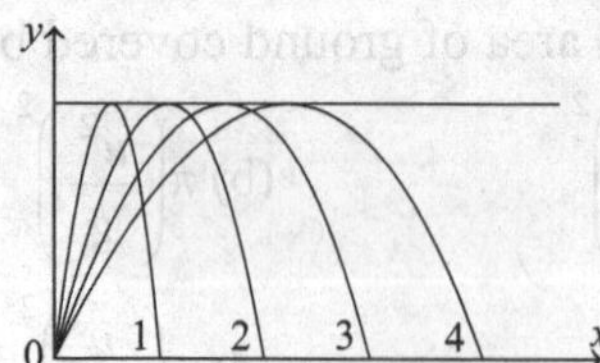

(a) 1, 2, 3, 4 (b) 2, 3, 4, 1
(c) 3, 4, 1, 2 (d) 4, 3, 2, 1

20. The range of a projectile, when thrown at an angle of 15° from the horizontal is 1.5 km. When thrown at angle of 45°, its range will be
(a) 3 km (b) 4.5 km
(c) 6 km (d) 9 km

21. If R is the maximum horizontal range for a particle, then maximum height it will reach during projectile motion will be
(a) R (b) $\frac{R}{2}$
(c) $2R$ (d) $\frac{R}{4}$

22. A particle is thrown with velocity u at an angle α from the horizontal. Another particle is thrown with the same velocity at an angle α from the vertical. The ratio of times of flight of two particles will be
(a) $\tan 2\alpha : 1$ (b) $\cot 2\alpha : 1$
(c) $\tan \alpha : 1$ (d) $\cot \alpha : 1$

23. A particles is moving with velocity $\mathbf{v} = k(y\hat{\mathbf{i}} + x\hat{\mathbf{j}})$, where k is a constant. The general equation for its path is
(a) $y = x^2$ + constant
(b) $y^2 = x$ + constant
(c) xy = constant
(d) $y^2 = x^2$ + constant

24. A ball is thrown from a point with a speed v_0 at an angle of projection θ. From the same point and the same instant, a person starts running with a constant speed $\frac{v_0}{2}$ to catch the ball. Will the person be able to catch the ball? If yes, what should be the angle of projection?
(a) Yes, 60° (b) Yes, 30°
(c) No (d) Yes, 45°

25. From the top of a tower at height h, a particle is projected horizontally with velocity u and another particle is thrown down with the same velocity u. If the time taken by these be t_1 and t_2, then
(a) $t_1 > t_2$ (b) $t_1 < t_2$
(c) $t_1 = t_2$ (d) $t_1 = 2t_2$

26. A gun is aimed at a target in a line of its barrel. The target is released and allowed to fall under gravity at the same instant the gun is fired. The bullet will
(a) pass above the target
(b) pass below the target
(c) hit the target
(d) certainty miss the target

27. It is possible to project a particle on a level ground with a given velocity in two possible ways so as to have the same range R. The product of corresponding times of flight is

(a) $\frac{R}{2g}$ (b) $\frac{2R}{g}$

(c) $\frac{R}{4g}$ (d) $\frac{4R}{g}$

28. The equation of motion of a projectile are given $x = 36t$ metre and $2y = 96t - 9.8t^2$ metre. The angle of projection is

(a) $\sin^{-1}\left(\frac{4}{5}\right)$ (b) $\sin^{-1}\left(\frac{3}{5}\right)$

(c) $\sin^{-1}\left(\frac{4}{3}\right)$ (d) $\sin^{-1}\left(\frac{3}{4}\right)$

29. When an object is shot from the bottom of a long smooth inclined plane kept at an angle 60° with horizontal, it can travel a distance x_1 along the plane. But when the inclination is decreased to 30° and the same object is shot with the same velocity, it can travel x_2 distance. Then, $x_1 : x_2$ will be

(a) $\sqrt{2}:1$ (b) $1:\sqrt{3}$

(c) $1:2\sqrt{3}$ (d) $1:\sqrt{2}$

30. For angles of projection of a projectile $(45° - \theta)$ and $(45° + \theta)$, the horizontal ranges described by the projectile are in the ratio of (both are projected with same speed)

(a) 1 : 3 (b) 1 : 2

(c) 2 :1 (d) 1 : 1

31. A particle moving with velocity of 4 m/s is subjected to an acceleration of 1.5 m/s^2 for 2 s, in a direction at right angles to its initial direction of motion. The magnitude of its resultant velocity will be

(a) 4 m/s (b) 5 m/s

(c) 8 m/s (d) 10 m/s

32. The trajectory of a projectile near the surface of the earth is given as $y = 2x - 9x^2$.
If it were launched at an angle θ_0 with speed v_0, then (Take, $g = 10\text{ ms}^{-2}$)

(a) $\theta_0 = \sin^{-1}\left(\frac{1}{\sqrt{5}}\right)$ and $v_0 = \frac{5}{3}\text{ ms}^{-1}$

(b) $\theta_0 = \cos^{-1}\left(\frac{2}{\sqrt{5}}\right)$ and $v_0 = \frac{3}{5}\text{ ms}^{-1}$

(c) $\theta_0 = \cos^{-1}\left(\frac{1}{\sqrt{5}}\right)$ and $v_0 = \frac{5}{3}\text{ ms}^{-1}$

(d) $\theta_0 = \sin^{-1}\left(\frac{2}{\sqrt{5}}\right)$ and $v_0 = \frac{3}{5}\text{ ms}^{-1}$

33. A projectile is projected with velocity of 25 m/s at an angle θ with the horizontal. After t seconds its inclination with horizontal becomes zero. If R represents horizontal range of the projectile, the value of θ will be [use, $g = 10\text{ m/s}^2$]

(a) $\frac{1}{2}\sin^{-1}\left(\frac{5t^2}{4R}\right)$ (b) $\frac{1}{2}\sin^{-1}\left(\frac{4R}{5t^2}\right)$

(c) $\tan^{-1}\left(\frac{4t^2}{5R}\right)$ (d) $\cot^{-1}\left(\frac{R}{20t^2}\right)$

34. A particle reaches its highest point when it has covered exactly one half of its horizontal range. The corresponding point on the path of its motion is characterised by

(a) negative slope and zero curvature

(b) zero slope and negative curvature

(c) zero slope and positive curvature

(d) positive slope and zero curvature

35. The position of a particle is given $\mathbf{r} = 3t\hat{\mathbf{i}} + 2t^2\hat{\mathbf{j}} + 5\hat{\mathbf{k}}$, where t is in seconds. Find the magnitude of velocity at $t = 1$ s.

(a) 3 m/s

(b) 7 m/s

(c) 5 m/s

(d) 10 m/s

36. A hiker stands on the edge of a cliff 490 m above the ground and throws a stone horizontally with an initial speed of 15 m/s. Neglecting air resistance, find (i) the time taken by the stone to reach the ground and (ii) speed by which it will strike the ground.

(a) 5 s, 99 m/s

(b) 10 s, 99 m/s

(c) 12 s, 90 m/s

(d) 8 s, 80 m/s

37. A cyclist starts from the centre O of a circular park of radius 1 km, reaches the edge P of the park, then cycles along the circumference and returns to the centre along QO as shown in figure.

If the round trip takes 10 min, what is the net displacement and average speed (in m and km/h)?

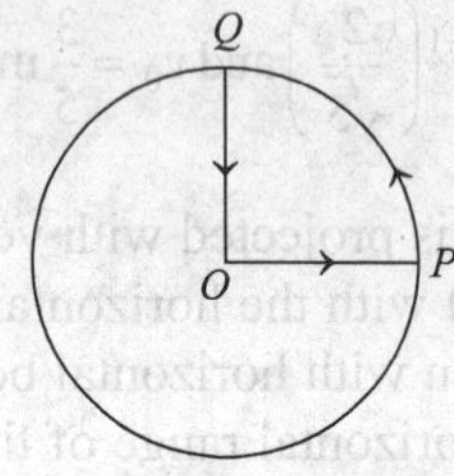

(a) 0, 1

(b) $\frac{\pi+4}{2}$, 0

(c) 21.4, $\frac{\pi+4}{2}$

(d) 0, 21.4

38. In a two dimensional motion, instantaneous speed v_0 is a positive constant. Then, which of the following are necessarily true?

(a) The average velocity is not zero at any time interval.

(b) Average acceleration must always vanish.

(c) Displacements in equal time intervals are equal.

(d) Equal path lengths are travelled in equal intervals.

39. A girl riding a bicycle with speed of 5 m/s towards north direction, observes rain falling vertically down. If she increases her speed to 10 m/s, rain appears to meet her at 45° to the vertical. What is the speed of the rain? In what direction does rain fall as observed by a ground based observer?

(a) $3\sqrt{2}$ m/s at 45° with vertical

(b) $5\sqrt{2}$ m/s at 60° with vertical

(c) $3\sqrt{2}$ m/s at 60° with vertical

(d) $5\sqrt{2}$ m/s at 45° with vertical

40. Two particles of same mass are projected in air with speed v_0 at angles θ_1 and θ_2, to the horizontal, respectively. If the height reached by the first particle is greater than that of the second, then mark incorrect choices.

(a) Angle of projection $\theta_1 > \theta_2$

(b) Time of flight $T_1 > T_2$

(c) Horizontal range $R_1 = R_2$

(d) Total energy $U_1 = U_2$

41. A ball is thrown from a roof top at an angle of 45° from the horizontal. It hits the ground a few seconds later, then during the motion,

(a) speed will be maximum at point of strike with ground

(b) speed will be maximum at highest point of path

(c) acceleration will not be constant

(d) acceleration will be minimum at highest point

42. A river is flowing due east with a speed 3m/s. A swimmer can swim in still water at a speed of 4 m/s. If swimmer starts swimming due north, what will be his resultant velocity (magnitude and direction)?

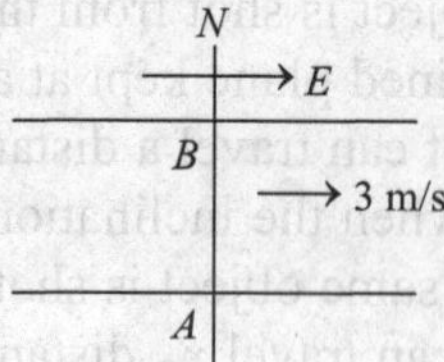

(a) 5 m/s, at 37° to N

(b) $\sqrt{7}$ m/s, at 37° to N

(c) 5 m/s, at 53° to N

(d) $\sqrt{7}$ n/s, at 53° to N

43. A body is projected with velocity u so that its horizontal range is twice the greatest height attained. The value of range is

(a) $\frac{3u^2}{4g}$

(b) $\frac{4u^2}{5g}$

(c) $\frac{4u^2}{3g}$

(d) $\frac{5u^2}{3g}$

44. A ball of mass m is thrown vertically up. Another ball of mass 2 m is thrown at an angle θ. If their time of ascents are equal, then the heights attained by them are in the ratio

(a) 1: sec θ

(b) 1 : cos θ

(c) 1 : 1

(d) 1 : θ

45. A body is projected at angle of 30° with horizontal. It's initial kinetic energy is 4 J. Kinetic energy of body at point where it's velocity **v** and acceleration **a** are such that $\mathbf{v} \cdot \mathbf{a} = 0$ will be

(a) 4 J (b) 3 J
(c) 2 J (d) 1 J

46. At maximum height if potential energy and kinetic energy of a projectile are equal, then it's angle of projection is

(a) 30° (b) 45°
(c) 60° (d) 37°

47. Two tall buildings are separated 20 m apart. A ball is thrown horizontally from a window 135 m above the ground in one building, so that it will enter a window 12.5 m above the ground. The ball must be thrown with a velocity of

(a) 8 ms^{-1}
(b) 4 ms^{-1}
(c) 2 ms^{-1}
(d) 1 ms^{-1}

48. At the highest point of the projectile, its velocity and acceleration are

(a) parallel to each other
(b) perpendicular to each other
(c) opposite to each other
(d) None of the above

49. Match the List I with List II.

	List-I		List-II
A.	Constant speed and varying velocity	1.	At highest point of body projected vertically up
B.	Zero displacement and finite distance	2.	Uniform circular motion
C.	Zero velocity and finite acceleration	3.	At any intermediate point of freely falling body
D.	Non-zero velocity and non-zero acceleration	4.	Body on reaching point of projection

	A	B	C	D
(a)	4	2	3	1
(b)	2	4	1	3
(c)	3	1	4	2
(d)	1	3	2	4

50. **Assertion** (A) Only vertical component of velocity of a projectile is known, time of fight can be calculated but horizontal range cannot be calculated.

Reason (R) Time of flight depends on horizontal component and range depends on vertical component of velocity projection.

In the light of above statements, choose the most appropriate answer from the options given below.

(a) Both A and R are correct and R is the correct explanation of A.
(b) Both A and R are correct but R is not the correct explanation of A.
(c) A is true but R is false.
(d) A is false but R is true.

Response Index

01 ⓐ ⓑ ⓒ ⓓ	14 ⓐ ⓑ ⓒ ⓓ	27 ⓐ ⓑ ⓒ ⓓ	40 ⓐ ⓑ ⓒ ⓓ
02 ⓐ ⓑ ⓒ ⓓ	15 ⓐ ⓑ ⓒ ⓓ	28 ⓐ ⓑ ⓒ ⓓ	41 ⓐ ⓑ ⓒ ⓓ
03 ⓐ ⓑ ⓒ ⓓ	16 ⓐ ⓑ ⓒ ⓓ	29 ⓐ ⓑ ⓒ ⓓ	42 ⓐ ⓑ ⓒ ⓓ
04 ⓐ ⓑ ⓒ ⓓ	17 ⓐ ⓑ ⓒ ⓓ	30 ⓐ ⓑ ⓒ ⓓ	43 ⓐ ⓑ ⓒ ⓓ
05 ⓐ ⓑ ⓒ ⓓ	18 ⓐ ⓑ ⓒ ⓓ	31 ⓐ ⓑ ⓒ ⓓ	44 ⓐ ⓑ ⓒ ⓓ
06 ⓐ ⓑ ⓒ ⓓ	19 ⓐ ⓑ ⓒ ⓓ	32 ⓐ ⓑ ⓒ ⓓ	45 ⓐ ⓑ ⓒ ⓓ
07 ⓐ ⓑ ⓒ ⓓ	20 ⓐ ⓑ ⓒ ⓓ	33 ⓐ ⓑ ⓒ ⓓ	46 ⓐ ⓑ ⓒ ⓓ
08 ⓐ ⓑ ⓒ ⓓ	21 ⓐ ⓑ ⓒ ⓓ	34 ⓐ ⓑ ⓒ ⓓ	47 ⓐ ⓑ ⓒ ⓓ
09 ⓐ ⓑ ⓒ ⓓ	22 ⓐ ⓑ ⓒ ⓓ	35 ⓐ ⓑ ⓒ ⓓ	48 ⓐ ⓑ ⓒ ⓓ
10 ⓐ ⓑ ⓒ ⓓ	23 ⓐ ⓑ ⓒ ⓓ	36 ⓐ ⓑ ⓒ ⓓ	49 ⓐ ⓑ ⓒ ⓓ
11 ⓐ ⓑ ⓒ ⓓ	24 ⓐ ⓑ ⓒ ⓓ	37 ⓐ ⓑ ⓒ ⓓ	50 ⓐ ⓑ ⓒ ⓓ
12 ⓐ ⓑ ⓒ ⓓ	25 ⓐ ⓑ ⓒ ⓓ	38 ⓐ ⓑ ⓒ ⓓ	
13 ⓐ ⓑ ⓒ ⓓ	26 ⓐ ⓑ ⓒ ⓓ	39 ⓐ ⓑ ⓒ ⓓ	

Performance Scanner

> 90% Excellent !	You have mastered this chapter. The concepts of this chapter are on your fingertips. Move on to the next chapter and maintain this momentum.
76-90% Very Good !	You have a good command over this chapter. Revise the chapter again after a few days and enhance your performance.
60-75% Good !	You have a wide scope to learn more from this chapter. Revise this chapter again.
<60% Not Satisfactory!	You have a long way ahead of you to master this chapter. Revise it thoroughly.

For Online Chapter Test **Scan the QR Code**

For Online Unit Test **Scan the QR Code**

Space for Rough Work

Test Booklet No. **3947104**

Test Booklet Code **CH4**

MEDACE

NEET (UG)

SELF ASSESSMENT KIT

Laws of Motion

Topics Covered

- Newton's Laws of Motion and Conservation of Momentum
- Equilibrium of Common Forces and Motion of Connected Bodies
- Friction and Circular Motion

Important Instructions

- This Booklet Contains – Three Topic Tests and One Test on Complete Chapter.
- Each question carries 4 Marks.
- For each correct response, the candidate will get 4 marks and for every incorrect response, 1 mark will be additionally deducted from total score.
- Use **Blue/Black** point pen only for filling the OMR.
- Rough work is to be done in the space provided for this purpose in the test booklet only.

Name of the Candidate (In Capitals) ______________________

____

Candidate's Signature ______________________

Invigilator's Signature ______________________

Facsimile signature stamp of center superintendent ______________________

Do not open this Booklet until you start attempting the Test

Topical Follow Thru

Test 1

Syllabus

- Force and Inertia, Newton's First Law of Motion
- Momentum & Newton's Second Law of Motion
- Impulse, Newton's Third Law of Motion & Law of Conservation of Momentum and its Applications

For deeper insight **Scan the QR Code**

Important Instructions

- The test is of 45 minutes duration and contains 25 Multiple Choice Questions. (Four options with a single correct answer).
- Choose the correct option and fill the OMR given on the last page of this test accordingly.
- At some instances, you may find more than 1 option may be correct, in such circumstances you have to judge the most appropriate answer as per conditions given in the question.

1. A body of mass 8 kg is accelerated upon by a constant force, travel a distance of 5 m in the first second and a distance of 3 m in the third second. The force acting on the body is

(a) 6 N (b) 8 N
(c) N (d) 4 N

2. A particle is moving with a constant speed along a straight line path. A force is not required to

(a) increase its speed
(b) decrease the momentum
(c) change its direction
(d) keep it moving with uniform velocity

3. The momenta of a body in two perpendicular directions at any time t are given by $p_x = 2t^2 + 6$ and $p_y = \frac{3t^2}{2} + 3$. The force acting on the body at $t = 3$ s is

(a) 15 units
(b) 10 units
(c) 20 units
(d) 5 units

4. A rocket with initial mass of 8000 kg ejects mass at a constant rate of 10 kg s^{-1} with a relative speed of 10 km/s vertically downward. The initial acceleration of the rocket is

(a) 2.5 ms^{-2} (b) 1.5 ms^{-2}
(c) 3 ms^{-2} (d) 4 ms^{-2}

5. If a bullet of mass 8 g moving with velocity 100 m/s, penetrates the wooden block upto 9 cm, then the average force imposed by the bullet on the block is

(a) 8300 N (b) 444.4 N
(c) 830 N (d) zero

6. A particle of mass 0.8 kg starting at origin at $t = 0$ with a speed of 10 m/s in the positive x-direction is subjected to a constant force $F = 8$ N towards the negative x-direction. The position of the particle after 25 s is

(a) −2875 m (b) −8000 m
(c) 4000 m (d) 6000 m

7. A particle of 2 kg strikes a wall with a velocity of 4 m/s at an angle of 60° with the normal of the wall. The particle reflects at the same angle. If it remain in contact with wall for 0.1s, then the force is

(a) 60 N (b) 80 N
(c) 100 N (d) $60\sqrt{2}$ N

8. A body of mass 5 kg starts from rest and a force is acting on the body as shown in figure. The speed of the body after 4 s is

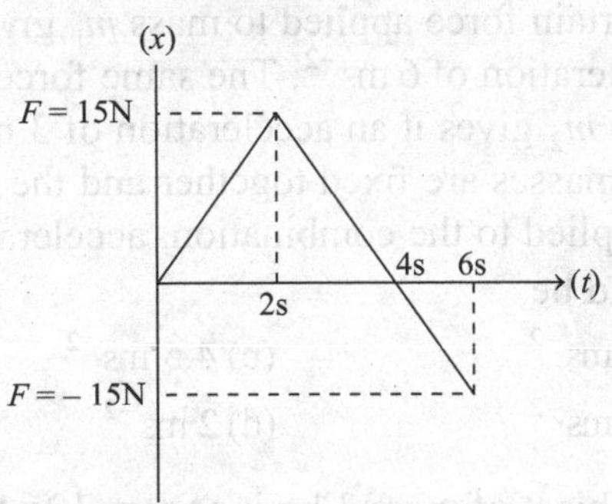

(a) 5 ms^{-1} (b) 3 ms^{-1}
(c) 6 ms^{-1} (d) 10 ms^{-1}

9. In an air collision between an aeroplane and a crow, the force experiened by the crow as compared to that of the aeroplane is
(a) very high (b) equal
(c) less (d) zero

10. A train is moving with velocity 20 m/s on which dust is falling at the rate of 50 kg/min. The extra force required to move this train with constant velocity will be
(a) 16.66 N (b) 1000 N
(c) 166.6 N (d) 1200 N

11. Sand is being dropped on a conveyer belt at the rate of $2M$ kg per second. The force necessary to keep the belt moving with a velocity of $2v$ m/s will be
(a) 4 Mv N (b) Mv N
(c) 2Mv N (d) zero

12. A bullet of mass 5 g is moving with velocity 100 m/s, penetrates the wooden block upto 6 cm. The average force imposed by the bullet on the block is
(a) 8300 N (b) 417 N
(c) 830 N (d) zero

13. The linear momentum p of a body moving in one-dimension varies with time according to the equation $p = a + bt^2$, where a and b are positive constants. The net force acting on the body is
(a) proportional to t^2
(b) a constant
(c) proportional to t
(d) inversely proportional to t

14. A vehicle of 100 kg is moving with a velocity of 5 m/s. To stop it in $\frac{1}{10}$ s, the required force in opposite direction is
(a) 5000 N (b) 500 N
(c) 50 N (d) 1000 N

15. A 100 g iron ball having velocity 10 m/s collides with a wall at an angle 30° and rebounds with the same speed at same angle. If the period of contact between the ball and wall is 0.1 s, then the force experienced by the wall is
(a) 10 N (b) 100 N
(c) 1.0 N (d) 0.1 N

16. A man of mass 90 kg is standing in an elevator whose cable broke suddenly. If the elevator falls, apparent weight of the man is
(a) 90 N
(b) 90 gN
(c) 0 N
(d) Any negative value

17. A particle moving with velocity v is acted by three forces shown by the vector triangle PQR. The velocity of the particle will

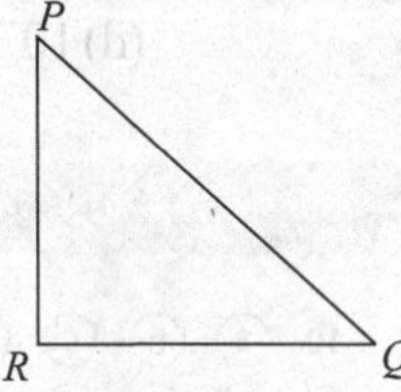

(a) increase
(b) decrease
(c) remain constant
(d) change according to the smallest force QR

18. An object with a mass 10 kg moves at a constant velocity of 10 m/s. A constant force then acts for 4 s on the object and gives it a speed of 2 m/s in opposite direction. The acceleration produced in it is
(a) 3 m/s^2 (b) –3 m/s^2
(c) 0.3 m/s^2 (d) –0.3 m/s^2

19. A player takes 0.1 s in catching a ball of mass 150 g moving with velocity of 20 m/s. The force imparted by the ball on the hands of the player is

(a) 0.3 N (b) 3 N
(c) 30 N (d) 300 N

20. Two bodies with kinetic energies in the ratio 4 : 1 are moving with equal linear momentum. The ratio of their masses is

(a) 1:2 (b) 1:1
(c) 4:1 (d) 1:4

21. A hammer with a head of mass M is to be used to drive nails horizontally into a wall. A force of F is required to penetrate the wall. Each blow should force the nail a distance x into the wall. What should be the velocity of the hammer's head to strike the nail?

(a) $\sqrt{\frac{Fx}{M}}$ (b) $\sqrt{\frac{Fx}{2M}}$
(c) $\sqrt{\frac{2Fx}{M}}$ (d) $\sqrt{\frac{2M}{Fx}}$

22. A ball of mass 250 g is moving with a speed of 2 ms^{-1} hits a wall normally. It rebounds with the same speed. If the two were in contact for 10^{-3} s, the average force exerted by the wall on the ball is

(a) 4×10^{-3} N (b) 2×10^{-3} N
(c) 10^{3} N (d) 10^{-2} N

23. A certain force applied to mass m_1 gives it an acceleration of 6 ms^{-2}. The same force applied to mass m_2 gives it an acceleration of 3 ms^{-2}. If the two masses are fixed together and the same force is applied to the combination, acceleration of it would be

(a) 9 ms^{-2} (b) 4.5 ms^{-2}
(c) 3 ms^{-2} (d) 2 ms^{-2}

24. An object of mass 3 kg is at rest. If a force $F=(6t^2\hat{i}+4t\hat{j})$ N is applied on the object, then the velocity of the object at $t=3$ s is

(a) $18\hat{i}+3\hat{j}$
(b) $18\hat{i}+6\hat{j}$
(c) $3\hat{i}+18\hat{j}$
(d) $18\hat{i}+4\hat{j}$

25. A particle of mass 1 kg moves along x-direction with a constant velocity 2 ms^{-1}. A force of 2 N is applied on along y-direction. Velocity of the body 4 s after the force is applied is

(a) $\sqrt{34}$ ms^{-1}
(b) $3\sqrt{34}$ ms^{-1}
(c) $4\sqrt{17}$ ms^{-1}
(d) $2\sqrt{17}$ ms^{-1}

Response Index

01	a	b	c	d	10	a	b	c	d	19	a	b	c	d
02	a	b	c	d	11	a	b	c	d	20	a	b	c	d
03	a	b	c	d	12	a	b	c	d	21	a	b	c	d
04	a	b	c	d	13	a	b	c	d	22	a	b	c	d
05	a	b	c	d	14	a	b	c	d	23	a	b	c	d
06	a	b	c	d	15	a	b	c	d	24	a	b	c	d
07	a	b	c	d	16	a	b	c	d	25	a	b	c	d
08	a	b	c	d	17	a	b	c	d					
09	a	b	c	d	18	a	b	c	d					

Performance Scanner

> 90% Excellent !	You have mastered these topics. The concepts of these topics are on your fingertips. Move on to the next test and maintain this momentum.
76-90% Very Good !	You have a good command over these topics. Revise these topics again after a few days and enhance your performance.
60-75% Good !	You have a wide scope to learn for this chapter. Revise these topics again.
<60% Not Satisfactory!	You have a long way ahead of you to master these topics. Revise it thoroughly.

Test 2

Syllabus
- Equilibrium of Concurrent Forces & Lami's Theorem
- Motion of Objects in Contact
- Tension in Strings

For deeper insight **Scan the QR Code**

Important Instructions
- The test is of 30 minutes duration and contains 15 Multiple Choice Questions (Four options with a single correct answer).
- Choose the correct option and fill the OMR given on the last page of this test accordingly.
- At some instances, you may find more than 1 option may be correct, in such circumstances you have to judge the most appropriate answer as per conditions given in the question.

1. An object is kept on a smooth inclined plane of height 1 unit and length l unit. The horizontal acceleration to be imparted to the inclined plane, so that the object is stationary relative to the inclined is

(a) $g\sqrt{l^2-1}$ (b) $g(l^2-1)$

(c) $\frac{g}{\sqrt{l^2-1}}$ (d) $\frac{g}{l^2-1}$

2. The resultant of two forces $3P$ and $2P$ is R. If the first force is doubled, then the resultant is also doubled. The angle between the two forces is

(a) 60° (b) 120°

(c) 70° (d) 180°

3. Statement I If all the forces working on a body are acting on the same point, then they are said to be concurrent.

Statement II In concurrent equilibrium, $\Sigma\mathbf{F}_{net}=0$

or $\Sigma\mathbf{F}_x=0, \Sigma\mathbf{F}_y=0, \Sigma\mathbf{F}_z=0$

Select the most appropriate answer from the options given below.

(a) Both Statement I and Statement II are true.

(b) Both Statement I and Statement II are false.

(c) Statement I is true but Statement II is false.

(d) Statement I is false but Statement II is true.

4. A body of mass 2.0 kg is placed on a smooth horizontal surface. Two forces $F_1=20$ N and $F_2=10\sqrt{3}$N are acting on the body in directions making angles of 30° and 60° to the surface.

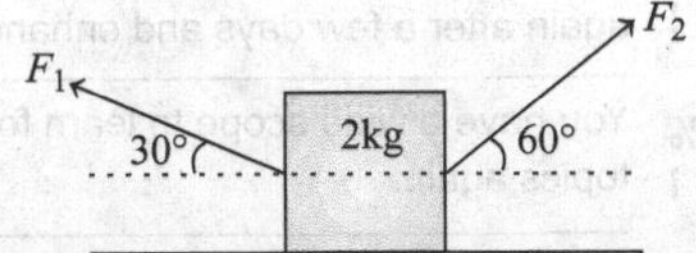

The reaction of the surface on the body will be

(a) 20 N (b) 25 N

(c) 5 N (d) zero

5. If two forces of 5 N each are acting along X and Y-axis, then the magnitude (in N) and direction of resultant is

(a) $-5\sqrt{2}, \frac{\pi}{3}$ (b) $5\sqrt{2}, \frac{\pi}{4}$

(c) $-5\sqrt{2}, \frac{\pi}{5}$ (d) $-5\sqrt{2}, \frac{\pi}{4}$

6. A uniform sphere of weight w having radius 3 m is being held by a string of length 5 m attached to a frictionless wall as shown in the figure. The tension in the string will be

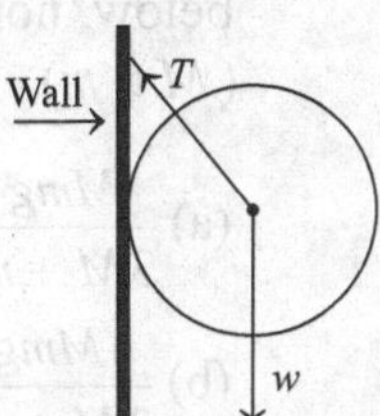

(a) $5w/4$ (b) $18w/5$

(c) $15w/16$ (d) $15w/6$

7. The pulleys and strings shown in the figure are smooth and of negligible mass. For the system to remain in equilibrium, the angle θ should be

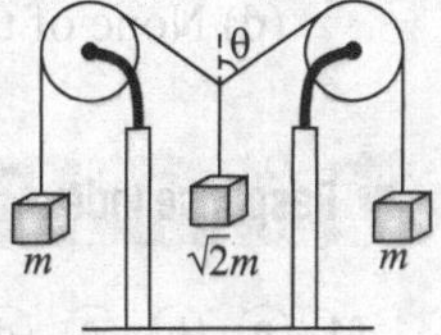

(a) 0° (b) 30°

(c) 45° (d) 60°

8. A mass M of 100 kg is suspended with the use of strings A, B and C as shown in figure, where W is vertical wall and R is a rigid horizontal rod. The tension in string B is

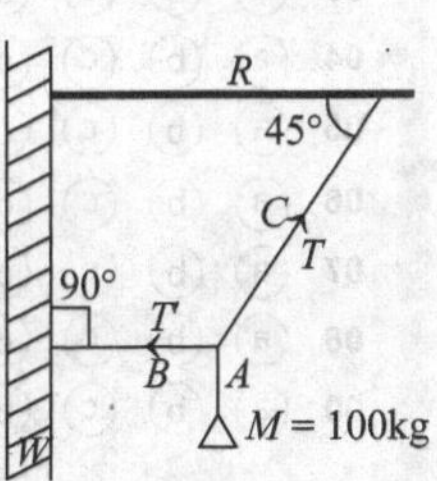

(a) $100\,g$ N
(b) zero
(c) $100\sqrt{2}\,g$ N
(d) $\frac{100}{\sqrt{2}}\,g$ N

9. Which of the following sets of concurrent forces may be in equilibrium
(a) $F_1 = 3\text{N}, F_2 = 5\text{N}, F_3 = 9\text{N}$
(b) $F_1 = 3\text{N}, F_2 = 5\text{N}, F_3 = 1\text{N}$
(c) $F_1 = 3\text{N}, F_2 = 5\text{N}, F_3 = 15\text{N}$
(d) $F_1 = 3\text{N}, F_2 = 5\text{N}, F_3 = 6\text{N}$

10. A smooth cylinder of mass M and radius R is resting on two corner edges A and B as shown in figure. The normal reaction at the edges A and B are related

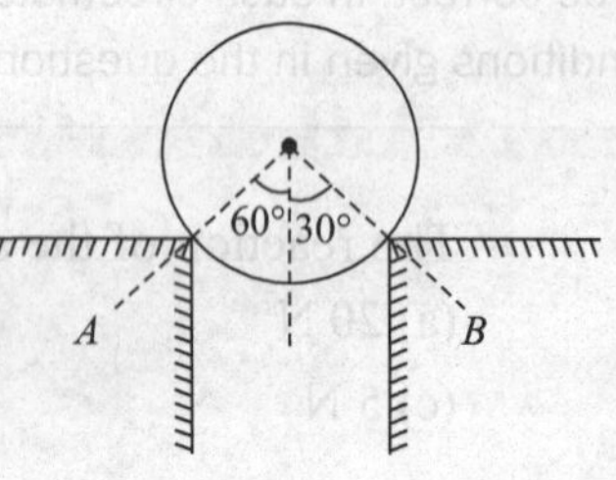

(a) $N_A = \sqrt{2}N_B$
(b) $N_B = \frac{2\sqrt{3}N_A}{5}$
(c) $N_A = \frac{N_B}{2}$
(d) $N_B = \sqrt{3}N_A$

11. In the system shown in the figure below, normal reaction on mass m is $(M > m)$

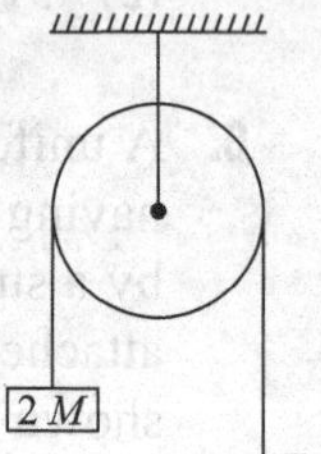

(a) $\frac{Mmg}{3M+m}$
(b) $\frac{4Mmg}{3M+m}$
(c) $\frac{3Mmg}{3M+m}$
(d) None of the above

12. Two masses 2 kg and 3 kg are attached to the end of a string passing over a pulley fixed at the top. The tension and acceleration are
(a) $\frac{7g}{8}; \frac{g}{8}$
(b) $\frac{21g}{8}; \frac{g}{8}$
(c) $\frac{21g}{8}; \frac{g}{5}$
(d) $\frac{12g}{5}; \frac{g}{5}$

13. A balloon is descending with a constant acceleration $g/8$. The mass of the balloon and its contents is M. What mass m of its contents should be released, so that the balloon starts ascending with the same acceleration? (Assume the volume of balloon as same)
(a) $2M/3$
(b) $2M/6$
(c) $2M/9$
(d) $2M/7$

14. A block of mass 2 kg is pulled by a force of 4N applied to the pulley as shown in the figure. The acceleration of the block and tension in the string (if it is massless) are

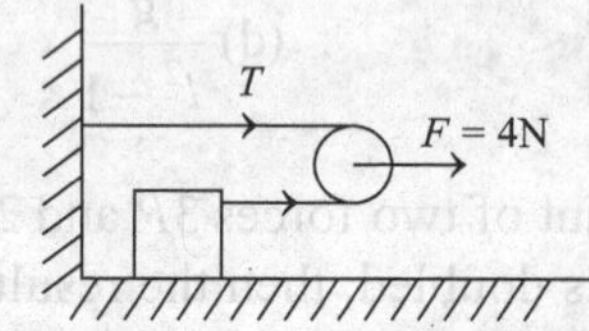

(a) 1 ms^{-2}, 4N
(b) 2 ms^{-2}, 2N
(c) 2 ms^{-2}, 4N
(d) 1 ms^{-2}, 2N

15. The minimum acceleration with which a person can slide down a rope whose breaking strength is 60% of his weight, is
(a) $g/5$
(b) $3g/5$
(c) $2g/5$
(d) $4g/5$

Response Index

01	a	b	c	d	10	a	b	c	d
02	a	b	c	d	11	a	b	c	d
03	a	b	c	d	12	a	b	c	d
04	a	b	c	d	13	a	b	c	d
05	a	b	c	d	14	a	b	c	d
06	a	b	c	d	15	a	b	c	d
07	a	b	c	d					
08	a	b	c	d					
09	a	b	c	d					

Performance Scanner

> 90% Excellent !	You have mastered these topics. The concepts of these topics are on your fingertips. Move on to the next test and maintain this momentum.
76-90% Very Good !	You have a good command over these topics. Revise these topics again after a few days and enhance your performance.
60-75% Good !	You have a wide scope to learn for these topics. Revise these topics again.
<60% Not Satisfactory!	You have a long way ahead of you to master these topics. Revise it thoroughly.

Test 3

Syllabus

- Static and Kinetic Friction, Laws of Friction and Rolling Friction
- Dynamics of Uniform Circular Motion
- Vehicle on a Level Circular Road
- Vehicle on a Banked Road
- Centripetal Force & Its Applications

For deeper insight **Scan the QR Code**

Important Instructions

- The test is of 45 minutes duration and contains 25 Multiple Choice Questions (Four options with a single correct answer).
- Choose the correct option and fill the OMR given on the last page of this test accordingly.
- At some instances, you may find more than 1 option may be correct, in such circumstances you have to judge the most appropriate answer as per conditions given in the question.

1. A boy of mass 80 kg is climbing a vertical pole at a constant speed. If the coefficient of friction between his palms and the pole is 0.8 and $g = 10\text{ m/s}^2$, the horizontal force that he is applying on the pole is

(a) 300 N (b) 400 N (c) 1000 N (d) 600 N

2. A uniform metal chain is placed on rough table, such that one end of chain hangs down over the edge of the table. When one-sixth of its length hanges over the edge, the chain starts sliding. The coefficient of static friction is

(a) $\frac{3}{4}$ (b) $\frac{1}{4}$

(c) $\frac{2}{3}$ (d) $\frac{1}{5}$

3. A lift is moving downwards with an acceleration equal to acceleration due to gravity. A body of mass m kept on the floor of the lift is pulled horizontally. If the coefficient of friction is μ, then the frictional resistance offered by the body is

(a) mg (b) μmg

(c) $2\mu mg$ (d) zero

4. A book of mass m is placed on a surface with vertical cross-section given by $y = \frac{x^3}{6}$. If the coefficient of friction is 0.5, the maximum height above the ground at which the book can be placed without slipping is

(a) (1/6) m (b) (2/3) m

(c) (1/3) m (d) (1/2) m

5. A mass of 1 kg is held against a wall by applying a force F perpendicular to the wall. If $\mu = 0.2$, then minimum value of F will be

(a) 980 N (b) 49 N

(c) 98 N (d) 490 N

6. **Assertion (A)** Static friction is a self-adjusting force.

Reason (R) Friction does not depend upon normal force on the body.

Select the most appropriate answer from the options given below.

(a) Both A and R are true and R is a correct explanation of A.

(b) Both A and R are true but R is not a correct explanation of A.

(c) A is true and R is false.

(d) A is false and R is true.

7. **Statement I** Use of ball bearings between two moving parts of machine is a common practice.

Statement II Ball bearings reduce vibrations and provide good stability.

Select the most appropriate answer from the options given below.

(a) Both Statement I and Statement II are true.

(b) Both Statement I and Statement II are false.

(c) Statement I is true but Statement II false.

(d) Statement I is false but Statement II is true.

8. A block of mass m which weight w, is held against a vertical wall by applying a horizontal force F. The minimum value of F needed to hold the block is
(a) less than w
(b) equal to w
(c) greater than w
(d) Data insufficient

9. An insect crawls up a hemisphere surface very slowly. The coefficient of friction between the insect and the surface is $\frac{1}{3}$. If the line joining the centre of the hemisphere surface to the insect makes an angle α with vertical, what will be the maximum value of α?

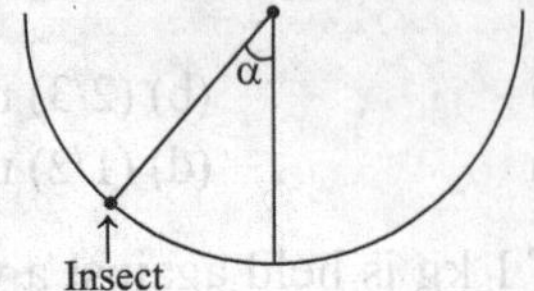

(a) $\cot \alpha = 3$
(b) $\tan \alpha = 3$
(c) $\sec \alpha = 3$
(d) $\text{cosec}\ \alpha = 3$

10. A block is lying static on the floor. The maximum value of static frictional force on the block is 20 N. If a horizontal force of 12 N is applied to the block, then the frictional force on the block will be
(a) 2N (b) 18N
(c) 12N (d) 10N

11. A marble block of mass 2 kg lying on ice when given a velocity of 6 m/s is stopped by a friction force in 10 s. The coefficient of friction is
(a) 0.02
(b) 0.03
(c) 0.06
(d) 0.3

12. Pulling force making an angle θ to the horizontal is applied on a block of weight w placed on a horizontal table. If the angle of friction is α, then the magnitude of force required to move the body is equal to
(a) $\frac{w\sin\alpha}{g\tan(\theta-\alpha)}$ (b) $\frac{w\cos\alpha}{\cos(\theta-\alpha)}$
(c) $\frac{w\sin\alpha}{\cos(\theta-\alpha)}$ (d) $\frac{w\tan\alpha}{\sin(\theta-\alpha)}$

13. If mass, speed and radius of rotation of a body moving on a circular path are increased by 60%, then to keep the body moving in a circular path, increase in the force required will be
(a) 256% (b) 156%
(c) 356% (d) 226%

14. A coin is placed on a disc. The coefficient of friction between the coin and the disc is μ. If the distance of the coin from the centre of the disc is r, the maximum angular velocity which can be given to the disc, so that the coin does not slip away, is
(a) $\sqrt{r/\mu g}$ (b) $\mu/\sqrt{rg}$
(c) $\mu g/r$ (d) $\sqrt{\mu g/r}$

15. A child of mass 5 kg is going round a merry-go-round that makes 1 rotation in 3.14 s. The radius of the merry-go-round is 2 m. The centrifugal force on the child will be
(a) 40 N (b) 100 N (c) 80 N (d) 50 N

16. A national roadways bridge over a canal is in the form of an arc of a circle of radius 49 m. The maximum speed with which a car can move without leaving the ground at highest point
(a) 19.6 m/s (b) 40 m/s
(c) 22 m/s (d) 70 m/s

17. A stone of mass 16 kg is tied to a string of 144 m long and it is whirled in a horizontal circle. The maximum tension the string can withstand is 16 N. The maximum velocity of revolution that can be given to the stone without breaking, will be
(a) 20 m/s (b) 16 m/s
(c) 14 m/s (d) 12 m/s

18. A particle of mass m is executing uniform circular motion on a path of radius r. If p is the magnitude of its linear momentum, the radial force acting on the particle is
(a) pmr (b) $\frac{rm}{p}$
(c) $\frac{mp^2}{r}$ (d) $\frac{p^2}{rm}$

19. A toy cart tied to the end of an unstretched string of length a, when revolved, moves in a horizontal circle of radius $2a$ with time period T. Now, the toy cart is speeded up until it moves a horizontal circle of radius $3a$ with a period T. If Hooke's law ($f = kx$) holds, then

(a) $T' = \sqrt{\frac{3}{2}}T$ (b) $T' = \left(\frac{\sqrt{3}}{2}\right)T$

(c) $T' = \left(\frac{3}{2}\right)T$ (d) $T' = T$

20. A block of mass m is pressed against a vertical wall by applying a force P at an angle θ to the horizontal as shown in figure. As a result, if that block is prevented from falling down and μ is coefficient of static friction between the block and the wall, the value of P is

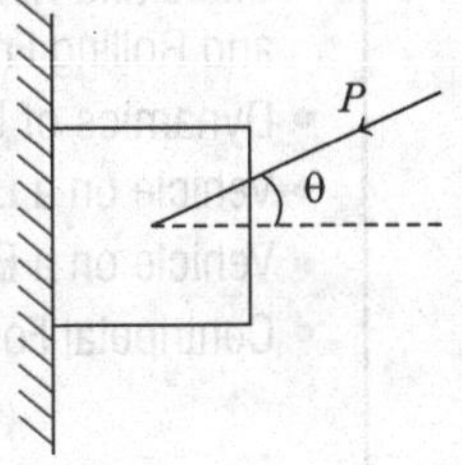

(a) $\frac{mg}{(\mu \sin\theta - \cos\theta)}$ (b) $\frac{mg}{(\mu \sin\theta + \cos\theta)}$

(c) $\frac{mg}{(\mu \cos\theta - \sin\theta)}$ (d) $\frac{mg}{(\mu \cos\theta + \sin\theta)}$

21. A smooth block is released at rest in a 45° inclination and slides to a distance of d. The time taken to slide down smooth incline is in n times as much to slide down a rough incline. The coefficient of friction is

(a) $\mu_k = 1 - \frac{1}{n^2}$ (b) $\mu_s = \sqrt{1 - \frac{1}{n^2}}$

(c) $\mu_s = 1 - \frac{1}{n^2}$ (d) $\mu_k = \sqrt{1 - \frac{1}{n^2}}$

22. A uniform chain hangs partly from the edge of a table. As a result, the remaining part on the table is in equilibrium. If $(1/n)$ th of the total length of the chain hangs down without sliding, coefficient of static friction between chain and table is

(a) $\frac{1}{n+1}$ (b) $\frac{1}{n-1}$

(c) $\frac{n}{n+1}$ (d) $\frac{n}{n-1}$

23. The coefficient of friction between an insect and bowl is μ and the radius of the bowl is r. The maximum height to which the insect can crawl in the bowl is

(a) $r\left(1 - \frac{1}{\sqrt{\mu^2+1}}\right)$ (b) $\frac{r}{\sqrt{\mu^2+1}}$

(c) $\frac{1}{\sqrt{\mu^2+1}}$ (d) r

24. A body of mass 1 kg lies on an inclined plane of angle 60° to the horizontal. If the coefficient of friction is 0.4, the frictional force along the inclined plane is

(a) 1.96 N (b) 0.98 N

(c) 0.49 N (d) 0.245 N

25. Match the List I with List II.

List I	List II
A. Friction is a	1. 0 and $\mu_k R$
B. Friction force is independent of	2. area of surface in contact
C. The value of static friction force lies between	3. non-conservative force
D. Magnitude of static friction is always greater than	4. kinetic friction

Codes

(a) A-3, B-2, C-1, D-4

(b) A-2, B-3, C-1, D-4

(c) A-4, B-3, C-1, D-2

(d) A-1, B-2, C-4, D-3

Response Index

01	a	b	c	d	10	a	b	c	d	19	a	b	c	d
02	a	b	c	d	11	a	b	c	d	20	a	b	c	d
03	a	b	c	d	12	a	b	c	d	21	a	b	c	d
04	a	b	c	d	13	a	b	c	d	22	a	b	c	d
05	a	b	c	d	14	a	b	c	d	23	a	b	c	d
06	a	b	c	d	15	a	b	c	d	24	a	b	c	d
07	a	b	c	d	16	a	b	c	d	25	a	b	c	d
08	a	b	c	d	17	a	b	c	d					
09	a	b	c	d	18	a	b	c	d					

Performance Scanner

> 90% Excellent !	You have mastered these topics. The concepts of these topics are on your fingertips. Move on to the next test and maintain this momentum.
76-90% Very Good !	You have a good command over these topics. Revise these topics again after a few days and enhance your performance.
60-75% Good !	You have a wide scope to learn for these topics. Revise these topics again.
<60% Not Satisfactory!	You have a long way ahead of you to master these topics. Revise it thoroughly.

Chapter Break Thru

Syllabus

- Force and Inertia, Newton's First Law of Motion
- Momentum & Newton's Second Law of Motion
- Impulse, Newton's Third Law of Motion & Law of Conservation of Momentum and its Applications
- Equilibrium of Concurrent Forces & Lami's Theorem
- Motion of Objects in Contact
- Tension in Strings
- Static and Kinetic Friction, Laws of Friction and Rolling Friction
- Dynamics of Uniform Circular Motion
- Vehicle on a Level Circular Road
- Vehicle on a Banked Road
- Centripetal Force & Its Applications

Important Instructions

- The test is of 1 hour duration and contains 50 Multiple Choice Questions (Four options with a single correct answer).
- Choose the correct option and fill the OMR given on the last page of this test accordingly.
- At some instances, you may find more than 1 option may be correct in such circumstances you have to judge the most appropriate answer as per the conditions given in the question.

1. A block of mass 10 kg is suspended by three strings as shown in the figure, the tension T_2 is

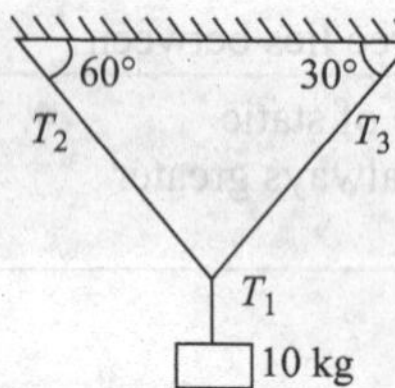

(a) 100 N (b) $\frac{100}{\sqrt{3}}$ N

(c) $\sqrt{3} \times 100$ N (d) $50\sqrt{3}$ N

2. Three blocks are placed at rest on a smooth inclined plane with force acting on m_1, parallel to the inclined plane. Then, the contact force between m_2 and m_3 is

(a) $\frac{(m_1 + m_2 + m_3)F}{m_3}$

(b) $\frac{m_3 F}{m_1 + m_2 + m_3}$

(c) $F - (m_1 + m_2)g$

(d) None of these

3. Four forces act on a point object, the object will be in equilibrium, if

(a) all of them are in the same plane

(b) they are opposite to each other in pairs

(c) the sum of x and y components of forces is zero

(d) they form a cyclic closed figure of 4 sides

4. A toy train consists of three identical compartment A, B and C. It is being pulled by a constant force F along C. The ratio of the tension in the string connecting AB and BC is

(a) 2:1 (b) 1:3 (c) 1:1 (d) 1:2

5. A body of mass 250 g falling in air with an acceleration 9.2 m/s^2. The frictional force on the body due to air resistance will be

(a) 0.05 N (b) 0.15 N

(c) 0.25 N (d) 0.35 N

6. A particle of mass m is in rest at the origin at time $t = 0$, it is subjected to a force $f(t) = F_0 e^{-bt}$ in the x-direction. Its speed $v(t)$ is depicted by which of the following curves?

(a) 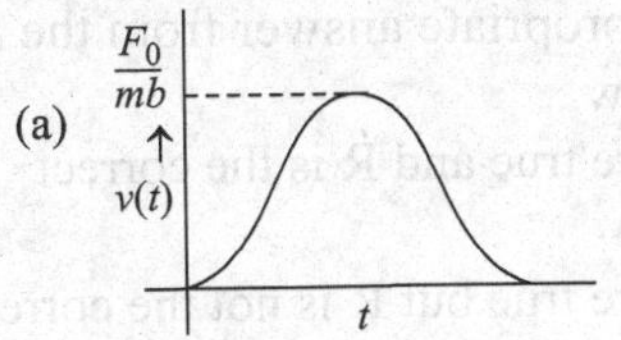

(b) 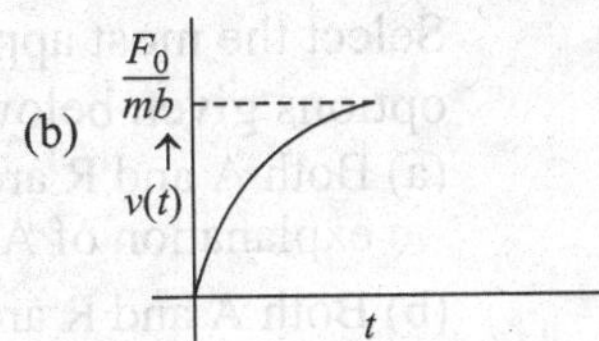

(c) 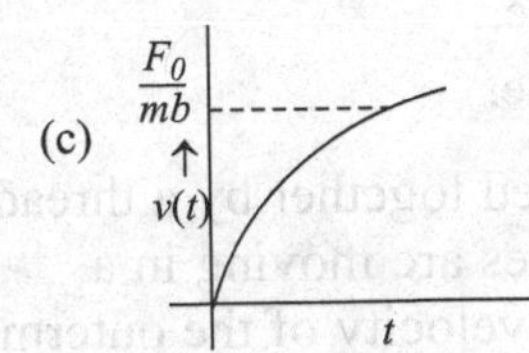

(d) 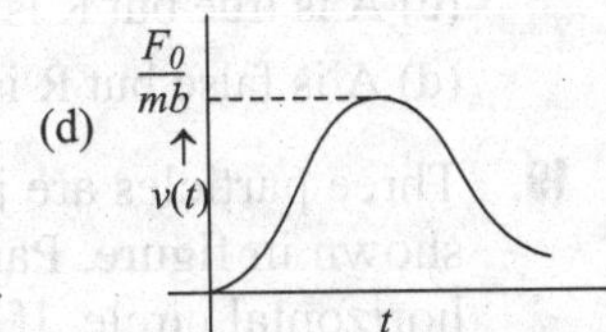

7. An aeroplane of mass M requires a speed v for take-off. The length of the runway is l and the coefficient of friction between runway and the tyres is μ. Assuming that the plane accelerates uniformly during the take-off, the minimum force required by the engine of the plane for take-off is

(a) $M\left(\mu g + \frac{v^2}{2l}\right)$ (b) $M\left(g + \frac{\mu v^2}{2l}\right)$

(c) $M\left(\mu g + \frac{v^2}{2\mu l}\right)$ (d) $M\left(g + \frac{v^2}{2\mu l}\right)$

8. A light rope passing over a smooth light pulley connects two blocks of masses m_1 and m_2. If the acceleration of the system is $g/8$, then the ratio of the masses is

(a) 8 : 1 (b) 9 : 7
(c) 4 : 3 (d) 5 : 3

9. Consider a car moving along a straight horizontal road with a speed of 82 km/h. If the coefficient of kinetic friction between the tyres and the road is 0.8, the shortest distance in which the car can be stopped is

(a) 30 m (b) 32.40 m
(c) 72 m (d) 20 m

10. A heavy uniform chain lies on horizontal table top. If the coefficient of friction between the chain and the table surface is 0.45, then the maximum fraction of length of chain that can hang over on edge of table is

(a) $\frac{0.45\,l}{1.45}$ (b) $\frac{0.42\,l}{1.42}$

(c) $\frac{0.82\,l}{1.82}$ (d) $\frac{0.62\,l}{1.62}$

11. A massive platform of mass M is moving with speed $v = 8\ \text{ms}^{-1}$. At $t = 0$, a body of mass $m (m << M)$ is gently placed on the platform. If the coefficient of friction between the body and platform is $\mu = 0.6$ and $g = 10\ \text{m/s}^2$, then

(a) the body covers a distance 3m on the platform in the direction of motion of the platform before coming to rest.
(b) the body covers a distance 3 m on the platform in the direction of motion of the platform.
(c) the body covers a distance 8 m on the platform in the direction of motion of the platform.
(d) the body covers a distance 5.4 m on the platform opposite to the direction of motion of platform before coming to rest.

12. The maximum tension that an inextensible ring of radius 1 m and mass density 0.1 kg m^{-1} can bear 40 N. The maximum angular velocity from which it can be rotated in a circular path is

(a) 20 rad/s (b) 18 rad/s
(c) 16 rad/s (d) 15 rad/s

13. An object is in equilibrium under four concurrent forces in the directions shown in figure, then magnitude of $\mathbf{F}_1$.

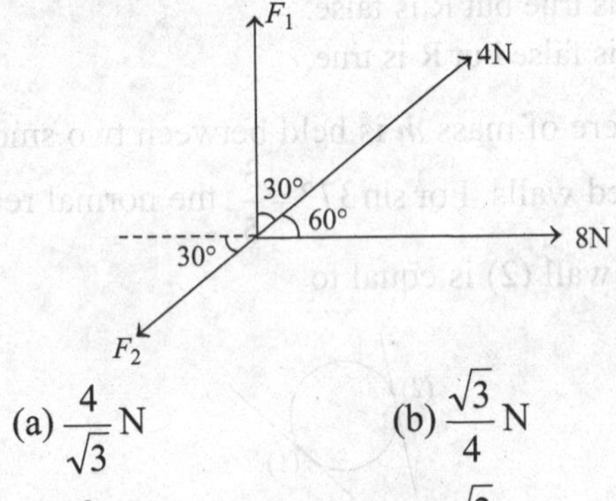

(a) $\frac{4}{\sqrt{3}}$ N (b) $\frac{\sqrt{3}}{4}$ N

(c) $\frac{3}{\sqrt{2}}$ N (d) $\frac{\sqrt{2}}{3}$ N

14. Two blocks are connected over a mass less pulley as shown in figure. The mass of block A is 10 kg and the coefficient of kinetic friction is 0.2. Block A slides down the incline at constant speed. The mass of block B in kg is

(a) 5.4 (b) 3.3
(c) 4.2 (d) 6.8

15. **Statement I** A rocket works on the principle of conservation of linear momentum.

Statement II Whenever, there is a change in momentum of one body, the same change occurs in the momentum of second body of the same system but in the opposite direction.

Select the most appropriate answer from the options given below.
(a) Both Statement I and Statement II are true.
(b) Both Statement I and Statement II are false.
(c) Statement I is true but Statement II is false.
(d) Statement I is false but Statement II is true.

16. **Assertion** (A) When a bullet is fired from a gun, the gunner should exert force on gun in the direction of motion of bullet.

Reason (R) The gun recoils when bullet is fired.

Select the most appropriate answer from the options given below.
(a) Both A and R are true and R is the correct explanation of A.
(b) Both A and R are true but R is not the correct explanation of A.
(c) A is true but R is false.
(d) A is false but R is true.

17. A sphere of mass m is held between two smooth inclined walls. For $\sin 37° = \frac{3}{5}$, the normal reaction of the wall (2) is equal to

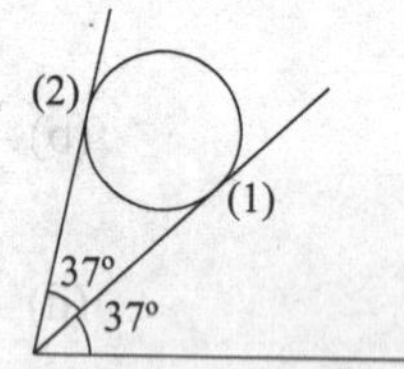

(a) $\frac{16\,mg}{25}$ (b) $\frac{25\,mg}{39}$
(c) $\frac{39\,mg}{21}$ (d) mg

18. **Assertion** (A) A body subjected to three forces cannot be in equilibrium.

Reason (R) If a large number of forces act on the same object, then the object will be in equilibrium.

Select the most appropriate answer from the options given below.
(a) Both A and R are true and R is the correct explanation of A.
(b) Both A and R are true but R is not the correct explanation of A.
(c) A is true but R is false.
(d) A is false but R is true.

19. Three particles are joined together by a thread as shown in figure. Particles are moving in a horizontal circle. If the velocity of the outermost particle is v_0, then the ratio of tension in the three sections of the strings is

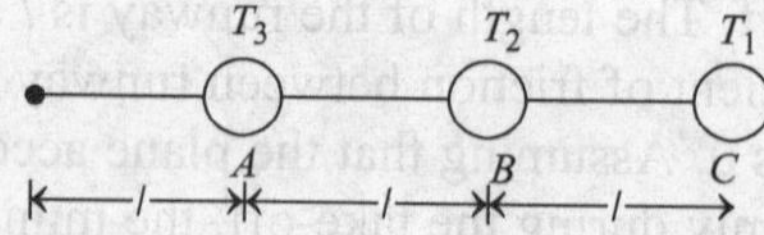

(a) 3 : 5 : 7 (b) 3 : 4 : 5
(c) 7 : 11 : 6 (d) 3 : 5 : 6

20. If a body of mass m is moving on a rough horizontal surface of coefficient of kinetic friction μ, the net electromagnetic force exerted by surface on the body is
(a) $mg\sqrt{1+\mu^2}$ (b) μmg
(c) mg (d) $mg\sqrt{1-\mu^2}$

21. A maximum speed that can be achieved without skidding by a car on a circular unbanked road of radius R and coefficient of static friction μ is
(a) μRg (b) $Rg\sqrt{\mu}$
(c) $\mu\sqrt{Rg}$ (d) $\sqrt{\mu Rg}$

22. Two masses M and $\frac{M}{2}$ are joined together by means of light inextensible string passes over a frictionless pulley as shown figure. When bigger mass is released, the small one will ascend with an acceleration of

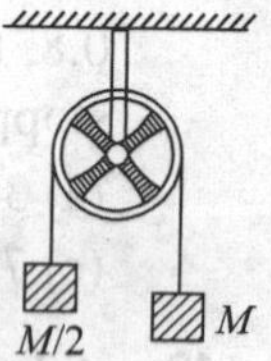

(a) g (b) $g/2$
(c) $g/3$ (d) $2g$

23. The pulleys and strings shown in figure are smooth and having negligible mass. For the system to the under equilibrium, the angle θ should be

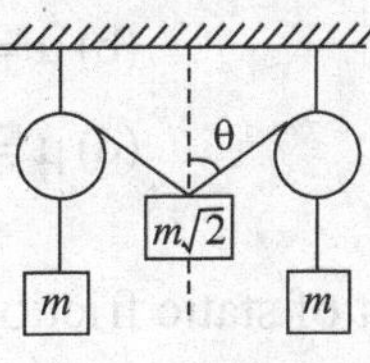

(a) 0° (b) 60°
(c) 45° (d) 30°

24. The mass of a body measured by a physical balance in a lift at rest is found to be *m*. If the lift is going up with an acceleration *a*, its mass will be measured as

(a) $m\left(1-\frac{a}{g}\right)$

(b) $m\left(1+\frac{a}{g}\right)$

(c) *m*

(d) zero

25. A 600 kg rocket is set for a vertical firing. If the exhaust speed is $1000\ ms^{-1}$, the mass of the gas ejected per second to supply the thrust needed to overcome the weight of rocket is

(a) $117.6\ kg\ s^{-1}$ (b) $58.6\ kg\ s^{-1}$
(c) $6\ kg\ s^{-1}$ (d) $76.4\ kg\ s^{-1}$

26. A block is kept on a frictionless inclined surface with angle of inclination α. If the incline is given an acceleration *a* to keep the block stationary, then *a* is equal to

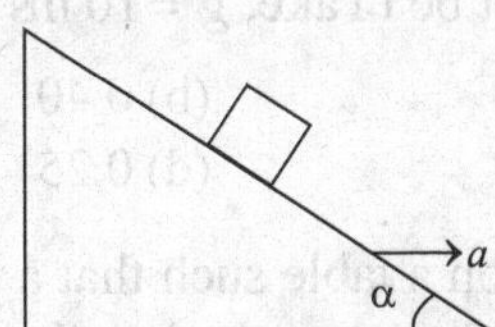

(a) *g* (b) $g \tan\alpha$
(c) $g / \tan\alpha$ (d) $g \operatorname{cosec}\alpha$

27. Match the List I with List II

	List-I		List-II
A.	Static friction	1.	constant for a given pair of surfaces
B.	Limiting friction	2.	independent of area of contact
C.	Kinetic friction	3.	self-adjusting
D.	Rolling friction	4.	has the least magnitude for a given normal reaction

The correct match is
(a) A → 1; B → 2; C → 3; D → 4
(b) A → 4; B → 2; C → 1; D → 3
(c) A → 3; B → 1; C → 2; D → 4
(d) A → 3; B → 4; C → 2; D → 1

28. A solid sphere of mass 2 kg is resting inside a cube as shown in the figure. The cube is moving with a velocity $\mathbf{v} = (5t\hat{i} + 2t\hat{j})$ m/s. Here, *t* is the time in second. All surfaces are smooth. The sphere is at rest with respect to the cube, then the total force exerted by the sphere on the cube is

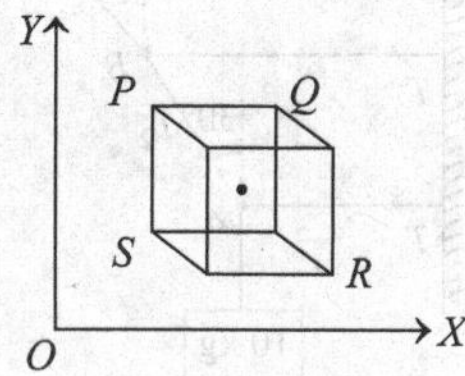

(a) $\sqrt{29}$ N (b) 29 N
(c) 26 N (d) $\sqrt{89}$ N

29. A block of mass 8 kg is kept on the floor. The coefficient of static friction is 0.4. If a force 2.5 N is applied on the block as shown in the figure, the frictional force between the block and the floor will be

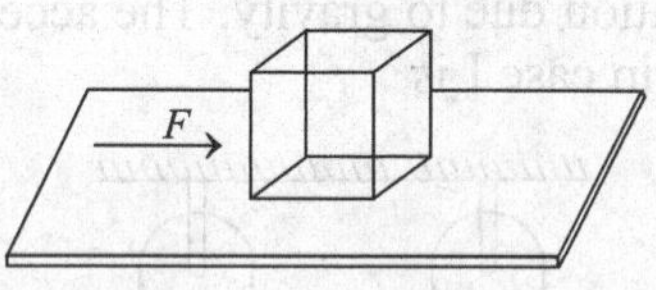

(a) 2.5 N (b) 2.8 N
(c) 7.84 N (d) 10 N

30. If μ_s, μ_k and μ_r are coefficients of static friction, kinetic friction and rolling friction, then
(a) $\mu_s < \mu_k < \mu_r$
(b) $\mu_k < \mu_r < \mu_s$
(c) $\mu_r < \mu_k < \mu_s$
(d) $\mu_r = \mu_k = \mu_s$

31. Three solids of masses m_1, m_2 and m_3 are connected with weightless string in succession and are placed on a frictionless table. If the mass m_3 is dragged with a force *T*, then tension in the string between m_2 and m_3 is

(a) $\frac{m_2}{m_1+m_2+m_3}T$ (b) $\frac{m_3}{m_1+m_2+m_3}T$

(c) $\frac{m_1+m_2}{m_1+m_2+m_3}T$ (d) $\frac{m_2+m_3}{m_1+m_2+m_3}T$

32. The system shown is in equilibrium. Find the magnitude of tension in string T_4. (Take, $g = 10 \text{ m/s}^2$)

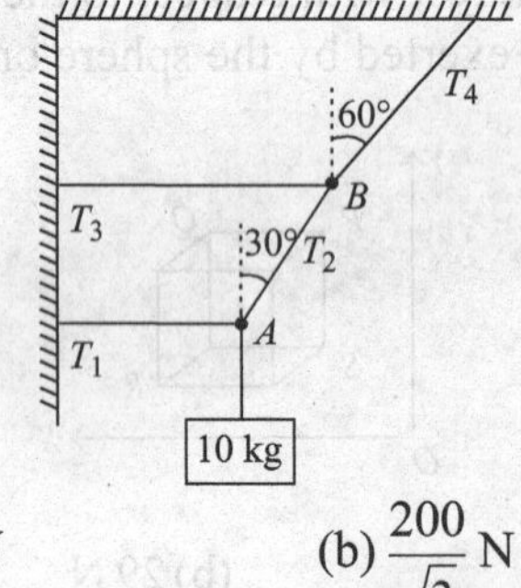

(a) 200 N (b) $\frac{200}{\sqrt{3}}$ N

(c) $200\sqrt{3}$ N (d) 100 N

33. The pulley arrangements shown in figure are identical and the mass of the rope being negligible. In case I, the mass m is lifted by attaching a mass $2m$ to the other end of the rope. In case II, the mass m is lifted by pulling the other end of the rope with a constant downward force $F = 2mg$, where g is acceleration due to gravity. The acceleration of mass m in case I is

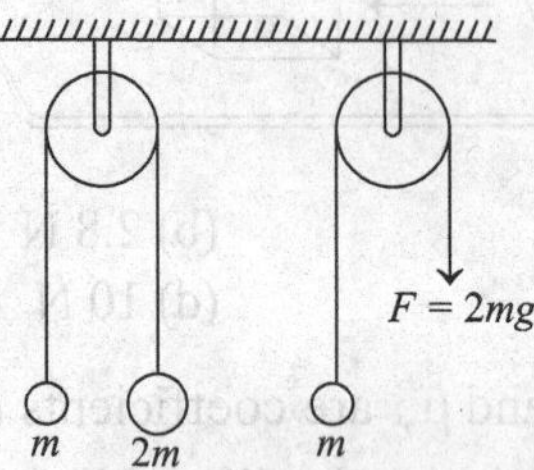

(a) zero

(b) more than that in case II

(c) less than that in case II

(d) equal to that in case II

34. The upper half of an inclined plane of inclination θ is perfectly smooth while the lower half is rough. A block starting from rest at the top of the plane will come to rest at the bottom, if the coefficient of friction between the block and the lower half of the plane is given by

(a) $\mu = 2 \tan\theta$ (b) $\mu = \tan\theta$

(c) $\mu = \frac{2}{\tan\theta}$ (d) $\mu = \frac{1}{\tan\theta}$

35. The coefficient of static friction μ_s, between block A of mass 2 kg and the tables as shown in the figure is 0.2. What would be the maximum mass value of block B so that the two blocks do not move? The string and the pulley are assumed to be smooth and massless. (Take, $g = 10 \text{ ms}^{-2}$)

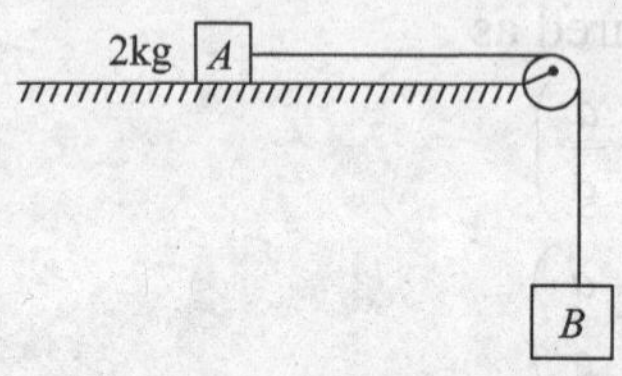

(a) 4.0 kg (b) 0.2 kg

(c) 0.4 kg (d) 2.0 kg

36. A horizontal force of 129.4 N is applied to a 10 kg block at rest on the horizontal surface. If the coefficient of kinetic friction is 0.3, the acceleration of the block is

(a) 1 m/s^2 (b) 2.5 m/s^2

(c) 10 m/s^2 (d) 5 m/s^2

37. A horizontal force of 1 N is needed to keep a block of mass 0.25 kg sliding on a horizontal surface with a constant speed. The coefficient of sliding friction must be (Take, $g = 10 \text{ ms}^{-2}$)

(a) 0.33 (b) 0.40

(c) 0.50 (d) 0.25

38. A rope lies on a table such that a part of it hangs down the table, when the length of hanging part is (1/3) rd of entire length, then rope just begins to slide. The coefficient of friction between the rope and the table is

(a) $\frac{2}{3}$ (b) $\frac{1}{2}$

(c) $\frac{1}{3}$ (d) $\frac{1}{6}$

39. A block of mass m lying on a rough horizontal plane is acted upon by a horizontal force P and another force Q inclined at an angle θ with the vertical. The block will remain in equilibrium if the minimum coefficient of friction between it and the surface is

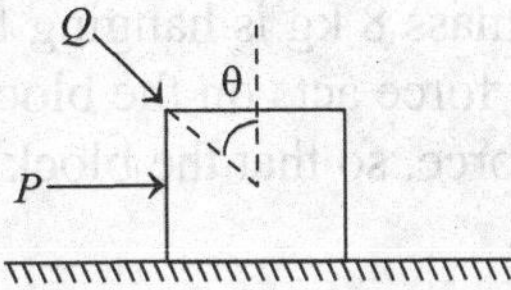

(a) $\frac{P+Q\sin\theta}{mg+Q\cos\theta}$ (b) $\frac{P\cos\theta+Q}{mg-Q\sin\theta}$

(c) $\frac{P+Q\cos\theta}{mg+Q\sin\theta}$ (d) $\frac{P\sin\theta+Q}{mg-Q\cos\theta}$

40. Two masses $M_2 = 10$ kg and $M_1 = 5$ kg are connected by a string passing over a pulley as shown in figure. If the coefficient of friction be 0.15, then the minimum weight that may be placed on M_2 to stop motion is

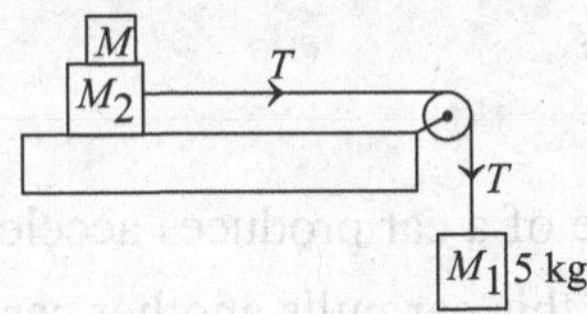

(a) 18.7 kg (b) 23.3 kg

(c) 32.5 kg (d) 44.3 kg

41. As shown in the figure, two blocks A and B are pushed against a wall with the force F. The wall is smooth but the surfaces between A and B are rough. Which of the following is true for the system of blocks to be at rest against the wall ?

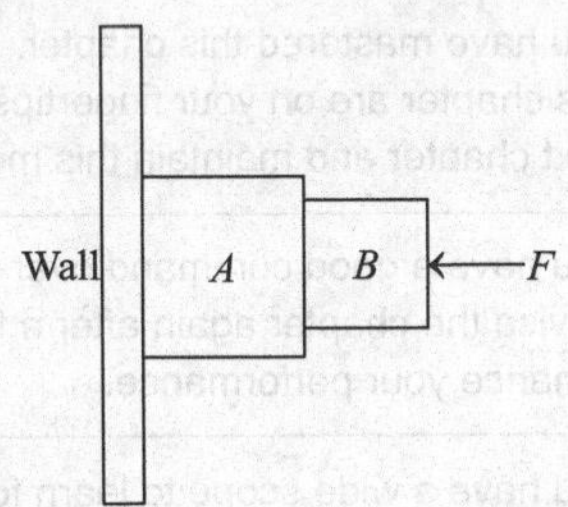

(a) F should be more than be weight of A plus B
(b) F should be equal to weight of A plus B
(c) F should be less than the weight of A plus B
(d) System cannot be in equilibrium

42. The minimum force required to start pushing a body up a rough (frictional coefficient μ) inclined plane is F_1 while the minimum force needed to prevent it from sliding down is F_2. If the inclined plane makes an angle θ from the horizontal such that $\tan\theta = 2\mu$, then the ratio of F_1/F_2 is

(a) 4 : 1 (b) 1 : 1

(c) 2 : 1 (d) 3 : 1

43. In the given figure, friction coefficient (μ) between wall and block is 0.5. For which of the following, value of F block is stationary?

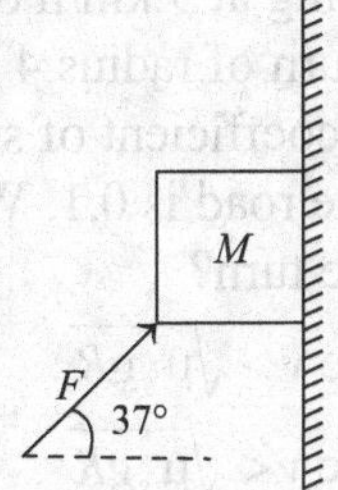

(a) $\frac{Mg}{2}$ (b) $6\,Mg$

(c) $3Mg$ (d) $\frac{7}{3}Mg$

44. The radius of the curved road on a national highway is R, and width of the road is b. The outer edge of the road is raised by h with respect to inner edge, so that a car with velocity v can pass safely over it. The value of h is

(a) $\frac{v^2 b}{R}$ (b) $\frac{v}{Rgb}$

(c) $\frac{v^2 R}{bg}$ (d) $\frac{v^2 b}{Rg}$

45. A particle of mass $m = 0.2$ kg is released from rest from a point A of a wedge of mass $M = 3.6$ kg and it is free to slide on a frictionless horizontal plane. The particle slides down the smooth face AB of the wedge. When the velocity of the wedge is 0.3 m/s, the velocity of the particle (in m/s) relative to the wedge is

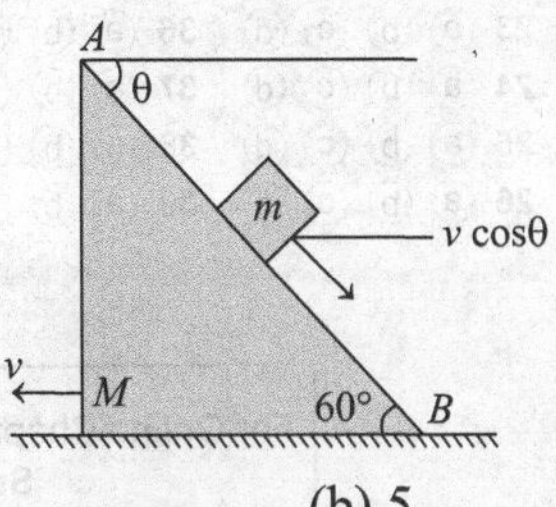

(a) 4.8 (b) 5

(c) 7.5 (d) 11.4

46. A mass is hanging on a spring balance which is kept in a stationary lift. If the lift is in upward motion, the spring balance will shown in its reading

(a) increase
(b) decrease
(c) no change
(d) depends upon rate of change of velocity of lift

47. A cyclist speeding at 9 km/h on a level road takes a sharp circular turn of radius 4 m without reducing the speed. The coefficient of static friction between the tyres and the road is 0.1. Will the cyclist slip while taking the turn?

(a) Yes, because $v > \sqrt{\mu_s gR}$
(b) Yes, because $v < \sqrt{\mu_s gR}$
(c) No, because $v \leq \sqrt{\mu_s gR}$
(d) No, because $v > \sqrt{\mu_s gR}$

48. A body of mass 3 kg is acted on by a force which varies as shown in the graph. The momentum acquired in 6s is

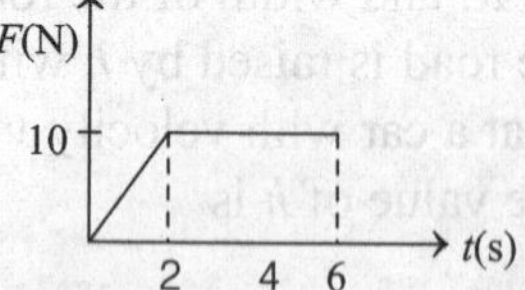

(a) zero (b) 5 N-s
(c) 30 N-s (d) 50 N-s

49. A block of mass 8 kg is hanging from a string and a horizontal force acts on the block. Find the horizontal force, so that the block will remain in equilibrium.

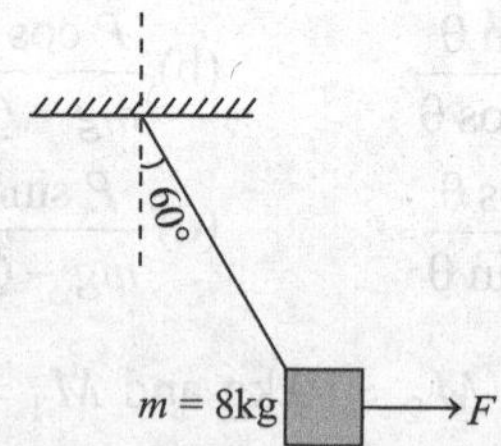

(a) $8\sqrt{3}$ kgf
(b) $8\sqrt{3}$ N
(c) $8\sqrt{3}$ dyne
(d) $\frac{8}{\sqrt{3}}$ kgf

50. The engine of a car produces acceleration of 4 m/s^2 in a car. If this car pulls another car of same mass, what will be the acceleration produced ?

(a) 8 m/s^2 (b) 2 m/s^2
(c) 4 m/s^2 (d) (1/2) m/s^2

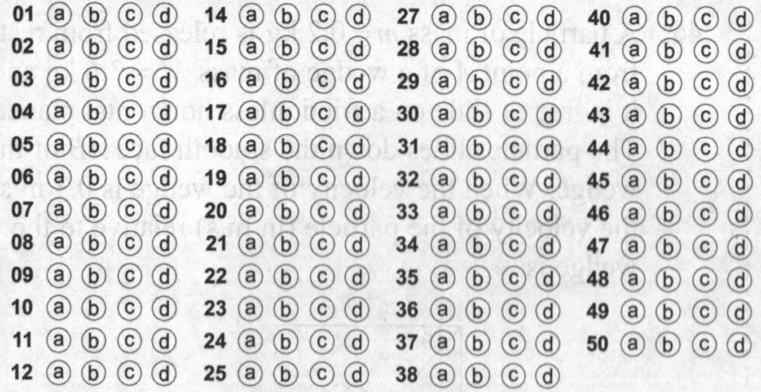

Response Index

01 ⓐ ⓑ ⓒ ⓓ	14 ⓐ ⓑ ⓒ ⓓ	27 ⓐ ⓑ ⓒ ⓓ	40 ⓐ ⓑ ⓒ ⓓ
02 ⓐ ⓑ ⓒ ⓓ	15 ⓐ ⓑ ⓒ ⓓ	28 ⓐ ⓑ ⓒ ⓓ	41 ⓐ ⓑ ⓒ ⓓ
03 ⓐ ⓑ ⓒ ⓓ	16 ⓐ ⓑ ⓒ ⓓ	29 ⓐ ⓑ ⓒ ⓓ	42 ⓐ ⓑ ⓒ ⓓ
04 ⓐ ⓑ ⓒ ⓓ	17 ⓐ ⓑ ⓒ ⓓ	30 ⓐ ⓑ ⓒ ⓓ	43 ⓐ ⓑ ⓒ ⓓ
05 ⓐ ⓑ ⓒ ⓓ	18 ⓐ ⓑ ⓒ ⓓ	31 ⓐ ⓑ ⓒ ⓓ	44 ⓐ ⓑ ⓒ ⓓ
06 ⓐ ⓑ ⓒ ⓓ	19 ⓐ ⓑ ⓒ ⓓ	32 ⓐ ⓑ ⓒ ⓓ	45 ⓐ ⓑ ⓒ ⓓ
07 ⓐ ⓑ ⓒ ⓓ	20 ⓐ ⓑ ⓒ ⓓ	33 ⓐ ⓑ ⓒ ⓓ	46 ⓐ ⓑ ⓒ ⓓ
08 ⓐ ⓑ ⓒ ⓓ	21 ⓐ ⓑ ⓒ ⓓ	34 ⓐ ⓑ ⓒ ⓓ	47 ⓐ ⓑ ⓒ ⓓ
09 ⓐ ⓑ ⓒ ⓓ	22 ⓐ ⓑ ⓒ ⓓ	35 ⓐ ⓑ ⓒ ⓓ	48 ⓐ ⓑ ⓒ ⓓ
10 ⓐ ⓑ ⓒ ⓓ	23 ⓐ ⓑ ⓒ ⓓ	36 ⓐ ⓑ ⓒ ⓓ	49 ⓐ ⓑ ⓒ ⓓ
11 ⓐ ⓑ ⓒ ⓓ	24 ⓐ ⓑ ⓒ ⓓ	37 ⓐ ⓑ ⓒ ⓓ	50 ⓐ ⓑ ⓒ ⓓ
12 ⓐ ⓑ ⓒ ⓓ	25 ⓐ ⓑ ⓒ ⓓ	38 ⓐ ⓑ ⓒ ⓓ	
13 ⓐ ⓑ ⓒ ⓓ	26 ⓐ ⓑ ⓒ ⓓ	39 ⓐ ⓑ ⓒ ⓓ	

Performance Scanner

> 90% Excellent !	You have mastered this chapter. The concepts of this chapter are on your fingertips. Move on to the next chapter and maintain this momentum.
76-90% Very Good !	You have a good command over this chapter. Revise the chapter again after a few days and enhance your performance.
60-75% Good !	You have a wide scope to learn for this chapter. Revise this chapter again.
<60% Not Satisfactory!	You have a long way ahead of you to master this chapter. Revise it thoroughly.

For Online Chapter Test **Scan the QR Code**

For Online Unit Test **Scan the QR Code**

Test Booklet No. **3947105**

Test Booklet Code **CH5**

MEDACE
NEET (UG)
SELF ASSESSMENT KIT

Work, Energy and Power

Topics Covered

- Work and Energy
- Work-Energy Theorem and Conservation of Energy
- Power, Vertical Circular Motion and Collision

Important Instructions

- This Booklet Contains – Three Topic Tests and One Test on Complete Chapter.
- Each question carries 4 Marks.
- For each correct response, the candidate will get 4 marks and for every incorrect response, 1 mark will be additionally deducted from total score.
- Use **Blue/Black** point pen only for filling the OMR.
- Rough work is to be done in the space provided for this purpose in the test booklet only.

Name of the Candidate (In Capitals) ____________________

____

Candidate's Signature ____________________

Invigilator's Signature

Facsimile signature stamp of center superintendent____________________

Do not open this Booklet until you start attempting the Test

Topical Follow Thru

Test 1

Syllabus
- Work Done by a Constant Force
- Work Done by a Variable Force
- Kinetic Energy
- Potential Energy

For deeper insight **Scan the QR Code**

Important Instructions
- The test is of 45 min duration and contains 25 Multiple Choice Questions (Four options with a single correct answer).
- Choose the correct option and fill the OMR given on the last page of this test accordingly.
- At some instances, you may find more than 1 option may be correct in such circumstances you have to judge the most appropriate answer as per the conditions given in the question.

1. A body of mass 1 kg is thrown upward with a velocity of 30 m/s. It momentarily comes to rest after attaining a height of 20 m. The energy is lost due to air friction is (Take, $g = 10\,\text{m/s}^2$)

(a) 220 J (b) 250 J
(c) 280 J (d) 300 J

2. A particle of mass 120 g is thrown vertically upward with a speed of 10 m/s. The work done by the force of gravity during the time, the particle goes up is

(a) −6 J (b) − 6.5 J
(c) −8 J (d) 6 J

3. Under the action of a force, a 2 kg body moves such that its position x as a function of time is given by

$$x = \frac{t^3}{3}$$

where, x is in metre and t is in second. The work done by the force in the first two second is

(a) 1600 J (b) 160 J
(c) 16 J (d) 1.6 J

4. Two springs of spring constants 2000 N/m and 4000 N/m respectively, are stretched with same force. They will have potential energy in the ratio

(a) 2 : 1 (b) 4 : 1
(c) 1 : 2 (d) 1 : 4

5. A position dependent force $F = (5 - 4x + 9x^2)$ N acts on a small body of mass 4 kg and displaces it from $x = 0$ to $x = 5$ m. The work done in joule is

(a) 330 (b) 350
(c) 250 (d) 270

6. **Statement I** Work done in moving a body over a closed loop is zero for every force in nature.
Statement II Work done does not depend on nature of force.
In the light of above statements, choose the most appropriate answer from the options given below.

(a) Both Statement I and Statement II are correct.
(b) Both Statement I and Statement II are incorrect.
(c) Statement I is correct but Statement II is incorrect.
(d) Statement I is incorrect but Statement II is correct.

7. A particle moves along the X-axis from $x = 0$ to $x = 5$ m under the influence of a force is given by $F = 7 - 2x + 3x^2$. The work done in this process (in J) is

(a) 70 (b) 270
(c) 55 (d) 135

8. A force acts on a 80 g particle in such a way that the position of the particle as a function of time is given by $x = 3t - 4t^2 + t^3$, where x is in metres and t is in second. The work done during the first 4 s is

(a) 14.08 J (b) 450 mJ
(c) 490 mJ (d) 530 mJ

9. The force constant of wire is k and that of another wire is $2k$. When both the wires are stretched through same distance, then the work done

(a) $W_2 = 2W_1^2$ (b) $W_2 = 2W_1$
(c) $W_2 = W_1$ (d) $W_2 = 0.5W_1$

10. A particle moves under the effect of a force $F = cx$ from $x = 0$ to $x = x_1$. The work done in the process is

(a) cx_1^2 (b) $\frac{1}{2}cx_1^2$
(c) cx_1 (d) zero

11. Two bodies P and Q have masses 20 kg and 5 kg, respectively. Each one is acted upon by a force of 4 kg wt. If they acquire the same kinetic energy in times t_P and t_Q, then the ratio t_P/t_Q is

(a) 1/2 (b) 2 (c) 2/5 (d) 5/6

12. A body having potential energy is given by $U = A - Bx^2$ (where, x is the displacement). The magnitude of force acting on the particle is

(a) constant
(b) proportional to x
(c) proportional to x^2
(d) inversely proportional to x

13. A man starts walking from a point on the surface of earth (assumed smooth) and reaches diagonally opposite point. Then, work done by him against gravity is

(a) zero
(b) positive
(c) negative
(d) Nothing can be said

14. If the momentum of a body is increased by 100%, then the percentage increase in the kinetic energy is

(a) 150% (b) 200%
(c) 225% (d) 300%

15. **Statement I** When a particle moves along a curved path, the work done by tangential forces only

$$W = \int F_t \cdot ds$$

Statement II Centripetal force is perpendicular to small displacement ds along curved path, therefore centripetal force does not perform any work.

In the light of above statements, choose the most appropriate answer from the options given below.

(a) Both Statement I and Statement II are correct.
(b) Both Statement I and Statement II are incorrect.
(c) Statement I is correct but Statement II is incorrect.
(d) Statement I is incorrect but Statement II is correct.

16. If a man increases his speed by 2 m/s, his kinetic energy is doubled, then original speed of the man is

(a) $(1 + 2\sqrt{2})$ m/s
(b) 4 m/s
(c) $(2 + 2\sqrt{2})$ m/s
(d) $(2 + \sqrt{2})$ m/s

17. A block is pulled by a constant horizontal force on a smooth surface. Work done on the block as a function of speed acquired by the block is represented by

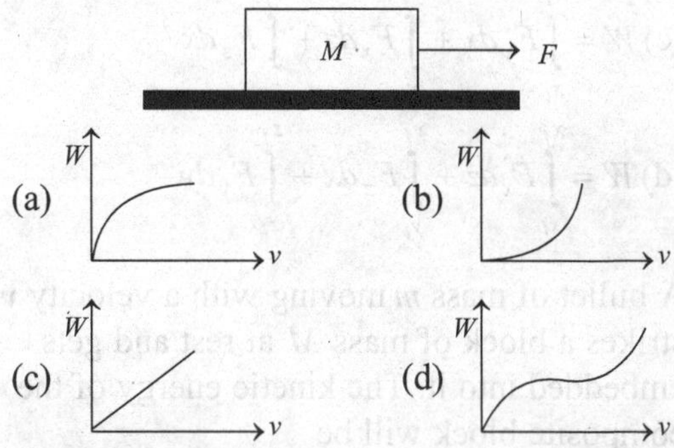

18. The work done by force acting on a body is as shown in the graph. The total work done in covering an initial distance of 20 m is

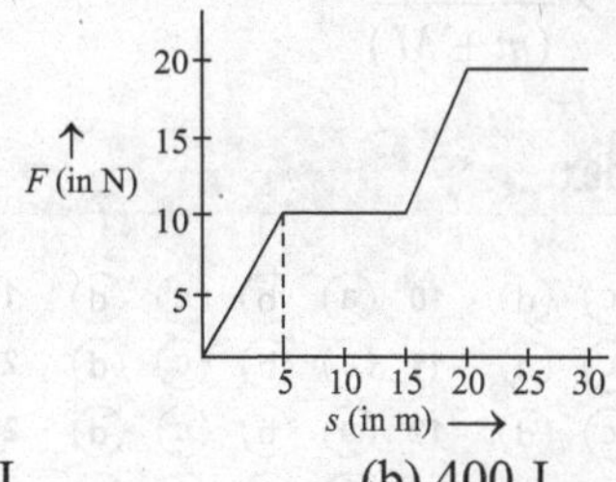

(a) 225 J (b) 400 J
(c) 200 J (d) 175 J

19. A force acts on a 2 kg object so that its position is given as a function of time as $x = 3t^2 + 5$. Then, the work done by this force in first 5 s is

(a) 900 J (b) 200 J (c) 800 J (d) 600 J

20. A force $\mathbf{F} = 6\hat{\mathbf{i}} + 2\hat{\mathbf{j}} - 3\hat{\mathbf{k}}$ acts on a particle and produces a displacement of $\mathbf{s} = 2\hat{\mathbf{i}} - 3\hat{\mathbf{j}} - x\hat{\mathbf{k}}$. If the work done is zero, the value of x is

(a) -2 (b) $\frac{1}{2}$ (c) 6 (d) 20

21. If force component is F_x as the system moves from x_i to x_f, then the area under curve between x_i and x_f. So work done will be

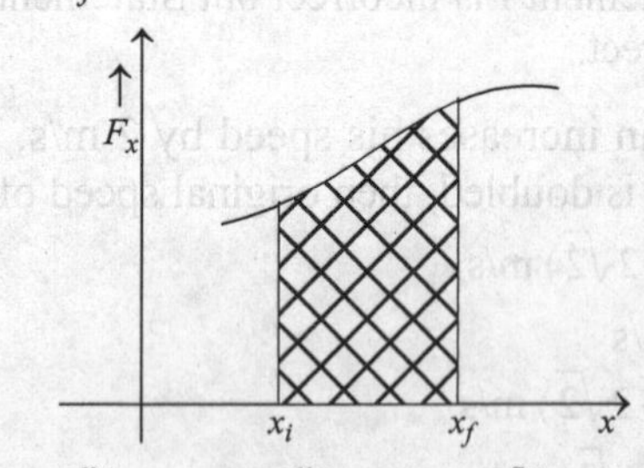

(a) $W = \int_{x_i}^{x_f} F_x dx + \int_{y_i}^{y_f} F_y dy + \int_{z_i}^{z_f} F_z dz$

(b) $W = \int_{x_i}^{x_f} F_z dx + \int_{y_i}^{y_f} F_y dz + \int_{z_i}^{z_f} F_x dx$

(c) $W = \int_{x_i}^{x_f} F_y dx + \int_{y_i}^{y_f} F_x dz + \int_{z_i}^{z_f} F_z dx$

(d) $W = \int_{x_i}^{x_f} F_x dz + \int_{y_i}^{y_f} F_z dx + \int_{z_i}^{z_f} F_y dy$

22. A bullet of mass m moving with a velocity v strikes a block of mass M at rest and gets embedded into it. The kinetic energy of the composite block will be

(a) $\frac{1}{2} mv^2 \times \frac{m}{(m+M)}$

(b) $\frac{1}{2} mv^2 \times \frac{M}{(m+M)}$

(c) $\frac{1}{2} mv^2 \times \frac{(M+m)}{M}$

(d) $\frac{1}{2} Mv^2 \times \frac{m}{(m+M)}$

23. A running man has 1/4 th kinetic energy that a boy of half his mass. Then, the velocity of the boy is

(a) 4 times the velocity of the man

(b) 2 times the velocity of the man

(c) equal to that of the man

(d) $2\sqrt{2}$ times the velocity of the man

24. A particle placed at the origin and force $F = kx$ is acting on it. If $U(0) = 0$, the graph of $U(x)$ *versus* x will be

(a) 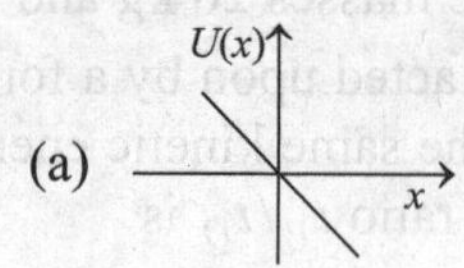

(b) 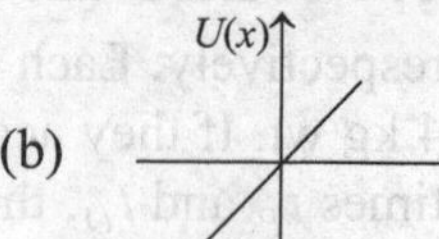

(c) 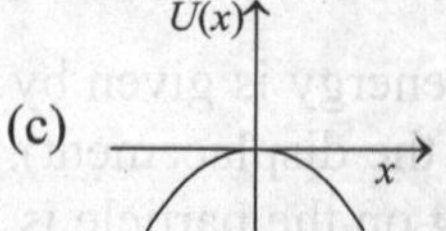

(d) 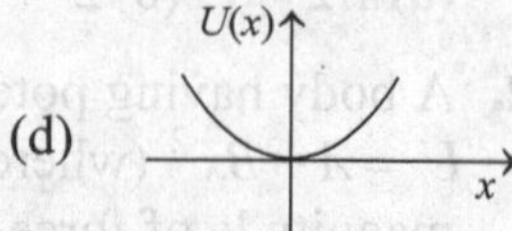

25. Potential energy of two particles which are interacting mutually is

$$U = \frac{A}{r^{12}} - \frac{B}{r^6}$$

If there is no other external force exists, then find equilibrium seperation between them.

(a) Zero (b) $\left(\frac{2A}{B}\right)^{\frac{1}{6}}$

(c) $\left(\frac{B}{2A}\right)^{\frac{1}{6}}$ (d) $\left(\frac{2B}{A}\right)^{\frac{1}{7}}$

Response Index

01	a	b	c	d	10	a	b	c	d	19	a	b	c	d
02	a	b	c	d	11	a	b	c	d	20	a	b	c	d
03	a	b	c	d	12	a	b	c	d	21	a	b	c	d
04	a	b	c	d	13	a	b	c	d	22	a	b	c	d
05	a	b	c	d	14	a	b	c	d	23	a	b	c	d
06	a	b	c	d	15	a	b	c	d	24	a	b	c	d
07	a	b	c	d	16	a	b	c	d	25	a	b	c	d
08	a	b	c	d	17	a	b	c	d					
09	a	b	c	d	18	a	b	c	d					

Performance Scanner

> 90% Excellent !	You have mastered these topics. The concepts of these topics are at your fingertips. Move on to the next test and maintain this momentum.
76-90% Very Good !	You have a good command over these topics. Revise them again after a few days and enhance your performance.
60-75% Good !	You have a wide scope to learn more in these topics. Revise them again.
<60% Not Satisfactory!	You have a long way ahead of you to master in these topics. Revise them thoroughly.

Test 2

Syllabus
- Work-Energy Theorem
- The Potential Energy of Spring
- Conservation of Energy
- Conservative and Non-Conservative Force

For deeper insight **Scan the QR Code**

Important Instructions
- The test is of 45 min duration and contains 25 Multiple Choice Questions (Four options with a single correct answer).
- Choose the correct option and fill the OMR given on the last page of this test accordingly.
- At some instances, you may find more than 1 option may be correct in such circumstances you have to judge the most appropriate answer as per the conditions given in the question.

1. A bullet ($m = 10$ g) strikes a hanging block of wood ($m = 10$ g) and get embedded in it.

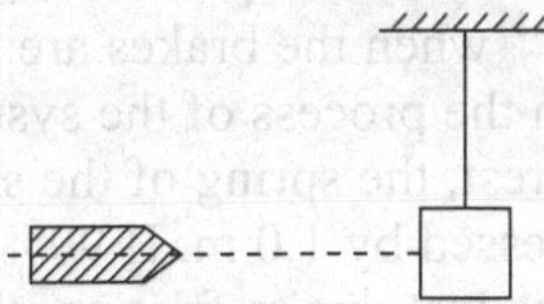

Loss of energy in this process is

(a) 0% (b) 50%
(c) 75% (d) 100%

2. A vehicle of mass 75 kg is moving in x-direction with a constant speed of 20 m/s. It is subjected to retarding force $F = -0.2x$ N, during its travel from $x = 10$ m to $x = 20$ m. The final kinetic energy of the vehicle is

(a) 15 kJ (b) 10 kJ
(c) 20 kJ (d) 25 kJ

3. A mass of 2 kg falls from a height of 40 cm on a spring of force constant 1960 N/m. The spring is compressed by

(a) 10 cm (b) 0.4 cm
(c) 0.1 cm (d) 0.04 cm

4. A spring gun of spring constant 90×10^2 N/cm is compressed 12 cm by a ball of mass 16 g. If the trigger is pulled, the velocity of the ball is

(a) 50 m/s (b) 90 m/s
(c) 40 m/s (d) 60 m/s

5. A body is allowed to fall from a height h above the ground. Then, match the following.

List-I	List-II
A. PE = KE	1. at height $h/2$
B. PE = 2 KE	2. constant at any point
C. KE = 2 PE	3. at height $2h/3$
D. PE + KE	4. at height $h/3$

(a) A → 1, B → 3, C → 4, D → 2
(b) A → 3, B → 1, C → 2, D → 4
(c) A → 2, B → 3, C → 1, D → 4
(d) A → 1, B → 4, C → 3, D → 2

6. **Assertion** (A) Work done by the gravitational force in moving a body through a certain distance remains the same whether the body moves uniformly or with decreasing acceleration.

Reason (R) Gravitational forces are conservative forces.

In the light of above statements, choose the most appropriate answer from the options given below.

(a) Both A and R are true and R is the correct explanation of A.
(b) Both A and R are true but R is not the correct explanation of A.
(c) A is true but R is false.
(d) A is false but R is true.

7. A particle of mass m moving with velocity v_0 strikes a simple pendulum of mass m and sticks to it. The maximum height attained by the pendulum will be

(a) $\frac{v_0^2}{8g}$ (b) $\sqrt{v_0 g}$

(c) $2\sqrt{\frac{v_0}{g}}$ (d) $\frac{v_0^2}{4g}$

8. Velocity-time graph of a moving car of mass 100 kg is shown below. The amount of work done on the moving car will be

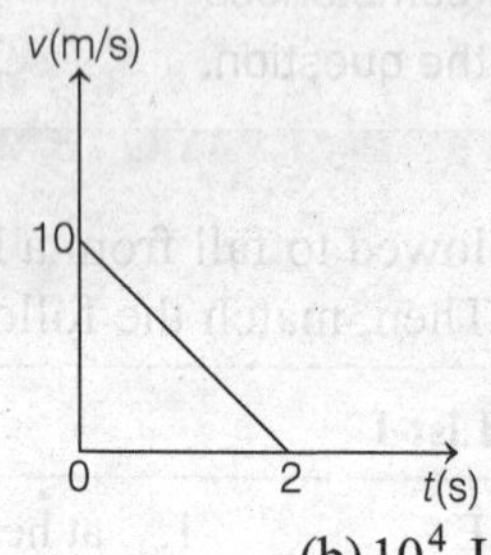

(a) -10^4 J (b) 10^4 J

(c) -5×10^3 J (d) 5×10^3 J

9. Conservative forces are those forces for which

(a) $\oint \mathbf{F}\cdot d\mathbf{r}=0$

(b) $\oint \mathbf{F}\cdot d\mathbf{r}\neq 0$

(c) the work done depends upon the path

(d) only the momentum remains constant

10. A body which is moving with 10 ms^{-1} is sliding up on a rough inclined plane having inclination of 30°. Find the height upto which it can go, if coefficient of friction of the inclined surface is 0.1.

(a) 4.26 m (b) 5.25 m (c) 6.25 m (d) 7.25 m

11. A 0.5 kg block is pushed with an initial speed of 3 m/s towards a spring over a track $ABCD$. The spring ($k = 4$N/m) is of length 1 m with one of end rigidly fixed to a support at point D.

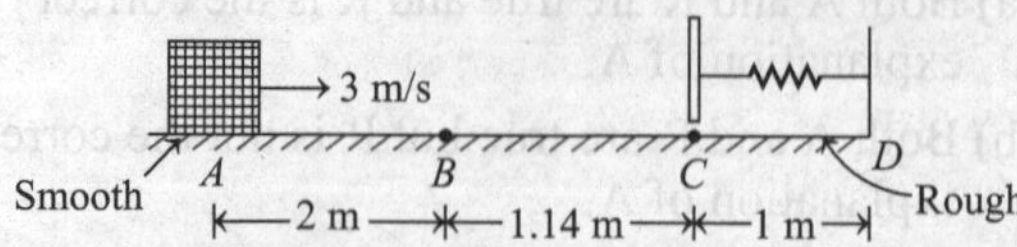

Part AB is smooth. For BD, $\mu_s = 0.22$ and $\mu_k = 0.2$. Total distance moved by the block before coming to rest for the first time is (Take, $g = 10$ ms^{-2})

(a) 3.44 m (b) 4.14 m

(c) 3.14 m (d) 8.28 cm

12. At a certain point, the PE and KE of a body of mass 0.1 kg moving vertically up are 3.6 J and 6.2 J. It rises to a maximum height of

(a) 0.1 m (b) 1 m

(c) 10 m (d) 100 m

13. An ideal spring with spring constant k is hung from the ceiling and a block of mass M is attached to its lower end. The mass is released with the spring initially unstretched. Then, the maximum extension in the spring is

(a) $\frac{4Mg}{k}$ (b) $\frac{2Mg}{k}$

(c) $\frac{Mg}{k}$ (d) $\frac{Mg}{2k}$

14. An engine is attached to a wagon through a shock absorber of length 1.5 m. The system with a total mass of 40000 kg is moving with a speed of 72 kmh^{-1} when the brakes are applied to bring it to rest. In the process of the system being brought to rest, the spring of the shock absorber gets compressed by 1.0 m. If 90% of energy of the wagon is lost due to friction, the spring constant is

(a) 16×10^5 N/m

(b) 12×10^5 N/m

(c) 12×10^4 N/m

(d) 16×10^4 N/m

15. A body of mass 0.1 kg moving with a velocity of 10 m/s hits a spring (fixed at the other end) of force constant 1000 N/m and comes to rest after compressing the spring. The compression of the spring is

(a) 0.01 m (b) 0.1 m

(c) 0.2 m (d) 0.5 m

16. An object of mass m is tied to a string of length l and a variable force F is applied on it which brings the string gradually at angle θ with the vertical. The work done by the force F is

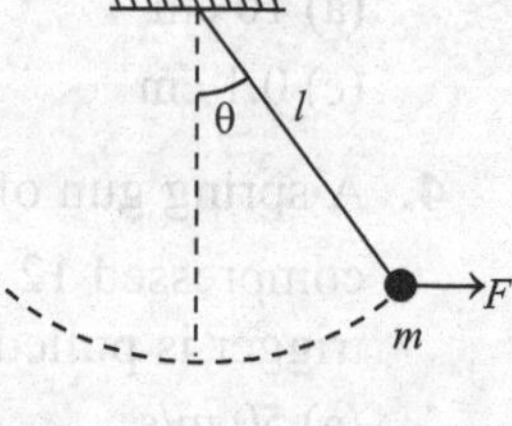

(a) $mg\,(1-\sin\theta)$

(b) $mgl\,(1-\cos\theta)$

(c) $mg\,(l-\cos\theta)$

(d) mgl

17. A bullet of mass m moving with velocity v strikes a suspended wooden block of mass M and remains embedded in it. If the block rises to a height h. The initial velocity of the bullet is

(a) $2gh$

(b) $\sqrt{2gh}$

(c) gh

(d) $\frac{gh}{2}$

18. A 0.8 kg ball is thrown up with an initial speed 14 m/s and reaches a maximum height 8.0 m. The energy dissipated by air drag acting on the ball during the ascent is

(a) 19.6 J (b) 4.9 J
(c) 10 J (d) 15.68 J

19. A machine which is 75% efficient, uses 12 J of energy in lifting 1 kg mass through a certain height. The mass is then allowed to fall through the same height. The velocity at the end of its fall is

(a) $\sqrt{9}$ (b) $\sqrt{27}$
(c) $\sqrt{18}$ (d) 18

20. A ball is projected vertically down with an initial velocity from a height of 20 m on to a floor.

During impact, it loses 50% of its energy and rebounds to the same height. The initial velocity of its projection is

(a) 20 m/s (b) 15 m/s
(c) 10 m/s (d) 5 m/s

21. A can of water having mass 10 kg is raised from a depth 20 m. When the can raises by 10 m, its velocity is 1 ms^{-1}. Work done is

(a) 980 J (b) 985 J
(c) 990 J (d) 975 J

22. A seed starts sliding from A on a frictionless wire with initial velocity of 4 ms^{-1}. Point A is at 5 m and point C is at 2.6 m above the ground. On reaching C its velocity will be (Take, $g = 10\ ms^{-2}$)

(a) 8 ms^{-1} (b) 4 ms^{-1}
(c) 2 ms^{-1} (d) zero

23. On piercing through a distance of 15 cm in a wooden block, a bullet loses half of its initial velocity. Before coming to rest, the further distance travelled by it is

(a) 15 cm (b) 10 cm
(c) 5 cm (d) 30 cm

24. A mass of 1 kg is acted upon by a single force $\mathbf{F} = (4\hat{\mathbf{i}} + 4\hat{\mathbf{j}})$ N. Under this force, it is displaced from (0, 0) to (1 m, 1 m). If initially, the speed of the particle was 2 ms^{-1}, its final speed should be

(a) 6 ms^{-1}

(b) 4.5 ms^{-1}

(c) 8 ms^{-1}

(d) 4 ms^{-1}

25. A sphere of mass m is dropped from a height h above the ground. On reaching the ground, it penetrates through a distance S in sand and finally stops. The average resistance offered by the sand to oppose the motion is

(a) $mg\left(+\frac{S}{h}\right)$ (b) $mg\ (h + S)$

(c) $mg\left(1 + \frac{h}{S}\right)$ (d) $mg\ \frac{h}{S}$

Response Index

01	a	b	c	d	10	a	b	c	d	19	a	b	c	d
02	a	b	c	d	11	a	b	c	d	20	a	b	c	d
03	a	b	c	d	12	a	b	c	d	21	a	b	c	d
04	a	b	c	d	13	a	b	c	d	22	a	b	c	d
05	a	b	c	d	14	a	b	c	d	23	a	b	c	d
06	a	b	c	d	15	a	b	c	d	24	a	b	c	d
07	a	b	c	d	16	a	b	c	d	25	a	b	c	d
08	a	b	c	d	17	a	b	c	d					
09	a	b	c	d	18	a	b	c	d					

Performance Scanner

> 90% Excellent !	You have mastered these topics. The concepts of these topics are at your fingertips. Move on to the next test and maintain this momentum.
76-90% Very Good !	You have a good command over these topics. Revise them again after a few days and enhance your performance.
60-75% Good !	You have a wide scope to learn more in these topics. Revise them again.
<60% Not Satisfactory!	You have a long way ahead of you to master in these topics. Revise them thoroughly.

Test 3

Syllabus

- Power
- Motion in a Vertical Circle
- Elastic & Inelastic Collisions in One & Two Dimensions

For deeper insight Scan the QR Code

Important Instructions

- The test is of 45 min duration and contains 25 Multiple Choice Questions (Four options with a single correct answer).
- Choose the correct option and fill the OMR given on the last page of this test accordingly.
- At some instances, you may find more than 1 option may be correct in such circumstances you have to judge the most appropriate answer as per the conditions given in the question.

1. A body is initially at rest. It undergoes one-dimensional motion with constant acceleration. The power delivered to it at time t is proportional to

(a) $t^{1/2}$
(b) t
(c) $t^{3/2}$
(d) t^2

2. **Statement I** In an elastic collision of two bodies, the momentum and energy of each body is conserved.

Statement II If two bodies stick to each other after colliding, the collision is said to be perfectly inelastic.

In the light of above statements, choose the most appropriate answer from the options given below.

(a) Both Statement I and Statement II are correct.
(b) Both Statement I and Statement II are incorrect.
(c) Statement I is correct but Statement II is incorrect.
(d) Statement I is incorrect but Statement II is correct.

3. A bullet of mass 0.02 kg travelling horizontally with velocity 250 ms^{-1} strikes a block of wood mass 0.23 kg which rests on a rough horizontal surface. After the impact, the block and bullet move together and come to rest after travelling a distance of 40 m. The coefficient of sliding friction of the rough surface is ($g = 9.8\ ms^{-2}$)

(a) 0.75 (b) 0.51
(c) 0.61 (d) 0.30

4. **Statement I** A quick collision between two bodies is more violent than slow collision, even when initial and final velocities are identical.

Statement II The ratio of change in momentum determines that force is small or large.

In the light of above statements, choose the most appropriate answer from the options given below.

(a) Both Statement I and Statement II are correct.
(b) Both Statement I and Statement II are incorrect.
(c) Statement I is correct but Statement II is incorrect.
(d) Statement I is incorrect but Statement II is corect.

5. An object of mass 8 kg moving with a velocity 10 m/s and collides with another body of the mass 28 kg at rest and comes to rest. The velocity of the second body due to collision is

(a) 2.85 m/s
(b) 5 m/s
(c) 7.5 m/s
(d) 10 m/s

6. A particle of mass M_1 collides elastically with another mass M_2 at rest. There is maximum transfer of energy when

(a) $M_1 > M_2$
(b) $M_1 < M_2$
(c) $M_1 = M_2$
(d) Same for all values of M_1 and M_2

7. A mass of 100 g strikes the wall with speed 5 m/s at an angle as shown in figure and it rebounds with the same speed. If the contact time is 2×10^{-3} s, then force applied on the mass by the wall is

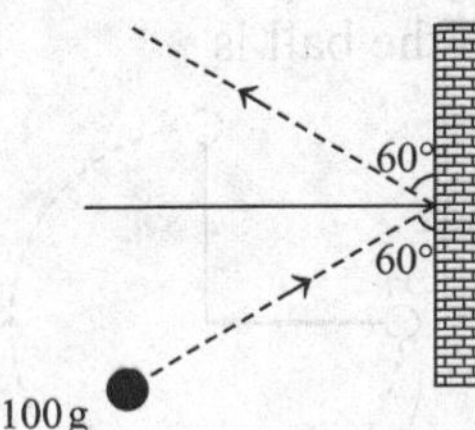

(a) $250\sqrt{3}$ N to right
(b) 250 N to right
(c) $250\sqrt{3}$ N to left
(d) 250 N to left

8. A space craft of mass M, moving with velocity v suddenly breaks in two pieces of same mass m. After the explosion, one of the mass m becomes stationary. The velocity of the other part of craft is

(a) $\frac{M-m}{m}v$ (b) v
(c) $\frac{Mv}{m}$ (d) $\frac{Mv}{M-m}$

9. A body of mass M moves with velocity v and collides elastically with another body of mass $m(M >> m)$ at rest, then the velocity of body of mass m is

(a) v (b) $2v$
(c) $v/2$ (d) zero

10. A body of mass m is at rest. Another body of same mass moving with velocity v makes head-on elastic collision, with the first body. After collision, the first body will start to move with velocity

(a) v
(b) $2v$
(c) remain at rest
(d) no predictable

11. A pendulum bob of mass m is suspended at rest. A constant horizontal force $F = mg$ starts acting on it, then the maximum angular deflection of the string will be

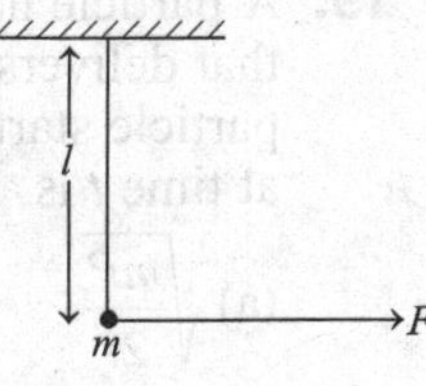

(a) 90° (b) 45°
(c) 30° (d) 0°

12. If the heart pushes 1 cc of blood in one second under pressure 4000 N/m^2, the power of heart is

(a) 0.04 W (b) 600 W
(c) 8×10^{-10} W (d) 0.004 W

13. A particle of mass M starting from rest undergoes uniform acceleration. If the speed acquired in time T is v, then power delivered to the particle is

(a) $\frac{M^2v^2}{T}$ (b) $\frac{Mv^2}{T}$
(c) $\frac{Mv^2}{T^2}$ (d) $\frac{1}{2}\frac{Mv^2}{T}$

14. A truck of mass 30000 kg moves upon an inclined plane of slope 1 in 100 at a speed of 40 kmph. The power of the truck is (Given, $g = 10$ ms^{-2})

(a) 25000 W (b) 33300 W
(c) 50000 W (d) 250000 W

15. A 80 kg man runs up a staircase in 12 s while a 70 kg man runs up the same staircase in 11 s. The rate of doing their work is

(a) 1.246 (b) 1.326
(c) 1.046 (d) 1.462

16. From an automatic gun, a man fires 380 bullets per minute with a speed of 360 km/h. If each weights 20 g, the power of the gun is

(a) 6.3×10^2 W (b) 6.9×10^{-2} W
(c) 150 W (d) 75 W

17. A man is cycling up a hill with a 1 in 20 slope at a speed of 7.2 km/h. The man and cycle together weight 100 kg. The ability of a guy is

(a) 200 W (b) 175 W
(c) 125 W (d) 98 W

18. A 800 N marine in basic training climbs a 12.0 m vertical rope at constant speed in 8.00 s. What is his, power output?

(a) 1.8 kW (b) 1.2 kW
(c) 2.2 kW (d) 2.8 kW

19. A particle having mass m is driven by a machine that delivers a constant power (P)W. If the particle starts from rest, the force on the particle at time t is

(a) $\sqrt{\frac{mP}{2t}}$ (b) $\frac{1}{2}\sqrt{\frac{mP}{t}}$

(c) $\sqrt{\frac{mP}{t}}$ (d) $\sqrt{\frac{2mP}{t}}$

20. A particle attached to a vertical string of length 1 m is projected horizontally with velocity $5\sqrt{2}$ m/s, then maximum height reached by the particle from the lower most point of its trajectory is

(a) 2 m (b) 4 m

(c) 6 m (d) 0 m

21. The power of a motor pump is 0.392 kW. The amount of water pumped by it to a height of 10 m in 60 s is

(a) 240 kg (b) 400 kg

(c) 480 kg (d) None of these

22. A pump of 200 W power is lifting 2 kg water from an average depth of 10 m. Velocity of water delivered by the pump is

(a) 4 ms^{-1} (b) 2.5 ms^{-1}

(c) 3 ms^{-1} (d) 2 ms^{-1}

23. When a belt moves horizontally at a constant speed of 1.5 ms^{-1}, gravel is falling on it at 5 kg s^{-1}. Then, the extra power needed to drive the belt is

(a) 7.5 W (b) 0.3 W

(c) 37.5 W (d) 11.25 W

24. A ball of mass m is attached to the end of a very light rod of length L. The other end of the rod is pivoted, so that the ball can move in a vertical circle. The rod is pulled aside to the horizontal and given a downward push as shown in figure, so that the rod swings down and just reaches the vertically upward position. Then, the initial speed imparted to the ball is

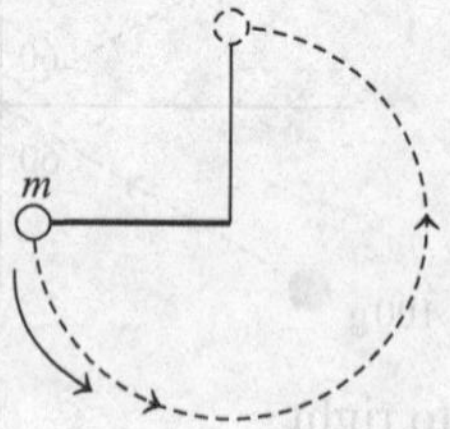

(a) $\sqrt{\frac{L}{g}}$ (b) $\sqrt{gL}$

(c) $\sqrt{2gL}$ (d) gL

25. A force of $2\hat{i}+3\hat{j}+4\hat{k}$ N acts on a particle for 4 s and displaced it by $3\hat{i}+4\hat{j}+5\hat{k}$ m. The power of the force is

(a) 4.5 W (b) 6.5 W

(c) 7.5 W (d) 9.5 W

Response Index

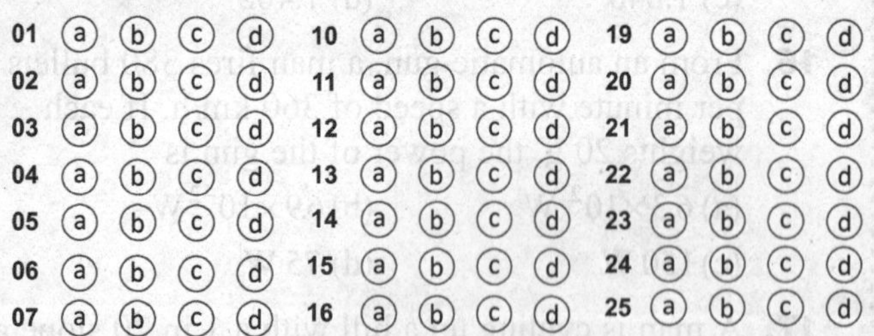

01	a	b	c	d	10	a	b	c	d	19	a	b	c	d
02	a	b	c	d	11	a	b	c	d	20	a	b	c	d
03	a	b	c	d	12	a	b	c	d	21	a	b	c	d
04	a	b	c	d	13	a	b	c	d	22	a	b	c	d
05	a	b	c	d	14	a	b	c	d	23	a	b	c	d
06	a	b	c	d	15	a	b	c	d	24	a	b	c	d
07	a	b	c	d	16	a	b	c	d	25	a	b	c	d
08	a	b	c	d	17	a	b	c	d					
09	a	b	c	d	18	a	b	c	d					

Performance Scanner

> 90% Excellent !	You have mastered these topics. The concepts of these topics are at your fingertips. Move on to the next test and maintain this momentum.
76-90% Very Good !	You have a good command over these topics. Revise them again after a few days and enhance your performance.
60-75% Good !	You have a wide scope to learn more in these topics. Revise them again.
<60% Not Satisfactory!	You have a long way ahead of you to master in these topics. Revise them thoroughly.

Chapter Break Thru

Syllabus	• Work Done by a Constant Force • Work Done by a Variable Force • Kinetic Energy • Potential Energy • Work-Energy Theorem • The Potential Energy of Spring	• Conservation of Energy • Conservative and Non-Conservative Force • Power • Motion in A Vertical Circle • Elastic & Inelastic Collisions in One & Two Dimensions

Important Instructions

- The test is of 1 hour duration and contains 50 multiple Choice Questions (Four options with a single correct answer).
- Choose the correct option and fill the OMR given on the last page of this test accordingly.
- At some instances, you may find more than 1 option may be correct in such circumstances you have to judge the most appropriate answer as per the conditions given in the question.

1. A simple pendulum swings with angular amplitude θ. The tension in the string when it is vertical, is twice the tension in extreme position. Then, the value of $\cos\theta$ is

(a) $\frac{3}{4}$ (b) $\frac{4}{3}$

(c) $\frac{4}{21}$ (d) $\frac{21}{4}$

2. A stone of mass m tied to a string length L is whirled in a vertical circle. If the string remains just stretched when the stone is at the top of circle, then tension in the string when the stone is at bottom of the circle, is

(a) $3\,mg$ (b) $6\,mg$

(c) $4\,mg$ (d) $2\,mg$

3. If a pendulum bob connected with a rod and $v_b < \sqrt{2gr}$, then velocity vanishes before tension T. The particle will oscillate below the diameter without leaving the circular path, but

(a) the particle will not rise upto the horizontal level.

(b) the particle will rise upto the horizontal level.

(c) the particle will remain at same position.

(d) None of the above

4. A machine gun fires 360 bullets per minute, with a velocity of 600 ms^{-1}. If the power of the gun is 5.4 kW, then mass of each bullet is

(a) 5 kg (b) 0.5 kg

(c) 5 g (d) 0.5 g

5. These diagrams represent the potential energy U of a diatomic molecule as a function of the interatomic distance r. Which diagram corresponds to stable molecules found in nature?

(a) 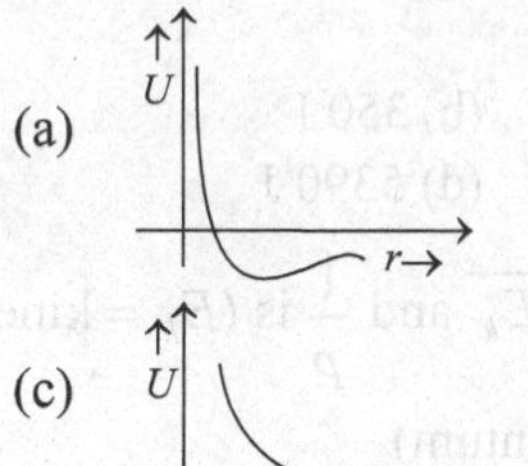

(b) 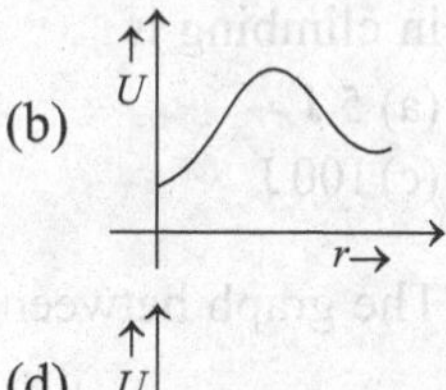

(c) U, r→

(d) U, r→

6. An athlete of mass 60 kg skips at the rate of 40 steps per minute through an average height of 25 cm. The power developed is

(a) 92 W

(b) 98 W

(c) 14 W

(d) 21 W

7. A body starts from rest and acquires a velocity v in time T. The instantaneous power delivered to the body in time t is proportional to

(a) $\frac{v}{T}t$ (b) $\frac{v^2}{T}t^2$

(c) $\frac{v^2}{T^2}t$ (d) $\frac{v^2}{T^2}t^2$

8. Statement I Mass and energy are not conserved separately, but are conserved as a single entity called mass-energy.

Statement II Mass and energy conservation can be obtained by Einstein's equation for energy.

In the light of above statements, choose the most appropriate answer from the options given below.

(a) Both Statement I and Statement II are incorrect.

(b) Both Statement I and Statement II are correct.

(c) Statement I is correct but Statement II is incorrect.

(d) Statement I is incorrect but Statement II is correct.

9. Work done by tension in a simple pendulum in one-third cycle is

(a) zero (b) $\frac{1}{2\pi}\sqrt{\frac{L}{g}}$

(c) $v\sin\left(\frac{\theta}{2}\right)$ (d) $\sqrt{mg}$

10. A 70 kg man with 40 kg load on his head climbs up 20 steps of 0.25 m height each. The work done in climbing is

(a) 5 J (b) 350 J

(c) 100 J (d) 5390 J

11. The graph between $\sqrt{E_k}$ and $\frac{1}{p}$ is (E_k = kinetic energy and p = momentum)

(a) 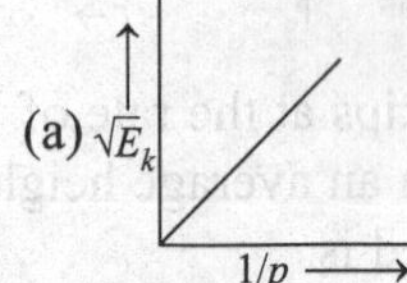

(b) 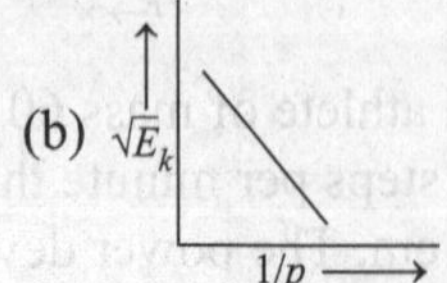

(c) 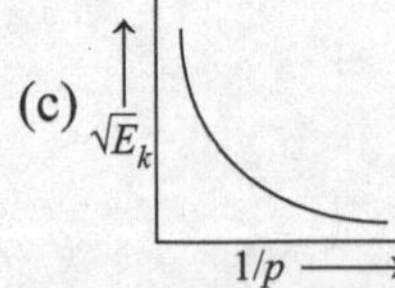

(d) 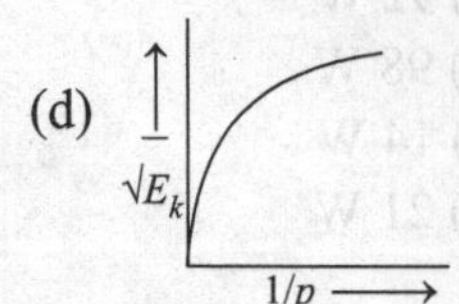

12. A force $F = kx^2$ acts on a particle at an angle of 60° with the X-axis. The work done in displacing the particle from x_1 to x_2 will be

(a) $\frac{kx^2}{2}$ (b) $\frac{k}{2}(x_2^2 - x_1^2)$

(c) $\frac{k}{6}(x_2^3 - x_1^3)$ (d) $\frac{k}{3}(x_2^3 - x_1^3)$

13. Statement I A man working on a horizontal road with a load on his head does no work.

Statement II No work is said to be done, if direction of force and displacement of load are perpendicular to each other.

In the light of above statements, choose the most appropriate answer from the options given below.

(a) Both Statement I and Statement II are incorrect.

(b) Both Statement I and Statement II are correct.

(c) Statement I is correct but Statement II is incorrect.

(d) Statement I is incorrect but Statement II is correct.

14. A body moves along the straight line by a machine delivering constant power. The distance moved by the body in time t is proportional to

(a) $t^{\frac{1}{2}}$ (b) t^2

(c) $t^{\frac{4}{3}}$ (d) $t^{\frac{3}{2}}$

15. A chain is lying on a frictionless table such that its one-fifth part is hanging at the edge. If the length of the chain is l and its mass is m, then the work done in pulling up the hanging part will be

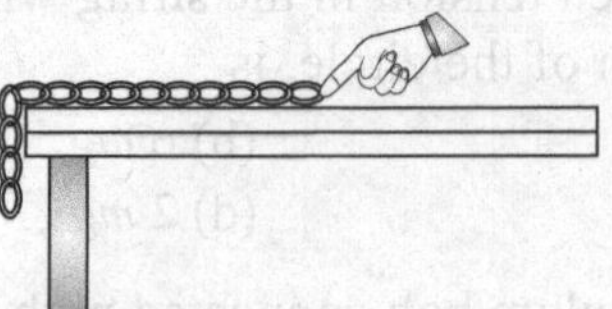

(a) $\frac{mgl}{10}$ (b) $\frac{mgl}{50}$

(c) $\frac{mgl}{5}$ (d) $\frac{mgl}{100}$

16. The relation between $U(r)$ and r for a diatomic molecule is given as $U(r) = \frac{a}{r^{12}} - \frac{b}{r^6}$. The energy of dissociation of the molecule is given as

(a) $\frac{b^2}{4a}$ (b) $\frac{b^2}{8a}$

(c) $\frac{4a}{b^2}$ (d) $\frac{8a}{b^2}$

17. A particle moves in a potential region by $U = 8x^2 - 4x + 400$ joule. Its state of equilibrium will be at

(a) $x = 25$ m (b) $x = 0.25$ m

(c) $x = 0.025$ m (d) $x = 2.5$ m

18. An engine of a train changes the velocity of a train of mass 2.05×10^6 kg from 5 m/s to 25 m/s in 5 min. The power of engine is

(a) 1.025 MW (b) 2.05 MW

(c) 5 MW (d) 6 MW

19. The $U(x)$-x curve for system is shown in the figure. Its force curve will be

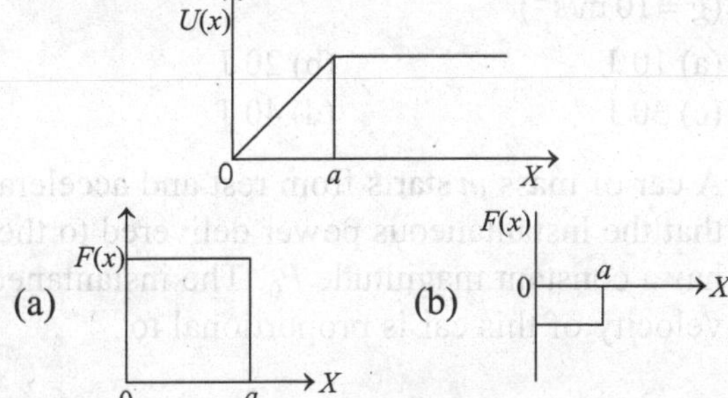

(a)

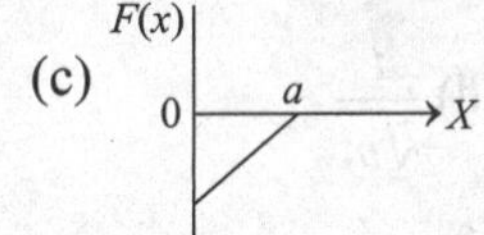

(b)

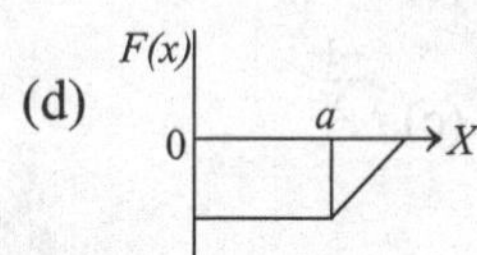

(c) (d)

20. The figure shows a particle sliding on a frictionless track, which terminates in a straight horizontal section.

If the particle starts slipping from the point A, how far away from the track will the particle hit the ground?

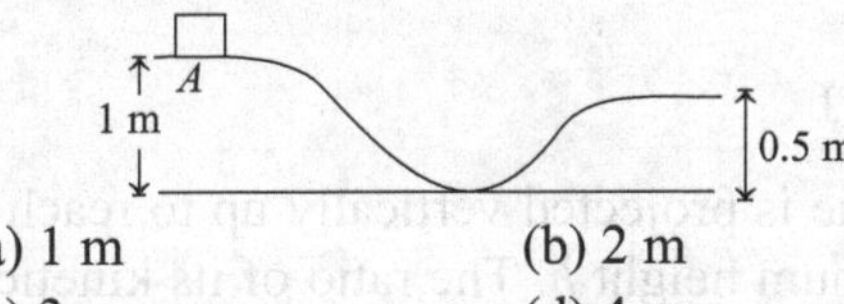

(a) 1 m (b) 2 m

(c) 3 m (d) 4 m

21. A simple pendulum hanging freely and at rest is vertical because in that position,

(a) kinetic energy is zero

(b) kinetic energy is minimum

(c) potential energy is zero

(d) potential energy is minimum

22. The kinetic energy of a body is four times its momentum. Its velocity is

(a) 2 ms^{-1} (b) 4 ms^{-1}

(c) 8 ms^{-1} (d) 16 ms^{-1}

23. The KE acquired by a body of mass m after travelling a fixed distance under the effect of constant force is

(a) inversely proportional to m

(b) directly proportional to m

(c) independent of m

(d) inversely proportional to $\sqrt{m}$

24. The ratio of the potential energies of the bob when it is at B and C as shown is

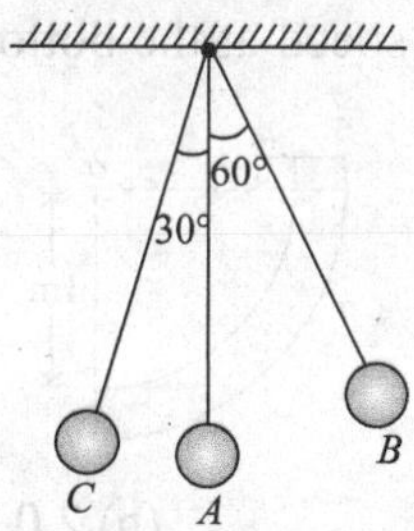

(a) $1:2$

(b) $1:(2-\sqrt{3})$

(c) $1:3$

(d) $1:\sqrt{3}$

25. A ball is dropped from 30 m on hitting the ground. If it loses 40% of its energy, it rebounds to a height equal to

(a) 12 m (b) 15 m

(c) 18 m (d) 16 m

26. A block of 5 kg moves in a straight line on a horizontal frictionless surface under the influence of a force that varies with position as shown in figure. If the block moves from the origin to $x = 8$ m, then the work done is

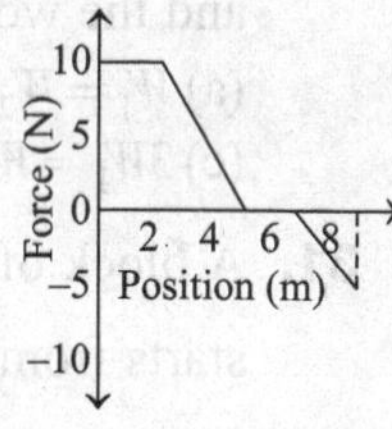

(a) 30 J

(b) 25 J

(c) 15 J

(d) –15 J

27. The energy (E) and momentum (p) of a free particle are graphically related by curve

(a) 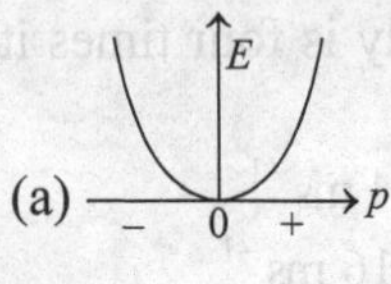
(b) 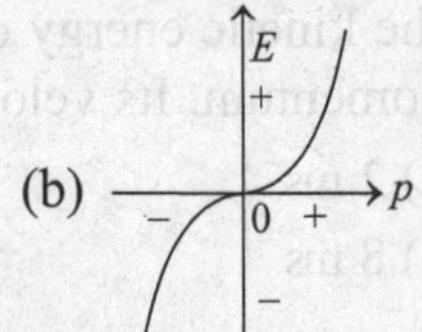

(c) 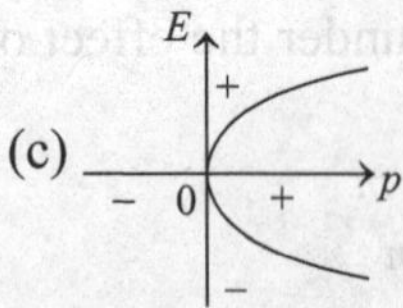
(d) 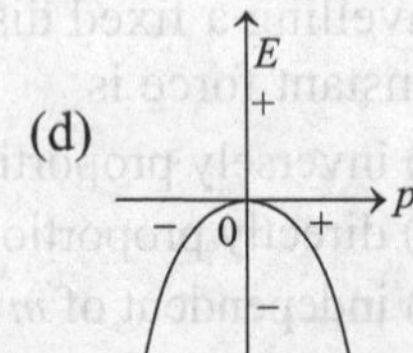

28. A body of mass 2 kg slides down a curved track which is quadrant of a circle of radius 1 metre. All the surfaces are frictionless. If the body starts from rest, its speed at the bottom of the track is

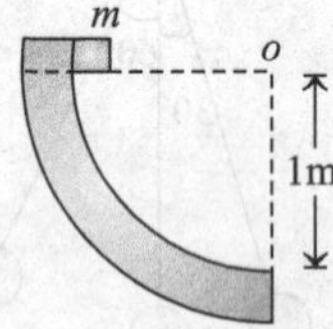

(a) 4.47 m/s (b) 2.0 m/s
(c) 3.13 m/s (d) 19.6 m/s

29. A body of mass 0.2 kg is gradully loaded to a spring, the length of the spring increases by 0.049 m. Then, the energy stored in the spring is
(a) 0.048 J (b) 0.48 J
(c) 4.8 J (d) 48 J

30. A spring from unstreched condition is first stretched to a length x and then again by a further length x. If the work done in the first case is W_1 and the work done in the second case is W_2, then
(a) $W_1 = W_2$ (b) $2W_1 = W_2$
(c) $3W_1 = W_2$ (d) $W_1 = 3W_2$

31. A block of mass m is kept on a platform which starts from rest with constant acceleration $\frac{g}{2}$ upward, as shown in figure. Work done by normal reaction on block in time t is

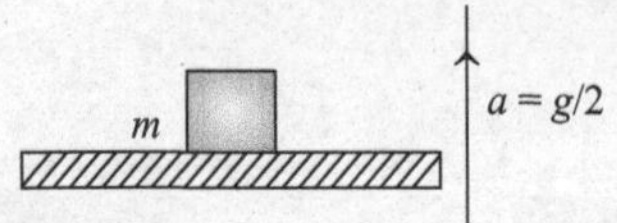

(a) zero (b) $\frac{3mg^2t^2}{8}$
(c) $-\frac{mg^2t^2}{8}$ (d) $\frac{mg^2t^2}{8}$

32. An engine pumps water continuously through a hose. Water leaves the hose with a velocity v and m is the mass per unit length of the water jet. What is the rate at which kinetic energy is imparted to water?
(a) $\frac{1}{2}m^2v^2$ (b) $\frac{1}{2}mv^3$
(c) mv^3 (d) $\frac{1}{2}mv^2$

33. A body of mass 1 kg is thrown upwards with a velocity 20 m/s. It momentarily comes to rest after attaining a height of 18 m. How much energy is lost due to air friction ?
($g = 10\ \text{m/s}^2$)
(a) 10 J (b) 20 J
(c) 30 J (d) 40 J

34. A car of mass m starts from rest and accelerates so that the instantaneous power delivered to the car has a constant magnitude P_0. The instantaneous velocity of this car is proportional to
(a) t^2P_0 (b) $t^{\frac{1}{2}}$
(c) $t^{\frac{-1}{2}}$ (d) $\frac{t}{\sqrt{m}}$

35. A uniform force of $(3\hat{i} + \hat{j})$ newton acts on a particle of mass 2 kg. Hence, the particle is displaced from position $(2\hat{i} + \hat{j})$ metre to position $(4\hat{i} + 3\hat{j} - \hat{k})$ metre. The work done by the force on the particle is
(a) 15 J
(b) 8 J
(c) 6 J
(d) 13 J

36. A stone is projected vertically up to reach a maximum height h. The ratio of its kinetic energy and potential energy, at a height $\frac{4h}{5}$ will be
(a) 5 : 4 (b) 4 : 5
(c) 1 : 4 (d) 4 : 1

37. A car is moving with a speed of 40 km/h. If the car engine generates 7 kW power, then the resistance in the path of motion of the car will be

(a) 360 N (b) 630 N
(c) 0 (d) 280 N

38. A stationary particle explodes into two particles of masses m_1 and m_2 which move in opposite directions with velocities v_1 and v_2. The ratio of their kinetic energies $\frac{E_1}{E_2}$ is

(a) $\frac{m_2}{m_1}$ (b) $\frac{m_1}{m_2}$ (c) 1 (d) $\frac{m_1 v_2}{m_2 v_1}$

39. The potential energy of a 1 kg particle freely moving along the X-axis is given by

$$V(x) = \left(\frac{x^4}{4} - \frac{x^2}{2}\right) \text{J}$$

The total mechanical energy of the particle 2 J. Then, the maximum speed (in m/s) is

(a) 2 (b) $\frac{3}{\sqrt{2}}$
(c) $\sqrt{2}$ (d) $\frac{1}{\sqrt{2}}$

40. A force $\mathbf{F} = (3xy - 5z)\hat{\mathbf{j}} + 4z\hat{\mathbf{k}}$ is applied on a particle. The work done by the force when the particle moves from point (0, 0, 0) point (2, 4, 0) as shown in figure.

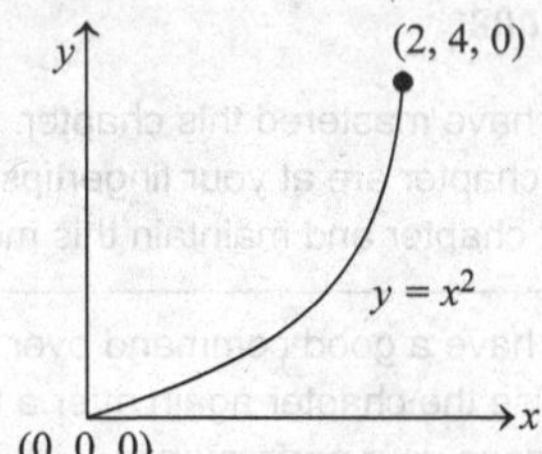

(a) $\frac{280}{5}$ units
(b) $\frac{140}{5}$ units
(c) $\frac{232}{5}$ units
(d) $\frac{192}{5}$ units

41. Compare work done by friction on paths 1 and 2 (friction coefficient is μ on both paths). If block of mass m_1 will move from A to B, then

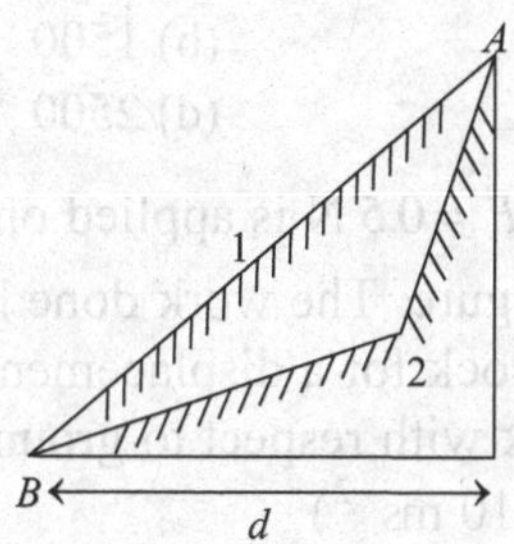

(a) $W_1 = W_2$
(b) $W_1 < W_2$
(c) $W_1 > W_2$
(d) Data is not sufficient

42. It is well known that a raindrop falls under the influence of the downward gravitational force and the opposing resistive force. Consider a drop of mass 1 g falling from a height 1 km. It hits the ground with a speed of 50.0 ms^{-1}. What is the work done by the gravitational force?

(a) 20 J (b) 10 J
(c) 100 J (d) 10.4 J

43. A bicyclist comes to a skidding stop in 10 m. During this process, the force on the bicycle due to the road is 200 N and is directly opposed to the motion. How much work is done by the road on the cycle?

(a) – 4000 J (b) – 200 J
(c) – 400 J (d) – 2000 J

44. A lift can carry a maximum mass of 1800 kg. It is moving up with a constant speed of 2 ms^{-1}. The frictional force opposing the motion is 4000 N. Determine the power delivered by the motor to the lift.

(a) 72 HP (b) 59 HP
(c) 52 HP (d) 49 HP

45. When a conservative force does positive work on a body, the potential energy of the body

(a) increases
(b) decreases
(c) remains unchange
(d) can't be predicted

46. The velocity of a ball of mass 200 grams at an instant $\mathbf{v} = (3\hat{\mathbf{i}} + 4\hat{\mathbf{j}})\ \text{cms}^{-1}$. Then, its kinetic energy (in ergs) will be ($1\ \text{J} = 10^7$ ergs)

(a) 1250 (b) 1500
(c) 2000 (d) 2500

47. A force of $F = 0.5$ N is applied on lower block as shown in figure. The work done by lower block on upper block for a displacement of 3 m of the upper block with respect to ground is (Take, $g = 10\ \text{ms}^{-2}$)

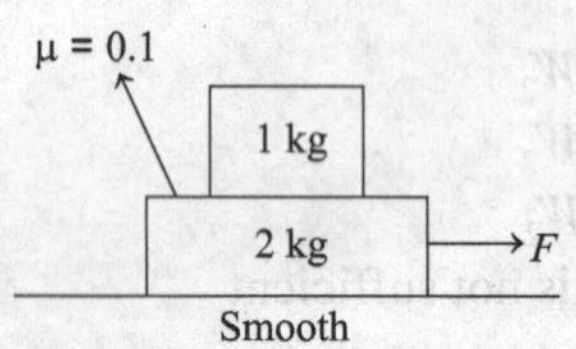

(a) -0.5 J (b) 0.5 J
(c) 2 J (d) -2 J

48. Two objects of different mass moving with same KE is stopped by the same break force. Then,

A. The lighter body is stopped in the short length.
B. The heavier body is stopped in long time.

(a) A is correct but B is wrong
(b) A is wrong but B is correct
(c) Both A and B are correct
(d) A and B are wrong

49. Match the pairs in the lists given below.

	List I		List II
A.	Gravitational force	1.	decreases
B.	Frictional force	2.	conservative force
C.	KE of freely falling body	3.	non-conservative force
D.	PE of freely falling body	4.	increases

The correct match is

(a) $A \rightarrow 2, B \rightarrow 4, C \rightarrow 3, D \rightarrow 1$
(b) $A \rightarrow 2, B \rightarrow 3, C \rightarrow 4, D \rightarrow 1$
(c) $A \rightarrow 2, B \rightarrow 3, C \rightarrow 1, D \rightarrow 4$
(d) $A \rightarrow 4, B \rightarrow 3, C \rightarrow 2, D \rightarrow 1$

50. **Assertion** (A) The power of a pump which raises 100 kg of water in 10 s to a height of 100 m is 10 kW.

Reason (R) The practical unit of power is horse power.

In the light of above statements, choose the most appropriate answer from the options given below.

(a) Both A and R are true and R is the correct explanation of A.
(b) Both A and R are true but R is not the correct explanation of A.
(c) A is true but R is false.
(d) A is false but R is true.

Response Index

01	ⓐ ⓑ ⓒ ⓓ	14	ⓐ ⓑ ⓒ ⓓ	27	ⓐ ⓑ ⓒ ⓓ	40	ⓐ ⓑ ⓒ ⓓ
02	ⓐ ⓑ ⓒ ⓓ	15	ⓐ ⓑ ⓒ ⓓ	28	ⓐ ⓑ ⓒ ⓓ	41	ⓐ ⓑ ⓒ ⓓ
03	ⓐ ⓑ ⓒ ⓓ	16	ⓐ ⓑ ⓒ ⓓ	29	ⓐ ⓑ ⓒ ⓓ	42	ⓐ ⓑ ⓒ ⓓ
04	ⓐ ⓑ ⓒ ⓓ	17	ⓐ ⓑ ⓒ ⓓ	30	ⓐ ⓑ ⓒ ⓓ	43	ⓐ ⓑ ⓒ ⓓ
05	ⓐ ⓑ ⓒ ⓓ	18	ⓐ ⓑ ⓒ ⓓ	31	ⓐ ⓑ ⓒ ⓓ	44	ⓐ ⓑ ⓒ ⓓ
06	ⓐ ⓑ ⓒ ⓓ	19	ⓐ ⓑ ⓒ ⓓ	32	ⓐ ⓑ ⓒ ⓓ	45	ⓐ ⓑ ⓒ ⓓ
07	ⓐ ⓑ ⓒ ⓓ	20	ⓐ ⓑ ⓒ ⓓ	33	ⓐ ⓑ ⓒ ⓓ	46	ⓐ ⓑ ⓒ ⓓ
08	ⓐ ⓑ ⓒ ⓓ	21	ⓐ ⓑ ⓒ ⓓ	34	ⓐ ⓑ ⓒ ⓓ	47	ⓐ ⓑ ⓒ ⓓ
09	ⓐ ⓑ ⓒ ⓓ	22	ⓐ ⓑ ⓒ ⓓ	35	ⓐ ⓑ ⓒ ⓓ	48	ⓐ ⓑ ⓒ ⓓ
10	ⓐ ⓑ ⓒ ⓓ	23	ⓐ ⓑ ⓒ ⓓ	36	ⓐ ⓑ ⓒ ⓓ	49	ⓐ ⓑ ⓒ ⓓ
11	ⓐ ⓑ ⓒ ⓓ	24	ⓐ ⓑ ⓒ ⓓ	37	ⓐ ⓑ ⓒ ⓓ	50	ⓐ ⓑ ⓒ ⓓ
12	ⓐ ⓑ ⓒ ⓓ	25	ⓐ ⓑ ⓒ ⓓ	38	ⓐ ⓑ ⓒ ⓓ		
13	ⓐ ⓑ ⓒ ⓓ	26	ⓐ ⓑ ⓒ ⓓ	39	ⓐ ⓑ ⓒ ⓓ		

Performance Scanner

> 90% Excellent !	You have mastered this chapter. The concepts of this chapter are at your fingertips. Move on to the next chapter and maintain this momentum.
76-90% Very Good !	You have a good command over this chapter. Revise the chapter again after a few days and enhance your performance.
60-75% Good !	You have a wide scope to learn more for this chapter. Revise this chapter again.
<60% Not Satisfactory!	You have a long way ahead of you to master this chapter. Revise it thoroughly.

For Online Chapter Test **Scan the QR Code**

For Online Unit Test **Scan the QR Code**

Test Booklet No. 3947106

Test Booklet Code CH6

MED ACE
NEET (UG)
SELF ASSESSMENT KIT

Rotational Motion

Topics Covered

- Centre of Mass and Moment of Inertia
- Moment of Force and Angular Momentum
- Rotational and Rolling Motion

Important Instructions

- This Booklet Contains – Three Topic Tests and One Test on Complete Chapter.
- Each question carries 4 Marks.
- For each correct response, the candidate will get 4 marks and for every incorrect response, 1 mark will be additionally deducted from total score.
- Use **Blue/Black** point pen only for filling the OMR.
- Rough work is to be done in the space provided for this purpose in the test booklet only.

Name of the Candidate (In Capitals) ____________________

____

Candidate's Signature ____________

Invigilator's Signature ____________

Facsimile signature stamp of center superintendent____________

Do not open this Booklet until you start attempting the Test

Topical Follow Thru

Test 1

Syllabus

- Centre of Mass of a two Particle Systems • Centre of Mass of a Rigid Body , Basic Concepts of Rotational Motion
- Parallel and Perpendicular Axes Theorems & Their Applications,
- Moment of Inertia, Radius of Gyration • Values of Moment of Inertia for Simple Geometrical Objects

For deeper insight **Scan the QR Code**

Important Instructions

- The test is of 45 minutes duration and contains 25 Multiple Choice Questions. (Four options with a single correct answer).
- Choose the correct option and fill the OMR given on the last page of this test accordingly.
- At some instances, you may find more than 1 option may be correct, in such circumstances you have to judge the most appropriate answer as per conditions given in the question.

1. Five particles of mass 2 kg are attached to the rim of a circular disc of radius 0.1 m and negligible mass. Moment of inertia of the system about the axis passing through the centre of the disc and perpendicular to its plane is

(a) 1 kg - m^2 (b) 0.1 kg - m^2

(c) 2 kg - m^2 (d) 0.2 kg - m^2

2. Two round discs of the same substance and thickness have radii 0.4 m and 0.8 m. Their moments of inertia about their axes will be in the ratio

(a) 1 : 16 (b) 1 : 27

(c) 1 : 9 (d) 1 : 3

3. Assertion (A) Moment of inertia depends on mass, distribution of mass and position of axis of rotation.

Reason (R) The moment of inertia of a body made up of number of particles (discrete distribution). For different masses,

$$I = m_1 r_1^2 + m_2 r_2^2 + \ldots.$$

In the light of above statements, choose the most appropriate answer from the options given below.

(a) Both A and R are true and R is the correct explanation of A.

(b) Both A and R are true but R is not the correct explanation of A.

(c) A is true but R is false.

(d) A is false but R is true.

4. A thin wire having length l and mass m is bent in the form of a rectangle $PQRS$ with $(PQ/QR) = 2$, then moment of inertia of thin wire about the side QR is

(a) $\frac{11}{252} ml^2$ (b) $\frac{8}{203} ml^2$

(c) $\frac{5}{136} ml^2$ (d) $\frac{7}{162} ml^2$

5. Three rods of the same mass are placed as shown in the figure. What will be the coordinate of centre of mass of the system?

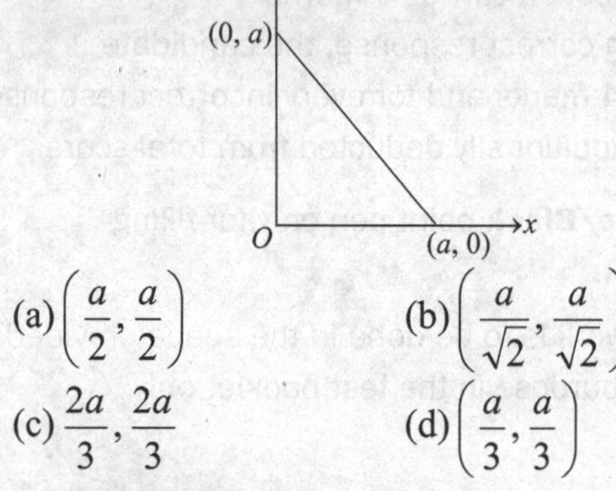

(a) $\left(\frac{a}{2}, \frac{a}{2}\right)$ (b) $\left(\frac{a}{\sqrt{2}}, \frac{a}{\sqrt{2}}\right)$

(c) $\frac{2a}{3}, \frac{2a}{3}$ (d) $\left(\frac{a}{3}, \frac{a}{3}\right)$

6. Figure represents the moment of inertia of the solid sphere about an axis parallel to the diameter of the solid sphere and at a distance x from it. Which one of the following represents the variations of I with x?

C

x

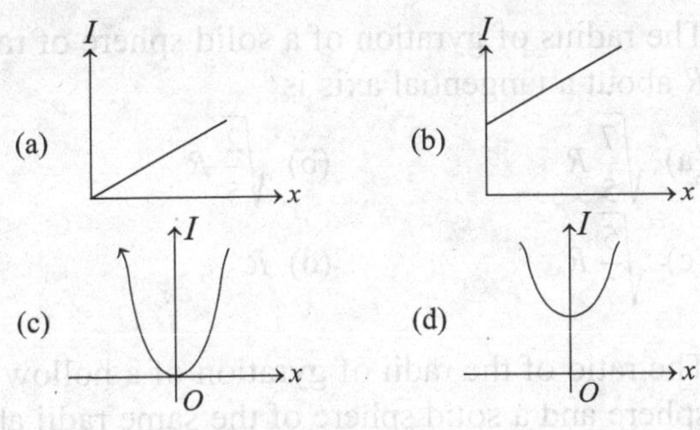

7. A portion of a ring of radius R has been removed as shown in figure. Mass of the remaining portion is m. Centre of the ring is at origin O. Let I_A and I_O be the moments of inertia passing through points A and O are perpendicular to the plane of the ring, then

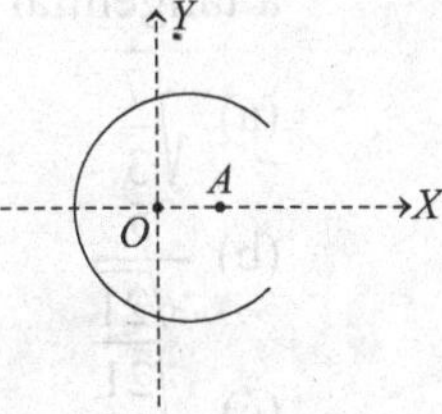

(a) $I_O = mR^2$ (b) $I_O = I_A$
(c) $I_O > I_A$ (d) $I_A > I_O$

8. In the context of rotational motion of a rigid body about a fixed axis, consider the motion of particles located at varying distances from the axis of rotation. Which of the following statements accurately describes the kinematic behaviour of these particles?
(a) same linear and angular velocity
(b) same linear and different angular velocity
(c) different linear velocities and same angular velocities
(d) different linear velocities and different angular velocities

9. The MI of thin uniform square plate of mass m and edge a about its diagonal is
(a) $\frac{ma^2}{12}$ (b) $\frac{ma^2}{6}$ (c) $\frac{ma^2}{4}$ (d) $\frac{ma^2}{3}$

10. Three stone bricks each of length l and mass M are arranged as shown from the wall. The distance of the centre of mass of the system from the wall is

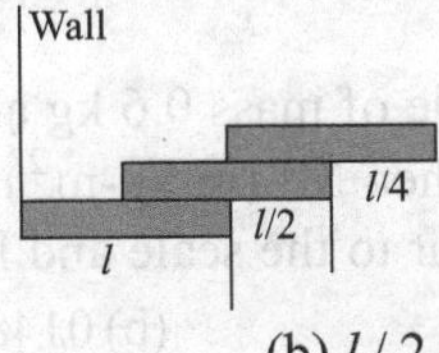

(a) $l/4$ (b) $l/2$
(c) $(3/2)\,l$ (d) $(11/12)\,l$

11. If the origin of coordinate system lies at the centre of mass, the sum of the moments of the system about the centre of mass
(a) greater than zero
(b) less than zero
(c) equal to zero
(d) is always zero

12. Consider a cube of uniform density ρ and side length a. The cube is positioned in a three-dimensional cartesian coordinate system with one vertex at the orgin (0,0,0) and edges aligned with the coordinate axes. Analyze the following statements regarding the position of the centre of mass of the cube and identify the correct one.
(a) edge of a cube
(b) the centre of one face
(c) centre of the intersection of diagonals of one face
(d) geometric centre of cube

13. The position of centre of mass of a system consisting of two particles of masses m_1 and m_2 separated by a distance L apart, from m_1 will be
(a) $\frac{m_1 L}{m_1 + m_2}$ (b) $\frac{m_2 L}{m_1 + m_2}$
(c) $\frac{m_2}{m_1} L$ (d) $\frac{L}{2}$

14. Mass is distributed uniformly over a thin square plate. If end points of a diagonal are (−2,0) and (2, 2), then the coordinates of the centre of mass
(a) (2, 1) (b) (2, 2)
(c) (1, 0) (d) (0, 1)

15. Four bodies of masses 2 kg, 3kg, 5kg and 8 kg are placed at the four corners of a square of side 2 m. The position of CM will be
(a) $\left(\frac{8}{9}, \frac{13}{9}\right)$ (b) $\left(\frac{7}{9}, \frac{11}{9}\right)$
(c) $\left(\frac{11}{9}, \frac{13}{9}\right)$ (d) $\left(\frac{11}{9}, \frac{8}{9}\right)$

16. Three identical spheres, each having mass 1 kg are kept as shown in figure, touching each other with their centres on a straight line. If their centres are marked A, B and C respectively, the distance of centre of mass of the system from A is

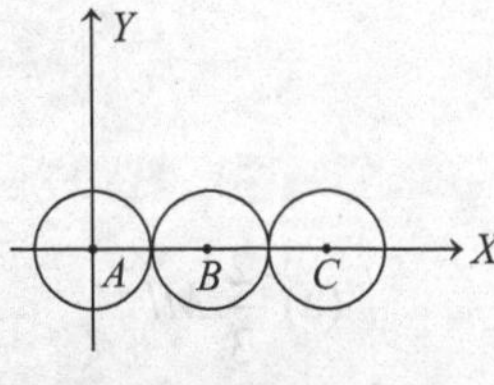

(a) $\frac{AB+AC+BC}{3}$ (b) $\frac{AB+AC}{3}$

(c) $\frac{AB+BC}{3}$ (d) $\frac{AC+BC}{3}$

17. The distance of the centre of mass of the T-shaped from O is

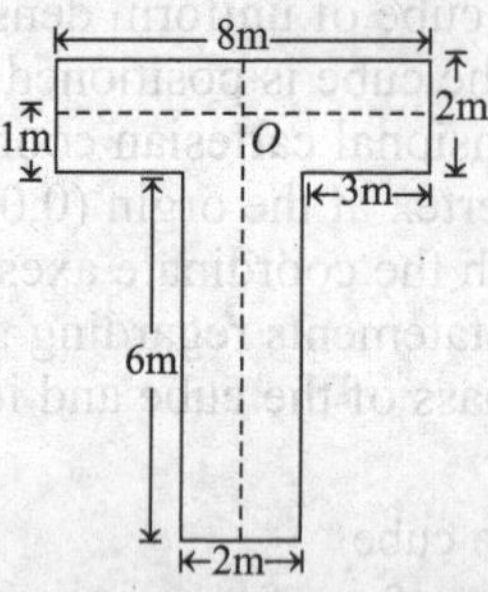

(a) 7 m (b) 1.7 m
(c) 3.4 m (d) 1 m

18. **Statement I** The value of radius of gyration of a body depends on axis of rotation.
Statement II Radius of gyration is root mean square distance of particle of the body from the axis of rotation.
In the light of above statements, choose the most appropriate answer from the options given below.

(a) Both Statement I and Statement II are correct.
(b) Both Statement I and Statement II are incorrect.
(c) Statement I is correct but Statement II is incorrect.
(d) Statement I is incorrect but Statement II is correct.

19. For the uniform T shaped structure, with mass $3M$, moment of inertia about an axis normal to the plane and passing through O would be

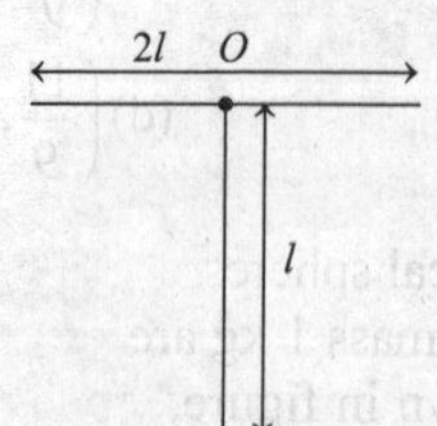

(a) $\frac{2}{3}Ml^2$ (b) Ml^2

(c) $\frac{Ml^2}{3}$ (d) $\frac{3}{2}Ml^2$

20. The radius of gyration of a solid sphere of radius R about a tangential axis is

(a) $\sqrt{\frac{7}{5}}R$ (b) $\sqrt{\frac{2}{5}}R$

(c) $\sqrt{\frac{5}{7}}R$ (d) R

21. The ratio of the radii of gyration of a hollow sphere and a solid sphere of the same radii about a tangential axis is

(a) $\sqrt{\frac{7}{3}}$

(b) $\frac{5}{\sqrt{21}}$

(c) $\sqrt{\frac{21}{5}}$

(d) $\frac{25}{9}$

22. A uniform rod of length L and mass M placed along the line $y=2x$ in a cartesian coordinate system, with its centre located at the origin (0,0,0). The rod lies in the xy-plane, making an angle $\theta=\tan^{-1}(2)$ with the x-axis. Analyze the following statements regarding the moment of inertia of the rod about different axes and identify the axis about which the moment of inertia is maximum.

(a) X-axis
(b) Y-axis
(c) Z-axis
(d) Data insufficient

23. Two bodies of mass 1 kg and 3 kg have position vectors $\hat{\mathbf{i}}+2\hat{\mathbf{j}}+\hat{\mathbf{k}}$ and $-3\hat{\mathbf{i}}-2\hat{\mathbf{j}}+\hat{\mathbf{k}}$, respectively. The magnitude of position vector of centre of mass of this system will be similar to the magnitude of vector.

(a) $\hat{\mathbf{i}}-2\hat{\mathbf{j}}+\hat{\mathbf{k}}$
(b) $-3\hat{\mathbf{i}}-2\hat{\mathbf{j}}+\hat{\mathbf{k}}$
(c) $-2\hat{\mathbf{i}}+2\hat{\mathbf{k}}$
(d) $-2\hat{\mathbf{i}}-\hat{\mathbf{j}}+2\hat{\mathbf{k}}$

24. A meter scale of mass 0.6 kg and breadth is negligible, then MI (in-kg-m^2) about an axis perpendicular to the scale and located at 20 cm is

(a) 0.074 (b) 0.148
(c) 0.104 (d) 0.208

25. A system of two particles with masses m_1 and m_2, separated by a distance d along a straight line. The centre of mass C of this system lies somewhere on this lines and divides the distance between the two particles into two segments. Determine which of the following statements correctly describes the relationship between the position of the centre of mass and the masses of the particles.

(a) in inverse ratio of square of masses of particles
(b) in direct ratio of square of masses of particles
(c) in inverse ratio of masses of particles
(d) in direct ratio of masses of particles

Response Index

01	a	b	c	d	10	a	b	c	d	19	a	b	c	d
02	a	b	c	d	11	a	b	c	d	20	a	b	c	d
03	a	b	c	d	12	a	b	c	d	21	a	b	c	d
04	a	b	c	d	13	a	b	c	d	22	a	b	c	d
05	a	b	c	d	14	a	b	c	d	23	a	b	c	d
06	a	b	c	d	15	a	b	c	d	24	a	b	c	d
07	a	b	c	d	16	a	b	c	d	25	a	b	c	d
08	a	b	c	d	17	a	b	c	d					
09	a	b	c	d	18	a	b	c	d					

Performance Scanner

> 90% Excellent !	You have mastered these topics. The concepts of these topics are at your fingertips. Move on to the next test and maintain this momentum.
76-90% Very Good !	You have a good command over these topics. Revise them again after a few days and enhance your performance.
60-75% Good !	You have a wide scope to learn more in these topics. Revise them again.
<60% Not Satisfactory!	You have a long way ahead of you to master in these topics. Revise them thoroughly.

Test 2

Syllabus

- Moment of Force, Torque and Angular Momentum
- Conservation of Angular Momentum and Its Applications
- Equilibrium of Rigid Body

For deeper insight **Scan the QR Code**

Important Instructions

- The test is of 45 minutes duration and contains 25 Multiple Choice Questions. (Four options with a single correct answer).
- Choose the correct option and fill the OMR given on the last page of this test accordingly.
- At some instances, you may find more than 1 option may be correct, in such circumstances you have to judge the most appropriate answer as per conditions given in the question.

1. When a body is projected at an angle with the horizontal in a uniform gravitational field of the earth, the angular momentum of the body about the point of projection, as it proceeds along its path

(a) remains constant
(b) increases
(c) decreases
(d) initially decreases and after its highest point increases

2. A particle of mass m is moving in YZ-plane with a uniform velocity v with its trajectory running parallel to + ve Y-axis and intersecting Z-axis at $z = a$ as shown in figure.

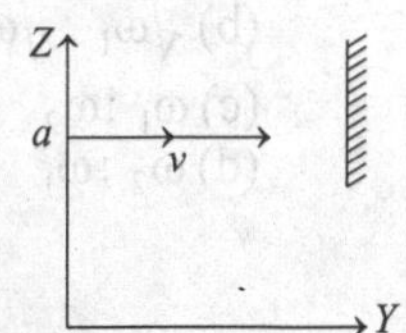

The change in its angular momentum about the origin as it bounces elastically from a wall at $y=$ constant is

(a) mva (b) $2\,mva$
(c) ymv (d) $2\,ymv$

3. A solid sphere is rotating in free space. If the radius a the sphere is increased keeping the mass same, which one of the following will not be affected?

(a) Angular momentum
(b) Moment of inertia
(c) Angular velocity
(d) Rotational kinetic energy

4. A particle system undergoing rotational motion about a fixed or variable axis. The total angular momentum **L** of the system is given by the vector sum of the angular momenta of all individual particles. Analyse the following statements regarding the conservation of angular momentum and identify the condition under which the total angular momentum of the system remains conserved.

(a) when no external force acts upon the system.
(b) when no external torque acts on the system.
(c) when no external impulse acts upon the system.
(d) when axis of rotation remains same.

5. A 4 kg mass is rotating on a circular path of radius 0.8 m with angular velocity of 44 rad/s. If radius of path becomes 1 m, then the value of angular velocity will be

(a) 27.16 rad/s
(b) 35.16 rad/s
(c) 19.28 rad/s
(d) 28.16 rad/s

6. The angular speed of a body changes from ω_1 to ω_2 without applying a torque but due to change in its moment of inertia. The ratio of radii of gyration in the two cases is

(a) $\sqrt{\omega_2} : \sqrt{\omega_1}$
(b) $\sqrt{\omega_1} : \sqrt{\omega_2}$
(c) $\omega_1 : \omega_2$
(d) $\omega_2 : \omega_1$

7. A body having mass m is rotating in a plane in circular path of radius r. Its angular momentum is L, then the centripetal force acting on the particle is

(a) L^2 / mr^3 (b) $L^2 m / r$
(c) $L^2 / m^2 r^2$ (d) L^2 / mr^2

8. **Statement I** Torque is equal to rate of change of angular momentum.

Statement II Angular momentum depends on moment of inertia and angular velocity.

In the light of above statements, choose the most appropriate answer from the options given below.

(a) Both Statement I and Statement II are correct.
(b) Both Statement I and Statement II are incorrect.
(c) Statement I is corect but Statement II is incorrect.
(d) Statement I is incorrect but Statement II is correct.

9. A body having mass m moves along line AC with velocity v as shown in figure. The angular momentum of the particle about O is

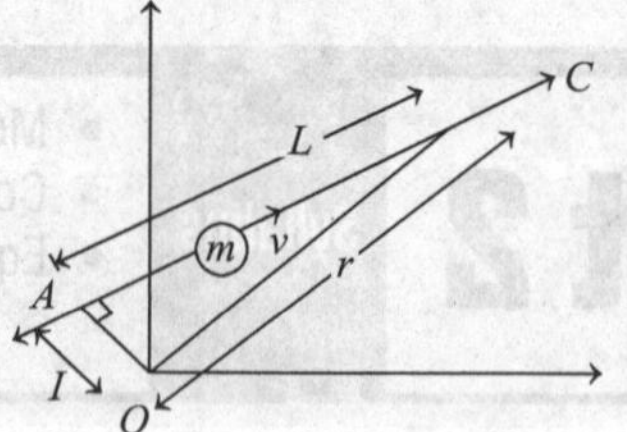

(a) mvL (b) mvl
(c) mvr (d) zero

10. A particle moving in a central force field, where the force always acts radially towards or away from the fixed central point. The particle exhibits rotational motion within a plane, and its trajectory is influenced solely by the central force. The angular momentum of the particle about the central point remains constant during its motion due to

(a) zero torque
(b) constant liner momentum
(c) constant force
(d) constant torque

11. A constant torque acting on a uniform circular wheel changes its angular momentum from A_0 to $4A_0$ in 4 s. The magnitude of this torque is

(a) $3A_0/4$ (b) A_0
(c) $4A_0$ (d) $12A_0$

12. A rod of weight W is supported by two parallel knife edges A and B and is in equilibrium in a horizontal position. The knives are at a distance d from each other. The centre of mass of the rod is at distance x from A. The normal reaction on A is

(a) $\frac{Wd}{x}$ (b) $\frac{W(d-x)}{x}$
(c) $\frac{W(d-x)}{d}$ (d) $\frac{Wx}{d}$

13. A wheel having moment of inertia $15\,\text{kg-m}^2$ about its vertical axis, rotates at the rate of 60 rpm about this axis. The torque which can stop the wheel's rotation in one minute would be

(a) $\frac{4\pi}{13}$ N-m (b) $\frac{\pi}{13}$ N-m
(c) $\frac{\pi}{2}$ N-m (d) $\frac{\pi}{3}$ N-m

14. A door 1.9 m wide requires a force of 6 N to be applied at the free end to open or close it. The force that is required at a point 0.8 m distant from the hinges for opening or closing the door is

(a) 1.2 N (b) 3.6 N
(c) 14.25 N (d) 4 N

15. A force of $-F\hat{\mathbf{k}}$ acts on O, the origin of the coordinate system. The torque about the point $(1,-1)$ is

(a) $-F(\hat{\mathbf{i}}+\hat{\mathbf{j}})$ (b) $F(\hat{\mathbf{i}}+\hat{\mathbf{j}})$
(c) $-F(\hat{\mathbf{i}}-\hat{\mathbf{j}})$ (d) $F(\hat{\mathbf{i}}-\hat{\mathbf{j}})$

16. A body of mass m moves in the XY-plane with a velocity v along the straight line PQ. If the angular momentum of the particle at point-P with respect to origin O is L_P and at point Q is L_Q, then

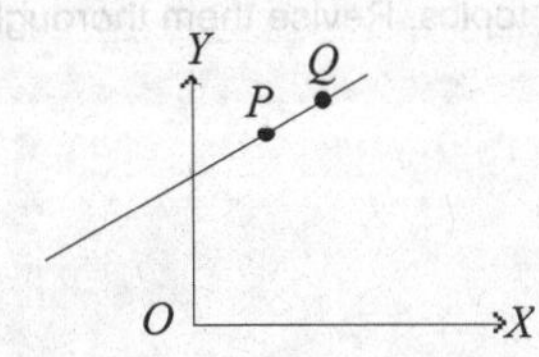

(a) $L_P > L_Q$
(b) $L_P = L_Q$
(c) The relationship between L_P and L_Q depends upon the slope of the line PQ
(d) $L_P < L_Q$

17. The graph between the angular momentum L and angular velocity ω will be

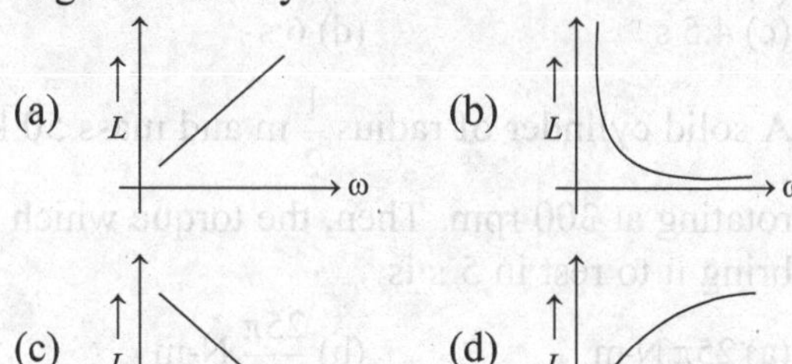

18. The diameter of a flywheel is 1m. It has a mass of 20 kg. It is rotating about its axis with a speed of 120 rotations in 1 min. Its angular momentum (in $\text{kg-m}^2/\text{s}$) is

(a) 13.4 (b) 31.4
(c) 41.4 (d) 43.4

19. **Statement I** The rate of change of angular momentum is directly proportional to external torque acting on the body.
Statement II The dimensional formula for torque is $[ML^2T^{-2}]$ and for $\tau_{ext} = \frac{dL}{dt} = I\frac{d\omega}{dt}$

In the light of above statements, choose the most appropriate answer from the options given below.

(a) Both Statement I and Statement II are correct.
(b) Both Statement I and Statement II are incorrect.
(c) Statement I is correct but Statement II is incorrect.
(d) Statement I is incorrect but Statement II is correct.

20. A rigid massless rod of length $3l$ has two masses attached at each end as shown in the figure. The rod is pivoted at point P on the horizontal axis (as shown in the figure). When released from initial horizontal position, its instantaneous angular acceleration will be

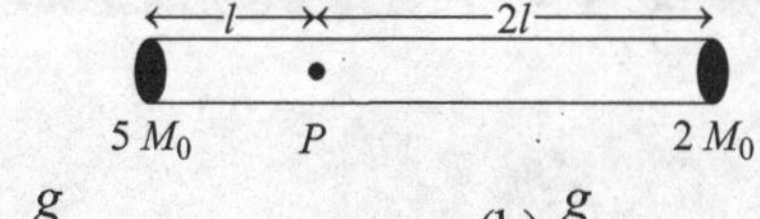

(a) $\frac{g}{13l}$ (b) $\frac{g}{2l}$
(c) $\frac{7g}{3l}$ (d) $\frac{g}{3l}$

21. A disc of moment of inertia 3 kg-m^2 is acted upon by a constant torque of 60 N-m. Initially if the disc is at rest, then the time after which the angular velocity of the disc will be 90 rad s^{-1} is

(a) 1.5 s (b) 3 s
(c) 4.5 s (d) 6 s

22. A solid cylinder of radius $\frac{1}{2}$ m and mass 50 kg is rotating at 300 rpm. Then, the torque which will bring it to rest in 5 s is

(a) 25π N-m (b) $\frac{25\pi}{2}$ N-m
(c) 50π N-m (d) 100π N-m

23. Two rigid bodies have the same angular momentum about their axes of symmetry. If the same torque is applied about their axes, the ratio of the times after which they will be stopped is

(a) 1:1
(b) 1:2
(c) 2:1
(d) Data is insufficient

24. A particle of mass 1 g is moving along a circular path of radius 1m with a velocity of 1 ms^{-1}, then its angular momentum is

(a) 1 kg m^2 s^{-1}
(b) 10^{-3} kg m^2 s^{-1}
(c) 10^{-2} kg m^2 s^{-1}
(d) 10^{-1} kg m^2 s^{-1}

25. A small mass m is attached to a massless string whose other end is fixed at P as shown in the figure. The mass is undergoing circular motion in the x-y plane with centre at O and constant angular speed ω. If the angular momentum of the system, calculated about O and P are denoted by $\mathbf{L}_O$ and $\mathbf{L}_P$ respectively, then

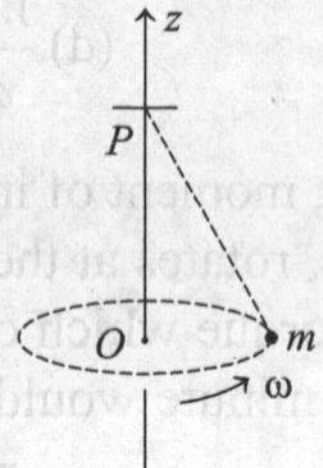

(a) $\mathbf{L}_O$ and $\mathbf{L}_P$ do not vary with time
(b) $\mathbf{L}_O$ varies with time while $\mathbf{L}_P$ remains constant
(c) $\mathbf{L}_O$ remains constant while $\mathbf{L}_P$ varies with time
(d) $\mathbf{L}_O$ and $\mathbf{L}_P$ both vary with time

■ **Response Index**

01	a	b	c	d	10	a	b	c	d	19	a	b	c	d
02	a	b	c	d	11	a	b	c	d	20	a	b	c	d
03	a	b	c	d	12	a	b	c	d	21	a	b	c	d
04	a	b	c	d	13	a	b	c	d	22	a	b	c	d
05	a	b	c	d	14	a	b	c	d	23	a	b	c	d
06	a	b	c	d	15	a	b	c	d	24	a	b	c	d
07	a	b	c	d	16	a	b	c	d	25	a	b	c	d
08	a	b	c	d	17	a	b	c	d					
09	a	b	c	d	18	a	b	c	d					

■ **Performance Scanner**

> 90% Excellent !	You have mastered these topics. The concepts of these topics are at your fingertips. Move on to the next test and maintain this momentum.
76-90% Very Good !	You have a good command over these topics. Revise them again after a few days and enhance your performance.
60-75% Good !	You have a wide scope to learn for these topics. Revise them again.
<60% Not Satisfactory!	You have a long way ahead of you to master in these topics. Revise them thoroughly.

Test 3

Syllabus
- Rigid Body Rotation and Equations of Rotational Motion
- Comparison of Linear and Rotational Motion
- Rolling Motion

For deeper insight **Scan the QR Code**

Important Instructions
- The test is of 30 minutes duration and contains 15 Multiple Choice Questions. (Four options with a single correct answer).
- Choose the correct option and fill the OMR given on the last page of this test accordingly.
- At some instances, you may find more than 1 option may be correct, in such circumstances you have to judge the most appropriate answer as per conditions given in the question.

1. **Statement I** A wheel moving down on a perfectly frictionless inclined plane will undergo slipping (not rolling motion).
Statement II For perfect rolling motion, work done against friction is zero.
In the light of above statements, choose the most appropriate answer from the options given below.
(a) Both Statement I and Statement II are correct.
(b) Both Statement I and Statement II are incorrect
(c) Statement I is correct but Statement II is incorrect.
(d) Statement I is incorrect but Statement II is correct.

2. A solid sphere rolls down two different inclined planes of same height inclination.
(a) In both cases, the speeds and time of descent will be same.
(b) The speeds will be same but time of descent will be different.
(c) The speeds will be different but time of descent will be same.
(d) Speeds and time of descent both will be different.

3. A uniform solid sphere rolls on a horizontal surface at 40 ms^{-1}. This rolls up an inclined having an angle of inclination at 30° with the horizontal. If the friction losses are negligible, then value of height h above the ground where the ball stops is
(a) 14.3 m
(b) 114.28 m
(c) 57.2 m
(d) 9.8 m

4. Two particles have their moments of inertia I and $4I$ respectively, about their axis of rotation. If their kinetic energies of rotation are equal, then their angular momentum will be in the ratio
(a) $1:\sqrt{2}$
(b) $\sqrt{2}:1$
(c) 2 : 1
(d) 1 : 2

5. **Statement I** In rolling, all points of a rigid body have the same linear speed.
Statement II The rotational motion does not affect the linear velocity of rigid body.
In the light of above statements, choose the most appropriate answer from the options given below.
(a) Both Statement I and Statement II are correct.
(b) Both Statement I and Statement II are incorrect.
(c) Statement I is correct but Statement II is incorrect.
(d) Statement I is incorrect but Statement II is correct.

6. A solid cylinder of mass M and radius R rolls without slipping down an inclined plane of length L and height h, then the speed of its centre of mass when the cylinder reaches its bottom

(a) $\sqrt{\frac{3}{4}gh}$ (b) $\sqrt{\frac{4}{3}gh}$

(c) $\sqrt{4gh}$ (d) $\sqrt{2gh}$

7. When a sphere rolls without slipping, the ratio of its kinetic energy of translation to its total kinetic energy is

(a) 1 : 7
(b) 1 : 2
(c) 1 : 1
(d) 5 : 7

8. A perfect spherical ball rolls on floor without slipping. The fraction of its total energy associated with rotation is

(a) 2/7 (b) 5/7
(c) 3/5 (d) 3/7

9. A man is standing on a rotating platform near the centre. He walks towards the circumference of platform and then comes back to his initial position, then

	List I		List II
A.	Moment of linear momentum is called	1.	$\Sigma\tau_{CM} \neq 0$ and $\Sigma F_{CM} = 0$
B.	For pure translatory motion	2.	$\Sigma\tau_{CM} \neq 0$ and $\Sigma F_{CM} \neq 0$
C.	For pure rotatory motion	3.	Angular momentum
D.	For rolling	4.	$\tau_{CM} = 0$

(a) A → 3, B → 4, C → 1, D → 2
(b) A → 4, B → 3, C → 2, D → 1
(c) A → 1, B → 3, C → 2, D → 4
(d) A → 2, B → 4, C → 1, D → 3

10. The ratio of rotational and translatory kinetic energies of a sphere is

(a) 2/9 (b) 2/7
(c) 2/5 (d) 7/2

11. If rotational kinetic energy is 50% of translational kinetic energy, then the body is

(a) ring
(b) solid cylinder
(c) hollow sphere
(d) solid sphere

12. A pot-maker rotates pot-making wheel of radius 5 m by applying a force of 2000 N tangentially because of this wheel complete exactly $1\frac{1}{2}$ revolution, the work done by him is

(a) 5654.86 J
(b) 4197.75 J
(c) 62800 J
(d) 5000 J

13. A solid sphere is rolling on a surface which is frictionless as shown in figure with a translational velocity v m/s. If solid sphere is to climb the inclined surface, then

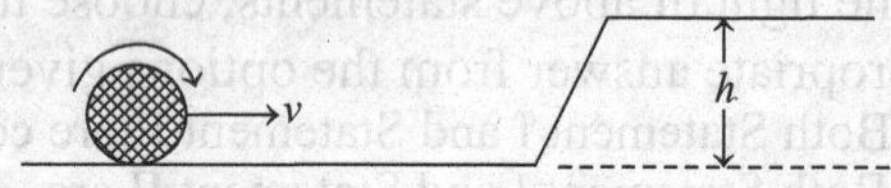

(a) $v \geq \sqrt{\frac{10}{7}gh}$

(b) $v \geq \sqrt{2gh}$

(c) $v = 0$

(d) $v = \frac{10}{7}gh$

14. Assertion (A) Total energy which is kinetic energy of a solid sphere is sum of translational and rotational kinetic energy.

Reason (R) For all solid bodies, total kinetic energy is always twice the translational kinetic energy.

In the light of above statements, choose the most appropriate answer from the options given below.

(a) Both A and R are true and R is the correct explanation of A.
(b) Both A and R are true but R is not the correct explanation of A.
(c) A is true but R is false.
(d) A is false but R is true.

15. Two bodies with moment of inertia I_1 and I_2 $(I_1 > I_2)$ have equal angular momentum. If the kinetic energy of rotation is E_1 and E_2, then

(a) $E_1 > E_2$
(b) $E_1 < E_2$
(c) $E_1 = E_2$
(d) $E_1 \geq E_2$

Response Index

01	ⓐ	ⓑ	ⓒ	ⓓ	11	ⓐ	ⓑ	ⓒ	ⓓ
02	ⓐ	ⓑ	ⓒ	ⓓ	12	ⓐ	ⓑ	ⓒ	ⓓ
03	ⓐ	ⓑ	ⓒ	ⓓ	13	ⓐ	ⓑ	ⓒ	ⓓ
04	ⓐ	ⓑ	ⓒ	ⓓ	14	ⓐ	ⓑ	ⓒ	ⓓ
05	ⓐ	ⓑ	ⓒ	ⓓ	15	ⓐ	ⓑ	ⓒ	ⓓ
06	ⓐ	ⓑ	ⓒ	ⓓ					
07	ⓐ	ⓑ	ⓒ	ⓓ					
08	ⓐ	ⓑ	ⓒ	ⓓ					
09	ⓐ	ⓑ	ⓒ	ⓓ					
10	ⓐ	ⓑ	ⓒ	ⓓ					

Performance Scanner

> 90% Excellent !	You have mastered these topics. The concepts of these topics are at your fingertips. Move on to the next test and maintain this momentum.
76-90% Very Good !	You have a good command over these topics. Revise them again after a few days and enhance your performance.
60-75% Good !	You have a wide scope to learn more in these topics. Revise them again.
<60% Not Satisfactory!	You have a long way ahead of you to master in these topics. Revise them thoroughly.

Chapter Break Thru

Syllabus

- Centre of Mass of a two Particle Systems • Centre of Mass of a Rigid Body , Basic Concepts of Rotational Motion
- Parallel and Perpendicular Axes Theorems & their Applications,
- Moment of Inertia, Radius of Gyration • Values of Moment of Inertia for Simple Geometrical Objects
- Moment of Force, Torque and Angular Momentum
- Conservation of Angular Momentum and Its Applications
- Equilibrium of Rigid Body
- Rigid Body Rotation and Equations of Rotational Motion
- Comparison of Linear and Rotational Motion
- Rolling Motion

Important Instructions

- The test is of 1 hour duration and contains 50 Multiple Choice Questions (Four options with a single correct answer).
- Choose the correct option and fill the OMR given on the last page of this test accordingly.
- At some instances, you may find more than 1 option may be correct in such circumstances you have to judge the most appropriate answer as per the conditions given in the question.

1. When a mass is rotating in a plane about a fixed point, its angular momentum is directed along

(a) radius
(b) tangent to the orbit
(c) line perpendicular to the plane of rotation
(d) line making an angle of 45° to the plane of rotation

2. Moment of inertia of a disc of radius R about a diametric axis is 35 kg - m^2. The moment of inertia of a disc about a parallel axis at a distance $R/2$ from the centre is

(a) 31.25 kg - m^2
(b) 37.5 kg - m^2
(c) 70 kg - m^2
(d) 62.5 kg - m^2

3. A particle performs uniform circular motion with an angular momentum L. If the frequency of a particle's motion is doubled and its kinetic energy is halved, the angular momentum becomes

(a) $2L$ (b) $4L$
(c) $L/2$ (d) $L/4$

4. From a uniform disc of radius R, a circular section of radius $\frac{R}{2}$ is removed.

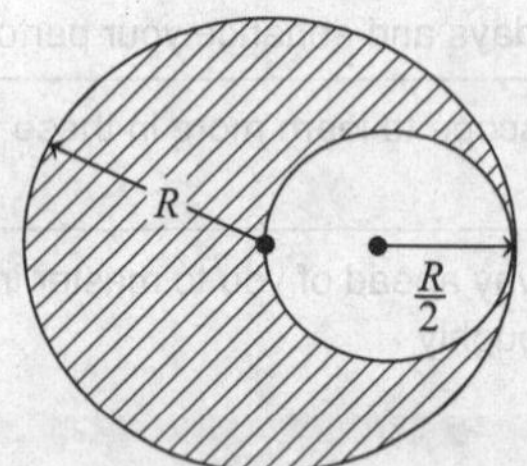

Distance of it's centre of mass and nearest point on circumference is

(a) $\frac{R}{6}$ (b) $\frac{3R}{6}$
(c) $\frac{5R}{6}$ (d) $\frac{2R}{3}$

5. The moment of inertia of a circular ring of radius R and mass M about centre and perpendicular to plane is MR^2, then moment of inertia about an axis which passes through tangentially and parallel to its plane will be

(a) MR^2 (b) $\frac{1}{2}MR^2$
(c) $\frac{3}{2}MR^2$ (d) $2MR^2$

6. Two coaxially aligned discs with moments of inertia I_1 and $I_1/2$, respectively, rotating about their common axis with initial angular velocities ω_1 and $\omega_1/2$. When these discs are brought into contact, friction acts at their interface, leading to a mutual exchange of angular momentum until they reach a common final angular velocity ω_f after some time. If E_f and E_i are the final and initial total energies, then $(E_f - E_i)$ is

(a) $-\frac{I_1\omega_1^2}{24}$ (b) $-\frac{I_1\omega_1^2}{12}$
(c) $\frac{3}{8}I_1\omega_1^2$ (d) $\frac{I_1\omega_1^2}{6}$

7. If the radius of a solid sphere is 35 cm, then radius of gyration when the axis is along a target is

(a) $7\sqrt{10}$ cm (b) $7\sqrt{35}$ cm
(c) $\frac{7}{5}$ cm (d) $\frac{2}{5}$ cm

8. The diameter of a flywheel increases by 1%. The percentage increase in moment of inertia about axis of symmetry

(a) 2% (b) 4% (c) 1% (d) 0.5%

9. Kepler's law of areas states that "A planet moving around sun sweeps out equal areas in equal time" is a consequence of

(a) law of conservation of energy
(b) law of conservation of angular momentum.
(c) law of conservation of kinetic energy
(d) work-energy theorem

10. **Statement I** If we apply force near the hinge, it is harder to open and shut the door.

Statement II Torque is maximum at hinge of the door.

In the light of above statements, choose the most appropriate answer from the options given below.

(a) Both Statement I and Statement II are incorrect.
(b) Both Statement I and Statement II are correct.
(c) Statement I is correct but Statement II is incorrect.
(d) Statement I is incorrect but Statement II is correct.

11. Two uniform thin identical rods AB and CD each of mass M and length L are joined as to form a cross as shown in figure. The moment of inertia of the cross about a bisection line EF is

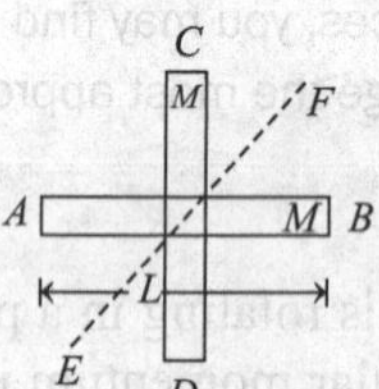

(a) $\frac{ML^2}{6}$ (b) $\frac{ML^2}{4}$
(c) $\frac{ML^2}{12}$ (d) $\frac{ML^2}{3}$

12. An electric motor has to provides a torque of 180 N-m to continuously rotating an oil mill at a constant angular speed of 200 rad s^{-1}.
If system is 75% efficient in supplying power to mill, then power delivered by motor is
(a) 36 kW (b) 48 kW
(c) 27 kW (d) 37 kW

13. If d is density of the material of a sphere of radius R, then its moment of inertia about its diameter is
(a) $\frac{8\pi}{15} dR^5$ (b) $\frac{4\pi}{3} dR^5$
(c) $\frac{2\pi}{5} dR^5$ (d) $\frac{3\pi}{4} dR^5$

14. Moment of inertia of a uniform ring about its diameter is I, then its moment of inertia about axis passing through its centre and perpendicular to its plane is
(a) $I/4$ (b) $I/2$
(c) I (d) $2I$

15. Moment of inertia of a rigid body about an axis through its centre of gravity is 10 kg - m^2. If mass of the body is 2 kg, then moment of inertia of the body about an axis parallel to the first axis and seperate by a distance of 1 m is
(a) 12 kg - m^2 (b) 8 kg - m^2
(c) 4 kg - m^2 (d) 2 kg - m^2

16. A flywheel having a radius of gyration of 2 m and mass 10 kg rotates at an angular speed of 5 rad s^{-1} about an axis perpendicular to it through its centre. The kinetic energy of rotation is
(a) 500 J (b) 2000 J
(c) 1000 J (d) 250 J

17. Three identical thin rods, each of mass m and length l are joined to form an equilateral triangular frame. The moment of inertia of the frame about an axis parallel to its one side and passing through the opposite vertex is
(a) $\frac{5}{2} ml^2$ (b) $\frac{5}{4} ml^2$
(c) $\frac{3}{2} ml^2$ (d) $\frac{5}{3} ml^2$

18. A tangential force acts at the top of a thin spherical shell of mass m and radius R. The acceleration of the shell, if it rolls without slipping is
(a) $\frac{2}{7}\frac{m}{F}$ (b) $\frac{6}{5}\frac{F}{m}$
(c) $\frac{5}{6}\frac{F}{m}$ (d) $\frac{7}{2}\frac{m}{F}$

19. Two particles of masses m_1 and m_2 are separated by a distance d, then moment of inertia of the system about an axis passing through centre of mass and perpendicular the line joining them is
(a) $\left(\frac{m_1 m_2}{m_1 + m_2}\right)\frac{d^2}{2}$ (b) $\left(\frac{m_1 m_2}{m_1 + m_2}\right) d$
(c) $\left(\frac{m_1 m_2}{m_1 + m_2}\right) d^2$ (d) $\left(\frac{2m_1 m_2}{m_1 + m_2}\right) d^2$

20. A fly wheel of mass 4 kg has moment of inertia 16 kg - m^2, then radius of gyration about the central axis perpendicular to its plane is
(a) 1m (b) 2 m
(c) 4 m (d) 16 m

21. A ring of mass m and radius r is melted and then molded into a sphere. The moment of inertia of the sphere will be
(a) two times that of the ring
(b) less than that of the ring
(c) equal to that of the ring
(d) four times that of the ring

22. As shown in the figure, a stick half of which is made of wood and the other half of iron is pivoted as shown (A). It is pivoted at wooden end and a force is applied to the other end at right angles to it (B). It is pivoted at iron end and the same force is applied to the other end at right angles to it, then angular acceleration produced is

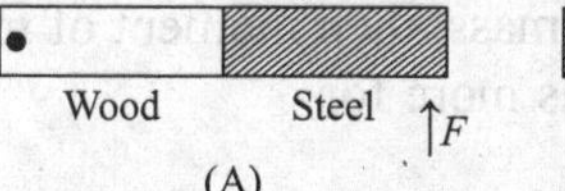

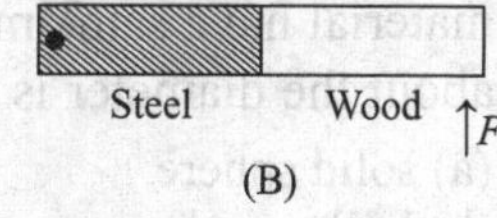

(a) more in case (A) than in (B)
(b) more in case (B) than in (A)
(c) equal in both cases
(d) we can not decide

23. A hollow sphere and solid sphere of the same radius rotate about their diameters with the same angular velocity and angular momentum, then the ratio of their masses is
(a) 3 : 8 (b) 5 : 8
(c) 3 : 5 (d) 5 : 3

24. A thin ring and a solid disc of same mass and radius are rolling with the same linear velocity, then ratio of their kinetic energies is

(a) 4:3 (b) 3:4 (c) 2:3 (d) 3:2

25. When a solid sphere rolls without slipping on a surface, its rotational kinetic energy is 40 J. Then, its total kinetic energy is

(a) 100 J (b) 70 J
(c) 140 J (d) 280 J

26. Two rigid bodies with their moments of inertia in the ratio 2 : 3 have same rotational kinetic energy, then ratio of their angular momenta is

(a) 2:3 (b) 3:2
(c) $\sqrt{2}:\sqrt{3}$ (d) $\sqrt{3}:\sqrt{2}$

27. A rod of length 15 m stands vertically on the ground. With one end hinged to the ground. When it falls on the ground such that it rotates without slipping, the velocity of the upper tip on striking the ground is (Take, $g = 10\ \text{ms}^{-2}$)

(a) 15 ms^{-1} (b) $15\sqrt{2}\text{ms}^{-1}$
(c) $\frac{15}{\sqrt{2}}\ \text{ms}^{-1}$ (d) $15\sqrt{3}\text{ms}^{-1}$

28. Moment of inertia of a rigid body about an axis passing through its centre of mass is I_0 and moment of inertia of the same body about another axis parallel to the first axis is I. Then,

(a) I is always equal to I_0
(b) I is always smaller than I_0
(c) I is always greater than I_0
(d) $0 < I < 1$

29. A solid sphere and hollow sphere of the same material have same mass, then moment of inertia about the diameter is more for

(a) solid sphere
(b) hollow sphere
(c) same for both
(d) None of the above

30. With the increase in temperature, moment of inertia of a solid sphere about the diameter is

(a) decreases
(b) increases
(c) does not change
(d) None of the above

31. An equilateral triangle ABC formed from a uniform wire has two small identical beads initially located at A. The triangle is set rotating about the vertical axis AO. Then, the beads are released from rest simultaneously and allowed to slide down, one along AB and other along AC as shown.

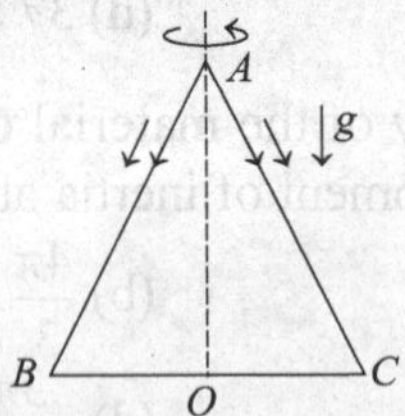

Neglecting frictional effects, the quantities that are conserved as beads slides down are

(a) angular velocity and total energy (kinetic and potential)
(b) total angular momentum and total energy
(c) angular velocity and moment of inertia about the axis of rotation
(d) total angular momentum and moment of inertia about the axis of rotation

32. Two rigid bodies have same angular momentum about their central axes, then which will have greater energy?

(a) Body having more moment of inertia
(b) Body having less moment of inertia
(c) Body will have same kinetic energy
(d) We cannot decide

33. A sphere is rolled on a rough horizontal surface. It gradually slows down and stops. The force of friction tries to

(a) decrease the linear velocity
(b) increase the angular velocity
(c) increase the linear momentum
(d) None of the above

34. A circular platform is free to rotate in a horizontal plane about a vertical axis passing through its centre. A tortoise is sitting at the edge of the platform. Now, the platform is given an angular velocity ω_0. When the tortoise move along a chord of the platform with a constant velocity (with respect to the platform). The angular velocity of the platform $\omega(t)$ will vary with time t as

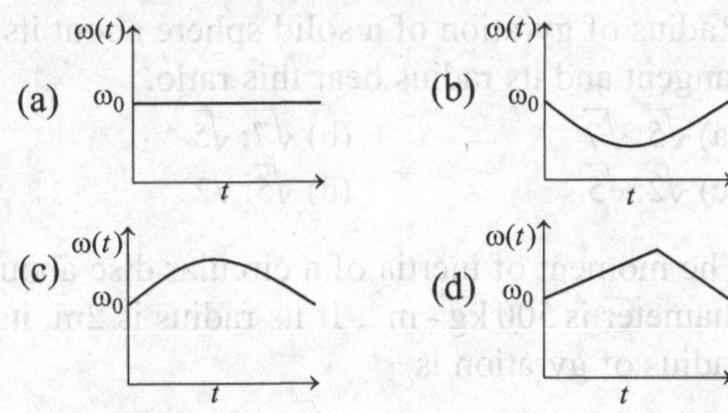

35. A circular plate rotating about its axis with angular speed ω is placed lightly (without any translational push) on a perfectly frictionless table. The radius of the disc is R. Let v_A, v_B and v_C be the magnitudes of linear velocities of the points A, B and C on the disc as shown below, then

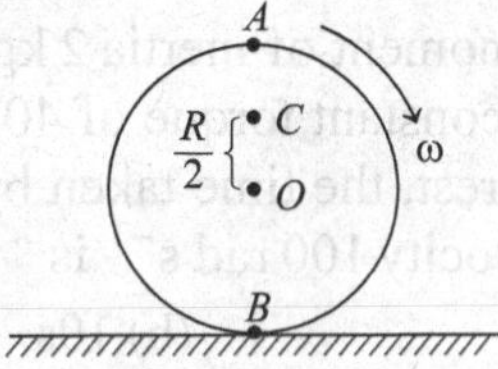

(a) $v_A > v_B > v_C$
(b) $v_A < v_B < v_C$
(c) $v_A = v_B > v_C$
(d) $v_A = v_B < v_C$

36. Match the List I with List II.

	List-I		List-II
A.	Moment of inertia	1.	$[ML^2T^{-1}]$
B.	Torque	2.	MR^2
C.	Angular momentum	3.	$(1/2)I\omega^2$
D.	Rotational KE of solid sphere	4.	$\mathbf{r} \times \mathbf{F}$

The correct match is

(a) A → 2; B → 4; C → 3; D → 1
(b) A → 1; B → 4; C → 3; D → 2
(c) A → 2; B → 4; C → 1; D → 3
(d) A → 1; B → 4; C → 2; D → 3

37. A wheel starting from rest is uniformly accelerated at 1 rad/s^2 for 2s. It is allowed to rotate uniformly for the next 4s and is finally brought to rest in the next 2s. The total angle rotated by the wheel is

(a) 20 rad (b) 8 rad
(c) 10 rad (d) 12 rad

38. Match the List I with List II.

	List-I		List-II
A.	Torque	1.	$(1/2)L\omega$
B.	Angular momentum	2.	zero
C.	Rotational KE	3.	$I\alpha$
D.	Work done by centripetal force	4.	$I\omega$

The correct match is

(a) A → 3; B → 2; C → 4; D → 1
(b) A → 1; B → 2; C → 3; D → 4
(c) A → 4; B → 3; C → 1; D → 2
(d) A → 3; B → 4; C → 1; D → 2

39. The rotational kinetic energy of a body is E and its moment of inertia is I. The angular momentum is

(a) EI (b) $2\sqrt{EI}$ (c) $\sqrt{2EI}$ (d) $\frac{E}{I}$

40. **Assertion** (A) Moment of inertia of a body is same, whatever be the axis of rotation.
Reason (R) Moment of inertia depends on mass and size of the body.
In the light of above statements, choose the most appropriate answer from the options given below.

(a) Both A and R are true and R is the correct explanation of A.
(b) Both A and R are true but R is not the correct explanation of A.
(c) A is true but R is false.
(d) A is false but R is true.

41. A circular loop of mass M and radius R hangs over a horizontal peg which is perpendicular to its plane, then its moment of inertia about the peg is

(a) $MR^2/2$ (b) MR^2
(c) $3MR^2/2$ (d) $2MR^2$

42. **Assertion** (A) The direction of position vector r is towards South and direction of force vector towards East, the direction of torque τ is vertically upwards.
Reason (R) If the position vector is along x-axis and force vector is along Y-axis, then direction of torque is along the Z-axis.

In the light of above statements, choose the most appropriate answer from the options given below.

(a) Both A and R are true and R is the correct explanation of A.
(b) Both A and R are true but R is not the correct explanation of A.
(c) A is true but R is false.
(d) A is false but R is true.

43. The moment of inertia of two spheres of equal masses about their diameters are the same. One is hollow, then ratio of their diameters

(a) 1:5 (b) $1:\sqrt{5}$ (c) $\pi:1$ (d) $\sqrt{5}:\sqrt{3}$

44. A disc has a diameter of 0.2 m and mass 0.1 kg. Its moment of inertia about an axis parallel to its plane and passing through a point on the rim will be

(a) 10^{-3} kg-m^2
(b) 1.5×10^{-3} kg-m^2
(c) 2×10^{-3} kg-m^2
(d) 1.25×10^{-3} kg-m^2

45. Two rings of the same mass and radius are placed such that their centres are at a common point and their planes are perpendicular to each other. The moment of inertia of the system about an axis passing the diameter of one of the rings is I, then moment of inertia of one ring of the system about the central axis and perpendicular to its plane would be

(a) $3I$ (b) $3I/2$
(c) $2I$ (d) $2I/3$

46. Radius of gyration of a solid sphere about its tangent and its radius bear this ratio.

(a) $\sqrt{5}:\sqrt{7}$ (b) $\sqrt{7}:\sqrt{5}$
(c) $\sqrt{2}:\sqrt{5}$ (d) $\sqrt{5}:\sqrt{2}$

47. The moment of inertia of a circular disc about its diameter is 500 kg - m^2. If its radius is 2m, its radius of gyration is

(a) 1m (b) 2m (c) $2\sqrt{2}$m (d) 4m

48. Moment of inertia of two spheres of same mass are equal. One of the sphere is solid and the other is hollow. If radius of the solid sphere is $\sqrt{15}$m, radius of the hollow sphere is

(a) 3m (b) $\sqrt{3}$m
(c) 6m (d) $\sqrt{6}$m

49. A disc of moment of inertia 2 kg - m^2 is acted upon by a constant torque of 40 N-m. If it is initially at rest, the time taken by it to acquire an angular velocity 100 rad s^{-1} is

(a) 20s (b) 10s
(c) 5s (d) 4s

50. A solid sphere is rotating with a constant angular velocity ω about its diameter. Its rotational kinetic energy is same as the kinetic energy acquired by it, if the same falls through a distance h under gravity. Radius of the sphere is

(a) $\sqrt{gh}/\omega$ (b) $\sqrt{2gh}/\omega$
(c) $\sqrt{3gh}/\omega$ (d) $\sqrt{5gh}/\omega$

Response Index

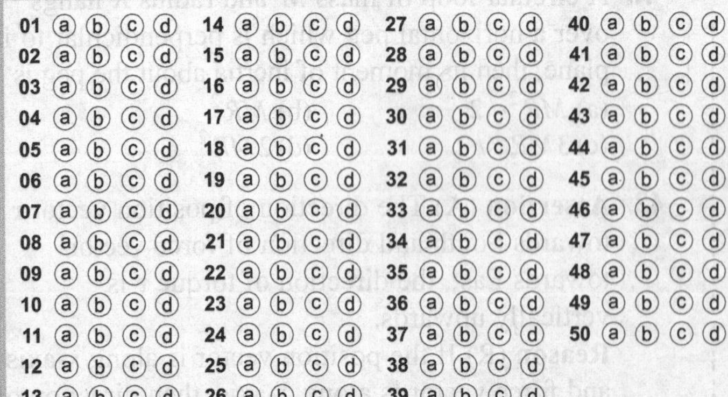

Performance Scanner

> 90% Excellent ! You have mastered this chapter. The concepts of this chapter are at your fingertips. Move on to the next chapter and maintain this momentum.

76-90% Very Good ! You have a good command over this chapter. Revise the chapter again after a few days and enhance your performance.

60-75% Good ! You have a wide scope to learn more for this chapter. Revise this chapter again.

<60% Not Satisfactory! You have a long way ahead of you to master this chapter. Revise it thoroughly.

For Online Chapter Test **Scan the QR Code**

For Online Unit Test **Scan the QR Code**

Test Booklet No. **3947107**

Test Booklet Code **CH7**

MEDACE
NEET (UG)
SELF ASSESSMENT KIT

Gravitation

Topics Covered

Universal Law of Gravitation and Acceleration Due to Gravity

Gravitational Potential and Gravitational Potential Energy

Kepler's Law and Motion of Satellite.

Important Instructions

- This Booklet Contains – Three Topic Tests and One Test on Complete Chapter.
- Each question carries 4 Marks.
- For each correct response, the candidate will get 4 marks and for every incorrect response, 1 mark will be additionally deducted from total score.
- Use **Blue/Black** point pen only for filling the OMR.
- Rough work is to be done in the space provided for this purpose in the test booklet only.

Name of the Candidate (In Capitals) ____________

____

Candidate's Signature ____________

Invigilator's Signature ____________

Facsimile signature stamp of center superintendent ____________

Do not open this Booklet until you start attempting the Test

Topical Follow Thru

Test 1

Syllabus
- The Universal Law of Gravitation
- Acceleration Due to Gravity and its Variation with Altitude and Depth

For deeper insight **Scan the QR Code**

Important Instructions
- The test is of 45 minutes duration and contains 25 Multiple Choice Questions. (Four options with a single correct answer).
- Choose the correct option and fill the OMR given on the last page of this test accordingly.
- At some instances, you may find more than 1 correct option, in such circumstances you have to judge the most appropriate answer as per conditions given in the question.

1. At what depth below the surface of the Earth, acceleration due to gravity will be half to its value 1600 km above the surface of the Earth?

(a) 4.3×10^6 m (b) 2.4×10^6 m

(c) 3.2×10^6 m (d) 1.6×10^6 m

2. Assertion (A) The force of attraction due to a hollow spherical shell of uniform density, on a point mass situated inside it is zero.

Reason (R) Various region of the spherical shell attract the point mass inside it in various directions. These forces cancel each other completely.

In the light of above statements, choose the most appropriate answer from the options given below.

(a) Both A and R are true and R is the correct explanation of A.

(b) Both A and R are true but R is not the correct explanation of A.

(c) A is true but R is false.

(d) A is false but R is true.

3. A spherical planet has a mass M_P and diameter D_P. A particle of mass m falling freely near the surface of this planet will experience an acceleration due to gravity, equal to

(a) $\frac{4GM_P}{D_P^2}$ (b) $\frac{GM_P m}{D_P^2}$

(c) $\frac{GM_P}{D_P^2}$ (d) $\frac{4GM_P m}{D_P^2}$

4. If g is the acceleration due to gravity on the surface of the earth, its value at a height equal to double the radius of the earth is

(a) g (b) $\frac{g}{2}$

(c) $\frac{g}{3}$ (d) $\frac{g}{9}$

5. A man is standing on an international space station, which is orbiting the earth at an altitude 520 km with a constant speed 7.6 km/s. If the man's mass is 50 kg, then his acceleration is

(a) 7.6 km/s^2 (b) 7.6 m/s^2

(c) 8.4 m/s^2 (d) 10 m/s^2

6. A body weighs 700 g wt on the surface of the earth. How much will it weigh on the surface of a planet whose mass is $\frac{1}{7}$ and radius is half that of the earth?

(a) 200 g wt (b) 400 g wt

(c) 50 g wt (d) 300 g wt

7. The masses of two planets are in ratio of $1:2$ and radii are in the ratio $1:2$. The ratio of acceleration due to gravity on the planets are

(a) $2:1$

(b) $1:2$

(c) $3:5$

(d) $5:3$

8. **Statement I** The difference in the value of acceleration due to gravity at pole and equator is proportional to square of angular velocity of the earth.

Statement II The value of acceleration due to gravity is minimum at the equator and maximum at the pole.

In the light of above statements, choose the most appropriate answer from the options given below.

(a) Both Statement I and Statement II are correct.

(b) Both Statement I and Statement II are incorrect.

(c) Statement I is correct but Statement II is incorrect.

(d) Statement I is incorrect but Statement II is correct.

9. A point mass m is placed at the centre of the square $ABCD$ of side a units as shown below. The resultant gravitational force on mass m due to masses m_1 and m_2 placed on the vertices of square is

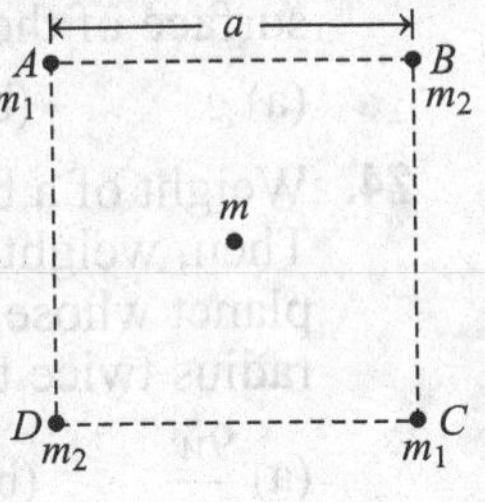

(a) $\dfrac{Gm_1 m_2}{(a\sqrt{2})^2}$ (b) $\dfrac{2Gm(m_1+m_2)}{a^2}$

(c) zero (d) $\dfrac{Gm(m_1+m_2)}{(a\sqrt{2})^2}$

10. If the acceleration due to gravity $g = 10\ \text{m/s}^2$ at the earth ($r = 6400$ km), then at height of 1600 km, the value of g will be (in m/s^2)

(a) 5 (b) 6.4 (c) 7.5 (d) 2.5

11. Two identical solid copper spheres of radius R are placed in contact with each other. The gravitational attraction between them is proportional to

(a) R^2 (b) R^{-2}

(c) R^4 (d) R^{-4}

12. Two identical spheres of radius R made of the same material are kept at a distance d apart. Then, the gravitational attraction between them is proportional to

(a) d^{-2} (b) d^2

(c) d^4 (d) d

13. The force between two objects of equal masses is F. If 25% mass of one object is transferred to the other object, then the new force will be

(a) $\dfrac{F}{4}$ (b) $\dfrac{3F}{4}$

(c) $\dfrac{15}{16}F$ (d) F

14. If the distance between two masses is doubled, then gravitational attraction between them

(a) is doubled

(b) becomes four times

(c) is reduced to half

(d) is reduced to a quarter

15. If R is the radius of the earth and g is the acceleration due to gravity on the earth's surface, the mean density of the earth is

(a) $\dfrac{4\pi G}{3gR}$ (b) $\dfrac{3\pi R}{4gG}$

(c) $\dfrac{3g}{4\pi RG}$ (d) $\dfrac{\pi RG}{12G}$

16. The depth d at which the value of acceleration due to gravity becomes $\dfrac{1}{n}$ times, the value at the surface is (R = radius of the earth)

(a) $\dfrac{R}{n}$ (b) $R\left(\dfrac{n-1}{n}\right)$

(c) $\dfrac{R}{n^2}$ (d) $R\left(\dfrac{n}{n+1}\right)$

17. The weight of an object in the coal mine, sea level and at the top of the mountain are w_1, w_2 and w_3 respectively, then

(a) $w_1 < w_2 > w_3$ (b) $w_1 = w_2 = w_3$

(c) $w_1 < w_2 < w_3$ (d) $w_1 > w_2 > w_3$

18. Suppose, the acceleration due to gravity at the earth's surface is $10\ \text{ms}^{-2}$ and at the surface of mars, it is $4.0\ \text{ms}^{-2}$. A 60 kg passenger goes from the earth to the mars in a spaceship moving with a constant velocity. Neglect all other objects in the sky. Which curve best

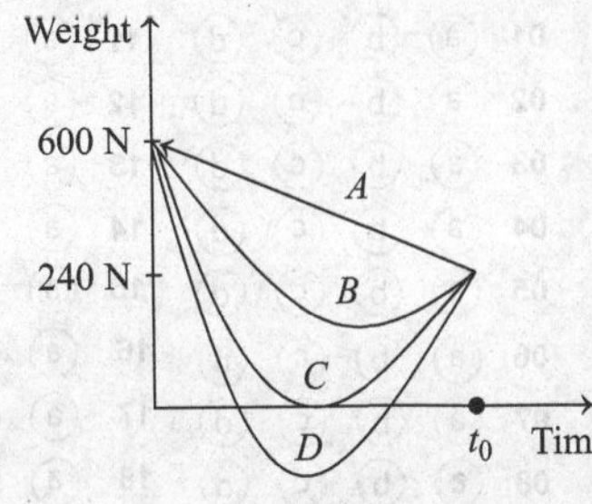

represents the weight (net gravitational force) of the passenger as a function of time?

(a) A (b) B

(c) C (d) D

19. If the earth is supposed to be a sphere of radius R, if $g_{30°}$ is value of acceleration due to gravity at latitude of 30° and g at the equator, the value of $g - g_{30°}$ is

(a) $\frac{1}{4}\omega^2 R$ (b) $\frac{3}{4}\omega^2 R$

(c) $\omega^2 R$ (d) $\frac{1}{2}\omega^2 R$

20. The rotation of the earth about its axis speeds up such that a man on the equator becomes weightless. In such a situation, what would be the duration of one day?

(a) $2\pi\sqrt{\frac{R}{g}}$ (b) $\frac{1}{2\pi}\sqrt{\frac{R}{g}}$

(c) $2\pi\sqrt{Rg}$ (d) $\frac{1}{2\pi}\sqrt{Rg}$

21. From a solid sphere of mass M and radius R, a solid sphere of radius $\frac{R}{2}$ is removed. Force on a point mass m placed at a distance of $2R$ from centre of sphere is

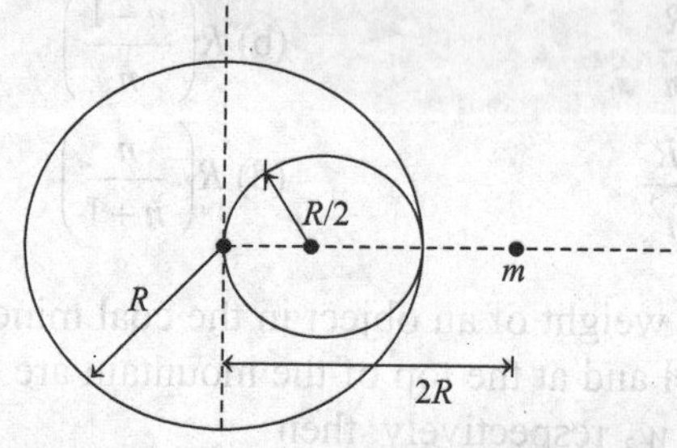

(a) $\frac{GMm}{36R^2}$ (b) $\frac{4}{36}\frac{GMm}{R^2}$

(c) $\frac{5}{36}\frac{GMm}{R^2}$ (d) $\frac{7}{36}\frac{GMm}{R^2}$

22. A point mass m is placed on axis of a large ring of radius R, at a distance R from centre of ring. If mass of ring is M, then force on mass m is

(a) $\frac{GMm}{R^2}$ (b) $\frac{GMm}{4R^2}$

(c) $\frac{GMm}{2\sqrt{2}R^2}$ (d) $\frac{GMm}{2R^2}$

23. Acceleration due to gravity on the surface of the earth is g. If the radius of the earth shrink to half the present value such that its mass does not change, then acceleration due to gravity on the surface of the earth would be

(a) g (b) $2g$ (c) $4g$ (d) $8g$

24. Weight of a body on the surface of the earth is w. Then, weight of the same body on the surface of a planet whose mass is double that of the earth and radius twice that of the earth will be

(a) $\frac{9w}{2}$ (b) $18w$ (c) $\frac{2w}{3}$ (d) $\frac{2w}{9}$

25. If R is the radius of earth the and ω is angular velocity with which it rotates about its axis, variation in the value of acceleration due to gravity at 45° latitude, if the earth stops its rotation will be

(a) increased by $R\omega^2$

(b) decreased by $R\omega^2$

(c) increased by $\frac{R\omega^2}{2}$

(d) decreased by $\frac{R\omega^2}{2}$

Response Index

01	a	b	c	d	11	a	b	c	d	21	a	b	c	d
02	a	b	c	d	12	a	b	c	d	22	a	b	c	d
03	a	b	c	d	13	a	b	c	d	23	a	b	c	d
04	a	b	c	d	14	a	b	c	d	24	a	b	c	d
05	a	b	c	d	15	a	b	c	d	25	a	b	c	d
06	a	b	c	d	16	a	b	c	d					
07	a	b	c	d	17	a	b	c	d					
08	a	b	c	d	18	a	b	c	d					
09	a	b	c	d	19	a	b	c	d					
10	a	b	c	d	20	a	b	c	d					

Performance Scanner

> 90% Excellent !	You have mastered these topics. The concepts of these topics are at your fingertips. Move on to the next test and maintain this momentum.
76-90% Very Good !	You have a good command over these topics. Revise these topics again after a few days and enhance your performance.
60-75% Good !	You have a wide scope to learn more for these topics. Revise these topics again.
<60% Not Satisfactory!	You have a long way ahead of you to master these topics. Revise it thoroughly.

Test 2

Syllabus
- Gravitational Potential
- Gravitational Potential Energy
- Escape Velocity

For deeper insight **Scan the QR Code**

Important Instructions
- The test is of 30 minutes duration and contains 15 Multiple Choice Questions. (Four options with a single correct answer).
- Choose the correct option and fill the OMR given on the last page of this test accordingly.
- At some instances, you may find more than 1 correct option, in such circumstances you have to judge the most appropriate answer as per conditions given in the question.

1. A ball released from a certain point and falls towards the earth from infinity, then velocity on reaching the earth would be

(a) infinity (b) $\sqrt{2gR}$
(c) $2\sqrt{gR}$ (d) zero

2. The potential energy of four particle each of mass 1 kg placed at the four vertices of a square of side length 1 m is

(a) $+4.0\,G$
(b) $-7.5\,G$
(c) $-5.4\,G$
(d) $+6.3\,G$

3. Dependence of intensity of gravitational field (E) of the earth with distance (r) from centre of the earth is correctly represented by

(a) 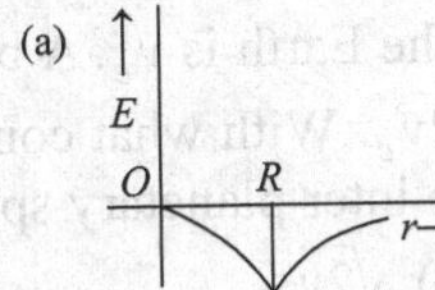

(b) 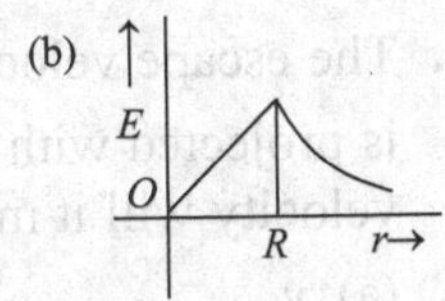

(c) 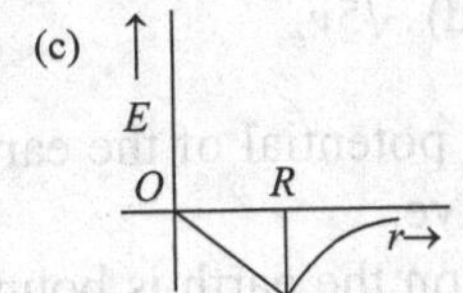

(d) 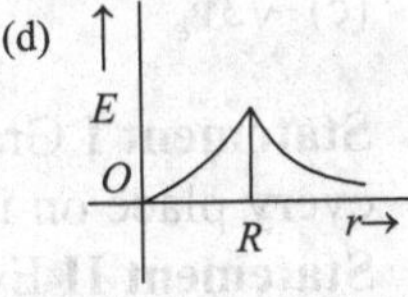

4. A satellite of mass m from the surface of the earth of mass M and radius R is to be put in a circular orbit at an altitude of $2R$, then minimum energy required to launch is

(a) $\frac{5GmM}{6R}$ (b) $\frac{GmM}{2R}$
(c) $\frac{2GmM}{3R}$ (d) $\frac{GmM}{3R}$

5. A particle of mass m is projected with a velocity $v = kv_e (k < 1)$ from the surface of the earth. (Here, v_e = escape velocity). The maximum height above the surface reached by the particle is

(a) $R\left(\frac{k}{1-k}\right)^2$ (b) $R\left(\frac{k}{1+k}\right)^2$
(c) $\frac{R^2k}{1+k}$ (d) $\frac{Rk^2}{1-k^2}$

6. An object is placed at height h above the earth's surface where, the gravitational potential is -5.12×10^7 J/kg and acceleration due to gravitation at this point is 6.4 ms^{-2}. Assume the radius of the earth is 6400 km, value of h is

(a) 1200 km
(b) 1600 km
(c) 1800 km
(d) 2400 km

7. Which of the following curve represents the variation of gravitational potential of a hollow sphere of radius R with distance r ?

(a) 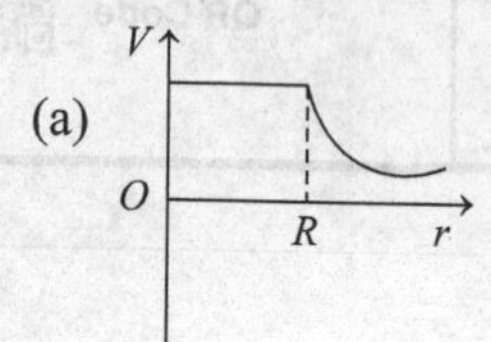

(b) 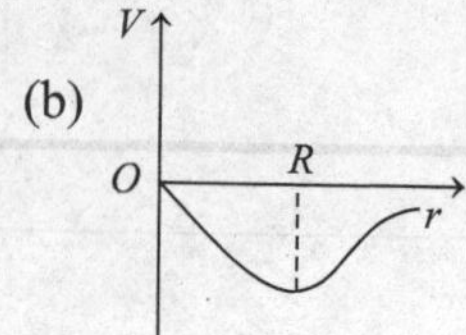

(c) 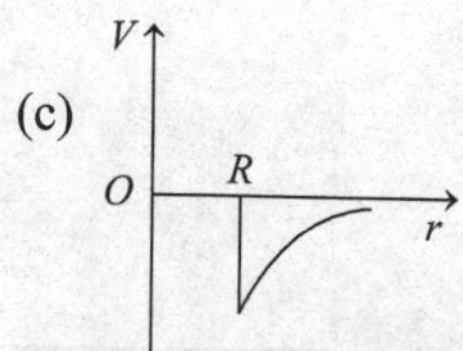

(d) 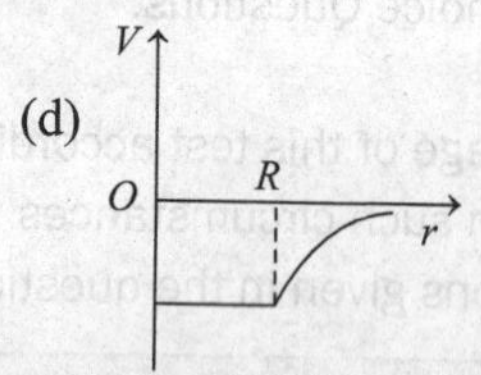

8. In some space, the gravitational field is zero. The gravitational potential in the region

(a) must be variable

(b) must be constant

(c) can not be zero

(d) must be zero

9. Two concentric spherical shells are as shown below in the figure.

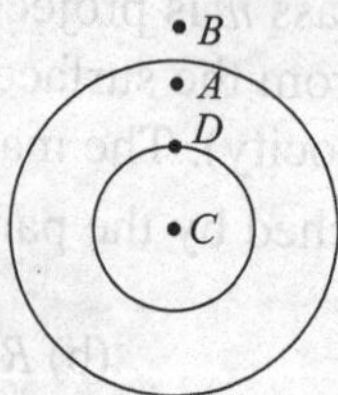

Match the List I with List II.

List I	List II
(A) Potential at A.	1. less than B
(B) Gravitational field at A.	2. potential remains constant
(C) As one moves from C to D	3. gravitational field decreases
(D) As one moves from D to A	4. zero

Choose the correct answer from the options given below.

(a) A-2, B-4, C-3, D-1

(b) A-1, B-2, C-3, D-4

(c) A-2, B-3, C-4, D-1

(d) A-3, B-4, C-1, D-2

10. A body is projected vertically upwards, from the surface of a planet of radius R with a velocity equal to half of the escape velocity for that planet. The maximum height attained by the body is

(a) $\frac{R}{3}$ (b) $\frac{R}{2}$

(c) $\frac{R}{4}$ (d) $\frac{R}{5}$

11 The variation of total energy (TE), kinetic energy (E) and potential energy (U) of a satellite with its distance r from the centre of the earth is correctly represented by which of the following curves

(a) 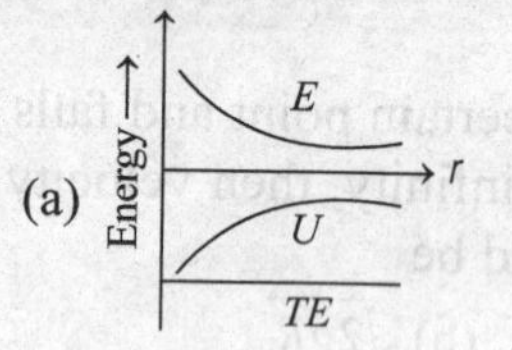

(b) 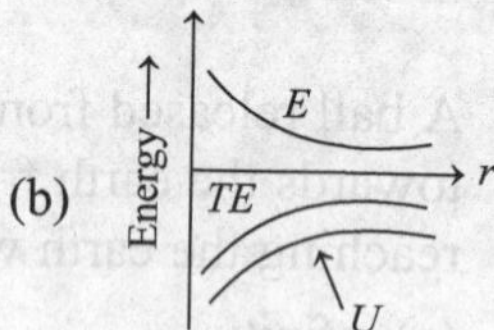

(c) 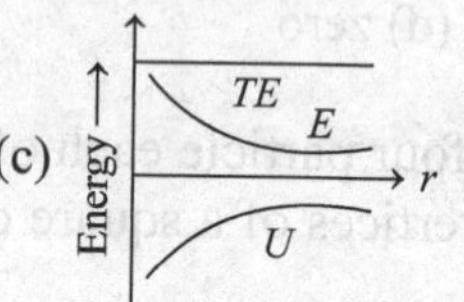

(d) 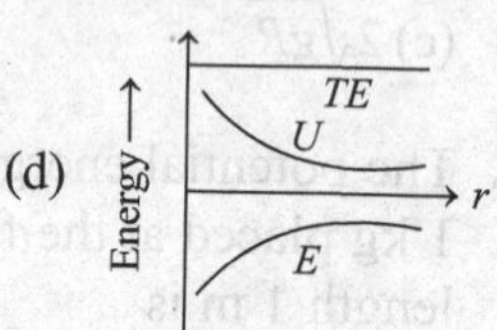

12. Energy required in moving a body of mass m from a distance $2R$ to $3R$ from centre of the Earth of mass M is

(a) $\frac{GMm}{12R^2}$ (b) $\frac{GMm}{3R^2}$

(c) $\frac{GMm}{8R}$ (d) $\frac{GMm}{6R}$

13. The escape velocity from the Earth is v_e. A body is projected with velocity $2v_e$. With what constant velocity will it move in the inter planetary space?

(a) v_e (b) $\sqrt{2}v_e$

(c) $\sqrt{3}v_e$ (d) $\sqrt{5}v_e$

14. **Statement I** Gravitational potential of the earth at every place on it, is negative.

Statement II Every body on the earth is bound by the attraction of the earth.

In the light of above statements, choose the most appropriate answer from the options given below.

(a) Both Statement I and Statement II are correct.

(b) Both Statement I and Statement II are incorrect.

(c) Statement I is correct but Statement II is incorrect.

(d) Statement I is incorrect but Statement II is correct.

15. The condition for a uniform spherical mass m of radius r to be a black hole is (G = gravitational constant and g = acceleration due to gravity)

(a) $\left(\frac{2Gm}{r}\right)^{\frac{1}{2}} \leq c$

(b) $\left(\frac{2Gm}{r}\right)^{\frac{1}{2}} = c$

(c) $\left(\frac{2Gm}{r}\right)^{\frac{1}{2}} \geq c$

(d) zero

Response Index

01	(a)	(b)	(c)	(d)	10	(a)	(b)	(c)	(d)
02	(a)	(b)	(c)	(d)	11	(a)	(b)	(c)	(d)
03	(a)	(b)	(c)	(d)	12	(a)	(b)	(c)	(d)
04	(a)	(b)	(c)	(d)	13	(a)	(b)	(c)	(d)
05	(a)	(b)	(c)	(d)	14	(a)	(b)	(c)	(d)
06	(a)	(b)	(c)	(d)	15	(a)	(b)	(c)	(d)
07	(a)	(b)	(c)	(d)					
08	(a)	(b)	(c)	(d)					
09	(a)	(b)	(c)	(d)					

Performance Scanner

> 90% Excellent !	You have mastered these topics. The concepts of these topics are on your fingertips. Move on to the next test and maintain this momentum.
76-90% Very Good !	You have a good command over these topics. Revise these topics again after a few days and enhance your performance.
60-75% Good !	You have a wide scope to learn more from this topics. Revise these topics again.
<60 Not Satisfactory!	You have a long way ahead of you to master these topics. Revise it thoroughly.

Test 3

Syllabus

- Kepler's Laws of Planetary Motion
- Motion of Satellites
- Time Period and Energy of Satellite
- Orbital Velocity

For deeper insight **Scan the QR Code**

Important Instructions

- The test is of 45 minutes duration and contains 25 Multiple Choice Questions. (Four options with a single correct answer).
- Choose the correct option and fill the OMR given on the last page of this test accordingly.
- At some instances, you may find more than 1 correct option, in such circumstances you have to judge the most appropriate answer as per conditions given in the question.

1. Two identical satellites are orbiting at distances R and $7R$ from the surface of the Earth, R being the radius of the Earth. The ratio of their

(a) kinetic energies is 4
(b) potential energies is 4
(c) total energies is 4
(d) All of the above

2. Ratio of total energy and kinetic energy of an earth's satellite is

(a) -1 (b) 1
(c) 2 (d) -2

3. The distance of neptune and saturn from the sun are nearly 10^{15} and 10^{14} m, respectively. Assuming that they move in circular orbits, their periodic times will be in the ratio

(a) $\sqrt{10}$
(b) 100
(c) $10\sqrt{10}$
(d) $\frac{1}{\sqrt{10}}$

4. A satellite of the earth revolves in a circular orbit at a height of 0.25×10^6 m above the surface of the earth. If the earth's radius is 6.38×10^6 m and $g=9.8\ \text{ms}^{-2}$, then the orbital speed of the satellite is

(a) 5.86 km s^{-1}
(b) 9.13 km s^{-1}
(c) 6.67 km s^{-1}
(d) 7.76 km s^{-1}

5. If the earth is at one-fourth of its present distance from the sun, then duration of the year will be

(a) half the present year
(b) one-eighth the present year
(c) one-fourth the present year
(d) one-sixth the present year

6. Assume average distance of the earth from the sun is B_1. If one year of the earth $=D$ days, one year of another planet whose average distance from the sun is B_2 will be

(a) $D\left(\frac{B_2}{B_1}\right)^{\frac{1}{2}}$ days

(b) $D\left(\frac{B_2}{B_1}\right)^{\frac{3}{2}}$ days

(c) $D\left(\frac{B_2}{B_1}\right)^{\frac{2}{3}}$ days

(d) $D\left(\frac{B_2}{B_1}\right)$ days

7. An unknown satellite is orbiting around the earth with total energy E. If the satellite's kinetic energy is made $2E$, then

(a) satellite escapes away
(b) period of revolution is doubled
(c) radius of the orbit is halved
(d) radius of the orbit is doubled

8. If r denotes the distance between the sun and the earth, then the angular momentum of the earth around the sun is proportional to

(a) $r^{\frac{3}{2}}$ (b) r
(c) $\sqrt{r}$ (d) r^2

9. The earth E moves in an elliptical orbit with the sun S at one of the foci as shown in figure. Its speed of motion will be maximum at the point

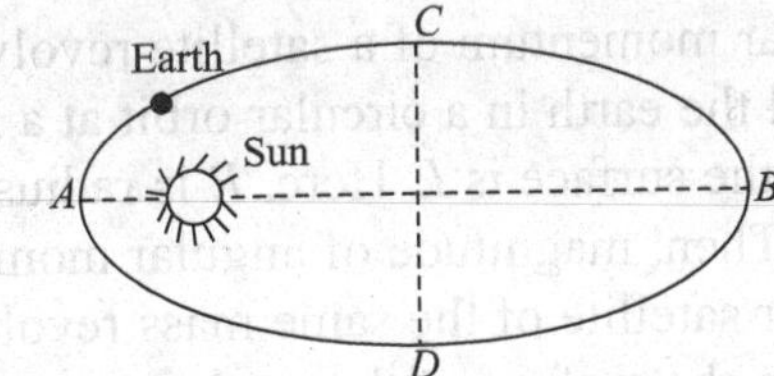

(a) C (b) A
(c) B (d) D

10. A satellite is revolving around the earth in a circular orbit having kinetic energy KE. Then, minimum kinetic energy required for it to escape into outer space is

(a) $\sqrt{2}$ KE (b) 2 KE
(c) $\frac{\text{KE}}{\sqrt{2}}$ (d) $\frac{\text{KE}}{2}$

11. Assume there are two satellites P and Q go around a planet Z in circular orbits having radii $9R$ and R respectively. If the speed of the satellite P is $3v$, the speed of the satellite Q will be

(a) $12v$ (b) $6v$
(c) $\frac{4}{3}v$ (d) $9v$

12. Statement I The velocity of satellite depends on its path.

Statement II The velocity of satellite always remains constant in an orbit.

In the light of above statements, choose the most appropriate answer from the options given below.

(a) Both Statement I and Statement II are correct.
(b) Both Statement I and Statement II are incorrect.
(c) Statement I is correct but Statement II is incorrect.
(d) Statement I is incorrect but Statement II is correct.

13. Statement I When orbit of a satellite is elliptical, its plane of rotation passes through the centre of the earth.

Statement II According to law of conservation of angular momentum, plane of rotation of satellite always remain same.

In the light of above statements, choose the most appropriate answer from the options given below.

(a) Both Statement I and Statement II are correct.
(b) Both Statement I and Statement II are incorrect.
(c) Statement I is correct but Statement II is incorrect.
(d) Statement I is incorrect but Statement II is correct.

14. If $g \propto \frac{1}{R^3}$ (instead of $\frac{1}{R^2}$), then the relation between time period of a satellite near the earth's surface and radius R will be

(a) $T^2 \propto R^3$ (b) $T \propto R^2$
(c) $T^2 \propto R$ (d) $T^2 \propto R^4$

15. Suppose a satellite is shifted towards the earth, then time period of satellite will be

(a) decreased
(b) increased
(c) unchanged
(d) Nothing can be said

16. Two stars of masses 3×10^{31} kg each and at distance 2×10^{11} m rotate in a plane about their common centre of mass O. A meteorite passes through O moving perpendicular to the star's rotational plane. In order to escape from the gravitational field of this double star, the minimum speed that meteorite should have at O is

(a) 2.8×10^5 m/s
(b) 3.8×10^4 m/s
(c) 2.4×10^4 m/s
(d) 1.4×10^5 m/s

17. The period of a satellite in a circular orbit of radius $4R$ is T, the period of another satellite in a circular orbit of radius $16R$ is

(a) $4T$ (b) $8T$
(c) $\frac{T}{4}$ (d) $\frac{T}{8}$

18. A body describes a circular motion under inverse square field, the time taken to complete one revolution T is related to the radius of the circular orbit as

(a) $T \propto r$ (b) $T \propto r^2$
(c) $T^2 \propto r^3$ (d) $T \propto r^4$

19. Assume the law of gravitational attraction suddenly changes and becomes an inverse cube law i.e., $F \propto \frac{1}{r^3}$, but still remaining a central force, then

(a) Kepler's law of areas still holds
(b) Kepler's law of period still holds
(c) Kepler's law of areas and period still holds
(d) neither the law of areas, nor the law of period still holds

20. The maximum and minimum distances of a comet from the sun are 9×10^{12} m and 8.1×10^{12} m. If its velocity when nearest to the sun is 50 m/s, then velocity (in m/s) when it is farthest, is

(a) 45 (b) 60
(c) 112 (d) 6

21. Imagine a light planet revolving around a massive star in circular orbit of radius R with a period of revolution T. If the gravitational force of attraction between the planet and the star is proportional to $R^{-\frac{5}{2}}$, then T^2 is proportional to

(a) R^3 (b) $R^{\frac{7}{2}}$ (c) $R^{\frac{5}{2}}$ (d) $R^{\frac{3}{2}}$

22. The distances of two planets from the sun are 10^{12} m and 10^{10} m respectively, then ratio of time periods of those planets is

(a) 10 (b) 100
(c) 1000 (d) $10\sqrt{10}$

23. The orbital velocity of a surface satellite of the earth is v. If another satellite is orbiting at an altitude equal to radius of the earth, its orbital velocity would be

(a) $\frac{v}{\sqrt{2}}$ (b) $\frac{v}{2}$ (c) $\sqrt{2}\,v$ (d) $2\,v$

24. Angular momentum of a satellite revolving around the earth in a circular orbit at a height R above the surface is L. Here, R is radius of the earth. Then, magnitude of angular momentum of another satellite of the same mass revolving very close to the surface of the earth is

(a) $\frac{L}{2}$ (b) $\frac{L}{\sqrt{2}}$ (c) $\sqrt{2}\,L$ (d) $2L$

25. A satellite of mass m is revolving in an orbit of radius $2R$. The minimum energy required to lift it into another orbit of radius $3R$ is (R is radius of the earth and g is acceleration due to gravity on its surface)

(a) $\frac{gRm}{4}$ (b) $\frac{gRm}{8}$
(c) $\frac{gRm}{12}$ (d) $\frac{gRm}{18}$

Response Index

01	a	b	c	d	11	a	b	c	d	21	a	b	c	d
02	a	b	c	d	12	a	b	c	d	22	a	b	c	d
03	a	b	c	d	13	a	b	c	d	23	a	b	c	d
04	a	b	c	d	14	a	b	c	d	24	a	b	c	d
05	a	b	c	d	15	a	b	c	d	25	a	b	c	d
06	a	b	c	d	16	a	b	c	d					
07	a	b	c	d	17	a	b	c	d					
08	a	b	c	d	18	a	b	c	d					
09	a	b	c	d	19	a	b	c	d					
10	a	b	c	d	20	a	b	c	d					

Performance Scanner

> 90% Excellent !	You have mastered these topics. The concepts of these topics are at your fingertips. Move on to the next test and maintain this momentum.
76-90% Very Good !	You have a good command over these topics. Revise these topics again after a few days and enhance your performance.
60-75% Good !	You have a wide scope to learn more for these topics. Revise these topics again.
<60% Not Satisfactory!	You have a long way ahead of you to master these topics. Revise it thoroughly.

Chapter Break Thru

Syllabus	• The Universal Law of Gravitation • Acceleration Due to Gravity and its Variation with Altitude and Depth • Gravitational Potential • Gravitational Potential Energy • Escape Velocity	• Kepler's Laws of Planetary Motion • Motion of Satellites • Time Period and Energy of Satellite • Orbital Velocity

Important Instructions

- The test is of 1 hour duration and contains 50 Multiple Choice Questions (Four options with a single correct answer).
- Choose the correct option and fill the OMR given on the last page of this test accordingly.
- At some instances, you may find more than 1 correct option, in such circumstances you have to judge the most appropriate answer as per conditions given in the question.

1. Two shining planets are at mean distances l_1 and l_2 from the sun and their rotational frequencies are f_1 and f_2 respectively, then

(a) $f_1^2 l_1^3 = f_2^2 l_2^3$ (b) $f_2^2 l_2^3 = f_1^2 l_1^3$

(c) $f_1^2 l_1^3 = f_1 l_1^2$ (d) $f_1^2 l_1 = f_2^2 l_2$

2. The period of the moon's rotation around the earth is 45 days. If moon's mass were 2 fold its present value and all other things remained unchanged, the period of the moon's rotation would be

(a) $45\sqrt{2}$ days

(b) $\frac{40}{\sqrt{2}}$ days

(c) 45×2 days

(d) 45 days

3. A body revolves around the sun 29 times faster than the earth. The ratio of their radii is

(a) 0.33 (b) 0.108

(c) 0.037 (d) 0.25

4. Two satellites are orbiting around the earth in the same circular orbit. The mass of the first satellite is 16 times to that of second satellite. Their period of revolutions are in the ratio

(a) 1:16 (b) 1:8

(c) 1:2 (d) 1:1

5. Match the following.

	List I		List II
A.	Universal gravitational constant	1.	g at equator, if earth stops rotating
B.	Increases by $R\omega^2$	2.	scalar
C.	g does not change at poles	3.	gravitational force
D.	Central force	4.	if earth stops rotating

The correct match is

(a) A — 1, B — 2, C — 3, D — 4

(b) A — 2, B — 1, C — 4, D — 3

(c) A — 1, B — 3, C — 2, D — 4

(d) A — 2, B — 4, C — 1, D — 3

6. The radii of two planets are respectively R_1 and R_2 and their densities are respectively ρ_1 and ρ_2. The ratio of the acceleration due to gravity at their surfaces is

(a) $g_1 : g_2 = \frac{\rho_1}{R_1^2} : \frac{\rho_2}{R_2^2}$

(b) $g_1 : g_2 = R_1 R_2 : \rho_1 \rho_2$

(c) $g_1 : g_2 = R_1 \rho_2 : R_2 \rho_1$

(d) $g_1 : g_2 = R_1 \rho_1 : R_2 \rho_2$

7. An earth's satellite is moved from one stable circular orbit to farther stable circular orbit. Which one of the following quantities increases?

(a) Linear orbital speed
(b) Gravitational force
(c) Centripetal acceleration
(d) Gravitational potential energy

8. The gravitational field due to a mass distribution is $E = \dfrac{K}{x^3}$ in the x-direction (K is a constant).

Taking the gravitational potential to be zero at infinity, its value at a distance x is

(a) $\dfrac{K}{x}$ (b) $\dfrac{K}{2x}$
(c) $\dfrac{K}{x^2}$ (d) $\dfrac{K}{2x^2}$

9. The change in potential energy, when a body of mass m is raised to a height nR from the earth's surface is (R = Radius of earth)

(a) $mgR\dfrac{n}{n-1}$
(b) $nmgR$
(c) $mgR\dfrac{n^2}{n^2+1}$
(d) $mgR\dfrac{n}{n+1}$

10. The escape velocity for a body projected vertically upwards from the surface of the earth is 11 km/s. If the body is projected at an angle of 45° with the vertical, the escape velocity will be

(a) $11\sqrt{2}$ km/s (b) 22 km/s
(c) 11 km/s (d) $11\sqrt{2}$ km/s

11. In the figure shown, the effective value of acceleration of the particle of mass m, placed at the origin is

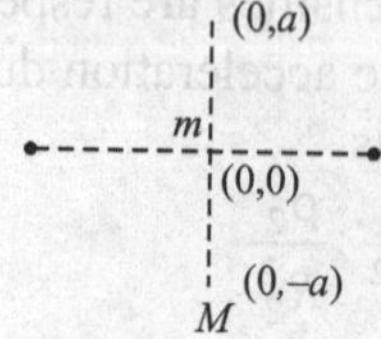

(a) zero
(b) less than zero
(c) greater than zero
(d) None of the above

12. Assuming the earth to have a constant density, point out which of the following curves shows the variation of acceleration due to gravity from the centre of the earth to the point far away from the surface of the earth?

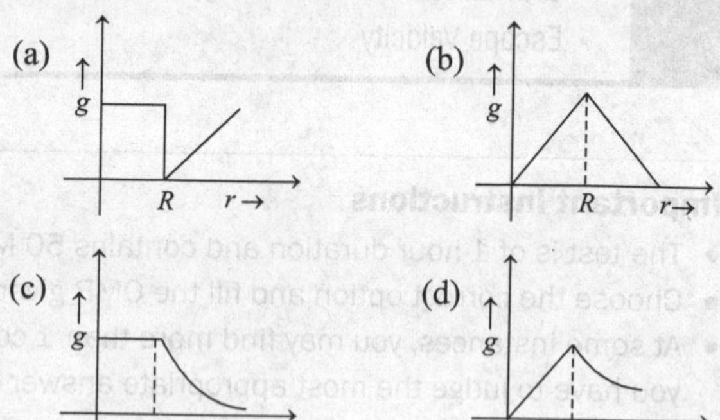

13. The magnitude of gravitational force on a particle of mass m placed at a distance x from the rod of mass M and length l as shown in the figure is

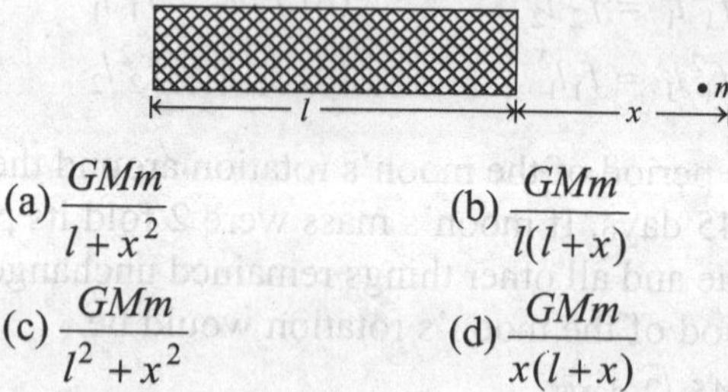

(a) $\dfrac{GMm}{l+x^2}$ (b) $\dfrac{GMm}{l(l+x)}$
(c) $\dfrac{GMm}{l^2+x^2}$ (d) $\dfrac{GMm}{x(l+x)}$

14. A satellite of mass m revolves in a circular orbit at a height h from the surface of the earth moreover the radius of the earth say R and acceleration due to gravity at the surface of the earth. Then, velocity of the satellite in the orbit is given by

(a) gR^2 (b) $\dfrac{gR^2}{R+h}$ (c) $\dfrac{gR}{R+h}$ (d) $\sqrt{\dfrac{gR^2}{R+h}}$

15. Two masses $2M$ and $18M$ are placed at a distance R from each other. Potential at a point where their net gravitational field is zero, will be

(a) $35\frac{GM}{R}$ (b) $64\frac{GM}{R}$

(c) $-64\frac{GM}{R}$ (d) $-35\frac{GM}{R}$

16. Kepler's third law states that the square of period of revolution (T) of a planet around the sun is proportional to third power of average distance r between sun and planet i.e. $T^2 = Kr^3$. Here, K is constant. If the mass of the sun and planet are M and m respectively, then as per Newton's law of gravitation force of attraction between them is $F = \frac{GMm}{r^2}$. The relation between G and K is described as

(a) $GMK = 4\pi^2$

(b) $K = G$

(c) $K = \frac{1}{G}$

(d) $GK = 4\pi^2$

17. Two moving satellites of same mass are launched in the same orbit around the earth, so as to rotate opposite to each other. If they collide and stick together as wreckage, then total energy will be

(a) $-\frac{2GMm}{r}$ (b) $-\frac{GMm}{r}$

(c) $\frac{GMm}{2r}$ (d) $\frac{GMm}{4r}$

18. **Statement I** Gravitational force is independent of the medium between the particles while electric and magnetic force depend on the nature of the medium between the particle.

Statement II Gravitational force is always attractive in nature while electric and magnetic force can be attractive or repulsive.

In the light of above statements, choose the most appropriate answer from the options given below.

(a) Both Statement I and Statement II are correct.

(b) Both Statement I and Statement II are incorrect.

(c) Statement I is correct but Statement II is incorrect.

(d) Statement I is incorrect but Statement II is correct.

19. **Assertion (A)** The square of the period of revolution of a planet is proportional to the cube of the semi-major axis of the ellipse.

Reason (R) Sun's gravitational field is inversely proportional to the square of its distance from the planet.

(a) Both A and R are true and R is the correct explanation of A.

(b) Both A and R are true but R is not the correct explanation of A.

(c) A is true but R is false.

(d) A is false but R is true.

20. Assuming the earth is supposed to be sphere of radius R and $g_{60°}$ is the value of acceleration due to gravity at latitude of 60° and g at the equator, the value of $g - g_{60°}$ is

(a) $\left(\frac{1}{4}\right)\omega^2 R$ (b) $\left(\frac{3}{4}\right)\omega^2 R$

(c) $\omega^2 R$ (d) $\left(\frac{1}{2}\right)\omega^2 R$

21. Two concentric shells have masses M and m and their radii are R and r respectively, where $R > r$. The gravitational potential at their common centre is

(a) $-\frac{GM}{R}$ (b) $\frac{-GM}{r}$

(c) $-G\left(\frac{M}{R} - \frac{m}{r}\right)$ (d) $-G\left(\frac{M}{R} + \frac{m}{r}\right)$

22. The escape velocity of a body on the surface of the earth is 11.2 km/s. If the earth's mass increases to twice its present value and radius of the earth becomes half, then escape velocity becomes

(a) 5.6 km/s (b) 11.2 km/s

(c) 22.4 km/s (d) 44.8 km/s

23. If the mass of the moon is $\frac{M}{81}$, where M is the mass of the earth, find the distance of the point where gravitational field due to the earth and the moon cancel each other, from the centre of the moon. Given that distance between centres of the earth and the moon is 60 R, where R is the radius of the earth.

(a) 4 R (b) 8 R
(c) 12 R (d) 6 R

24. A satellite of mass m revolves around the earth of radius R at height x from its surface. If g is the acceleration due to gravity on the surface of the earth, the orbital speed of the satellite is

(a) gx (b) $\frac{gR}{R-x}$

(c) $\frac{gR^2}{R+x}$ (d) $\left(\frac{gR^2}{R+x}\right)^{1/2}$

25. Which of the following is the evidence to show that there must be a force acting on the earth and directed towards the sun?

(a) Deviation of the falling bodies towards east
(b) Revolution of the earth around the sun
(c) Phenomenon of day and night
(d) Apparent motion of sun around the earth

26. If the earth stops rotating, the value of g at the equator will

(a) increase
(b) remain same
(c) decrease
(d) may increase or decrease

27. Let g be the acceleration due to gravity at the earth's surface and K be the rotational kinetic energy of the earth. Suppose the earth's radius decreases by 2% keeping all other quantities same, then

(a) g decreases by 2% and K decreases by 4%
(b) g decreases by 4% and K increases by 2%
(c) g increases by 4% and K increases by 4%
(d) g decreases by 4% and K increases by 4%

28. The depth at which the effective value of acceleration due to gravity is $\frac{g}{4}$ is

(a) R (b) $\frac{3R}{4}$ (c) $\frac{R}{2}$ (d) $\frac{R}{4}$

29. A planet has twice the radius but the mean density is $\frac{1}{4}$ th as compared to the earth. What is the ratio of escape velocity from the earth to that from the planet?

(a) 3:1 (b) 1:2 (c) 1:1 (d) 2:1

30. Two satellites of masses m_1 and m_2 $(m_1 > m_2)$ are revolving around the earth in circular orbits of radius r_1 and r_2 $(r_1 > r_2)$ respectively. Which of the following statement is true regarding their speeds v_1 and v_2?

(a) $v_1 = v_2$ (b) $v_1 < v_2$
(c) $v_1 > v_2$ (d) $\frac{v_1}{r_1} = \frac{v_2}{r_2}$

31. The period of a satellite in a circular orbit around a planet is independent of

(a) mass of the planet
(b) radius of the planet
(c) mass of the satellite
(d) all the three parameters (a), (b) and (c)

32. In a satellite, if the time of revolution is T, then KE is proportional to

(a) $\frac{1}{T}$ (b) $\frac{1}{T^2}$

(c) $\frac{1}{T^3}$ (d) $\frac{1}{T^{2/3}}$

33. A planet moves around the sun. At a given point P, it is closest from the sun at a distance d_1 and has a speed v_1. At another point Q, when it is farthest from the sun at a distance d_2, its speed will be

(a) $\frac{d_1^2 v_1}{d_2^2}$ (b) $\frac{d_2 v_1}{d_1}$

(c) $\frac{d_1 v_1}{d_2}$ (d) $\frac{d_2^2 v_1}{d_1^2}$

34. Kepler's second law regarding constancy of areal velocity of a planet is a consequence of the law of conservation of

(a) energy
(b) angular momentum
(c) linear momentum
(d) kinetic energy

35. An asteroid of mass m is approaching the earth, initially at a distance $10\ R_E$ with speed v_i. It hits the earth with a speed v_f (R_E and M_E are radius and mass of earth), then

(a) $v_f^2 = v_i^2 + \frac{2Gm}{R_E}\left(1+\frac{1}{10}\right)$

(b) $v_f^2 = v_i^2 + \frac{2GM_E}{R_E}\left(1+\frac{1}{10}\right)$

(c) $v_f^2 = v_i^2 + \frac{2GM_E}{R_E}\left(1-\frac{1}{10}\right)$

(d) $v_f^2 = v_i^2 + \frac{2Gm}{R_E}\left(1-\frac{1}{10}\right)$

36. A satellite of mass M is orbiting in an orbit of radius R. Work done by gravity per revolution on the satellite is given by

(a) $\frac{MgR}{2}$ (b) MgR

(c) $Mg \times 2\pi R$ (d) zero

37. If a rocket is fired with a speed $v = 2\sqrt{gr}$ near the earth's surface and coasts upwards, its speed in the intersteller space is

(a) $4\sqrt{gr}$ (b) $\sqrt{2gr}$

(c) $\sqrt{gr}$ (d) $\sqrt{4gr}$

38. The variation in the speed of the planets in their orbits about the sun can be explained on the basis of the conservation of

(a) linear momentum

(b) angular momentum

(c) total energy

(d) angular kinetic energy

39. A particle would take a time t to move down a straight tube from the surface of earth (supposed to be a homogeneous sphere) to its centre. If gravity were to remain constant, then the time would be t'. The ratio of t/t' will be

(a) $\frac{\pi}{2\sqrt{2}}$ (b) $\frac{\pi}{\sqrt{2}}$

(c) $\sqrt{2}\pi$ (d) $\frac{\pi}{\sqrt{2}}$

40. If three uniform spheres, each having mass M and radius r, are kept in such a way that each touches the other two, the magnitude of the gravitational force on any sphere due to the other two is

(a) $\frac{GM^2}{4r^2}$ (b) $\frac{2GM^2}{r^2}$

(c) $\frac{2GM^2}{4r^2}$ (d) $\frac{\sqrt{3}\,GM^2}{4r^2}$

41. If three particles each of mass M are placed at the corners of an equilateral triangle of side a, the potential energy of the system and the work done if the side of the triangle is changed from a to $2a$, are

(a) $\frac{3GM}{a^2}, \frac{3GM}{2a}$ (b) $-\frac{3GM^2}{a}, \frac{3GM^2}{2a}$

(c) $-\frac{3GM^2}{a^2}, \frac{3GM^2}{4a^2}$ (d) $-\frac{3GM^2}{a}, \frac{3GM}{2a}$

42. How much work per kilogram need to be done to shift a 1 kg mass from the surface of the earth to infinity? [Take acceleration due to gravity = g and radius of the earth = R]

(a) $\frac{g}{R}$ (b) $\frac{R}{g}$ (c) gR (d) $\frac{g}{R^2}$

43. A thin rod of length L is bent to form a semi-circle. The mass of rod is M. What will be the gravitational potential at the centre of the circle?

(a) $-\frac{GM}{L}$ (b) $-\frac{GM}{2\pi L}$

(c) $-\frac{\pi GM}{2L}$ (d) $-\frac{\pi GM}{L}$

44. If M is mass of the earth, R is radius of the earth, then what is the gravitational potential at a distance $\frac{R}{2}$ from its centre

(a) $-\frac{GM}{R}$ (b) $-\frac{3}{2}\frac{GM}{R}$

(c) $\frac{-8GM}{11R}$ (d) $-\frac{11GM}{8R}$

45. A projectile is fired vertically upwards. It escapes from the earth, when fired with velocity v. If it is to be fired at 45° to the horizontal, what should be its velocity to enable it to escape from the gravitational pull of the earth?

(a) $\sqrt{2}\,v$

(b) $\frac{v}{\sqrt{2}}$

(c) v

(d) Some other velocity

46. A man covers 60 m distance in one minute on the surface of the earth. The distance he will cover on the surface of moon per minute is $\left(\text{assuming } g_{\text{moon}} = \frac{g_{\text{earth}}}{6}\right)$

(a) 60 m
(b) 60×6 m
(c) $\frac{60}{6}$ m
(d) $\sqrt{60}$ m

47. A satellite is moving around the earth with a speed v in a circular orbit of radius r. If the orbit radius is decreased by 1%, its speed will

(a) increase by 1%
(b) increase by 0.5%
(c) decrease by 1%
(d) decrease by 0.5%

48. By what percentage the energy of a satellite has to be increased to shift it from an orbit of radius r to $3/2r$?

(a) 66.7%
(b) 33.3%
(c) 75%
(d) 20.3%

49. The escape velocity of a body from the surface of earth is 11.2 km/s. It is thrown up with a velocity 4 times the velocity of escape. The velocity of the body when it has escaped the gravitational pull of earth (neglecting presence of all other heavenly bodies) is

(a) 4×11.2 km/s
(b) $\sqrt{15} \times 11.2$ km/s
(c) zero
(d) 3×11.2 km/s

50. **Assertion** (A) If the earth were to stop rotating about its axis, g would increase.

Reason (R) This is because, $g' = g - R\omega^2 \cos^2 \lambda$ where the symbols have standard meaning.

In the light of above statements, choose the most appropriate answer from the options given below.

(a) Both A and R are true and R is the correct explanation of A.
(b) Both A and R are true but R is not the correct explanation of A.
(c) A is true but R is false.
(d) A is false but R is true.

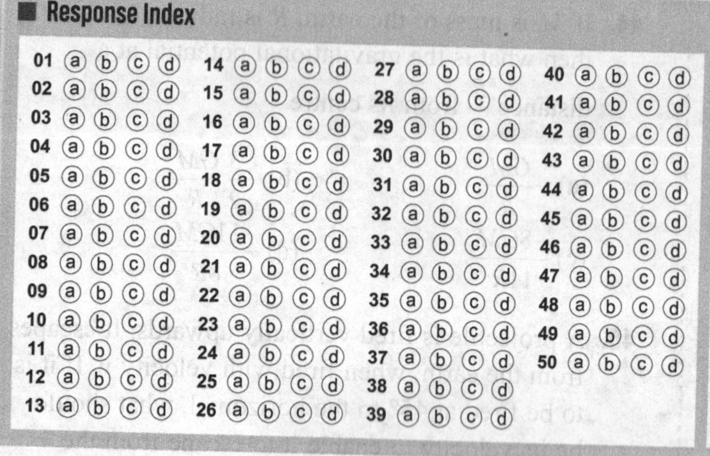

Response Index

01	ⓐ ⓑ ⓒ ⓓ	14	ⓐ ⓑ ⓒ ⓓ	27	ⓐ ⓑ ⓒ ⓓ	40	ⓐ ⓑ ⓒ ⓓ
02	ⓐ ⓑ ⓒ ⓓ	15	ⓐ ⓑ ⓒ ⓓ	28	ⓐ ⓑ ⓒ ⓓ	41	ⓐ ⓑ ⓒ ⓓ
03	ⓐ ⓑ ⓒ ⓓ	16	ⓐ ⓑ ⓒ ⓓ	29	ⓐ ⓑ ⓒ ⓓ	42	ⓐ ⓑ ⓒ ⓓ
04	ⓐ ⓑ ⓒ ⓓ	17	ⓐ ⓑ ⓒ ⓓ	30	ⓐ ⓑ ⓒ ⓓ	43	ⓐ ⓑ ⓒ ⓓ
05	ⓐ ⓑ ⓒ ⓓ	18	ⓐ ⓑ ⓒ ⓓ	31	ⓐ ⓑ ⓒ ⓓ	44	ⓐ ⓑ ⓒ ⓓ
06	ⓐ ⓑ ⓒ ⓓ	19	ⓐ ⓑ ⓒ ⓓ	32	ⓐ ⓑ ⓒ ⓓ	45	ⓐ ⓑ ⓒ ⓓ
07	ⓐ ⓑ ⓒ ⓓ	20	ⓐ ⓑ ⓒ ⓓ	33	ⓐ ⓑ ⓒ ⓓ	46	ⓐ ⓑ ⓒ ⓓ
08	ⓐ ⓑ ⓒ ⓓ	21	ⓐ ⓑ ⓒ ⓓ	34	ⓐ ⓑ ⓒ ⓓ	47	ⓐ ⓑ ⓒ ⓓ
09	ⓐ ⓑ ⓒ ⓓ	22	ⓐ ⓑ ⓒ ⓓ	35	ⓐ ⓑ ⓒ ⓓ	48	ⓐ ⓑ ⓒ ⓓ
10	ⓐ ⓑ ⓒ ⓓ	23	ⓐ ⓑ ⓒ ⓓ	36	ⓐ ⓑ ⓒ ⓓ	49	ⓐ ⓑ ⓒ ⓓ
11	ⓐ ⓑ ⓒ ⓓ	24	ⓐ ⓑ ⓒ ⓓ	37	ⓐ ⓑ ⓒ ⓓ	50	ⓐ ⓑ ⓒ ⓓ
12	ⓐ ⓑ ⓒ ⓓ	25	ⓐ ⓑ ⓒ ⓓ	38	ⓐ ⓑ ⓒ ⓓ		
13	ⓐ ⓑ ⓒ ⓓ	26	ⓐ ⓑ ⓒ ⓓ	39	ⓐ ⓑ ⓒ ⓓ		

Performance Scanner

> 90% Excellent !	You have mastered this chapter. The concepts of this chapter are on your fingertips. Move on to the next chapter and maintain this momentum.
76-90% Very Good !	You have a good command over this chapter. Revise the chapter again after a few days and enhance your performance.
60-75% Good !	You have a wide scope to learn for this chapter. Revise this chapter again.
<60% Not Satisfactory!	You have a long way ahead of you to master this chapter. Revise it thoroughly.

For Online Chapter Test **Scan the QR Code**

For Online Unit Test **Scan the QR Code**

Test Booklet No. 3947108

Test Booklet Code CH8

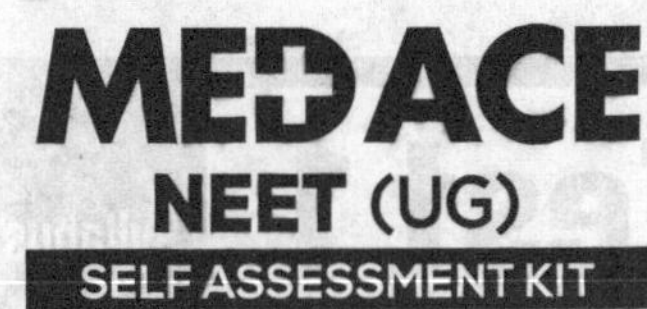

Mechanical Properties of Solids

Topics Covered

Stress and Strain, Elastic Modulus

Stress-Strain Curve and Energy in Stretched Wire

Important Instructions

- This Booklet Contains – Two Topic Tests and One Test on Complete Chapter.
- Each question carries 4 Marks.
- For each correct response, the candidate will get 4 marks and for every incorrect response, 1 mark will be additionally deducted from total score.
- Use **Blue/Black** point pen only for filling the OMR.
- Rough work is to be done in the space provided for this purpose in the test booklet only.

Name of the Candidate (In Capitals)

____

____

Candidate's Signature _______________

Invigilator's Signature _______________

Facsimile signature stamp of center superintendent_______________

Do not open this Booklet until you start attempting the Test

Topical Follow Thru

Test 1

Syllabus

- Stress and Strain, Hooke's Law, Young's Modulus, Bulk Modulus and Shearing Modulus

For deeper insight **Scan the QR Code**

Important Instructions

- The test is of 45 minutes duration and contains 25 Multiple Choice Questions. (Four options with a single correct answer).
- Choose the correct option and fill the OMR given on the last page of this test accordingly.
- At some instances, you may find more than 1 option may be correct, in such circumstances you have to judge the most appropriate answer as per the conditions given in the question.

1. A steel rod of 2.0 m long has a cross-section area of 0.5 cm^2. This rod is now hung by one end from a support and a 500 kg weight is hung from the rod's lower end. The stress and the strain are, respectively

(Take, $Y = 20 \times 10^{10}\ Nm^{-2}$)

(a) 9.8×10^7 Pa, 9.0×10^{-4}
(b) 1.8×10^8 Pa, 4.9×10^{-4}
(c) 9.8×10^7 Pa, 4.9×10^{-4}
(d) 1.8×10^8 Pa, 9.0×10^{-4}

2. A force F is required to break a wire having radius R. The force required to break another wire of same material and radius $2R$ will be

(a) $\frac{F}{2}$ (b) $2F$ (c) $4F$ (d) $\frac{F}{4}$

3. Two wires of equal length and cross-sectional area suspended as shown in figure. Their Young's modulii are Y_1 and Y_2, respectively. The equivalent Young's modulus will be

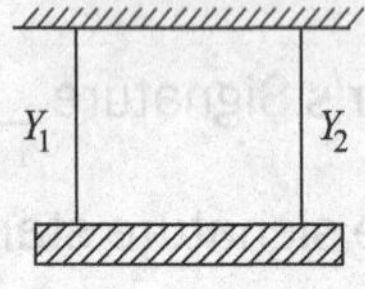

(a) $Y_1 + Y_2$ (b) $\frac{Y_1 + Y_2}{2}$

(c) $\frac{Y_1 Y_2}{Y_1 + Y_2}$ (d) $\sqrt{Y_1 Y_2}$

4. If the ratio of lengths, radii and Young's modulii of two wires of different material in the figure are A, B and C respectively, then the corresponding ratio of increase in their lengths would be

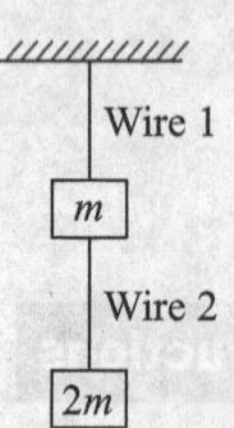

(a) $\frac{2AC}{B^2}$ (b) $\frac{3A}{2B^2C}$

(c) $\frac{3C}{2AB^2}$ (d) $\frac{2A^2C}{B}$

5. Three blocks A, B and C each of mass 4 kg are attached as shown in figure. Both the wires have equal cross-sectional area $5 \times 10^{-7}\ m^2$. The surface is smooth. Find the longitudinal strain in each wire, if Young's modulus of both the wires is $2 \times 10^{11}\ N/m^2$. (Take, $g = 10\ m/s^2$).

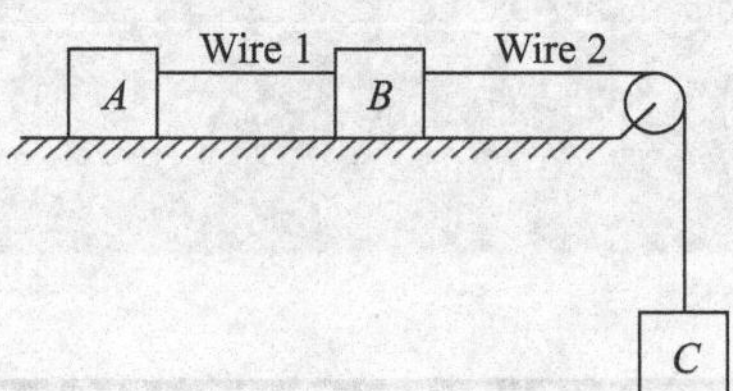

(a) $\frac{4}{3}\times10^{-4}$, $\frac{8}{3}\times10^{-4}$
(b) $\frac{3}{8}\times10^{-4}$, $\frac{3}{4}\times10^{-4}$
(c) $\frac{4}{3}\times10^{-4}$, $\frac{3}{8}\times10^{-4}$
(d) $\frac{8}{3}\times10^{-4}$, $\frac{3}{4}\times10^{-4}$

6. The length of a metallic wire is L_1 when the tension in the wire is T_1 and is L_2 when the tension is T_2. The natural length of the wire is
(a) $\frac{L_1T_2 - L_2T_1}{T_2 - T_1}$
(b) $\frac{L_1T_1 - L_2T_2}{T_2 + T_1}$
(c) $\frac{L_1T_2 - L_2T_1}{T_2 + T_1}$
(d) $\frac{L_2T_2 - L_1T_1}{T_2 - T_1}$

7. A metal rod has a radius of 10 mm and a length of 1.0 m. A 100 kN force stretches it along its length. Calculate stress on the metal rod. (Take, $Y = 2.0\times10^{11}$ N/m^2)
(a) 3.18×10^8 N/m^2
(b) 5.2×10^6 N/m^2
(c) 5.2×10^8 N/m^2
(d) 3.18×10^6 N/m^2

8. On applying a stress of 5×10^9 N/m^2, the length of an elastic wire is increased to double. Young's modulus of the material of wire is
(a) 2.5×10^9 N/m^2
(b) 10^{10} N/m^2
(c) 5×10^9 N/m^2
(d) 5×10^8 N/m^2

9. A steel wire of length L and density d and Young's modulus Y is hanging from a support. The elongation in the length of wire at which wire will break
(a) $\frac{L^2dg}{4Y}$ (b) $\frac{2L^2dg}{Y}$
(c) $\frac{L^2dg}{2Y}$ (d) $\frac{L^2dg}{Y}$

10. A brass rod of length 5 m and cross- sectional area 5.0 cm^2 is attached end-to-end to a steel rod of length L and cross-sectional area 1.0 cm^2. The compound rod is subjected to equal and opposite pulls of magnitude 5×10^4 N at its ends. If the elongations of the two rods are equal, then the length of the steel rod L is ($Y_{Brass} = 1.0\times10^{11}$ N/m^2 and $Y_{Steel} = 2.0\times10^{11}$ N/m^2)
(a) 1.5 m (b) 1.8 m
(c) 1 m (d) 2 m

11. The diameter of a metal rod is 4 mm and Young's modulus of this metal is 9×10^{10} N/m^2. The force required to stretch it by 0.1% of its length is
(a) 360π N (b) 36 N
(c) $144\pi\times10^3$ N (d) $36\pi\times10^5$ N

12. A 10 kg motor rests on four cylindrical rubber blocks. Each block has a height of 5 cm and a cross-sectional area of 16 cm^2. The shear modulus of rubber is 2×10^6 N/m^2. A sideways force of 800 N is applied to the motor. The distance that the motor moves sideways is
(a) 0.156 cm (b) 1.56 cm
(c) 0.31 cm (d) 0.204 cm

13. **Statement I** Reciprocal of bulk modulus of elasticity is called compressibility.
Statement II It is difficult to twist a long rod as compared to small rod.
In the light of the above statements, choose the most appropriate answer from the options given below.
(a) Both Statement I and Statement II are incorrect.
(b) Both Statement I and Statement II are correct.
(c) Statement I is correct but Statement II is incorrect.
(d) Statement I is incorrect but Statement II is correct.

14. A square brass plate of side 2.0 m × 1 m and thickness 0.01 m is subjected to a force F on its smaller opposite edges, causing a displacement of 0.04 cm. If the shear modulus of brass is 0.4×10^{11} N/m^2, the value of the force F is
(a) 4×10^3 N (b) 400 N
(c) 4×10^4 N (d) 3.2×10^5 N

15. The compressibility of a material is
(a) the fractional change in volume per unit change in pressure
(b) the change in pressure per unit change in volume strain
(c) product of volume and its pressure
(d) None of the above

16. A metal block is experiencing an atmospheric pressure of 2×10^5 N/m^2, when the same block is placed in a vacuum chamber, the fractional change in its volume is (the bulk modulus of metal is 1.25×10^{11} N/m^2)
(a) 4×10^{-7}
(b) 2×10^{-7}
(c) 8×10^{-7}
(d) 16×10^{-7}

17. The bulk modulus of a liquid, if its volume changes from 100 L to 99 L under a pressure of 100 atm is (Take, 1 atm $=10^5$ Nm^{-2})
(a) 2×10^7 Nm^{-2}
(b) 1×10^9 Nm^{-2}
(c) 2×10^9 Nm^{-2}
(d) 2×10^{10} Nm^{-2}

18. A sphere of radius 10 cm and mass 25 kg is attached to the lower end of a steel wire of length 5m and diameter 4 mm which is suspended from the ceiling of a room. The point of support is 521 cm above the floor. When the sphere is set swinging as a simple pendulum, its lowest point just grazes the floor. Calculate the velocity of the ball as its lowest position.
Young's modulus of steel$=20\times10^{10}$ Nm^{-2}
Unstretched length of wire $=500$ cm
Radius of the steel wire $=0.05$ cm
(a) 23. 31 m/s
(b) 25.3 m/s
(c) 31.26 m/s
(d) 24.1 m/s

19. The metal cube of side 20 cm is subjected to a shearing stress of 10^6 Nm^{-2}. The modulus of rigidity, if the top of the cube is displaced by 0.05 cm with respect to its bottom, is
(a) 4×10^8 Nm^{-2}
(b) 10^5 Nm^{-2}
(c) 1×10^7 Nm^{-2}
(d) 4×10^5 Nm^{-2}

20. **Statement I** Bulk modulus of elasticity (K) represents incompressibility of the material.
Statement II The compressibility of solids is less than that of gases and liquids.
In the light of above statements, choose the most appropriate answer from the options given below.
(a) Both Statement I and Statement II are correct.
(b) Both Statement I and Statement II are incorrect.
(c) Statement I is correct but Statement II is incorrect.
(d) Statement I is incorrect but Statement II is correct.

21. A solid ball of radius R made of a metal of bulk modulus B surrounded by a liquid in a cylindrical container. A massless piston of area A floats on the surface of the liquid. Find the fractional decrease in the radius of the sphere $\left(\frac{\Delta R}{R}\right)$ when a mass m is placed on the piston to compress the liquid.
(a) $\frac{mg}{AB}$
(b) $\frac{mg}{4AB}$
(c) $\frac{mg}{3AB}$
(d) $\frac{mg}{2AB}$

22. A sphere contracts in volume by 0.02% when taken to the bottom of sea 2 km deep. Bulk modulus of the material of sphere is
(a) 9.8×10^6 N/m^2
(b) 1.2×10^{10} N/m^2
(c) 9.8×10^{10} N/m^2
(d) 9.8×10^{11} N/m^2

23. Two blocks of masses 3 kg and 5 kg are connected by a metal wire going over a smooth pulley. The breaking stress of the metal is $\frac{24}{\pi} \times 10^2$ N-m^{-2}.

What is the minimum radius of the wire? (Take, $g = 10$ ms^{-2})

(a) 125 cm
(b) 1250 cm
(c) 12.5 cm
(d) 1.25 cm

24. A rigid bar of mass M is supported symmetrically by three wires each of length L. Those at each end are of copper and the middle one is of iron. The ratio of their diameters, if each is to have the same tension, is equal to

(a) $\frac{\sqrt{Y_{copper}}}{Y_{iron}}$
(b) $\sqrt{\frac{Y_{iron}}{Y_{copper}}}$
(c) $\frac{Y^2_{iron}}{Y^2_{copper}}$
(d) $\frac{Y_{iron}}{Y_{copper}}$

25. A bar of cross-section area A is subjected to equal and opposite tensile forces at its end. Consider a plane section of the bar, whose normal makes an angle θ with axis (axis is along the length) of the bar. Match the List I with List II.

	List I		List II
A.	Shearing stress on plane section	1.	$\frac{F}{A}\cos^2\phi$
B.	Tensile stress on plane section	2.	0°
C.	The tensile stress is maximum for θ =	3.	$\frac{F}{A}\sin\theta\cos\theta$
D.	The shearing stress is maximum for θ =	4	45°

Choose the correct answer from the options given below.

(a) A-1, B-3, C-2, D-4
(b) A-3, B-1, C-2, D-4
(c) A-1, B-3, C-2, D-4
(d) A-3, B-1, C-4, D-2

Response Index

01	a	b	c	d	10	a	b	c	d	19	a	b	c	d
02	a	b	c	d	11	a	b	c	d	20	a	b	c	d
03	a	b	c	d	12	a	b	c	d	21	a	b	c	d
04	a	b	c	d	13	a	b	c	d	22	a	b	c	d
05	a	b	c	d	14	a	b	c	d	23	a	b	c	d
06	a	b	c	d	15	a	b	c	d	24	a	b	c	d
07	a	b	c	d	16	a	b	c	d	25	a	b	c	d
08	a	b	c	d	17	a	b	c	d					
09	a	b	c	d	18	a	b	c	d					

Performance Scanner

> 90% Excellent !	You have mastered these topics. The concepts of these topics are at your fingertips. Move on to the next test and maintain this momentum.
76-90% Very Good !	You have a good command over these topics. Revise them again after a few days and enhance your performance.
60-75% Good !	You have a wide scope to learn more in these topics. Revise them again.
<60% Not Satisfactory!	You have a long way ahead of you to master in these topics. Revise them thoroughly.

Test 2

Syllabus

- Stress-Strain Curve
- Energy Stored in a Deformed Body
- Thermal Stress & Strain
- Energy in Stretched Wire

For deeper insight **Scan the QR Code**

Important Instructions

- The test is of 45 minutes duration and contains 25 Multiple Choice Questions. (Four options with a single correct answer).
- Choose the correct option and fill the OMR given on the last page of this test accordingly.
- At some instances, you may find more than 1 option may be correct, in such circumstances you have to judge the most appropriate answer as per conditions given in the question.

1. A brass bar of length 0.2 m and cross-sectional area 1 cm^2 when compressed with a load of 5 kg-wt along its length, the increase in elastic potential energy is (Take, $Y = 1 \times 10^{11}$ N/m^2 and $g = 9.8\ m/s^2$)

(a) 2.4×10^{-5} J

(b) 1.3×10^{-4} J

(c) 13×10^{-3} J

(d) 5×10^{7} J

2. If the potential energy of a spring is P on stretching it by 2 cm, its potential energy when it is stretched by 10 cm will be

(a) $\frac{P}{25}$ (b) $5P$

(c) $\frac{P}{5}$ (d) $25\ P$

3. Two wires of the same material (Young's modulus = Y) and same length L but radii R and $2R$ respectively, are joined end-to-end and a weight w is suspended from the combination as shown in the figure. The elastic potential energy in the system is

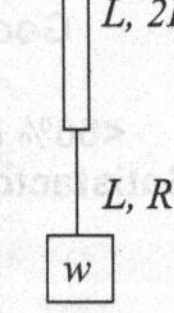

(a) $\frac{3w^2L}{4\pi R^2 Y}$ (b) $\frac{3w^2L}{8\pi R^2 Y}$

(c) $\frac{5w^2L}{8\pi R^2 Y}$ (d) $\frac{w^2L}{\pi R^2 Y}$

4. When the load on a wire increased slowly from 5 kg-wt to 10 kg-wt, the elongation in the wire increases from 0.5 mm to 1.0 mm. The work done during the extension of the wire is (Take, $g = 9.8\ m/s^2$)

(a) 3.6×10^{-2} J

(b) 3.6×10^{-3} J

(c) 7.2×10^{-3} J

(d) 7.2×10^{-2} J

5. If a spring of spring constant k is stretched by length of x, under tension T. Then, the energy stored is

(a) $\frac{2T^2}{k}$ (b) $\frac{2T}{k^2}$

(c) $\frac{T^2}{2k}$ (d) $\frac{k}{2T}$

6. The given graph shows stress *versus* strain curve for the materials I and II. From the curves, we conclude that

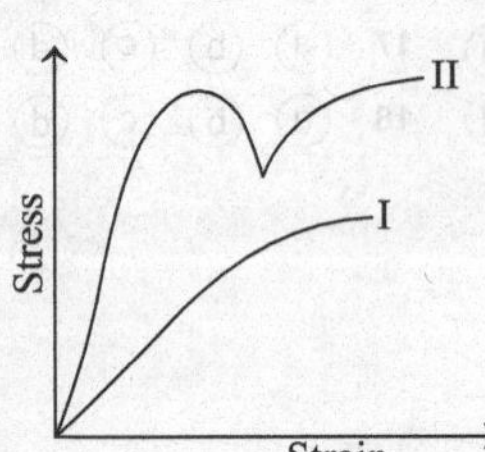

(a) material I is brittle but material II is ductile

(b) material I is ductile and material II is brittle

(c) both materials I and II are ductile

(d) both materials I and II are brittle

7. The increase in energy of a metal bar of length L and cross-sectional area A when compressed with a load M along its length is (where, Y = Young's modulus of the material of metal bar)

(a) $\frac{FL}{2AY}$ (b) $\frac{F^2L}{2AY}$

(c) $\frac{FL}{AY}$ (d) $\frac{F^2L^2}{2AY}$

8. If work done in stretching a wire by 2 mm is 4 J, the work necessary for stretching another wire of same material but with double the radius and half the length by 2 mm (in joule), is

(a) 32 (b) 4

(c) 8 (d) 16

9. Length and radius of two wires is same and subjected to the same load. One wire is made of steel and another is of copper. If Young's modulus of steel is twice that of copper, then the ratio of elastic energy stored per unit volume of steel to that of copper wire is

(a) 3 : 1 (b) 2 : 1

(c) 1 : 3 (d) 1 : 2

10. Identify the specific mechanical property of metals that facilitates their ability to undergo substantial plastic deformation under tensile stress, enabling them to be drawn into a thin wire beyond their elastic limit without experiencing rupture of fracture. What is this property called?

(a) elasticity

(b) ductility

(c) malleability

(d) hardness

11. Aluminium of fixed volume V is drawn into wire of length L. When this wire is subjected to a constant force F, the extension produced in the wire is ΔL. Which of the following graphs is a straight line?

(a) ΔL *versus* $\frac{1}{L}$

(b) ΔL *versus* L^2

(c) ΔL *versus* $\frac{1}{L^2}$

(d) ΔL *versus* L

12. A metal wire of Young's modulus Y have L longitudinal strain, then energy stored in the material of the wire per unit volume is

(a) Y^2L

(b) $2Y^2L$

(c) $\frac{Y^2L}{2}$

(d) $\frac{YL^2}{2}$

13. Stress-strain curve for four metals are given in graph. The minimum Young's modulus of elasticity is for metal

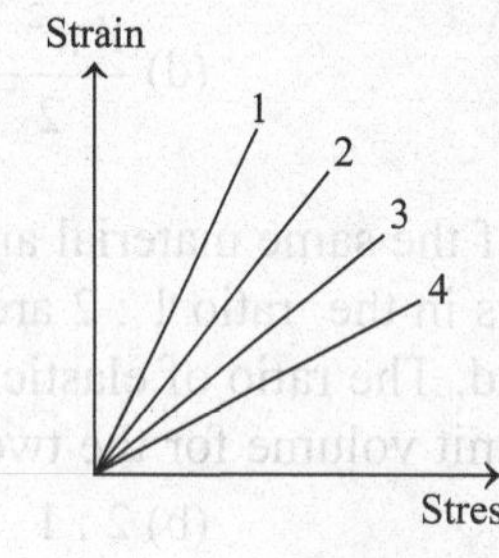

(a) 3 (b) 4

(c) 2 (d) 1

14. The load *versus* elongation graph for four wires of the same materials is as shown in the figure. The thickest wire is represented by the line

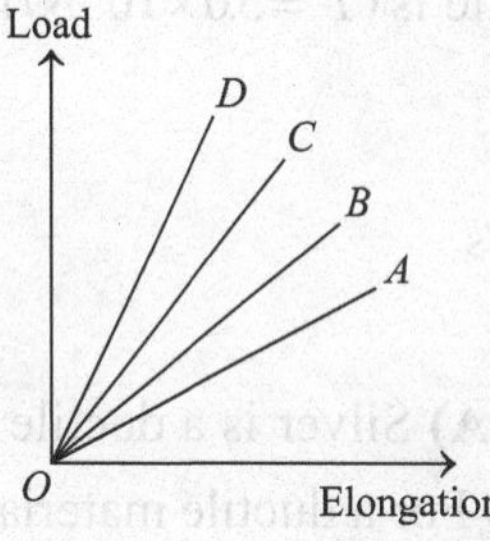

(a) OC (b) OD

(c) OA (d) OB

15. When weight of 10 kg is hung on a wire, the extension of 2 m takes place, then work done will be [Take, $g = 10 \text{ m/s}^2$]

(a) 75 J

(b) 60 J

(c) 50 J

(d) 100 J

16. A steel wire length 4 m is stretched through 2 mm. The cross sectional area of the wire is 2 mm^2. If Young's modulus of steel is 2×10^{11} Nm^{-2}, then the elastic potential energy stored in the wire is

(a) 2 J (b) 0.2 J
(c) 2.5 J (d) 0.3 J

17. A wire of length L and area of cross section A is made of material of Young's modulus Y. It is stretched by an amount x. The work done in stretching the wire is

(a) $\frac{Yx^2A}{2L}$ (b) $\frac{2Yx^2A}{L}$
(c) $\frac{YxA}{2L}$ (d) $\frac{Yx^2A}{2}$

18. Two wires of the same material and same length but diameters in the ratio 1 : 2 are stretched by the same load. The ratio of elastic potential energy per unit volume for the two wires is

(a) 1 : 1 (b) 2 : 1
(c) 4 : 1 (d) 16 : 1

19. A rubber cord of catapult has cross-section area 25 mm^2 and total unstretched length 10 cm. It is stretched to 5 cm and then released to project a missile of mass 5.0 g. The velocity of projection of the missile is ($Y = 5.0 \times 10^8 N/m^2$)

(a) 20 m/s
(b) 200 m/s
(c) 141.5 m/s
(d) 250 m/s

20. Assertion (A) Silver is a ductile material.

Reason (R) For a ductile material, yield point and breaking point are separated by larger distance than for brittle materials on the stress-strain curve.

In the light of above statements, choose the correct answer from the options given below.

(a) Both A and R are true and R is the correct explanation of A.
(b) Both A and R are true but R is not the correct explanation of A.
(c) A is true but R is false.
(d) A is false but R is true

21. The stress-strain graphs for materials A and B are shown in Figs. (i) and (ii) (given, $\theta < \alpha$).

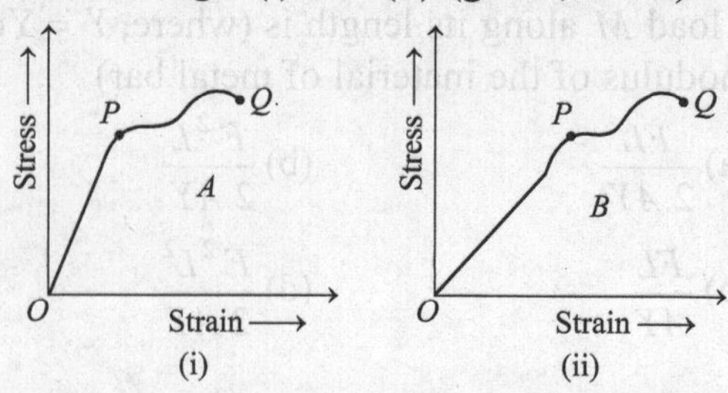

The graphs are drawn to the same scale. Which of the two is the stronger material?

(a) A
(b) B
(c) Both A and B
(d) None of the above

22. In plotting stress *versus* strain curves for two materials P and Q, a student by mistake puts strain on the Y-axis and stress on the X-axis as shown in the figure.

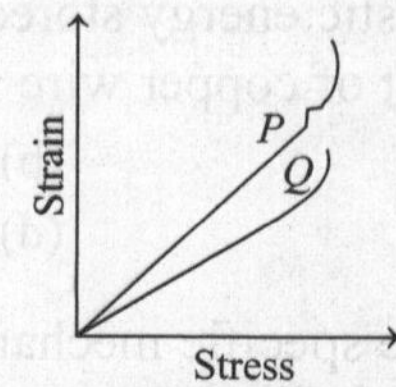

(a) P has more tensile strength than Q
(b) P is more ductile than Q
(c) P is more brittle than Q
(d) The Young's modulus of P is more than that of Q

23. Diagram shows the stress-strain graph for a metal wire. In the graph, the region in which Hooke's law is obeyed, the ultimate strength and fracture points are represented by

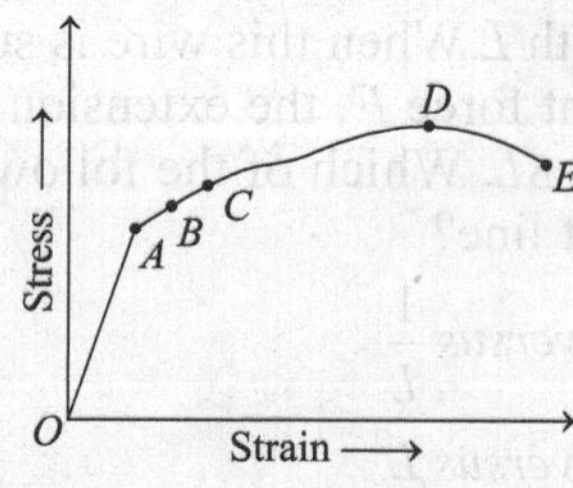

(a) OB, D, E (b) OB, C, D
(c) OA, C, D (d) OA, D, E

24. Figure shows the strain-stress curve for a given material. What are (i) Young's modulus and (ii) approximate yield strength for this material?

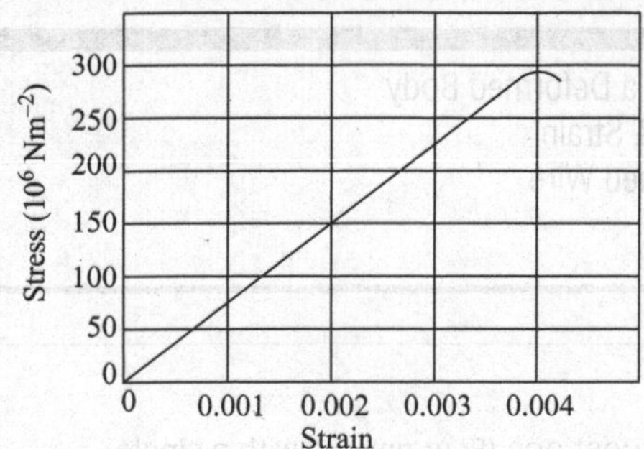

(a) 5×10^5 Nm^{-2}, 3×10^6 Nm^{-2}

(b) 2×10^{-6} Nm^{-2}, 4×10^4 Nm^{-2}

(c) 7.5×10^{10} Nm^{-2}, 3×10^8 Nm^{-2}

(d) 7.5×10^{10} Nm^{-2}, 3×10^6 Nm^{-2}

25. The strain-stress curves of three wires of different materials are shown in the figure. P, Q and R are elastic limits of the wires.

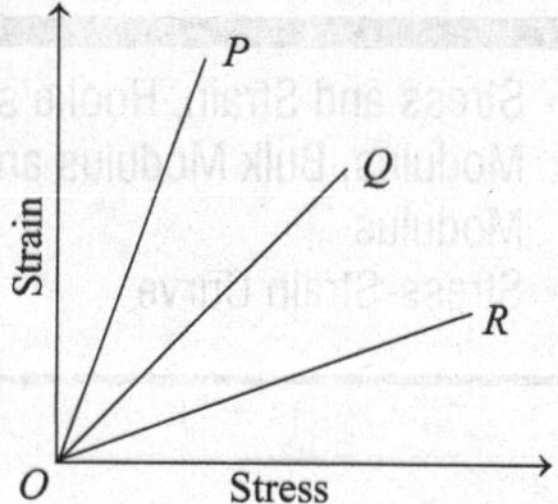

The figure shows that

(a) elasticity of wire P is maximum

(b) elasticity of wire Q is maximum

(c) tensile strength of R is maximum

(d) None of the above

Response Index

01	ⓐ ⓑ ⓒ ⓓ	10	ⓐ ⓑ ⓒ ⓓ	19	ⓐ ⓑ ⓒ ⓓ
02	ⓐ ⓑ ⓒ ⓓ	11	ⓐ ⓑ ⓒ ⓓ	20	ⓐ ⓑ ⓒ ⓓ
03	ⓐ ⓑ ⓒ ⓓ	12	ⓐ ⓑ ⓒ ⓓ	21	ⓐ ⓑ ⓒ ⓓ
04	ⓐ ⓑ ⓒ ⓓ	13	ⓐ ⓑ ⓒ ⓓ	22	ⓐ ⓑ ⓒ ⓓ
05	ⓐ ⓑ ⓒ ⓓ	14	ⓐ ⓑ ⓒ ⓓ	23	ⓐ ⓑ ⓒ ⓓ
06	ⓐ ⓑ ⓒ ⓓ	15	ⓐ ⓑ ⓒ ⓓ	24	ⓐ ⓑ ⓒ ⓓ
07	ⓐ ⓑ ⓒ ⓓ	16	ⓐ ⓑ ⓒ ⓓ	25	ⓐ ⓑ ⓒ ⓓ
08	ⓐ ⓑ ⓒ ⓓ	17	ⓐ ⓑ ⓒ ⓓ		
09	ⓐ ⓑ ⓒ ⓓ	18	ⓐ ⓑ ⓒ ⓓ		

Performance Scanner

> 90% Excellent !	You have mastered these topics. The concepts of these topics are at your fingertips. Move on to the next test and maintain this momentum.
76-90% Very Good !	You have a good command over these topics. Revise them again after a few days and enhance your performance.
60-75% Good !	You have a wide scope to learn more in these topics. Revise them again.
<60% Not Satisfactory!	You have a long way ahead of you to master in these topics. Revise them thoroughly.

Chapter Break Thru

Syllabus

- Stress and Strain, Hooke's Law, Young's Modulus, Bulk Modulus and Shearing Modulus
- Stress-Strain Curve
- Energy Stored in a Deformed Body
- Thermal Stress & Strain
- Energy in Stretched Wire

Important Instructions

- The test is of 45 min duration and contains 30 Multiple Choice Questions (Four options with a single correct answer).
- Choose the correct option and fill the OMR given on the last page of this test accordingly.
- At some instances, you may find more than 1 correct option, in such circumstances you have to judge the most appropriate answer as per conditions given in the question.

1. Two wires each of radius 0.2 cm and negligible mass, one made of steel and the other made of brass are loaded as shown in the figure. The elongation of the steel wire is .... (Young's modulus for steel $=2\times10^{11}$ Nm $^{-2}$ and $g=10$ ms $^{-2}$)

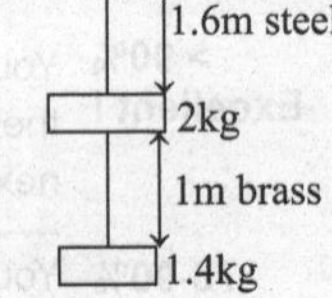

(a) 20×10^{-6} m (b) 20×10^{-5} m
(c) 28×10^{-6} m (d) 28×10^{-5} m

2. The length of a wire becomes l_1 and l_2 when 100 N and 120 N tensions are applied, respectively. If $10l_2=11l_1$, the natural length of wire will be

(a) $\frac{l_1}{2}$ (b) $\frac{l_2}{2}$
(c) $\frac{l_1}{4}$ (d) $\frac{l_2}{4}$

3. Two wires of different materials have same diameter and length are connected end to end and a force is applied, which stretches their combined length by 1 cm. The wires will have

(a) same stress and strain
(b) same strain but different stresses
(c) same stress but different strains
(d) different stresses and strains

4. A metal wire with a radius 4 cm supports a load. If the maximum stress is not to exceed 2×10^{6} Nm $^{-2}$, the maximum load on the cable can support is

(a) $4\pi\times10^{5}$ N (b) $4\pi\times10^{4}$ N
(c) $32\pi\times10^{5}$ N (d) $32\pi\times10^{2}$ N

5. The Young's modulus of metal wire of length L and radius r is Y. If the length is reduced to $\frac{2}{3}L$ and radius is $\frac{4}{5}r$, then the Young's modulus will be

(a) $\frac{Y}{2}$ (b) Y
(c) $2Y$ (d) $\frac{2}{3}Y$

6. The area of a cross-section of steel wire is 1 cm^2 and Young's modulus of steel is 2×10^{11} Nm^{-2}. The force required to stretch by 0.01% of its length is

(a) 1000 N (b) 2000 N
(c) 4000 N (d) 5000 N

7. A metal wire of length L and radius r is clamped at one end. On stretching the other end of the wire with a force F, the increase in its length is l. If another wire of same material but of length $\frac{L}{2}$ and radius $\frac{r}{2}$ is stretched with a force $\frac{F}{2}$, the increase in its length will be

(a) $\frac{l}{4}$ (b) $\frac{l}{2}$
(c) l (d) $2l$

8. The stress *versus* strain graph for wires of two different materials A and B are as shown in the figure. If Y_A and Y_B are the Young's modulii of these materials, then

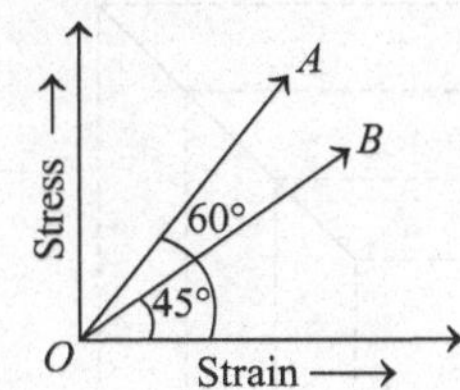

(a) $Y_B = 2Y_A$ (b) $Y_A = Y_B$
(c) $Y_B = \frac{Y_A}{\sqrt{3}}$ (d) $Y_A = 3Y_B$

9. A stress of 10^6 N/m^2 is required for breaking a material. If the density of the material is 3×10^3 kg/m^3, then what should be the length of the wire made of material so that it breaks by its own weight?
(a) 20 m (b) 30 m
(c) 34 m (d) 28 m

10. Three metal bars having lengths $2l$, $3l$ and $4l$ and areas of cross-section $A, 2A$ and $3A$ are joined rigidly end to end. Compound rod is subjected to a stretching force F. The increase in length of rod is (Young's modulus of material is Y and bars are massless)
(a) $\frac{13Fl}{2AY}$ (b) $\frac{Fl}{AY}$ (c) $\frac{29Fl}{6AY}$ (d) $\frac{3Fl}{AY}$

11. A metal wire is stretched by 0.05 m by a certain force F. Another wire of the same material whose diameter and length are double to the original wire is stretched by the same force, then its elongation will be
(a) 0.005 m (b) 0.01 m
(c) 2.0 cm (d) 2.5 cm

12. The following four wires are made of copper. Which of these will have the largest extension when the same tension is applied?
(a) Length = 50 m, diameter = 0.5 cm
(b) Length = 100 m, diameter = 1 cm
(c) Length = 200 m, diameter = 2 cm
(d) Length = 300 m, diameter = 3 cm

13. A metal wire having length L and cross-sectional area A is stretched by a tension T. According to Hooke's law of elasticity, if stress is increased, then the ratio of stress to strain
(a) increases
(b) decreases
(c) becomes zero
(d) remains constant

14. A metal wire of length L, Young's modulus Y and cross-sectional area A is hanging from a support. The breaking stress of this wire depends on
(a) length (L) of the wire
(b) cross-sectional area (A) of the wire
(c) Young's modulus (Y) of the wire
(d) elongation of the wire

15. A metal wire of mass m and length L is applying a force F on it, the increase in length is l and the density of the material of wire is d, then the Young's modulus of the material of the metal wire will be
(a) $\frac{Fdl}{ml}$ (b) $\frac{FL}{mdl}$
(c) $\frac{Fml}{dl}$ (d) $\frac{FdL^2}{ml}$

16. **Statement I** Steel is more elastic than rubber.
Statement II Steel and brass are more elastic than copper and aluminium.
In the light of above statements, choose the most appropriate answer from the options given below
(a) Both Statement I and Statement II are correct.
(b) Both Statement I and Statement II are incorrect.
(c) Statement I is correct but Statement II is incorrect.
(d) Statement I is incorrect but Statement II is correct.

17. A rod of length L and mass M is rotated in a horizontal plane about one of it's end at constant angular speed ω. Change in length of rod will be

(a) $\frac{M\omega^2 L^2}{AY}$ (b) $\frac{M\omega^2 L^2}{2AY}$

(c) $\frac{M\omega^2 L^2}{3AY}$ (d) $\frac{M\omega^2 L^2}{4AY}$

18. A metal wire can support a maximum load of w before reaching its elastic limit. How much load can another wire, made out of identical metal, but with a radius two-third the radius of the first wire, support before reaching its elastic limit?

(a) w (b) $\frac{w}{2}$

(c) $\frac{w}{4}$ (d) $\frac{4w}{9}$

19. Two metal wires A and B are stretched by same force. If, for A and B, $Y_A : Y_B = 2:1$, $r_A : r_B = 3:1$ and $l_A : l_B = 2:1$, then ratio of their extension $\left(\frac{\Delta l_A}{\Delta l_B}\right)$ will be

(a) 10 : 13
(b) 1 : 9
(c) 8 : 9
(d) 6 : 5

20. A metal bar is subjected to axial forces as shown. If Y is the modulus of elasticity of the bar and A is its cross-sectional area. Its elongation will be

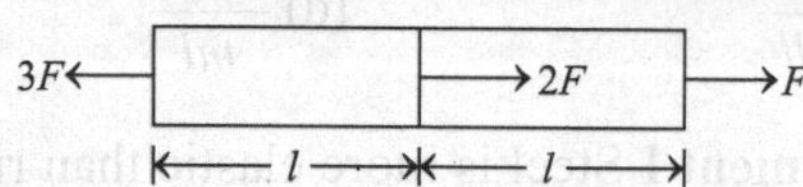

(a) $\frac{Fl}{AY}$ (b) $\frac{2Fl}{AY}$

(c) $\frac{3Fl}{AY}$ (d) $\frac{4Fl}{AY}$

21. The Young's modulus of brass is half that of steel.Two wires of the same length and of the same area of cross-section, one of brass and another of steel are suspended from the same roof. If we want the lower ends of the wires to be at the same level, then the weights added to the brass and steel wires must be in the ratio of

(a) 1 : 1
(b) 1 : 2
(c) 2 : 1
(d) 4 : 1

22. The given graph shows the extension (Δl) of a metal wire of length 3 m suspended from the top of a root at one end with a load w connected to the other end. If the cross-sectional area of the wire is 2×10^{-6} m^2, calculate the Young's modulus of the material of the wire.

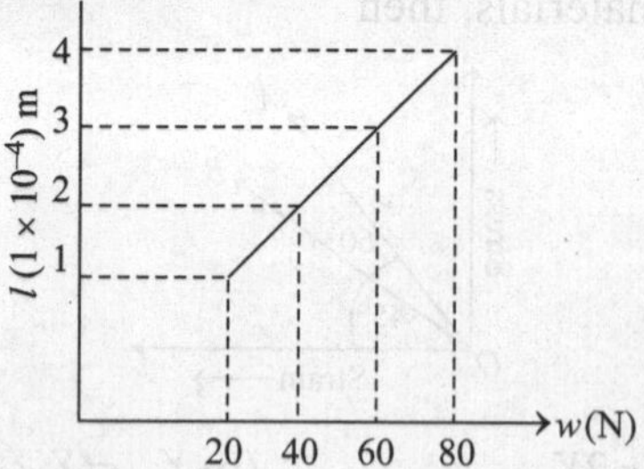

(a) 3×10^{11} N/m^2
(b) 2×10^{-11} N/m^2
(c) 2×10^{11} N/m^2
(d) 2×10^{-13} N/m^2

23. A steel wire of length 5 m and cross-sectional area 7×10^{-5} m^2 stretches by the same amount as a copper wire of length 3 m and cross-sectional area of 8×10^{-5} m^2 under a given load. The ratio of the Young's modulus of steel to that of copper is

(a) 1.3 (b) 1.5 (c) 1.7 (d) 1.9

24. Two exactly similar wires of steel and copper are stretched by equal force. If the difference in their elongation is 1 cm, the elongation in both steel and copper wires respectively (Given, Young's modulus for steel $= 2 \times 10^{12}$ dyne cm^{-2} and for copper $= 12 \times 10^{11}$ dyne cm^{-2})

(a) 1.5 cm, 2.5 cm
(b) 2.5 cm, 5.5 cm
(c) 0.75 cm, 5.0 cm
(d) 2.5 cm, 0.75 cm

25. A wire of length 4 m is made of a material of Young's modulus 20×10^{11} Pa. When the wire is extended by 1 mm, the stress developed in the wire is

(a) 5×10^{-1} Nm^{-2}
(b) 5×10^{8} Nm^{-2}
(c) 5×10^{9} Nm^{-2}
(d) 5×10^{10} Nm^{-2}

26. Two wires of the same material and same mass are stretched by the same force. Their lengths are in the ratio 2:3. Then, their elongations are in the ratio

(a) 3:2 (b) 2:3 (c) 4:9 (d) 9:4

27. Assertion (A) If radius of cylindrical wire is doubled, then this wire can bear four times stress.

Reason (R) By doubling the radius, area of cross-section will become four times.

In the light of above statements, choose the most appropriate answer from the options given below.

(a) Both A and R are true and R is the correct explanation of A.
(b) Both A and R are true but R is not the correct explanation of A.
(c) A is true but R is false.
(d) A is false but R is true.

28. A steel wire of cross-sectional area A and length $2l$ is clamped firmly at two points A and B which are separated by $2l$ apart and in the same plane. A body is hung from the middle point of the wire such that the middle point shifts by a distance x lower from the original position. Calculate mass of the body. If Y is Young's modulus of material of wire.

(a) $\frac{YAx^2}{gl^3}$ (b) $\frac{YAx}{gl}$
(c) $\frac{YAl^3}{gx^3}$ (d) $\frac{YAx^3}{gl^3}$

29. A structural steel rod has a radius of 10 mm and a length of 1 m. A 100 kN force F stretches it along its length. Given, $Y = 2\times10^{11}$ Nm^{-2}, then match List I (physical quantity) with List II (value).

	List I		List II
A.	Stress (in Nm^{-2})	1.	1.59
B.	Elongation (in mm)	2.	1.59×10^{-3}
C.	Strain	3.	0.16
D.	Change in length (in percent)	4.	3.18×10^{8}

Choose the correct answer from the options given below.

(a) A-4, B-1, C-2, D-3
(b) A-2, B-1, C-4, D-3
(c) A-4, B-3, C-2, D-1
(d) A-3, B-4, C-2, D-1

30. One face of an aluminium cube of side length 1m is fixed to a vertical wall.

A load is attached to it's other opposite face.
For all sections parallel to wall, choose incorrect option.

(a) Stress is same at all section.
(b) Stress is not same at all section.
(c) Strain is same at all sections.
(d) Modulus of rigidity is same at all sections.

Response Index

01 ⓐ ⓑ ⓒ ⓓ 02 ⓐ ⓑ ⓒ ⓓ 03 ⓐ ⓑ ⓒ ⓓ 04 ⓐ ⓑ ⓒ ⓓ 05 ⓐ ⓑ ⓒ ⓓ 06 ⓐ ⓑ ⓒ ⓓ 07 ⓐ ⓑ ⓒ ⓓ 08 ⓐ ⓑ ⓒ ⓓ 09 ⓐ ⓑ ⓒ ⓓ 10 ⓐ ⓑ ⓒ ⓓ 11 ⓐ ⓑ ⓒ ⓓ 12 ⓐ ⓑ ⓒ ⓓ 13 ⓐ ⓑ ⓒ ⓓ
14 ⓐ ⓑ ⓒ ⓓ 15 ⓐ ⓑ ⓒ ⓓ 16 ⓐ ⓑ ⓒ ⓓ 17 ⓐ ⓑ ⓒ ⓓ 18 ⓐ ⓑ ⓒ ⓓ 19 ⓐ ⓑ ⓒ ⓓ 20 ⓐ ⓑ ⓒ ⓓ 21 ⓐ ⓑ ⓒ ⓓ 22 ⓐ ⓑ ⓒ ⓓ 23 ⓐ ⓑ ⓒ ⓓ 24 ⓐ ⓑ ⓒ ⓓ 25 ⓐ ⓑ ⓒ ⓓ 26 ⓐ ⓑ ⓒ ⓓ
27 ⓐ ⓑ ⓒ ⓓ 28 ⓐ ⓑ ⓒ ⓓ 29 ⓐ ⓑ ⓒ ⓓ 30 ⓐ ⓑ ⓒ ⓓ

Performance Scanner

> 90% Excellent !	You have mastered this chapter. The concepts of this chapter are on your fingertips. Move on to the next chapter and maintain this momentum.
76-90% Very Good !	You have a good command over this chapter. Revise the chapter again after a few days and enhance your performance.
60-75% Good !	You have a wide scope to learn more from this chapter. Revise this chapter again.
<60% Not Satisfactory!	You have a long way ahead of you to master this chapter. Revise it thoroughly.

For Online Chapter Test **Scan the QR Code**

Space for Rough Work

Space for Rough Work

Space for Rough Work

MEDACE
NEET (UG)
SELF ASSESSMENT KIT

Test Booklet No. **3947109**

Test Booklet Code **CH9**

Mechanical Properties of Fluids

Topics Covered

Fluid Statics

Fluid Dynamics

Viscosity and Surface Tension

Important Instructions

- This Booklet Contains – Three Topic Tests and One Test on Complete Chapter.
- Each question carries 4 Marks.
- For each correct response, the candidate will get 4 marks and for every incorrect response, 1 mark will be additionally deducted from total score.
- Use **Blue/Black** point pen only for filling the OMR.
- Rough work is to be done in the space provided for this purpose in the test booklet only.

Name of the Candidate (In Capitals)

____

____

Candidate's Signature ____________

Invigilator's Signature ____________

Facsimile signature stamp of center superintendent____________

Do not open this Booklet until you start attempting the Test

Topical Follow Thru

Test 1

Syllabus
- Pressure Due to a Fluid Column
- Pascal's Law and its Applications
- Effect of Gravity on Fluid Pressure

For deeper insight **Scan the QR Code**

Important Instructions
- The test is of 45 min duration and contains 25 Multiple Choice Questions (Four options with a single correct answer).
- Choose the correct option and fill the OMR given on the last page of this test accordingly.
- At some instances, you may find more than 1 option may be correct in such circumstances you have to judge the most appropriate answer as per the conditions given in the question.

1. Two pistons of a hydraulic machine have diameters 20 cm and 2 cm. The force exerted on the larger piston when 50 kg-wt is placed on the smaller piston and when the smaller piston moves in through 5 cm, then the distance other piston moves out is

(a) 5×10^4 N, 0.01 cm
(b) 5×10^4 N, 0.05 cm
(c) 3×10^4 N, 0.05 cm
(d) 3×10^4 N, 0.01 cm

2. A cylinder containing water is closed by a smooth piston of mass m. If A is the cross-sectional area of the piston and p_0 is the atmospheric pressure, then the pressure of the water just below the piston is

(a) $p_0-\frac{mg}{A}$ (b) $p_0+\frac{mg}{A}$
(c) $\frac{mg}{A}$ (d) p_0

3. Two liquids of densities ρ and 4ρ having volumes $2V$ and V are mixed together. The density of the mixture is

(a) $\frac{\rho}{2}$ (b) $\frac{3\rho}{2}$
(c) 2ρ (d) $\frac{5\rho}{2}$

4. Find density of ethyl alcohol. Using information given in the diagram below.

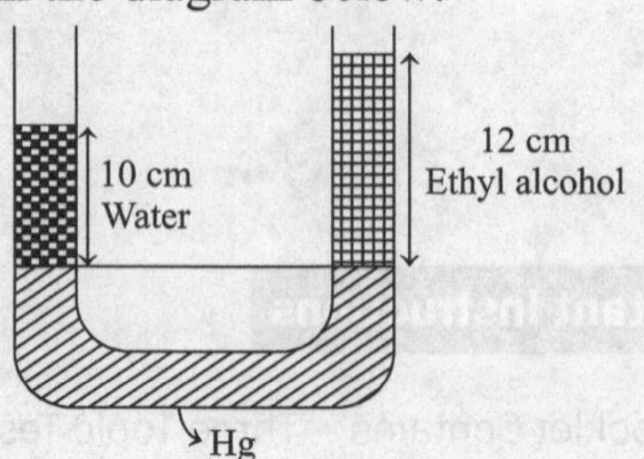

(a) $0.83\ \text{gcm}^{-3}$ (b) $0.5\ \text{gcm}^{-3}$
(c) $1.83\ \text{gcm}^{-3}$ (d) $0.12\ \text{gcm}^{-3}$

5. Preeti is wearing point heels shoes, balances her whole body on a single heel. Her total weight is 50 kg and the heel is circular with a diameter 1 cm. The pressure exerted by the heel on the horizontal floor is (Take, $g=10\ \text{m/s}^2$)

(a) 6.4×10^4 Pa (b) 6.4×10^5 Pa
(c) 6.4×10^6 Pa (d) 6.4×10^7 Pa

6. A column of water having length of 5 m is open to the atmosphere, the pressure exerted at the bottom of the column is ($\rho=1\times10^3\ \text{kg/m}^3, g=10\ \text{m/s}^2$)

(a) 1.5×10^5 Pa
(b) 1×10^5 Pa
(c) 1.5×10^7 Pa
(d) 1×10^7 Pa

7. A cylinder of height 15 cm and radius 7 cm is immersed in water, the buoyant force acting on it is [Take, density of water $=1\times10^3$ kg/m^3 gravity $=10$ m/s^2]

(a) 60 N (b) 45 N
(c) 23 N (d) 46 N

8. Three vessels 1, 2 and 3 of different shapes contain water upto the same height as shown in the figure. p_1, p_2 and p_3 be the pressures exerted by the water at the bottom of the vessels 1, 2 and 3 respectively. Then,

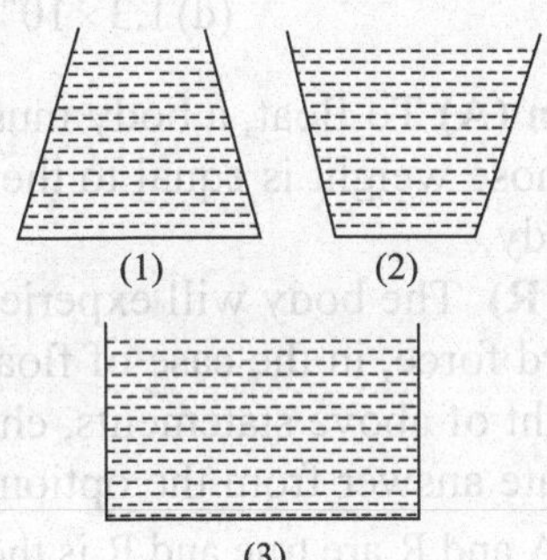

(a) $p_1 \geq p_2 \geq p_3$ (b) $p_3 > p_2 > p_1$
(c) $p_1 = p_2 = p_3$ (d) $p_2 > p_3 > p_1$

9. Statement I Pressure of water is very large at the bottom of a dam.
Statement II Pascal's law is the working principle of hydraulic lift.
In the light of the above statements, choose the most appropriate answer from the options given below.

(a) Both Statement I and Statement II are correct.
(b) Statement I is correct but Statement II is incorrect.
(c) Statement I is incorrect but Statement II is correct.
(d) Both Statement I and Statement II are incorrect.

10. An open pan A filled with a liquid (density ρ_l) is placed on a vertical rod, maintaining equilibrium. A block of density ρ is placed on one side of the pan as shown. Depth of liquid is more than height of the block.

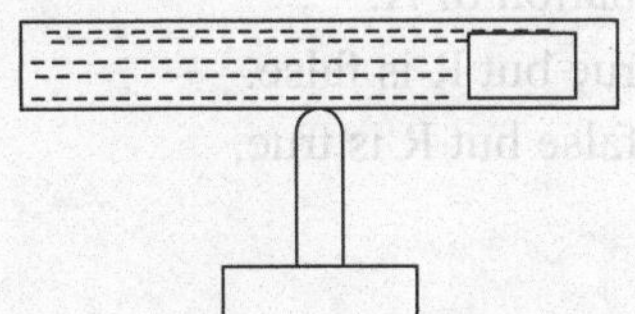

(a) Equilibrium will be maintained only, if $\rho > \rho_l$
(b) Equilibrium will be maintained only, if $\rho \leq \rho_l$
(c) Equilibrium will be maintained for all relations between ρ and ρ_l
(d) Equilibrium will not be maintained in any cases

11. The total weight of a piece of wood is 6 kg. In the floating state in water its $\frac{1}{3}$ part remains inside the water. On this floating piece of wood what maximum weight is to be put such that the whole of the piece of wood is to be drowned in the water?

(a) 15 kg
(b) 14 kg
(c) 10 kg
(d) 12 kg

12. A vessel contains oil (density $=0.8$ g/cm^3) over mercury (density $=13.6$ g/cm^3). A homogeneous sphere floats with half of its volume immersed in mercury and the other half on oil. The density of the material of the sphere in gm/cm^3 is

(a) 3.3 (b) 6.4
(c) 7.2 (d) 12.8

13. A hydraulic lift has limbs of areas A_1 and A_2 ($A_1 >> A_2$). A piston creates a force F_2 in small limb to balance a large force F_1. Which of the following statement is correct?

(a) $F_2 \propto \frac{A_1}{A_2}$.
(b) Work done by F_1 > Work done by F_2.
(c) Pressure in small area limb is more than pressure in large area limb.
(d) If piston of small area limb has velocity v_2 and piston of large area limb as velocity v_1, then $\frac{v_2}{v_1} = \frac{A_1}{A_2}$.

14. An iceberg is floating in ocean. What fraction of its volume is above the water? (Given, density of ice $=900$ kg/m^3 and density of ocean water $=1030$ kg/m^3)

(a) $\frac{90}{103}$ (b) $\frac{13}{103}$
(c) $\frac{10}{103}$ (d) $\frac{1}{103}$

15. A solid sphere of density $\eta(>1)$ times lighter than water is suspended in a water tank by a string tied to its base as shown in figure. If the mass of the sphere is m, then the tension in the string is given by

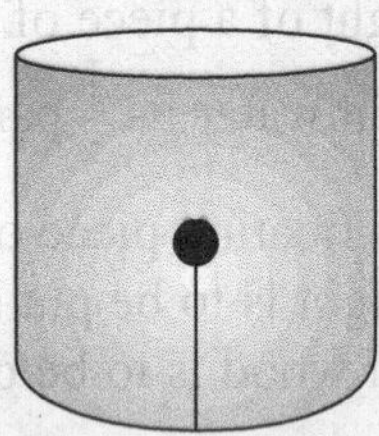

(a) $\left(\frac{\eta-1}{\eta}\right)mg$ (b) $\eta\, mg$

(c) $\frac{mg}{\eta-1}$ (d) $(\eta-1)\,mg$

16. A boy can reduce the pressure in his lungs to 750 mm of mercury. Using a straw he can drink water from a glass upto the maximum depth of (atmospheric pressure = 760 mm of mercury, density of mercury $= 13.6\,\text{g cm}^{-3}$)

(a) 13.6 cm
(b) 9.8 cm
(c) 10 cm
(d) 76 cm

17. A wooden block, with a coin placed on its top, floats in water as shown in figure, the distance l and h are shown there. After sometime, the coin falls into the water. Then

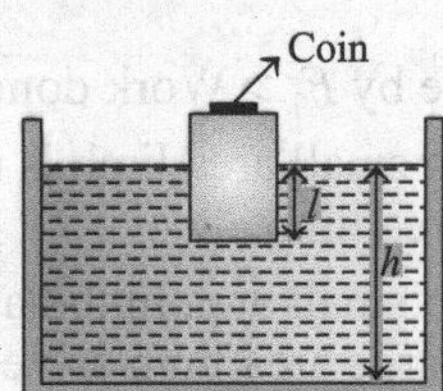

(a) l decreases and h increases
(b) l increases and h decreases
(c) Both l and h increases
(d) Both l and h decreases

18. Figure shows a hydraulic press with the larger piston of diameter 35 cm at a height of 1.5 m relative to the smaller piston of diameter 10 cm. The mass on the smaller piston is 20 kg. The force exerted on the load by the larger piston is (The density of oil in the press is 750 kgm^{-3} and Take, $g = 9.8\,\text{ms}^{-2}$)

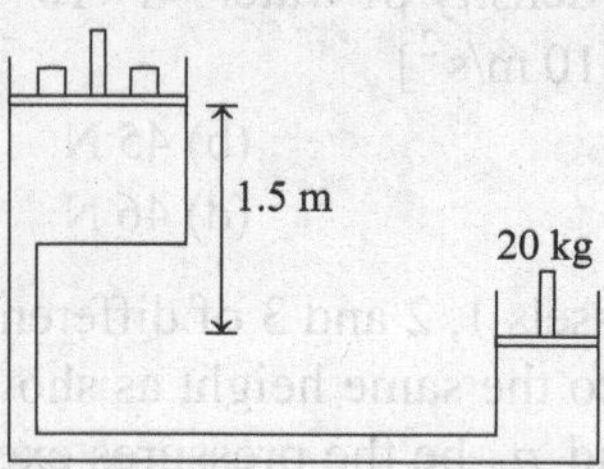

(a) 1.3×10^3 N (b) 1.3×10^2 N

(c) 1.3 N (d) 1.3×10^4 N

19. **Assertion (A)** To float, a body must displace liquid whose weight is equal to the actual weight of the body.

Reason (R) The body will experiences no net downward force, in the case of floating.

In the light of above statements, choose the most appropriate answer from the options given below.

(a) Both A and R are true and R is the correct explanation of A.
(b) Both A and R are true but R is not the correct explanation of A.
(c) A is true but R is false.
(d) A is false but R is true.

20. Two solids A and B float in water. It is observed that A floats with half its volume immersed and B floats with 2/3 of its volume immersed. Compare the densities of A and B.

(a) 4 : 3 (b) 2 : 3

(c) 3 : 4 (d) 1 : 3

21. **Assertion (A)** Paper pins are made to have pointed end.

Reason (R) Because pointed pins have very small area due to which even for small applied force, it exerts large pressure on the surface.

In the light of above statements, choose the most appropriate answer from the options given below.

(a) Both A and R are true and R is the correct explanation of A.
(b) Both A and R are true but R is not the correct explanation of A.
(c) A is true but R is false.
(d) A is false but R is true.

22. The fraction of a floating object of volume V_0 and density d_0 above the surface of a liquid of density d will be

(a) $\frac{d_0}{d}$ (b) $\frac{dd_0}{d+d_0}$

(c) $\frac{d-d_0}{d}$ (d) $\frac{dd_0}{d-d_0}$

23. If pressure at half the depth of a lake is equal to 2/3 pressure at the bottom of the lake then what is the depth of the lake

(a) 10 m
(b) 20 m
(c) 60 m
(d) 30 m

24. If two liquids of same masses but densities ρ_1 and ρ_2 respectively are mixed, then density of mixture is given by

(a) $\rho = \frac{\rho_1 + \rho_2}{2}$ (b) $\rho = \frac{\rho_1 + \rho_2}{2\rho_1\rho_2}$

(c) $\rho = \frac{2\rho_1\rho_2}{\rho_1 + \rho_2}$ (d) $\rho = \frac{\rho_1\rho_2}{\rho_1 + \rho_2}$

25. An ornament weighing 50 g in air, weights only 46 g in water. Assume that, some copper is mixed with gold to prepare the ornament. The amount of copper in it is (Specific gravity of gold is 20 and that of copper is 10)

(a) 10 g (b) 20 g
(c) 30 g (d) 50 g

Response Index

01	a	b	c	d	11	a	b	c	d	21	a	b	c	d
02	a	b	c	d	12	a	b	c	d	22	a	b	c	d
03	a	b	c	d	13	a	b	c	d	23	a	b	c	d
04	a	b	c	d	14	a	b	c	d	24	a	b	c	d
05	a	b	c	d	15	a	b	c	d	25	a	b	c	d
06	a	b	c	d	16	a	b	c	d					
07	a	b	c	d	17	a	b	c	d					
08	a	b	c	d	18	a	b	c	d					
09	a	b	c	d	19	a	b	c	d					
10	a	b	c	d	20	a	b	c	d					

Performance Scanner

> 90% Excellent !	You have mastered these topics. The concepts of these topics are at your fingertips. Move on to the next test and maintain this momentum.
76-90% Very Good !	You have a good command over these topics. Revise these topics again after a few days and enhance your performance.
60-75% Good !	You have a wide scope to learn more for these topics. Revise these topics again.
<60% Not Satisfactory!	You have a long way ahead of you to master these topics. Revise it thoroughly.

Test 2

Syllabus
- Streamline and Turbulent Flow
- Critical Velocity
- Bernoulli's Principle and its Applications

For deeper insight **Scan the QR Code**

Important Instructions
- The test is of 30 min duration and contains 15 Multiple Choice Questions (Four options with a single correct answer).
- Choose the correct option and fill the OMR given on the last page of this test accordingly.
- At some instances, you may find more than 1 option may be correct in such circumstances you have to judge the most appropriate answer as per the conditions given in the question.

1. A manometer connected to a closed tap reads $2.0 \times 10^5 \text{N/m}^2$. When the valve is opened, the reading of manometer falls to $1.5 \times 10^5 \text{ N/m}^2$. Then velocity of flow of water is

(a) 25 m/s
(b) 10 m/s
(c) 2 m/s
(d) $2\sqrt{10}$ m/s

2. Figure shows two holes in a wide tank containing a liquid column. The water streams coming out of these holes strike the ground at the same point. The height of liquid column in the tank is

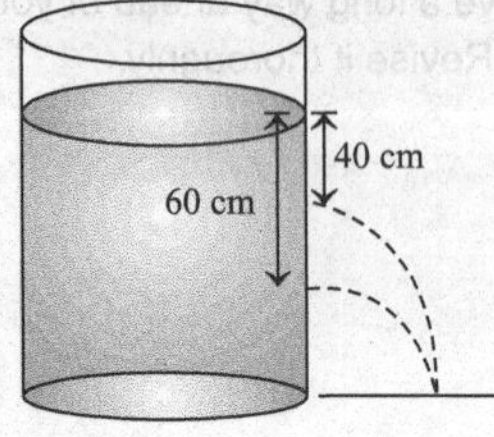

(a) 100 cm
(b) 80 cm
(c) 90 cm
(d) 980 cm

3. A water tank filled with water having total 1000 L water and total pressure at bottom of tank is 3 atm. There is a small hole in the bottom of tank, then the velocity of flow of water is
(Take, 1 atm $= 10^5 \text{ N/m}^2$)

(a) $3\sqrt{50}$ m/s
(b) $2\sqrt{100}$ m/s
(c) $3\sqrt{100}$ m/s
(d) $2\sqrt{50}$ m/s

4. A wind with speed 50 m/s blows parallel to the roof of a house. The area of the roof is 200 m^2. Assuming that the pressure inside the house is atmospheric pressure, the force exerted by the wind on the roof and the direction of the force will be ($\rho_{\text{air}} = 1.2 \text{ kg/m}^2$)

(a) 4.8×10^3 N, downwards
(b) 3.0×10^5 N, upwards
(c) 2.4×10^5 N, upwards
(d) 2.4×10^5 N, downwards

5. The figure shows a liquid of given density flowing steadily in horizontal tube of the section. Cross-sectional areas at A is 1.5 cm^2 and B is 25 mm^2, if speed of liquid at B is 60 cm/s, then $(p_A - p_B)$ is

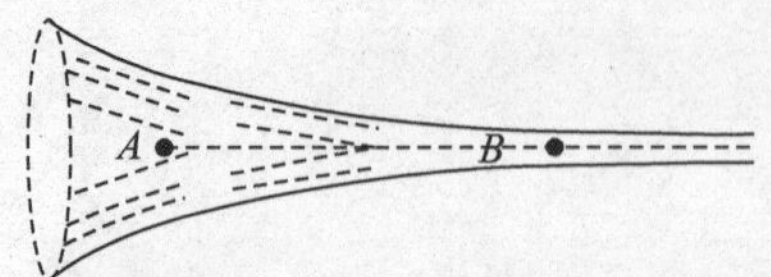

(Given, p_A and p_B are liquid pressure at A and B points. Density, $\rho = 1000 \text{ kg m}^{-3}$ A and B are on the axis of tube

(a) 36 Pa
(b) 135 Pa
(c) 175 Pa
(d) 27 Pa

6. A horizontal pipe carries water in streamline flow. At a point where the cross-section area is 15 cm^2 the velocity of water is 1 m/s and pressure is 2500 Pa. The pressure due to water at another point where the cross-section area is 7.5 cm^2 is

(a) 250 Pa
(b) 2500 Pa
(c) 500 Pa
(d) 3000 Pa

7. When a body falls in air, the resistance of air depends to a great extent on the shape of the body, three bodies *A, B* and *C* of different shapes are given. Identify the combination of air resistances which truly represents the physical situation. (The cross-sectional areas are same).

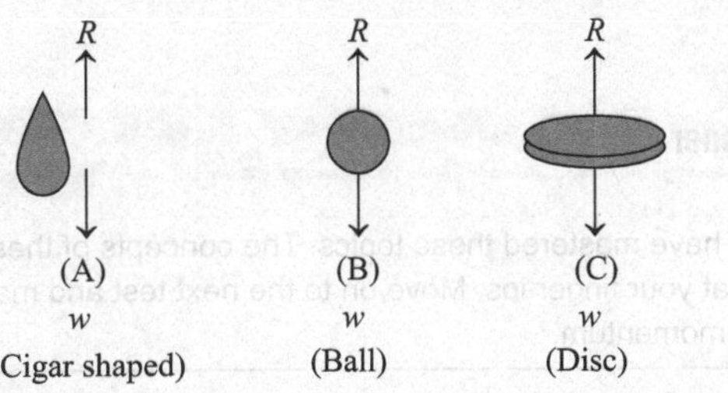

(a) A < B < C
(b) B < C < A
(c) C < B < A
(d) A > B > C

8. Statement I The stream of water flowing at high speed from a garden hose pipe tends to spread like a fountain when held vertically up, but tends to narrow down when held vertically down.

Statement II In any steady flow of an incompressible fluid, the volume flow rate of the fluid remains constant.

Select the most appropriate answer from the options given below.
(a) Both Statement I and Statement II are true.
(b) Both Statement I and Statement II are false.
(c) Statement I is true but Statement II false.
(d) Statement I is false but Statement II is true.

9. Air is blown through a pipe *AB* at a rate of $15\,\text{L/min}$. The cross-sectional area of the broad portion of the pipe *AB* is $2\,\text{cm}^2$ and that of the narrow portion is $0.5\,\text{cm}^2$. The difference in water level *h* is (density of air = $1.32\,\text{kg/m}^3$)

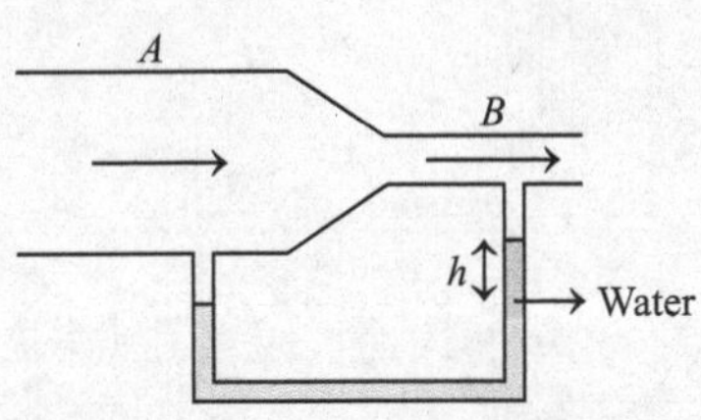

(a) 16 mm
(b) 1.5 mm
(c) 10 mm
(d) 3.2 mm

10. A cylinder of height 45 m is completely filled with water. The velocity of efflux of water through a small hole on the side wall of the cylinder near its bottom is (Take, $g = 10\,\text{m/s}^2$)

(a) 20 m/s (b) 30 m/s (c) 45 m/s (d) 10 m/s

11. Water from a tap emerges vertically down with an initial speed of $1.0\,\text{ms}^{-1}$. The cross-sectional area of tap is $10^{-4}\,\text{m}^2$. Assume that the pressure is constant throughout the stream of water and that the flow is steady. The cross-sectional area of the stream 0.15 m below the tap is

(a) $5.0\times10^{-4}\,\text{m}^2$
(b) $1.0\times10^{-5}\,\text{m}^2$
(c) $5.0\times10^{-5}\,\text{m}^2$
(d) $2.0\times10^{-5}\,\text{m}^2$

12. Air flows horizontally with a speed $v = 106\,\text{km/h}$. A house has plane roof of area $A = 20\,\text{m}^2$. If the density of air is $1.3\,\text{kg/m}^3$, then magnitude of aerodynamic lift of the roof is

(a) $1.13\times10^4\,\text{N}$
(b) $5.0\times10^4\,\text{N}$
(c) $127\times10^5\,\text{N}$
(d) $3.127\times10^4\,\text{N}$

13. The cylindrical tube of a spray pump has radius *R*, one end of which has a fine holes, each of radius *r*. If the speed of the liquid in the tube is *v*, the speed of the ejection of the liquid through the holes is

(a) $\dfrac{vR^2}{nr^2}$
(b) $\dfrac{vR^2}{n^3r^2}$
(c) $\dfrac{v^2R}{nr}$
(d) $\dfrac{vR^2}{n^2r^2}$

14. A hole is made at the bottom of the tank filled with water (density $1000\,\text{kgm}^{-3}$). If the total pressure at the bottom of the tank is 3 atm (1 atm $=10^5\,\text{Nm}^{-2}$), then the velocity of efflux is

(a) $\sqrt{200}\,\text{ms}^{-1}$
(b) $\sqrt{400}\,\text{ms}^{-1}$
(c) $\sqrt{500}\,\text{ms}^{-1}$
(d) $\sqrt{800}\,\text{ms}^{-1}$

15. A large tank filled with water to a height h is to be emptied through a small hole at the bottom. The ratio of time taken for the level of water to fall from h to $\frac{h}{2}$ and $\frac{h}{2}$ to zero is

(a) $\sqrt{2}$

(b) $\frac{1}{\sqrt{2}}$

(c) $\sqrt{2}-1$

(d) $\frac{1}{\sqrt{2}-1}$

Response Index

01	(a)	(b)	(c)	(d)	11	(a)	(b)	(c)	(d)
02	(a)	(b)	(c)	(d)	12	(a)	(b)	(c)	(d)
03	(a)	(b)	(c)	(d)	13	(a)	(b)	(c)	(d)
04	(a)	(b)	(c)	(d)	14	(a)	(b)	(c)	(d)
05	(a)	(b)	(c)	(d)	15	(a)	(b)	(c)	(d)
06	(a)	(b)	(c)	(d)					
07	(a)	(b)	(c)	(d)					
08	(a)	(b)	(c)	(d)					
09	(a)	(b)	(c)	(d)					
10	(a)	(b)	(c)	(d)					

Performance Scanner

> 90% Excellent !	You have mastered these topics. The concepts of these topics are at your fingertips. Move on to the next test and maintain this momentum.
76-90% Very Good !	You have a good command over these topics. Revise them again after a few days and enhance your performance.
60-75% Good !	You have a wide scope to learn more in these topics. Revise them again.
<60 Not Satisfactory!	You have a long way ahead of you to master in these topics. Revise them thoroughly.

Test 3

Syllabus

- Viscosity
- Terminal Velocity
- Stoke's Law
- Surface Energy and Surface Tension
- Angle of Contact
- Excess Pressure Across a Curved Surface
- Applications of Surface Tension, Drops Bubbles and Capillary Rise.

For deeper insight **Scan the QR Code**

Important Instructions

- The test is of 30 min duration and contains 15 Multiple Choice Questions (Four options with a single correct answer).
- Choose the correct option and fill the OMR given on the last page of this test accordingly.
- At some instances, you may find more than 1 option may be correct in such circumstances you have to judge the most appropriate answer as per the conditions given in the question.

1. 64 small water drops of equal radii combine to form a big drop. The ratio of final surface energy to the total initial surface energy is

(a) 16 : 1
(b) 1 : 16
(c) 4 : 1
(d) 1 : 4

2. A big drop of water has radius R. Energy needed in breaking this into n drops of radii r is given by

(a) $4\pi T(nr^2 - R^2)$
(b) $\frac{4\pi}{T}(nr^2 - R^2)$
(c) $\frac{4}{3}\pi T(R^2 - nr^2)$
(d) $\frac{4\pi}{T}(nr^2 + R^2)$

3. The pressure inside a small air bubble of 0.1 mm radius situated just below the water surface is (Take, surface tension of water, $T = 7.2 \times 10^{-2}$ N/m and atmospheric pressure, $p_0 = 1.013 \times 10^5$ N/m^2)

(a) 10^4 N/m^2 (b) 10^5 N/m^2
(c) 10^6 N/m^2 (d) 10^7 N/m^2

4. Water flows through a tube of radius 1.5 cm at a rate of 0.5 L/min. Viscosity of water is 10^{-3} Pa.s and density 10^3 kg m^{-3}. Now, choose correct option.

(a) Flow is streamlined
(b) Flow is turbulent
(c) Flow is unstable
(d) Can-not be concluded

5. Water rises in a capillary tube to a height of 2 cm. In another capillary tube whose radius is half of it, the rise in water is

(a) 2 cm (b) 3 cm
(c) 4 cm (d) 5 cm

6. Two equal drops of water are falling through air with a steady velocity v. If the drops are coalesced, then new velocity of the combination of drops will be

(a) $2^{1/3}v$
(b) $4^{2/3}v$
(c) $4^{1/3}v$
(d) $-2^{2/3}v$

7. Two flat iron plates of same thickness A and B of sides 6 cm × 4 cm and 8 cm × 3 cm respectively, are taken and put over a flat table over which some water is poured. The ratio of force needed to lift the plates (with considering weight of plates) is

(a) 1 : 11
(b) 11 : 2
(c) 10 : 11
(d) 12 : 11

8. Two water droplets merge with each other and forms a large droplet. In this process,

(a) energy is released
(b) energy is absorbed
(c) neither released nor absorbed
(d) some mass is converted into energy

9. A rectangular liquid film is extended from 10 cm × 20 cm to 20 cm × 25 cm. If the work done in this process is 5×10^{-3} J, then the value of surface tension of the liquid is

(a) 0.012 N/m
(b) 0.045 N/m
(c) 0.083 N/m
(d) 0.063 N/m

10. Statement I For liquids, which wet the walls of a vessel, the angle of contact is acute.
Statement II The liquid that wets the solid surface has convex mensiscus.
In the light of above statements, choose the most appropriate answer from the options given below.

(a) Both Statement I and Statement II are correct.
(b) Both Statement I and Statement II are incorrect.
(c) Statement I is correct but Statement II is incorrect.
(d) Statement I is incorrect but Statement II is correct.

11. An air bubble of radius 1 cm rises with terminal velocity 0.21 cm/s in liquid column. If the density of liquid is 1.47×10^3 kg/m^3, then the value of coefficient of viscosity of liquid ignoring the density of air, will be

(a) 1.71×10^4 poise
(b) 1.82×10^4 poise
(c) 1.78×10^4 poise
(d) 1.52×10^4 poise

12. Match the List I with List II.

List I		List II
A. When a single drop splits into *n*-identical drops, then	1.	zero
B. When *n* identical drops combine to form a single drop, then	2.	increase in temperature
C. The surface tension of a liquid drop decreases for	3.	energy absorbed
D. The surface tension of water at boiling temperatrue is	4.	energy released

Choose the correct answer from given options

(a) A - (3), B - (4), C - (2), D - (1)
(b) A - (3), B - (4), C - (1), D - (2)
(c) A - (4), B - (3), C - (2), D - (1)
(d) A - (4), B - (2), C - (1), D - (2)

13. If a ball of steel (density $\rho = 7.8 \text{ gcm}^{-3}$) attains a terminal velocity of 10 cms^{-1} when falling in a tank of water (coefficient of viscosity $\eta_{\text{water}} = 8.5 \times 10^{-4}$ Pa-s) then its terminal velocity in glycerin ($\rho = 1.2 \text{ g cm}^{-3}$, $\eta = 13.2$ Pa-s) would be nearly

(a) $1.6 \times 10^{-5} \text{ cms}^{-1}$
(b) $6.25 \times 10^{-4} \text{ cms}^{-1}$
(c) $6.45 \times 10^{-4} \text{ cms}^{-1}$
(d) $1.5 \times 10^{-5} \text{ cms}^{-1}$

14. Which of the following is the velocity time graph of a small spherical body falling through a long columns of a viscous liquid ?

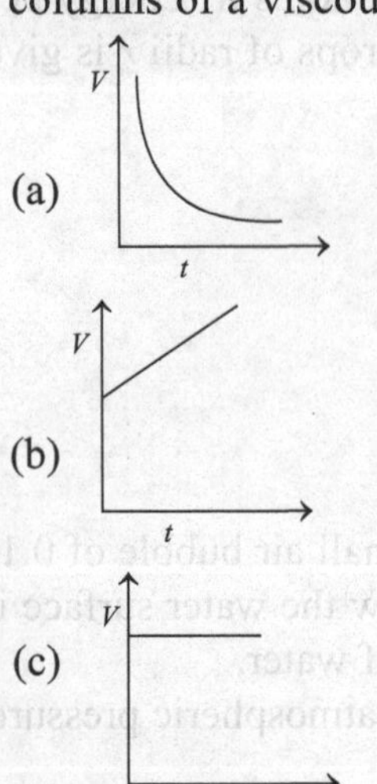

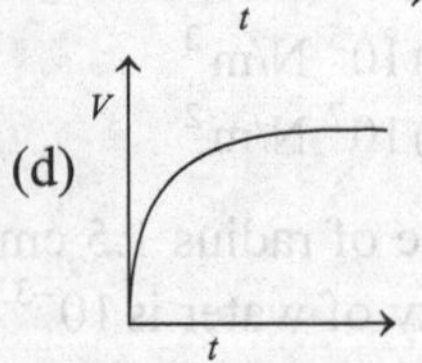

15. A certain number of spherical drops of a liquid of radius r coalesce to form a single drop of radius R and volume V. If T is the surface tension of the liquid, then

(a) energy $= 4VT\left(\frac{1}{r}-\frac{1}{R}\right)$ is released

(b) energy $= 3VT\left(\frac{1}{r}+\frac{2}{R}\right)$ is absorbed

(c) energy $= 3VT\left(\frac{1}{r}-\frac{1}{R}\right)$ is released

(d) energy is neither released nor absorbed

Response Index

01	a	b	c	d	11	a	b	c	d
02	a	b	c	d	12	a	b	c	d
03	a	b	c	d	13	a	b	c	d
04	a	b	c	d	14	a	b	c	d
05	a	b	c	d	15	a	b	c	d
06	a	b	c	d					
07	a	b	c	d					
08	a	b	c	d					
09	a	b	c	d					
10	a	b	c	d					

Performance Scanner

> 90% Excellent !	You have mastered these topics. The concepts of these topics are at your fingertips. Move on to the next test and maintain this momentum.
76-90% Very Good !	You have a good command over these topics. Revise them again after a few days and enhance your performance.
60-75% Good !	You have a wide scope to learn more in these topics. Revise them again.
<60% Not Satisfactory!	You have a long way ahead of you to master in these topics. Revise them thoroughly.

Chapter Break Thru

Syllabus	
• Pressure Due to a Fluid Column • Pascal's Law and its Applications • Effect of Gravity on Fluid Pressure • Streamline and Turbulent Flow • Critical Velocity • Bernoulli Principle and its Applications • Viscosity	• Terminal Velocity • Stoke's Law • Surface Energy and Surface Tension • Angle of Contact • Excess Pressure Across a Curved Surface • Applications of Surface Tension, Drops Bubbles and Capillary Rise.

Important Instructions

- The test is of 45 min duration and contains 30 Multiple Choice Questions (Four options with a single correct answer).
- Choose the correct option and fill the OMR given on the last page of this test accordingly.
- At some instances, you may find more than 1 correct option, in such circumstances you have to judge the most appropriate answer as per conditions given in the question.

1. To get maximum upthrust of the wing of a fan, the structure of the wing of a fan must be

(a) (b)

(c) (d)

2. In the following figure, the flow of liquid through a horizontal pipe is shown. Three tubes *A*, *B* and *C* are connected to the pipe. The radii of the tubes *A*, *B* and *C* at the junction are respectively 5 cm, 2 cm and 5 cm. It can be said that the

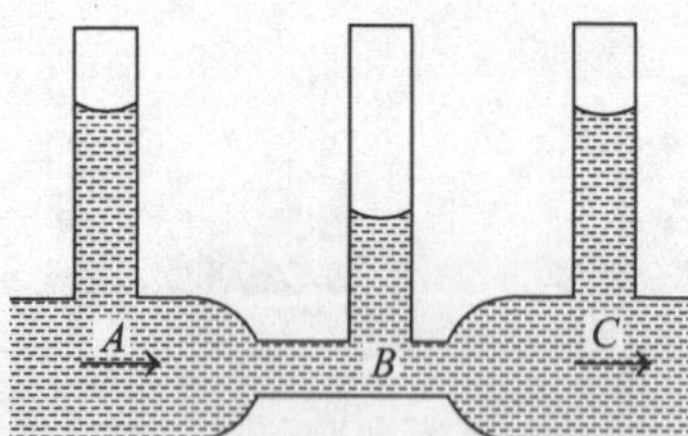

(a) height of the liquid in the tube *A* is maximum
(b) height of the liquid in the tubes *A* and *B* is the same
(c) height of the liquid in all the three tubes is the same
(d) height of the liquid in the tubes *A* and *C* is the same

3. The tube shown in figure is of uniform cross-section. Water flows through it at a constant speed in the direction shown by arrows, then water exerts on the tube is

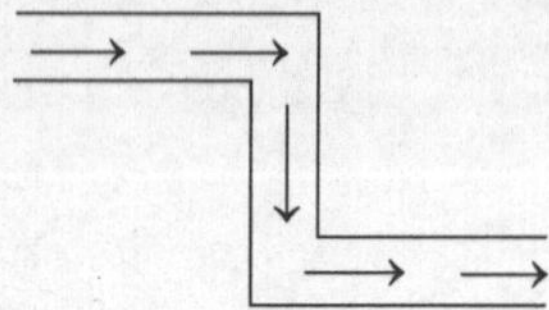

(a) a net force to the right
(b) a net force to the left
(c) a clockwise torque
(d) an anti-clockwise torque

4. An incompressible liquid travels as shown in figure. The speed of the fluid in the lower branch will be

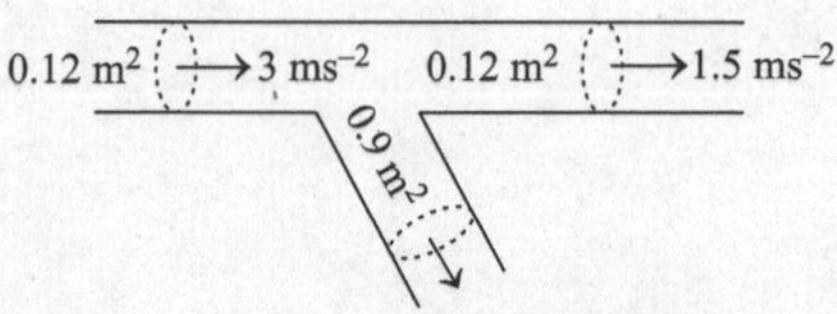

(a) $1\ ms^{-1}$ (b) $1.5\ ms^{-1}$
(c) 20 cm/s (d) 35 cm/s

5. 27 drops of water, each of radius 3 mm are falling through air at a terminal velocity of 9 cms^{-1}. If they coalesce to form a single drop, then the terminal velocity of combined drop will be
(a) 32 $cm\ s^{-1}$
(b) 41 $cm\ s^{-1}$
(c) 81 $cm\ s^{-1}$
(d) 64 $cm\ s^{-1}$

6. A piece of gold weight 50 g in air and 42 g in liquid. If there is a cavity inside the piece of gold, then its volume is (Density of gold = 19.3 g/cc)
(a) 2.4 cm^3 (b) 5.4 cm^3
(c) 3.2 cm^3 (d) 3.0 cm^3

7. Match the List I with List II.

	List I		List II
A.	Hydraulic lift	1.	Archimedes principle
B.	A razor blade can be made to float on water surface in a tray.	2.	Pascal's law
C.	The dam of water reservoir is made thick at the bottom level.	3.	Surface tension
D.	Ship is floating on ocean water.	4.	Pressure

Choose the correct answer from given options
(a) A - (2), B - (3), C - (4), D - (1)
(b) A - (4), B - (3), C - (4), D - (1)
(c) A - (4), B - (1), C - (3), D - (4)
(d) A - (1), B - (2), C - (3), D - (4)

8. The terminal velocity of a ball has radius 4 cm in a viscous liquid is 25 $cm\ s^{-1}$. What would be the terminal velocity, if the radius of the ball were halved?
(a) 80 cms^{-1}
(b) 40 cms^{-1}
(c) 6.25 cms^{-1}
(d) 5 cms^{-1}

9. Two identical bubbles each of radius r and of same surface tension T combine to form a new soap bubble of radius R. Temperature inside the both bubbles are same. If the atmospheric pressure is p_0, then find the surface tension T of the soap solution in terms of p_0, r and R. Assume process is isothermal.
(a) $\frac{p_0(2r^3 - R^3)}{4(R^2 - 2r^2)}$
(b) $\frac{p_0(2r^3 + 3R^3)}{4(R^2 - 2r^2)}$
(c) $\frac{p_0(r^3 - R^3)}{2(R^2 + 2r^2)}$
(d) $\frac{p_0(2r^3 - R^3)}{2(R^2 + 2r^2)}$

10. A body floats with 2/3 of its volume outside when immersed in water. The same body floats with 3/4 of its volume inside when immersed in some other liquid. The density of the other liquid (in gcm^{-3}) is
(Density of water $= 1000\ kg/m^3$)
(a) $\frac{9}{4}$ (b) $\frac{4}{9}$
(c) $\frac{8}{9}$ (d) $\frac{8}{3}$

11. **Assertion (A)** Pascal's law is the working principle of a hydraulic lift.
Reason (R) Pressure is equal to thrust per unit area.
In the light of above statements, choose the most appropriate answer from the options given below.
(a) Both A and R are true and R is the correct explanation of A.
(b) Both A and R are true but R is not the correct explanation of A.
(c) A is true but R is false.
(d) A is false but R is true.

12. Which of three balls will cover maximum horizontal distance

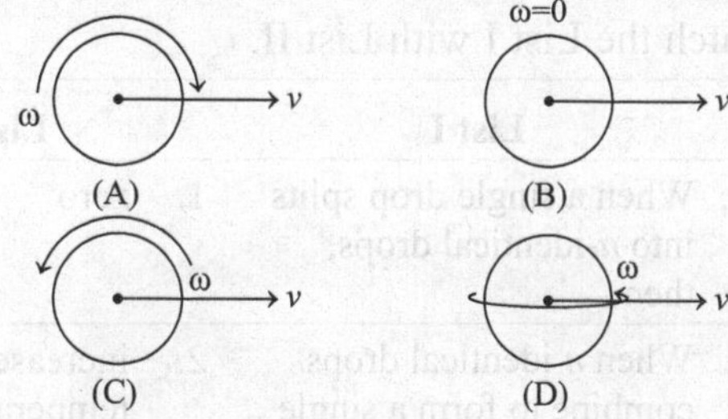

All balls are thrown from same height horizontally giving same angular speed and same linear speed.

8. Two water droplets merge with each other and forms a large droplet. In this process,
(a) energy is released
(b) energy is absorbed
(c) neither released nor absorbed
(d) some mass is converted into energy

9. A rectangular liquid film is extended from $10 \text{ cm} \times 20 \text{ cm}$ to $20 \text{ cm} \times 25 \text{ cm}$. If the work done in this process is $5 \times 10^{-3} \text{J}$, then the value of surface tension of the liquid is
(a) 0.012 N/m
(b) 0.045 N/m
(c) 0.083 N/m
(d) 0.063 N/m

10. **Statement I** For liquids, which wet the walls of a vessel, the angle of contact is acute.
Statement II The liquid that wets the solid surface has convex mensiscus.
In the light of above statements, choose the most appropriate answer from the options given below.
(a) Both Statement I and Statement II are correct.
(b) Both Statement I and Statement II are incorrect.
(c) Statement I is correct but Statement II is incorrect.
(d) Statement I is incorrect but Statement II is correct.

11. An air bubble of radius 1 cm rises with terminal velocity 0.21 cm/s in liquid column. If the density of liquid is $1.47 \times 10^3 \text{ kg/m}^3$, then the value of coefficient of viscosity of liquid ignoring the density of air, will be
(a) 1.71×10^4 poise
(b) 1.82×10^4 poise
(c) 1.78×10^4 poise
(d) 1.52×10^4 poise

12. Match the List I with List II.

List I	List II
A. When a single drop splits into n-identical drops, then	1. zero
B. When n identical drops combine to form a single drop, then	2. increase in temperature
C. The surface tension of a liquid drop decreases for	3. energy absorbed
D. The surface tension of water at boiling temperatrue is	4. energy released

Choose the correct answer from given options
(a) A - (3), B - (4), C - (2), D - (1)
(b) A - (3), B - (4), C - (1), D - (2)
(c) A - (4), B - (3), C - (2), D - (1)
(d) A - (4), B - (2), C - (1), D - (2)

13. If a ball of steel (density $\rho = 7.8 \text{ gcm}^{-3}$) attains a terminal velocity of 10 cms^{-1} when falling in a tank of water (coefficient of viscosity $\eta_{water} = 8.5 \times 10^{-4}$ Pa-s) then its terminal velocity in glycerin ($\rho = 1.2 \text{ g cm}^{-3}$, $\eta = 13.2$ Pa-s) would be nearly
(a) $1.6 \times 10^{-5} \text{ cms}^{-1}$
(b) $6.25 \times 10^{-4} \text{ cms}^{-1}$
(c) $6.45 \times 10^{-4} \text{ cms}^{-1}$
(d) $1.5 \times 10^{-5} \text{ cms}^{-1}$

14. Which of the following is the velocity time graph of a small spherical body falling through a long columns of a viscous liquid ?

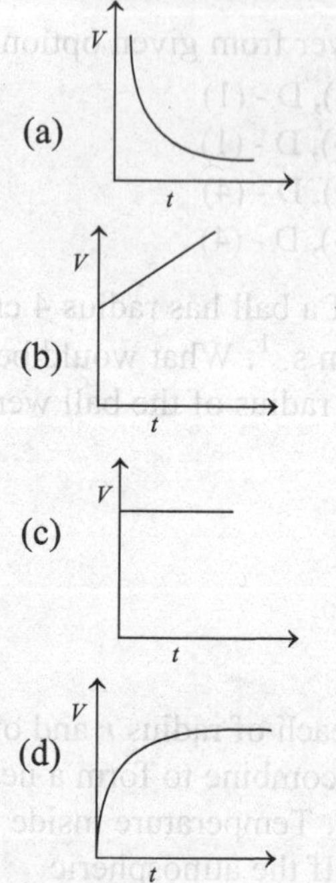

15. A certain number of spherical drops of a liquid of radius r coalesce to form a single drop of radius R and volume V. If T is the surface tension of the liquid, then

(a) energy $= 4VT\left(\frac{1}{r}-\frac{1}{R}\right)$ is released

(b) energy $= 3VT\left(\frac{1}{r}+\frac{2}{R}\right)$ is absorbed

(c) energy $= 3VT\left(\frac{1}{r}-\frac{1}{R}\right)$ is released

(d) energy is neither released nor absorbed

■ Response Index

01	(a)	(b)	(c)	(d)	11	(a)	(b)	(c)	(d)
02	(a)	(b)	(c)	(d)	12	(a)	(b)	(c)	(d)
03	(a)	(b)	(c)	(d)	13	(a)	(b)	(c)	(d)
04	(a)	(b)	(c)	(d)	14	(a)	(b)	(c)	(d)
05	(a)	(b)	(c)	(d)	15	(a)	(b)	(c)	(d)
06	(a)	(b)	(c)	(d)					
07	(a)	(b)	(c)	(d)					
08	(a)	(b)	(c)	(d)					
09	(a)	(b)	(c)	(d)					
10	(a)	(b)	(c)	(d)					

■ Performance Scanner

> 90% Excellent !	You have mastered these topics. The concepts of these topics are at your fingertips. Move on to the next test and maintain this momentum.
76-90% Very Good !	You have a good command over these topics. Revise them again after a few days and enhance your performance.
60-75% Good !	You have a wide scope to learn more in these topics. Revise them again.
<60% Not Satisfactory!	You have a long way ahead of you to master in these topics. Revise them thoroughly.

In the light of the above statements, choose the most appropriate answer from the options given below.

(a) Both Statement I and Statement II are correct.
(b) Both Statement I and Statement II are incorrect.
(c) Statement I is correct but Statement II is incorrect.
(d) Statement I is incorrect but Statement II is correct.

29. A mercury drop is divided into 64 equal droplets. The pressure difference between inner and outer sides of the big drop

(a) will be the same as for smaller droplet
(b) will be half of that for smaller droplet
(c) will be one-fourth of that for smaller droplet
(d) will be twice of that for smaller droplet

30. Water rises to a height of 25 cm in a glass capillary tube. If the area of cross-section of the tube is reduced to half of the former value, the height of water rise will be

(a) 20 cm
(b) 35.35 cm
(c) 2.5 cm
(d) 17.35 cm

Response Index

01	a	b	c	d	11	a	b	c	d	21	a	b	c	d
02	a	b	c	d	12	a	b	c	d	22	a	b	c	d
03	a	b	c	d	13	a	b	c	d	23	a	b	c	d
04	a	b	c	d	14	a	b	c	d	24	a	b	c	d
05	a	b	c	d	15	a	b	c	d	25	a	b	c	d
06	a	b	c	d	16	a	b	c	d	26	a	b	c	d
07	a	b	c	d	17	a	b	c	d	27	a	b	c	d
08	a	b	c	d	18	a	b	c	d	28	a	b	c	d
09	a	b	c	d	19	a	b	c	d	29	a	b	c	d
10	a	b	c	d	20	a	b	c	d	30	a	b	c	d

Performance Scanner

> 90% Excellent !	You have mastered this chapter. The concepts of this chapter are at your fingertips. Move on to the next chapter and maintain this momentum.
76-90% Very Good !	You have a good command over this chapter. Revise the chapter again after a few days and enhance your performance.
60-75% Good !	You have a wide scope to learn more for this chapter. Revise this chapter again.
<60% Not Satisfactory!	You have a long way ahead of you to master this chapter. Revise it thoroughly.

For Online Chapter Test **Scan the QR Code**

Test Booklet No. **3947110**

Test Booklet Code **CH10**

MEDACE
NEET (UG)
SELF ASSESSMENT KIT

Thermal Properties of Matter

Topics Covered

Thermometry and Thermal Expansion

Calorimetry and Heat transfer

Important Instructions

- This Booklet Contains – Two Topic Tests and One Test on Complete Chapter.
- Each question carries 4 Marks.
- For each correct response, the candidate will get 4 marks and for every incorrect response, 1 mark will be additionally deducted from total score.
- Use **Blue/Black** point pen only for filling the OMR.
- Rough work is to be done in the space provided for this purpose in the test booklet only.

Name of the Candidate (In Capitals) ____________________

____

Candidate's Signature ____________________

Invigilator's Signature ____________________

Facsimile signature stamp of center superintendent ____________________

Do not open this Booklet until you start attempting the Test

Topical Follow Thru

Test 1

Syllabus
- Heat
- Temperature
- Thermal Expansion of Solids, Liquids and Gases

For deeper insight **Scan the QR Code**

Important Instructions
- The test is of 30 minutes duration and contains 15 Multiple Choice Questions. (Four options with a single correct answer).
- Choose the correct option and fill the OMR given on the last page of this test accordingly.
- At some instances, you may find more than 1 option may be correct, in such circumstances you have to judge the most appropriate answer as per the conditions given in the question.

1. 1 degree rise on celsius scale is equal to how many degree rise on fahrenheit scale?

(a) 1 (b) 1.8
(c) 0.56 (d) 10

2. A solid ball of metal has a concentric spherical cavity within it. If the ball is heated, the volume of the cavity will

(a) increase
(b) decrease
(c) remain unaffected
(d) None of these

3. At what temperature a gold ring of diameter 6.230 cm be heated, so that it can be fitted on a wooden bangle of diameter 6.241 cm? Both the diameters have been measured at room temperature (27° C).

(Given, coefficient of linear thermal expansion of gold, $\alpha_L = 1.4 \times 10^{-5}\ K^{-1}$)

(a) 125.7°C
(b) 91.7°C
(c) 425.7°C
(d) 152.7°C

4. If 10g of oxygen are subjected to a pressure of 3 atm at a temperature of 10°C. Heating at a constant pressure, the gas is expanded to 10L. With reference to the given situation, match the List I (physical quantity) with List II (value) and select the correct answer from the codes given below. ($R = 0.0821$ atm-litre K^{-1} mol^{-1})

	List I		List II
A.	The volume of the gas before expansion (in litres)	1.	4.13
B.	The temperature of the gas after expansion (in kelvin)	2.	1.0
C.	The density of gas before expansion (in gL^{-1})	3.	2.42
D.	The density of gas after expansion (in gL^{-1})	4.	1169.4

	A	B	C	D
(a)	3	4	2	1
(b)	4	3	1	2
(c)	3	4	1	2
(d)	4	2	3	1

5. A steel scale is calibrated for 27°C. The error in a reading of 50 cm at 30°C is [$\alpha_{steel} = 1.2 \times 10^{-5} /°C$]

(a) 0.018 mm
(b) 0.18 mm
(c) 0.0018 mm
(d) 0.16 mm

6. The freezing point on a thermometer is marked as –20° and the boiling point as 130°. A temperature of human body (34°C) on this thermometer will be read as

(a) 31°
(b) 51°
(c) 20°
(d) None of the above

7. **Statement I** A solid and hollow sphere of same diameter and same material when heated through the same temperature, will expand by same amount.

Statement II The change in volume is independent of the mass but depends on volume.

In the light of the above statements, choose the most appropriate answer from the options given below.

(a) Both Statement I and Statement II are correct.
(b) Both Statement I and Statement II are incorrect.
(c) Statement I is correct but Statement II is incorrect.
(d) Statement I is incorrect but Statement II is correct.

8. The coefficient of linear expansion of crystal in one direction is α and that in every direction perpendicular to it is β. The coefficient of cubical expansion is

(a) $\alpha + \beta$
(b) $2\alpha + \beta$
(c) $\alpha + 2\beta$
(d) None of the above

9. In the given figure, which strip have higher coefficient of linear expansion?

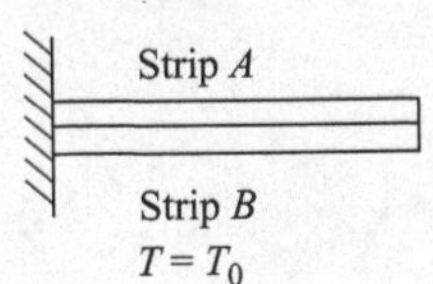

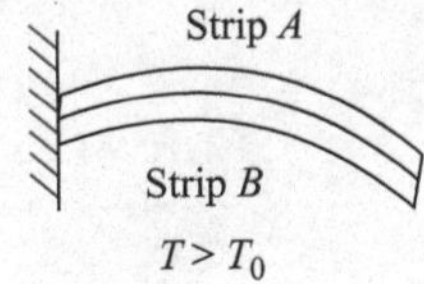

(a) Strip-A
(b) Strip-B
(c) Both have equal
(d) Cannot be decided from given data

10. A rod of metal M_1 of length 50 cm elongates by 1 mm when it is heated from 0°C to 100°C. Another rod of metal M_2 of length 80 cm elongates by 0.8 mm for the same rise in temperature. The coefficients of linear expansion of M_1 and M_2 are in the ratio

(a) 3 : 2 (b) 2 : 1
(c) 3 : 1 (d) 4 : 3

11. A pendulum clock is 5 s fast at temperature 15°C and 10 s slow at 30°C, find the temperature at which clock gives correct time.

(a) 25°C (b) 23°C (c) 20°C (d) 18°C

12. A rod of length 500 mm and coefficient of linear expansion $\alpha = 10^{-4}$ per degree is placed symmetrically between fixed walls separated by 501 mm. The Young's modulus of the rod is 10^{11} N/m^2. If the temperature is increased by 40°C, then the stress developed in the rod is (in N/m^2)

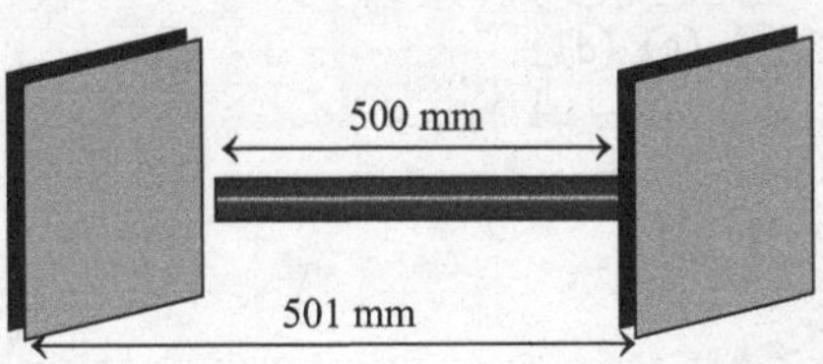

(a) 10
(b) 10^8
(c) 2×10^8
(d) Cannot be calculated

13. A metal rod of silver at 0°C is heated to 100°C. Its length is increased by 0.19 cm. Coefficient of cubical expansion of the silver rod is

(a) 5.7×10^{-5}/°C
(b) 0.63×10^{-5}/°C
(c) 1.9×10^{-5}/°C
(d) 16.1×10^{-5}/°C

14. A glass flask of volume 1.5 L at 0°C is filled, level full of mercury at this temperature. The flask and mercury are now heated to 110°C. Then, mercury will spill out in amount of (if coefficient of volume expansion of mercury is 1.82×10^{4}/°C and linear expansion of glass is 0.1×10^{-4}/°C)

(a) 21.2 cc
(b) 25 cc
(c) 1.52 cc
(d) 2.12 cc

15. A thin rod of negligible mass and cross-section of $4\times10^{-6}\ m^2$ suspended vertically from one end, has a length of 2 m at 150°C. The rod is cooled to 0°C, but prevented from contracting by attaching a mass at the lower end. The value of this mass is (Young's modulus $=10^{11}\ N/m^2$, Coefficient of linear expansion $=10^{-5}\ K^{-1}$ and $g=10\ m/s^2$)

(a) 20 kg
(b) 60 kg
(c) 40 kg
(d) 50 kg

Response Index

01	a	b	c	d	11	a	b	c	d
02	a	b	c	d	12	a	b	c	d
03	a	b	c	d	13	a	b	c	d
04	a	b	c	d	14	a	b	c	d
05	a	b	c	d	15	a	b	c	d
06	a	b	c	d					
07	a	b	c	d					
08	a	b	c	d					
09	a	b	c	d					
10	a	b	c	d					

Performance Scanner

> 90% Excellent !	You have mastered these topics. The concepts of these topics are at your fingertips. Move on to the next test and maintain this momentum.
76-90% Very Good !	You have a good command over these topics. Revise them again after a few days and enhance your performance.
60-75% Good !	You have a wide scope to learn more in these topics. Revise them again.
<60% Not Satisfactory!	You have a long way ahead of you to master in these topics. Revise them thoroughly.

Test 2

Syllabus

- Specific Heat Capacity
- Calorimetry
- Change of State
- Latent Heat
- Heat transfer-Conduction, Convection and Radiation

For deeper insight **Scan the QR Code**

Important Instructions

- The test is of 45 minutes duration and contains 25 Multiple Choice Questions. (Four options with a single correct answer).
- Choose the correct option and fill the OMR given on the last page of this test accordingly.
- At some instances, you may find more than 1 option may be correct, in such circumstances you have to judge the most appropriate answer as per the conditions given in the question.

1. Heat energy of 184 kJ is given to ice of mass 600 g at $-12°C$. Specific heat of ice is 2222.3 J $kg^{-1°}C^{-1}$ and latent heat of ice is 336 kJ kg^{-1}.

A. Final temperature of system will be 0°C.
B. Final temperature of the system will be greater than 0°C.
C. The final system will have a mixture of ice and water in the ratio of 5 : 1.
D. The final system will have a mixture of ice and water in the ratio of 1: 5.
E. The final system will have water only.

Choose the correct answer from the options given below

(a) A and C Only
(b) A and D Only
(c) B and D Only
(d) A and E Only

2. 500 g of water and 100 g of ice at 0°C are in a calorimeter whose water equivalent is 40 g. 10 g of steam at 100°C is added to it. Then, water in the calorimeter is (Latent heat of ice = 80 cal/g, latent heat of steam = 540 cal/g)

(a) 580 g (b) 590 g
(c) 600 g (d) 610 g

3. A block of ice at –10°C is slowly heated and converted to steam at 100°C. Which of the following curves represents the phenomenon qualitatively?

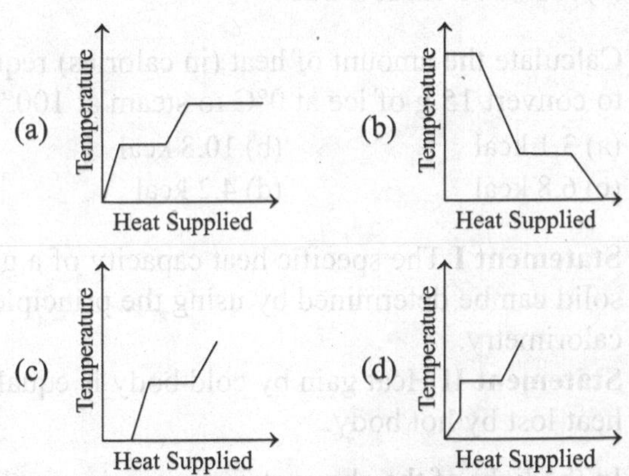

4. If two rods A and B of equal length L, and different areas of cross-section A_1 and A_2 have one end each at temperature T_1 and T_2, have equal rates of flow of heat, then

(a) $A_1 = A_2$
(b) $\frac{A_1}{A_2} = \frac{K_1}{K_2}$
(c) $\frac{A_1}{A_2} = \frac{K_2}{K_1}$
(d) $K_1 = K_2$

5. **Assertion** (A) Two conducting rods of same material and same lengths are joined end to end as shown in figure. Heat current H is flowing through them as shown. Temperature difference across rod-1 is more than the temperature difference across rod-2.

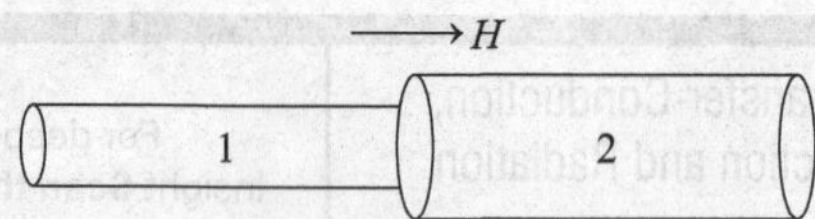

Reason (R) Thermal resistance of rod-1 is less compared to rod-2.

In the light of the above statements, choose the most appropriate answer from the options given below.

(a) Both A and R are true and R is the correct explanation of A.
(b) Both A and R are true but R is not the correct explanation of A.
(c) A is true but R is false.
(d) A is false but R is true.

6. Calculate the amount of heat (in calories) required to convert 15 g of ice at 0°C to steam at 100°C.

(a) 3.1 kcal (b) 10.8 kcal
(c) 6.8 kcal (d) 4.2 kcal

7. **Statement I** The specific heat capacity of a given solid can be determined by using the principle of calorimetry.
Statement II Heat gain by cold body is equal to heat lost by hot body.

In the light of the above statements, choose the most appropriate answer from the options given below.

(a) Both Statement I and Statement II are incorrect.
(b) Both Statement I and Statement II are correct.
(c) Statement I is correct but Statement II is incorrect.
(d) Statement I is incorrect but Statement II is correct.

8. The portion BC of the indicator diagram representing the state of matter denotes

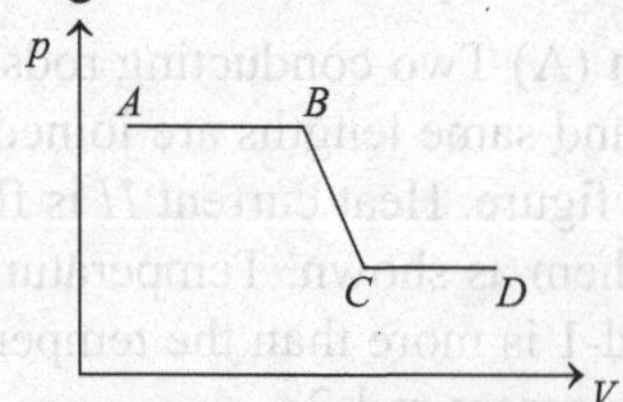

(a) gaseous state of matter
(b) liquid state of matter
(c) change from liquid to gaseous state
(d) change from gaseous to liquid state

9. Two identical vessels are filled with equal amounts of ice. The vessels are made of steel and copper, respectively. If the ice melts in both vessels in times t_1 and t_2 respectively, then their thermal conductivities are in the ratio

(a) $\frac{t_1}{t_2}$ (b) $\frac{t_2}{t_1}$
(c) $t_2^2 : t_1^2$ (d) $t_1^2 : t_2^2$

10. Two rigid boxes containing different ideal gases are placed on a table. Box A contains one mole of nitrogen at temperature T_0, while Box B contains one mole of helium at temperature (7/3) T_0. The boxes are, then put into thermal contact with each other and heat flows between them until the gases reach a common final temperature (ignore the heat capacity of boxes). Then, the final temperature of the gases T_f, in terms of T_0 is

(a) $T_f = \frac{7}{3} T_0$ (b) $T_f = \frac{3}{2} T_0$
(c) $T_f = \frac{5}{2} T_0$ (d) $T_f = \frac{3}{7} T_0$

11. If 5 m is the length, A is the area of cross-section and K is the thermal conductivity, then the thermal resistance of the block is given by

(a) $\frac{Kl}{A}$ (b) $\frac{5}{KA}$
(c) $\frac{AK}{l}$ (d) $\frac{A}{Kl}$

12. 540 g of ice at 0°C is mixed with 540 g of water at 80°C. The final temperature of the mixture is

(a) 0°C (b) 40°C
(c) 80°C (d) less than 0°C

13. Sun rays are allowed to fall on a lens of diameter 20 cm. They are brought to focus on a calorimeter containing 20 g of ice. If the absorption by the lens is negligible, the time required to melt all the ice is (Take, solar constant $= 1.9$ cal min^{-1}cm^{-2} and $L = 80$ calg^{-1})

(a) 6.4 min (b) 3.2 min
(c) 7.2 min (d) 2.7 min

14. Work done in converting one gram of ice at -10°C into steam at 100°C is

(a) 3045 J (b) 6056 J
(c) 721 J (d) 616 J

15. A calorimeter contains 10 g of water at 20°C. The temperature falls to 15°C in 10 min. When calorimeter contains 20 g of water at 20°C, it takes 15 min for the temperature to become 15°C. The water equivalent of the calorimeter is

(a) 5 g (b) 10 g
(c) 25 g (d) 50 g

16. Two metal cubes A and B of same size are arranged as shown in the figure. The extreme ends of the combination are maintained at the indicated temperatures. The arrangement is thermally insulated. The coefficients of thermal conductivity of A and B are 300 W/m°C and 200 W/m°C, respectively. After steady state is reached, the temperature of the interface will be

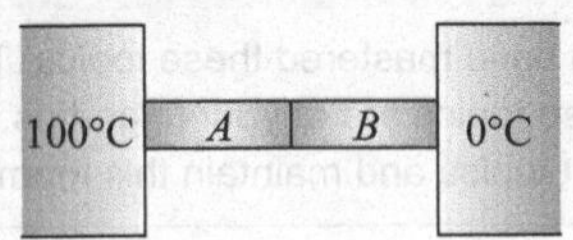

(a) 45°C
(b) 90°C
(c) 30°C
(d) 60°C

17. 2 kg of ice at –20°C is mixed with 5 kg of water at 20°C in an insulating vessel having a negligible heat capacity. Calculate the final mass of water remaining in the container. It is given that the specific heats of water and ice are 1 kcal $kg^{-1}°C^{-1}$ and 0.6 kcal $kg^{-1}°C^{-1}$ while the latent heat of fusion of ice is 80 kcal/kg.

(a) 7 kg (b) 6 kg
(c) 4 kg (d) 2 kg

18. The temperature of the body is increased from 20°C to 60°C, the ratio of energy emitted per second $P_2 : P_1$ is

(a) 1 : 3
(b) 1.6 :1
(c) 1:27
(d) 1:9

19. An iron cylindrical rod having temperature T_1 and T_2 at its ends. The rate of flow of heat is Q_1 cal/s. If all the linear dimensions are half keeping temperature constant, then rate of flow of heat Q_2 will be

(a) $4Q_1$
(b) $2Q_1$
(c) $\frac{Q_1}{4}$
(d) $\frac{Q_1}{2}$

20. A hammer of mass 1 kg having speed of 30 m/s, hits an iron nail of mass 250 g. If specific heat of iron is 0.105 cal/g°C and half the energy is converted into heat, then raise in temperature of nail is

(a) 7.1°C (b) 9.2°C (c) 10.5°C (d) 2.0°C

21. Two similar rods are joined as shown in figure. Then, temperature of junction is (assume no heat loss through lateral surface of rod and temperatures at the ends are shown in steady state)

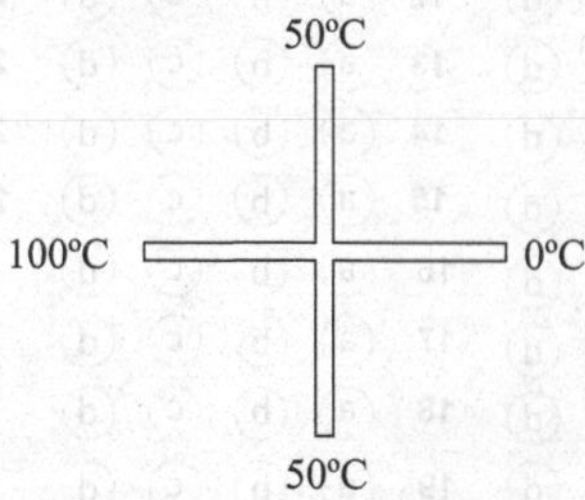

(a) 50°C (b) 75°C
(c) 66.6°C (d) 33.3°C

22. If some quantity of water having mass m at a temperature θ (in °C) is poured on to a larger mass M of ice which is at its melting point. If c is the specific heat capacity of water and L the specific latent heat of fusion of ice, then the mass of ice melted is given by

(a) $\frac{ML}{m\theta}$ (b) $\frac{mcL}{\theta}$
(c) $\frac{mc\theta}{ML}$ (d) $\frac{mc\theta}{L}$

23. A wall has two layers A and B, each made of different material. Both the layers have the same thickness. The thermal conductivity for A is twice that of B and, under steady condition, the temperature difference across the wall is 36°C. The temperature difference across the layer A is

(a) 6°C (b) 12°C (c) 24°C (d) 18°C

24. Three liquids with masses m_1, m_2 and m_3 are thoroughly mixed. If their specific heats are c_1, c_2 and c_3 and their temperatures T_1, T_2 and T_3 respectively, then the temperature of the mixture is

(a) $\dfrac{c_1T_2 + c_2T_2 + c_3T_3}{m_1c_1 + m_2c_2 + m_3c_3}$

(b) $\dfrac{m_1c_1T_1 + m_2c_2T_2 + m_3c_3T_3}{m_1c_1 + m_2c_2 + m_3c_3}$

(c) $\dfrac{m_1c_1T_1 + m_2c_2T_2 + m_3c_3T_3}{m_1T_1 + m_2T_2 + m_3T_3}$

(d) $\dfrac{m_1T_1 + m_2T_2 + m_3T_3}{c_1T_1 + c_2T_2 + c_3T_3}$

25. A metal of mass m kg requires a power input of P watts to remain in the molten state at its melting point. When the power is turned off, the sample completely solidifies in time t second, then the latent heat of fusion of the substance is

(a) $\dfrac{Pt^2}{m}$ (b) $\dfrac{Pt}{m}$

(c) $\dfrac{m}{P+2}$ (d) $\dfrac{Pm}{t}$

Response Index

01	a	b	c	d	11	a	b	c	d	21	a	b	c	d
02	a	b	c	d	12	a	b	c	d	22	a	b	c	d
03	a	b	c	d	13	a	b	c	d	23	a	b	c	d
04	a	b	c	d	14	a	b	c	d	24	a	b	c	d
05	a	b	c	d	15	a	b	c	d	25	a	b	c	d
06	a	b	c	d	16	a	b	c	d					
07	a	b	c	d	17	a	b	c	d					
08	a	b	c	d	18	a	b	c	d					
09	a	b	c	d	19	a	b	c	d					
10	a	b	c	d	20	a	b	c	d					

Performance Scanner

> 90% Excellent !	You have mastered these topics. The concepts of these topics are at your fingertips. Move on to the next topics and maintain this momentum.
76-90% Very Good !	You have a good command over these topics. Revise these topics again after a few days and enhance your performance.
60-75% Good !	You have a wide scope to learn more for these topics. Revise these topics again.
<60 Not Satisfactory!	You have a long way ahead of you to master these topics. Revise it thoroughly.

Chapter Break Thru

Syllabus	• Heat • Temperature • Thermal expansion of Solids, Liquid and Gases • Specific Heat Capacity • Calorimetry	• Change of State • Latent Heat • Heat transfer-conduction, convection and Radiation

Important Instructions

- The test is of 45 min duration and contains 30 Multiple Choice Questions (Four options with a single correct answer).
- Choose the correct option and fill the OMR given on the last page of this test accordingly.
- At some instances, you may find more than 1 correct option, in such circumstances you have to judge the most appropriate answer as per conditions given in the question.

1. The temperature of a body on kelvin scale is found to be x K. When it is measured by fahrenheit thermometer, it is found to be x°F, then the value of x is

(a) 40
(b) 313
(c) 574.25
(d) 301.25

2. When a bimetallic strip is heated, it

(a) does not bend at all.
(b) gets twisted in the form of an helix.
(c) bends in the form of an arc with the more expandable metal outside.
(d) bends in the form of an arc with the more expandable metal inside.

3. When a metal ball is heated, the maximum percentage increase will occur in its

(a) density
(b) radius
(c) volume
(d) area

4. **Assertion** (A) If equal amount of heat is added to equal masses of different substances, the resulting change in temperature is also equal.

Reason (R) Every substance requires a unique value of heat to change its temperature per unit mass, per degree centigrade (or per kelvin).

In the light of the above statements, choose the most appropriate answer from the options given below.

(a) Both A and R are true and R is the correct explanation of A.
(b) Both A and R are true but R is not the correct explanation of A.
(c) A is true but R is false.
(d) A is false but R is true.

5. A solid sphere of metal at 1°C is lying at the bottom of a bucket full of water at 1°C. If then temperature of the water is increased to 4°C, the buoyant force on the sphere due to water will

(a) increase
(b) be unchanged
(c) decrease
(d) increase or decrease depending on the numerical values of coefficient of expansion of water and iron

6. 80 g of water at 30°C are poured on a large block of ice at 0°C. The mass of ice that melts is

(a) 30 g (b) 80 g (c) 1600 g (d) 150 g

7. On a new scale of temperature (which is linear) and called the W scale, the freezing and boiling points of water are 39°W and 239°W, respectively. What will be the temperature on the new scale, corresponding to a temperature of 39°C on the Celsius scale?

(a) 78°W (b) 117°W
(c) 200°W (d) 139°W

8. A steel wire *AB* of length 85 cm at 10°C is fixed rigidly at points *A* and *B* in an aluminium frame as shown in figure. If the temperature of the system is raised to 110°C, what extra stress will be produced in the wire relative to aluminium frame? Assume that coefficients of linear expansion for aluminium and steel are $23\times10^{-6}/°C$ and $11\times10^{-6}/°C$ respectively and Young's modulus for steel is 2×10^{11} Pa.

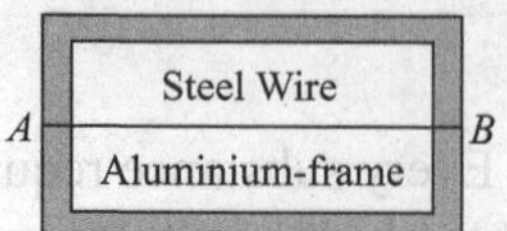

(a) 4.6×10^8 Pa (b) 2.4×10^8 Pa
(c) 3.6×10^8 Pa (d) 2.2×10^8 Pa

9. The graph between two temperature scales *A* and *B* as shown in figure. Between upper fixed point and lower fixed point, there are 150 equal divisions on scale *A* and 100 on scale *B*. The relationship for conversion between the two scales is given by

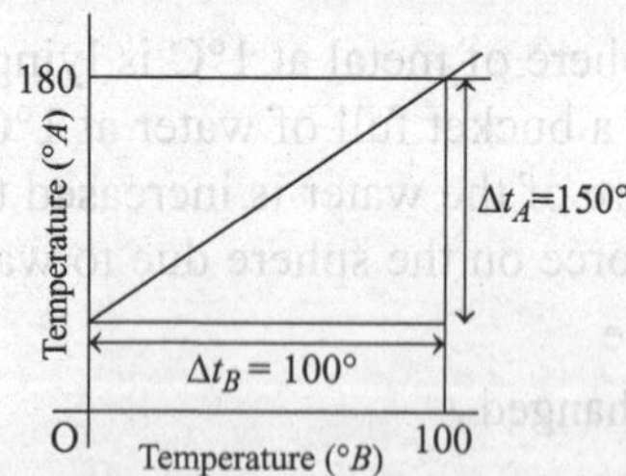

(a) $\dfrac{t_A-180}{100}=\dfrac{t_B}{150}$

(b) $\dfrac{t_A-30}{150}=\dfrac{t_B}{100}$

(c) $\dfrac{t_B-180}{150}=\dfrac{t_A}{100}$

(d) $\dfrac{t_B-40}{100}=\dfrac{t_A}{180}$

10. **Statement I** In change of state from solid to liquid, the temperature decreases until the entire amount of the solid substance melts.

Statement II The phenomena of refreezing is called melting.

In the light of the above statements, choose the most appropriate answer from the options given below.

(a) Both Statement I and Statement II are incorrect.
(b) Both Statement I and Statement II are correct.
(c) Statement I is correct and Statement II is incorrect.
(d) Statement I is incorrect and Statement II is correct.

11. Two liquids are at 30°C and 20°C. When mixed in equal masses, the temperature of the mixture is found to be 25°C. The ratio of specific heats of these liquids are

(a) 3 : 2 (b) 1 : 1 (c) 2 : 3 (d) 4 : 3

12. An electric heater is heated up and after that the electric supply being cut-off. The electric heater element cools down to the temperature of its surroundings, but it will not cool further because

(a) supply is cut-off
(b) it has high resistance
(c) surroundings are radiating
(d) elements and surroundings have the same temperature

13. 20 g of ice at −20 °C is mixed into a calorimeter containing 20 g of water at 15°C. The specific heat of water is twice that of ice. Heat capacity of the calorimeter has to be neglected. When equilibrium is reached, the calorimeter will contain

(a) 20 g ice and 20 g water
(b) 35 g water and 5 g ice
(c) 40 g of water
(d) 40 g of ice

14. The temperature gradient in a rod of 1 m length is 70°C/m. If the temperature of hotter end of the rod is 30°C, then the temperature of the cooler end is

(a) 40°C (b) −10°C (c) 10°C (d) −40°C

15. The sun rays are allowed to fall on a lens of diameter 20 cm. They are then brought to focus on a calorimeter containing 20 g of ice. If the absorption by the lens is negligible, the time required to melt all the ice is (solar constant $=1.9$ cal/min/cm^2 and $L=80$ cal/g)

(a) 6.4 min (b) 3.2 min
(c) 7.2 min (d) 2.7 min

16. On heating a liquid of coefficient of cubical expansion γ in a steel container having coefficient of linear expansion $\frac{\gamma}{3}$, the level of liquid in the container will

(a) rise
(b) fall
(c) remain almost stationary
(d) It is difficult to say

17. Steam is passed into 54 g of water at 30°C till the temperature of mixture becomes 90°C. If the latent heat of steam is 530 cal/g, the mass of the mixture will be

(a) 80 g (b) 60 g
(c) 50 g (d) 24 g

18. The radius of a metal sphere at room temperature T is R and the coefficient of linear expansion of the metal is α. The sphere is heated a little by a temperature ΔT, so that its new temperature is $T+\Delta T$. The increase in the volume of the sphere is approximately,

(a) $2\pi R\,\alpha\,\Delta T$ (b) $\pi R^2 \alpha \Delta T$
(c) $4\pi R^3 \alpha \Delta T/3$ (d) $4\pi R^3 \alpha \Delta T$

19. Hailstone at 0°C falls from a height of 1 km on an insulating surface converting whole of its kinetic energy into heat. What part of it will melt $(g=10\,\text{m/s}^2)$

(a) $\frac{1}{29.3}$
(b) $\frac{1}{8}$
(c) $\frac{1}{33} \times 10^{-4}$
(d) All of it will melt

20. Two identical conducting rods are first connected independently to two vessels, one containing water at 100°C and the other containing ice at 0°C. In the second case, the rods are joined end to end and connected to the same vessels. Let q_1 and q_2 g/s be the rate of melting of ice in two cases, respectively. The ratio of $\frac{q_1}{q_2}$ is

(a) $\frac{1}{2}$ (b) $\frac{2}{1}$
(c) $\frac{4}{1}$ (d) $\frac{1}{4}$

21. Match the List I with List II and choose the correct combination from the options given below.

	List I		List II
A.	The temperature of an iron piece is increased from 20° to 70°. What is change in its temperature on the Fahrenheit scale (in °F)?	1.	20
B.	At what temperature (in °C) do the Celsius and Fahrenheit readings have the same numerical value?	2.	90
C.	100 g ice at 0°C is converted into steam at 100°C. Find total heat (in kcal) required ($L_f = 80$ cal/g, $s_w = 1$ cal/g°C, $L_v = 540$ cal/g)	3.	– 40
D.	A ball is dropped on a floor from a height of 5 m. After the collision it rises upto a height of 3 m. Assume that 50% of the mechanical energy lost goes as thermal energy into the ball. Calculate the rise in temperature (in milli centigrade) of the ball in the collision. ($s_{\text{ball}} = 500$ J/K, $g=10\,\text{m/s}^2$)	4.	72

	A	B	C	D
(a)	2	3	4	1
(b)	2	4	3	1
(c)	4	3	2	1
(d)	1	2	3	4

22. A pendulum clock keeps correct time at $\theta°$C. Its mean coefficient of linear expansion is α/°C, then the loss in seconds per day by the clock if the temperature rises by $t°$C is

(a) $\dfrac{\frac{1}{2}\alpha t \times 864000}{1-\frac{\alpha t}{2}}$

(b) $\frac{1}{2}\alpha t \times 86400$

(c) $\dfrac{\frac{1}{2}\alpha t \times 86400}{\left(1-\frac{\alpha t}{2}\right)^2}$

(d) $\dfrac{\frac{1}{2}\alpha t \times 86400}{1+\frac{\alpha t}{2}}$

23. Three rods of equal length l are joined to form an equilateral triangle PQR. O is the mid-point of PQ. Distance OR remains same for small change in temperature. Coefficient of linear expansion for PR and RQ is same, *i.e.* α_2 but that for PQ is α_1.

Then,

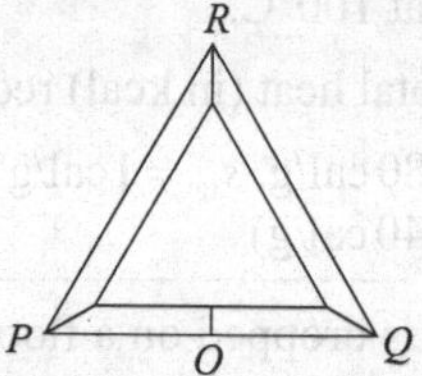

(a) $\alpha_2 = 3\alpha_1$
(b) $\alpha_2 = 4\alpha_1$
(c) $\alpha_1 = 3\alpha_2$
(d) $\alpha_1 = 4\alpha_2$

24. Coefficient of linear expansion of copper and steel rods are α_1 and α_2. Lengths of copper and steel rods are L_1 and L_2, respectively. If $L_2 - L_1$ is maintained same at all temperatures, which one of the following relations holds good?

(a) $\dfrac{L_1}{L_2} = \dfrac{\alpha_2}{\alpha_1}$ (b) $\dfrac{L_1}{L_2} = \sqrt{\dfrac{\alpha_2}{\alpha_1}}$

(c) $\dfrac{L_2}{L_1} = \dfrac{\alpha_1^2}{\alpha_2^2}$ (d) $\dfrac{L_2}{L_1} = \sqrt{\dfrac{\alpha_1}{\alpha_2}}$

25. In an industrial process, 10 kg of water per hour is to be heated from 20°C to 80°C. To do this, steam at 150°C is passed from a boiler into a copper coil immersed in water. The steam condenses in the coil and is returned to the boiler as water at 90°C, how many kg of steam is required per hour?

(Take, specific heat of steam $= 1$ cal per g°C, latent heat of vaporisation $= 540\,\text{cal g}^{-1}$)

(a) 1 g
(b) 1 kg
(c) 10 g
(d) 10 kg

26. An ice block at 0°C and of mass 200 g is dropped from height h such that the loss in gravitational potential energy of block is exactly equal to the heat required to just completely melt the ice. Taking latent heat of fusion of ice $= 80$ cal/g, acceleration due to gravity $= 10\,\text{m/s}^2$ and mechanical equivalent of heat $= 4.2$ J/cal. The value of h is

(a) 72 m
(b) 28 km
(c) 48 m
(d) 33.6 km

27. Five rods of same dimensions are arranged as shown in the figure. They have thermal conductivities K_1, K_2, K_3, K_4 and K_5. When points A and B are maintained at different temperatures, no heat flows through the centre rod if

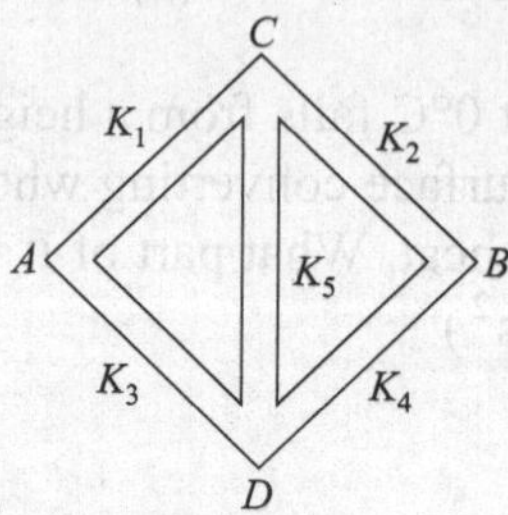

(a) $K_1 = K_4$ and $K_2 = K_3$
(b) $K_1K_4 = K_2K_3$
(c) $K_1K_2 = K_3K_4$
(d) $\dfrac{K_1}{K_4} = \dfrac{K_2}{K_3}$

28. A sphere and a cube of same material and same volume are heated upto same temperature and allowed to cool in the same surroundings. The ratio of the amounts of radiations will be

(a) 1 : 1 (b) $\frac{4\pi}{3}:1$

(c) $\left(\frac{\pi}{6}\right)^{1/3}:1$ (d) $\frac{1}{2}\left(\frac{4\pi}{3}\right)^{2/3}:1$

29. The coefficient of thermal conductivity of copper, mercury and glass are K_c, K_m and K_g respectively, such that $K_c > K_m > K_g$. If the same quantity of heat is to flow per second per unit area of each and corresponding temperature gradients are X_c, X_m and X_g, then

(a) $X_c = X_m = X_g$
(b) $X_c > X_m > X_g$
(c) $X_c < X_m < X_g$
(d) $X_m < X_c < X_g$

30. Two bodies of equal mass m at 0°C, are heated uniformly under identical conditions. The temperature of first body with latent heat L_1 and specific heat c_1 changes as graph 1. The temperature of second body with latent heat L_2 and specific heat capacity c_2 changes as graph 2. Which of the following option is correct?

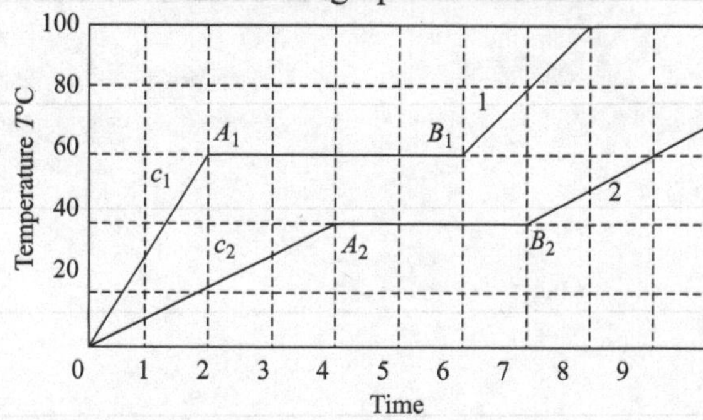

(a) $L_1 > L_2; c_1 < c_2$
(b) $L_1 < L_2; c_1 < c_2$
(c) $L_1 > L_2; c_1 > c_2$
(d) $L_1 < L_2; c_1 > c_2$

Response Index

01	a	b	c	d	11	a	b	c	d	21	a	b	c	d
02	a	b	c	d	12	a	b	c	d	22	a	b	c	d
03	a	b	c	d	13	a	b	c	d	23	a	b	c	d
04	a	b	c	d	14	a	b	c	d	24	a	b	c	d
05	a	b	c	d	15	a	b	c	d	25	a	b	c	d
06	a	b	c	d	16	a	b	c	d	26	a	b	c	d
07	a	b	c	d	17	a	b	c	d	27	a	b	c	d
08	a	b	c	d	18	a	b	c	d	28	a	b	c	d
09	a	b	c	d	19	a	b	c	d	29	a	b	c	d
10	a	b	c	d	20	a	b	c	d	30	a	b	c	d

Performance Scanner

> 90% Excellent !	You have mastered this chapter. The concepts of this chapter are at your fingertips. Move on to the next chapter and maintain this momentum.
76-90% Very Good !	You have a good command over this chapter. Revise the chapter again after a few days and enhance your performance.
60-75% Good !	You have a wide scope to learn more for this chapter. Revise this chapter again.
<60% Not Satisfactory!	You have a long way ahead of you to master this chapter. Revise it thoroughly.

For Online Chapter Test **Scan the QR Code**

For Online Unit Test **Scan the QR Code**

Space for Rough Work

Space for Rough Work

Space for Rough Work

Test Booklet No. **3947111**

Test Booklet Code **CH11**

MEDACE

NEET (UG)

SELF ASSESSMENT KIT

Thermodynamics

Topics Covered

Thermodynamic Terms and First Law of Thermodynamics

Thermodynamic Processes and Second Law of Thermodynamics

Important Instructions

- This Booklet Contains – Two Topic Tests and One Test on Complete Chapter.
- Each question carries 4 Marks.
- For each correct response, the candidate will get 4 marks and for every incorrect response, 1 mark will be additionally deducted from total score.
- Use **Blue/Black** point pen only for filling the OMR.
- Rough work is to be done in the space provided for this purpose in the test booklet only.

Name of the Candidate (In Capitals) ______________________

____

Candidate's Signature ______________

Invigilator's Signature ______________

Facsimile signature stamp of center superintendent______________

Do not open this Booklet until you start attempting the Test

Topical Follow Thru

Test 1

Syllabus

- Thermal Equilibrium & Zeroth Law of Thermodynamics
- Concept of Temperature, Heat, Work & Internal Energy
- First Law of Thermodynamics

For deeper insight **Scan the QR Code**

Important Instructions

- The test is of 30 min duration and contains 15 Multiple Choice Questions (Four options with a single correct answer).
- Choose the correct option and fill the OMR given on the last page of this test accordingly.
- At some instances, you may find more than 1 option may be correct, in such circumstances you have to judge the most appropriate answer as per the conditions given in the question.

1. An ideal gas is taken through the cycle $A \to B \to C \to A$ as shown in the figure. If the net heat supplied to the gas in the cycle is 15 J, then the work done by the gas in the process $C \to A$ is

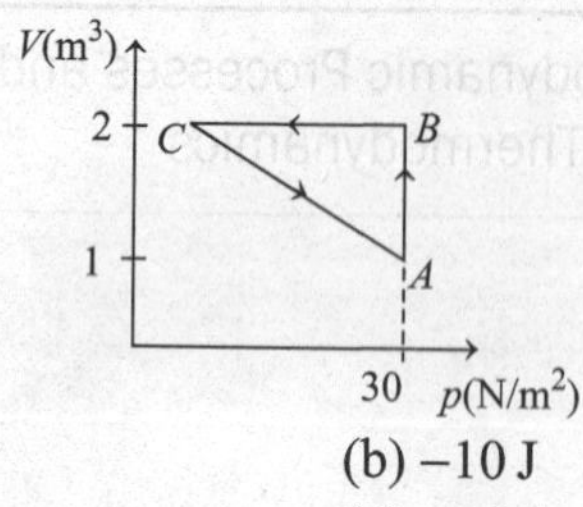

(a) −5 J (b) −10 J
(c) −15 J (d) −20 J

2. A system changes from the state (p_1, V_1) to (p_2, V_2) as shown in the figure below. What is the work done by the system?

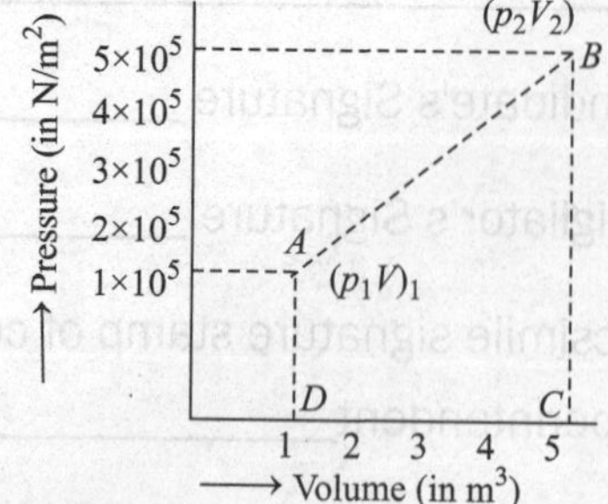

(a) 7.5×10^5 J
(b) 7.5×10^5 ergs
(c) 12×10^5 J
(d) 6×10^5 J

3. The internal energy of an ideal diatomic gas corresponding to volume V and pressure p is $U = 1.5\, pV$. The gas expands from 1 L to 2 L at a constant pressure of one atmosphere. The heat supplied to gas is

(a) 100 J (b) 250 J
(c) 350 J (d) 50 J

4. If the heat of 110 J is added to a gaseous system and it acquires internal energy of 40 J, then the amount of internal work done is

(a) 60 J (b) 70 J
(c) 110 J (d) 40 J

5. The first law of thermodynamics can be interpreted as a fundamental principle that encapsulates which of the following complex thermodynamic concepts?

(a) The principle asserting that the equivalent kinetic energy of a thermodynamic system remains invariant.

(b) The law governing the conservation of total energy within an isolated thermodynamic system, accounting for both internal energy and work interactions.

(c) The assertion that heat cannot spontaneously transfer from a colder to a hotter body without the involvement of external work, in accordance with the Clausius statement.

(d) The criterion that establishes the necessary conditions for a thermodynamic system to achieve and maintain equilibrium.

6. An ideal gas is taken from state A to state B through optional path I, II, III, and IV as shown in the p-V diagram. Let Q, W and U represent the heat supplied, work done and change in internal energy of the gas respectively. Then,

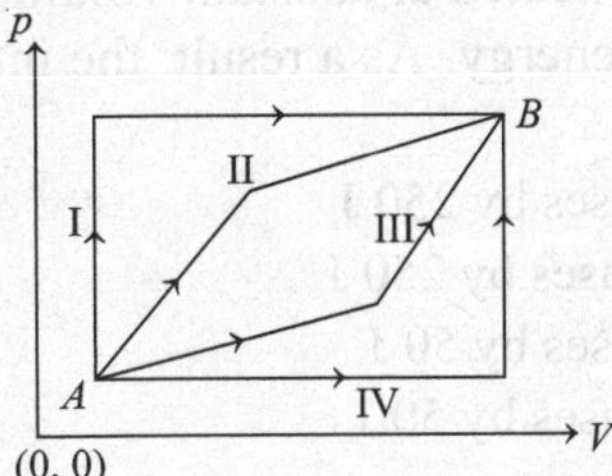

(a) $Q_{\text{I}} - Q_{\text{IV}} = W_{\text{I}} - W_{\text{IV}}$
(b) $Q_{\text{II}} - W_{\text{II}} > Q_{\text{III}} - W_{\text{III}}$
(c) $W_{\text{I}} < W_{\text{II}} < W_{\text{III}} < W_{\text{IV}}$
(d) $Q_{\text{I}} < Q_{\text{II}} < Q_{\text{III}} < Q_{\text{IV}}$

7. A source supplies heat to a system at the rate of 1000 W. If the system performs work at a rate of 200 W. The rate at which internal energy of the system increases is
(a) 600 W
(b) 500 W
(c) 800 W
(d) 1200 W

8. Some of the thermodynamic parameters are state variables while some are process variables. Some grouping of the parameters are given. Choose the correct one.
(a) State variables : Temperature, number of moles.
Process variables : Internal energy, work done by the gas.
(b) State variables : Volume, temperature.
Process variables : Internal energy, work done by the gas.
(c) State variables : Work done by the gas, heat rejected by the gas.
Process variables : Temperature, volume.
(d) State variables : Internal energy, volume.
Process variables: Work done by the gas, heat absorbed by the gas.

9. Statement I The heat supplied to a system is always equal to the increase in its internal energy.
Statement II When a system changes from one thermal equilibrium to another, some heat is absorbed by it.

In the light of above statements, Choose the most appropriate option from the options given below.
(a) Both Statement I and Statement II are correct.
(b) Both Statement I and Statement II are incorrect.
(c) Statement I is correct but Statement II is incorrect.
(d) Statement I is incorrect but Statement II is correct.

10. A thermally insulated rigid container contains an ideal gas heated by a filament of resistance 100 W through a current of 1 A for 5 min, then change in internal energy is
(a) 0 (b) 10 kJ
(c) 20 kJ (d) 30 kJ

11. Find the work done by the gas in the process ABC.

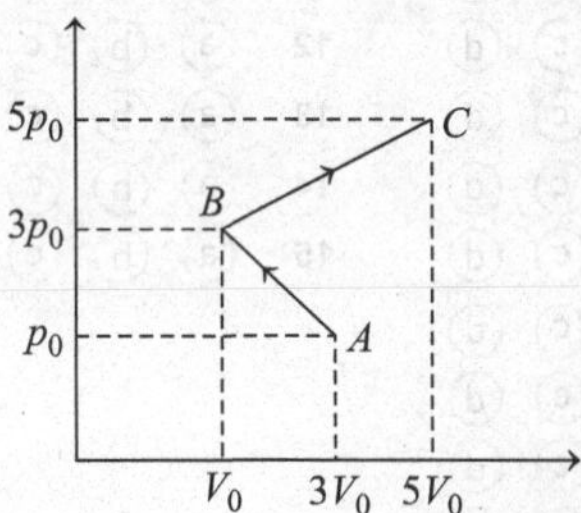

(a) $\frac{3}{2} p_0 V_0$
(b) $\frac{5}{2} p_0 V_0$
(c) $\frac{12}{3} p_0 V_0$
(d) $12\, p_0 V_0$

12. 1 g of a liquid is converted to vapour at 3×10^5 Pa pressure. If 10% of the heat supplied is used for increasing the volume by 1600 cm^3 during this phase change, increase in internal energy in the process will be
(a) 4.32×10^8 J (b) 432000 J
(c) 4320 J (d) 4800 J

13. A system is provided with 200 cal of heat and the work done by the system on the surroundings is 40 J.

Then, its internal energy
(a) increases by 600 J
(b) decreases by 800 J
(c) increases by 800 J
(d) decreases by 50 J

14. Assertion (A) We cannot change the temperature of a body without supplying (or extracting) heat to (or from) it.

Reason (R) According to principle of conservation of energy, total energy of a system remains conserved.

In the light of above statements, choose the most appropriate option from the options given below.

(a) Both A and R are true and R is the correct explanation of A.

(b) Both A and R are true but R is not the correct explanation of A.

(c) A is true but R is false.

(d) A is false but R is true.

15. A gas is compressed from a volume of $2\,m^3$ to a volume of $1m^3$ at a constant pressure of $100\ N/m^2$, then it is heated at constant volume by supplying 150 J of energy. As a result, the internal energy of the gas

(a) increases by 250 J

(b) decreases by 250 J

(c) increases by 50 J

(d) decreases by 50 J

Response Index

01	(a)	(b)	(c)	(d)	11	(a)	(b)	(c)	(d)
02	(a)	(b)	(c)	(d)	12	(a)	(b)	(c)	(d)
03	(a)	(b)	(c)	(d)	13	(a)	(b)	(c)	(d)
04	(a)	(b)	(c)	(d)	14	(a)	(b)	(c)	(d)
05	(a)	(b)	(c)	(d)	15	(a)	(b)	(c)	(d)
06	(a)	(b)	(c)	(d)					
07	(a)	(b)	(c)	(d)					
08	(a)	(b)	(c)	(d)					
09	(a)	(b)	(c)	(d)					
10	(a)	(b)	(c)	(d)					

Performance Scanner

> 90% Excellent !	You have mastered these topics. The concepts of these topics are at your fingertips. Move on to the next test and maintain this momentum.
76-90% Very Good !	You have a good command over these topics. Revise them again after a few days and enhance your performance.
60-75% Good !	You have a wide scope to learn more in these topics. Revise them again.
<60% Not Satisfactory!	You have a long way ahead of you to master in these topics. Revise them thoroughly.

Test 2

Syllabus

- Thermodynamics Processes : Isothermal and Adiabatic Processes
- Second Law of Thermodynamics : Reversible & Irreversible Process

For deeper insight **Scan the QR Code**

Important Instructions

- The test is of 45 min duration and contains 25 Multiple Choice Questions (Four options with a single correct answer).
- Choose the correct option and fill the OMR given on the last page of this test accordingly.
- At some instances, you may find more than 1 option may be correct in such circumstances you have to judge the most appropriate answer as per the conditions given in the question.

1. An ideal gas is initially contained in a vessel with a volume of 1 L, and the gas exerts a pressure equivalent to 72 cm of mercury. The gas is then isothermally compressed to a final volume of 900 cm^3. Determine the resulting pressure of the gas after compression, expressed in cm of mercury.

(a) 8 cm Hg (b) 7 cm Hg
(c) 6 cm Hg (d) 4 cm Hg

2. Consider an ideal gas undergoing a heating process at constant pressure. How does the isothermal compressibility of the gas respond to this change in temperature?

(a) remains constant
(b) increases linearly with temperature
(c) decreases linearly with temperature
(d) decreases inversely with temperature

3. The ratio of work done by an ideal monoatomic gas to the heat supplied by the gas in an isobaric process is

(a) $\frac{5}{7}$ (b) $\frac{3}{5}$
(c) $\frac{2}{7}$ (d) $\frac{2}{3}$

4. One mole of an ideal gas at temperature T_1 expands slowly according to the law p/V = constant. Its final temperature is T_2. The work done by the gas is

(a) $R(T_2 - T_1)$
(b) $2R(T_2 - T_1)$
(c) $\frac{R}{2}(T_2 - T_1)$
(d) $\frac{2R}{3}(T_2 - T_1)$

5. In adiabatic expansion of 1 mole of a gas, the internal energy decreases by 40 J. Work done during this process is

(a) – 50 J
(b) – 40 J
(c) 40 J
(d) 50 J

6. An ideal gas *A* and a real gas *B* have their volumes increased from *V* to 2*V* under isothermal conditions. The increase in internal energy

(a) will be zero in both *A* and *B*
(b) will be non-zero in both *A* and *B*
(c) of *B* will be more than that of *A*
(d) of *A* will be more than that of *B*

7. An ideal gas has initial volume *V* and pressure *p*. If volume of the gas is doubled, then in which of the following processes work done will be minimum?

(a) Isothermal
(b) Isobaric
(c) Adiabatic
(d) Same in all given processes

8. Identity the graph (s) which correctly represents an isotherm at temperatures T_1 and $(T_2 > T_1)$.

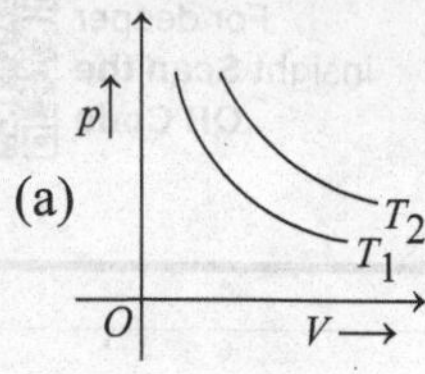
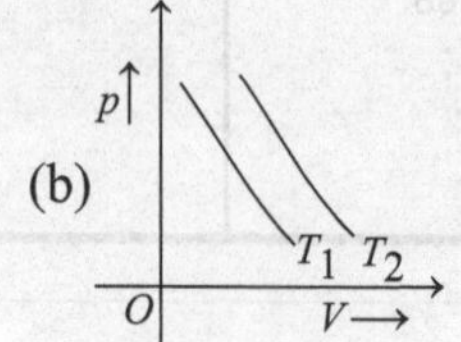
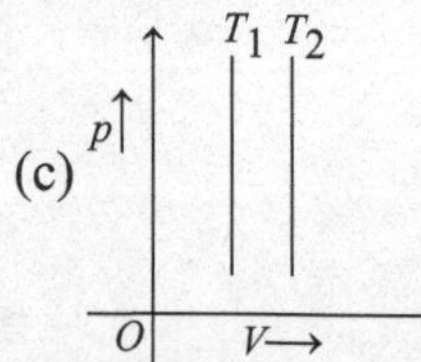
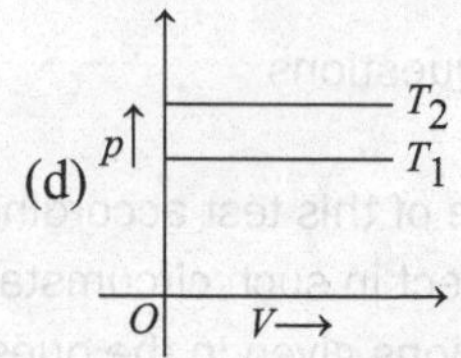

9. One mole of an ideal gas expands at a constant temperature of 300 K from an initial volume of 10 L to a final volume of 20 L. The work done in expanding the gas is ($R = 8.31$ J/mol-K)

(a) 750 J (b) 1728 J
(c) 1500 J (d) 3456 J

10. Match the Column I with Column II.

Column I	Column II
A. Cyclic process	1. $\Delta U < 0$
B. Isobaric process	2. $\Delta Q = \Delta W$
C. Isochoric process	3. $\Delta W = nR\Delta T$
D. Adiabatic process	4. $\Delta Q = \Delta U$

Choose the correct answer from the given options.

(a) A - 4, B - 3, C - 2, D - 1
(b) A - 4, B - 3, C - 1, D - 2
(c) A - 3, B - 4, C - 2, D-1
(d) A - 2, B - 3, C - 4, D - 1

11. 2 moles of an ideal gas undergo from an initial state A to final state B *via* two different processes. If during first, it undergoes isothermal expansion from volume V_0 to $2V_0$ and then its volume is decreased from $2V_0$ to V_0 at constant pressure. The correct *p-V* diagram representing two processes is

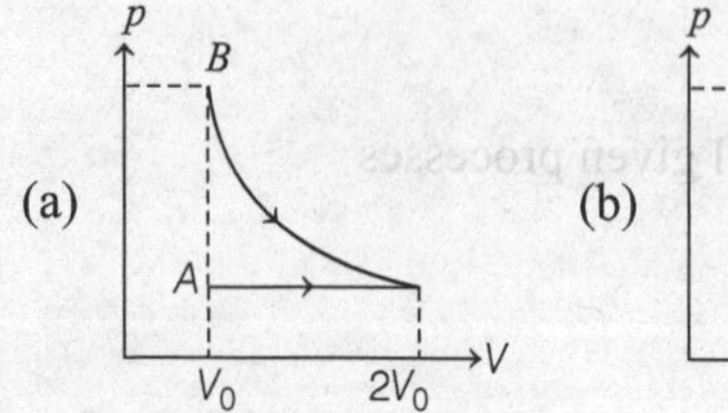
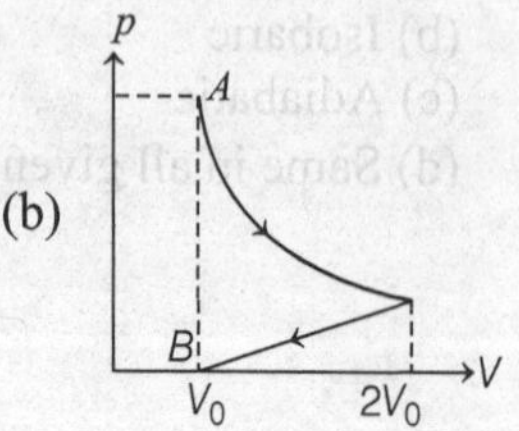
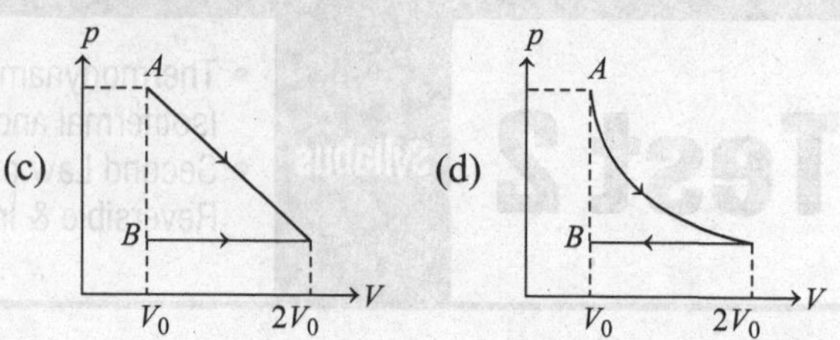

12. A tubeless tyre pumped to a pressure 8 atm at 27°C suddenly bursts. The final temperature is $\left(\gamma = \frac{3}{2}\right)$

(a) – 73° C
(b) – 123°C
(c) – 27° C
(d) 150°C

13. A container having 1 mole of a gas at a temperature 27°C has a movable piston which maintains at constant pressure in container of 1 atm. The gas is compressed until temperature becomes 127°C. The work done is (C_p for gas is 7.03 cal/mol K)

(a) 703 J (b) 814 J
(c) 121 J (d) 2035 J

14. The specific heat of hydrogen gas at constant pressure is $C_p = 3.4 \times 10^3$ cal / kg°C and at constant volume is $C_V = 2.4 \times 10^3$ cal / kg°C. If one kilogram hydrogen gas is heated from 10°C to 20°C at constant pressure, the external work done on the gas to maintain it at constant pressure is

(a) 10^5 cal
(b) 10^4 cal
(c) 10^3 cal
(d) 5×10^3 cal

15. Assertion (A) Air quickly leaking out of a balloon becomes cooler.

Reason (R) The leaking air undergoes adiabatic expansion.

In the light of above statements, choose the most appropriate option from the options given below.

(a) Both A and R are true and R is the correct explanation of A.

(b) Both A and R are true but R is not the correct explanation of A.

(c) A is true but R is false.

(d) A is false but R is true.

16. In an adiabatic process, $R = \frac{4}{3}C_V$. The pressure of the gas will be proportional to

(a) $T^{5/3}$ (b) $T^{7/2}$ (c) $T^{7/4}$ (d) $T^{5/6}$

17. Assertion (A) It is not possible for a system, unaided by an external agency to transfer heat from a body at lower temperature to another body at higher temperature.

Reason (R) According to Clausius statement, no process is possible whose sole result is the transfer of heat from a cooled object to a hotter object.

In the light of above statements, choose the most appropriate option from the options given below.

(a) Both A and R are true and R is the correct explanation of A.

(b) Both A and R are true but R is not the correct explanation of A.

(c) A is true but R is false.

(d) A is false but R is true.

18. Statement I The bulk modulus of an isobaric process is always zero.

Statement II For isobaric process, $p_1V_1 = p_2V_2$

In the light of above statements, choose the most appropriate option from the options given below.

(a) Both Statement I and Statement II are correct.

(b) Statement I is correct but Statement II is incorrect.

(c) Statement I is incorrect but Statement II is correct.

(d) Both Statement I and Statement II are incorrect.

19. A thermodynamic system is taken through the cycle *ABCD* as shown in the figure. Heat rejected by the gas during the cycle is

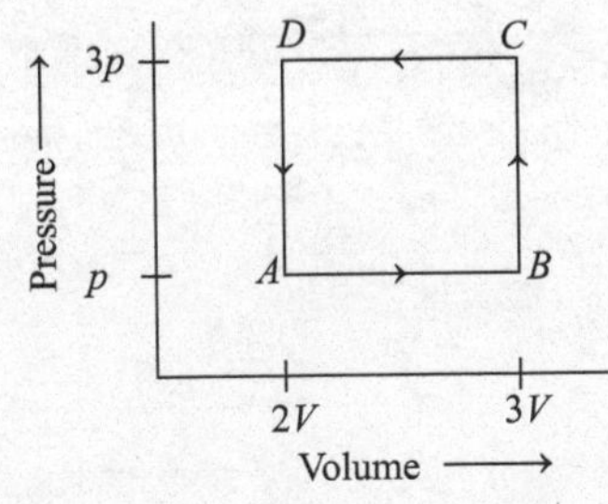

(a) $3\,pV$ (b) $2\,pV$

(c) $\frac{5}{3}pV$ (d) $\frac{3}{2}pV$

20. The figures given below show different process for a given amount of an ideal gas. For which of the following processes, work done on a system is positive?

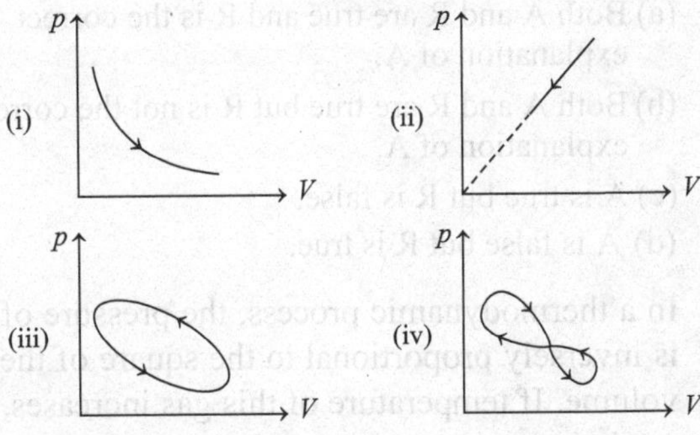

(a) Only IV

(b) Only III

(c) I, II, IV

(d) II, IV

21. An ideal gas of 2 mole undergoes a cyclic process as shown in the *p*-*V* graph . In which of the following processes, internal energy of gas increase?

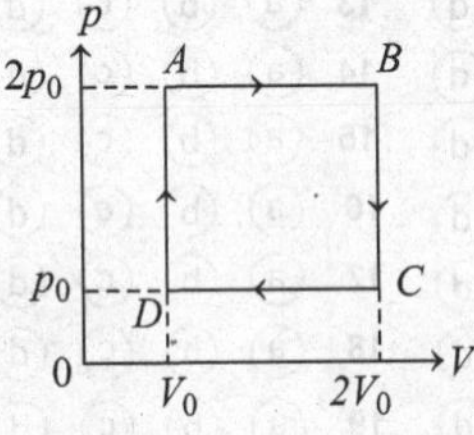

(a) *AB* and *BC*

(b) *AB* and *CD*

(c) *AB* and *DA*

(d) *BC* and *DA*

22. 1 mole of a monoatomic ideal gas is taken through process pT = constant. On increasing temperature from T_0 to $2T_0$, the work done by gas is W_0. The work done by gas if temperature is increased further $2T_0$ to $3T_0$, is

(a) $\frac{2}{3}W_0$ (b) W_0

(c) $\frac{3}{2}W_0$ (d) $(\sqrt{3}-\sqrt{2})W_0$

23. Assertion (A) A room can be cooled by switching ON the air conditioner in a closed room.

Reason (R) Heat flows from lower temperature to higher temperature (room).

In the light of above statments, choose the most appropriate option from the options given below.

(a) Both A and R are true and R is the correct explanation of A.

(b) Both A and R are true but R is not the correct explanation of A.

(c) A is true but R is false.

(d) A is false but R is true.

24. In a thermodynamic process, the pressure of a gas is inversely proportional to the square of the volume. If temperature of this gas increases, then work done

(a) may be negative

(b) is negative

(c) is positive

(d) may be positive

25. For an ideal gas, the graph between log T and log V for an adiabatic process has been in the following figure, then the gas is (where, T and V are in the SI unit)

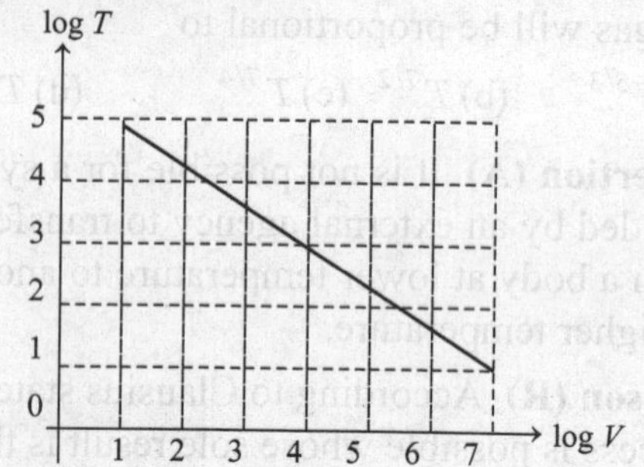

(a) monoatomic

(b) diatomic

(c) triatomic linear

(d) a mixture of monoatomic and diatomic

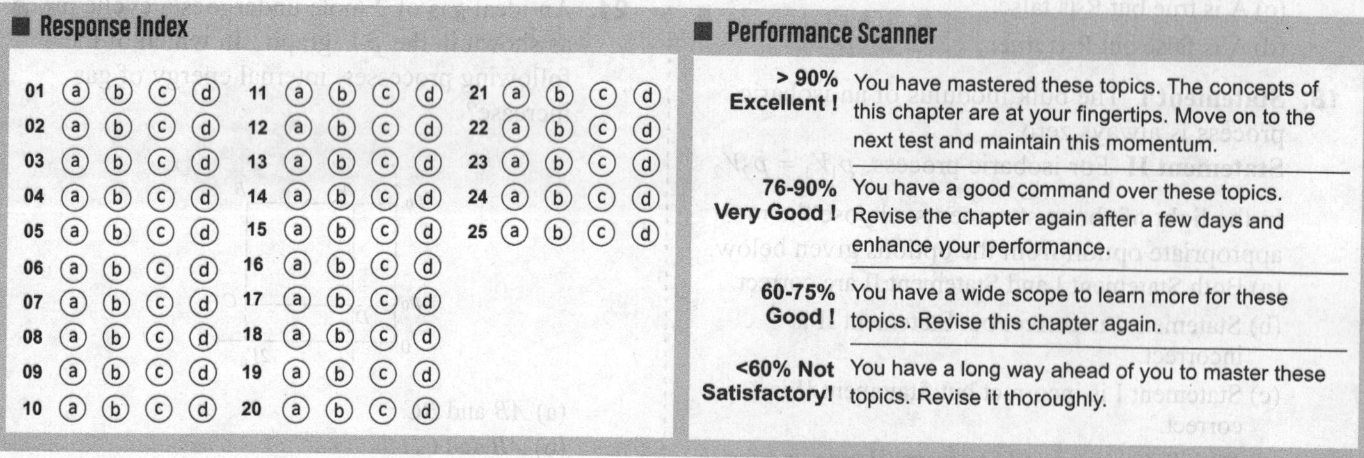

Chapter Break Thru

Syllabus	• Thermal Equilibrium & Zeroth Law of Thermodynamics • Concept of Temperature, Heat, Work & Internal Energy • First Law of Thermodynamics	• Thermodynamics Processes : Isothermal and Adiabatic Processes • Second Law of Thermodynamics : Reversible & Irreversible Process

Important Instructions

- The test is of 45 min duration and contains 30 Multiple Choice Questions (Four options with a single correct answer).
- Choose the correct option and fill the OMR given on the last page of this test accordingly.
- At some instances, you may find more than 1 correct option, in such circumstances you have to judge the most appropriate answer as per conditions given in the question.

1. Heat is supplied to a monoatomic gas at constant pressure. The ratio of $\Delta Q : \Delta U : \Delta W$ is

(a) 7 : 2 : 5
(b) 5 : 3 : 2
(c) 7 : 5 : 2
(d) 7 : 2 : 5

2. Which of the following figure shows that the change in internal energy of the system is zero?

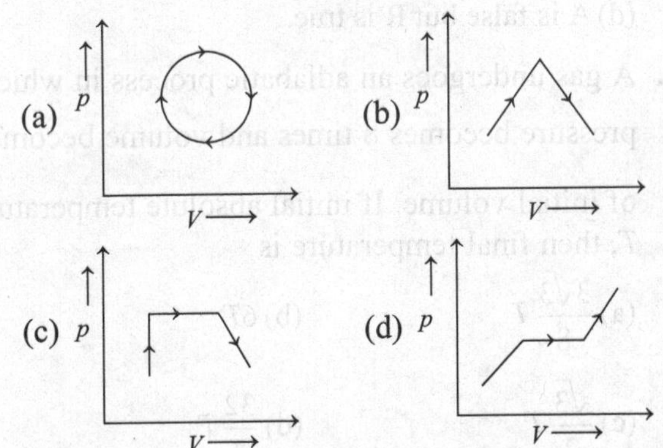

3. Which one of the following gases possesses the largest internal energy?

(a) 2 moles of helium occupying 1 m^3 at 300 K
(b) 56 kg of nitrogen at 107 Nm^{-2} at 300 K
(c) 8 g of oxygen at 8 atm at 300 K
(d) 6×10^{26} molecules of argon occupying 40 m^3 at 900 K

4. In the following indicator diagram, the net amount of work done will be

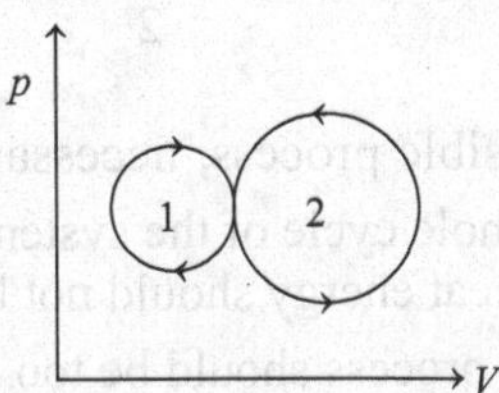

(a) positive
(b) negative
(c) zero
(d) infinity

5. Statement I Thermodynamics processes are irreversible in nature.

Statement II Most of the process are dissipative in nature.

In the light of the above statements, choose the most appropriate answer from the options given below

(a) Both Statement I and Statement II are correct.
(b) Statement I is correct but Statement II is incorrect.
(c) Statement I is incorrect but Statement II is correct.
(d) Both Statement I and Statement II are incorrect.

6. For an ideal gas graph is shown for three processes, process 1, 2 and 3 are respectively.

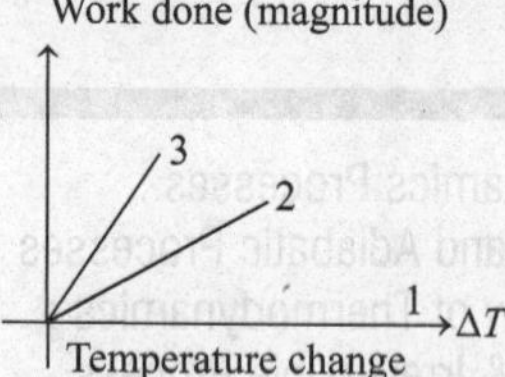

(a) Isobaric, adiabatic isochoric
(b) Adiabatic, isobaric, isochoric
(c) Isochoric, adiabatic, isobaric
(d) Isochoric, isobaric, adiabatic

7. The slopes of isothermal and adiabatic curves are related as

(a) isothermal curve slope = adiabatic curve slope
(b) isothermal curve slope = $\gamma \times$ adiabatic curve slope
(c) adiabatic curve slope = $\gamma \times$ isothermal curve slope
(d) adiabatic curve slope = $\frac{1}{2} \times$ isothermal curve slope

8. For a reversible process, necessary condition is

(a) In the whole cycle of the system, the loss of any type of heat energy should not be zero
(b) That the process should be too fast
(c) That the process should be slow so that the working substance should not remain in thermal and mechanical equilibrium with the surroundings
(d) The loss of energy should be zero and it should be quasi-static

9. Three moles of an ideal monoatomic gas perform a cycle shown in figure. The gas temperatures in different states are $T_1 = 200\,\text{K}, T_2 = 400\,\text{K}$, $T_3 = 1600\,\text{K}$ and $T_4 = 800\,\text{K}$. The work done by the gas during the cycle is (Take, $R = 25/3$ J/mol-K)

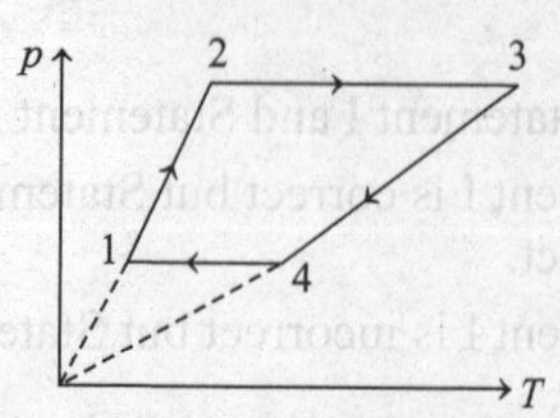

(a) 5 kJ (b) 25 kJ
(c) 15 kJ (d) 20 kJ

10. The state of an ideal gas is changed through an isothermal process at temperature T_0 as shown in figure. The work done by gas in going from state B and C is double the work done by gas in going from state A to B. If the pressure in the state B is $p_0/2$, then the pressure of the gas in state C is

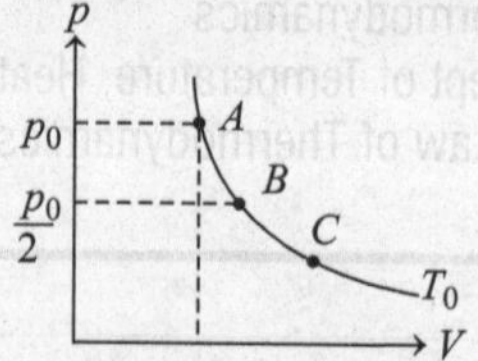

(a) $\frac{p_0}{2}$ (b) $\frac{p_0}{4}$
(c) $\frac{p_0}{6}$ (d) $\frac{p_0}{8}$

11. Assertion (A) Zeroth law of thermodynamics explain the concept of energy.

Reason (R) Internal energy is dependent on temperature.

In the light of above statements, choose the most appropriate option from the options given below.

(a) Both A and R are true and R is the correct explanation of A.
(b) Both A and R are true but R is not the correct explanation of A.
(c) A is true but R is false.
(d) A is false but R is true.

12. A gas undergoes an adiabatic process in which pressure becomes 8 times and volume becomes $\frac{3}{4}$ of initial volume. If initial absolute temperature is T, then final temperature is

(a) $\frac{3\sqrt{3}}{8}T$ (b) $6T$
(c) $\frac{\sqrt{3}}{2}T$ (d) $\frac{32}{3}T$

13. Helium gas is supplied heat Q very slowly keeping the pressure constant. The work done by the gas is

(a) $\frac{1}{3}Q$ (b) $\frac{3}{2}Q$
(c) $\frac{Q}{3}$ (d) $\frac{2}{3}Q$

14. A container of volume 1 m^3 is divided into two equal compartments by a partition. One of these compartments contains an ideal gas at 300 K. The other compartment is vacuum. The whole system is thermally isolated from its surroundings. The partition is removed and the gas expands to occupy the whole volume of the container. Its temperature now would be

(a) 300 K
(b) 239 K
(c) 200 K
(d) 100 K

15. If a cylinder containing a gas at high pressure explodes, the gas undergoes

(a) reversible adiabatic change and fall of temperature
(b) reversible adiabatic change and rise of temperature
(c) irreversible adiabatic change and fall of temperature
(d) irreversible adiabatic change and rise of temperature

16. When a system is taken from state A to B along the path ACB, it absorbs 86 cal of heat and work done is 30 cal. Along the path ADB, $Q = 86$ cal. What is the work done (in cal) along ADB?

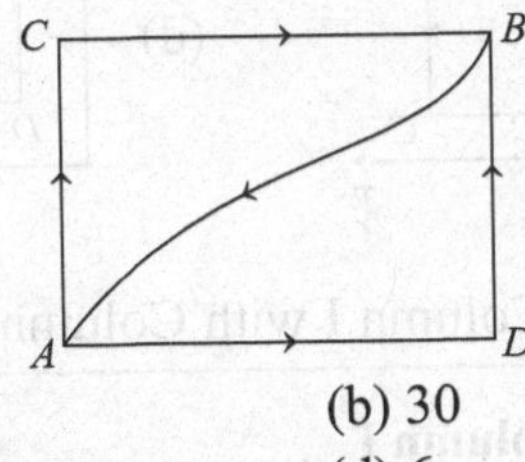

(a) 56 (b) 30
(c) 16 (d) 6

17. Pressure *versus* density graph of an ideal gas is shown in figure.

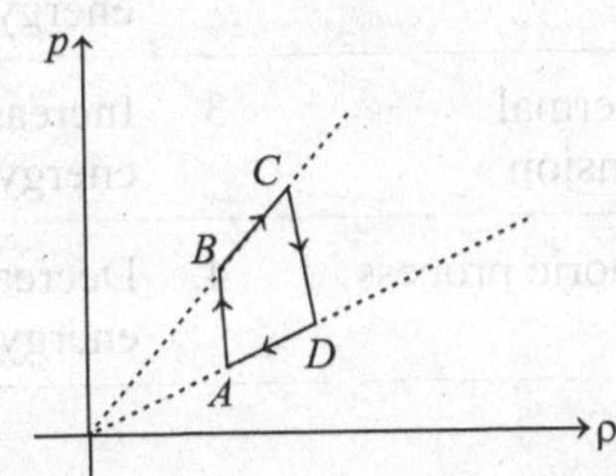

(a) During the process AB, work done by the gas is positive
(b) During the process AB, work done by the gas is negative
(c) During the process BC, internal energy of the gas is increasing
(d) During process BC, internal energy is constant

18. 540 cal of heat convert 1 cubic centimeter of water at 100° C into 1671 cubic centimeter of steam at 100°C at a pressure of one atmosphere, then the work done against the atmospheric pressure is nearly

(a) 540 cal (b) 40 cal
(c) zero cal (d) 500 cal

19. An ideal gas is expanding such that $pT^2 =$ constant. The coefficient of volume expansion of the gas is

(a) $1/T$ (b) $2/T$
(c) $3/T$ (d) $4/T$

20. A gas expand with temperature according to the relation $V = kT^{\frac{2}{3}}$, then the work done when temperature changes by 24°C is

(a) 16 R (b) 20 R
(c) 24 R (d) 30 R

21. In the following p-V adiabatic curve two isothermals at temperatures T_1 and T_2 as shown in figure. The value of $\frac{V_a}{V_d}$ will be

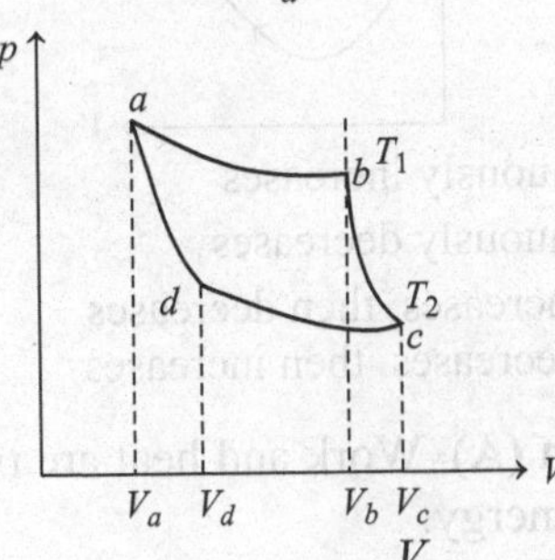

(a) $\frac{V_b}{V_c}$ (b) $\frac{V_c}{V_b}$
(c) $\frac{V_d}{V_a}$ (d) $V_b V_c$

22. For a thermodynamic process, $\delta Q = -50$ cal and $W = -20$ cal. If the initial internal energy is -30 cal, then final internal energy will be

(a) 191.20 cal (b) -60 cal
(c) 100 cal (d) -100 cal

23. The cyclic processes for 1 mole of an ideal gas on three different *p-V* diagrams have been shown below. The work done are W_1, W_2 and W_3 respectively,

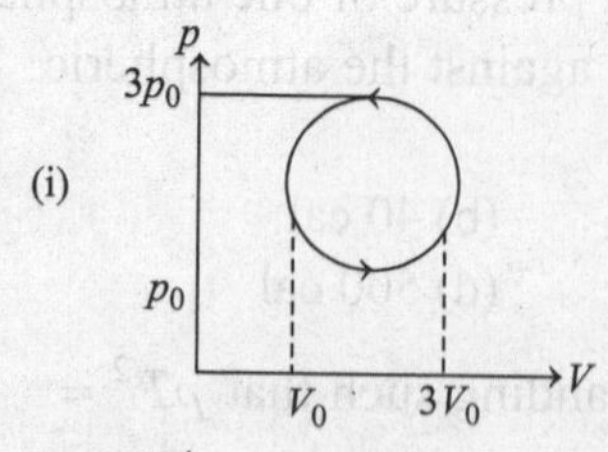

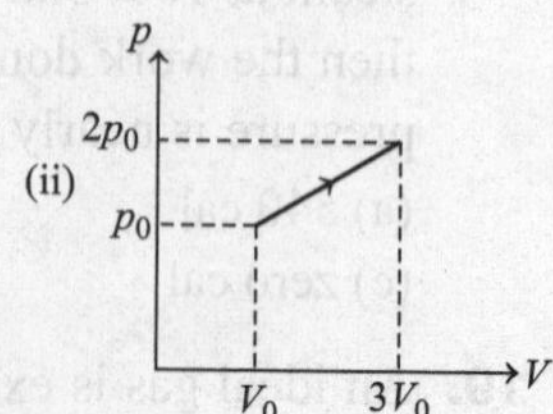

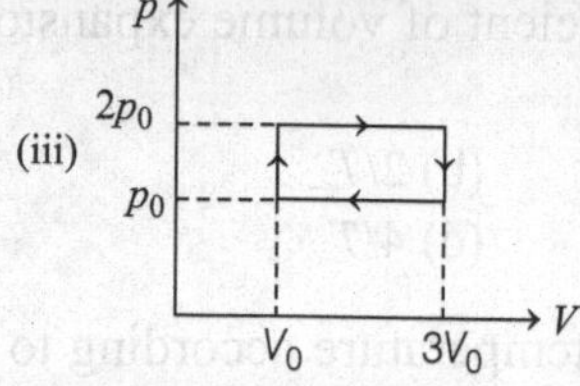

(a) $W_1 > W_2 > W_3$
(b) $W_2 > W_1 > W_3$
(c) $W_3 > W_2 > W_1$
(d) $W_2 > W_3 > W_1$

24. Consider a process shown in the figure. During this process, the work done by the system

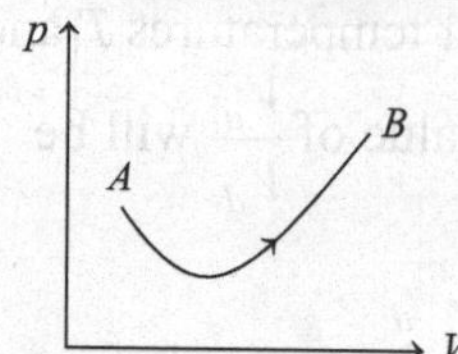

(a) continuously increases
(b) continuously decreases
(c) first increases, then decreases
(d) first decreases, then increases

25. Assertion (A) Work and heat are two equivalent form of energy.
Reason (R) Work is the transfer of mechanical energy irrespective of temperature difference, whereas heat is the transfer of thermal energy because of temperature different only.

In the light of above statements, choose the most appropriate option from the options given below.
(a) Both A and R are true and R is the correct explanation of A.
(b) Both A and R are true but R is not the correct explanation of A.
(c) A is true but R is false.
(d) A is false but R is true.

26. A cyclic process *ABCD* is shown in the figure *p-V* diagram. Which of the following curves represent the same process?

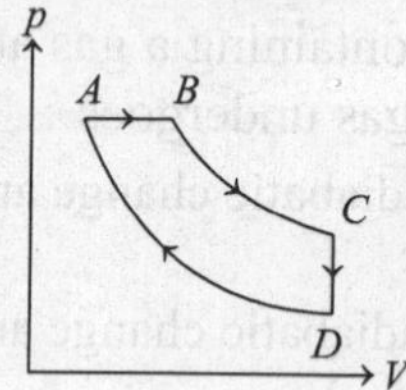

(a)
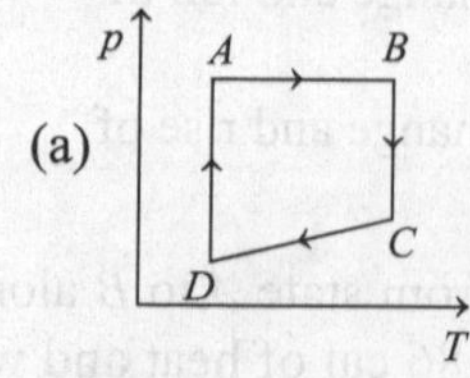

(b)
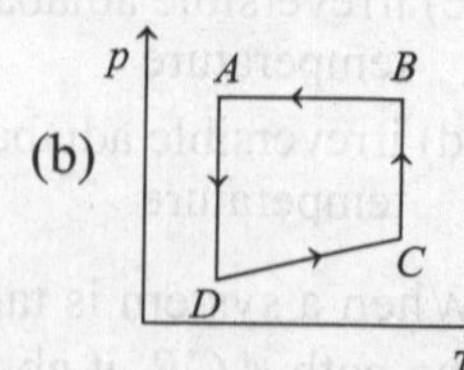

(c)
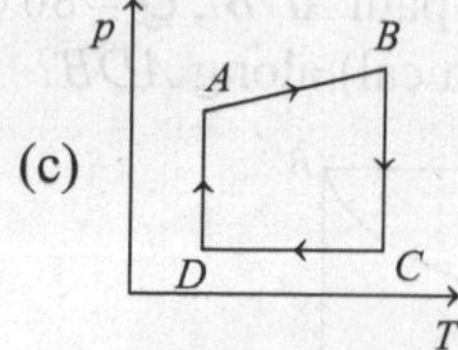

(d)
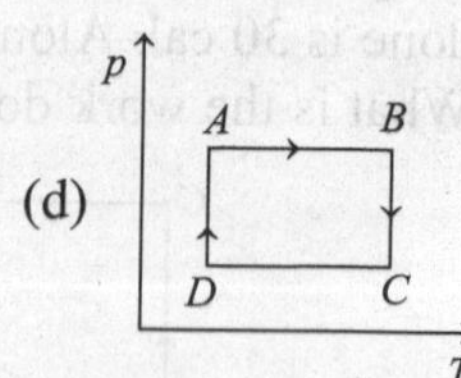

27. Match the Column I with Column II.

Column I	Column II
A. Adiabatic expansion	1. No work done
B. Isobaric expansion	2. Constant internal energy
C. Isothermal expansion	3. Increase in internal energy
D. Isochoric process	4. Decrease in internal energy

Choose the correct answer from the given options.

(a) A - 4, B - 3, C - 2, D-1

(b) A - 4, B - 3, C - 1, D- 2

(c) A - 1, B - 2, C - 3, D- 4

(d) A - 2, B - 3, C - 1, D- 4

28. The volume of air increases by 5% in its adiabatic expansion. The percentage decrease in its pressure will be

(a) 5% (b) 6%

(c) 7% (d) 8%

29. In the following figure, four curves A, B, C and D are shown. The curves are

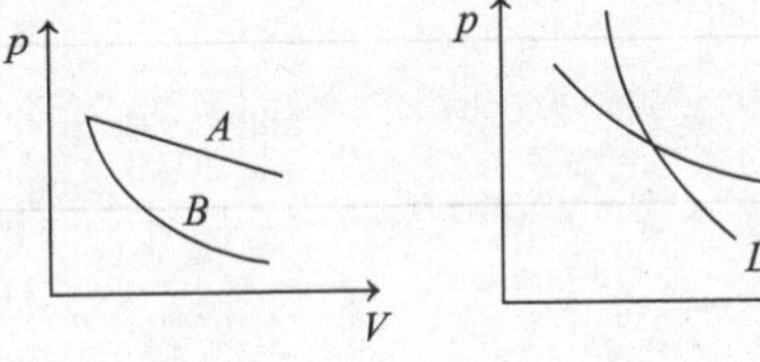

(a) isothermal for A and D while adiabatic for B and C

(b) adiabatic for A and C while isothermal for B and D

(c) isothermal for A and B while adiabatic for C and D

(d) isothermal for A and C while adiabatic for B and D

30. A diatomic ideal gas is heated at constant volume until the pressure is doubled and again heated at constant pressure until volume is doubled. The average molar heat capacity for whole process is

(a) $\frac{13R}{6}$

(b) $\frac{19R}{6}$

(c) $\frac{23R}{6}$

(d) $\frac{17R}{6}$

Response Index

01 ⓐ ⓑ ⓒ ⓓ	14 ⓐ ⓑ ⓒ ⓓ	27 ⓐ ⓑ ⓒ ⓓ
02 ⓐ ⓑ ⓒ ⓓ	15 ⓐ ⓑ ⓒ ⓓ	28 ⓐ ⓑ ⓒ ⓓ
03 ⓐ ⓑ ⓒ ⓓ	16 ⓐ ⓑ ⓒ ⓓ	29 ⓐ ⓑ ⓒ ⓓ
04 ⓐ ⓑ ⓒ ⓓ	17 ⓐ ⓑ ⓒ ⓓ	30 ⓐ ⓑ ⓒ ⓓ
05 ⓐ ⓑ ⓒ ⓓ	18 ⓐ ⓑ ⓒ ⓓ	
06 ⓐ ⓑ ⓒ ⓓ	19 ⓐ ⓑ ⓒ ⓓ	
07 ⓐ ⓑ ⓒ ⓓ	20 ⓐ ⓑ ⓒ ⓓ	
08 ⓐ ⓑ ⓒ ⓓ	21 ⓐ ⓑ ⓒ ⓓ	
09 ⓐ ⓑ ⓒ ⓓ	22 ⓐ ⓑ ⓒ ⓓ	
10 ⓐ ⓑ ⓒ ⓓ	23 ⓐ ⓑ ⓒ ⓓ	
11 ⓐ ⓑ ⓒ ⓓ	24 ⓐ ⓑ ⓒ ⓓ	
12 ⓐ ⓑ ⓒ ⓓ	25 ⓐ ⓑ ⓒ ⓓ	
13 ⓐ ⓑ ⓒ ⓓ	26 ⓐ ⓑ ⓒ ⓓ	

Performance Scanner

> 90% Excellent !	You have mastered this chapter. The concepts of this chapter are at your fingertips. Move on to the next chapter and maintain this momentum.
76-90% Very Good !	You have a good command over this chapter. Revise the chapter again after a few days and enhance your performance.
60-75% Good !	You have a wide scope to learn more for this chapter. Revise this chapter again.
<60% Not Satisfactory!	You have a long way ahead of you to master this chapter. Revise it thoroughly.

For Online Chapter Test **Scan the QR Code**

For Online Unit Test **Scan the QR Code**

Space for Rough Work

Space for Rough Work

Space for Rough Work

Test Booklet No. **3947112**

Test Booklet Code **CH12**

MED ACE
NEET (UG)
SELF ASSESSMENT KIT

Kinetic Theory of Gases

Topics Covered

Kinetic Theory of Gases and Ideal Gas Law

Degree of Freedom and Equipartition of Energy

Important Instructions

- This Booklet Contains – Two Topic Tests and One Test on Complete Chapter.
- Each question carries 4 Marks.
- For each correct response, the candidate will get 4 marks and for every incorrect response, 1 mark will be additionally deducted from total score.
- Use **Blue/Black** point pen only for filling the OMR.
- Rough work is to be done in the space provided for this purpose in the test booklet only.

Name of the Candidate (In Capitals)

____

____

Candidate's Signature ____________

Invigilator's Signature ____________

Facsimile signature stamp of center superintendent____________

Do not open this Booklet until you start attempting the Test

Topical Follow Thru

Test 1

Syllabus

- Equation of State of a Perfect Gas
- Work done on Compressing a Gas
- Kinetic Theory of Gases-Assumptions, the Concept of Pressure
- Kinetic Interpretation of Temperature
- RMS Speed of Gas Molecules
- Avogadro's Number

For deeper insight **Scan the QR Code**

Important Instructions

- The test is of 45 minutes duration and contains 25 Multiple Choice Questions. (Four options with a single correct answer).
- Choose the correct option and fill the OMR given on the last page of this test accordingly.
- At some instances, you may find more than 1 option may be correct, in such circumstances you have to judge the most appropriate answer as per the conditions given in the question.

1. The quantity $\frac{pV}{kT}$ for an ideal gas represent
(k = Boltzmann's constant)
(a) number of moles of the gas
(b) total mass of the gas
(c) number of molecules in the gas
(d) density of the gas

2. If the ratio of vapour density for hydrogen and oxygen is $\frac{1}{16}$, then under constant pressure, the ratio of their rms velocities will be
(a) $\frac{4}{1}$
(b) $\frac{1}{4}$
(c) $\frac{1}{16}$
(d) $\frac{16}{1}$

3. In a closed vessel, pressure increases by 0.4% when temperature increases by 1°C. What is the initial temperature?
(a) 250 K
(b) 250°C
(c) 26 K
(d) 25°C

4. Match the List I (relation of p, V and T) with List II (related laws) and select the correct answer from the codes given below.

	List I		List II
A.	$pV = k_B NT$	1.	Dalton's law
B.	$p \propto 1/V, T = \text{constant}$	2.	Boyle's law
C.	$V \propto T, p = \text{constant}$	3.	Ideal gas equation
D.	$p = p_1 + p_2 + ...$	4.	Charles' law

Choose the correct answer from the options given below.
(a) A-3, B-2, C-1, D-4
(b) A-3, B-4, C-1, D-2
(c) A-3, B-2, C-4, D-1
(b) A-1, B-2, C-3, D-4

5. An ideal gas at 27°C has a pressure of 760 mm of Hg. The gas is compressed until its volume becomes $\frac{3}{4}$ of initial volume. The final pressure of the gas will be (Here, temperature is constant)
(a) 1013.3 mm of Hg
(b) 997 mm of Hg
(c) 1440 mm of Hg
(d) 817.6 mm of Hg

6. A thin balloon filled with air at 27°C has a volume of 3.0 L. If on placing it in a cooled room its volume becomes 2.7 L, then temperature of the room is

(a) 300 K
(b) 270 K
(c) 250 K
(d) 273 K

7. The variation of pV with V of fixed mass of an ideal gas at constant temperature is graphically represented by the curve

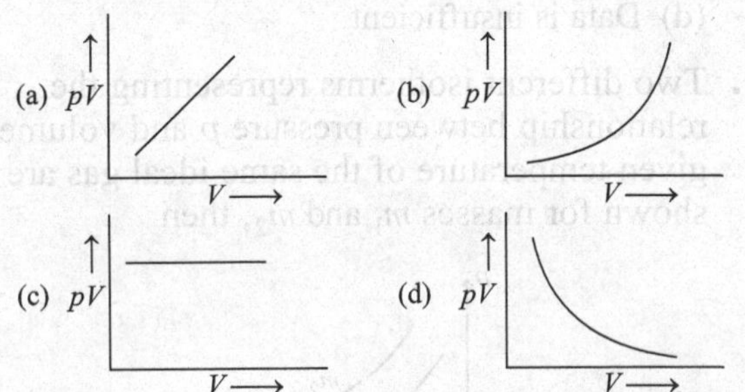

8. Pressure *versus* temperature graph of an ideal gas of equal number of moles of different volumes are plotted as shown in figure. Choose the correct alternative.

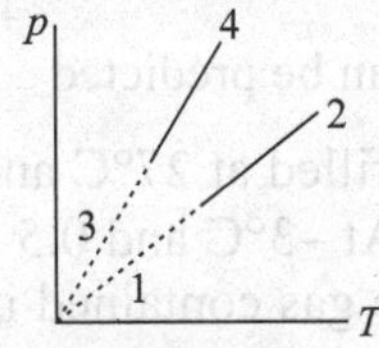

(a) $V_1 = V_2; V_3 = V_4$ and $V_2 > V_3$
(b) $V_1 = V_2; V_3 = V_4$ and $V_2 < V_3$
(c) $V_1 = V_2 = V_3 = V_4$
(d) $V_4 > V_3 > V_2 > V_1$

9. The equation of state for 16 g of oxygen at a pressure p and temperature T, when occupying a volume V, will be

(a) $pV = \left(\frac{5}{32}\right)RT$
(b) $pV = 5RT$
(c) $pV = \left(\frac{5}{2}\right)RT$
(d) $2pV = RT$

10. The pressure p, volume V and temperature T of a gas in the jar A and the other gas in the jar B at pressure $2p$, volume $\frac{V}{4}$ and temperature $2T$. The ratio of the number of molecules in the jars A and B will be

(a) 1:1 (b) 1:2 (c) 2:1 (d) 4:1

11. Two gases A and B having the same temperature T, pressure of gas A is $2p$, pressure of gas B is $3p$ and same volume V are mixed. If the mixture is at the same temperature T and occupies a volume V, then pressure of the mixture is

(a) $2p$ (b) $5p$
(c) $\frac{p}{2}$ (d) $4p$

12. If 450 ml of a gas at 77°C is cooled to –23°C at constant pressure, then its final volume will be

(a) 254 ml
(b) 321.4 ml
(c) 135 ml
(d) 242.8 ml

13. When the temperature of a gas in a metal box is increased from 27°C to 127°C, the initial pressure of 4 atm changes to

(a) 1.0 atm
(b) 1.6 atm
(c) 2.4 atm
(d) 5.3 atm

14. A flask is filled with 13 g of an ideal gas at 27°C and its temperature is raised to 52°C. The mass of the gas that has to be released to maintain the temperature of the gas in the flask at 52°C and the pressure remaining the same is

(a) 2.5 g (b) 2.0 g
(c) 1.5 g (d) 1.0 g

15. The kinetic energy of a gas at 27°C is KE. At what temperature, the KE of a gas molecule become halved?

(a) 150 °C
(b) – 123 °C
(c) – 123 K
(d) 13.5 °C

16. A cylinder contains hydrogen gas at pressure of 249 kPa and temperature 27°C. Its density is ($R = 8.3\ \text{J mol}^{-1}\ \text{K}^{-1}$)

(a) $0.2\ \text{kg/m}^3$
(b) $0.1\ \text{kg/m}^3$
(c) $0.02\ \text{kg/m}^3$
(d) $0.5\ \text{kg/m}^3$

17. If intermolecular force just vanishes, then volume occupied by 2.25 kg of water is

(a) $2.8 \times 10^3\ \text{m}^3$
(b) $2.8 \times 10^{-3}\ \text{m}^3$
(c) $2.8\ \text{m}^3$
(d) $2.8 \times 10^6\ \text{m}^3$

18. Consider a sample of gas that contains only 12 molecules with speeds (in cms^{-1}), 6, 2, 4, 6, 6, 4, 1, 8, 5, 3, 7 and 8, respectively. This sample is contained in a box of size 1 cm × 1 cm × 1 cm. The ratio of rms to mean speed of molecules is

(a) 2.05 (b) 1.09 (c) 1.54 (d) 2.05

19. An ideal gas is initially at temperature T and volume V. Its volume is increased by ΔV due to an increase in temperature ΔT, pressure remaining constant.

The quantity $\delta = \Delta V / (V\ \Delta T)$ varies with temperature as

(a) 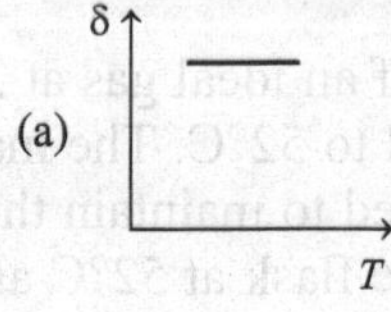

(b) 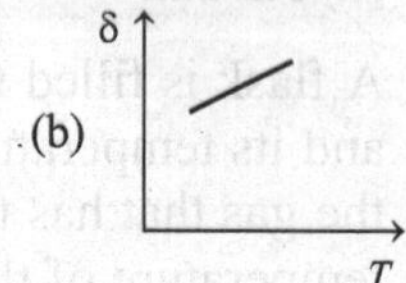

(c) 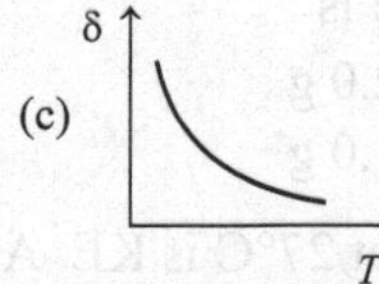

(d) 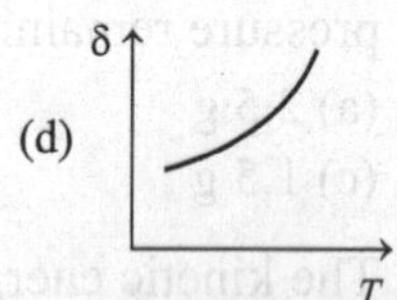

20. Volume *versus* temperature graphs for a given mass of an ideal gas are shown in figure. At two different values of constant pressure, what can be inferred about relation between p_1 and p_2?

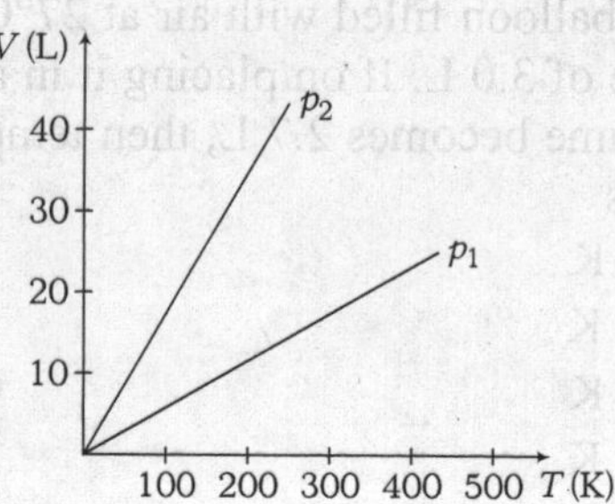

(a) $p_1 > p_2$
(b) $p_1 = p_2$
(c) $p_1 < P_2$
(d) Data is insufficient

21. Two different isotherms representing the relationship between pressure p and volume V at a given temperature of the same ideal gas are shown for masses m_1 and m_2, then

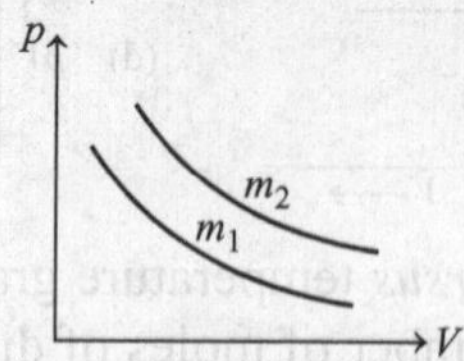

(a) $m_1 > m_2$
(b) $m_1 = M_2$
(c) $m_1 < m_2$
(d) Nothing can be predicted

22. A balloon is filled at 27°C and 1 atm pressure by $500\ \text{m}^3$ He. At –3°C and 0.5 atm pressures, the volume of He gas contained in balloon will be

(a) $700\ \text{m}^3$
(b) $900\ \text{m}^3$
(c) $1000\ \text{m}^3$
(d) $500\ \text{m}^3$

23. If Maxwell distribution is valid and v_p denotes the most probable speed, v_{av} is the average speed and v_{rms} is the root mean square speed, then

(a) $v_{av} < v_p < v_{rms}$
(b) $v_{av} < v_{rms} < v_p$
(c) $v_p < v_{av} < v_{rms}$
(d) $v_p < v_{rms} < v_{av}$

24. Which one of the following pair is incorrect?

(a) $v_{rms} \rightarrow 1.73\sqrt{\frac{kT}{m}}$

(b) $v_{mean} \rightarrow 2.23\sqrt{\frac{kT}{m}}$

(c) Average velocity $\rightarrow 0$

(d) $v_{mp} \rightarrow 1.41\sqrt{\frac{kT}{m}}$

25. Some gas at 300 K is enclosed in a container. Now, the container is placed on a fast moving train. While the train is in motion, the temperature of the gas

(a) rises above 300 K

(b) falls below 300 K

(c) remains unchanged

(d) becomes unsteady

Response Index

01	a	b	c	d	11	a	b	c	d	21	a	b	c	d
02	a	b	c	d	12	a	b	c	d	22	a	b	c	d
03	a	b	c	d	13	a	b	c	d	23	a	b	c	d
04	a	b	c	d	14	a	b	c	d	24	a	b	c	d
05	a	b	c	d	15	a	b	c	d	25	a	b	c	d
06	a	b	c	d	16	a	b	c	d					
07	a	b	c	d	17	a	b	c	d					
08	a	b	c	d	18	a	b	c	d					
09	a	b	c	d	19	a	b	c	d					
10	a	b	c	d	20	a	b	c	d					

Performance Scanner

> 90% Excellent !	You have mastered these topics. The concepts of these topics are at your fingertips. Move on to the next test and maintain this momentum.
76-90% Very Good !	You have a good command over these topics. Revise these topics again after a few days and enhance your performance.
60-75% Good !	You have a wide scope to learn more for these topics. Revise these topics again.
<60% Not Satisfactory!	You have a long way ahead of you to master these topics. Revise it thoroughly.

Test 2

Syllabus
- Degrees of Freedom
- Law of Equipartition of
- Applications to Specific Heat Capacities of Gases
- Mean Free Path

For deeper insight **Scan the QR Code**

Important Instructions
- The test is of 45 minutes duration and contains 25 Multiple Choice Questions. (Four options with a single correct answer).
- Choose the correct option and fill the OMR given on the last page of this test accordingly.
- At some instances, you may find more than 1 option may be correct, in such circumstances you have to judge the most appropriate answer as per the conditions given in the question.

1. For a molecule of an ideal gas, the number density is $2\sqrt{2} \times 10^8 \text{ cm}^{-3}$ and the mean free path is $\frac{10^{-2}}{\pi}$ cm. The diameter of the gas molecule is

(a) 5×10^{-4} cm
(b) 0.5×10^{-4} cm
(c) 2.5×10^{-4} cm
(d) 4×10^{-4} cm

2. A gas mixture consists of 2 mol of oxygen and 4 mol of argon at temperature T. Neglecting all vibrational modes, the total internal energy of the system is

(a) $4RT$
(b) $15RT$
(c) $9RT$
(d) $11RT$

3. In a close container having a mixture of H_2 and He, then

(a) hydrogen has more mean translational KE
(b) helium has more mean translational KE
(c) both have same mean translational KE
(d) None of the above

4. A gas has molar heat capacity $C = 37.55$ J mol^{-1}K^{-1}, in this process pT = constant. The number of degree of freedom of the molecule of gas is

(a) 2 (b) 3
(c) 5 (d) 7

5. **Statement I** Degree of freedom of a diatomic gas does not depend on temperature.

Statement II Degree of freedom of a monoatomic gas is 3 for all temperatures.

In the light of above statements, choose the most appropriate answer from the options given below.

(a) Both Statement I and Statement II are incorrect.
(b) Both Statement I and Statement II are correct.
(c) Statement I is correct but Statement II is incorrect.
(d) Statement I is incorrect but Statement II is correct.

6. Energy of 10 non-rigid diatomic molecules at temperature T is

(a) $70\, k_B T$
(b) $\frac{7}{2} RT$
(c) $35 k_B T$
(d) $35RT$

7. A gas mixture consists of 8 moles of argon and 6 moles of oxygen at temperature T. Neglecting all vibrational modes, the total internal energy of the system is

(a) 21 RT
(b) 29 RT
(c) 27 RT
(d) 20 RT

8. Time interval between two successive collisions of a gas molecule is given by

(a) $\frac{\lambda}{v_{\text{rms}}}$ (b) $\frac{\lambda}{v_{\text{mean}}}$

(c) $\frac{\lambda}{v_{\text{mp}}}$ (d) $\frac{\lambda}{\sqrt{v_{\text{mean}}^2 + v_{\text{mp}}^2}}$

9. A polyatomic gas with n degree of freedom has a mean energy per molecule given by

(a) $\frac{3}{2} n kT$

(b) $\frac{nkT}{N_A}$

(c) $\frac{1}{2} nkT$

(d) $\frac{nkT}{3N_A}$

10. **Statement I** In a diatomic molecule, the rotational energy at a temperature have same value for all molecules.

Statement II The ratio of C_p/C_V for an ideal gas with monoatomic molecule is $\frac{7}{5}$.

In the light of above statements, choose the most appropriate answer from the options given below.

(a) Both Statement I and Statement II are incorrect.

(b) Both Statement I and Statement II are correct.

(c) Statement I is correct but Statement II is incorrect.

(d) Statement I is incorrect but Statement II is incorrect.

11. 40 cal of heat to raise the temperature of 1 mol of an ideal monoatomic gas from 20°C to 30°C at a constant pressure. The amount of heat required to raise its temperature over the same interval at a constant volume ($R = 2$ cal/mol/K) is

(a) 20 cal (b) 40 cal

(c) 60 cal (d) 80 cal

12. 1 mole of a gas with $\gamma = \frac{7}{5}$ is mixed with 1 mole of a gas with $\gamma = \frac{5}{3}$, then the value of γ for the resulting mixture is

(a) $\frac{7}{5}$ (b) $\frac{2}{5}$

(c) $\frac{3}{2}$ (d) $\frac{12}{7}$

13. The molar specific heat at a constant pressure of an ideal gas is $\frac{5}{2}R$. The ratio of specific heat at constant pressure to that at constant volume is

(a) $\frac{8}{7}$

(b) $\frac{5}{3}$

(c) $\frac{3}{5}$

(d) $\frac{7}{8}$

14. For nitrogen gas, $C_p - C_V = A$ and for hydrogen gas, $C_p - C_V = B$, so the relation between A and B is

(a) $A = 14B$

(b) $14A = B$

(c) $A = B$

(d) $A = 4B$

15. The mean free path of molecule of oxygen is proportional to (r = radius of oxygen molecule)

(a) r^2 (b) $\frac{1}{r^2}$

(c) $\sqrt{r}$ (d) $\frac{1}{\sqrt{r}}$

16. 1 mol of an ideal diatomic gas undergoes a transition from A to B along a path AB as shown in the figure.

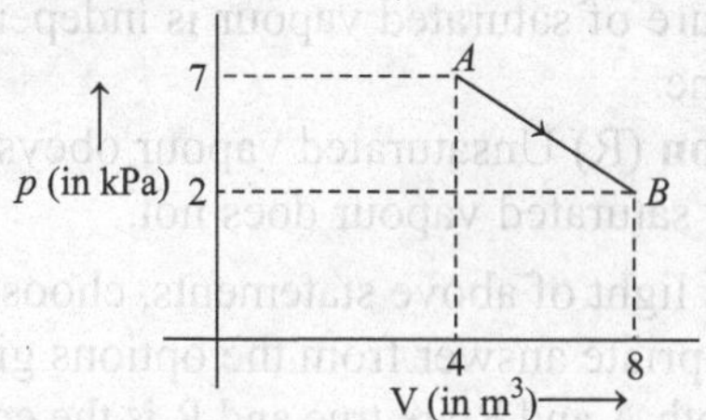

The change in internal energy of the gas during the transition is

(a) – 20 kJ

(b) –30 kJ

(c) –12 kJ

(d) –18 kJ

17. The specific heats C_p and C_V of a gas of diatomic molecules, A are given (in units of J $mol^{-1} K^{-1}$) by 29 and 22, respectively. Another gas of diatomic molecules B, has the corresponding values 30 and 21. If they are treated as ideal gases, then

(a) A has a vibrational mode but B has none.
(b) Both A and B have a vibrational mode each.
(c) A has one vibrational mode and B has two.
(d) A is rigid but B has a vibrational mode.

18. The specific heat ratio γ of oxygen, helium and another ideal diatomic gas X (whose molecules are not rigid but have vibrational mode also) are respectively equal to

(a) $\frac{5}{3}, \frac{5}{3}, \frac{7}{5}$
(b) $\frac{5}{3}, \frac{7}{5}, \frac{9}{7}$
(c) $\frac{7}{5}, \frac{5}{3}, \frac{9}{7}$
(d) $\frac{7}{5}, \frac{5}{3}, \frac{7}{5}$

19. Let total internal energy of a gas contained in a cubical box of side l is E.

Then, total momentum transferred to one of face of cube in 3 seconds is

(a) $2El$ (b) $\frac{1}{2}El$
(c) $3El$ (d) $\frac{1}{3}El$

20. **Assertion** (A) At constant temperature, the pressure of saturated vapour is independent of volume.
Reason (R) Unsaturated vapour obeys gas law while saturated vapour does not.
In the light of above statements, choose the most appropriate answer from the options given below.
(a) Both A and R are true and R is the correct explanation of A.
(b) Both A and R are true but R is not the correct explanation of A.
(c) A is true but R is false.
(d) A is false but R is true.

21. A ring shaped tube contains two ideal gases with equal masses and relative molar masses $M_1 = 32$ and $M_2 = 28$. The gases are separated by one fixed partition P and another movable stopper S which can move freely without friction inside the ring.

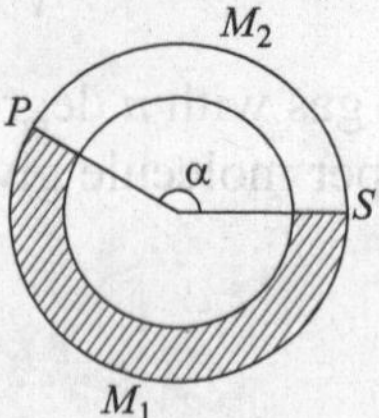

The angle α in equilibrium as shown in the figure (in degrees) is
(a) 291
(b) 219
(c) 129
(d) 192

22. For an ideal gas, the specific heat at constant pressure is C_p the specific heat at constant volume is C_V and molecular weight is M, then which relation is correct?

(a) $C_p - C_V = \frac{R}{M}$
(b) $C_p - C_V = MR$
(c) $C_p - C_V = \frac{R}{M^2}$
(d) $C_p - C_V = MR$

23. A gas mixture consists of 5 moles of oxygen and 7 moles of argon at temperature T. Assuming the gases to be ideal and the oxygen bond to be rigid, the total internal energy (in units of RT) of the mixture is
(a) 23 (b) 13
(c) 11 (d) 20

24. The following sets of values for C_V and C_p of a gas has been reported by different students. The units are cal/g-mole-K. Which of these sets are most reliable?
(a) $C_V = 3, C_p = 5$ (b) $C_V = 4, C_p = 6$
(c) $C_V = 3, C_p = 2$ (d) $C_V = 3, C_p = 4.2$

25. As adiabatic vessel contains $n_1 = 3$ moles of diatomic gas. Moment of inertia of each molecule is $I = 2.76 \times 10^{-46}$ kg-m^2 and root-mean-square angular velocity is $\omega_0 = 5 \times 10^{12}$ rad/s. Another adiabatic vessel contains $n_2 = 5$ moles of a monatomic gas at a temperature 470 K. Assume gases to be ideal, calculate root-mean-square angular velocity of diatomic molecules when the two vessels are connected by a thin tube of negligible volume. (Boltzmann constant, $k = 1.38 \times 10^{-23}$ J/molecule)

(a) 6×10^{12} rad/s (b) 8×10^{12} rad/s
(c) 6×10^{10} rad/s (d) 8×10^{10} rad/s

Response Index

01	a	b	c	d	11	a	b	c	d	21	a	b	c	d
02	a	b	c	d	12	a	b	c	d	22	a	b	c	d
03	a	b	c	d	13	a	b	c	d	23	a	b	c	d
04	a	b	c	d	14	a	b	c	d	24	a	b	c	d
05	a	b	c	d	15	a	b	c	d	25	a	b	c	d
06	a	b	c	d	16	a	b	c	d					
07	a	b	c	d	17	a	b	c	d					
08	a	b	c	d	18	a	b	c	d					
09	a	b	c	d	19	a	b	c	d					
10	a	b	c	d	20	a	b	c	d					

Performance Scanner

> 90% Excellent !	You have mastered these topics. The concepts of these topics are at your fingertips. Move on to the next topic and maintain this momentum.
76-90% Very Good !	You have a good command over these topic. Revise the topics again after a few days and enhance your performance.
60-75% Good !	You have a wide scope to learn more for these topics. Revise these topics again.
<60% Not Satisfactory!	You have a long way ahead of you to master these topics. Revise it thoroughly.

Chapter Break Thru

Syllabus

- Equation of State of a Perfect Gas
- Work done on Compressing a Gas
- Kinetic Theory of Gases-Assumptions, the Concept of Pressure
- Kinetic Interpretation of Temperature
- RMS Speed of Gas Molecules
- Avogadro's Number
- Degrees of Freedom
- Law of Equipartition of Energy Capacities
- Applications of Specific Heat Capacities of Gases
- Mean Free Path

Important Instructions

- The test is of 45 min duration and contains 30 Multiple Choice Questions (Four options with a single correct answer).
- Choose the correct option and fill the OMR given on the last page of this test accordingly.
- At some instances, you may find more than 1 option may be correct, in such circumstances you have to judge the most appropriate answer as per the conditions given in the question.

1. Sound travels in a mixture of two moles of helium and n moles of hydrogen. If rms speed of gas molecules in the mixture is $\sqrt{2}$ times the speed of sound, then the value of n will be

(a) 1 (b) 2
(c) 3 (d) 4

2. On any planet, the presence of atmosphere implies (c_{rms} = root-mean-square velocity of molecules and v_e = escape velocity)

(a) $c_{\text{rms}} << v_e$
(b) $c_{\text{rms}} > v_e$
(c) $c_{\text{rms}} = v_e$
(d) $c_{\text{rms}} = 0$

3. A gas is filled in a cylinder. Its temperature is increased by 20% on kelvin scale and volume is reduced to 90%. The percentage of the gas has to leak for pressure to remain constant is

(a) 25% (b) 40%
(c) 20% (d) 30%

4. **Statement I** The mean free path of molecules of a gas is proportional to $\sqrt{T}$.

Statement II The mean free path of molecules of a gas is inversely proportional to pressure p.

In the light of above statements, choose the most appropriate answer from the options given below.

(a) Both Statement I and Statement II are incorrect.
(b) Both Statement I and Statement II are correct.
(c) Statement I is correct but Statement II is incorrect.
(d) Statement I is incorrect but Statement II is correct.

5. Which of the following statements about kinetic theory of gases is incorrect?

(a) The molecules of a gas are in continuous random motion.
(b) The molecules continuously undergo inelastic collisions.
(c) The molecules do not interact with each other except during collisions.
(d) The collisions amongst the molecules are of short duration.

6. The temperature at which rms velocity of helium molecules is equal to the rms velocity of hydrogen molecules at NTP, is

(a) 512 K (b) 480 K (c) 502 K (d) 546 K

7. pV *versus* T graph of equal masses of H_2, He and O_2 is shown in figure. Choose the correct alternative.

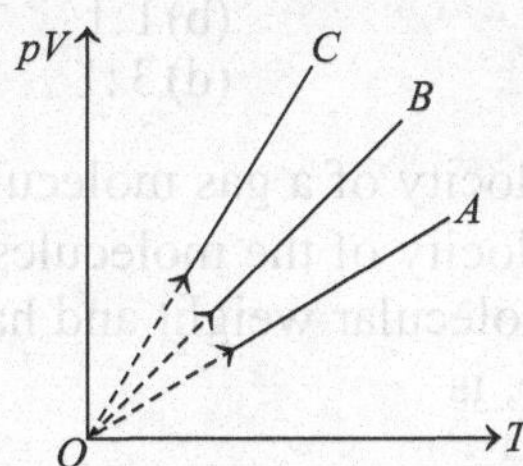

(a) A corresponds to H_2, B to He and C to O_2
(b) A corresponds to He, B to H_2 and C to O_2
(c) A corresponds to He, B to O_2 and C to H_2
(d) A corresponds to O_2, B to H_2 and C to He

8. Let $\bar{u}$, v_{rms} and $\bar{u}_p$ respectively denote the mean speed, root mean square speed and most probable speed of the molecules in an ideal monoatomic gas at absolute temperature T, the mass of a molecule in m. Then,

(a) $u_p >> u_{rms}$

(b) The average kinetic energy of a molecule is $\frac{3}{4} m\bar{u}_p^2$

(c) no molecule can have speed greater than $\sqrt{2}\bar{v}_{rms}$

(d) no molecule can have speed less than $\bar{u}_p/\sqrt{2}$

9. A diatomic gas with degree of freedom 5 has a mean energy per molecule is

(a) $\frac{nkT}{N}$ (b) $\frac{nkT}{2N}$
(c) $\frac{5}{2}kT$ (d) $\frac{3}{2}kT$

10. Read the given statements and decide which is/are correct on the basis of kinetic theory of gases.

I. Energy of one molecule at absolute temperature is zero.
II. RMS speeds of different gases are same at same temperature.
III. For one gram of all ideal gas, kinetic energy is same at same temperature.
IV. For one mole of all ideal gases, kinetic energy is same.

(a) I and III
(b) I and IV
(c) IV
(d) II and III

11. The root mean square velocity of the molecules in a sample of helium is $\frac{5}{7}$th that molecules in a sample of hydrogen. If the temperature of hydrogen gas is 0°C, then that of helium sample is near about

(a) 5 °C (b) 0°C
(c) 273°C (d) 100 K

12. The graph which represents the variation of mean kinetic energy of molecules with temperature t°C is

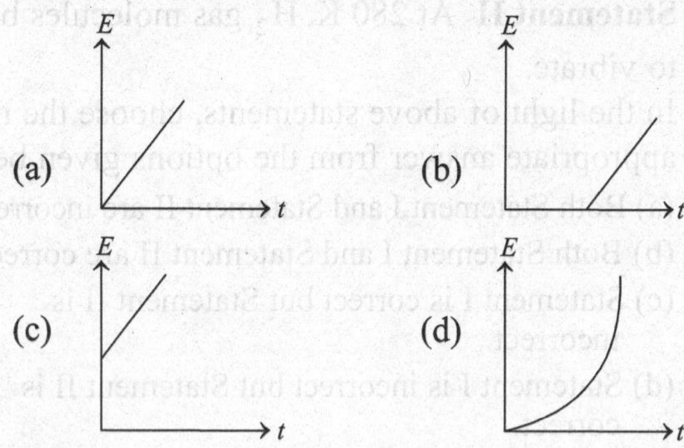

13. Match List I with List II and choose the correct combination from the options given.

	List I		List II
A.	Root mean square speed of gas molecules	1.	$\frac{1}{3}nm\bar{v}^2$
B.	Pressure exerted by ideal gas	2.	$\sqrt{\frac{3RT}{M}}$
C.	Average kinetic energy of a molecule	3.	$\frac{5}{2}RT$
D.	Total internal energy of 1 mole of a diatomic gas	4.	$\frac{3}{2}k_BT$

(a) A - 3, B -1, C -4, D -2
(b) A - 2, B -3, C -4, D -1
(c) A -2, B -1, C -4, D -3
(d) A -3, B -2, C -1, D -4

14. From the following statements, concerning ideal gas at any given temperature T. Select the incorrect statement.

(a) The coefficient of volume expansion at constant pressure is same for all ideal gases.
(b) In a gaseous mixture, the average translational kinetic energy of the molecules of each component is same.

(c) The mean free path of molecules increases with the decrease in pressure.

(d) The average translational kinetic energy per molecule of oxygen gas is $3kT$ (k being Boltzmann constant).

15. **Statement I** Below 50 K temperature for H_2 gas, value of specific heat (C_V) is $\frac{3}{2}R$ and above 250 K, its value of specific heat (C_V) becomes $\frac{5}{2}R$.

Statement II At 280 K, H_2 gas molecules begin to vibrate.

In the light of above statements, choose the most appropriate answer from the options given below

(a) Both Statement I and Statement II are incorrect.

(b) Both Statement I and Statement II are correct.

(c) Statement I is correct but Statement II is incorrect.

(d) Statement I is incorrect but Statement II is correct.

16. 1000 L of an ideal gas is heated at constant pressure from 327°C such that its volume becomes 500 L. The final temperature is

(a) 54 K (b) 400 K
(c) 300 K (d) 600 K

17. A closed vessel A of volume 300 cc contains helium. Total kinetic energy of all molecules of He in this container is 1600 J. Another closed vessel B of same volume contains oxygen at double the pressure. Total kinetic energy of all molecules of O_2 in container B is

(a) 4000 J (b) 6000 J
(c) 3000 J (d) 3200 J

18. A perfect gas having the ratio of specific heats γ, the number of degree of freedom for this gas is

(a) $\frac{2}{\gamma-1}$ (b) $\frac{9}{2}(\gamma-1)$
(c) $\frac{3}{2}(\gamma-1)$ (d) $\frac{25}{2}(\gamma-1)$

19. Two containers A and B are partially filled with water and closed. The volume of A is twice that of B and it contains double the amount of water in B. If both are at the same temperature, then water vapour in the containers will have pressure in the ratio of

(a) 1:2 (b) 1:1
(c) 2:1 (d) 3:1

20. The rms velocity of a gas molecule is 300 ms^{-1}. The rms velocity of the molecules of gas with twice the molecular weight and half the absolute temperature, is

(a) 300 ms^{-1}

(b) 600 ms^{-1}

(c) 75 ms^{-1}

(d) 150 ms^{-1}

21. **Assertion** (A) If a gas chamber containing a gas is moved translationally, then temperature of gas will increase.

Reason (R) Total kinetic energy of the chamber will increase by the translational motion

In the light of above statements, choose the most appropriate answer from the options given below.

(a) Both A and R are true and R is the correct explanation of A.

(b) Both A and R are true but R is not the correct explanation of A.

(c) A is true but R is false.

(d) A is false but R is true.

22. Calculate the ratio of the mean free paths of the molecules of two gases having molecular diameters 1.5 Å and 2.5 Å. The gases may be considered under identical conditions of temperature, pressure and volume.

(a) 3 : 5

(b) 15 : 4

(c) 4 : 3

(d) 25 : 9

23. The root mean square speed of the molecules of a diatomic gas is v. When the temperature is doubled, the molecules dissociate into two atoms. The new root mean square speed of the atom is

(a) $\sqrt{2}v$ (b) v
(c) $2v$ (d) $4v$

24. A cylindrical vessel contains two non-reactive gases helium (monoatomic) and nitrogen (diatomic). The ratio of their partial pressure is 5 : 3. The ratio of number of molecules is

(a) 2 : 3 (b) 5 : 3
(c) 1 : 1 (d) 1 : 2

25. A container has n_1 moles of a monoatomic gas and n_2 moles of a diatomic gas. The molar specific heat capacity at constant volume (C_0) of the mixture is found to be $2R$, then the ratio $\frac{n_1}{n_2}$ is

(a) $\frac{3}{5}$ (b) $\frac{5}{3}$

(c) 1 (d) $\frac{7}{5}$

26. A cubical vessel contains 1 g molecule atoms of argon at a pressure of 2 atm and temperature 27°C. Assume that atoms are moving with rms velocity, then the number of collisions per unit area per second, which the molecules make with the wall of the vessel is

(a) 1.17×10^{-29} (b) 1.05×10^{29}

(c) 1.17×10^{29} (d) 3.5×10^{27}

27. Which one of the following graphs shows the correct variation of heat capacity (C) with temperature (T) of solids?

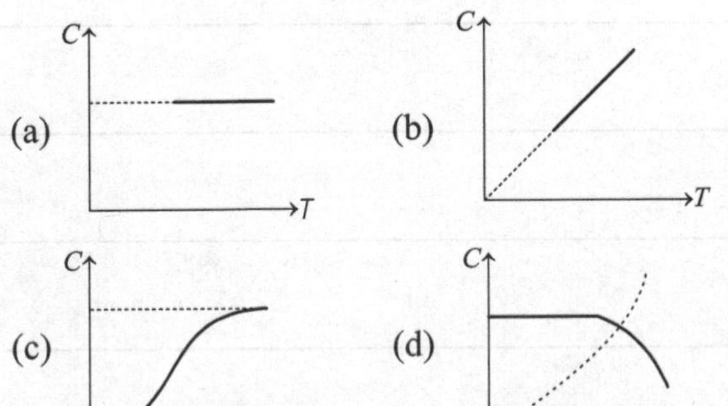

28. Two molecules of a gas have speeds of 12×10^6 ms^{-1} and 4×10^6 ms^{-1}, respectively. What is the root mean square speed of these molecules?

(a) $\sqrt{21} \times 10^6$ m/s (b) $\sqrt{41} \times 10^6$ m/s

(c) 8.5×10^6 m/s (d) $4\sqrt{5} \times 10^6$ m/s

29. A certain mass of a gas was heated in a constant volume vessel. Its p-T curve is plotted and denoted by 1. Similarly, another mass of the gas was heated in the same vessel and its p-T curve is represented by 2. The ratio of masses of the gas in the two experiment is

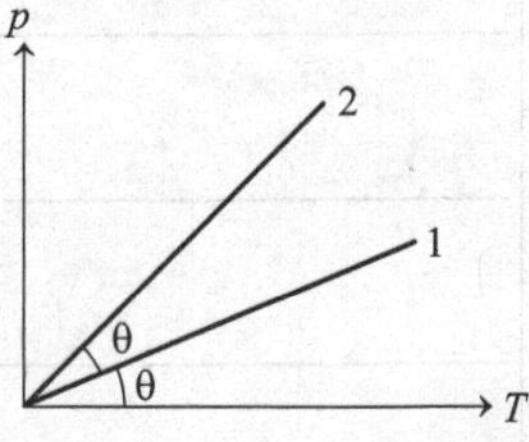

(a) $\frac{\sin\theta}{\cos 2\theta}$ (b) $\tan\theta$

(c) $\tan\theta \tan 2\theta$ (d) $\tan\theta \cot 2\theta$

30. The specific heats, C_p and C_V of a gas of diatomic molecules A, are given (in units of J mol^{-1} K^{-1}) by 29 and 22, respectively. Another gas of diatomic molecules, B has the corresponding values 30 and 21. If they are treated as ideal gases, then

(a) A has a vibrational mode but B has none

(b) both A and B have a vibrational mode each

(c) A has one vibrational mode and B has two

(d) A is rigid but B has a vibrational mode

Response Index

01	a	b	c	d	11	a	b	c	d	21	a	b	c	d
02	a	b	c	d	12	a	b	c	d	22	a	b	c	d
03	a	b	c	d	13	a	b	c	d	23	a	b	c	d
04	a	b	c	d	14	a	b	c	d	24	a	b	c	d
05	a	b	c	d	15	a	b	c	d	25	a	b	c	d
06	a	b	c	d	16	a	b	c	d	26	a	b	c	d
07	a	b	c	d	17	a	b	c	d	27	a	b	c	d
08	a	b	c	d	18	a	b	c	d	28	a	b	c	d
09	a	b	c	d	19	a	b	c	d	29	a	b	c	d
10	a	b	c	d	20	a	b	c	d	30	a	b	c	d

Performance Scanner

> 90% Excellent !	You have mastered this chapter. The concepts of this chapter are at your fingertips. Move on to the next chapter and maintain this momentum.
76-90% Very Good !	You have a good command over this chapter. Revise the chapter again after a few days and enhance your performance.
60-75% Good !	You have a wide scope to learn more for this chapter. Revise this chapter again.
<60% Not Satisfactory!	You have a long way ahead of you to master this chapter. Revise it thoroughly.

For Online Chapter Test **Scan the QR Code**

For Online Unit Test **Scan the QR Code**

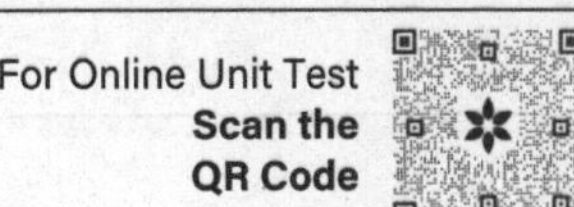

Space for Rough Work

Space for Rough Work

Space for Rough Work

Test Booklet No. 3947113

Test Booklet Code CH13

MEDACE
NEET (UG)
SELF ASSESSMENT KIT

Oscillations

Topics Covered

Simple Harmonic Motion and its Characteristics

Energy in SHM

Simple Pendulum

Important Instructions

- This Booklet Contains – Three Topic Tests and One Test on Complete Chapter.
- Each question carries 4 Marks.
- For each correct response, the candidate will get 4 marks and for every incorrect response, 1 mark will be additionally deducted from total score.
- Use **Blue/Black** point pen only for filling the OMR.
- Rough work is to be done in the space provided for this purpose in the test booklet only.

Name of the Candidate (In Capitals) ____________

Candidate's Signature ____________

Invigilator's Signature ____________

Facsimile signature stamp of center superintendent ____________

Do not open this Booklet until you start attempting the Test

Topical Follow Thru

Test 1

Syllabus
- Oscillations and Periodic Motion-Time Period, Frequency, Displacement as a Function of Time.
- SHM and its Equations
- Phase

For deeper insight **Scan the QR Code**

Important Instructions
- The test is of 45 min duration and contains 25 Multiple Choice Questions (Four options with a single correct answer).
- Choose the correct option and fill the OMR given on the last page of this test accordingly.
- At some instances, you may find more than 1 option may be correct in such circumstances you have to judge the most appropriate answer as per the conditions given in the question.

1. A simple pendulum performs simple harmonic motion about $X = 0$ with an amplitude A and time period T. The speed of the pendulum at $X = A/4$ will be

(a) $\frac{\pi A\sqrt{3}}{T}$ (b) $\frac{\sqrt{15}}{2}\frac{A\pi}{T}$

(c) $\frac{\pi A\sqrt{3}}{2T}$ (d) $\frac{3\pi^3 A}{T}$

2. Assertion (A) Acceleration is proportional to the displacement. This condition is not sufficient for motion in simple harmonic.

Reason (R) In simple harmonic motion, direction of displacement is also considered.

In the light of above statements, choose the most appropriate answer from the options given below.

(a) Both A and R are true and R is the correct explanation of A.

(b) Both A and R are true but R is not the correct explanation of A.

(c) A is true but R is false.

(d) A is false but R is true.

3. Average acceleration of a particle executing SHM in one complete vibration is

(a) $\frac{A\omega}{2}$ (b) $A\omega$ (c) $\frac{A\omega^2}{2}$ (d) 0

4. For a particle executing simple harmonic motion, its displacement equation is $x = (\sin\omega t - \cos\omega t)$, then the initial phase and amplitude of the particle respectively, are

(a) zero, 1 m (b) $\frac{\pi}{4}, \sqrt{2}$ m

(c) $-\frac{\pi}{4}, \sqrt{2}$ m (d) $\frac{\pi}{2}, \sqrt{2}$ m

5. A particle executes SHM on a straight line path. The amplitude of oscillation is 2 cm. When the displacement of the particle from the mean position is 1 cm, the numerical value of magnitude of acceleration is equal to the numerical value of magnitude of velocity. Then, what will be the angular velocity of SHM?

(a) $\frac{\sqrt{3}}{2}$ rad/s (b) $\frac{3}{2}$ rad/s

(c) $\frac{3}{\sqrt{2}}$ rad/s (d) $\sqrt{3}$ rad/s

6. A particle executing SHM of amplitude 4 cm and $T = 5$ s. The time taken by it to move from positive extreme position to half of the amplitude is

(a) 5 s (b) $\frac{1}{3}$ s (c) $\frac{5}{6}$ s (d) $\frac{2}{3}$ s

7. The function $\sin^2 \frac{\omega t}{2}$ represents

(a) a simple harmonic motion with a period $\frac{2\pi}{\omega}$.

(b) a simple harmonic motion with a period $\frac{\pi}{\omega}$.

(c) a periodic, but not simple harmonic motion with a period $\frac{2\pi}{\omega}$.

(d) a periodic, but not simple harmonic motion with a period $\frac{\pi}{\omega}$.

8. Statement I If displacement of particle is $x = A\sin(\omega t + \phi)$, then force on particle is $F = -m\omega^2 A \cdot \sin(\omega t + \phi)$.

Statement II Force on a particle executing simple harmonic motion is periodic in nature.

In the light of the above statements, choose the most appropriate answer from the options given below.

(a) Both Statement I and Statement II are correct.

(b) Both Statement I and Statement II are incorrect.

(c) Statement I is correct but Statement II is incorrect.

(d) Statement I is incorrect but Statement II is correct.

9. A particle is performing simple harmonic motion along X-axis with amplitude 5 cm and time period 1.2 s. The minimum time taken by the particle to move from $x = 2.5$ cm to $x = +5$ cm and back again is

(a) 0.6 s (b) 0.4 s
(c) 0.3 s (d) 0.2 s

10. The displacement-time equation of a particle executing SHM is $x = A\sin(\omega t + \frac{\phi}{2})$. At time $t = 0$, position of the particle is $x = \frac{A}{2}$ and it is moving along negative x-direction. Then, the angle ϕ can be

(a) $\frac{\pi}{2}$ (b) $\frac{\pi}{3}$
(c) $\frac{\pi}{6}$ (d) $\frac{5\pi}{3}$

11. Two simple harmonic motions are represented by equations $y_1 = 4\sin\left(10t + \frac{\phi}{3}\right)$ and $y_2 = 5\cos 10t$.

What is the phase difference between their velocities?

(a) $\frac{\phi}{3}$ (b) $\frac{-\phi}{3}$
(c) $\left(\frac{\phi}{3} + \frac{\pi}{2}\right)$ (d) $\left(\frac{\phi}{3} - \frac{\pi}{2}\right)$

12. Assertion (A) For an oscillatory motion, the equilibrium position can be represented by saying that it is a point for periodic motion, where net external force on the body is zero.

Reason (R) For an oscillatory motion, if the body is displaced from the equilibrium position, a restoring force will arise that will try to bring back the body to equilibrium position.

In the light of above statements, choose the most appropriate answer from the options given below.

(a) Both A and R are true and R is the correct explanation of A.

(b) Both A and R are true but R is not the correct explanation of A.

(c) A is true but R is false.

(d) A is false but R is true.

13. Displacement *versus* time curve for a particle executing SHM is shown in figure. Choose the correct statements.

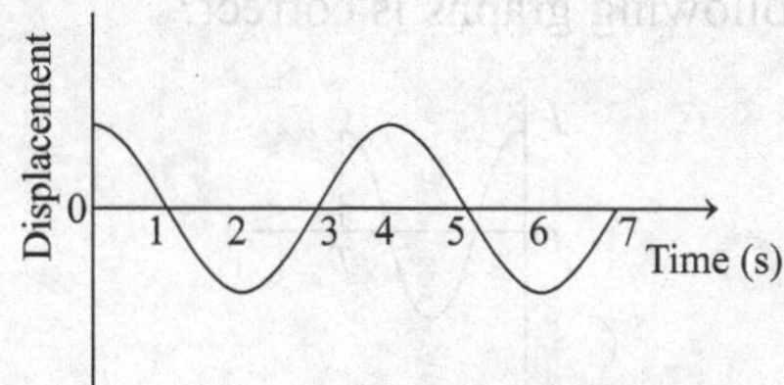

(a) Phase of the oscillator is same at $t = 0$ s and $t = 2$ s.

(b) Phase of the oscillator is same at $t = 2$ s and $t = 6$ s.

(c) Phase of the oscillator is same at $t = 1$ s and $t = 7$ s.

(d) Phase of the oscillator is same at $t = 3$ s and $t = 5$ s.

14. The period of a particle executing SHM is 8 s. At $t=0$, it is at the mean position. The ratio of the distances covered by the particle in the 1st second to the 2nd second is

(a) $\frac{1}{\sqrt{2}+1}$ (b) $\sqrt{2}$

(c) $\frac{1}{\sqrt{2}}$ (d) $\sqrt{2}+1$

15. The acceleration-displacement graph of a particle executing simple harmonic motion is shown in figure. The time period of simple harmonic motion is

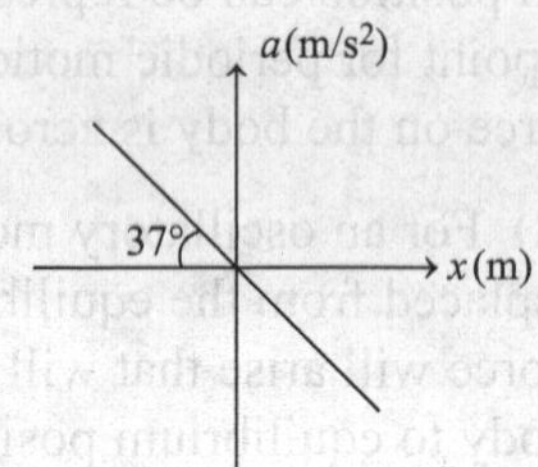

(a) $\frac{4\pi}{\sqrt{3}}$ s

(b) $\frac{2\pi}{\sqrt{3}}$ s

(c) The given graph doesn't represent simple harmonic motion.

(d) Information is insufficient.

16. A body is performing simple harmonic motion with amplitude a and time period T. Variation of its acceleration (f) with time (t) is shown in figure. If at time t, velocity of body is v, which of the following graphs is correct?

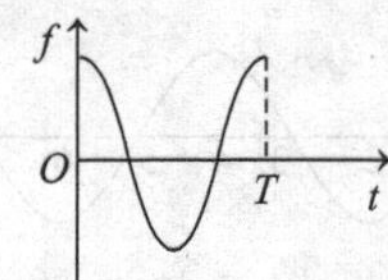

(a) 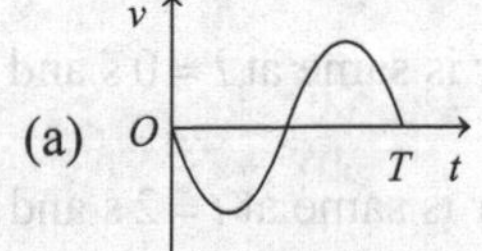

(b) 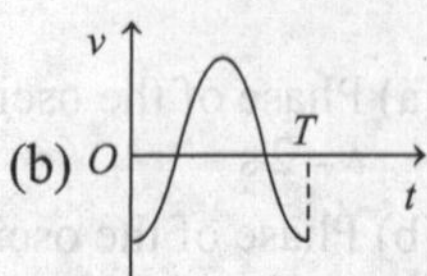

(c) 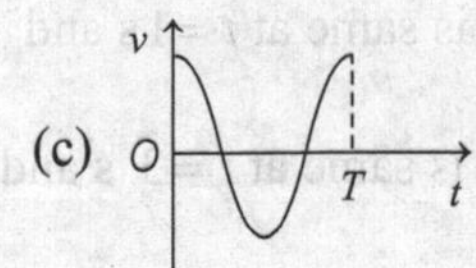

(d) 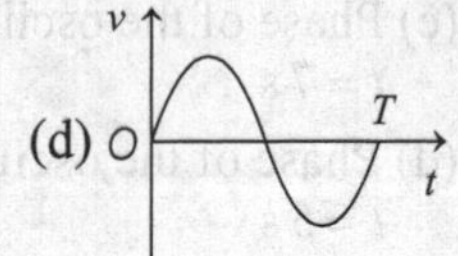

17. If a is the acceleration and v is the velocity of a particle executing SHM, then a^2-v^2 graph will look like

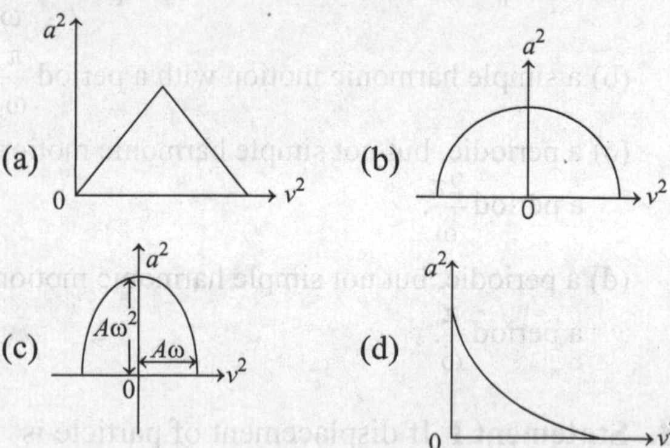

18. The velocity v of a particle of mass m moving along a straight line changes with time t as $\frac{d^2v}{dt^2} = -Kv$, where K is a positive constant.

Which of the following statement is correct?

(a) The particle does not perform SHM.

(b) The particle performs SHM with time period $2\pi\sqrt{\frac{m}{K}}$

(c) The particle performs SHM with frequency $\frac{\sqrt{K}}{2\pi}$.

(d) The particle performs SHM with time period $\frac{2\pi}{K}$.

19. A particle moves along a straight line to follow the equation $3ax^2 + 2bv^2 = k$, where a, b and k are constants and x and v are x-coordinate and velocity of the particle, respectively. Then, the amplitude will be

(a) $\sqrt{\frac{k}{2b}}$ (b) $\sqrt{\frac{2b}{k}}$

(c) $\sqrt{\frac{k}{a}}$ (d) $\sqrt{\frac{k}{3a}}$

20. A particle executing simple harmonic motion along Y-axis has its motion described by the equation $y = A\sin(\omega t) + B$. What is the minimum distance of the particle from the X-axis during its motion?

(a) A (b) $B + A$ (c) B (d) $B - A$

21. A particle moves with simple harmonic motion in a straight line. In first τ s, after starting from rest, it travels a distance a and in next τ s, it travels $2a$, in same direction, then

(a) amplitude of motion is $3a$
(b) time period of oscillations is 8π
(c) amplitude of motion is $4a$
(d) time period of oscillations is 6π

22. If $x = a\sin\left(\omega t + \dfrac{\pi}{6}\right)$ and $x' = a\cos\omega t$, then what is the phase difference between the two waves?

(a) $\dfrac{\pi}{3}$ (b) $\dfrac{\pi}{6}$
(c) $\dfrac{\pi}{2}$ (d) π

23. If the displacement equation of a particle be represented by $y = A\sin PT + B\cos PT$, then the particle executes

(a) a uniform circular motion
(b) a uniform elliptical motion
(c) a SHM
(d) an rectilinear motion

24. The displacement of a particle varies with time as $x = 12\sin\omega t - 16\sin^3\omega t$ (in cm). If its motion is SHM, then its maximum acceleration is

(a) $12\omega^2$ (b) $36\omega^2$
(c) $144\omega^2$ (d) $\sqrt{192}\,\omega^2$

25. The displacements of a particle varies according to the relation $x = 3\sin 100t + 8\cos^2 50t$. Which of the following is/are correct about this motion?

(a) The motion of the particle is not SHM.
(b) The amplitude of the SHM of the particle is 5 units.
(c) The amplitude of the resultant SHM is $\sqrt{73}$ units.
(d) The maximum displacement of the particle from origin in 8 units.

Response Index

01	a	b	c	d	10	a	b	c	d	19	a	b	c	d
02	a	b	c	d	11	a	b	c	d	20	a	b	c	d
03	a	b	c	d	12	a	b	c	d	21	a	b	c	d
04	a	b	c	d	13	a	b	c	d	22	a	b	c	d
05	a	b	c	d	14	a	b	c	d	23	a	b	c	d
06	a	b	c	d	15	a	b	c	d	24	a	b	c	d
07	a	b	c	d	16	a	b	c	d	25	a	b	c	d
08	a	b	c	d	17	a	b	c	d					
09	a	b	c	d	18	a	b	c	d					

Performance Scanner

> 90% Excellent !	You have mastered these topics. The concepts of these topics are at your fingertips. Move on to the next test and maintain this momentum.
76-90% Very Good !	You have a good command over these topics. Revise them again after a few days and enhance your performance.
60-75% Good !	You have a wide scope to learn more in these topics. Revise them again.
<60% Not Satisfactory!	You have a long way ahead of you to master in these topics. Revise them thoroughly.

Test 2

Syllabus
- Energy in SHM-Kinetic and Potential Energies

For deeper insight **Scan the QR Code**

Important Instructions
- The test is of 30 min duration and contains 15 Multiple Choice Questions (Four options with a single correct answer).
- Choose the correct option and fill the OMR given on the last page of this test accordingly.
- At some instances, you may find more than 1 option may be correct in such circumstances you have to judge the most appropriate answer as per the conditions given in the question.

1. The mass of a particle is 2 kg and it is moving along X-axis. The period of its small oscillation is $\frac{\pi}{3}$. What is its potential energy?

(a) $-72\sin x$ (b) $-16\sin x$
(c) $-36\sin x$ (d) $-72\cos x$

2. A particle is executing simple harmonic motion with frequency f. The frequency at which its kinetic energy changes into potential energy is

(a) $f/2$
(b) f
(c) $2f$
(d) $4f$

3. When a mass M is attached to the spring force constant k, then the spring stretches by l. If the mass oscillates with amplitude l, what will be maximum potential stored in the spring?

(a) $\frac{kl}{2}$ (b) $2kl$
(c) $\frac{1}{2}Mgl$ (d) Mgl

4. Consider the following statements.
The total energy of particle executing simple harmonic motion depends on its
(1) amplitude (2) period
(3) displacement of these statements

(a) (1) and (2) are correct
(b) (2) and (3) are correct
(c) (1) and (3) are correct
(d) (1), (2) and (3) are correct

5. **Assertion (A)** The graph of total energy of a particle in SHM w.r.t. position is a straight line with zero slope.

Reason (R) Total energy of particle in SHM remains constant throughout its motion.
In the light of above statements, choose the most appropriate answer from the options given below.

(a) Both A and R are true and R is the correct explanation of A.
(b) Both A and R are true but R is not the correct explanation of A.
(c) A is true but R is false.
(d) A is false but R is true.

6. The variation of potential energy of harmonic oscillator is as shown in figure. The spring constant is

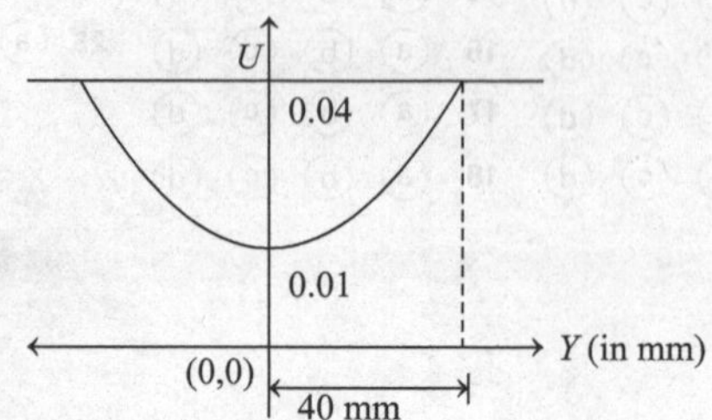

(a) 1×10^2 N/m
(b) 37.5 N/m
(c) 0.667×10^2 N/m
(d) 3×10^2 N/m

7. A block is attached to a spring and executing simple harmonic motion with amplitude A on smooth horizontal surface. At what value of x, average potential energy and average kinetic energy are equal for one time period?

(a) $\frac{A}{2}$
(b) $\frac{A}{\sqrt{2}}$
(c) At all values of x
(d) For no value of x

8. Starting from the origin, a body oscillates simple harmonically with a period of 4 s. After what time will its kinetic energy be 75% of the total energy?

(a) $\frac{1}{4}$ s (b) $\frac{1}{3}$ s
(c) $\frac{1}{12}$ s (d) $\frac{1}{6}$ s

9. For a particle executing simple harmonic motion, the kinetic energy K is given by $K = K_0 \cos^2 \omega t$. The maximum value of potential energy is

(a) K_0 (b) zero
(c) $\frac{K_0}{2}$ (d) $\frac{K_0}{4}$

10. A body is executing SHM. At a displacement x, its potential energy is E_1 and at a displacement, y its potential energy is E_2. The potential energy E at displacement $(x - y)$ is

(a) $\sqrt{E} = \sqrt{E_1} - \sqrt{E_2}$
(b) $\sqrt{E} = \sqrt{E_1} + \sqrt{E_2}$
(c) $E = E_1 + E_2$
(d) $E = E_1 + E_2$

11. Figure shows the kinetic energy K of a simple pendulum *versus* its angle θ from the vertical. The pendulum bob has mass 0.4 kg. The length of the pendulum is equal to
$(g = 10 \text{ m/s}^2)$

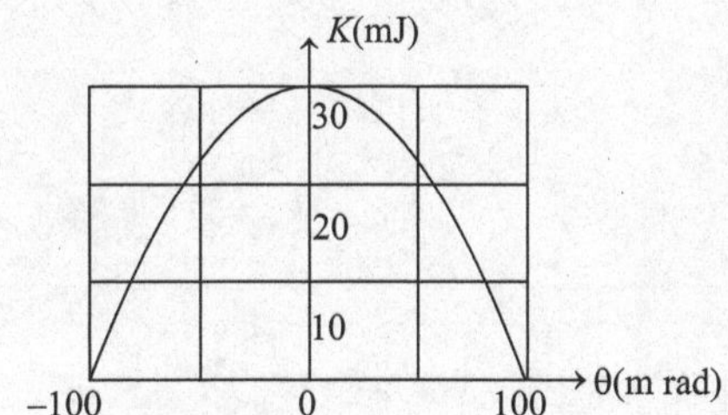

(a) 2.0 m (b) 1.8 m
(c) 1.5 m (d) 1.2 m

12. A particle of mass m oscillates with simple harmonic motion between points x_1 and x_2, the equilibrium position being O. The graph for the kinetic energy of the particle will be

(a) 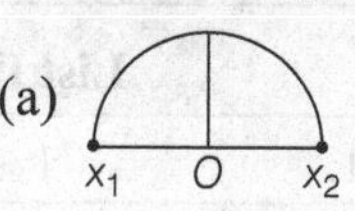

(b) 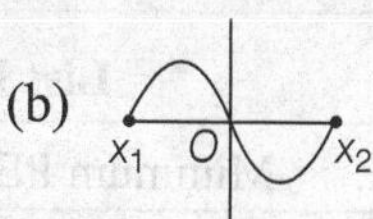

(c) 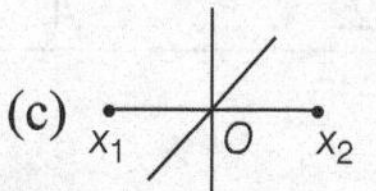

(d) 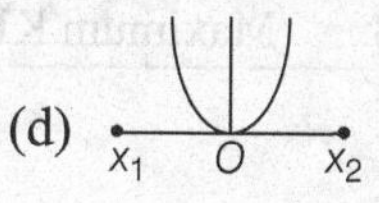

13. **Statement I** If the amplitude of a simple harmonic oscillator is doubled, its total energy becomes four times.

Statement II The total energy is directly proportional to the square of amplitude of vibration of the harmonic oscillator.

In the light of above statements, choose the most appropriate answer from the options given below.

(a) Both Statement I and Statement II are correct.
(b) Both Statement I and Statement II are incorrect.
(c) Statement I is correct but Statement II is incorrect.
(d) Statement I is incorrect but Statement II is correct

14. The angular velocity and the amplitude of a simple pendulum is ω and a, respectively. At a displacement x from the mean position, if its kinetic energy is T and potential energy is V, then the ratio of T to V is

(a) $\frac{x^2\omega^2}{(a^2 - x^2\omega^2)}$
(b) $\frac{x^2}{(a^2 - x^2)}$
(c) $\frac{(a^2 - x^2\omega^2)}{x^2\omega^2}$
(d) $\frac{(a^2 - x^2)}{x^2}$

15. Potential energy of a particle in SHM along X-axis is given by $U = 4 + (x-1)^2$ J, here U is in joule and x is in metre. If the mass of particle is 8 kg and total mechanical energy is 20 J, then match List I with List II.

	List I		List II
A.	Minimum PE	1.	1
B.	Maximum KE	2.	4
C.	Angular frequency	3.	16
D.	Amplitude of oscillation	4.	2

Codes

	A	B	C	D
(a)	1	2	3	4
(b)	2	3	1	4
(c)	3	4	2	1
(d)	2	3	4	1

Response Index

01	ⓐ	ⓑ	ⓒ	ⓓ	11	ⓐ	ⓑ	ⓒ	ⓓ
02	ⓐ	ⓑ	ⓒ	ⓓ	12	ⓐ	ⓑ	ⓒ	ⓓ
03	ⓐ	ⓑ	ⓒ	ⓓ	13	ⓐ	ⓑ	ⓒ	ⓓ
04	ⓐ	ⓑ	ⓒ	ⓓ	14	ⓐ	ⓑ	ⓒ	ⓓ
05	ⓐ	ⓑ	ⓒ	ⓓ	15	ⓐ	ⓑ	ⓒ	ⓓ
06	ⓐ	ⓑ	ⓒ	ⓓ					
07	ⓐ	ⓑ	ⓒ	ⓓ					
08	ⓐ	ⓑ	ⓒ	ⓓ					
09	ⓐ	ⓑ	ⓒ	ⓓ					
10	ⓐ	ⓑ	ⓒ	ⓓ					

Performance Scanner

> 90% Excellent !	You have mastered these topics. The concepts of these topics are at your fingertips. Move on to the next test and maintain this momentum.
76-90% Very Good !	You have a good command over these topics. Revise them again after a few days and enhance your performance.
60-75% Good !	You have a wide scope to learn more in these topics. Revise them again.
<60% Not Satisfactory!	You have a long way ahead of you to master in these topics. Revise them thoroughly.

Test 3

Syllabus

- Some Systems Executing SHM
- Simple Pendulum–Derivation of Expression for Its Time Period.
- Oscillations of a Spring–Restoring Force and Force Constant.

For deeper insight Scan the QR Code

Important Instructions

- The test is of 30 min duration and contains 15 Multiple Choice Questions (Four options with a single correct answer).
- Choose the correct option and fill the OMR given on the last page of Booklet accordingly.
- At some instances, you may find more than 1 option may be correct in such circumstances you have to judge the most appropriate answer as per the conditions given in the question.

1. A pendulum has time period T. If it is taken on to another planet having acceleration due to gravity half and mass 9 times that of the earth, then its time period on the other planet will be

(a) $\sqrt{T}$ (b) T

(c) $T^{1/3}$ (d) $\sqrt{2}T$

2. An object is attached to the bottom of a light vertical spring and set vibrating. The maximum speed of the object is 20 cm/s and the time period is 1.57×10^{-3} s. Amplitude of the oscillation is

(a) 15 cm (b) 0.01 cm

(c) 1.5 cm (d) 0.005 cm

3. A mass M is attached to a horizontal spring of force constant k fixed one side to a rigid support as shown in figure. The mass oscillates on a frictionless surface with time period T and amplitude A. When the mass is in equilibrium position, another mass m is gently placed on it. What will be the new amplitude of oscillations?

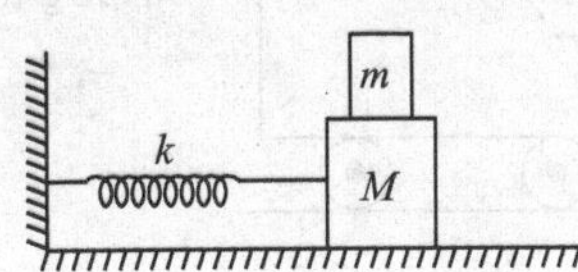

(a) $\sqrt{\frac{(M+m)}{M}}A$ (b) $\sqrt{\frac{(M-m)}{M}}A$

(c) $\sqrt{\frac{M}{(M+m)}}A$ (d) $\sqrt{\frac{M}{(M-m)}}A$

4. One end of long metallic wire of length L is tied to the ceiling. The other end is tied to massless spring of spring constant K. A mass m hangs freely from the free end of the spring. The area of cross-section and Young's modulus of the wire are A and Y, respectively. If the mass is slightly pulled down and released, it will oscillate with a time period T equal to

(a) $2\pi\left(\frac{m}{K}\right)$ (b) $2\pi\left\{\frac{(YA+KL)m}{YAK}\right\}^{1/2}$

(c) $2\pi\frac{mYA}{KL}$ (d) $2\pi\frac{mL}{YA}$

5. A particle moves with simple harmonic motion in a straight line. In first τ s, after starting from rest, it travels a distance a, and in next τ s, it travels $2a$, in the same direction, then

(a) amplitude of motion is $3a$

(b) amplitude of motion is $4a$

(c) time period of oscillations is 8τ

(d) time period of oscillations is 6τ

6. The period of simple pendulum, whose bob is a hollow metallic sphere, is T. The period is T_1 when the bob is filled with sand, T_2 when it is filled with mercury and T_3 when it is half filled with water. Which of the following is true?

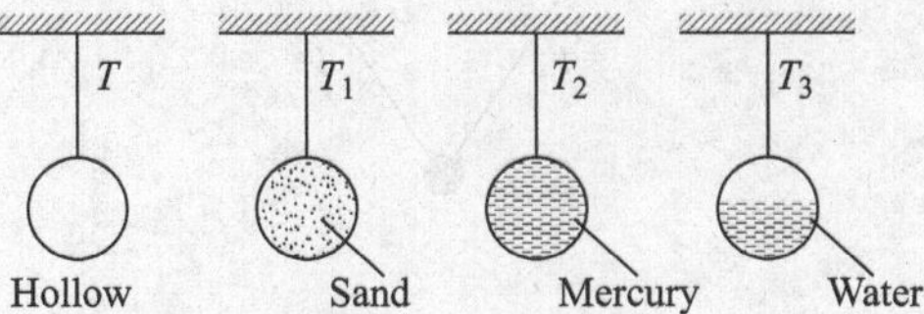

(a) $T = T_1 = T_2 > T_3$
(b) $T_1 = T_2 = T_3 > T$
(c) $T > T_3 > T_1 = T_2$
(d) $T = T_1 = T_2 < T_3$

7. **Assertion (A)** For an oscillating simple pendulum, the tension in the string is maximum at the mean position and minimum at the extreme position.

Reason (R) The velocity of oscillating bob in simple harmonic motion is maximum at the mean position.

In the light of above statements, choose the most appropriate answer from the options given below.
(a) Both A and R are true and R is the correct explanation of A.
(b) Both A and R are true but R is not the correct explanation of A.
(c) A is true but R is false.
(d) A is false but R is true.

8. In case of a simple pendulum, square of time period *versus* length is depicted by

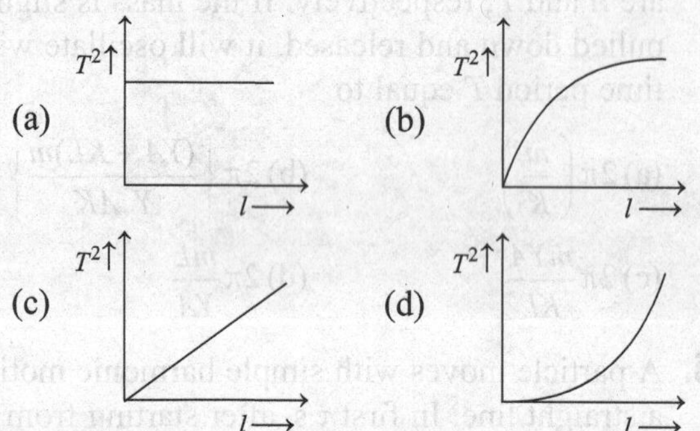

9. Two light strings, each of length l, are fixed at points M and N on a fixed horizontal rod xy. A small bob is tied by both strings and in equilibrium, the strings are making angle 45° with the rod. If the bob is slightly displaced normal to the plane of the strings and released, then frequency of the resulting small oscillation will be

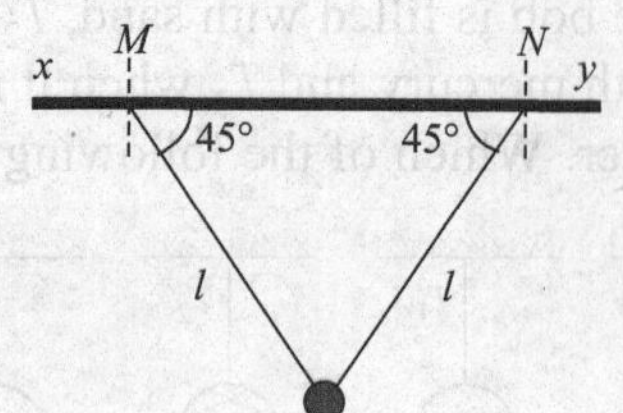

(a) $2\pi\sqrt{\frac{2\sqrt{2}l}{g}}$ (b) $2\pi\sqrt{\frac{2l}{g}}$
(c) $2\pi\sqrt{\frac{l}{g}}$ (d) $2\pi\sqrt{\frac{l}{\sqrt{2}g}}$

10. **Statement I** Time period of a simple pendulum depends on amplitude.

Statement II The graph between length of the pendulum and time period is a parabola.

In the light of the above statements, choose the most appropriate answer from the options given below.
(a) Both Statement I and Statement II are correct.
(b) Both Statement I and Statement II are incorrect.
(c) Statement I is correct but Statement II is incorrect.
(d) Statement I is incorrect but Statement II is correct.

11. A simple pendulum is suspended from the ceiling of a lift. When the lift is at rest, its time period is T. With what acceleration should the lift be accelerated upwards in order to reduce its period to $T/2$? (Take, g is acceleration due to gravity)
(a) $2g$ (b) $3g$
(c) $4g$ (d) g

12. A simple pendulum of 30 cm long is suspended from the roof of a cart accelerating in the horizontal direction with constant acceleration $\sqrt{8}\ g\ \text{m/s}^2$. The period of small oscillations of the pendulum about its equilibrium position is ($g = \pi^2\ \text{m/s}^2$)

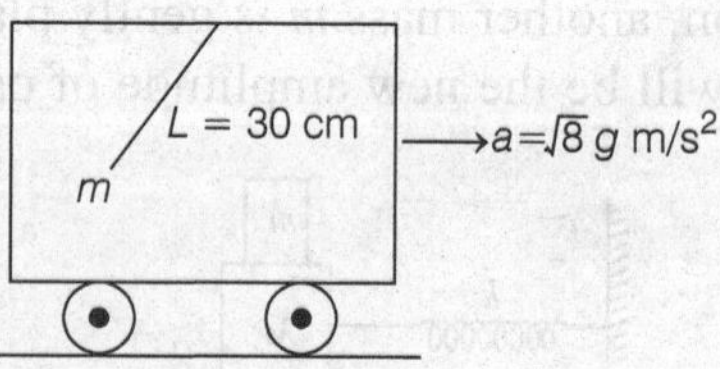

(a) 1.0 s
(b) $\sqrt{10}$ s
(c) 1.53 s
(d) $2\sqrt{10}$ s

13. The metallic bob of a simple pendulum has the relative density ρ. The time period of this pendulum is T. If the metallic bob is immersed in water, then the new time period will be

(a) $T\left(\frac{1-\rho}{\rho}\right)$ (b) $T\frac{\sqrt{\rho}}{\sqrt{\rho-1}}$

(c) $T\sqrt{\frac{\rho-1}{\rho}}$ (d) $T\sqrt{\frac{\rho}{\rho-1}}$

14. A man measures the period of a simple pendulum inside a stationary lift and finds it to be T second. If the lift accelerates upwards with an acceleration $g/4$, then the period of the pendulum will be

(a) T (b) $\frac{T}{4}$

(c) $\frac{2T}{\sqrt{5}}$ (d) $2T\sqrt{5}$

15. An object of mass m is suspended from a spring and it executes SHM with frequency n. If the mass is increased 4 times, the new frequency will be

(a) $2n$ (b) $n/2$ (c) n (d) $n/4$

Response Index

01	a	b	c	d	11	a	b	c	d
02	a	b	c	d	12	a	b	c	d
03	a	b	c	d	13	a	b	c	d
04	a	b	c	d	14	a	b	c	d
05	a	b	c	d	15	a	b	c	d
06	a	b	c	d					
07	a	b	c	d					
08	a	b	c	d					
09	a	b	c	d					
10	a	b	c	d					

Performance Scanner

> 90% Excellent !	You have mastered these topics. The concepts of these topics are at your fingertips. Move on to the next test and maintain this momentum.
76-90% Very Good !	You have a good command over these topics. Revise them again after a few days and enhance your performance.
60-75% Good !	You have a wide scope to learn more in these topics. Revise them again.
<60% Not Satisfactory!	You have a long way ahead of you to master in these topics. Revise them thoroughly.

Chapter Break Thru

Syllabus	• Oscillations and Periodic Motion-Time Period Frequency, Displacement as a Function of Time. • SHM and its Equation • Phase • Energy in SHM	• Simple Pendulum-Derivation of Expression for its Time Period. • Oscillations of a Spring, Restoring Force and Force Constant.

Important Instructions

- The test is of 45 min duration and contains 30 Multiple Choice Questions (Four options with a single correct answer).
- Choose the correct option and fill the OMR given on the last page of this test accordingly.
- At some instances, you may find more than 1 option may be correct, in such circumstances you have to judge the most appropriate answer as per the conditions given in the question.

1. The amplitude of a particle executing SHM with frequency of 60 Hz is 0.01 m. The maximum value of the acceleration of the particle is

(a) $144\pi^2$ m/s^2

(b) 144 m/s^2

(c) $\frac{144}{\pi^2}$ m/s^2

(d) $288\pi^2$ m/s^2

2. A system exhibiting SHM must possess

(a) inertia only

(b) elasticity as well as inertia

(c) elasticity, inertia and an external force

(d) elasticity only

3. A particle executes simple harmonic motion (amplitude $= A$) between $x = -A$ and $x = +A$. The time taken for it to go from 0 to $A/2$ is T_1 and to go from $A/2$ to A is T_2. Then,

(a) $T_1 < T_2$

(b) $T_1 > T_2$

(c) $T_1 = T_2$

(d) $T_1 = 2T_2$

4. The oscillation of a body on a smooth horizontal surface is represented by the equation,

$$X = A\cos(\omega t)$$

where, X = displacement at time t and ω = frequency of oscillation.
Which one of the following graphs shows correctly the variation of velocity v with time t?

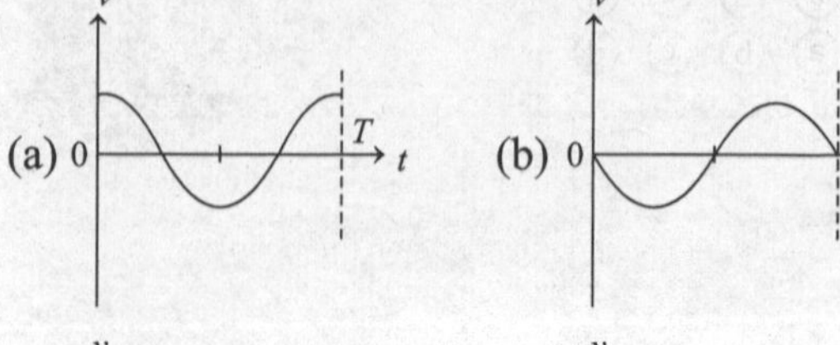

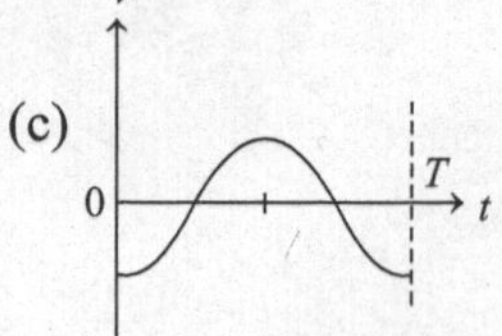

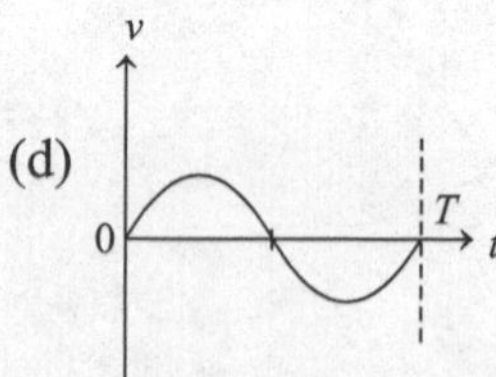

Here, v = velocity at time t and T = time period.

5. Two particles P and Q start from origin and execute simple harmonic motion along X-axis with same amplitude but with periods 4 s and 8 s, respectively. The ratio of the velocities of P and Q when they meet is

(a) 1 : 2

(b) 2 : 1

(c) 1 : 8

(d) 4 : 2

6. A body of mass 0.01 kg executes simple harmonic motion (SHM) about $x = 0$ under the influence of a force as shown below. The period of the SHM is

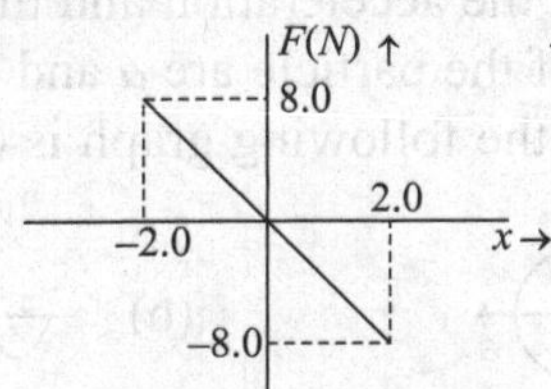

(a) 1.05 s (b) 0.52 s
(c) 0.25 s (d) 0.30 s

7. The graph shows the variation of displacement of a particle executing SHM with time. We infer from this graph that

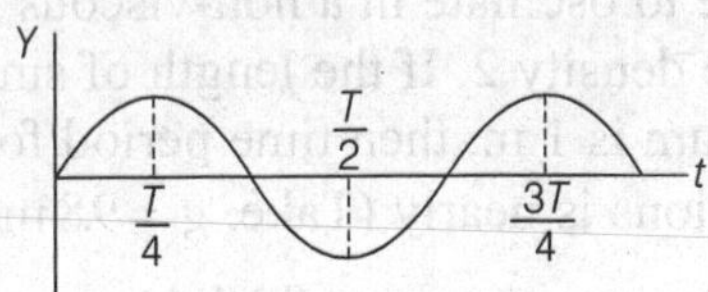

(a) the force is zero at time $3T/4$
(b) the velocity is maximum at time $T/2$
(c) the acceleration is maximum at time T
(d) the PE is equal to total energy at time $T/2$

8. A block executes SHM of time period 2 s and amplitude 8 cm. The time taken by it to travel 3 cm from negative extremity of oscillation is
$\left[\text{Use, } \sin^{-1}\left(\frac{5}{8}\right) = 0.435,\ \cos^{-1}\left(\frac{5}{8}\right) = 0.9\right]$

(a) 0.467 s (b) 0.534 s
(c) 0.286 s (d) 0.7 s

9. The displacement equation of a particle performing SHM along X-axis is $x(t) = 20\sin\left[\frac{\pi}{3}(15t + 0.5)\right]$ cm and the displacement of another particle performing SHM along Y-axis is $y(t) = 8[\sin 10\pi t + 0.75\cos 10\pi t]$ cm. The ratio of their amplitudes and time periods are respectively

(a) $\frac{A_x}{A_y} = \frac{2}{1}, \frac{T_x}{T_y} = \frac{2}{1}$
(b) $\frac{A_x}{A_y} = 1, \frac{T_x}{T_y} = 2$
(c) $\frac{A_x}{A_y} = 2, \frac{T_x}{T_y} = 1$
(d) $\frac{A_x}{A_y} = 1, \frac{T_x}{T_y} = 1$

10. **Assertion (A)** All oscillatory motions are necessarily periodic motion but all periodic motions are not oscillatory.

Reason (R) Simple pendulum is an example of oscillatory motion.

In the light of above statements, choose the most appropriate answer from the options given below.

(a) Both A and R are true and R is the correct explanation of A.
(b) Both A and R are true but R is not the correct explanation of A.
(c) A is true but R is false.
(d) A is false but R is true.

11. Match List I (figure) with List II (time period).

List I	List II
A. (m, spring)	1. $2\pi\sqrt{\frac{m}{2k}}$
B. (l)	2. $2\pi\sqrt{\frac{2m}{k}}$
C. (k, m, k)	3. $2\pi\sqrt{\frac{m}{k}}$
D. (k, k, m)	4. $2\pi\sqrt{\frac{l}{g}}$

Codes

	A	B	C	D
(a)	3	4	1	2
(b)	1	2	3	4
(c)	2	1	4	3
(d)	3	1	2	4

12. If a spring has time period T, and is cut into n equal parts, then the frequency of each part will be

(a) $T\sqrt{n}$
(b) $\sqrt{n} / T$
(c) n/T
(d) $1/T$

13. A mass M is suspended from a spring of negligible mass. The spring is pulled a little and then released so that the mass executes SHM of time period T. If the mass is increased by m, time period becomes $7T / 3$, then the ratio of $2m/ M$ is

(a) $\frac{40}{9}$ (b) $\frac{49}{9}$
(c) $\frac{25}{9}$ (d) $\frac{80}{9}$

14. A man of mass 60 kg is standing on a platform executing SHM in the vertical plane. The displacement from the mean position varies as $y = 5\sin\omega t$ m. The maximum value of ω, for which man always keeps in touch with platform is nearly

(a) 1.4 rad/s (b) 0.14 rad/s
(c) 14 rad/s (d) 1.96 rad/s

15. Three massless springs whose constants are $2k$, k and $2k$, respectively are attached to a mass M kept on a frictionless plane (as shown in figure). If the mass M is displaced in the horizontal direction, then the frequency of oscillation of the system is

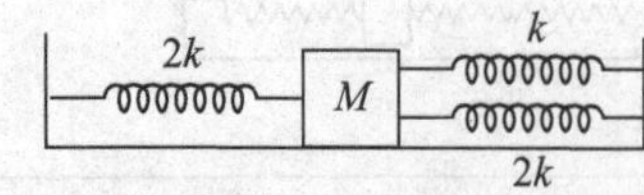

(a) $\frac{1}{2\pi}\sqrt{\frac{k}{4M}}$ (b) $\frac{1}{2\pi}\sqrt{\frac{5k}{M}}$
(c) $\frac{1}{2\pi}\sqrt{\frac{k}{7M}}$ (d) $\frac{1}{2\pi}\sqrt{\frac{7k}{M}}$

16. In figure, S_1 and S_2 are identical springs. The oscillation time period of the mass m is T. If one spring is removed, the time period will become

S_1 [m] S_2

(a) T (b) $2T$
(c) $T\sqrt{2}$ (d) $T / \sqrt{2}$

17. A particle is performing a linear simple harmonic motion. If the acceleration and the corresponding velocity of the particle are a and v, respectively. Which of the following graph is correct?

(a) 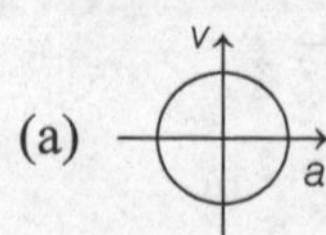

(b) 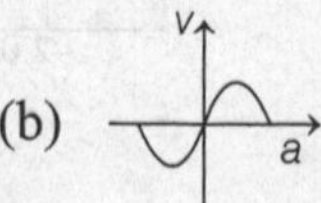

(c) 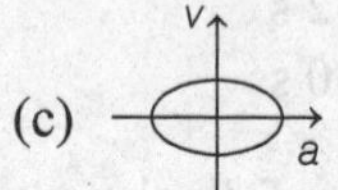

(d) 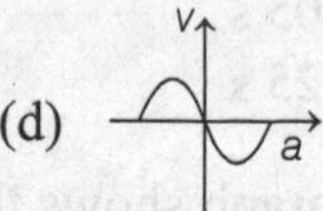

18. The bob of a pendulum having relative density 4 is made to oscillate in a non-viscous fluid of relative density 2. If the length of simple pendulum is 1 m, then time period for small oscillations is nearly (Take, $g = 9.8\text{ m/s}^2$)

(a) 2.83 s (b) 1.41 s
(c) 2 s (d) 1.72 s

19. If displacement x and velocity v are related as $4v^2 = 25 - 2x^2$ in a SHM, then time period of given SHM is

(a) π (b) $2\sqrt{2}\pi$
(c) 4π (d) 6π

20. The bob of a simple pendulum is displaced from its equilibrium position O to a position Q which is at height h above O and the bob is then released.

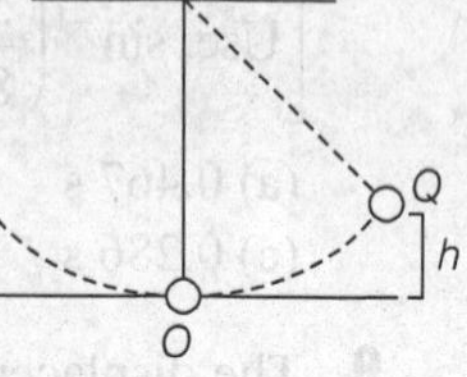

Assuming the mass of the bob to be m and time period of oscillations to be 4.0 s, the tension in the string when the bob passes through O is

(a) $m\left(g + \pi\sqrt{\frac{gh}{2}}\right)$
(b) $m(g + \sqrt{\pi^2 gh})$
(c) $m\left(g + \sqrt{\frac{\pi^2}{2} g h}\right)$
(d) $m\left(g + \sqrt{\frac{\pi^2}{3} gh}\right)$

21. A block of mass 2.5 kg attached to a spring of stiffness 100 N/m is executing SHM with an amplitude of 100 cm. When the block is passing through its mean position, a piece of mass 0.5 kg of block gets detached from it and immediately come to rest. However, the other part continues SHM, then its maximum velocity is

(a) 7.9 m/s
(b) 2.5 m/s
(c) 0.632 m/s
(d) 6.32 m/s

22. **Statement I** The graph between velocity and displacement for a harmonic oscillator is a parabola.

Statement II Velocity does not change uniformly with displacement in harmonic motion.

In the light of the above statements, choose the most appropriate answer from the options given below.

(a) Both Statement I and Statement II are incorrect.
(b) Both Statement I and Statement II are correct.
(c) Statement I is correct but Statement II is incorrect.
(d) Statement I is incorrect but Statement II is correct.

23. A linear harmonic oscillator of force constant 2×10^6 N/m and amplitude 0.01 m has a total mechanical energy of 160 joules. Its

(a) maximum potential energy is 100 J
(b) maximum KE is 100 J
(c) maximum PE is 60 J
(d) minimum PE is zero

24. A clock which keeps correct time at 25°C, is subjected to 35°C. If coefficient of linear expansion of the pendulum is 12×10^{-6}/°C. How much will it gain or loose in time?

(a) 10.3 s/day
(b) 5.18 s/day
(c) 5 s/day
(d) 6 min/day

25. When the displacement of a particle executing SHM is one-fourth of its amplitude, what fraction of the total energy is the kinetic energy?

(a) $\frac{16}{15}$ (b) $\frac{15}{16}$ (c) $\frac{5}{4}$ (d) $\frac{3}{4}$

26. A simple pendulum has time period T_1. The point of suspension is now moved upward according to equation $y = 2Kt^2$, where $K = 1\ \text{m/s}^2$. If new time period is T_2, then the ratio $\frac{T_2^2}{T_1^2}$ will be

(a) 2/3 (b) 5/7
(c) 6/5 (d) 49/25

27. Three simple harmonic motions in the same direction having the same amplitude a and same period are superposed. If each differs in phase from the next by 45°, then choose the correct statement.

(a) The resultant amplitude is $(1+\sqrt{2})\,a$.
(b) The phase of the resultant motion relative to the first is 90°.
(c) The energy associated with the resulting motion is $(3-2\sqrt{2})$ times the energy associated with any single motion.
(d) The resulting motion is not simple harmonic.

28. A uniform rod of length 2.0 m is suspended through an end and is set into oscillation with small amplitude under gravity. The time period of oscillation is approximately

(a) 1.60 s (b) 1.80 s
(c) 2.0 s (d) 2.40 s

29. A girl weighing 50 kg is standing on a platform that oscillates vertically with a frequency of 2 Hz and amplitude 5 cm.

Let N_2 is reaction of platform at it's lowest position and N_1 is reaction at topmost position then $|N_2 - N_1|$ is nearly

(a) zero (b) 400 N
(c) 200 N (d) 800 N

30. The phase difference between two particles executing SHM of the same amplitudes and frequency along same straight line while passing one another when going in opposite directions with equal displacement from their respective starting point is $\pi / 3$. The phase of one particle is $5\pi / 6$. If amplitude is A, then the displacement at this instant is

(a) $A / 3$

(b) $2A / 3$

(c) $\sqrt{3}A / 2$

(d) $A / 2$

■ **Response Index**

01	ⓐ	ⓑ	ⓒ	ⓓ	14	ⓐ	ⓑ	ⓒ	ⓓ	27	ⓐ	ⓑ	ⓒ	ⓓ
02	ⓐ	ⓑ	ⓒ	ⓓ	15	ⓐ	ⓑ	ⓒ	ⓓ	28	ⓐ	ⓑ	ⓒ	ⓓ
03	ⓐ	ⓑ	ⓒ	ⓓ	16	ⓐ	ⓑ	ⓒ	ⓓ	29	ⓐ	ⓑ	ⓒ	ⓓ
04	ⓐ	ⓑ	ⓒ	ⓓ	17	ⓐ	ⓑ	ⓒ	ⓓ	30	ⓐ	ⓑ	ⓒ	ⓓ
05	ⓐ	ⓑ	ⓒ	ⓓ	18	ⓐ	ⓑ	ⓒ	ⓓ					
06	ⓐ	ⓑ	ⓒ	ⓓ	19	ⓐ	ⓑ	ⓒ	ⓓ					
07	ⓐ	ⓑ	ⓒ	ⓓ	20	ⓐ	ⓑ	ⓒ	ⓓ					
08	ⓐ	ⓑ	ⓒ	ⓓ	21	ⓐ	ⓑ	ⓒ	ⓓ					
09	ⓐ	ⓑ	ⓒ	ⓓ	22	ⓐ	ⓑ	ⓒ	ⓓ					
10	ⓐ	ⓑ	ⓒ	ⓓ	23	ⓐ	ⓑ	ⓒ	ⓓ					
11	ⓐ	ⓑ	ⓒ	ⓓ	24	ⓐ	ⓑ	ⓒ	ⓓ					
12	ⓐ	ⓑ	ⓒ	ⓓ	25	ⓐ	ⓑ	ⓒ	ⓓ					
13	ⓐ	ⓑ	ⓒ	ⓓ	26	ⓐ	ⓑ	ⓒ	ⓓ					

■ **Performance Scanner**

> 90% Excellent !	You have mastered this chapter. The concepts of this chapter are at your fingertips. Move on to the next chapter and maintain this momentum.
76-90% Very Good !	You have a good command over this chapter. Revise the chapter again after a few days and enhance your performance.
60-75% Good !	You have a wide scope to learn more for this chapter. Revise this chapter again.
<60% Not Satisfactory!	You have a long way ahead of you to master this chapter. Revise it thoroughly.

For Online Chapter Test **Scan the QR Code**

MEDACE
NEET (UG)
SELF ASSESSMENT KIT

Test Booklet No. 3947114

Test Booklet Code CH14

Waves

Topics Covered

Mechanical Waves and Speed of Sound Waves

Progressive Waves, Superposition of Waves and Beats

Standing Waves, Vibration of Air Columns and Strings

Important Instructions

- This Booklet Contains – Three Topic Tests and One Test on Complete Chapter.
- Each question carries 4 Marks.
- For each correct response, the candidate will get 4 marks and for every incorrect response, 1 mark will be additionally deducted from total score.
- Use **Blue/Black** point pen only for filling the OMR.
- Rough work is to be done in the space provided for this purpose in the test booklet only.

Name of the Candidate (In Capitals)

____

____

Candidate's Signature ______________

Invigilator's Signature ______________

Facsimile signature stamp of center superintendent______________

Do not open this Booklet until you start attempting the Test

Topical Follow Thru

Test 1

Syllabus
- Longitudinal and Transverse Waves
- Speed of Travelling Wave

For deeper insight **Scan the QR Code**

Important Instructions
- The test is of 30 min duration and contains 15 Multiple Choice Questions (Four options with a single correct answer).
- Choose the correct option and fill the OMR given on the last page of this test accordingly.
- At some instances, you may find more than 1 option may be correct in such circumstances you have to judge the most appropriate answer as per the conditions given in the question.

1. When tension in string is 400 N, wave speed is 300 m/s.

To make wave speed 315 m/s increase in tension required is nearly

(a) 10% (b) 15%
(c) 5% (d) 7%

2. Statement I Sound would travel faster on a hot summer day than on a cold winter day.

Statement II Velocity of sound is directly proportional to the square of its absolute temperature.

In the light of the above statements, choose the most appropriate answer from the options given below.

(a) Both Statement I and Statement II are correct.
(b) Both Statement I and Statement II are incorrect.
(c) Statement I is correct but Statement II is incorrect.
(d) Statement I is incorrect but Statement II is correct.

3. Speed of sound in air is $v = \sqrt{\frac{E}{\rho}}$. Ratio of speed obtained by Laplace and that by Newton is

(a) $\sqrt{\frac{3}{5}}$ (b) $\sqrt{\frac{4}{5}}$
(c) $\sqrt{\frac{7}{5}}$ (d) $\sqrt{\frac{9}{5}}$

4. A string of mass 25 kg, length 20 m is under a tension of 2000 N.

Time taken by a pulse to reach end of string when it is plucked at the middle point is

(a) 1 s (b) 1/2 s
(c) 1/4 s (d) 1/3 s

5. A 20 m long steel wire has mass 10 g. If the wire is under a tension of 125 N, the speed of transverse waves on the wire is

(a) 100 ms^{-1}
(b) 200 ms^{-1}
(c) 400 ms^{-1}
(d) 500 ms^{-1}

6. Assertion (A) Transverse waves are not produced in liquids and gases.

Reason (R) Sound waves are longitudinal waves.

In the light of above statements, choose the most appropriate answer from the options given below.

(a) Both A and R are true and R is the correct explanation of A.
(b) Both A and R are true but R is not the correct explanation of A.
(c) A is true but R is false.
(d) A is false but R is true.

7. The following figure depicts a wave travelling in a medium. Which pair of particles are in phase?

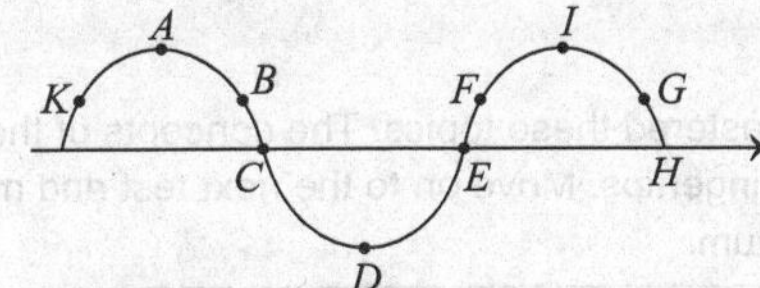

(a) K and B
(b) H and D
(c) C and E
(d) K and F

8. Ratio of wavelengths of audible range for humans $\lambda_{max}/\lambda_{min}$ is
(a) 10
(b) 100
(c) 1000
(d) 10,000

9. The string of length L is stretched by x when the speed of transverse wave along it is v_1. The string is further stretched by Δx when the speed of transverse wave along it is $v_1\sqrt{5}$. Find Δx.
(a) $(\sqrt{2}-1)x$
(b) $x\sqrt{5}$
(c) $0.8x$
(d) $(\sqrt{5}-1)x$

10. Two small boats are 20 m apart on a lake. Each pops up and down with a period of 2.0 s due to wave motion on the surface of water. When one boat is at its highest point, the other boat is at its lowest point. Both boats are always within a single cycle of the waves. The speed of the waves is
(a) 2.5 m/s
(b) 5.0 m/s
(c) 14 m/s
(d) 20 m/s

11. A uniform rope of length L and mass m_1 hangs vertically from a rigid support. A block of mass m_2 is attached to the free end of the rope. A transverse pulse of wavelength λ_1 is produced at the lower end of the rope.

The wavelength of the pulse when it reaches the top of the rope is λ_2, the ratio $\frac{\lambda_2}{\lambda_1}$ is

(a) $\sqrt{\frac{m_1}{m_2}}$
(b) $\sqrt{\frac{m_1+m_2}{m_2}}$
(c) $\sqrt{\frac{m_2}{m_1}}$
(d) $\sqrt{\frac{m_1+m_2}{m_1}}$

12. At what temperature, speed of sound will be three times of it's value at 0°C?
(a) 1632°C
(b) 2356°C
(c) 1224°C
(d) 2184°C

13. Two solid bars having Young's modulus Y_1 and Y_2 is in the ratio of $Y_1/Y_2 = 4$. If the bars are made up of materials with same density, then the ratio of the speeds of longitudinal waves in the solid bars i.e. v_1/v_2 is
(a) 2
(b) 1
(c) 3
(d) 4

14. Two strings of copper are stretched to the same tension. If their cross-section area are in the ratio 1 : 4, then the respective wave velocities will be in the ratio

(a) 4 : 1 (b) 2 : 1
(c) 1 : 2 (d) 1 : 4

15. The ratio of the speed of sound in nitrogen gas to that in helium gas, at 300 K is

(a) $\sqrt{\dfrac{2}{7}}$ (b) $\sqrt{\dfrac{1}{7}}$
(c) $\dfrac{\sqrt{3}}{5}$ (d) $\dfrac{\sqrt{6}}{5}$

Response Index

01	a	b	c	d	11	a	b	c	d
02	a	b	c	d	12	a	b	c	d
03	a	b	c	d	13	a	b	c	d
04	a	b	c	d	14	a	b	c	d
05	a	b	c	d	15	a	b	c	d
06	a	b	c	d					
07	a	b	c	d					
08	a	b	c	d					
09	a	b	c	d					
10	a	b	c	d					

Performance Scanner

> 90% Excellent !	You have mastered these topics. The concepts of these topics are at your fingertips. Move on to the next test and maintain this momentum.
76-90% Very Good !	You have a good command over these topics. Revise them again after a few days and enhance your performance.
60-75% Good !	You have a wide scope to learn more in these topics. Revise them again.
<60% Not Satisfactory!	You have a long way ahead of you to master in these topics. Revise them thoroughly.

Test 2

Syllabus
- Displacement Relation for a Progressive Wave
- Principle of Superposition of Waves
- Reflection of Waves
- Beats

For deeper insight **Scan the QR Code**

Important Instructions
- The test is of 30 min duration and contains 15 Multiple Choice Questions (Four options with a single correct answer).
- Choose the correct option and fill the OMR given on the last page of this test accordingly.
- At some instances, you may find more than 1 option may be correct in such circumstances you have to judge the most appropriate answer as per the conditions given in the question.

1. A transverse wave described by equation $y = 0.5 \sin(2x + 60t)$ (where, x and t are in metres and seconds, respectively) is travelling along a wire of area of cross-section 1mm^2 and density 9000 kg/m^3. What is the tension in the string?

(a) 8.1 N (b) 7.2 N
(c) 30 N (d) 14.4 N

2. Figure here shows an incident pulse P reflected from a rigid support. Which one of A, B, C and D represents the reflected pulse correctly?

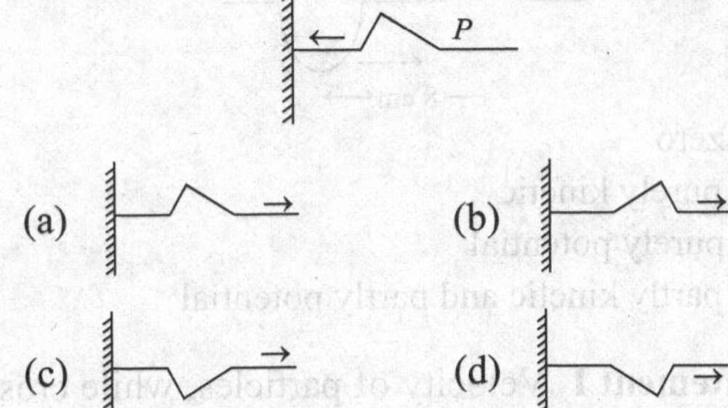

3. Two periodic waves of intensities I_1 and I_2 pass through a region at the same time in the same direction. The difference between the maximum and minimum intensities is

(a) $(\sqrt{I_1} - \sqrt{I_2})^2$
(b) $2(I_1 - I_2)$
(c) $I_1 - I_2$
(d) $4\sqrt{I_1 I_2}$

4. Two pulses travel in mutually opposite direction in a string with a speed of 2.5 cm/s. Initially the pulses are 10 cm apart. What will be the shape of the string after 2s ?

(a) 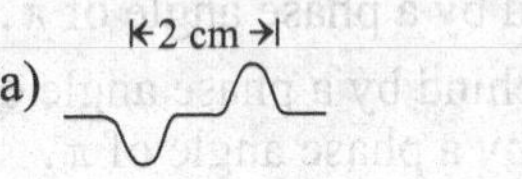

(b) 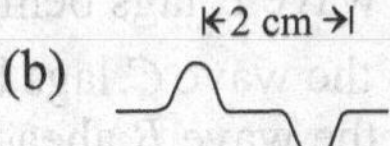

(c)
(d) 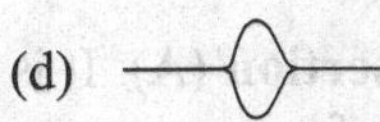

5. A progressive wave is represented by the equation

$$y = y_0 \sin \frac{2\pi}{\lambda}(vt - x)$$

For what value of λ, the maximum particle velocity equal to three times the wave velocity?

(a) $\lambda = 2\pi y_0$
(b) $\lambda = 2\pi y_0 / 3$
(c) $\lambda = \pi y_0 / 2$
(d) $\lambda = \pi y_0$

6. Equation of motion in the same direction is given by $y_1 = A \sin(\omega t - kx)$, $y_2 = A \sin(\omega t - kx - \theta)$. Half of the amplitude of the medium particle will be

(a) $A \cos \frac{\theta}{2}$ (b) $A \cos \theta$
(c) $\sqrt{2} A \cos \frac{\theta}{2}$ (d) $\sqrt{2} A \cos \theta$

7. The figure shows four progressive waves A, B, C and D with their phases expressed with respect to the wave A. It can be concluded from the figure that

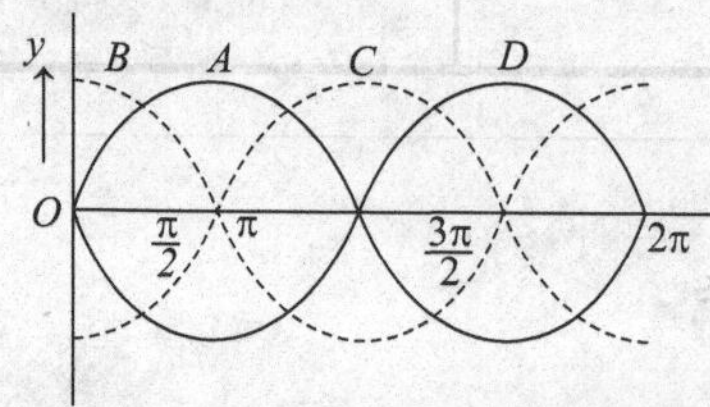

(a) the wave C is ahead by a phase angle of $\frac{\pi}{2}$ and the wave B lags behind by a phase angle of $\frac{\pi}{2}$.

(b) the wave C lags behind by a phase angle of $\frac{\pi}{2}$ and the wave B is ahead by a phase angle of $\frac{\pi}{2}$.

(c) the wave C is ahead a phase angle of π and the wave B lags behind by a phase angle of π.

(d) the wave C lags behind by a phase angle of π and the wave B ahead by a phase angle of π.

8. Assertion (A) It is not possible to have interference between the waves produced by two violins.

Reason (R) For interference of two waves, the phase difference between the waves must remain constant.

In the light of above statements, choose the most appropriate answer from the options given below.

(a) Both A and R are true and R is the correct explanation of A.

(b) Both A and R are true but R is not the correct explanation of A.

(c) A is true but R is false.

(d) A is false but R is true.

9. An unknown frequency x produces 12 beats/s with a frequency of 250 Hz and 8 beats with 270 Hz source, then x is

(a) 258 Hz (b) 242 Hz
(c) 262 Hz (d) 282 Hz

10. The equations of a travelling and stationary waves are $y_1 = a\sin(\omega t - kx)$ and $y_2 = a\sin kx \cos\omega t$, respectively. The phase difference between two points $x_1 = \frac{\pi}{5k}$ and $x_2 = \frac{5\pi}{3k}$ are ϕ_1 and ϕ_2 respectively for two waves, where k is the wave number. The ratio of ϕ_1 / ϕ_2 is

(a) 6 / 7 (b) 15/22
(c) 22/15 (d) 13/12

11. Assertion (A) To hear distinct beats, difference in frequencies of two sources should be less than 10.

Reason (R) More the number of beats per second, more difficult to hear them.

In the light of above statements, choose of most appropriate answer from the options given below.

(a) Both A and R are true and R is the correct explanation of A.

(b) Both A and R are true but R is not the correct explanation of A.

(c) A is true but R is false.

(d) A is false but R is true.

12. Two pulses in a stretched string whose centres are initially 8 cm apart are moving towards each other as shown in the figure. The speed of each pulse is 2 cm/s. After 2 s, the total energy of the pulses will be

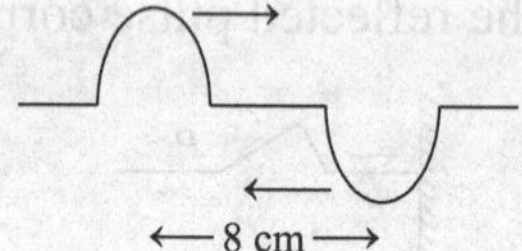

(a) zero

(b) purely kinetic

(c) purely potential

(d) partly kinetic and partly potential

13. Statement I Velocity of particles, while crossing mean position in case of stationary waves varies from maximum at anti-nodes and zero at nodes.

Statement II All particles between two successive nodes cross the mean position together.

In light of above statements, choose the most appropriate answer from the options given below.

(a) Both Statement I and Statement II are correct.

(b) Both Statement I and Statement II are incorrect.

(c) Statement I is correct and Statement II is incorrect.

(d) Statement I is incorrect and Statement II is correct.

14. Three waves of equal frequency having amplitudes 10 mm, 4 mm and 7 mm arrives at a given point with successive phase difference of $\frac{\pi}{2}$.

The amplitude of the resulting wave (in mm) is given by

(a) 7 (b) 6
(c) 5 (d) 4

15. Two loudspeakers L_1 and L_2 driven by a common oscillator and amplifier, are arranged as shown in figure. The frequency of the oscillator is gradually increased from zero and the detector at M records a series of maxima and minima. If the speed of sound is 340 ms^{-1}, then the frequency at which the first maximum is observed is

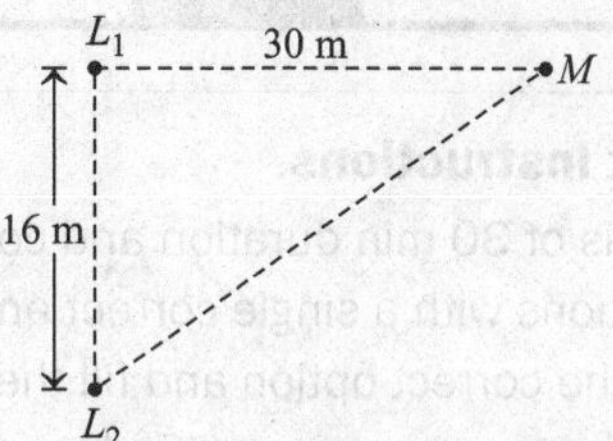

(a) 85 Hz (b) 330 Hz
(c) 496 Hz (d) 220 Hz

Response Index

01	a	b	c	d	11	a	b	c	d
02	a	b	c	d	12	a	b	c	d
03	a	b	c	d	13	a	b	c	d
04	a	b	c	d	14	a	b	c	d
05	a	b	c	d	15	a	b	c	d
06	a	b	c	d					
07	a	b	c	d					
08	a	b	c	d					
09	a	b	c	d					
10	a	b	c	d					

Performance Scanner

> 90% Excellent !	You have mastered these topics. The concepts of these topics are at your fingertips. Move on to the next test and maintain this momentum.
76-90% Very Good !	You have a good command over these topics. Revise them again after a few days and enhance your performance.
60-75% Good !	You have a wide scope to learn more in these topics. Revise them again.
<60% Not Satisfactory!	You have a long way ahead of you to master in these topics. Revise them thoroughly.

Test 3

Syllabus
- Standing Waves in String and Organ Pipes
- Fundamental Mode and Harmonics

For deeper insight **Scan the QR Code** 

Important Instructions

- The test is of 30 min duration and contains 15 Multiple Choice Questions (Four options with a single correct answer).
- Choose the correct option and fill the OMR given on the last page of this test accordingly.
- At some instances, you may find more than 1 option may be correct in such circumstances you have to judge the most appropriate answer as per the conditions given in the question.

1. n_1 is the frequency of the pipe closed at one end and n_2 is the frequency of the pipe open at both ends. If both are joined end-to-end, find the fundamental frequency of closed pipe, so formed.

(a) $\dfrac{n_1 n_2}{n_2 + 2n_1}$ (b) $\dfrac{n_1 n_2}{2n_2 + n_1}$

(c) $\dfrac{n_1 + 2n_2}{n_2 n_1}$ (d) $\dfrac{2n_1 + n_2}{n_2 n_1}$

2. For a standing wave, $y = 10\sin\left(\dfrac{\pi}{18}x\right)\cos(84\pi t)$ m

The distance (in metre) between a node and the next anti-node is

(a) 8.5 (b) 9

(c) 18 (d) 19

3. A string of length 3 m is fixed at both ends. If this string vibrates in its third normal mode with a frequency of 600 Hz, then the waves would travel on it with a velocity of

(a) 1200 m/s

(b) 250 m/s

(c) 600 m/s

(d) 1400 m/s

4. An open pipe is suddenly closed with the result that the second overtone of the closed pipe is observed to be higher in frequency by 200 Hz than the first overtone of the original pipe. The fundamental frequency of the open pipe will be

(a) 400 Hz (b) 300 Hz

(c) 150 Hz (d) 200 Hz

5. The equation for the vibration of a string fixed at both ends vibrating in its third harmonic is given by $y = 4\text{ cm}\sin[(0.9\text{ cm}^{-1})x]\cos[(600\pi\text{s}^{-1})t]$ The length of the string is

(a) 24.6 cm (b) 12.5 cm

(c) 10.5 cm (d) 15.7 cm

6. **Assertion (A)** The frequencies of the first three harmonics in a closed pipe bear a ratio $1:3:5$.

Reason (R) Frequency is an odd multiple of $\dfrac{v}{4l}$, where l is the length of the pipe.

In the light of above statements, choose of most appropriate answer from the options given below.

(a) Both A and R are true and R is the correct explanation of A.

(b) Both A and R are true but R is not the correct explanation of A.

(c) A is true but R is false.

(d) A is false but R is true.

7. A cylindrical tube, open at both ends, has a fundamental frequency f_0 in air. The tube is dipped vertically into water such that half of its length is inside water. The fundamental frequency of the air column now is

(a) $\dfrac{3f_0}{4}$

(b) f_0

(c) $\dfrac{f_0}{2}$

(d) $2f_0$

8. Spacing between two successive nodes in a standing wave on a string is x. If frequency of the standing wave is kept unchanged but tension in the string is trippled , then new spacing between successive nodes will become

(a) $x/\sqrt{2}$ (b) $\frac{\sqrt{3}}{2}x$

(c) $x/2$ (d) $2x$

9. An organ pipe P_1, closed at one end vibrating in its first harmonic and another pipe P_2, open at both ends vibrating in its third harmonic, are in resonance with a given tuning fork. The ratio of the lengths of P_1 and P_2 is

(a) 8/3 (b) 1/6

(c) 1/2 (d) 1/3

10. The fundamental frequency of a closed organ pipe of length 40 cm is equal to the second overtone of an organ pipe open at both the ends. The length of organ pipe open at both the ends is

(a) 80 cm (b) 100 cm

(c) 120 cm (d) 240 cm

11. **Assertion (A)** Sound produced by an open organ pipe is richer than the sound produced by a closed organ pipe.

Reason (R) Outside air can enter the pipe from both ends, in case of open organ pipe.

In the light of above statements, choose of most appropriate answer from the options given below.

(a) Both A and R are true and R is the correct explanation of A.

(b) Both A and R are true but R is not the correct explanation of A.

(c) A is true but R is false.

(d) A is false but R is true.

12. A glass tube 1 m long and open at both ends is immersed vertically in a water tank completely. A tuning fork of 720 Hz is vibrated and kept at the upper end of the tube and the tube is gradually raised out of water. The total number of resonances heard before the tube comes out of water, taking velocity of sound air 340 m/s is

(a) 12 (b) 5 (c) 8 (d) 4

13. A source of sound placed at the open end of a resonance column sends an acoustic wave of pressure amplitude ρ_0 inside the tube. It the atmospheric pressure is ρ_A, then the ratio of minimum and maximum pressure at the closed end of the tube will be

(a) $\frac{(\rho_A+\rho_0)}{(\rho_A-\rho_0)}$ (b) $\frac{(\rho_A+2\rho_0)}{(\rho_A-2\rho_0)}$

(c) $\frac{\rho_A-\rho_0}{\rho_A+\rho_0}$ (d) $\frac{\left(\rho_A+\frac{1}{2}\rho_0\right)}{\left(\rho_A-\frac{1}{2}\rho_0\right)}$

14. Two identical flutes produce fundamental notes of frequency 300 Hz at 27°C. If the temperature of air in one flute is increased to 33°C, the number of the beats heard per second will be

(a) 1 (b) 2 (c) 3 (d) 4

15. For a certain organ pipe, three successive resonance frequencies are observed at 425, 595 and 765 Hz. The speed of sound in air is 340 ms^{-1}. The pipe is a

(a) closed pipe of length 1 m

(b) closed pipe of length 2 m

(c) open pipe of length 1 m

(d) open pipe of length 2 m

Response Index

01	a	b	c	d	11	a	b	c	d
02	a	b	c	d	12	a	b	c	d
03	a	b	c	d	13	a	b	c	d
04	a	b	c	d	14	a	b	c	d
05	a	b	c	d	15	a	b	c	d
06	a	b	c	d					
07	a	b	c	d					
08	a	b	c	d					
09	a	b	c	d					
10	a	b	c	d					

Performance Scanner

> 90% Excellent !	You have mastered these topics. The concepts of these topics are at your fingertips. Move on to the next test and maintain this momentum.
76-90% Very Good !	You have a good command over these topics. Revise them again after a few days and enhance your performance.
60-75% Good !	You have a wide scope to learn more in these topics. Revise them again.
<60% Not Satisfactory!	You have a long way ahead of you to master in these topics. Revise them thoroughly.

Chapter Break Thru

Syllabus

- Longitudinal and Transverse Waves
- Speed of Travelling Wave
- Displacement Relation for a Progressive Wave
- Principle of Superposition of Waves
- Reflection of Waves
- Beats
- Standing Waves in String and Organ Pipes
- Fundamental Mode and Harmonics

Important Instructions

- The test is of 45 min duration and contains 30 Multiple Choice Questions (Four options with a single correct answer).
- Choose the correct option and fill the OMR given on the last page of this test accordingly.
- At some instances, you may find more than 1 option may be correct, in such circumstances you have to judge the most appropriate answer as per the conditions given in the question.

1. The equation of wave on a string of linear mass density 0.04 kg-m^{-1} is given by $y = 0.02\sin\left[2\pi\left(\frac{1}{0.04} - \frac{x}{0.50}\right)\right]$. The tension in the string is

(a) 4.0 N (b) 12.5 N
(c) 0.5 N (d) 6.25 N

2. A progressive sound wave of frequency 500 Hz is travelling through air with a speed of 350 ms^{-1}. A compression maximum appears at a place at a given instant. The minimum time interval after which the rarefaction maximum occurs at the same point, is

(a) 200 s (b) $\frac{1}{250}$ s
(c) $\frac{1}{500}$ s (d) $\frac{1}{1000}$ s

3. The displacement equation of a travelling wave is as follows $y = 4\cos 2\pi(5t - 0.0040x + 0.25)$, where x and y are in cm and t in seconds. The phase difference between oscillatory motion of two points separated by a distance of 2 m is

(a) $16\pi \times 10^{-3}$ rad
(b) 1.6π rad
(c) 1.6×10^{-3} rad
(d) $1.6\pi \times 10^{-3}$ rad

4. Equation of a transverse wave travelling along a rope is given by $y = 10\sin(At - Bx)$, where x and y are expressed in cm and t in seconds. If maximum velocity of the particle and wave velocity are 40 cm/s and 2 m/s respectively, then value of A and B respectively are

(a) 4 s^{-1}, 2 m/s (b) 20 cm/s, 4 s^{-1}
(c) 400 s^{-1}, 2 m/s (d) 4 s^{-1}, 0.2 m/s

5. Wavelengths of two notes in air are 1 m and $1\frac{1}{169}$ m. Each note produces 2 beat/s with a third note of a fixed frequency. The speed of sound in air is

(a) 330 m/s (b) 340 m/s
(c) 350 m/s (d) 328 m/s

6. **Assertion (A)** Transverse waves travel through air in an organ pipe.

Reason (R) Air possesses only volume elasticity.

In the light of above statements, choose of most appropriate answer from the options given below.

(a) Both A and R are true and R is the correct explanation of A
(b) Both A and R are true but R is not the correct explanation of A.
(c) A is true but R is false.
(d) A is false but R is true.

7. A string is stretched between fixed points separated by 75.0 cm. It is observed to have resonant frequencies of 420 Hz and 315 Hz. There are no other resonant frequency between these two, then the lowest resonant frequency for this string is
(a) 105 Hz
(b) 1.05 Hz
(c) 1050 Hz
(d) 10.5 Hz

8. Ratio of frequencies that are possible on a metal rod fixed at one end is
(a) 1 : 2 : 3 : ....
(b) 1 : 3 : 5 : ....
(c) 1 : 4 : 8 : ....
(d) 1 : 5 : 9 : ....

9. Two waves are represented by the equations $y_1 = a\sin(\omega t + kx + 0.62)$ m and $y_2 = a\cos(\omega t + kx)$ m, where x is in metre and t is in second. The phase difference between them is
(a) 1.25 rad (b) 1.57 rad
(c) 0.57 rad (d) 0.95 rad

10. S_1 and S_2 are two coherent sources of sound having no initial phase difference. The velocity of sound is 340 m/s. A minima will be formed on the line passing through S_2 and perpendicular to the line joining S_1 and S_2, if the frequency of both the sources is

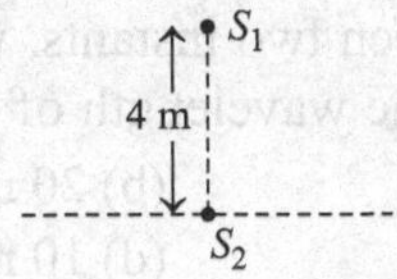

(a) 50 Hz (b) 60 Hz
(c) 70 Hz (d) 40 Hz

11. A steel rod 200 cm long is clamped at its middle. The fundamental frequency of longitudinal vibrations of the rod is given as 2 kHz, the speed of sound in steel is
(a) 800 km/s
(b) 400 km/s
(c) 4 km/s
(d) 8 km/s

12. Two tuning forks have frequencies 376 Hz and 384 Hz, respectively. When they are sounded together, they produce 4 beats. After hearing the maximum sound, how long will it take to hear the minimum sound?
(a) $\frac{1}{2}$ s (b) $\frac{1}{4}$ s
(c) $\frac{1}{8}$ s (d) $\frac{1}{16}$ s

13. A fork A has frequency 3% more than the standard fork and B has a frequency 6% less than the frequency of same standard fork. The forks A and B, when sounded together produced 10 beats/s. The frequency of fork A is
(a) 116.4 Hz
(b) 114.4 Hz
(c) 122.4 Hz
(d) 238.8 Hz

14. Three similar wires of frequency n_1, n_2 and n_3 are joined to make one wire. Its frequency will be
(a) $n = n_1 + n_2 + n_3$
(b) $\frac{1}{n} = \frac{1}{n_1} + \frac{1}{n_2} + \frac{1}{n_3}$
(c) $\frac{1}{\sqrt{n}} = \frac{1}{\sqrt{n_1}} + \frac{1}{\sqrt{n_2}} + \frac{1}{n_3}$
(d) $\frac{1}{n} = \frac{1}{n_1^2} + \frac{1}{n_2^2} + \frac{1}{n_3^2}$

15. A uniform wire of length L, diameter D and density ρ is stretched by a tension $4T$. The correct relation between its fundamental frequency f, length L and diameter D is
(a) $f \propto \frac{1}{LD}$ (b) $f \propto \frac{1}{L\sqrt{D}}$
(c) $f \propto \frac{1}{D^2}$ (d) $f \propto \frac{1}{LD^2}$

16. The frequency of a stretched uniform wire under tension is in resonance with the fundamental frequency of a closed tube. If the tension in the wire is increased by 10 N, it is in resonance with the first overtone of the closed tube. The initial tension in the wire is
(a) $\frac{5}{4}$ N (b) 4 N
(c) 8 N (d) $\frac{10}{3}$ N

17. Two vibrating strings of same length, same cross-section area and stretched to same tension is made of materials with densities ρ and 4ρ. Each string is fixed at both ends. If v_1 represents the fundamental mode of vibration of the one made with density ρ and v_2 for another, then v_1 / v_2 is

(a) $\frac{1}{2}$ (b) 2

(c) $\sqrt{2}$ (d) $\frac{1}{\sqrt{2}}$

18. Statement I When we start filling an empty bucket with water, the pitch of sound produced goes on decreasing.

Statement II The frequency of man voice is usually higher than that of woman.

In the light of above statements, choose of most appropriate answer from the options given below.

(a) Both Statement I and Statement II are correct.

(b) Both Statement I and Statement II are incorrect.

(c) Statement I is correct and Statement II are incorrect.

(d) Statement I is incorrect and Statement II are correct.

19. Two tuning fork when sounded together, produce 6 beat/s. One of the fork is in unison with 27 cm length of sonometer wire and other with 29 cm length of the same wire. The frequencies of the two tuning forks are

(a) 87, 81 Hz (b) 42, 39 Hz

(c) 81, 78 Hz (d) 84, 81 Hz

20. The transverse displacement of a string (clamped at its both ends) is given by

$y = 0.04 \sin\left(\frac{\pi}{3}x\right)\cos(60\pi t)$, where x and y are is in metres and t is in seconds. If the length of the string is 2.0 m and its mass is 2×10^{-2} kg, then tension in the string is

(a) 648 N (b) 324 N (c) 216 N (d) 162 N

21. A sound wave $y = A_0 \sin(\omega t - kx)$ is reflected from a rigid wall with 25% of its amplitude. The equation of the reflected wave is

(a) $y = \frac{5}{10} A_0 \sin(\omega t + kx)$

(b) $y = -\frac{1}{4} A_0 \sin(\omega t + kx)$

(c) $y = \frac{64}{100} A_0 \sin(\omega t - kx)$

(d) $y = \frac{25}{10} A_0 \cos(\omega t - kx)$

22. Consider the three waves z_1, z_2 and z_3 as $z_1 = A\sin(2kx - \omega t)$, $z_2 = A\sin(2kx + \omega t)$ and $z_3 = A\sin(2ky - \omega t)$. Which of the following represent standing wave?

(a) $z_1 + z_2$ (b) $z_2 + z_3$

(c) $z_3 + z_1$ (d) $z_1 + z_2 + z_3$

23. A number of tuning forks are arranged in the order of increasing frequency and any two successive tuning forks produce 4 beats/s, when sounded together. If the last tuning fork has a frequency octane higher than that of the first tuning fork and the frequency of first tuning fork is 256 Hz, then the number of tuning fork is

(a) 63 (b) 64

(c) 65 (d) 66

24. Two sinusoidal waves with same wavelengths and amplitudes travel in opposite directions along a string with a speed 20 ms^{-1}. If the minimum time interval between two instants, when the string is flat is 0.1 s, the wavelength of the waves is

(a) 25 m (b) 20 m

(c) 4 m (d) 10 m

25. The amplitude of a wave disturbance propagating in the positive x-direction is given by $y = \frac{1}{1+x^2}$ at $t = 0$ and $y = \frac{1}{2+x^2-2x}$ at $t = 2$ s, where x and y are in metre. Assuming that the shape of the wave

disturbance does not change during the propagation, the speed of the wave is
(a) 0.5 m/s
(b) 1 m/s
(c) 1.5 m/s
(d) 2 m/s

26. Two string A and B produce 5 beats per seconds. Tension in B is increased and beat frequency observed is 3 per second.
If frequency of A is 427 Hz, then initial frequency of B in Hz is
(a) 432 (b) 422
(c) 427 (d) 417

27. Three sound waves of equal amplitudes have frequencies $(v-1)$, v and $(v+1)$. They superpose to give beats. The number of beats produced per second will be
(a) 3 (b) 2
(c) 1 (d) 4

28. A wave disturbance in a medium is described by $y(x,t)=0.2\cos\left(50\pi t+\frac{\pi}{2}\right)\cos(10\pi x)$, where x and y are in metres and t in seconds.
(a) A displacement node occurs at $x=0.15$ m
(b) An anti-node occurs at $x=0.3$ m
(c) The wavelength of the wave is 0.2 m
(d) The speed of the wave of 8.0 m/s

29. Following is given the equation of a stationary wave (all in SI units)

$$y=(0.06)\sin(2\pi x)\cos(5\pi t)$$

Match the Column I with Column II.

Column I	Column II
A. Amplitude of constituent wave	1. 0.06
B. Position of node at $x=\ldots$ m	2. 0.5
C. Position of antinode at $x=\ldots$ m	3. 0.25
D. Amplitude at $x=\frac{3}{4}$ m	4. 0.03

Choose the correct answer from the options given below.
(a) A-2, B-1, C-3, D-4 (b) A-1, B-4, C-2, D-3
(c) A-4, B-2, C-3, D-1 (d) A-2, B-3, C-4, D-1

30. The frequencies of two sound sources are 258 Hz and 261 Hz. At $t=0$, the intensity of sound is maximum. Then, the phase difference at the time $t=\frac{1}{9}$ s will be
(a) $\frac{2\pi}{3}$ (b) π
(c) $\frac{\pi}{2}$ (d) $\frac{\pi}{4}$

Response Index

01 ⓐ ⓑ ⓒ ⓓ	14 ⓐ ⓑ ⓒ ⓓ	27 ⓐ ⓑ ⓒ ⓓ
02 ⓐ ⓑ ⓒ ⓓ	15 ⓐ ⓑ ⓒ ⓓ	28 ⓐ ⓑ ⓒ ⓓ
03 ⓐ ⓑ ⓒ ⓓ	16 ⓐ ⓑ ⓒ ⓓ	29 ⓐ ⓑ ⓒ ⓓ
04 ⓐ ⓑ ⓒ ⓓ	17 ⓐ ⓑ ⓒ ⓓ	30 ⓐ ⓑ ⓒ ⓓ
05 ⓐ ⓑ ⓒ ⓓ	18 ⓐ ⓑ ⓒ ⓓ	
06 ⓐ ⓑ ⓒ ⓓ	19 ⓐ ⓑ ⓒ ⓓ	
07 ⓐ ⓑ ⓒ ⓓ	20 ⓐ ⓑ ⓒ ⓓ	
08 ⓐ ⓑ ⓒ ⓓ	21 ⓐ ⓑ ⓒ ⓓ	
09 ⓐ ⓑ ⓒ ⓓ	22 ⓐ ⓑ ⓒ ⓓ	
10 ⓐ ⓑ ⓒ ⓓ	23 ⓐ ⓑ ⓒ ⓓ	
11 ⓐ ⓑ ⓒ ⓓ	24 ⓐ ⓑ ⓒ ⓓ	
12 ⓐ ⓑ ⓒ ⓓ	25 ⓐ ⓑ ⓒ ⓓ	
13 ⓐ ⓑ ⓒ ⓓ	26 ⓐ ⓑ ⓒ ⓓ	

Performance Scanner

> 90% Excellent !	You have mastered this chapter. The concepts of this chapter are at your fingertips. Move on to the next chapter and maintain this momentum.
76-90% Very Good !	You have a good command over this chapter. Revise the chapter again after a few days and enhance your performance.
60-75% Good !	You have a wide scope to learn more for this chapter. Revise this chapter again.
<60% Not Satisfactory!	You have a long way ahead of you to master this chapter. Revise it thoroughly.

For Online Chapter Test **Scan the QR Code**

For Online Unit Test **Scan the QR Code**

Space for Rough Work

Space for Rough Work

Space for Rough Work

MEDACE
NEET (UG)
SELF ASSESSMENT KIT

Test Booklet No. **3947115**

Test Booklet Code **SPT1**

Syllabus Part Thru 1
(Based on 11th Syllabus)

Chapters Covered

- Units and Measurement
- Motion in a Straight Line
- Motion in a Plane
- Laws of Motion
- Work, Power and Energy
- Rotational Motion
- Gravitation

Important Instructions

- The test is of 45 minutes and the Test Booklet contains 45 multiple choice questions (four options with a single correct answer) from Physics.
- Candidates are advised to read all questions before they start attempting the question paper.
- Each question carries 4 marks. For each correct response, the candidate will get 4 marks. For each incorrect response, one mark will be deducted from the total scores. The maximum marks are 180.
- In the event of candidate marking more than one option, then one mark will be deducted.
- Use **Blue/Black Point Pen** only for writing particular on this page/ marking response on Answer Sheet.

Name of the Candidate (In Capitals) ____________________

____

Candidate's Signature ____________________

Invigilator's Signature ____________________

Facsimile signature stamp of center superintendent____________________

Do not open this Booklet until you start attempting the Test

Physics (Q. No. 1-45)

1. Assuming that the mass m of the largest stone that can be moved by a flowing river depends upon the velocity v of the water, its density ρ and the acceleration due to gravity g. Then, m is directly proportional to

(a) v^3 (b) v^4
(c) v^5 (d) v^6

2. A thin metal disc of radius 0.25 m and mass 2 kg starts from rest and rolls down an inclined plane. If its rotational kinetic energy is 4 J at the foot of the inclined plane, then its linear velocity at the same point is

(a) 1.2 ms^{-1} (b) $2\sqrt{2}$ ms^{-1}
(c) 20 ms^{-1} (d) 2 ms^{-1}

3. Assertion (A) An air bubble rises up in a water tank, then its potential energy increases.

Reason (R) Gravitation potential energy of a body for small height above the earth's surface is mgh.

In the light of above statements, choose the most appropriate answer from the options given below.

(a) Both A and R are true and R is the correct explanation of A.
(b) Both A and R are true but R is not the correct explanation of A.
(c) A is true but R is false.
(d) A is false but R is true

4. Resultant of two equal magnitude vectors has a magnitude as that of any of vector. Angle between vectors is

(a) 0° (b) 90° (c) 120° (d) 135°

5. Two particles, each of mass 1 kg and at a distance of 1m from origin are as shown.

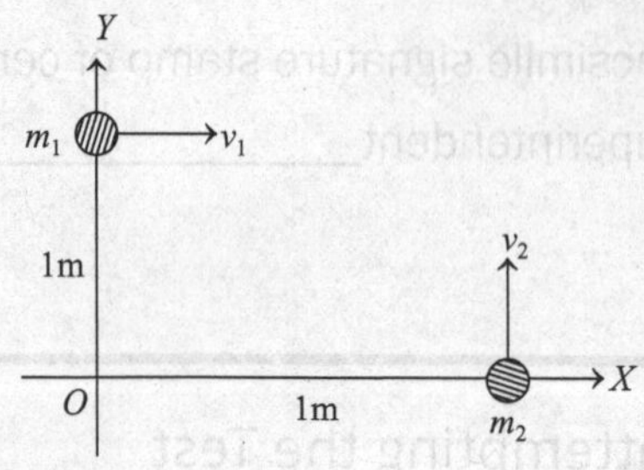

If $|\mathbf{v}_1| = |\mathbf{v}_2| = 1$ m/s, then angular momentum of system of particles given is

(a) zero (b) 2 kg m^2 s^{-1}
(c) -2 kg m^2 s^{-1} (d) $\sqrt{2}$ kg m^2 s^{-1}

6. Moment of inertia of a solid cylinder of length L and diameter D about an axis passing through its centre of gravity and perpendicular to its geometric axis is

(a) $M\left(\frac{D^2}{4}+\frac{L^2}{12}\right)$

(b) $M\left(\frac{L^2}{16}+\frac{D^2}{8}\right)$

(c) $M\left(\frac{D^2}{4}+\frac{L^2}{6}\right)$

(d) $M\left(\frac{L^2}{12}+\frac{D^2}{16}\right)$

7. Forces F_1, F_2 and F_3 are acting on a point mass of 2 kg as shown.

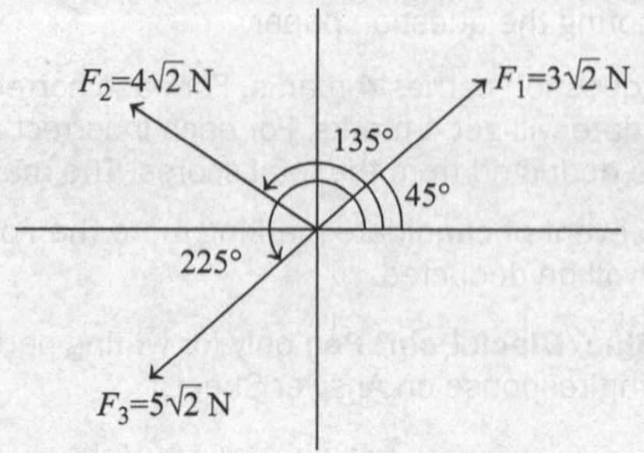

Acceleration of mass is

(a) π m/s^2 (b) 2π m/s^2
(c) 3π m/s^2 (d) $\frac{3}{2}\pi$ m/s^2

8. A marble block of mass 2 kg lying on ice when given a velocity of 6 ms^{-1} is stopped by friction in 10 s. Then, the coefficient of friction is

(a) 0.02 (b) 0.03
(c) 0.06 (d) 0.01

9. A fireman of mass 60 kg slides down a pole. He is pressing the pole with a force of 600 N. The coefficient of friction between the hands and the pole is 0.5, with what acceleration will the fireman slide down? (Take, $g = 10 \text{ m/s}^2$)

(a) 1 m/s^2 (b) 2.5 m/s^2
(c) 10 m/s^2 (d) 5 m/s^2

10. A disc of mass 10 g is kept floating horizontally in air by firing bullets, each of mass 5 g, with the same velocity at the same rate of 10 bullets per second. The bullets rebound with the same speed in positive direction. The velocity of each bullet at the time of impact is

(a) 196 cms^{-1} (b) 98 cms^{-1}
(c) 49 cms^{-1} (d) 392 cms^{-1}

11. A batsman hits back a ball straight in the direction of the bowler without changing its initial speed of 12 ms^{-1}. If the mass of the ball is 0.15 kg, the impulse (in N-s) imparted to the ball is

(a) 1.5 (b) 3.6
(c) 9.4 (d) 7.3

12. The dimensions of $\frac{a}{b}$ in the equation $p = \frac{a - t^2}{bx}$, where p is pressure, x is distance and t is time, are

(a) $[M^2LT^{-3}]$ (b) $[MT^{-2}]$
(c) $[LT^{-3}]$ (d) $[ML^3T^{-1}]$

13. Which one of the following is not correct?

(a) Dimensional formula of thermal conductivity (K) is $[M^1L^1T^{-3}K^{-1}]$.
(b) Dimensional formula of potential (V) is $[M^1L^2T^3A^{-1}]$.
(c) Dimensional formula of permeability of free space (μ_0) is $[M^1L^1T^{-2}A^{-2}]$.
(d) Dimensional formula of RC is $[M^0L^0T]$.

14. Time period of revolution of a nearest satellite around a planet of radius R is T. Period of revolution around another planet, whose radius is $3R$ but having same density is

(a) T (b) $3T$
(c) $9T$ (d) $3\sqrt{3}\,T$

15. If W_1, W_2 and W_3 represent the work done in moving a particle from A to B along three different paths 1, 2 and 3 respectively (as shown) in a gravitional field of point mass m, then

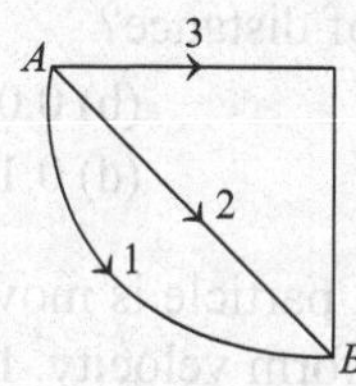

(a) $W_1 = W_2 = W_3$
(b) $W_1 > W_2 > W_3$
(c) $W_1 > W_2 < W_3$
(d) $W_1 < W_2 < W_3$

16. The gravitational potential difference between the surface of a planet and a point 20 m above it is 14 J kg^{-1}. The work done in moving a 2.0 kg mass by 8.0 m on a slope of 60° from the horizontal, is equal to

(a) 7 J (b) 9.7 J
(c) 16 J (d) 32 J

17. A particle moves along a curve of unknown shape but the magnitude of the force is constant and always acts along tangent to the curve. The force is

(a) conservative
(b) non-conservative
(c) conservative as well as non-conservative
(d) neither conservative nor non-conservative

18 Two satellites A and B have their masses in the ratio 3 : 1 are orbiting in circular orbits of radii r and $4r$. Then, ratio of total mechanical energy of A and B is

(a) 1 : 3
(b) 3 : 1
(c) 3 : 4
(d) 12 : 1

19. A block of mass 5 kg is resting on a smooth surface. At what angle a force of 20 N be acted on the body, so that it will acquire a kinetic energy of 40 J after moving 4 m?

(a) 30° (b) 45°
(c) 60° (d) 120°

20. The vernier scale of a travelling microscope has 50 divisions which coincide with 49 main scale divisions. If each main scale division is 0.5 mm, then what is the minimum inaccuracy in the measurement of distance?

(a) 0.02 mm (b) 0.05 mm
(c) 0.01 mm (d) 0.1 mm

21. **Statement I** A particle is moving on a straight line with a uniform velocity. Its angular momentum is always zero.

Statement II The momentum is zero when particle moves with a uniform velocity.

In the light of above statements, choose the most appropriate answer from the options given below.

(a) Both Statement I and Statement II are correct.
(b) Both Statement I and Statement II are incorrect.
(c) Statement I is correct but Statement II is incorrect.
(d) Statement I is incorrect but Statement II is correct.

22. If E = energy, G = gravitational constant, I = impulse and M = mass, then dimensions of $\frac{GIM^2}{E^2}$ are same as that of

(a) time (b) mass
(c) length (d) force

23. A bullet of mass 0.04 kg moving with a speed of 90 ms^{-1} enters a heaavy wooden block and is stopped after a distance of 60 cm. The average resistive force exerted by the block on the bullet is

(a) 100 N (b) 270 N
(c) 50 N (d) 298 N

24. A ball falling freely from a height of 4.9 m/s, hits a horizontal surface. If $e = \frac{3}{4}$, then the ball will hit the surface second time after

(a) 1.0 s (b) 1.5 s
(c) 2.0 s (d) 3.0 s

25. A particle of mass 10 g moves along a circle of radius 6.4 cm with a constant tangential acceleration. What is the magnitude of this acceleration, if the kinetic energy of the particle becomes 8×10^{-4} J by the end of the second revolution after the beginning?

(a) 0.1 m/s^2 (b) 0.6 m/s^2
(c) 0.8 m/s^2 (d) 1.6 m/s^2

26. In going from one city to another, a car travels 75 km north, 60 km north-west and 20 km east. The magnitude of displacement between the two cities is (Take, $\frac{1}{\sqrt{2}} = 0.7$)

(a) 170 km (b) 137 km (c) 119 km (d) 140 km

27. Two forces F_1 and F_2 are acting on a particle as shown in the figure. The acceleration of the particle is along X-axis. The value of force F_1 is (Take, $\sin 37° = \frac{3}{5}$)

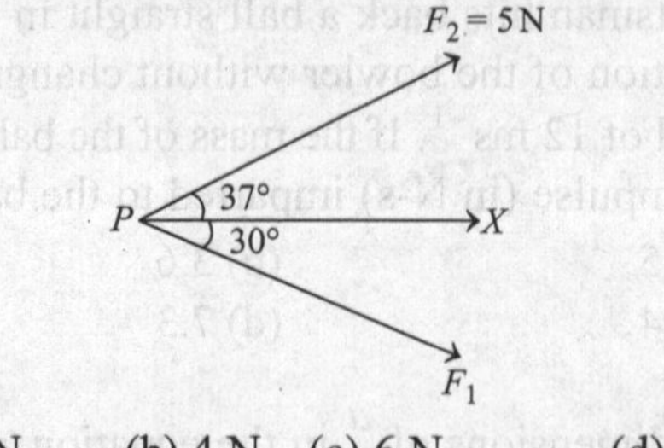

(a) 2 N (b) 4 N (c) 6 N (d) 8 N

28. The resultant of three vectors **OA**, **OB** and **OC** shown in the figure is

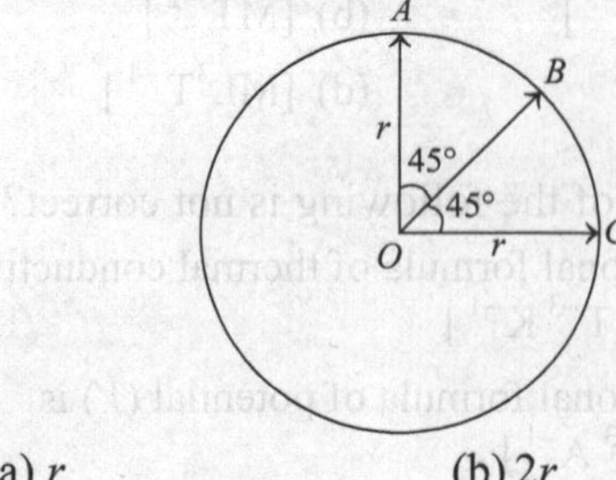

(a) r (b) $2r$
(c) $r(1+\sqrt{2})$ (d) $r(\sqrt{2}-1)$

29. A car is going north at $10\sqrt{2}$ ms^{-1} turns right through an angle of 90° without changing the speed. The change in velocity of car is

(a) 20 ms^{-1} in south-east direction
(b) $20\sqrt{2}$ ms^{-1} in south-east direction
(c) 20 ms^{-1} in north-east direction
(d) 20 ms^{-1} in north-west direction

30. You measure two quantities as $A = 1.0 \text{ m} \pm 0.2 \text{ m}$, $B = 2.0 \text{ m} \pm 0.2 \text{ m}$. We should report correct value for $\sqrt{AB}$ as

(a) $1.4 \text{ m} \pm 0.4 \text{ m}$
(b) $1.41 \text{ m} \pm 0.15 \text{ m}$
(c) $1.4 \text{ m} \pm 0.3 \text{ m}$
(d) $1.4 \text{ m} \pm 0.2 \text{ m}$

31. In a village game, three boys A, B and C are in motion. The velocity of boy A seen by boy B is 1 ms^{-1} towards the north-east direction. The velocity of the boy B seen by boy C is 1 ms^{-1} towards the north-west direction. The direction of velocity of boy C seen by boy A is

(a) 1 ms^{-1} towards south
(b) 1 ms^{-1} towards east
(c) $\sqrt{2} \text{ ms}^{-1}$ towards south
(d) $\sqrt{2} \text{ ms}^{-1}$ towards north

32. The value of $\hat{\mathbf{i}} \times (\hat{\mathbf{i}} \times \mathbf{a}) + \hat{\mathbf{j}} \times (\hat{\mathbf{j}} \times \mathbf{a}) + \hat{\mathbf{k}} \times (\hat{\mathbf{k}} \times \mathbf{a})$ is

(a) $\mathbf{a}$
(b) $\mathbf{a} \times \hat{\mathbf{k}}$
(c) $-2\,\mathbf{a}$
(d) $-\mathbf{a}$

33. **Assertion** (A) A sphere is placed in pure rolling condition over a rough inclined surface. Then, force of friction will act in downward direction.

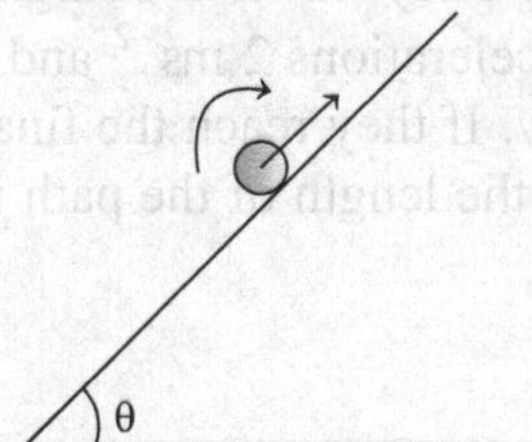

Reason (R) Angular acceleration (actually retardation) due to friction is anti-clockwise.

In the light of above statements, choose the most appropriate answer from the options given below.

(a) Both A and R are true and R is the correct explanation of A.
(b) Both A and R are true but R is not the correct explanation of A.
(c) A is true but R is false.
(d) A is false but R is true.

34. A thin uniform rod of length l and mass m is swinging freely about a horizontal axis passing through its end. Its maximum angular speed is ω. Its centre of mass rises to a maximum height of

(a) $\frac{1}{3}\frac{l^2\omega^2}{g}$ (b) $\frac{1}{6}\frac{l\omega}{g}$ (c) $\frac{1}{2}\frac{l^2\omega^2}{g}$ (d) $\frac{1}{6}\frac{l^2\omega^2}{g}$

35. In List-I, some straight line graphs are given and in List-II, corresponding signs of slopes and intercepts are given. Match the types of graphs of List-I corresponding to signs of slopes and intercepts in List-II and select the correct option from the codes given below.

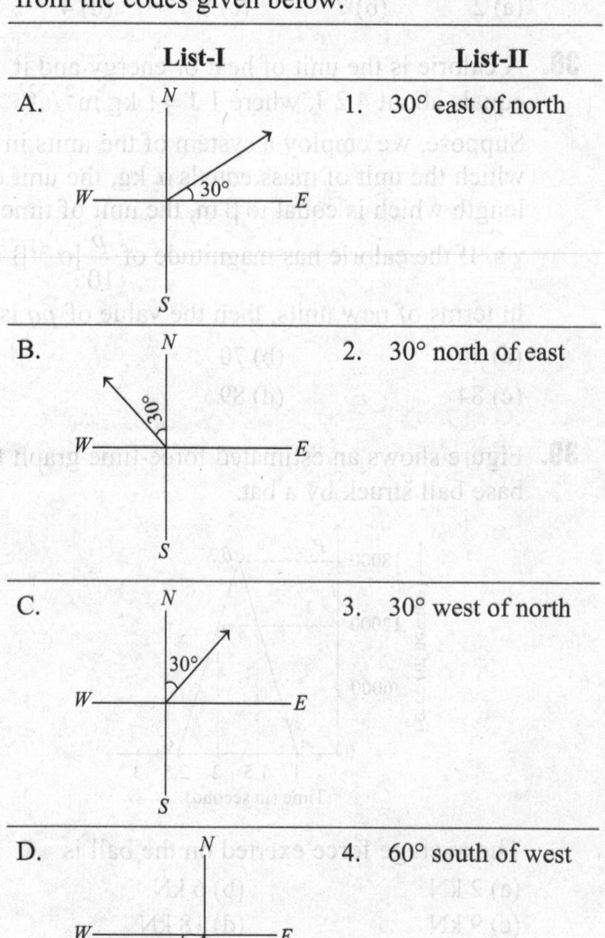

	List-I		List-II
A.		1.	30° east of north
B.		2.	30° north of east
C.		3.	30° west of north
D.		4.	60° south of west

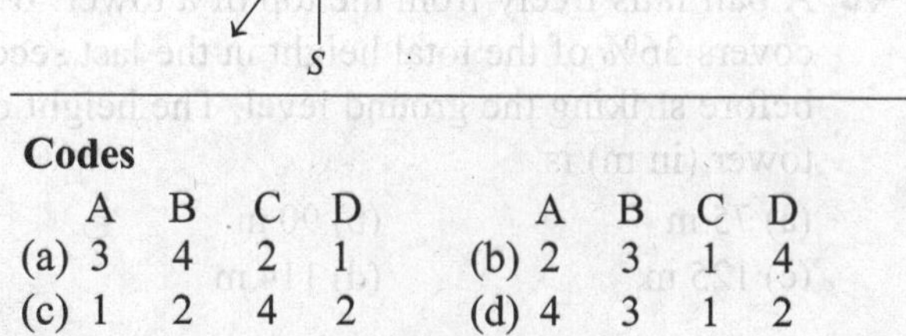

Codes

	A	B	C	D		A	B	C	D
(a)	3	4	2	1	(b)	2	3	1	4
(c)	1	2	4	2	(d)	4	3	1	2

36. A man moves 20 m north, then 10 m east and then $10\sqrt{2}$ m south-west. His displacement is
(a) 20 m north
(b) $10\sqrt{2}$ m north-west
(c) 10 m north
(d) $10\sqrt{2}$ m south-east

37. Infinite number of bodies, each of mass 2 kg are situated on X-axis at a distance 1m, 2m, 4m, 8m, ... respectively from the origin. If the resulting gravitational potential due to this system at the origin is found to be $-xG$, then the value of x is
(a) 2 (b) 7 (c) 8 (d) 4

38. A calorie is the unit of heat or energy and it equals about 4.2 J, where 1 J = 1 kg m^2/s^2. Suppose, we employ a system of the units in which the unit of mass equals α kg, the unit of length which is equal to β m, the unit of time is γ s. If the calorie has magnitude of $\frac{p}{10}[\alpha^{-1}\beta^{-1}\gamma^{q}]$ in terms of new units, then the value of pq is
(a) 40 (b) 70
(c) 84 (d) 89

39. Figure shows an estimated force-time graph for a base ball struck by a bat.

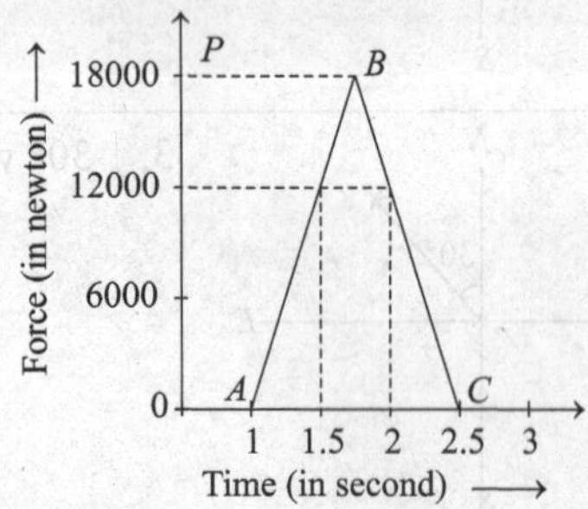

The average force exerted on the ball is
(a) 2 kN (b) 6 kN
(c) 9 kN (d) 18 kN

40 A ball falls freely from the top of a tower. It covers 36% of the total height in the last second before striking the ground level. The height of tower (in m) is
(a) 75 m (b) 90 m
(c) 125 m (d) 114 m

41. A block of mass 5 kg is suspended by a massless rope of length 2 m from the ceiling. A force of 50 N is applied in the horizontal direction at the mid-point P of the rope, as shown in figure.

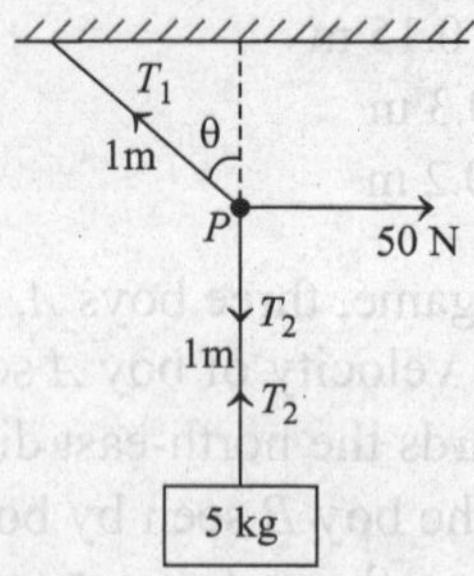

I. The tension T_1 in the rope is $50\sqrt{2}$ N.
II. The tension T_2 in the rope is 50 N.
III. The angle made by the rope with the vertical in equilibrium is 30°.
IV. The angle made by the rope with the vertical in equilibrium is 45°.

Choose the correct statements from the options given below.
(a) II and III
(b) I, II and III
(c) I, II and IV
(d) I, II, III and IV

42. Two cars start off a race with velocities 2 ms^{-1} and 4 ms^{-1}. They travel in straight line with uniform accelerations 2 ms^{-2} and 1ms^{-2} respectively. If they reach the final point at the same time, the length of the path is
(a) 40 m
(b) 24 m
(c) 20 m
(d) 30 m

43. A rope ladder of length 100 m is attached to a balloon of mass m. As the man of mass m climbs the ladder into the balloon basket, the balloon comes down by a vertical distance of 50 m. Then, the increase in potential energy of man divided by the increase in potential energy of balloon is
(a) 4 (b) 2
(c) 8 (d) 6

44. If g is the acceleration due to gravity on the earth's surface, the gain in the potential energy of an object of mass m raised from the surface of the earth to a height equal to the radius R of the earth, is

(a) $2\,mgR$

(b) $\frac{1}{2}\,mgR$

(c) $\frac{1}{4}\,mgR$

(d) mgR

45. Four point masses, each of value m, are placed at the corners of a square $ABCD$ of side l. The moment of inertia of the system about an axis passing through A and parallel to BD is

(a) $\sqrt{3}\,ml^2$

(b) $3\,ml^2$

(c) ml^2

(d) $2\,ml^2$

For Online Syllabus Part Test
Scan the QR Code

Response Index

01 ⓐ ⓑ ⓒ ⓓ	14 ⓐ ⓑ ⓒ ⓓ	27 ⓐ ⓑ ⓒ ⓓ	40 ⓐ ⓑ ⓒ ⓓ
02 ⓐ ⓑ ⓒ ⓓ	15 ⓐ ⓑ ⓒ ⓓ	28 ⓐ ⓑ ⓒ ⓓ	41 ⓐ ⓑ ⓒ ⓓ
03 ⓐ ⓑ ⓒ ⓓ	16 ⓐ ⓑ ⓒ ⓓ	29 ⓐ ⓑ ⓒ ⓓ	42 ⓐ ⓑ ⓒ ⓓ
04 ⓐ ⓑ ⓒ ⓓ	17 ⓐ ⓑ ⓒ ⓓ	30 ⓐ ⓑ ⓒ ⓓ	43 ⓐ ⓑ ⓒ ⓓ
05 ⓐ ⓑ ⓒ ⓓ	18 ⓐ ⓑ ⓒ ⓓ	31 ⓐ ⓑ ⓒ ⓓ	44 ⓐ ⓑ ⓒ ⓓ
06 ⓐ ⓑ ⓒ ⓓ	19 ⓐ ⓑ ⓒ ⓓ	32 ⓐ ⓑ ⓒ ⓓ	45 ⓐ ⓑ ⓒ ⓓ
07 ⓐ ⓑ ⓒ ⓓ	20 ⓐ ⓑ ⓒ ⓓ	33 ⓐ ⓑ ⓒ ⓓ	
08 ⓐ ⓑ ⓒ ⓓ	21 ⓐ ⓑ ⓒ ⓓ	34 ⓐ ⓑ ⓒ ⓓ	
09 ⓐ ⓑ ⓒ ⓓ	22 ⓐ ⓑ ⓒ ⓓ	35 ⓐ ⓑ ⓒ ⓓ	
10 ⓐ ⓑ ⓒ ⓓ	23 ⓐ ⓑ ⓒ ⓓ	36 ⓐ ⓑ ⓒ ⓓ	
11 ⓐ ⓑ ⓒ ⓓ	24 ⓐ ⓑ ⓒ ⓓ	37 ⓐ ⓑ ⓒ ⓓ	
12 ⓐ ⓑ ⓒ ⓓ	25 ⓐ ⓑ ⓒ ⓓ	38 ⓐ ⓑ ⓒ ⓓ	
13 ⓐ ⓑ ⓒ ⓓ	26 ⓐ ⓑ ⓒ ⓓ	39 ⓐ ⓑ ⓒ ⓓ	

Performance Scanner

> 90% Excellent !	You have mastered the first half of NEET syllabus (11th). The concepts of this syllabus are on your fingertips. Maintain this momentum.
76-90% Very Good !	You have a good command over the first half of NEET syllabus (11th). Revise it again after a few days and enhance your performance.
60-75% Good !	You have a wide scope to learn for the first half of NEET syllabus (11th). Revise it again.
<60% Not Satisfactory!	You have a long way ahead of you to master the first half of NEET syllabus (11th). Revise it thoroughly.

Space for Rough Work

Test Booklet No. **3947116**

Test Booklet Code **SPT2**

MEDACE
NEET (UG)
SELF ASSESSMENT KIT

Syllabus Part Thru 2

(Based on 11th Syllabus)

Chapters Covered

- Mechanical Properties of Solids
- Mechanical Properties of Fluids
- Thermal Properties of Matter
- Thermodynamics
- Kinetic Theory of Gases
- Oscillations
- Waves

Important Instructions

- The test is of 45 minutes and the Test Booklet contains 45 multiple choice questions (four options with a single correct answer) from Physics.
- Candidates are advised to read all questions before they start attempting the question paper.
- Each question carries 4 marks. For each correct response, the candidate will get 4 marks. For each incorrect response, one mark will be deducted from the total scores. The maximum marks are 180.
- In the event of candidate marking more than one option, then one mark will be deducted.
- Use **Blue/Black Point Pen** only for writing particular on this page/ marking response on Answer Sheet.

Name of the Candidate (In Capitals) ____________________

____

Candidate's Signature ____________

Invigilator's Signature ____________

Facsimile signature stamp of center superintendent____________

Do not open this Booklet until you start attempting the Test

Physics (Q. No. 1-45)

1. 640 cc of a gas having $\gamma = 5/3$ is suddenly compressed to 80 cc. If the initial pressure is p, then the final pressure will be

(a) $8p$ (b) $32p$
(c) $16p$ (d) $64p$

2. A body A is at a temperature T_A and a body B is at a temperature T_B such that $T_A > T_B$. Bodies A and B are connected. Which of the following statements is/are correct related to two bodies?

I. Body A is hotter than body B.
II. Heat flows from A to B.
III. Heat flows from B to A.

(a) Both I and II
(b) Only I
(c) Both II and III
(d) Both I and II

3. A gas at 27°C in a cylinder has a volume of 4 L and pressure 100 Nm^{-2}. Gas is first compressed at constant temperature, so that the pressure is 150 Nm^{-2}. Then, change in volume is

(a) −1.8 L (b) −1.333 L
(c) −1.2 L (d) −1.777 L

4. Two rods of different materials having coefficients of linear expansion α_1 and α_2 and Young's modulii of elasticity Y_1 and Y_2 respectively, are fixed between two rigid massive walls. The rods are heated such that they undergo the same increase in temperature without bending. If $\alpha_1 : \alpha_2 = 2:3$, then the thermal stress developed in the two rods will be equal if $Y_1 : Y_2$ is equal to

(a) 2 : 3 (b) 3 : 2
(c) 1 : 2 (d) 2 : 1

5. Two wires made of same material are subjected to forces in the ratio 1 : 4. Their lengths are in the ratio 2 : 1 and diameters in the ratio 1 : 3. The ratio of their extensions is

(a) 1 : 3 (b) 2 : 5
(c) 9 : 2 (d) 1 : 2

6. The stress-strain curves for brass, steel and rubber are shown in the figure. The lines A, B and C are for

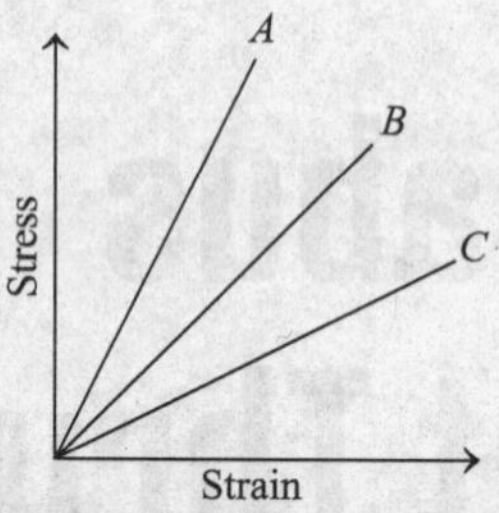

(a) Rubber, brass and steel respectively
(b) Brass, steel and rubber respectively
(c) Steel, brass and rubber respectively
(d) Steel, rubber and brass respectively

7. A tall cylinder is filled with viscous oil. A round pebble is dropped from the top with zero initial velocity. From the plot shown in figure, indicate the one that represents the velocity v of the pebble as a function of time t.

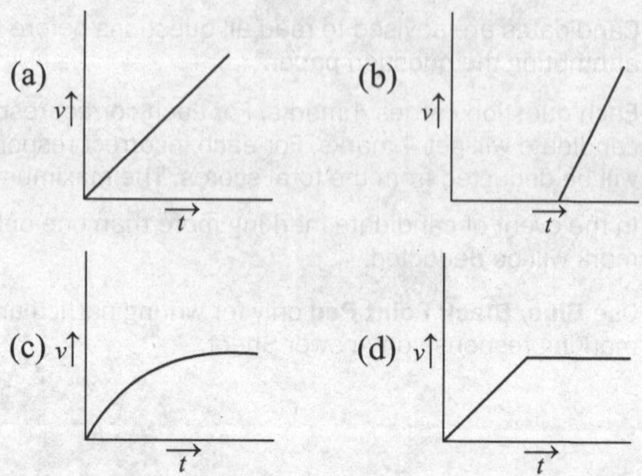

8. Find the minimum force required to drag a hard polythene plate of area 2 m^2 on a thin film of oil of thickness 0.25 cm and $\eta = 15$ poise. Assume the speed of the plate is 10 cms^{-1}.

(a) 2.4×10^7 dyne (b) 1.8×10^7 dyne
(c) 1.2×10^7 dyne (d) 6.0×10^7 dyne

9. The pressure produced by the block standing on one side (as shown in figure) is p. If the size of its length, width and height is doubled, the new pressure will be

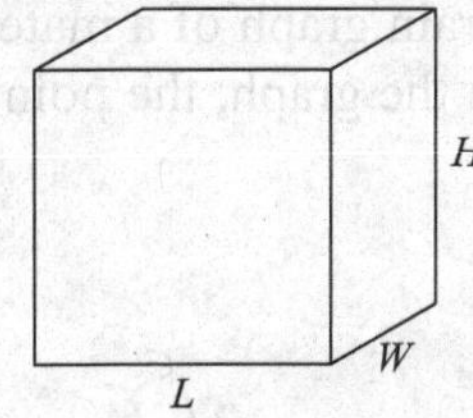

(a) $\frac{p}{2}$ (b) $4p$
(c) $2p$ (d) $8p$

10. In a vehicle lifter, the enclosed gas exerts a force F on a small piston having a diameter of 8 cm. This pressure is transmitted to a second piston of diameter 24 cm. If the mass of the vehicle to be lifted is 1400 kg, then value of F is
(a) 1200 N (b) 1800 N
(c) 1600 N (d) 700 N

11. **Statement I** Longitudinal waves can be propagated through solids and fluids both.

Statement II Solids as well as fluids have non-zero bulk modulus i.e., they can sustain compressive stress.

In the light of above statements, choose the most appropriate answer from the options given below.
(a) Both Statement I and Statement II are correct.
(b) Both Statement I and Statement II are incorrect.
(c) Statement I is correct but Statement II is incorrect.
(d) Statement I is incorrect but Statement II is correct.

12. A body is moving in a room in gravity free space with a velocity of 20 m/s perpendicular to the two walls separated by 5 m. There is no friction and the collisions with the walls are elastic. The motion of the body is
(a) not periodic
(b) periodic but not simple harmonic
(c) periodic and simple harmonic
(d) period with variable time periods

13. 2 kg particle undergoes SHM according to $x = 1.5 \sin\left(\frac{\pi}{4}t + \frac{\pi}{6}\right)$, where x is in metre and t in second. The total mechanical energy of the particle is
(a) 1.39 J (b) 1.72 J
(c) 2.39 J (d) 2.72 J

14. If the initial tension on a stretched string is tripled, then the ratio of the initial and final speed of a transverse wave along the string is
(a) $\sqrt{3}:1$ (b) $1:\sqrt{3}$
(c) $3\sqrt{3}:1$ (d) $1:9$

15. In the equation for a stationary wave given by $y = 5\cos\frac{\pi x}{25}\sin 100\pi t$. Here, x is in cm and t in s.

A node will not occur at distance x equal to
(a) 25 cm
(b) 62.5 cm
(c) 12.5 cm
(d) 37.5 cm

16. A gas mixture consists of 2 moles of oxygen and 4 moles of argon at temperature T. Neglecting all vibrational modes, the total internal energy of the system is
(a) $4RT$
(b) $15RT$
(c) $9RT$
(d) $11RT$

17. **Assertion** (A) Spring balance does not give correct measurement when it has been used for a long time.

Reason (R) Spring does not get longer time to regain its original configuration after use to long time.

In the light of above statements, choose the most appropriate answer from the options given below.
(a) Both A and R are true and R is the correct explanation of A.
(b) Both A and R are true but R is not the correct explanation of A.
(c) A is true but R is false.
(d) A is false but R is true.

18. The p-V graph of a system undergoing thermodynamic transformation is shown in figure. The work done by the system in going from $a \to b \to c$ is 50 J and 20 cal heat is given to the system. The change in internal energy between a and c is

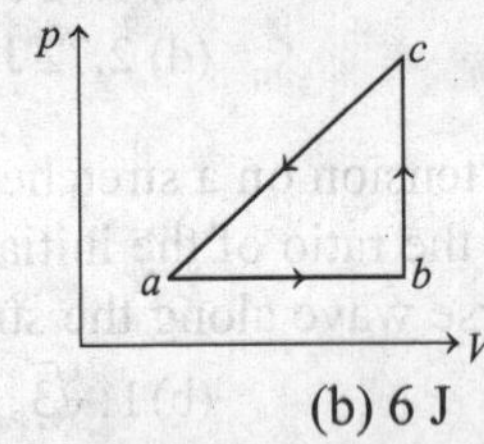

(a) 10 J (b) 6 J
(c) 30 J (d) 34 J

19. Figure given below shows a progressive wave with equation $y = A \sin(\omega t - kx)$

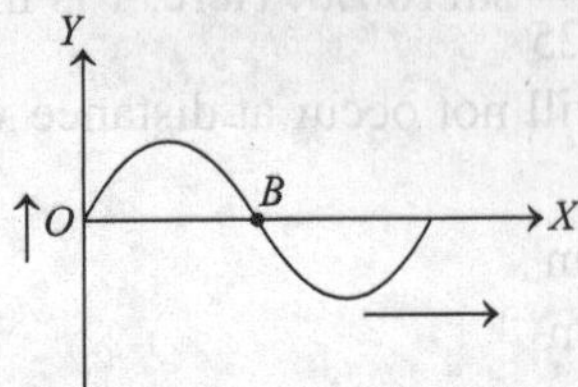

The slope of the curve at B is
(a) ωx (b) kx
(c) kA (d) ωk

20. Two moles of a gas at temperature T and volume V are heated to twice its volume at constant pressure. If $C_p/C_V = \gamma$, then increase in internal energy of the gas is

(a) $\frac{RT}{\gamma - 1}$ (b) $\frac{2RT}{\gamma - 1}$
(c) $\frac{2RT}{3(\gamma - 1)}$ (d) $\frac{2T}{\gamma - 1}$

21. Statement I The stress-strain curves vary from material to material.

Statement II A rubber can be pulled to several times its original length and still returns to its original shape.

In the light of above statements, choose the most appropriate answer from the options given below.
(a) Both Statement I and Statement II are correct.
(b) Both Statement I and Statement II are incorrect.
(c) Statement I is correct but Statement II is incorrect.
(d) Statement II is correct but Statement I is incorrect.

22. The stress-strain graph of a material is shown in the figure. In the graph, the point of proportional limit is

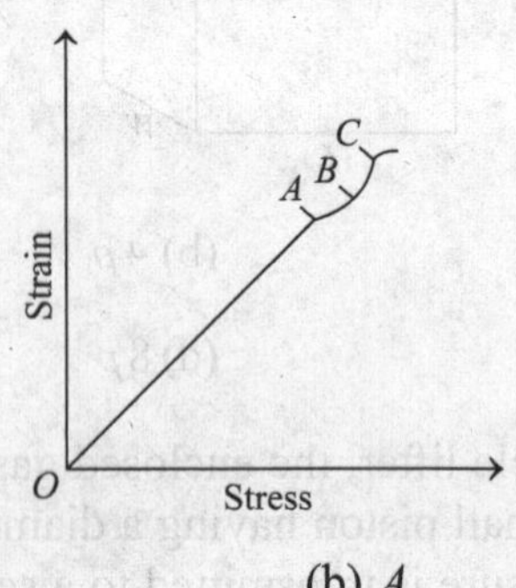

(a) O (b) A
(c) B (d) C

23. A cylindrical tank has a hole of 1 cm^2 in its bottom. If the water is allowed to flow into the tank from a tube above it at the rate of 70 cm^3/s, then the maximum height upto which water can rise in the tank is
(a) 2.5 cm (b) 5 cm
(c) 10 cm (d) 0.25 cm

24. For the given equation of transverse wave travelling in a rope is $y = 5\sin(4.0t - 0.02x)$, where y and x are expressed in cm and time in second.

Match the List I with List II (all in given system of units)

	List I		List II
A.	Amplitude of wave	1.	100π
B.	Frequency of wave	2.	5
C.	Velocity of wave	3.	0.637
D.	Wavelength of wave	4.	200

Choose the correct answer from given options.
(a) A-2, B-3, C-4, D-1
(b) A-2, B-2, C-3, D-4
(c) A-1, B-3, C-1, D-4
(d) A-2, B-1, C-3, D-4

25. The number of degree of freedom in a gas is 5. Then molar heat capacity at constant pressure is

(a) 32 J mol^{-1} K^{-1}
(b) 29 J mol^{-1} K^{-1}
(c) 30 J mol^{-1} K^{-1}
(d) 25 J mol^{-1} K^{-1}

26. Assertion (A) Specific heat of a gas at constant pressure is greater than its specific heat at constant volume.

Reason (R) At constant pressure, some heat is spent in expansion of the gas.

In the light of the above statements, choose the correct answer from the options given below.

(a) Both A and R are true and R is the correct explanation of A.
(b) Both A and R are true but R is not the correct explanation of A.
(c) A is true but R is false.
(d) A is false but R is true.

27. An ideal gas undergoes a process whose process equation is

$$p = \frac{a}{\left[1+\left(\frac{V}{b}\right)^2\right]}$$

where, a and b are constants. When volume of gas $V = b$, the temperature of the gas will be

(a) $\frac{ab}{2R}$ (b) $\frac{ab}{R}$
(c) ab (d) zero

28. Statement I Nitrogen is the most common constituent of atmosphere while helium is found only in traces.

Statement II Helium molecules have speeds exceeding the earth's escape speed.

In the light of the above statements, choose the most appropriate answer from the options given below.

(a) Both Statement I and Statement II are incorrect.
(b) Both Statement I and Statement II are correct.
(c) Statement I is correct but Statement II is incorrect.
(d) Statement I is incorrect but Statement II is correct.

29. The pressure p, volume V and temperature T of a gas in the jar A and the other gas in the jar B at pressure $2p$, volume $\frac{V}{4}$ and temperature $2T$, then the ratio of the number of molecules in the jar A and B will be

(a) 1 : 1 (b) 1 : 2 (c) 2 : 1 (d) 4 : 1

30. A 1 m long wire is stretched without tension at 30°C between two rigid supports. What strain will be produced in the wire if the temperature falls to 0°C?

(a) 36×10^{-5} (b) 64×10^{-5}
(c) 0.78 (d) 0.32

31. The displacement of a particle varies with time according to the relation $y = a \sin \omega t + b \cos \omega t$, then

(a) the motion is oscillatory but not SHM
(b) the motion is SHM with amplitude $a + b$
(c) the motion is SHM with amplitude $a^2 + b^2$
(d) the motion is SHM with amplitude $\sqrt{a^2 + b^2}$

32. A plane is in level flight at constant speed and each of its wings has an area $10 m^2$. If the speed of air on upper and lower surfaces are 80 m/s and 70 m/s, respectively, then the mass of the plane is ($g = 10 m/s^2$ and $\rho_{air} = 1 kg/m^3$)

(a) 2500 kg (b) 1500 kg
(c) 3000 kg (d) 4000 kg

33. A gaseous mixture enclosed in a vessel consists of 1g mole of a gas $A\left(\gamma = \frac{5}{3}\right)$ and some amount of gas $B\left(\gamma = \frac{7}{5}\right)$ at a temperature T. The gases A and B do not react with each other and are assumed to be ideal. Find number of gram moles of the gas B, if γ for the gaseous mixture is $\left(\frac{19}{13}\right)$.

(a) 2 g mol (b) 3 g mol
(c) 5 g mol (d) 1 g mol

34. A progressive wave as shown in the figure below, is travelling with speed of 330 m/s.

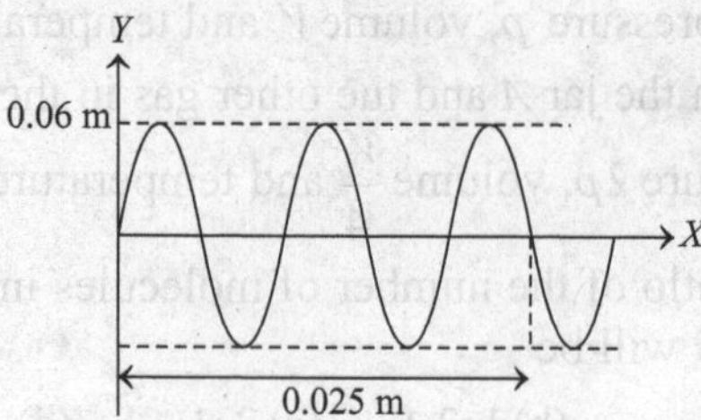

Then, the equation of wave propagation in positive x-direction will be

(a) $Y = 0.12 \sin 2\pi (4000t - 12x)$
(b) $Y = 0.12 \sin 2\pi (3300t - 12.25x)$
(c) $Y = 0.06 \sin 2\pi (4000t - 40x)$
(d) $Y = 0.06 \sin 2\pi (33000t - 100x)$

35. A large horizontal surface moves up and down in SHM with an amplitude of 1 cm. If a mass of 10 kg (which is placed on the surface) is to remain continuously in contact with it, then the maximum frequency of SHM will be

(a) 5 Hz (b) 0.5 Hz
(c) 1.5 Hz (d) 10 Hz

36. A capillary tube of radius 0.25 mm is submerged vertically in water, so that 25 mm of its length is outside the water. The radius of curvature of the meniscus will be [Take, surface tension of water $= 75 \times 10^{-3}\ \text{Nm}^{-1}$]

(a) 0.3 mm (b) 0.6 mm
(c) 0.9 mm (d) 1.2 mm

37. A spring is stretched by 10 cm by a force of 25 N. What is the time period of the oscillations when a mass of 4 kg is suspended by it?

(a) 0.2 s (b) 0.5 s (c) 0.8 s (d) 1 s

38. Corresponding to the process $ABCA$ as shown in figure, what is the heat given to the gas?

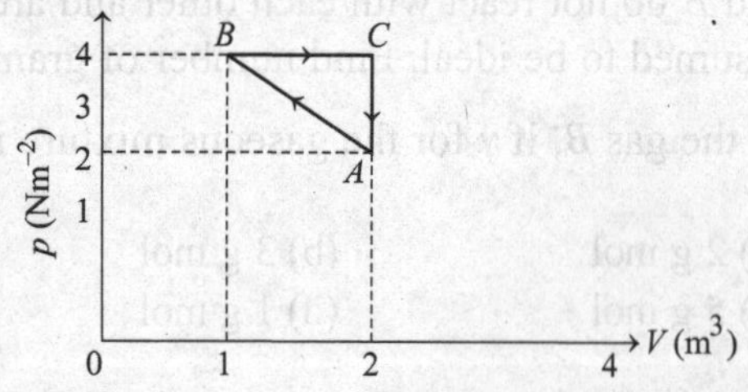

(a) 1 J (b) $\frac{3}{2}$ J
(c) $\frac{1}{2}$ J (d) Zero

39. Pressure inside two soap bubble are 1.01 and 1.02 atmospheres. Ratio between their volume is

(a) 102 : 101 (b) $(102)^3 : (101)^3$
(c) 8 : 1 (d) 2 : 1

40. The ratio of specific heats $\frac{C_p}{C_V}$ of a diatomic gas molecule that has translational, rotational and vibrational motion is

(a) $\frac{7}{9}$ (b) $\frac{5}{3}$
(c) $\frac{3}{5}$ (d) $\frac{9}{7}$

41. A wall has two layers A and B each made of different materials. The layer A is 10 cm thick and B is 20 cm thick. The thermal conductivity of A is thrice that of B. Under thermal equilibrium, temperature difference across the wall is 35°C. The difference of temperature across the layer A is

(a) 20°C
(b) 10°C
(c) 15°C
(d) 5°C

42. A cylindrical metallic rod in thermal contact with two reservoirs of heat at its two ends conducts an amount of heat Q in time t. The metallic rod is melted and the material is formed into a rod of half the radius of the original rod. What is the amount of heat conducted by the new rod when it is placed in thermal contact with the two reservoirs for time t?

(a) $\frac{Q}{4}$ (b) $\frac{Q}{16}$
(c) $2Q$ (d) $\frac{Q}{2}$

43. On centigrade or Celsius scale (°C), the temperature of a body increases by 30° C. The increase in temperature on Fahrenheit scale (°F) is

(a) 50° (b) 40°
(c) 30° (d) 54°

44. In a new scale N of temperature, the freezing point of water is 200° N and boiling point is 800°N. The Celsius and new temperature scale reading will be same at

(a) –50°C
(b) 100°C
(c) 50°C
(d) –100°C

45. What will be the force constant of the spring system shown in figure?

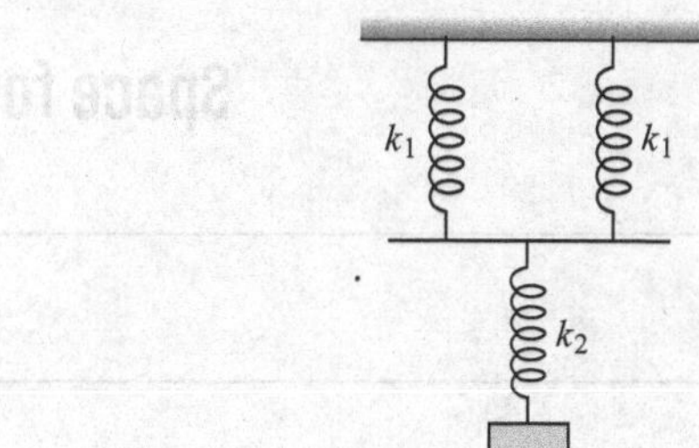

(a) $\frac{k_1}{2}+k_2$ (b) $\left(\frac{1}{2k_1}+\frac{1}{k_2}\right)^{-1}$

(c) $\frac{1}{2k_1}+\frac{1}{k_2}$ (d) $\left(\frac{2}{k_1}+\frac{1}{k_2}\right)^{-1}$

For Online Syllabus Part Test **Scan the QR Code**

Response Index

01 ⓐ ⓑ ⓒ ⓓ	14 ⓐ ⓑ ⓒ ⓓ	27 ⓐ ⓑ ⓒ ⓓ	40 ⓐ ⓑ ⓒ ⓓ
02 ⓐ ⓑ ⓒ ⓓ	15 ⓐ ⓑ ⓒ ⓓ	28 ⓐ ⓑ ⓒ ⓓ	41 ⓐ ⓑ ⓒ ⓓ
03 ⓐ ⓑ ⓒ ⓓ	16 ⓐ ⓑ ⓒ ⓓ	29 ⓐ ⓑ ⓒ ⓓ	42 ⓐ ⓑ ⓒ ⓓ
04 ⓐ ⓑ ⓒ ⓓ	17 ⓐ ⓑ ⓒ ⓓ	30 ⓐ ⓑ ⓒ ⓓ	43 ⓐ ⓑ ⓒ ⓓ
05 ⓐ ⓑ ⓒ ⓓ	18 ⓐ ⓑ ⓒ ⓓ	31 ⓐ ⓑ ⓒ ⓓ	44 ⓐ ⓑ ⓒ ⓓ
06 ⓐ ⓑ ⓒ ⓓ	19 ⓐ ⓑ ⓒ ⓓ	32 ⓐ ⓑ ⓒ ⓓ	45 ⓐ ⓑ ⓒ ⓓ
07 ⓐ ⓑ ⓒ ⓓ	20 ⓐ ⓑ ⓒ ⓓ	33 ⓐ ⓑ ⓒ ⓓ	
08 ⓐ ⓑ ⓒ ⓓ	21 ⓐ ⓑ ⓒ ⓓ	34 ⓐ ⓑ ⓒ ⓓ	
09 ⓐ ⓑ ⓒ ⓓ	22 ⓐ ⓑ ⓒ ⓓ	35 ⓐ ⓑ ⓒ ⓓ	
10 ⓐ ⓑ ⓒ ⓓ	23 ⓐ ⓑ ⓒ ⓓ	36 ⓐ ⓑ ⓒ ⓓ	
11 ⓐ ⓑ ⓒ ⓓ	24 ⓐ ⓑ ⓒ ⓓ	37 ⓐ ⓑ ⓒ ⓓ	
12 ⓐ ⓑ ⓒ ⓓ	25 ⓐ ⓑ ⓒ ⓓ	38 ⓐ ⓑ ⓒ ⓓ	
13 ⓐ ⓑ ⓒ ⓓ	26 ⓐ ⓑ ⓒ ⓓ	39 ⓐ ⓑ ⓒ ⓓ	

Performance Scanner

> 90% Excellent !	You have mastered the second half of NEET syllabus (11th). The concepts of this syllabus are on your fingertips. Maintain this momentum.
76-90% Very Good !	You have a good command over the second half of NEET syllabus (11th). Revise it again after a few days and enhance your performance.
60-75% Good !	You have a wide scope to learn more from the second half of NEET syllabus (11th). Revise it again.
<60% Not Satisfactory!	You have a long way ahead of you to master the second half of NEET syllabus (11th). Revise it thoroughly.

Space for Rough Work

Test Booklet No. 3947117

Test Booklet Code NSS 1

MEDACE

NEET (UG)

SELF ASSESSMENT KIT

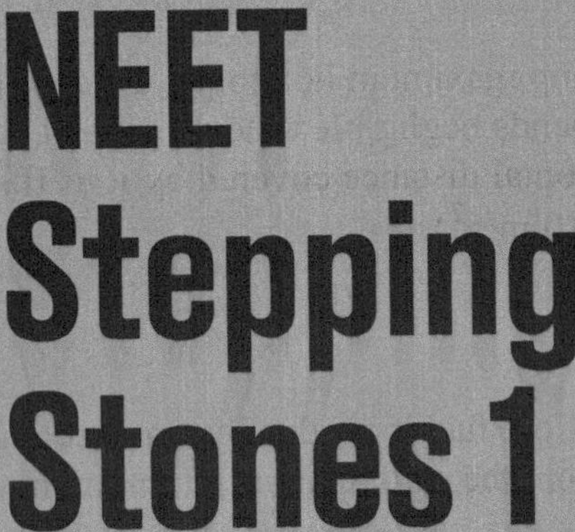

NEET Stepping Stones 1

(Based on Complete 11th Syllabus)

Name of the Candidate (In Capitals)

____

____

____

Candidate's Signature ____________

Invigilator's Signature ____________

Facsimile signature stamp of center superintendent____________

Important Instructions

- The test is of 45 minutes and the Test Booklet contains 45 multiple choice questions (four options with a single correct answer) from Physics.
- Candidates are advised to read all questions before they start attempting the question paper.
- Each question carries 4 marks. For each correct response, the candidate will get 4 marks. For each incorrect response, one mark will be deducted from the total scores. The maximum marks are 180.
- In the event of candidate marking more than one option then one mark will be deducted.
- Use **Blue/Black Point Pen** only for writing particular on this page/ marking response on Answer Sheet.

Do not open this Booklet until you start attempting the Test

Physics (Q. No. 1-45)

1. At 0°C, pressure measured by barometer is 760 mm. What will be the pressure at 100°C?

(a) 760 mm (b) 730 mm
(c) 780 mm (d) 1038 mm

2. Let A and B are two quantities and let $[A]=[M^{\alpha}L^{\beta}T^{\gamma}]$ and $[B]=[M^{\beta}L^{\gamma}T^{\alpha}]$, then which of these functions has a physical meaning?

(a) $A \times B$ (b) $A+B$
(c) $A-B$ (d) $-A+B$

3. If C_p and C_V represent the specific heats of a gas at constant pressure and volume respectively, then which among the following relation is incorrect for ratio $\frac{C_p}{C_V}$?
(R is gas constant).

(a) $1+\frac{R}{C_V}$ (b) $\frac{1}{1-\frac{R}{C_p}}$

(c) $\frac{C_p-R}{C_V+R}$ (d) $\frac{C_p}{C_p-R}$

4. An ideal gas undergoes a process such that $pT^2=(C)$ constant, coefficient of volume expansion of gas is

(a) $\frac{1}{T}$ (b) $\frac{2}{T}$
(c) $\frac{3}{T}$ (d) $\frac{4}{T}$

5. On increasing the temperature, the elasticity of the material in general

(a) increases
(b) decreases
(c) remains same
(d) may increase or decrease depends on the nature of material

6. A frog can jump maximum horizontal distance of 30 cm. If it spends negligible time on ground, then the horizontal distance covered by it in 10 s is (Take, $g=10\ \text{m/s}^2$)

(a) 3.06 m (b) 6.12 m
(c) 12.24 m (d) 18.37 m

7. Statement I More fuel is needed by a rocket to go to the moon from the earth than its return journey.

Statement II Distance of zero gravitational potential point is less from the moon than from the earth.

In the light of above statements, choose the most appropriate answer from the options given below.

(a) Both Statement I and Statement II are incorrect.
(b) Both Statement I and Statement II are correct.
(c) Statement I is correct and Statement II is incorrect.
(d) Statement I is incorrect and Statement II is correct.

8. The linear velocity of a particle executing circular motion, varies with time as $\mathbf{v}=(4t\,\hat{\mathbf{i}}+t^2\,\hat{\mathbf{j}})$ m/s, where t is in second. The tangential acceleration of particle at $t=2$ s, is

(a) $\frac{3}{\sqrt{5}}\ \text{m/s}^2$ (b) $\frac{4}{\sqrt{5}}\ \text{m/s}^2$
(c) $\frac{6}{\sqrt{5}}\ \text{m/s}^2$ (d) $\frac{12}{\sqrt{5}}\ \text{m/s}^2$

9. Two solid spheres A and B are made of metals of different densities ρ_A and ρ_B, respectively. If their masses are equal, then the ratio of their moments of inertia (I_B/I_A) about their respective diameters is

(a) $\left(\frac{\rho_B}{\rho_A}\right)^{2/3}$

(b) $\left(\frac{\rho_A}{\rho_B}\right)^{2/3}$

(c) $\frac{\rho_A}{\rho_B}$

(d) $\frac{\rho_B}{\rho_A}$

10. Which of the following graphs can possibly represent one-dimensional motion of a particle?

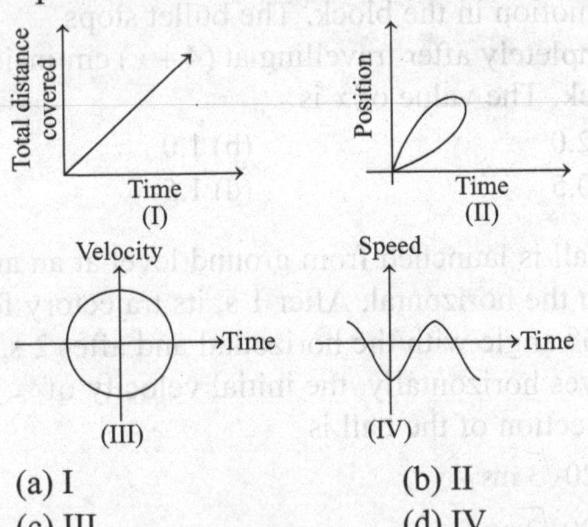

(a) I (b) II
(c) III (d) IV

11. The motor of an engine is rotating about its axis with an angular velocity of 100 rev min^{-1}. It comes to rest in 15 s after being switched OFF. Assuming constant angular deceleration, what are the number of revolutions made by it before coming to rest?

(a) 12.5 (b) 40
(c) 32.6 (d) 15.6

12. There is a hole in the bottom of tank having water. If total pressure at bottom is 3 atm (1 atm $=10^5$ N/m^2), then the velocity of water flowing from hole is

(a) $\sqrt{400}$ m/s
(b) $\sqrt{600}$ m/s
(c) $\sqrt{60}$ m/s
(d) $\sqrt{40}$ m/s

13. At what temperature, hydrogen molecules will escape from the earth's surface?

(Take, radius of the earth $=6.4\times10^6$ m, mass of hydrogen molecule $=0.34\times10^{-26}$ kg, Boltzmann constant $=1.38\times10^{-23}$ JK^{-1} and acceleration due to gravity $=9.8\ ms^{-2}$)

(a) 10 K (b) 10^2 K
(c) 10^3 K (d) 10^4 K

14. Which of the following statements given below are correct for a mono-atomic gas?

I. $C_V = \frac{3}{2}R$ II. $C_p = \frac{5}{2}R$

III. $\frac{C_p}{C_V} = \frac{5}{3}$ IV. $C_p - C_V = 2R$

(a) III only (b) II only
(c) I, II and III (d) I only

15. A body of mass 0.5 kg travels in a straight line with speed $v = 5x^{3/2}$. Work done by force in displacing body from $x = 0$ m to $x = 2$ m is

(a) 12.5 J (b) 25 J
(c) 50 J (d) 100 J

16. **Assertion** (A) Total internal energy of oxygen gas at a given temperature is E. Out of this energy $\frac{3}{5}E$ is translational kinetic energy and $\frac{2}{5}E$ is rotational kinetic energy.

Reason (R) Potential energy of an ideal gas is zero.

In the light of above statements, choose the most appropriate answer from the options given below.

(a) Both A and R are true and R is the correct explanation of A.
(b) Both A and R are true but R is not the correct explanation of A.
(c) A is true but R is false.
(d) A is false but R is true.

17. A car weighing 1400 kg is moving at a speed of 54 kmph up a hill when the motor stops, it is just able to reach the destination which is at a height of 10 m above the point. Then, the work done against friction (negative of the work done by the friction) is (take, $g = 10\ ms^{-2}$)

(a) 10 kJ (b) 15 kJ
(c) 17.5 kJ (d) 25 kJ

18. In a cylindrical container, a solid sphere with radius R, composed of a material with bulk modulus B, is surrounded by a liquid. A weight m is placed on a massless piston of area A, floating on the liquid's surface, to compress the liquid. The fractional change in the radius of the sphere $\frac{dR}{R}$ is

(a) $\frac{mg}{AB}$ (b) $\frac{mg}{2AB}$
(c) $\frac{mg}{3AB}$ (d) $\frac{mg}{4AB}$

19. If the length of the pendulum in a pendulum clock increases by 0.1%, then the error in time per day is

(a) 86.4 s (b) 4.32 s
(c) 43.2 s (d) 8.64 s

20. A particle executes linear simple harmonic motion with an amplitude of 4 cm. When the particle is at 2 cm from the mean position, the magnitude of its velocity is equal to that of its acceleration. Then, its time period in seconds is

(a) $\frac{\sqrt{5}}{\pi}$ (b) $\frac{\sqrt{5}}{2\pi}$
(c) $\frac{4\pi}{\sqrt{6}}$ (d) $\frac{2\pi}{\sqrt{3}}$

21. A book with numerous printing errors presents four distinct formulas describing the displacement y of a particle engaged in periodic motion.

i. $y = a\sin vt$

ii. $y = \left(\frac{a}{T}\right)\sin\left(\frac{t}{a}\right)$

iii. $y = \left(\frac{a}{\sqrt{2}}\right)\left(\sin\frac{2\pi t}{T} + \cos\frac{2\pi t}{T}\right)$

iv. $y = a\sin\frac{2\pi t}{T}$

where, a = maximum displacement of the particle,
v = speed of the particle
T = time period of motion.

The wrong formula on the dimensional grounds is

(a) i and ii (b) i and iv
(c) ii and iii (d) i, ii and iv

22. In a calorimeter, 19 g of water initially at 30°C and 5 g of ice initially at −20°C are combined. The final temperature of the mixture is

(Given, specific heat capacity of ice = 0.5 cal / g°C and latent heat of fusion of ice = 80 cal / g)

(a) 5°C (b) −5°C
(c) 0°C (d) 10°C

23. An ideal gas ($\gamma = 1.5$) is expanded adiabatically. How many times the gas has to be expanded to reduce the root mean square velocity of the molecules by 2 times?

(a) 4 times (b) 16 times
(c) 8 times (d) 2 times

24. The velocity of the bullet becomes one third after it penetrates 4 cm in a wooden block. Assume that the bullet is facing constant resistance during its motion in the block. The bullet stops completely after travelling at $(4 + x)$ cm inside the block. The value of x is

(a) 2.0 (b) 1.0
(c) 0.5 (d) 1.5

25. A ball is launched from ground level at an angle θ with the horizontal. After 1 s, its trajectory forms a 45° angle with the horizontal and after 2 s, it moves horizontally, the initial velocity of projection of the ball is

(a) $20\sqrt{3}\ \text{ms}^{-1}$
(b) $20\sqrt{2}\ \text{ms}^{-1}$
(c) $10\sqrt{3}\ \text{ms}^{-1}$
(d) $10\sqrt{5}\ \text{ms}^{-1}$

26. Two projectiles A and B thrown with speeds in the ratio $1:\sqrt{2}$ acquired the same height. If A is thrown at an angle of 45° with the horizontal, then angle of projection of B will be

(a) 0° (b) 30°
(c) 45° (d) 60°

27. A gas is compressed isothermally to half of its initial volume. The same gas is compressed separately through an adiabatic process until its volume is again reduced to half. Then,

(a) compressing the gas through adiabatic process will require more work to be done.

(b) compressing the gas isothermally or adiabatically will require the same amount of work.

(c) the case (whether compression through isothermal or through adiabatic process) which requires more work will depend upon the atomicity of the gas.

(d) compressing the gas isothermally will require more work to be done.

28. A particle of mass 10 g is projected at an angle of 30° with horizontal. Velocity of projection is 2 m/s. Angular momentum of particle with respect to point of projection when the particle has least kinetic energy is nearly

(a) 0.9×10^{-3} SI units

(b) 0.5×10^{-3} SI units

(c) 0.3×10^{-3} SI units

(d) 0.2×10^{-3} SI units

29. A bag is gently dropped on a conveyor belt moving at a speed of 2 m/s. The coefficient of friction between the conveyor belt and bag is 0.4. Initially the bag slips on the belt before it stops due to friction. The distance travelled by the bag on the belt during slipping motion, is (Take, $g = 10$ m/s^2))

(a) 2 m (b) 0.5 m
(c) 3.2 m (d) 0.8 ms

30. A drop of liquid occupying a volume of 0.04cm^3, spreads between two glass slides to form a thin layer covering an area of 20cm^2. To separate the slides, a force of 16×10^5 dyne is required perpendicular to the surfaces. The surface tension of the liquid is (in dyne/cm)

(a) 70 (b) 80
(c) 90 (d) 96

31. Statement I If percentage increase in momentum is x, then percentage increase in kinetic energy is always of $2x$ percent.

Statement II If percentage increase in momentum is 100%, then kinetic energy of body will increase by 300%.

In the light of above statements, choose the most appropriate answer from the options given below.

(a) Both Statement I and Statement II are correct.

(b) Both Statement I and Statement II are incorrect.

(c) Statement I is correct and Statement II is incorrect.

(d) Statement I is incorrect and Statement II is correct.

32. An average force of 125 N is applied on a machine gun firing bullets each of mass 10 g at the speed of 250 m/s to keep it in position. The number of bullets fired per second by the machine gun is

(a) 25 (b) 5
(c) 50 (d) 100

33. Two strings A and B, made of same materials are stretched by same tension. The radius of string A is double the radius of B. A transverse wave travels on A with speed v_A and on B with speed v_B. The ratio of $\frac{v_A}{v_B}$ is

(a) $\frac{1}{2}$ (b) 2
(c) $\frac{1}{4}$ (d) 4

34. A particle is moving with a uniform speed in a circular orbit of radius R in a central force inversely proportional to the nth power of R. If the period of rotation of the particle is T, then

(a) $T \propto R^{n/2}$

(b) $T \propto R^{3/2}$ for any value of n

(c) $T \propto R^{\frac{n}{2}+1}$

(d) $T \propto R^{\frac{n+1}{2}}$

35. The x-t graph for motion of a car is given below. According to the graph which of the given statement(s) is /are correct.

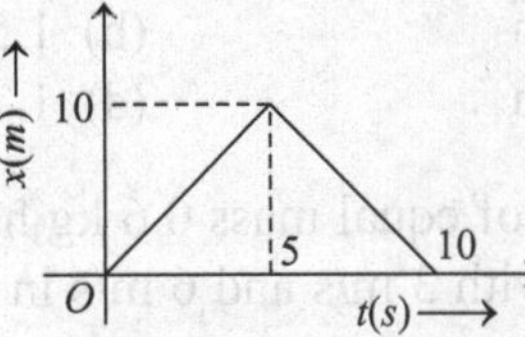

I. The instantaneous speed during the interval $t = 5$ s to $t = 10$ s is negative at all time instants during the interval.

II. The velocity and the average velocity for the interval $t = 0$ s to $t = 5$ s are equal and positive.

III. The car changes its direction of motion at $t = 5$s

IV. The instantaneous speed and the instantaneous velocity is positive at all time instants during the interval $t = 0$s to $t = 5$s.

(a) I, II, III and IV
(b) II and III
(c) II, III and IV
(d) I and II

36. If 10 g of oxygen is subjected to a pressure of 3 atm at a temperature of 10°C. Heating at a constant pressure, the gas is expanded to 10L. With reference to the given situation, match the Column I (physical quantity) with Column II (value) and select the correct answer from the codes given below.
($R = 0.0821$ atm-litre K^{-1} mol^{-1})

Column I	Column II
A. The volume of the gas before expansion (in litres)	1. 4.13
B. The temperature of the gas after expansion (in kelvin)	2. 1.0
C. The density of gas before expansion (in gL^{-1})	3. 2.42
D. The density of gas after expansion (in gL^{-1})	4. 1169.4

	A	B	C	D
(a)	3	4	2	1
(b)	4	3	1	2
(c)	3	4	1	2
(d)	4	2	3	1

37. Young's moduli of two wires *A* and *B* are in the ratio 7 : 4. Wire *A* is 2 m long and has radius *R*. Wire *B* is 1.5 m long and has radius 2 mm. If the two wires stretch by the same length for a given load, then the value of *R* is close to

(a) 1.3 mm (b) 1.5 mm
(c) 1.9 mm (d) 1.7 mm

38. Two balls of equal mass 0.6 kg have a head-on collision with 3 m/s and 6 m/s in opposite directions. If the coefficient of restitution is $\frac{1}{2}$, then magnitude of impulse exerted by each ball is

(a) 4.05 N-s (b) 2.4 N-s
(c) 6.5 N-s (d) 2.0 N-s

39. A particle undergoing simple harmonic motion has its displacement described by the equation.

$$y = 5\sin\left(4t + \frac{\pi}{3}\right)$$

Given that, *T* is the time period and the mass of the particle is 2 g, then kinetic energy of the particle at $t = \frac{T}{4}$ is

(a) 0.8 J (b) 0.3 J
(c) 0.4 J (d) 0.2 J

40. If *M* is the mass of water that rises in a capillary tube of radius *r*, then mass of water which will rise in a capillary tube of radius 2*r* is

(a) 2*M* (b) 4*M*
(c) $\frac{M}{2}$ (d) *M*

41. A graph of the square of the velocity against the square of the acceleration of a given simple harmonic motion is

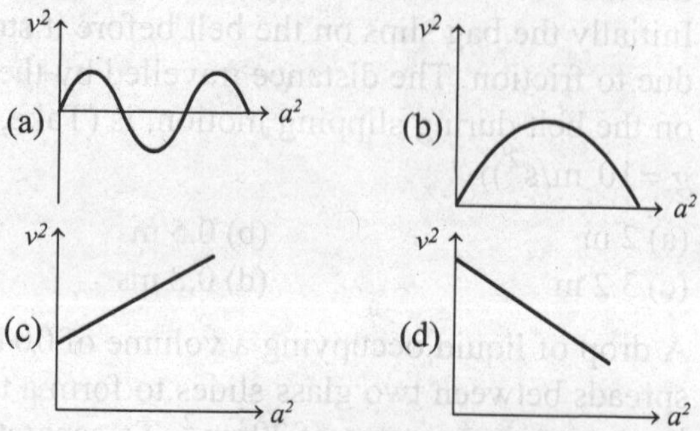

42. A block of mass *m* attached to a massless spring is performing oscillatory motion of amplitude *A* on a frictionless horizontal plane. If half of the mass of the block breaks off when it is passing through its equilibrium point, the amplitude of oscillation for the remaining system become *fA*. The value of *f* is

(a) $\frac{1}{\sqrt{2}}$ (b) 1
(c) $\frac{1}{2}$ (d) $\sqrt{2}$

43. A string 2.0 m long and fixed at its ends is driven by a 240 Hz vibrator. This string vibrates in its third harmonic mode. The speed of the wave and its fundamental frequency is

(a) 180 m/s, 80 Hz (b) 320 m/s, 80 Hz
(c) 320 m/s, 120 Hz (d) 180 m/s, 120 Hz

44. A solid metallic cube having total surface area 24 m^2 is uniformly heated. If its temperature is increased by 10°C, calculate the increase in volume of the cube.
(Given, $\alpha = 5.0 \times 10^{-4}$ °C^{-1})

(a) 2.4×10^6 cm^3
(b) 1.2×10^5 cm^3
(c) 6.0×10^4 cm^3
(d) 4.8×10^5 cm^3

45. Same gas is filled in two vessels of the same volume at the same temperature. If the ratio of the number of molecules is 1 : 4, then

A. The rms velocity of gas molecules in two vessels will be the same.
B. The ratio of pressure in these vessels will be 1 : 4.
C. The ratio of pressure will be 1 : 1.
D. The rms velocity of gas molecules in two vessels will be in the ratio of 1 : 4.

(a) A and C only (b) B and D only
(c) A and B only (d) C and D only

Response Index

01 ⓐ ⓑ ⓒ ⓓ	14 ⓐ ⓑ ⓒ ⓓ	27 ⓐ ⓑ ⓒ ⓓ	40 ⓐ ⓑ ⓒ ⓓ
02 ⓐ ⓑ ⓒ ⓓ	15 ⓐ ⓑ ⓒ ⓓ	28 ⓐ ⓑ ⓒ ⓓ	41 ⓐ ⓑ ⓒ ⓓ
03 ⓐ ⓑ ⓒ ⓓ	16 ⓐ ⓑ ⓒ ⓓ	29 ⓐ ⓑ ⓒ ⓓ	42 ⓐ ⓑ ⓒ ⓓ
04 ⓐ ⓑ ⓒ ⓓ	17 ⓐ ⓑ ⓒ ⓓ	30 ⓐ ⓑ ⓒ ⓓ	43 ⓐ ⓑ ⓒ ⓓ
05 ⓐ ⓑ ⓒ ⓓ	18 ⓐ ⓑ ⓒ ⓓ	31 ⓐ ⓑ ⓒ ⓓ	44 ⓐ ⓑ ⓒ ⓓ
06 ⓐ ⓑ ⓒ ⓓ	19 ⓐ ⓑ ⓒ ⓓ	32 ⓐ ⓑ ⓒ ⓓ	45 ⓐ ⓑ ⓒ ⓓ
07 ⓐ ⓑ ⓒ ⓓ	20 ⓐ ⓑ ⓒ ⓓ	33 ⓐ ⓑ ⓒ ⓓ	
08 ⓐ ⓑ ⓒ ⓓ	21 ⓐ ⓑ ⓒ ⓓ	34 ⓐ ⓑ ⓒ ⓓ	
09 ⓐ ⓑ ⓒ ⓓ	22 ⓐ ⓑ ⓒ ⓓ	35 ⓐ ⓑ ⓒ ⓓ	
10 ⓐ ⓑ ⓒ ⓓ	23 ⓐ ⓑ ⓒ ⓓ	36 ⓐ ⓑ ⓒ ⓓ	
11 ⓐ ⓑ ⓒ ⓓ	24 ⓐ ⓑ ⓒ ⓓ	37 ⓐ ⓑ ⓒ ⓓ	
12 ⓐ ⓑ ⓒ ⓓ	25 ⓐ ⓑ ⓒ ⓓ	38 ⓐ ⓑ ⓒ ⓓ	
13 ⓐ ⓑ ⓒ ⓓ	26 ⓐ ⓑ ⓒ ⓓ	39 ⓐ ⓑ ⓒ ⓓ	

Performance Scanner

> 90% Excellent !	You have mastered the NEET syllabus (11th). The concepts of this syllabus are on your fingertips. Maintain this momentum.
76-90% Very Good !	You have a good command over the NEET syllabus (11th). Revise it again after a few days and enhance your performance.
60-75% Good !	You have a wide scope to learn for the NEET syllabus (11th). Revise it again.
<60% Not Satisfactory!	You have a long way ahead of you to master the NEET syllabus (11th). Revise it thoroughly.

Space for Rough Work

Test Booklet No. **3947118**

Test Booklet Code **NSS 2**

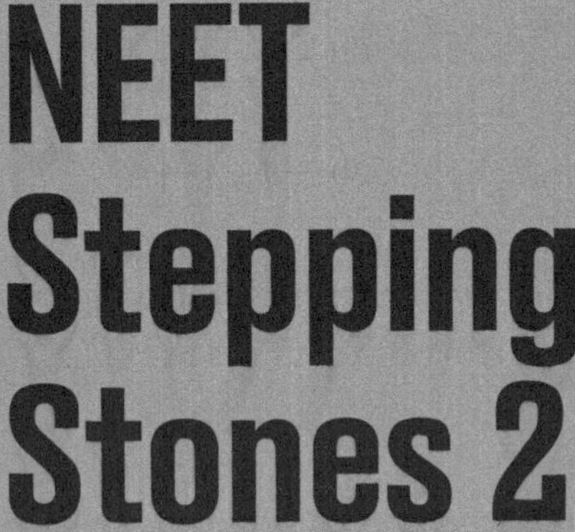

(Based on Complete 11th Syllabus)

Name of the Candidate (In Capitals)

____

____

____

Candidate's Signature ____________

Invigilator's Signature ____________

Facsimile signature stamp of center superintendent____________

Important Instructions

- The test is of 45 minutes and the Test Booklet contains 45 multiple choice questions (four options with a single correct answer) from Physics.
- Candidates are advised to read all questions before they start attempting the question paper.
- Each question carries 4 marks. For each correct response, the candidate will get 4 marks. For each incorrect response, one mark will be deducted from the total scores. The maximum marks are 180.
- In the event of candidate marking more than one option then one mark will be deducted.
- Use **Blue/Black Point Pen** only for writing particular on this page/ marking response on Answer Sheet.

Do not open this Booklet until you start attempting the Test

Physics (Q. No. 1-45)

1. A particle when hung from a spring stretches it by 1 cm on earth's surface. Radius of earth is 6400 km. At a place 800 km above earth's surface, stretch of spring will be
(a) 1 cm
(b) 8 cm
(c) 0.1 cm
(d) 0.79 cm

2. van der Waals' gas equation is

$$\left(p+\frac{a}{V^2}\right)(V-b)=RT$$

where, p = pressure, V = volume,
R = molar gas constant and
T = absolute temperature
Dimensions of ab are
(a) $[ML^6T^{-2}]$
(b) $[ML^5T^{-2}]$
(c) $[ML^8T^{-2}]$
(d) $[M^2L^5T^{-2}]$

3. A bead of mass m enters at end A of a U-shaped wire and leaves from B and friction is zero. Magnitude of force exerted by bead on wire is

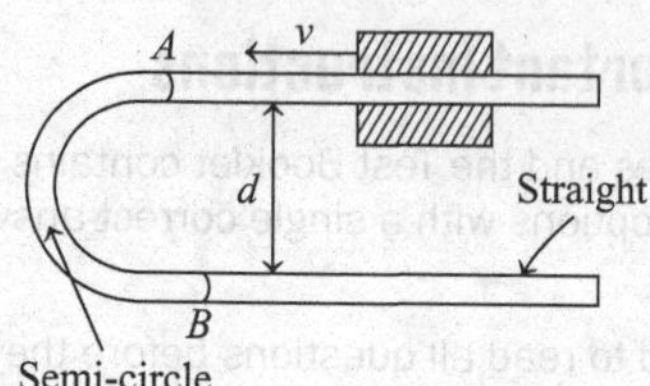

(a) zero
(b) $\frac{4mv^2}{\pi d}$
(c) $\frac{2mv^2}{\pi d}$
(d) Depends on mass of wire

4. A wave pulse on a string at $t=0$ is as shown.

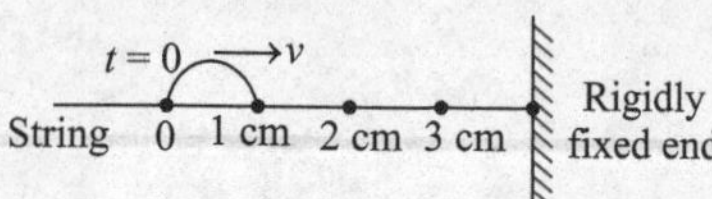

Pulse is moving towards fixed end with speed $v=1$ cm/s.

Wave on string at $t=4.5$ s is

(a) (b) 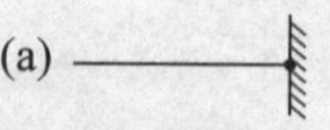
(c) (d)

5. An ideal gas $\left(\frac{C_p}{C_V}=\gamma\right)$ undergoes following cyclic process.

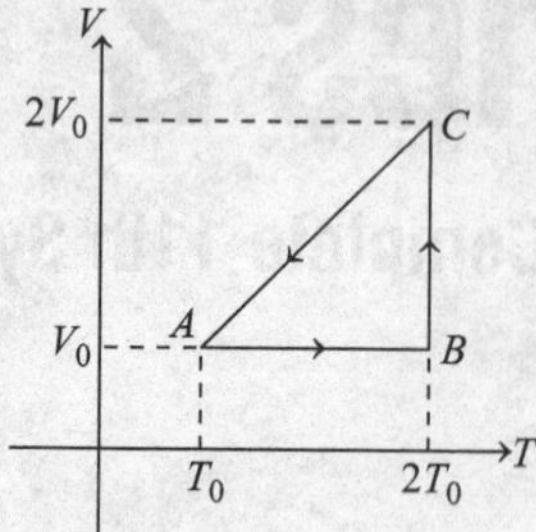

Cycle efficiency is
(a) $\frac{2\ln 2-1}{\left[\frac{\gamma}{(\gamma-1)}\right]}$
(b) $\frac{1-2\ln 2}{\left[\frac{\gamma}{(\gamma-1)}\right]}$
(c) $\frac{2\ln 2+1}{\left[\frac{\gamma}{(\gamma-1)}\right]}$
(d) $\frac{2\ln 2-1}{\left[\frac{\gamma}{(\gamma+1)}\right]}$

6. Consider the following two statements.
Statement I Sum of 12.0 + 0.038 will not have three significant figures.
Statement II For a given quantity, the numerical value (n) is directly proportional to its unit (u).
In the light of above statements, choose the most appropriate answer from the options given below.
(a) Both Statement I and Statement II are correct.
(b) Both Statement I and Statement II are incorrect.
(c) Statement I is correct and Statement II is incorrect.
(d) Statement I is incorrect and Statement II is correct.

7. A metal sheet with two rectangular shaped holes is shown in the figure.

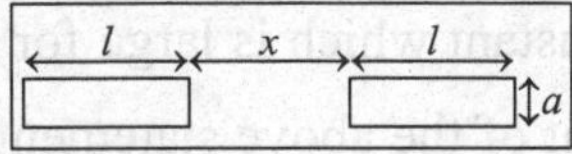

If the temperature of the metal sheet is increased, then
(a) l, x and a will increase
(b) l and a increase but x decreases
(c) l increases but x and a decrease
(d) l, x and a will decrease

8. A particle is projected from ground at an angle θ with the vertical such that its horizontal range R is related to its time of flight T as $R = 10\frac{\sqrt{3}}{2}T^2$. The value of projection angle θ is (Take, $g = 10\ \text{m/s}^2$)
(a) 30° (b) 45° (c) 60° (d) 53°

9. A particle of mass m is executing SHM according to the equation $y = 4\sin\left(4t + \frac{\pi}{3}\right)$ cm, where t is in second and has time period T. The ratio of kinetic energy to total energy at $t = \frac{T}{4}$ s is
(a) 1 : 4 (b) 3 : 4 (c) 1 : 2 (d) 3 : 8

10. If kinetic energy, potential energy, vibrational energy and total energy of a gas are denoted by E_K, E_P, E_V and E_T respectively, then which of these energy(s) is/are zero at 0 K temperature?
(a) E_K only (b) E_K and E_V
(c) E_K, E_V, E_T (d) All

11. A steel bar has radius $R = 9.5$ mm and length $L = 81$ cm. A force $F = 6.2 \times 10^4$ N stretches it along its length, then stress in the bar is
(a) $0.95 \times 10^8\ \text{N/m}^2$ (b) $1.1 \times 10^8\ \text{N/m}^2$
(c) $2.2 \times 10^8\ \text{N/m}^2$ (d) $3.2 \times 10^8\ \text{N/m}^2$

12. A ball is moving in a straight line through a fluid which is spinning around its own centre of mass as shown below.

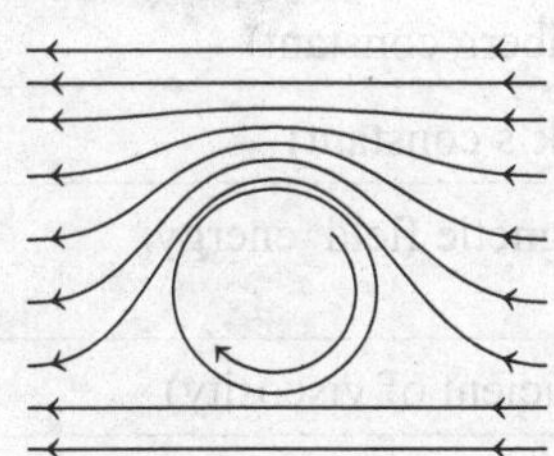

The ball experiences
(a) an upward force
(b) a downward force
(c) a leftward force
(d) a rightward force

13. A clock with a metal pendulum beating seconds keeps correct time at 0°C. If it loses 14.5 s a day at 25°C, the coefficient of linear expansion of metal pendulum is
(a) 1.34×10^{-5} /°C
(b) 2.34×10^{-5} /°C
(c) 7.24×10^{8} /°C
(d) 7.24×10^{-8} /°C

14. The kinetic energy of a particle moving in a straight line is varying with time as $K = 20t^2$. The force acting on the particle is
(a) constant
(b) increasing
(c) decreasing
(d) first increases and then decreases

15. The maximum height reached by a projectile is 64 m. If the initial velocity is halved, what will be the new maximum height of the projectile?
(a) 20 m (b) 16 m
(c) 25 m (d) 40 m

16. A parachutist after bailing out falls 50 m without friction. When parachute opens, it decelerates at $2\ \text{ms}^{-2}$. He reaches the ground with a speed of $3\ \text{ms}^{-1}$. At what height, did he bail out?
(a) 91 m (b) 182 m
(c) 293 m (d) 111 m

17. A metal wire when subjected under tension, its length becomes l and when tension is T', the length is now l'. The unstretched length of the metal wire was
(a) $\frac{T'l + Tl'}{T' + T}$
(b) $\sqrt{ll'}$
(c) $\frac{l + l'}{2}$
(d) $\frac{T'l - Tl'}{T' - T}$

18. A wooden block, initially at rest on the ground, is pushed by a force which increases linearly with time t. Which of the following curve best describes acceleration of block with time?

(a) 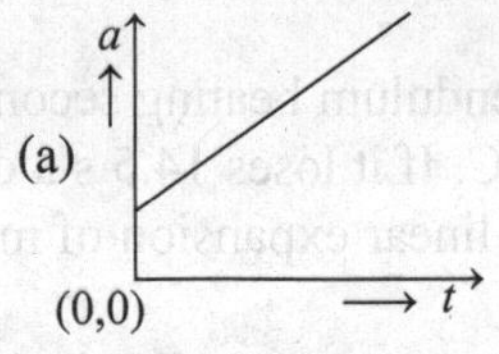

(b) 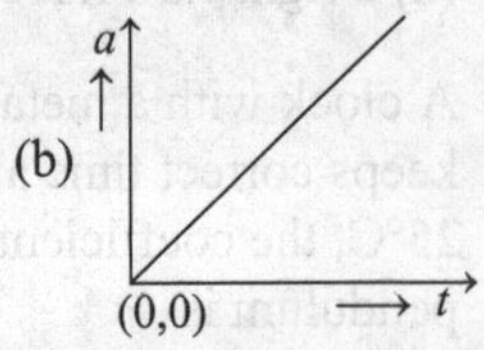

(c) 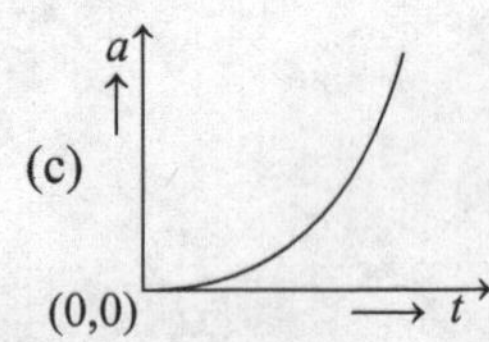

(d) 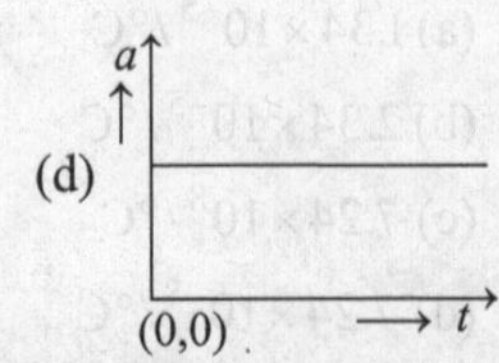

19. In a capillary tube, water rises to a height of 2.0 cm. In another capillary tube whose radius is one third of it, how much the water will rise?

(a) 6 cm (b) 3 cm
(c) 4 cm (d) 2 cm

20. Given below are two statements.

Statement I The limiting force of static friction depends on the area of contact and independent of materials.

Statement II The limiting force of kinetic friction is independent of the area of contact and depends on materials.

In the light of the above statements, choose the most appropriate answer from the options given below.

(a) Both Statement I and Statement II are correct.
(b) Both Statement I and Statement II are incorrect.
(c) Statement I is correct but Statement II is incorrect.
(d) Statement I is incorrect but Statement II is correct.

21. In a system, two particles of masses $m_1 = 3$ kg and $m_2 = 2$ kg are placed at certain distance from each other. The particle of mass m_1 is moved towards the centre of mass of the system through a distance 2 cm. In order to keep the centre of mass of the system at the original position, by what distance the particle of mass m_2 should move towards the centre of mass?

(a) 5 cm (b) 3 cm
(c) 10 cm (d) 1 cm

22. **Assertion** (A) The periodic time of a hard spring is less as compared to that of a soft spring.
Reason (R) The time period depends upon the spring constant which is large for hard spring.

In the light of the above statements, choose the most appropriate answer from the options given below.

(a) Both Assertion (A) and Reason (R) are true and Reason (R) is a correct explanation of Assertion (A).
(b) Both Assertion (A) and Reason (R) are true but Reason (R) is not a correct explanation of Assertion (A).
(c) Assertion (A) is true and Reason (R) is false.
(d) Assertion (A) is false and Reason (R) is true.

23. Energy of all molecules of a monoatomic gas having a volume V and pressure p is $\frac{3}{2}pV$. Ratio of total translational kinetic energy of all molecules to total energy of all molecules of a diatomic gas at same pressure and volume is

(a) $\frac{3}{2}$ (b) $\frac{3}{5}$
(c) $\frac{5}{3}$ (d) $\frac{5}{2}$

24. A heavy iron bar of weight w is having its one end on the ground and the other on the shoulder of a person. The bar makes an angle θ with the horizontal. The weight experienced by the person is

(a) w (b) $w\cos\theta$
(c) $w\sin\theta$ (d) $\frac{w}{2}$

25. A body of mass 1000 kg is moving horizontally with a velocity 6 m/s. If 200 kg extra mass is added, then the final velocity (in m/s) is

(a) 3 (b) 6 (c) 5 (d) 2

26. Match List I with List II.

List I	List II
A. R_H (Rydberg constant)	1. kg $m^{-1}s^{-1}$
B. h (Planck's constant)	2. kg m^2s^{-1}
C. μ_B (Magnetic field energy density)	3. m^{-1}
D. η (Coefficient of viscosity)	4. kg $m^{-1}s^{-2}$

Choose the most appropriate answer from the options given below.

	A	B	C	D
(a)	2	3	4	1
(b)	3	2	4	1
(c)	4	2	1	3
(d)	3	2	1	4

27. The instantaneous velocity of a particle moving in a straight line is given as $v = \alpha t + \beta t^2$, where α and β are constants. The distance travelled by the particle between 1s and 2s is

(a) $3\alpha + 7\beta$ (b) $\frac{3}{2}\alpha + \frac{7}{3}\beta$

(c) $\frac{\alpha}{2} + \frac{\beta}{3}$ (d) $\frac{3}{2}\alpha + \frac{7}{2}\beta$

28. Air is streaming past a horizontal aeroplane wing such that its speed is 120 m/s over the upper surface and 90 m/s at the lower surface. If the density of air is 1.3 kg/m^3 and the wing is 10 m long and has an average width of 2 m, then the difference of the pressure of the two sides of the wing is

(a) 40.95 N/m^2

(b) 409.5 N/m^2

(c) 4095 N/m^2

(d) 40950 N/m^2

29. *p-V* diagram of a diatomic gas is a straight line passing through origin. The molar heat capacity of the gas in the process will be

(a) $4R$ (b) $2.5R$

(c) $3R$ (d) $\frac{4R}{3}$

30. As shown in the figure, a particle is moving with constant speed π m/s. Considering its motion from A to B, the magnitude of the average velocity is

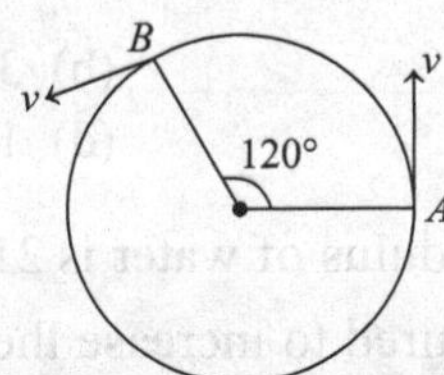

(a) π m/s (b) $\sqrt{3}$ m/s

(c) $1.5\sqrt{3}$ m/s (d) $2\sqrt{3}$ m/s

31. The period of a particle executing SHM is 8 s. At $t = 0$, it is at the mean position. The ratio of the distances covered by the particle in the 1st second to the 2nd second is

(a) $\frac{1}{\sqrt{2}+1}$ (b) $\sqrt{2}$

(c) $\frac{1}{\sqrt{2}}$ (d) $\sqrt{2}+1$

32. Three bodies A, B and C have equal kinetic energies and their masses are 400 g, 1.2 kg and 1.6 kg, respectively. The ratio of their linear momenta is

(a) $1:\sqrt{3}:\sqrt{2}$

(b) $\sqrt{2}:\sqrt{3}:1$

(c) $1:\sqrt{3}:2$

(d) $\sqrt{3}:\sqrt{2}:1$

33. A liquid of specific heat 0.2 at a temperature 48°C must be mixed with 100 g of a liquid of specific heat of 0.5 at a temperature 20°C, so that the final temperature of the mixture becomes 40°C. Number of grams is

(a) 175 (b) 300

(c) 295 (d) 625

34. 1 mole of a gas sample at temperature T is expanded adiabatically to double its volume. If adiabatic constant for the gas is $\gamma = \frac{3}{2}$, the work done by the gas in the process is

(a) $\frac{R}{T}[1-\sqrt{2}]$ (b) $\frac{T}{R}[\sqrt{2}-1]$

(c) $RT\,[2+\sqrt{2}]$ (d) $RT\,[2-\sqrt{2}]$

35. A planet takes 200 days to complete one revolution around the sun. If the distance of the planet from sun is reduced to one-fourth of the original distance, how many days will it take to complete one revolution?

(a) 25 (b) 20

(c) 100 (d) 50

36. What will be the length of second pendulum at a height of $h = 2R$ from the surface of earth, where R is the radius of earth? (Take acceleration due to gravity on the surface of earth, $g = \pi^2$ m/s^2)

(a) $\frac{4}{9}$ m (b) $\frac{1}{9}$ m

(c) $\frac{2}{9}$ m (d) $\frac{8}{9}$ m

37. The position, velocity and acceleration of a particle moving with a constant acceleration can be represented by

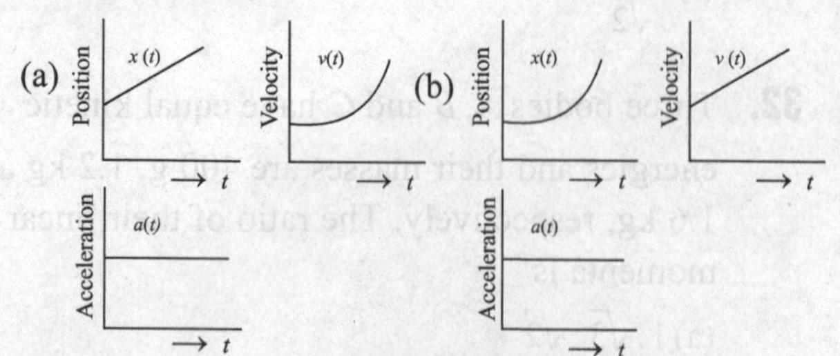

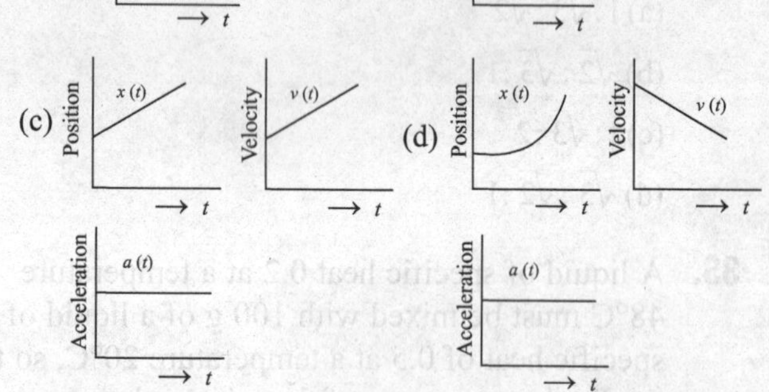

38. Position of a particle is given by the following equation,

$$x = t^3 - 6t^2 + 9t$$

Ratio of distance and displacement of body in first five seconds will be

(a) 1 (b) 2

(c) $\frac{3}{7}$ (d) $\frac{7}{5}$

39. A body of mass M thrown horizontally with velocity v from the top of the tower of height H touches the ground at a distance of 100 m from the foot of the tower. If a body of mass $2M$ thrown at a velocity $\frac{v}{2}$ from the top of the tower of height $4H$, at what distance from the base of the tower will it touch the ground?

(a) 50 m

(b) 70 m

(c) 100 m

(d) 130 m

40. Simple harmonic motion is followed by a particle along the X-axis. If the distances x_1 and x_2 from the mean position, the velocities of the particle are v_1 and v_2 respectively, then the time period of its oscillation is given as

(a) $T = 2\pi\sqrt{\frac{x_2^2 + x_1^2}{v_1^2 - v_2^2}}$

(b) $T = 2\pi\sqrt{\frac{x_2^2 + x_1^2}{v_1^2 + v_2^2}}$

(c) $T = 2\pi\sqrt{\frac{x_2^2 - x_1^2}{v_1^2 + v_2^2}}$

(d) $T = 2\pi\sqrt{\frac{x_2^2 - x_1^2}{v_1^2 - v_2^2}}$

41. A bubble underwater oscillates with period T, which is directly proportional to $p^{-5/6}\, d^{1/2}\, E^{\gamma}$, where p is pressure, d is density and E is energy. The value of γ is

(a) $\frac{1}{3}$ (b) $\frac{1}{5}$

(c) $\frac{1}{6}$ (d) $\frac{1}{7}$

42. A block takes t time to slide down on a smooth surface at 45° inclined plane but same identical block takes twice as much time to slide down on a rough surface inclined at 45°. The coefficient of kinetic friction between the block and rough inclined plane is

(a) 1.141 (b) 0.25

(c) 0.75 (d) 0.173

43. Two bodies of masses 5 kg and 3 kg respectively are connected to two ends of a light string passing over horizontal frictionless pulley. The tension in the string is (Take, $g = 9.8\ \text{m/s}^2$)

(a) 60 N (b) 36.75 N

(c) 73.50 N (d) 18 N

44. The bulk modulus of water is $2.1 \times 10^{19}\ \text{N/m}^2$. The pressure required to increase the density of water by 0.1% is

(a) $2.1 \times 10^3\ \text{N/m}^2$

(b) $2.1 \times 10^6\ \text{N/m}^2$

(c) $2.1 \times 10^5\ \text{N/m}^2$

(d) $2.1 \times 10^7\ \text{N/m}^2$

45. A wheel of radius r consists of a thin uniform rim of mass m and six thin spokes of mass m. The moment of inertia of the wheel about axis passing through point P and perpendicular to the plane is

(a) $3mr^2$ (b) $4mr^2$

(c) $6mr^2$ (d) $10\ mr^2$

Response Index

01 ⓐ ⓑ ⓒ ⓓ	14 ⓐ ⓑ ⓒ ⓓ	27 ⓐ ⓑ ⓒ ⓓ	40 ⓐ ⓑ ⓒ ⓓ
02 ⓐ ⓑ ⓒ ⓓ	15 ⓐ ⓑ ⓒ ⓓ	28 ⓐ ⓑ ⓒ ⓓ	41 ⓐ ⓑ ⓒ ⓓ
03 ⓐ ⓑ ⓒ ⓓ	16 ⓐ ⓑ ⓒ ⓓ	29 ⓐ ⓑ ⓒ ⓓ	42 ⓐ ⓑ ⓒ ⓓ
04 ⓐ ⓑ ⓒ ⓓ	17 ⓐ ⓑ ⓒ ⓓ	30 ⓐ ⓑ ⓒ ⓓ	43 ⓐ ⓑ ⓒ ⓓ
05 ⓐ ⓑ ⓒ ⓓ	18 ⓐ ⓑ ⓒ ⓓ	31 ⓐ ⓑ ⓒ ⓓ	44 ⓐ ⓑ ⓒ ⓓ
06 ⓐ ⓑ ⓒ ⓓ	19 ⓐ ⓑ ⓒ ⓓ	32 ⓐ ⓑ ⓒ ⓓ	45 ⓐ ⓑ ⓒ ⓓ
07 ⓐ ⓑ ⓒ ⓓ	20 ⓐ ⓑ ⓒ ⓓ	33 ⓐ ⓑ ⓒ ⓓ	
08 ⓐ ⓑ ⓒ ⓓ	21 ⓐ ⓑ ⓒ ⓓ	34 ⓐ ⓑ ⓒ ⓓ	
09 ⓐ ⓑ ⓒ ⓓ	22 ⓐ ⓑ ⓒ ⓓ	35 ⓐ ⓑ ⓒ ⓓ	
10 ⓐ ⓑ ⓒ ⓓ	23 ⓐ ⓑ ⓒ ⓓ	36 ⓐ ⓑ ⓒ ⓓ	
11 ⓐ ⓑ ⓒ ⓓ	24 ⓐ ⓑ ⓒ ⓓ	37 ⓐ ⓑ ⓒ ⓓ	
12 ⓐ ⓑ ⓒ ⓓ	25 ⓐ ⓑ ⓒ ⓓ	38 ⓐ ⓑ ⓒ ⓓ	
13 ⓐ ⓑ ⓒ ⓓ	26 ⓐ ⓑ ⓒ ⓓ	39 ⓐ ⓑ ⓒ ⓓ	

Performance Scanner

> 90% Excellent !	You have mastered the NEET syllabus (11th). The concepts of this syllabus are on your fingertips. Maintain this momentum.
76-90% Very Good !	You have a good command over the NEET syllabus (11th). Revise it again after a few days and enhance your performance.
60-75% Good !	You have a wide scope to learn for the NEET syllabus (11th). Revise it again.
<60% Not Satisfactory!	You have a long way ahead of you to master the NEET syllabus (11th). Revise it thoroughly.

Space for Rough Work

Test Booklet No. **3947119**

Test Booklet Code **NSS 3**

MEDACE
NEET (UG)
SELF ASSESSMENT KIT

NEET Stepping Stones 3

(Based on Complete 11th Syllabus)

Name of the Candidate (In Capitals)

____

____

____

Candidate's Signature ______________

Invigilator's Signature ______________

Facsimile signature stamp of center superintendent______________

Important Instructions

- The test is of 45 minutes and the Test Booklet contains 45 multiple choice questions (four options with a single correct answer) from Physics.
- Candidates are advised to read all questions before they start attempting the question paper.
- Each question carries 4 marks. For each correct response, the candidate will get 4 marks. For each incorrect response, one mark will be deducted from the total scores. The maximum marks are 180.
- In the event of candidate marking more than one option then one mark will be deducted.
- Use **Blue/Black Point Pen** only for writing particular on this page/ marking response on Answer Sheet.

Do not open this Booklet until you start attempting the Test

Physics (Q. No. 1-45)

1. A body is thrown vertically upwards. If air resistance is taken into account and the time of ascent is t_1 and time of descent is t_2, then which of the following is true ?

(a) $t_1 = t_2$ (b) $t_1 < t_2$
(c) $t_1 > t_2$ (d) $t_1 \geq t_2$

2. Select the correct option about harmonic progressive wave.

(a) All particles have same phase at given instant of time.
(b) All particles have different amplitudes.
(c) All particles have different phase at a given instant of time.
(d) All particles have same momentum at a given instant of time.

3. **Statement I** Newton's laws are not valid in non-inertial frame of reference.

Statement II A non-inertial frame has a non-zero velocity.

In the light of above statements, choose the most appropriate answer from the options given below:

(a) Both Statement I and Statement II are correct.
(b) Both Statement I and Statement II are incorrect.
(c) Statement I is correct but Statement II is incorrect.
(d) Statement I is incorrect but Statement II is correct.

4. A body is released from a point distance r from the centre of earth. If R is the radius of the earth and $r > R$, then the velocity of the body at the time of striking the earth will be

(a) $\sqrt{2gr}$ (b) $\sqrt{2gR}$
(c) $\sqrt{\frac{2gRr}{r-R}}$ (d) $\sqrt{\frac{2gR(r-R)}{r}}$

5. A block of mass m is given an initial velocity v over a rough surface, then time taken by block to stop, is

(a) directly proportional to mass of block
(b) inversely proportional to mass of block
(c) inversely proportional to square of mass
(d) independent of mass of block

6. A cable that can support a maximum load of 320 kg is cut into two equal parts. The maximum load that can be supported by either part is

(a) 80 kg (b) 160 kg
(c) 320 kg (d) 640 kg

7. A planet moves around the sun. Its closest distance from sun is d_1 and at this point speed is v_1. At farthest point from sun, its distance is d_2, speed of planet at farthest point will be

(a) $\frac{d_1^2 v_1}{d_2^2}$ (b) $\frac{d_2 v_1}{d_1}$
(c) $\frac{d_1 v_1}{d_2}$ (d) $\frac{d_2^2 v_1}{d_1}$

8. A gas is heated at constant pressure. Fraction of heat that can be used to do external work is $\left(\gamma = \frac{C_p}{C_V}\right)$

(a) $\frac{1}{\gamma}$ (b) $1 - \frac{1}{\gamma}$
(c) $1 - \frac{1}{\gamma^2}$ (d) $\gamma - 1$

9. A hollow sphere of mass 3 kg and radius 50 cm rolls down without slipping on inclined plane of height 20 m. When it reaches at the bottom, its rotational kinetic energy is ($g = 10 \text{ m/s}^2$)

(a) 600 J (b) 240 J
(c) 360 J (d) 171.4 J

10. Conservation of mechanical energy holds true when on system
(a) only conservative forces act
(b) only non-conservative forces act
(c) total work done of non-conservative force is zero
(d) total work done of both conservative and non-conservative forces is zero

11. A particle is projected with some initial velocity at an angle θ with the horizontal from the ground. If the particle remains in air for 4 s, then its maximum possible horizontal range is
(Take, $g = 10 \text{ m/s}^2$)
(a) 40 m (b) 60 m
(c) 80 m (d) 100 m

12. The time period of particle executing SHM is doubled by keeping maximum velocity constant, then
(a) amplitude becomes half
(b) maximum acceleration becomes double
(c) total energy becomes four times
(d) total energy becomes double

13. The value of coefficient of volume expansion of glycerin is $5 \times 10^{-4} \text{ K}^{-1}$. The fractional change in the density of glycerin for a rise of 50°C in its temperature is
(a) 0.010 (b) 0.015
(c) 0.020 (d) 0.025

14. Let h = Planck's constant, ε = permittivity,
μ = permeability and R = Rydberg's constant.
Then, dimensions of quantity $\dfrac{h \times \sqrt{\varepsilon\mu}}{R}$ are same as that of
(a) Reynold's number (b) energy density
(c) moment of inertia (d) thermal conductivity

15. **Statement I** Fundamental frequency of a narrow organ pipe is more than a broad diameter organ pipe of same length.
Statement II If we apply Laplace end correction, then fundamental frequency of a closed organ pipe is more than $\dfrac{v}{4l}$.

In the light of above statements, choose the most appropriate answer from the options given below.
(a) Both Statement I and Statement II are correct.
(b) Both Statement I and Statement II are incorrect.
(c) Statement I is correct but Statement II is incorrect.
(d) Statement I is incorrect but Statement II is correct.

16. A particle at the end of a spring executes SHM with a period t_1 while corresponding to period of another spring is t_2. If the period of oscillation with the two springs in series is T, then
(a) $T = t_1 + t_2$ (b) $T^2 = t_1^2 + t_2^2$
(c) $T^{-1} = t_1^{-1} + t_2^{-1}$ (d) $\dfrac{1}{T^2} = \dfrac{1}{t_1^2} + \dfrac{1}{t_2^2}$

17. A column of air and a tuning fork produces 4 beats/s. When sounding together, the tuning fork gives the lower note. The temperature of air is 15°C. When the temperature falls to 10°C, the two produce 3 beats/s. Find the frequency of the tuning fork.
(a) 112.67 Hz (b) 110.76 Hz
(c) 100 Hz (d) 973 Hz

18. What should be the minimum coefficient of static friction between the plane and the cylinder, for the cylinder not a slip on an inclined plane?
(a) $\dfrac{1}{3}\tan\theta$ (b) $\dfrac{1}{3}\sin\theta$
(c) $\dfrac{2}{3}\tan\theta$ (d) $\dfrac{2}{3}\sin\theta$

19. At 27° C two moles of an ideal monoatomic gas occupy a volume V. The gas expands adiabatically to volume $2V$. What will be the final temperature and change in internal energy of the gas?
(a) 175K, – 2767.25 J (b) 189 K, – 2767.23 J
(c) 189 K, – 2677.23 J (d) 175, – 2677.23 J

20. Two balls A and B are thrown vertically upward from the same location on the surface of earth with velocities $2\sqrt{\dfrac{gR}{3}}$ and $\sqrt{\dfrac{2gR}{3}}$ respectively, where R is the radius of earth and g is the acceleration due to gravity. The ratio of the maximum heights attained by A to attained by B is

(a) 7 (b) 5 (c) $4\sqrt{2}$ (d) 4

21. 1 kg of steam at 200°C is converted into 20° C ice. If Q_1 is the heat released to convert steam at 200°C to 100°C steam, Q_2 is the heat released to convert steam at 100°C to water at 100°C, Q_3 is the heat released to convert water at 100°C to water at 0°C, Q_4 is heat released to convert water at 0°C to ice at 0°C and Q_5 is the heat released to convert ice at 0°C to ice at – 20°C, then match List I with List II.

	List I		List II
A	$Q_1 + Q_2$	1.	180 kcal
B.	$Q_1 + Q_3$	2.	150 kcal
C.	$Q_2 + Q_5$	3.	590 kcal
D	$Q_3 + Q_4$	4.	550 kcal

Choose the correct answer from the options given below.

	A B C D		A B C D
(a)	1 4 3 2	(b)	3 2 4 1
(c)	3 1 4 2	(d)	4 3 2 1

22. A 2 kg block slides on a horizontal floor at a speed of 4m/s. It then strikes an uncompressed spring and compresses it untill the block comes to a stop. The kinetic friction force between the block and the floor is 15 N and the spring constant is 10000 N/m. By how much does the spring compress?

(a) 11.2 cm (b) 5.5 cm (c) 2.7 cm (d) 8.8 cm

23. An airplane is flying at an altitude of 490 m with a horizontal velocity of 150 m/s. To deliver a bag of food directly to soldiers on the ground, how far in advanced should the bag be released from the airplane?

(a) 2000 m (b) 1250 m (c) 2500 m (d) 1500 m

24. In a system of units, a unit mass is 10 kg, length is 1 km and time is 1 min. What will be the value of 1 J in this system of unit?

(a) 3.6 (b) 36×10^{-2}

(c) 36×10^{-5} (d) 36×10^{2}

25. The displacement of a particle is represented by the equation $y = \sin^3 \omega t$. The motion is

(a) non-periodic

(b) periodic but not simple harmonic

(c) simple harmonic with period $2\pi/\omega$

(d) simple harmonic with period π/ω

26. **Assertion** (A) The internal energy of a real gas is a function of both temperature and volume.

Reason (R) Internal kinetic energy of real gases depends on temperature and internal potential energy depends on volume.

In the light of above statements, choose the most appropriate answer from the option given below.

(a) Both A and R are true and R is the correct explanation of A.

(b) Both A and R are true but R is not the correct explanation of A.

(c) A is true but R is false.

(d) A is false but R is true.

27. A spherical ball of radius 3.0×10^{-4} m and density 10^4 kg/m^3 falls freely under gravity through a distance h before entering a tank of water. If after entering the water, the velocity of the ball does not change, then find the value of h. (Viscosity of water = 9.8×10^{-6} N-s/m^2)

(a) 1.65×10^3 m (b) 1.75×10^3 m

(c) 1.60×10^3 m (d) 1.50×10^3 m

28. A uniform metal wire having Young's modulus 2×10^{11} N/m^2 is subjected to longitudinal stress of 5×10^7N/m^2. If the overall volume change in the wire is 0.02%, the fractional decrease in the radius of the wire is

(a) 0.25×10^{-4} (b) 0.25×10^{5}

(c) 0.5×10^{-4} (d) 1×10^{5}

29. 8 g of steam at 100°C is added to 40 g of water at 50°C in a container of negligible mass. Assuming no heat is lost to surrounding, then the mass of water in container at thermal equilibrium is (Take, latent heat of vaporisation = 540 cal/g and specific heat of water = 1 cal/g-°C)

(a) 38 g (b) 40 g (c) 42 g (d) 43.7 g

30. A block weighing 200 N is pulled at a constant speed along a rough horizontal surface by a force of 100 N which is applied at an angle of 30° above the horizontal. Determine the coefficient friction between the block and the surface.

(a) 0.85 (b) 0.58 (c) 0.45 (d) 0.75

31. A person throws a ball at a height of 1.2 m above the ground at an angle of 45°. Its horizontal range is 110 m. The ball is lifted towards the field line where a fence of 7.5 m is located 100 m from the person who throws the ball. What will be the velocity of projection of the ball?

(a) $\frac{110}{\sqrt{10.88}}$ (b) $\frac{(110)^2}{10.88}$

(c) $\frac{110}{108.8}$ (d) $\frac{110}{\sqrt{108.8}}$

32. A body is moving in a straight line covers $\frac{1}{3}$ rd of the total distance with velocity v_1. The remaining distance is covered with velocity v_2 for half time and with a velocity v_3 for other half of the time. What is the mean velocity averaged over the entire duration of the motion?

(a) $\frac{3v_1(v_2+v_3)}{v_1+v_2+v_3}$ (b) $\frac{3v_1(v_2+v_3)}{4v_1+v_2+v_3}$

(c) $\frac{v_1(v_2+v_3)}{v_1+v_2+v_3}$ (d) $\frac{3v_1(v_2+v_3)}{2v_1+v_2+v_3}$

33. The linear momentum of a sphere of mass of 2 kg varies with time t as $p = 3t^2 + 4$, where p and t are in SI units. It follows that the sphere moving with

(a) constant acceleration (b) variable acceleration

(c) constant speed (d) constant velocity

34. An ideal monoatomic gas at temperature 27° C and pressure 10^6 N/m^2 occupies 10 L volume. 10000 cal of heat is added to the system without changing the volume. Calculate the final temperature of the gas.
(Given, $R = 8.31$ J/mol-K and $J = 4.18$ J/cal)

(a) 1000 K (b) 1133 K

(c) 1240 K (d) 1300 K

35. A steel cable of radius 1.5 cm can support a chair lift. If the maximum stress is not to exceed 10^8 N / m^2, what will be the maximum load the cable can support?

(a) 7.5×10^4 N (b) 7.1×10^4 N

(c) 5.8×10^4 N (d) 8.2×10^4 N

36. Two wires of same material having radius in ratio 2 : 1 and lengths in ratio 1 : 4. If same force is applied on them, then ratio of their change in length will be

(a) 1 : 1 (b) 1 : 2

(c) 1 : 4 (d) 1 : 16

37. A truck accelerates from rest at a constant rate a for a certain period of time, then decelerates at a constant rate b until it comes to rest. If total time elapsed is t, then what is the maximum velocity acquired by the truck?

(a) $\left(\frac{ab}{a+b}\right)t$ (b) $\left(\frac{a+b}{ab}\right)t$

(c) $\left(\frac{a}{a+b}\right)t$ (d) $\left(\frac{a^2+b^2}{ab}\right)t$

38. A ball is projected vertically upward from the top of a building and takes time t_1 to reach the ground. If the ball is thrown vertically downward from the same point with same initial speed, it takes time t_2 to reach the ground. If the ball is allowed to fall freely from same point what will be the time taken to reach the ground?

(a) $\frac{t_1+t_2}{2}$ (b) $\frac{t_1-t_2}{2}$

(c) $\sqrt{\frac{t_1}{t_2}}$ (d) $\sqrt{t_1 t_2}$

39. Starting from rest a car accelerates at the rate of a through a distance s, then continues at constant speed for time t and then decelerate at the rate of $\frac{a}{2}$ to come to rest. If total distance travelled is $15s$, then

(a) $s = ft$ (b) $s = \frac{1}{7}at^2$

(c) $s = \frac{1}{5}at^2$ (d) $s = \frac{at^2}{72}$

40. When a body of mass m is raised to a height h above the Earth's surface, its weight decreases by 1%. If the body is taken to a depth h into a mine, what will be the change in its weight?

(a) decreases by 2% (b) increases by 2%

(c) decreases by 0.5% (d) increases by 0.5%

41. Maximum kinetic energy of a particle of mass 1 kg in SHM is 8 J. Time period of SHM is 4 s. Maximum potential energy during the motion is 10 J, then

(a) amplitude of oscillations is approximately 4.53 m

(b) minimum potential energy of the particle is 4 J

(c) maximum acceleration of the particle is approximately 6.3 ms^{-2}

(d) minimum kinetic energy of the particle is 2 J

42. The root mean square speed of molecules of a gas is 1260 m/s. The average speed of the gas molecules is

(a) 1161 m/s

(b) 1671 m/s

(c) 912 m/s

(d) 1040 m/

43. Three identical metal rods A, B and C are placed end to end and a temperature difference is maintained between their ends. If the thermal conductivity of $B\,(K_B)$ is twice that of C (K_C) and half that of $A(K_A)$, then the effective thermal conductivity of the arrangement is

(a) $\frac{K_A}{7}$ (b) $\frac{6}{7}K_B$

(c) $\frac{7}{3}K_B$ (d) $7K_C$

44. Match the process in Column I with the predictions of first law given in Column II.

Column I	Column II
A. Isothermal	1. $Q = W = \Delta E_{int} = 0$
B. Adiabatic	2. $\Delta E_{int} = -W$
C. Isobaric	3. $\Delta E_{int} = 0, Q = W$
D. Free expansion	4. $\Delta E_{int} + W = \Delta E_{int} + p\Delta V$

Codes

A B C D

(a) 3 2 4 1 (b) 2 3 1 4

(c) 4 3 2 1 (d) 4 2 3 1

45. A particle is moving on circular path of radius 2 m with uniform speed of 10 m/s. At $t = 0$ s, the particle is at point P as shown in figure. The direction of acceleration vector at $t = \frac{3\pi}{10}$ s is

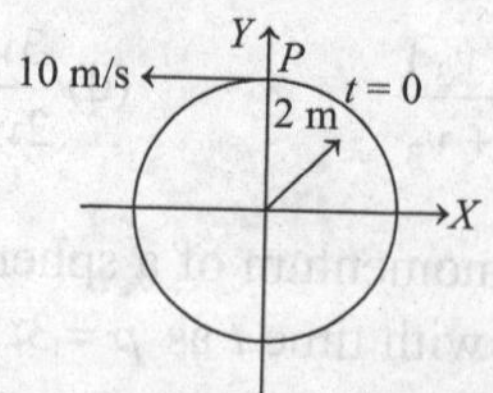

(a) along $\hat{i}$ (b) along $(-\hat{i})$

(c) along $\hat{j}$ (d) along $\left(\frac{\hat{i}-\hat{j}}{\sqrt{2}}\right)$

■ **Response Index**

01 ⓐ ⓑ ⓒ ⓓ	14 ⓐ ⓑ ⓒ ⓓ	27 ⓐ ⓑ ⓒ ⓓ	40 ⓐ ⓑ ⓒ ⓓ
02 ⓐ ⓑ ⓒ ⓓ	15 ⓐ ⓑ ⓒ ⓓ	28 ⓐ ⓑ ⓒ ⓓ	41 ⓐ ⓑ ⓒ ⓓ
03 ⓐ ⓑ ⓒ ⓓ	16 ⓐ ⓑ ⓒ ⓓ	29 ⓐ ⓑ ⓒ ⓓ	42 ⓐ ⓑ ⓒ ⓓ
04 ⓐ ⓑ ⓒ ⓓ	17 ⓐ ⓑ ⓒ ⓓ	30 ⓐ ⓑ ⓒ ⓓ	43 ⓐ ⓑ ⓒ ⓓ
05 ⓐ ⓑ ⓒ ⓓ	18 ⓐ ⓑ ⓒ ⓓ	31 ⓐ ⓑ ⓒ ⓓ	44 ⓐ ⓑ ⓒ ⓓ
06 ⓐ ⓑ ⓒ ⓓ	19 ⓐ ⓑ ⓒ ⓓ	32 ⓐ ⓑ ⓒ ⓓ	45 ⓐ ⓑ ⓒ ⓓ
07 ⓐ ⓑ ⓒ ⓓ	20 ⓐ ⓑ ⓒ ⓓ	33 ⓐ ⓑ ⓒ ⓓ	
08 ⓐ ⓑ ⓒ ⓓ	21 ⓐ ⓑ ⓒ ⓓ	34 ⓐ ⓑ ⓒ ⓓ	
09 ⓐ ⓑ ⓒ ⓓ	22 ⓐ ⓑ ⓒ ⓓ	35 ⓐ ⓑ ⓒ ⓓ	
10 ⓐ ⓑ ⓒ ⓓ	23 ⓐ ⓑ ⓒ ⓓ	36 ⓐ ⓑ ⓒ ⓓ	
11 ⓐ ⓑ ⓒ ⓓ	24 ⓐ ⓑ ⓒ ⓓ	37 ⓐ ⓑ ⓒ ⓓ	
12 ⓐ ⓑ ⓒ ⓓ	25 ⓐ ⓑ ⓒ ⓓ	38 ⓐ ⓑ ⓒ ⓓ	
13 ⓐ ⓑ ⓒ ⓓ	26 ⓐ ⓑ ⓒ ⓓ	39 ⓐ ⓑ ⓒ ⓓ	

■ **Performance Scanner**

> 90% Excellent !	You have mastered the NEET syllabus (11th). The concepts of this syllabus are on your fingertips. Maintain this momentum.
76-90% Very Good !	You have a good command over the NEET syllabus (11th). Revise it again after a few days and enhance your performance.
60-75% Good !	You have a wide scope to learn for the NEET syllabus (11th). Revise it again.
<60% Not Satisfactory!	You have a long way ahead of you to master the NEET syllabus (11th). Revise it thoroughly.

Space for Rough Work

Space for Rough Work

Test Booklet No. **3947120**

Test Booklet Code **NSS 4**

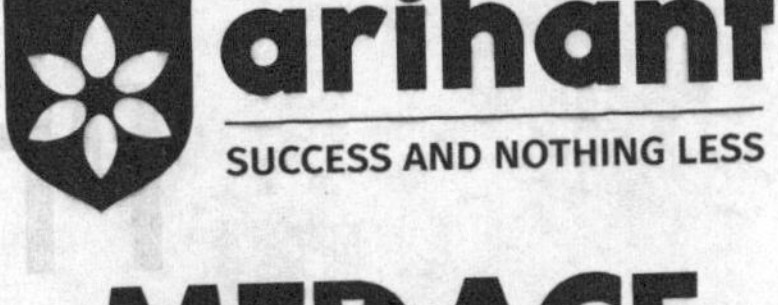

MEDACE

NEET (UG)

SELF ASSESSMENT KIT

NEET Stepping Stones 4

(Based on Complete 11th Syllabus)

Name of the Candidate (In Capitals)

____

____

____

Candidate's Signature ______________

Invigilator's Signature ______________

Facsimile signature stamp of center superintendent______________

Important Instructions

- The test is of 45 minutes and the Test Booklet contains 45 multiple choice questions (four options with a single correct answer) from Physics.
- Candidates are advised to read all questions before they start attempting the question paper.
- Each question carries 4 marks. For each correct response, the candidate will get 4 marks. For each incorrect response, one mark will be deducted from the total scores. The maximum marks are 180.
- In the event of candidate marking more than one option then one mark will be deducted.
- Use **Blue/Black Point Pen** only for writing particular on this page/ marking response on Answer Sheet.

Do not open this Booklet until you start attempting the Test

Physics (Q. No. 1-45)

1. A ball is dropped from a spacecraft revolving around the earth at a height of 150 km. What will happen to the ball?

(a) It will continue to move with the same speed along the original orbit of spacecraft.

(b) It will fall down to earth with speed of 2 km/s.

(c) It will fall down to earth with speed of 5 km/s.

(d) It will go very far in space.

2. A particle moves in a straight line with a constant acceleration. It changes its velocity from 15 m/s to 25 m/s while passing through a distance 150 m in t s. The value of t is

(a) 9 (b) 8.5

(c) 7.5 (d) 10

3. Five moles of hydrogen gas $\left(\gamma = \frac{7}{5}\right)$, initially at standard temperature and pressure, are compressed adiabatically until the temperature matches 400°C. Determine the increase in internal energy of the gas expressed in kJ.

(a) 45.5 (b) 41.5

(c) 40.2 (d) 49.2

4. A rectangular film of liquid is extended from 16 cm^2 to 40 cm^2. If the work done is 5×10^{-4} J, the value of the surface tension of liquid is

(a) 0.1 N/m (b) 0.2 N/m

(c) 0.3 N/m (d) 0.5 N/m

5. T is the time period of simple pendulum on the earth's surface. Its time period becomes $x\,T$ when taken to a height R (equal to earth's radius) above the earth's surface. Then, the value of x will be

(a) 2 (b) $\frac{1}{2}$ (c) 4 (d) $\frac{1}{4}$

6. Which of the following equations can be derived using method of dimensional analysis?

(a) $N = N_0 \cdot e^{-\lambda t}$

(b) $y = A \sin(\omega t + kx)$

(c) $E = \frac{1}{2}mv^2 + \frac{1}{2}I\omega^2$

(d) None of the above

7. A particle executes linear SHM with an amplitude of 5 cm. When the particle is at 3 cm from the mean position, the magnitude of its velocity is equal to that of its acceleration. Then, its time period (in s) is

(a) 5.8

(b) 4.7

(c) 6.2

(d) 3.2

8. An ideal gas initially at pressure p_1 undergoes isothermal expansion from volume V_1 to V_2 followed by adiabatic compression back to its final pressure of p_3. The total work done during the entire process is W. What will be the relation between the variables?

(a) $p_3 = p_1$ $W = 0$

(b) $p_3 > p_1, W < 0$

(c) $p_3 < p_1, W < 0$

(d) $p_3 > p_1$ $W > 0$

9. The period of revolution of a planet A around the sun is 27 times that of B. The distance of A from the sun is how many times greater than that of B from the sun ?

(a) 4

(b) 6

(c) 9

(d) 12

10. Which of these graphs correctly shows change of kinetic energy K of a small steel ball dropping in a deep water lake?

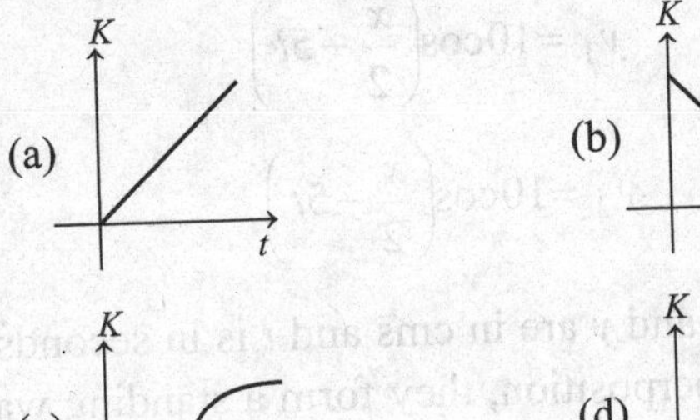

11. Statement I Without any external force, there is no change in velocity.

Statement II Force = mass × acceleration in all reference frames.

In light of above statements, choose the most appropriate answer from the options given below:

(a) Both Statement I and Statement II are correct.

(b) Both Statement I and Statement II are incorrect.

(c) Statement I is correct but Statement II is incorrect.

(d) Statement I is incorrect but Statement II is correct.

12. A disc rolls without slipping and climbs on a rough inclined surface and come back as shown in the figure. During the motion on inclined surface,

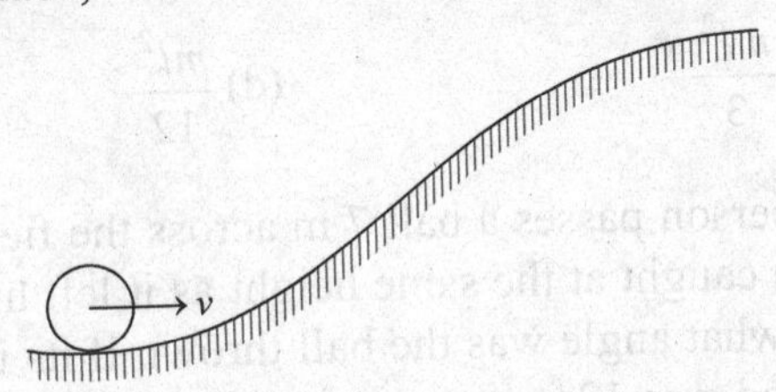

(a) friction is downward during the upward journey

(b) friction is upward during the upward journey

(c) friction is zero

(d) Information is insufficient to determine the direction

13. A large glass surface is 2 mm thick. The outside temperature is −20°C and the inside temperature is 25°C. If the thermal conductivity of glass is 0.8 W/m-K, then the temperature at the mid-point of the window is

(a) 0 °C (b) 2.5 °C

(c) −2.5 °C (d) 22.5 °C

14. Assertion (A) Specific heat capacity and molar specific heat capacity both have same units.

Reason (R) Specific heat capacity and molar specific heat capacity both do not depend on mass.

In the light of above statements choose the most appropriate answer from the options given below.

(a) Both A and R are true and R is the correct explanation of A.

(b) Both A and R are true but R is not the correct explanation of A.

(c) A is true but R is false.

(d) A is false but R is true.

15. Heat is evolved in a resistance on passing current upto definite time. Measurement for current, time and resistance suffer practical errors of magnitudes 1%, 2% and 2%, respectively. The maximum percentage error in the heat evolved will be

(a) 6% (b) 8%

(c) 5% (d) 3%

16. A metal rod of length l and with end face radii r_1 and r_2 is stretched by equal forces F applied at both ends, shown in the figure. Given that Y is the Young's modulus of the metal, determine the extension produced in the length of the rod.

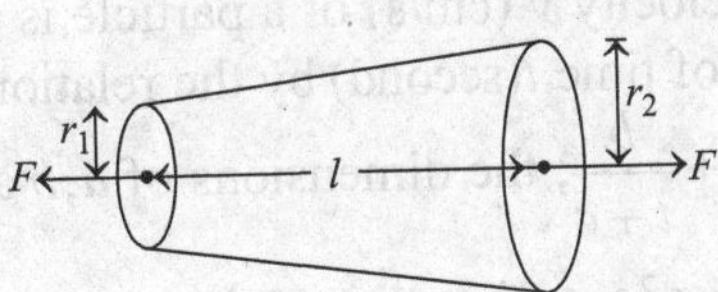

(a) $\dfrac{lF}{\pi r_1^2 Y}$ (b) $\dfrac{lF}{\pi^2 r_1 r_2 Y}$

(c) $\dfrac{lF}{\pi r_2^2 Y}$ (d) $\dfrac{lF}{\pi r_1 r_2 Y}$

17. An ideal gas undergoes the cycle $A \rightarrow B \rightarrow C \rightarrow A$, as illustrated in the figure. If the net heat supplied to the gas during the entire cycle is 5 J, then the work done by gas during the process from C to A is

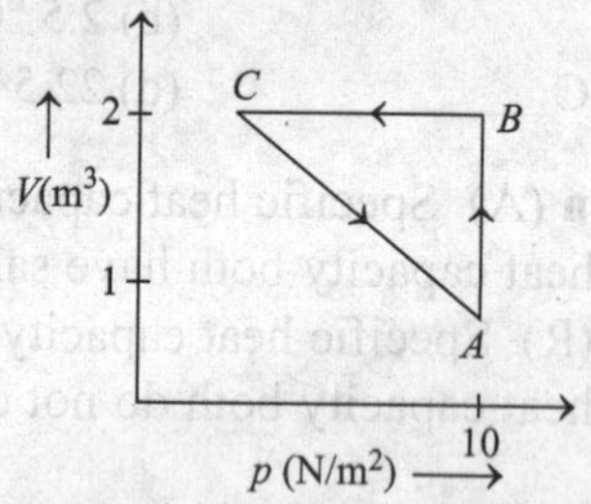

(a) –15 J (b) –5 J
(c) – 20 J (d) –10 J

18. A copper rod of cylindrical shape has length 1 m and a cross-sectional area of 2 cm^2. The rod is insulated along its curved surface. If one end of the rod is placed in a stream chamber while the other end is in contact with ice at 0°C, determine the temperature at a point located 60 cm from the colder end of the rod. (Take thermal conductivity of copper = 386 J/m°C)

(a) 40°C (b) 60°C
(c) 70°C (d) 80°C

19. A series of tuning forks are arranged in increasing order of frequency and any two successive tuning forks produce 4 beats/s when sounded together. If the last tuning fork has a frequency that is an octave higher than the first tuning fork and the frequency of the first tuning fork is 256 Hz, then the total number of tuning forks in the series is

(a) 76 (b) 65 (c) 67 (d) 71

20. The velocity v (cm/s) of a particle is given in terms of time t(second) by the relation $v = at + \frac{b}{t+c}$; the dimensions of a, b and c are

(a) $a = [L^2], b = [T], c = [LT^2]$
(b) $a = [L], b = [LT], c = [T]^2$
(c) $a = [L^2T], b = [LT], c = [L]$
(d) $a = [LT^{-2}], b = [L], c = [T]$

21. Two electromagnetic waves are travelling in opposite direction along X-axis and their wave equations are given as

$$y_1 = 10\cos\left(\frac{x}{2} + 5t\right)$$

and $$y_2 = 10\cos\left(\frac{x}{2} - 5t\right)$$

where, x and y are in cms and t is in seconds. After superposition, they form a standing wave. What is the distance between nodes and anti-nodes?

(a) 3.14 cm (b) 4.51 cm
(c) 1 cm (d) 2 cm

22. The coefficient of linear expansion of a crystal in one direction is α_1 and in the direction perpendicular to it is α_2. What is the coefficient of volume expansion for the crystal?

(a) $\alpha_1 + 2\alpha_2$
(b) $2\alpha_1 + 2\alpha_2$
(c) $2\alpha_1 + \alpha_2$
(d) $\alpha_1 + \alpha_2$

23. Three thin metal rods, each with a mass m and length l, are melded together to form an equilateral triangle. What is the moment of inertia of this triangular structure about an axis that passes through its centre of mass and is perpendicular to the plane of triangle?

(a) $\frac{ml^2}{2}$ (b) $\frac{ml^2}{6}$
(c) $\frac{ml^2}{3}$ (d) $\frac{ml^2}{12}$

24. A person passes a ball 7 m across the field, where it is caught at the same height as it left his hand. At what angle was the ball thrown if its initial speed was 12 m/s, assuming that the smaller of the two possible angles was used?

(a) 10° (b) 12.4°
(c) 14.2° (d) 15.4°

25. Third overtone of a closed organ pipe is in unison with fourth harmonic of an open organ pipe. Find the ratio of length of organ pipes.

(a) 7 : 8 (b) 3 : 4

(c) 1 : 2 (d) 5 : 6

26. What will the dimensions of mass, if energy (E), velocity (v) and force (F) are taken as the fundamental quantities?

(a) $[Ev^{-2}]$ (b) $[Fv^{-3}]$

(c) $[Ev^2]$ (d) $[Fv^{-1}]$

27. To compress one kilomole of a gas adiabatically, 146 kJ of work is done, causing the temperature of the gas to increase by 7°C. Given that, $R = 8.3$ J/mole-K, identify the gas.

(a) Monoatomic

(b) Triatomic

(c) A mixture of monoatomic and diatomic

(d) Diatomic

28. When heat Q is supplied to a diatomic gas of rigid molecules, at constant volume, its temperature increases by ΔT. The heat required to produce the same change in temperature, at a constant pressure is

(a) $\frac{2}{3}Q$ (b) $\frac{5}{3}Q$

(c) $\frac{3}{2}Q$ (d) $\frac{7}{5}Q$

29. Water is conveyed through a pipe of inner radius 5 cm at a rate of 1000 litres per minute to a place 5 km far away. The coefficient of viscosity of water is 0.001 $Nm^{-2}s$, the required pressure difference (in 10^4 Nm^{-2}) is

(a) 3.4 (b) 1.2

(c) 2.7 (d) 4.3

30. A bird is flying horizontally at a speed of 3 m/s when the fish in her talons wiggles lose and falls into the lake 5 m below. What will be the velocity of fish relative to the water when it hits the water?

(a) 12.24 m/s (b) 10.3 m/s

(c) 9.90 m/s (d) 13.3 m/s

31. A ball is thrown vertically upwards with a velocity u from the balloon descending with velocity v (constant). The ball will pass by the balloon after time

(a) $\frac{|u-v|}{2g}$ (b) $\frac{u+v}{2g}$

(c) $\frac{2|u-v|}{g}$ (d) $\frac{2(u+v)}{g}$

32. Match the List I (examples of different types of motion) with List II (types of motion)

List I	List II
A. Circular motion of a rigid body about a common axis	1. Projectile
B. Motion of a pendulum	2. Rectilinear
C. Motion of a car on a straight road	3. Oscillatory
D. Motion of a ball thrown by a boy at an angle with horizontal	4. Rotational

Choose the correct option from the codes given below.

Codes

	A	B	C	D
(a)	2	3	4	1
(b)	4	3	2	1
(c)	3	4	1	2
(d)	4	3	1	2

33. The potential energy of a particle of mass 0.5 kg in moving along the X-axis is given by $U = 2(1 - \cos 5x)$ J, where x is in metres. The time period of small oscillations is

(a) $\frac{\pi}{\sqrt{5}}$ s (b) $\sqrt{5}\,\pi$s

(c) $\frac{\pi}{5}$ s (d) $\frac{\pi}{10}$ s

34. The bottom end of a cubical block of side 5×10^{-2} m is fixed. A force of 10^5N tangential to the top face displaces it by 1.2×10^{-4} m. The rigidity modulus is

(a) 6×10^{-10} Nm^{-2}

(b) 6×10^{-9} Nm^{-2}

(c) 1.67×10^{10} Nm^{-2}

(d) 10^{11} Nm^{-2}

35. If the earth shrinks to n times of its radius without changing its mass, then duration of the day will be

(a) nT (b) $\frac{T}{n}$

(c) n^2T (d) $\frac{T}{n^2}$

(where, T = duration of day before shrinking)

36. Two bodies have their moments of inertia I and $2I$ respectively, about their axis of rotation. If their kinetic energies of rotation are equal, their angular velocities will be in the ratio

(a) $2:1$ (b) $1:2$

(c) $\sqrt{2}:1$ (d) $1:\sqrt{2}$

37. Two balls of masses m_1 and m_2 are moving with velocities $v_1\hat{\mathbf{i}}$ and $v_2\hat{\mathbf{i}}$ undergoes a collinear collision. After collision, velocities of m_1 and m_2 are $v_3\hat{\mathbf{i}}$ and $v_4\hat{\mathbf{i}}$ respectively. If $m_2 = 0.5\, m_1$ and $v_3 = 0.5\, v_1$, then value of v_1 is

(a) $v_4 + v_2$ (b) $v_4 - \frac{v_2}{4}$

(c) $v_4 - \frac{v_2}{2}$ (d) $v_4 - v_2$

38. **Statement I** Waves produced by a motor boat sailing in water are both longitudinal and transverse waves.

Statement II The longitudinal and transverse waves cannot be produced simultaneously.

In the light of above statements, choose the most appropriate answer from the options given below.

(a) Both Statement I and Statement II are correct.

(b) Both Statement I and Statement II are incorrect.

(c) Statement I is correct but Statement II is incorrect.

(d) Statement I is incorrect but Statement II is correct.

39. A 15 g mass of nitrogen gas is enclosed in a vessel at a temperature 27°C. Amount of heat transferred to the gas, so that rms velocity of molecules is doubled is about (Take, $R = 8.3$ J/K-mol)

(a) 10 kJ (b) 0.9 kJ

(c) 14 kJ (d) 6 kJ

40. The p-V graph of three different gases A, B and C during adiabatic expansion has been plotted. The gases A, B and C can be respectively

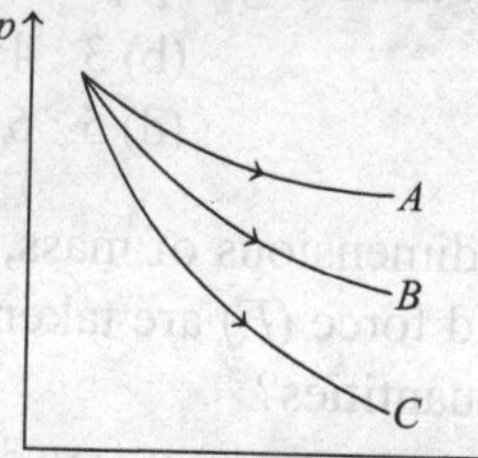

(a) monoatomic, diatomic, polyatomic

(b) polyatomic, diatomic, monoatomic

(c) diatomic, triatomic (linear), triatomic (non-linear)

(d) monoatomic, triatomic (linear), triatomic (non-linear)

41. If a rubber ball falls from a height h and rebounds upto the height of $\frac{h}{2}$. The percentage loss of total energy of the initial system as well as velocity of ball before it strikes the ground, respectively, are

(a) 50%, $\sqrt{\frac{gh}{2}}$ (b) 40%, $\sqrt{2gh}$

(c) 50%, $\sqrt{2gh}$ (d) 50%, $\sqrt{gh}$

42. A 2 kg shell is moving at 4 m/s and suddenly explodes into equal fragments. The fragments travel in directions inclined to the original line of motion with equal velocities. If the explosion imparts a total of 48 J of translational kinetic energy to the fragments, equally divided between them, what are the magnitude and direction of velocity of each fragment?

(a) 6 m/s, 45°

(b) 2 m/s, 45°

(c) 2 m/s, 60°

(d) 8 m/s, 60°

43. A particle of mass m is suspended from a ceiling through a string of length L. The particle moves in a horizontal circle of radius r such that $r = \frac{L}{\sqrt{2}}$.

The speed of particle will be

(a) $\sqrt{rg}$ (b) $\sqrt{2rg}$

(c) $2\sqrt{rg}$ (d) $\sqrt{\frac{rg}{2}}$

44. A liquid with a density ρ and surface tension T rises to a height h in a capillary tube with a radius r. What is the potential energy of the liquid in the capillary tube?

(a) $\frac{2\pi T^2}{\rho g}$ (b) $\frac{\pi T^2}{\rho g}$

(c) $\frac{4\pi T^2}{\rho g}$ (d) $\frac{\pi^2 T^2}{\rho g}$

45. A particle is moving in XY-plane, such that its position co-ordinates at time t are given by $x = 3t$ and $y = 3t(1-4t)$. The time at which velocity vector makes an angle of 45° with acceleration vector is

(a) 4 s (b) $\frac{1}{4}$ s

(c) 45 s (d) $\frac{1}{3}$ s

Response Index

01 ⓐ ⓑ ⓒ ⓓ	14 ⓐ ⓑ ⓒ ⓓ	27 ⓐ ⓑ ⓒ ⓓ	40 ⓐ ⓑ ⓒ ⓓ
02 ⓐ ⓑ ⓒ ⓓ	15 ⓐ ⓑ ⓒ ⓓ	28 ⓐ ⓑ ⓒ ⓓ	41 ⓐ ⓑ ⓒ ⓓ
03 ⓐ ⓑ ⓒ ⓓ	16 ⓐ ⓑ ⓒ ⓓ	29 ⓐ ⓑ ⓒ ⓓ	42 ⓐ ⓑ ⓒ ⓓ
04 ⓐ ⓑ ⓒ ⓓ	17 ⓐ ⓑ ⓒ ⓓ	30 ⓐ ⓑ ⓒ ⓓ	43 ⓐ ⓑ ⓒ ⓓ
05 ⓐ ⓑ ⓒ ⓓ	18 ⓐ ⓑ ⓒ ⓓ	31 ⓐ ⓑ ⓒ ⓓ	44 ⓐ ⓑ ⓒ ⓓ
06 ⓐ ⓑ ⓒ ⓓ	19 ⓐ ⓑ ⓒ ⓓ	32 ⓐ ⓑ ⓒ ⓓ	45 ⓐ ⓑ ⓒ ⓓ
07 ⓐ ⓑ ⓒ ⓓ	20 ⓐ ⓑ ⓒ ⓓ	33 ⓐ ⓑ ⓒ ⓓ	
08 ⓐ ⓑ ⓒ ⓓ	21 ⓐ ⓑ ⓒ ⓓ	34 ⓐ ⓑ ⓒ ⓓ	
09 ⓐ ⓑ ⓒ ⓓ	22 ⓐ ⓑ ⓒ ⓓ	35 ⓐ ⓑ ⓒ ⓓ	
10 ⓐ ⓑ ⓒ ⓓ	23 ⓐ ⓑ ⓒ ⓓ	36 ⓐ ⓑ ⓒ ⓓ	
11 ⓐ ⓑ ⓒ ⓓ	24 ⓐ ⓑ ⓒ ⓓ	37 ⓐ ⓑ ⓒ ⓓ	
12 ⓐ ⓑ ⓒ ⓓ	25 ⓐ ⓑ ⓒ ⓓ	38 ⓐ ⓑ ⓒ ⓓ	
13 ⓐ ⓑ ⓒ ⓓ	26 ⓐ ⓑ ⓒ ⓓ	39 ⓐ ⓑ ⓒ ⓓ	

Performance Scanner

> 90% Excellent !	You have mastered the NEET syllabus (11th). The concepts of this syllabus are on your fingertips. Maintain this momentum.
76-90% Very Good !	You have a good command over the NEET syllabus (11th). Revise it again after a few days and enhance your performance.
60-75% Good !	You have a wide scope to learn for the NEET syllabus (11th). Revise it again.
<60% Not Satisfactory!	You have a long way ahead of you to master the NEET syllabus (11th). Revise it thoroughly.

Space for Rough Work

Test Booklet No. **3947121**

Test Booklet Code **NSS 5**

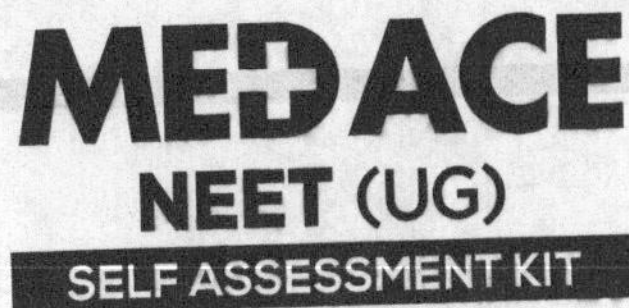

SELF ASSESSMENT KIT

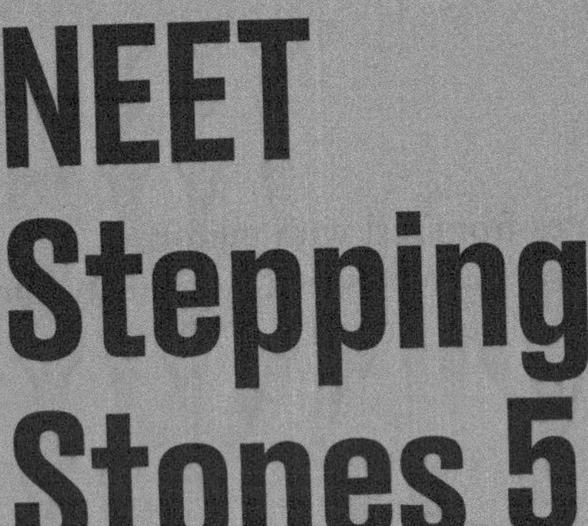

NEET Stepping Stones 5

(Based on Complete 11th Syllabus)

Name of the Candidate (In Capitals)

____

____

____

Candidate's Signature ______________

Invigilator's Signature ______________

Facsimile signature stamp of center superintendent______________

Important Instructions

- The test is of 45 minutes and the Test Booklet contains 45 multiple choice questions (four options with a single correct answer) from Physics.
- Candidates are advised to read all questions before they start attempting the question paper.
- Each question carries 4 marks. For each correct response, the candidate will get 4 marks. For each incorrect response, one mark will be deducted from the total scores. The maximum marks are 180.
- In the event of candidate marking more than one option then one mark will be deducted.
- Use **Blue/Black Point Pen** only for writing particular on this page/ marking response on Answer Sheet.

Do not open this Booklet until you start attempting the Test

Physics (Q. No. 1-45)

1. The motion of a particle is described by the equation $x = a + bt^2$, where $a = 15$ cm and $b = 3$ cm/s^2. Its instantaneous velocity at time 3 s will be
(a) 36 cm/s
(b) 18 cm/s
(c) 16 cm/s
(d) 32 cm/s

2. A cylinder contains 3 moles of oxygen and 1 mole of argon gas at room temperature of 27°C. Total internal energy of the system is
(a) 3600R
(b) 5500R
(c) 2700R
(d) 3200R

3. If the elastic limit of a typical rock on the top of mountain is 3.43×10^8 Nm^{-2} and material density is 3×10^3 kg/m^3, then maximum height of rock is ($g = 9.8$ m/s^2)
(a) 1.167 km
(b) 5.83 km
(c) 11.667 km
(d) 23.33 km

4. **Statement I** The average kinetic energy per degree of freedom per molecule at a given temperature increases as degree of freedom increases.
Statement II The ratio of molar specific heat at constant pressure to that at constant volume increases as the atomicity increases.
In light of above statements, choose the most appropriate answer from the options given below.
(a) Both Statement I and Statement II are correct.
(b) Both Statement I and Statement II are incorrect.
(c) Statement I is correct and Statement II is incorrect.
(d) Statement I is incorrect and Statement II is correct.

5. Dimensions of gyromagnetic ratio are
(a) [MLTA]
(b) [M^{-1}LTA]
(c) [ML^0TA]
(d) [$M^{-1}L^0$TA]

6. A car accelerates from rest with uniform acceleration. The graph between its velocity and displacement has been plotted

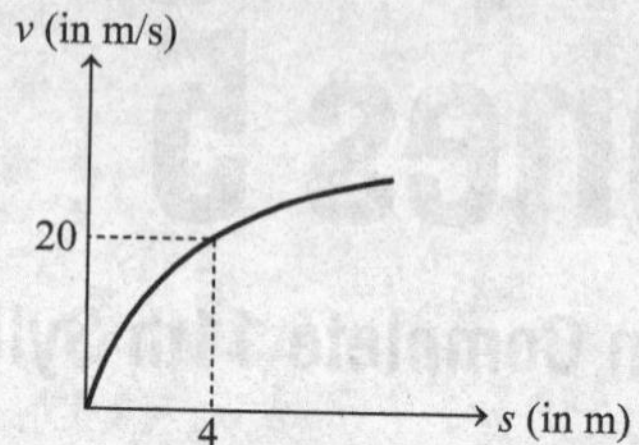

The acceleration of car is
(a) 2.5 m/s^2
(b) 5 m/s^2
(c) 50 m/s^2
(d) 20 m/s^2

7. An open organ pipe of length L is sounded together with another open organ pipe of length $(L + l)$ in their fundamental modes. If speed of sound in air is v, then number of beats heard per second is $(l << L)$
(a) $\dfrac{vl}{2L^2}$
(b) $\dfrac{vL^2}{2l}$
(c) $\dfrac{vl^2}{2(L + l)}$
(d) $\dfrac{vl}{2L(L + l)}$

8. **Assertion** (A) When certain mass of wood and same mass of metal left in sun for sometime, iron piece is hotter to touch.
Reason (R) Iron absorbs more heat than wood.

In the light of above statements, choose the most appropriate answer from the options given below.

(a) Both A and R are true and R is the correct explanation of A.

(b) Both A and R are true but R is not the correct explanation of A.

(c) A is true but R is false.

(d) A is false but R is true.

9. A ball of mass m strikes a rough horizontal surface with speed u at an angle θ with the normal and it rebounds with the speed v at an angle ϕ with the normal. If the ball remain in contact for time Δt, then average normal force on the ball due to horizontal surface is

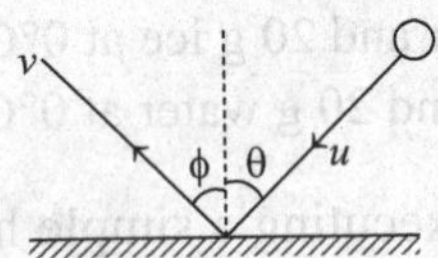

(a) $\frac{m(v\cos\phi - u\cos\theta)}{\Delta t}$

(b) $\frac{m(v\sin\phi - u\sin\theta)}{\Delta t}$

(c) $\frac{m(v\cos\phi + u\cos\theta)}{\Delta t}$

(d $\frac{m(v\sin\phi + u\sin\theta)}{\Delta t}$

10. The potential energy of a satellite of mass m in a circular orbit is $U = -x$. Escape speed of satellite in this orbit is

(a) $v_e = \sqrt{\frac{2x}{m}}$

(b) $v_e = \sqrt{\frac{x}{2m}}$

(c) $v_e = \sqrt{\frac{x}{m}}$

(d) $v_e = 2\sqrt{\frac{x}{m}}$

11. **Assertion** (A) The motion of the centre of mass describes the translational part of the motion.
Reason (R) Translational motion always means straight line motion.

In the light of above statements, choose the most appropriate answer from the options given below.

(a) Both A and R are true and R is the correct explanation of A.

(b) Both A and R are true but R is not the correct explanation of A.

(c) A is true but R is false.

(d) A is false but R is true.

12. A monoatomic gas ($\gamma = 5/3$) is suddenly compressed to $\frac{1}{8}$ of its original volume adiabatically, then the pressure of the gas will change to

(a) $\frac{24}{5}$

(b) 8

(c) $\frac{40}{3}$

(d) 32 times of its initial pressure

13. A steel scale measures the length of a copper wire as 50.0 cm when both are at 25° C (the calibration temperature for scale). The scale read for the length of the wire when both are at 40° C is (Take, $\alpha_{steel} = 11 \times 10^{-6}$ per °C and $\alpha_{copper} = 17 \times 10^{-6}$ per °C)

(a) 80.0096 cm (b) 80.0272 cm
(c) 10 mm (d) 50.0075 cm

14. Suppose the torque acting on a body is given by $\tau = KL + (MI/\omega)$, where L = angular momentum, I = moment of inertia and ω = angular speed. The dimensional formula for KM is same as that for

(a) time^{-4} (b) time^{-2}
(c) time^{2} (d) time^{4}

15. A wave is represented by $y_1 = 10\cos(5x + 25t)$, where x is measured in metre and t in second. A second wave given by $y_2 = 20\cos\left(5x + 25t + \frac{\pi}{3}\right)$, interferes with the first wave. The resultant wave is

(a) $y=10\sqrt{5}\cos[5x+25t+\tan^{-1}(\sqrt{2})]$
(b) $y=10\sqrt{7}\cos\left[5x+25t+\tan^{-1}\left(\left(\frac{\sqrt{3}}{2}\right)\right)\right]$
(c) $y=10\sqrt{7}\cos[5x+25t+\tan^{-1}(\sqrt{2})]$
(d) $y=10\sqrt{5}\cos\left[5x+25t+\tan^{-1}\left(\left(\frac{\sqrt{3}}{2}\right)\right)\right]$

16. To what height (h) should a cylindrical vessel of radius (R) be filled with a homogeneous liquid to make the force with which the liquid presses on the curved side wall of the vessel equal to the force exerted by the liquid on the bottom of the vessel?
(a) $h=R$
(b) $h=\sqrt{2}R$
(c) $h=\frac{R}{2}$
(d) $h=2R$

17. If retardation produced by air resistance is $g/10$, then time of flight of projectile will nearly
(a) increases by 1% (b) decreases by 1%
(c) remain same (d) decreases by 2%

18. An Iron block of mass 4 kg, fall from height 10 m. After colliding with the ground it loses 25% energy to surrounding, then the temperature rise of the block is (Here, $c_{iron}=470\,J/kg°C$)
(a) 5.3×10^{-2}°C
(b) 273°C
(c) 2.0×10^{-3}°C
(d.) 480°C

19. Rate of change of weight near the earth's surface varies with height h as
(a) h (b) h^0
(c) h^{-1} (d) $h^{1/2}$

20. A wave is travelling along a string is given as $y(x,t)=\frac{1}{1000}\sin(40x-4t)$, where numerical values are in SI units. Wave velocity is
(a) 100 cm/s (b) 20 cm/s
(c) 10 cm/s (d) 50 cm/s

21. A solid sphere of radius R acquires a terminal velocity v_1 when falling (due to gravity) through a viscous fluid having a coefficient of viscosity η. The sphere is broken into 27 identical solid spheres. If each of these spheres acquires a terminal velocity, v_2 when falling through the same fluid, the ratio (v_1/v_2) equals
(a) 9 (b) 1/27
(c) 1/9 (d) 27

22. 100 g ice at 0°C is mixed with 10 g steam at 100°C. Final mixture contains
(a) only water at 0°C
(b) only ice at 0°C
(c) 90 g water and 20 g ice at 0°C
(d) 90 g ice and 20 g water at 0°C

23. A body is executing a simple harmonic motion such that its potential energy is U_1 at x and U_2 at y. When the displacement is $x+y$, the potential energy will be
(a) U_1+U_2
(b) $\sqrt{U_1^2+U_2^2}$
(c) $U_1+U_2+2\sqrt{U_1U_2}$
(d) $\sqrt{U_1U_2}$

24. A bullet is fired from a gun with velocity v at an angle θ from the horizontal to hit the vertical target at a distance R from the point of projection, then the height from the ground level where the bullet hits the target is
(a) $R\tan\theta-\frac{gR^2}{2u^2\tan^2\theta}$
(b) $R\tan\theta-\frac{gR^2}{2u^2\cos^2\theta}$
(c) $R\tan\theta-\frac{gR^2}{2u^2\sin^2\theta}$
(d) $R\sin\theta-\frac{gR^2}{2u^2\sin^2\theta}$

25. If Earth has a mass nine times and radius twice to that of a planet P, then $\frac{v_e}{3}\sqrt{x}\ ms^{-1}$ will be the minimum velocity required by a rocket to pull out of gravitational force of P, where v_e is escape velocity on earth. The value of x is

(a) 18 (b) 1

(c) 2 (d) 3

26. A platform of mass m and counterweight of $M+m$ (where, $M=3m$) are connected by a light cord which passes over two smooth pulleys (see figure). A man of mass M is standing on the platform which is at rest. If the man leaps vertically upwards (and out of platform) with velocity $10\ \text{ms}^{-1}$, find the distance through which the platform will descend.

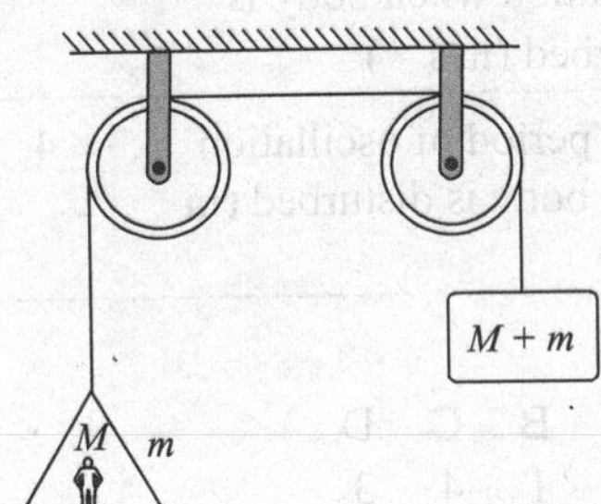

(a) 1 m (b) 2 m

(c) 3 m (d) 4 m

27. A particle is located at (3 m, 4 m) and moving with velocity $\mathbf{v}=(4\hat{\mathbf{i}}-3\hat{\mathbf{j}})\ \text{ms}^{-1}$. Find its angular velocity about origin at this instant.

(a) $-\frac{1}{2}\hat{\mathbf{k}}$ (b) $-\frac{3}{4}\hat{\mathbf{k}}$

(c) $-\hat{\mathbf{k}}$ (d) $-\frac{2}{3}\hat{\mathbf{k}}$

28. A load of 4 kg is suspended from a ceiling through a steel wire of length 20 m and radius 2 mm. It is found that the length of the wire increases by 0.031 mm, as equilibrium is achieved. If $g=(3.1\times\pi)\ \text{ms}^{-2}$, the value of Young's modulus of the material of the wire (in Nm^{-2}) is

(a) 2×10^{12} (b) 4×10^{11}

(c) 2×10^{11} (d) 0.02×10^{9}

29. First overtone frequency of a closed organ pipe is equal to the first overtone frequency of an open organ pipe. Further nth harmonic of closed organ pipe is also equal to the mth harmonic of open pipe, where n and m are

(a) 7, 3 (b) 9, 6

(c) 7, 5 (d) 5, 4

30. A bullet of mass 15 g strikes a wooden plank with a velocity of 540 m/s and energies from it with a velocity of 360 m/s. If the thickness of the plank is 20 cm.

The workdone by the bullet against resisting force of the plank is

(a) 1300 J (b) 245 J

(c) 1215 J (d) 1548 J

31. A body having a moment of inertia about its axis of rotation equal to 3 kg-m^2 is rotating with angular velocity of 3 rad s^{-1}. Kinetic energy of this rotating body is same as that of a body of mass 27 kg moving with a velocity v. The value of v is

(a) $1\ \text{ms}^{-1}$ (b) $0.5\ \text{ms}^{-1}$

(c) $2\ \text{ms}^{-1}$ (d) $1.5\ \text{ms}^{-1}$

32. A wire of length 1m and radius 1mm is subjected to a load. The extension is x. The wire is melted and then drawn into a wire of square cross-section of side 2 mm. Its extension under the same load will be

(a) $\frac{\pi^2 x}{8}$ (b) $\frac{\pi^2 x}{16}$

(c) $\frac{\pi^2 x}{2}$ (d) $\frac{x}{2\pi}$

33. A gas obeys $pV^{3/2}=$ constant. If this gas is compressed quickly to half of its initial volume, then final temperature of the gas is

(a) $\sqrt{2}\,T$ (b) $2\,T$

(c) $2\sqrt{2}\,T$ (d) $4\,T$

34. You measure two quantities as $A=1.0\ \text{m}\pm2.0\ \text{m}$, $B=2.0\ \text{m}\pm0.2\ \text{m}$. We should report correct value for $\sqrt{AB}$ as

(a) 1.4 m ± 0.4 m

(b) 1.41 m ± 0.15 m

(c) 1.4 m ± 0.3 m

(d) 1.4 m ± 0.2 m

35. The maximum velocity of a body undergoing simple harmonic motion is $0.04\ ms^{-1}$ and its acceleration at 0.02 m from the mean position is $0.06\ ms^{-2}$. Its amplitude and time period, respectively are

(a) 3.21×10^{-2} m, 3.23 s
(b) 1.92×10^{-2} m, 2.82 s
(c) 3.14×10^{-2} m, 3.82 s
(d) 2.31×10^{-2} m, 3.63 s

36. A uniform rope of length l is placed on a rough table such that a part of its length l_1, overhangs from the edge of the table. If μ is the coefficient of static friction between the plane surface of the table and rope, then the maximum value of l, which can overhang from the edge of the table without slipping is

(a) $\frac{\mu}{1+\mu} l$
(b) $\frac{l}{\mu}$
(c) $l\mu$
(d) $\frac{l}{1+\mu}$

37. A particle moves in a circular path such that its speed v varies with distance s as $v = \alpha\sqrt{s}$, where α is positive constant. Find the acceleration of the particle after traversing a distance s.

(a) $\alpha^2\sqrt{\frac{1}{4}+\frac{s^2}{R^2}}$
(b) $\alpha^2\sqrt{\frac{1}{8}+\frac{s^2}{R^2}}$
(c) $\alpha^2\sqrt{\frac{1}{9}+\frac{s^2}{R^2}}$
(d) $\alpha^2\sqrt{\frac{1}{10}+\frac{s^2}{R^2}}$

38. A block of mass m moves with a velocity v_0 towards a stationary block of mass M (connected to a spring) on a smooth horizontal surface (see figure). If spring constant is k, what is the maximum compression in the spring?

(a) $v_0\sqrt{\frac{mM}{2k(m+M)}}$
(b) $v_0\sqrt{\frac{mM}{k(m+M)}}$
(c) $v_0\sqrt{\frac{2mM}{k(m+M)}}$
(d) None of these

39. A spring compressed by 30 cm develops a restoring force of 30 N. A body of 5 kg is placed over it. Match the different quantities given in Column I with the respective value in Column II. [Take, $g = 10\ m/s^2$]

	Column I		Column II
A.	Force constant of spring (in N/m)	1.	50
B.	Displacement under the weight of body (in cm)	2.	100
C.	Angular frequency of oscillation when body is disturbed (in s^{-1})	3.	$2\sqrt{5}$
D.	Time period of oscillation when body is disturbed (in rad/s)	4.	$\frac{\pi}{\sqrt{5}}$

Codes

	A	B	C	D
(a)	2	1	4	3
(b)	1	3	2	4
(c)	2	4	3	1
(d)	2	1	3	4

40. During an adiabatic process, the pressure of a mixture of monoatomic and diatomic gases is found to be proportional to the cube of the temperature. The value of C_P/C_V is

(a) 3/2
(b) 4/5
(c) 1/2
(d) 1

41. The radius of the circle, the periodic revolution, the initial position and sense of revolution are indicated in the given figure. The simple harmonic motion of X-projection of the radius vector of the revolving particle P is

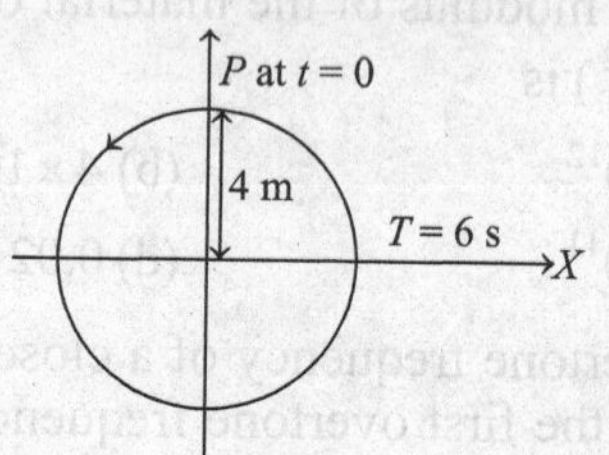

(a) $x = 4\sin\left(\frac{\pi}{3}t + \pi\right)$
(b) $x = 4\cos\left(\frac{\pi}{3}t + \pi\right)$
(c) $x = 4\sin\left(\frac{2\pi}{3}t - \pi\right)$
(d) $x = 4\cos\left(\frac{2\pi}{3} - \pi\right)$

42. In a certain process pV^n = constant, the heat Q given to a monoatomic gas leads to a change in internal energy of a gas which is equal to $\frac{Q}{4}$. The value of n is

(a) 7/9
(b) 2
(c) 3/5
(d) 6/7

43. A small block of mass 100 g moves with uniform speed in a horizontal circular groove, with vertical side walls of radius 25 cm. If the block takes 2 s to complete one round, then the normal contact force by the side wall of the groove is

(a) 0.462
(b) 0.785
(c) 0.846
(d) 0.246

44. A block of mass 5 kg is placed at rest on a table of rough surface. Now, if a force of 30N is applied in the direction parallel to surface of the table, the block slides through a distance of 50 m in an interval of time 10s. Coefficient of kinetic friction is (Given, $g = 10\ \text{ms}^{-2}$)

(a) 0.50
(b) 0.75
(c) 0.25
(d) 0.60

45. A solid sphere of mass M and radius R is divided into two unequal parts. The first part has a mass of $7M/8$ and is converted into a uniform disc of radius $2R$. The second part is converted into a uniform solid sphere. Let I_1 be the moment of inertia of the disc about its axis and I_2 be the moment of inertia of the new sphere about its axis. The ratio I_1/I_2 is given by

(a) 285
(b) 185
(c) 65
(d) 140

Response Index

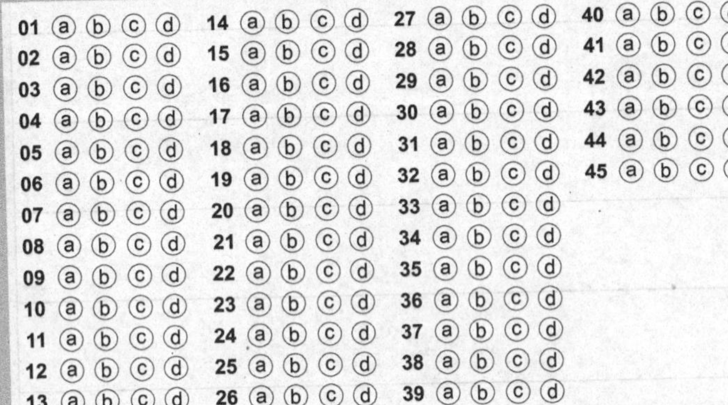

Performance Scanner

> 90% Excellent ! You have mastered the NEET syllabus (11th). The concepts of this syllabus are on your fingertips. Maintain this momentum.

76-90% Very Good ! You have a good command over the NEET syllabus (11th). Revise it again after a few days and enhance your performance.

60-75% Good ! You have a wide scope to learn for the NEET syllabus (11th). Revise it again.

<60% Not Satisfactory! You have a long way ahead of you to master the NEET syllabus (11th). Revise it thoroughly.

Space for Rough Work

MEDACE

NEET (UG)

SELF ASSESSMENT KIT

Exactly as per the Latest Pattern of NTA

Released on 25 Jan 2025

PHYSICS - XIth

Hints, Solutions & Mind Maps Booklet

MEDACE

NEET (UG) SELF ASSESSMENT KIT

Exactly as per the Latest Pattern of NTA

Released on 25 Jan 2025

PHYSICS - XIth

Hints, Solutions & Mind Maps Booklet

Authors

Sunny Kumar,

Anshuman & Kajal

ARIHANT PRAKASHAN (SERIES), MEERUT

卐 **Administrative & Production Offices**

Regd. Office

'Ramchhaya' 4577/15, Agarwal Road, Darya Ganj, New Delhi -110002
Tele: 011- 47630600, 43518550

卐 **Head Office**

Kalindi, TP Nagar, Meerut (UP) - 250002
Tel: 0121-7156203, 7156204

卐 **Sales & Support Offices**

Agra, Ahmedabad, Bengaluru, Bareilly, Chennai, Delhi, Guwahati, Hyderabad, Jaipur, Jhansi, Kolkata, Lucknow, Nagpur & Pune.

卐 **PRICE** ₹1200.00

卐 **PO No :** TXT-59-T063621-03-25

Published by Arihant Publications (India) Ltd.

For further information about the books published by Arihant, log on to www.arihantbooks.com or e-mail at info@arihantbooks.com

PHYSICS XIth

CONTENT LIST

Hints & Solutions

Ch-01 Units and Measurement

Topical Follow Thru

Test-1

1. (c) We know that,

$$F = ma \quad \text{...(i)}$$

As, $a = \frac{v}{t} = \frac{s}{t \times t} = st^{-2}$ ...(ii) $\left[\because v = \frac{s}{t}\right]$

From Eqs. (i) and (ii),we get

$\Rightarrow \quad F = mst^{-2}$

Let x kg be unit of mass, then putting the values, we get

$\Rightarrow \quad F = (x) \times 20000 \times (200)^{-2}$

$\Rightarrow \quad 1000 = \frac{x \times 20000}{(200)^2}$

$\Rightarrow \quad x = 2000\,\text{kg}$

or $\quad x = 2 \times 10^3\,\text{kg}$

2. (a) Let length of side of the cube be a, then volume of the cube $= a^3$

Also, surface area of the cube $= 6a^2$

Given, surface area of cube

= volume of cube

$\Rightarrow \quad 6a^2 = a^3$

$\Rightarrow \quad a = 6\,\text{cm}$

Thus, volume of the cube

$= (6)^3 = 216\,\text{cm}^3$

3. (d) As, $\frac{\text{mass} \times \text{pressure}}{\text{density}}$

$$= \frac{[\text{M}]\,[\text{ML}^{-1}\text{T}^{-2}]}{[\text{ML}^{-3}]} = [\text{ML}^2\text{T}^{-2}]$$

which is the dimensional formula of work.

So, $\frac{\text{mass} \times \text{pressure}}{\text{density}}$ denotes work.

4. (a) As, $[\text{W}] = [\tau] = [\text{M}^1\text{L}^2\text{T}^{-2}]$

and $[\text{L}] = [h] = [\text{M}^1\text{L}^2\text{T}^{-1}]$

Hence, both statements are correct.

5. (a) Given that, $[p]^{x/2}[Q]^{y/3}[c]^{z/2}$

$$[\text{ML}^{-1}\text{T}^{-2}]^{x/2}[\text{MT}^{-3}]^{y/3}[\text{LT}^{-1}]^{z/2} = [\text{M}^0\text{L}^0\text{T}^0]$$

Comparing the coefficients, we get

$\frac{x}{2} + \frac{y}{3} = 0 \Rightarrow 3x + 2y = 0$ ...(i)

$-\frac{x}{2} - \frac{y}{3} + z/2 = 0$ ...(ii)

$-x - y - z/2 = 0$ ...(iii)

On solving the equations, we get

$x = 2,\ y = -3,\ z = 2$

The values x, y, z which satisfies the three equations are $2, -3, 2$

6. (a) Consider the given potential

$$U = \frac{A\sqrt{x}}{x^2 + B}$$

Dimension of B must be equal to

$$[x^2] = [\text{L}^2]$$

Write the expression of A.

$$A = \frac{U(x^2 + B)}{\sqrt{x}}$$

$$[A] = \frac{[U][x^2]}{[\sqrt{x}]} = \frac{[\text{ML}^2\text{T}^{-2}][\text{L}^2]}{[\text{L}^{1/2}]}$$

$$= [\text{ML}^{7/2}\text{T}^{-2}]$$

$$\frac{[A]}{[B]} = \frac{[\text{ML}^{7/2}\text{T}^{-2}]}{[\text{L}^2]} = [\text{ML}^{3/2}\text{T}^{-2}]$$

7. (d) The dimensions of K must be equal to $p, \frac{1}{2}\rho V^2$ or ρgh.

Hence,

$\frac{[p]}{[K]} = [\text{M}^0\text{L}^0\text{T}^0]$, dimensionless.

Angle is also dimensionless, correct option is (d).

8. (a) Dimensional formula of z must be equal to ct^3.

$$[z] = [ct^3]$$

$$[\text{L}] = [c][\text{T}^3]$$

$$[c] = [\text{LT}^{-3}]$$

9. (b) $[E] = [\text{ML}^2\text{T}^{-2}], [m] = [\text{M}]$

$[L] = [\text{ML}^2\text{T}^{-1}]$,

$$[G] = \frac{[\text{MLT}^{-2}][\text{L}^2]}{[\text{M}^2]}$$

$$= [\text{M}^{-1}\text{L}^3\text{T}^{-2}]$$

$$\left[\frac{EL^3}{m^5G^2}\right] = \frac{[\text{ML}^2\text{T}^{-2}][\text{ML}^2\text{T}^{-1}]^3}{[\text{M}]^5[\text{M}^{-1}\text{L}^3\text{T}^{-2}]^2}$$

$$= [\text{ML}^2\text{T}^{-1}]$$

It is dimensional formula of angular momentum L.

10. (c) According to question, we have

$$f = k\rho^a r^b S^c$$

($\because K$ = dimensionless constant)

$$[f] = [\rho^a r^b S^c]$$

$$[\text{T}^{-1}] = [\text{ML}^{-3}]^a[\text{L}]^b[\text{ML}^0\text{T}^{-2}]^c$$

$$[\text{T}^{-1}] = [\text{M}^{a+c}\text{L}^{-3a+b}\text{T}^{-2c}]$$

On comparing, we get

$a + c = 0$

$-3a + b = 0$

and $\quad -2c = -1$

$c = \frac{1}{2}$

$\Rightarrow \quad a = -\frac{1}{2}$ and $b = -\frac{3}{2}$

$$f = k\sqrt{\frac{S}{\rho r^3}}$$

11. (b) Here, $\frac{K\theta}{\alpha Z}$ should be dimensionless.

$$\alpha = \frac{K\theta}{Z}$$

$\Rightarrow \quad [\alpha] = \frac{[\text{ML}^2\text{T}^{-2}\text{K}^{-1}][\text{K}]}{[\text{L}]}$

$$= [\text{MLT}^{-2}]$$

$$p = \frac{\beta}{\alpha}$$

$\Rightarrow [\beta] = [p\alpha] = [MLT^{-2}][MLT^{-2}]$
$= [M^2L^2T^{-4}]$

12. (a) In the given equation, $\frac{\alpha Z}{K\theta}$ should be dimensionless.

$\therefore \quad \alpha = \frac{K\theta}{Z}$

$\Rightarrow \quad [\alpha] = \frac{[ML^2T^{-2}K^{-1}][K]}{[L]}$
$= [MLT^{-2}]$

and $\quad p = \frac{\alpha}{\beta}$

$\Rightarrow [\beta] = \left[\frac{\alpha}{p}\right] = \frac{[MLT^{-2}]}{[ML^{-1}T^{-2}]}$
$= [M^0L^2T^0]$

13. (c) [Rydberg constant] $\propto \frac{1}{\lambda}(m^{-1})$

[Energy density] = [Pressure] (Pa)

[Thermal capacity] = J/kg

[Surface tension]
$= [\text{Surface energy}] = J/m^2$

14. (b) Given equation,

$F = \frac{\alpha}{\beta + \sqrt{\rho}}$

$\Rightarrow \quad F\beta + F\sqrt{\rho} = \alpha$

$\therefore \quad [F\beta] = [F\sqrt{\rho}] = [\alpha]$

From $[\alpha] = [F\sqrt{\rho}] = [F][\rho]^{\frac{1}{2}}$

$= [M^1L^1T^{-2}][M^{\frac{1}{2}}L^{-\frac{3}{2}}]$

$[\alpha] = \left[M^{\frac{3}{2}}L^{-\frac{1}{2}}T^{-2}\right]$

Similarly, from $[F\beta] = [F\sqrt{\rho}]$

or $\quad [\beta] = [\rho]^{\frac{1}{2}}$

$[\beta] = \left[M^{\frac{1}{2}}L^{-\frac{3}{2}}\right]$

15. (c) A is true but R is false

$\left(p + \frac{a}{V^2}\right)(V - b) = \text{constant}$

As we can add (or subtract) physical quantities of same dimensions,

$[p] = \left[\frac{a}{V^2}\right] \Rightarrow [a] = [p][V^2]$

Also, $[V] = [b]$

So, $[a]\cdot[b] = [p][V^2]\cdot[V]$
$= [p][V^3] = \frac{[F]}{[L^2]}\cdot[L^3]^3$
$= [F]\cdot[L^7]$

So, unit of $a \cdot b = N\text{-}m^7$.

Any two physical quantities can be multiplied or divided irrespective of their dimensions. Hence, Reason is false.

16. (c) According to the principle of homogeneity of dimensions, only those terms can be added or subtracted, which have same dimensional formula but we can multiply or divide the physical quantities which have different dimensional formulae and gives new physical quantity with non-zero dimensions.

In the question, it is given that P and Q have different dimensional formula. So, both quantities cannot be added (i.e. $P + Q$) but dividing P by Q, we can have new physical quantity.

Also we know that, exponents and trigonometric angles are dimensionless. So, given term $\frac{P}{Q}$ must be a valid quantity, which can represent a new physical quantity with its own dimensional formula.

17. (d) As given, $X = \varepsilon_0 L \frac{\Delta V}{\Delta t}$

According to the principle of homogeneity, for the equation to be correct, the dimensional formula of both sides should be same. i.e.

Dimensional formula of X =

Dimensional formula of $\varepsilon_0 L \frac{\Delta V}{\Delta t}$

or $\quad [X] = \left[\varepsilon_0 L \frac{\Delta V}{\Delta t}\right]$

$= \frac{[\varepsilon_0][L][\Delta V]}{[\Delta t]} \quad \ldots \text{(i)}$

As we know that,

$[\varepsilon_0] = [M^{-1}L^{-3}T^4A^2]$

$[L] = [L^1]$

$[\Delta V] = [M^1L^2T^{-3}A^{-1}]$

$[\Delta t] = [T]$

Putting all values, in Eq. (i), we get

$[X] = \frac{[M^{-1}L^{-3}T^4A^2][L][M^1L^2T^{-3}A^{-1}]}{[T]}$

$= [M^0L^0T^0A]$

which is equivalent to dimensional formula of current.

18. (a) We have, $[c] = [LT^{-1}]$

$[G] = [M^{-1}L^3T^{-2}]$

and $\quad [h] = [ML^2T^{-1}]$

Now, mass, $m \propto c^x G^y h^z$

Then,

$[M] = [LT^{-1}]^x \cdot [M^{-1}L^3T^{-2}]^y \cdot [ML^2T^{-1}]^z$

Equating powers of similar quantities on both sides, we have

$x = \frac{1}{2}, y = -\frac{1}{2}$ and $z = \frac{1}{2}$

$\therefore \quad m \propto \left[c^{\frac{1}{2}}G^{-\frac{1}{2}}h^{\frac{1}{2}}\right]$

19. (d) Friction, $f = \mu N$

$\Rightarrow \quad \mu = \frac{f}{N}$

$[\mu] = \left[\frac{f}{N}\right] = \left[\frac{MLT^{-2}}{MLT^{-2}}\right]$

= Dimensionless

20. (c) By putting the dimensions of each quantity both sides, we get

$[T^{-1}] = [M^{x+y}T^{-2y}]$

Now, comparing the dimensions of quantities in both sides, we get

$x + y = 0$

21. (d) Dimensions of $B = [M^0L^0T^0]$

Dimensions of $e = [AT]$

Dimensions of ε_0
$= [A^2M^{-1}L^{-3}T^4]$

Dimensions of $h = [ML^2T^{-1}]$

Dimensions of $c = [LT^{-1}]$

$\therefore [M^0L^0T^0] = \dfrac{[AT]^2}{[A^2M^{-1}L^{-3}T^4]^n[ML^2T^{-1}][LT^{-1}]}$

or $[M^0L^0T^0] = [A^{2-2n}M^{n-1}L^{3n-3}T^{2-4n+2}]$

Comparing the coefficients of M, we get

$n-1=0$

$n=1$

22. (a) Here $[\alpha]=[T^1]$

and $[\beta]=[L^1]$

So, $\left[\dfrac{\beta}{\alpha}\right]=[L^1T^{-1}]$, which is equal to velocity.

23. (c) Let power of dimensions of surface tension be a in K, b in v, c in T, then

$[\text{Surface tension}] = [K]^a[v]^b[T]^c$

$[M^1L^0T^{-2}] = [M^1L^2T^{-2}]^{a}[LT^{-1}]^b[T]^c$

$[M^1L^0T^{-2}] = [M^aL^{2a+b}T^{-2a-b+c}]$

On comparing both sides of the above equation, we get

$a=1$

$2a+b=0$

$2\times1+b=0$

or $b=-2$

and $-2a-b+c=-2$

$-2\times1-(-2)+c=-2$

$c=-2$

Hence, [surface tension] $= [Kv^{-2}T^{-2}]$

24. (c) Electromotive force has unit of voltage (potential), while eV represents energy.

25. (a) $T^2 = kR^3$ (Given)

$\therefore\ k=\dfrac{T^2}{R^3}$,

where, k is Kepler's constant

$\Rightarrow k=\dfrac{[T^2]}{[L^3]}$

$\Rightarrow [k]=[T^2L^{-3}]$

Test-2

1. (a) The percentage error in Y is given by

$$\Rightarrow \frac{\Delta Y}{Y}\times100 = 3\left(\frac{\Delta P}{P}\right)\times100+\frac{1}{3}\left(\frac{\Delta Q}{Q}\right)\times100 +4\left(\frac{\Delta R}{R}\right)\times100+\frac{1}{2}\left(\frac{\Delta S}{S}\right)\times100$$

Substituting given values in above expression,

$$=3\times2\%+\frac{1}{3}\times9\%+4\times7\%+\frac{1}{2}\times4\%$$

$$=6\%+3\%+28\%+2\%=39\%$$

2. (d) In addition or subtraction, the final result should retain same number decimal places as the number with the least decimal place.

In multiplication or division, the final result should retain same significant figures as the original number with the least significant figures.

Hence, option (d) is correct from the point of view of significant figures.

3. (a) Resistivity, $\rho=\dfrac{RA}{l}$

or $\rho=\dfrac{R\pi\left(\dfrac{d}{2}\right)^2}{l}=\dfrac{\pi Rd^2}{4l}$

$$\therefore \frac{\Delta\rho}{\rho}=\frac{\Delta R}{R}+\frac{2\Delta d}{d}+\frac{\Delta l}{l}$$

$$=\frac{2}{65}+2\left(\frac{1\times10^{-3}}{10.5\times10^{-3}}\right)+\left(\frac{0.2\times10^{-3}}{7\times10^{-3}}\right)$$

$$=0.225$$

$$\therefore \frac{\Delta\rho}{\rho}\times100\%=0.225\times100\%$$

$$=22.5\%$$

4. (d) Density $=\dfrac{m}{V}=\dfrac{2.436}{3.62}=0.67292$

Round-off to 3 significant figures because there are 3 significant figures in 3.62.

Density $=0.673\ \text{g/cm}^3$

5. (a) The measurement, $l=0.600$ m is the most accurate because of greatest significant figures (3).

All zeroes between two non-zero numbers are significant, hence 1.0201 has 5 significant figures. If a number is less than 1, then zeroes after first non-zero numbers is significant. Hence, 0.1020 has 4 significant figures.

6. (a) More precise value is that one which contains more decimal places. Hence, (a) is the correct option.

7. (c) Closer the measured value more accurate is the reading. Hence, 3.13 g is the most accurate value and instrument C should be used to measure.

8. (a) Surface area,

$$S=2\pi r^2=2\times3.14\times(2.5)^2 = 39.25\ \text{cm}^2$$

Now, $\dfrac{\Delta S}{S}=2\cdot\dfrac{\Delta r}{r}$

$$\Delta S=2\cdot\frac{\Delta r}{r}\cdot S = \frac{2\times0.6\times39.25}{2.5}=18.84\ \text{cm}^2$$

Therefore, $S=(39.25\pm18.84)\ \text{cm}^2$

9. (a) $n(\text{VSD})=(n-1)\text{MSD}$

Therefore,

$$1\ \text{VSD}=\frac{(n-1)}{n}\text{MSD} \quad ...(i)$$

Least count (LC) = 1 MSD − 1 VSD

$$=1\ \text{MSD}-\frac{(n-1)}{n}\text{MSD} \quad \text{[From Eq. (i)]}$$

$$=\frac{1}{n}\text{MSD}$$

Since, given, 1 MSD $=\dfrac{1}{n}$ cm

Therefore, LC $=\dfrac{1}{n}\times\dfrac{1}{n}$ cm $=\dfrac{1}{n^2}$ cm

10. (b) A measurement is said to be more accurate, when it has a lesser value of relative error. However, a measurement is said to be more precise when it has a lesser value of absolute error, i.e. measured by an instrument that has a smaller least count.

Therefore, we conclude that a most precise measurement may be most accurate but not necessarily and *vice-versa* is not true.

11. (b) Given that, $x = \frac{a^m}{b^n}$

If the relative error in measurement of a and b are $\pm \frac{\Delta a}{a}$ and $\pm \frac{\Delta b}{b}$, respectively. Then, on solving the above expression, we get

$$\frac{\Delta x}{x} = m\left(\pm \frac{\Delta a}{a}\right) + n\left(\pm \frac{\Delta b}{b}\right)$$

where, m and n may be any real number (positive, negative, rational or irrational).

The values of Δa and Δb should not be comparable to their respective quantity or we can say that $\frac{\Delta a}{a}$ and $\frac{\Delta b}{b}$ should be very small. Thus, the above relation is valid when $\Delta a << a$ and $\Delta b << b$.

Here, the values of Δa and Δb denote change in quantities a and b but absolute error is always taken as positive because error cannot be negative.

12. (c) Given, $x = \frac{a\sqrt{b}}{c^{3/2} d^4}$

Maximum percentage error in x,

$$\frac{\Delta x}{x} \times 100 = \frac{\Delta a}{a} \times 100 + \frac{1}{2}\frac{\Delta b}{b} \times 100 + \frac{3}{2}\frac{\Delta c}{c} \times 100 + \frac{4\,\Delta d}{d} \times 100 \quad \ldots(i)$$

Given that, $\frac{\Delta a}{a} \times 100 = 2\%$

$$\frac{\Delta b}{b} \times 100 = 3\%$$

$$\frac{\Delta c}{c} \times 100 = 1\%$$

$$\frac{\Delta d}{d} \times 100 = 0.5\%$$

Substituting given values in Eq. (i), we get

$$\frac{\Delta x}{x} \times 100 = 2\% + \frac{1}{2} \times 3\% + \frac{3}{2} \times 1\% + 4 \times 0.5\%$$

Thus, $\frac{\Delta x}{x} \times 100 = 7\%$

13. (c) A is true but R is false.

$$V_T = \frac{2}{9\eta}|\sigma - \rho| r^2 g$$

$$V_T \propto r^2$$

$$\%\text{ error is } V_T = 2 \times \left(\frac{0.1}{5} \times 100\right) = 4\%$$

14. (b) All the non-zero digits are significant digits and the trailing zero (zero to the right of the last non-zero digit) in a number with a decimal point are significant, so 20.000 has 5 significant figures.

When the number is expressed in exponential form, the exponential term does not affect the number of significant figure. So, 6.23×10^1 has 3 significant figures.

15. (b) Given that, initial temperature, $T_i = (30.4 \pm 0.2)°\text{C}$

Final temperature,

$$T_f = (51.5 \pm 0.4)°\text{C}$$

$\therefore$ Rise in temperature,

$$T = T_f - T_i = 51.5 - 30.4 = 21.1°\text{C}$$

$$\Delta T = \pm(\Delta T_i + \Delta T_f) = \pm(0.2 + 0.4) = \pm 0.6°\text{C}$$

$\therefore$ Rise in temperature

$$= (21.1 \pm 0.6)°\text{C}$$

16. (d) Here, $A = (1.0 \pm 0.2)\,\text{m}$

$$B = (2.0 \pm 0.2)\,\text{m}$$

Let $X = (AB)^{\frac{1}{2}}$

$\Rightarrow$ $X = (1 \times 2)^{\frac{1}{2}} = 1.414\,\text{m}$

Rounding off to two significant digits, we get

$$X = 1.4\,\text{m}$$

Now, $\frac{\Delta X}{X} = \frac{1}{2}\left[\frac{\Delta A}{A} + \frac{\Delta B}{B}\right] = \frac{1}{2}\left[\frac{0.2}{1.0} + \frac{0.2}{2.0}\right]$

$$\frac{\Delta X}{X} = 0.15$$

or $\Delta X = 0.15X = (0.15)(1.414) = 0.2121$

Rounding off to one significant digit,

$$\Delta X = 0.2\,\text{m}$$

Hence, $(AB)^{\frac{1}{2}} = (1.4 \pm 0.2)\,\text{m}$

17. (a) From the given figure,

Least count (LC) of vernier caliper

$$= \frac{1}{10} = 0.1\,\text{mm}$$

Here, vernier scale is on the left hand side from main scale, so zero error will be negative.

$\therefore$ Zero error = (Number of divisions on vernier scale − Number of divisions that coincides with a main scale division) × LC

$$= -(10 - 4) \times 0.1$$

$\Rightarrow$ Zero error = − 0.6 mm

As, zero correction = − zero error

$$= -(-0.6)\,\text{mm} = 0.6\,\text{mm}$$

18. (d) Given, $\frac{\Delta R}{R} \times 100 = 1\%$

$$\frac{\Delta I}{I} \times 100 = 2\%$$

and $\frac{\Delta t}{t} \times 100 = 3\%$

We know that, heat produced due to current flowing through a resistor R,

$$H = I^2 Rt$$

$$\Rightarrow \frac{\Delta H}{H} = \frac{2\Delta I}{I} + \frac{\Delta R}{R} + \frac{\Delta t}{t}$$

$$\Rightarrow \frac{\Delta H}{H} \times 100 = 2\left(\frac{\Delta I}{I} \times 100\right) + \frac{\Delta R}{R} \times 100 + \frac{\Delta t}{t} \times 100$$

$$= 2 \times 2\% + 1\% + 3\% = 8\%$$

19. (d) Percentage error in A

$$= 2\frac{\Delta a}{a} + \frac{1}{3}\frac{\Delta b}{b} + \frac{1}{2}\frac{\Delta c}{c}$$

$$= \left(2 \times 1 + \frac{1}{3} \times 2 + \frac{1}{2} \times 2\right)\% = 3.7\%$$

20. (d) Here, $\frac{1}{f} = \frac{1}{v} - \frac{1}{u}$

$$\therefore f = \frac{uv}{u - v}, \frac{\Delta f}{f} = \frac{\Delta u}{u} + \frac{\Delta v}{v} + \frac{\Delta(u + v)}{u + v}$$

$$= \frac{\Delta u}{u} + \frac{\Delta v}{v} + \frac{\Delta u}{u + v} + \frac{\Delta v}{u + v}$$

21. (b) Given, $A = (3.01 \pm 0.1)\,\text{m}$,

$$B = (2.0 \pm 0.2)\,\text{m}$$

Let $y = \sqrt[4]{A/B}$

$$= \sqrt[4]{\frac{3.0}{2.0}} = 1.10668$$

Rounding off to two significant digits

$$Y = 1.12\,\text{m}$$

$$\frac{\Delta Y}{Y} = \frac{1}{4}\left[\frac{\Delta A}{A} + \frac{\Delta B}{B}\right]$$

$$= \frac{1}{4}\left(\frac{0.1}{3.0} + \frac{0.2}{2.0}\right)$$

$$\Delta Y = \frac{1}{4}\left(\frac{0.8}{6.0}\right)Y = \frac{0.8}{4(6.0)}(1.12)$$

$$= 0.037\,\text{m}$$

Rounding off to one significant digit

$$\Delta Y = 0.04\,\text{m}$$

Thus, correct value for

$$\sqrt[4]{AB} = Y + \Delta Y = (1.1 \pm 0.04)\,\text{m}$$

22. (d) Given that, $a = b^{\alpha} c^{\beta} / d^{\gamma/2} e^{3\delta}$

So, maximum error in a is given by

$$\left(\frac{\Delta a}{a} \times 100\right)_{\max}$$

$$= \alpha \cdot \left(\frac{\Delta b}{b} \times 100\right) + \beta \cdot \left(\frac{\Delta c}{c} \times 100\right) + \frac{\gamma}{2}\left(\frac{\Delta d}{d} \times 100\right) + 3\delta \cdot \left(\frac{\Delta e}{e} \times 100\right)$$

$$= (\alpha b_1 + \beta c_1 + \frac{\gamma}{2} d_1 + 3\delta e_1)\%$$

23. (d) $d = \dfrac{\lambda}{2\sin\theta}$

In $d = \ln\lambda - \ln 2 - \ln\sin\theta$

$$\frac{\Delta(d)}{d} = 0 - 0 - \frac{1}{\sin\theta} \times \cos\theta\,(\Delta\theta)$$

Fractional error $= \left|\dfrac{\Delta d}{d}\right| = (\cot\theta)\Delta\theta$

Absolute error, $\Delta d = (d\cot\theta)\Delta\theta$

$$= \left(\frac{\lambda}{2\sin\theta}\right)\left(\frac{\cos\theta}{\sin\theta}\right)\Delta\theta$$

Now, given that $\Delta\theta$ = constant

As θ increases, $\sin\theta$ increases, $\cos\theta$ and $\cot\theta$ decrease.

$\therefore$Both fractional and absolute erorrs decrease.

24. (c) As, $KE = \dfrac{1}{2}mv^2$

$$\Rightarrow KE_1 = \frac{1}{2}mv^2$$

$$KE_2 = \frac{1}{2}m\left(v + \frac{30}{100}v\right)^2$$

$$= \frac{1}{2}m\left(\frac{13}{10}v\right)^2$$

$$= \frac{169}{100}\left(\frac{1}{2}mv^2\right)$$

$$\Rightarrow KE_2 = \frac{169}{100}(KE_1)$$

$$\Rightarrow \Delta KE = \frac{69}{100}(KE_1)$$

$$\Rightarrow \frac{\Delta KE}{KE_1} \times 100\% = 69\%$$

25. (b) Here, $R_1 = (300 \pm 3)\,\Omega$,

$R_2 = (500 \pm 4)\,\Omega$

$\therefore$ The equivalent resistance of series combination,

$$R_s = R_1 + R_2$$

$$= (300 + 500) = 800\,\Omega$$

and error in equivalent resistance,

$$\Delta R = \Delta R_1 + \Delta R_2$$

$$= (3 + 4)\,\Omega = 7\,\Omega$$

$\therefore$ Equivalent resistance along with error $= (800 \pm 7)\,\Omega$

Chapter Break Thru

1. (c) As we know that, exponentials are always dimensionless, so

$$[\alpha x] = [M^0L^0T^0]$$

or $[\alpha][x] = [M^0L^0T^0]$

or $[\alpha][L] = [M^0L^0T^0]$

or $[\alpha] = [M^0L^{-1}T^0]$

2. (d) According to the principle of homogeneity, each term in an expression should have same dimensional formula.

$$\Rightarrow [p] = [\alpha V^2]$$

or $[\alpha] = \dfrac{[p]}{[V]^2} = \dfrac{[ML^{-1}T^{-2}]}{[L^3]^2}$

$$= [ML^{-7}T^{-2}]$$

3. (a) 29MSD = 30VSD

and 1 MSD = 0.5°

$$LC = 1\,MSD - 1\,VSD$$

$$= \frac{1}{30}MSD - \frac{1}{30} \times 0.5°$$

$$= \frac{1}{60}\text{ degree or 1 min}$$

4. (b) The dimensional formulae of the given physical quantities are as follows

$$[P] = [M^1L^2T^{-3}]$$
$$[c] = [LT^{-1}]$$
$$[G] = [M^{-1}L^3T^{-2}]$$
$$[R] = [L]$$
$$[\omega] = [T^{-1}]$$

Given expression,

$$P = kc^xG^yM^2R^4\omega^6$$

The dimensional formula of both sides should be identical in accordance with principle of homogeneity.

i.e. $[P] = [kc^xG^yM^2R^4\omega^6]$

$$\Rightarrow [P] = [k][c]^x[G]^y[M]^2[R^4][\omega]^6$$

$$\Rightarrow [M^1L^2T^{-3}] = [M^0L^0T^0][LT^{-1}]^x[M^{-1}L^3T^{-2}]^y[M]^2[L]^4[T^{-1}]^6$$

$$\Rightarrow [M^1L^2T^{-3}] = [M^{2-y}L^{x+3y+4}T^{-x-2y-6}]$$

Comparing the powers on both sides, we get

$2 - y = 1$ or $y = 1$

or $x + 3y + 4 = 2$

or $x + 3 \times 1 + 4 = 2$ or $x = -5$

$\therefore$ Sum, $x + y = -5 + 1$

$$x + y = -4$$

5. (d) The dimensional formulae of physical quantities given in options are as follows :

Reynolds' number $= [M^0L^0T^0]$ and

Friction coefficient $= [M^0L^0T^0]$

Latent heat $= [M^0L^2T^{-2}]$

and Gravitational potential $= [M^0L^2T^{-2}]$

Activity $= [T^{-1}]$

and Frequency $= [T^{-1}]$

Planck's constant $= [M^1L^2T^{-1}]$

Torque $= [M^1L^2T^{-2}]$

It is clear that the dimensional formulae of Planck's constant and torque are different.

6. (c) Magnetic pole strength,

$m = \text{A-m}$

Magnetic flux density

$B = \text{Wb/A}^2$

Intensity of magnetisation,

$I = \frac{m}{V} = \text{A/m}$

Permeability of medium

$= \text{wb/A-m} = \text{T-m/A}$

7. (c) The number of significant figures of a measurement cannot be increased by changing the unit. Thus, for the given measurement of state highway in km and metre, the number of significant figures will be same and equal to 3.
Thus, Statement I is correct but Statement II is incorrect.

8. (b) Dimensional formula of c, G and h are as follows

$[c] = [LT^{-1}]$

$[G] = [M^{-1}L^3T^{-2}]$

$[h] = [ML^2T^{-1}]$

Consider, $t \propto c^x G^y h^z$

$\Rightarrow \ [T] = [LT^{-1}]^x [M^{-1}L^3T^{-2}]^y [ML^2T^{-1}]^z$

$\Rightarrow \ [M^0L^0T^1]$

$= L^{x+3y+2z}\, M^{-y+z}\, T^{-x-2y-z}$

Equating dimension of length,

$x + 3y + 2z = 0$

Equating dimension of mass,

$-y + z = 0$

Equation dimension of time,

$-x - 2y - z = 1$

On solving, we get

$x = -\frac{5}{2}, y = \frac{1}{2}, \ z = \frac{1}{2}$

$[T] = [c^{-5/2}G^{1/2}h^{1/2}]$

9. (d) As we know, if the unit is increasing, then the numerical value is decreasing and if the unit is decreasing, then the numerical value is increasing. Hence,

$\therefore \quad n \propto \frac{1}{u}$

10. (c) bt must have dimension of L
$\Rightarrow b$ must have dimension of L/T i.e. ms^{-1}.

11. (d) The unit of LHS $= m^1s^{-1}$
The unit of RHS = coulomb

$\left(\frac{\text{Newton}}{\text{Coulomb}}\right)^y$ (kilogram)^z (second).

But unit of LHS = unit of RHS
Coulomb does not come in LHS

$\therefore \frac{\text{Coulomb}^1}{\text{Coulomb}^y} = \text{unitless}$

$\Rightarrow \quad \frac{1}{y} = 1$

12. (d) Let total energy,

$E = kp^a A^b t^c$ ...(i)

where, k is a dimensionless constant of proportionality. Equating dimensions on both sides of Eq. (i), we get

$[ML^2T^{-2}]$

$= [MLT^{-1}]^a [M^0L^2T^0]^b [M^0L^0T]^c$

$\Rightarrow [ML^2T^{-2}] = [M^a L^{a+2b} T^{-a+c}]$

Applying the principle of homogeneity of dimensions, we get

$a = 1$ ...(ii)

$a + 2b = 2$ ...(iii)

$-a + c = -2$ ...(iv)

On solving Eqs. (ii), (iii) and (iv) we get

$a = 1, b = \frac{1}{2}, c = -1$

$\therefore$ The dimensional formula of energy, $[E] = [p^1 A^{1/2} t^{-1}]$

13. (b) Plane angle

$= \frac{\text{Arc}}{\text{Radius}} = \text{dimensionless}$

All unitless quantities are dimensionless but *vice-versa* is not true.

14. (b) Let, $[G] \propto c^x g^y p^z$

By substituting the following dimensions, we get

$[G] = [M^{-1}L^3T^{-2}]$, $[c] = [LT^{-1}]$,

$[g] = [LT^{-2}]$

$[p] = [ML^{-1}T^2]$

and by comparing the powers of both sides, $x = 0$, $y = 2$, $z = -1$

$\Rightarrow \quad \frac{x}{y} = \frac{0}{2} = 0$

15. (d) The sum of the numbers can be calculated as 672.961 arithmetically. The number with least decimal places is 226.3 is correct to only one decimal place.

16. (a) It is clear that

$[1 - p^2] = [M^0L^0T^0]$

Hence, $[p] = [M^0L^0T^0]$

17. (a) Critical velocity $v_c \propto [\eta^x \rho^y r^z]$

$\Rightarrow [LT^{-1}] \propto$

$[M^1L^{-1}T^{-1}]^x [M^1L^{-3}]^y [L^1]^z$

$\Rightarrow [LT^{-1}] \propto$

$[M^{x+y}][L^{-x-3y+z}][T^{-x}]$

Taking comparison on both sides, we get

$x + y = 0, -x - 3y + z = 1, -x = -1$

$\Rightarrow \quad x = 1, y = -1, z = -1$

$\frac{x}{y} + z = -2$

18. (b) Let $v^4 \propto \sigma^a \rho^b \lambda^c$

Equating dimensions on both sides,

$[M^0L^1T^{-1}]^4 \propto [MT^{-2}]^a [ML^{-3}]^b [L]^c$

$\Rightarrow [LT^{-1}]^4 \propto [M]^{a+b} [L]^{-3b+c} [T]^{-2a}$

Equating the powers of M, L, T on both sides, we get

$a + b = 0$

$-3b + c = 4$

$-2a = -4$

Solving, we get

$a = 2, b = -2, \ c = -2$

$\therefore \quad v \propto \sigma^2 \rho^{-2} \lambda^{-2}$

$\therefore \quad v^2 \propto \frac{\sigma^2}{(\rho\lambda)^2}$

19. (d) $a + b = 1.00$, so number of significant figures is 3.
$a - b = 0.64$, so number of significant figures is 2. In case of multiplication and division, result will contain least number of significant figures. In 0.82 and 0.18, there are two significant figures.

20. (b) Given, $\frac{\Delta x}{x}\times 100 =$

$$a\left(\frac{\Delta M}{M}\times 100\right)+b\left(\frac{\Delta L}{L}\times 100\right)+c\left(\frac{\Delta T}{T}\times 100\right)$$

$$= a\alpha + b\beta + c\gamma$$

21. (c) Given, $Y = \frac{4MgL}{\pi D^2 l}$

So, maximum permissible error in Y

$$\frac{\Delta Y}{Y}\times 100 = \left(\frac{\Delta M}{M}+\frac{\Delta g}{g}+\frac{\Delta L}{L}+\frac{2\Delta D}{D}+\frac{\Delta l}{l}\right)\times 100$$

$$=\left(\frac{1}{301}+\frac{1}{981}+\frac{1}{283}+2\times\frac{1}{141}+\frac{1}{9}\right)\times 100$$

$$= 13.3\%$$

22. (c) Here, $nA\left(\frac{\Delta V}{\Delta x}\right) =$ Force $= [\text{MLT}^{-2}]$

and $\frac{1}{\sqrt{LC}} = \omega =$ Angular frequency $= [\text{T}^{-1}]$

$CV^2 =$ Energy $= [\text{ML}^2\text{T}^{-2}]$

$\frac{1}{\sqrt{\varepsilon_0\mu_0}} =$ speed of light $= [\text{LT}^{-1}]$

23. (a) RC is time constant of the circuit,

$RC = T$

$$\because C = \frac{q}{V} = \frac{[\text{AT}]^2}{[\text{ML}^2\text{T}^{-2}]} = [\text{M}^{-1}\text{L}^{-2}\text{T}^4\text{A}^2]$$

$$R = \frac{V}{I} = \frac{[\text{ML}^2\text{T}^{-2}]}{[\text{AT}]\,[\text{A}]} = [\text{ML}^2\text{T}^{-3}\text{A}^{-2}]$$

$\therefore$ Dimensional formula of CR

$$= [\text{M}^{-1}\text{L}^{-2}\text{T}^4\text{A}^2][\text{ML}^2\text{T}^{-3}\text{A}^{-2}] = [\text{M}^0\text{L}^0\text{T}^1\text{A}^0]$$

24. (d) Dimensional formula of stress, energy density and modulus of elasticity is $[\text{ML}^{-1}\text{T}^{-2}]$.

Dimensional formula of thermal capacity is $[\text{ML}^2\text{T}^{-2}\text{K}^{-1}]$

25. (b) The value of constants cannot be found using dimensional formula. Therefore, gravitational force formula cannot be derived by dimensional formula because G is gravitational constant.

26. (a) $\sqrt{\mu_0\varepsilon_0} = \frac{1}{c}$ and $\frac{F}{qB} = v$

$$\Rightarrow \sqrt{\mu_0\varepsilon_0}\times\frac{F}{qB} = \frac{v}{c} = \frac{[\text{L}^1\text{T}^{-1}]}{[\text{L}^1\text{T}^{-1}]} = [\text{M}^0\text{L}^0\text{T}^0]$$

27. (c) 1 N $= 10^5$ dyne

$1\ \text{m}^2 = 10^4\ \text{cm}^2$

$\Rightarrow 1\text{N/ m}^2 = 10\,\text{dyne/cm}^2$

$\therefore 1.9\times 10^{11}\ \text{N-m}^{-2} = 1.9\times 10^{12}\ \text{dyne/cm}^2$

28. (b) As, $T = 2\pi\sqrt{\frac{l}{g}}$ or $g = \frac{4\pi^2 l}{T^2}$

$$\Rightarrow \frac{\Delta g}{g} = \frac{\Delta l}{l} + 2\frac{\Delta T}{T}$$

$$\Rightarrow \frac{\Delta g}{g} = \left(\frac{1/10}{20}\right) + 2\left(\frac{1}{90}\right) = \frac{1}{200}+\frac{2}{90}$$

$$\Rightarrow \frac{\Delta g}{g}\times 100\% = \left(\frac{1}{200}+\frac{2}{90}\right)\times 100\% = 2.7\%$$

29. (a) As, $[Y] \propto v^a A^b F^c$

$\therefore\ [\text{ML}^{-1}\text{T}^{-2}] = [\text{LT}^{-1}]^a\,[\text{LT}^{-2}]^b\,[\text{MLT}^{-2}]^c$

$[\text{ML}^{-1}\text{T}^{-2}] = [\text{M}^c\text{L}^{a+b+c}\text{T}^{-a-2b-2c}]$

On comparing and solving, we get

$a = -4,\ b = 2,\ c = 1$

Hence, $Y = [\text{FA}^2\text{v}^{-4}]$

30. (d) Given, $T \propto p^a d^b E^c$

We have

$[\text{M}^0\text{L}^0\text{T}] = [\text{ML}^{-1}\text{T}^{-2}]^a [\text{ML}^{-3}]^b [\text{ML}^2\text{T}^{-2}]^c$

On comparing dimensions of similar terms, we have

$[\text{M}^0\text{L}^0\text{T}] = [\text{M}^{a+b+c}\text{L}^{-a-3b+2c}\text{T}^{-2a-2c}]$

On comparing powers of M, we have

$0 = a + b + c$ ...(i)

On comparing powers of L, we have

$0 = -a - 3b + 2c$ ...(ii)

On comparing powers of T, we have

$1 = -2a - 2c$ ...(iii)

On solving Eqs. (i), (ii) and (iii), we get

$$a = -\frac{5}{6},\ b = \frac{1}{2},\ c = \frac{1}{3}$$

Ch-02 Motion in a Straight Line

Topical Follow Thru

Test-1

1. (c) Initial velocity of the stone is 12 m/s downward under gravity,

$$\therefore \quad h = ut + \frac{1}{2}gt^2$$

$$= 12\times 10 + \frac{1}{2}\times 10\times (10)^2$$

$$= 120 + 500 = 620\,\text{m}$$

2. (b) In first 10 s,

$$s_1 = 0 + \frac{1}{2}a\times(10)^2 = 50a \quad \ldots(\text{i})$$

In the next 10 s,

$$s_2 = vt + \frac{1}{2}at^2$$

where, v is the velocity after 10 s.

$$\therefore \quad v = u + at = 0 + a\times 10 = 10a$$

Thus, $s_2 = 10a\times 10 + \frac{1}{2}a\times(10)^2$

$$= 100a + 50a$$

$$= 150a \quad \ldots(\text{ii})$$

From Eqs. (i) and (ii), we get

$$\frac{s_1}{s_2} = \frac{50a}{150a}$$

$$\Rightarrow \quad s_1 = \frac{s_2}{3}$$

3. (a) Let the time to attain maximum velocity v is t_1 and the particle comes to rest after total time $t_1 + t_2$, then

$$v = 0 + 4t_1 \quad \ldots(\text{i})$$

$$v = 0 - 2t_2 \quad \ldots(\text{ii})$$

Solving Eqs. (i) and (ii), we get

$$t_2 = 2t_1$$

Also, $t_1 + t_2 = 12$ (given)

$$t_1 = 4\,\text{s and } t_2 = 8\,\text{s}$$

and $v = 4t_1 = 4\times 4 = 16\,\text{m/s}$

4. (c) Let v be the maximum velocity for the first kilometre of accelerated motion, $\frac{1}{t_1} = \left(\frac{0+v}{2}\right) \Rightarrow 2 = vt_1$

For the uniform motion, $3 = vt_2$

For the retarded motion,

$$\frac{2}{t_3} = \left(\frac{v+0}{2}\right) \Rightarrow 4 = vt_3$$

From the above three equations

$$9 = v(t_1 + t_2 + t_3)$$

$$\Rightarrow \quad v = \frac{9}{10/60} = 54\,\text{kmph}$$

5. (b) Here $s_1 = \frac{1}{2}a_1 t_1^2$

and $s_2 = \frac{1}{2}a_2 t_2^2$

$$v = a_1 t_1 \text{ and } v = a_2 t_2$$

$$\frac{s_1}{s_2} = \frac{a_1 t_1^2}{a_2 t_2^2} = \frac{vt_1}{vt_2} = \frac{t_1}{t_2} = \frac{a_2}{a_1}$$

6. (b) Given, $t = 2x^2 + 3x$

$$\frac{dt}{dx} = 4x + 3$$

$$v = \frac{dx}{dt} = \frac{1}{4x+3}$$

$$a = v\cdot\frac{dv}{dx}$$

$$= \frac{1}{(4x+3)}\cdot\left(\frac{-1\times 4}{(4x+3)^2}\right)$$

$$a = \frac{-4}{(4x+3)^3}$$

$$a = -4v^3$$

$$a \propto v^3$$

7. (a) Let the time taken during retardation $(-2a)$ be t and time taken during acceleration $(+a)$ be $(9-t)$ s.

$$\because \quad v = u + at$$

$$v = 0 + a(9-t) = a(9-t)$$

A ——(9 − t)—— B ——(t)—— C

and $v' = v - (2a)t$

$$\Rightarrow \quad 0 = a(9-t) - 2at$$

$$\Rightarrow \quad 3at = 9a \Rightarrow t = 3\,\text{s}$$

8. (d) Let height of Minaret is H and boy takes time T to fall from peak to bottom.

(Figure: H, T; $(H-40)$m, $(T-2)$s; 40m, 2 s)

Height, $H = \frac{1}{2}gT^2 \quad \ldots(\text{i})$

In last 2 s, boy travels distance of 40 m. So in $(T-2)$ s, distance travelled $= (H-40)$ m

$$(H-40) = \frac{1}{2}g(T-2)^2 \quad \ldots(\text{ii})$$

By solving Eqs. (i) and (ii), we get

$$T = 3\,\text{s and } H = 45\,\text{m}$$

9. (b) Distance covered in first 5 s,

$$h_1 = ut + \frac{1}{2}at^2 = 0 + \frac{1}{2}a(5)^2 \quad [\because u = 0]$$

$$\Rightarrow \quad h_1 = \frac{25a}{2} \quad \ldots(\text{i})$$

Distance covered in first 10 s,

$$s_2 = 0 + \frac{1}{2}a(10)^2 = \frac{100a}{2}$$

So, distance covered in second 5 s,

$$h_2 = s_2 - h_1$$

$$= \frac{100a}{2} - \frac{25a}{2} = \frac{75a}{2} \quad \ldots(\text{ii})$$

Distance covered in first 15 s,

$$s_3 = 0 + \frac{1}{2}a(15)^2 = \frac{225a}{2}$$

So, distance covered in last 5 s,

$$h_3 = s_3 - s_2$$

$$= \frac{225a}{2} - \frac{100a}{2} = \frac{125a}{2} \quad \ldots(\text{iii})$$

Using Eqs. (i), (ii) and (iii), we get

$$\frac{h_1}{\frac{25a}{2}} = \frac{h_2}{\frac{75a}{2}} = \frac{h_3}{\frac{125a}{2}}$$

$$\Rightarrow \quad h_1 = \frac{h_2}{3} = \frac{h_3}{5}$$

10. (a) Equation for X-axis depends on time as $\sqrt{x} = t + 1$ ...(i)

Squaring on both sides in Eq. (i),

$$x = (t+1)^2 = t^2 + 2t + 1$$

Differentiating it w.r.t. time, we get

$\therefore$ Velocity, $v = \frac{dx}{dt} = 2t + 2$

Thus, velocity increases linearly with time.

11. (b) As, $v^2 = u^2 + 2as$

$$a = \frac{v^2 - u^2}{2s} = \frac{(20)^2 - (10)^2}{2 \times 135}$$

$$= \frac{300}{270} = \frac{10}{9} \text{ m/s}$$

Also, $v = u + at$

$$\Rightarrow \quad 20 - 10 = \frac{10}{9} t$$

$$\Rightarrow \quad 10 \times \frac{9}{10} = t \Rightarrow t = 9 \text{ s}$$

12. (b) According to question,

$$a = \alpha t + \beta$$

As $a = \frac{dv}{dt} \Rightarrow \alpha t + \beta = \frac{dv}{dt}$

At $t = 0$, velocity $v = 0$

$$\int_0^v dv = \int_0^t (\alpha t + \beta) dt$$

$$\Rightarrow \quad v = \frac{\alpha t^2}{2} + \beta t$$

13. (a) Distance covered in 5th second,

$$s_{5\text{th}} = u + \frac{a}{2}(2n-1)$$

$$= 0 + \frac{a}{2}(2 \times 5 - 1) = \frac{9a}{2}$$

and distance covered in 5 s,

$$s_5 = ut + \frac{1}{2}at^2$$

$$= 0 + \frac{1}{2} \times a \times 25$$

$$s_5 = \frac{25a}{2}$$

$$\frac{s_5\text{th}}{s_5} = \frac{9}{25}$$

14. (c) Given,

Initial velocity of a body, $u = 0$

Let s be the distance covered by a body in time t,

$$s = ut + \frac{1}{2}at^2$$

or $\quad s = \frac{1}{2}at^2$

$$s \propto t^2$$

15. (a) Using, $s_n = u + \frac{a}{2}(2n-1)$

$$= \frac{a}{2}(2n-1) \quad (\because u = 0)$$

Thus, $\frac{s_4}{s_3} = \frac{2 \times 4 - 1}{2 \times 3 - 1} = \frac{7}{5}$

16. (b) The distance covered in nth second is given by

$$s_n = u + \frac{a}{2}(2n-1)$$

For $n = 3$, $s_3 = 6$ m, we get

$$s_3 = u + \frac{a}{2}(2 \times 3 - 1) = u + \frac{5a}{2}$$

$$\Rightarrow \quad 6 = u + \frac{5a}{2} \quad \text{...(i)}$$

Similarly, for distance of 12 m in 6th second,

$$s_6 = u + \frac{11}{2}a$$

$$\Rightarrow \quad 12 = u + \frac{11}{2}a \quad \text{...(ii)}$$

From Eqs. (i) and (ii), we get

$$6 - \frac{5a}{2} = 12 - \frac{11a}{2}$$

$$\Rightarrow \quad a = \frac{6}{6} \times 2 = 2 \text{ ms}^{-2}$$

and $\quad u = 6 - \frac{5a}{2} = 6 - \frac{10}{2} = 1 \text{ ms}^{-1}$

Distance travelled in next 3s,

$$s = s_9 - s_6$$

$$= \left(ut + \frac{1}{2}at^2\right)_{t=9\text{s}} - \left(ut + \frac{1}{2}at^2\right)_{t=6\text{s}}$$

Substituting $u = 1 \text{ ms}^{-1}$ and $a = 2 \text{ ms}^{-2}$, we get

$$s = \left(1 \times 9 + \frac{1}{2} \times 2 \times 81\right) - \left(1 \times 6 + \frac{1}{2} \times 2 \times 36\right)$$

$$s = 90 - 42 = 48 \text{ cm}$$

17. (c) It is given that, $v = \frac{t^2}{10} + 20$

Differentiating both sides w.r.t. time, we get

$$\frac{dv}{dt} = \frac{2t}{10} + 0 = \frac{t}{5}$$

$\therefore$ Acceleration,

$$a = \frac{dv}{dt} = \frac{t}{5} \neq \text{constant}$$

Hence, it is a case of non-uniform acceleration.

18. (c) Change in velocity, $\frac{dv}{dt} = bt$

$$\Rightarrow \quad dv = bt\,dt$$

$$\Rightarrow \quad v = \frac{bt^2}{2} + k_1$$

At $t = 0$ and $v = v_0 \Rightarrow k_1 = v_0$

Then we get $v = \frac{1}{2}bt^2 + v_0$

Now, integrating again, we get

$$x = \frac{1}{6}bt^3 + v_0 t + k_2$$

Again,

at $\quad t = 0, x = 0, k_2 = 0$

Hence, $x = \frac{1}{6}bt^3 + v_0 t$

19. (b) Let, $PQ = s$

Average speed

$$= \frac{s + s}{\left(\frac{s}{20}\right) + \left(\frac{s}{30}\right)}$$

$$= 24 \text{ km/h}$$

20. (a) $\because$ Velocity

$$v = \frac{dx}{dt} = 0 - 5 + 12t$$

At $\quad t = 0,$

$$v = -5 \text{ m/s}$$

21. (b) Given, $d = 4 + 9t - 5t^2$

(a) Initial acceleration

$$\frac{d}{dt}(d) = v = 9 - 10t$$

$$\frac{d}{dt}(v) = a = -10 \text{ unit}$$

(b) Velocity at $t = 3$ s,

$$v_{t=3} = 9 - 10 \times 3 = -21 \text{ unit}$$

(c) Distance travelled in 2 s,

$$dE_2 = 4 + 9 \times 2 - 5 \times (2)^2$$
$$= 2 \text{ unit}$$

(d) Displacement at 1s.,

$$= 4 + 9 - 5 = 8 \text{ unit}$$

22. (b) Times of flight,

$$t_1 = 5\text{ s}, t_2 = 3\text{ s}$$
$$t = \sqrt{\frac{2h}{g}}$$
$$\Rightarrow \quad h = \frac{1}{2} g t^2$$
$$h_1 - h_2 = \frac{1}{2} g (t_1^2 - t_2^2)$$
$$= \frac{1}{2} \times 9.8 (25 - 9)$$
$$= 8 \times 9.8 = 78.4 \text{ m}$$

23. (d) Total distance $= s + s = 2s$

Total displacement = zero

Total time = 2 + 3 = 5 h

So, average speed $= \frac{2s}{5}$

but average velocity = 0

24. (a) In case of uniform velocity, both magnitude and direction of distance and displacement will be same. So, all three options are correct.

25. (a) A body can have zero velocity but still have acceleration.

For example, when a ball thrown upwards reaches its highest point, its velocity is zero, but still have downward acceleration due to gravity.

Test-2

1. (b) In region bc, x = constant

$\Rightarrow \quad v = 0$, also $a = 0$

2. (d) Since, $a = -$ constant

Hence, its displacement is given by $x = c - c' t^2$

Hence, graph (d) is correct.

3. (d) Upto time t_1, $x \propto t$

or v = constant

After time t_1, x = constant or $v = 0$

4. (b) Distance travelled = Area of v-t graph

$$= \left(\frac{1}{2} \times 1 \times 20\right) + (1 \times 20)$$
$$+ \left[\frac{1}{2} \times 1 \times (20 + 10)\right] + 1 \times 10$$
$$= 10 + 20 + 15 + 10 = 55 \text{ m}$$

5. (c) $v = u + at \quad \Rightarrow v \propto t$

$$s = ut + \frac{1}{2} a t^2 \Rightarrow s \propto t^2$$

6. (d) Area of graph in 1st and 4th quadrant is same, so net displacement is zero.

Particle changes direction of motion at $t = T$.

Initial and final speeds are same.

7. (a) $v_{\text{av}} = \frac{\int v dt}{\int dt}$

$$= \frac{\text{Area of } v\text{-}t \text{ curve}}{\text{Total time}}$$

Here, area of v-t curve

$$= \left[\frac{25}{2} - \frac{25}{2}\right] = 0$$

8. (b)

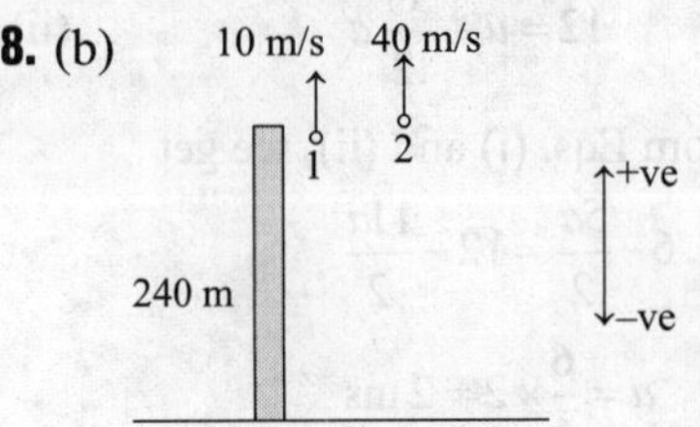

Let us first find the time of collision of two particles with the ground

$$S = ut + \frac{1}{2} a t^2$$
$$-240 = 10 t_1 - \frac{1}{2} \times 10 \times t_1^2$$

Solving, we get positive value of $t_1 = 8\text{ s}$

Similarly, $-240 = 40 t_2 - \frac{1}{2} \times 10 \times t_2^2$

On solving this equation, we get positive value of $t_2 = 12\text{ s}$

From 0 to 8 s, both particles are moving under gravity. Their absolute accelerations are same (equal to g). So, relative acceleration is zero or relative motion is uniform. So, relative position will change (or increase) linearly. At 8 s, first particle reaches with ground. Its acceleration has become zero. The second particle has reached its initial position and is moving downwards so, relative position will now decrease. The particle is still in air. So, its acceleration is g, or relative acceleration is g.

Hence, graph is parabola.

9. (c)

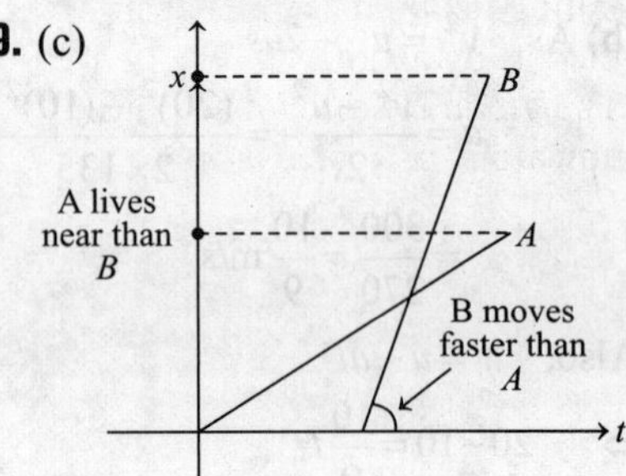

Given, slope of $B >$ slope of A. So, B is fast.

Projection of A on X-axis is less than projection of B. So, A lives near to school.

Therefore, option (c) is correct.

10. (a) Displacement = Area of half ellipse

$$= \frac{\pi}{2} ab = \frac{\pi}{2} (v_m) \left(\frac{t_0}{2}\right)$$
$$= \frac{\pi}{2} v_m t_0$$

Average speed $= \frac{\text{Displacement}}{\text{Time}}$

$$= \frac{\frac{\pi}{4} v_m t_0}{t_0}$$
$$= \frac{\pi}{4} v_m$$

At $t = 0$ and $t = t_0$, acceleration which is slope of v-t graph will be infinite, so such motion is practically impossible. Both A and B are correct statements.

11. (d) For upward motion,

$$v = u_0 - (g + a) t$$

Negative acceleration, magnitude of velocity decreases with time linearly for downward motion, after reaching max height.

$$v=(g-a)t$$

Magnitude of acceleration is decreases i.e. slope of the curve decreased, direction of motion is negative with increasing speed. Correct option is (d).

12. (a) It is evident that when ball is thrown upwards, its velocity continuously decreases and at peak point, it becomes zero and while falling down, its velocity starts increasing again.

The graph for thrown an object upward is projected as

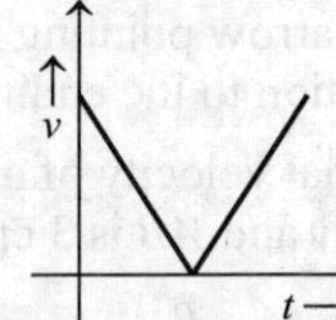

13. (c) In uniform motion, the object moves with uniform velocity, the magnitude of its velocity at different instant. i.e. At $t=0$, $t=1\,\text{s}$, $t=2\,\text{s}$ will always be constant.

Hence, Statement I is correct but Statement II is incorrect.

14. (d) Time taken

$$=\frac{\text{Total length}}{\text{Relative velocity}}$$

$$=\frac{80+80}{10+15}=\frac{160}{25}$$

$$=6.4\ \text{s}$$

15. (c)

(a) For $t=0\,\text{s}$ to $t=2\,\text{s}$, the motion is in positive direction as the velocity is positive and the acceleration is positive, since the slope of the straight line is positive.

(b) For $t=2\text{s}$ to $t=4\,\text{s}$, the object is moving in positive direction, till time $t_1=2\,\text{s}$, and then turns back with the same negative acceleration till $t=4\,\text{s}$.

(c) For $t=4\,\text{s}$ to $t=6\,\text{s}$, the object is moving in negative direction, since the velocity is negative. The acceleration is positive, since the slope of the straight line is positive.

(d) Displacement for overall journey ($t=0\,\text{s}$ to $t=6\,\text{s}$) = Total area under v-t graph considering the area below time axis as negative = [Area under v-t curve for $t=0$ to $t=3\,\text{s}$] + [Area under v-t curve for $t=3\,\text{s}$ to $t=6\,\text{s}$] = Area of triangle (OAB) + Area of triangle (BCD)

$$=\frac{1}{2}\times 3\times 5+\frac{1}{2}\times 3\times(-5)=0$$

16. (b) Both Statement I and Statement II are incorrect.

The displacement of a body moving in straight line with constant acceleration is given by,

$$s=ut+\frac{1}{2}at^2$$

This is a equation of parabola, not straight line. Therefore, the displacement-time graph is a parabola. This displacement-time graph will be straight line, if and only if acceleration of body is zero or body is moving with uniform velocity.

17. (a) Area (1) $=\frac{1}{2}\times 10\times 5=25$

Area (2) (area of lower triangle)

$$=\frac{1}{2}\times 3\times 6=9$$

Distance $=25+9=34$ m

18. (a) In the acceleration-time graph,

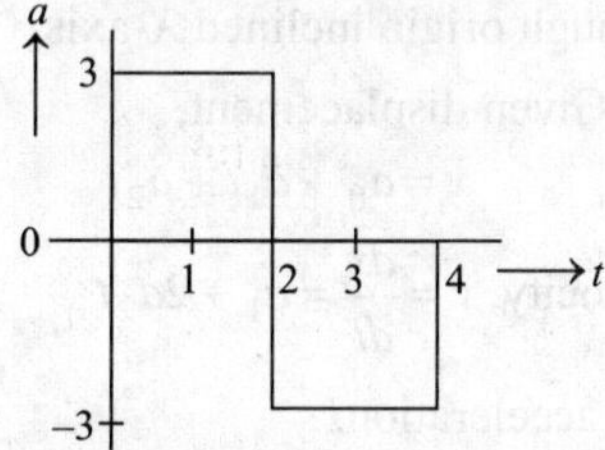

Taking the motion from 0 to 2 s

$u=0$, $a=3\,\text{ms}^{-2}$, $t=2\text{s}$, $v=?$

By using,

$v=u+at=0+3\times 2=6\,\text{ms}^{-1}$

Taking the motion from 2 s to 4 s given apply $v=u+at$

Now, $u=6\,\text{ms}^{-1}$, $a=-3\,\text{ms}^{-2}$, $t=2\text{s}$

$v=6+(-3)(2)=0\,\text{ms}^{-1}$

19. (b) As, $v=u+at$

where, $u=0\Rightarrow v=at$

The graph (b) is correct as $v=0$ at $t=0$ and it is a straight line graph.

$y=mx$, $y=v$, $m=a$ and $t=x$

20. (a) Relative speed of train 1 w.r.t. wind, $v_1=v-u$

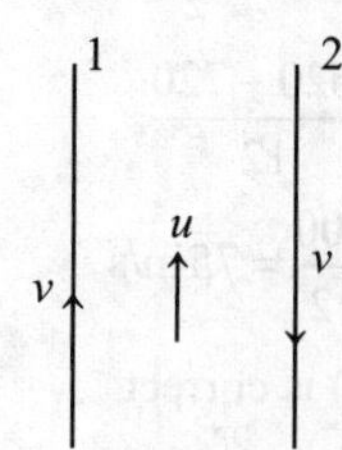

For second train, relative velocity,

$$v_2=v+u$$

According to question,

$$\frac{v_1}{v_2}=\frac{1}{2}=\frac{v-u}{v+u}$$

$$\Rightarrow\quad v+u=2v-2u$$

$$\Rightarrow\quad v=3u$$

21. (a) Distance covered by the car in first 4 s,

$$s=0+\frac{1}{2}at^2$$

$$\Rightarrow\quad s=\frac{1}{2}at^2$$

This is the equation for parabola with slope increasing with time. After 4 s, the velocity is uniform which means position-time graph will be straight line with non-zero positive slope.

22. (a) For the given particle, the graph should be

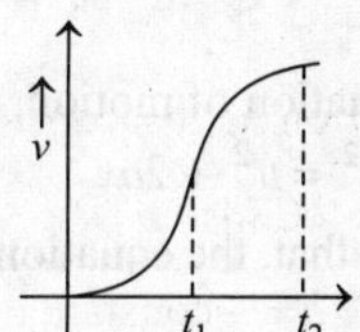

As acceleration is always positive, the velocity keep increasing exponentially.

23. (b) For ball 1

$$h=\frac{1}{2}gt^2$$

$$= \frac{1}{2} \times 10 \times (18)^2 = 1620\,\text{m}$$

For ball 2

($h = 1620$ m, $u = ?$, $t = 18 - 6\,\text{s} = 12\,\text{s}$)

$$h = ut + \frac{1}{2}gt^2$$

$$1620 = u \times 12 + \frac{1}{2} \times 10(12)^2$$

$$u = \frac{1620 - 720}{12}$$

$$= \frac{900}{12} = 75\,\text{m/s}$$

Option (b) is correct.

24. (a) Let their speeds be v_1 and v_2 and $v_1 < v_2$, when both persons approach one another, relative distance between them decreases with the speed $v_1 - (-v_2) = v_1 + v_2 = 6\,\text{m/s}$.
If both move in the same direction, then the relative distance between them increases with the speed $v_1 - v_2$.
Since, $v_1 < v_2$,
we use $v_2 - v_1 = 4\,\text{m/s}$
Solving these two equations, we get
$v_1 = 1\,\text{m/s}$
and $v_2 = 5\,\text{m/s}$

25. (a) v^2 *versus* x graph is shown below.

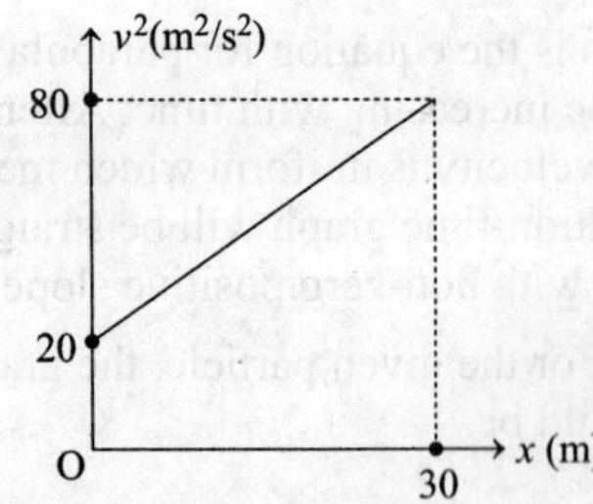

Using equation of motion,

$$v^2 = u^2 + 2ax \quad \text{...(i)}$$

We know that, the equation of straight line.

$$y = mx + c \quad \text{...(ii)}$$

Comparing Eqs. (i) and (ii),

$$\text{Slope, } m = 2a = \frac{80 - 20}{30 - 0} = \frac{60}{30} = 2$$

Now, the acceleration,
$a = 2/2 = 1\,\text{m/s}^2$

Chapter Break Thru

1. (d) ($s = t^3 - 6t^2 + 3t + 4$) m

$$\Rightarrow v = \frac{ds}{dt} = 3t^2 - 12t + 3$$

and $a = 6t - 12$

At $a = 0$, $t = 2$ s

$$v_{\text{at } t = 2\text{s}} = 3(2)^2 - 12(2) + 3$$

$$= 12 - 24 + 3 = -9\,\text{m/s}$$

2. (a) Distance covered = Area enclosed by v-t graph
= Area of triangle between 0 s to 4 s

$$= \frac{1}{2} \times 4 \times 8 = 16\,\text{m}$$

3. (a) At time t,
Velocity of P, $v_P = u - gt$ (upward)
Velocity of Q, $v_Q = gt$ (downward)
If we assume that, height h is smaller than or equal to the maximum height reached by P.

Thus, $v_{PQ} = v_P + v_Q$
$= u - gt + gt = u$

4. (a) By using, $v = u + at$
where, initial velocity is $u = 0$.
Then, $v = at \quad (\because a = g)$
Comparing with $y = mx + c$
It represents a straight line passing through origin inclined X-axis.

5. (c) Given displacement,

$$x = a_0 + a_1 t + a_2 t^2$$

$$\text{Velocity, } v = \frac{dx}{dt} = a_1 + 2a_2 t$$

So, acceleration,

$$a = \frac{dv}{dt} = \frac{d^2x}{dt^2} = 2a_2$$

6. (d) Given, $a = 19.6\,\text{m/s}^2 = 2g$
Resultant velocity of rocket after 5 s, $v = 2g \times 5 = 10g$ m/s
Height achieved after 5 s,

$$h_1 = \frac{1}{2} \times 2g \times 25 = 245\,\text{m}$$

On switching OFF the engine, it goes upto height h_2, where velocity becomes zero.

$$(0) = (10g)^2 - 2gh_2 \Rightarrow h_2 = 490\,\text{m}$$

Total height $= 245 + 490 = 735$ m

7. (a) From $s = \int_0^3 v\,dt = \int_0^3 kt\,dt$

$$= \left[\frac{1}{2}kt^2\right]_0^3 = \frac{1}{2} \times 2 \times 9$$

$$= 9\,\text{m}$$

8. (d) The definition of displacement is a change of an object's position. Hence, it is not the vector sum of area under velocity-time graph. It is a vector quantity with a magnitude and direction. The system for it is an arrow pointing from the initial location to the ending place.

9. (a) Let initial velocity of a body at point A be v and AB is 3 cm.

A v B C
3 cm x
v/2

From $v^2 = u^2 - 2as$

$$\Rightarrow \left(\frac{v}{2}\right)^2 = v^2 - 2a \times 3$$

$$\text{or} \quad a = \frac{v^2}{8}$$

Let on penetrating 3 cm in a wooden block, the body moves x distance from B to C.

So, for B to C, $u = \frac{v}{2}$, $v = 0$

$$s = x, a = \frac{v^2}{8}$$

$$\therefore (0)^2 = \left(\frac{v}{2}\right)^2 - 2 \cdot \frac{v^2}{8} \cdot x$$

$$\Rightarrow x = 1\,\text{cm}$$

Note Here, it is assumed that retardation is uniform.

10. (a) The v-x equation from the given graph can be written as

$$v = \left(-\frac{v_0}{x_0}\right)x + v_0 \Rightarrow \frac{dv}{dx} = -\frac{v_0}{x_0}$$

$$\text{Now,} \quad a = v \cdot \frac{dv}{dx}$$

$$\Rightarrow a = \left(\frac{v_0}{x_0}\right)^2 x - \frac{v_0^2}{x_0}$$

(a linear equation in a and x)

Thus, a-x graph is a straight line with positive slope and negative intercept.

11. (d) In case of acceleration,

$$v = \alpha t_1 \Rightarrow t_1 = \frac{v}{\alpha}$$

In case of retardation,

$$0 = v - \beta t_2 \Rightarrow t_2 = \frac{v}{\beta}$$

$$t = t_1 + t_2 = \frac{v}{\alpha} + \frac{v}{\beta} = \left(\frac{\alpha+\beta}{\alpha\beta}\right) v$$

$$\Rightarrow v = \left(\frac{\alpha\beta}{\alpha+\beta}\right) t$$

12. (d) Height = Area of v-t curve

$$= \frac{1}{2} \times 2 \times 3.6 + 8 \times 3.6 + \frac{1}{2} \times 2 \times 3.6$$

$$= 3.6 + 28.8 + 3.6$$

$$= 36.0 \text{ m}$$

13. (c) $s_n = u + \frac{a}{2}(2n-1)$

Here, $u = 0$

$$\Rightarrow a = \frac{2 \times s_n}{(2n-1)} = \frac{2 \times 1.2}{12-1}$$

$$= \frac{24}{11} = 0.218 \text{ m/s}^2$$

14. (a) $s_4 = 24 = 4u + \frac{1}{2}a(4)^2$

$\Rightarrow 24 = 4u + 8a$ ...(i)

Given, $s_8 - s_4 = 64$

$\Rightarrow s_8 = 64 + s_4 = 64 + 24 = 88$

$\Rightarrow s_8 = 88 = 8u + \frac{1}{2}a(8)^2$

$\Rightarrow 8u + 32a = 88$ ...(ii)

On solving Eqs. (i) and (ii), we get

$u = 1 \text{ m/s}$ and $a = \frac{5}{2} \text{ m/s}^2$

15. (b) Since, speed of particle is decreasing, acceleration must be negative.

16. (b) $s_n = u + \frac{a}{2}(2n-1)$

$$x_1 = \frac{5}{2}a \text{ and } x_2 = \frac{9}{2}a$$

$$\Rightarrow x_1 : x_2 = 5 : 9$$

17. (d) $h = \frac{v^2}{2g}$ or $h \propto \frac{1}{g}$

$$\frac{h_B}{h_A} = \frac{g_A}{g_B}$$

$$\Rightarrow h_B = \left(\frac{g_A}{g_B}\right) h_A = \frac{2}{9} \text{ m}$$

18. (b) $h = \frac{v^2}{2g} = \frac{19.6 \times 19.6}{2 \times 9.8} = 19.6 \text{ m}$

19. (c) $v^2 = 2gh \Rightarrow v \propto \sqrt{h}$

Since, h is same for all,

$v_1 : v_2 : v_3 = 1:1:1$

20. (b) $v = u - gt$

$$\Rightarrow u = 10 \times 6 = 60 \text{ m/s}$$

$$\Rightarrow s_1 = 60 - \frac{10}{2}(1)^2 = 55 \text{ m}$$

Velocity at $t = 6$s is 0 m/s.

Hence, to calculate distance travelled by object in 7th second, use $u = 0$ m/s, $t = 1$s, $a = -10 \text{ m/s}^2$, in the expression $s = ut + \frac{1}{2}at^2$

$$s_7 = 0 - \frac{10}{2} \times (1)^2 = 5 \text{ m}$$

$$s_1 : s_7 = 55 : 5 = 11 : 1$$

21. (b) $t \propto \sqrt{\frac{2h}{g}}$

$$\Rightarrow \frac{t_1}{t_2} = \sqrt{\frac{h_1}{h_2}}$$

22. (a) $s_3 - s_2 = \frac{9.8}{2}(3)^2 - \frac{9.8}{2}(2)^2$

$$= 24.5 \text{ m}$$

23. (b) Here, $-h = ut - \frac{1}{2}gt^2$

$$\Rightarrow t^2 - \frac{2u}{g}t - \frac{2h}{g} = 0$$

For higher u, t will be higher.

$t_P < t_Q < t_R$

24. (c) $t = \sqrt{\frac{2h}{g}}$

$$t_1 = \sqrt{\frac{2}{g}}$$

$$t_{2\text{-}1} = t_2 - t_1$$

$$= \sqrt{\frac{4}{g}} - \sqrt{\frac{2}{g}} = \sqrt{\frac{2}{g}}(\sqrt{2}-1)$$

$$t_{3\text{-}2} = t_3 - t_2$$

$$= \sqrt{\frac{6}{g}} - \sqrt{\frac{4}{g}} = \sqrt{\frac{2}{g}}(\sqrt{3}-\sqrt{2})$$

$$\Rightarrow t_1 : t_{2\text{-}1} : t_{3\text{-}2}$$

$$= 1 : (\sqrt{2}-1) : (\sqrt{3}-\sqrt{2})$$

25. (d) $s = \frac{1}{2}gt^2 = h$

$$s' = \frac{1}{2}g\left(\frac{t}{2}\right)^2 = \frac{1}{4}(s) \text{ or } \frac{1}{4}(h)$$

Height from ground

$$= h - \frac{h}{4} = \frac{3h}{4}$$

26. (b) s (in first 3 s)

$$= \frac{1}{2}g(3)^2 = \frac{9}{2}g$$

$$s_n = u + \frac{g}{2}(2n-1)$$

$$\frac{g}{2}(2n-1) = \frac{9}{2}g$$

$$2n - 1 = 9$$

$$\Rightarrow n = 5 \text{ s}$$

27. (b) $u^2 = 2gh$

$$\Rightarrow \frac{h_2}{h_1} = \left(\frac{u_2}{u_1}\right)^2 = 4$$

$\therefore h_2 = 4h_1$ $[\because h_1 = h]$

$h_2 = 4h$

28. (a) $s_1 = 20t - \frac{1}{2}gt^2$

$$s_2 = \frac{1}{2}gt^2 + 20t$$

$$s_1 + s_2 = 40$$

$\Rightarrow 40t = 40$ or $t = 1$s

$$s_1 = 20 - \frac{1}{2} \times 10 = 15 \text{ m}$$

(from ground)

29. (b) For rising, $a_{\text{eff}} = g + \frac{F}{m}$

For fall, $a_{\text{eff}} = g - \frac{F}{m}$

So, rising time will lesser than falling time.

30. (b) $v_A = 90$ km/h

$= \frac{90 \times 5}{18} = 25$ m/s

$v_B = 54$ km/h

$= \frac{54 \times 5}{18} = 15$ m/s

$v_{BA} = v_B - v_A$

$= 15 - (-25)$

(Move opposite to each other)

$= 15 + 25 = 40$ m/s

Time of crossing $= \frac{\text{Length of train}}{\text{Relative velocity}}$

$8 = \frac{l}{40}$

$l = 8 \times 40$

$= 320$

$l = 320$ m

31. (a) At maximum height for any object thrown vertically upward,

$v = 0 \; a = g$

In case of reversal of direction, body momentary comes at rest.

32. (b) Velocity of train A,

$v_A = 108$ km/h

$= 108 \times \frac{5}{18}$ m/s

$= 30$ m/s

Velocity of train B,

$v_B = 72$ km/h

$= 72 \times \frac{5}{18} = 20$ m/s

According to given situation, time taken to cross the tunnel by train B – time taken to cross the tunnel by train $A = 35$ s

$\Rightarrow \quad \frac{L + 4l}{20} - \frac{L + l}{30} = 35$

$\Rightarrow \quad \frac{60l + 4l}{20} - \frac{60l + l}{30} = 35$

$(\because L = 60l)$

$\Rightarrow \quad \frac{180l + 12l - 120l - 2l}{60} = 35$

$\Rightarrow \quad l = 30$ m

$\therefore$ Length of the tunnel,

$L = 60l = 60 \times 30$

$= 1800$ m

33. (c) According to question,

$v^2 = u^2 + 2as$

If $u = 0$, then $v^2 \propto s$

i.e. Graph should be parabola symmetric to displacement axis.

34. (d) Length of trucks T_1 and T_2,

$T_1 = T_2 = 40$ m

Speed of T_1 truck $= 20$ m/s

Speed of T_2 truck $= 10$ m/s

Relative velocity

$= 10 + 20 = 30$ m/s

and total length $= 40 + 40 = 80$ m

Thus, time $= \frac{\text{total length}}{\text{relative velocity}}$

$= \frac{80}{30} = 2.67$ s

35. (a) Time taken by particle when go up and down,

$t = \sqrt{\frac{2h}{g + a}}$

where, t is time taken and h is height of the particle.

36. (b) The speed of eagle relative to bullet train

$= 22 + 12 = 34$ m/s

Time taken, $t = \frac{160}{34} = 4.7$ s

37. (c) As we know, negative slope of graph shows that the body is moving towards the negative direction.

38. (c) We know that,

Acceleration, $a = \frac{dv}{dt}$

$dv = a \cdot dt$

Then, $\int dv = \int a \cdot dt$

$v = \int (At^2 + B) dt$

$v = \frac{1}{3} At^3 + Bt$

Thus, velocity of the body after time $t = \frac{1}{3} At^3 + Bt$

39. (d) When two particles move towards each other, then

$v_1 + v_2 = 8$ m/s ...(i)

But when these particles move in the same direction, then

$v_1 - v_2 = 2$ m/s ...(ii)

From Eqs. (i) and (ii), we get

$v_1 = 5$ m/s, $v_2 = 3$ m/s

40. (a) Given,

Displacement in first $(p - 1)$ second is s_1 and displacement in first p second is s_2, then displacement in $(p^2 - p + 1)$th second = ?

By using, $s = ut + \frac{1}{2} at^2$

$s_1 = \frac{1}{2} a(p - 1)^2$

$s_2 = \frac{1}{2} ap^2 \quad [\because u = 0]$

$\because \quad S_n = u + \frac{a}{2}(2n - 1)$

$S_{(p^2 - p + 1)\text{th}} = \frac{a}{2}[2(p^2 - p + 1) - 1]$

$= \frac{a}{2}[2p^2 - 2p + 1]$

It is clear that

$S_{(p^2 - p + 1)^{\text{th}}} = s_1 + s_2$

41. (d) Let v be the final velocity acquired in this case when accelerated for time t_1. Let t_2 be the time for which it retards, s_1 and s_2 be the distances covered in these two cases, then $v^2 = 2a_1 s_1 = 2a_2 s_2$

$\Rightarrow \quad s_1 = \frac{v^2}{2a_1} = \frac{v^2}{10}$

and $s_2 = \frac{v^2}{2a_2} = \frac{v^2}{20}$

Here $s_1 + s_2 = 1500$ m

$\Rightarrow \frac{v^2}{10} + \frac{v^2}{20} = 1500$

$\Rightarrow \quad v = 100 \text{ ms}^{-1}$

Similarly, $v = a_1 t_1 = a_2 t_2$

$\Rightarrow \quad 100 = 5t_1 = 10t_2$

$\Rightarrow \quad t_1 = 20\,\text{s}$ and $t_2 = 10\,\text{s}$

$\Rightarrow \quad t_1 + t_2 = 30\,\text{s}$

42. (a) From $s_n = \frac{g}{2}(2n-1)$

$$25 = \frac{10}{2}(2n-1)$$

$\Rightarrow 2n - 1 = 5$ and $n = 3$

So, total time of fall is 3s.

Height of the tower,

$h = \frac{1}{2}gt^2 = \frac{1}{2} \times 10 \times 9 = 45\,\text{m}$

43. (b) For the 1st drop, $s_1 = \frac{1}{2}gt_1^2$

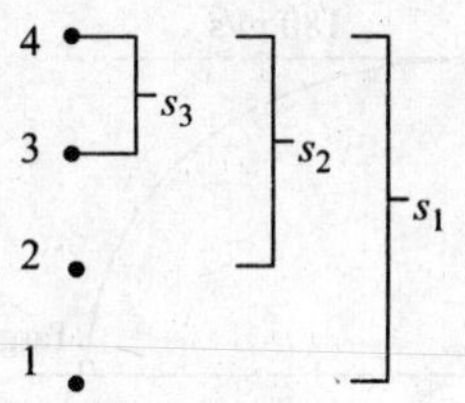

$$9 = \frac{1}{2}gt_1^2$$

$$\Rightarrow \quad t_1 = 3\sqrt{\frac{2}{g}}$$

As the drops are falling at regular intervals of time, for the second and third drops, we have

$t_2 = 2\sqrt{\frac{2}{g}}$ and $t_3 = \sqrt{\frac{2}{g}}$

$s_3 = \frac{1}{2}gt_3^2 = 1\,\text{m}$

Then $s_2 = \frac{1}{2}gt_2^2 = 4\,\text{m}$

and $s_1 = \frac{1}{2}gt^2 = 9\,\text{m}$

Now $s_1 - s_2 = 9 - 4 = 5\,\text{m}$,

$s_2 - s_3 = 4 - 1 = 3\,\text{m}$,

$s_3 - s_4 = 1 - 0 = 1\,\text{m}$

44. (a) After he observed the ball, it would rise to a height h above that level which is given by

$$h = \frac{u^2}{2g} = \frac{5 \times 5}{2 \times 10} = 1.25\,\text{m}$$

Before that, it has already travelled 10 m.

So, the total height travelled by it is $10 + 1.25 = 11.25\,\text{m}$

45. (c) Distance travelled in 2 s,

$y = \frac{1}{2}gt^2 = \frac{1}{2} \times 10 \times 4 = 20\,\text{m}$

Velocity acquired after 2 s,

$$v = gt = 10 \times 2 = 20\,\text{ms}^{-1}$$

As there is no acceleration, that body would travel the remaining distance $(100 - 20 = 80\,\text{m})$ with uniform velocity of $20\,\text{ms}^{-1}$.

Time taken for the remaining journey is $\frac{80}{20} = 4\,\text{s}$

i.e. Total time of motion is $2 + 4 = 6\,\text{s}$

46. (c) We have, $h = \frac{1}{2}gt^2$

If it falls through a distance y in $\frac{2t}{3}$,

$$y = \frac{1}{2}g\left(\frac{2t}{3}\right)^2 = \frac{4}{9} \cdot \frac{1}{2}gt^2 = \frac{4h}{9}$$

Then height of the body from the ground is $(h - y) = h - \frac{4h}{9} = \frac{5h}{9}$

47. (d) When a body is projected vertically up with velocity u, after time t its height above ground,

$h = ut - \frac{1}{2}gt^2$

$\frac{1}{2}gt^2 - ut + h = 0$

This is a quadratic equation in t. If t_1 and t_2 are the roots of this equation, product of the roots

$$t_1 t_2 = \frac{h}{\frac{g}{2}} = \frac{2h}{g}$$

48. (c) If h is height of the tower and t is the time taken by the stone to reach the ground,

$$-h = ut - \frac{1}{2}gt^2$$

$$\Rightarrow \quad -h = (14.7 \times 5) - \left(\frac{1}{2} \times 9.8 \times 25\right)$$

$$= 73.5 - 122.5$$

$$= -49$$

So, the height of the tower is 49 m.

49. (d) The graph in (A) shows an object moving with $v > 0$ initially, but decelerating $(a < 0)$.

The graph in (B) shows decreasing position x, indicating $v < 0$ and possibly $a = 0$.

The graph in (C) represents zero displacement, meaning the object stops moving.

The graph in (D) indicates positive velocity $v > 0$ and acceleration $a > 0$

The correct answer is (d) A-3, B-2, C-4, D-1.

50. (c) If the total time of fall is n seconds, distance travelled in the nth second,

$$s_n = \frac{g}{2}(2n-1)$$

If h is the total distance travelled,

$$h = \frac{1}{2}gn^2$$

But $\quad s_n = 36\%$ of h

i.e. $\frac{g}{2}(2n-1) = \frac{36}{100}\frac{1}{2}gn^2$

$\Rightarrow 2n - 1 = \frac{36n^2}{100} = \frac{9n^2}{25}$

$\Rightarrow 50n - 25 = 9n^2$

$\Rightarrow 9n^2 - 50n + 25 = 0$

$\Rightarrow (9n - 5)(n - 5) = 0$

i.e. $\quad n = 5$ and $h = \frac{1}{2}gn^2$

$= \frac{1}{2} \times 9.8 \times 25 = 122.5\,\text{m}$

Ch-03 Motion in a Plane

Topical Follow Thru

Test-1

1. (d) $T = \dfrac{2u_y}{g}$ ...(i)

$\therefore u_y = \dfrac{gT}{2}$

$h_A = u_y t_A - \dfrac{1}{2} g t_A^2$

$= u_y \left(\dfrac{2u_y}{3g}\right) - \dfrac{1}{2} g \left(\dfrac{2u_y}{3g}\right)^2$

$= \dfrac{4}{9} \dfrac{u_y^2}{g}$

$= \left(\dfrac{4}{9g}\right)\left(\dfrac{gT}{2}\right)^2 = \dfrac{gT^2}{9}$ [using Eq. (i)]

$h_B = u_y \left(\dfrac{5}{9} \times \dfrac{2u_y}{g}\right) - \dfrac{1}{2}$

$\times g \times \left(\dfrac{5}{6} \times \dfrac{2u_y}{g}\right)^2$

$= \dfrac{5}{18} \dfrac{u_y^2}{g} = \dfrac{5}{18g}\left(\dfrac{gT}{2}\right)^2 = \dfrac{5}{12} gT^2$

$\therefore \quad h_A - h_B = \dfrac{gT^2}{24}$

2. (d) Given, $\mathbf{A} = 5\hat{\mathbf{i}} + 7\hat{\mathbf{j}} - 3\hat{\mathbf{k}}$

$\mathbf{B} = 2\hat{\mathbf{i}} + 2\hat{\mathbf{j}} - c\hat{\mathbf{k}}$

As we know, scalar product of perpendicular vector must be zero. Therefore,

$\mathbf{A} \cdot \mathbf{B} = A_x B_x + A_y B_y + A_z B_z = 0$

Thus, $10 + 14 + 3c = 0$

or $c = -8$

3. (c) The maximum height achieves $= h$

The velocity with which the object is thrown upward, $v = \sqrt{2gh}$

As, range of projectile,

$R = \dfrac{v^2 \sin 2\theta}{g}$

Maximum distance can be covered, when $\theta = 45°$

Thus, $\sin 2\theta = 1$

$\therefore \quad R = \dfrac{v^2}{g}$

Therefore, $R = \dfrac{2gh}{g} = 2h$

4. (c) As, horizontal range is three times of greatest height.

$R = 3 \times H_{max}$

$\dfrac{2u^2 \sin\theta \cos\theta}{g} = 3\left(\dfrac{u^2 \sin^2\theta}{2g}\right)$

$\dfrac{\sin\theta}{\cos\theta} = \dfrac{4}{3} \Rightarrow \tan\theta = \dfrac{4}{3}$

$\theta = \tan^{-1}\left(\dfrac{4}{3}\right)$

5. (a) $T/2 = 2 + 1 = 3$ s

or $T = 6$ s

$\therefore \quad \dfrac{2u_y}{g} = 6$

$\therefore \quad u_y = 30$ m/s

Further, $\tan 30° = \dfrac{v_y}{v_x} = \dfrac{u_y - gt}{u_x}$

$\Rightarrow \quad \dfrac{1}{\sqrt{3}} = \dfrac{30 - 20}{u_x}$

$\left\{\because \tan 30° = \dfrac{1}{\sqrt{3}}\right\}$

or $u_x = 10\sqrt{3}$ m/s

or $u = \sqrt{u_x^2 + u_y^2}$

$= 20\sqrt{3}$ m/s

$\tan\theta = \dfrac{u_y}{u_x} = \dfrac{30}{10\sqrt{3}} = \sqrt{3}$

or $\theta = 60°$

6. (a) Maximum range, $R_{max} = \dfrac{u^2}{g}$

$u = \sqrt{g \times R_{max}}$

$u = \sqrt{(9.8)(0.6)} = \sqrt{5.88}$

$u = 2.4$ m/s

7. (d) Maximum range,

$R_{max} = \dfrac{u^2}{g} = \dfrac{(45)^2}{10} = 202.5$ m

8. (b) The direction of vector $\lambda\mathbf{A}, (\lambda < 0)$ is opposite to the direction of vector **A**.

If a vector is multiplied by zero, then the result obtained is a vector quantity.

$0 \cdot \mathbf{A} = \mathbf{0}$

9. (d)

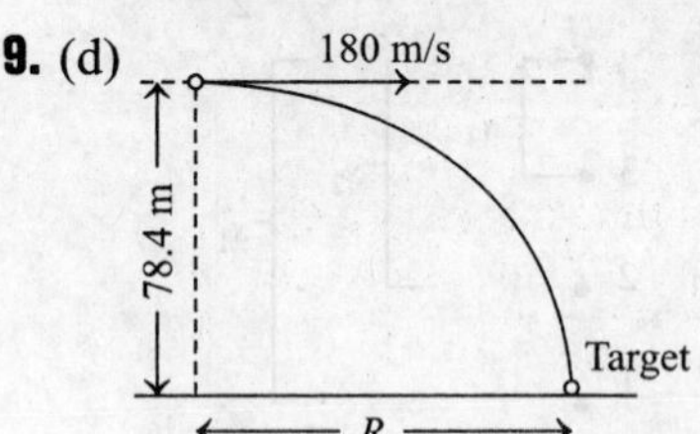

Time of flight

$= \sqrt{\dfrac{2h}{g}} = \sqrt{\dfrac{2 \times 78.4}{9.8}} = 4$ s

Horizontal range, $R = 180 \times 4$

$= 720$ m

10. (a) As, $R = \dfrac{u^2 \sin 2\theta}{g}$

For $R = R_{max}$,

$\sin 2\theta = 1$ or $\theta = 45°$

11. (d) As, **A** and **B** are perpendicular to each other

$\therefore |\mathbf{A} - \mathbf{B}|$

$= \sqrt{A^2 + B^2 - 2AB\cos 90°}$

$= \sqrt{A^2 + B^2}$

Now, unit vector along $|\mathbf{A} - \mathbf{B}|$ will be

$= \dfrac{\mathbf{A} - \mathbf{B}}{\sqrt{A^2 + B^2}}$

Component of **A** + **B** in direction of **A** – **B**,

$\mathbf{R} = (\mathbf{A} + \mathbf{B}) \cdot \dfrac{(\mathbf{A} - \mathbf{B})}{\sqrt{A^2 + B^2}}$

$= \dfrac{A^2 - B^2}{\sqrt{A^2 + B^2}}$

12. (c) Given,

$$\tan\theta = \frac{v_y}{v_x} = \frac{gt}{v_x} = \frac{10\times 10}{800} = \frac{1}{8}$$

i.e. $\theta = \tan^{-1}\left(\frac{1}{8}\right)$ with horizontal.

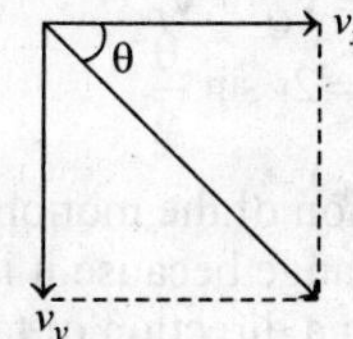

13. (a) By using,

Time of flight, $T = \frac{2v\sin\theta}{g}$

$$T = \frac{2\times 20\times \sin 30^\circ}{10} = 2\text{ s}$$

Total time taken by the ball,

$$t = \frac{d}{v} = \frac{40}{20\sin 30^\circ} = \frac{40}{20\times\frac{1}{2}} = 4\text{ s}$$

So, the ratio is $4:2 = 2:1$

14. (b) Given, $h = 150 - 27.5 = 122.5$ m

$$t = \sqrt{\frac{2\times 122.5}{9.8}} = 5\text{ s}$$

Hence, $u = \frac{R}{t} = \frac{50}{5} = 10\text{ ms}^{-1}$

15. (a) Here, angle with the horizontal is 45°.

$$\tan 45^\circ = \frac{H}{x}$$

Vertical range = Height

$$\because \quad t = \sqrt{\frac{2h}{g}} = \sqrt{\frac{2\times 40}{10}} = 2.8\text{ s}$$

$$u = \frac{\text{Vertical range}}{t}$$

$$u = \frac{40}{2.8} = 14.2\text{ m/s} \simeq 14\text{ m/s}$$

16. (c) The average velocity of the particle between projection point to highest point,

$$v_{av} = \frac{\text{Displacement}}{\text{Time}}$$

$$v_{av} = \frac{\sqrt{H^2 + \frac{R^2}{4}}}{\frac{T}{2}} = \frac{\sqrt{4H^2 + R^2}}{T}$$

$$\because H = \frac{v^2\sin^2\theta}{2g}, R = \frac{v^2\sin 2\theta}{g}$$

and $T = \frac{2v\sin\theta}{g}$

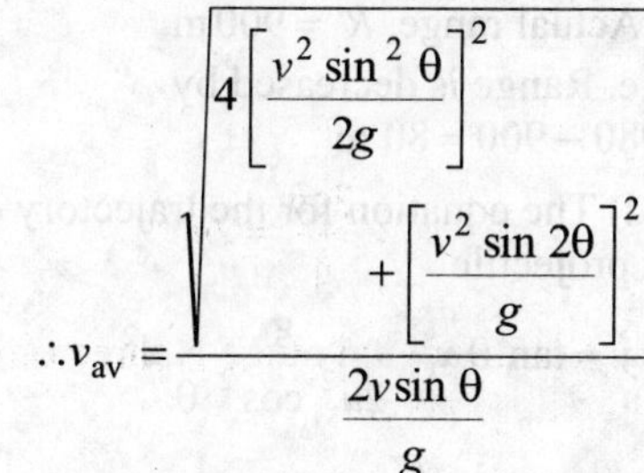

$$\therefore v_{\text{av}} = \frac{\sqrt{4\left[\frac{v^2\sin^2\theta}{2g}\right]^2 + \left[\frac{v^2\sin 2\theta}{g}\right]^2}}{\frac{2v\sin\theta}{g}}$$

$$= \frac{\frac{v^2}{g}[(\sin^2\theta)^2 + (\sin 2\theta)^2]^{\frac{1}{2}}}{\frac{2v\sin\theta}{g}}$$

$$v_{\text{av}} = \frac{v}{2}\sqrt{1 + 3\cos^2\theta}$$

17. (a) Given, $\mathbf{A} = 3\hat{\mathbf{i}} + 4\hat{\mathbf{j}}$

$$\mathbf{B} = 7\hat{\mathbf{i}} + 24\hat{\mathbf{k}}$$

Magnitude,

$$B\hat{\mathbf{A}} = \sqrt{(7)^2 + (24)^2}\left(\frac{3\hat{\mathbf{i}} + 4\hat{\mathbf{j}}}{5}\right)$$

$$= 25\left(\frac{3\hat{\mathbf{i}} + 4\hat{\mathbf{j}}}{5}\right) = 15\hat{\mathbf{i}} + 20\hat{\mathbf{j}}$$

18. (c) Given,

$$\mathbf{A} = 2\hat{\mathbf{i}} + 3\hat{\mathbf{j}} + 8\hat{\mathbf{k}}$$

$$\mathbf{B} = 4\hat{\mathbf{i}} - 4\hat{\mathbf{j}} + \alpha\hat{\mathbf{k}}$$

Here,

$$(2\hat{\mathbf{i}} + 3\hat{\mathbf{j}} + 8\hat{\mathbf{k}})\cdot(4\hat{\mathbf{i}} - 4\hat{\mathbf{j}} + \alpha\hat{\mathbf{k}}) = 0$$

$$\Rightarrow \quad 8 - 12 + 8\alpha = 0$$

$$\Rightarrow \quad \alpha = \frac{1}{2}$$

19. (c) Range is maximum when angle of projection is 45°.

$$H = \frac{v^2\sin^2 45^\circ}{g} = \frac{v^2}{4g} \quad \text{...(i)}$$

Vertical component of velocity at half of the maximum height,

$$v_y'^2 = v^2\sin^2 45^\circ - 2g\cdot\frac{H}{2}$$

$$= \frac{v^2}{2} - \frac{v^2}{4}$$

$$v_y'^2 = \frac{v^2}{4}$$

$$v_y' = \frac{v}{2}$$

At half of the maximum height, horizontal components of velocity remains constant.

So, net velocity at half of the maximum height.

$$v = \sqrt{v_x^2 + v_y'^2}$$

$$v = \sqrt{\left(\frac{v}{\sqrt{2}}\right)^2 + \left(\frac{v}{2}\right)^2}$$

$$\left[\begin{array}{l}\text{For maximum range, } \theta = 45^\circ \\ \therefore\ v_x = v\cos 45^\circ = \frac{v}{\sqrt{2}}\end{array}\right]$$

$$v = \frac{\sqrt{3}\,v}{2}$$

(ii) Velocity at the maximum height

$$v = v\cos 45^\circ = \frac{v}{\sqrt{2}}$$

because vertical component of velocity is zero at highest point.

(iii) At projection point,

$$v_i = v\cos 45^\circ\,\hat{\mathbf{i}} + v\sin 45^\circ\,\hat{\mathbf{j}}$$

At the point, when the body strikes the ground

$$v_f = v\cos 45\,\hat{\mathbf{i}} - v\sin 45^\circ\,\hat{\mathbf{j}}$$

$$\Delta v = \mathbf{v}_f + (-\mathbf{v}_i)$$

$$\Delta v = 2v\sin 45^\circ\,(-\hat{\mathbf{j}})$$

$$|\Delta\mathbf{v}| = 2v\sin 45^\circ = v\sqrt{2}$$

(iv) Average velocity

$$= \frac{\text{Total displacement}}{\text{Total time}}$$

$$= \frac{\sqrt{\left(\frac{R}{2}\right)^2 + H^2}}{\frac{v\sin\theta}{g}} = \frac{\sqrt{R^2 + 4H^2}}{\frac{2v\sin\theta}{g}}$$

$$v_{\text{av}} = \frac{\sqrt{\left(\frac{v^2}{g}\right)^2 + 4\left(\frac{v^2}{4g}\right)^2}}{\frac{\sqrt{2}\,v}{g}}$$

$$= \frac{\frac{v^2}{g}\sqrt{1+\frac{1}{4}}}{\frac{v\sqrt{2}}{g}}$$

$$v_{av} = \frac{v\sqrt{5}}{2\sqrt{2}} = \frac{v}{2}\sqrt{\frac{5}{2}}$$

20. (a)

(a) Range becomes equal at complimentary angle.

Hence, $\beta = 90° - \alpha$

(b) $h_1 = \frac{u^2 \sin^2 \alpha}{2g}$

$h_2 = \frac{u^2 \cos^2 \alpha}{2g}$ (as $\beta = 90 - \alpha$)

$$\therefore 4\sqrt{h_1 h_2} = \frac{2u^2 \sin\alpha \cos\alpha}{g}$$

$$= \frac{u^2 \sin 2\alpha}{g} = R$$

(c) $\frac{t_1}{t_2} = \frac{(2u \sin\alpha)/g}{(2u\cos\alpha/g)} = \tan\alpha$

(d) $\sqrt{\frac{h_1}{h_2}} = \tan\alpha$

21. (a) Time of flight, $T = \frac{2u\sin\theta}{g}$

$$\Rightarrow T^2 = \frac{4u^2 \sin^2\theta}{g^2}$$

Horizontal range, $R = \frac{u^2 \sin 2\theta}{g}$

$$\frac{T^2}{R} = \frac{4u^2 \sin^2\theta}{g^2} \times \frac{g}{u^2 \sin 2\theta}$$

$$= \frac{4\sin\theta}{g\, 2\cos\theta} = \frac{2\tan\theta}{g}$$

or $\tan\theta = \frac{gT^2}{2R}$

22. (d) Comparing the equations with the standard forms for a projectile,

$x = u\cos\theta t$ and $y = u\sin\theta\, t - \frac{1}{2}gt^2$,

$u\cos\theta = 40\sqrt{3}$ and $u\sin\theta = 40$

Then, $u = \sqrt{40^2 + (40\sqrt{3})^2}$

$= 80\,\text{ms}^{-1}$

$$\tan\theta = \frac{40}{40\sqrt{3}} = \frac{1}{\sqrt{3}} \Rightarrow \theta = 30°$$

23. (b) If there is no air resistance, expected horizontal range,

$$R = \frac{u^2 \sin 2\theta}{g} = \frac{98 \times 98}{9.8} = 980\,\text{m}$$

Actual range, $R' = 900\,\text{m}$

i.e. Range is decreased by $980 - 900 = 80$ m

24. (d) The equation for the trajectory of a projectile

$$y = \tan\theta\, x - \frac{g}{2u^2\cos^2\theta}x^2$$

$$y = x\tan\theta\left(1 - \frac{gx}{u^2\, 2\tan\theta\cos^2\theta}\right)$$

$$= x\tan\theta\left(1 - \frac{gx}{u^2 \sin 2\theta}\right)$$

$$= x\tan\theta\left(1 - \frac{x}{R}\right) \text{(here, } R \text{ is range)}$$

If the given equation is converted into this form

$$y = px - qx^2 = px\left(1 - \frac{qx}{p}\right)$$

On comparison, we get

$$R = \frac{p}{q}$$

i.e. Horizontal range is $\frac{p}{q}$.

25. (d) Velocity on reaching the ground,

$$v = \sqrt{u^2 + 2gh}$$

$$v = \sqrt{29 + 2 \times 9.8 \times 10}$$

$$= \sqrt{225} = 15\,\text{ms}^{-1}$$

Test-2

1. (c)

Velocity at point P,

$$\mathbf{v}_P = -v\sin\left(90° - \frac{\theta}{2}\right)\hat{\mathbf{i}} + v\cos\left(90° - \frac{\theta}{2}\right)\hat{\mathbf{j}}$$

Velocity at point Q,

$$\mathbf{v}_Q = -v\sin\left(90° - \frac{\theta}{2}\right)\hat{\mathbf{i}} - v\cos\left(90° - \frac{\theta}{2}\right)\hat{\mathbf{j}}$$

Thus, change in velocity,

$$\Delta\mathbf{v} = \mathbf{v}_Q - \mathbf{v}_P$$

$$\Rightarrow |\Delta\mathbf{v}| = 2v\sin\frac{\theta}{2}$$

2. (c) Direction of the motion will always change because it is always directed in a direction of tangent to circle.

3. (b) Given, $R = 12$ cm and $T = 100$ s

Angular speed, $\omega = \frac{2\pi}{T} = \frac{2\pi \times 7}{100}$

$= 0.44$ rad/s

Linear speed, $v = \omega R = 0.44 \times 12$

$= 5.3$ cm/s

The direction of velocity v is along the tangent to the circle at every point. The acceleration is directed towards the centre of the circle. Since, this direction changes continuously, hence acceleration here is not constant vector.

The magnitude of acceleration,

$$a = \omega^2 R = (0.44)^2 \times 12 = 2.3\,\text{cm/s}^2$$

Thus, the statement given in option (b) is correct, rest are incorrect.

4. (b) Given, rotated an angle, $\theta = \omega t$

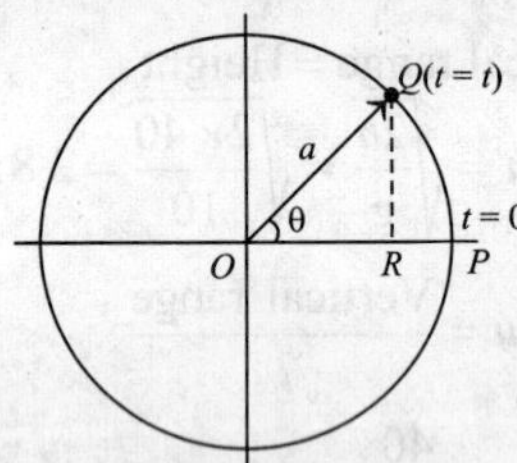

Displacement,

$$s = PQ = \sqrt{QR^2 + PR^2}$$

$$= \sqrt{(a\sin\omega t)^2 + (a - a\cos\omega t)^2}$$

or $s = 2a\sin\frac{\omega t}{2}$

5. (c) Given, $r = 35 \times 10^{-2}$ m,

$f = 2\,\text{s}^{-1}$

$\omega = 2\pi f = 4\pi$ rad/s

Acceleration $= \omega^2 r$

$= (4\pi)^2 \times 35 \times 10^{-2}$
$= 16 \times 35 \times 10^{-2}\, \pi^2$
$= 5.6\pi^2 \text{ m/s}^2$

6. (b) Angular velocity of particle A about point P,

$$\omega_P = \frac{v}{r_{PQ}} = \frac{v}{2a}$$

Angular velocity of particle A about point C,

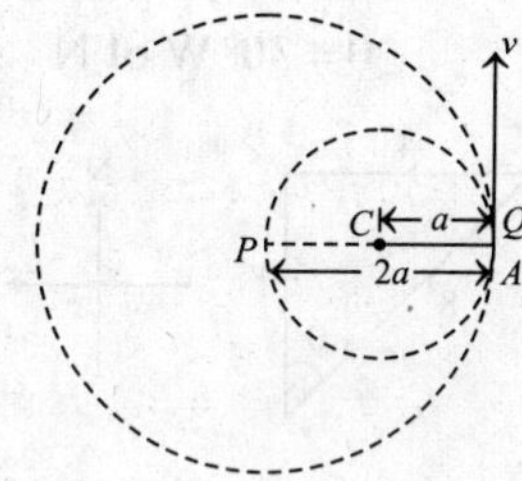

$$\omega_C = \frac{v}{a}$$

Ratio, $\dfrac{\omega_P}{\omega_C} = \dfrac{v/2a}{v/a} = \dfrac{1}{2}$

7. (b) Given that, tangential acceleration,

$$a_t = r\alpha = 4 \text{ m/s}^2$$

Radial acceleration,

$$a_r = \omega^2 r = \frac{v^2}{r} = \frac{60 \times 60}{1200} = 3 \text{ m/s}^2$$

Hence, resultant acceleration of the car

$$a = \sqrt{a_t^2 + a_r^2} = \sqrt{4^2 + 3^2}$$
$$= 5 \text{ m/s}^2$$

8. (a) Here, $r = 400 \text{ cm} = 4 \text{ m}$

Frequency, $\nu = \dfrac{14}{22}$ Hz

$\therefore \quad \omega = 2\pi\nu = 2 \times \dfrac{22}{7} \times \dfrac{14}{22}$
$= 4 \text{ rad s}^{-1}$

The acceleration of the stone,

$$a_c = \omega^2 r = (4)^2 (4) = 64 \text{ ms}^{-2}$$

9. (a) It is only in case of parabolic motion that the direction and magnitude of the acceleration remains same. In uniform circular motion, though magnitude of acceleration remains constant but direction changes from moment to moment.

10. (c) Displacement, velocity and acceleration change continuously with respect to time because of change in direction but speed remains constant with time.

11. (a) Particle is moving in a circle of radius a and centre $(a, 0)$ with constant angular velocity ω. At time $t = 0$, particle is at origin and it starts rotating clockwise. At time t, it has rotated an angle θ given by $\theta = \omega t$

$$y = a \sin\theta = \sin \omega t$$

and $\quad x = a - a\cos\theta$
$= a(1 - \cos \omega t)$

$\therefore \quad \mathbf{r} = a(1 - \cos\omega t)\hat{\mathbf{i}} + a \sin \omega t \hat{\mathbf{j}}$

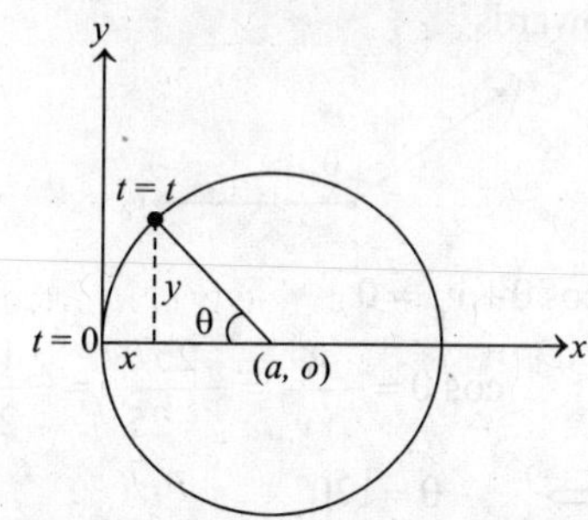

12. (d) Acceleration is rate of change of velocity with respect to time but in circular motion, the speed of the body is constant but velocity changes continuously as its direction changes. Thus, statement I is incorrect but statement II is correct. So, radial acceleration always towards the centre.

13. (c) Here, $r = 100 \text{ cm} = 1 \text{ m}$

Frequency, $\nu = \dfrac{16}{22}$ Hz

$$\omega = 2\pi\nu = 2 \times \frac{22}{7} \times \frac{16}{22} = 4.56 \text{ Hz}$$

Acceleration,

$$a_c = \omega^2 r = (4.56)^2 (1)$$
$$= 20.79 \text{ m/s}^2$$

14. (c) Given,

Radius of circular path, $r = 8$ m

Uniform speed, $v = 8$ m/s

acceleration, $a = ?$

When the particle completes half revolution, change in velocity is given by

$$\Delta v = 8 \text{ m/s} - (-8 \text{ m/s}) = 16 \text{ m/s}$$

Time taken, $t = \dfrac{\pi r}{v} = \dfrac{\pi \times 8}{8} = \pi$ s

Average acceleration,

$$= \frac{\Delta v}{t} = \frac{16}{\pi} \text{ m/s}^2$$

15. (c) Speed, $v = 60$ m/s

Radius of circular path or road $= 700$ m

By using, $a_r = \dfrac{v^2}{r} = \dfrac{(60)^2}{700}$

$= \dfrac{3600}{700} = 5.14 \text{ m/s}^2$

Tangential acceleration

$= 2 \text{ m/s}^2$

Resultant acceleration,

$$a^2 = a_r^2 + a_t^2 + 2a_r a_t \cos\theta$$

Here, $\theta = 90°$

$a^2 = (5.14)^2 + (2)^2 + 0$
$= 26.4 + 4 = 30.4$
$a = \sqrt{30.4} = 5.5/36$
$a \cong 5.5 \text{ m/s}^2$

Test-3

1. (d) As, $\mathbf{v}_Q = \mathbf{v}_{QP} + \mathbf{v}_P$

$= (5\hat{\mathbf{i}} + 12\hat{\mathbf{j}}) + (3\hat{\mathbf{i}} - 4\hat{\mathbf{j}})$

$\mathbf{v}_Q = 8\hat{\mathbf{i}} + 8\hat{\mathbf{j}}$

2. (b) As per figure.

$v_{mR} = 2$ m/s

$v_R = \sqrt{3}$ m/s

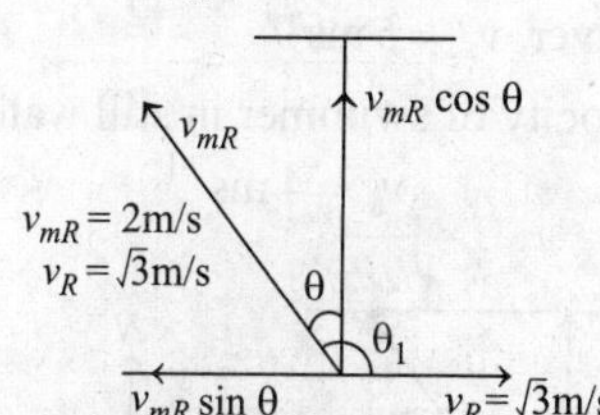

The velocity component acting opposite to that of the velocity of water current is given as

$$v_{mR} \sin\theta = v_R$$
$$2 \times \sin\theta = \sqrt{3}$$
$$\sin\theta = \frac{\sqrt{3}}{2}$$

$\Rightarrow \quad \theta = 60°$

The angle between the speed of man and the water current is given as

$$\theta_1 = 60° + 90°$$

Hence, 150° with water current.

3. (b) Horizontal component of rain's velocity will be equal to velocity of wind which is 4 m/s in north direction. If cyclist goes towards north with velocity 4 m/s, then with respect to him, rain's horizontal component of velocity will be zero and he will see only vertical component.

4. (c) Given, $\mathbf{v}_w = 40\hat{\mathbf{i}}, \mathbf{v}_c = 40\hat{\mathbf{j}}$

Here, we have to look for velocity of wind with respect to car.

So, $\mathbf{v}_{w/C} = \mathbf{v}_w - \mathbf{v}_c$

$$= 40\hat{\mathbf{i}} - 40\hat{\mathbf{j}}$$

This is in south-east direction.

5. (b) With respect to the man on ground, the stone has horizontal velocity (equal to that of the bus) as well as vertical velocity, so it would appear to move along a parabolic path.

6. (c)

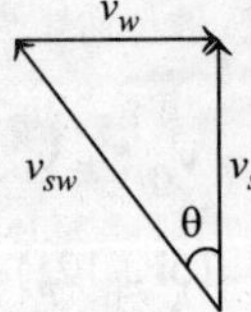

In this case, as $v_W > v_{SW}$ as sin θ cannot be greater than 1, he cannot reach directly opposite bank in this way.

7. (b) Given, velocity of water flowing in river, $v_r = 5\,\text{ms}^{-1}$

Velocity of swimmer in still water,

$$v_s = 4\,\text{ms}^{-1}$$

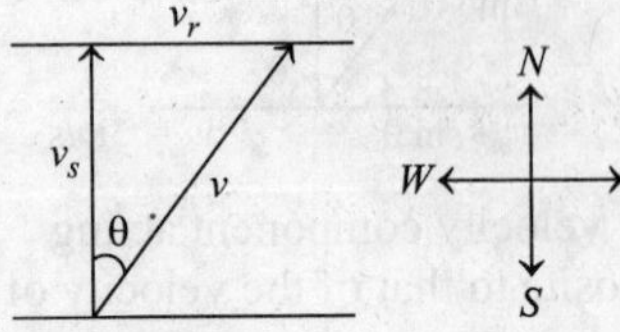

From figure,

The resultant velocity of the swimmer

$$v = \sqrt{v_s^2 + v_r^2} = \sqrt{(4)^2 + (5)^2}$$

$$= \sqrt{16+25}$$

$$= \sqrt{41} = 6.40\,\text{ms}^{-1}$$

8. (d) For shortest possible time to cross river, $T = \frac{336}{1} = 336\,\text{s}$

9. (c) Given,

$$\mathbf{v}_c = -5\hat{\mathbf{j}}$$

$$\mathbf{v}_{bc} = -2\sqrt{6}\,\hat{\mathbf{i}}$$

$$\mathbf{v}_b = \mathbf{v}_{bc} + \mathbf{v}_c = -2\sqrt{6}\hat{\mathbf{i}} - 5\hat{\mathbf{j}}$$

Thus, $|\mathbf{v}_b| = \sqrt{4 \times 6 + 25} = 7\,\text{m/s}$

10. (a) Given, $v_c = 45$ km/h $= \frac{25}{2}$ m/s

For the resultant motion to be upwards

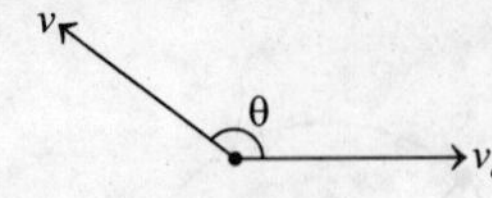

$$v\cos\theta + v_c = 0$$

$$\cos\theta = -\frac{v_C}{v} = -\frac{25/2}{25} = -\frac{1}{2}$$

$$\Rightarrow \quad \theta = 120°$$

11. (a) The situation can be drawn as follows,

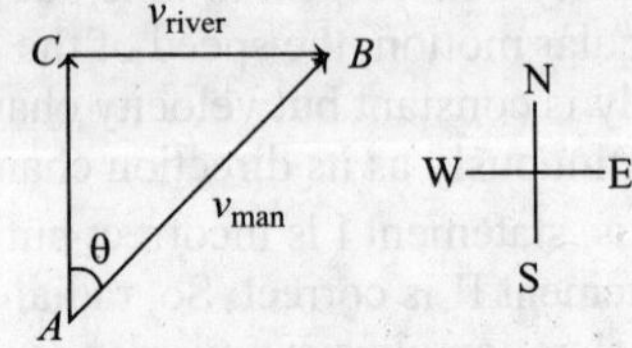

Here, AC is the shortest distance for the person to cross the river

∴ Time taken by person,

$$t = \frac{AC}{v_{\text{man}}\cos\theta}$$

and for minimum t. θ should be 0°. Thus, the direction in which the swimmer should more will be in north direction.

12. (d) Resultant velocity,

$$= \sqrt{20^2 + 15^2} = 25\,\text{km/h}$$

13. (c) As we know, the earth rotates west to east.

The velocity of train 2 increases,

$$a_C = \frac{v^2}{R}.$$

Thus, centripetal acceleration of train 2 is more.

Therefore, $\frac{a_1}{a_2} < 1$

14. (b) At the opposite, the boat should start at an angle θ with north such that $\sin\theta = \frac{4}{8}$ or θ = 30°. The real velocity of boat will be

$$v = \sqrt{8^2 - 4^2} = \sqrt{48}$$

$$\theta = 30° \text{ W of N}$$

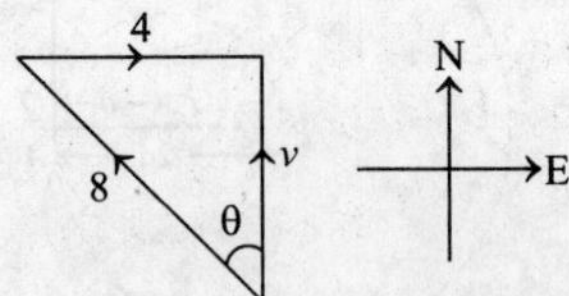

15. (b) Here, $\mathbf{v}_P - \mathbf{v}_Q = v\left(\frac{\hat{\mathbf{i}} + \hat{\mathbf{j}}}{\sqrt{2}}\right)$

and $\quad \mathbf{v}_Q - \mathbf{v}_R = v\left(\frac{-\hat{\mathbf{i}} + \hat{\mathbf{j}}}{\sqrt{2}}\right)$

Adding,

$$\Rightarrow \quad \mathbf{v}_P - \mathbf{v}_R = \frac{2v}{\sqrt{2}}\hat{\mathbf{j}}$$

$$\Rightarrow \quad \mathbf{v}_R - \mathbf{v}_P = -\sqrt{2}v\hat{\mathbf{j}}$$

$$= \sqrt{2}v(-\hat{\mathbf{j}})$$

So, R will be moving towards south as seen by P.

16. (c) Velocity of the rain $\mathbf{v}_r$ and velocity of wind $\mathbf{v}_w$.

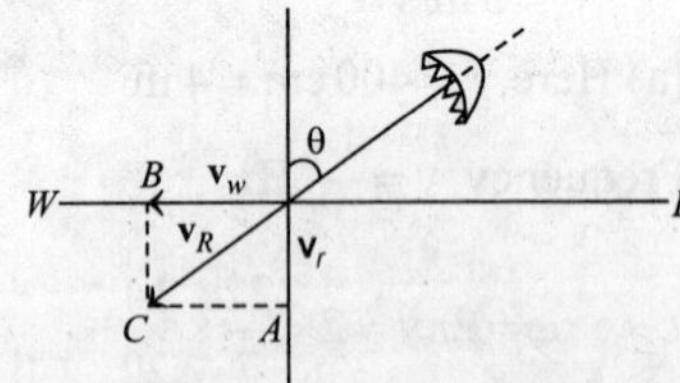

If θ is the angle which resultant velocity $\mathbf{v}_R$ makes with the vertical, then $\tan\theta = \frac{v_w}{v_r} = \frac{12}{35}$

or $\quad \theta = \tan^{-1}\left(\frac{12}{35}\right)$

17. (c) $|\mathbf{v}_{QP}| = \sqrt{10^2 + 10^2}$

$$= 10\sqrt{2}\,\text{km/h}$$

Shortest distance,

$$OQ = 100 \sin 45° = 50\sqrt{2} \text{ km}$$

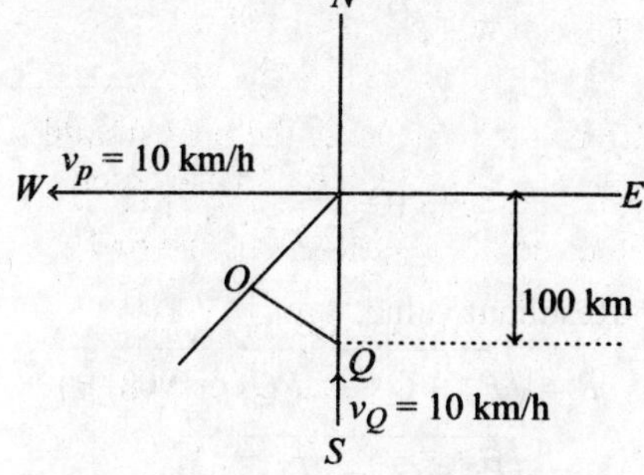

Time taken to reach the shortest distance between P and Q

$$= \frac{50\sqrt{2}}{|\mathbf{v}_{QP}|} = \frac{50\sqrt{2}}{10\sqrt{2}} = 5 \text{ h}$$

18. (b) Velocity of rain is at 30° with vertical. So, its horizontal component is $v_R \sin 30° = \frac{v_R}{2}$. When man starts walking with 10 km/h rain appears vertical. So, horizontal component $\frac{v_R}{2}$ is balanced by his speed of 10 km/h. Thus,

$$\frac{v_R}{2} = 10 \quad \text{or} \quad v_R = 20 \text{ km/h}$$

19. (b) Considering the initial position of ship A as origin.

After time t, coordinates of ships B and A are

$(80 - 10t, 150)$ and $(30t, 50t)$.

$$[v_B = -10\hat{\mathbf{i}}]$$

So, distance between A and B after time t is

$$d = \sqrt{(80 - 10t - 30t)^2 + (150 - 50t)^2}$$

$$\Rightarrow d^2 = (80 - 40t)^2 + (150 - 50t)^2$$

Distance is minimum when

$$\frac{d}{dt}(d^2) = 0$$

$$\frac{d}{dt}[(80 - 40t)^2 + (150 - 50t)^2] = 0$$

$$\Rightarrow 2(80 - 40t)(-40) + 2(150 - 50t)(-50) = 0$$

After solving, we get

$$t = 2.6 \text{ h}$$

20. (d)

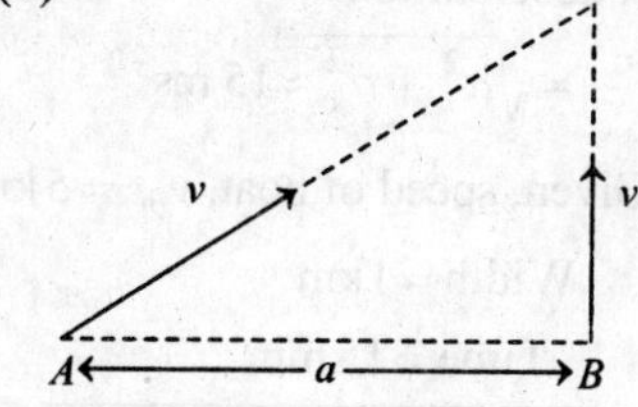

According to the diagram,

$$AC = vt$$
$$AB = a$$
$$BC = v_1 t$$

$$\Rightarrow \quad AC^2 = AB^2 + BC^2$$

$$v^2t^2 = a^2 + v_1^2 t^2$$

$$\Rightarrow (v^2 - v_1^2)t^2 = a^2$$

or

$$t = \frac{a}{\sqrt{v^2 - v_1^2}}$$

21. (b)

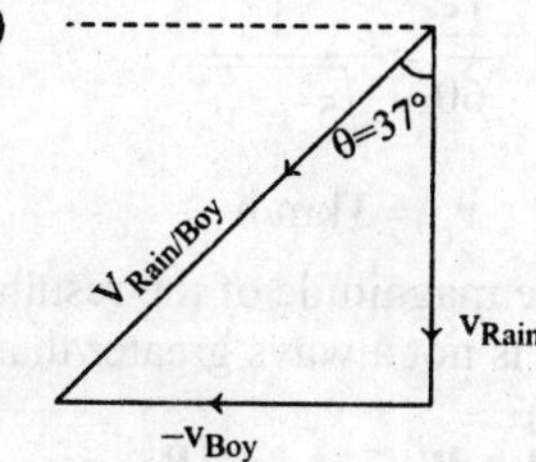

$$\tan \theta = \frac{v_{boy}}{v_{rain}}$$

$$\Rightarrow \tan 37° = \frac{3}{4} = \frac{v_{boy}}{20}$$

So, $v_{boy} = 15$ m/s

22. (b) $\mathbf{v}_x = -v\hat{\mathbf{j}}$

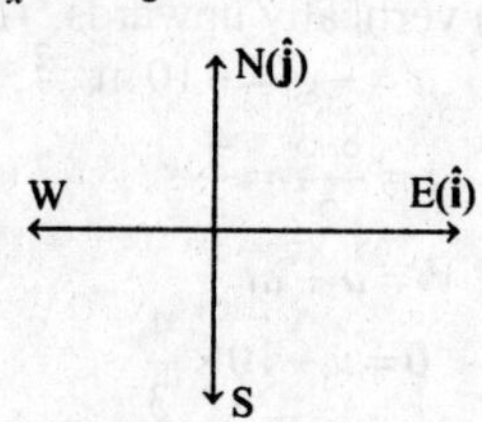

$$\therefore \quad \mathbf{v}_Y = \mathbf{v}_{YX} + \mathbf{v}_X = -v\hat{\mathbf{i}} + v\hat{\mathbf{j}}$$

$$\therefore |\mathbf{v}_Y| = \sqrt{2}v$$

Direction of $\mathbf{v}_Y$ is North-West.

23. (c) If x is horizontal distance covered by the first particle, the distance covered by the second particle is $(R - x)$.

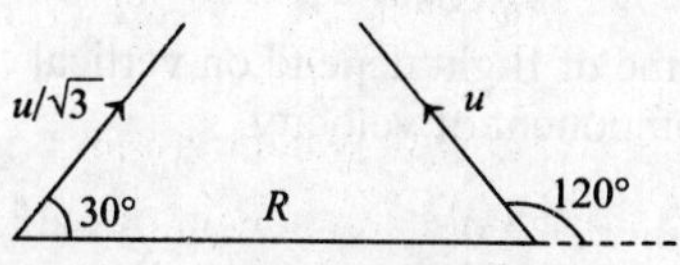

For the given condition,

$$x = \frac{u}{\sqrt{3}} \cos 30° \, t$$

$$(R - x) = u \cos 60° \, t$$

On adding these, we get

$$R = \frac{ut}{2} + \frac{ut}{2}$$

$$\Rightarrow \quad t = \frac{R}{u}$$

24. (c) $t = \dfrac{d}{v_r \cos 30°} = \dfrac{2d}{\sqrt{3}\, v_r}$

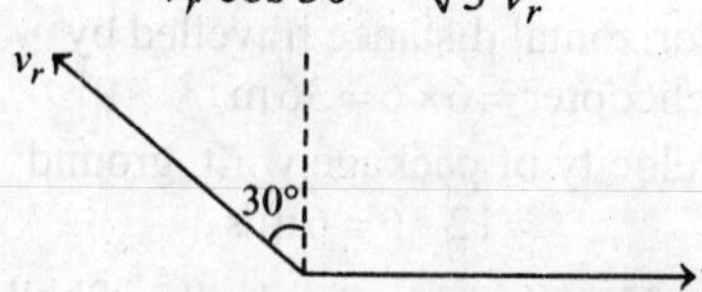

Now, drift $\frac{d}{2} = (v - v_r \sin 30°)\, t$

$$= (v - v_r/2)\left(\frac{2d}{\sqrt{3}\, v_r}\right)$$

$$\therefore \sqrt{3}\, v_r = 4v - 2v_r$$

$$\therefore \quad v_r = \left(\frac{4}{2 + \sqrt{3}}\right) v$$

$$= 4(2 - \sqrt{3})\, v$$

25. (a) $y_1 = x_1 \tan \theta - \frac{1}{2} g t^2$

$$y_2 = x_2 \tan \theta - \frac{1}{2} g t^2$$

$$\Rightarrow (y_2 - y_1) = (x_2 - x_1) \tan \theta$$

$$\Rightarrow \quad y_{rel} \propto x_{rel}$$

Path will be straight line.

Chapter Break Thru

1. (a) Given, distance = 250 m

$$t = \sqrt{\frac{2h}{g}}, \; x = vt = v\sqrt{\frac{2h}{g}}$$

$$x' = \frac{v}{2}\sqrt{\frac{2(4h)}{g}} = x = 250 \text{ m}$$

2. (b) Here, $v_0 \sin\theta = v$

$$v_0 \cos\theta = u$$

Time of flight depend on vertical component of velocity,

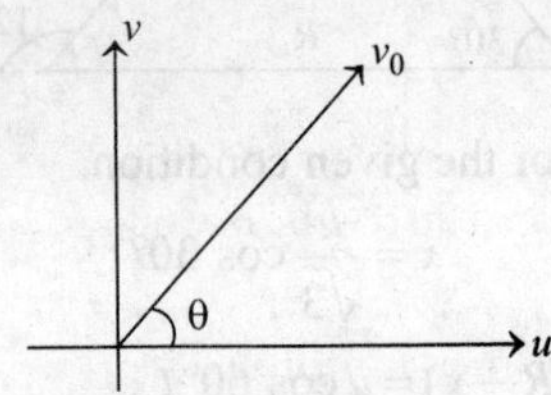

$$T = \frac{2v_0 \sin\theta}{g} = \frac{2v}{g}$$

3. (c) Time taken by package to reach the ground,

$$T = \sqrt{\frac{2\times 180}{10}} = 6\,\text{s}$$

Horizontal distance travelled by helicopter $= 6\times 6 = 36\,\text{m}$

Velocity of package w.r.t. ground $= 12 - 6 = 6\,\text{m/s}$

4. (b) Components of velocity of ball relative to lift are

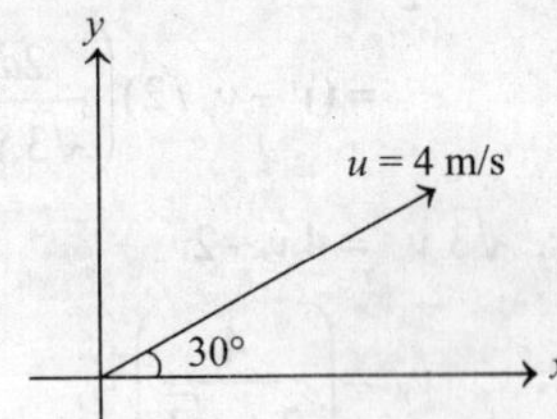

$$u_x = 4\cos 30° = 2\sqrt{3}\,\text{m/s}$$

$$u_y = 4\sin 30° = 2\,\text{m/s}$$

Acceleration of ball relative to lift,

$a = 10 + 2 = 12\,\text{m/s}^2$ in negative y-direction on vertically downwards.

Hence, time of flight,

$$T = \frac{2u_y}{12} = \frac{u_y}{6} = \frac{2}{6} = \frac{1}{3}\,\text{s}$$

5. (c) Speed, $v = \frac{ds}{dt} = 3t^2$

$$a_t = \frac{dv}{dt} = 6t$$

$\therefore$ Tangential acceleration at $t = 2$ s,

$$a_t = 6\times 2 = 12\,\text{ms}^{-2}$$

and at $t = 2\,\text{s}, v = 3(2)^2 = 12\,\text{ms}^{-1}$

$\therefore$ Centripetal acceleration,

$$a_c = \frac{v^2}{R} = \frac{144}{16}\,\text{ms}^{-2} = 9\,\text{ms}^{-2}$$

$\therefore$ Net acceleration

$$= \sqrt{a_t^2 + a_c^2} \approx 15\,\text{ms}^{-2}$$

6. (a) Given, speed of boat, $v_{br} = 5\,\text{km/h}$

Width = 1 km

Time = 15 min

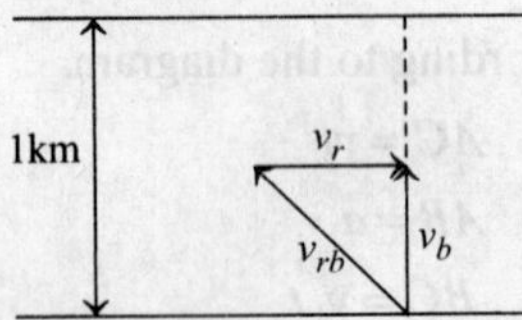

Time of crossing

$$= \frac{\text{Width of water river}}{\text{Velocity of boat perpendicular river flow}}$$

Now, $t = \frac{1}{v_b} = \frac{1}{\sqrt{v_{br}^2 - v_r^2}}$

$$\frac{15}{60} = \frac{1}{\sqrt{5^2 - v_r^2}}$$

$$v_r = 3\,\text{km/h}$$

7. (d) The magnitude of the resultant vector is not always greater than $(a+b)$.

i.e. $|\mathbf{A}+\mathbf{B}| \le |\mathbf{A}| + |\mathbf{B}|$

$\Rightarrow \quad |\mathbf{A}+\mathbf{B}| \le a + b$

8. (c) The time taken by cart to cover 80 m,

$$\frac{s}{v} = \frac{80}{30} = \frac{8}{3}\,\text{s}$$

The projectile must be fired (relative to cart) vertically upwards.

$$a = -g = -10\,\text{ms}^{-2}, v' = 0$$

and $\quad t = \frac{8/3}{2} = \frac{4}{3}\,\text{s}$

$\therefore \quad v' = u + at$

or $\quad 0 = u - 10\times\frac{4}{3}$

or $\quad u = \frac{40}{3}\,\text{ms}^{-1}$

9. (a) When component of velocity is perpendicular to the plane remains the same but in opposite direction $u\sin\theta = 20\sin 30° = 10\,\text{m/s}$

10. (b) As,

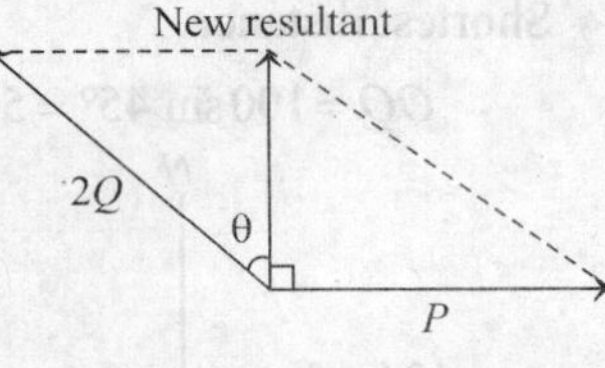

$$\sin\theta = \frac{P}{2Q}$$

Resultant value,

$$R = \sqrt{P^2 + Q^2 + 2PQ\cos(90°+\theta)}$$

$$= \sqrt{P^2 + Q^2 - 2PQ\sin\theta}$$

$$= \sqrt{P^2 + Q^2 - P^2}$$

Thus, $\quad R = Q$

11. (d) If both horizontal range and maximum height are equal, then

$$H_{max} = R$$

$$\frac{u^2\sin^2\theta}{2g} = \frac{2u^2\sin\theta\cos\theta}{g}$$

Thus, $\quad \tan\theta = 4$

$$\theta = \tan^{-1}(4)$$

12. (b) Here, $r = 18$ cm

Frequency, $\nu = \frac{7}{100}$ Hz

The angular speed of the insect,

$$\omega = 2\pi\nu = 2\pi\times\frac{7}{100} = 0.44\,\text{rads}^{-1}$$

The linear speed of the insect,

$$v = \omega r = 0.44\times 18 = 7.92\,\text{cms}^{-1}$$

13. (d) As per,

$$\mathbf{AB} = \mathbf{r}_B - \mathbf{r}_A$$

$$= (4\hat{\mathbf{i}} + 5\hat{\mathbf{j}} + 6\hat{\mathbf{k}}) - (3\hat{\mathbf{i}} + 4\hat{\mathbf{j}} + 5\hat{\mathbf{k}})$$

$$= \hat{\mathbf{i}} + \hat{\mathbf{j}} + \hat{\mathbf{k}}$$

$$\mathbf{CD} = \mathbf{r}_D - \mathbf{r}_C$$

$$= (4\hat{\mathbf{i}} + 6\hat{\mathbf{j}}) - (7\hat{\mathbf{i}} + 9\hat{\mathbf{j}} + 3\hat{\mathbf{k}})$$

$$= -3\hat{\mathbf{i}} - 3\hat{\mathbf{j}} - 3\hat{\mathbf{k}}$$

$\therefore \mathbf{AB} \downarrow\uparrow \mathbf{CD}$

14. (d) The range is same for angle of projection, θ or $90 - \theta$.

$$\text{Range }(R) = \frac{u^2\sin 2\theta}{g}$$

Height $(h) = \frac{u^2 \sin^2 \theta}{2g}$

For h_1, $R_1 = \frac{u^2 \sin^2 \theta}{2g}$

and for h_2, $R_2 = \frac{u^2 \cos^2 \theta}{2g}$

Thus, $\sqrt{h_1 h_2} = \frac{u^2 \sin\theta \cos\theta}{2g}$

$= \frac{1}{4}\left[\frac{u^2 \sin 2\theta}{g}\right] = \frac{R}{4}$

$\Rightarrow R = 4\sqrt{h_1 h_2} = 4\sqrt{4h^2} = 8h$

15. (b) As we know,

Range $= \frac{u^2 \sin 2\theta}{g}$ ...(i)

Range is maximum, when $\sin 2\theta = 1$

From Eq. (i), $R_{max} = \frac{u^2}{g}$

Maximum area covered

$= \pi(R_{max})^2$

$= \pi\left(\frac{u^2}{g}\right)^2$

16. (c) Two balls will meet if,

$(50\cos 37°)\, t_A = 120$ or $t_A = 3$ s

Vertical component of A is also $50 \sin 37°$ or 30 ms^{-1}, so they will meet if thrown simultaneously.

$h_A = h_B = 30 \times 3 - \frac{1}{2} \times 10 \times (3)^2$

$= 45$ m

17. (c) In projectile, the speed of release and landing are the same but velocities are not same. Hence, Statement I is correct but Statement II is incorrect.

18. (c) Stone has a initial horizontal velocity which is same as that of train. In acquire a vertical component under the force of gravity.

Since it has a constant horizontal speed and a constant vertical acceleration. So, the trajectory is parabolic.

19. (d) $R = \frac{u^2 \sin 2\theta}{g} = \frac{2u_x u_y}{g}$

$\therefore$ Range $\propto$ horizontal initial velocity component (u_x)

In path 4 range is maximum as football has maximum horizontal velocity component in this path.

20. (a) Since, range,

$R = \frac{2u^2 \sin\theta \cos\theta}{g}$

$\therefore \frac{R_2}{R_1} = \frac{2\sin\theta_2 \cos\theta_2}{2\sin\theta_1 \cos\theta_1}$

$= \frac{\sin 2\theta_2}{\sin 2\theta_1} = \frac{\sin 90°}{\sin 30°} = 2$

$\Rightarrow R_2 = 2R_1 = 3$ km

21. (d) For maximum range, $\sin 2\theta = 1$

or $\theta = 45°$

$\Rightarrow h = \frac{u^2 \sin^2 45°}{2g}$

$= \frac{1}{2}\frac{u^2}{2g} = \frac{u^2}{4g}$

and $R = \frac{u^2 \sin 90°}{g} = \frac{u^2}{g}$

$\Rightarrow h = \frac{R}{4}$

22. (c) Here, $T_1 = \frac{2u \sin\alpha}{g}$

$T_2 = \frac{2u \sin(90° - \alpha)}{g}$

$\Rightarrow \frac{T_1}{T_2} = \frac{\sin\alpha}{\sin(90° - \alpha)} = \tan\alpha : 1$

23. (d) $v_x = \frac{dx}{dt} = ky$

$v_y = \frac{dy}{dt} = kx$

$\Rightarrow \frac{dy}{dx} = \frac{x}{y}$ or $y dy = x dx$

$\Rightarrow \int y dy = \int x dx$

$y^2 = x^2 +$ constant

24. (a) Range of projectile $= \frac{v_0^2 \sin 2\theta}{g}$

Distance travelled by person

$= \frac{v_0}{2} t = \frac{v_0}{2} \times \frac{2v_0 \sin\theta}{g}$

For possibility $\frac{v_0^2 \sin 2\theta}{g} = \frac{v_0^2 \sin\theta}{g}$

or $\sin 2\theta = \sin\theta$

or $\cos\theta = \frac{1}{2}$ or $\theta = 60°$

25. (a) $t = \sqrt{\frac{2h}{g}}$ or $h = \frac{1}{2} g t_1^2$

and $h = u t_2 + \frac{1}{2} g t_2^2$

$\Rightarrow \frac{1}{2} g t_1^2 = \frac{1}{2} g t_2^2 + u t_2$

$\Rightarrow \frac{1}{2} g (t_1 - t_2)(t_1 + t_2) = u t_2$

$\Rightarrow t_1 - t_2 = \frac{2u t_2}{g(t_1 + t_2)} \Rightarrow t_1 > t_2$

26. (c) Since, both bullet and target are falling under gravity, both will fall at same distance.

Hence, bullet will hit the target.

27. (b) $R = \frac{v^2 \sin 2\theta}{g}$

Given, $R_1 = R_2$ and $v_1 = v_2$

So, $\sin 2\theta_1 = \sin 2\theta_2$

$2\theta_1 = 180° - 2\theta_2$

$\theta_1 = 90° - \theta_2$

Now, $T_1 \times T_2 = \frac{2u \sin\theta}{g} \times \frac{2u \sin(90° - \theta)}{g}$

$= \frac{2R}{g}$

28. (a) Equation of projectile

$x = 36t$

$\Rightarrow u\cos\theta = 36$

$2y = 96t - 9.8t^2$

$y = 48t - \frac{1}{2} \times 9.8 \times t^2$

$\Rightarrow u\sin\theta = 48$

$\Rightarrow \frac{u\sin\theta}{u\cos\theta} = \frac{48}{36} = \frac{4}{3}$

$\Rightarrow \quad \tan\theta = \frac{4}{3}$ or $\sin\theta = \frac{4}{5}$

$\Rightarrow \quad \theta = \sin^{-1}\left(\frac{4}{5}\right)$

29. (b) The motion of object shot in two cases can be depicted as below

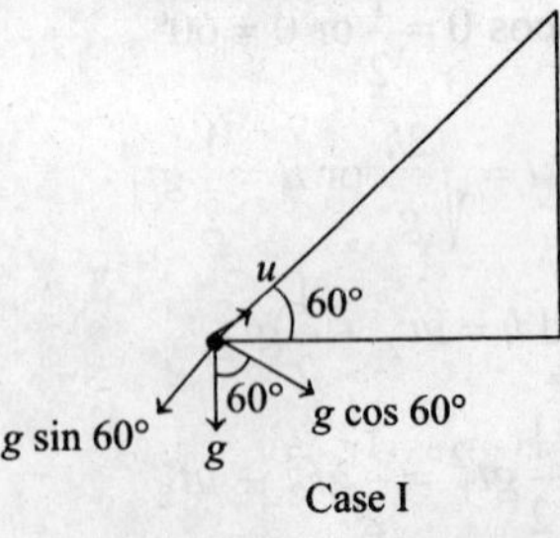

Case I

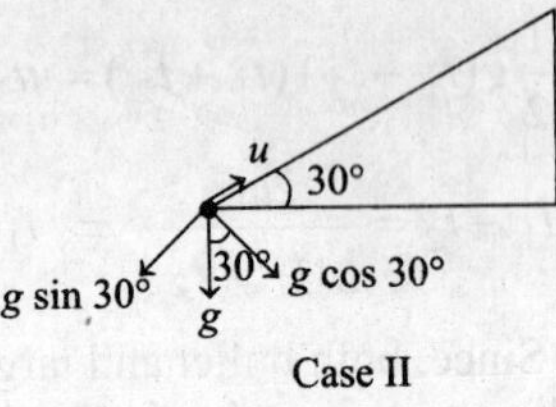

Case II

Using third equation of motion,

$$v^2 = u^2 - 2gh \quad \dots \text{(i)}$$

As the object stops finally, so

$$v = 0$$

For inclined motion,

$$g = g\sin\theta \text{ and } h = x$$

Substituting these values in Eq. (i), we get

$$\Rightarrow \quad u^2 = 2g\sin\theta\, x$$

$$\Rightarrow \quad x = \frac{u^2}{2g\sin\theta}$$

For case (I), $x_1 = \frac{u^2}{2g\sin 60°}$

For case (II), $x_2 = \frac{u^2}{2g\sin 30°}$

$$\Rightarrow \quad \frac{x_1}{x_2} = \frac{u^2}{2g\sin 60°} \times \frac{2g\sin 30°}{u^2}$$

$$= \frac{1}{2} \times \frac{2}{\sqrt{3}} = \frac{1}{\sqrt{3}} \text{ or } 1 : \sqrt{3}$$

30. (d) $\frac{R_2}{R_1} = \frac{u^2 \sin 2(45° - \theta)}{2g} \div \frac{u^2 \sin 2(45° + \theta)}{2g}$

$$\frac{R_2}{R_1} = \frac{\sin 2(45° - \theta)}{\sin 2(45° + \theta)} = \frac{\cos 2\theta}{\cos 2\theta}$$

$$\frac{R_2}{R_1} = 1:1$$

31. (b) $v_1 = 4$ m/s

$$v_2 = 0 + (1.5) \times 2 = 3 \text{ m/s}$$

As, v_1 and v_2 are perpendicular.

$$\Rightarrow \quad v^2 = v_1^2 + v_2^2 \Rightarrow v = 5 \text{ m/s}$$

32. (c) Given, $g = 10\text{ m/s}^2$

Equation of trajectory of the projectile,

$$y = 2x - 9x^2$$

In projectile motion, equation of trajectory is given by

$$y = x\tan\theta_0 - \frac{g x^2}{2v_0^2\cos^2\theta_0}$$

Comparing these equations, we get

$$\tan\theta_0 = 2$$

$$\therefore \quad \cos\theta_0 = \frac{1}{\sqrt{5}}$$

and $\quad \frac{g}{2v_0^2\cos^2\theta_0} = 9$

or $\quad v_0^2 = \frac{g}{9 \times 2\cos^2\theta_0}$

$$\therefore \quad v_0^2 = \frac{10 \times (\sqrt{5})^2}{2 \times (1)^2 \times 9}$$

$$= \frac{10 \times 5}{2 \times 9}$$

$$\Rightarrow \quad v_0^2 = \frac{25}{9} \text{ or } v_0 = \frac{5}{3} \text{ m/s}$$

and $\quad \theta_0 = \cos^{-1}\left(\frac{1}{\sqrt{5}}\right)$

33. (d) Velocity of projectile,

$$v = 25 \text{ m/s}, g = 10 \text{ m/s}^2$$

Since, after t seconds, its inclination becomes 0°, i.e. $\theta = 0°$, hence it concludes that projectile reaches at maximum height after t seconds.

$$\therefore \quad t = \frac{\text{time of flight}}{2}$$

$$= \frac{2u\sin\theta}{2g}$$

$$\Rightarrow \quad t = \frac{u\sin\theta}{g} \quad z$$

$$\Rightarrow \quad u = \frac{tg}{\sin\theta} \quad \dots \text{(i)}$$

Again we know that, horizontal range,

$$R = \frac{u^2\sin 2\theta}{g}$$

$$= \frac{\frac{t^2 g^2}{\sin^2\theta} \times 2\sin\theta\cos\theta}{g}$$

[From Eq. (i)]

$$\Rightarrow \quad R = 2t^2 g\cot\theta$$

$$\Rightarrow \quad \frac{1}{\cot\theta} = \frac{2t^2 g}{R} = \frac{2t^2 \times 10}{R}$$

$$= \frac{20t^2}{R}$$

$$\Rightarrow \quad \cot\theta = \frac{R}{20t^2}$$

$$\Rightarrow \quad \theta = \cot^{-1}\left(\frac{R}{20t^2}\right)$$

34. (c) At the highest point, the target is parallel to X-axis. Hence, slope at this point is zero. Moreover, the curve is convex upwards, hence curvature is positive at this point.

35. (c) Given, $\mathbf{r} = 3t\hat{\mathbf{i}} + 2t^2\hat{\mathbf{j}} + 5\hat{\mathbf{k}}$

$$\Rightarrow \quad \mathbf{v} = \frac{d\mathbf{r}}{dt} = 3\hat{\mathbf{i}} + 4t\hat{\mathbf{j}}$$

At $t = 1$ s,

$$\mathbf{v} = (3\hat{\mathbf{i}} + 4\hat{\mathbf{j}}) \text{ m/s}$$

$$\Rightarrow |\mathbf{v}| = \sqrt{3^2 + 4^2} = 5 \text{ m/s}$$

36. (b) Time, $t = \sqrt{\frac{2h}{g}} = \sqrt{\frac{2 \times 490}{9.8}}$

$$= \sqrt{100} = 10 \text{ s}$$

Speed, $v_x = 15$ m/s

$$v_y = 0 + 9.8 \times 10 = 98 \text{ m/s}$$

$$v^2 = v_x^2 + v_y^2$$

$$v = \sqrt{225 + 9604}$$

$$= \sqrt{9829}$$

$$\approx 99 \text{ m/s}$$

37. (d) Displacement is zero.

$$\text{Distance} = r + \frac{\pi r}{2} + r$$

$$= 2r + \frac{\pi r}{2} = 2 \times 1 + \frac{3.14}{2}$$

$$= \frac{7.14}{2} \text{km}$$

$$\text{Average speed} = \frac{7.14}{2} \div \frac{1}{6}$$

$$= 21.42 \text{ km/h}$$

38. (d) Speed is constant (v_0).

Distance travelled $r = v_0 t$

$\therefore r \propto t$

Hence, equal path lengths are travelled in equal interval.

39. (d) **Case I**

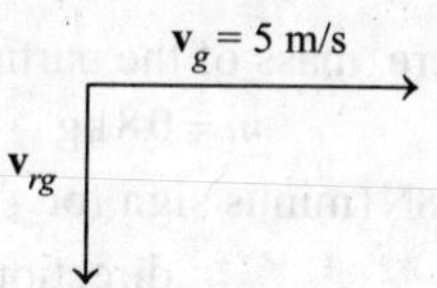

Here, $v_g = 5\hat{\mathbf{i}}$ m/s

Let, $\mathbf{v}_r = a\hat{\mathbf{i}} + b\hat{\mathbf{j}}$

$$\mathbf{v}_{rg} = \mathbf{v}_r - \mathbf{v}_g$$

$$\mathbf{v}_{rg} = (a-5)\hat{\mathbf{i}} + b\hat{\mathbf{j}}$$

Since, $\mathbf{v}_{rg}$ is downward,

$$\mathbf{v}_x = 0 \Rightarrow a = 5$$

Case II

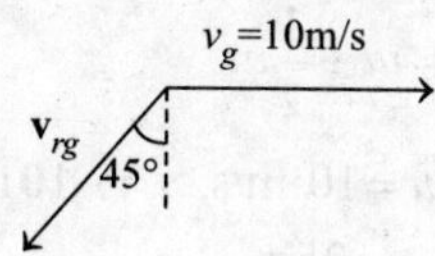

$$\mathbf{v}_{rg} = \mathbf{v}_r - \mathbf{v}_g = a\hat{\mathbf{i}} + b\hat{\mathbf{j}} - 10\hat{\mathbf{i}}$$

$$= (a-10)\hat{\mathbf{i}} + b\hat{\mathbf{j}} = -5\hat{\mathbf{i}} + b\hat{\mathbf{j}}$$

Here, $\tan 45° = \frac{v_y}{v_x} = \frac{b}{-5}$

$\Rightarrow \quad b = -5$

Therefore, $\mathbf{v}_{rg} = 5\hat{\mathbf{i}} - 5\hat{\mathbf{j}}$

or $\quad v_{rg} = 5\sqrt{2}$ m/s

40. (c) Height, reached by the particle is directly proportional to the vertical component of the initial velocity $v_0 \sin\theta$. So, angle of projection $\theta_1 > \theta_2$.

Time of flight is proportional to $\sin\theta$. So, if $\theta_1 > \theta_2$ then $T_1 > T_2$.

$$R \propto u^2 \sin 2\theta$$

$$\frac{R_2}{R_1} = \frac{\sin 2\theta_2}{\sin 2\theta_1}$$

Since, $\theta_1 \neq \theta_2$ (and $\theta_1, \theta_2 < 90°$) then $R_2 \neq R_1$.

Both particle have the same mass and initial speed. So, total mechanical energy will be same for both particle.

41. (a) As the ball falls under the influence of gravity, its speed increases, reaching the maximum value just before it strikes the ground.

At the highest point, the vertical component of the speed is zero, so the speed is minimum, not maximum.

The only force acting on the ball is gravity (assuming no air resistance), so the acceleration is constant and equal to g (9.8 m/s^2) downward throughout the motion.

The acceleration due to gravity is constant throughout the motion, including at the highest point.

42. (a) $v_r = 3\hat{\mathbf{i}}$

$$v_s = 4\hat{\mathbf{j}}$$

$$|\mathbf{v}_{rs}| = \sqrt{3^2 + 4^2} = 5 \text{ m/s}$$

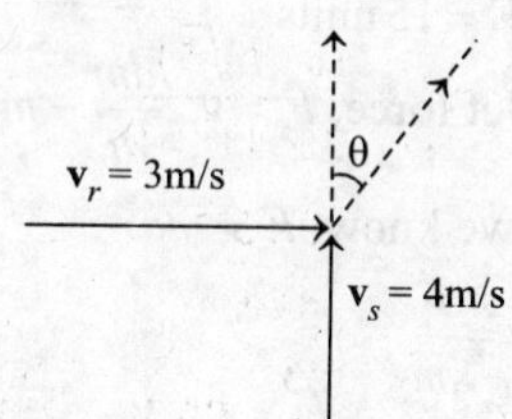

$$\tan\theta = \frac{3}{4} \Rightarrow \theta = 37° \text{ from north}$$

43. (b) Let θ is angle of projection, H is maximum height and R is horizontal range.

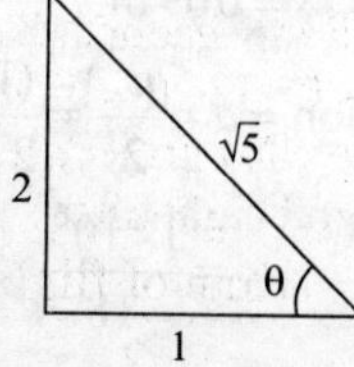

According to question, $R = 2H$

$$\frac{u^2 \sin 2\theta}{g} = \frac{2 \cdot u^2 \sin^2\theta}{2g}$$

$$\Rightarrow \quad \tan\theta = \frac{2}{1}$$

Then, $\sin\theta = \frac{2}{\sqrt{5}}, \cos\theta = \frac{1}{\sqrt{5}}$

$$\text{Horizontal range } R = \frac{u^2 \sin 2\theta}{g}$$

$$= \frac{u^2\, 2\sin\theta\cos\theta}{g}$$

$$= \frac{u^2 \times 2 \times (2/\sqrt{5}) \times (1/\sqrt{5})}{g}$$

$$= \frac{4u^2}{5g}$$

44. (c) Time of ascent for the first body,

$$t_1 = \frac{u_1}{g}$$

Time of ascent for the second body,

$$t_2 = \frac{u_2 \sin\theta}{g}$$

As $t_1 = t_2$, $u_1 = u_2 \sin\theta$

Ratio of maximum height attained,

$$h_1 : h_2 = \frac{u_1^2}{2g} : \frac{(u_2 \sin\theta)^2}{2g} = 1:1$$

45. (b) When $\mathbf{v} \cdot \mathbf{a} = 0$, object is at top most point of it's trajectory.

At top most point, kinetic energy is

$$K = \frac{1}{2} m(u \cos 30°)^2$$

$$= \frac{3}{4}\left(\frac{1}{2} mu^2\right) = \frac{3}{4} \times 4 = 3 \text{ J}$$

46. (b) Given, PE and KE at max height are equal.

$$\therefore mg\left(\frac{u^2 \sin^2\theta}{2g}\right) = \frac{1}{2} m(u^2 \cos^2\theta)$$

$$\Rightarrow \sin^2\theta = \cos^2\theta$$

or $\quad \theta = 45°$

47. (b) Vertical displacement of the ball,

$$y = (13.5 - 12.5) = 122.5 \text{ m}$$

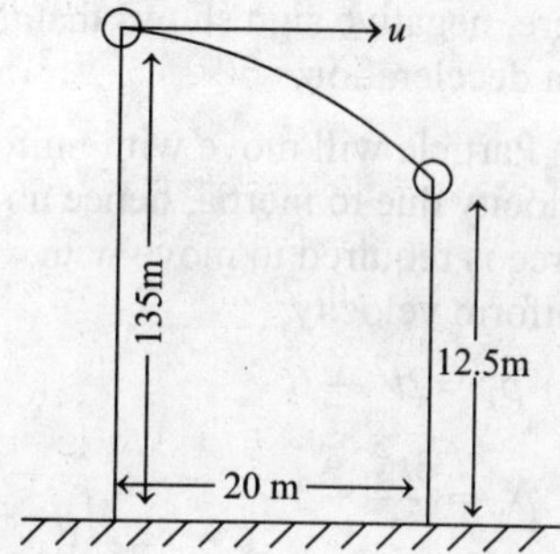

Time taken for this motion,

$$t=\sqrt{\frac{2y}{g}}=\sqrt{\frac{2\times 122.5}{9.8}}=5\text{ s}$$

Horizontal displacement $x = ut$
where, u is velocity of projection.

$$20 = u\times 5$$

$$\Rightarrow \quad u = 4\text{ ms}^{-1}$$

48. (b) At highest point,

$$\mathbf{v}=\mathbf{u}_x = u\cos\theta(\hat{\mathbf{i}})$$

$$\mathbf{a}=\mathbf{a}_y=-g(\hat{\mathbf{j}})$$

$$\Rightarrow \mathbf{v}\perp\mathbf{a}$$

49. (b) A. Uniform circular motion $\rightarrow$ Speed = constant, $\mathbf{v}\neq$ constant.

B. Body on reaching at point of projection $\rightarrow$ displacement = 0 distance $\neq 0$.

C. At highest point in vertical projection $\rightarrow v_y = 0,\ a = g$.

D. During free fall $\rightarrow v\neq 0\ a = g,\ v = gt$.

50. (c) $T=\dfrac{2u_y}{g}$

and $R=\dfrac{2u_x u_y}{g}$

So, time of flight depends on vertical components of velocity, but range depends on both components of velocity.
Hence, A is true but R is false.

Ch-04 Laws of Motion

Topical Follow Thru

Test-1

1. (b) The force is constant, i.e. the acceleration is constant but distance decreasing with time. Therefore,

By 1st second,

$$u\times 1+\left(\frac{1}{2}\right)a\times 1=5 \quad \text{...(i)}$$

By 3rd second, $u\times 3+\left(\frac{1}{2}\right)a\times 9$

$$-\left(u\times 2+\left(\frac{1}{2}\right)a\times 4\right)=3$$

$$\Rightarrow \quad u\times 1+\left(\frac{1}{2}\right)a\times 5=3 \quad \text{...(ii)}$$

From Eqs. (i) and (ii), we get

$$\left(\frac{1}{2}\right)a\times 4=-2\Rightarrow a=-1\text{m/s}^2$$

$\therefore$ Constant force

$$F = ma$$

$$F = 8\times(-1) = -8\text{N}$$

Here, negative sign shows that there is a deceleration.

2. (d) Particle will move with uniform velocity due to inertia, hence no force is required to move with uniform velocity.

3. (a) $p_x = 2t^2+6$

$$p_y=\frac{3t^2}{2}+3$$

$$\mathbf{p}=(2t^2+6)\hat{\mathbf{i}}+\left(\frac{3t^2}{2}+3\right)\hat{\mathbf{j}}$$

$$\mathbf{F}=\frac{d\mathbf{p}}{dt}$$

$$\mathbf{F}=4t\hat{\mathbf{i}}+3t\hat{\mathbf{j}}$$

$$|\mathbf{F}|=\sqrt{(4t)^2+(3t)^2}$$

$$|\mathbf{F}|=5t$$

At $t = 3$ s,

$$F = 5\times 3$$

$$F = 15\text{ units}$$

4. (a) Net force, $F = v_r\dfrac{dm}{dt}-mg$

As we know, $F = ma$

$$a=\frac{F}{m}$$

$$a=\frac{10\times 10^3\times 10-8000\times 10}{8000}$$

$$a=\frac{20}{8}=2.5\text{ ms}^{-2}$$

5. (b) Given, $u = 100$ m/s, $v = 0$,

$$s = 0.09\text{ m}$$

$$\text{Retardation}=a=\frac{u^2}{2s}=\frac{(100)^2}{2\times 0.09}$$

$$=\frac{1\times 10^6}{18}$$

$$\therefore \text{Force}=ma=\frac{8\times 10^{-3}\times 1\times 10^6}{18}$$

$$=\frac{8000}{18}=444.4\text{ N}$$

6. (a) Here, mass of the particle,

$$m = 0.8\text{ kg}$$

$F = -8$N (minus sign for direction of force)

$\therefore$ Acceleration,

$$a=\frac{F}{m}=\frac{-8\text{N}}{0.8\text{kg}}=-10\text{ m/s}^2$$

The position of the particle at any time t is given by

$$x = x_0+ut+\frac{1}{2}at^2$$

The position of the particle at $t = 0$ is 0, therefore $x_0 = 0$

$$\therefore \quad x = ut+\frac{1}{2}at^2$$

Here, $u = 10$ m/s, $a = -10\text{ m/s}^2$,

$$t = 25\text{ s}$$

Position of the particle at $t = 25$ s,

$$x = 10\times 25+\frac{1}{2}(-10)(25)^2$$

$$= 250-3125 = -2875\text{ m}$$

7. (b)

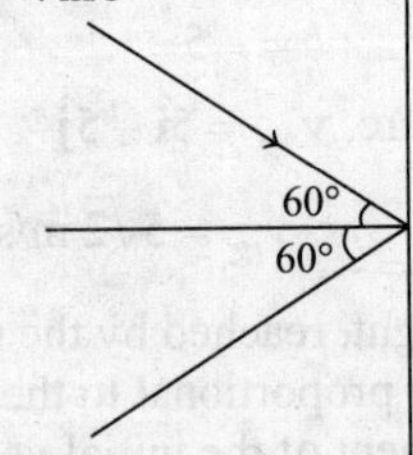

$$\Delta p = 2\,mu\cos 60°$$

$$= 2 \times 2 \times 4 \times \frac{1}{2}$$

$$= 8 \text{ kg ms}^{-1}$$

$$F = \frac{\Delta p}{\Delta t}$$

$$F = \frac{8}{0.1}$$

$$F = 80 \text{N}$$

8. (c) Area under graph,

$$\Delta p = \frac{1}{2} F \times t$$

$$= \frac{1}{2} \times 15 \times 4$$

$$= 30 \text{kg ms}^{-1}$$

$$\Delta p = (mv - mu)$$

$$30 = 5(v - 0)$$

$$30 = 5v$$

$$v = 6 \text{m/s}$$

9. (b) According to Newton's third law, force on each of colliding masses will be same but they experience unequal accelerations and acceleration is inversely proportional to the mass of the object.

10. (a) Given, $v = 20 \text{m/s}$,

$$\frac{dm}{dt} = 50 \text{kg/min}$$

$$= \frac{50}{60} \text{kg/s}$$

$$F_{\text{extra}} = v \frac{dm}{dt}$$

$$= 20 \times \frac{5}{6} = \frac{100}{6} = 16.66 \text{N}$$

11. (a) $\frac{dm}{dt} = 2 M \text{ kg/s}$

$$v = 2v \text{ m/s}$$

$$F = v \frac{dm}{dt} = 2 \times 2Mv$$

$$= 4 Mv \text{ N}$$

12. (b) $\therefore v^2 = u^2 - 2as$

$$\Rightarrow \quad a = \frac{u^2}{2s} \Rightarrow \text{Force} = \frac{mu^2}{2s}$$

$$F = \frac{5}{1000} \times \frac{100 \times 100 \times 100}{2 \times 6}$$

$$= \frac{5000}{12} \simeq 417 \text{N}$$

13. (c) Given, $p = a + bt^2$

$$\Rightarrow \quad F = \frac{dp}{dt} = 2bt$$

or $\quad F \propto t$

14. (a) Given, $m = 100 \text{kg}$, $v = 5 \text{m/s}$,

$$t = \frac{1}{10} \text{s}$$

$$F = m \frac{\Delta v}{\Delta t}$$

$$= 100 \times \frac{(5-0)}{1/10} = 5000 \text{N}$$

15. (a) Given, $m = \frac{1}{10} \text{kg}$, $v = 10 \text{ m/s}$,

$$\theta = 30°$$

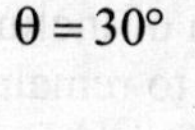

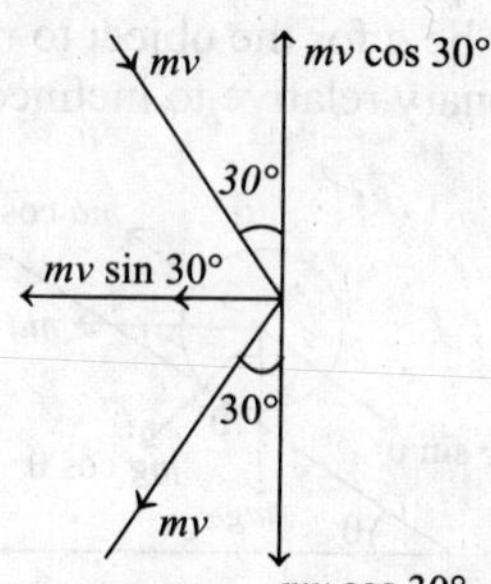

$$v_1 = v \sin \theta,$$

$$v_2 = -v \sin \theta$$

$$\Rightarrow v_1 = 10 \times \frac{1}{2},$$

$$v_2 = -10 \times \frac{1}{2}$$

$$|\Delta v| = |v_1 - v_2| = 10$$

Now, $F = \frac{m\Delta v}{\Delta t} = \frac{\frac{1}{10} \times (10)}{0.1}$

$$\Rightarrow \quad F = 10 \text{N (magnitude)}$$

16. (c) Given that,

$$M = 90 \text{kg}$$

$$a = g$$

The force exerted by the floor on a man = actual weight of man − net upward force on a man

$$F = ma - mg$$

$$F = mg - mg$$

$$F = 0 \text{N}$$

Hence, the force exerted by the floor on a man is zero.

17. (c) As, forces are forming closed loop in same order.

So, $m \frac{dv}{dt} = 0 \Rightarrow v = \text{constant}$

18. (b) $a = \frac{\Delta v}{\Delta t}$

$$= \frac{(-2-10)}{4} = -3 \text{ m/s}^2$$

19. (c) Force imparted = rate of change of momentum

$$F = \frac{\Delta p}{\Delta t}$$

or $\quad F = \frac{p_1 - p_2}{\Delta t}$

or $\quad F = \frac{m(v_1 - v_2)}{\Delta t}$

Here, mass of body

$$m = 150 \text{ g} = 0.150 \text{ kg},$$

$$v_1 = 20 \text{m/s}, \ v_2 = 0$$

Time taken,

$$\Delta t = 0.1 \text{s}$$

$$\therefore \quad F = \frac{0.150 \times (20 - 0)}{0.1}$$

$$= 30 \text{N}$$

20. (d) $\frac{K_1}{K_2} = \frac{4}{1}$

$$\Rightarrow \frac{p_1^2}{2m_1} \times \frac{2m_2}{p_2^2} = \frac{4}{1}$$

$$\Rightarrow \frac{m_2}{m_1} = \frac{4}{1} \text{ or } \frac{m_1}{m_2} = \frac{1}{4}$$

$$(p_1 = p_2)$$

21. (c) When the hammer strikes the nail, the reaction force on the hammer retards the hammer.

Retardation = F / M

Distance travelled by the nail = x

From $v^2 - u^2 = 2as$

$$u = \sqrt{2as} \text{ (as, } v = 0)$$

$$\Rightarrow \quad u = \sqrt{\frac{2Fx}{M}}$$

22. (c) Average force

= Rate of change in momentum

$$F = \frac{mv - (-mv)}{\Delta t} = \frac{2mv}{\Delta t}$$

$$= \frac{2 \times 0.25 \times 2}{10^{-3}} = 10^3 \text{ N}$$

23. (d) If F is the force applied,

$F = m_1 a_1 = m_2 a_2 = (m_1 + m_2) a$

$\Rightarrow m_1 = \frac{F}{a_1}, m_2 = \frac{F}{a_2}$

and $(m_1 + m_2) = \frac{F}{a}$

$\Rightarrow \frac{F}{a_1} + \frac{F}{a_2} = \frac{F}{a}$

$\Rightarrow a = \frac{a_1 a_2}{a_1 + a_2}$

$= \frac{6 \times 3}{6+3} = 2 \text{ ms}^{-2}$

24. (b) According to Newton's second law,

i.e. $F = \frac{dp}{dt}$

or $F = m\frac{dv}{dt}$ ...(i)

Given, $m = 3$ kg

$F = (6t^2\hat{i} + 4t\hat{j})$N

Substituting these values in Eq. (i), we get

$(6t^2\hat{i} + 4t\hat{j}) = 3\frac{dv}{dt}$

or $dv = \frac{1}{3}(6t^2\hat{i} + 4t\hat{j})\,dt$

Now, taking integration of both sides, we get

$\int dv = \int_0^t \frac{1}{3}(6t^2\hat{i} + 4t\hat{j})\,dt$

$v = \frac{1}{3}\int_0^t (6t^2\hat{i} + 4t\hat{j})\,dt$

but $t = 3$ s (given)

$\therefore v = \frac{1}{3}\int_0^3 (6t^2\hat{i} + 4t\hat{j})\,dt$

or $v = \frac{1}{3}\left[\frac{6t^3}{3}\hat{i} + \frac{4t^2}{2}\hat{j}\right]_0^3$

$= 18\hat{i} + 6\hat{j}$

25. (d) Velocity of the particle along x-direction, $v_x = 2 \text{ ms}^{-1}$

Acceleration along y-direction

$= 2 \text{ ms}^{-2}$

Velocity of the particle along y-direction after 4 s,

$v_y = at = 2 \times 4 = 8 \text{ ms}^{-1}$

Resultant velocity

$= \sqrt{(v_x)^2 + (v_y)^2}$

$= \sqrt{4 + 64}$

$= \sqrt{68} \text{ ms}^{-1}$

$= 2\sqrt{17} \text{ ms}^{-1}$

Test-2

1. (c) As we know, $\sin\theta = \frac{1}{l}$

Let required acceleration of inclined plane be a for the object to remain stationary relative to inclined plane.

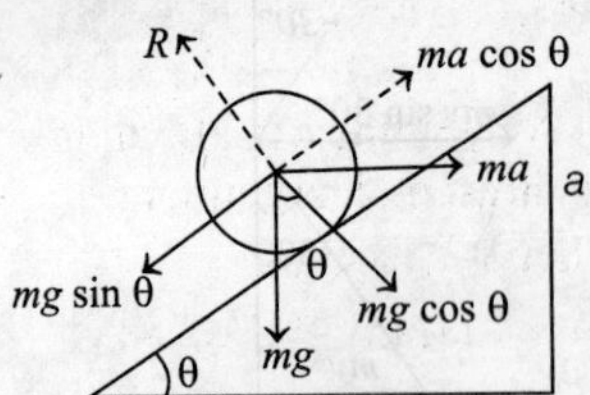

We have, $ma\cos\theta = mg\sin\theta$

$a = g\tan\theta$

Thus, $a = g\frac{1}{\sqrt{l^2 - 1}}$

2. (b) $R^2 = (3P)^2 + (2P)^2 + 2 \times 3P \times 2P\cos\theta$ ...(i)

Now, $(2R)^2 = (6P)^2 + (2P)^2 + 2 \times 6P \times 2P\cos\theta$ ...(ii)

By solving Eqs (i) and (ii), we have

$\cos\theta = -\frac{1}{2}$

$\Rightarrow \theta = 120°$

3. (a) If vector sum all forces acting on a body is zero, then body is in equilibrium.

4. (d) Let vertical force,

$F_1 \sin 30° + F_2 \sin 60°$

$= 20 \times \frac{1}{2} + 10\sqrt{3}\left(\frac{\sqrt{3}}{2}\right) = 25$N

This is greater than mg, so contact of the body with surface will be lost and reaction will be zero.

5. (b) Here,

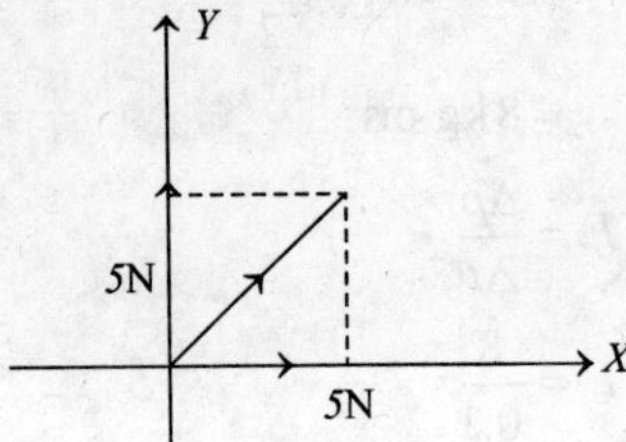

Resultant force,

$|F| = \sqrt{5^2 + 5^2}$

$= 5\sqrt{2}$N

where, $\tan\theta = \frac{5}{5} = 1$

$\theta = \tan^{-1}(1)$

Thus, $\theta = \frac{\pi}{4}$

6. (a) Free body diagram of sphere, Here, weight

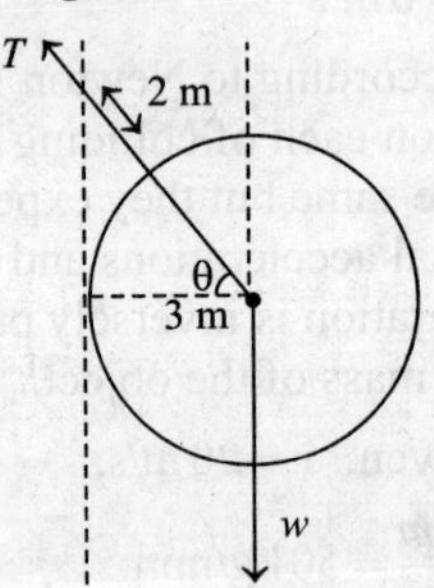

$w = T\sin\theta$

and $\cos\theta = \frac{3}{5} \Rightarrow \theta = 53°$

$\Rightarrow T = \frac{w}{\sin 53°}$

$\Rightarrow$ Tension $(T) = \frac{5}{4}w$

7. (c)

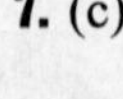

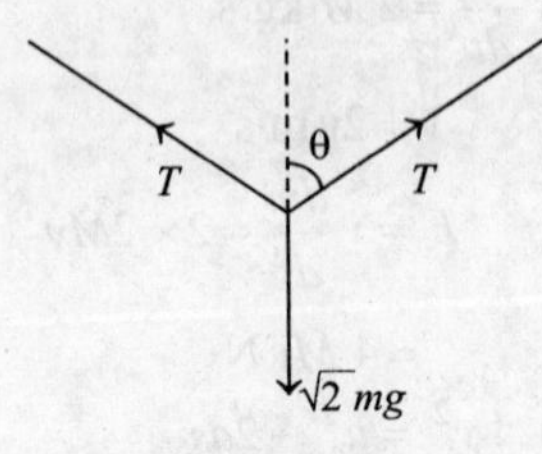

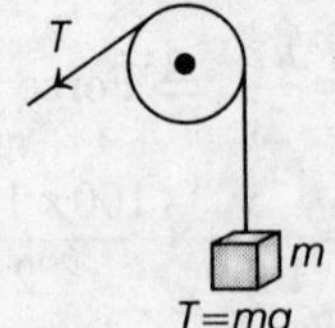

$$2T\cos\theta = \sqrt{2}\,mg$$

$$T\cos\theta = \frac{1}{\sqrt{2}}mg$$

$$\Rightarrow \quad mg\cos\theta = \frac{1}{\sqrt{2}}mg$$

$$\Rightarrow \quad \cos\theta = \frac{1}{\sqrt{2}}$$

or $\theta = 45°$

8. (c) Using Lami's theorem,

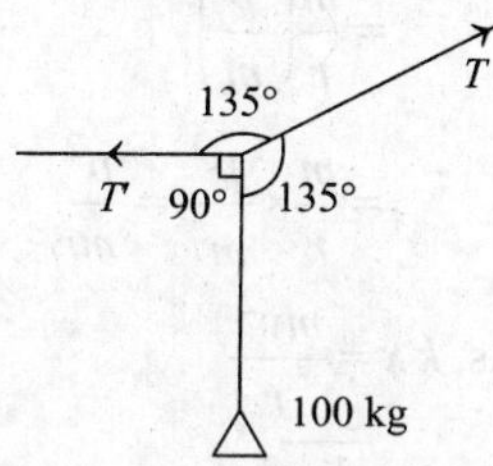

$$\frac{T'}{\sin 135°} = \frac{T}{\sin 90°} = \frac{100g}{\sin 135°}$$

$$T' = 100g \text{ N}$$

$$T = 100\sqrt{2}\,g \text{ N}$$

9. (d) For three forces to be in equilibrium, if they must form a cyclic traingle and their magnitudes must be follow triangle in equality. So, sum of magnitudes of any two forces must be greater than third.

10. (d) $N_A\cos 60° + N_B\cos 30° = Mg$

and $N_B\sin 30° = N_A\sin 60°$

or $N_B = \sqrt{3}\,N_A$

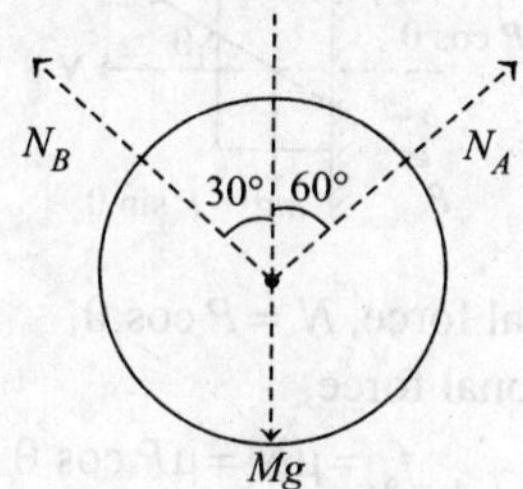

11. (b) Here,

$T-(M+m)g = (M+m)a$ ...(i)

and $2Mg - T = 2Ma$ ...(ii)

Adding Eqs. (i) and (ii), we get

$(M-m)g = (3M+m)a$

or $a = \left(\dfrac{M-m}{3M+m}\right)g$

In system of M and m,

$$R - mg = ma$$

$$\Rightarrow \quad R = m(g+a)$$

$$= mg\left(1+\frac{M-m}{3M+m}\right)$$

$$\Rightarrow \quad R = \frac{4Mmg}{3M+m}$$

12. (d) $3g - T = 3a$ ...(i)

$T - 2g = 2a$ ...(ii)

$$\Rightarrow \quad g = 5a \text{ or } a = \frac{g}{5}$$

Also, $T = 3g - \dfrac{3g}{5} = \dfrac{12}{5}g$

13. (c) As volume of balloon is constant, the thrust on it is constant.

When it descends,

$$Mg - F = Ma$$

When it ascends,

$$F-(M-m)g = (M-m)a$$

On adding these two equations, we get

$$Mg - Mg + mg = 2Ma - ma$$

$$\Rightarrow m(a+g) = 2Ma$$

$$\Rightarrow \quad m = \frac{2Ma}{(a+g)}$$

Here, $a = g/8$

$$\Rightarrow \quad m = \frac{2Mg/8}{(g/8+g)} = \frac{2M}{9}$$

14. (d) Here, tension in the string,

$$T = F/2 = 2\text{N}$$

For the block, $T = ma \Rightarrow 2 = 2a$

$$\Rightarrow \quad a = 1\text{ ms}^{-2}$$

15. (c) Here, tension in the rope,

$$T = \frac{60}{100}mg = \frac{3mg}{5}$$

$$mg - ma = T$$

$$g - a = \frac{3g}{5}$$

$$\Rightarrow \quad a = \frac{2g}{5}$$

Test -3

1. (c) Given, $\mu = 0.8$

Let F be horizontal force that the body is applying on the pole .

Frictional force, $f = \mu N = mg$

$$N = \frac{mg}{\mu} = \frac{80\times 10}{0.8} = 1000\text{N}$$

$$\Rightarrow \quad F = N = 1000\text{N}$$

2. (d)

$$\mu_s = \frac{\text{Length of the chain hanging from the table}}{\text{Length of the chain lying on the table}}$$

$$\frac{\frac{l}{6}}{l-\frac{l}{6}} = \frac{\frac{1}{6}}{\frac{5}{6}} = \frac{1}{5}$$

3. (d) Frictional force is directly proportional to the normal contact force between the bodies under consideration in the given question. The lift is falling with acceleration equal to g, there is zero normal contact force between the bodies.

4. (a) Here,

$$\frac{dy}{dx} = \tan\theta = \mu \text{ in limiting case}$$

$$\Rightarrow \frac{dy}{dx} = \frac{3x^2}{6} = \frac{1}{2} \Rightarrow x \pm 1$$

So, $y = \dfrac{1}{6}$ m

5. (b) Given, minimum value of F will be determined by

$$F = \frac{mg}{\mu} = \frac{1\times 9.8}{0.2} = 49\text{ N}$$

6. (c) Static friction is a self- adjusting force because force of static friction is equal and opposite to applied force.

Frictional force $= \mu$N

i.e. Friction depends on normal force.

7. (c) Ball bearing are used to reduce friction and provide good stability which make moving parts of machine easy to operate.

8. (c) Here, applied horizontal force F acts as normal reaction.

For holding the block,

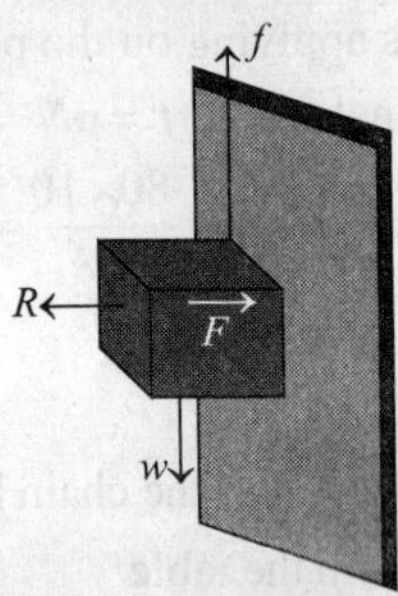

Force of friciton = Weight of the block

$$f = w \Rightarrow \mu R = w$$

$$\Rightarrow \quad \mu F = w$$

$$\Rightarrow \quad F = \frac{w}{\mu}$$

As, $\mu < 1$

$\therefore \quad F > w$

9. (a)

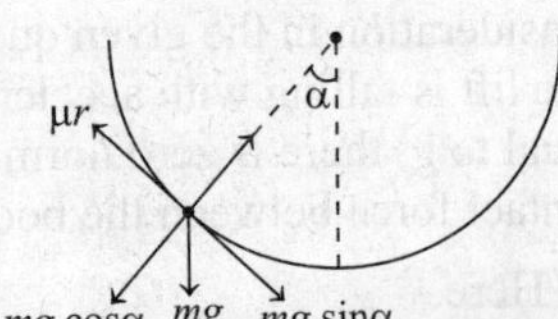

$$\mu R = mg \sin \alpha$$

$$\mu\, mg \cos \alpha = mg \sin \alpha$$

$$\cot \alpha = \frac{1}{\mu}$$

$$\cot \alpha = 3$$

10. (c) The limiting force of friciton,

$f_s = 20\text{N}$

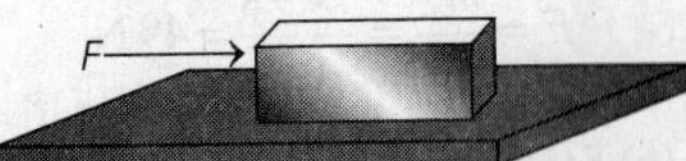

As $F = 12\text{N} < f_s$, therefore block does not move. As static friction is a self-adjusting force, therefore the frictional force on the block is 12 N.

11. (c) We know that, $F = ma$

$$\mu mg = ma$$

Now, $v = u + at \Rightarrow 0 = 6 + 10a$

$$a = -0.6 \text{ ms}^{-2}$$

So, $\mu = \frac{a}{g}$

$$\mu = \frac{0.6}{10}$$

$$\mu = 0.06$$

12. (c) The magnitude of force required to move the body is equal to

$$\frac{w \sin \alpha}{\cos(\theta - \alpha)}$$

13. (b) $F = \frac{mv^2}{r}$

$$F' = \frac{1.6\, m \times (1.6v)^2}{1.6 \times r}$$

$$F' = \frac{mv^2}{r} \times (1.6)^2 = 2.56\, F$$

% Force increased

$$= \frac{F' - F}{F} \times 100$$

$$= \frac{2.56F - F}{F} \times 100\%$$

$$= 1.56 \times 100\% = 156\%$$

14. (d)

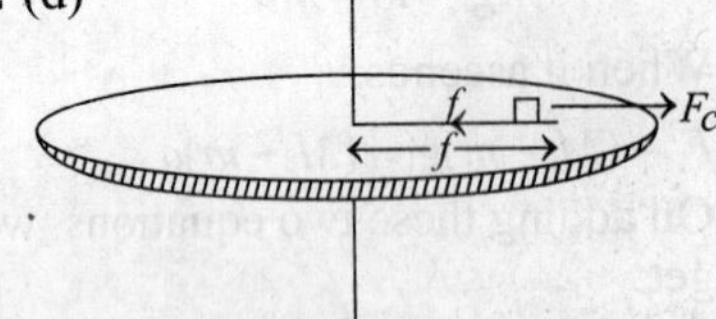

Force on the coin is centripetal force which is provided by the friction.

So, $\quad f = F_c$

$$\mu mg = \frac{mv^2}{r} \text{ and } v = r\omega$$

$$\Rightarrow \quad \mu mg = mr\omega^2$$

$\therefore$ Angular speed upto which coin holds,

$$\omega = \sqrt{\mu g / r}$$

15. (a) Given, $m = 5\,\text{kg}$, $R = 2\,\text{m}$

Time t for 1 rev = 3.14s or πs

θ for 1 rev = 2π rad

Therefore, $\omega = \frac{\theta}{t} = \frac{2\pi}{\pi} = 2 \text{ rad/s}$

Centrifugal force, $F = mR\omega^2$

$$F = 5 \times 2 \times 2^2$$

$$F = 40\,\text{N}$$

16. (c) Radius of circle $(r) = 49\,\text{m}$

$$v_{\max} = \sqrt{gR}$$

$$= \sqrt{9.8 \times 49} = 22 \text{ m/s}$$

17. (d) Mass of stone, $m = 16\,\text{kg}$

Length, $l = 144\,\text{m}$

Maximum tension,

$$T = \frac{mv^2}{r} = 16\,\text{N}$$

$$= \frac{16 \times v^2}{144} = 16 \Rightarrow v = 12 \text{ m/s}$$

18. (d) Radial force $= \frac{mv^2}{r}$

$$= \frac{m}{r}\left(\frac{p}{m}\right)^2$$

$$= \frac{m}{r} \times \frac{p^2}{m^2} = \frac{p^2}{mr}$$

19. (b) As, $kx = \frac{mv^2}{r}$

$$v = \sqrt{\frac{kxr}{m}}$$

$$\Rightarrow \quad T = \frac{2\pi r}{v} = 2\pi\sqrt{\frac{mr}{kx}}$$

$$\therefore \quad T \propto \sqrt{\frac{r}{x}}$$

$$T' = T\sqrt{\frac{r'x}{rx'}}$$

$$= T\sqrt{\frac{3a \times a}{2a \times 2a}} = \frac{\sqrt{3}}{2}T$$

20. (c) P is resolved into rectangular components as shown.

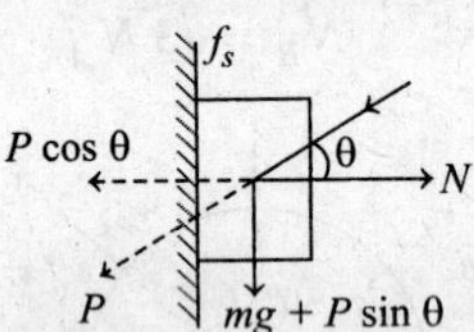

Normal force, $N = P \cos \theta$

Frictional force,

$$f_s = \mu N = \mu P \cos \theta$$

As the block is prevented from sliding down,

$$mg + P \sin \theta = f_s = \mu P \cos \theta$$

$$\Rightarrow P(\mu \cos \theta - \sin \theta) = mg$$

$$P = \frac{mg}{(\mu \cos \theta - \sin \theta)}$$

21. (a) When the surface is smooth, the effective acceleration with which the block slides down is $g \sin \theta$. If the block takes time t_1 to slide a distance d, then $d = \frac{1}{2}(g \sin \theta)t_1^2$ ...(i)

When the surface is rough having kinetic friction coefficient 'μ_k' between the block and the incline, then the effective acceleration will be $= g \sin \theta - \mu_k g \cos \theta$

If this time the distance d is covered in time t_2, then

$$d = \frac{1}{2} g (\sin \theta - \mu_k \cos \theta) t_2^2$$

$$= \frac{1}{2} g (\sin 45° - \mu_k \cos 45°) t_2^2$$

$$= \frac{g}{2\sqrt{2}} (1 - \mu_k) n^2 t_1^2 \quad ...(ii)$$

$[\because t_2 = nt_1 \text{ (given)}]$

From Eqs. (i) and (ii), we get

$$\frac{g}{2\sqrt{2}} (1 - \mu_k) n^2 t_1^2 = \left(\frac{1}{2} g \sin 45°\right) t_1^2$$

$$(1 - \mu_k) n^2 = 1$$

$$\mu_k = 1 - \frac{1}{n^2}$$

22. (b) If M is mass of the chain and l is the length, weight of the hanging part is equal to static friction on the part resting on the table.

l/n

$$\frac{Mg}{n} = \mu Mg\left(1 - \frac{1}{n}\right)$$

$$\Rightarrow \quad \frac{1}{n} = \mu\left(\frac{n-1}{n}\right) \Rightarrow \quad \mu = \frac{1}{n-1}$$

23. (a) $mg \sin \theta = \mu\, mg \cos \theta$

r, θ, N, μN, h, $mg \sin \theta$, mg, $mg \cos\theta$

$$\Rightarrow \tan \theta = \mu \text{ and } \cos \theta = \frac{1}{\sqrt{\mu^2 + 1}}$$

$$\cos \theta = \frac{r - h}{r}$$

$$\Rightarrow \quad h = r(1 - \cos \theta)$$

$$= r\left(1 - \frac{1}{\sqrt{\mu^2 + 1}}\right)$$

24. (a) Frictional force $= \mu\, mg \cos \theta$

$(\because N = mg \cos \theta)$

$$= 0.4 \times 1 \times 9.8 \times \frac{1}{2} \text{ (as, } \theta = 60°)$$

$$= 1.96 \text{ N}$$

25. (a) A—3, B—2, C—1, D—4

A. Friction is a non-conservative force.

B. Friction force is independent to area of surface in contact.

C. The value of static friction force lies between 0 and $\mu_k R$, where μ is the coefficient of kinetic friction and R is normal reaction.

D. Magnitude of static friction is always greater than kinetic friction as well as rolling friction.

Chapter Break Thru

1. (d) As given, mass $m = 10$ kg,

Then, tension,

$$T_3 \sin 60° = T_2 \sin 30°$$

$$T_3 = \frac{T_2}{\sqrt{3}}$$

Now, $T_2 \cos 30° + T_3 \cos 60° = T_1 = 100$

$$\frac{\sqrt{3}}{2} T_2 + \frac{T_2}{\sqrt{3}} \times \frac{1}{2} = 100$$

$$\Rightarrow \quad \frac{4T_2}{2\sqrt{3}} = 100$$

or $\quad T_2 = 50\sqrt{3}$ N

2. (b) Acceleration of a system

$$a = \frac{\text{Net pushing force}}{\text{Total mass}}$$

$$\text{or } a = \frac{F - (m_1 + m_2 + m_3) g \sin \theta}{(m_1 + m_2 + m_3)}$$

Equation of motion for mass m_3,

$$N - m_3 g \sin \theta = m_3 a$$

$$\text{or} \quad N = m_3 g \sin \theta + m_3 \left(\frac{F - (m_1 + m_2 + m_3) g \sin \theta}{(m_1 + m_2 + m_3)}\right)$$

$$= \frac{m_3 F}{m_1 + m_2 + m_3}$$

3. (d) The equilibrium condition is gained, when the net force acting on the body will zero and closed polygon of 4 sides will give the resultant force as zero.

4. (d) Here,

A, B, C; m —T_1— m —T_2— m → F

$$\text{Acceleration, } a = \frac{F}{3m} \Rightarrow T_1 = \frac{F}{3} \text{N}$$

$$T_2 - T_1 = \frac{F}{3}$$

$$T_2 = \frac{2F}{3} \Rightarrow \text{So, } T_1 : T_2 = 1 : 2$$

5. (b) Let, F is the frictional force. Now, equation of motion for the body is,

$$mg - F = ma$$

$$\Rightarrow \quad F = mg - ma = m(g - a)$$

$$\Rightarrow \quad F = 0.25(9.8 - 9.2) = 0.15 \text{ N}$$

6. (b) From, $F = ma = F_0 e^{-bt}$

$$\Rightarrow \quad \frac{dv}{dt} = \frac{F_0}{m} e^{-bt}$$

$$\Rightarrow \quad \int_0^v dv = \frac{F_0}{m} \int_0^t e^{-bt} dt$$

$$v = \frac{F_0}{m} \left[\frac{e^{-bt}}{-b}\right]_0^t$$

$$\Rightarrow \quad v = \frac{F_0}{mb} (1 - e^{-bt})$$

7. (a) Using equation of motion,

$$v^2 = u^2 + 2as$$

$$a = \frac{v^2}{2l} \quad (\because u = 0 \text{ and } s = l)$$

Force required to produce acceleration a,

$$F = Ma = \frac{Mv^2}{2l}$$

Force required to overcome the friction,

$$F = \mu N = \mu Mg$$

Total force required,

$$F = \mu Mg + \frac{Mv^2}{2l} = M\left(\mu g + \frac{v^2}{2l}\right)$$

8. (b) Here,

Acceleration is given by

$$a = \left(\frac{m_1 - m_2}{m_1 + m_2}\right) g$$

$$\frac{g}{8} = \left(\frac{m_1 - m_2}{m_1 + m_2}\right) g$$

$$\frac{m_1}{m_2} = \frac{9}{7}$$

9. (b) Here, $s = \frac{v^2}{2\mu g}$

$$s = \frac{\left(82 \times \frac{5}{18}\right)^2}{2 \times 0.8 \times 10}$$

$$= \frac{(22.77)^2}{16}$$

$$= 32.40\ \text{m}$$

10. (a) Force of friction of chain = Weight of hanging chain

$$\mu(l - x)\rho g = x\rho g$$

or $\mu(l - x) = x$

$$\mu l = (\mu + 1)x$$

or $x = \mu l / (1 + \mu)$

$$x = \frac{0.45l}{0.45 + 1} = \frac{0.45l}{1.45}$$

11. (d) Acceleration of m,

$$a = \frac{\mu mg}{m} = \mu g$$

Initial acceleration,

$$a_{mM} = a - 0 = a$$

and initial relative velocity,

$$v_{mM} = 0 - v = v$$

Hence, stopping distance

$$S_{mM} = \frac{v^2}{2\mu g} = \frac{(8)^2}{2 \times 0.6 \times 9.8}$$

$$S_{mM} = \frac{64}{0.12 \times 9.8} = 5.442$$

12. (a) Let us take an angle which subtends angle $2(d\theta)$ at centre. Tangential component of T cancel out each other, while inward component provide the necessarly centripetal force, thus

$$2T \sin(d\theta) = (dm)R\omega^2$$

$$= (\pi 2R \cdot d\theta)(R\omega^2)$$

The linear mass density to small angles, $\sin d\theta = d\theta$

$$2Td\theta = 2\lambda R^2 \omega^2 d\theta$$

or $T = \lambda R^2 \omega^2$

$$\omega_{max} = \sqrt{\frac{T_{max}}{\lambda} \cdot \frac{1}{R}}$$

$$= \sqrt{\frac{40}{0.1} \times \frac{1}{1}}$$

$$\omega_{max} = 20\ \text{rad/s}$$

13. (a)

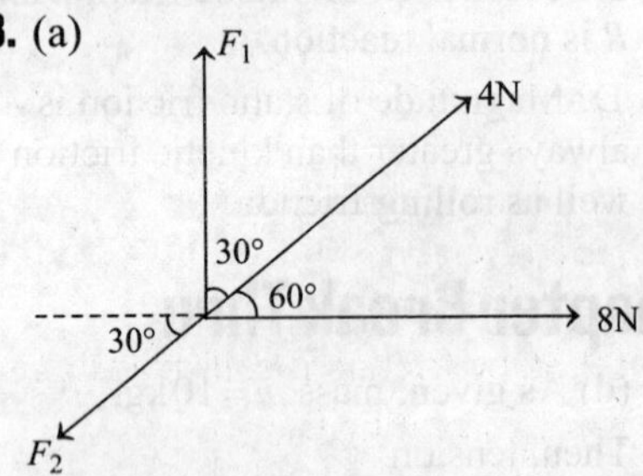

Case I

$$\Sigma F_x = 0$$

$\therefore\ 8 + 4\cos 60° - F_2 \cos 30° = 0$

or $8 + 2 - F_2 \frac{\sqrt{3}}{2} = 0$ or $F_2 = \frac{20}{\sqrt{3}}$ N

Case II

$$\Sigma F_y = 0$$

$\therefore\ F_1 + 4\sin 60° - F_2 \sin 30° = 0$

or $F_1 + \frac{4\sqrt{3}}{2} - \frac{F_2}{2} = 0$

or $F_1 = \frac{F_2}{2} - 2\sqrt{3}$

$$= \frac{10}{\sqrt{3}} - 2\sqrt{3}$$

or $F_1 = \frac{4}{\sqrt{3}}$ N

14. (b) Net pulling force on the system should be zero as velocity is constant. Hence, $m_A g \sin 30°$ $= \mu m_A g \cos 30° + m_B g$

$$m_B = \left(\frac{m_A}{2}\right) - \left(\frac{\mu m_A \sqrt{3}}{2}\right)$$

$$= 10\left[\frac{1}{2} - 0.2 \times \frac{\sqrt{3}}{2}\right] = 3.3\ \text{kg}$$

15. (c) The major principle of rocket is conservation of linear momentum. Statement II is true only when net external force on system is zero and system contains only two bodies.

16. (a) To hold a gun, gunner should exert force because it comes back due to action-reaction. The fired bullet recoils gun due to reaction.

17. (d) $N_1 \sin 37° = N_2 \sin 74°$

$\Rightarrow\ N_1 = 2N_2 \cos 37°$

Now, $N_1 \cos 37° - N_2 \cos 74° = mg$

$\Rightarrow 2N_2 \cos^2 37° - N_2(2\cos^2 37° - 1) = mg$

$\Rightarrow 2N_2\left(\frac{16}{25}\right) - N_2\left(\frac{32}{25} - 1\right) = mg$

$\Rightarrow\ N_2 = mg$

18. (c) If vector sum of three forces is zero, then the body will be in equililbrium.

19. (d) Angular velocity (ω) is same for all particles.

$\therefore\ T_C = m\omega^2(3l)$

$$T_B = T_C + m\omega^2(2l) = m\omega^2(5l)$$

$$T_A = T_B + m\omega^2(l) = m\omega^2(6l)$$

$\therefore\ T_C : T_B : T_A = 3 : 5 : 6$

20. (a) As we know,

Kinetic friction = μ

When a body of mass m is moving with rough horizontal surface,

$\therefore\ F_{net} = \sqrt{F_1^2 + F_2^2}$

$$= \sqrt{(mg)^2 + (\mu mg)^2}$$

$$F_{net} = mg\sqrt{1 + \mu^2}$$

21. (d) In the given condition, the required centripetal force is provided by frictional force between the road and tyre

$$\frac{mv^2}{R} = \mu mg$$

$$\Rightarrow v = \sqrt{\mu gR}$$

22. (c) Given, mass of heavier object, $m_1 = M$ and mass of the lighter object $m_2 = \frac{M}{2}$

$$\because \quad a = \left(\frac{m_1 - m_2}{m_1 + m_2}\right)g \quad \text{...(i)}$$

Putting these value in Eq. (i),

$$a = \left(\frac{M - \frac{M}{2}}{M + \frac{M}{2}}\right)g$$

$$a = \left(\frac{\frac{2M - M}{2}}{\frac{2M + M}{2}}\right)g$$

$$\Rightarrow a = g/3$$

23. (c) In equilibrium,

For mass $\sqrt{2}m$,

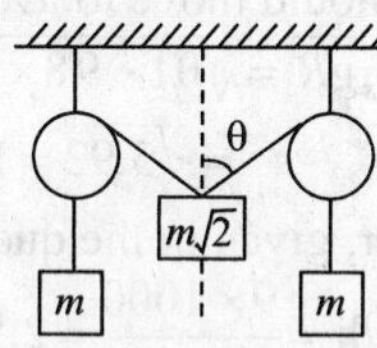

$$T\cos\theta + T\cos\theta = \sqrt{2}mg$$

and for mass m,

$$T = mg$$

$$2T\cos\theta = 2mg\cos\theta = \sqrt{2}mg$$

$$\Rightarrow \quad \theta = \frac{\pi}{4} = 45°$$

24. (c) Mass measured by physical balance remains unaffected due to variation in acceleration due to gravity.

25. (c) Thrust on the rocket,

$$F = -u\frac{dm}{dt}$$

where, u is relative velocity of exhaust gases with respect to the rocket. $\frac{dm}{dt}$ is rate of combustion of fuel at that instant.

$$\therefore \quad F = -u\frac{dm}{dt} = mg$$

$$\Rightarrow \quad -\frac{dm}{dt} = \frac{mg}{u}$$

Here, $\quad m = 600$ kg, $u = 1000$ ms^{-1}

$$\therefore \quad -\frac{dm}{dt} = \frac{600 \times 10}{1000} = 6 \text{ kg s}^{-1}$$

26. (b) Let the mass of a block is m. It will remain stationary, if force acting on it are in equilibrium i.e.

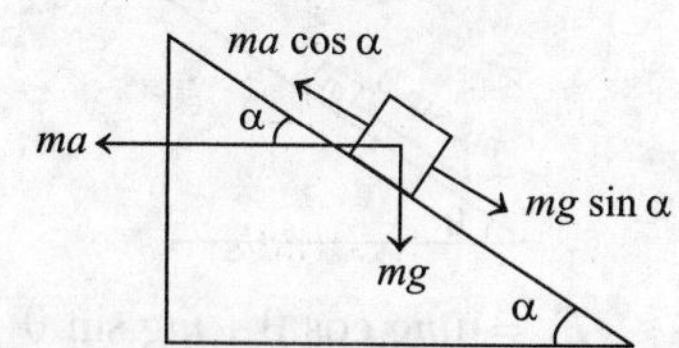

Here, ma is pseudo force on block, mg = weight.
From the above equation,

$$ma\cos\alpha = mg\sin\alpha$$

$$\Rightarrow \quad a = g\tan\alpha$$

27. (c) Static friction is self-adjusting in nature. Limiting friction $= \mu_s\ mg$

Kinetic friction (and static/kinetic friction) is independent of area of contact.

Rolling friction has least magnitude.

28. (c) Given that,

$$\mathbf{v} = (5t\,\hat{\mathbf{i}} + 2t\,\hat{\mathbf{j}}) \text{ m/s}$$

$$\therefore \quad \mathbf{a} = a_x\hat{\mathbf{i}} + a_y\hat{\mathbf{j}} = 5\hat{\mathbf{i}} + 2\hat{\mathbf{j}}$$

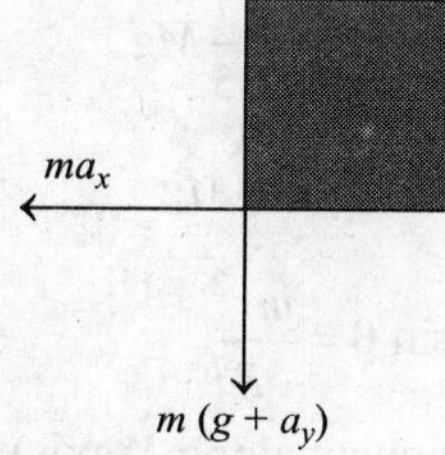

$$\mathbf{F} = ma_x\hat{\mathbf{i}} + m(g + a_y)\hat{\mathbf{j}}$$

$$|\mathbf{F}| = m\sqrt{a_x^2 + (g + a_y)^2} = 26\text{N}$$

29. (a) Applied force = 2.5 N

Limiting friction $= \mu mg$

$$= 0.4 \times 8 \times 9.8 = 31.36\text{ N}$$

For the given condition, applied force is very smaller than limiting friction,

Static friction on a body = Applied force = 2.5 N

30. (c) $\mu_r < \mu_k < \mu_s$

31. (c)

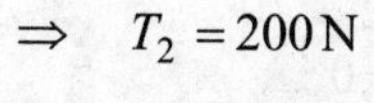

Here, $T' = (m_1 + m_2) \times \frac{T}{m_1 + m_2 + m_3}$

32. (a) Using Lami's theorem at point A.

$$\frac{100}{\sin 120°} = \frac{T_2}{\sin 90°}$$

$$\Rightarrow \quad T_2 = 200\text{N}$$

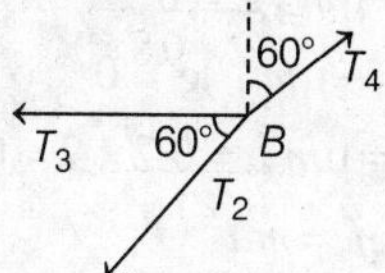

Using Lami's theorem at point B,

$$\frac{T_4}{\sin 60°} = \frac{T_2}{\sin 150°}$$

$$\Rightarrow \quad T_4 = \frac{T_2}{\sin 150°} \times \sin 60°$$

$$\Rightarrow \quad T_4 = T_2 = 200\text{N}$$

33. (c)

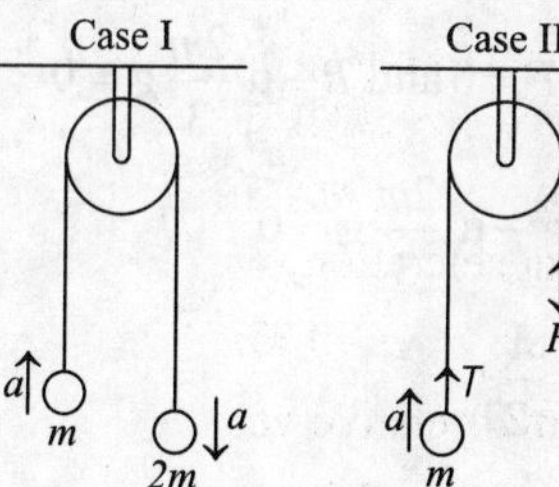

$$2mg - T = 2ma$$

$$T = F = 2mg$$

$$T - mg = ma \quad \Rightarrow a = g$$

$$2mg + mg = ma \Rightarrow a = g/3$$

Clearly, $a_{\text{I}} < a_{\text{II}}$

34. (a) In first half (AB)

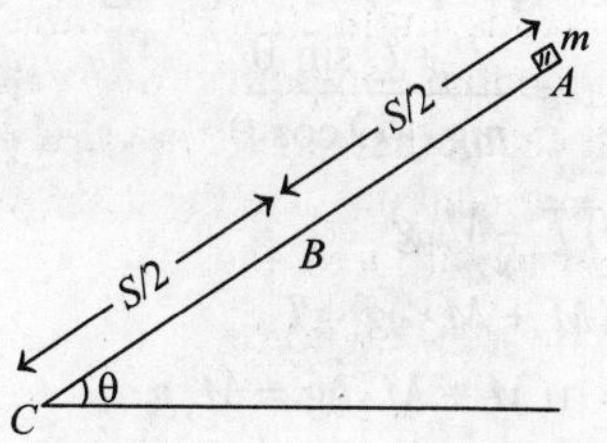

$a = g\sin\theta$

$\Rightarrow v^2 = 0 + 2g\sin\theta \times \frac{s}{2}$

$= s\,g\sin\theta$

In second half,

$a = g(\sin\theta - \mu\cos\theta)$

$0 = v^2 + 2g(\sin\theta - \mu\cos\theta)\frac{s}{2}$

$\Rightarrow s g\sin\theta = -s g(\sin\theta - \mu\cos\theta)$

$\Rightarrow 2\sin\theta = \mu\cos\theta$

or $\mu = 2\tan\theta$

35. (c) $m_B g - T = 0$

$T - \mu m_A g = 0$

$\Rightarrow (m_B - \mu m_A)g = 0$

or $m_B = \mu m_A = 0.2 \times 2 = 0.4$ kg

36. (c) $F - f = ma$

$\Rightarrow 129.4 - 0.3 \times 10 \times 9.8 = 10a$

$\Rightarrow 10a = 100$ or $a = 10\,\text{m/s}^2$

37. (b) $F_{net} = 0 \Rightarrow F - \mu mg = 0$

or $\mu = \frac{F}{mg} = \frac{1}{0.25 \times 10} = \frac{1}{2.5} = 0.4$

38. (b)

$\frac{m}{3}g - T = 0$ and $T - \mu\frac{2m}{3}g = 0$

$\Rightarrow \frac{m}{3}g - \mu\frac{2m}{3}g = 0$

$\Rightarrow \mu = \frac{1}{2}$

39. (a)

$R = mg + Q\cos\theta$

$\mu(mg + Q\cos\theta) = P + Q\sin\theta$

$\mu = \frac{P + Q\sin\theta}{mg + Q\cos\theta}$

40. (b) $T = M_1 g$

$\mu(M + M_2)g = T$

$\Rightarrow \mu(M + M_2)g = M_1 g$

or $M + M_2 = \frac{M_1}{\mu}$

$\Rightarrow M = \frac{M_1}{\mu} - M_2$

$= \frac{5}{0.15} - 10$

$= \frac{500 - 150}{15} = \frac{350}{15}$

$= 23.33$ kg

41. (d) Since, $\mu = 0$, No force is available to balance gravity.

42. (d)

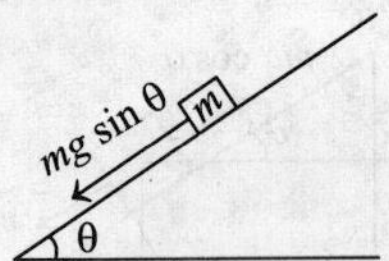

$F_1 = \mu mg\cos\theta + mg\sin\theta$

$F_2 = mg\sin\theta - \mu\,mg\cos\theta$

$\frac{F_1}{F_2} = \frac{\mu\cos\theta + \sin\theta}{\sin\theta - \mu\cos\theta}$

$= \frac{\mu + \tan\theta}{\tan\theta - \mu}$

$= \frac{3\mu}{\mu} = 3:1$

43. (d) $F\sin 37° = Mg + \mu Mg\cos 37°$

$F \times \frac{3}{5} = Mg\left[1 + \frac{1}{2} \times \frac{4}{5}\right]$

$= Mg\left[1 + \frac{2}{5}\right]$

$F \times \frac{3}{5} = \frac{7}{5}Mg$

or $F = \frac{7}{3}Mg$

44. (d) $N\sin\theta = \frac{mv^2}{R}$

(component along X-axis)

and $N\cos\theta = mg$

(components along Y-axis)

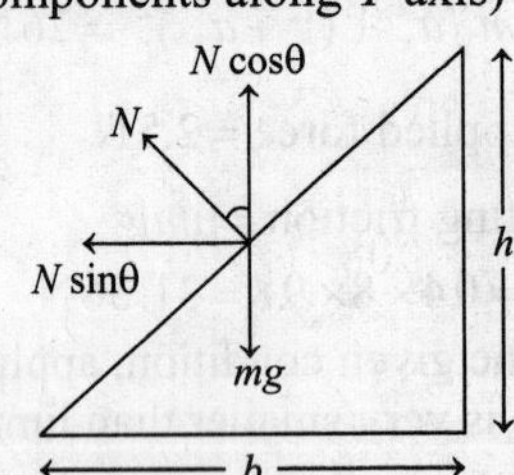

$\tan\theta = \frac{v^2}{Rg} = \frac{h}{b}$

$h = \frac{bv^2}{Rg}$

45. (d) Let the velocity of m w.r.t. to M is v.

By momentum conservation law, along X-axis,

$-Mv + m(v\cos 60° - v) = 0$

$-3.6 \times 0.3 + 0.2\left(v \times \frac{1}{2} - 0.3\right) = 0$

$-5.4 + \frac{v}{2} - 0.3 = 0$

$\frac{v}{2} - 5.7 = 0$

$v = 5.7 \times 2 = 11.4$ m/s

46. (d) If $v =$ constant, weight will remain same ($g_{eff} = g$)

If v is increasing, weight will increase ($g_{eff} = g + a$)

If v is decreasing, weight will decrease ($g_{eff} = g - a$)

47. (a) Here, $v = 9$ km/h, $R = 4$ m,

$\mu_s = 0.1$

$\therefore$ Maximum velocity with which the cyclist should move to avoid slipping

$\sqrt{\mu_s gR} = \sqrt{0.1 \times 9.8 \times 4}$

$= \sqrt{3.92} = 1.97$ m/s

However, given in the question,

$v = 9\,\text{km/h} = \frac{9 \times 1000}{60 \times 60} = 2.5$ m/s

Here, $v > \sqrt{\mu_s gR}$

So, cyclist will slip while taking the turn.

48. (d) $\int dP = \int F dt$

$=$ Area of F-t graph

$= \frac{1}{2} \times 10 \times 2 + 4 \times 10 = 50$ N-s

49. (a)

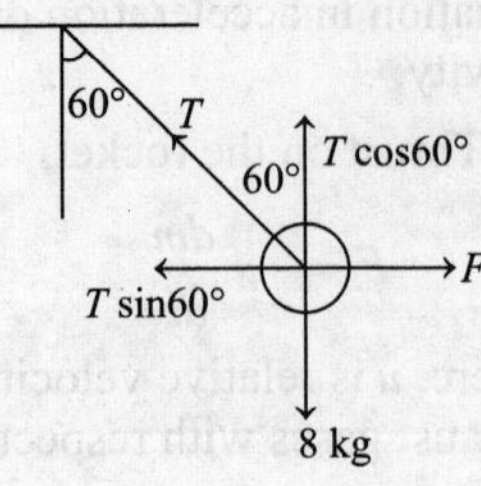

[$\because$ 1 kgf = gravitational force on 1 kg mass = 9.8 N]

$$\frac{T\sin 60^\circ}{T\cos 60^\circ}=\frac{F}{mg}$$

$$\frac{\sqrt{3}/2}{1/2}=F/8g$$

$$F=8\sqrt{3}g=8\sqrt{3}\times 9.8\text{ N}$$

$$=8\sqrt{3}\text{ kgf}$$

50. (b) $a=\frac{F}{m+m}$

$$=\frac{m\times 4}{m+m}=2\text{ m/s}^2$$

Ch-05 Work, Energy and Power

Topical Follow Thru

Test-1

1. (b) Initial energy of body

$$=\frac{1}{2}mv^2$$

$$=\frac{1}{2}\times 1\times(30)^2=450\text{ J}$$

A part of this energy consumes in doing work against gravitational force and remaining part consumes in doing work against air friction,

i.e. $W_T=W_{\text{grav}}+W_{\text{air ficition}}$

$\Rightarrow$ $450=1\times 10\times 20+W_{\text{air fricition}}$

$\Rightarrow$ $W_{\text{air ficition}}=450-200=250\text{ J}$

2. (a) Maximum height reached by the particle,

$$H_{\max}=\frac{u^2}{2g}=\frac{(10)^2}{2\times 10}=5\text{ m}$$

Workdone $=\mathbf{F}\cdot\mathbf{d}=Fd\cos\theta$

$$=mg\times H_{\max}\times\cos(180^\circ)$$

$$=0.12\times 10\times 5\times(-1)=-6\text{ J}$$

3. (c) Function of time is given by

$$x=\frac{t^3}{3}$$

$$\frac{dx}{dt}=t^2$$

$\Rightarrow$ $v=t^2$

$$a=\frac{dv}{dt}=2t$$

But, $W=\int F\cdot dx=\int ma\cdot dx=m\int_0^2(2t)(t^2dt)$

$$=2m\int_0^2 t^3\,dt=2\times 2\left|\frac{t^4}{4}\right|_0^2=16\text{ J}$$

4. (a) $U=\frac{F^2}{2K}$

$\Rightarrow U\propto\frac{1}{K}$ (If forces are same.)

$$\Rightarrow\frac{U_1}{U_2}=\frac{K_2}{K_1}$$

$$\therefore\ \frac{U_1}{U_2}=\frac{4000}{2000}=\frac{2}{1}$$

5. (b) $W=\int_0^5 F\cdot dx$

$$=\int_0^5(5-4x+9x^2)dx$$

$$=[5x-2x^2+3x^3]_0^5$$

$$=25-50+375=350\text{ J}$$

6. (b) Work done in the motion of a particle over a closed loop will be zero, when moving under the action of conservative force. So, work done depends on the nature of force.

7. (d) Work done in the process (in J),

$$W=\int_0^5(7-2x+3x^2)dx$$

$$=|7x-x^2+x^3|_0^5$$

$$=|7\times 5-(5)^2+(5)^3|$$

$$=35-25+125$$

$$W=135\text{ J}$$

8. (a) $v=\frac{dx}{dt}=3-8t+3t^2$

$\therefore v_0=3$ m/s and $v_4=19$ m/s

$W=$ change in KE

$$=\frac{1}{2}m(v_4^2-v_0^2)$$

$$=\frac{1}{2}\times 0.08\times(19^2-3^2)$$

$$=14.08\text{ J}$$

9. (b) Here, $W=\frac{1}{2}kx^2$

If both wires are stretched through same distance, then $W\propto k$,

As, $k_2=2k_1$

So, $W_2=2W_1$

10. (b) Here, force $F=cx$

From position $x=0$ to $x=x_1$,

$$W=\int_0^{x_1}F\cdot dx=\int_0^{x_1}cx\cdot dx=c\left[\frac{x^2}{2}\right]_0^{x_1}$$

$$W=\frac{1}{2}cx_1^2$$

11. (b) According to question,

$$\frac{1}{2}m_Pv_P^2=\frac{1}{2}m_Qv_Q^2$$

$$\Rightarrow\ \frac{v_P}{v_Q}=\sqrt{\frac{m_Q}{m_P}}=\sqrt{\frac{5}{20}}=\frac{1}{2}$$

Using impulse momentum,

$$\frac{F\Delta t_P}{F\Delta t_Q}=\frac{m_P\Delta v_P}{m_Q\Delta v_Q}$$

$$\Rightarrow\frac{\Delta t_P}{\Delta t_Q}=\frac{20}{5}\times\frac{1}{2}=2$$

12. (b) Here, potential energy,

$$U=A-Bx^2$$

Then, $F=-\frac{dU}{dx}=2Bx$

Thus, $F\propto x$

13. (a) As we know, surface is smooth, so work done against friction is zero. Thus, the displacement and force of gravity are perpendicular, so work done against gravity is zero.

14. (d) The percentage increase in the kinetic energy,

$$E = \frac{p^2}{2m}$$

$$\Rightarrow E_2 = E_1\left(\frac{p_2}{p_1}\right)^2 = E_1\left(\frac{2p}{p}\right)^2$$

$$\Rightarrow E_2 = 4E_1 = E_1 + 3E_1$$
$$= E + 300\% \text{ of } E.$$

15. (a)

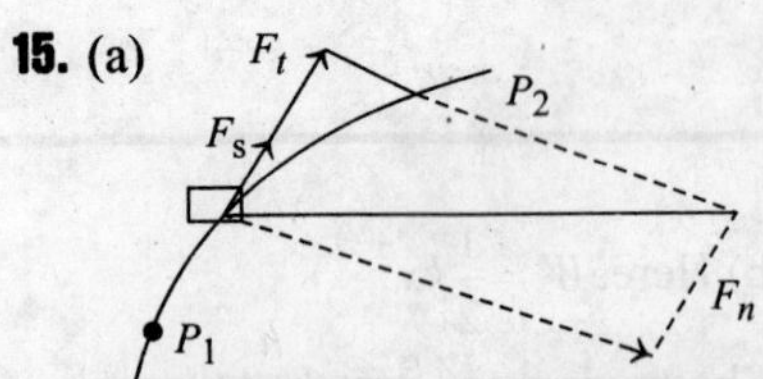

The work done by tangential forces,

$W = \int F_t \cdot ds$

For curved path, centripetal force is perpendicular to small displacement ds.
Thus, centripetal force does not perform any work.

16. (c) Initial kinetic energy,

$$E = \frac{1}{2}mv^2 \quad \text{...(i)}$$

Final kinetic energy

$$2E = \frac{1}{2}m(v+2)^2 \quad \text{...(ii)}$$

By solving Eqs. (i) and (ii), we get

$$v = (2 + 2\sqrt{2})\,\text{m/s}$$

17. (b) The work done on the block as function of speed is

$$\frac{dW}{dt} = Fv = F(at)$$

$$W = \int Fat \cdot dt = Fa\frac{t^2}{2}$$

$$W \propto t^2$$

18. (c)

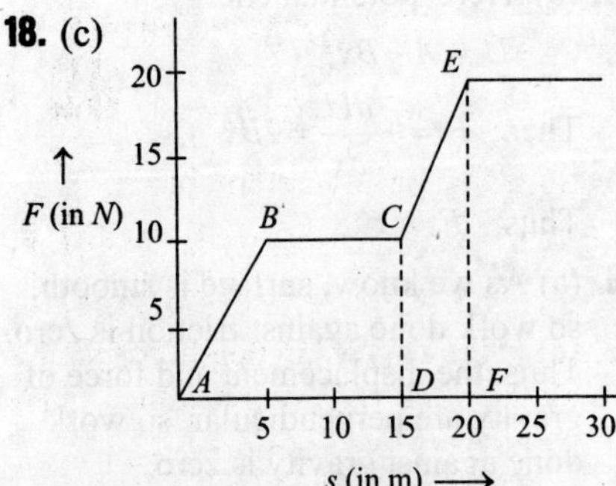

Work done, W = area under F-s graph

= area of trapezium $ABCD$ + area of trapezium $CEFD$

$$= \frac{1}{2}\times(10+15)\times 10 + \frac{1}{2}\times(10+20)\times 5$$

$$= 125 + 75 = 200\,\text{J}.$$

19. (a) Here, $x = 3t^2 + 5$

Velocity, $v = \frac{dx}{dt}$

$$\Rightarrow \quad v = \frac{d}{dt}(3t^2+5) \Rightarrow v = 6t$$

at $\quad t = 0,\ v = 0$

at $t = 5$ s, $v = 30$ m/s

Work done $= \frac{1}{2}mv^2$

$$= \frac{1}{2}(2)(30)^2 = 900\,\text{J}$$

20. (a) $W = \mathbf{F}\cdot\mathbf{s}$

$$= (6\hat{\mathbf{i}} + 2\hat{\mathbf{j}} - 3\hat{\mathbf{k}})\cdot(2\hat{\mathbf{i}} - 3\hat{\mathbf{j}} - x\hat{\mathbf{k}})$$

$$\Rightarrow \quad W = 12 - 6 + 3x$$

Given, $W = 0$

$\Rightarrow \ 6 + 3x = 0$ or $x = -2$

21. (a) The work done under the area of curve between x_i and x_f will be

$$W = \int_{x_i}^{x_f} F_x dx + \int_{y_i}^{y_f} F_y dy + \int_{z_i}^{z_f} F_z dz$$

22. (a) By conservation of momentum,

$mv + M\times 0 = (m+M)v'$

Velocity of composite block,

$$v' = \left(\frac{m}{m+M}\right)v$$

Kinetic energy block

$$= \frac{1}{2}(M+m)v'^2$$

$$= \frac{1}{2}(M+m)\left(\frac{m}{M+m}\right)^2 v^2$$

$$= \frac{1}{2}mv^2\left(\frac{m}{m+M}\right)$$

23. (d) If M and m are masses of the man and boy respectively and v' and v are their velocities

$$\frac{1}{2}Mv'^2 = \frac{1}{4}\times\frac{1}{2}mv^2$$

$$\Rightarrow Mv'^2 = \frac{1}{4}\times\frac{M}{2}v^2$$

$$\Rightarrow \quad v^2 = 8v'^2 \Rightarrow \ v = 2\sqrt{2}\,v'$$

24. (c) Potential energy,

$$U = -\int F dx = -\int kx dx$$

$$U = -k\frac{x^2}{2}$$

This is the equation of parabola symmetric to U-axis in negative direction.

25. (b) Force between particles is

$F = -\frac{dU}{dr}$ and at equilibrium, $F = 0$.

So, $\frac{dU}{dr} = 0 \Rightarrow \frac{12A}{r^{13}} = \frac{6B}{r^7}$

$$\Rightarrow \quad r = \left(\frac{2A}{B}\right)^{1/6}$$

Test-2

1. (b) Conservation of momentum gives

$$mu = (m+m)v$$

$$u = 2v \text{ or } v = \frac{u}{2}$$

Loss of energy $= \frac{1}{2}mu^2 - \frac{1}{2}(2m)v^2$

$$= \frac{1}{2}mu^2 - m\cdot\left(\frac{u}{2}\right)^2$$

$$= \frac{1}{2}mu^2 - \frac{1}{4}mu^2$$

$$= \frac{1}{4}mu^2$$

$$\therefore \text{Loss \%} = \frac{\frac{1}{2}mu^2 - \frac{1}{4}mu^2}{\frac{1}{2}mu^2}\times 100$$

$$= 50\%$$

2. (a) According to work-energy theorem,

Work done, W = Change in KE of vehicle

$$\Rightarrow \quad W = K_f - K_i$$

$$\Rightarrow \quad Fdx = K_f - \frac{1}{2}mv_i^2$$

$$\Rightarrow \quad Fdx = K_f - \frac{1}{2}\times 75\times 20^2$$

$$\Rightarrow \quad Fdx = K_f - 15000$$

$$\Rightarrow \quad \int_{10}^{20}(-0.2x)\,dx = K_f - 15000$$

$$\Rightarrow \quad \left[-0.2\cdot\frac{x^2}{2}\right]_{10}^{20} = K_f - 15000$$

$$[-0.1x^2]_{10}^{20} = K_f - 15000$$

$\Rightarrow -0.1\times 20^2 + 0.1\times 10^2 = K_f - 15000$

$\Rightarrow \quad -40+10 = K_f - 15000$

$\Rightarrow \quad K_f = 14970\text{ J}$

$= 14.97\times 10^3$ J

$= 14.97 \simeq 15$ kJ

3. (a) Mass, $m = 2$ kg

Height, $h = 40$ cm

Force constant, $k = 1960$ N/m

The spring is compressed by, is determined by using

$$\frac{1}{2}kx^2 = mg(h+x)$$

$$\frac{1}{2}\times 1960\times x^2 = 2\times 9.8(0.40+x)$$

$$980x^2 = 7.84 + 19.6x$$

$$980x^2 - 19.6x - 7.84 = 0$$

On solving, we get

$$x = 10\text{ cm}$$

4. (b) Loss in potential energy of spring = Gain in kinetic energy of ball

$$\frac{1}{2}kx^2 = \frac{1}{2}mv^2$$

$$\frac{90}{10^{-2}}\times(12\times 10^{-2})^2 = 16\times 10^{-3}v^2$$

$$\Rightarrow \quad v = 90\text{ m/s}$$

5. (a) At $\frac{h}{2}$, PE $= \frac{mgh}{2}$

KE = TE – PE

$$= mgh - \frac{mgh}{2} = \frac{mgh}{2}$$

Hence, PE = KE

$\therefore$ A → 1.

TE = PE + KE is constant everywhere in free fall.

$\therefore$ D → 2.

At height $\frac{h}{3}$, PE $= \frac{mgh}{3}$

$$\text{KE} = mgh - \frac{mgh}{3} = \frac{2mgh}{3} = 2\text{ PE}$$

$\therefore$ C → 4.

At height $\frac{2h}{3}$, PE $= \frac{2mgh}{3}$

$$\text{KE} = \frac{mgh}{3} = \frac{\text{PE}}{2}$$

or PE = 2KE

$\therefore$ B → 3.

6. (a) Workdone = mgh (independent of type of motion)

Gravitational force is conservative force.

Hence, $\Delta W = -\Delta U$ (valid only for conservative forces)

$$= -[0 - mgh]$$

$$\Rightarrow \quad \Delta W = mgh$$

7. (a) Initial momentum of particle $= mv_0$

Final momentum of system (particle + pendulum) = $2mv$

By law of conservation of momentum,

$\Rightarrow mv_0 = 2mv$

$\Rightarrow v = \frac{v_0}{2}$

Initial kinetic energy of the system

$$= \frac{1}{2}(2m)v^2 = \frac{1}{2}(2m)\left(\frac{v_0}{2}\right)^2$$

If the system rises up to height h then PE = $2mgh$

By the law of conservation of energy,

$$\frac{1}{2}(2m)\left(\frac{v_0}{2}\right)^2 = 2mgh \Rightarrow h = \frac{v_0^2}{8g}$$

8. (c) According to given graph,

Initial velocity of car, $v_i = 10$ m/s

Final velocity of car, $v_f = 0$ m/s

$\therefore$ According to work-energy theorem,

Work done on the car

= Change in kinetic energy of car

$$= \frac{1}{2}m(v_f^2 - v_i^2)$$

$$= \frac{1}{2}\times 100\times(0^2 - 10^2)$$

$$= \frac{1}{2}\times 100\times(-100)$$

$$= -5\times 10^3\text{ J}$$

9. (a) Work done under conservative force in a closed path is zero.

10. (a) According to work-energy theorem,

Kinetic energy = Work against gravity + Work against friction

Thus, using the figure given below, we have

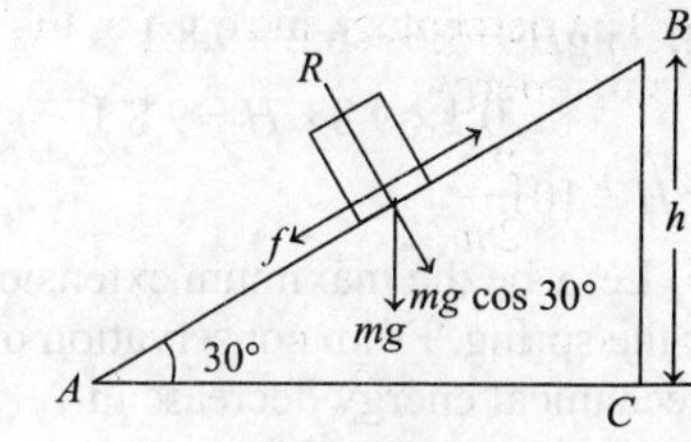

$$\frac{1}{2}mv^2 = mgh + \mu R\cdot AB$$

$$\Rightarrow \frac{1}{2}mv^2 = mgh$$

$$+\mu\, mg\cos 30°\cdot\frac{h}{\sin 30°}$$

$$\left[\because AB = \frac{h}{\sin 30°} \text{ and } R = mg\cos 30°\right]$$

$$\Rightarrow \frac{1}{2}\times m\times(10)^2 = mgh$$

$$+\mu mg\cot 30°\times h$$

$$\Rightarrow \quad h = \frac{50}{11.732} = 4.26\text{ m}$$

11. (a) Loss of energy of block = Work done against friction + Energy stored in spring

Let x = Spring's full compression, then

$$\mu_k(mg)(BC+x) = \frac{1}{2}mv^2 - \frac{1}{2}kx^2$$

V=0

A B C x D

$\Rightarrow 0.2\,(0.5)\,(10)\,(1.14+x)$

$$= \frac{1}{2}(0.5)(3^2) - \frac{1}{2}(4)(x^2)$$

$\Rightarrow \quad 2(1.14+x) = 0.5\times 9 - 4x^2$

$\Rightarrow \quad 2.28 + 2x = 4.5 - 4x^2$

or $2x^2 + x - 0.61 = 0$

$\Rightarrow \quad x = 0.3$ m

So, distance covered by block

$= AB + BC + x$

$= 2 + 1.14 + 0.3 = 3.44$ m

12. (c) If the maximum height reached by the body is H, on reaching, its PE $= mgH$.

This should be equal to the total energy at any instant.

i.e. $mgH = 3.6 + 6.2 = 9.8$ J

$$0.1 \times 9.8 \times H = 9.8 \text{ J}$$

or $H = 10$ m

13. (b) Let x be the maximum extension of the spring. From conservation of mechanical energy decrease in gravitational potential energy = increase in elastic potential energy

$$\therefore \; Mg\,x = \frac{1}{2}kx^2 \quad \text{or} \quad x = \frac{2Mg}{k}$$

14. (a) By work-energy theorem,

$$(\text{WD})_{\text{total}} = K_f - K_i = \frac{1}{2}m(v^2 - u^2)$$

$$= \frac{1}{2} \times 40000 \left[0^2 - \left(72 \times \frac{5}{18} \right)^2 \right]$$

$$= -800 \times 10^4 \text{ J}$$

Now, because 90% of total energy is lost.

$$\therefore (\text{WD})_{\text{net}} = (1 - 0.9) \times (\text{WD})_{\text{total}}$$

$$\therefore (\text{WD})_{\text{net}} = -0.1 \times 800 \times 10^4 \text{ J}$$

As, $\text{WD} = \int F dx = -\int k \cdot x dx$

$$= -\frac{1}{2}kx^2$$

$$\therefore \; -0.1 \times 800 \times 10^4 = -\frac{k \cdot (1)^2}{2}$$

$$= 16 \times 10^5 \text{ N/m}$$

15. (b) Here, $\frac{1}{2}mv^2 = \frac{1}{2}kx^2$

$$\Rightarrow \; x = v\sqrt{\frac{m}{k}} \Rightarrow x = 10\sqrt{\frac{0.1}{1000}} = 0.1 \text{ m}$$

16. (b) In this case, three forces are acting on the object

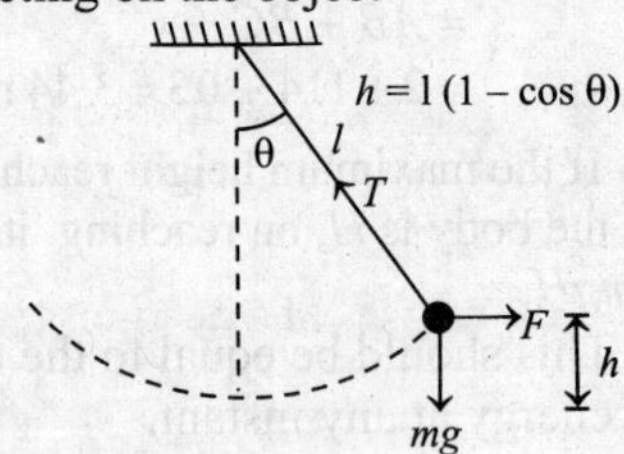

(i) Tension (T),

(ii) Weight (mg) and

(iii) Applied force (F)

Using work-energy theorem,

$$W_{\text{net}} = \Delta \text{KE}$$

$$\text{or } W_T + W_{mg} + W_F = 0 \quad \ldots\text{(i)}$$

as $\Delta\,\text{KE} = 0$

because $K_i = K_f = 0$

Further, $W_T = 0$, as tension is always perpendicular to displacement.

$$W_{mg} = -mgh$$

$$\text{or} \quad W_{mg} = -mgl\,(1 - \cos\theta)$$

Substituting these values in Eq. (i), we get

$$W_F = mgl\,(1 - \cos\theta)$$

17. (b) Initial kinetic energy of the block when the bullet strikes

$$= \frac{1}{2}(m + M)v^2$$

Due to this kinetic energy, the block will rise to a height h. Its potential energy $= (m + M)gh$

So, from the law of conservation of energy,

$$\frac{1}{2}(M + m)v^2 = (M + m)gh$$

$$\Rightarrow \; \frac{v^2}{2} = gh$$

Initial velocity of the bullet,

$$v = \sqrt{2gh}$$

18. (d) If there is no air drag, then maximum height,

$$H = \frac{u^2}{2g} = \frac{14 \times 14}{2 \times 9.8} = 10 \text{ m}$$

Due to air drag, ball reaches up to height 8 m only.

So, loss in energy is given as

$$= mg(10 - 8)$$

$$= 0.8 \times 9.8 \times 2 = 15.68 \text{ J}$$

19. (c) Potential energy of the mass at a height above the earth's surface

$$= \frac{75}{100} \times 12 = 9 \text{ J}$$

Now, kinetic energy of the mass at the end of fall $= \frac{1}{2}mv^2$

Applying law of conservation of energy,

$$\frac{1}{2}mv^2 = 9$$

$$\Rightarrow \; v = \sqrt{\frac{2 \times 9}{m}}$$

$$= \sqrt{\frac{18}{1}} = \sqrt{18} \text{ ms}^{-1}$$

20. (a) Let a ball is projected vertically downward with velocity v from height h.

Total energy at point

$$A = \frac{1}{2}mv^2 + mgh$$

During collision, loss of energy is 50% and the ball rises up to same height.

It means it posses only potential energy at same level.

$$50\% \left(\frac{1}{2}mv^2 + mgh \right) = mgh$$

$$\Rightarrow \; \frac{1}{2}\left(\frac{1}{2}mv^2 + mgh \right) = mgh$$

$$\Rightarrow \; v = \sqrt{2gh} = \sqrt{2 \times 10 \times 10}$$

$$\Rightarrow \; v = 20 \text{ m/s}$$

21. (b) Work done = Change in (KE + PE)

= Gain in KE + Gain in PE

$$W = \frac{1}{2} \times 10 \times 1^2 + 10 \times 9.8 \times 10$$

$$= 5 + 980 = 985 \text{ J}$$

22. (a) From conservation of energy,

Total energy at A = Total energy at C

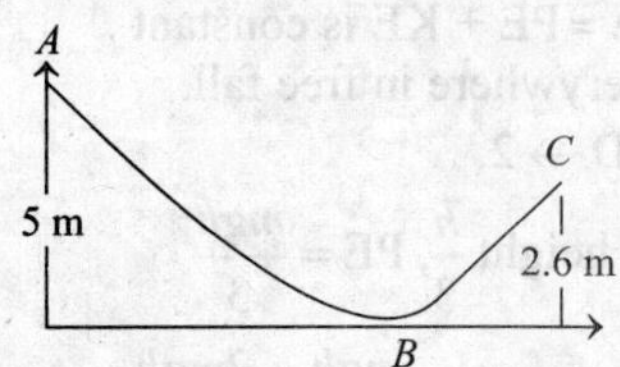

$$m \times 10 \times 5 + \frac{1}{2}m \times 4^2 = m \times 10 \times 2.6 + \frac{1}{2}mv^2$$

$$\Rightarrow \; \frac{1}{2}mv^2 = m \times 10\,(5 - 2.6) + \frac{1}{2}m \times 4^2$$

$$\Rightarrow \quad \frac{v^2}{2} = 10 \times 2.4 + 8$$

$$= 24 + 8 = 32$$

$$\Rightarrow \quad v = \sqrt{64} = 8 \text{ ms}^{-1}$$

23. (c) From work-energy theorem,

$FS = \Delta \text{KE}$ in $S \propto$ loss in KE

$$K_1 = \frac{1}{2} mv^2,$$

$$K_2 = \frac{1}{2} m\left(\frac{v}{2}\right)^2 = \frac{1}{8} mv^2$$

Now, work done over 15 cm is

$$W_1 = K_2 - K_1 = \frac{3}{8} mv^2$$

Resistive force, $F = \frac{W_1}{d_1} = \frac{mv^2}{0.4}$

Work done to stop,

$$W_2 = -\frac{1}{8} mv^2$$

$$-\frac{1}{8} mv^2 = -\frac{MV^2}{0.4} \times S_2$$

$$S_2 = \frac{0.4}{8} = 0.05 \text{ m}$$

$$S = 5 \text{ cm}$$

24. (b) Given, force,

$$\mathbf{F} = (4\hat{\mathbf{i}} + 4\hat{\mathbf{j}}) \text{N}$$

$$\mathbf{r}_1 = 0\hat{\mathbf{i}} + 0\hat{\mathbf{j}}$$

$$\mathbf{r}_2 = \hat{\mathbf{i}} + \hat{\mathbf{j}}$$

$$\Delta \mathbf{r} = \mathbf{r}_2 - \mathbf{r}_1 = \hat{\mathbf{i}} + \hat{\mathbf{j}}$$

Initial speed, $v_1 = 2 \text{ ms}^{-1}$

From work-energy theorem, we have

$$\Delta W = \Delta K$$

$$\Rightarrow \mathbf{F} \cdot \Delta \mathbf{r} = \frac{1}{2} m(v_2^2 - v_1^2)$$

$$\Rightarrow (4\hat{\mathbf{i}} + 4\hat{\mathbf{j}}) \cdot (\hat{\mathbf{i}} + \hat{\mathbf{j}}) = \frac{1}{2} \times 1(v_2^2 - 4)$$

$$\Rightarrow \quad 4 + 4 = \frac{1}{2}(v_2^2 - 4)$$

$$\Rightarrow \quad v_2^2 = 20$$

$$\Rightarrow \quad v_2 \simeq 4.5 \text{ ms}^{-1}$$

25. (c) PE at the point of release = KE on reaching ground

$$\Rightarrow mgh = \frac{1}{2} mv^2$$

The forces acting on the sphere during penetration are weight mg downward and resistance R upward.

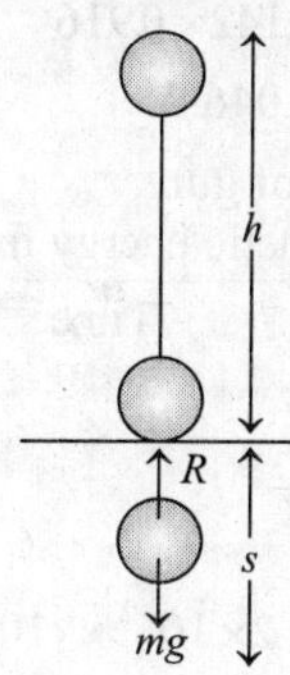

From work-energy theorem,

$$(R - mg) S = \frac{1}{2} mv^2 = mgh$$

$$\Rightarrow RS = mg(h + S)$$

$$\Rightarrow R = mg\left(1 + \frac{h}{S}\right)$$

Test-3

1. (b) Power delivered to the body

$$P = F.v = mav$$

Since, body undergoes one-dimensional motion and is initially at rest, so

$$v = 0 + at$$

$$\therefore \quad P = ma^2 t$$

or $\quad P \propto t$

2. (d) In an elastic collision, both the momentum and kinetic energy remain conserved but this rule is not for individual bodies, but for the system of bodies before and after the collision. Collision in which there occurs some loss of kinetic energy, is called inelastic collision.

3. (b) After impact, the mass and block move together and come to rest after a distance of 40 m.

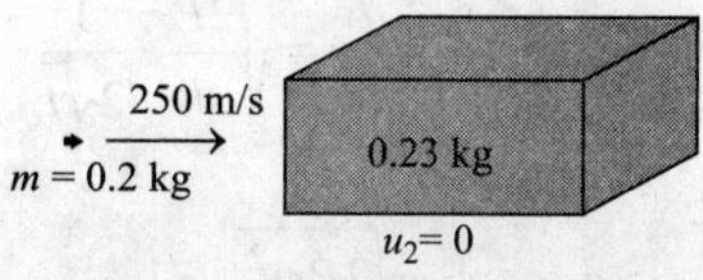

By using conservation of momentum,

$$m_1 u_1 + m_2 u_2 = m_1 v_1 + m_2 v_2$$

$$\Rightarrow 0.02 \times 250 + 0.23 \times 0 = 0.02v + 0.23v$$

$$\Rightarrow \quad 5 = v(0.25)$$

$$\Rightarrow \quad \frac{500}{25} = v$$

$$\Rightarrow \quad v = 20 \text{ ms}^{-1}$$

Now, according conservation of energy,

$$\frac{1}{2} Mv^2 = \mu Rd$$

$$\frac{1}{2} \times 0.25 \times 400 = \mu \times 0.25 \times 9.8 \times 40$$

$$\Rightarrow \quad \mu = 0.51$$

4. (a) In a quick collision, the t is small. As $F \times t =$ constant, force involved is large.

5. (a) Momentum conservation,

$$8 \times 10 + 28 \times 0 = 8 \times 0 + 28 \times v$$

$$\Rightarrow \quad 80 = 28v$$

$$\Rightarrow \quad v = 2.85 \text{ m/s}$$

6. (c) When $M_1 = M_2$, velocities are exchanged. So, total energy of M_1 is transferred to M_2.

7. (c) Given, $m = 0.1 \text{ kg}$, $v = 5 \text{ m/s}$, $\theta = 60°$

Force is equal to rate of change of momentum,

Initial momentum,

$$\mathbf{p}_i = mv\sin\theta\hat{\mathbf{i}} + mv\cos\theta\hat{\mathbf{j}}$$

Final momentum,

$$\mathbf{p}_f = -mv\sin\theta\hat{\mathbf{i}} + mv\cos\theta\hat{\mathbf{j}}$$

$$\mathbf{F} = \frac{\Delta \mathbf{p}}{\Delta t} = \frac{-2 \times 0.1 \times 5 \sin 60°}{2 \times 10^{-3}}$$

Force on the ball, $\mathbf{F} = -250\sqrt{3}$ N

Here, negative sign indicates direction of force.

8. (d) By the principle of conservation of linear momentum,

$$Mv = mv_1 + mv_2$$

$$\Rightarrow \quad Mv = 0 + (M - m)v_2$$

$$v_2 = \frac{Mv}{M - m}$$

9. (b) When target is very light and at rest, then after head on elastic collision, it moves with double speed of projectile i.e., the velocity of body of mass m will be $2v$.

10. (a) If the masses in a head-on elastic collision are the same, their velocities switch places.

Consequently, the first body begins to move with velocity v after the collision.

11. (a) As we know,
Pendulum bob of mass m is suspended at rest, then

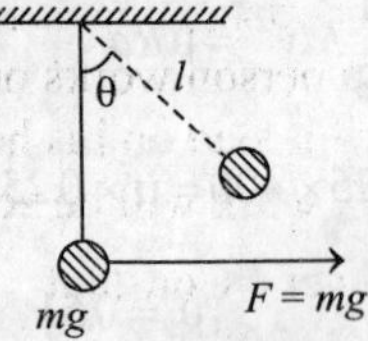

Let angular deflection be θ and velocity be v. From work-energy theorem,

$$\frac{1}{2}mv^2 = -mg(1-\cos\theta) + Fl\sin\theta$$
$$= mgl[-1+\cos\theta+\sin\theta]$$

When $v = 0$, then maximum angular deflection $\theta = 90°$.

12. (d) Power $= \dfrac{\text{Work done}}{\text{Time}}$

$$= \frac{\text{Pressure} \times \text{Volume}}{\text{Time}}$$
$$= \frac{4000 \times 1\times 10^{-6}}{1} = 4\times 10^{-3}$$
$$= 0.004 \text{ W}$$

13. (d) Power delivered,

$$P = \mathbf{F}\cdot\mathbf{v} = mav$$
$$P = Mv\frac{dv}{dT}$$
$$\Rightarrow \quad PT = \frac{Mv^2}{2} \quad \text{Or } P = \frac{1}{2}\frac{Mv^2}{T}$$

14. (b) As truck is moving on an inclined plane, only component of weight ($mg\sin\theta$) will oppose the upward motion.

Power = Force × Velocity

$$= mg\sin\theta \times v$$
$$= 30000\times 10\times\left(\frac{1}{100}\right)\times\frac{40\times 5}{18}$$
$$= 33333.33 \text{ W}$$
$$\approx 33300 \text{ W}$$

15. (c) Given, mass of a man,

$$m_1 = 80 \text{ kg}$$

Mass of other man, $m_2 = 70$ kg

$$P = \frac{mgh}{t} \Rightarrow \frac{P_1}{P_2} = \frac{m_1}{m_2}\times\frac{t_2}{t_1}$$

[As, h = constant]

$$\therefore \frac{P_1}{P_2} = \frac{80}{70}\times\frac{11}{12}$$
$$= 1.142\times 0.916$$
$$= 1.046 \text{ W}$$

16. (a) Power of gun

$$= \frac{\text{Total kinetic energy fired by bullet}}{\text{Time}}$$
$$= \frac{n\times\frac{1}{2}mv^2}{t}$$
$$= \frac{380\times\frac{1}{2}\times 2\times 10^{-2}\times(100)^2}{60}$$
$$= 6.3\times 10^2 \text{ W}$$

17. (d) Given, speed, $v = 7.2$ km/h

$$= 7.2\times\frac{5}{18} = 2 \text{ m/s}$$

Slope is given 1 in 20, so $\sin\theta = \dfrac{1}{20}$

When a man and cycle move up, then component of weight opposes its motion.

i.e. $F = mg\sin\theta$

$$P = F\times v = mg\sin\theta\, v$$
$$= 100\times 9.8\times\left(\frac{1}{20}\right)\times 2$$
$$= 98 \text{ W}$$

18. (b) Power $= \dfrac{W}{t} = \dfrac{mgh}{t} = \dfrac{800\times 12}{8}$

$$= 1.2 \text{ kW}$$

19. (a) Power is given by,

$$P = \frac{dW}{dt}$$
$$W = P\times t = \frac{1}{2}mv^2$$

So, $\sqrt{\dfrac{2Pt}{m}} = v$

Hence, $a = \dfrac{dv}{dt} = \sqrt{\dfrac{2P}{m}}\cdot\dfrac{1}{2\sqrt{t}}$

So, force

$$F = ma = \sqrt{\frac{2Pm^2}{m}}\cdot\frac{1}{2\sqrt{t}}$$
$$= \sqrt{\frac{Pm}{2t}}$$

20. (a) Minimum velocity of lowest point for completing circle is

$$u_{\min} = \sqrt{5gl}$$

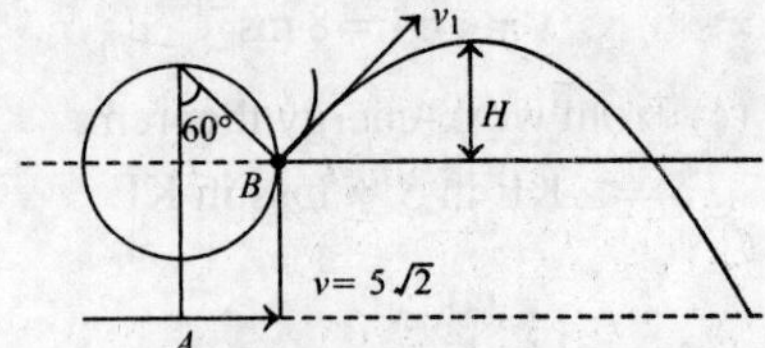

$$u = 5\sqrt{2} \text{ m/s}, \; l = 1 \text{ m}$$
$$u = u_{\min} = \sqrt{5gl}$$
$$= \sqrt{5\times 10\times 1}$$
$$= 5\sqrt{2} \text{ m/s}$$

Condition to complete the whole circle is satisfied

$$H_{\max} = 2l = 2 \text{ m}$$

21. (a) Power $= \dfrac{\text{Work}}{\text{Time}} = \dfrac{mgh}{t}$

$$0.392\times 10^3 = \frac{m\times 9.8\times 10}{60}$$
$$\Rightarrow \quad m = 240 \text{ kg}$$

22. (d) Power $= \dfrac{\text{Work}}{\text{Time}}$

Work = Gain in PE + Gain in KE

$$200\times 1 = 2\times 9.8\times 10 + \frac{1}{2}\times 2\times v^2$$

On solving, we get

$$\Rightarrow \quad v = 2 \text{ ms}^{-1}$$

23. (d) $P = \left(\dfrac{dm}{dt}\right)v^2$

$$= 5\times(1.5)^2 = 11.25 \text{ W}$$

24. (c) Using, $\Delta K = \Delta W$

$$\frac{1}{2}mv^2 - 0 = mgl$$
$$\Rightarrow \quad v^2 = 2gl$$
$$\Rightarrow \quad v = \sqrt{2gl}$$

25. (d) Here, $\mathbf{v} = \dfrac{\Delta\mathbf{x}}{\Delta t} = \dfrac{3\hat{\mathbf{i}}+4\hat{\mathbf{j}}+5\hat{\mathbf{k}}}{4}$

So, power = $\mathbf{F}\cdot\mathbf{v}$

$$= \frac{(2\hat{\mathbf{i}}+3\hat{\mathbf{j}}+4\hat{\mathbf{k}})\cdot(3\hat{\mathbf{i}}+4\hat{\mathbf{j}}+5\hat{\mathbf{k}})}{4}$$
$$= \frac{6+12+20}{4} = 9.5 \text{ W}$$

Chapter Break Thru

1. (a) At extreme position, $v=0$

At vertical position,

$$T_1 = mg\cos\theta$$

From work-energy theorem

$$T_2 = mg + 2mg(1-\cos\theta)$$

Given, $T_2 = 2T_1$

i.e., $mg(3-2\cos\theta) = 2mg\cos\theta$

$$= 3-2\cos\theta = 2\cos\theta$$

$$\Rightarrow \cos\theta = \frac{3}{4}$$

2. (b) According to work-energy theorem,

$$\frac{1}{2}mu^2 - mgL(1-\cos\theta) = \frac{1}{2}mv^2$$

$$\Rightarrow v = \sqrt{u^2 - 2gL(1-\cos\theta)}$$

and tension,

$$T - mg\cos\theta = \frac{mv^2}{L}$$

$$T = mg\cos\theta + \frac{m}{L}(u^2 - 2gL(1-\cos\theta))$$

$$T = \frac{mu^2}{L} - 2mg + 3mg\cos\theta$$

Here, $\theta = 0°$ at bottom

and $u = \sqrt{5gL}$

$$T = \frac{m\sqrt{(5gL)^2}}{L} - 2mg + 3mg(1)$$

Thus, $T = 6mg$

3. (a) If $v_b < \sqrt{2gr}$, then the particle will not rise upto the horizontal level.

4. (c) Here, $n = \frac{360}{60} = 6$ bullets/s

Velocity, $v = 600\,\text{ms}^{-1}$

$M = ?$

Power of gun = Power of bullets

$$5.4\times 10^3 = \frac{1}{2}(nm)v^2$$

$$2\times 5400 = 6\times m\times (600)^2$$

$$m = \frac{2\times 5400}{6\times 600\times 600}$$

$$m = \frac{1}{200}\text{ kg}$$

$$m = \frac{1000}{200}\times 10^{-3}\text{ kg}$$

$$m = 5\times 10^{-3}\text{ kg}$$

$$m = 5\text{ g}$$

5. (a) For stable equilibrium, U = min. Thus, graph (a) is correct for stable nature of molecules.

6. (b) $W = mgh = 60\times 9.8\times (25/100)$

$$= 147\text{ J}$$

Energy in one minute

$$= 147\times 40 = 5880$$

$$P = \frac{5880}{60} = 98\text{ W}$$

7. (c) Power $= \frac{\text{Work done}}{\text{Time}} = \frac{v^2t^2}{T^2t}$

$$\text{Power} \propto \frac{v^2t}{T^2}$$

8. (b) Both Statement I and Statement II are correct.

By using Einstein equation for energy which is $E = mc^2$

where, E is energy of particle.

m = mass of the object/ particle

c = speed of light in vacuum.

9. (a) In simple pendulum, tension is always perpendicular to displacement. Hence, work done is zero.

10. (d) Total height climbed

Total height = number of steps × height of each step

$$= 20\times 0.25 = 5\text{ m}$$

Force $= mg = (70+40)\times 9.8$

$$= 1078\text{ N}$$

Now, work done is given by

$$W = f\times h$$

$$= 1078\times 5 = 5390\text{ J}$$

So, the work done in climbed in 5390 J.

11. (c) $E_k = \frac{p^2}{2m}$

or $\sqrt{E_k} \propto p$ or $\sqrt{E_k} \propto \frac{1}{\left(\frac{1}{p}\right)}$

Cleary, the graph will be rectangular hyperbola.

12. (c) $F = kx^2$

$$W = \int_{x_1}^{x_2} \mathbf{F}\cdot d\mathbf{x} = \int_{x_1}^{x_2} kx^2\,dx\cos 60°$$

$$W = \frac{k}{2}\left[\frac{x^3}{3}\right]_{x_1}^{x_2}$$

$$= \frac{k}{6}[x_2^3 - x_1^3]$$

13. (b) Work done, $W = \mathbf{F}\cdot\mathbf{s} = Fs\cos\theta$, when a person works on a horizontal road with load on his head, then $\theta = 90°$, work will be zero.

14. (d) Power = Constant

$$\Rightarrow mv\frac{dv}{dt} = \text{Constant}$$

$$\Rightarrow \int mv\,dv = \int dt$$

$$\Rightarrow \frac{mv^2}{2} \propto t \text{ or } v \propto \sqrt{t}$$

$$\Rightarrow \frac{dx}{dt} \propto \sqrt{t}$$

$$\Rightarrow \int dx \propto \int \sqrt{t}\,dt$$

$$\Rightarrow x \propto t^{\frac{3}{2}}$$

15. (b)

$\frac{l}{10}$

$\frac{m}{5}$

$$w = mgh$$

$$= \frac{m}{5}\times g\times \frac{l}{10}$$

$$w = \frac{mgl}{50}$$

16. (a) Given, $U(r) = \frac{a}{r^{12}} - \frac{b}{r^6}$

At dissociation, $F = 0$, $r = r_0$

Here, $F = \frac{-\partial U}{\partial r} = \frac{-12a}{r_0^{13}} + \frac{6b}{r_0^7} = 0$

$$\Rightarrow \frac{12a}{r_0^{13}} = \frac{6b}{r_0^7} \Rightarrow r_0^6 = \frac{2a}{b}$$

Putting this value in equation of potential energy, we get

$$U(r) = \frac{ab^2}{4a^2} - \frac{b\times b}{2a}$$

$$= \frac{b^2}{4a} - \frac{b^2}{2a} = \frac{-b^2}{4a}$$

17. (b) Given, $U = 8x^2 - 4x + 400$

In equilibrium, $F = 0$

$$\Rightarrow \frac{\partial U}{\partial x} = 16x - 4 = 0$$

or $x = \frac{4}{16}$

$\Rightarrow \quad x = 0.25 \text{ m}$

18. (b) Work done in process $= \Delta K$

$$= \frac{1}{2} \times 2.05 \times 10^6 \ [625 - 25]$$

$$= 300 \times 2.05 \times 10^6$$

$$\text{Power} = \frac{W}{t} = \frac{300 \times 2.05}{300} \times 10^6$$

$$= 2.05 \text{ MW}$$

19. (b) From $x = 0$ to $x = a$,

$$F = -\frac{\partial U}{\partial x} = -\text{ Constant}$$

For $x > a$,

$$F = \frac{-\partial U}{\partial x} = 0$$

20. (a) The given figure is

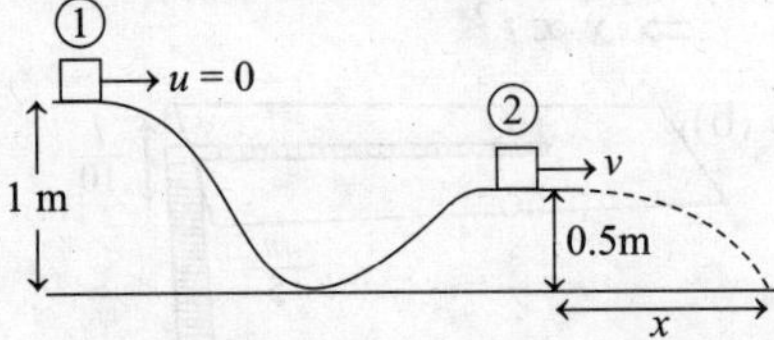

From law of conservation of energy, $mg(1) = \frac{1}{2} mv^2 + mg\,(0.5)$

$\Rightarrow \quad v^2 = 2g(1 - 0.5) = g$

Also, $\quad t = \frac{x}{v}$

$\because \quad y = \frac{1}{2} gt^2$

$\Rightarrow 0.5 = \frac{gx^2}{2\,v^2} = \frac{10x^2}{2(10)}$

$\Rightarrow x^2 = 1 \Rightarrow \quad x = 1 \text{m}$

21. (d) A body tries to remain in state of its minimum potential energy.

22. (c) $K = 4p$

But $K = \frac{1}{2} pv$

$\Rightarrow 4p = \frac{1}{2} pv$ or $v = 8 \text{ m/s}$

23. (c) For constant force

$$\Delta K = \Delta W$$

$$= \text{Force} \times \text{Displacement}$$

Since, force and displacement are constant

$\Rightarrow \quad \Delta K = \text{constant}$

24. (b) Potential energy $= mgl\,(1 - \cos\theta)$

$$\therefore \text{Ratio of PE} = \frac{(1 - \cos 60^\circ)}{(1 - \cos 30^\circ)}$$

$$= \frac{1 - \frac{1}{2}}{1 - \frac{\sqrt{3}}{2}} = \frac{\frac{1}{2}}{\frac{2 - \sqrt{3}}{2}}$$

$$= 1 : (2 - \sqrt{3})$$

25. (c) % loss of energy

$$= \frac{mg\,(h_1 - h_2)}{mgh_1} \times 100$$

$$\Rightarrow \quad 40 = \frac{(30 - h_2)}{30} \times 100$$

$\Rightarrow \quad h_2 = 18 \text{ m}$

26. (b) Work done = Area under F-x curve

$$= 10 \times 2 + \frac{1}{2} \times 10 \times 2 - \frac{1}{2} \times 5 \times 2$$

$$= 20 + 10 - 5 = 25 \text{ J}$$

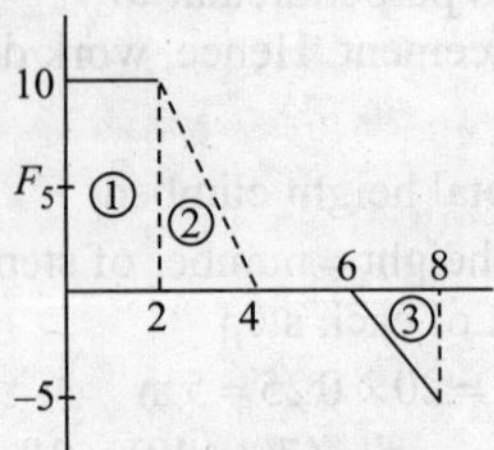

27. (a) $E = \frac{p^2}{2m} \Rightarrow E \propto p^2$

Clearly, (a) graph will be correct.

28. (a) $\frac{1}{2} mv^2 - 0^2 = mg(1)$

$\Rightarrow \quad v^2 = 2g = 20$

$\Rightarrow \quad v = 4.47 \text{ m/s}$

29. (a) $mg = kx \Rightarrow k = \frac{mg}{x}$

Energy stored $= \frac{1}{2} kx^2$

$$= \frac{1}{2} mgx$$

$$= \frac{1}{2} \times 0.2 \times 9.8 \times 0.049$$

$$= 0.048 \text{ J}$$

30. (c) $W_1 = \frac{1}{2} k\,(x^2 - 0^2)$

$$= \frac{1}{2} kx^2$$

$$W_2 = \frac{1}{2} k\,((2x)^2 - x^2)$$

$$= \frac{1}{2} kx^2 \times 3$$

$\Rightarrow \quad W_2 = 3W_1$

31. (b) Normal reaction,

$$N = m\left(g + \frac{g}{2}\right) = \frac{3}{2} mg$$

Displacement, $x = \frac{1}{2} at^2$

$$= \frac{1}{2} \times \frac{1}{2} gt^2 = \frac{1}{4} gt^2$$

Workdone $= N \times$ Displacement

$\Rightarrow \quad W = \frac{3}{8} mg^2 t^2$

32. (b) Rate of mass per second

$$\frac{dm}{dt} = \frac{dm}{dx} \cdot \frac{dx}{dt} = mv$$

Rate of KE $= \frac{1}{2} v^2 \frac{dm}{dt}$

$$= \frac{1}{2} v^2 (mv) = \frac{1}{2} mv^3$$

33. (b) $m = 1 \text{kg}$, $v = 20 \text{ m/s}$, $h = 18 \text{ m}$

$$\text{KE} = \frac{1}{2} mv^2 = 200 \text{ J}$$

$$\text{PE} = mgh = 1 \times 10 \times 18 = 180 \text{ J}$$

So, loss in energy = 200 J – 180 J

= 20 J

34. (b) Power, $P_0 = \text{constant}$

$$mv \frac{dv}{dt} = c$$

$$\Rightarrow \int v\, dv \propto \int dt$$

$\Rightarrow v^2 \propto t$ or $v \propto t^{\frac{1}{2}}$

35. (b) Displacement

$$= (4 - 2)\,\hat{\mathbf{i}} + (3 - 1)\,\hat{\mathbf{j}} - \hat{\mathbf{k}}$$

$$= 2\hat{\mathbf{i}} + 2\hat{\mathbf{j}} - \hat{\mathbf{k}}$$

Workdone $= \mathbf{F} \cdot \mathbf{d}$

$$= (3\hat{\mathbf{i}} + \hat{\mathbf{j}}) \cdot (2\hat{\mathbf{i}} + 2\hat{\mathbf{j}} - \hat{\mathbf{k}})$$

$$= 6 + 2 = 8 \text{ J}$$

36. (c) At ground, total energy $= \frac{1}{2} mv^2$

At maximum height, total energy $= mgh$

at $y = \frac{4h}{5}$,

$$PE = mg\left(\frac{4}{5}h\right) = \frac{4}{5} mgh$$

$$KE = TE - PE$$

$$= mgh - \frac{4}{5} mgh = \frac{1}{5} mgh$$

$\therefore$ KE : PE = 1 : 4

37. (b) $F = \frac{P}{v} = \frac{7000 \times 18}{40 \times 5}$

$$\left(v = 40 \times \frac{5}{18} \text{ m/s}\right)$$

$$\Rightarrow F = \frac{700 \times 18}{4 \times 5}$$

$$= 35 \times 18 = 630 \text{ N}$$

38. (a) $\frac{E_1}{E_2} = \frac{\frac{1}{2} m_1 v_1^2}{\frac{1}{2} m_2 v_2^2}$

$$= \frac{(m_1 v_1)^2 m_2}{m_1 (m_2 v_2)^2} = \frac{m_2}{m_1}$$

$$(\because m_1 v_1 = m_2 v_2)$$

39. (b) Speed (or KE) will be maximum when PE is minimum.

$$\Rightarrow \frac{\partial V(x)}{\partial x} = 0$$

$$\Rightarrow x^3 - x = 0$$

$$\Rightarrow x = \pm 1$$

at $x = 1$

$$\Rightarrow V(x) = \left(\frac{1}{4} - \frac{1}{2}\right) \text{J}$$

$$= -\frac{1}{4} \text{J}$$

$$KE = TE - PE = 2 + \frac{1}{4} = \frac{9}{4} \text{J}$$

Now, $\frac{9}{4} = \frac{1}{2} mv^2$

$$\Rightarrow v = \frac{3}{\sqrt{2}} \text{ m/s} \quad [\because m = 1 \text{kg}]$$

40. (d) $\mathbf{F} = (3xy - 5z)\,\hat{\mathbf{j}} + 4z\hat{\mathbf{k}}$

$$\mathbf{F} = (3y^{\frac{3}{2}} - 5z)\,\hat{\mathbf{j}} + 4z\hat{\mathbf{k}}$$

$$(y = x^2)$$

$$W = \int F_y \, dy = \int_0^4 3y^{\frac{3}{2}} \, dy$$

$$W = \left[\frac{3y^{\frac{5}{2}} \times 2}{5}\right]_0^4$$

$$= \frac{6}{5}[4^{\frac{5}{2}}] = \frac{6}{5} \times 32 = \frac{192}{5} \text{ units}$$

41. (b) Friction is a non-conservative force. Work done by friction depends on path length. As length of path 2 is more than that of path 1, so $W_2 > W_1$

42. (b) PE $= mgh$

$$= \frac{1}{10^3} \times 10 \times 10^3 = 10 \text{ J}$$

= Workdone by gravitational force

43. (d) $W = \mathbf{F} \cdot d\mathbf{x}$

$$= Fdx \cos 180° = 200 \times 10 \times (-1)$$

$$= -2000 \text{ J}$$

44. (b) $m = 1800 \text{ kg}$, $v = 2 \text{ m/s}$

$$g_{\text{eff}} = g + a$$

$$\Rightarrow g_{\text{eff}} = g + \frac{4000}{1800}$$

$$= 10 + \frac{20}{9} = \frac{110}{9} \text{ m/s}^2$$

$$P = \mathbf{F} \cdot \mathbf{v}$$

$$= 1800 \times \frac{110}{9} \times 2 \text{ W}$$

$$P = \frac{200 \times 110 \times 2}{746} \text{ HP}$$

$$\approx 59 \text{ HP}$$

45. (b) Work is done on body. So, its speed (KE) will increase. Hence, PE will decrease.

46. (d) $KE = \frac{1}{2} m\mathbf{v} \cdot \mathbf{v}$ or $\frac{1}{2} mv^2$

$$= \frac{1}{2} \times 200 \times (3^2 + 4^2)$$

$$= 100 \times 25$$

$$= 2500 \text{ ergs}$$

47. (b) Maximum acceleration of 1 kg block, $a_{\text{max}} = \mu g = 1 \text{ ms}^{-2}$

Common acceleration without relative motion between two blocks, $a = \frac{0.5}{3} \text{ ms}^{-2}$

Since, $a < a_{\text{max}}$

So, there will be no relative motion and blocks will move with acceleration $\frac{0.5}{3} \text{ ms}^{-2}$.

Force of friction by lower block on upper block,

$$f = ma = (1)\left(\frac{0.5}{3}\right) = \frac{1}{6} \text{ N}$$

(towards right)

$\therefore$ Work done,

$$W = f \times s = 0.5 \text{ J}$$

48. (b) A heavier body is stopped at lower (short) distance due to greater inertia.

Heavier body takes longer time to stop due to inertia of motion.

49. (b) Gravitational force is conservative $\left(\mathbf{F}_g \propto \frac{1}{r^2}\hat{\mathbf{i}}\right)$

Frictional force is non-conservative.

KE of free falling body increases due to increment in speed.

PE of free falling body decrease (mgh).

50. (b) $P = \frac{mgh}{t}$

$$= \frac{100 \times 10 \times 100}{10}$$

$$= 10 \text{ kW}$$

Practically, power is measured in horse power and 1 HP = 746 W.

Ch-06 Rotational Motion

Topical Follow Thru

Test-1

1. (b) As the mass of disc is negligible. Therefore, only moment of inertia of five particles will be considered.

$$I = \Sigma mr^2 = 5\,mr^2$$

$$= 5 \times 2 \times (0.1)^2 = 0.1 \text{ kg - m}^2$$

2. (a) As, moment of inertia of a disc,

$$I = \frac{1}{2}MR^2 = \frac{1}{2} \times (\pi R^2 t \times \rho) \times R^2$$

$\Rightarrow \quad I \propto R^4$ (as t and ρ are same)

$$\therefore \quad \frac{I_1}{I_2} = \left(\frac{R_1}{R_2}\right)^4 = \left(\frac{0.4}{0.8}\right)^4 = \frac{1}{16}$$

3. (a) Moment of inertia of particle, $I = mr^2$. So, it depends on mass as well as on position of axis of rotation.

4. (d) As per question,

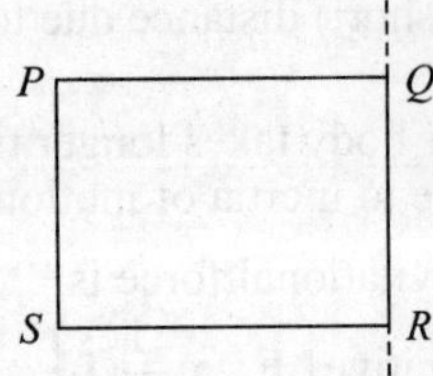

$$\frac{PQ}{QR} = 2$$

$$PQ = SR = \frac{l}{3} \text{ and } QR = PS = \frac{l}{6}$$

Similarly, $m_{PQ} = m_{SR} = \dfrac{m}{3}$

and $m_{QR} = m_{PS} = \dfrac{m}{6}$

Now, MI about side QR,

$$I = I_{PQ} + I_{SR} + I_{PS} + I_{QR}$$

$$= \frac{1}{3}m_{PQ} \times \left(\frac{l}{3}\right)^2 + \frac{1}{3}m_{SR}\left(\frac{l}{3}\right)^2 + m_{PS} \times \left(\frac{l}{3}\right)^2 + 0$$

$$= \frac{ml^2}{81} + \frac{ml^2}{81} + \frac{1}{54}ml^2$$

$$= \frac{2}{81}ml^2 + \frac{1}{54}ml^2 = \frac{7}{162}ml^2$$

5. (d) Here, the coordinate of CM of inclined rod is $(a/2, a/2)$.

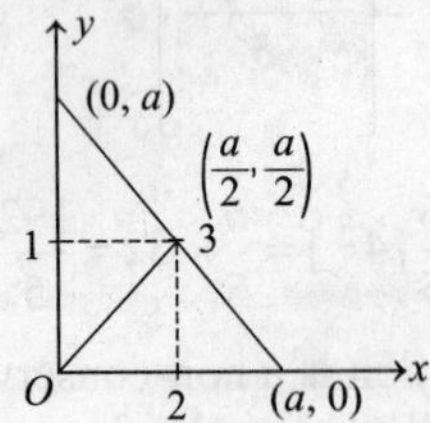

$$\because x_{CM} = \frac{m_1x_1 + m_2x_2 + m_3x_3}{m_1 + m_2 + m_3}$$

$$= \frac{m \times 0 + m\left(\frac{a}{2}\right) + m\left(\frac{a}{2}\right)}{m + m + m} = \frac{a}{3}$$

Similarly, $y_{CM} = \dfrac{a}{3}$

6. (d) Moment of inertia,

$$I = I_{CM} + mx^2$$

i.e. I-x graph is a parabola not passing through origin.

7. (d) Whole mass has equal distance from the centre O, hence $I_0 = mR^2$. Further, centre of mass of the remaining portion will be to the left of point O. More the distance of axis from centre of mass, more is the moment of inertia. Hence, $I_A > I_O$.

8. (c) As the body is rigid, therefore angular velocity of all particles will be same, i.e. $\omega =$ constant but different linear velocities.

As $\mathbf{v} = \omega \times \mathbf{r}$

and $\mathbf{r}$ is different for all particles.

9. (a) We know that, for square plate

$$I_x = I_y = \frac{ma^2}{12}$$

$$I_x + I_y = I_z$$

(perpendicular axes theorem) ...(i)

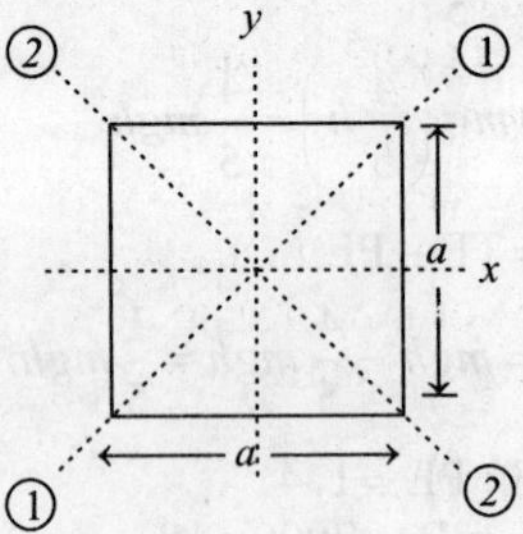

Diagonals of square are perpendicular.

$$I_{1-1} + I_{2-2} = I_z$$

$$I_{1-1} + I_{2-2} = I_x + I_y = I_z$$

By symmetry $I_{1-1} = I_{2-2}$

$$I_{1-1} = I_{2-2} = I_x = I_y = \frac{ma^2}{12}$$

For any axis passing through the centre of plate and lying in the XY-plane, moment of inertia $I = \dfrac{ma^2}{12}$.

10. (d)

From figure,

$$x_1 = \frac{l}{2}, x_2 = \frac{l}{2} + \frac{l}{2} = l$$

$$x_3 = \frac{l}{2} + \frac{l}{4} + \frac{l}{2} = \frac{5l}{4}$$

$$\therefore \quad X_{CM} = \frac{m_1x_1 + m_2x_2 + m_3x_3}{m_1 + m_2 + m_3}$$

$$= \frac{M \times \frac{l}{2} + M \times l + M \times \frac{5l}{4}}{M + M + M}$$

$$= \frac{\frac{11}{4}Ml}{3M} = \frac{11l}{12}$$

11. (d) If the origin of the coordinate system is at the centre of mass then $\mathbf{R}_{CM} = 0$, which implies that $\sum_i m_i \mathbf{r}_i = 0$

Here, $m_i\mathbf{r}_i$ represents the moment of a mass about the origin on the centre of mass.

12. (d) As the cube is a symmetrical body of uniform density. Hence, the centre of mass has to be at the geometric centre of the cube.

13. (b) As, $X_{CM} = \dfrac{m_1 \times 0 + m_2 L}{m_1 + m_2}$

$$= \frac{m_2 L}{m_1 + m_2}$$

$$Y_{CM} = \frac{m_1 \times 0 + m_2 \times 0}{m_1 \times m_2} = 0$$

$$Z_{CM} = \frac{m_1 \times 0 + m_2 \times 0}{m_1 \times m_2} = 0$$

i.e., the centre of mass is at distance $\dfrac{m_2 L}{(m_1 + m_2)}$ from m_1 internally on the line joining the two particles.

14. (d) Coordinate of the centre of mass

$$= \left(\frac{x_1 + x_2}{2}, \frac{y_1 + y_2}{2}\right)$$

$$= \left(\frac{-2+2}{2}, \frac{0+2}{2}\right) = (0, 1)$$

15. (a) The coordinates of the corners of the square are (0, 0) (2, 0) (2, 2) (0, 2). Hence,

$$X_{CM} = \frac{m_1 x_1 + m_2 x_2 + m_3 x_3 + m_4 x_4}{m_1 + m_2 + m_3 + m_4}$$

$$= \frac{2 \times 0 + 3 \times 2 + 5 \times 2 + 8 \times 0}{2 + 3 + 5 + 8}$$

$$= \frac{16}{18} = \frac{8}{9}\text{ m}$$

$$Y_{CM} = \frac{m_1 y_1 + m_2 y_2 + m_3 y_3 + m_4 y_4}{m_1 + m_2 + m_3 + m_4}$$

$$= \frac{2 \times 0 + 3 \times 0 + 5 \times 2 + 8 \times 2}{18}$$

$$= \frac{26}{18} = \frac{13}{9}\text{ m}$$

16. (b) From centre of mass of three identical sphere,

$$X_{CM} = \frac{1 \times 0 + 1 \times AB + 1 \times AC}{1 + 1 + 1}$$

$$= \frac{AB + AC}{3}$$

17. (b) Take parts 1 and 2 as two bodies of a system.

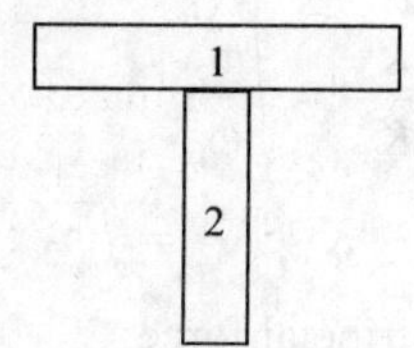

$$m_1 = l \times b \times \sigma = 8 \times 2 \times \sigma = 16\,\sigma$$

$$m_2 = l \times b \times \sigma = 6 \times 2 \times \sigma = 12\sigma$$

From, $y_1 = 0\text{ m}$, $y_2 = 1 + 3 = 4\text{ m}$

$$\therefore Y_{CM} = \frac{m_1 y_1 + m_2 y_2}{m_1 + m_2}$$

$$= \frac{16\sigma \times 0 + 12\sigma \times 4}{16\sigma + 12\sigma}$$

$$= 1.7\text{ m}$$

18. (a) Radius of gyration is given by

$$K = \sqrt{\frac{r_1^2 + r_2^2 + \ldots r_n^2}{n}}$$

Thus, it depends on axis of rotation.

19. (b) $I = 3\left[\dfrac{Ml^2}{3}\right] = Ml^2$

20. (a) K = radius of gyration

$$= \sqrt{\frac{I}{m}} = \sqrt{\frac{\frac{7}{5}mR^2}{m}} = \sqrt{\frac{7}{5}}R$$

21. (b) For hollow sphere,

$$K_H = \sqrt{\frac{I}{m}} = \sqrt{\frac{\frac{2}{3}mR^2 + mR^2}{m}}$$

$$= \sqrt{\frac{5}{3}}R$$

For solid sphere,

$$K_S = \sqrt{\frac{I}{m}} = \sqrt{\frac{\frac{2}{5}mR^2 + mR^2}{m}} = \sqrt{\frac{7}{5}}R$$

$$\therefore \quad \frac{K_H}{K_S} = \sqrt{\frac{25}{21}} = \frac{5}{\sqrt{21}}$$

22. (c) The given situation of rod is shown below.

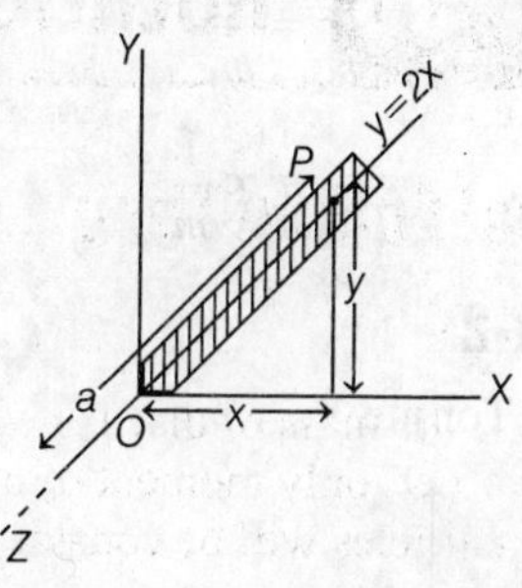

Suppose a mass particle situated at point $P(x, y)$.

Hence, distance of mass particle from X-axis $= x$, distance of mass particle from Y-axis $= y$ and distance of mass particle from Z-axis,

$$a = \sqrt{x^2 + y^2}$$

Clearly, $a > x$

$a > y$

Since, moment of inertia,

$I \propto (\text{distance})^2$

Hence, moment of inertia of the rod is maximum about Z-axis.

23. (a) Position of CM of system will be

$$\mathbf{r}_{CM} = \frac{m_1\mathbf{r}_1 + m_1\mathbf{r}_2}{m_1 + m_2}$$

$$= \frac{1(\hat{\mathbf{i}} + 2\hat{\mathbf{j}} + \hat{\mathbf{k}}) + 3(-3\hat{\mathbf{i}} - 2\hat{\mathbf{j}} + \hat{\mathbf{k}})}{1 + 3}$$

$$= -2\hat{\mathbf{i}} - \hat{\mathbf{j}} + \hat{\mathbf{k}}$$

$$\Rightarrow |\mathbf{r}_{CM}| = |-2\hat{\mathbf{i}} - \hat{\mathbf{j}} + \hat{\mathbf{k}}|$$

$$= \sqrt{2^2 + 1^2 + 1^2} = \sqrt{6}$$

Only option (a) has a magnitude $\sqrt{6}$.

$$\because \sqrt{1^2 + 2^2 + 1^2} = \sqrt{6}$$

24. (c)

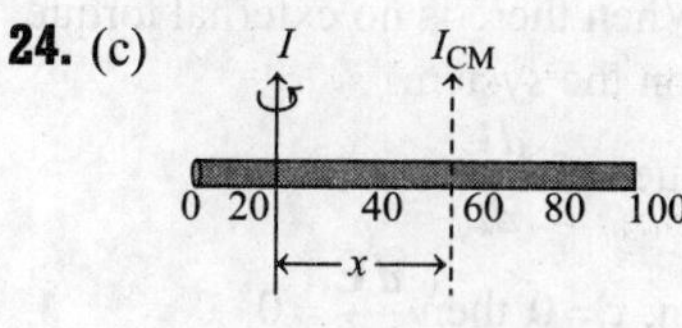

$$I = I_{CM} + mx^2 = \frac{ml^2}{12} + mx^2$$

$$= m\left(\frac{(1)^2}{12} + (0.3)^2\right)$$

$$= 0.6\left(\frac{1}{12} + 0.09\right) = 0.104\text{ kg-m}^2$$

25. (c) Here, $m_1 r_1 = m_2 r_2$

$$\Rightarrow \quad \frac{r_1}{r_2} = \frac{m_2}{m_1}$$

$$\therefore \quad r \propto \frac{1}{m}$$

Test-2

1. (b) Torque, $\tau_0 = mg \times r_\perp$

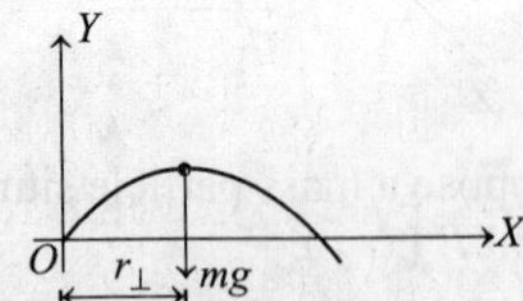

As, $r_\perp$ is continuously increasing or torque is continuously increasing on the particle.

Hence, angular momentum is continuously increasing.

2. (b) The initial velocity is $\mathbf{v}_i = v\hat{\mathbf{e}}_y$ and after reflection from the wall, the final velocity is $\mathbf{v}_f = -v\hat{\mathbf{e}}_y$. The trajectory is described as position vector $\mathbf{r} = y\hat{\mathbf{e}}_y + a\hat{\mathbf{e}}_z$.

Hence, the change in angular momentum

$= \mathbf{r} \times m(\mathbf{v}_f - \mathbf{v}_i)$

$= (y\hat{\mathbf{e}}_y + a\hat{\mathbf{e}}_z) \times (-mv\hat{\mathbf{e}}_y - mv\hat{\mathbf{e}}_y)$

$= (y\hat{\mathbf{e}}_y + a\hat{\mathbf{e}}_z) \times (-2mv\hat{\mathbf{e}}_y)$

$[\because \hat{\mathbf{e}}_y \times \hat{\mathbf{e}}_y = 0 \text{ and } \hat{\mathbf{e}}_z \times \hat{\mathbf{e}}_y = -\hat{\mathbf{e}}_x]$

$= 2mva\hat{\mathbf{e}}_x$

3. (a) In free space, there will be no torque acting on the sphere, therefore the angular momentum of the sphere will not be affected.

$$\tau = \frac{dL}{dt} = 0$$

i.e. $L = \text{constant}$

4. (b) When there is no external torque acts on the system.

$$\text{Torque, } \tau = \frac{d\mathbf{L}}{dt}$$

$$\text{When, } \tau = 0, \text{ then } \frac{d\mathbf{L}}{dt} = 0$$

$\Rightarrow L = \text{constant}$ is conserved.

5. (d) Given,

Path of radius, $R_1 = 0.8$ m

Angular velocity = 44 rad/s

Path of radius, $R_2 = 1$ m

Angular momentum,

$$L = mR^2\omega = \text{constant}$$

$$\frac{\omega_2}{\omega_1} = \left(\frac{R_1}{R_2}\right)^2 = \left(\frac{0.8}{1}\right)^2 = 0.64$$

$$\omega_2 = 44 \times 0.64 = 28.16 \text{ rad/s}$$

6. (a) Angular speed of a body changes $\omega_1 \to \omega_2$ (without torque)

Ratio of radii of gyration,

$$L = I\omega = MK^2\omega = \text{constant}$$

$$\therefore \quad \frac{K_1}{K_2} = \sqrt{\frac{\omega_2}{\omega_1}}$$

Thus, $\quad K_1 : K_2 = \sqrt{\omega_2} : \sqrt{\omega_1}$

7. (a) Centripetal force,

$$F = \frac{mv^2}{r} = \frac{m}{r} \times \frac{L^2}{m^2 r^2} = \frac{L^2}{mr^3}$$

8. (a) As we know,

$$\text{Torque } (\tau) = \frac{d\mathbf{L}}{dt} \text{ and } L = I\omega$$

Hence, both statements are correct.

9. (b) Angular momentum = Linear momentum × Perpendicular distance of line of action of linear momentum from axis of rotation $= mv \times l$

10. (a) Central force passes through axis of rotation, so torque is zero. If no external force is acting on a particle, the angular momentum of a particle is constant.

11. (a) Here,

Change in angular momentum,

$$\Delta L = L_f - L_i = 4A_0 - A_0 = 3A_0$$

Time take, $\Delta T = 4$ s

$$\text{Torque,} \quad \tau = \frac{3A_0}{4}$$

12. (c) Equating torque about centre of mass,

$$N_A x = N_B (d - x)$$

$$N_A + N_B = mg$$

Solving, we get

$$N_A = \frac{W(d - x)}{d}$$

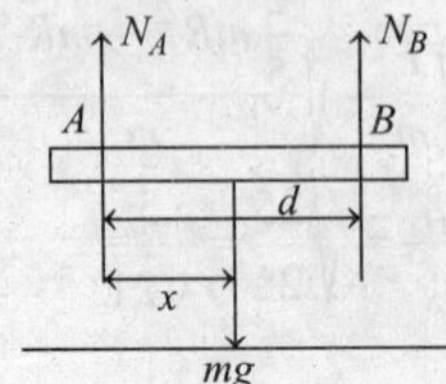

13. (c) As we know,

$$\alpha = \frac{2\pi(n_2 - n_1)}{t}$$

$$= \frac{2\pi\left(0 - \frac{60}{60}\right)}{60} = \frac{-2\pi}{60}$$

$$= \frac{-\pi}{30} \text{ rad/s}^2$$

$$\therefore \quad \tau = I\alpha = -\frac{15 \times \pi}{30} = -\frac{\pi}{2} \text{ N-m}$$

Negative sign indicates that the torque is applied in opposite direction to stop the wheel's.

14. (c) Torque = Force × Perpendicular distance

$$\tau = 1.9 \times 6 = 11.4 \text{ N-m}$$

Force required,

$$F = \frac{\tau}{d} = \frac{11.4}{0.8} = 14.25 \text{ N}$$

15. (b) Force, $\mathbf{F} = -F\hat{\mathbf{k}}$

Torque about the point (1, – 1),

$$\mathbf{r} = (\hat{\mathbf{i}} - \hat{\mathbf{j}})$$

i.e. $\tau = \mathbf{r} \times \mathbf{F} = (\hat{\mathbf{i}} - \hat{\mathbf{j}}) \times (-F\hat{\mathbf{k}})$

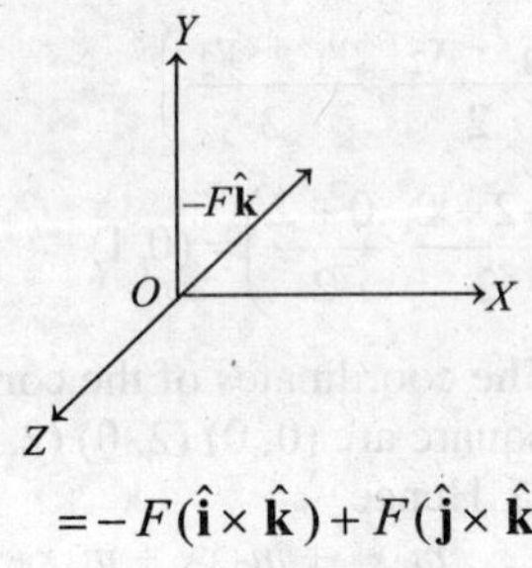

$$= -F(\hat{\mathbf{i}} \times \hat{\mathbf{k}}) + F(\hat{\mathbf{j}} \times \hat{\mathbf{k}})$$

$$= -F(-\hat{\mathbf{j}}) + F(\hat{\mathbf{i}}) = F\hat{\mathbf{j}} + F\hat{\mathbf{i}}$$

Thus, $\tau = F(\hat{\mathbf{i}} + \hat{\mathbf{j}})$

16. (b) Angular momentum = Linear momentum × Perpendicular distance

$$L_P = p_P \times d$$

and $L_Q = p_Q \times d$

As, linear momentum are equal.

i.e., $p_P = p_Q = mv$

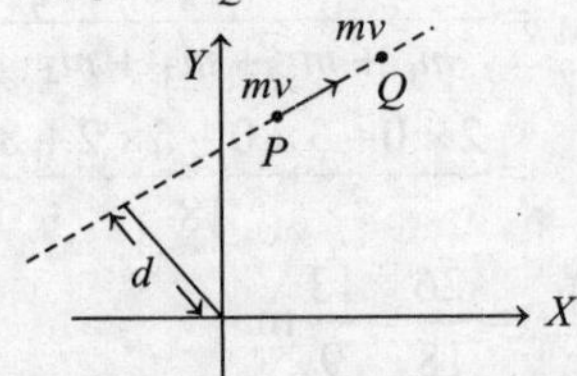

Therefore, $\quad L_P = L_Q$

17. (a) Angular momentum is the product of moment of inertia and angular velocity ω

$L = I \times \omega \quad \therefore \quad L \propto \omega$

Thus, graph between L and ω will be straight line with constant slope.

18. (b) As, $L = I\omega = \left(\frac{1}{2}Mr^2\right)\omega$

Here, $\omega = 2\pi n = 2\pi \times \frac{120}{60}$

$= 4\pi$ rad/s

$\therefore \quad L = \frac{1}{2} \times 20 \times (0.5)^2 \times 4\pi$

$= 10\pi = 31.4$ kg.m^2/s

19. (a) Both Statement I and Statement II are correct.

$\tau_{ext} = I \cdot \frac{d^2\theta}{dt^2} = I\alpha$

$\tau_{ext} = |\mathbf{r} \times \mathbf{F}|$

Dimension of $\tau = \text{MLT}^{-2} \times \text{L}$

$= [\text{ML}^2\text{T}^{-2}]$

20. (a) We know that, $\tau = I\alpha$ thus,

$\alpha = \frac{\tau}{I} = \frac{(5M_0 g)l - (2M_0 g)(2l)}{(5M_0)l^2 + (2M_0)(2l)^2}$

$= \frac{g}{13l}$

21. (c) As, $\alpha = \frac{\omega_2 - \omega_1}{t} = \frac{90 - 0}{t} = \frac{90}{t}$

and $\tau = I\alpha$

$\Rightarrow 60 = 3 \times \frac{90}{t} \Rightarrow t = 4.5$ s

22. (b) Moment of inertia,

$I = \frac{MR^2}{2} = \frac{50 \times (1/2)^2}{2}$

$= \frac{50}{8}$ kg - m^2

Angular acceleration

$\alpha = \frac{\omega_2 - \omega_1}{t} = \frac{0 - 300 \times 2\pi}{60 \times 5}$

$= -2\pi$ rad s^{-2} (negative sign indicates retardation)

Torque, $\tau = I\alpha = \frac{50}{8} \times 2\pi$

$= \left(\frac{25\pi}{2}\right)$ N-m

23. (a) We know that, torque = rate of change of angular momentum.

So, change of angular momentum = torque × time

Here, change in angular momentum is same for path.

i.e. $\tau_1 t_1 = \tau_2 t_2$ as $\tau_1 = \tau_2$, $t_1 = t_2$

24. (b) Angular momentum, $L = mvr$

$= \frac{1}{1000} \times 1 \times 1$

$= 10^{-3}$ kg m^2 s^{-1}

25. (c) Angular momentum of a particle about a point is given by

$\mathbf{L} = \mathbf{r} \times \mathbf{p} = m(\mathbf{r} \times \mathbf{v})$

For $\mathbf{L}_O$

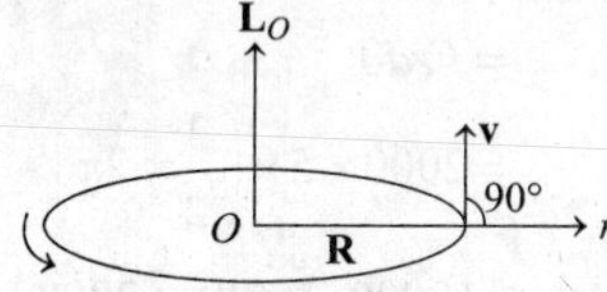

$|\mathbf{L}| = (mvr \sin \theta)$

$= m(R\omega)(R)\sin 90° =$ constant

Direction of $\mathbf{L}_O$ is always upwards. Therefore, complete $\mathbf{L}_O$ is constant, both in magnitude as well as direction.

For $\mathbf{L}_P$

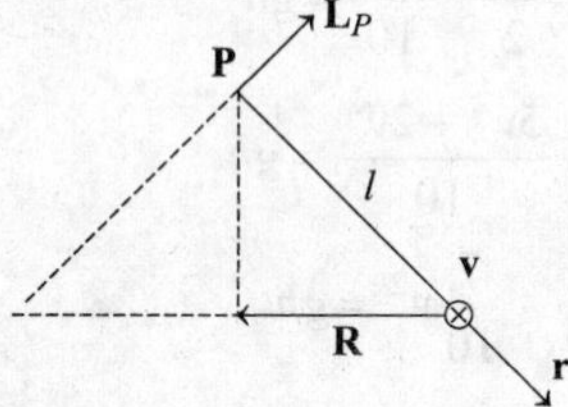

$|\mathbf{L}_P| = (mvr \sin \theta)$

$= (m)(R\omega)(l)\sin 90° = (mRl\omega)$

Magnitude of $\mathbf{L}_P$ will remain constant but direction of $\mathbf{L}_P$ keeps on changing.

Test-3

1. (a) Rolling occurs only on account of friction which is a tangential force capable of providing torque when the inclined plane is perfectly smooth, it will simply slip under the effect of its own weight. Once the perfect rolling begins, force of friction becomes zero. Here, the work done against friction is zero.

2. (b) As, $v = \sqrt{\frac{2gh}{1 + \frac{I}{MR^2}}}$

Hence, velocity is independent of the inclination of the plane and depends only on height h through which body descends.

But, $t = \frac{1}{\sin\theta}\sqrt{\frac{2h}{g}\left(1 + \frac{I}{MR^2}\right)}$

it also depend upon inclination. Thus, greater inclination lesser will be the time of descend.

3. (b) Using law of conservation of energy, $\frac{1}{2}Mv^2 + \frac{1}{2}I\omega^2 = Mgh$

$\frac{1}{2}Mv^2 + \frac{1}{2} \times \frac{2}{5}MR^2 \frac{v^2}{R^2} = Mgh$

$\left(\frac{1}{2} + \frac{1}{5}\right)Mv^2 = Mgh$

$\frac{7}{10}v^2 = 9.8 \times h$

or $h = \frac{7}{10} \times \frac{(40)^2}{9.8}$, $h = 0.7 \times \frac{1600}{9.8}$

$h = 0.7 \times 163.26 = 114.28$ m

4. (d) Here, $L = \sqrt{2IE}$

If E are equal, then $\frac{L_1}{L_2} = \sqrt{\frac{I_1}{I_2}} = \sqrt{\frac{I}{4I}}$

$\frac{L_1}{L_2} = \frac{1}{\sqrt{4}} = \frac{1}{2}$

5. (b) In rolling, all points of rigid body have the same angular speed but different linear speed.

6. (b)

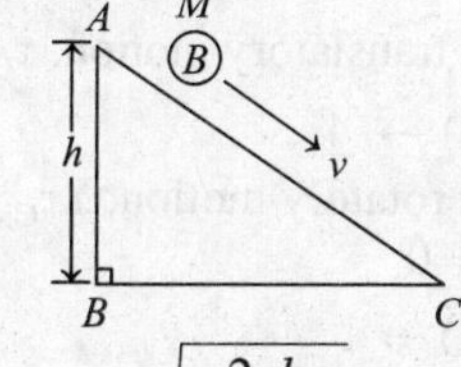

Here, $v = \sqrt{\frac{2gh}{1 + \frac{K^2}{R^2}}}$

$= \sqrt{\frac{2gh}{1 + \frac{1}{2}}} = \sqrt{\frac{4}{3}gh}$

7. (d) Given, $\frac{K_T}{K}=\frac{\frac{1}{2}mv^2}{\frac{1}{2}mv^2+\frac{1}{2}I\omega^2}$

$$=\frac{\frac{1}{2}mv^2}{\frac{1}{2}mv^2+\frac{1}{2}\times\frac{2}{5}mr^2\times\frac{v^2}{r^2}}$$

$(\because I=\frac{2}{5}mr^2$ and $v=r\omega)$

$$\therefore \quad \frac{K_T}{K}=\frac{1}{1+\frac{2}{5}}=\frac{5}{7}$$

Thus, $K_T : K = 5:7$

8. (a) Total energy,

$$K=K_R+K_T=\frac{1}{2}I\omega^2+\frac{1}{2}mv^2$$

$$=\frac{1}{2}\left(\frac{2}{5}mr^2\right)\omega^2+\frac{1}{2}mr^2\omega^2$$

$$=\frac{1}{5}mr^2\omega^2+\frac{1}{2}mr^2\omega^2$$

$$=\frac{7}{10}mr^2\omega^2$$

Now, rotational kinetic energy

$$K_R=\frac{1}{2}I\omega^2=\frac{1}{5}mr^2\omega^2$$

$$\therefore \quad \frac{K_R}{K}=\frac{\frac{1}{5}mr^2\omega^2}{\frac{7}{10}mr^2\omega^2}=\frac{2}{7}$$

9. (a) A→3, B→4, C→1, D→2

Moment of linear momentum is called angular momentum and it is an axial vector.

$\therefore$ (A) → 3

In pure translatory motion, $\tau_{CM}=0$

$\therefore$ (B) → 4

In pure rotatory motion, $\Sigma\tau_{CM}\neq 0$ but $\Sigma F_{CM}=0$

$\therefore$ (C) → 1

In rolling motion, $\Sigma\tau_{CM}\neq 0$ and $\Sigma F_{CM}\neq 0$

$\therefore$ (D) → 2

10. (c) Here,

$$\frac{\text{Rotational kinetic energy}}{\text{Translatory kinetic energy}}=\frac{\frac{1}{2}mv^2\frac{k^2}{R^2}}{\frac{1}{2}mv^2}=\frac{k^2}{R^2}=\frac{2}{5}$$

$$\left\{\because I_{\text{sphere}}=\frac{2}{5}MR^2\right\}$$

11. (b) Kinetic energy for rotational motion,

$$K_R=50\%\ K_T$$

$$\frac{1}{2}mv^2\left(\frac{K^2}{R^2}\right)=\frac{50}{100}\times\frac{1}{2}mv^2$$

$$\therefore \quad \frac{K^2}{R^2}=\frac{1}{2}$$

i.e. Body will be solid cylinder.

12. (c) Work done,

$$W=\tau\times d\theta$$

$$=Frd\theta$$

$$=2000\times5\times\left(\frac{3}{2}\times2\pi\right)$$

$$=10000\times6.28=62800\text{ J}$$

13. (a) From conservation of energy,

Potential energy = Translational KE + Rotational KE

$$mgh=\frac{1}{2}mv^2+\frac{1}{2}\left(\frac{2}{5}\right)mR^2\frac{v^2}{R^2}$$

$$\frac{v^2}{2}+\frac{2v^2}{10}=gh$$

$$\frac{5v^2+2v^2}{10}=gh$$

or $\quad \frac{7}{10}v^2=gh$

$$v^2=\frac{10}{7}gh$$

or $\quad v\geq\sqrt{\frac{10}{7}gh}$

14. (c) Total kinetic energy

$$K_M=K_R+K_T$$

This equation is correct for any body which is rolling without slipping. For the ring and hollow cylinder only $K_R=K_P$

i.e. $K_M=2K_T$

15. (b) As $I_1>I_2$

For constant angular momentum

$$I\propto\frac{1}{\omega} \qquad [\because L=I\omega]$$

So, $\omega_1<\omega_2$

Hence, $\frac{1}{2}I_1\omega_1^2<\frac{I_2\omega_2^2}{2}$

or $\quad E_1<E_2$

Chapter Break Thru

1. (c) Angular momentum is given by

$$\mathbf{L}=\mathbf{r}\times m\mathbf{v}$$

where, **r** is directed towards the axis of rotation and **v** acts tangentially. Thus cross-product is along the direction perpendicular to the plane of rotation.

2. (c) Moment of inertia of a disc about a parallel axis

$$I_{R/2}=I_{CM}+md^2$$

$$=35+m\left(\frac{R}{2}\right)^2$$

$$\left(\because I_{CM}=\frac{mR^2}{4}=35\text{ kg - m}^2\right)$$

$$=35+\frac{mR^2}{4}=70\text{ kg - m}^2$$

3. (d) Kinetic energy, $E=\frac{1}{2}I\omega^2$

$$=\frac{1}{2}L\times2\pi n$$

$$\therefore \quad E\propto L\times n$$

$$\Rightarrow \quad \frac{L_2}{L_1}=\frac{E_2}{E_1}\times\frac{n_1}{n_2}$$

$$\frac{L_2}{L_1}=\left[\frac{(E_1/2)}{E_1}\right]\times\left[\frac{n_1}{2n_1}\right]$$

$$L_2\Rightarrow\frac{L_1}{4}=\frac{L}{4}$$

4. (c)

CM
O_1
O_2
$R/6$

Remaining portion of disc can be considered as a combination of two masses.

M at O_1 and $\frac{M}{2}$ at O_2

$\therefore$ x-coordinate of CM is

$$x=\frac{M\times O-\frac{M}{4}\times\frac{R}{2}}{M-\frac{M}{4}}=\frac{-R}{6}$$

So, distance of CM of given disc and nearest point on circumference

$$=R-\frac{R}{6}=\frac{5R}{6}$$

5. (c)

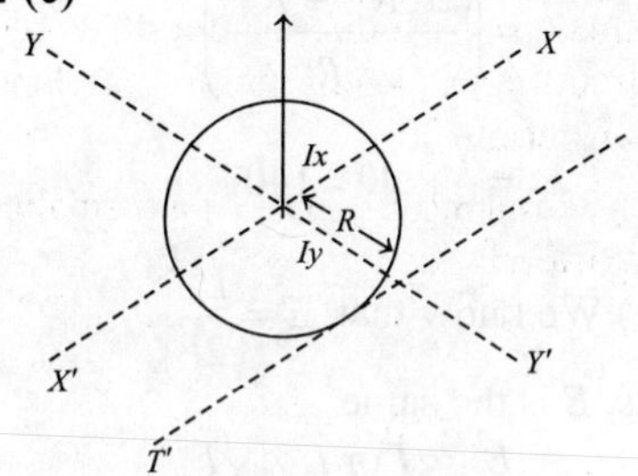

According to theorem of perpendicular, $I_z=I_x+I_y$

As $I_x=I_y$

$\therefore$ $2I_x$ or $2I_y=I_z$

or I_x or $I_y=\frac{I_z}{2}=\frac{MR^2}{2}$

Now, according to theorem of parallel,

$$I_{TT'}=I_x+MR^2$$

$$=\frac{MR^2}{2}+MR^2=\frac{3}{2}MR^2$$

6. (a) $E_i=\frac{1}{2}I_1\omega_1^2+\frac{1}{2}\left(\frac{I_1}{2}\right)\left(\frac{\omega_1}{2}\right)^2$

$$=\frac{9}{16}I_1\omega_1^2 \quad \ldots(i)$$

Now, using angular momentum conservation law (assuming angular velocity after contact is ω)

Initial angular momentum = Final angular momentum

$$I_1\omega_1+\left(\frac{I_1}{2}\right)\left(\frac{\omega_1}{2}\right)=I_1\omega'+\frac{I_1}{2}\omega'$$

Using Eq. (i),

$\Rightarrow$ $\omega'=\frac{5}{6}\omega_1$

Now, final kinetic energy is

$$E_f=\frac{1}{2}I_1\omega'^2+\frac{1}{2}\left(\frac{I_1}{2}\right)\omega'^2$$

$$=\frac{1}{2}I_1\left(\frac{5}{6}\omega_1\right)^2+\frac{1}{4}I_1\left(\frac{5}{6}\omega_1\right)^2$$

$$=\frac{25}{48}I_1\omega_1^2$$

Hence, change in KE,

$$=\frac{25}{48}I_1\omega_1^2-\frac{9}{16}I_1\omega_1^2$$

$$=-\frac{1}{24}I_1\omega_1^2$$

7. (b) Moment of inertia,

$$I=I_{CM}+MR^2$$

$$=\frac{2}{5}MR^2+MR^2$$

$$=\frac{7}{5}MR^2$$

$$MK^2=\frac{7}{5}MR^2$$

$$\therefore \quad K=\sqrt{\frac{7}{5}}R=\sqrt{\frac{7}{5}}\times 35\,\text{cm}$$

$$=7\sqrt{35}\,\text{cm}$$

8. (a) The moment of inertia of a flywheel, $I=MR^2$

Taking log both sides, we get

$$\log I=\log M+2\log R$$

Differentiating it, we get

$$\frac{dI}{I}=0+2\frac{dR}{R}$$

$$100\times\frac{dI}{I}=2\left[\frac{dR}{R}\times 100\right]$$

$\therefore$% increase in moment of inertia

$$=2\times 1=2\%$$

9. (b) Areal velocity of a planet is $\frac{\Delta A}{\Delta t}=\frac{L}{2m}$

As there is no external torque, L is constant for a planet in it's orbit.

10. (c) Torque = Force × Perpendicular distance of line of action from the axis of rotation.

So, we need a maximum torque for easy opening or shutting the door by applying minimum force. But the force is maximum and torque is minimum near the hinge. Thus, Statement I is correct but Statement II is incorrect.

11. (a) Moment of inertia of rod AB about the centre and perpendicular to plane, $I_{AB}=\frac{ML^2}{12}$

Moment of inertia of rod CD about the centre and perpendicular to plane.

$$I_{CD}=\frac{ML^2}{12}$$

Now, MI of the cross about line EF,

$$I_{EF}=I_{AB}+I_{CD}$$

$$=\frac{ML^2}{12}+\frac{ML^2}{12}=\frac{ML^2}{6}$$

12. (b) Power required by mill,

$$P=\tau\omega=180\times 200=36\,\text{kW}$$

Let 36 kW = 75% of x,

then $x=\frac{4\times 36}{3}\,\text{kW}=48\,\text{kW}$

$\therefore$ Motor must deliver 48 kW.

13. (a) We know that, $I=\frac{2}{5}MR^2$

But, mass = density × volume

$$=d\times\frac{4}{3}\pi R^3$$

Then, $I=\frac{2}{5}\times d\times\frac{4}{3}\pi R^3\times R^2$

$$=\frac{8\pi}{15}dR^5$$

14. (d) Assuming the ring in the XY-plane,

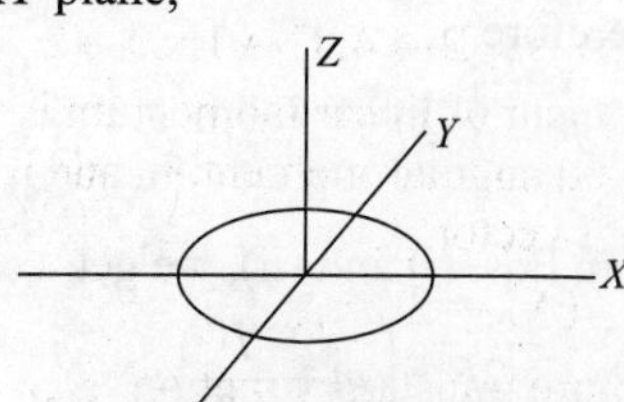

$I_x=I_y=I$ (given)

From perpendicular axes theorem,

$$I_z=I_x+I_y=2I$$

15. (a) From parallel axes theorem,

$$I=I_G+Mr^2$$

$$=10+2\times 1^2$$

$$=12\,\text{kg-m}^2$$

16. (a) $\therefore$ $I=mK^2=10(2)^2=40\,\text{kg-m}^2$

Kinetic energy of rotation,

$$K_R = \frac{1}{2} I\omega^2$$

$$= \frac{1}{2}(40)(5)^2 = 500\,\text{J}$$

17. (b) Moment of inertia of each of rod AC and BC about the given axis OO',

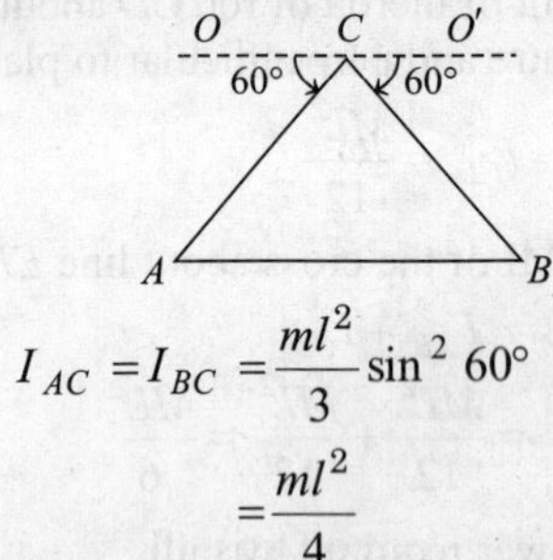

$$I_{AC} = I_{BC} = \frac{ml^2}{3}\sin^2 60°$$

$$= \frac{ml^2}{4}$$

and MI of AB about given axis OO',

$$I_{AB} = m\left(\frac{\sqrt{3}}{2}\right)^2 = \frac{3}{4}ml^2$$

Hence, $I = I_{AC} + I_{BC} + I_{AB}$

$$= \frac{ml^2}{4} + \frac{ml^2}{4} + \frac{3}{4}ml^2$$

$$= \frac{5}{4}ml^2$$

18. (b) For translational motion between shell and horizontal surface,

$$F + f = ma \quad \ldots\text{(i)}$$

For rotational motion,

$$FR - fR = I\alpha = I \times \frac{a}{R} \quad (\because a = R\alpha)$$

Therefore,

$$F - f = I \times \frac{a}{R^2} \quad \ldots\text{(ii)}$$

From Eqs. (i) and (ii), we get

$$2F = \left(m + \frac{I}{R^2}\right)a$$

$$\left(m + \frac{2}{3}m\right)a = \frac{5}{3}ma$$

$$\left(\because I_{\text{shell}} = \frac{2}{3}MR^2\right)$$

$$F = \frac{5}{6}ma$$

Thus, $a = \dfrac{6F}{5m}$

19. (c) If r_1 and r_2 are the distances of particles and masses m_1 and m_2, respectively, from their centre of mass.

$$r_1 = \frac{m_2 d}{m_1 + m_2}$$

and $r_2 = \dfrac{m_1 d}{m_1 + m_2}$

$$I = m_1 r_1^2 + m_2 r_2^2$$

$$= \frac{m_1 m_2 d^2 (m_1 + m_2)}{(m_1 + m_2)^2}$$

$$= \left(\frac{m_1 m_2}{m_1 + m_2}\right)d^2$$

20. (b) As, $I = MK^2$

and $K = \sqrt{\dfrac{I}{M}} = \sqrt{\dfrac{16}{4}} = 2\,\text{m}$

21. (b) $I_{\text{ring}} > I_{\text{sphere}}$ also, radius of sphere is again, lesser than that of ring.

22. (b) We know that, $\tau = I\alpha$ and $\tau = Fl$, where l is length of the stick. Here, τ is the same.

$\Rightarrow I\alpha$ is same or α is inversely proportional to I.

Moment of inertia is less in case B, so angular acceleration is more in case B.

23. (c) For hollow sphere,

$$L_1 = I_1\omega = \frac{2}{3}M_1R^2\omega$$

For solid sphere,

$$L_2 = I_2\omega = \frac{2}{5}M_2R^2\omega$$

Given, $L_1 = L_2$

$$\frac{2}{3}M_1R^2\omega = \frac{2}{5}M_2R^2\omega \Rightarrow \frac{M_1}{M_2} = \frac{3}{5}$$

24. (a) Kinetic energy of a rolling body is $\dfrac{1}{2}Mv^2\left(1 + \dfrac{K^2}{R^2}\right)$

For ring, KE $= \dfrac{1}{2}Mv^2(1+1)$

$$(\because K^2 = R^2)$$

For disc, KE $= \dfrac{1}{2}Mv^2(1 + 1/2)$

$$(\because K^2 = R^2/2)$$

Then, ratio of their kinetic energies is $2 : 3/2 = 4 : 3$

25. (c) We know that,

Rotational KE

$$= \left(\frac{K^2}{K^2 + R^2}\right) \times \text{total energy}$$

Total kinetic energy $= \left(\dfrac{K^2 + R^2}{K^2}\right) \times$ rotational KE

For sphere, $K^2 = \dfrac{2}{5}R^2$

Then, total KE

$$= \left(\frac{2/5R^2 + R^2}{2/5R^2}\right) \times 40$$

$$= \frac{7}{2} \times 40 = 140\,\text{J}$$

26. (c) We know that, $E = \dfrac{L^2}{2I}$

As, E is the same

$$L^2 \propto I \text{ or } L \propto \sqrt{I}$$

So, ratio of their angular momenta is $\sqrt{2} : \sqrt{3}$.

27. (b) When the rod is vertical, it posses PE. As it rotates and falls on to the ground, its PE converts into KE.

$$mg\frac{l}{2} = \frac{1}{2}I\omega^2$$

then $mg\dfrac{l}{2} = \dfrac{1}{2}\dfrac{ml^2}{3}\omega^2 \quad \left(\because I = \dfrac{ml^2}{3}\right)$

and $\omega = \sqrt{\dfrac{3g}{l}}$

Hence, $v = l\omega = \sqrt{3gl} \quad (\because v = \omega r)$

$$= \sqrt{3 \times 10 \times 15} = 15\sqrt{2}\ \text{ms}^{-1}$$

28. (c) $I = I_0 + md^2$

(parallel axes theorem)

$$I > I_0$$

29. (b) $I_{\text{Hollow}} > I_{\text{Solid}}$

$$\because \frac{2}{3}MR^2 > \frac{2}{5}MR^2$$

30. (b) Radius of sphere increase with increases in temperature.

$\therefore$ I increases

31. (b) Net external torque on the system is zero. Therefore, angular momentum is conserved. Force acting on the system are only conservative. Therefore, total mechanical energy of the system is also conserved.

32. (b) $L = \text{constant} \Rightarrow I_1\omega_1 = I_2\omega_2$

Kinetic energy $= \frac{1}{2}I\omega^2 = \frac{1}{2}\frac{(I\omega)^2}{I}$

$\Rightarrow \text{KE} \propto \frac{1}{I}$ Hence, body with less moment of inertia will have greater KE.

33. (d) In pure rolling, work done by friction is zero.

Friction is preventing slipping at point of contact.

So, it neither increasing nor decreasing angular or linear velocity.

Rolling sphere stops due to torque of normal reaction.

34. (c) Since, there is no external torque, angular momentum will remain conserved. The moment of inertia will first decrease till the tortoise moves from A to C and then increase as it moves from C and D. Therefore, ω will initially increase and then decrease.

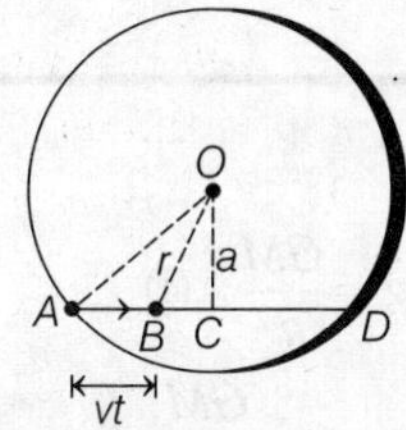

Let R be the radius of platform, m the mass of tortoise and M is the mass of platform.

Moment of inertia when the tortoise is at A

$$I_1 = mR^2 + \frac{MR^2}{2}$$

and moment of inertia when the tortoise is at B

$$I_2 = mr^2 + \frac{MR^2}{2}$$

Here, $r^2 = a^2 + [\sqrt{R^2 - a^2} - vt]^2$

From conservation of angular momentum

$$\omega_0 I_1 = \omega(t) I_2$$

Substituting the values, we can see that variation of $\omega(t)$ is non-linear.

35. (c) Velocity at a point on the circular plate (disc) $v = R\omega$, where r is the distance of point from O.

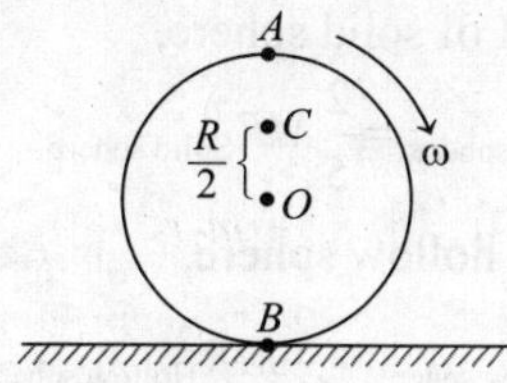

Since, $R_A = R_B$

$v_A = v_B$

Also, $R_C < R_A$ or R_B

$\Rightarrow v_A = v_B > v_C$

36. (c) Moment of inertia $= MR^2$

Torque $= \mathbf{r} \times \mathbf{F}$

Rotational kinetic energy $= \frac{1}{2}I\omega^2$

Angular momentum

$$= [MR^2\omega] = [\text{M}^1\text{L}^2\text{T}^{-1}]$$

37. (d) $t = 0\text{ s}$ to $t = 2\text{ s}$

[uniform angular acceleration]

$$\theta_1 = \omega_0 t + \frac{1}{2}\alpha t^2$$

$$= 0 + \frac{1}{2} \times 1 \times (2)^2$$

$$= 2\text{ rad}$$

$$\omega_1 = \omega_0 + \alpha t$$

$$= 0 + 1 \times 2 = 2\text{ rad/s}$$

$t = 2\text{ s}$ to $t = 6\text{ s}$

[uniform angular velocity]

$$\theta_2 = \omega_1(6 - 2)$$

$$= 2(4) = 8\text{ rad}$$

$t = 6\text{ s}$ to $t = 8\text{ s}$

[uniform angular acceleration]

$$\theta_3 = \omega_1 t - \frac{1}{2}\alpha t^2$$

$$= 2 \times 2 - \frac{1}{2} \times 1 \times (2)^2$$

$$= 4 - 2 = 2\text{ rad}$$

Total angle $= \theta_1 + \theta_2 + \theta_3$

$$= 2 + 8 + 2$$

$$= 12\text{ rad}$$

38. (d) Torque $= I\alpha$

Angular momentum $= I\omega$

Rotational kinetic energy

$$= \frac{1}{2}I\omega^2 = \frac{1}{2}L\omega$$

Work done by centripetal force $= 0$

39. (c) Rotational kinetic energy,

$$E = \frac{1}{2}I\omega^2$$

$$\Rightarrow \omega = \sqrt{\frac{2E}{I}}$$

Now, angular momentum,

$$L = I\omega = \sqrt{2EI}$$

40. (d) MI depends on axis of rotation, mass, size and shape of body.

41. (d) According to parallel axes theorem, $I = I_g + MR^2$

$$\Rightarrow I = MR^2 + MR^2 = 2MR^2$$

42. (a) $\mathbf{r} = r\hat{\mathbf{i}}$ and $\mathbf{F} = F\hat{\mathbf{j}}$, then

$$\tau = \mathbf{r} \times \mathbf{F} = r\hat{\mathbf{i}} \times F\hat{\mathbf{j}} = (rF)\hat{\mathbf{k}}$$

43. (d) MI of a solid sphere of mass M, about its diameter is $I_1 = \frac{2}{5}MR_1^2$

MI of a hollow sphere of mass M, about its diameter is $I_2 = \frac{2}{3}MR_2^2$

Given that, $I_1 = I_2$

$$\Rightarrow \frac{R_1^2}{5} = \frac{R_2^2}{3}$$

$$\therefore \frac{R_1}{R_2} = \sqrt{\frac{5}{3}}$$

44. (d) As, $I = \frac{5}{4}MR^2 = \frac{5}{4} \times 0.1 \times (0.1)^2$

$$= 1.25 \times 10^{-3}\text{ kg-m}^{-2}$$

45. (d) MI of the system,

$$I = \frac{MR^2}{2} + MR^2 = \frac{3}{2}MR^2$$

$$\Rightarrow MR^2 = \frac{2I}{3}$$

But MI of one ring of the system about the central axis and perpendicular to its plane is

$$I' = MR^2 = \frac{2I}{3}$$

46. (b) MI of a solid sphere about its tangent, $I = \frac{7}{5}MR^2$

$\Rightarrow \quad MK^2 = \frac{7}{5}MR^2$

$\Rightarrow \quad K^2 = \frac{7}{5}R^2$

or $\quad K = \sqrt{\frac{7}{5}}R$

$\therefore$ Ratio of radius of gyration of solid sphere to its radius

$= \frac{\sqrt{(7/5)}R}{R} = \sqrt{\frac{7}{5}} = \sqrt{7} : \sqrt{5}$

47. (a) Given that, $\frac{MR^2}{4} = 500$

$\Rightarrow M = \frac{500 \times 4}{(2)^2} = 500\,\text{kg}$

$\therefore$ Radius of gyration,

$K = \frac{I}{M} = \frac{500}{500} = 1\,\text{m}$

48. (a) MI of solid sphere,

$I_{\text{Solid sphere}} = \frac{2}{5}MR^2_{\text{Solid sphere}}$

MI of hollow sphere,

$I_{\text{Hollow sphere}} = \frac{2}{3}MR^2_{\text{Hollow sphere}}$

Given that,

$\frac{2}{5}MR^2_{\text{Solid sphere}} = \frac{2}{3}MR^2_{\text{Hollow sphere}}$

$\Rightarrow \quad \frac{1}{5} \times (\sqrt{15})^2 = \frac{1}{3}R^2_{\text{Hollow sphere}}$

$\therefore R_{\text{Hollow sphere}} = 3\,\text{m}$

49. (c) As, $\tau = I\alpha = 2\left[\frac{\omega_f - \omega_i}{t}\right]$

$\Rightarrow t = \frac{2 \times 100}{40} = 5\,\text{s}$

50. (d) Rotational KE $= \frac{1}{2}I\omega^2$

i.e. $\frac{1}{2} \times M \times 2gh$

$= \frac{1}{2} \times \frac{2}{5}MR^2 \times \omega^2$

$\Rightarrow \quad 5gh = R^2\omega^2$

$\Rightarrow \quad R^2 = \frac{5gh}{\omega^2}$

or $R = \frac{\sqrt{5gh}}{\omega}$

Ch-07 Gravitation

Topical Follow Thru

Test-1

1. (a) $g\left(1 - \frac{d}{R}\right) = \frac{1}{2}\frac{g}{\left(1 + \frac{h}{R}\right)^2}$

or $\quad 1 - \frac{d}{R} = \frac{1}{2\left(1 + \frac{1600}{6400}\right)^2} = \frac{16}{50}$

$\frac{d}{R} = \frac{34}{50}$

$\therefore \quad d = (6.4 \times 10^6)\left(\frac{34}{50}\right)$

$= 4.352 \times 10^6\,\text{m}$

2. (a) A point P (mass m) is situated inside the hollow spherical shell is shown in the figure.

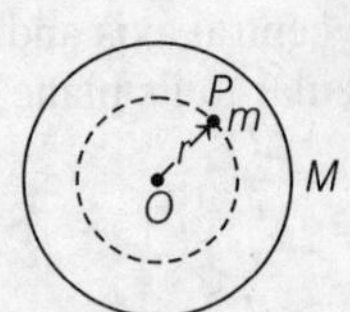

For point P inside the hollow spherical shell,

$F_P = \text{zero}$

The force of gravitation due to various region of the spherical shell be attractive and hence from symmetry, it can be seen that these forces cancel each other completely. Therefore, both Assertion and Reason are true and Reason is the correct explanation of Assertion.

3. (a) Gravitational attraction force on a particle B,

$$F_g = \frac{GM_P m}{\left(\frac{D_P}{2}\right)^2}$$

Acceleration of particle due to gravity

$$a = \frac{F_g}{m} = \frac{4GM_P}{D_P^2}$$

4. (d) Acceleration due to gravity on the earth is given by

$$g = \frac{GM}{R^2} \quad \text{...(i)}$$

$$g' = \frac{GM}{(R + 2R)^2} \quad \text{...(ii)}$$

$$= \frac{1}{9}\frac{GM}{R^2}$$

From Eqs. (i) and (ii), we get

$\Rightarrow \quad g' = \frac{g}{9}$

5. (c) Acceleration due to gravity at an altitude h is

$g_h = \frac{gR_e^2}{(R_e + h)^2}$, where R_e is the radius of the earth

$\Rightarrow g_h = \frac{9.8 \times (6400 \times 10^3)^2}{(6400 \times 10^3 + 520 \times 10^3)^2}$

$= 8.4\,\text{m/s}^2$

6. (b) We know that, $g = \frac{GM}{R^2}$

On the planet,

$$g_P = \frac{\frac{GM}{7}}{\frac{R^2}{4}} = \frac{4}{7}g$$

Hence, weight on the planet

$$= 700 \times \frac{4}{7} = 400 \text{ g wt}$$

7. (a) Acceleration due to gravity is given as, $g = \frac{GM}{R^2}$

$$\frac{g'}{g} = \frac{M'}{M} \times \frac{R^2}{R'^2}$$

$$= \frac{1}{2} \times \frac{4}{1} = \frac{2}{1} = 2:1$$

8. (a) The value of acceleration due to gravity is maximum at poles and minimum at equators i.e.,

$$g_p - g_e = g - g + R\omega^2 = R\omega^2$$

Thus, the value of ω is maximum at equator and hence, g is minimum at equator.

9. (c) A point mass m is located at the centre of the square $ABCD$. Let gravitational force between m and m_1 is F_1.

i.e. $|\mathbf{F}_1| = \left[\frac{Gmm_1}{(a/\sqrt{2})^2}\right]$

and between m and m_2 is F_2.

i.e. $|\mathbf{F}_2| = \left[\frac{Gmm_2}{(a/\sqrt{2})^2}\right]$ as shown below.

Along BD, there are two forces of same magnitude F_2 acting between m and m_2 (on B or D)

$$\mathbf{F}_{\text{net }(BD)} = \mathbf{F}_2 - \mathbf{F}_2 = 0$$

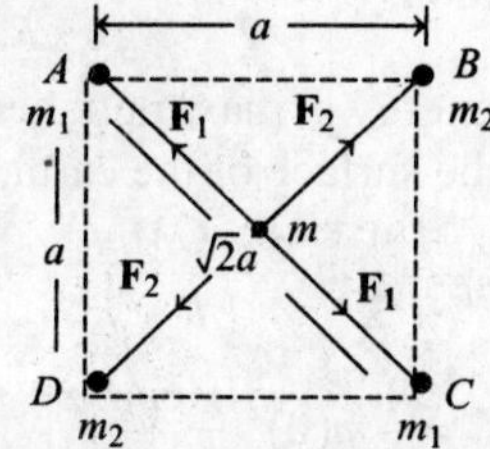

Similarly, net gravitational force along AC,

$$\mathbf{F}_{\text{net }(AC)} = \mathbf{F}_1 - \mathbf{F}_1 = 0$$

$\therefore$ Net force on m is $|\mathbf{F}_{\text{net}}|$ = zero

10. (a) The value of g at the height h from the surface,

$$g' = g\left(1 - \frac{2h}{R}\right) = 10\left(1 - \frac{2 \times 1600}{6400}\right)$$

$$= 5 \text{ ms}^{-2}$$

11. (c) Here, force,

$$F = \frac{GMm}{(2R)^2} = \frac{G \times \left(\frac{4}{3}\pi R^3 \rho\right)^2}{4R^2} \quad [m = M]$$

$$= \frac{4}{9}\pi^2 \rho^2 R^4 G$$

$$\therefore \quad F \propto R^4$$

12. (a) According to Newton's law of gravitation,

$$F \propto \frac{1}{d^2} \Rightarrow F \propto d^{-2}$$

13. (c) From Newton's law of gravitation,

$$F = \frac{GM_1M_2}{R^2} = \frac{G}{R^2} \times 100 \times 100$$

(Let $M_1 = M_2 = 100$)

$$\frac{G}{R^2} = \frac{F}{10000}$$

As 25% of mass M_1 is transferred to M_2

So, $M_1 = 75$, $M_2 = 125$

$$F' = \frac{G}{R^2} \times 125 \times 75$$

$$= \frac{G}{R^2} \times 9375$$

$$F' = \frac{F}{10000} \times 9375 = \frac{15}{16}F$$

14. (d) Gravitational force of attraction between two masses,

$$F \propto \frac{1}{r^2}$$

If r becomes double, then F reduces to $\frac{F}{4}$.

15. (c) Here, $g = \frac{GM}{R^2}$ and $M = \frac{4}{3}\pi R^3 \rho$

$$\therefore \quad g = \frac{4}{3} \times \frac{\pi R^3 \times G\rho}{R^2}$$

Thus, $\rho = \frac{3g}{4\pi RG}$

16. (b) Acceleration due to gravity at depth d is given by

$$g' = g\left(1 - \frac{d}{R}\right)$$

$$\frac{g}{n} = g\left(1 - \frac{d}{R}\right)$$

$$\Rightarrow \quad d = \left(\frac{n-1}{n}\right)R$$

17. (a) As we know, at depth d,

$$g' = g\left(1 - \frac{d}{R}\right)$$

At height h, $g' = g\left(1 - \frac{2h}{R}\right)$

At sea level, $g' = g$

So, we can say that, value of g decreases when we move either in coal mine or at the top of mountain.

18. (c) Initially, the weight of the passenger at the earth's surface, $w = mg = 60 \times 10 = 600$ N.

Finally, the weight of the passenger at the surface of mars $= 60 \times 4 = 240$ N and during the flight in between somewhere its weight will be zero because the gravitational pull of the earth and mars will be equal. Only the curve (C) represents the weight $= 0$.

So, (c) is correct option.

19. (b) Acceleration due to gravity at latitude λ is given by

$$g' = g - R\omega^2 \cos^2 \lambda$$

At 30°,

$$g_{30°} = g - R\omega^2 \cos^2 30° = g - \frac{3}{4}R\omega^2$$

$$\therefore \quad g - g_{30°} = \frac{3}{4}\omega^2 R$$

20. (a) At equator,

$$g' = g - R\omega^2 = 0$$

$$\therefore \quad \omega = \sqrt{\frac{g}{R}}$$

$$\Rightarrow \quad \frac{2\pi}{T} = \sqrt{\frac{g}{R}}$$

$$\Rightarrow \quad T = 2\pi\sqrt{\frac{R}{g}}$$

21. (d) Force due to remaining sphere = Force due to solid sphere of radius R − Force due to sphere of radius $\frac{R}{2}$

$$= \frac{GMm}{(2R)^2} - \frac{G(M/8)m}{\left(\frac{3R}{2}\right)^2}$$

$$= \frac{7}{36}\frac{GMm}{R^2}$$

22. (c)

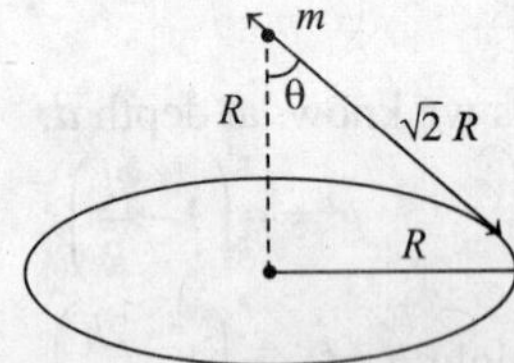

Force due to a small mass dM of ring is

$$dF = \frac{G(dM)m}{(\sqrt{2}R)^2}$$

∴Resultant force on mass m is

$$F = \int dF \cos\theta$$

$$= \int \frac{G(dM)m}{2R^2}\cdot\left(\frac{R}{\sqrt{2}R}\right)$$

$$= \frac{1}{2\sqrt{2}}\frac{GMm}{R^2}$$

23. (c) In the first case, $g = \frac{GM}{R^2}$

In the next case,

$$g' = \frac{GM}{\left(\frac{R}{2}\right)^2} = \frac{4GM}{R^2} = 4g$$

24. (d) On the surface of the earth,

$$w = \frac{GMm}{R^2}$$

On the surface of the planet,

$$w' = \frac{G(2M)m}{(R+2R)^2} = \frac{2}{9}\frac{GMm}{R^2} = \frac{2w}{9}$$

25. (c) Present value at 45° latitude is

$$g' = g - R\omega^2\cos^2 45°$$

i.e., $g' = g - \frac{R\omega^2}{2}$

If the earth stops its rotation, $\omega = 0$

then $g'' = g$ i.e., $g'' = g' + \frac{R\omega^2}{2}$

It means acceleration due to gravity increases by $\frac{R\omega^2}{2}$.

Test-2

1. (b) Let, mass of the earth = M

Mass of particle = m

Velocity with which particle moves = v

Radius of the earth = R

Force acting on particle = F

The work is stored as potential energy in the body. Thus,

$$(\text{PE})_{\text{surface}} = -\frac{GMm}{R}$$

Using conservation of mechanical energy at the surface of earth and at infinity,

$$0 = (\text{KE})_{\text{surface}} + (\text{PE})_{\text{surface}}$$

$$0 = \frac{1}{2}mv^2 + \left(-\frac{GMm}{R}\right)$$

$$v^2 = \frac{2GM}{R} \text{ or } v^2 = \frac{2GMR}{R^2}$$

Since, $\frac{GM}{R^2} = g$

∴ $v = \sqrt{2gR}$.

2. (c)

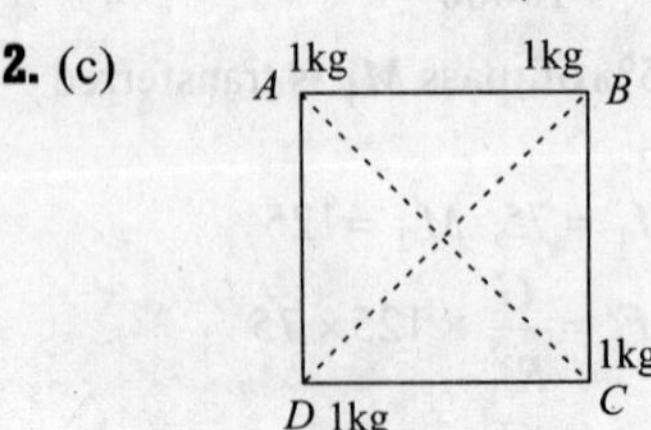

$$AC = BD = \sqrt{1^2 + 1^2} = \sqrt{2}\text{ m}$$

$$U = \left(\frac{-G\times1\times1}{AB}\right) + \left(\frac{-G\times1\times1}{AC}\right) + \left(\frac{-G\times1\times1}{AD}\right) + \left(\frac{-G\times1\times1}{BC}\right) + \left(\frac{-G\times1\times1}{BD}\right) + \left(\frac{-G\times1\times1}{CD}\right)$$

$$= \left(\frac{-G\times1\times1}{1}\right) + \left(\frac{-G\times1\times1}{\sqrt{2}}\right) + \left(\frac{-G\times1\times1}{1}\right) + \left(\frac{-G\times1\times1}{1}\right) + \left(\frac{-G\times1\times1}{\sqrt{2}}\right) + \left(\frac{-G\times1\times1}{1}\right)$$

$$= -4G - \frac{2G}{\sqrt{2}} = -2G\left(2 + \frac{1}{\sqrt{2}}\right)$$

$$= -5.4\,G$$

3. (b) Here, $E_{\text{in}} = +\frac{GMr}{R^3}$

and $E_{\text{out}} = +\frac{GM}{r^2}$

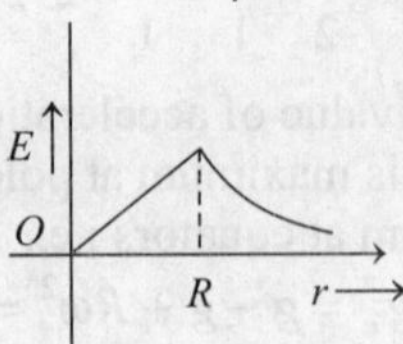

This graph is followed for both E_{in} and E_{out}, $E_{\text{in}} \propto \frac{1}{R^3}$ and $E_{\text{out}} \propto \frac{1}{r^2}$.

4. (a) The minimum energy will be $E_f - E_i$, so

$$E_i = -\frac{GMm}{R}$$

Total energy, $E_f = \frac{-GmM}{2(R+2R)}$

$$= \frac{-GmM}{2\times3R} = \frac{-GmM}{6R}$$

Then, $E_f - E_i = \frac{5GMm}{6R}$

5. (d) Given, the mass of particle = m

Velocity = kv_e

Initial energy at the time of projection, $E_i = \frac{1}{2}mv^2 - \frac{GMm}{R}$

Final energy at maximum height h from the surface of the earth,

$$E_f = \frac{1}{2}mv^2 - \frac{GMm}{R+h}$$

$$= \frac{1}{2}m(0)^2 - \frac{GMm}{R+h}$$

Using law of conservation of energy,

$$E_i = E_f$$

$$\Rightarrow \frac{1}{2}mv^2 - \frac{GMm}{R} = -\frac{GMm}{R+h}$$

$\Rightarrow \frac{1}{2}m(kv_e)^2 - \frac{GMm}{R} = \frac{-GMm}{R+h}$

$\Rightarrow \frac{1}{2}mk^2\left(\frac{2GM}{R}\right) - \frac{GMm}{R} = -\frac{GMm}{R+h}$

$\left(\because v_e = \sqrt{\frac{2GM}{R}}\right)$

$\Rightarrow \frac{k^2}{R} - \frac{1}{R} = \frac{-1}{R+h}$

$\Rightarrow \frac{1}{R+h} = \frac{1}{R} - \frac{k^2}{R}$

$\Rightarrow \frac{R}{1-k^2} = R+h$

$\Rightarrow h = \frac{R}{1-k^2} - R$

$\Rightarrow h = R\left(\frac{1}{1-k^2} - 1\right)$

$\Rightarrow h = R\left(\frac{1-1+k^2}{1-k^2}\right)$

$\Rightarrow h = R\left(\frac{k^2}{1-k^2}\right)$

6. (b) Given, gravitational potential,

$V = -5.12 \times 10^7$ J/kg

Acceleration due to gravity,

$g = 6.4 \text{ m/s}^2$

Let r be the distance of the given point from the centre of the earth.

Thus, $V = -5.12 \times 10^7 = \frac{-GM}{r}$ ...(i)

$g = 6.4 = \frac{GM}{r^2}$ ...(ii)

From Eqs. (i) and (ii), we get

$\frac{GM \times r^2}{GM \times r} = \frac{5.12 \times 10^7}{6.4}$

$\Rightarrow r = 0.8 \times 10^7$ m

$r = 8000$ km

Now, the height of the point from the earth's surface,

$h = r - R = 8000 - 6400 = 1600$ km

7. (d) For a hollow sphere,

$V_{\text{inside}} = -\frac{GM}{R}, V_{\text{outside}} = -\frac{GM}{r}$

i.e. $V \propto \frac{1}{r}$

8. (b) As, $g = -\frac{dV}{dr}$

Hence, g is gravitational field and V is gravitational potential.

Hence, the gravitational potential in the region must be constant.

9. (a) Inside a shell, gravitational potential, $V = -\frac{GM}{R} = $ constant.

Gravitational field at $A = 0$.

As r increases, V increases and E decreases. So, as one moves from C to D gravitational field decreases.

10. (a) According to law of conservation of energy,

TE at surface = TE at height

$(\text{KE} + \text{PE})_{\text{at surface}} = \text{PE}_{\text{at height}}$

$\frac{1}{2}m\left(\frac{v_e}{2}\right)^2 - \frac{GMm}{R} = -\frac{GMm}{R+H}$

$\frac{1}{2}m\left(\frac{1}{2}\sqrt{\frac{2GM}{R}}\right)^2 - \frac{GMm}{R} = -\frac{GMm}{R+H}$

$\frac{1}{2} \times m \times \frac{1}{4} \times \frac{2GM}{R} - \frac{GMm}{R} = \frac{-GMm}{R+H}$

$\frac{GMm}{4R} - \frac{GMm}{R} = \frac{-GMm}{R+H}$

$GMm\left(\frac{1}{4R} - \frac{1}{R}\right) = \frac{-GMm}{R+H}$

$\frac{-3}{4R} = \frac{-1}{R+H}$

$\Rightarrow -3R - 3H = -4R$

$\Rightarrow 3H = R$

$\Rightarrow H = \frac{R}{3}$

11. (b) The variation of total energy TE, kinetic energy E and potential energy U is given

$U = -\frac{GMm}{r}$

$E = \frac{GMm}{2r}$

$TE = -\frac{GMm}{2r}$

Since, both TE and U are negative and varies by $\frac{1}{r}$. The correct graph will be represented as in option (b).

12. (d) Change in potential energy in displacing a body from r_1 to r_2 is given by

$\Delta U = GMm\left[\frac{1}{r_1} - \frac{1}{r_2}\right]$

$= GMm\left(\frac{1}{2R} - \frac{1}{3R}\right)$

$= \frac{GMm}{6R}$

13. (c) $U_i + K_i = U_f + K_f$

$-\frac{GMm}{R} + \frac{1}{2}m(2v_e)^2 = 0 + \frac{1}{2}mv^2$

or $-\frac{GM}{R} + 2v_e^2 = \frac{1}{2}v^2$

or $-\frac{2GM}{R} + \frac{8GM}{R} = v^2$

$\left(\because v_e = \sqrt{2gR} \text{ and } gR = \frac{GM}{R}\right)$

or $v = \sqrt{\frac{6GM}{R}} = \sqrt{3\left(\frac{2GM}{R}\right)}$

$= \sqrt{3(2gR)} = \sqrt{3}v_e$

14. (a) At the earth's surface, gravitational potential energy is negative because the gravitational field performs work in bringing a mass from infinity. Also, every object is bound by the force of attraction of the earth.

15. (c) As we know that, escape velocity for that body is given as

$v_e = \sqrt{\frac{2Gm}{r}}$

The condition for a uniform spherical mass m of radius r to be a black hole is that its v_e should be more than or equal to speed of light i.e.,

$v_e = \sqrt{\frac{2Gm}{r}} \geq c$

Test-3

1. (d) $r_1 = R + R = 2R$

and $r_2 = 7R + R = 8R$

Now, $K = \frac{GMm}{2r}$

$\frac{K_1}{K_2} = \frac{r_2}{r_1} = 4$

$U = -\frac{GMm}{r}$

$$\frac{U_1}{U_2} = \frac{r_2}{r_1} = 4$$

and $E = -\dfrac{GMm}{2r}$

or $\dfrac{E_1}{E_2} = \dfrac{r_2}{r_1} = 4$

2. (a) Kinetic energy

$$= \frac{1}{2}mv_0^2 = \frac{GMm}{2r}$$

Total energy $= K + U = \dfrac{-GMm}{2r}$

So, ratio $= -1$

3. (c) From Kepler's third law, $T^2 \propto R^3$

Thus, $\dfrac{T_1}{T_2} = \left(\dfrac{R_1}{R_2}\right)^{\frac{3}{2}} = \left(\dfrac{10^{15}}{10^{14}}\right)^{\frac{3}{2}}$

$$= (1000)^{\frac{1}{2}} = 10\sqrt{10}$$

4. (d) The orbital velocity of the satellite,

$$v = \sqrt{\frac{GM}{(R+h)}}$$

Here, $h = 0.25 \times 10^6$ m

R (radius of earth) $= 6.38 \times 10^6$ m

$$\therefore v = \sqrt{\frac{(6.67 \times 10^{-11}) \times (6 \times 10^{24})}{(6.38 \times 10^6) + (0.25 \times 10^6)}}$$

$= 7.76$ km/s

5. (b) From Kepler's third law, $T^2 \propto r^3$

$$\therefore \left(\frac{T'}{T}\right)^2 = \left(\frac{1}{4}\right)^3$$

$$\Rightarrow T' = \frac{1}{8}T$$

6. (b) According to Kepler's third law,

$$T^2 \propto r^3 \text{ or } T \propto r^{\frac{3}{2}}$$

$$\therefore \frac{D'}{D} = \left(\frac{B_2}{B_1}\right)^{\frac{3}{2}}$$

or $D' = D\left(\dfrac{B_2}{B_1}\right)^{\frac{3}{2}}$

7. (a) As we know, kinetic energy of the satellite orbiting the earth is

$$E = \frac{1}{2}mv^2$$

$$\Rightarrow v = \sqrt{\frac{2E}{m}}$$

When $E = 2E$, then $v' = \sqrt{2}v$

$$2E = \frac{1}{2}m(v')^2$$

$$2E = \frac{1}{2}m(\sqrt{2}v)^2$$

When the kinetic energy of satellite is made $2E$, satellite escapes away.

8. (c) Angular momentum is given as

$$L = M_E v_0 r$$

$$\Rightarrow L = M_E \sqrt{\frac{GM_s}{r}}\, r \qquad \left(\because v_0 = \sqrt{\frac{GM_s}{r}}\right)$$

$$\Rightarrow L = [M_E^2\, GM_s r]^{\frac{1}{2}}$$

Thus, $L \propto \sqrt{r}$

9. (b) Speed of the earth will be maximum when its distance from the sun is minimum because $mvr =$ constant.

10. (b) For a satellite revolving around the earth,

$$\frac{mv_0^2}{r} = \frac{GMm}{r^2} \Rightarrow v_0 = \sqrt{\frac{GM}{r}}$$

$$\therefore \quad \text{KE} = \frac{1}{2}mv_0^2 = \frac{1}{2}\frac{GMm}{r}$$

Now, $\dfrac{1}{2}mv_e^2 = \dfrac{GMm}{r}$

or $v_e^2 = \dfrac{2GM}{r}$

$$\text{KE}_e = \frac{1}{2}mv_e^2 = \frac{1}{2} \times \frac{m \times 2GM}{r}$$

or $\text{KE}_e = 2\,\text{KE}$

11. (d) Given,

Satellite P has orbital radius $= 9R$

Satellite Q has orbital radius $= R$

Speed of the satellite $P = 3v$

Speed of the satellite $Q = ?$

The orbital velocity is given below,

$$v = \sqrt{\frac{GM}{R}}$$

Thus, $\dfrac{v_P}{v_Q} = \sqrt{\dfrac{R_Q}{R_P}}$

$$\Rightarrow \frac{v_P}{v_Q} = \sqrt{\frac{R}{9R}} = \frac{1}{3}$$

$$\therefore \frac{v_P}{v_Q} = \frac{3v}{v_Q} = \frac{1}{3}$$

$$\Rightarrow v_Q = 9v$$

12. (c) If the orbital path of a satellite is circular, then its speed is constant and if the orbital path of a satellite is elliptical, then its speed in its orbit is not constant. In that case, its areal velocity is constant. Speed of satellite depends on distance between its axis of rotation and itself.

13. (a) No torque is acting on the planet, its angular momentum remains constant in magnitude as well as direction.

Hence, though orbit of a satellite is elliptical, its plane of rotation passes through centre of the earth.

14. (d) Given, $g \propto \dfrac{1}{R^3}$

Then, gravitational force provides the required centripetal force,

$$m\omega^2 R = \frac{GMm}{R^3} \Rightarrow \frac{4\pi^2}{T^2} = \frac{GM}{R^4}$$

$$T^2 \propto R^4$$

15. (a) As we know, square of time period is directly proportional to the cube of the radius of the orbit. Thus, option (a) is correct.

16. (a) Let us assume that stars are moving in XY-plane with origin as their centre of mass as shown in the figure below.

Given,

Mass of each star $= 3 \times 10^{31}$ kg

Diameter of circle, $2R = 2 \times 10^{11}$ m

$$\Rightarrow R = 10^{11} \text{ m}$$

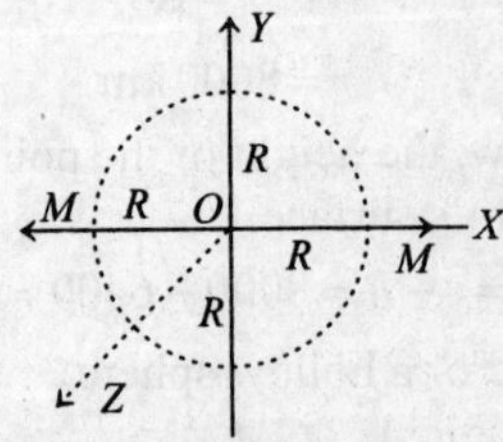

Potential energy of meteorite at O, origin $\hat{\mathbf{j}}$ is,

$$U_{total} = -\frac{2GMm}{r}$$

If v is the velocity of meteorite at O, then kinetic energy K of the meteorite is

$$K = \frac{1}{2}mv^2$$

To escape from dual star system, total mechanical energy of the meteorite at infinite distance from stars must be atleast zero.

By conservation of energy, we have

$$\frac{1}{2}mv^2 - \frac{2GMm}{R} = 0$$

$$\Rightarrow v^2 = \frac{4GM}{R}$$

$$= \frac{4 \times 6.67 \times 10^{-11} \times 3 \times 10^{31}}{10^{11}}$$

$$= 2.83 \times 10^5 \text{ m/s}$$

17. (b) From Kepler's law,

$$\frac{T_1}{T_2} = \left(\frac{R_1}{R_2}\right)^{\frac{3}{2}}$$

$$= \left(\frac{4R}{16R}\right)^{\frac{3}{2}} = \left(\frac{R}{4R}\right)^{\frac{3}{2}}$$

$$\frac{T_1}{T_2} = \left(\frac{1}{4}\right)^{\frac{3}{2}}$$

$$T_2 = 8T_1 \quad [\text{Here, } T_1 = T]$$

18. (c) Time taken to complete one revolution T is related to the radius of circular orbit as $T^2 \propto r^3$.

19. (d) If the law of gravitational attraction become cube law, then

$$F = \frac{GMm}{r^3} = \frac{mv^2}{r}$$

or $$v = \sqrt{\frac{GM}{r^2}} = \frac{\sqrt{GM}}{r}$$

$\therefore$ Time period,

$$T = \frac{2\pi r}{v} = \frac{2\pi r^2}{\sqrt{GM}} \Rightarrow T^2 \propto r^4$$

i.e. law of periods does not hold true. It means planets will not have an elliptical orbit and circular orbit, also may not be possible as gravitational force obey inverse square law not cube law. So, Kepler's 2nd law (law of areas) will also not be valid.

20. (a) By conservation of angular momentum, $mvr = \text{constant}$

$$v_{min} \times r_{max} = v_{max} \times r_{min}$$

$$\therefore \quad v_{min} = \frac{50 \times 8.1 \times 10^{12}}{9 \times 10^{12}}$$

$$\Rightarrow \quad v_{min} = 45 \text{ m/s}$$

21. (b) Gravitational force = Centripetal force

$$\frac{GMm}{R^{\frac{5}{2}}} = MR\omega^2 = mR\frac{4\pi^2}{T^2}$$

or $$T^2 = \left(\frac{4\pi^2}{GM}\right)R^{\frac{7}{2}}$$

$$\Rightarrow \quad T^2 \propto R^{\frac{7}{2}}$$

22. (c) We know that, $T^2 \propto r^3$

and $$\frac{T_1^2}{T_2^2} = \frac{r_1^3}{r_2^3} = \left(\frac{10^{12}}{10^{10}}\right)^3 = 10^6$$

then $$\frac{T_1}{T_2} = 10^3 : 1 = 1000$$

23. (a) The orbital velocity of a satellite in circular orbit of radius of a planet having mass M is given by

$$v = \sqrt{\frac{GM}{R}} \quad \ldots \text{(i)}$$

Let the radius of the earth be R

For a satellite orbiting at an altitude equal to radius of earth, $R_2 = R$.

$$\Rightarrow v_2 = \sqrt{\frac{GM}{R+R}} = \sqrt{\frac{GM}{2R}}$$

$$v_2 = \sqrt{\frac{1}{2}}\,v = \frac{v}{\sqrt{2}}$$

24. (b) For the first satellite, $L = mvr$

$$L = m\sqrt{\frac{GM}{2R}}\,2R$$

For the second satellite, $L' = mv'r'$

$$L' = m\sqrt{\frac{GM}{R}}\,R$$

$$\frac{L'}{L} = \frac{1}{\sqrt{2}}$$

$$\Rightarrow \quad L' = \frac{L}{\sqrt{2}}$$

25. (c) Total energy of the satellite in the first orbit is $E_1 = \frac{-GMm}{4R}$

Total energy of the satellite in the second orbit is $E_2 = \frac{-GMm}{6R}$

Then, energy required is

$$E_2 - E_1 = \frac{GMm}{2R}\left[\frac{1}{2} - \frac{1}{3}\right] = \frac{GMm}{12R}$$

but $\frac{GM}{R} = gR$

$$\therefore \quad E_2 - E_1 = \frac{gRm}{12}$$

Chapter Break Thru

1. (a) From Kepler's third law,

$$\frac{T^2}{R^3} = \frac{T^2}{l^3} = \frac{1}{f^2 l^3} = \text{constant}$$

$$f_1^2 l_1^3 = f_2^2 l_2^3$$

2. (d) Time period does not depend upon the mass of the satellite. Thus, the rotation around the earth of 45 days will not be effected, if the moon's mass becomes 2 fold.

3. (b) Given, $\omega_{body} = 29\omega_{earth}$

From Kepler's third law,

$$T^2 \propto r^3 \Rightarrow \omega^2 \propto \frac{1}{r^3}$$

$$\Rightarrow \quad \omega \propto \frac{1}{r^{\frac{3}{2}}}$$

$$\therefore \quad r \propto \frac{1}{\omega^{\frac{2}{3}}}$$

$$\Rightarrow \frac{r_{body}}{r_{earth}} = \left(\frac{\omega_{earth}}{\omega_{body}}\right)^{\frac{2}{3}} = \left(\frac{1}{29}\right)^{\frac{2}{3}}$$

$$= 0.108$$

4. (d) Time period of a satellite is the time taken by satellite to go once around the earth.

$$T = \frac{2\pi(R+h)^{\frac{3}{2}}}{R\sqrt{g}}$$

T is independent to mass of the satellite, so ratio of their period will be 1 : 1.

5. (b) Universal gravitational constant is scalar quantity.

$$g_{\text{equator}} = g - \omega^2 R$$

if $\omega = 0$

$\Rightarrow$ $g_{\text{equator}} = g$

if $\omega = 0$

$\Rightarrow$ $g_{\text{pole}} = g$

Gravitational force, $F \propto f(r)\,\hat{\mathbf{r}}$, so it is central force.

6. (d) Acceleration due to gravity is given as

$$g = \frac{4}{3}\pi\rho G R$$

$\therefore$ Ratio will be $\dfrac{g_1}{g_2} = \dfrac{R_1 \rho_1}{R_2 \rho_2}$

7. (d) Gravitational potential energy is given as

$$U = -\frac{GMm}{r}$$

$\therefore$ $U_1 = \dfrac{-GMm}{r_1}, U_2 = -\dfrac{GMm}{r_2}$

As, $r_2 > r_1$

$U_1 > U_2$ or $U_2 < U_1$

But U is negative, potential energy becomes less negative.

Thus, gravitational potential energy increases.

8. (d) Gravitational potential,

$$V = -\int \mathbf{E}\cdot dx = \frac{K}{2x^2} + C$$

at $x = \infty, V = 0$

$\Rightarrow$ $C = 0$

$\Rightarrow$ $V = \dfrac{K}{2x^2}$

9. (d) At surface of earth (taking centre as reference) at height nR,

$$U_1 = -\frac{GMm}{R}$$

and $U_2 = -\dfrac{GMm}{(1+n)R}$

$\Rightarrow$ $\Delta U = U_2 - U_1 = \dfrac{GMmn}{(n+1)R}$

$$= \frac{mgnR}{n+1}$$

10. (c) The escape velocity is independent to the angle of projection. Hence, the body when projected at an angle 45° to the horizontal, the escape velocity remains the same i.e., 11 km/s.

11. (a) Resultant gravitational force on mass m is zero, hence acceleration is zero.

12. (d) For earth having constant density,

for $r < R, g \propto r$

and for $r > R, g \propto \dfrac{1}{r^2}$

Thus, the correct graph is depicted in options (d).

13. (d) Consider a small length element dr of mass dm at a distance r from m

$\therefore$ $\lambda = \dfrac{M}{l}$

and $dm = \lambda \cdot dr$

$$\frac{M}{l}\cdot dr = dm$$

dr, r, m, l, x

$$dF = \frac{Gm\cdot dm}{r^2} = \frac{GmM}{l}\cdot\frac{1}{r^2}\cdot dr$$

$\therefore$ $F = \dfrac{GmM}{l}\displaystyle\int_x^{l+x}\frac{1}{r^2}\cdot dr$

$$= \frac{GmM}{l}\cdot\left[-\frac{1}{r}\right]_x^{l+x}$$

$$= \frac{GmM}{l}\left(\frac{1}{x} - \frac{1}{l+x}\right) = \frac{GmM}{x(l+x)}$$

14. (d) Given,

Mass of satellite $= m$

Height $= h$

Acceleration due to gravity $= g$

Velocity of the satellite, $v = \sqrt{\dfrac{gR^2}{R+h}}$

15. (d) Let at a distance x from 2 m, the field intensity is zero.

Hence, $E_{2M} = E_{18M}$

$$\frac{G(2M)}{(2x)^2} = \frac{G(18M)}{(R-x)^2}$$

$$36x^2 = (R-x)^2$$

$$6x = R - x$$

$$x = \frac{R}{7}$$

Now, potential at x,

$$V_x = \frac{-G(2M)}{x} + \frac{-G(18M)}{R-x}$$

$$= -\frac{2GM}{R/7} - \frac{18GM}{6R/7}$$

$$= -35\frac{GM}{R}$$

16. (a) Newton's law of gravitation,

$$F = \frac{Gm_1 m_2}{r^2}$$

where, time period,

$$T^2 = \frac{4\pi^2}{GM}r^3$$

So, $K = \dfrac{4\pi^2}{GM}$

$$GMK = 4\pi^2$$

17. (a) Energy of each satellite $= -\dfrac{GMm}{2r}$

Total energy of the system before collision,

$$E_i = E_1 + E_2 = 2E = -2\times\frac{GMm}{2r}$$

Velocity of satellite after collision,

$mv - mv = 2mv$ i.e. $v = 0$

$$E_f = -\frac{GM(2m)}{r}$$

$$= -\frac{2GMm}{r}$$

18. (a) Both Statement I and Statement II are correct and gravitational force is independent of the medium between the particles while electric and magnetic field depend upon nature of medium and particle.

19. (a) $T^2 \propto R^3$ (Kepler's law)

(Derived from gravitational force)

$$E = -\frac{GM}{R^2} \Rightarrow E \propto \frac{1}{R^2}$$

20. (a) Given,

Radius of the earth $= R$

Acceleration due to gravity, $g = g_{60°}$

At latitude λ,

$$g' = g - R\omega^2\cos^2\lambda$$

At 60°, $g_{60°} = g - R\omega^2\cos^2 60°$

$$= g - \frac{1}{4}R\omega^2$$

$$= \frac{1}{4}\omega^2 R$$

21. (d) The gravitational potential at centre due to bigger sphere,

$$V_1 = -\frac{GM}{R}$$

The gravitational potential due to smaller sphere, $V_2 = \frac{-Gm}{r}$

Thus, $V = V_1 + V_2 = -G\left(\frac{M}{R} + \frac{m}{r}\right)$

22. (c) Given that,

Escape velocity of a body on the earth surface, $v_e = 11.2$ km/s

New mass of the earth, $M_e' = 2M_e$

New radius of the earth $R_e' = 0.5 R_e$

Escape velocity, $v_e = \sqrt{\frac{2GM_e}{R_e}}$

Therefore, $\frac{v_e}{v_e'} = \sqrt{\frac{M_e}{R_e} \times \frac{0.5 R_e}{2M_e}}$

or $v_e' = 2v_e = 22.4$ km/s

23. (d) Equating gravitational field intensities, $\frac{\frac{GM}{81}}{r^2} = \frac{GM}{(60R - r)^2}$

Solving, we get

$60R - r = 9r$

$\Rightarrow r = 6R$

24. (d) For the satellite, the gravitational force provides the necessary centripetal force,

$$\frac{GM_e m}{(R+x)^2} = \frac{mv_0^2}{(R+x)}$$

$$v = \sqrt{\frac{GM_e}{R+x}} = \sqrt{\frac{GM_e}{R^2} \times \frac{R^2}{R+x}}$$

and $\frac{GM_e}{R^2} = g$

$$\therefore \quad v_0 = \sqrt{\frac{gR^2}{R+x}}$$

25. (b) The earth revolves around the sun due to gravitation pull of the sun. Due to this gravitational attraction between this celestial body, centripetal force is generated which binds the solar system together. Hence, revolution of earth around the sun is the evidence to show that threre must be force acting on earth and directed towards the sun.

26. (a) $g_{\text{eff}} = g - \omega^2 R \cos^2 \lambda$

Clearly, when $\omega = 0$, g_{eff} will increase.

27. (c) Acceleration due to gravity,

$$g = \frac{Gm}{R^2}$$

$$\frac{\Delta g}{g} = -2\frac{\Delta R}{R}$$

$$\frac{\Delta g}{g} \times 100 = -2\left(\frac{\Delta R}{R} \times 100\right)$$

Substituting the percentage decrease in radius, we get

$$\therefore \frac{\Delta g}{g} \times 100 = (-2)(-2) = +4\%$$

Now, rotational kinetic energy,

$$K = \frac{1}{2}\frac{L^2}{I}$$

But $\quad I = \frac{2}{5} MR^2$

$$K = \frac{5}{4}\frac{L^2}{MR^2}$$

$$\frac{\Delta K}{K} \times 100 = -2\left(\frac{\Delta R}{R} \times 100\right)$$

$$= (-2)(-2) = +4\%$$

So, both g and K increases by 4%.

28. (b) $\quad g_d = g\left[1 - \frac{d}{R}\right]$

Given, $g_d = \frac{g}{4}$

$$\Rightarrow \frac{g}{4} = g\left[1 - \frac{d}{R}\right]$$

$$\Rightarrow \frac{d}{R} = 1 - \frac{1}{4} \Rightarrow d = \frac{3}{4} R$$

29. (c) Escape velocity,

$$v_e = \sqrt{\frac{2GM}{R}}$$

$$\Rightarrow v_e \propto \sqrt{\rho R^2}$$

$$\Rightarrow \frac{v_{e,2}}{v_{e,1}} = \sqrt{\frac{\rho_2 R_2^2}{\rho_1 R_1^2}} = \left(\frac{1}{4} \times 4\right)^{1/2} = 1:1$$

30. (b) Orbital speed is given by

$$v_0 = \sqrt{\frac{GM}{r}}$$

(Here, M = mass of earth)

$$\Rightarrow \frac{v_2}{v_1} = \sqrt{\frac{r_1}{r_2}}$$

$$\Rightarrow v_2 > v_1$$

31. (c) According to Kepler's laws,

$$T^2 \propto R^3$$

and T is given by

$$T = \frac{4\pi^2}{GM_e} R^3$$

Clearly, T is independent of mass of satellite.

32. (d) $\frac{mv^2}{r} = \frac{GMm}{r^2}$

$$\frac{1}{2}mv^2 = \frac{GMm}{2r} \propto \frac{1}{T^{2/3}}$$

33. (c) Using angular momentum conservation,

$$mv_1 d_1 = mv_2 d_2$$

$$\Rightarrow v_1 d_1 = v_2 d_2$$

$$\Rightarrow v_2 = \frac{v_1 d_1}{d_2}$$

34. (b) $\frac{dA}{dt} = \text{constant}$

$$\Rightarrow \frac{dr^2\theta}{dt} = \text{constant}$$

$$\Rightarrow r^2\omega = \text{constant}$$

$$\Rightarrow m\omega r^2 = \text{constant}$$

$$\Rightarrow mvr = \text{constant}$$

or angular momentum = constant

35. (c) The kinetic energy of an asteroid of mass m and speed v_i,

$$K_i = \frac{1}{2}mv_i^2 \quad \text{...(i)}$$

The potential energy of asteroid at a distance 10 R_E,

$$U_i = -\frac{GM_E m}{10R_E} \quad \text{...(ii)}$$

where, M_E is mass of the earth.

$\therefore$ Initial energy of the asteroid is

$$E_i = K_i + U_i = \frac{1}{2}mv_i^2 - \frac{GM_E m}{10R_E}$$

As it hits the earth with a speed of v_f (R_E and M_E are radius and mass of earth), then final energy of the asteroid,

$$E_f = \frac{1}{2}mv_f^2 - \frac{GM_E m}{R_E}$$

According to law of conservation of energy, $E_i = E_f$

$$\frac{1}{2}mv_i^2 - \frac{GM_E m}{10R_E} = \frac{1}{2}mv_f^2 - \frac{GM_E m}{R_E}$$

$$\Rightarrow v_f^2 - \frac{2GM_E}{R_E} = v_i^2 - \frac{2GM_E}{10R_E}$$

$$\Rightarrow \quad v_f^2 = v_i^2 + \frac{2GM_E}{R_E}\left(1 - \frac{1}{10}\right)$$

36. (d) Since, gravitational force is a conservative force and work done by this force is independent of the path followed and only depends upon initial and final positions. Thus, $W = 0$ as the final and initial positions of satellite is same for one revolution of an orbit.

37. (b) Using energy conservation,

$$\frac{1}{2}mv_e^2 + \text{KE} = \frac{1}{2}mv^2$$

$$\Rightarrow \quad \text{KE} = \frac{1}{2}m(4gr) - \frac{1}{2}m(2gr)$$

$$= \frac{1}{2}m(2gr)$$

$$\Rightarrow \frac{1}{2}mv'^2 = \frac{1}{2}m(2gr)$$

$$\Rightarrow \quad v' = \sqrt{2gr}$$

38. (b) $v_1 r_1 = v_2 r_2$

39. (c) The force on particle for varying g is given by

$$F = \frac{GMmx}{R^3} = m\omega^2 x$$

$$\Rightarrow \quad \omega^2 = \frac{GM}{R^3}$$

$$\left(\frac{2\pi}{t}\right)^2 = \frac{GM}{R^3} \quad \left(\because \omega = \frac{2\pi}{t}\right)$$

$$\Rightarrow \quad t = 2\pi\sqrt{\frac{R^3}{GM}}$$

When g is constant,

$$s = \frac{1}{2}gt'^2$$

(for initial velocity, $u = 0$)

$$\Rightarrow \quad R = \frac{1}{2}\left(\frac{GM}{R^2}\right)(t')^2 \quad \left(\because g = \frac{GM}{R^2}\right)$$

$$\Rightarrow \quad (t')^2 = \frac{2R^3}{GM}$$

$$\Rightarrow \quad t' = \sqrt{2}\sqrt{\frac{R^3}{GM}}$$

$$\therefore \quad \frac{t}{t'} = \frac{2\pi\sqrt{R^3/GM}}{\sqrt{2}\sqrt{R^3/GM}}$$

$$= \frac{2\pi}{\sqrt{2}} = \sqrt{2}\,\pi$$

40. (d) $F_A^2 = F_{AB}^2 + F_{AC}^2 + 2F_{AB}F_{AC}\cos 60°$

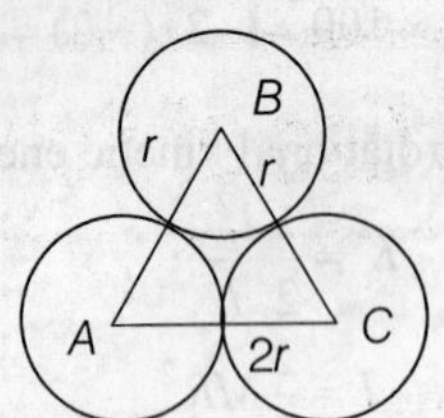

$$\Rightarrow F_A^2 = \left(\frac{GM^2}{4r^2}\right)^2 + \left(\frac{GM^2}{4r^2}\right)^2 + 2\left(\frac{GM^2}{4r^2}\right)^2 \frac{1}{2}$$

$$= 3\left(\frac{GM^2}{4r^2}\right)^2$$

$$\Rightarrow \quad F_A = \frac{\sqrt{3}\,GM^2}{4r^2}$$

41. (b) Potential energy in given situation,

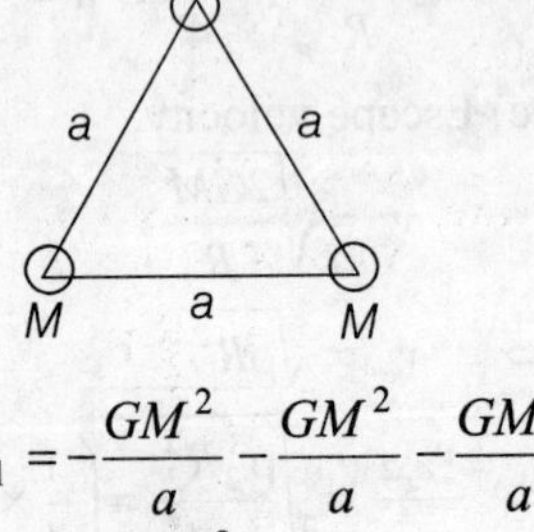

$$U_1 = -\frac{GM^2}{a} - \frac{GM^2}{a} - \frac{GM^2}{a}$$

$$= -\frac{3GM^2}{a}$$

Similarly, potential energy in new situation,

$$U_2 = -\frac{3GM^2}{2a}$$

$$\Delta U = U_2 - U_1$$

$$= \left(\frac{-3}{2}\frac{GM^2}{a} + \frac{3GM^2}{a}\right)$$

$$= \frac{GM^2}{a}\left(3 - \frac{3}{2}\right) = \frac{3}{2}\frac{GM^2}{a}$$

Work done, $\Delta W = \Delta U = \dfrac{3GM^2}{2a}$

42. (c) Let work done on the surface of earth is W,

Using energy conservation,

$$W - \frac{GM(1)}{R} = 0$$

$$W = \frac{GM}{R} = \frac{GM}{R^2}R = gR$$

43. (d) Here, $L = \pi r$

or $\quad r = \dfrac{L}{\pi}$

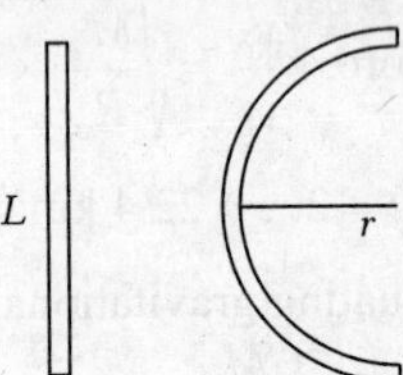

Gravitational potential at the centre of the circle,

$$V = -\frac{GM}{r} = -\frac{\pi GM}{L}$$

44. (d) Gravitational potential inside the earth,

$$V_{\text{in}} = \frac{-GM}{2R}\left[3 - \left(\frac{r}{R}\right)^2\right]$$

$$= \frac{-GM}{2R}\left[3 - \left(\frac{1}{2}\right)^2\right]$$

$$\Rightarrow V_{\text{in}} = -\frac{11}{8}\frac{GM}{R}$$

45. (c) Escape velocity does not depend on firing angle.

46. (a) Here, man travels 60 m in one minute on the surface of the earth which means he has a velocity of 1 m/s but this velocity is along the surface of the earth, so it is not affected by the acceleration due to gravity of the earth because that is perpendicular to the surface, so he will have same velocity on any other planet and will cover same distance.

47. (b) $\frac{mv^2}{r} = \frac{GmM}{r^2}$

$\Rightarrow$ $v^2 r = \text{constant}$

$\Rightarrow$ $v^2 \propto \frac{1}{r} \Rightarrow 2\frac{\Delta v}{v} = -\frac{\Delta r}{r}$

or $\frac{\Delta v}{v} = -\frac{1}{2}\frac{\Delta r}{r} = 0.5\%$

(increment)

48. (b) Potential energy at $r = r$,

$$U_r = \frac{-GMm}{r}$$

PE at $r = \frac{3}{2}r$,

$$U_{\frac{3r}{2}} = -\frac{GMm}{\frac{3}{2}r} = -\frac{2}{3}\frac{GMm}{r}$$

Change in PE $= U_{\frac{3r}{2}} - U_r = \frac{1}{3}\frac{GMm}{r}$

$$\frac{\Delta U}{U} = \frac{1}{3} \text{ or } 33.33\%$$

49. (b) $v = 4v_e$

$$-\frac{GMm}{R} + \frac{1}{2}m(4v_e)^2 = \frac{1}{2}mv^2$$

$$-\frac{v_e^2}{2} + \frac{16}{2}v_e^2 = \frac{1}{2}v^2$$

$\Rightarrow$ $v^2 = 15v_e^2$

$\Rightarrow$ $v = \sqrt{15} \times 11.2 \text{ km/s}$

50. (a) Due to rotating of earth, effective acceleration due to gravity,

$$g' = g - \omega^2 R\cos^2\lambda$$

So, if ω becomes zero,

$g' = g$ (g' will increase)

Ch-08 Mechanical Properties of Solids

Topical Follow Thru

Test-1

1. (c) Given, length $(l) = 2.0 \text{ m}$

Area of cross-section (A)

$$= 0.5 \text{ cm}^2$$
$$= 5 \times 10^{-5} \text{ m}^2$$

$\therefore$ Stress $= \frac{F}{A} = \frac{mg}{A} = \frac{500 \times 9.8}{5 \times 10^{-5}}$

$$= 9.8 \times 10^7 \text{ Pa}$$

$\therefore$ Strain $= \frac{\Delta l}{l} = \frac{\text{Stress}}{Y}$

$$= \frac{9.8 \times 10^7}{20 \times 10^{10}} = 4.9 \times 10^{-4}$$

2. (c) From the Young's modulus of elasticity,

$$\frac{F}{A} = Y\frac{\Delta l}{l}$$

Here, Y and $\frac{\Delta l}{l}$ are constants.

$$\frac{F}{A} = \text{constant}$$

$$F \propto A \Rightarrow F \propto r^2$$
$$F' = 4F$$

3. (b)

Y_1 k_1 k_2 Y_2

From the figure, we have

$$k_{eq} = k_1 + k_2$$

$\therefore$ $\frac{Y2A}{l} = \frac{Y_1 A}{l} + \frac{Y_2 A}{l}$

$$\left[\because k = \frac{F}{\Delta l} = \frac{YA}{l}\right]$$

$\Rightarrow$ $2Y = Y_1 + Y_2$

$\Rightarrow$ $Y = \frac{Y_1 + Y_2}{2}$

4. (b) According to question,

$$\frac{l_1}{l_2} = A, \frac{r_1}{r_2} = B, \frac{Y_1}{Y_2} = C$$

$\therefore$ $\Delta l_1 = \frac{(3mg)l_1}{A_1 Y_1}$ $\left(\because \Delta l = \frac{Fl}{AY}\right)$

and $\Delta l_2 = \frac{(2mg)l_2}{A_2 Y_2}$

Now, $\frac{\Delta l_1}{\Delta l_2} = \frac{3l_1}{A_1 Y_1} \times \frac{A_2 Y_2}{2l_2}$

$$= \frac{3l_1 r_2^2 Y_2}{2l_2 r_1^2 Y_1}$$

$$= \frac{3}{2}\frac{A}{B^2 C}$$

5. (a) Tension in wire $1 = T_1$

Tension in wire $2 = T_2$

$$4g - T_2 = 4a \quad \text{... (i)}$$
$$T_2 - T_1 = 4a \quad \text{... (ii)}$$
$$T_1 = 4a \quad \text{... (iii)}$$

Here, acceleration,

$$a = \frac{40}{12} = \frac{10}{3} \text{ m/s}^2$$

$\therefore$ $T_1 = \frac{40}{3} \text{ N}, T_2 = \frac{80}{3} \text{ N}$

Therefore, strain in wire 1 is

$$= \frac{40}{3 \times 5 \times 10^{-7} \times 2 \times 10^{11}} = \frac{4}{3} \times 10^{-4}$$

and strain in wire 2 is

$$= \frac{80}{3 \times 5 \times 10^{-7} \times 2 \times 10^{11}}$$
$$= \frac{8}{3} \times 10^{-4}$$

6. (a) Suppose L be the natural length of the wire.

Young's modulus is given by

$$Y = \frac{FL}{A\Delta L}$$

In the first case, $F = T_1$, $\Delta L = L_1 - L$

$\therefore$ $Y = \frac{T_1 L}{A(L_1 - L)}$ ...(i)

In the second case,

$$F = T_2, \ \Delta L = L_2 - L$$

$\therefore$ $Y = \frac{T_2 L}{A(L_2 - L)}$ ...(ii)

From Eqs. (i) and (ii), we get

$$\frac{T_1 L}{A(L_1 - L)} = \frac{T_2 L}{A(L_2 - L)}$$

or $T_1(L_2-L)=T_2(L_1-L)$

or $L(T_2-T_1)=L_1T_2-L_2T_1$

or $L=\dfrac{L_1T_2-L_2T_1}{T_2-T_1}$

7. (a) Given, radius $(r)=10\,\text{mm}=10^{-2}\,\text{m}$

Length $(l)=1\,\text{m}$

Force $(F)=100\,\text{kN}=10^5\,\text{N}$

As we know that,

$$\text{Stress}=\frac{F}{A}=\frac{F}{\pi r^2}=\frac{10^5}{3.14\times(10^{-2})^2}=3.18\times10^8\,\text{N/m}^2$$

8. (c) Given, stress $=5\times10^9\,\text{N/m}^2$

$l_1=l,\ l_2=2l_1=2l$

$\therefore$ Change in length, $\Delta l=l_2-l_1=2l-l=l$

$\therefore$ Young's modulus, $Y=\dfrac{\text{Stress}}{\text{Strain}}$

$$=\frac{5\times10^9}{\left(\frac{\Delta l}{l}\right)}=\frac{5\times10^9}{\left(\frac{l}{l}\right)}=5\times10^9\,\text{N/m}^2$$

9. (d) As we know that,

$$Y=\frac{\text{Stress}}{\text{Strain}}=\frac{FL}{A\Delta l}$$

$$\Delta l=\frac{FL}{AY}=\frac{ALdgL}{AY}\quad[\because m=ALd]$$

$$=\frac{L^2dg}{Y}$$

10. (d) Given, $l_B=5\,\text{m}$

$A_B=5\,\text{cm}^2=5\times10^{-4}\,\text{m}^2$

$l_S=L=1\times10^{-4}\,\text{m}^2$

$A_S=1\,\text{cm}^2$

Here, $\Delta l_B=\Delta l_s$

$$\frac{Fl_B}{A_BY_B}=\frac{Fl_S}{A_SY_S}$$

$$l_S=\frac{A_SY_S}{A_BY_B}l_B=\frac{1\times10^{-4}\times2\times10^{11}}{5\times10^{-4}\times1\times10^{11}}\times5$$

$L=2\,\text{m}$

11. (a) Given, $d=4\,\text{mm}=4\times10^{-3}\,\text{mm}$

$\therefore\quad r=2\times10^{-3}\,\text{m}$

$Y=9\times10^{10}\,\text{N/m}^2$

$$\Rightarrow\quad \frac{F}{A}=Y\frac{\Delta l}{l}$$

$$\Rightarrow\quad F=AY\frac{\Delta l}{l}$$

$$=\pi(2\times10^{-3})^2\times9\times10^{10}\times0.001$$

$$=\pi\times4\times10^{-6}\times9\times10^7$$

$$=360\pi\,\text{N}$$

12. (c) Given, mass of motor $(m)=10\,\text{kg}$

Height of rubber blocks

$(h)=5\,\text{cm}=5\times10^{-2}\,\text{m}$

Cross-sectional area $(A)=16\,\text{cm}^2=16\times10^{-4}\,\text{m}^2$

Shear modulus $(\eta)=2\times10^6\,\text{N/m}^2$

Shearing force $(F_0)=800\,\text{N}$

Force applied on each block is given by

$$F=\frac{F_0}{n}=\frac{800}{4}\,\text{N}$$

Let x be the distance by which motor moves sideways, then from the formula of shearing stress, we have

$$\frac{F}{A}=\eta\frac{x}{h}$$

$$\frac{800}{4\times16\times10^{-4}}=2\times10^6\times\frac{x}{5\times10^{-2}}$$

$$\frac{200}{16\times10^{-4}}=\frac{2\times10^6\times x}{5\times10^{-2}}$$

$$\Rightarrow\quad x=\frac{200\times5\times10^{-2}}{16\times10^{-4}\times2\times10^6}$$

$$=3.1\times10^{-3}\,\text{m}=0.31\,\text{cm}$$

13. (c) As we know that,

$$\text{elasticity}\propto\frac{1}{\text{compressibility}}$$

$\therefore$ Statement I is correct.

As we know, for twisting, angle of shear,

$$\phi\propto\frac{1}{L}$$

It means, L is always responsible for shear angle and if L is more, then ϕ will be small.

14. (d) Given, side of plate $(l_1)=2\,\text{m}$

Thickness $(H)=0.01\,\text{m}$

Height $(h)=1\,\text{m}$

As we know that, $F=\eta A\dfrac{x}{h}$

To cause displacement of 0.04 cm, the force

$$=0.4\times10^{11}\times2\times0.01\times\frac{0.04\times10^{-2}}{1}$$

$$[\because A=l_1\times H=(2\times0.1)\,\text{m}^2]$$

$$=3.2\times10^5\,\text{N}$$

15. (a) As we know that,

$$\frac{1}{K}=\text{compressibility}=\left(-\frac{\Delta V}{V}\right)\times\frac{1}{p}$$

Therefore, the compressibility of a material is the fractional change in volume per unit change in pressure.

16. (d) Fractional change in volume during compression is given by

$$\frac{\Delta V}{V}=\frac{\Delta p}{|B|}=\frac{2\times10^5}{1.25\times10^{11}}=1.6\times10^{-7}$$

17. (b) According to bulk modulus,

$$B=-\frac{p}{\Delta V/V}$$

Here, $p=100\,\text{atm}=100\times10^5\,\text{Nm}^{-2}=10^7\,\text{Nm}^{-2}$

$\Delta V=(99-100)\,\text{L}=-1.0\,\text{L}$

$V=100\,\text{L}$

$$\therefore\quad B=-\frac{10^7}{(-1.0/100)}=1\times10^9\,\text{Nm}^{-2}$$

18. (c) $\because \Delta l=521-500-20=1\,\text{cm}=0.01\,\text{m}$

$$\because\quad T-mg=mv^2/R$$

$$\therefore\quad T=m\left(g+\frac{v^2}{R}\right)$$

$$\Delta l=\frac{Tl}{AY}$$

$$=\frac{m\left(g+\frac{v^2}{l}\right)l}{(\pi d^2/4)Y}=\frac{mg\,l+mv^2}{(\pi d^2/4)Y}$$

$$\therefore\quad v=\sqrt{\frac{\pi d^2\Delta lY}{4m}-gl}$$

$$= \sqrt{\frac{(3.14)(4\times10^{-3})^2\ (0.01)}{(2\times10^{11})}\ \frac{}{4\times25} - 9.8\times5}$$

$= 31.26\,\text{m/s}$

19. (a) Given, $l = 20\,\text{cm} = 20\times10^{-2}$ m

$\Delta l = 0.05$ cm $= 0.05\times10^{-2}$ m

Shearing stress $= 10^6\ \text{N/m}^2$

Shearing strain $= \Delta l / l$

$$= \frac{0.05\times10^{-2}}{20\times10^{-2}} = 0.0025$$

$$\therefore\ \eta = \frac{\text{Shearing stress}}{\text{Shearing strain}} = \frac{10^6}{0.0025}$$

$= 4\times10^8\ \text{N/m}^2$

20. (a) Bulk modulus of elasticity measures how good the body is to regain its original volume on being compressed. Therefore, it represents incompressibility of the material,

$K = \frac{-pV}{\Delta V}$, where p is increase in pressure, ΔV is change in volume.

The molecules in liquids and in gases are bound with their neighbours but not as strong as in solids, they are poorly coupled to their neighbours. Therefore, compressibility of solids is less than that of gases and liquids.

21. (c) As we know that,

$$\text{Pressure, } p = \frac{\text{Force}}{\text{Area}} = \frac{mg}{A}$$

and bulk modulus,

$$B = \left(\frac{p}{\frac{\Delta V}{V}}\right)$$

$$\therefore\quad -\frac{\Delta V}{V} = \frac{p}{B}$$

$$-\frac{\Delta V}{V} = \frac{mg}{AB} \quad \ldots\text{(i)}$$

$$\because\quad V = \frac{4}{3}\pi R^3$$

$$\therefore\quad \frac{\Delta V}{V} = \frac{3\Delta R}{R}$$

Using Eq. (i), we get

$$-\frac{\Delta R}{R} = \frac{mg}{3AB}$$

Negative sign indicates decrease in radius.

22. (c) Here, $\frac{\Delta V}{V} = \frac{0.02}{100} = 2\times10^{-4}$

and pressure, $p = \rho gh$

$= 10^3\times9.8\times2\times10^3$

$= 19.6\times10^6$

$= 1.96\times10^7\ \text{N/m}^2$

Now, bulk modulus $= \frac{p}{\Delta V / V}$

$$= \frac{1.96\times10^7}{2\times10^{-4}} = 0.98\times10^{11}$$

$= 9.8\times10^{10}\ \text{N/m}^2$

23. (c) Given, $m_1 = 3$ kg, $m_2 = 5$ kg

$$\therefore\ T = \frac{2m_1m_2g}{m_1+m_2} = \frac{2\times3\times5\times10}{8} = \frac{75}{2}$$

$$\text{Stress} = \frac{T}{A} = \frac{T}{\pi r^2}$$

$$\Rightarrow\quad \frac{24}{\pi}\times10^2 = \frac{75}{2\times\pi r^2}$$

$$\Rightarrow\quad r^2 = \frac{3}{8\times24}$$

$$\Rightarrow\quad r = 0.125\,\text{m} = 12.5\,\text{cm}$$

24. (b) We know that, Young's modulus,

$$Y = \frac{\text{Stress}}{\text{Strain}} = \frac{F/A}{\Delta L/L} = \frac{F}{A}\times\frac{L}{\Delta L}$$

$$= \frac{F}{\pi(D/2)^2}\times\frac{L}{\Delta L} = \frac{4\,FL}{\pi D^2\Delta L}$$

$$\Rightarrow\quad D^2 = \frac{4\,FL}{\pi\Delta LY}$$

$$\Rightarrow\quad D = \sqrt{\frac{4\,FL}{\pi\Delta LY}}$$

As, F and $\frac{L}{\Delta L}$ are constants.

Hence, $D \propto \sqrt{\frac{1}{Y}}$

Now, we can find ratio as

$$\frac{D_{\text{copper}}}{D_{\text{iron}}} = \sqrt{\frac{Y_{\text{iron}}}{Y_{\text{copper}}}}$$

25. (b) The resolved part of F along the normal is the tensile stress on this plane and the resolved part parallel to the plane is the shearing stress on the plane as shown below.

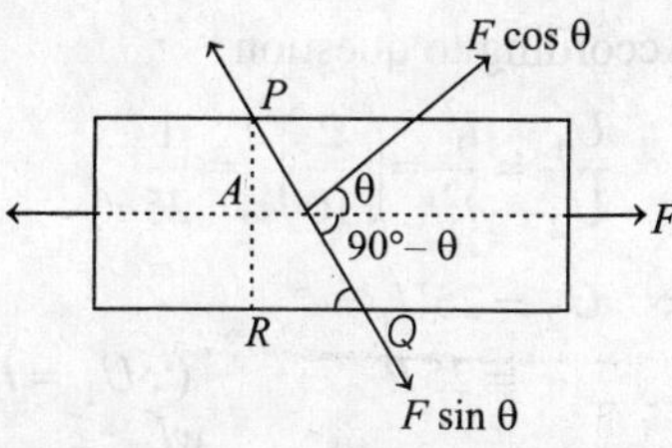

Given, cross-section area of bar $= A$

Let cross-section area of plane $= A'$, then

From ΔPQR,

$$\frac{A}{A'} = \sin(90^\circ - \theta) = \cos\theta$$

$$\therefore\ \text{Area, } A' = \frac{A}{\cos\theta} = A\sec\theta$$

A. Shearing stress $= \frac{\text{Force}}{\text{Area}} = \frac{F\sin\theta}{A\sec\theta}$

$$= \frac{F}{A}\sin\theta\cos\theta$$

B. Tensile stress $= \frac{\text{Force}}{\text{Area}}$

$$= \frac{F\cos\theta}{A\sec\theta} = \frac{F}{A}\cos^2\theta$$

(area of plane section $= A\sec\theta$)

C. Tensile stress or strength will be maximum when $\cos^2\theta$ is maximum, i.e. $\cos\theta = 1$ or $\theta = 0^\circ$.

D. Shearing stress will be maximum when $\sin 2\theta$ is maximum, i.e. or $2\theta = 90^\circ$, i.e. $\theta = 45^\circ$.

Hence, A-3, B-1, C-2, D-4.

Test-2

1. (a) As we know that,

$$k = \frac{AY}{l} = \frac{1\times10^{-4}\times1\times10^{11}}{0.2}$$

$= 5\times10^7$

Increase in elastic potential energy,

$$\Delta U = \frac{F^2}{2k} = \frac{(5\times9.8)^2}{2\times5\times10^7}$$

$$= \frac{49\times49}{10^8}$$

$= 2.4\times10^{-5}$ J

2. (d) Elastic potential energy is given by

$$U = \frac{1}{2}\left(\frac{YA}{L}\right)l^2$$

$$\therefore\quad U \propto l^2$$

According to question,

$$\frac{U_1}{U_2} = \frac{l_1^2}{l_2^2} = \left(\frac{2}{10}\right)^2 = \frac{1}{25}$$

$$\Rightarrow U_2 = 25U_1$$

$$= 25P \quad (\because U_1 = P)$$

3. (c) We have, $\Delta l_1 = \frac{wL}{(4\pi R^2)Y}$ and

$$\Delta l_2 = \frac{wL}{\pi R^2 Y}$$

The elastic potential energy in the system,

$$U = \frac{1}{2}k_1(\Delta l_1)^2 + \frac{1}{2}k_2(\Delta l_2)^2$$

$$= \frac{1}{2}\times\frac{Y(4\pi R^2)}{L}\times\left[\frac{wL}{4\pi R^2 Y}\right]^2 + \frac{1}{2}\times\frac{Y(\pi R^2)}{L}\times\left[\frac{wL}{\pi R^2 Y}\right]^2$$

$$\left(\because k = \frac{YA}{L}\right)$$

$$= \frac{5w^2L}{8\pi R^2 Y}$$

4. (a) The work done in stretching the wire from x_1 to x_2 elongation is given by

$$W = \frac{1}{2}[F_2x_2 - F_1x_1]$$

Given, $x_1 = 0.5$ mm, $x_2 = 1.0$ mm,

$F_1 = 5$ kg-wt,

$F_2 = 10$ kg-wt,

$$W = \frac{1}{2}[10\times 9.8\times 1.0\times 10^{-3} - 5\times 9.8 \times 0.5\times 10^{-3}]$$

$$= \frac{1}{2}\times 10^{-3}[98 - 24.5]$$

$$= 36.75\times 10^{-3}$$

$$= 3.6\times 10^{-2} \text{ J}$$

5. (c) Energy stored $= \frac{1}{2}\times$ Stress $\times$ Strain $\times$ Volume

$$= \frac{1}{2}\times\frac{T}{A}\times\frac{x}{l}\times Al = \frac{1}{2}\times Tx$$

$$= \frac{1}{2}T\cdot\frac{T}{k} \quad (\because T = kx)$$

$$= \frac{1}{2}\frac{T^2}{k}$$

6. (a) In ductile materials, yield point exists while in brittle materials, yield point does not exists. Therefore, material I is brittle and material II is ductile.

7. (b) Energy $= \frac{1}{2}\times$ stress $\times$ strain $\times$ volume

$$= \frac{1}{2}\frac{(\text{stress})^2}{Y}\times\text{volume}$$

$$= \frac{1}{2}\frac{\left(\frac{F}{A}\right)^2}{y}\times L.A$$

$$\left[\text{as stress} = \frac{F}{A}, \text{ volume} = L\times A\right]$$

or $\quad$ energy $(E) = \frac{F^2L}{2AY}$

8. (a) As we know that, $k = \frac{AY}{l}$

According to question,

$$k' = \frac{A'Y}{l'} = \frac{4AY}{l/2} = 8k$$

$$[\because A' = 4A, l' = l/2]$$

Now, as we know,

$$U = \frac{1}{2}k\Delta l^2$$

$$\frac{U}{4} = \frac{k'}{k} = \frac{8k}{k}$$

$$\Rightarrow \quad U = 32 \text{ J}$$

9. (d) $W = \frac{1}{2}\times$ Stress $\times$ Strain

$$= \frac{1}{2}\times\frac{(\text{Stress})^2}{Y}\left(\because Y = \frac{\text{Stress}}{\text{Strain}}\right)$$

$$W \propto \frac{1}{Y}$$

($\because$ Stress is same in both the cases)

$$\frac{W_{\text{steel}}}{W_{\text{copper}}} = \frac{Y_{\text{copper}}}{Y_{\text{steel}}} = \frac{1}{2}$$

10. (b) Metal can be readily drawn into thin wire shape beyond the elastic limit because these are ductile.

11. (b) Young's modulus, $Y = \frac{\text{Stress}}{\text{Strain}}$

or $\quad Y = \frac{F/A}{\Delta L/L} = \frac{FL}{A\Delta L}$

$$\Rightarrow \quad \Delta L = \frac{FL}{AY} \quad \text{...(i)}$$

Volume of wire, $V = AL$

or $\quad A = \frac{V}{L} \quad$ ...(ii)

Substituting the value of A in Eq. (i), we get

$$\Delta L = \frac{FL^2}{VY}$$

$$\Rightarrow \quad \Delta L \propto L^2$$

[here, F, V and Y are constants]

Hence, the graph of ΔL *versus* L^2 will give a straight line.

12. (d) Energy stored per unit volume

$$= \frac{1}{2}\times\text{Stress}\times\text{Strain}$$

From the definition of Young's modulus of wire,

$$Y = \frac{\text{Stress}}{\text{Strain}}$$

$$\Rightarrow \quad \text{Stress} = Y\times\text{Strain}$$

Therefore, $U = \frac{1}{2}\times$ Young's modulus $\times$ (Strain)^2

$$= \frac{1}{2}\times Y\times L^2 = \frac{YL^2}{2}$$

13. (b) The ratio of stress to the strain is called Young's modulus. Therefore, the slope of graph gives the value of Y. Since, line 4 has minimum slope, so the Young's modulus of line 4 is minimum.

14. (b) Elongation of the wire,

$$Y = \frac{FL}{\Delta LA}$$

$$\therefore \quad Y = \frac{FL}{\Delta L\pi R^2} \quad [\because A = \pi R^2]$$

$$\therefore \quad \Delta L \propto \frac{1}{R^2}$$

[$\because Y, L$ and F are constants]

i.e. For the same load, thickest wire will show minimum elongation. So, line OD represents the thickest wire.

15. (d) As we know that,

$$\text{Work done } (W) = \frac{1}{2}Fl = \frac{1}{2}mgl$$

Here, $m = 10$ kg, $g = 10$ m/s^2,

$l = 2$ m

$$\Rightarrow \quad W = \frac{1}{2}\times 10\times 10\times 2 = 100 \text{ J}$$

16. (b) Given, $l = 4$ m,

$\Delta l = 2\text{ mm} = 2\times 10^{-3}$ m

$A = 2\text{ mm}^2 = 2\times 10^{-6}\text{ m}^2$

$Y = 2\times 10^{11}\text{ Nm}^2$

Energy density is given by

$$u = \frac{1}{2} Y \times (\text{Strain})^2$$

$$= \frac{1}{2} Y \times \left(\frac{\Delta l}{l}\right)^2$$

$$= \frac{1}{2} \times 2\times 10^{11} \left[\frac{2\times 10^{-3}}{4}\right]^2$$

$$= 2.5\times 10^4\text{ Jm}^{-3}$$

Now, the elastic potential energy stored is given by

$U =$ Energy density $\times$ Volume

$$= u \times A \times l$$

$$= 2.5\times 10^4 \times 2\times 10^{-6} \times 4$$

$$= 0.2\text{ J}$$

17. (a) If a force F is applied along the length L of wire for stretching by an amount x, then Young's modulus is given by

$$Y = \frac{\text{stress}}{\text{strain}} = \frac{FL}{Ax}$$

where, A = area of cross-sectional.

$$\Rightarrow \quad F = \frac{YA}{L} x$$

The work done in stretching the wire is given by

$$W = \int_0^x F \cdot dx = \int_0^x \frac{YA}{L} x$$

$$= \frac{YA}{L}\left[\frac{x^2}{2}\right]_0^x = \frac{YAx^2}{2L}$$

18. (d) We know that, elastic potential energy per unit volume,

$$U = \frac{1}{2} \times \frac{(\text{Stress})^2}{Y}$$

$$\Rightarrow \quad U \propto (\text{Stress})^2$$

$$\therefore \quad \frac{U_1}{U_2} = \frac{(\text{Stress})_1^2}{(\text{Stress})_2^2}$$

$$\therefore \quad \frac{U_1}{U_2} = \frac{(F_1 / A_1)^2}{(F_2 / A_2)^2} = \left(\frac{F_1}{F_2}\right)^2 \left(\frac{A_2}{A_1}\right)^2$$

As, both the wires are stretched by the same load. Therefore,

$$\frac{U_1}{U_2} = \left(\frac{A_2}{A_1}\right)^2 = \left(\frac{d_2^2}{d_1^2}\right)^2$$

$$= \left(\frac{2^2}{1^2}\right)^2 = \frac{16}{1}$$

$$\Rightarrow \quad U_1 : U_2 = 16 : 1$$

19. (d) Potential energy stored in the rubber cord of catapult will be converted into kinetic energy of mass.

$$\frac{1}{2} mv^2 = \frac{1}{2} \frac{YA\,l^2}{L}$$

Here, $l = 5\times 10^{-2}$ m, $A = 25\times 10^{-6}\text{ m}^2$,

$L = 10\times 10^{-2}$ m, $m = 5\times 10^{-3}$ kg

$$\Rightarrow \quad v = \sqrt{\frac{Y A\, l^2}{mL}}$$

$$= \sqrt{\frac{5\times 10^8 \times 25\times 10^{-6} \times (5\times 10^{-2})^2}{5\times 10^{-3} \times 10\times 10^{-2}}}$$

$$= 250\text{ m/s}$$

20. (b) Both A and R are true but R is not the correct explanation of A.

Ductility is the property of metals to get drawn into thin wires and such metals have considerable distance between the points representing elastic limit and breaking point compared to brittle material.

Below the curves for ductile and brittle metal has been compared.

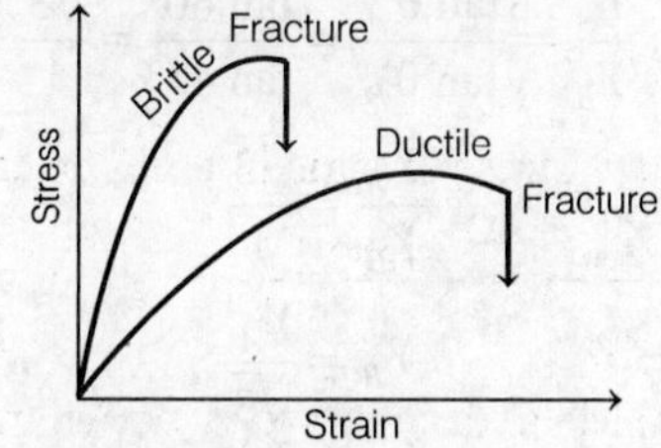

21. (b) From the given figure, we can say that, the slope of the linear portion of the stress-strain curve is greater for material B. Hence, Young's modulus of B is greater than that of material A. Material B can withstand more load without breaking, so it is stronger than material A and its ultimate stress is higher.

22. (b) From the given graph, P has more strain for same stress as on Q, so P is more ductile than Q.

23. (d) In the region OA, the graph is linear showing that stress is proportional to the strain. Thus, in this region, Hooke's law is obeyed. The point D on the graph is known as ultimate tensile strength.

The point E on the graph is known as fracture point.

24. (c) The slope of straight line portion of strain-stress curve for a given material represents its Young's modulus.

(i) Young's modulus of the given material (Y)

= Slope of strain-stress curve

$$Y = \frac{150\times 10^6}{0.002} = 75\times 10^9$$

$$= 7.5\times 10^{10}\text{ Nm}^{-2}$$

(ii) Yield strength of the given material = Maximum stress that material can sustain

$$= 300\times 10^6$$

$$= 3\times 10^8\text{ Nm}^{-2}$$

25. (d) As stress is shown on X-axis and strain on Y-axis.

So, we can say that,

$$Y = \cot\theta = \frac{1}{\tan\theta} = \frac{1}{\text{slope}}$$

So, elasticity of wire P is minimum and of wire R is maximum.

Chapter Break Thru

1. (a) Steel wire is elongated due to a load of mass

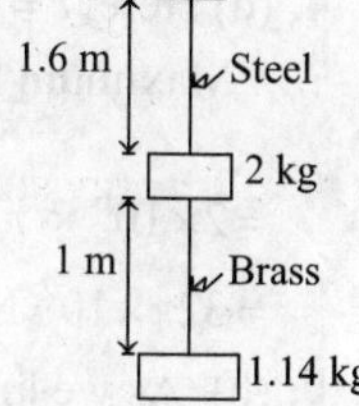

$$m = 2 + 1.14$$

$$= 3.14\text{ kg}$$

$$= \pi\text{ kg}$$

Now using,

$$Y = \frac{Fl}{A\Delta l}$$

$$\Rightarrow \Delta l = \frac{F\cdot l}{Y\cdot A}$$

$$= \frac{\pi(1.6)\,g}{2\times 10^{11}\times \pi\times (0.2\times 10^{-2})^2}$$

$$= \frac{\pi\times 1.6\,g}{2\times 10^{11}\times \pi\times (0.2)^2\times 10^{-4}}$$

$$= \frac{\pi\times 16\times 10^{-1}\times 10}{2\times 10^{11}\times \pi\times 2^2\times 10^{-2}\times 10^{-4}}$$

$$= 20\times 10^{-6}\text{ m}$$

2. (a) We know that,

$$F = kx \Rightarrow F = \frac{YA}{l_0}\cdot x$$

When $F = 100$ N

$$100 = K(l_1 - l_0) \quad \text{...(i)}$$

When $F = 120$ N

$$120 = K(l_2 - l_0) \quad \text{...(ii)}$$

So, $\frac{120}{100} = \frac{k(l_2 - l_0)}{k(l_1 - l_0)}$

Given, $10 l_2 = 11 l_1,\ l_2 = 1\cdot 1 l_1$

$$\frac{120}{100} = \frac{(1\cdot 1 l_1 - l_0)}{l_1 - l_0}$$

$$1\cdot 2 l_1 - 1\cdot 2 l_0 = 1\cdot 1 l_1 - l_0$$

$$0\cdot 1 l_1 = 0\cdot 2 l_0 \Rightarrow l_0 = \frac{l_1}{2}$$

3. (c) As we know that,

$$\text{Stress} = \frac{\text{Force}}{\text{Area}}$$

Here, force and area of cross-section of wires same, therefore stress has to be same.

$$\text{Strain} = \frac{\text{Stress}}{Y}$$

So, strain depends on Y.
Therefore, strain has to be different.

4. (d) Here, $r = 4\text{ cm} = 4\times 10^{-2}$ m

Maximum load = Maximum stress × Area of cross-section

$$= 2\times 10^6\times \pi\times (4\times 10^{-2})^2$$

$$= 32\pi\times 10^2\text{ N}$$

5. (b) As we know that, the Young's modulus depends upon the nature of the material not on its length and cross-section area. Therefore, the Young's modulus will remain the same as before.

6. (b) Given, $A = 1\text{ cm}^2 = 1\times 10^{-4}\text{ m}^2$,

$$Y = 2\times 10^{11}\text{ N/m}^2$$

$$\frac{\Delta L}{L} = 0.01\% = \frac{0.01}{100} = 1\times 10^{-4}$$

As, $Y = \frac{FL}{A\Delta L}$

$$\therefore\quad F = \frac{YA\Delta L}{L}$$

$$= 2\times 10^{11}\times 1\times 10^{-4}\times 1\times 10^{-4}$$

$$= 2\times 10^{11}\times 10^{-8}$$

$$= 2\times 10^3 = 2000\text{ N}$$

7. (c) Let Y be the Young's modulus of the material of the wire, then for first wire,

$$Y = \frac{F/\pi r^2}{l/L} = \frac{FL}{\pi r^2 l} \quad \text{...(i)}$$

As both the wires are made of the same material, so their Young's modulus is same.

Let the extension produced in second wire be l', then

$$Y = \frac{\frac{F}{2}\Big/\pi\left(\frac{r}{2}\right)^2}{\frac{l'}{L/2}} = \frac{FL}{\pi r^2 l'} \quad \text{...(ii)}$$

Equating Eqs. (i) and (ii), we get

$$\frac{FL}{\pi r^2 l} = \frac{FL}{\pi r^2 l'}$$

or $l' = l$

8. (c) From the graph,

$$\frac{\text{Stress}}{\text{Strain}} = Y = \text{slope of graph}$$

Here, $\theta_A = 60°,\ \theta_B = 45°$

$$\therefore\quad \frac{Y_A}{Y_B} = \frac{\tan\theta_A}{\tan\theta_B} = \frac{\tan 60°}{\tan 45°} = \frac{\sqrt{3}}{1}$$

$$\Rightarrow\quad \frac{Y_A}{Y_B} = \frac{\sqrt{3}}{1}$$

$$\Rightarrow\quad Y_B = \frac{Y_A}{\sqrt{3}}$$

9. (c) Let L be the length of the wire of cross-sectional area A and density ρ

Weight of the wire $= mg$

$$= V\times \rho\times g$$

$$= AL\rho g$$

Now, stress $= \frac{\text{weight}}{\text{cross-sectional area}}$

$$= \frac{AL\rho g}{A}$$

$$10^6 = L\rho g$$

$$L = \frac{10^6}{\rho g}$$

$$= \frac{10^6}{3\times 10^3\times 9.8} = 34\text{ m}$$

10. (c) Change in length of compound metal bar,

$$\Delta l = \Delta l_1 + \Delta l_2 + \Delta l_3$$

$$\Delta l = \frac{FL_1}{A_1 Y} + \frac{FL_2}{A_2 Y} + \frac{FL_3}{A_3 Y}$$

$$= \frac{F(2l)}{AY} + \frac{F(3l)}{2AY} + \frac{F(4l)}{3AY}$$

$$= \frac{Fl}{AY}\left[\frac{2}{1} + \frac{3}{2} + \frac{4}{3}\right] = \frac{29Fl}{6AY}$$

11. (d) From Young's modulus formula, we have

$$l = \frac{FL}{\pi r^2 Y}$$

$$\therefore\quad l \propto \frac{L}{r^2}$$

($\because$ Y and F are constants)

$$\because\quad \frac{l_2}{l_1} = \frac{L_2}{L_1}\times \left(\frac{r_1}{r_2}\right)^2 = 2\times \left(\frac{1}{2}\right)^2 = \frac{1}{2}$$

$$\Rightarrow\quad l_2 = \frac{l_1}{2} = \frac{0.05}{2} = 0.025\text{ m}$$

$$= 2.5\text{ cm}$$

12. (a) As we know,

Extension of the wire, $\Delta l = \frac{L}{D^2}$

So, for wire 1,

$$\Delta l_1 = \frac{50}{(0.5\times 10^{-2})^2}$$

$$= \frac{50}{0.25\times 10^{-4}} = 2\times 10^6$$

For wire 2,

$$\Delta l_2 = \frac{100}{(1\times 10^{-2})^2} = 1\times 10^6$$

For wire 3,

$$\Delta l_3 = \frac{200}{(2\times 10^{-2})^2} = 5\times 10^5$$

For wire 4,

$$\Delta l_4 = \frac{300}{(3\times 10^{-2})^2} = 3.3\times 10^5$$

Hence, maximum extension is in wire 1.

13. (d) The ratio of stress to strain is constant for material of the given body and is called modulus of elasticity, E.

Thus, $Y = \frac{\text{Stress}}{\text{Strain}} = \text{Constant}$

It depends only on nature of material. Hence, if stress is increased, then the ratio of stress to strain remains constant.

14. (c) The breaking stress of a metal wire does not depend on its geometrical properties like as length or cross-sectional area, etc. It depends on Young's modulus of the wire.

15. (d) Let m be the mass of the wire, L be the length, d be the density of wire and l be the change in length.

Then, $Y = \frac{FL}{Al} = \frac{FL}{\frac{V}{L}l}$ $\quad (\because V = A \times L)$

$= \frac{FdL^2}{ml}$ $\quad (\because m = V \times d)$

16. (c) Elasticity is the property to return to its original shape after being deformed by an external force. Elasticity is measured by Young's modulus which is 200 GPa for steel and 0.1 GPa for rubber. Hence, steel is more elastic than rubber.
Steel is more elastic than copper and aluminium but brass is not.
Therefore, Statement I is correct but Statement II is incorrect.

17. (c)

x ← L–x → T ← ε → com

Centripetal pull or, tension in rod at a section distant x from axis of rotation is

$$T = mr\omega^2 = \frac{M}{L}(L-x)\cdot\left(x + \frac{L-x}{2}\right)\omega^2$$

$$= \frac{M\omega^2(L^2 - x^2)}{2L}$$

So, change in length dl of section at distance x is $dl = \frac{m\omega^2(L^2 - x^2)}{2LAy}\cdot dx$

So, change in length of complete rod

$$= \int_0^L dl = \int_0^L \frac{M\omega^2(L^2 - x^2)}{2LAY}\cdot dx$$

$$= \frac{M\omega^2}{2LAY}\left(\int_0^L L^2\cdot dx - \int_0^L x^2 dx\right)$$

$$= \frac{M\omega^2 L^2}{3AY}$$

18. (d) As we know that, breaking stress remains constant.

$\therefore$ Stress $= \frac{w}{A} = \frac{w}{\pi r^2}$ ...(i)

Now, $r' = \frac{2}{3}r$, then

$$\text{Stress} = \frac{w'}{\pi r'^2}$$

$$= \frac{w'}{\pi\left(\frac{2}{3}r\right)^2} = \frac{9w'}{4\pi r^2} \quad \text{...(ii)}$$

From Eqs. (i) and (ii), we get

$$\frac{9w'}{4\pi r^2} = \frac{w}{\pi r^2}$$

$$\Rightarrow \quad w' = \frac{4w}{9}$$

19. (b) As we know that,

$$Y = \frac{Fl}{A\Delta l}$$

$$Y_A = \frac{F_A l_A}{A_A \cdot \Delta l_A} \quad \text{...(i)}$$

and $\quad Y_B = \frac{F_B L_B}{A_B \Delta l_B} \quad$ ...(ii)

Dividing Eq. (ii) by Eq. (i), we get

$$\frac{Y_B}{Y_A} = \frac{F_B l_B}{A_B \Delta l_B} \times \frac{A_A \Delta l_A}{F_A l_A}$$

$$\Rightarrow \quad \frac{\Delta l_A}{\Delta l_B} = \frac{Y_B}{Y_A} \times \frac{F_A}{F_B} \times \frac{A_B}{A_A} \times \frac{l_A}{l_B}$$

$$= \frac{1}{2} \times 1 \times \frac{1}{9} \times \frac{2}{1}$$

$$= \frac{2}{18} = \frac{1}{9}$$

20. (d) Given, axial force $= 4F$

$$p = 4F$$

$$\because \quad \sigma = \frac{p}{A}$$

According to Hooke's law,

$$\sigma = \frac{Y\Delta l}{l}$$

$$\therefore \quad \frac{p}{A} = \frac{Y\Delta l}{l}$$

$$\Rightarrow \quad \Delta l = \frac{pl}{AY} = \frac{4Fl}{AY}$$

21. (b) As we know,

Young's modulus, $Y = \frac{w}{A\Delta l}$

l, A and Δl are the same for both the wires.

$$Y \propto w$$

$$\frac{Y_b}{Y_s} = \frac{w_b}{w_s} = \frac{1}{2}$$

$$\therefore \quad \frac{w_b}{w_s} = 1:2$$

22. (a) Given, $L = 3\,\text{m}$

$A = 2 \times 10^{-6}\ \text{m}^2$

From the graph, $l = 10^{-4}$ m

$F = 20\,\text{N}$

As we know that, $Y = \frac{FL}{Al}$

$$= \frac{20 \times 3}{2 \times 10^{-6} \times 10^{-4}}$$

$$= 3.0 \times 10^{11}\ \text{N/m}^2$$

23. (d) For copper wire, $L_C = 3\,\text{m}$,

$A_C = 8 \times 10^{-5}\,\text{m}^2$

For steel wire, $L_S = 5\,\text{m}$,

$A_S = 7 \times 10^{-5}\ \text{m}^2$

As, Young's modulus,

$$Y = \frac{(F/A)}{(\Delta L/L)}$$

As, applied force F and extension ΔL are same for steel and copper wires.

$$\therefore \quad \frac{F}{\Delta L} = \frac{Y_S A_S}{L_S} = \frac{Y_C A_C}{L_C}$$

where, the subscripts C and S refers to copper and steel, respectively.

$$\therefore \quad \frac{Y_S}{Y_C} = \frac{L_S}{L_C} \times \frac{A_C}{A_S}$$

$$= \frac{(5) \times (8 \times 10^{-5})}{(3) \times (7 \times 10^{-5})}$$

$$= 1.9$$

24. (a) Elongation insteel wire will be

$$\Delta l_S = \frac{Fl}{Y_S A}$$

Elongation in copper wire will be

$$\Delta l_C = \frac{Fl}{Y_C A}$$

According to question,

$$\Delta l_S - \Delta l_C = 1\text{cm}$$

$$\Rightarrow \frac{Fl}{A}\left(\frac{1}{Y_S} - \frac{1}{Y_C}\right) = 1$$

$$\Rightarrow \frac{Fl}{A} = \frac{Y_C Y_S \times 1}{(Y_C - Y_S)}$$

$$\Rightarrow \frac{Fl}{A} = 30\times 10^{11}$$

$$\therefore \Delta l_S = \left(\frac{Fl}{A}\right)\times\frac{1}{Y_S}$$

$$= \frac{30\times 10^{11}}{2\times 10^{12}} = 1.5 \text{ cm}$$

$$\text{and } \Delta l_C = \left(\frac{Fl}{A}\right)\times\frac{1}{Y_C} = \frac{30\times 10^{11}}{12\times 10^{11}}$$

$$= 2.5 \text{ cm}$$

25. (b) $Y = \frac{\text{Stress}}{\text{Strain}}$

$\Rightarrow$ Stress $= Y \times$ Strain

$$= 20\times 10^{11} \times \frac{1\times 10^{-3}}{4}$$

$$= 5\times 10^{8} \text{ Nm}^{-2}$$

26. (c) Elongation of wire when stretched by a force, i.e. $e = \frac{Fl}{AY}$

$$\Rightarrow e \propto \frac{l}{A}$$

As the mass is same, volume is also same.

i.e. $A_1 l_1 = A_2 l_2$ or $l \propto \frac{1}{A}$

or $A \propto \frac{1}{l}$

Then $e \propto l^2$ and $\frac{e_1}{e_2} = \frac{l_1^2}{l_2^2} = \frac{4}{9}$

27. (d) A is false but R is true.

$$\text{Stress} = \frac{\text{Restoring force}}{\text{Area}}$$

$$S = \frac{\text{Force}}{\pi r^2} = \frac{F}{\pi r^2} \quad \text{...(i)}$$

When the radius of cylindrical wire is doubled,

$$S' = \frac{F}{\pi (2r)^2}$$

$$\Rightarrow S' = \frac{F}{4\pi r^2} = \frac{S}{4} \quad \text{[from Eq. (i)]}$$

Now, $A = \pi r^2$ ...(ii)

By doubling the radius, area of cross-section,

$$A' = \pi (2r)^2 = 4\pi r^2$$

$$\Rightarrow a' = 4A \quad \text{[From Eq. (ii)]}$$

Therefore, area of cross-section will become four times.

28. (d) Let T be the tension in the wire. For equilibrium, $2T \sin\theta = mg$

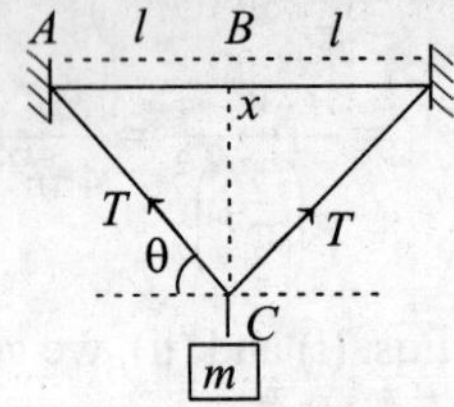

Here, $\sin\theta \approx \tan\theta = \frac{x}{l}$

(as, θ is very small)

$$\Rightarrow \frac{2Tx}{l} = mg \Rightarrow m = \frac{2Tx}{gl}$$

$$\text{From } Y = \frac{\text{Stress}}{\text{Strain}} = \frac{\left(\frac{T}{A}\right)l}{\sqrt{l^2 + x^2} - l}$$

$$Y = \frac{\left(\frac{T}{A}\right)l}{l\left(1 + \frac{x^2}{l^2}\right)^{1/2} - l}$$

$$Y = \frac{\left(\frac{T}{A}\right)l}{l\left(1 + \frac{1}{2}\frac{x^2}{l^2}\right) - l}$$

$$\Rightarrow Y = \frac{2Tl^2}{x^2 A}$$

$$\Rightarrow 2T = \frac{Yx^2 A}{l^2}$$

$$\Rightarrow m = \frac{Yx^2 A}{l^2}\frac{x}{gl} = \frac{YAx^3}{gl^3}$$

29. (a) Given, $r = 10\,\text{mm} = 0.01$ m,

$l = 1$m,

$F = 100\,\text{kN} = 10^5$ N,

$Y = 2.0\times 10^{11}$ Nm^{-2}

$$\text{Stress} = \frac{F}{A} = \frac{F}{\pi r^2}$$

$$= \frac{10^5 \text{ N}}{\left(\frac{22}{7}\right)\times (0.01 \text{ m})^2}$$

$$= 3.18\times 10^{8} \text{ Nm}^{-2}$$

As, $Y = \frac{F}{A}\cdot\frac{l}{\Delta L}$

$\therefore$ Elongation,

$$\Delta L = \frac{F}{A}\cdot\frac{l}{Y}$$

$$= \frac{3.18\times 10^8 \times 1}{2\times 10^{11}}$$

$$= 1.59\times 10^{-3} \text{ m}$$

$$= 1.59 \text{ mm}$$

$$\text{Strain} = \frac{\Delta l}{l} = \frac{1.59\times 10^{-3} \text{ m}}{1 \text{ m}}$$

$$= 1.59\times 10^{-3}$$

Change in percent $= 0.16\%$

30. (b)

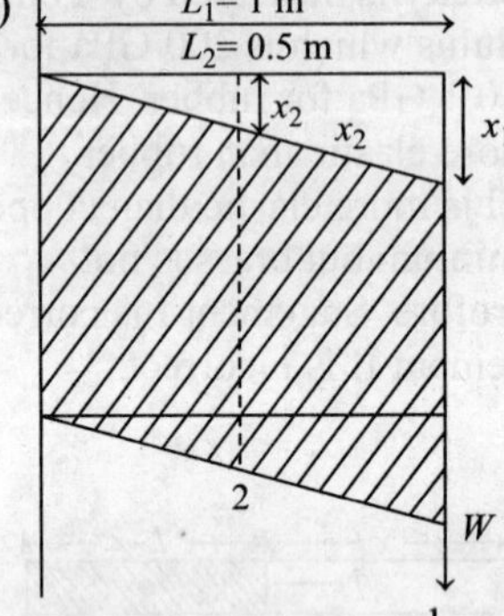

Strain at section 1,

$$\varepsilon_1 = \frac{x_1}{L_1}$$

Strain at section 2,

$$\varepsilon_2 = \frac{x_2}{L_2} = \frac{x_1/2}{L_1/2}\left\{\because \frac{x_1}{x_2} = \frac{L_1}{L_2} = 2\right.$$

$$= \frac{x_1}{L_1}$$

Stress at section 1 = stress at section 2

$= Y\cdot\varepsilon_1 = Y\varepsilon_2$

Ch-09 Mechanical Properties of Fluids

Topical Follow Thru

Test-1

1. (b) For smaller piston, area

$A_1 = \pi \times (1)^2$

For larger piston, area

$A_2 = \pi \times (10)^2$

$\therefore$ Force exerted on the larger piston,

$$F_2 = \frac{A_2}{A_1} \times F_1$$

$$= \frac{\pi(10)^2}{\pi(1)^2} \times 50 \times 10$$

$$= 100 \times 50 \times 10 \simeq 5 \times 10^4 \text{ N}$$

This is the force exerted on the larger piston. The liquids are considered incompressible. Therefore, volume covered by movement of smaller piston inwards equal to the outward movement of larger piston.

$$\therefore \quad L_1 A_1 = L_2 A_2$$

$$\Rightarrow \quad L_2 = \left(\frac{A_1}{A_2}\right) L_1 = \frac{\pi(1)^2}{\pi(10)^2} \times 5$$

$$= \frac{1}{100} \times 5 = 0.05 \text{ cm}$$

So, the distance moved out by the larger piston is 0.05 cm.

2. (b) As we know that,

$$pA = p_0 A + mg$$

$$p = p_0 + \frac{mg}{A}$$

3. (c) Given, density of first liquid, $\rho_1 = \rho$

Density of second liquid, $\rho_2 = 4\rho$

Volume of first liquid, $V_1 = 2V$

Volume of second liquid, $V_2 = V$

Density of the mixture is given as

$$\rho_{mix} = \frac{\rho_1 V_1 + \rho_2 V_2}{V_1 + V_2}$$

$$= \frac{\rho \cdot 2V + 4\rho \cdot V}{2V + V}$$

$$= \frac{6\rho V}{3V} = 2\rho$$

4. (a) Pressure at left arm of U-tube,

$$p_1 = p_0 + \rho_1 g h_1$$

$$= p_0 + \rho_1 10(10 \times 10^{-2})$$

or $\quad p_1 = p_0 + \rho_1$

Pressure at right arm of U-tube,

$$p_2 = p_0 + \rho_2 10(12 \times 10^{-2})$$

or $\quad p_2 = p_0 + 1.2\, \rho_2$

$\therefore \quad p_1 = p_2$

$\Rightarrow p_0 + \rho_1 = p_0 + 1.2\rho_2$

$\therefore$ Density of ethyl alcohol,

$$\rho_2 = \frac{\rho_1}{1.2} = \frac{1000}{1.2} = 833.3 \text{ kg/m}^3$$

$$= 0.83 \text{ gcm}^{-3}$$

5. (c) Given, $m = 50$ kg,

$D = 1 \text{ cm} = 10^{-2}$ m, $g = 10 \text{ ms}^{-2}$

$\therefore$ Pressure exerted by the heel on the horizontal floor is

$$p = \frac{F}{A} = \frac{mg}{\pi(D/2)^2} = \frac{4mg}{\pi D^2}$$

$$= \frac{4 \times 50 \times 10}{3.14 \times (10^{-2})^2}$$

$$= 6.4 \times 10^6 \text{ Pa}$$

6. (a) Given, $h = 5$ m

$$\rho = 1 \times 10^3 \text{ kg/m}^3$$

$$g = 10 \text{ m/s}^2$$

$\therefore$ Pressure at the bottom of the column,

$$p = p_a + \rho g h$$

$$= 1 \times 10^5 + 1 \times 10^3 \times 10 \times 5$$

$$= 1 \times 10^5 + 0.5 \times 10^5$$

$$= 1.5 \times 10^5 \text{ Pa}$$

7. (c) Given, height of the cylinder, h

$= 15 \text{ cm} = 15 \times 10^{-2}$ m

Radius of cylinder, r

$= 7 \text{ cm} = 7 \times 10^{-2}$ m

$\therefore$ Volume of the cylinder,

$$V = \pi r^2 h$$

$$= \frac{22}{7} \times (7 \times 10^{-2})^2 \times 15 \times 10^{-2}$$

$$= 2310 \times 10^{-6} = 2.3 \times 10^{-3} \text{ m}^3$$

Now, Buoyant force $= V\rho g$

$$= 2.3 \times 10^{-3} \times 1 \times 10^3 \times 10$$

$$= 23 \text{ N}$$

8. (c) As we know, pressure $= h\rho g$

Pressure at the bottom is independent of the area of the base of the vessel. It depends on the height of water upto which the vessel is filled with water. As in all the three vessels, level of water are the same, therefore pressure at the bottom in all the vessels will also be the same.

Hence, $p_1 = p_2 = p_3$

9. (a) With increase in depth, the pressure increases from the formula $p \propto h$.

Therefore, the pressure of water is very large at bottom of a dam.

A hydraulic lift is an arrangement used to multiply the force. When a force is applied, hydraulic pressure is transmitted in all directions. This is the working principle of Pascal's law.

Hence, both Statement I and Statement II are correct.

10. (b) As long as $\rho \le \rho_l$ pressure at the bottom of the pan would be same everywhere.

11. (d) Weight of submerged part of the block,

$$w = \frac{1}{3} v \rho_w g \quad \text{...(i)}$$

where, ρ_w = density of water.

Excess weight = Weight of water having $\frac{2}{3}$ volume of the block, we get

$$w' = \frac{2}{3} v \rho_w g \quad \text{...(ii)}$$

Dividing Eq. (ii) by Eq. (i),

$$\frac{w'}{w} = \frac{2/3}{1/3}$$

$$\therefore \ w' = 2w$$

$$\Rightarrow w' = 2 \times 6 = 12 \text{ kg}$$

12. (c) As the sphere floats in the liquid, therefore its weight will be equal to the upthrust force on it.

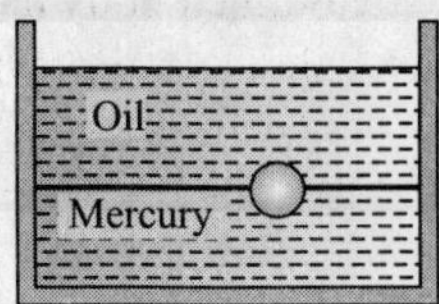

Weight of sphere $= \frac{4}{3}\pi R^3 \rho g$ ...(i)

Upthrust due to oil and mercury

$= \frac{2}{3}\pi R^3 \times \sigma_{oil} g + \frac{2}{3}\pi R^3 \sigma_{Hg} g$ ...(ii)

Equating Eqs. (i) and (ii), we get

$$\frac{4}{3}\pi R^3 \rho g = \frac{2}{3}\pi R^3 0.8g + \frac{2}{3}\pi R^3 \times 13.6g$$

$\Rightarrow 2\rho = 0.8 + 13.6 = 14.4$

$\Rightarrow \rho = 7.2$

13. (d) By Pascal's law

$\Rightarrow \frac{F_1}{A_1} = \frac{F_2}{A_2}$

$\Rightarrow F_2 \propto A_2/A_1$

Also, $V_1 = V_2$

$\Rightarrow A_1 x_1 = A_2 x_2$

$\Rightarrow A_1 \frac{d}{dt} x_1 = A_2 \frac{d}{dt} x_2$

$\Rightarrow A_1 v_1 = A_2 v_2$

$\Rightarrow \frac{v_2}{v_1} = \frac{A_1}{A_2}$

As pressure is same in both the limbs, so work done by force F_1 is equal to that of F_2.

Thus, the statement given in option (d) is correct, rest are incorrect.

14. (b) Let V be the volume of iceberg and x be the fraction of volume above water.

Using law of floatation, weight of floating body = weight of liquid displaced by part of the floating body inside the liquid.

Therefore, $V\rho_{ice} g = (1-x)V\rho_{water} g$.

Using the value of ρ_{ice} and ρ_{water}, we get $(1-x) = \frac{900}{1030}$

$\Rightarrow x = \frac{13}{103}$

15. (d) Here, $T + mg = F_b$

$\therefore T = F_b - mg$

$= V\rho_w g - mg$

$= \frac{m}{(\rho_w/\eta)}\rho_w g - mg$

$= (\eta - 1)mg$

16. (a) Pressure difference between lungs and atmosphere $= (760 - 750)$ mm of Hg $= 10$ mm of Hg $= 1$ cm of Hg.

Let the boy can suck water from depth h, then pressure difference

$h\rho_{water} g = 1$ cm of Hg or

$h \times 1\text{g cm}^{-3} \times 980\text{cm s}^{-2}$

$= 1\text{cm} \times 13.6\text{ gcm}^{-3} \times 980\text{cms}^{-2}$

$\therefore h = 13.6$ cm.

The boy can suck water from the depth of 13.6 cm

17. (d) As the block moves up with the fall of coin l decreases, similarly h will also decreases because when the coin is in water, it displaces water equal to its own volume only.

18. (a) Pressure on the smaller piston

$= \frac{20 \times 9.8}{\pi \times (5 \times 10^{-2})^2}\text{Nm}^{-2}$

Pressure on the larger piston

$= \frac{F}{\pi \times (17.5 \times 10^{-2})^2}\text{Nm}^{-2}$

The difference between the two pressures $= h\rho g$

where, $h = 1.5$ m

and $\rho = 750\text{ kgm}^{-3}$

Thus, $\frac{20 \times 9.8}{\pi \times (5 \times 10^{-2})^2} - \frac{F}{\pi \times (17.5 \times 10^{-2})^2}$

$= 1.5 \times 750 \times 9.8$

which gives, $F = 1.3 \times 10^3$ N

Note Atmospheric pressure is common to both pistons and has been ignored.

19. (a) Net force = Actual weight − Upthrust force

= Actual weight − Weight of liquid displaced.

The body will rise above the surface of liquid to such an extent that the weight of the liquid displaced by the immersed part of the body (i.e. upward thrust) becomes equal to the weight of the body. In this special case, the density of solid body is less than the density of liquid.

20. (c) If two different bodies A and B are floating in the same liquid, then

$$\frac{\rho_A}{\rho_B} = \frac{(f_{in})_A}{(f_{in})_B} = \frac{1/2}{2/3} = \frac{3}{4}$$

21. (a) As we know, $p = \frac{F}{A}$

So, smaller the area, larger the pressure exerted by a force.

Hence, both A and R are true and R is the correct explanation of A.

22. (c) For the floatation, $V_0 d_0 g = V_{in} dg$

$\Rightarrow V_{in} = V_0 \frac{d_0}{d}$

$V_{out} = V_0 - V_{in} = V_0 - V_0 \frac{d_0}{d}$

$= V_0\left[\frac{d - d_0}{d}\right]$

$\frac{V_{out}}{V_0} = \frac{d - d_0}{d}$

23. (b) Pressure at bottom of the lake

$= p_0 + h\rho g$

Pressure at half the depth of a lake

$= p_0 + \frac{h}{2}\rho g$

According to given condition,

$p_0 + \frac{1}{2}h\rho g = \frac{2}{3}(p_0 + h\rho g)$

$\Rightarrow \frac{1}{3}p_0 = \frac{1}{6}h\rho g$

$\Rightarrow h = \frac{2p_0}{\rho g} = \frac{2 \times 10^5}{10^3 \times 10} = 20$ m

24. (c) As we know,

$\rho = \frac{\text{Total mass}}{\text{Total volume}}$

$= \frac{2m}{V_1 + V_2} = \frac{2m}{m\left(\frac{1}{\rho_1} + \frac{1}{\rho_2}\right)}$

$\rho = \frac{2\rho_1\rho_2}{\rho_1 + \rho_2}$

25. (c) Let m be the mass of the copper in ornament, then, mass of gold in it is $(50 - m)$.

Volume of copper, $V_1 = \frac{m}{10}$

$\left(\because \text{Volume} = \frac{\text{Mass}}{\text{Density}}\right)$

and volume of gold,

$V_2 = \frac{50-m}{20}$

When immersed in water

$(\rho_w = 1 \text{gcm}^{-3})$

Decrease in weight = Upthrust

$\therefore (50-46)g = (V_1 + V_2)\rho_w g$

or $4 = \frac{m}{10} + \frac{50-m}{20}$

or $80 = 2m + 50 - m$

$\therefore m = 30 \text{ g}$

Test-2

1. (b) Bernoulli's theorem for unit mass of liquid,

$\frac{p}{\rho} + \frac{1}{2}v^2 = \text{constant}$

As the liquid starts flowing, its pressure energy decreases

$\frac{1}{2}v^2 = \frac{p_1 - p_2}{\rho} = \frac{2.0\times10^5 - 1.5\times10^5}{10^3}$

$\Rightarrow v^2 = \frac{2\times 0.5\times 10^5}{10^3}$

$\Rightarrow v^2 = 100$

$\Rightarrow v = 10 \text{ m/s}$

2. (a) As we know that, range,

$R = 2\sqrt{h(H-h)}$

$\because$ Range of both holes are same.

$\therefore 2\sqrt{h_1(H-h_1)} = 2\sqrt{h_2(H-h_2)}$

$h_1(H-h_1) = h_2(H-h_2)$

$60(H-60) = 40(H-40)$

$60H - 3600 = 40H - 1600$

$20H = 3600 - 1600$

$20H = 2000$

$H = 100 \text{ cm}$

3. (b) Pressure at the bottom of tank,

$p = h\rho g = 3\times10^5 \text{ N/m}^2$

Pressure due to liquid column,

$p_l = 3\times10^5 - 1\times10^5$

$= 2\times10^5 \text{ N/m}^2$

Now, velocity of water

$v = \sqrt{\frac{2p_l}{\rho}} = \sqrt{\frac{2\times2\times10^5}{10^3}}$

$= 2\sqrt{100}$ m/s

4. (b) Applying Bernoulli's theorem just above and just below the roof,

$p + \frac{1}{2}\rho v^2 = p_0 + 0$

$(p_0 - p) = \frac{1}{2}\rho v^2 = \Delta p$

Hence lift of the roof

$F = \Delta\rho\cdot A$

$= \frac{1}{2}\rho A v^2 = \frac{1}{2}\times 1.2\times 200\times (50)^2$

$= 3.0\times 10^5$ N, upwards

5. (c) Given, $v_2 = 60 \text{ cm/s} = 0.6 \text{ m/s}$

$A_1 = 1.5 \text{ cm}^2 = 1.5\times 10^{-4} \text{m}^{-2}$

$A_2 = 25 \text{ mm}^2$

$= 25\times 10^{-6} \text{ m}^2$

According to equation of continuity,

$A_1 v_1 = A_2 v_2$

$\Rightarrow v_1 = \frac{A_2 v_2}{A} = \frac{25\times10^{-6}\times 0.6}{1.5\times10^{-4}}$

$= 0.1 \text{ m/s}$

$\therefore$ According to Bernoulli's principle,

$p_A - p_B = \frac{1}{2}\rho(v_2^2 - v_1^2)$

$= \frac{1}{2}\times 1000[(0.6)^2 - (0.1)^2]$

$= 500\,[0.35] = 175.00$

$= 175 \text{ Pa}$

6. (b) Since, the cross-section area is halved, velocity will be doubled.

Here, $p_1 = 2500 \text{ Pa}$, $v_1 = 1 \text{ m/s}$

$v_2 = 2 \text{ m/s}$

Now, $p_2 + \frac{1}{2}\rho v_2^2 = p_1 + \frac{1}{2}\rho v_1^2$

$\Rightarrow p_2 + \frac{1}{2}\times 10^3\times 2\times 2$

$= 2500 + \frac{1}{2}\times 10^3\times 2\times 2$

$p_2 + 2000 = 2500 + 2000$

$p_2 = 2500 \text{ Pa}$

7. (a) A streamlined body has less resistance due to air, so cigar shaped body has less air resistance and disc shaped body has maximum air resistance.

8. (a) From continuity equaiton,

$Av = \text{constant}$

or $A \propto \frac{1}{v}$

9. (b) $Q = A_1 v_1 = A_2 v_2$

$= 15 \text{ L/min}$

$= \frac{15\times 10^{-3}}{60} = 2.5\times10^{-4} \text{ m}^3\text{/s}$

$v_1 = \frac{2.5\times10^{-4}}{2\times10^{-4}} = 1.25 \text{ m/s}$

$v_2 = \frac{2.5\times10^{-4}}{0.5\times10^{-4}} = 5.0 \text{ m/s}$

Now, difference in pressure = difference in kinetic energy

$h\rho_w g = \frac{1}{2}\rho_{\text{air}}(v_2^2 - v_1^2)$

or $h = \frac{\rho_{\text{air}}}{2\rho_w g}(v_2^2 - v_1^2)$

$= \frac{1.32}{2\times10^3\times 10}[(5)^2 - (1.25)^2]$

$= 1.5\times10^{-3} \text{ m} \approx 1.5 \text{ mm}$

10. (b) Given, $h = 45$ m

Velocity of efflux, $v = \sqrt{2gh}$

$= \sqrt{2\times10\times45}$

$= \sqrt{900} = 30 \text{ m/s}$

11. (c) Decrease in potential energy = Increase in kinetic energy

$\therefore \rho g h = \frac{1}{2}\rho(v_f^2 - v_i^2)$

or $2(10)(0.15) = v_f^2 - (1.0)^2$

or $v_f = 2 \text{ m/s}$

Now, from continuity equation,

$A_1 v_1 = A_2 v_2$ or $A \propto \frac{1}{v}$

Velocity has become two times. Hence, area of cross-section will remain half.

$A_1 v_1 = A_2 v_2$

$10^{-4}\times 1 = A_2\times 2$

$A_2 = \frac{1\times10^{-4}}{2} = 0.5\times10^{-4} \text{ m}^2$

$A_2 = 5\times10^{-5} \text{ m}^2$

12. (a) Air flows just above the roof and there is no air flow just below the roof inside the room. Therefore $v_1 = 0$ and $v_2 = v$. Applying Bernoulli's theorem at the points inside and outside the roof, we obtain

$(1/2)\rho v_1^2 + \rho g h_1 + p_1$

$= (1/2)\rho v_2^2 + \rho g h_2 + p_2$

Since, $h_1 = h_2 = h$, $v_1 = 0$ and $v_2 = v$

$\therefore\ p_1 = p_2 + (1/2)\rho v^2$

$\Rightarrow\ p_1 - p_2 = \Delta p = (1/2)\rho v^2$

Since, the area of the roof is A the aerodynamic lift exerted on it

$= F = (\Delta p)A$

$$\Rightarrow\quad F = \frac{1}{2}\rho A v^2$$

where, ρ (density of air) $= 1.3\ \text{kg/m}^3$

$A = 20\text{m}^2$, $v = 29.44$ m/s

$\Rightarrow\ F = \{(1/2)\times 1.3\times 20\times (29.44)^2\}$

$F \simeq 1.13\times 10^4$ N

13. (a) Inflow rate of volume of the liquid = Outflow rate of volume of the liquid

$\pi R^2 v = n\pi r^2 (v)$

$$\Rightarrow\quad v = \frac{\pi R^2 v}{n\pi r^2} = \frac{vR^2}{nr^2}$$

14. (b) Using Torricelli's law,

Velocity, $v = \sqrt{2gh}$ ...(i)

and $p_2 - p_1 = \rho g(h_2 - h_1)$

Here, $h_2 = h$ and $h_1 = 0$ then

$p_2 - p_1 = \rho g h$

$$h = \frac{p_2 - p_1}{\rho g} \quad \text{...(ii)}$$

From Eq. (i) and Eq. (ii), we get

$$v = \sqrt{\frac{2g\times(p_2 - p_1)}{\rho g}}$$

$$= \sqrt{\frac{2\times(3\times 10^5 - 1\times 10^5)}{1000}}$$

$$= \sqrt{\frac{4\times 10^5}{1000}} = \sqrt{400}\ \text{m/s}$$

15. (c) As, $t = k(\sqrt{h_1} - \sqrt{h_2})$

$\therefore\quad t_1 = k(\sqrt{h} - \sqrt{h/2})$

and $t_2 = k(\sqrt{h/2} - 0)$

$$\therefore\quad \frac{t_1}{t_2} = \sqrt{2} - 1$$

Test-3

1. (d) As volume remains constant therefore $R = n^{1/3} r$

$$= \frac{\text{Surface energy of one big drop}}{\text{Surface energy of } n \text{ drops}}$$

$$= \frac{4\pi R^2 T}{n\times 4\pi r^2 T}$$

$$= \frac{R^2}{nr^2} = \frac{n^{2/3} r^2}{nr^2} = \frac{1}{n^{1/3}}$$

$$= \frac{1}{(64)^{1/3}} = \frac{1}{4} = 1:4$$

2. (a) As we know,

energy needed = increment in surface energy

= surface energy of n small drops − surface energy of one big drop

$= n4\pi r^2 T - 4\pi R^2 T$

$= 4\pi T(nr^2 - R^2)$

3. (b) Given, surface tension of water,

$T = 7.2\times 10^{-2}$ N/m

Radius of air bubble, $R = 0.1$ mm $= 10^{-4}$ m

The excess pressure inside the air bubble is given by

$$p_2 - p_1 = \frac{2T}{R}$$

$\therefore$ Pressure inside the air bubble,

$$p_2 = p_1 + \frac{2T}{R}$$

$$= (1.013\times 10^5) + \frac{2\times 7.2\times 10^{-2}}{10^{-4}}$$

$= 1.027\times 10^5\ \text{N/m}^2$

$\simeq 10^5\ \text{N/m}^2$

4. (a) Velocity of flow,

$$v = \frac{\Delta V/\Delta t}{A} = \frac{0.5\times 10^{-3}}{\pi r^2 (60)}\cdot\frac{\text{m}}{\text{s}}$$

Now Reynold's number for flow

$$R = \frac{\rho v D}{\eta} = \frac{1000\times 0.5\times 10^{-3}\times 2r}{\pi r^2\times 60\times\eta}$$

[Here, $r = 1.5$ cm]

$= 796$

As $R < 1000$ so, flow is streamlined.

5. (c) We know that, rise of liquid in capillary tube is given as

$$h = \frac{2T\cos\theta}{r\rho g}$$

$$\therefore\quad hr = \frac{2T\cos\theta}{\rho g} = \text{constant}$$

$\Rightarrow\quad hr = \text{constant}$

$\Rightarrow\ h_1 r_1 = h_2 r_2$

$$\Rightarrow\quad h_2 = \frac{h_1 r_1}{r_2} = 2\times\frac{r_1}{r_1/2}\quad\left(\because r_2 = \frac{r_1}{2}\right)$$

$= 4$ cm

6. (c) Let r be the radius of each drop. The terminal velocity of the drop is given as

$$v = \frac{2r^2(\rho - \sigma)g}{9\eta} \quad \text{...(i)}$$

When two drops are coalesced to form a new big drop of radius R, then

$R = 2^{1/3}\cdot r$

$\therefore$New terminal velocity of coalesced drop,

$$v' = \frac{2}{9}\left[\frac{(2^{1/3} r)^2(\rho - \sigma)g}{\eta}\right] \quad \text{...(ii)}$$

From Eqs. (i) and (ii), we get

$$\frac{v'}{v} = 2^{2/3} \Rightarrow v' = 2^{2/3} v = 4^{1/3} v$$

7. (c) Force needed to lift = Force of surface tension

$\Rightarrow\quad F = 2(l + b)\times S$

[S = surface tension of liquid]

$$\therefore\text{Ratio}\ \frac{F_A}{F_B} = \frac{(l+b)_A}{(l+b)_B}$$

$$= \frac{6+4}{8+3} = \frac{10}{11}$$

8. (a) When two droplets merge with each other, the surface area decreases.
So, excess energy is liberated.

9. (c) We know that liquid film has two surfaces, hence increase in surface area.

$$\Delta A = 2[(20\times 25)-(10\times 20)]\times 10^{-4}$$
$$= 2(300)\times 10^{-4}$$
$$= 6\times 10^{-2}\text{ m}^2$$

Since, $W = T\Delta A$

$$\Rightarrow \quad T = \frac{W}{\Delta A} = \frac{5\times 10^{-3}}{6\times 10^{-2}}$$
$$= 0.083\text{ N/m}$$

10. (c) For liquids, which wet the walls of a vessel, the angle of contact is acute. The liquid that wets the solid surface has concave meniscus because adhesive force is greater than the cohesive force.

11. (d) Using the formula of the terminal velocity of a body falling through a viscous medium

$$v = \frac{2r^2(\rho-\sigma)g}{9\eta}$$
$$\Rightarrow \quad \eta = \frac{2r^2(\rho-\sigma)g}{9v}$$

where ρ is the density of material of body and σ is the density of medium.
In case of the air bubble $\rho = 1\text{ kg/m}^3$ and $\sigma = 1.47\times 10^3$ kg/ms the air bubble rises up $\eta = \frac{2r^2\sigma g}{9v}$

$$= \frac{2\times (10^{-2})^2\times 1.47\times 10^3\times 9.8}{9\times 0.21\times 10^{-2}}$$
$$= 1.52\times 10^3\text{ decapoise}$$
$$= 1.52\times 10^4\text{ poise}$$

12. (a) A. When a single drop splits, then its total surface tension will be increase. Therefore, energy is absorbed in this process.
B. When n drops combine to form a single drop, then energy is released.
C. The surface tension of a liquid drop decreases for increases in temperature.
D. The surface tension of water at boiling point is zero.

Hence, A $\to$ 3, B $\to$ 4, C $\to$ 2, D $\to$ 1.

13. (b) As we know, $v \propto \frac{\rho-\rho_0}{\eta}$

$$\therefore \quad \frac{v_2}{v_1} = \frac{\rho-\rho_{02}}{\rho-\rho_{01}}\times\frac{\eta_1}{\eta_2}$$
$$v_2 = \frac{7.8-1.2}{7.8-1}\times\frac{8.5\times 10^{-4}\times 10}{13.2}$$
$$= 6.25\times 10^{-4}\text{ cms}^{-1}$$

14. (d) Initially velocity increases with respect to time and becomes constant after sometime, this constant velocity is called terminal velocity.

15. (c) As surface area decreases, so energy is released,
Energy released
$\Delta E = 4\pi R^2 T[n^{1/3}-1]$
(where $R = n^{1/3} r$)

$$= 4\pi R^3 T\left[\frac{1}{r}-\frac{1}{R}\right]$$
$$= 3VT\left[\frac{1}{r}-\frac{1}{R}\right]$$

Chapter Break Thru

1. (a) Air streams have to cover a larger distance above the surface as compared to the air streams below the surface. So, velocity above the surface is large and consequently the pressure is less. On the other hand, velocity below the surface is small and consequently the pressure is large. This explains maximum upthrust in figure (a).

2. (d) As cross-section areas of both the tubes A and C are same and tube is horizontal. Hence, according to equation of continuity $v_A = v_C$ and therefore according to Bernoulli's theorem $p_A = p_C$ i.e. height of liquid is same in both the tubes A and C.

3. (c) The force exerted by water at the bends is shown in figure. Water undergoes change in momentum at these points and hence these exert force on each other.
The two forces form a couple exerting a clockwise torque.

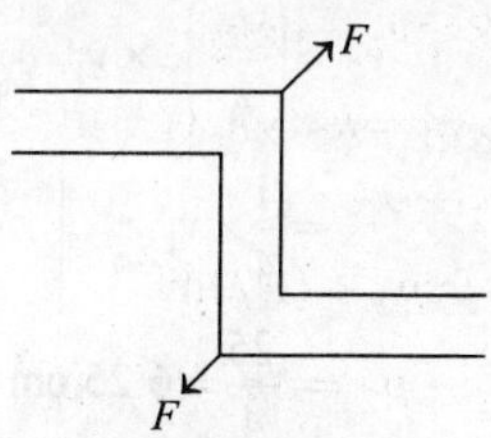

4. (c) Let us assume that the speed of fluid in the lower branch is v, then from the equation of continuity,

$$0.9v + 0.12\times 1.5 = 0.12\times 3$$
$$\Rightarrow \quad 0.9v = 0.12\times 3 - 0.12\times 1.5$$
$$\Rightarrow \quad 0.9v = 0.18$$
$$\Rightarrow \quad v = \frac{0.18}{0.9} = 0.2\text{ m/s}$$
$$= 20\text{ cm/s}$$

5. (c) Let the radius of bigger drop is R and of smaller drop is r, then

$$\frac{4}{3}\pi R^3 = 27\times\frac{4}{3}\times\pi r^3$$

or $\quad R = 3r$

Terminal velocity, $v \propto r^2$

$$\therefore \quad \frac{v'}{v} = \frac{R^2}{r^2} = \left(\frac{3r}{r}\right)^2 = 9$$

or $\quad v' = 9v = 9\times 9$
$$= 81\text{ cms}^{-1}$$

6. (b) Let V_C be the volume of cavity and V be the actual volume of gold piece [excluding volume of cavity, $\rho = 1.2\text{ kg/m}^3$]

$$\therefore \quad V = \frac{50}{19.3} = 2.6\text{ cm}^3$$

Now, loss in weight of gold in water
= Thrust due to water
$$\Rightarrow 50-42 = [V+V_C]\rho\omega g$$
$$8 = (2.6+V_C)1$$
$$V_C = 5.4\text{ cm}^3$$

7. (a) A - (2), B - (3), C - (4), D - (1).

8. (c) As we know that, terminal velocity $v_t \propto r^2$

$$\frac{v_2}{v_1} = \left(\frac{r_2}{r_1}\right)^2$$

$$v_2 = \left(\frac{r_2}{r_1}\right)^2 \times v_1$$

$$= \frac{1}{4} \times v_1 \quad \left[\because \frac{r_2}{r_1} = \frac{1}{2}\right]$$

$$= \frac{25}{4} = 6.25 \text{ cm/s}$$

9. (a) Total number of moles of air in the two soap bubbles = Number of moles of air in the resulting bubble

$$\frac{2pV}{RT} = \frac{p'V'}{RT}$$

$$2pV = p'V'$$

$$2\left(p_0 + \frac{4T}{r}\right)\frac{4}{3}\pi r^3 = \left(p_0 + \frac{4T}{R}\right)\frac{4}{3}\pi R^3$$

$$2\left(p_0 + \frac{4T}{r}\right)r^3 = \left(p_0 + \frac{4T}{R}\right)R^3$$

$$\therefore \quad T = \frac{p_0(R^3 - 2r^3)}{8r^2 - 4R^2}$$

$$= \frac{p_0(2r^3 - R^3)}{4(R^2 - 2r^2)}$$

10. (b) Let density of body be σ, then according to question,

$$\frac{\sigma}{\rho_w} = 1 - \frac{2}{3} = \frac{1}{3} \quad \text{...(i)}$$

$$\text{and } \frac{\sigma}{\rho_l} = \frac{3}{4} \quad \text{...(ii)}$$

From Eqs. (i) and (ii), we get

$$\frac{\rho_l}{\rho_w} = \frac{4}{9} \Rightarrow \rho_l = \frac{4}{9}\rho_w$$

∴ density of water

$$\rho_w = 1 \text{ g cm}^{-1}$$

$$= \frac{4}{9} \times 1 = \frac{4}{9} \text{ g cm}^{-3}$$

11. (a) According to Pascal's law, if gravity effect is neglected, the pressure at every point of liquid in equilibrium is same.

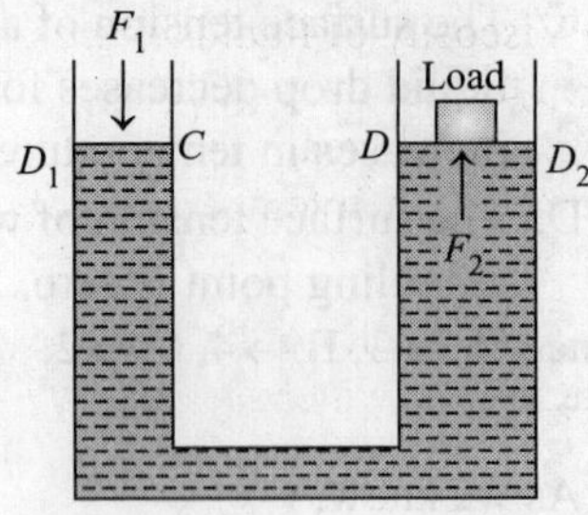

$$p_1 = p_2$$

$$\text{i.e.} \quad \frac{F_1}{a_1} = \frac{F_2}{a_2}$$

$$\text{or} \quad F_2 = \frac{a_2}{a_1} F_1$$

$F_2 >> F_1$, as $a_2 >> a_1$

This shows that small force (F_1) applied on the smaller piston (of area a_1) will be appearing as a very large force on the larger piston.

12. (c) Ball *C* further rises up due to lowering of pressure in upper part. So, it will taken more time to fall down and it will cover maximum range.

13. (c) Volume of log of wood,

$$V = \frac{\text{mass}}{\text{density}} = \frac{100}{600} = 0.16 \text{ m}^3$$

Let *x* be the weight that can be put on the log of wood, so weight of the body = $(100 + x) \times 10$ N.

Weight of displaced liquid

$$= V\sigma g = (0.16 \times 10^3 \times 10) \text{ N}$$

The body will just sink in liquid, if the weight of the body will be equal to the weight of displaced liquid.

$$\therefore \quad (100 + x) \times 10 = 0.16 \times 10^3 \times 10$$

$$\Rightarrow \quad 100 + x = 160$$

$$\therefore \quad x = 60 \text{ kg}$$

14. (b) The given situation is shown in the U-tube below

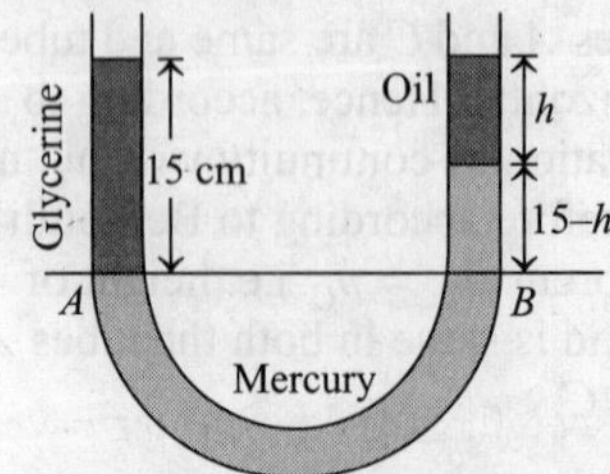

At the condition of equilibrium,

Pressure at point *A* = Pressure at point *B*

$$p_A = p_B$$

$$15 \times 1.3 \times g = h \times 0.8 \times g + (15 - h) \times 13.6 \times g$$

$$19.5 = 0.8h + 204 - 13.6h$$

$$12.8h = 184.5$$

$$h = 14.4 \text{ cm}$$

15. (a) According to Bernoulli's theorem,

$$p + \frac{1}{2}\rho v^2 = a \text{ (constant)}$$

i.e. When velocity is large, the pressure is less in streamline flow of an ideal liquid through a horizontal tube.

16. (c) The rise of liquid column in capillary is given by

$$h = \frac{2T \cos\theta}{r\rho g}$$

∴ For water,

$$h_w = \frac{2 \times T_w \times \cos 0°}{r \times 1 \times g} \quad \text{...(i)}$$

Similarly, for mercury,

$$h_m = -\frac{2 \times T_m \times \cos 135°}{r \times 13.6 \times g} \quad \text{...(ii)}$$

$$\therefore \quad \frac{h_w}{h_m} = \frac{2 \times T_w \times 1}{r \times 1 \times g} \times \frac{r \times 13.6 \times g \times \sqrt{2}}{2 \times T_m \times 1}$$

$$[\because \cos 135° = -1/\sqrt{2}]$$

$$\Rightarrow \quad \frac{20}{6.84} = \frac{T_w}{T_m} \times 13.6 \times \sqrt{2}$$

$$\therefore \quad \frac{T_w}{T_m} = \frac{20}{6.84 \times 13.6 \times 1.414} = \frac{1}{6.5}$$

Therefore, $T_w : T_m = 1 : 6.5$

17. (d) From Bernoulli's principle in the horizontal streamline motion of a liquid, the sum of pressure (p) and kinetic energy per unit volume of the liquid at any point is constant,

Hence $p + \frac{1}{2}\rho v^2 = \text{constant}$

It is clear from this equation that a flowing liquid where the velocity of flow is less, the pressure is large and *vice-versa*. Hence, arteries carrying blood become narrow resulting in increase in the blood pressure.

18. (c) When the whole container is accelerated the liquid is pushed side of the container, but the volume of whole liquid remains the same,

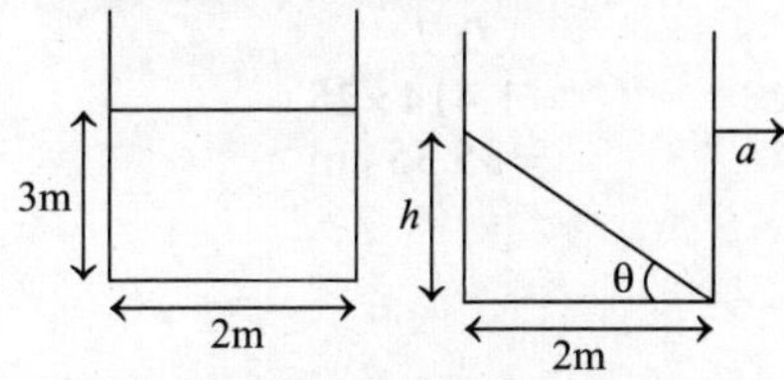

$$2\times 3=\frac{1}{2}\times h\times 2 \Rightarrow h=6\,\text{m}$$

$$\therefore \quad \tan\theta=\frac{6}{2}=\frac{a}{g}$$

$$\Rightarrow \quad a=\frac{6}{2}g=3g$$

19. (c) As, $\frac{\Delta p}{\Delta x}=\rho a=\rho g$

(in horizontal direction)

Pressure decreases in the direction of acceleration in horizontal.

$\therefore p_D < p_C \Rightarrow p_C - p_D = \rho g L$

$\frac{\Delta p}{\Delta x}=\rho g$ (in vertical direction)

Pressure increases with depth in vertical direction.

$\therefore \quad p_A - p_C = \rho g L$

20. (a) From the figure, we have

$\delta g R(\cos\theta+\sin\theta)=\rho g R$

$(\cos\theta-\sin\theta)$

$\Rightarrow \delta\cos\theta+\delta\sin\theta=\rho\cos\theta$

$-\rho\sin\theta$

$\Rightarrow \sin\theta(\delta+\rho)=\cos\theta(\rho-\delta)$

$$\Rightarrow \quad \tan\theta=\frac{\rho-\delta}{\rho+\delta}$$

$$\theta=\tan^{-1}\left(\frac{\rho-\delta}{\rho+\delta}\right)$$

21. (b) Given, $A=4\,\text{m}^2$

$v=1.5$ m/s

$x=2$ mm $=2\times10^{-3}$ m

$\eta=16$ N-sm^{-2}

Now, $F=\frac{\eta\cdot Av}{x}=\frac{16\times4\times1.5}{2\times10^{-3}}$

$=48000$ N

22. (b) Viscosity of liquids decreases when temperature of liquids increases whereas viscosity of gases increases when temperature of gases increases.

23. (d) The velocity of ball before entering the water surface,

$$v=\sqrt{2gh}=\sqrt{2g\times10}$$

When ball enters into water, due to upthrust of water, the velocity of ball decreases (or retarded).

$$\text{Retardation, } a=\frac{\text{Apparent weight}}{\text{Mass of ball}}$$

$$=\frac{V(\rho-\sigma)g}{V\rho}=\left(\frac{\rho-\sigma}{\rho}\right)g$$

$$=\left(\frac{0.5-1}{0.5}\right)\times g=-g$$

If h be the depth upto which ball sink, then

$$0-v^2=2(-g)\times h$$

$$\Rightarrow \quad 2g\times10=2gh \therefore h=10\,\text{cm}$$

24. (d) Pressure at bottom of the lake $=p_0+h\rho g$

Pressure at surface of a lake $=p_0$

According to given condition,

$$p_0=\frac{2}{3}(p_0+h\rho g)$$

$$\Rightarrow \quad \frac{1}{3}p_0=h\rho g$$

$$h=\frac{p_0}{3\rho g}=\frac{10^5}{3\times10^3\times10}$$

$$=\frac{10}{3}=3.3\,\text{m}$$

25. (b) Suppose, weight of gold in air is x g.

Weight of aluminium in air is y g.

Density of gold $=d_1$

Density of aluminium $=d_2$

(where, $d_1>d_2$)

Volume of gold $=\frac{x}{d_1}$ and volume of aluminium $=\frac{y}{d_2}$

As weight of gold in water = weight of aluminium in water

$$\left(x-\frac{x}{d_1}\times1\right)g=\left(y-\frac{y}{d_2}\times1\right)g$$

$$\frac{x}{y}=\frac{\left(1-\frac{1}{d_2}\right)}{\left(1-\frac{1}{d_1}\right)}<1$$

or $x<y$ or $y>x$

i.e. Weight of aluminium in air is more than that of gold in air.

26. (a) As we know that,

Force = Area of base × Pressure due to liquid column of height h

$=\pi r^2\times h\rho g$

$=\pi r^2\times20\times\rho g \quad [\because h=20\,\text{m}]$

$=20\pi r^2\rho g$

27. (c) Since, volume remains constant.

$$\frac{4}{3}\pi R^3=10^6\times\frac{4}{3}\pi r^3$$

[No. of small drops $=10^6$]

$$\therefore \quad r=\frac{R}{10^2}$$

$\therefore$ Change in surface energy

= Increase in surface area × Surface tension

$$=(10^6\times4\pi r^2-4\pi R^2)\times T$$

$$=4\pi\left(10^6\times\frac{R^2}{10^4}-R^2\right)\times T$$

$$=396\pi R^2 T$$

28. (b) Angle of contact decreases with increase in temperature. The surface tension of a liquid also decreases with increase in temperature.

29. (c) Suppose, R = radius of water drop and r = radius of droplets

$$\therefore \quad \frac{4}{3}\pi R^3=64\times\frac{4}{3}\pi r^3$$

(Since, volume remains constant)

$$\therefore \quad r=\frac{R}{4}$$

Pressure difference from mercury drop of radius R,

$$p_R=\frac{4T}{R}$$

Pressure difference from droplet of radius r,

$$p_r = \frac{4T}{r} = \frac{4T}{R/4} = \frac{16T}{R}$$

$$p_r = 4\left(\frac{4T}{R}\right) = 4p_R$$

$$\Rightarrow \quad p_R = \frac{p_r}{4}$$

Therefore, pressure difference between inner and outer surfaces of bigger drop will be one-fourth of that for smaller droplet.

30. (b) Here, area reduced to half of the initial value.

$$\therefore \quad A_2 = \frac{A_1}{2}$$

$$\pi r_2^2 = \frac{\pi r_1^2}{2}$$

$$r_2 = \frac{r_1}{\sqrt{2}}$$

$$\Rightarrow \quad \frac{r_2}{r_1} = \frac{1}{\sqrt{2}}$$

From ascent formula, we have

$$h \propto \frac{1}{r}$$

$$\frac{h_2}{h_1} = \frac{r_1}{r_2}$$

$$h_2 = \left(\frac{r_1}{r_2}\right) h_1 = \sqrt{2} \times 25$$

$$= 1.414 \times 25$$

$$= 35.35 \text{ cm}$$

Ch-10 Thermal Properties of Matter

Topical Follow Thru

Test-1

1. (b) We know, $F = 1.8°C + 32$

Then, for water,

Freezing point $= 0°C = 32°F$

Boiling point $= 100°C = 212°$ on F

Therefore, 180 degree rise on fahrenheit scale is equal to 100 degree rise on celsius scale. We see, 1.8 degree rise on fahrenheit scale is equal to 1 degree rise on celsius scale.

2. (a) When the ball is heated, expansion of ball and cavity both occurs, hence volume of cavity increases.

3. (d) For gold ring required change in diameter is

$$\Delta l = d_{\text{final}} - d_{\text{initial}}$$

$$\because d_{\text{final}} = l_2,\ d_{\text{initial}} = l_1$$

$$= 6.241 - 6.230$$

$$= 0.011 \text{ cm}$$

Initial temperature,

$$T_1 = 27°C = 300 \text{ K}$$

Let, final temperature $= T_2$

Now, $\Delta l = l_1 \alpha_L \Delta T$

$$\Rightarrow 0.011 = 6.230 \times 1.4 \times 10^{-5} \times \Delta T$$

$$\Rightarrow \quad \Delta T = 126.11 \text{ K}$$

or $\quad T_2 = T_1 + 126.11$

$$= 426.11 \text{ K}$$

$$= 426.11 - 273.15$$

$$= 152.96°C$$

$$\approx 152.7°C$$

4. (c) Initial condition,

Given, $m = 10$ g

$\Rightarrow$ Number of moles, $n = \dfrac{M}{M_0} = \dfrac{10}{32}$

$\Rightarrow \quad p_1 = 3$ atm

$$T_1 = 10°C = 10 + 273$$

$$= 283 \text{ K}$$

A. Let volume of the gas before expansion $= V_1$

From ideal gas equation,

$$p_1 V_1 = nRT_1$$

$$\Rightarrow V_1 = \frac{nRT_1}{p_1}$$

$$= \frac{10 \times 0.0821 \times 283}{32 \times 3}$$

$$= 2.42 \text{ L}$$

B. At constant pressure, applying Charles' law,

$$\frac{V_1}{T_1} = \frac{V_2}{T_2} \quad \ldots \text{(i)}$$

Given, $V_2 = 10$ L, $T_2 = ?$

Using Eq. (i), we get

$$T_2 = \left(\frac{V_2}{V_1}\right) \times T_1 = \left(\frac{10}{2.42}\right) \times 283 \text{ K}$$

$$= 1169.4 \text{ K}$$

C. Density before expansion,

$$d_1 = \frac{\text{Mass}}{V_1} = \frac{10}{2.42} = 4.13 \text{ gL}^{-1}$$

D. Density after expansion,

$$d_2 = \frac{\text{Mass}}{V_2} = \frac{10}{10} = 1 \text{ gL}^{-1}$$

Hence, A $\rightarrow$ 3, B $\rightarrow$ 4, C $\rightarrow$ 1 and D $\rightarrow$ 2.

5. (a) Error, $\Delta L = L\alpha\, \Delta T$

$$= 50 \times 1.2 \times 10^{-5} \times 3$$

$$= 0.0018 \text{ cm or } 0.018 \text{ mm}$$

6. (a) $100°C = 150°$ of the thermometer

$\therefore \quad 1°C = 1.5°$ of the thermometer

or $\quad 34°C = 51°$ of the thermometer

$\therefore$ Thermometer will read

$-20° + 51° = 31°$ of the thermometer

7. (a) The change in volume depends on original volume, so when heated through the same temperature, both solid and hollow sphere will expand by the same amount.

8. (c) $V = V_0(1 + \gamma\Delta\theta)$

$$L^3 = L_0(1 + \alpha\Delta\theta)L_0^2(1 + \beta\Delta\theta)^2$$

$$= L_0^3(1 + \alpha\Delta\theta)(1 + \beta\Delta\theta)^2$$

Since, $L_0^3 = V_0$

and $L^3 = V$

Hence, $1 + \gamma\Delta\theta = (1 + \alpha\Delta\theta)(1 + \beta\Delta\theta)^2$

$$\simeq (1 + \alpha\Delta\theta)(1 + 2\beta\Delta\theta)$$

$$\cong (1+\alpha_1 \Delta\theta + 2\beta\Delta\theta)$$
$$\Rightarrow \gamma = \alpha + 2\beta$$

9. (a) When both strips A and B are heated, the length of strip-A is more than strip-B. Hence, strip-A has higher coefficient of linear expansion.

10. (b) For M_1,

$$\alpha_1 = \frac{\Delta L}{L\Delta\theta} = \frac{0.01}{50\times 100}$$
$$= 2\times 10^{-6}\,{}^\circ C^{-1}$$

For M_2,

$$\alpha_2 = \frac{\Delta L}{L\Delta\theta} = \frac{0.008}{80\times 100}$$
$$= 1\times 10^{-6}\,{}^\circ C^{-1}$$
$$\therefore \alpha_1 : \alpha_2 = 2:1$$

11. (c) Let temperature at which clock gives correct time is T.

$$5 = \frac{1}{2}\alpha(T-15)t_1 \quad ...(i)$$
$$10 = \frac{1}{2}\alpha(30-T)t_1 \quad ...(ii)$$

On dividing Eq. (i) by Eq. (ii), we get

$$\frac{1}{2} = \frac{T-15}{30-T}$$
$$\Rightarrow T = 20^\circ C$$

12. (c) The change in length of rod due to increase in temperature in absence of walls is

$$\Delta l = l\alpha\,\Delta T$$
$$= 500\times 10^{-4}\times 40\,\text{mm}$$
$$= 2\,\text{mm}$$

But the rod can expand upto 501 mm only.

At that temperature, its natural length is = 502 mm.

$\therefore$ Compression = 1 mm

$\therefore$ Mechanical stress

$$= Y\times\frac{\Delta l}{l}$$
$$= 10^{11}\times\frac{1}{500}$$
$$= 2\times 10^{8}\ \text{N/m}^2$$

13. (a) $\alpha = \dfrac{\Delta L}{L_0(\Delta\theta)} = \dfrac{0.19}{100(100-0)}$

$$= 1.9\times 10^{-5}/^\circ C$$

Now, $\gamma = 3\alpha = 3\times 1.9\times 10^{5}/^\circ C$

$$= 5.7\times 10^{-5}/^\circ C$$

14. (b) Due to volume expansion of both liquid and vessel, the change in volume of liquid relative to container is given by $\Delta V = V_0[\gamma_L - \gamma_g]\Delta\theta$

Given, $V_0 = 1500\,\text{cc}$,

$$\alpha_g = 0.1\times 10^{-4}/^\circ C$$
$$\therefore \gamma_g = 3\alpha_g = 3\times 0.1\times 10^{-4}/^\circ C$$
$$= 0.3\times 10^{-4}/^\circ C$$
$$\therefore \Delta V = 1500[1.82\times 10^{-4} - 0.3\times 10^{-4}]\times 110 = 25\,\text{cc}$$

15. (b) Strain, $\varepsilon = \dfrac{\Delta l}{l}$

$$\varepsilon = \frac{\Delta l}{l} = \alpha\Delta T$$
$$= (10^{-5})(150) = 1.5\times 10^{-3}$$

Stress = Y (Strain)

Stress $= 10^{11}\times 1.5\times 10^{-3}$

$$= 1.5\times 10^{8}\,\text{N/m}^2$$

$\Rightarrow$ Required force = Stress × Area

$$= (1.5\times 10^{8})(4\times 10^{-6})$$
$$= 6\times 10^{2} = 600\,\text{N}$$

$\therefore$ Mass to be attached $= \dfrac{600}{10} = 60\,\text{kg}$

Test-2

1. (b)

ice −12°C	→ $\Delta Q = 184\times 10^3$ J	?

First ice absorbs heat and it's temperature rises to 0°C.

Now using, $\Delta Q = mc\Delta T$

We have,

$$\Delta Q = (600\times 10^{-3})(2222.3)(12)$$
$$= 16000.56\,\text{J}$$
$$\approx 16\,\text{kJ}$$

Now, ice at 0°C starts melting. Let m kg of ice melts due to remaining heat.

Heat available = (184 − 16) kJ

$$= 168\,\text{kJ}$$

Now using, $\Delta Q = mL$, we have

$$168 = m(336)$$
$$\Rightarrow m = 0.5\,\text{kg} = 500\,\text{g}$$

As out of 600 g of ice, 500 g is converted into water, final mixture contains 100 g ice and 500 g water.

2. (b) As 1 g of steam at 100°C melts 8 g of ice at 10 g of steam will melt 8×10 g of ice at 0°C.

Water in calorimeter

$$= 500 + 80 + 10 = 590\,\text{g}$$

3. (a) Initially on heating, the temperature rises from −10 to 0°C, then ice melts and temperature does not rise. After the whole ice has melted, temperature begins to rise until it reaches 100°C, then it becomes constant as at the boiling point will not rise.

4. (c) $\dfrac{\Delta Q_1}{\Delta t} = \dfrac{\Delta Q_2}{\Delta t} \quad (\because L_1 = L_2)$

$$\Rightarrow K_1A_1\frac{T_1 - T_2}{L_1} = K_2A_2\frac{T_1 - T_2}{L_2}$$
$$\therefore \frac{A_1}{A_2} = \frac{K_2}{K_1}$$

5. (c) $R = \dfrac{l}{KA}$ or $R \propto \dfrac{1}{A}$

$$\therefore R_1 > R_2$$

Further, $\Delta T = H\times R$ or $\Delta T \propto R$

$$\therefore (\Delta T)_1 > (\Delta T)_2$$

6. (b) Ice at 0°C converts into steam at 100°C in following steps.

Step I Ice at 0°C to water at 0°C

$$Q_1 = mL = 15\times 80 = 1200\,\text{cal}$$

Step II Water at 0°C to water at 100°C

$$Q_2 = mc_w\Delta\theta$$
$$= 15\times 1\times 100 = 1500\,\text{cal}$$

Step III Water at 100°C to steam at 100°C

$$Q_3 = mL = 15\times 540 = 8100\,\text{cal}$$

Total heat required

$$= Q_1 + Q_2 + Q_3$$
$$= 1200 + 1500 + 8100$$
$$= 10.8\,\text{kcal}$$

7. (b) Calorimetry means measurement of heat, the heat lost by the hot body is equal to the heat gained by the cold body provided no heat is allowed to escape to the surroundings.
Hence, both statements are correct.

8. (c) The volume of matter in portion *BC* of the curve is increasing. But the pressure is decreasing.
Therefore, it shows the change from liquid to gaseous state.

9. (b) We know,

$$mL = \frac{KA(\theta_1 - \theta_2)t}{d}$$

In the given problem, Kt = constant

$$\therefore \quad \frac{K_1}{K_2} = \frac{t_2}{t_1}$$

10. (b) When two gases are mixed together, then
Heat lost by the helium gas = Heat gained by the nitrogen gas

$$n_B \times (c_v)_{He} \times \left(\frac{7}{3}T_0 - T_f\right) = n_A \times (c_v)_{N_2} \times (T_f - T_0)$$

Box *A*	Box *B*
1 mole N_2, Temperature = T_0	1 mole He, Temperature = $\frac{7}{3}T_0$

$$\Rightarrow 1 \times \frac{3}{2}R \times \left(\frac{7}{3}T_0 - T_f\right) = 1 \times \frac{5}{2}R \times (T_f - T_0)$$

By solving, we get

$$T_f = \frac{3}{2}T_0$$

11. (b) Here, $Q = \frac{KA(\theta_1 - \theta_2)t}{l}$

or $\frac{Q}{t} = \frac{\theta_1 - \theta_2}{\frac{l}{KA}}$

Compare with, $I = \frac{V}{R}$

So, thermal resistance $= \frac{l}{KA}$

$$= \frac{5}{KA} \qquad [\because l = 5\text{ m}]$$

12. (a) Heat taken by ice to melt at 0°C is

$$Q_1 = mL = 540 \times 80 = 43200 \text{ cal}$$

Heat given by water to cool upto 0°C is

$$Q_2 = ms\,\Delta\theta = 540 \times 1 \times (80 - 0) = 43200 \text{ cal}$$

Hence, heat given by water is just sufficient to melt the whole ice and final temperature of mixture is 0°C.

13. (d) Heat required to melt whole ice is

$$Q = mL = 20 \times 80 = 1600 \text{ cal}$$

Energy incident per minute is

$$P = 1.9 \times \frac{\pi}{4} \times d^2 = 1.9 \times \frac{\pi}{4} \times (20)^2 = 597 \text{ cal min}^{-1}$$

Therefore, time required to melt whole ice is $t = \frac{Q}{P} \approx 2.7$ min

14. (a) Ice (−10° C) converts into steam as follows

Ice −10°C → ($Q_1 = mc_i\Delta\theta$) → Ice 0°C → ($Q_2 = mL_f$) → Water at 0°C → ($Q_3 = mc_w\Delta T$) → Water at 100°C → ($Q_4 = mL_v$) → Steam 100°C

(Here, c_i = specific heat of ice, c_w = specific heat of water)

Total heat required,

$$Q = Q_1 + Q_2 + Q_3 + Q_4$$

$$\Rightarrow Q = 1 \times 0.5(10) + 1 \times 80 + 1 \times 1 \times (100 - 0) + 1 \times 540 = 725 \text{ cal}$$

Hence, work done,

$$W = JQ = 4.2 \times 725 = 3045 \text{ J}$$

15. (b) Let water equivalent be *x*.

$$\therefore (10 + x)\,c\,\frac{\Delta T}{\Delta t} = -k\left(\frac{T_1 + T_2}{2} - T_0\right)$$

where, *c* is the specific heat of water, ΔT = change in temperature and Δt = time at which temperature falls

$$\therefore (10 + x)\,c\,\frac{(20 - 15)}{10} = -k\left(\frac{20 + 15}{2} - T_0\right) \quad \ldots\text{(i)}$$

and

$$(20 + x)\,c\,\frac{(20 - 15)}{15} = -k\left(\frac{20 + 15}{2} - T_0\right) \quad \ldots\text{(ii)}$$

From Eqs. (i) and (ii), we get

$$\frac{10 + x}{10} = \frac{20 + x}{15}$$

$$\Rightarrow 150 + 15x = 200 + 10x$$

$$\Rightarrow 5x = 50$$

$$\Rightarrow x = 10 \text{ g}$$

16. (d) Temperature of interface,

$$T = \frac{K_1\theta_1 + K_2\theta_2}{K_1 + K_2} = \frac{300 \times 100 + 200 \times 0}{300 + 200} = 60°\text{C}$$

17. (b) Initially, ice will absorb heat to raise its temperature to 0°C, then its melting takes place.
If m_i = initial mass of ice, m'_i = mass of ice that melts and m_W = initial mass of water
By law of mixture, heat gained by ice = heat lost by water

$$\Rightarrow m_1 \times c \times (20) + m'_i \times L = m_W c_W (20)$$

$$\Rightarrow 2 \times 0.5\,(20) + m_i \times 80 = 5 \times 1 \times 20$$

$$\Rightarrow m'_i = 1 \text{ kg}$$

So, final mass of water = initial mass of water + mass of ice that melts = 5 + 1 = 6 kg

18. (b) As we know that,
Energy per second,

$$P \propto T^4$$

$$\therefore \quad \frac{P_2}{P_1} = \frac{T_2^4}{T_1^4} = \left(\frac{T_2}{T_1}\right)^4 = \left(\frac{60 + 273}{20 + 273}\right)^4 = (1.13)^4 \simeq 1.6$$

19. (d) Rate of heat flow,

$$\left(\frac{Q}{T}\right) = \frac{k\pi r^2(\theta_1 - \theta_2)}{L} \propto \frac{r^2}{L}$$

$\therefore \quad \dfrac{Q_1}{Q_2} = \left(\dfrac{r_1}{r_2}\right)^2 \left(\dfrac{L_2}{L_1}\right)$

$= \left(\dfrac{2}{1}\right)^2 \times \dfrac{1}{2} = \dfrac{2}{1}$

$Q_2 = \dfrac{Q_1}{2}$

20. (d) $W = JQ$

$\Rightarrow \dfrac{1}{2}\left(\dfrac{1}{2} Mv^2\right) = J(m.c.\Delta\theta)$

$\Rightarrow \dfrac{1}{4} \times 1 \times (30)^2$

$= 4.2(250 \times 0.105 \times \Delta\theta)$

$\Rightarrow \dfrac{900}{4} = 4.2\,[26.25\Delta\theta]$

$\Rightarrow \quad \Delta\theta = \dfrac{900}{4 \times 4.2 \times 26.25} = 2.0°C$

21. (a) Let θ be the temperature of junction.

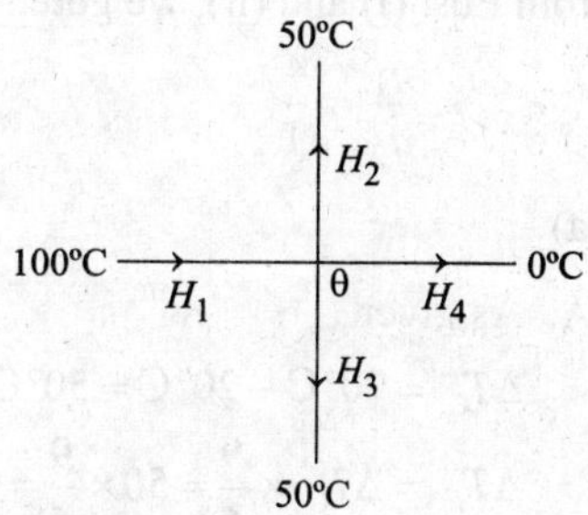

H_1, H_2, H_3 and H_4 be the heat currents. Then,

$H_1 = H_2 + H_3 + H_4$

or $\dfrac{100-\theta}{R} = \dfrac{\theta - 50}{R} + \dfrac{\theta - 50}{R} + \dfrac{\theta - 0}{R}$

(where, R = thermal resistance of each part of two rods)

Solving the above equations, we get

$\theta = 50°C$

22. (d) By the principle of mixture, heat given out by water = heat absorbed by the melted ice

$\Rightarrow \quad mc\,(\theta - 0) = M'L$

$\Rightarrow \quad M' = \dfrac{mc\theta}{L}$

23. (b) $K_A = 2K_B$

$\Rightarrow R_A = \dfrac{R_B}{2} \quad \left(\because R = \dfrac{l}{KA}\right)$

Suppose, $R_A = R$, then $R_B = 2R$

Heat current,

$H = \dfrac{36}{R + 2R} = \dfrac{36}{3R} = \dfrac{12}{R}$

$\therefore$ Temperature difference across A

$= H \times R_A = \dfrac{12}{R} \times R = 12°C$

24. (b) Let the final temperature be $T°$ C.

Total heat supplied by the three liquids in coming down to 0°C

$= m_1 c_1 T_1 + m_2 c_2 T_2 + m_3 c_3 T_3 \quad$ ...(i)

Total heat used by three liquids in raising temperature from 0°C to T°C

$= m_1 c_1 T + m_2 c_2 T + m_3 c_3 T \quad$ ...(ii)

By equating (i) and (ii), we get

$(m_1 c_1 + m_2 c_2 + m_3 c_3)\,T$

$= m_1 c_1 T_1 + m_2 c_2 T_2 + m_3 c_3 T_3$

$\Rightarrow T = \dfrac{m_1 c_1 T_1 + m_2 c_2 T_2 + m_3 c_3 T_3}{m_1 c_1 + m_2 c_2 + m_3 c_3}$

25. (b) Heat lost in t, $s = mL$ or heat lost per $s = \dfrac{mL}{t}$. This must be the heat supplied for keeping the substance in molten state per s.

$\therefore \quad \dfrac{mL}{t} = P$

or $\quad L = \dfrac{Pt}{m}$

Chapter Break Thru

1. (c) $\dfrac{F - 32}{9} = \dfrac{K - 273}{5}$

$\Rightarrow \quad \dfrac{x - 32}{9} = \dfrac{x - 273}{5}$

$\Rightarrow \quad x = 574.25$

2. (c) When a bimetallic strip is heated, it bends in the form of an arc with the more expandable metal outside.

3. (c) When a metal ball is heated, its size increases. As, volume $\propto$ (radius)^3 and area $\propto$ (radius)^2, so percentage increase will be largest in its volume. Density will decrease with rise in temperature.

4. (d) If equal amount of heat is added to equal masses of different substances, then the resulting temperature changes will not be the same.

It implies that every substance has a unique value for the amount of heat absorbed or rejected to change the temperature of unit mass of it by one unit.

Therefore, A is false but R is true.

5. (a) As the temperature of water is increased from 1°C to 4°C, the density of water increases (remember anomalous behaviour of water), also the volume of sphere increases. Therefore, buoyant force on sphere due to water will increase.

6. (a) If m g ice melts, then

heat lost = heat gain

$80 \times 1 \times (30 - 0) = m \times 80$

$\Rightarrow \quad m = 30\text{ g}$

7. (b) Freezing temperature $= T_f = 39°$ W

Boiling temperature $= T_b = 239°$ W

We know that,

$\dfrac{T_b - T_f}{100°\text{ C} - 0°\text{ C}} = \dfrac{T - 39°\text{ C}}{39°\text{ C}}$

$\dfrac{239 - 39}{100} = \dfrac{T - 39°\text{ C}}{39°\text{ C}}$

$\dfrac{200}{100} = \dfrac{T - 39°\text{ C}}{39°\text{ C}}$

$78°\text{ W} = T - 39°\text{ W}$

$\Rightarrow \quad T = 117°\text{ W}$

8. (b) As on heating, aluminium frame will expand more than the steel wire, thermal strain in steel wire relative to aluminium frame will be,

$\left(\dfrac{\Delta L}{L}\right) = (\alpha_{Al} - \alpha_S)\,\Delta\theta$

[as $\Delta L = L\alpha\,\Delta\theta$]

i.e. Thermal strain

$= (23 - 11) \times 10^{-6} \times (110 - 10)$

$= 1.2 \times 10^{-3}$

But, thermal stress = $Y \times$ strain

[as Y = stress/strain]

So, thermal stress

$= 2 \times 10^{11} \times 1.2 \times 10^{-3}$

$= 2.4 \times 10^8$ Pa

9. (b) It is clear from the graph that lowest point for scale A is 30° and lowest point for scale B is 0°. Highest point for the scale A is 180° and for scale B is 100°. Hence, correct relation is

$$\frac{t_A-(\text{LFP})_A}{(\text{UFP})_A-(\text{LFP})_A}=\frac{t_B-(\text{LFP})_B}{(\text{UFP})_B-(\text{LFP})_B}$$

where, LFP = lower fixed point
and UFP = upper fixed point

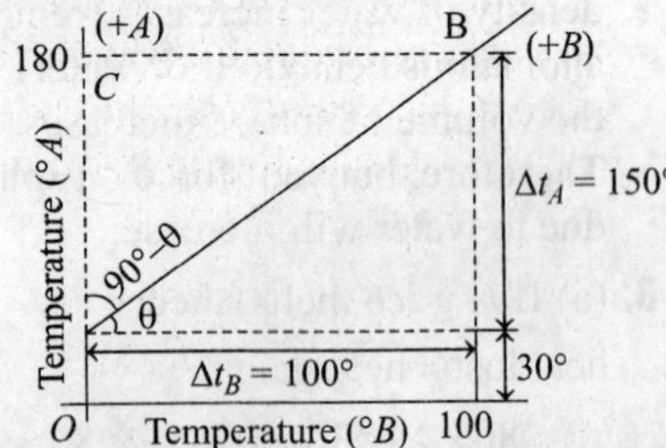

$$\Rightarrow \frac{t_A-30}{180-30}=\frac{t_B-0}{100-0}$$

$$\Rightarrow \frac{t_A-30}{150}=\frac{t_B}{100}$$

10. (a) Both the solid and liquid states of the substances co-exist in thermal equilibrium during the change of state from solid to liquid. The phenomena of refreezing is called regelation.

11. (b) Let the specific heats of both liquids are s_1 and s_2.

$$\therefore \quad m_1s_1(30-25)=m_2s_2(25-20)$$

$$[\because m_1=m_2=m]$$

$$\Rightarrow \quad ms_1(5)=ms_2(5)$$

$$\Rightarrow \quad \frac{s_1}{s_2}=\frac{1}{1}=1:1$$

12. (d) When element and surrounding have the same temperature, there will be no temperature difference, hence heat will not flow from the filament and its temperature remains constant.

13. (a) As we know, $Q = mc\Delta\theta$

$$\therefore Q_1 = 20\times 1\times 15 = 300\,\text{cal}$$

$$Q_2 = 20\times 0.5\times[0-(-20)]+20\times 80$$

$$= 200+1600 = 1800\,\text{Cal}$$

Here, $Q_1 < Q_2$,

So, ice will not melt completely.

As heat given by water in cooling up to 0°C is only just sufficient to increase the temperature of ice from − 20°C to 0°C, hence mixture in equilibrium will consist of 20 g of ice and 20 g of water at 0°C.

14. (d) As, we know,

$$\frac{30-\theta}{1}=70$$

$$\Rightarrow \quad \theta = 30-70$$

$$= -40°\text{C}$$

15. (d) Heat required to melt whole ice is

$$Q = mL = 20\times 80 = 1600\,\text{cal}$$

Energy incident per minute is

$$P = 1.9\times\frac{\pi}{4}\times d^2$$

$$= 1.9\times\frac{\pi}{4}\times(20)^2$$

$$= 597\ \text{cal/min}$$

Therefore, time required to melt whole ice is $t=\dfrac{Q}{P}\approx 2.7\,\text{min}$.

16. (c) As coefficient of cubical expansion of liquid equals coefficient of cubical expansion of steel container, the level of liquid will not change on heating.

17. (b) Let m be mass of steam convert into water.

$$\therefore \ 54\times 1\times(90-30)$$

$$= m(530)+m\times 1\times(100-90)$$

$$\Rightarrow 54\times 60 = m(530+10)$$

$$\Rightarrow \quad m=\frac{54\times 60}{540}=6\,\text{g}$$

Total mass of water = 54 + 6 = 60 g

18. (d) The radius of the sphere is R. As the temperature increases, radius of the sphere increases as shown in figure.

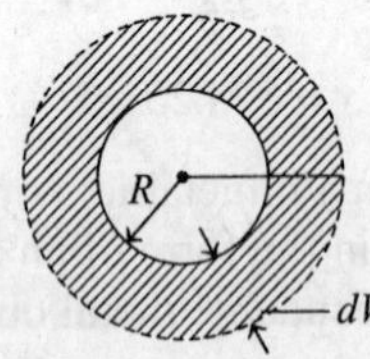

Original volume, $V=\dfrac{4}{3}\pi R^3$

Coefficient of linear expansion = α

∴ Coefficient of volume expansion = 3α

$$\therefore \quad \frac{1}{V}\frac{dV}{dT}=3\alpha$$

$$\Rightarrow \quad dV = 3V\alpha dT \approx 4\pi R^3\alpha\Delta T$$

= Increase in the volume

19. (a) Suppose m' kg ice melts out of m kg, then by using

$$W = JQ \Rightarrow mgh = J(m'L)$$

Hence, fraction of ice melts

$$=\frac{m'}{m}=\frac{gh}{JL}=\frac{9.8\times 1000}{4.18\times 80}=\frac{1}{29.3}$$

20. (c) Initially, the rods are in parallel.

$$\Rightarrow \quad \frac{Q}{t}=\frac{(\theta_1-\theta_2)}{R}$$

$$\Rightarrow \quad \left(\frac{Q}{t}\right)_1=\frac{mL}{t}$$

$$= q_1L=\frac{(100-0)}{R/2} \quad \text{...(i)}$$

Finally, when rods are in series.

$$\Rightarrow \quad \left(\frac{Q}{t}\right)_2=\frac{mL}{t}=q_2L$$

$$=\frac{(100-0)}{2R} \quad \text{...(ii)}$$

From Eqs. (i) and (ii), we get

$$\frac{q_1}{q_2}=\frac{4}{1}$$

21. (a)

A. As given,

$$\Delta T_C = 70°\text{C}-20°\text{C} = 50°\text{C}$$

$$\Delta T_F = \Delta T_C\times\frac{9}{5}=50\times\frac{9}{5}=90°\text{F}$$

B. As we know, $F=\dfrac{9}{5}C+32$

Let, $C = F = x$, then

$$x=\frac{9}{5}x+32$$

$$\Rightarrow \quad 5x = 9x+160$$

$$\Rightarrow \quad 4x = -160$$

$$\Rightarrow \quad x = -40°\text{C}$$

C. Heat to melt ice,

$$Q_1 = m\times L_f = 100\times 80$$

$$= 8000\,\text{cal}$$

Heat to raise temperature of water from 0° to 100°C.

$$Q_2 = M\times C\times\Delta T = 100\times 1\times 100$$

$$= 10000\,\text{cal}$$

Heat to convert water at 100°C to steam at 100°C.

$Q_3 = m \times L_v$
$= 100 \times 540 = 54000$ cal

Total heat required :
$Q_{total} = Q_1 + Q_2 + Q_3$
$= 8000 + 10000 + 54000$
$= 72000$ cal $= 72$ kcal

D. Initial mechanical energy
$E_i = mgh = m \times 10 \times 5$

Mechanical energy after collision,
$E_f = mgh = m \times 10 \times 3$

Energy lost,
$\Delta E = E_i - E_f$
$= m \times 10 \times (5-3) = m \times 10 \times 2$

Thermal energy into the ball,
$\Delta E_{thermal} = \frac{1}{2} \Delta E = m \times 10$

Temperature rise,
$\Delta T = \frac{\Delta E_{thermal}}{500 \times m} = \frac{m \times 10}{500 \times m} = \frac{1}{50}$

$\Delta T = 0.02$ °C
$\Delta T = 20$ m°C

22. (b) Loss in time per second
$= \frac{\Delta T}{T} = \frac{1}{2} \alpha \Delta\theta = \frac{1}{2} \alpha (t - 0)$

$\Rightarrow$ Loss in time per day,
$\Delta t = \frac{1}{2} \alpha t \times (24 \times 60 \times 60)$
$= \frac{1}{2} \alpha t \times 86400$

23. (d) In ΔOPR,
$(OR)^2 = (PR)^2 - (PO)^2$
$= l^2 - \left(\frac{l}{2}\right)^2$

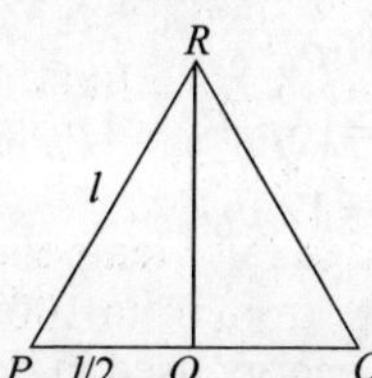

$\Rightarrow (OR)^2 = [l(1 + \alpha_2 t)]^2 - \left[\frac{l}{2}(1 + \alpha_1 t)\right]^2$

$l^2 - \frac{l^2}{4} = l^2 (1 + \alpha_2^2 t^2 + 2\alpha_2 t) - \frac{l^2}{4}(1 + \alpha_1^2 t^2 + 2\alpha_1 t)$

Neglecting $\alpha_2^2 t^2$ and $\alpha_1^2 t^2$, we get
$0 = l^2 (2\alpha_2 t) - \frac{l^2}{4}(2\alpha_1 t)$
$\Rightarrow \quad 2\alpha_2 = \frac{2\alpha_1}{4}$
$\Rightarrow \quad \alpha_1 = 4\alpha_2$

24. (a) Change in length for both rods should be same.
$\therefore \Delta L_1 = \Delta L_2$
$L_1 \alpha_1 \Delta T = L_2 \alpha_2 \Delta T$
$L_1 \alpha_1 = L_2 \alpha_2$
$\frac{L_1}{L_2} = \frac{\alpha_2}{\alpha_1}$

25. (b) Suppose m gram steam is required per hour.
Heat is released by steam in following three steps:

(i) When steam at 150°C $\xrightarrow[Q_1]{}$ steam at 100 °C
$Q_1 = mc_{steam} \Delta\theta$
$= m \times 1 (150 - 100) = 50m$ cal

(ii) When steam at 100°C $\xrightarrow[Q_2]{}$ water at 100°C
$Q_2 = mL_V = m \times 540 = 540m$ cal

(iii) When water at 100°C $\xrightarrow[Q_2]{}$ water at 90°C
$Q_3 = mc_w \Delta\theta = m \times 1 \times (100 - 90)$
$= 10m$ cal

Hence, total heat given by the steam,
$Q = Q_1 + Q_2 + Q_3$
$= 600m$ cal ...(i)

Heat taken by 10 kg water,
$Q' = mc_w \Delta\theta$
$= 10 \times 10^3 \times 1 \times (80 - 20)$
$= 600 \times 10^3$ cal

As, $Q = Q' \Rightarrow 600m = 600 \times 10^3$
$\Rightarrow \quad m = 10^3$ g $= 1$ kg

26. (d) From given statement,
$mgh = mL$ or $gh = L$

$\Rightarrow \quad 10 \times h = \frac{80 \times 4.2}{10^{-3}}$
or $h = 33.6 \times 10^3$ m $= 33.6$ km

27. (b) As we know that, thermal resistance is given as $R = \frac{L}{KA}$

So, simply here, apply the concept of Wheatstone bridge for which no current will flow across the central rod and mathematically, it is given as $R_1 R_4 = R_2 R_3$.
Here, ratio of L/A is constant
$\therefore \quad K_1 K_4 = K_2 K_3$

28. (c) $Q = \sigma At (T^4 - T_0^4)$ if T, T_0, σ and t are same for both bodies, then
$\frac{Q_{sphere}}{Q_{cube}} \frac{A_{sphere}}{A_{cube}} = \frac{4\pi r^2}{6a^2}$ ...(i)

But according to problem,
Volume of sphere = Volume of cube
$\Rightarrow \frac{4}{3}\pi r^3 = a^3$
$\Rightarrow \quad a = r\left(\frac{4}{3}\pi\right)^{1/3}$

Substituting the value of a in Eq. (i), we get
$\frac{Q_{sphere}}{Q_{cube}} = \frac{4\pi r^2}{\left\{6\left(\frac{4}{3}\pi\right)^{1/3} r\right\}^2}$
$= \left(\frac{\pi}{6}\right)^{1/3} : 1$

29. (c) As we know that,
$Q = -KA\left(\frac{dT}{dx}\right)$
where, $\left(\frac{dT}{dx}\right)$ = Temperature gradient
$= X$
$\therefore \quad X \propto \frac{1}{K}$

So, here, $K_c > K_m > K_g$
$\therefore \quad X_c < X_m < X_g$

30. (a) If heat is supplied at constant rate P, then $Q = P\Delta\tau$
and as during change of state,
$Q = ml$

so, $mL = P\Delta t$

i.e. $L = \left[\frac{P}{m}\right]\Delta t$

$= \frac{P}{m}$ (length of line AB)

Hence, $L_1 > L_2$

i.e., The ratio of latent heat of fusion of the two substances are in the ratio 3 : 4.

In the portion OA, the substance is in solid state and its temperature is changing,

$\Delta Q = mc\Delta T$

and $\Delta Q = P\Delta t$

So, $\frac{\Delta T}{\Delta t} = \frac{P}{mc}$ or slope

$= \frac{P}{mS} = \left[\text{as } \frac{\Delta T}{\Delta t} = \text{slope}\right]$

Hence, $c_1 < c_2$

Ch-11 Thermodynamics

Topical Follow Thru

Test-1

1. (c) $dU_{\text{cyclic}} = 0$

$\Rightarrow \Delta Q_{\text{cyclic}} = \Delta W_{\text{cyclic}}$

$\Rightarrow \Delta Q_{\text{cyclic}} = W_{AB} + W_{BC} + W_{CA}$

$\Rightarrow +15 = +30(2-1) + 0 + W_{CA}$

$\Rightarrow 15 = 30 + 0 + W_{CA}$

$\Rightarrow W_{CA} = -15\,\text{J}$

2. (c) Work done = Area of graph $ABCD$ Area

$= \frac{1}{2} \times 4(1\times 10^5 + 5\times 10^5)$

$= 2\times 6\times 10^5 = 12\times 10^5\,\text{J}$

3. (b) Given,

$U = 1.5\,pV$

So, $\Delta U = 1.5\,p\Delta V$ $\quad(\because \Delta V = 1\text{L})$

Also, $W = p\Delta V$

So, $Q = \Delta U + W = 2.5\,p\Delta V$

$= 2.5(1\times 10^5)(2-1)\times 10^{-3}$

$= 250\,\text{J}$

4. (b) Given, $\Delta Q = 110\,\text{J}, \Delta U = 40\,\text{J}$

From first law of thermodynamics,

$\Delta Q = \Delta U + \Delta W$

$\Delta W = \Delta Q - \Delta U$

$= 110 - 40 = 70\,\text{J}$

5. (b) The law governing the conservation of total energy within an isolated thermodynamic system, accounting for both internal energy and work interactions.

6. (a) Work done by gas in all four processes is positive and in order

$W_{\text{I}} > W_{\text{II}} > W_{\text{III}} > W_{\text{IV}}$

$\Rightarrow$ (c) is false

The change in internal energy U is same for all processes.

$\therefore \quad Q_{\text{I}} = U + W_{\text{I}}$ ...(i)

$Q_{\text{II}} = U + W_{\text{II}}$ ...(ii)

$Q_{\text{III}} = U + W_{\text{III}}$ ...(iii)

$Q_{\text{IV}} = U + W_{\text{IV}}$ ...(iv)

From Eqs. (i) and (iv), we get

$\therefore \quad Q_{\text{I}} - Q_{\text{IV}} = W_{\text{I}} - W_{\text{IV}}$

$\Rightarrow$ (a) is true

7. (c) From the first law of thermodynamics,

$dQ = dU + dW$

Also, we can write this as,

$\frac{dQ}{dt} = \frac{dU}{dt} + \frac{dW}{dt}$

$1000 = \frac{dU}{dt} + 200$

$\frac{dU}{dt} = 800\,\text{W}$

8. (d) Internal energy and volume depend on states.

So, there are state variables.

Work done by the gas and heat absorbed by the gas are process variables.

9. (d) According to first law of thermodynamics,

$\Delta Q = \Delta U + \Delta W$

$= \Delta U + p\Delta V$

If heat supplies in such a manner that volume does not change $\Delta V = 0$ i.e. isochoric process, then whole of the heat energy supplied to the system will increase internal energy only. But in any other process, it is not possible. Also, heat may or may not be absorbed or released when state of thermal equilibrium changes.

10. (d) Volume of the ideal gas is constant, so $W = p\Delta V = 0$, using First law of thermodynamics,

$\Delta Q = \Delta U$

$\Rightarrow \Delta U = i^2 Rt$

$= 1^2 \times 100\times 5\times 60$

$= 30\times 10^3 = 30\,\text{kJ}$

11. (d) Here,

$W_{AB} = -\left[2p_0V_0 + \frac{2p_0 \times 2V_0}{2}\right]$

$= -[2p_0V_0 + 2p_0V_0] = -4p_0V_0$

$W_{BC} = (3p_0)(4V_0) + \frac{(2p_0)\times(4V_0)}{2}$

$= 12p_0V_0 + 4p_0V_0$

$= 16p_0V_0$

$\therefore W_{ABC} = 16p_0V_0 - 4p_0V_0$

$= 12\,p_0V_0$

12. (c) Total energy used in doing work

$= p\Delta V = 3\times 10^5 \times 1600\times 10^{-6}$

$= 480\,\text{J}$

If only 10% energy = 480 J, is used in doing work.

Then, total energy = 4800 J
Therefore, the rest 90% of the remaining energy is used in increasing internal energy.
So, increase in internal energy = 90% of 4800 J

$$= \frac{90}{100} \times 4800\,\text{J} = 4320\,\text{J}$$

13. (c) Given, $dQ = +200$ cal
$= 200 \times 4.2 = 840$ J
and $dW = +40$ J
From first law of thermodynamics,

$$dQ = dU + dW$$
$$dU = dQ - dW = 840 - 40 = 800\,\text{J}$$

So, the internal energy of the system increases by 800 J.

14. (d) We can change the temperature of a body without supplying (or extracting) heat to (or from) it. For example, in an adiabatic compression, temperature rises and in an adiabatic expansion, temperature false, although no heat is given or taken from the system in the respective changes.

15. (a) As we know, $\Delta Q = \Delta U + \Delta W$
(First law of thermodynamics)
$\Rightarrow \Delta Q = \Delta U + p\Delta V$
or $150 = \Delta U + 100(1-2)$
$= \Delta U - 100$
$\therefore \Delta U = 150 + 100 = 250$ J
Thus the internal energy of the gas increases by 250 J.

Test-2

1. (a) For isothermal process,

$$p_1V_1 = p_2V_2$$
$$\Rightarrow \quad p_2 = \frac{p_1V_1}{V_2} = \frac{72 \times 1000}{900} = 80\,\text{cm}$$
$$\Delta p = p_2 - p_1 = (80 - 72)\,\text{cm} = 8\,\text{cm}$$

2. (a) The isothermal compressibility k_T is defined as

$$k_T = -\frac{1}{V}\left(\frac{\partial V}{\partial p}\right)_T$$

For an ideal gas

$$pV = nRT \Rightarrow V = \frac{nRT}{p}$$

Taking the derivative with respect to pressure at constant temperature.

$$\left(\frac{\partial V}{\partial p}\right)_T = -\frac{nRT}{p^2}$$

Substituting in Eq. (i), we get

$$k_T = \frac{1}{p}$$

Therefore k_T remains invarient throughout the process.

3. (d) As we know,

$$\Delta U = nC_V\Delta T = n\left(\frac{3}{2}\right)R\Delta T$$
$$\Delta Q = nC_p\Delta T = n\left(\frac{5}{2}\right)R\Delta T$$
$$W = \Delta Q - \Delta U = \frac{5n}{2}R\Delta T - \frac{3n}{2}R\Delta T$$
$$= nR\Delta T$$

Thus, $\frac{W}{\Delta U} = \frac{2}{3}$

4. (c) $pV^{-1} = \text{constant}$
In the process, $pV^n = \text{constant}$

$$W = \left(\frac{R}{1-n}\right)\Delta T$$

Here, $n = -1$

$$\therefore \quad W = \frac{R}{2}\Delta T = \frac{R}{2}(T_2 - T_1)$$

5. (c) In adiabatic expansion, $\Delta Q = 0$
$\therefore \Delta W = -\Delta U = -(-40) = 40$ J

6. (c) For ideal gas, there is no interaction between particles.
$\therefore \quad \Delta U = 0$
But for real gas, there is interaction between the particles i.e. $\Delta U \neq 0$
$\therefore$ The increase in internal energy for real gas is non-zero but for ideal gas, it is zero.

7. (c) The p-V graph of all given processes in doubling the volume is shown in the graph given below

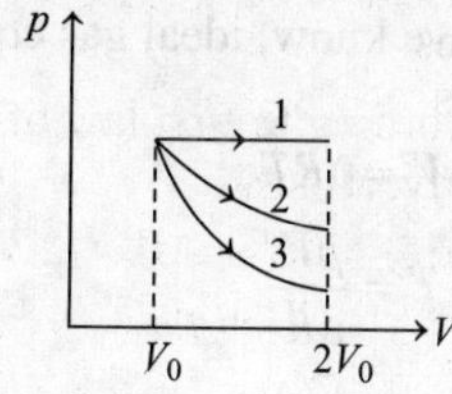

Here, process-1 is isobaric, process-2 is isothermal and process-3 is adiabatic. The minimum area of p-V graph on V-axis is for process-3.

8. (a) For isothermal process, $pV = \text{constant}$.
Therefore, p-V graph is a rectangular hyperbola.
Since, $T_2 > T_1$
$\Rightarrow (pV)_{\text{at } T_2} > (pV)_{\text{at } T_1}$
Thus, the graph given in option (a) correctly represents the given situation.

9. (b) $W_{\text{iso}} = nRT\log_e\frac{V_2}{V_1}$

$$= 1 \times 8.31 \times 300 \log_e\frac{20}{10}$$
$$= 1728\,\text{J}$$

10. (d) In cyclic process, $\Delta Q = \Delta W$
In isobaric process, $\Delta W = nR\Delta T$
In isochoric process, $\Delta Q = \Delta U$
In adibatic process, $\Delta U < 0$
A - 2, B - 3, C - 4, D - 1.

11. (d) At first, the gas undergoes isothermal expansion from V_0 to $2V_0$. For such a process, the equation of gas will be $pV = \text{constant}$
This means pressure is inversely proportional to volume. Thus, p-V curve for such a process will be as shown below.

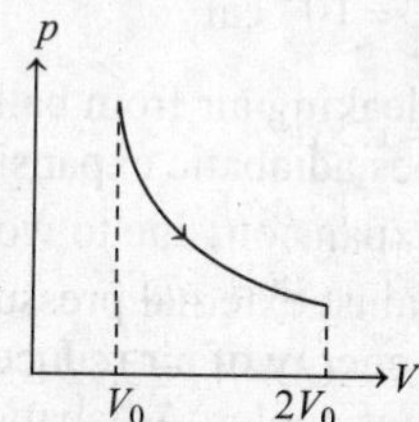

After that, its volume is decreased or reduced from $2V_0$ to V_0 at constant pressure. Thus, the final p-v Curve for this ideal gas will be as follows

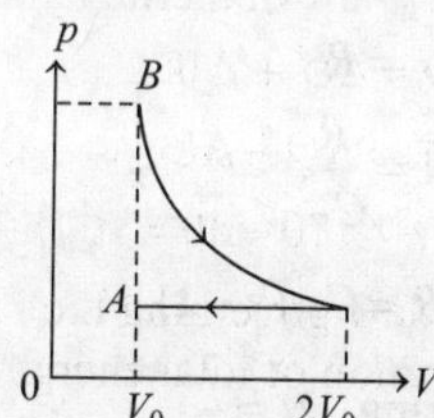

12. (b) As we know,

$$T_1^{\gamma}p_1^{1-\gamma} = T_2^{\gamma}p_2^{1-\gamma}$$

$$\left(\frac{T_2}{T_1}\right)^{\gamma} = \left(\frac{p_2}{p_1}\right)^{\gamma-1}$$

$$\left(\frac{T_2}{300}\right)^{\frac{3}{2}} = \left(\frac{1}{8}\right)^{\frac{3}{2}-1}$$

$$\left(\frac{T_2}{300}\right)^{\frac{3}{2}} = \left(\frac{1}{8}\right)^{\frac{1}{2}}$$

$$\frac{T_2}{300} = \left(\frac{1}{8}\right)^{\frac{1}{3}}$$

$$T_2 = \frac{300}{2} = 150\text{ K} = -123^\circ\text{C}$$

13. (b) At constant pressure,

$$W = p\Delta V = \mu R \Delta T$$
$$= 1 \times 8.31 \times 100$$
$$= 831 \approx 814\text{ J}$$

14. (b) From first law of thermodynamics, $\Delta Q = \Delta U + \Delta W$

Work done at constant pressure,

$\Delta W_p = \Delta Q_p - \Delta U = \Delta Q_p - \Delta Q_V$

(as we know $\Delta Q_V = \Delta U$)

Also, $\Delta Q_p = mC_p \Delta T$

and $\Delta Q_V = mC_V \Delta T$

$\Rightarrow \Delta W_p = m(C_p - C_V)\Delta T$

$\Rightarrow \Delta W_p = 1 \times (3.4 \times 10^3 - 2.4 \times 10^3) \times 10$

$= 10^4$ cal

15. (a) The leaking air from balloon undergoes adiabatic expansion. In this expansion, due to work done against external pressure, the internal energy of air reduces. Thus, it becomes cooler. Adiabatic expansion produces cooling.

16. (c) Here, $R = \frac{4}{3} C_V$

We know that,

$C_p - C_V = R$

or $\gamma - 1 = \frac{R}{C_V}$

or $R = C_V(\gamma - 1)$

Comparing, $\gamma = \frac{7}{3}$

$$p^{1-\gamma} T^{\gamma} = \text{constant} = K$$

or $p \propto T^{(\gamma/\gamma-1)}$,

Given, $\gamma = \frac{7}{3}$

$\Rightarrow \frac{\gamma}{(\gamma - 1)} = \frac{7}{4}$

So, $p \propto T^{\frac{7}{4}}$

17. (a) The Assertion (A) and Reason (R) both describe the clausius statement of the second law of thermodynamics, which states that heat cannot spontaneously transfer from a cooler to a hotter body without external work. Thus R correctly explains A.

18. (b) For isobaric process,

$\Delta p = 0$ i.e. $p =$ Constant

$\therefore$ Bulk modulus,

$$= \frac{\Delta p}{\frac{-\Delta V}{V}} = 0 \qquad [\because \Delta p = 0]$$

and for isobaric process,

$$\frac{V_1}{T_1} = \frac{V_2}{T_2}$$

Hence, Statement I is correct but Statement II is incorrect.

19. (b) From the first law of thermodynamics

$$\Delta Q = \Delta U + \Delta W$$

For cyclic process,

$$\Delta U = 0$$

Hence, $Q = W$

Work done,

$W =$ area under p-V diagram

$\Rightarrow Q = -(2p)(V)$

$= -2pV$

So, heat rejected by the gas during this cycle is $2pV$.

20. (b) When volume of gas increases, the work done on the gas is negative and *vice-versa*.

In case (III), ideal gas is taken through cyclic process in anti-clockwise direction, so work done on the gas is positive.

21. (c) As we know, ideal gas equation is given as

$$pV = \mu RT$$

or $T = \frac{pV}{\mu R}$

From the given diagram,

Temperature at point A,

$$T_A = \frac{p_A V_A}{\mu R} = \frac{(2p_0)(V_0)}{2R} = \frac{p_0 V_0}{R}$$

Temperature at point B,

$$T_B = \frac{p_B V_B}{\mu R} = \frac{(2p_0)(2V_0)}{2R} = \frac{2p_0 V_0}{R}$$

Temperature at point C,

$$T_C = \frac{p_C V_C}{\mu R} = \frac{(p_0)(2V_0)}{2R} = \frac{p_0 V_0}{R}$$

Temperature at point D,

$$T_D = \frac{p_D V_D}{\mu R} = \frac{p_0 V_0}{2R}$$

The change in internal energy of gas, $\Delta U = \mu C_V \Delta T$

If ΔT is positive, then ΔU will increase.

Among all the given processes, temperature increases for AB and DA processes. Thus, in processes AB and DA, the internal energy of gas increases.

22. (b) Here, $pT = p_1 T_1 = p_2 T_2 = k$

From ideal gas equation, $pV = \mu RT$

or $T = \frac{pV}{R}$ $\quad (\because \mu = 1)$

Given, $pT =$ constant

$\therefore p\left(\frac{pV}{R}\right) = k \quad \left(\because T = \frac{pV}{R}\right)$

or $p^2 V = kR$

or $p = \sqrt{\frac{kR}{V}}$

As, work done by gas,

$$W = \int_{V_1}^{V_2} p\,dV$$

$$W_0 = \int_{V_1}^{V_2} \sqrt{\frac{kR}{V}}\,dV$$

$$= \sqrt{kR} \int_{V_1}^{V_2} \frac{dV}{\sqrt{V}}$$

$= \sqrt{kR}\ [2\sqrt{V}]_{V_1}^{V_2}$

$= 2\sqrt{kR}[\sqrt{V_2} - \sqrt{V_1}]$

$= 2[RT_2 - RT_1]$

$W_0 = 2R(T_2 - T_1)$ ...(ii)

For first case,

$T_1 = T_0, T_2 = 2T_0$

$W_0 = 2R[2T_0 - T_0]$

$W_0 = 2RT_0$

For second case,

$T_1 = 2T_0, T_2 = 3T_0$

$W = 2R(3T_0 - 2T_0) = 2RT_0$

$W = W_0$

23. (c) An air conditioner can cool a room when it is turned ON in a closed environment by removing heat from the room and expelling it outside. According to the second law of thermodynamics, heat naturally flows from a higher temperature to a lower temperature.

24. (b) Given, $p \propto \frac{1}{V^2}$

$p = \frac{k}{V^2}$

$\Rightarrow \quad pV^2 = k$

$\therefore \quad pV \cdot V = k \Rightarrow TV = k'$

Since, temperature increases therefore volume decreases. Hence, the work done by the gas should be negative.

25. (a) For adiabatic process,

$TV^{\gamma-1} = \text{constant}$

$\log TV^{\gamma-1} = \text{constant}$

$\log T + \log V^{\gamma-1} = \text{constant}$

or $\log T + (\gamma - 1)\log V = \text{constant}$

The above equation represents a straight line equation whose slope is equal to $-(\gamma - 1)$.

As from the given graph, slope

$\frac{\Delta y}{\Delta x} = \frac{5-1}{1-7} = \frac{4}{-6} = -\frac{2}{3}$

$\therefore \quad -\frac{2}{3} = -(\gamma - 1)$ or $\gamma = \frac{5}{3}$

The value of γ for monoatomic gas is $\frac{5}{3}$.

Chapter Break Thru

1. (b) As, $\Delta Q = \mu C_p \Delta T$

$= \frac{5}{2}\mu RT \left[\because C_p = \frac{5}{2}R\right]$

$\Delta U = \mu C_V \Delta T$

$= \frac{3}{2}\mu RT \quad \left[\because C_V = \frac{3}{2}R\right]$

and, $\quad \Delta W = \Delta Q - \Delta U = \mu RT$

$\therefore \quad \Delta Q : \Delta U : \Delta W = 5:3:2$

2. (a) For a cyclic process, the change in internal energy of the system is always zero.

3. (b) $\Delta U = \mu C_V \Delta T = \frac{m}{M} C_V \Delta T$

$= \frac{N}{N_A} C_V \Delta T$

$\Delta U_{He} = 2 \times \frac{3}{2} R \times 300$

$= 900R$

$\Rightarrow (\Delta U)_N = \frac{56 \times 10^3}{14} \times \frac{5}{2} R \times 300$

$= 3 \times 10^6$

$\Delta U_O = \frac{8}{32} \times \frac{5R}{2} \times 300 = 187.5R$

and $(\Delta U)_{Ar} = \frac{6 \times 10^{26}}{6 \times 10^{23}} \times \frac{3}{2} R \times 900$

$= 13.5 \times 10^6 R$

$\Rightarrow (\Delta U)_N > (\Delta U)_{Ar} > (\Delta U)_{He} > (\Delta U)_O$

4. (b) The cyclic process 1 is clockwise whereas process 2 is anti-clockwise. Clockwise area represents positive work and anti-clockwise area represents negative work. Since, negative area (2) > positive area (1), hence net work done is negative.

5. (a) In a perfectly reversible system, there is no loss of energy.

But there always occurs a loss of energy due to energy last in working against the dissipative force.

It is impossible by any means to recover the whole energy lost in doing work against dissipative forces. Normally, all process are dissipative in nature.

6. (d) For isochoric process, $dV = 0$

$W = 0$ for process 1

For isobaric, $W = p\Delta V = nR\Delta T$

For adiabatic, $W = \frac{nR\Delta T}{\gamma - 1}$ $0 < \gamma - 1 < 1$

As work done in case of adiabatic process is more, so process 3 is adiabatic and process 2 is isobaric.

7. (c)

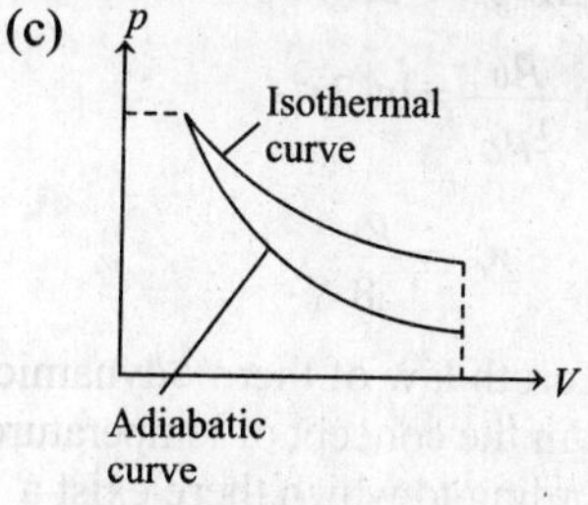

$\frac{\text{Slope of adiabatic curve}}{\text{Slope of isothermal curve}}$

$= \frac{(dp/dV)_{adi}}{(dp/dV)_{iso}} = +\gamma$

So slope to adiabatic curve is γ $\left(= \frac{C_p}{C_V}\right)$ times of isothermal curve, as clear also from figure.

8. (d) The loss of energy should be zero and it should be quesi-static.

This means that the process must occur infinitely slowly to ensure the system remains in equilibrium with its surrounding, preventing any loss of energy.

For a reversible process, $\int \frac{dQ}{T} = 0$

9. (c) Process $1 \to 2$ and process $3 \to 4$ are isochoric processes.

$W_{12} = 0, W_{34} = 0, W_{23} = nR(T_3 - T_2)$

$= 3R(1600 - 400) = 3600R$

$W_{41} = nR(T_1 - T_4)$

$= 3R(200 - 800) = -1800R$

$W = (3600 - 1800)R = 1800R$

$= 15\text{kJ}$

10. (d) Work done by gas in going isothermally from state A to B is

$\Delta W_{AB} = nRT \ln \frac{p_A}{p_B}$

$= nRT \ln 2$ ...(i)

Work done by gas in going isothermally from state B to C is

$$\Delta W_{BC} = nRT \ln \frac{p_B}{p_C}$$

$$= nRT \frac{p_0}{2p_C} \quad \text{...(ii)}$$

It is given that

$$\Delta W_{BC} = 2\Delta W_{AB}$$

$$\ln \frac{p_0}{2p_C} = \ln(2)^2$$

$$\therefore \quad p_C = \frac{p_0}{8}$$

11. (d) Zeroth law of thermodynamics explain the concept of temperature. According to which there exist a scalar quantity called temperature, which is property of all thermodynamic system.
Internal energy depends on temperature.

12. (b) For adiabatic process,

$$p_i V_i^\gamma = p_f V_f^\gamma$$

$$p_0 V_0^\gamma = 8p_0\left(\frac{3}{4}V_0\right)^\gamma$$

$$1 = 8\left(\frac{3}{4}\right)^\gamma \quad \text{...(i)}$$

Also, from $T_i V_i^{\gamma-1} = T_f V_f^{\gamma-1}$

$$TV_0^{\gamma-1} = T_2\left(\frac{3}{4}V_0\right)^{\gamma-1} \quad \text{...(ii)}$$

Multiplying by V_0 on both sides of Eq. (ii), we get

$$TV_0^\gamma = T_2\left(\frac{3}{4}V_0\right)^{\gamma-1} V_0$$

Multiplying the above equation by $\left(\frac{3}{4}\right)$, we get

$$\text{or} \quad \frac{3}{4}TV_0^\gamma = T_2\left(\frac{3}{4}V_0\right)^{\gamma-1}\left(\frac{3}{4}V_0\right)$$

$$\text{or} \quad TV_0^\gamma = \frac{4}{3}T_2\left(\frac{3}{4}V_0\right)^\gamma$$

$$\text{or} \quad T = \frac{4}{3}\left(\frac{3}{4}\right)^\gamma T_2 \quad \text{....(iii)}$$

On dividing Eq. (i) by Eq. (iii), we get

$$\frac{1}{T} = \frac{8\left(\frac{3}{4}\right)^\gamma}{\frac{4}{3}\left(\frac{3}{4}\right)^\gamma T_2}$$

$$\frac{1}{T} = \frac{6}{T_2}$$

$$\Rightarrow \quad T_2 = 6T$$

13. (d) Helium is a monoatomic gas.

$$\therefore \quad \frac{\Delta U}{Q} = \frac{1}{3}$$

$$\Delta U = \frac{Q}{3}$$

From the first law of thermodynamics,

$$Q = \Delta U + W$$

$$\therefore \quad W = Q - \Delta U$$

$$= Q - \frac{Q}{3} = \frac{2Q}{3}$$

14. (a) In free expansion, temperature remains the same.

15. (c) Gas cylinder suddenly explodes is an irreversible adiabatic change and work done against expansion reduces the temperature.

16. (b) Internal energy during path ACB,

$$\Delta U = Q - W$$

$$= 86 - 30 = 56 \text{ cal}$$

Work done along ADB,

$$W = Q - \Delta U$$

$$= 86 - 56 = 30 \text{ cal}$$

17. (d) In process AB, density is constant. Hence, volume is constant. Therefore, work done will be zero.
In process BC, $p \propto \rho$ but $\rho \propto \frac{1}{V}$

$$\therefore \quad p \propto \frac{1}{V}$$

or the process is isothermal.
Hence internal energy is constant.

18. (b) Amount of heat given = 540 cal
Change in volume, $\Delta V = 1670$ cc
Atmospheric pressure

$$p = 1.01 \times 10^6 \text{ dyne/cm}^2$$

Work done against atmospheric pressure,

$$W = p\Delta V = \frac{1.01 \times 10^6 \times 1670}{4.2 \times 10^7}$$

$$\approx 40 \text{ cal}$$

19. (c) $\because pT^2 = \text{constant}$

$$\Rightarrow \left(\frac{nRT}{V}\right) \cdot T^2 = \text{constant}$$

On differentiating the above equation, we get

$$\frac{3T^2}{V} \cdot dT - \frac{T^3}{V^2} dV = 0$$

$$\Rightarrow \quad 3dT = \frac{T}{V} dV \quad \text{... (i)}$$

$$\because \quad dV = V\gamma dT$$

$$\Rightarrow \quad \gamma = \frac{dV}{VdT} \quad \text{... (ii)}$$

From, Eqs. (i) and (ii), we get

$$\frac{dV}{VdT} = \frac{3}{T}$$

20. (a) Here, $W = \int p dV = \int \frac{RT}{V} dV$

$$\because \quad V = kT^{2/3}$$

$$dV = \frac{2}{3} kT^{-\frac{1}{3}} dT$$

$$\therefore \quad \frac{dV}{V} = \frac{2}{3}\frac{dT}{T}$$

$$\text{Hence, } W = \int_{T_1}^{T_2} \frac{2}{3}\frac{RT}{T} dT$$

$$= \frac{2}{3} R(T_2 - T_1)$$

$$= \frac{2}{3} \times R \times 24 = 16R$$

21. (a) For adiabatic process

$$TV^{\gamma-1} = \text{constant}$$

For bc curve, $T_1 V_b^{\gamma-1} = T_2 V_C^{\gamma-1}$

$$\text{or} \quad \frac{T_2}{T_1} = \left(\frac{V_b}{V_c}\right)^{\gamma-1} \quad \text{...(i)}$$

For ad curve,

$$T_1 V_a^{\gamma-1} = T_2 V_a^{\gamma-1}$$

$$\text{or} \quad \frac{T_2}{T_1} = \left(\frac{V_a}{V_b}\right)^{\gamma-1} \quad \text{...(ii)}$$

From Eqs. (i) and (ii), we get

$$\frac{V_b}{V_c} = \frac{V_a}{V_d}$$

22. (b) $\delta Q = W + \delta U$

$-50 = -20 + (U_f - U_i)$

$U_f = -60\,\text{cal}$

23. (a) The work done by a gas in a thermodynamic process is equal to area of p-V diagram under the X-axis.

For diagram (i),

$$W_1 = \pi\left(\frac{3V_0 - V_0}{2}\right)\left(\frac{3p_0 - p_0}{2}\right)$$

$$= \pi p_0 V_0 = 3.14\,p_0 V_0$$

For diagram (ii),

$W_2 =$ Area of trapezium

$$= \frac{1}{2} \times (3V_0 - V_0) \times (p_0 + 2p_0)$$

$$= 3p_0 V_0$$

For diagram (iii),

$W_3 =$ Area of rectangle

$$= (3V_0 - V_0)(2p_0 - p_0) = 2p_0 V_0$$

It is clear that, $W_1 > W_2 > W_3$

24. (a) As the volume is continuously increasing and the work of expansion is always positive, so the work done by the system continuously increases.

25. (a) Heat is similar to work because both represent ways of transferring energy. Work is the transfer of mechanical energy irrespective of temperature difference. Heat is transfer of thermal energy due to temperature difference.

26. (a) AB is isobaric process, BC is isothermal process, CD is isometric process and DA is isothermal process. These process are correctly represented by graph (a).

27. (a) A - 4, B - 3, C - 2, D - 1.

28. (c) $pV^\gamma = K$

or $p\gamma V^{\gamma-1} dV + dp \cdot V^\gamma = 0$

or $\dfrac{dp}{p} = -\gamma \dfrac{dV}{V}$

or $\dfrac{dp}{p} \times 100 = -\gamma\left(\dfrac{dV}{V} \times 100\right)$

$= -1.4 \times 5 = -7$

So, the decrease in presure in 7%.

29. (d) Adiabatic curves are more stepper than isothermal curves.

30. (b) Let initial pressure, volume, temperature be $p_0 V_0, T_0$ indicated by state A in p-V diagram. The gas is then isochorically taken to state $B(2p_0, V_0, 2T_0)$ and then taken from state B to state $C(2p_0, 2V_0, 4T_0)$ isobarically. Total heat absorbed by 1 mole of gas $\Delta Q = C_V(2T_0 - T_0) + C_p(4T_0 - 2T_0)$

$$= \frac{5}{2}RT_0 + \frac{7}{2}R \times 2T_0$$

$$= \frac{19}{2}RT_0$$

Total change in temperature from state A and C, $\Delta T = 3T_0$

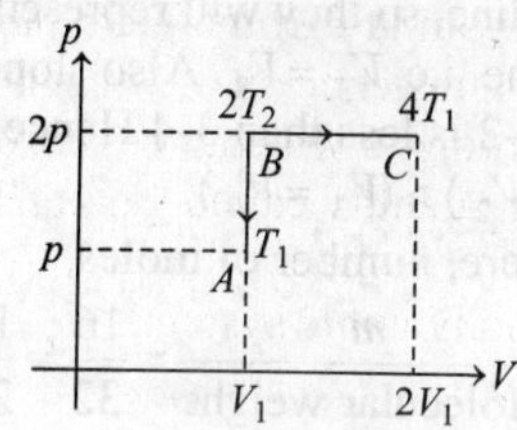

$\therefore$ Molar heat capacity

$$= \frac{\Delta Q}{\Delta T} = \frac{\frac{19}{2}RT_0}{3T_0}$$

$$= \frac{19}{6}R$$

Ch-12 Kinetic Theory of Gases

Topical Follow Thru

Test-1

1. (c) $\dfrac{pV}{kT} = \dfrac{nR}{k} = \dfrac{nR}{R/N_A} = nN_A = N$

$=$ number of molecules in the gas

2. (a) $v_{\text{rms}} = \sqrt{\dfrac{3p}{\rho}}$

$\Rightarrow \dfrac{v_1}{v_2} = \sqrt{\dfrac{\rho_2}{\rho_1}} = \sqrt{\dfrac{16}{1}} = \dfrac{4}{1}$

3. (a) As, $\dfrac{p}{T} =$ constant

$\dfrac{\Delta p}{p} = \dfrac{\Delta T}{T}$

$T = p\dfrac{\Delta T}{\Delta p} = \dfrac{\Delta T}{(\Delta p/p)}$

$= \dfrac{1}{0.4/100} = 250\,\text{K}$

4. (c) A $\rightarrow$ 3, B $\rightarrow$ 2, C $\rightarrow$ 4, D $\rightarrow$ 1

5. (a) Here, temperature $=$ constant.

So, $p_1 V_1 = p_2 V_2$

$p_2 = \dfrac{p_1 V_1}{V_2}$

Given, $p_1 = 760\,\text{mm}$

and $V_2 = \dfrac{3}{4}V_1$

$\Rightarrow \dfrac{V_1}{V_2} = \dfrac{4}{3}$

$\therefore p_2 = \dfrac{760 \times 4}{3}$

$= 1013.3$ mm of Hg

6. (b) Here, pressure is constant,

$\therefore \dfrac{V_2}{V_1} = \dfrac{T_2}{T_1}$

$T_2 = \dfrac{V_2}{V_1} T_1$

Given, $T_1 = 27°\,\text{C} = 300\,\text{K}$

$V_1 = 3.0\,\text{L}$

$V_2 = 2.7\,\text{L}$, then

$T_2 = \dfrac{2.7}{3.0} \times 300$

$= 270\,\text{K}$

7. (c) As we know,

$pV = nRT$

Here, temperature is constant

i.e. $pV =$ constant

Therefore, option (c) is correct.

8. (a) From ideal gas equation,

$$pV = \mu RT$$

$\Rightarrow$ Slope of pt curve, $\frac{p}{T} = \frac{\mu R}{V}$

$\Rightarrow$ Slope $\propto \frac{1}{V}$

It means line of smaller slope represent greater volume of gas. For the given problem, in figure, points 1 and 2 are on the same line, so they will represent same volume, i.e. $V_1 = V_2$.

Similarly points 3 and 4 are on the same line, so they will represent same volume. i.e. $V_3 = V_4$. Also slope of line 1-2 is less than 3-4 Hence, $(V_1 = V_2) > (V_3 = V_4)$

9. (d) Here, number of moles,

$$n = \frac{m}{\text{Molecular weight}} = \frac{16}{32} = \frac{1}{2}$$

So, for ideal gas equation,

$$pV = nRT$$

$$pV = \frac{1}{2}RT$$

$$2pV = RT$$

10. (d) $pV = NkT$

$$\Rightarrow \frac{N_A}{N_B} = \frac{p_A V_A}{p_B V_B} \times \frac{T_B}{T_A}$$

$$\Rightarrow \frac{N_A}{N_B} = \frac{p \times V \times (2T)}{2p \times \frac{V}{4} \times T} = \frac{4}{1}$$

11. (b) Here, $p_1 = 2p$

and $p_2 = 3p$

From Dalton's law of partial pressure, $p_{\text{total}} = p_1 + p_2$

$$= 2p + 3p = 5p$$

12. (b) As we know,

$V \propto T$ at constant pressure,

$$\Rightarrow \frac{V_1}{V_2} = \frac{T_1}{T_2}$$

$$V_2 = \frac{V_1 T_2}{T_1}$$

Here, $V_1 = 450\,\text{ml}$, $T_2 = -23°C$

$$= 273 - 23 = 250\,\text{K}$$

$$T_1 = 77°C = 273 + 77 = 350\,\text{K}$$

$$V_2 = \frac{450 \times 250}{350} = 321.4\,\text{ml}$$

13. (d) Here, V = constant

$T_1 = 27°C = 300$ K

$T_2 = 127°C = 400$ K

$p_1 = 4$ atm

Now, $\frac{p_2}{p_1} = \frac{T_2}{T_1}$

$$p_2 = \frac{T_2}{T_1} \times p_1 = \frac{400}{300} \times 4 = 5.3\,\text{atm}$$

14. (d) $pV = mrT$

Since, p, V and $r \to$ remains same

Hence, $m \propto \frac{1}{T}$

$$\Rightarrow \frac{m_1}{m_2} = \frac{T_2}{T_1}$$

$$\Rightarrow \frac{13}{m_2} = \frac{(273 + 52)}{(273 + 27)} = \frac{325}{300}$$

i.e. Mass released $= 13\,\text{g} - 12\,\text{g}$

$$= 1\,\text{g}$$

15. (b) As we know that, kinetic energy of gas $\propto$ temperature

$$\text{KE} \propto T$$

$$\therefore \frac{(\text{KE})_2}{(\text{KE})_1} = \frac{T_2}{T_1}$$

$$T_2 = \frac{(\text{KE})_2}{(\text{KE})_1} \times T_1 = \frac{300}{2}$$

$$(\because T_1 = 27°C = 300\,\text{K})$$

$$= 150\,\text{K} = -123\,°C$$

16. (a) Given, pressure,

$$p = 249\,\text{kPa} = 249 \times 10^3\,\text{Pa}$$

Temperature, $T = 27°C$

$$= 273 + 27 = 300\,\text{K}$$

As, from ideal gas equation,

$$pV = nRT$$

$$\Rightarrow pV = \frac{m}{M}RT \quad \left[\text{as, } n = \frac{m}{M}\right]$$

$$\Rightarrow pVM = mRT$$

$$\Rightarrow pM = \frac{m}{V}RT = \rho RT \quad \left[\text{as, } \frac{m}{V} = \rho\right]$$

$$\Rightarrow \rho = \frac{pM}{RT} = \frac{249 \times 10^3 \times 2 \times 10^{-3}}{8.3 \times 300}$$

[$\because$ for hydrogen gas, $M = 2$ g $= 2 \times 10^{-3}$ kg]

$$\Rightarrow \rho = 0.2\,\text{kg/m}^3$$

17. (c) At STP, $T = 273\,\text{K}$, $p = 10^5\,\text{N/m}^2$

No. of moles of water in 2.25 kg,

$$n = \frac{2.25\,\text{kg}}{18\,\text{g}} = \frac{2.25\,\text{kg}}{1.8 \times 10^{-2}}$$

$$= 125\,\text{moles}$$

Now, using ideal gas equation,

$$pV = nRT$$

We have, $V = \frac{nRT}{p}$

$$= \frac{125 \times 8.3 \times 273}{10^5}$$

$$= 2.8\,\text{m}^3$$

18. (b) Ratio of rms to mean speed of molecules $= \frac{5.45}{5} = 1.09$

19. (c) From ideal gas equation,

$$pV = nRT \quad \text{...(i)}$$

or $$p\Delta V = nR\Delta T \quad \text{...(ii)}$$

On dividing Eq. (ii) by Eq. (i), we get

$$\frac{\Delta V}{V} = \frac{\Delta T}{T}$$

$$\Rightarrow \frac{\Delta V}{V\,\Delta T} = \frac{1}{T} = \delta \quad \text{(given)}$$

$$\therefore \delta = \frac{1}{T}$$

So, the graph between δ and T will be rectangular hyperbola.

20. (a) We know for an ideal gas,

$$pV = nRT$$

$$\Rightarrow V = \left(\frac{nR}{p}\right)T$$

where, p = pressure,

V = volume,

n = number of moles of gases,

R = gas constant

and T = temperature.

Slope of V-T graph,

$$m = \frac{dV}{dT} = \frac{nR}{p}$$

$$\Rightarrow m \propto \frac{1}{p} \quad (\because nR = \text{constant})$$

$$\Rightarrow p \propto \frac{1}{m}$$

Hence, $\frac{p_1}{p_2} = \frac{m_2}{m_1} > 1$

where, m_1 is slope of the graph corresponding to p_1 and m_2 is slope corresponding to p_2.

$$\Rightarrow \quad p_2 < p_1 \text{ or } p_1 > p_2$$

21. (c) $pV = \mu RT = \frac{m}{M} RT$

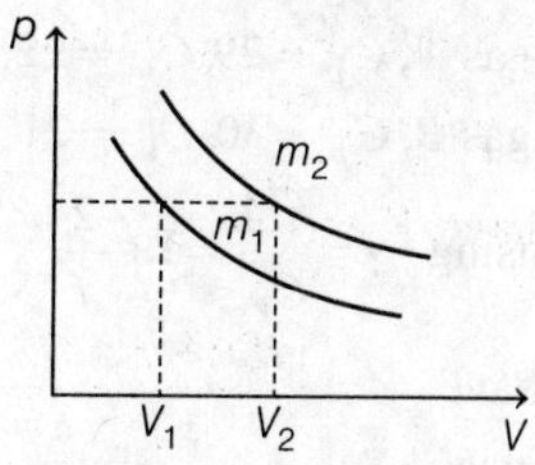

For 1st plot, $p = \frac{m_1}{M} \frac{RT}{V_1}$ ...(i)

For 2nd plot, $p = \frac{m_2}{M} \frac{RT}{V_2}$ ...(ii)

From Eqs. (i) and (ii), we get

$$\frac{m_1}{m_2} = \frac{V_1}{V_2} \Rightarrow m \propto V$$

As, $V_2 > V_1 \Rightarrow m_1 < m_2$

22. (b) As, $\frac{p_1 V_1}{T_1} = \frac{p_2 V_2}{T_2}$

or $V_2 = \frac{p_1 V_1 T_2}{p_2 T_1}$

$\therefore$ Volume of He,

$$V_2 = \frac{1 \times 500 \times (273 - 3)}{0.5 \times (273 + 27)}$$

$$= \frac{1 \times 500 \times 270}{0.5 \times 300} = 900 \text{ m}^3$$

23. (c) $v_{\text{rms}} = \sqrt{\frac{3RT}{M}}, v_{\text{av}} = \sqrt{\frac{8RT}{\pi M}}$

and $v_p = \sqrt{\frac{2RT}{M}}$

$$\Rightarrow v_{\text{rms}} : v_{\text{av}} : v_p = \sqrt{3} : \sqrt{\frac{8}{\pi}} : \sqrt{2}$$

$$\therefore \quad v_{\text{rms}} > v_{\text{av}} > v_p$$

24. (b) As we know that,

$$v_{\text{mean}} = \frac{|\mathbf{v}_1| + |\mathbf{v}_2| + \ldots |\mathbf{v}_n|}{N}$$

$$= \sqrt{\frac{8p}{\pi \rho}}$$

$$= \sqrt{\frac{8RT}{\pi m_w}} = \sqrt{\frac{8kT}{\pi m}} = 1.59 \sqrt{\frac{kT}{m}}$$

25. (c) The kinetic energy of gas molecules is the internal property, which is independent of the motion of frame. The temperature depends on the kinetic energy, so it will remain unchanged, when the container is kept in a moving train.

Test-2

1. (a) Mean free path,

$$\lambda = \frac{1}{\sqrt{2} \pi n d^2}$$

$$\Rightarrow d^2 = \frac{1}{\sqrt{2} \pi n \lambda}$$

$$= \frac{1 \times \pi}{\sqrt{2} \times \pi \times 2\sqrt{2} \times 10^8 \times 10^{-2}}$$

$$\Rightarrow d^2 = \frac{1}{4 \times 10^6}$$

$$\Rightarrow \quad d = \frac{1}{2} \times 10^{-3} \text{ cm}$$

$$\Rightarrow \quad d = 5 \times 10^{-4} \text{ cm}$$

2. (d) Total internal energy of system

$$= U_{\text{oxygen}} + U_{\text{argon}}$$

$$= \mu_1 \frac{f_1}{2} RT + \mu_2 \frac{f_2}{2} RT$$

$$= 2 \times \frac{5}{2} RT + 4 \times \frac{3}{2} RT$$

$$= 5RT + 6RT = 11RT$$

[as $f_1 = 5$ (for oxygen) and $f_2 = 3$ (for argon)]

3. (c) As, H_2 has 5 degree of freedom and He has 3 degree of freedom. So, the mean energy of H_2 will be greater than He.

However, mean translational KE for both will be same.

$$\text{KE} = \frac{3}{2} kT$$

4. (c) Given, $C = 37.55 \text{ J mol}^{-1} \text{ K}^{-1}$

Also, $pT = \text{constant } (K)$ ... (i)

According to ideal gas equation,

$$pV = RT$$

$$\Rightarrow \quad p = \frac{RT}{V} \quad \text{... (ii)}$$

Putting the value of p in Eq. (i), we get

$$\frac{RT}{V} \times T = K$$

$$\Rightarrow \quad V = \frac{RT^2}{K}$$

On differentiating above equation both sides, we get

$$\frac{dV}{dT} = \frac{2RT}{K} \quad \text{... (iii)}$$

But $\frac{T}{K} = \frac{1}{p}$ [from Eq. (i)]

Hence, Eq. (iii) becomes

$$\frac{dV}{dT} = \frac{2R}{p}$$

So, $C = C_V + \frac{pdV}{dT}$

or $C = C_V + \frac{p \times 2R}{p} = C_V + 2R$

or $C_V = C - 2R$ ... (iv)

As $C_V = \frac{nR}{2}$, where n = number of degrees of freedom.

Putting the value of C_V in Eq. (iv), we get

$$\frac{nR}{2} = C - 2R$$

$$n = \frac{2(C - 2R)}{R} = \frac{2\,(37.55 - 2 \times 8.3)}{8.3}$$

$$= 5.048 \simeq 5$$

5. (d) Statement I is incorrect but Statement II is correct.

Degree of freedom of a diatomic gas depends on temperature because when a diatomic gas dissociates into atoms, it behaves like monoatomic gas. Degree of freedom of monoatomic gas is 3 for all temperatures.

6. (c) Degree of freedom of non-rigid diatomic molecules,

$$= 5 + 2(3N - 5)$$

$$= 5 + 2(3 \times 2 - 5)$$

$$= 5 + 2 = 7$$

$$f = 7$$

Energy of one molecule $= \frac{f}{2} k_B T$

$\therefore$ Energy of 10 molecules

$$= 10\left(\frac{f}{2} k_B T\right)$$

$$= 10 \times \frac{7}{2} k_B T = 35 k_B T$$

7. (c)Argon is monoatomic, its degree of freedom is 3.

Oxygen is diatomic with 5 degree of freedom.

Total internal energy of mixture

= Internal energy of Ar + Internal energy of O_2

$$= 8\times\frac{3}{2}RT + 6\times\frac{5}{2}RT$$
$$= (12+15)RT$$
$$= 27RT$$

8. (b) Mean relaxation time or average time duration between two successive collisions is

$$\tau = \frac{\text{mean relaxation time}}{\text{mean velocity}}$$
$$= \frac{\lambda}{v_{\text{mean}}}$$

9. (c) According to law of equipartition of energy, the energy per degree of freedom is $\frac{1}{2}kT$.

For a polyatomic gas with degree of freedom $n = \frac{n}{2}kT$

10. (c) At a given temperature, the rotational energy of diatomic molecules are fixed and same for all. It is $\frac{2}{3}$rd of translational kinetic energy of each molecule.

For monoatomic gases, $f = 3$ and the ratio of C_p/C_V is

$$= 1+\frac{2}{f} = 1+\frac{2}{3} = \frac{5}{3}$$

11. (a) At constant pressure,

$$(\Delta Q)_p = \mu C_p \Delta T$$
$$= 1\times C_p \times (30-20) = 40$$
$$\Rightarrow C_p = 4\frac{\text{calorie}}{\text{mole}\times\text{kelvin}}$$
$$\therefore C_V = C_p - R = 4-2$$
$$= 2\frac{\text{calorie}}{\text{mole}\times\text{kelvin}}$$

Now, $(\Delta Q)_V = \mu C_V \Delta T$

$$= 1\times 2\times(30-20) = 20\,\text{cal}$$

12. (c) $\gamma_{\text{mix}} = \dfrac{\dfrac{\mu_1\gamma_1}{\gamma_1-1}+\dfrac{\mu_2\gamma_2}{\gamma_2-1}}{\dfrac{\mu_1}{\gamma_1-1}+\dfrac{\mu_2}{\gamma_2-1}}$ ...(i)

Here $\mu_1 = \mu_2 = 1;\ \gamma_1 = \frac{7}{5}$

and $\gamma_2 = \frac{5}{3}$

On putting the values in Eq. (i) and solving, we get

$$\gamma_{\text{mix}} = \frac{3}{2}$$

13. (b) Given, $C_p = \frac{5}{2}R$

As we know that,

$$C_V = C_p - R$$
$$= \frac{5}{2}R - R = \frac{3}{2}R$$
$$\therefore \frac{C_p}{C_V} = \frac{\frac{5}{2}R}{\frac{3}{2}R} = \frac{5}{3}$$

14. (c) Here, both nitrogen and hydrogen gases are diatomic gases.

From Mayer's formula for all gases,

$$C_p - C_V = R$$
$$\therefore A = B$$

15. (b) Mean free path of a gas,

$$\lambda_m = \frac{1}{\sqrt{2}\,\pi d^2 n}$$

where, d is diameter of molecule of gas

$$\because d = 2r$$
$$\therefore \lambda_m \propto \frac{1}{r^2}$$

16. (b) Change in internal energy from $A \rightarrow B$.

$$\Delta U = \frac{f}{2}nR\Delta T$$
$$= \frac{f}{2}nR(T_f - T_i)$$
$$= \frac{5}{2}(p_f V_f - p_i V_i)$$
$$= \frac{5}{2}(2\times10^3\times8 - 7\times10^3\times4)$$
$$= \frac{5}{2}(16-28)\times10^3\ \text{J}$$
$$= \frac{5}{2}\times(-12)\times10^3\ \text{J}$$
$$\Delta U = -30\,\text{kJ}$$

17. (a) Now, in given case,

For gas A, $C_p = 29$, $C_V = 22$

For gas B, $C_p = 30$, $C_V = 21$

By using $\gamma = \frac{C_p}{C_V} = 1+\frac{2}{f}$,

we have

For gas A,

$$1+\frac{2}{f} = \frac{29}{22} \approx 1.3$$
$$\Rightarrow f = 6.67 \approx 7$$

So, gas A has vibrational mode of degree of freedom.

For gas B,

$$1+\frac{2}{f} = \frac{30}{21} \approx 1.4$$
$$\Rightarrow f = 5$$

18. (c) For oxygen, $f = 5$

$$\gamma = 1+\frac{2}{f} = 1+\frac{2}{5} = \frac{7}{5}$$

For helium, $f = 3$

$$\gamma = 1+\frac{2}{f} = 1+\frac{2}{3} = \frac{5}{3}$$

For gas X, $f = 7$

$$\gamma = 1+\frac{2}{f} = 1+\frac{2}{7} = \frac{9}{7}$$

So, $\left(\frac{7}{5}, \frac{5}{3}, \frac{9}{7}\right)$

19. (a) Pressure $= \frac{2E}{3V} = \frac{2}{3}\frac{E}{l^3}$

Force on any of wall

$$= P\times A = \frac{2}{3}\frac{E}{l^3}\times l^2$$

Momentum transferred in 3 seconds.

$$= F\times\Delta t = 2El$$

20. (b) Saturated vapours does not follow gas law as the pressure is independent of volume, whereas unsaturated vapour obeys gas law.

21. (d) Pressure on both sides should be same.

$$\Rightarrow \frac{n_1 RT}{V_1} = \frac{n_2 RT}{V_2}$$

$$\Rightarrow \frac{m}{M_1 V_1} = \frac{m}{M_2 V_2}$$

$$\Rightarrow \frac{m}{32(360° - \alpha)V} = \frac{m}{28\alpha V}$$

$$\Rightarrow 28\alpha = 32(360° - \alpha)$$

$$\Rightarrow \alpha = \frac{32 \times 360}{60}$$

or $\alpha = 192°$

22. (a) According to Mayer's formula,

$\because \quad C_p - C_V = R$

$\therefore \quad MC_p - MC_V = R$

$$C_p - C_V = \frac{R}{M}$$

23. (a) Internal energy of a gas mixture = Sum of internal energies of its components

Also, internal energy of a gas is given by

$$U = \frac{f}{2}(nRT)$$

Here, gases are oxygen (diatomic, $f = 5$) and argon (monoatomic $f = 3$).

So, total internal energy of the mixture,

$$U = \left(\frac{f}{2}nRT\right)_{O_2} + \left(\frac{f}{2}nRT\right)_{Ar}$$

$$= \frac{5}{2} \times 5 \times RT + \frac{3}{2} \times 7 \times RT = 23RT$$

24. (a) $C_p - C_V = R = 2.\dfrac{\text{cal}}{\text{g-mol-K}}$

where is correct for option (a) and (b). Further the ratio $\dfrac{C_p}{C_V}(=\gamma)$

should equal to some standard value corresponding to that of either, mono, di or tri-atomic gases. From the point of view, option (a) is correct because $\left(\dfrac{C_p}{C_V}\right)_{\text{mono}} = \dfrac{5}{3}$

25. (a) We know that, according to law of equipartition of energy, each gas molecule has $(1/2)kt$ energy associated with each of its degrees of freedom. As a diatomic gas molecule has two rotational degrees of freedom, final temperature of the system,

$$T_l = \frac{f_1 n_1 T_1 + f_2 n_2 T_2}{f_1 n_1 + f_2 n_2} \quad \ldots\text{(i)}$$

Using $\frac{1}{2}I\omega_{\text{rms}}^2 = kT_1$

$$T_1 = 250\text{ K}$$

Here for diatomic gas,

$$f_1 = 5, n_1 = 3$$

and $T_1 = 250$ K

For monatomic gas,

$f_2 = 3, n_2 = 5$ and $T_2 = 470$ K

Thus from Eq. (i), we get

$$T_f = \frac{5 \times 3 \times 250 + 3 \times 5 \times 470}{5 \times 3 + 3 \times 5}$$

$$= 360\text{ K}$$

Thus, final mixture of the two gases is at temperature 360 K. If final rms angular velocity of diatomic gas molecule is $\omega_{\text{rms}} f$ according to law of equipartition of energy, we have

$$\frac{1}{2}I\omega_{\text{rms}}^2 f = kT$$

or $\omega_{\text{rms}} f = \sqrt{\dfrac{2kT}{I}}$

$$= \sqrt{\frac{2 \times 1.38 \times 10^{-23} \times 360}{2.76 \times 10^{-46}}}$$

$$\omega_{\text{rms}} f = 6 \times 10^{12} \text{ rad/s}$$

Chapter Break Thru

1. (b) For diatomic gas of H_2,

$$C_{p_2} = \frac{7}{2}R, C_{V_2} = \frac{5}{2}R$$

For monoatomic gas of He,

$$C_{p_1} = \frac{5}{2}R, C_{V_1} = \frac{3}{2}R$$

Specific heat ratio,

$$\gamma = \frac{n_1 C_{p_1} + n_2 C_{p_2}}{n_1 C_{V_1} + n_2 C_{V_2}}$$

$$= \frac{2 \times \frac{5}{2}R + n \times \frac{7}{2}R}{2 \times \frac{3}{2}R + n \times \frac{5}{2}R}$$

$$\gamma = \frac{10 + 7n}{6 + 5n} \quad \ldots\text{(i)}$$

It is given that, $v_{\text{rms}} = \sqrt{2} \times v_{\text{sound}}$

$$\Rightarrow \sqrt{\frac{3RT}{M}} = \sqrt{2} \times \sqrt{\frac{\gamma RT}{M}}$$

$$\Rightarrow \gamma = \frac{3}{2}$$

From Eq. (i), $\dfrac{3}{2} = \dfrac{10 + 7n}{6 + 5n}$

$$\Rightarrow n = 2$$

2. (a) Since, $c_{\text{rms}} << v_e$, hence molecules do not escape out.

3. (a) $pV = nRT \quad \ldots\text{(i)}$

$$p\left(\frac{90V}{100}\right) = n_1 R\left(T + \frac{20}{100}T\right)$$

or $\dfrac{9}{10}pV = \dfrac{6}{5}n_1 RT \quad \ldots\text{(ii)}$

Dividing Eq. (ii) by Eq. (i), we get

$$\frac{6n_1}{5n} = \frac{9}{10}$$

$$n_1 = \frac{3}{4}n$$

$$\% \text{ of gas leaked} = \frac{n - n_1}{n} \times 100$$

$$= \left(1 - \frac{3}{4}\right) \times 100 = 25\%$$

4. (d) As we know that, mean free path of molecules of a gas,

$$\lambda = \frac{1}{\sqrt{2}\, n\pi d^2}$$

$\because \quad pV = NkT$

$$p = \frac{N}{V}kT$$

$$p = nkT \qquad \left[\because \frac{N}{V} = n\right]$$

$$n = \frac{p}{kT}$$

$$\therefore \quad \lambda = \frac{kT}{\sqrt{2}\,\pi d^2 p}$$

Hence, $\lambda \propto T$ and $\lambda \propto \dfrac{1}{p}$

5. (b) According to the kinetic theory of gases, the molecules of a gas are in continuous random motion because gas is not in a fixed state.

The molecules do not interact of in contact with each others except collisions.

It is experimentally proved that the collision amongst the molecules are

of short duration because collision occurs very fast.
So, the statement that the molecule continuously undergo inelastic collision is wrong or incorrect. Because it is not sure that collision is elastic or inelastic. It depends on the conditions.

6. (d) As we know that,

$$v_{\text{rms}} = \sqrt{\frac{3RT}{M}}$$

$$\therefore \quad T \propto M$$

$$\therefore \quad \frac{T'}{T} = \frac{4}{2} = 2 \text{ or } T' = 2T$$

or $\quad T = 2 \times 273\,\text{K} = 546\,\text{K}$

7. (a) A corresponds to H_2, B to He and C to O_2.

$$pV = \mu RT = \frac{m}{M}RT$$

$$\Rightarrow \quad \frac{pV}{T} \propto \frac{1}{M}$$

$(\because M = \text{molecular mass})$

From graph,

$$\left(\frac{pV}{T}\right)_A < \left(\frac{pV}{T}\right)_B < \left(\frac{pV}{T}\right)_C$$

$$\Rightarrow \quad M_A > M_B > M_C$$

8. (b) $v_{\text{rms}} = \sqrt{\frac{3RT}{M}}$,

$$u_p = \sqrt{2\frac{RT}{M}} = 0.816\, v_{\text{rms}}$$

$$\bar{u} = \sqrt{\frac{8RT}{\pi M}} = 0.92\, v_{\text{rms}}$$

$$\Rightarrow \quad u_p < v_{\text{rms}}$$

Further, $E_{\text{av}} = \frac{1}{2}mv_{\text{rms}}^2$

$$= \frac{1}{2}m\frac{3}{2}u_p = \frac{3}{4}mu_p$$

9. (c) According to law of equipartition of energy, the energy per degree of freedom is $\frac{1}{2}kT$.

For diatomic gas with degree of freedom 5, the mean energy per molecule $= \frac{1}{2}nkT = \frac{1}{2} \times 5\,kT = \frac{5}{2}kT$

10. (c) Kinetic energy of one mole of ideal gas does not depend on the molecular weight $\left(E = \frac{3}{2}RT\right)$. Hence, Statement IV is correct.

11. (a) We know that,

$$v_{\text{rms}} = \sqrt{\frac{3RT}{M}}$$

Now, the root mean square velocity of helium,

$$v_{\text{rms}}\,(\text{He}) = \sqrt{\frac{3R \times T}{M}} \qquad \text{...(i)}$$

Now, the root mean square velocity of hydrogen,

$$v_{\text{rms}}\,(\text{H}) = \sqrt{\frac{3R \times 273}{M}} \qquad \text{...(ii)}$$

From Eqs. (i) and (ii), we get

$$\frac{v_{\text{rms}}\,(\text{He})}{v_{\text{rms}}\,(\text{H})} = \frac{\sqrt{\frac{3R \times T}{4}}}{\sqrt{\frac{3R \times 273}{2}}}$$

$$\frac{5}{7} = \sqrt{\frac{T \times 2}{273 \times 4}}$$

$$\frac{25}{49} = \frac{T \times 2}{273 \times 4}$$

$$T = \frac{273 \times 25 \times 4}{49 \times 2}$$

$$T \simeq 278\,\text{K}$$

$$T = 278 - 273$$

$$T = 5°\text{C}$$

12. (c) Mean KE of gas molecule,

$$E = \frac{3}{2}kT = \frac{3}{2}k(t + 273)$$

where, T = temperature is in kelvin and t = in centigrade

$$\therefore \quad E = \frac{3}{2}kt + \frac{3}{2} \times 273\,\text{K}$$

(k = Boltzmann's constant)
By comparing this equation with standard equation of straight line $y = mx + c$, we get

$$m = \frac{3}{2}k$$

and $\quad c = \frac{3}{2}273k$

So, the graph between E and t will be a straight line with positive intercept on E-axis and positive slope with t-axis.

13. (c) A → 2, B → 1, C → 4, D → 3

14. (d) Coefficient of volume expansion at constant pressure is $\frac{1}{273}$ for all gases. The average translational KE is same for molecule of all gases and for each molecules it is $\frac{3}{2}KT$

Mean free path, $\lambda = \frac{KT}{\sqrt{2}\pi d^2 p}$

(as p decreases, λ increases)
The average translational kinetic energy per molecule of oxygen gas is $\frac{3}{2}kT$. Hence, statement IV is incorrect.

15. (c) At about 60 K or less, temperature is low and gas molecules have only translatory motion, hence its degree of freedom is 3.

So, $C_V = \frac{f}{2}R = \frac{3}{2}R$

Above 60 K, molecules begin to rotate and at 250 K, rotational energy attains its classical value. At 250 K, gas molecules have 3 translatory and 2 rotatory degrees of freedom. i.e. $f = 5$

So, $C_V = \frac{5}{2}R$.

At 280 K, H_2 gas molecules do not begin to vibrate because it is too low temperature.

16. (c) At constant pressure,

$$T \propto V$$

$$\frac{T_2}{T_1} = \frac{V_2}{V_1}$$

Here, $T_1 = 600\,\text{K}$

$V_1 = 1000\,\text{L}$

$V_2 = 500\,\text{L}$

$$\therefore \quad T_2 = \frac{V_2}{V_1} \times T_1$$

$$= \frac{500}{1000} \times 600$$

$$= 300\,\text{K}$$

17. (d) As we know that,

Total $\quad \text{KE} = \frac{3}{2}NkT$

Put $\quad T = \frac{pV}{R}$

$$\text{KE} = \frac{3}{2}\frac{NkpV}{R}$$

$$\therefore \quad \text{KE} \propto pV$$

$$\Rightarrow \frac{KE_1}{KE_2} = \frac{p_1V_1}{p_2V_2}$$

$$KE_2 = \frac{p_2V_2}{p_1V_1} \times KE_1$$

$$= \frac{2pV}{pV} \times 1600$$

$$= 3200\,J$$

18. (a) As we know that,
The ratio of specific heats of a gas is represent as

$$\gamma = 1 + \frac{2}{f}$$

$$\Rightarrow \quad f = \frac{2}{\gamma - 1}$$

19. (b) The pressure of vapour does not depend on the mass of substance. It depends on the temperature of containers. Here, both are at same temperature, so the ratio of vapour pressure is 1 : 1.

20. (d) Given, $v_{rms} = 300\,ms^{-1}$
Root mean square velocity,

$$v_{rms} = \sqrt{\frac{3k_BT}{m}} \quad \ldots(i)$$

$$v'_{rms} = \sqrt{\frac{3k_B\,(T/2)}{2m}} = \frac{1}{2}\sqrt{\frac{3k_BT}{m}}$$

$$= \frac{v_{rms}}{2} \quad \text{[from Eq. (i)]}$$

$$= \frac{300}{2} = 150\,ms^{-1}$$

21. (d) The translational motion of the gas chamber increases the total kinetic energy of the chamber but it does not contribute to the internal energy of the system. So, the temperature of gas in the chamber remains same. Therefore, A is false but R is true.

22. (d) Mean free path of a molecule is given by

$$l = \frac{1}{\sqrt{2}d^2 n\pi}$$

where, n = number of molecules/volume and d = diameter of the molecule.

Now, we can write $l \propto \frac{1}{d^2}$

Given, $d_1 = 1.5\,Å$, $d_2 = 2.5\,Å$

As $l_1 \propto \frac{1}{d_1^2}$ and $l_2 \propto \frac{1}{d_2^2}$

$$\Rightarrow \text{So, } \frac{l_1}{l_2} = \left(\frac{d_2}{d_1}\right)^2 = \left(\frac{2.5}{1.5}\right)^2 = \frac{25}{9}$$

Hence, $l_1 : l_2 = 25 : 9$

23. (b) As we know that,

$$v_{rms} = \sqrt{\frac{3RT}{M}}$$

Here, $(v_{rms})_1 = v$

$$T_2 = 2T_1 \Rightarrow \frac{T_2}{T_1} = 2$$

$$M_2 = 2M_1 \Rightarrow \frac{M_2}{M_1} = 2$$

$$\therefore \quad \frac{(v_{rms})_2}{(v_{rms})_1} = \sqrt{\frac{T_2}{T_1} \times \frac{M_1}{M_2}}$$

$$\Rightarrow \quad \frac{(v_{rms})_2}{v} = \sqrt{2 \times \frac{1}{2}} \Rightarrow (v_{rms})_2 = v$$

24. (b) As partial pressure of a gas in a mixture is the pressure, it would exert for the same volume and temperature, if it alone occupied the vessel. Therefore, for same V and T, p_1 and p_2 be partial pressures.
From ideal gas equations,

$$p_1V = \mu_1 RT$$

and $p_2V = \mu_2 RT$

Here, 1 and 2 refer to helium gas and nitrogen gas, respectively.

Now, $\frac{p_1}{p_2} = \frac{\mu_1}{\mu_2}$

or $\frac{\mu_1}{\mu_2} = \frac{p_1}{p_2} = \frac{5}{3}$

$$\therefore \quad \frac{\mu_1}{\mu_2} = \frac{5}{3} \quad \left(\because \frac{p_1}{p_2} = \frac{5}{3}\right)$$

25. (c) Average number of degree of freedom per molecule,

$$f = \frac{\text{Total number of degree of freedom}}{\text{Total number of molecule}}$$

$$= \frac{n_1N_Af_1 + n_2N_Af_2}{n_1N_A + n_2N_A}$$

$$= \frac{n_1f_1 + n_2f_2}{n_1 + n_2}$$

Here, $f_1 = 3$, $f_2 = 5$

and $\gamma = 1 + \frac{2}{f}$

Also, $\gamma = \frac{C_p}{C_V} = \frac{3R}{2R} = 1.5$

$$\Rightarrow \quad 1.5 = 1 + \frac{2}{f} \Rightarrow f = 4$$

Hence, $\frac{3n_1 + 5n_2}{n_1 + n_2} = 4$

which, on solving $\frac{n_1}{n_2} = 1$

26. (d) Rms speed of atoms,

$$v_{rms} = \sqrt{\frac{3RT}{M_w}}$$

Here, $T = 27°C$ or 300 K

$M_w = 40\,g$ or 40×10^{-3} kg

$R = 8.31\,J/kg\text{-}K$

$$\therefore \quad v_{rms} = \sqrt{\frac{3 \times 8.31 \times 300}{40 \times 10^{-3}}}$$

$$= 432.40\,m/s$$

As, pressure = force per unit area or pressure = rate of change in momentum per unit area

= (Number of molecules striking) × (Rate of change in momentum of one atom per unit area)

$$= N \times \frac{m[v_{rms} - (-v_{rms})]}{At}$$

(Here, m is mass of one atom of Ar)

$$\Rightarrow \quad p = \left(\frac{N}{At}\right) 2mv_{rms}$$

$$= n\,2mv_{rms}$$

(Here, n = number of atoms striking per unit area per second)

or $n = \frac{p}{2mv_{rms}}$

Given, $p = 2$ atm

$$= 2 \times 1.01 \times 10^5\ Pa$$

$$m = \frac{40}{6.023 \times 10^{23}}\,g$$

$$= 6.6412 \times 10^{-26}\ kg$$

$$n = \frac{2 \times 1.01 \times 10^5}{2 \times 6.6412 \times 10^{-26} \times 432.40}$$

$$n = 3.5 \times 10^{27}$$

27. (c) At high temperatures (greater than 250 K), heat capacity is nearly constant and equals to $3R$. At low temperatures, the heat capacities decrease. At $T = 0\,K$, C tends to zero. The correct variation of heat capacity with temperature is shown in the figure given below

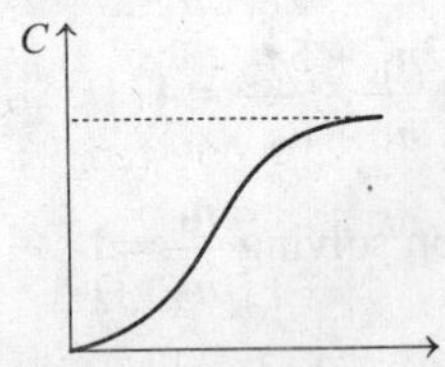

28. (d) For n-molecules, we know that

$$v_{rms} = \sqrt{\frac{v_1^2 + v_2^2 + v_3^2 + \ldots + v_n^2}{n}}$$

[v_{rms} = root mean square velocity]

where, $v_1, v_2, v_3, \ldots, v_n$ are individual velocities of n molecules of the gas.

For two molecules,

$$v_{rms} = \sqrt{\frac{v_1^2 + v_2^2}{2}}$$

[$v_1, v_2 \cdot v_3 \ldots v_n$ are individual velocity]

Given, $v_1 = 12 \times 10^6$ m/s

and $v_2 = 4 \times 10^6$ m/s

$$\therefore v_{rms} = \sqrt{\frac{(12 \times 10^6)^2 + (4 \times 10^6)^2}{2}}$$

$$= 4\sqrt{5} \times 10^6 \text{ m/s}$$

29. (d) From the ideal gas equation,

$$p = \left(\frac{\mu R}{V}\right)T = \left(\frac{mR}{MV}\right)T \quad \ldots\text{(i)}$$

$$\left(\because \mu = \frac{m}{M}\right)$$

The constant volumes are straight lines with slope $\frac{mR}{MV}$. The slope of lines is proportional to the mass of the gas.

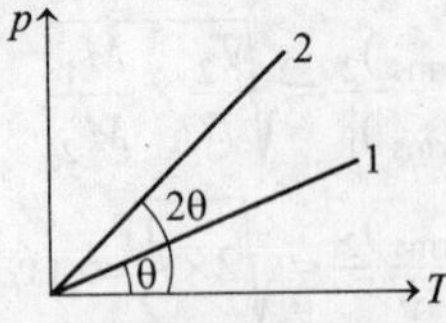

From Eq. (i), we get

$$\frac{(\text{slope})_1}{(\text{slope})_2} = \frac{m_1}{m_2} = \frac{\tan\theta}{\tan 2\theta}$$

$$= \frac{\tan\theta}{\tan 2\theta}$$

$$\frac{(\text{slope})_1}{(\text{slope})_2} = \tan\theta \cot 2\theta$$

$$\left(\because \cot x = \frac{1}{\tan x}\right)$$

30. (a) Now, in given case,

For gas A, $C_p = 29$, $C_V = 22$

For gas B, $C_p = 30$, $C_V = 21$

By using,

$$\gamma = \frac{C_p}{C_V} = 1 + \frac{2}{f}$$

For gas A,

$$1 + \frac{2}{f} = \frac{29}{22}$$

$$\Rightarrow f = 6.29 \approx 7$$

So, gas A has vibrational mode of degree of freedom.

For gas B,

$$1 + \frac{2}{f} = \frac{30}{21} \approx 14 \Rightarrow f \approx 4$$

Hence, gas B does not have any vibrational mode of degree of freedom.

Ch-13 Oscillations

Topical Follow Thru

Test-1

1. (b) Velocity of a particle executing SHM is given by

$$v = \omega\sqrt{a^2 - x^2} = \frac{2\pi}{T}\sqrt{A^2 - \frac{A^2}{16}}$$

$$= \frac{2\pi}{T}\sqrt{\frac{15A^2}{16}} = \frac{\sqrt{15}\,A\pi}{2T}$$

2. (a) In SHM, the acceleration is always in a direction opposite to that of the displacement, i.e. proportional to $(-y)$.

3. (d) Displacement = 0 in one complete oscillation.

$\Rightarrow$ Average velocity

$$= \frac{\text{Displacement}}{T} = 0$$

Average acceleration

$$= \frac{\text{Average velocity}}{T} = 0$$

4. (c) As given, displacement,

$$x = (\sin\omega t - \cos\omega t)$$

Multiplying and dividing by $\sqrt{2}$ in RHS, we get

$$x = \frac{\sqrt{2}}{\sqrt{2}}(\sin\omega t - \cos\omega t)$$

$$= \sqrt{2}\left(\sin\omega t \times \frac{1}{\sqrt{2}} - \cos\omega t \times \frac{1}{\sqrt{2}}\right)$$

$$= \sqrt{2}\left[\sin\omega t \cos\frac{\pi}{4} - \cos\omega t \sin\frac{\pi}{4}\right]$$

$$= \sqrt{2}\left[\sin\left(\omega t - \frac{\pi}{4}\right)\right]$$

Comparing the above equation with the general equation for the displacement of a particle executing SHM $x = A\sin(\omega t + \phi)$, we get

Phase, $\phi = -\frac{\pi}{4}$

Amplitude, $A = \sqrt{2}$ m

5. (d) The speed of particle at a distance $x = 1$ cm from mean position is

$$v = \omega\sqrt{A^2 - x^2}$$

$$= \omega\sqrt{2^2 - 1^2} = \sqrt{3}\omega \quad \ldots\text{(i)}$$

The magnitude of acceleration at $x = 1$ cm is

$$a = \omega^2 x = \omega^2 \quad \ldots\text{(ii)}$$

From Eqs. (i) and (ii), we get

$$\omega^2 = \sqrt{3}\omega \Rightarrow \omega = \sqrt{3} \text{ rad/s}$$

6. (c) Equation of motion, $y = a\cos\omega t$

$$\Rightarrow \frac{a}{2} = a\cos\omega t$$

$\Rightarrow \cos \omega t = \frac{1}{2} \Rightarrow \omega t = \frac{\pi}{3}$

$\Rightarrow \frac{2\pi t}{T} = \frac{\pi}{3}$

$\Rightarrow t = \frac{\frac{\pi}{3} \times T}{2\pi} = \frac{5}{3 \times 2} = \frac{5}{6}\text{ s}$

7. (c) $y = \frac{1 - \cos\left(\frac{2\omega t}{2}\right)}{2} = \frac{1 - \cos \omega t}{2}$

Period, $T = \frac{2\pi}{\omega}$

This function is periodic but not executing simple harmonic motion. As $a \neq -\omega^2 y$

8. (a) Force = Mass × Acceleration
$= m(-\omega^2 x)$
$= -m\omega^2 A \sin(\omega t + \phi)$

Force is periodic as $\sin(\omega t + \phi)$ is periodic.

9. (b) Time taken by particle to move from $x = 0$ (mean position) to $x = 5$ (extreme position) $= \frac{T}{4} = \frac{1.2}{4} = 0.3$ s.

Let t be the time taken by the particle to move from $x = 0$ to $x = 2.5$ cm.

$x = a \sin \omega t$

$\Rightarrow 2.5 = 5 \sin \frac{2\pi}{T} t$

$\Rightarrow \frac{1}{2} = \sin \frac{2\pi}{1.2} t$

$\Rightarrow \frac{\pi}{6} = \frac{2\pi}{1.2} t \Rightarrow t = 0.1\text{s}$

Hence, time to move from $x = 2.5$ to $x = 5$ will be equal to $0.3 - 0.1 = 0.2$ s.

Hence, total time to move from $x = 2.5$ to $x = 5$ and back again $= 2 \times 0.2 = 0.4$ s.

10. (d) At $t = 0, x = \frac{A}{2}$

$\frac{A}{2} = A \sin \frac{\phi}{2}$

or $\frac{\phi}{2} = \frac{\pi}{6}$ or $\frac{5\pi}{6}$

$\Rightarrow \phi = \frac{\pi}{3}$ or $\frac{5\pi}{3}$

$u = \frac{dx}{dt} = A\omega \cos\left(\omega t + \frac{\phi}{2}\right)$

At $t = 0, u = A\omega \cos \frac{\phi}{2}$

Now, $\cos \frac{\pi}{3} = \frac{1}{2}$

and $\cos \frac{5\pi}{3} = -\frac{1}{2}$

As u is negative at $t = 0$, ϕ must be $\frac{5\pi}{3}$.

11. (d) $y_1 = 4 \sin\left(10t + \frac{\phi}{3}\right)$

$y_2 = 5 \cos 10t$

$\therefore v_1 = \frac{dy_1}{dt} = 40 \cos\left(10t + \frac{\phi}{3}\right)$

and $v_2 = \frac{dy_2}{dt} = -50 \sin 10t$

$= 50 \cos\left(10t + \frac{\pi}{2}\right)$

Phase difference between v_1 and v_2

$= \left(\frac{\phi}{3} - \frac{\pi}{2}\right)$

12. (a) In oscillatory or vibratory motion, an object moves about an equilibrium position due to a restoring force.

When the body is at equilibrium position, no net external force acts on it, i.e. $F_{net} = 0$. Therefore, if it is left there at rest, it remains there forever.

If the body is then given then a small displacement from that position, a force comes into play, i.e. restoring force which tries to bring the body back to the equilibrium point giving rise to oscillation or vibrations.

13. (b) It is clear from the curve that points corresponding to $t = 2$ s and $t = 6$ s are separated by a distance λ belongs to one time period. Hence, these points must be in same phase.

14. (d) $\omega = \frac{2\pi}{T} = \frac{\pi}{4}$ s.

Therefore, $y = A \sin \frac{\pi}{4} t$. Now, put $t = 1$ s and then $t = 2$ s, we get

$y_1 = 8 \sin \frac{\pi}{4} = \frac{8}{\sqrt{2}}$,

$y_2 = 8 \sin \frac{\pi}{\sqrt{2}} = 8$

$\therefore \frac{y_1}{y_2 - y_1} = \frac{\frac{8}{\sqrt{2}}}{8 - \frac{8}{\sqrt{2}}}$

$= \frac{1}{\sqrt{2} - 1} = \sqrt{2} + 1$

15. (a) $\frac{da}{dx} - \tan 37° = -\frac{3}{4}$

$\Rightarrow a = -\frac{3}{4} x = -\omega^2 x$

So, $\omega^2 = \frac{3}{4} \Rightarrow \frac{2\pi}{T} = \frac{\sqrt{3}}{2}$

$\Rightarrow T = \frac{4\pi}{\sqrt{3}}$ s

16. (d) Acceleration of a particle executing SHM is always directed towards the mean position and its magnitude is directly proportional to that of displacement from mean position.

Since, acceleration of the particle at initial moment is maximum possible and negative, therefore the particle is at right extreme position at this moment.

When the particle is released, it starts to move to the left. It means, velocity starts to increase from zero initial value to negative value and its magnitude becomes maximum possible at mean position (at $t = T/4$).

17. (c) The equation giving relation between acceleration and speed as function of distance from mean position is

$a = -\omega^2 x$ ...(i)

$v = \omega\sqrt{A^2 - x^2}$ ...(ii)

From Eq. (i) and Eq. (ii), we get

$v^2 = \omega^2\left(A^2 - \frac{a^2}{\omega^4}\right)$

$v^2 = \omega^2 A^2 - \frac{a^2}{\omega^2}$

$\frac{a^2}{\omega^2} + v^2 = \omega^2 A^2$

$\frac{a^2}{(A\omega^2)^2} + \frac{v^2}{(A\omega)^2} = 1$

This is the equation of an ellipse in the a^2 - v^2 plane.

So, the a^2 *versus* v^2 graph will be an ellipse.

18. (c) Here, $\frac{d^2v}{dt^2} = -Kv$

This equation has standard solution
$v = v_0 \sin(\sqrt{K}t + \theta)$
where, $\omega = \sqrt{K}$

Hence, the particle executes SHM with angular frequency $\omega = \sqrt{K}$ or frequency, $f = \frac{\sqrt{K}}{2\pi}$

19. (d) $3ax^2 + 2bv^2 = k$

$\Rightarrow \quad 2bv^2 = k - 3ax^2$

$\Rightarrow \quad v^2 = \frac{k}{2b} - \frac{3}{2}\frac{a}{b}x^2$

Compare with $v^2 = A^2\omega^2 - \omega^2x^2$, we get

$$\omega^2 = \frac{3a}{2b} \text{ and } A^2\omega^2 = \frac{k}{2b}$$

$$A = \sqrt{\frac{A^2\omega^2}{\omega^2}} = \sqrt{\frac{k/2b}{3a/2b}} = \sqrt{\frac{k}{3a}}$$

20. (d) Particle is performing SHM along $y = B$. A is the amplitude of particle. So, maximum and minimum distance of the particle from the X-axis is $A + B$ and $B - A$ respectively.

21. (d) In SHM, a particle starts from rest, we have
i.e. $x = A\cos\omega t$, at $t = 0, x = A$
When $t = \tau$, then
$$x = A - a \qquad \ldots\text{(i)}$$
When $t = 2\tau$, then
$$x = A - 3a \qquad \ldots\text{(ii)}$$
On comparing Eqs. (i) and (ii), we get
$$A - a = A\cos\omega\tau$$
$$A - 3a = A\cos 2\omega\tau$$
As, $\cos 2\omega\tau = 2\cos^2\omega\tau - 1$

$$\Rightarrow \frac{A - 3a}{A} = 2\left(\frac{A - a}{A}\right)^2 - 1$$
$$= \frac{2A^2 + 2a^2 - 4Aa - A^2}{A^2}$$
$$A^2 - 3aA = A^2 + 2a^2 - 4Aa$$
$\Rightarrow 2a^2 = aA \Rightarrow A = 2a$

Now, $A - a = A\cos\omega\tau \quad [\because \tau = t]$
$\Rightarrow \quad \cos\omega t = 1/2$

$\Rightarrow \quad \frac{2\pi}{T}t = \frac{\pi}{3}$

$\Rightarrow \quad T = 6\pi$

22. (a) $x = a\sin\left(\omega t + \frac{\pi}{6}\right)$

and $x' = a\cos\omega t = a\sin\left(\omega t + \frac{\pi}{2}\right)$

$$\therefore \Delta\phi = \left(\omega t + \frac{\pi}{2}\right) - \left(\omega t + \frac{\pi}{6}\right) = \frac{\pi}{3}$$

23. (c) $y = A\sin PT + B\cos PT$
Let $A = r\cos\theta, B = r\sin\theta$
$\Rightarrow y = r\sin(PT + \theta)$ which is the equation of SHM.

24. (b) $x = 12\sin\omega t - 16\sin^3\omega t$
$= 4[3\sin\omega t - 4\sin^3\omega t]$
$= 4[\sin 3\omega t]$
(by using, $\sin 3\theta = 3\sin\theta - 4\sin^3\theta$)
$\therefore$Maximum acceleration,
$a_{max} = (3\omega)^2 \times 4 = 36\omega^2$

25. (a) Displacement,
$x = 3\sin 100t + 8\cos^2 50t$
$= 3\sin 100t + 4(1 - \cos 100t)$
$= 3\sin 100t - 4\cos 100t + 4$
Velocity, $v = \frac{dx}{dt}$
$\Rightarrow v = 300\cos 100t + 400\sin 100t$
Acceleration, $a = \frac{dv}{dt}$
$\Rightarrow a = 30000\sin 100t + 40000\cos 100t$
As acceleration a is not proportional to displacement x. So, this is not SHM.

Test-2

1. (d) $T = \frac{\pi}{3}$

$\Rightarrow \quad \frac{2\pi}{\omega} = \frac{\pi}{3}$

$\Rightarrow \quad \omega = 6$

As, $a = -\omega^2x = -36x = -36\sin x$
(for small oscillation, $\sin x = x$)
$F = ma = -72\sin x \; [\because m = 2\text{ kg}]$
$\therefore \quad U = -\int F\cdot dx = -72\cos x$

2. (c) For a particle performing SHM, the KE reaches its maximum value two times. So, we can say that if the frequency of SHM is of then its frequency will be 2 times that is $2f$ when its kinetic energy changes to potential energy.

3. (c) $Mg = kl$
when mass is further stretched to l.
Net potential energy of spring
$$= \frac{1}{2}k\Delta x^2$$
$$\Rightarrow U_{max} = \frac{1}{2}kl^2 = \frac{1}{2}Mgl$$

4. (a) $E = \frac{1}{2}mA^2\omega^2$
$$= \frac{1}{2}mA^2\left[\frac{4\pi^2}{T^2}\right] \Rightarrow E \propto \frac{A^2}{T^2}$$
The total energy of particle is due ectly proportional to A^2 and inversely proportional to T^2.

5. (a) The total energy of SHM = Kinetic energy of particle + Potential energy of particle. The variation of total energy of the particle in SHM with time is shown in the graph.

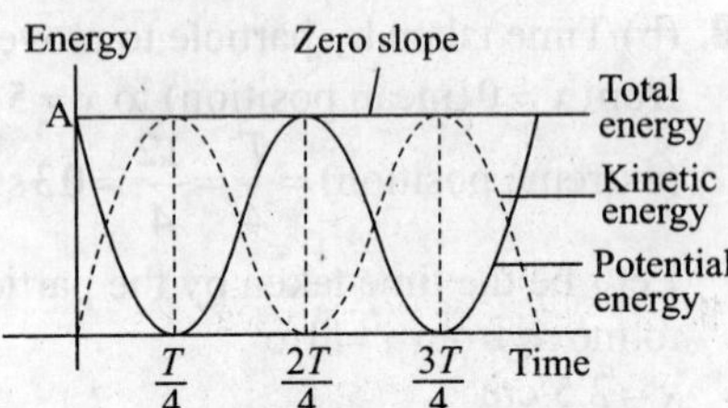

6. (b) Total potential energy = 0.04 J
Resting potential energy = 0.01 J
Change in potential energy
$$= (0.04 - 0.01) = 0.03\text{ J}$$
$$= \frac{1}{2}m\omega^2A^2 = \frac{1}{2}kA^2$$
$$\Rightarrow 0.03 = \frac{1}{2} \times k \times \left(\frac{40}{1000}\right)^2$$
$$\Rightarrow \quad k = 0.06 \times 625\text{ N/m}$$
$$= 37.5\text{ N/m}$$

7. (c) The average potential energy of a block for one complete period is given as
$$U_{avg} = \frac{1}{4}m\omega^2A^2$$
Also, average kinetic energy is given as
$$K_{avg} = \frac{1}{4}m\omega^2A^2$$
It means both energies are equal for one time period and it is independent of x. So, for all values of x, average value of both energies are equal.

8. (b) Total energy of particle performing SHM $= \frac{1}{2} m\omega^2 a^2$

Kinetic energy of particle performing SHM

$$= \frac{1}{2} m\omega^2 a^2 \cos^2\left(\frac{2\pi}{T}\right)t$$

According to problem, kinetic energy = 75% of total energy, so

$$\frac{1}{2} m\omega^2 a^2 \cos^2\left(\frac{2\pi}{T}\right)t = \frac{3}{4}\left(\frac{1}{2} m\omega^2 a^2\right)$$

$$\Rightarrow \cos^2\left(\frac{2\pi}{T}\right)t = \frac{3}{4}$$

$$\Rightarrow \cos\left(\frac{2\pi}{T}\right)t = \frac{\sqrt{3}}{2}$$

$$\Rightarrow \left(\frac{2\pi}{T}\right)t = \frac{\pi}{6}$$

$$\Rightarrow t = \frac{T}{12}\ \text{s}$$

In the problem, $T = 4$ s

$$\therefore \quad t = \frac{1}{3}\ \text{s}$$

9. (a) Since, maximum value of $\cos^2 \omega t$ is 1.

$\therefore \quad K_{\max} = K_0 \cos^2 \omega t = K_0$

Also, $K_{\max} = \text{PE}_{\max} = K_0$

10. (a) $E_1 = \frac{1}{2} Kx^2$

$$\Rightarrow x = \sqrt{\frac{2E_1}{K}},$$

$$E_2 = \frac{1}{2} Ky^2 \Rightarrow y = \sqrt{\frac{2E_2}{K}}$$

And $\quad E = \frac{1}{2} K(x-y)^2$

$$\Rightarrow x - y = \sqrt{\frac{2E}{K}}$$

$$\Rightarrow \sqrt{\frac{2E_1}{K}} - \sqrt{\frac{2E_2}{K}} = \sqrt{\frac{2E}{K}}$$

$$\Rightarrow \sqrt{E_1} - \sqrt{E_2} = \sqrt{E}$$

11. (c) As we can see from the graph,

$$\frac{1}{2} mv_m^2 = 30 \times 10^{-3}$$

$$\Rightarrow \frac{1}{2}(0.4)\, v_m^2 = 30 \times 10^{-3}$$

$$\Rightarrow v_m = \sqrt{0.150}\ \text{m/s}$$

$$\Rightarrow A\omega = \sqrt{0.150}\ \text{m/s}$$

$$\Rightarrow L\theta_m \cdot \sqrt{\frac{g}{L}} = \sqrt{0.150}\ \text{m/s}$$

$$\Rightarrow \sqrt{gL} = \frac{\sqrt{0.150}}{100 \times 10^{-3}}$$

$$\Rightarrow L = \frac{0.150}{0.1} = 1.5\ \text{m}$$

12. (a) Kinetic energy of particle performing SHM is given by $\frac{1}{2} m\omega(A^2 - x^2)$.

Here, A is the amplitude and x is the position of the particle.

It varies parabolically such that, at mean position it becomes maximum and zero at extreme position.

13. (a) Total energy of the harmonic oscillator,

$$E = \frac{1}{2} m\omega^2 a^2$$

i.e., $E \propto a^2$.

Therefore, $\frac{E'}{E} = \left(\frac{2a}{a}\right)^2$ or $E' = 4E$

14. (d) Kinetic energy,

$$T = \frac{1}{2} m\omega^2 (a^2 - x^2)$$

and potential energy,

$$V = \frac{1}{2} m\omega^2 x^2$$

$$\therefore \quad \frac{T}{V} = \frac{a^2 - x^2}{x^2}$$

15. (b) Given, $U = 4 + (x-1)^2$ J

As force, $F = -\frac{dU}{dx}$

$$= -\frac{d}{dx}[4 + (x-1)^2]$$

$$= -(0 + 2(x-1))$$

$$= -2(x-1)$$

Acceleration, $a = \frac{F}{m} = \frac{-2(x-1)}{2}$

$$(\because m = 2\ \text{kg})$$

$$a = -(x-1)$$

On comparing with standard equation of SHM, $a = -\omega^2 (x - x_0)$, we get

$$\omega^2 = 1 \text{ or } \omega = 1\ \text{rad/s}$$

At $x = 1$ m, minimum potential energy,

$$U_{\min} = 4 + (0)^2 = 4\ \text{J}$$

At mean position, potential energy is minimum and kinetic energy is maximum and sum of both energies is equal to total mechanical energy. So, we may write

$$\text{TE} = U_{\min} + \text{KE}_{\max}$$

$$\text{KE}_{\max} = \text{TE} - U_{\min} = 20 - 4 = 16\ \text{J}$$

Maximum kinetic energy of a particle in SHM is given as

$$\text{KE}_{\max} = \frac{1}{2} m\omega^2 A^2$$

Putting the values of $\text{KE}_{\max}$, m and ω^2 in the above expression, we get

$$16 = \frac{1}{2} \times 8 \times 1^2 \times A^2$$

or $\quad A^2 = 16/4$

or $\quad A = 2$ m

Test-3

1. (d) $T = 2\pi\sqrt{\frac{l}{g}} \Rightarrow T \propto \frac{1}{\sqrt{g}}$

$$\Rightarrow \frac{T_p}{T} = \sqrt{\frac{g_e}{g_p}} = \frac{\sqrt{2}}{1} \Rightarrow T_P = \sqrt{2}T$$

2. (d) Maximum velocity, $v_{\max} = a\omega$

or $\quad v_{\max} = a\left(\frac{2\pi}{T}\right)$

$$\Rightarrow a = \frac{v_{\max} T}{2\pi} = \frac{20 \times 1.57 \times 10^{-3}}{2 \times 3.14}$$

$$= 5 \times 10^{-3} \text{ or } 0.005\ \text{cm}$$

3. (c) $(M)(\omega A) = (M+m)\, v$ $\quad (P_i = P_f)$

$$\therefore \quad v = \frac{M\omega A}{(M+m)} = \omega' A'$$

$$\therefore \quad A' = \left(\frac{M}{M+m}\right)\frac{\omega}{\omega'}$$

Now, $\quad \omega = \sqrt{\frac{k}{m}}$

or $\quad \omega \propto \frac{1}{\sqrt{m}}$

$$\therefore \quad \frac{\omega}{\omega'} = \sqrt{\frac{M+m}{M}}$$

$$\therefore \quad A' = \left(\sqrt{\frac{M}{m+M}}\right)A$$

and $\quad K = 0$

4. (b) The wire may be treated as a string for which force constant

$$k_1 = \frac{\text{Force}}{\text{Extension}} = \frac{YA}{L} \quad \left(\because Y = \frac{F}{A} \times \frac{L}{\Delta L}\right)$$

Spring constant of the spring $k_2 = K$.
Here, spring constant of the combination (series)

$$k_{eq} = \frac{k_1 k_2}{k_1 + k_2} = \frac{(YA/L)K}{(YA/L)+K} = \frac{YAK}{YA + KL}$$

$\because$ Time period, $T = 2\pi\sqrt{\frac{m}{k}}$

$$= 2\pi\left[\frac{(YA+KL)m}{YAK}\right]^{1/2}$$

5. (d) $A(1-\cos\omega\tau) = a$

$A(1-\cos 2\omega\tau) = 3a$

$$\cos\omega\tau = \left(1 - \frac{a}{A}\right)$$

$$\cos 2\omega\tau = \left(1 - \frac{3a}{A}\right)$$

$$2\left(1-\frac{a}{A}\right)^2 - 1 = 1 - \frac{3a}{A}$$

[Using $\cos 2\theta = 2\cos^2\theta - 1$]
Solving the equation

$$\frac{a}{A} = \frac{1}{2}$$

$$A = 2a$$

$$\cos\omega\tau = \frac{1}{2}$$

$$\omega\tau = \frac{\pi}{3}$$

$$T = \frac{2\pi}{\omega} = 6\tau$$

6. (d) Time period of pendulum does not depend upon mass but it depends upon length (distance between point of suspension and centre of mass). In first three cases, centre of masses are same, so $T = T_1 = T_2$. But in last case, centre of mass lowers which in turn increases the length. So, in this case, time period will be more than the other cases.

7. (a) In simple pendulum, when bob is in deflection position, the tension in the string is $T = mg\cos\theta + \frac{mv^2}{l}$.

So, tension is maximum at mean position.
At mean position, $\theta = 0$ and velocity v is maximum.

8. (c) $T \propto \sqrt{l} \Rightarrow T^2 \propto l$

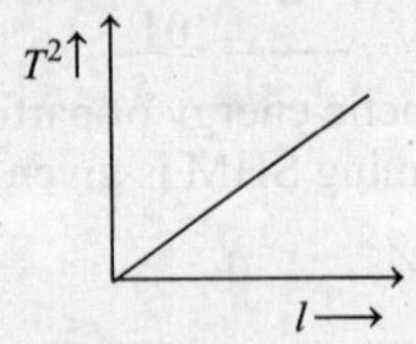

9. (d) Resulting torque on the bob,

$$\tau = mg\frac{l}{\sqrt{2}}\sin\theta$$

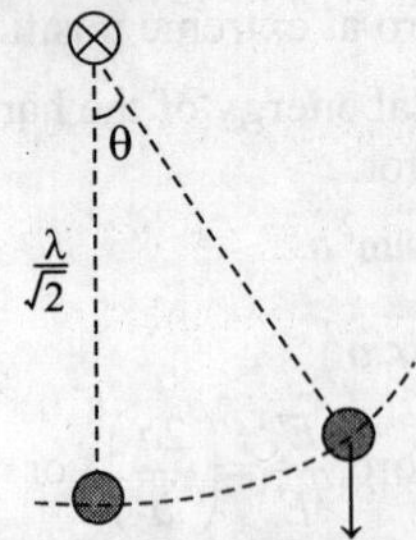

MI of bob about axis xy, $(I) = \frac{ml^2}{2}$

For small θ, angular acceleration,

$$\alpha = \frac{\tau}{I}$$

$$\Rightarrow \quad \alpha = \frac{\sqrt{2}g}{l}\theta$$

$$\Rightarrow \quad \frac{\alpha}{\theta} = \frac{\sqrt{2}g}{l} = \omega^2$$

$$\Rightarrow \quad \omega = \sqrt{\frac{\sqrt{2}g}{l}}$$

$$\Rightarrow \quad T = 2\pi\sqrt{\frac{l}{\sqrt{2}g}}$$

10. (d) $T = 2\pi\sqrt{\frac{l}{g}}$

$$\Rightarrow \quad l = \left(\frac{g}{4\pi^2}\right)T^2$$

$$\Rightarrow \quad l \propto T^2$$

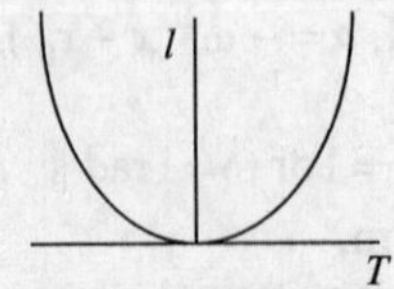

11. (b) Time period of a simple pendulum which is initially at rest is given by

$$T = 2\pi\sqrt{\frac{l}{g}} \quad \ldots\text{(i)}$$

When the lift is moving up with an acceleration a, then time period becomes

$$T' = 2\pi\sqrt{\frac{l}{g+a}}$$

Given, $T' = \frac{T}{2}$

$$\Rightarrow \quad T' = \frac{T}{2} = 2\pi\sqrt{\frac{l}{g+a}} \quad \ldots\text{(ii)}$$

On dividing Eq. (ii) by Eq. (i), we get

$$\frac{1}{2} = \sqrt{\frac{g}{g+a}}$$

$$\Rightarrow \quad a = 3g$$

12. (d) With respect to the cart, equilibrium position of the pendulum is shown.

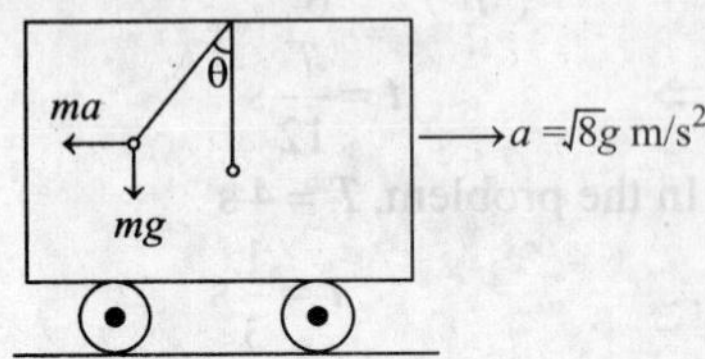

If displaced by small angle θ from this position, then it will execute SHM about this equilibrium position, time period of which is given by

$$T = 2\pi\sqrt{\frac{L}{g_{eff}}}$$

Here, $g_{eff} = \sqrt{g^2 + (\sqrt{8}g)^2}$

$$\Rightarrow \quad g_{eff} = 3g$$

$$\Rightarrow \quad T = 2\pi\sqrt{\frac{30}{3g}} = 2\pi\sqrt{\frac{30}{3\pi^2}}$$

$[\because g \approx \pi^2]$

$$= 2\sqrt{10}\text{ s}$$

13. (d) Effective weight of bob when it is immersed in water

$$= mg - \frac{mg}{\rho} = mg\left(\frac{\rho-1}{\rho}\right)$$

$$\Rightarrow g_{eff} = g\left(\frac{\rho-1}{\rho}\right)$$

$$\frac{T'}{T} = \sqrt{\frac{g}{g_{eff}}}$$

$$\Rightarrow \quad T' = T\sqrt{\frac{\rho}{(\rho-1)}}$$

14. (c) In stationary lift, $T = 2\pi\sqrt{\frac{l}{g}}$

In upward motion of lift,

$$T' = 2\pi\sqrt{\frac{l}{(g+a)}}$$

(a = acceleration of life)

$$\Rightarrow \frac{T'}{T} = \sqrt{\frac{g}{g+a}}$$

$$= \sqrt{\frac{g}{\left(g + \frac{g}{4}\right)}} = \sqrt{\frac{4}{5}}$$

$$\Rightarrow T' = \frac{2T}{\sqrt{5}}$$

15. (b) $f = \frac{1}{2\pi}\sqrt{\frac{k}{m}} \Rightarrow f \propto \frac{1}{\sqrt{m}}$

$\therefore f' = \frac{f}{2}$ or $\frac{n}{2}$ $\quad (\because \sqrt{m'} = \sqrt{4m})$

Chapter Break Thru

1. (a) Maximum acceleration

$$= A\omega^2 = A \times 4\pi^2 v^2$$
$$= 0.01 \times 4 \times (\pi)^2 \times (60)^2$$
$$= 144\pi^2 \text{ m/s}^2$$

2. (b) A system executing SHM must possess elasticity as will as inertia. Inertia means mass, and elasticity means spring constant.

3. (a) When $x = 0$, $\omega t_1 = 0$, $\therefore t_1 = 0$

When $x = a/2$, $\omega t_2 = \pi/6$, $\therefore t_2 = \pi/6\omega$

When $x = a$, $\omega t_3 = \pi/2$, $\therefore t_3 = \pi/2\omega$

Time taken from 0 to $a/2$ will be

$$T_1 = t_2 - t_1 = \pi/6\omega$$

Time taken from $a/2$ to will be

$$T_2 = t_3 - t_2$$
$$= \frac{\pi}{2\omega} - \frac{\pi}{6\omega} = \frac{\pi}{3\omega}$$

4. (c) Displacement, $X = A\cos(\omega t)$ (given)

Velocity, $v = \frac{dX}{dt} = -A\omega\sin(\omega t)$

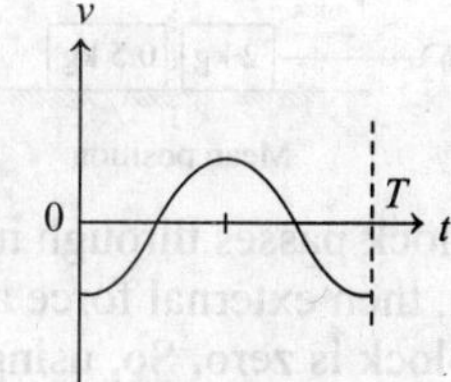

Hence, graph (c) correctly depicts the variation of velocity v with time t.

5. (b) The particles will meet at the mean position when P completes one oscillation and Q completes half oscillation.

So, $\frac{v_P}{v_Q} = \frac{A\omega_P}{A\omega_Q} = \frac{T_Q}{T_P} = \frac{8}{4} = \frac{2}{1}$ or 2 : 1

6. (d) From graph, slope,

$$K = \frac{F}{x} = \frac{8}{2} = 4$$

$$T = 2\pi\sqrt{\frac{m}{K}}$$

$$\Rightarrow \quad T = 2\pi\sqrt{\frac{0.01}{4}} = 0.30\text{ s}$$

7. (d) At time $\frac{T}{2}$; $v = 0$

$\therefore$ Total energy = Potential energy

8. (c) Consider that the block starts its motion from negative extreme position.

As we know, displacement,

$$x = A\sin(\omega t + \theta) \quad \dots \text{(i)}$$

At $t = 0$, $x = -A$

$\therefore \quad -A = A\sin(\omega \times 0 + \theta)$

$\Rightarrow \quad \sin\theta = -1$

or $\quad \sin\theta = \sin\frac{3\pi}{2}$ or $\theta = \frac{3\pi}{2}$

Given that, $A = 8$ cm, $T = 2$ s

$$\omega = \frac{2\pi}{T} = \frac{2\pi}{2} = \pi \text{ rad/s}$$

Putting the values of A, ω, θ in Eq. (i), we get

$$x = 8\sin\left(\pi t + \frac{3\pi}{2}\right)\text{ cm}$$

or $\quad x = -8\cos\pi t$ cm $\quad \dots$ (ii)

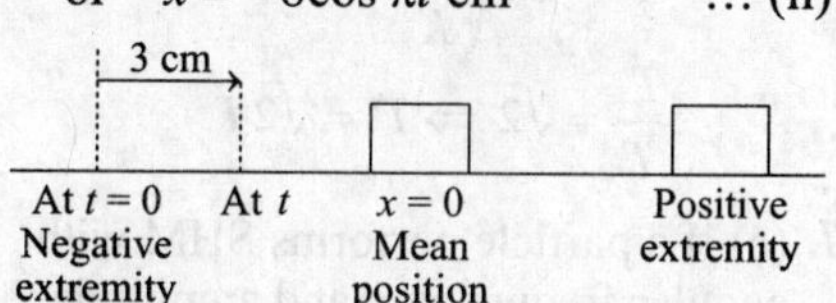

At time t, position of block

$$= -8 + 3 = -5\text{ cm}$$

From Eq. (ii), we get

$$-5 = -8\cos\pi t$$

or $\cos\pi t = \frac{5}{8} = 0.9$

$$\therefore \quad t = \frac{0.9}{\pi} = \frac{0.9}{3.14}$$
$$= 0.286\text{ s}$$

9. (a) Given, $x(t) = 20\sin\frac{\pi}{3}(15t + 0.5)$ cm

$$\Rightarrow x(t) = 20\sin\left(5\pi t + \frac{\pi}{6}\right)\text{cm}$$

$\therefore$ Amplitude, $A_x = 20$ cm

Time period, $T_x = \frac{2\pi}{\omega_x} = \frac{2\pi}{5\pi} = \frac{2}{5}$ s

Also, $y(t) = 8[\sin 10\pi t + 0.75\cos 10\pi t]$ cm

$$= 8\sin 10\pi t + 6\cos 10\pi t$$

$$= \frac{\sqrt{8^2 + 6^2}}{\sqrt{8^2 + 6^2}}[8\sin 10\pi t + 6\cos 10\pi t]$$

$$= \left[10\sin 10\pi t \times \frac{8}{10} + 10\cos 10\pi t \times \frac{6}{10}\right]$$

$$= 10\left[\sin 10\pi t \times \frac{4}{5} + \cos 10\pi t \times \frac{3}{5}\right]$$

$$= 10[\sin 10\pi t\cos 37° + \cos 10\pi t\sin 37°]$$

$y(t) = 10\sin(10\pi t + 37°)$ cm

$\therefore$ Amplitude, $A_y = 10$ cm

Time period, $T_y = \frac{2\pi}{\omega_y} = \frac{2\pi}{10\pi} = \frac{1}{5}$ s

Ratio, $\frac{A_x}{A_y} = \frac{20}{10} = \frac{2}{1}$

and $\quad \frac{T_x}{T_y} = \frac{2/5}{1/5} = \frac{2}{1}$

10. (b) Both A and R are true but R is not the correct explanation of A.

11. (a) Figure (A) is a simple mass-spring system. The time period for a mass spring system is

$$T = 2\pi\sqrt{\frac{m}{k}}$$

Figure (B) is a simple pendulum. The time period for a simple pendulum is

$$T = 2\pi\sqrt{l/g}$$

In figure (C), let us displace the block in towards left through displacement x.

Resultant force,

$$F = F_1 + F_2$$
$$= (k_1 + k_2)x$$
$$= 2kx \qquad (\because k_1 = k_1 \cdot k)$$

Acceleration $\left(\frac{F}{m}\right)=\frac{2kx}{m}$

Time period, $T=2\pi\sqrt{\frac{\text{displacement}}{\text{acceleration}}}$

$$=2\pi\sqrt{\frac{x}{\frac{2kx}{m}}}=2\pi\sqrt{\frac{m}{kx}}$$

In figure (D) spring are in series combination. Let equivalent spring constant be k_{eq}

So, $\frac{1}{k_{eq}}=\frac{1}{k_1}+\frac{1}{k_2}$

$$=k_{eq}=\frac{k_1k_2}{k_1+k_2}=\frac{k^2}{2k}=\frac{k}{2}$$

Time period,

$$T=2\pi\sqrt{\frac{m}{k_{eq}}}$$

$$T=2\pi\sqrt{\frac{m}{k/2}}$$

$$T=2\pi\sqrt{\frac{2m}{k}}$$

12. (b) When spring is cut into n equal parts, then spring constant of each part will be nk and so using $T\propto\frac{1}{\sqrt{k}}$, time period will be $T/\sqrt{n}$ and frequency is $\sqrt{n}f$ because $f=\frac{1}{T}$.

$\therefore$ Frequency $=\sqrt{n}f$

$$=\frac{\sqrt{n}}{T}$$

13. (d) $T\propto\sqrt{m}\Rightarrow\frac{T_2}{T_1}=\sqrt{\frac{m_2}{m_1}}$

$$\Rightarrow\frac{7T}{3\cdot T}=\sqrt{\frac{M+m}{m}}$$

$$\Rightarrow\frac{49}{9}=\frac{M+m}{M}$$

$$\Rightarrow\frac{m}{M}=\frac{40}{9}$$

$$\Rightarrow\frac{2m}{M}=\frac{80}{9}$$

14. (a)

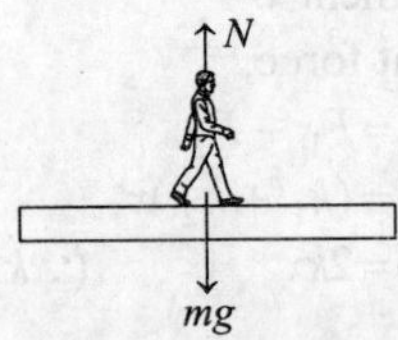

As platform moves from top extreme position.

From given FBD, we have $mg-N=ma$ or $N=m(g-a)$

In this case, N decreases as a increases. At the extreme position, acceleration is maximum $(=\omega^2A)$.

So, N is minimum when the block is about to leave but still in contact with platform , then N becomes zero.

$\therefore\quad 0=m(g-\omega^2A)$

or $\quad g-\omega^2A=0$

or $\quad \omega^2=\frac{g}{A}$

or $\quad \omega=\sqrt{\frac{g}{A}}=\sqrt{\frac{9.8}{5}}$

$$=1.4\text{ rad/s}$$

15. (b) The two springs on right hand side of mass M are in parallel. Their effective spring constant is $(k+2k)=3k$.

Equivalent spring constants of value $2k$ and $3k$ are in parallel and their net value of spring constant of all the three springs is $3k+2k=5k$.

$\therefore$ Frequency of mass, $n=\frac{1}{2\pi}\sqrt{\frac{5k}{M}}$

16. (c) Effective force constant,

$$K_{eff}=2K$$

$$T=2\pi\sqrt{\frac{m}{2K}}$$

When one spring is removed, K_{eff} becomes K and new time period will be

$$T'=2\pi\sqrt{\frac{m}{K}}$$

$\therefore\quad\frac{T'}{T}=\sqrt{2}\Rightarrow T'=\sqrt{2}T$

17. (c) If a particle performs SHM with angular frequency ω and amplitude A, then its displacement from mean position will be equal to $x=a\sin\omega t$. If its initial phase is equal to zero, then its velocity will be

$$v=\frac{dx}{dt}=A\omega\cos\omega t\quad\ldots\text{(i)}$$

and acceleration will be

$$a=\frac{dv}{dt}=-A\omega^2\sin(\omega t)\quad\ldots\text{(ii)}$$

From these equations, $\cos\omega t=\frac{v}{A\omega}$

$$\sin\omega t=\frac{a}{-A\omega^2}$$

Squaring and adding both equations,

$$\frac{v^2}{A^2\omega^2}+\frac{a^2}{A^2\omega^4}=1\quad\ldots\text{(iii)}$$

If v is taken on Y-axis and a on X-axis, then it will be an ellipse.

18. (a) Given that, relative density of simple pendulum, $\rho=4$

Relative density of non-viscous fluid, $\sigma=2$

Length, $l=1$ m

As time period,

$$T=2\pi\sqrt{\frac{l}{g\left(1-\frac{\sigma}{\rho}\right)}}$$

$$=2\times3.14\sqrt{\frac{1}{9.8\left(1-\frac{2}{4}\right)}}=2.83\text{ s}$$

19. (b) Given, $4v^2=25-2x^2$

Differentiating with respect to t on both sides,

$$8va=-4xv\Rightarrow a=-\frac{x}{2}$$

Motion is simple harmonic.

So, $\quad\omega^2=1/2$

and $\quad T=2\pi\sqrt{2}=2\sqrt{2}\pi$

20. (a) Tension in the string when bob passes through lowest point,

$$T=mg+\frac{mv^2}{r}=mg+mv\omega^2$$

$[\because v=r\omega]$

Putting $v=\sqrt{2gh}$ and

$$\omega=\frac{2\pi}{T}=\frac{2\pi}{4.0}=\frac{\pi}{2}$$

we get, $T=m\left(g+\pi\sqrt{\frac{gh}{2}}\right)$

21. (a) According to question,

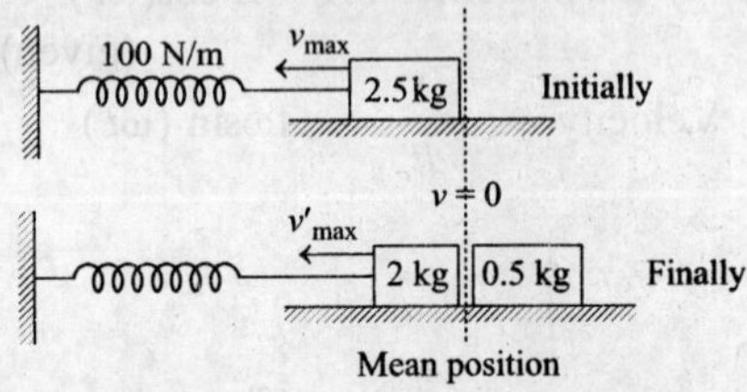

When block passes through mean position, then external force acting on the block is zero. So, using the principle of conservation of momentum,

$$p_i = p_f$$
$$mv_{max} = m' v'_{max}$$

where, v'_{max} is new maximum velocity of the block of mass 2 kg.

or $v'_{max} = \frac{mv_{max}}{m'}$

or $v'_{max} = \frac{m}{m'} A\sqrt{\frac{k}{m}}$

Here, $m = 2.5\,\text{kg}$, $m' = 2\,\text{kg}$

$k = 100\,\text{N/m}$, $A = 1\,\text{m}$

$$\therefore\ v'_{max} = \frac{2.5}{2} \times 1 \times \sqrt{\frac{100}{2.5}} = 7.9\,\text{m/s}$$

22. (d) In SHM, $v = \omega\sqrt{a^2 - y^2}$

or $v^2 = \omega^2 a^2 - \omega^2 y^2$.

Dividing both sides by $\omega^2 a^2$, we get

$$\frac{v^2}{\omega^2 \alpha^2} + \frac{y^2}{a^2} = 1$$

This is the equation of an ellipse. Hence, the graph between v and y is an ellipse not parabola.

23. (b) Harmonic oscillator has some initial elastic potential energy and amplitude of harmonic variation of energy is

$$\frac{1}{2}Ka^2 = \frac{1}{2} \times 2 \times 10^6 (0.01)^2 = 100\,\text{J}$$

This is the maximum kinetic energy of the oscillator. Thus, $K_{max} = 100$ J.

24. (b) Time period

$$T \propto \sqrt{l} \Rightarrow \frac{\Delta T}{T} = \frac{1}{2}\frac{\Delta l}{l} = \frac{1}{2}\alpha\Delta\theta$$

Also according to thermal expansion,

$$l' = l(1 + \alpha\Delta\theta)$$
$$\frac{\Delta l}{l} = \alpha\Delta\theta$$

Hence, $\frac{\Delta T}{T} = \frac{1}{2}\frac{\Delta l}{l} = \frac{1}{2}\alpha\Delta\theta$

$$= \frac{1}{2} \times 12 \times 10^{-6} \times (35 - 25)$$
$$= 6 \times 10^{-5}$$

$\Rightarrow \Delta T = 6 \times 10^{-5} \times 86400$ s/day

$\therefore\ \Delta T \approx 5.18$ s/day

25. (b) For SHM, the kinetic energy is given by

$$K = \frac{1}{2}m\omega^2 (A^2 - x^2)$$

At $x = \frac{A}{4}$,

$$K = \frac{1}{2}m\omega^2\left[A^2 - \left(\frac{A}{4}\right)^2\right] = \frac{1}{2}\left(\frac{15}{16}m\omega^2 A^2\right)$$

Total energy of the particle,

$$E = \frac{1}{2}m\omega^2 A^2$$

$$\therefore\ \frac{K}{E} = \frac{\frac{1}{2}\left(\frac{15}{16}m\omega^2 A^2\right)}{\frac{1}{2}m\omega^2 A^2}$$

$$\Rightarrow\ \frac{K}{E} = \frac{15}{16}$$

26. (b) $y = 2Kt^2 \Rightarrow \frac{d^2y}{dt^2} = a_y = 4K$

$a_y = 4 \times 1 = 4\,\text{m/s}^2$ $(\because K = 1\,\text{m/s}^2)$

Now, $T_1 = 2\pi\sqrt{\frac{l}{g}}$

and $T_2 = 2\pi\sqrt{\frac{l}{(g + a_y)}}$

Dividing, $\frac{T_1}{T_2} = \sqrt{\frac{g + a_y}{g}}$

Considering, $g = 10$ m/s

$$\Rightarrow\ \frac{T_1}{T_2} = \sqrt{\frac{7}{5}} \Rightarrow \frac{T_1^2}{T_2^2} = \frac{7}{5}$$

$$\Rightarrow\ \frac{T_2^2}{T_1^2} = \frac{5}{7}$$

27. (a) Let simple harmonic motions be represented by

$$y_1 = a\sin\left(\omega t - \frac{\pi}{4}\right);\ y_2 = a\sin\omega t$$

and $y_3 = a\sin\left(\omega t + \frac{\pi}{4}\right)$

On superimposing, resultant SHM will be

$$y = a\left[\sin\left(\omega t - \frac{\pi}{4}\right) + \sin\omega t + \sin\left(\omega t + \frac{\pi}{4}\right)\right]$$

$$= a\left[2\sin\omega t\cos\frac{\pi}{4} + \sin\omega t\right]$$

$$= [a(1 + \sqrt{2})\sin\omega t]$$

Thus, resultant amplitude, $A = (1 + \sqrt{2})a$.

28. (d) This is the special case of physical pendulum and in this case

$$T = 2\pi\sqrt{\frac{2l}{3g}}$$

$$\Rightarrow\ T = 2 \times 3.14\sqrt{\frac{2 \times 2}{3 \times 9.8}} = 2.31\,\text{s}$$

$$\approx 2.4\,\text{s}$$

29. (d) At lowest position, platform is moving up, so reaction is

$$N_2 = mg + ma$$
$$= mg + m\omega^2 A$$

At topmost position platform is moving down so reaction,

$$N_1 = mg - m\omega^2 A$$

$$\therefore N_2 - N_1 = 2m\omega^2 A$$
$$= 2m(2\pi f)^2 A$$
$$= 2 \times 50(2 \times 3.14 \times 2)^2 \times 5 \times 10^{-2}$$
$$= 100 \times 157 \times 5 \times 10^{-2}$$
$$= 788 \simeq 800\,\text{N}$$

30. (c) Phase difference,

$$\delta = \frac{\pi}{3} = \delta_2 - \delta_1$$

$$\frac{\pi}{3} = \delta_2 - \frac{5\pi}{6}$$

$$\Rightarrow\ \delta_2 = \frac{7\pi}{6}$$

$$\sin\delta_1 = \sin\delta_2 = \frac{\sqrt{3}}{2}$$

Displacement is measured from starting point ($t = 0$).

So, $x = A\sin(\omega t + \delta_1)$

$$A\sin\left(0 + \frac{\pi}{3}\right) = \frac{A\sqrt{3}}{2}$$

Ch-14 Waves

Topical Follow Thru

Test-1

1. (a) Wave speed, $v=\sqrt{\frac{T}{\mu}}$

$$\Rightarrow \quad \Delta T = 2T\cdot\frac{\Delta v}{v}$$
$$=2\times 400\times\frac{15}{300}$$
$$=40\,\text{N}$$

Percentage change in tension

$$\Rightarrow \frac{\Delta T}{T}\times 100 = 10\%$$

2. (c) Statement I is correct but Statement II is incorrect because velocity of sound is directly proportional to the square root of absolute temperature.

3. (c) Ratio is $\sqrt{r}$, $r=\frac{7}{5}$ for air.

4. (c) Speed of transverse wave over string is

$$v=\sqrt{\frac{T}{\mu}}=\sqrt{\frac{2000}{25/20}}$$
$$=40\,\text{ms}^{-1}$$

Time taken by pulse to reach other end

$$=\frac{10}{40}=0.25\,\text{s}=\frac{1}{4}\,\text{s}$$

5. (d) Given, length $(L)=20\,\text{m}$

Mass $(M)=10\,\text{g}=10^{-2}\,\text{kg}$

Tension $(T)=125\,\text{N}$

Mass per unit length of the wire,

$$\mu=\frac{M}{L}=\frac{10^{-2}}{20}=5\times 10^{-4}\,\text{kg/m}$$

Speed of the transverse wave on the wire,

$$v=\sqrt{\frac{T}{\mu}}$$
$$=\sqrt{\frac{125}{5\times 10^{-4}}}=5\times 10^{2}\,\text{m/s}$$
$$\Rightarrow \quad v=500\,\text{m/s}$$

6. (d) A is false but R is true.

Waves on water surface are transverse waves. Sound waves in air are longitudinal in nature.

7. (d) Both points K and F are moving up and are at the same distance from equilibrium position at the instant shown.

Hence, K and F are in phase.

8. (c) Wavelength, $\lambda=\frac{v}{f}$

$$\Rightarrow \quad \frac{\lambda_{max}}{\lambda_{min}}=\frac{u/f_{min}}{v/f_{max}}$$
$$=\frac{f_{max}}{f_{min}}=\frac{20,000}{20}$$
$$=1000$$

9. (c) $v=\sqrt{\frac{T}{\mu}}\Rightarrow v\propto\sqrt{T}$

Also, stress $\propto$ strain

Hence, tension $\propto$ deformation

$$T\propto \Delta l$$

Hence, $\frac{T_1}{T_2}=\frac{x}{x+\Delta x}=\left(\frac{v_1}{v_2}\right)^2$

$$\frac{x}{x+\Delta x}=(\sqrt{5})^2$$
$$\Rightarrow x=5x+5\Delta x$$
$$\Rightarrow \quad \Delta x=-\frac{4}{5}x=-0.8x$$
$$|\Delta x|=0.8x$$

10. (d) Distance between boats $=20\,\text{m}$

Wavelength $(\lambda)=2\times$ Distance between the boats

$$\Rightarrow \lambda=40\,\text{m}$$

Time period, $T=2\,\text{s}$

$$\therefore \quad v=\frac{\lambda}{T}=\frac{40}{2}=20\,\text{m/s}$$

11. (b) From figure, tension, $T_1=m_2g$

$$T_2=(m_1+m_2)g$$

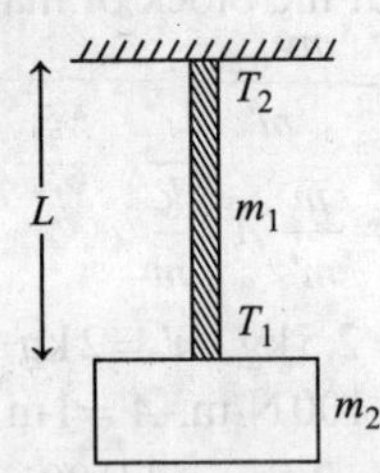

As we know, velocity $\propto\sqrt{T}$

So, $\quad \lambda\propto\sqrt{T}$

$$\frac{\lambda_1}{\lambda_2}=\frac{\sqrt{T_1}}{\sqrt{T_2}}$$
$$\frac{\lambda_2}{\lambda_1}=\sqrt{\frac{m_1+m_2}{m_2}}$$

12. (d) As, $v\propto\sqrt{T}$

$$\Rightarrow \quad \frac{v_2}{v_1}=\sqrt{\frac{T_2}{T_1}}=3$$
$$\Rightarrow \sqrt{\frac{273+T}{273}}=3$$
$$\Rightarrow \quad T=2184^\circ\text{C}$$

13. (a) The speed of wave in a bar,

$$v=\sqrt{\frac{Y}{\rho}}$$

So, the ratio of the speed of longitudinal waves in the solid bars is

$$\frac{v_1}{v_2}=\sqrt{\frac{Y_1\rho_2}{Y_2\rho_1}}$$

Since, solid bars are made up of the materials with same density,

i.e. $\quad \rho_1=\rho_2$

$$\Rightarrow \quad \frac{v_1}{v_2}=\sqrt{\frac{Y_1}{Y_2}}=\sqrt{4}=2$$
$$\left[\text{given, } \frac{Y_1}{Y_2}=4\right]$$

14. (b) $v=\sqrt{\frac{T}{\mu}}=\sqrt{\frac{T}{\rho s}}$ or $v\propto\frac{1}{\sqrt{s}}$

So, $\frac{v_1}{v_2}=\sqrt{\frac{s_2}{s_1}}\Rightarrow\sqrt{\frac{4}{1}}=\frac{2}{1}$

15. (c) Velocity of sound in gas,

$$v=\sqrt{\frac{\gamma RT}{M}}$$

$$\Rightarrow \quad v\propto\sqrt{\frac{\gamma}{M}}$$

$$\Rightarrow \quad \frac{v_{N_2}}{v_{He}}=\sqrt{\frac{\gamma_{N_2}}{\gamma_{He}}\times\frac{M_{He}}{M_{N_2}}}$$

$$=\sqrt{\frac{\frac{7}{5}\times 4}{\frac{5}{3}\times 28}}=\frac{\sqrt{3}}{5}$$

Test-2

1. (a) Compare $y=0.5\sin(2x+60t)$ with $y=y_0\sin(kx+\omega t)$, we get $k=2$ and $\omega=60$.

Velocity of wave,

$$v=\frac{\omega}{k}=\frac{60}{2}=30\,\text{m/s}$$

Now, velocity of wave in terms of tension and mass per unit length,

$$v=\sqrt{\frac{T}{\mu}}$$

$$\Rightarrow \quad T=\mu v^2=A\rho v^2 \quad (\because \mu=A\rho)$$

Here, A is area of cross-section, ρ is the density and v is the wave speed.

$$T=(1\times10^{-6})\,(9000)(30)^2$$

$$=8.1\,\text{N}$$

2. (d) When pulse is reflected from a rigid support, the pulse is inverted both lengthwise and sidewise. Hence, the wave will get inverted after reflectlion.

3. (d) By using,

$$I_{max}=I_1+I_2+2\sqrt{I_1I_2}$$

$$I_{min}=I_1+I_2-2\sqrt{I_1I_2}$$

$\therefore$ Difference of maximum and minimum intensities

$$=4\sqrt{I_1I_2}$$

4. (c) After two seconds each wave travel a distance of $2.5\times2=6\,\text{cm}$. i.e. Distance between the pulses is 2 cm because total distance covered by both waves is $2\times5\,\text{cm}=10\,\text{cm}$ and initial distance was 10 cm.

5. (b) On comparing the given equation with standard equation

$y=a\sin\frac{2\pi}{\lambda}(vt-x)$, it is clear that the wave speed $(v)_{wave}=v$ and maximum particle velocity

$(v_{max})_{particle}=a\omega=y_0\times$ coefficient of t

$$=y_0\times\frac{2\pi v}{\lambda}$$

$$\frac{y_0\,2\pi v}{\lambda}=3v$$

$$[\because (v_{max})_{particle}=3v]$$

$$\Rightarrow \quad \lambda=\frac{2}{3}y_0\pi$$

6. (a) The resultant amplitude is given by

$$A_R=\sqrt{A^2+A^2+2AA\cos\theta}$$

$$=\sqrt{2A^2(1+\cos\theta)}$$

$$=2A\cos\theta/2$$

$$(\because 1+\cos\theta=2\cos^2\theta/2)$$

$$\frac{A_R}{2}=A\cos\frac{\theta}{2}$$

7. (b) Equation of A, B, C and D are

$$y_A=A\sin\omega t$$

$$y_B=A\sin(\omega t+\pi/2)$$

$$y_C=A\sin(\omega t-\pi/2)$$

$$y_D=A\sin(\omega t-\pi)$$

It is clear that wave C lags behind by a phase angle of $\frac{\pi}{2}$ and the wave B is ahead a phase angle at $\frac{\pi}{2}$.

8. (a) Since, the initial phase difference between the two waves coming from different violins changes, therefore the waves produced by two different violins does not interfere because two waves interfere only when the phase difference between them remain constant throughout.

9. (c) Since, source of frequency x gives 12 beats/s with frequency 250 Hz, its possible frequencies are 238 or 262. As source of frequency x gives 8 beats/s with a frequency 270 Hz, its possible frequencies are 262 or 278 Hz. Therefore, the only possible frequency of x which gives 12 beats/s with frequency 250 Hz and 8 beats/s with 270 Hz is 262 Hz.

10. (b) $\Delta x=x_2-x_1=\left(\frac{5}{3}-\frac{1}{5}\right)\frac{\pi}{k}=\frac{22\pi}{15k}$

$$\sin kx_1=\sin k\left(\frac{\pi}{5k}\right)=\sin\frac{\pi}{5}\neq0$$

$$\sin kx_2=\sin k\frac{5\pi}{3k}=\sin\frac{5\pi}{3}\neq0$$

x_1 and x_2 are not the nodes

$$\frac{2\pi}{k}>\Delta x>\frac{\pi}{k}$$

$$\Rightarrow \quad \lambda>\Delta x>\frac{\lambda}{2}$$

$$\text{For } \phi_1=\pi, \phi_2=k(\Delta x)=k\left(\frac{22\pi}{15k}\right)$$

$$=\frac{22\pi}{15}$$

$$\frac{\phi_1}{\phi_2}=\frac{\pi}{22\pi/15}=\frac{15}{22}$$

11. (b) According to the property of persistence of hearing, the impression of a sound heard persists on our mind for $\frac{1}{10}$ s. Therefore, number of beats per second should be less than 10. Hence, difference in frequencies of two sources must be less than 10.

12. (b) After 2 s, the each wave travels a distance $=2\times2=4$ m.

These two pulse will superimpose. The wave shape is shown in figure. As the spring is in normal condition, thus potential energy is zero. From the law of conservation of energy. Thus, energy is purely kinetic energy.

13. (a) A standing wave is as shown below.

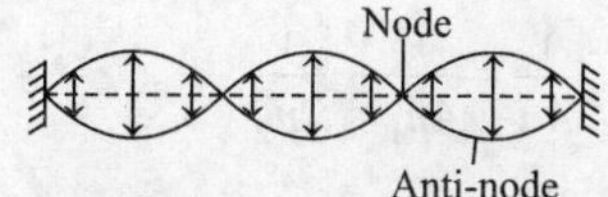

As all particles vibrate together, they cross mean position simultaneously.

In stationary wave, a node is place of zero amplitude and an anti-node is a place of maximum amplitude and velocity is directly proportional to amplitude, hence velocity is maximum at the position of anti-node and zero at node.

14. (c) The waves 1 and 3 reach out of phase, hence resultant phase difference between them is π.

$\therefore$ Resultant amplitude of 1 and $3 = 10 - 7 = 3$ mm.

This wave has phase difference of $\frac{\pi}{2}$ with 4 mm.

$\therefore$ Resultant amplitude

$$= \sqrt{3^2 + 4^2} = 5 \text{ mm}$$

15. (a) Path difference between the wave reaching at M,

$$\Delta x = L_2P - L_1P$$
$$= \sqrt{30^2 + 16^2} - 30$$
$$= 4 \text{ m}$$

For maximum, $\Delta x = (2n)\frac{\lambda}{2}$

For first maximum ($n = 1$),

$$4 = 2(1)\frac{\lambda}{2} \Rightarrow \lambda = 4 \text{ m}$$

$$\Rightarrow \quad n = \frac{v}{\lambda} = \frac{340}{4} = 85 \text{ Hz}$$

Test-3

1. (a) Frequency of closed pipe,

$$n_1 = \frac{v}{4l_1} \Rightarrow l_1 = \frac{v}{4n_1}$$

Frequency of open pipe,

$$n_2 = \frac{v}{2l_2}$$

$$\Rightarrow \quad l_2 = \frac{v}{2n_2}$$

When both pipes are joined, then length of closed pipe

$$l = l_1 + l_2$$

$$\frac{v}{4n} = \frac{v}{4n_1} + \frac{v}{2n_2}$$

or $\frac{1}{2n} = \frac{1}{2n_1} + \frac{1}{n_2}$

or $\frac{1}{2n} = \frac{n_2 + 2n_1}{2n_1 n_2}$

or $n = \frac{n_1 n_2}{n_2 + 2n_1}$

2. (b) $y = 10 \sin\left(\frac{\pi}{18}x\right)\cos(84\pi t)$

Here, $y = 2A\cos\left(\frac{2\pi x}{\lambda}\right)\sin\left(\frac{2\pi vt}{\lambda}\right)$

$$y = 2A\sin\left(\frac{2\pi x}{\lambda}\right)\cos\left(\frac{2\pi vt}{\lambda}\right)$$

So, $\frac{2\pi}{\lambda} = \frac{\pi}{18}$

$$\Rightarrow \quad \lambda = 36 \text{ m}$$

Distance between a node and anti-node $\frac{\lambda}{4} = \frac{36}{4} = 9$ m

3. (a) For string, $\lambda = \frac{2l}{p}$

where, p = number of loops = order of vibration

Hence, for third mode $p = 3$

$$\Rightarrow \quad \lambda = \frac{2l}{3}$$

Hence, $v = n\lambda = 600 \times \frac{2(3)}{3} = 1200$ m/s

4. (a) Given, $n_3 - n_2 = 200$

$$5 \times \frac{v}{4l} - \frac{v}{l} = 200$$

or $\frac{v}{l}\left(\frac{5}{4} - 1\right) = 200$

$$\Rightarrow \quad \frac{v}{4l} = 200 \text{ or } \frac{v}{2l} = 400$$

Fundamental frequency of open pipe

$$\frac{v}{2l} = 400 \text{ Hz}$$

5. (c) Wave number, $k = \frac{2\pi}{\lambda} = 0.9 \text{ cm}^{-1}$

$$\frac{\lambda}{2} = \frac{\pi}{0.9} \text{cm}$$

$$\therefore \quad l = \frac{3\lambda}{2} = 3\left(\frac{\pi}{0.9}\right) = 10.5 \text{ cm}$$

6. (a) In closed pipe, frequencies of its harmonics are in ratio $1:3:5:7$ ...... and fundamental frequency is given as $n = \frac{v}{\lambda} = \frac{v}{4l}$

7. (b) Here, $n_{\text{open}} = \frac{v}{2l_{\text{open}}}$

$$n_{\text{closed}} = \frac{v}{4l_{\text{closed}}}$$
$$= \frac{v}{4\left(\frac{l_{\text{open}}}{2}\right)} = \frac{v}{2l_{\text{open}}}$$

$$\left(\text{As, } l_{\text{closed}} = \frac{l_{\text{open}}}{2}\right)$$

i.e. Frequency remains unchanged.

8. (b) Spacing between successive nodes $= \frac{\lambda}{2}$ (using $v = n\lambda$)

Velocity of standing wave,

$$v = \sqrt{\frac{T}{\mu}}$$

$$\lambda \propto v \propto \sqrt{\frac{T}{\mu}}$$

Now, $\frac{\lambda'}{\lambda} = \frac{\sqrt{3T}}{\sqrt{T}}$

$$\Rightarrow \quad \lambda' = \sqrt{3}\lambda$$

$$\frac{\lambda'}{2} = \sqrt{3} \cdot \frac{\lambda}{2} = \frac{\sqrt{3}}{2}x$$

9. (b) For the first harmonic of closed organ pipe P_1, frequency, $f_c = \frac{v}{4l_1}$

For the third harmonic open organ pipe P_2,

$$f_o = \frac{3v}{2l_2}$$

Given, $f_c = f_o$

$$\frac{v}{4l_1} = \frac{3v}{2l_2}$$

$$\frac{l_1}{l_2} = \frac{1}{6}$$

10. (d) Fundamental frequency of closed organ pipe,

$$f_c = \frac{v}{4l_c}$$

Fundamental frequency of open organ pipe,

$$f_o = \frac{v}{2l_o}$$

Second overtone frequency of open organ pipe, $f_o' = 3 \times f_o$

$$= \frac{3v}{2l_o}$$

From question,

$$\frac{v}{4l_c} = \frac{3v}{2l_0}$$

$$l_o = 6l_c = 6 \times 40 = 240\,\text{cm}$$

11. (b) Sound produced by an open organ pipe is richer because it contains all harmonics and frequency of fundamental note in an open organ pipe is twice the fundamental frequency in a closed organ pipe of same length . Reason is also correct, but is not explaining the Assertion.

12. (b) Suppose, N resonance occurred before tube coming out.

Hence, by using $l = \frac{(2N-1)v}{4n}$

$$\Rightarrow \quad 1 = \frac{(2N-1)340}{4 \times 720}$$

$$\Rightarrow \quad N = \left(\frac{4 \times 720}{340} + 1\right)\frac{1}{2} \approx 5$$

13. (c) The maximum pressure at closed end will be the sum of atmospheric pressure and acoustic wave pressure.

So, $\rho_{max} = \rho_A + \rho_0$

and $\rho_{min} = \rho_A - \rho_0$

Thus, $\frac{\rho_{min}}{\rho_{max}} = \frac{\rho_A - \rho_0}{\rho_A + \rho_0}$

14. (c) Velocity of sound increases, if the temperature increases. So, with $v = n\lambda$, if v increases n will increase at 27°C , $v_1 = n\lambda$ and at 33°C, $v_2 = (n+x)\lambda$.

Now using, $v \propto \sqrt{T}$ $\left(\because v = \sqrt{\frac{\gamma RT}{M}}\right)$

$$\frac{v_2}{v_1} = \sqrt{\frac{T_2}{T_1}} = \frac{n+x}{n}$$

$$\Rightarrow \frac{300+x}{300} = \sqrt{\frac{(273+33)}{(273+27)}}$$

$$= \sqrt{\frac{306}{300}} = \sqrt{\frac{300+6}{300}}$$

$$\Rightarrow 1 + \frac{x}{300} = \left(1 + \frac{6}{300}\right)^{1/2}$$

$$= \left(1 + \frac{1}{2} \times \frac{6}{300}\right)$$

$$\Rightarrow \quad x = 3 \qquad [\because (1+x)^n = 1 + nx]$$

15. (a) $f_1 : f_2 : f_3 = 425 : 595 : 765$

$$= 5 : 7 : 9$$

Since, these are odd harmonics, pipe is closed.

Further, $5\left(\frac{v}{4l}\right) = 425$

$$\therefore \quad l = \frac{425 \times 4}{5v} = \frac{425 \times 4}{5 \times 340} = 1\,\text{m}$$

Chapter Break Thru

1. (d) $T = \mu v^2 = \mu \frac{\omega^2}{k^2}$

$$= 0.04 \frac{(2\pi / 0.04)^2}{(2\pi / 0.50)^2} = 6.25\,\text{N}$$

2. (d) $T = \frac{1}{500}\,\text{s}$

$$t = \frac{T}{2} = \frac{1}{1000}\,\text{s}$$

3. (b) Equation for a travelling wave is given as

$$y = 4\cos 2\pi(5t - 0.0040x + 0.25)$$

$$= 4\cos(10\pi t - 0.008\pi x + 0.5\,\pi)$$

where, propagation constant,

$$k = 0.008\,\pi\,\text{cm}^{-1}$$

Amplitude, $a = 4$ cm

Angular frequency, $\omega = 10\pi$ rad/s

Phase difference is given by the relation,

$$\Delta\phi = k\Delta x$$

For $\Delta x = 2\,\text{m}$ or 200 cm,

$$\Delta\phi = 0.008\pi \times 200$$

$$= 1.6\pi\,\text{rad}$$

4. (a) As, maximum velocity of particle,

$$v_{max} = a\omega$$

$$\Rightarrow \quad \omega = \frac{v_{max}}{a}$$

or $A = \frac{40}{10} = 4\,\text{s}^{-1}$

Similarly, wave velocity, $v = \frac{\omega}{k}$

or $k = \frac{\omega}{v}$

$$\Rightarrow \quad B = \frac{A}{v} = \frac{4}{2}$$

$$= 2\,\text{m/s}$$

5. (b) Given, $\lambda_1 = 1\,\text{m}$, $\lambda_2 = \frac{170}{169}\,\text{m}$

We know that, $f = \frac{v}{\lambda}$

$$f_1 = \frac{v}{1}, \; f_2 = \frac{169v}{170}$$

$$f_1 - f_2 = 2$$

$$\frac{v}{170} = 2 \Rightarrow v = 340\,\text{m/s}$$

6. (d) Since, transverse wave can propagate through medium which posses elasticity of shape. Air posses only volume elasticity, therefore transverse wave cannot propagate through air.

7. (a) Given $\frac{mv}{2l} = 315$

and $(n+1)\frac{v}{2l} = 420$

$$\Rightarrow \quad \frac{n+1}{n} = \frac{420}{315} \Rightarrow n = 3$$

$$f_{\text{lowest}} = \frac{315}{n} = \frac{315}{3}$$

$$\Rightarrow \quad \frac{v}{2l} = 105\,\text{Hz}$$

The lowest reasonant frequency is when $n = 1$. Therefore, lowest resonant frequency = 105 Hz

8. (b) Modes of vibrations are

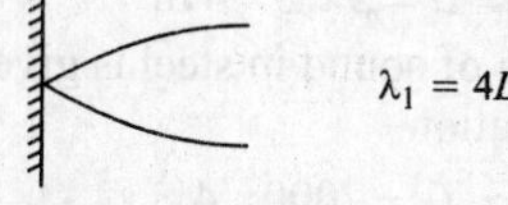

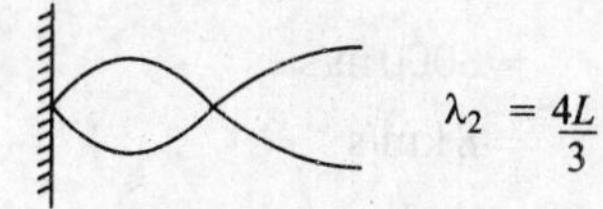

$$\therefore f_1 : f_2 : f_3 \ldots\ldots = 1 : 3 : 5 : \ldots\ldots$$

9. (d) $y_1 = a\sin(\omega t + kx + 0.62)$ m

and $y_2 = a\cos(\omega t + kx)$ m

or $y_2 = a\sin\left(\frac{\pi}{2} + \omega t + kx\right)$ m

Phase difference,

$$\Delta\phi = \phi_2 - \phi_1 = \frac{\pi}{2} - 0.62$$

$$= 1.57 - 0.62 = 0.95 \text{ rad}$$

10. (d) For minimum, $\Delta x = (2n-1)\frac{\lambda}{2}$

The maximum possible path difference = distance between the sources = 4 m

For no minima case,

$$\frac{\lambda}{2} > 4 \Rightarrow \lambda > 8$$

$$\therefore \quad f = \frac{v}{\lambda} < \frac{340}{8} = 42.5 \text{ Hz}$$

$\therefore$ If $f < 42.5$ Hz, no minimum will formed.

11. (d) When the rod is clamped at its middle, a node (N) is formed at its centre and anti-nodes (A) are formed at its two ends as shown in the figure.

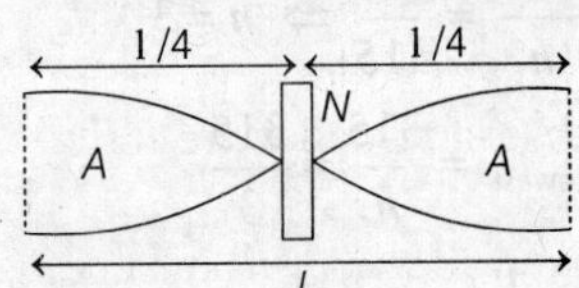

The distance between two successive anti-nodes is $\frac{\lambda}{4} + \frac{\lambda}{4} = \frac{\lambda}{2}$

$$\therefore \quad l = \frac{\lambda}{2}$$

or $\lambda = 2l = 2 \times 2 = 4$ m

The speed of sound in steel is given by the relation,

$$v = f\lambda = 2000 \times 4$$

$$= 8000 \text{ m/s}$$

or $= 8$ km/s

12. (d) Beat period,

$$T = \frac{1}{n_1 - n_2} \text{ s}$$

$$= \frac{1}{384 - 376} = \frac{1}{8} \text{ s}$$

Hence, minimum time interval between maxima and minima,

$$t = \frac{T}{2} = \frac{1}{16}$$

13. (b) The frequency of A,

$$n_A = n + \frac{3}{100}n$$

and the frequency of B,

$$n_B = n - \frac{6}{100}n$$

According to question,

$$n_A - n_B = 10$$

$$\therefore \quad \left(n + \frac{3}{100}n\right) - \left(n - \frac{6}{100}n\right) = 10$$

or $\frac{9}{100}n = 10$

$$\Rightarrow \quad n = \frac{1000}{9} \text{ Hz}$$

The frequency of A,

$$n_A = \left(n + \frac{3}{100}n\right)$$

$$= \frac{1000}{9} + \frac{3}{100} \times \frac{1000}{9}$$

$$= 114.4 \text{ Hz}$$

14. (b) As we know, $n = \frac{1}{2l}\sqrt{\frac{T}{m}}$

$$\Rightarrow \quad n_1 l_1 = n_2 l_2 = n_3 l_3 = k$$

$$l_1 + l_2 + l_3 = l$$

$$\Rightarrow \frac{k}{n_1} + \frac{k}{n_2} + \frac{k}{n_3} = \frac{k}{n}$$

$$\Rightarrow \quad \frac{1}{n} = \frac{1}{n_1} + \frac{1}{n_2} + \frac{1}{n_3}$$

15. (a) The fundamental frequency,

$$f = \frac{1}{2L}\sqrt{\frac{T}{\mu}}$$

where, μ is the mass per unit length of the wire.

$$f = \frac{1}{2L}\sqrt{\frac{T}{\rho\pi\frac{D^2}{4}}}$$

$$= \frac{1}{2L}\sqrt{\frac{4T}{\rho\pi D^2}} = \frac{1}{LD}\sqrt{\frac{T}{\pi\rho}}$$

or $\quad f \propto \frac{1}{LD}$

16. (a) According to problem,

$$\frac{1}{2L}\sqrt{\frac{T}{m}} = \frac{v}{4L} \quad \text{...(i)}$$

and $\frac{1}{2L}\sqrt{\frac{T+10}{m}} = \frac{3v}{4L}$ ...(ii)

Dividing Eq. (i) by Eq. (ii), we get

$$\sqrt{\frac{T}{T+10}} = \frac{1}{3}$$

$$\Rightarrow \quad \frac{T+10}{T} = 9$$

$$\Rightarrow \quad T = \frac{10}{8} = \frac{5}{4} \text{ N}$$

17. (b) Velocity of sound is inversely proportional to the square root of density of the medium. i.e.

$$\Rightarrow \quad \frac{v_1}{v_2} = \sqrt{\frac{\rho_2}{\rho_1}}$$

$$= \sqrt{\frac{4\rho}{\rho}} = 2$$

18. (b) A bucket can be treated as a pipe closed at one end. The frequency of the note produced $= \frac{v}{2L}$, here L equal to depth of water level from the open end. As the bucket is filled with water L decreases, hence frequency increases. Therefore, frequency or pitch of sound produced goes on increasing. Also, the frequency of woman voice is usually higher than that of man.

19. (a) $\frac{\nu_1}{\nu_2} = \frac{l_2}{l_1}$

$$\Rightarrow \frac{\nu_1}{\nu_2} = \frac{29}{27}$$

$$\nu_1 - \nu_2 = 6$$

or $\frac{29}{27}\nu_2 - \nu_2 = 6$

$$\nu_2 = \frac{27}{2} \times 6 = 81 \text{ Hz}$$

$$\nu_1 = \nu_2 + 6 = 87 \text{ Hz}$$

or $\quad \nu_1 = 87$ Hz

20. (b) Given that,

$$y = 0.04\sin\left(\frac{\pi}{3}x\right)\cos(60\pi t)$$

So, wavelength,

$$\lambda = \frac{2\pi}{k} = \frac{2\pi}{\pi/3} = 6 \text{ m}$$

Frequency, $f = \frac{\omega}{2\pi} = \frac{60\pi}{2\pi} = 30\,\text{Hz}$

Speed, $v = f\lambda$

$= 30 \times 6 = 180\,\text{m/s}$

The speed of a wave in a string is given by

$$v = \sqrt{\frac{T}{\mu}}$$

or $T = v^2 \times \mu$

or $T = \frac{v^2 m}{l} \quad \left(\because \mu = \frac{m}{l}\right)$

$= \frac{(180)^2 \times 2 \times 10^{-2}}{2}$

$T = 324\,\text{N}$

21. (b) In case of a sound wave, the reflection at a rigid boundary will take place with a phase reversal of π but the reflection at an open boundary takes place without any phase change.

$\therefore$ The reflected wave is

$$y = \frac{25}{100} A_0 \sin(\omega t + kx)$$

$$= -\frac{1}{4} A_0 \sin(\omega t + kx).$$

22. (a) Wave, $z_1 = A\sin(2kx - \omega t)$ is travelling towards positive x-direction.

Wave, $z_2 = A\sin(2kx + \omega t)$ is travelling towards negative x-direction.

Wave, $z_3 = A\sin(2ky - \omega t)$ is travelling towards positive y-direction.

Since, waves, z_1 and z_2 are travelling along the same line, so they will produce stationary wave.

23. (c) Remember that octane is twice of the fundamental. If f is the frequency of first tuning fork, then the frequency of last tuning fork must be $2f$. Since, any two successive fork produce 4 beats/s.

Frequency of 2nd fork,

$$f + 4 = f + 1 \times 4$$

that of 3rd fork is $f + 8 = f + 2 \times 4$

that of 4th fork is $f + 12 = f + 3 \times 4$

and

Nth fork $= f + (N - 1) \times 4$

Given that,

$$f + (N-1)4 = 2f$$

$$(N-1)4 = f = 256$$

$$N - 1 = 64$$

$$N = 65$$

24. (c) Minimum time interval between two instants when the string is flat

$$= \frac{T}{2} = 0.1\,\text{s}$$

$\Rightarrow \quad T = 0.2\,\text{s}$

Hence, $\lambda = v \times T = 20 \times 0.2 = 4\,\text{m}$

25. (a) At $t = 0$, $y = \frac{1}{1 + x^2}$

or $x = \sqrt{\frac{1-y}{y}} = x_1$

At $t = 2\,\text{s}$,

$$y = \frac{1}{2 + x^2 - 2x} = \frac{1}{1 + (x-1)^2}$$

or $(x-1)^2 = \frac{1-y}{y}$

or $x = 1 + \sqrt{\frac{1-y}{y}} = x_2$

$\therefore$ Speed of the wave

$$v = \frac{\Delta x}{\Delta t} = \frac{x_2 - x_1}{t_2 - t_1}$$

$$= \frac{1}{2-0} = 0.5\,\text{m/s}$$

26. (b) Possible frequency of

$$B = 427 \pm 5 = 432 \text{ or } 422\,\text{Hz}$$

Now, when tension in B is increased, it's frequency increases and beat frequency decreases.

So, original frequency of B will be 422 Hz.

27. (b) Maximum number of beats $= (v + 1) - (v - 1) = 2$

28. (a) $y = 0.02\cos(10\pi x)$

$$\cos\left(50\pi t + \frac{\pi}{2}\right)$$

At node, amplitude $= 0$

$\Rightarrow \cos(10\pi x) = 0 \Rightarrow 10\pi x = \frac{\pi}{2}, \frac{3\pi}{2}$

$\Rightarrow x = \frac{1}{20} = 0.05\,\text{m}, 0.15\,\text{m}$

At anti-node, amplitude is maximum

$\Rightarrow \cos(10\pi x) = \pm 1$

$\Rightarrow x = 0, \pi, 2\pi$

$\Rightarrow \quad x = 0, 0.1\,\text{m}, 0.2\,\text{m}$

Now $\lambda = 2 \times$ Distance between two nodes or anti-nodes $= 2 \times 0.1 = 0.2$

and $\frac{2\pi v t}{\lambda} = 50\pi t$

$$v = 25\lambda = 25 \times 0.2 = 5\,\text{m/s}$$

29. (c) General equation for stationary wave,

$$y = 2A\sin(kx)\cos(\omega t)$$

Comparing it with given equation, we get

$\therefore \quad 2A = 0.06 \Rightarrow A = 0.03$

Position of nodes is given by 0.5 m, whereas anti-nodes are formed at 0.25 m.

Amplitude will remain same, i.e. 0.06.

Hence, A-4, B-2, C-3 and D-1.

30. (a) Time interval between two consecutive beats,

$$T = \frac{1}{n_1 - n_2} = \frac{1}{261 - 258}$$

$$= \frac{1}{3}\,\text{s, so } t = \frac{1}{9} = \frac{T}{3}\,\text{s}$$

By using, time difference

$$= \frac{T}{2\pi} \times \text{phase difference}$$

$\Rightarrow \quad \frac{T}{3} = \frac{T}{2\pi} \times \phi$

$\Rightarrow \quad \phi = \frac{2\pi}{3}$

SPT1 Syllabus Part Thru 1

1. (d) Here, $m \propto v^a \rho^b g^c$.

Writing the dimensions on both sides

$[M] = [LT^{-1}]^a \ [ML^{-3}]^b \ [LT^{-2}]^c$

$[M] = [M^b L^{a-3b+c} T^{-a-2c}]$

$\therefore \quad b = 1$

$a - 3b + c = 0$

$-a - 2c = 0$

Solving these equations, we get

$a = 6$

Hence, $m \propto v^6$

2. (b) Here, $r = 0.25$ m and $m = 2$ kg

Rotational KE

$$= \frac{1}{2} I\omega^2 = \frac{1}{2} \times \left(\frac{1}{2} mr^2\right)\omega^2$$

$$\Rightarrow \quad 4 = \frac{1}{4} mv^2 = \frac{1}{4} \times 2v^2$$

$$\therefore \quad v = \sqrt{8} = 2\sqrt{2} \text{ ms}^{-1}$$

3. (d) Air bubble is held against buoyant force at bottom of tank. As it rises, its potential energy decreases.

4. (c) Using $R = \sqrt{P^2 + Q^2 + 2PQ\cos\theta}$

we have,

$x^2 = x^2 + x^2 + 2x^2 \cos\theta$

(Given $|\mathbf{P}| = |\mathbf{Q}| = |\mathbf{R}| = x$ (let))

So, $\cos\theta = -\frac{1}{2}$

or $\theta = 120°$

5. (a) Angular momentum $= \mathbf{r} \times \mathbf{p}$

$\therefore \quad \mathbf{l}_1 = \hat{\mathbf{j}} \times mv_1 \hat{\mathbf{i}} = \hat{\mathbf{j}} \times \hat{\mathbf{i}} = -\hat{\mathbf{k}}$

and $\mathbf{l}_2 = \hat{\mathbf{i}} \times \hat{\mathbf{j}} = \hat{\mathbf{k}}$

Total angular momentum of system,

$\mathbf{l} = \mathbf{l}_1 + \mathbf{l}_2 = \hat{\mathbf{k}} + (-\hat{\mathbf{k}}) = 0$

6. (d) Moment of inertia of a solid cylinder about an axis passing through its centre of gravity and perpendicular to geometric axis,

$$I = M\left(\frac{L^2}{12} + \frac{r^2}{4}\right)$$

$$= M\left(\frac{L^2}{12} + \frac{D^2}{16}\right) \quad \left(\because r = \frac{D}{2}\right)$$

7. (a) Resolving forces along X and Y axis, we have

$$P = \Sigma F_x = F_1 \cos 45° + F_2 \cos 135° + F_3 \cos 225°$$

$$= 3\sqrt{2} \times \frac{1}{\sqrt{2}} + 4\sqrt{2} \times \frac{(-1)}{\sqrt{2}} + 5\sqrt{2} \times \frac{-1}{\sqrt{2}}$$

$$= -6\hat{\mathbf{i}}$$

and $Q = \Sigma F_y = 3\sqrt{2} \sin 45° + 4\sqrt{2} \sin 135° + 5\sqrt{2} \sin 225°$

$$= 3\sqrt{2} \times \frac{1}{\sqrt{2}} + 4\sqrt{2} \times \frac{1}{\sqrt{2}} + 5\sqrt{2} \times \frac{-1}{\sqrt{2}}$$

$$= 3 + 4 - 5 = 2\hat{\mathbf{j}}$$

Net force on particle, $\mathbf{R} = -6\hat{\mathbf{i}} + 2\hat{\mathbf{j}}$

Magnitude of resultant

$$= \sqrt{6^2 + 2^2} = \sqrt{40} \text{ N}$$

Acceleration,

$$a = \frac{R}{m} = \frac{\sqrt{40}}{2} = \sqrt{10} \text{ ms}^{-2}$$

$$= \pi \text{ ms}^{-2}$$

8. (c) Let coefficient of friction be μ, then retardation will be μg. From equation of motion, $v = u + at$

$\Rightarrow \quad 0 = 6 - \mu g \times 10$

or $\mu = \frac{6}{100} = 0.06$

9. (d) Net downward acceleration,

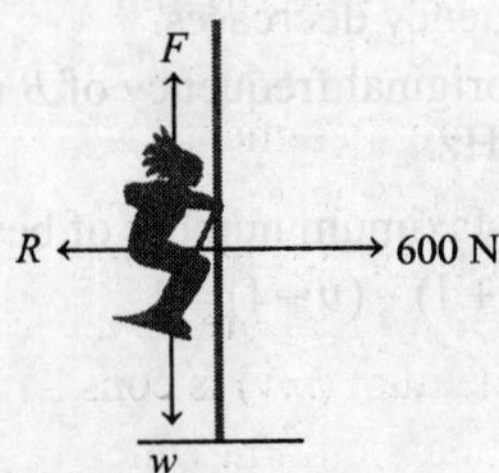

$$a = \frac{\text{Weight} - \text{Frictional force}}{\text{Mass}}$$

$$= \frac{mg - \mu R}{m}$$

$$= \frac{60 \times 10 - 0.5 \times 600}{60}$$

$$= \frac{300}{60} = 5 \text{ m/s}^2$$

10. (b) Here, $2mnv = Mg$

$$\therefore \quad v = \frac{Mg}{2mn}$$

or $$v = \frac{10 \times 980}{2 \times 5 \times 10}$$

$$= \frac{9800}{100} = 98 \text{ cms}^{-1}$$

11. (b) Change in momentum $= m\Delta v$

Given, $m = 0.15$ kg

$\therefore \quad \Delta p = 0.15[12 - (-12)]$

$= 3.6$ N-s

in the direction from the batsman to the bowler.

12. (b) Given, $p = \frac{a - t^2}{bx}$, where p pressure, t-time and x-distance

$$[pbx] = [a] = [t^2]$$

Dimensions of $\frac{a}{b} = [px] = [MT^{-2}]$

13. (b) Dimensional formula of potential $[V] = [ML^2T^{-3}A^{-1}]$

Hence, option (b) is incorrect.

14. (a) Centripetal force,

$mR\omega^2 =$ Gravitational force, $\frac{GmM}{R^2}$

$$\omega^2 = \frac{GmM}{mR^3}$$

$$= G \times \frac{4}{3} \times \frac{\pi R^3 \rho}{R^3}$$

$$= G \cdot \frac{4}{3} \pi\rho$$

$$\Rightarrow \quad \omega = \sqrt{\frac{4\pi G\rho}{3}}$$

or $$\frac{2\pi}{T} = \sqrt{\frac{4\pi G\rho}{3}}$$

$\therefore \quad T \propto \sqrt{\frac{1}{\rho}}$

i.e. time period of nearest satellite does not depend upon the radius of planet, it only depends upon the density and it is same, so time period will be same.

15. (a) Since, the gravitational field is conservative field, hence the work done in taking a particle from one point to another in a gravitational field is path independent.

Hence, $W_1 = W_2 = W_3$.

16. (b) Let the change in height is Δh.

$$\Delta h = d \sin \theta$$

$$\Delta h = 8.0 \times \sin 60°$$

$$= 8.0 \times \frac{\sqrt{3}}{2} = 4\sqrt{3} \text{ m}$$

$$\simeq 6.39 \text{ m}$$

The change in gravitational potential energy is

$$\Delta U = m\Delta V \times \frac{\Delta h}{20}$$

$$= 2.0 \times 14 \times \frac{6.93}{20}$$

$$\simeq 9.70 \text{ J}$$

The work done is

$$W = \Delta U \approx 9.70 \text{ J}$$

17. (b) In this case, the force is always tangent to the curve and its magnitude is constant, which suggests that the work done by the force depends on the path taken and not just on the initial and final positions, making it non-conservative force.

18. (d) Energy of satellite is given by

$$E = -\frac{GMm}{2r}$$

$$\Rightarrow \quad E \propto \frac{m}{r}$$

$$\Rightarrow \quad \frac{E_A}{E_B} = \frac{m_A}{m_B} \times \frac{r_B}{r_A}$$

$$= \frac{3}{1} \times \frac{4r}{r}$$

$$\left[\because \frac{m_A}{m_B} = \frac{3}{1}, \frac{r_B}{r_A} = \frac{4r}{r}\right]$$

$$\Rightarrow \quad \frac{E_A}{E_b} = \frac{12}{1}$$

Therefore, ratio of total mechanical energy is 12 : 1.

19. (c) According to work energy theorem,

work done, W = change in kinetic energy

$$\Rightarrow Fs \cos \theta = \frac{1}{2} mv^2 - \frac{1}{2} mu^2$$

Given, $m = 5$ kg

$F = 20$ N

$s = 4$ m

Initial KE, $\frac{1}{2} mu^2 = 0$

Final KE, $\frac{1}{2} mv^2 = 40$ J

$$\therefore \quad Fs \cos \theta = 40$$

$$\Rightarrow \quad \cos \theta = \frac{40}{80} = \frac{1}{2}$$

$$\Rightarrow \quad \theta = 60°$$

20. (c) In question, it is given that

50 VSD = 49 MSD

$$1 \text{ VSD} = \frac{49}{50} \text{ MSD}$$

Minimum inaccuracy

= least count error

= 1 MSD − 1VSD

$$= 1 \text{ MSD} - \frac{49}{50} \text{ MSD}$$

$$= \frac{1}{50} \text{ MSD}$$

Given, 1 MSD = 0.5 mm

Hence, minimum inaccuracy

$$= \frac{1}{50} \times 0.5 \text{ mm}$$

$$= \frac{1}{100} = 0.01 \text{ mm}$$

21. (b) Both Statement I and Statement II are incorrect.

As a particle is moving with uniform velocity, therefore its linear momentum (mv) is constant.

But about a point which is not on the line of motion, the moment of momentum, i.e. angular momentum can be non-zero.

22. (a) The SI unit in which G is measured = N-m^2/kg^2

$\therefore$ Its dimensions will be

$$\frac{[\text{MLT}^{-2}][\text{L}^2]}{[\text{M}^2]} = [\text{M}^{-1}\text{L}^3\text{T}^{-2}]$$

$\because$ Impulse = Force × Time

$$= [\text{MLT}^{-2}][\text{T}] = [\text{MLT}^{-1}]$$

$\because$ Dimensions for energy = $[\text{ML}^2\text{T}^{-2}]$

Now, put the dimensions of G, I, M and E in $\frac{GIM^2}{E^2}$

$$= \frac{[\text{M}^{-1}\text{L}^3\text{T}^{-2}][\text{MLT}^{-1}][\text{M}^2]}{[\text{ML}^2\text{T}^{-2}]^2}$$

$$= \frac{[\text{M}^{-1}\text{L}^3\text{T}^{-2}][\text{MLT}^{-1}][\text{M}^2]}{[\text{M}^2\text{L}^4\text{T}^{-4}]}$$

$$= \frac{[\text{M}^2\text{L}^4\text{T}^{-3}]}{[\text{M}^2\text{L}^4\text{T}^{-4}]} = [\text{T}^1] = [\text{T}]$$

The equation $\frac{GIM^2}{E^2}$ has dimensions of time.

23. (b) The retardation a of the bullet is given by

$$a = -\frac{u^2}{2s} = \frac{-90 \times 90}{2 \times 0.6} \text{ ms}^{-2}$$

$$= -6750 \text{ ms}^{-2}$$

The retarding force by the second law of motion is

$$F = ma = 0.04 \times 6750$$

$$= 270 \text{ N}$$

24. (b) Velocity on hitting the surface

$$= \sqrt{2 \times 9.8 \times 4.9}$$

$$= 9.8 \text{ m/s}$$

Velocity after first bounce

$$v = \frac{3}{4} \times 9.8$$

Time taken from first bounce to the second bounce $= \frac{2v}{g}$

$$= 2 \times \frac{3}{4} \times 9.8 \times \frac{1}{9.8} = 1.5 \text{ s}$$

25. (a) As we know,

$$\text{KE} = \frac{1}{2} mv^2$$

$$= 8 \times 10^{-4} \text{ J}$$

$$\therefore\ v^2 = \frac{8 \times 2 \times 10^{-4}}{m}$$

$$= \frac{16 \times 10^{-4}}{0.01}$$

$$= 16 \times 10^{-2} \quad \ldots(i)$$

By third equation of motion,

$$v^2 = u^2 + 2a_t s$$

$$\Rightarrow v^2 = 2a_t s \quad [\because u = 0]$$

$$\text{or } v^2 = 2a_t(4\pi r)$$

($\because$ particle covers 2 revolutions)

$$\Rightarrow a_t = \frac{v^2}{8\pi r} = \frac{16 \times 10^{-2}}{8 \times 3.14 \times 6.4 \times 10^{-2}}$$

[from Eq. (i)]

$$\therefore\ a_t \simeq 0.1 \text{ m/s}^2$$

26. (c)

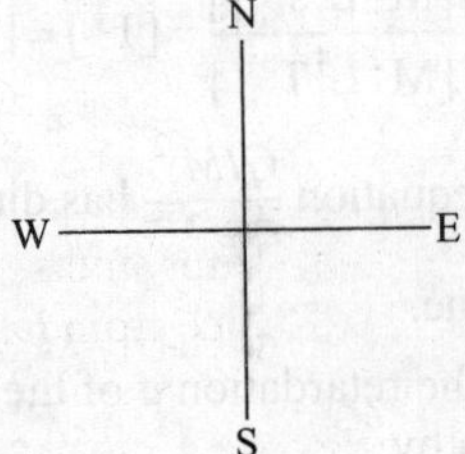

The displacement between the two cities is

$$\mathbf{s} = 75\hat{\mathbf{j}} + [60\cos 45°\ \hat{\mathbf{j}} - 60\sin 45°\ \hat{\mathbf{i}}] + 20\hat{\mathbf{i}}$$

$$= \left(20 - 60 \times \frac{1}{\sqrt{2}}\right)\hat{\mathbf{i}} + \left(60 \times \frac{1}{\sqrt{2}} + 75\right)\hat{\mathbf{j}}$$

$$= -22\hat{\mathbf{i}} + 117\hat{\mathbf{j}}$$

Magnitude,

$$|\mathbf{s}| = \sqrt{(22)^2 + (117)^2}$$

$$= \sqrt{484 + 1689} \approx 119 \text{ km}$$

27. (c) According to Newton's 2nd law of motion, the resultant force on a particle is in the direction of acceleration of the particle.

Here, the acceleration of particle is along X-axis. So, net force will be along X-axis.

Hence, $\Sigma F_Y = 0$

$$\therefore F_2 \sin 37° - F_1 \sin 30° = 0$$

$$\Rightarrow \frac{3}{5}F_2 = \frac{F_1}{2}$$

$$\Rightarrow F_1 = \frac{6}{5} \times F_2$$

$$= \frac{6}{5} \times 5 \text{ N} = 6 \text{ N}$$

28. (c) From figure, **OC** and **OA** are equal in magnitude and are inclined to each other at an angle of 90°. So, their resultant is $\sqrt{2}r$.

The resultant is mid-way between **OC** and **OA**, i.e. along **OB**.

Now, both r and $\sqrt{2}r$ are along the same line and in same direction.

$\therefore$ Resultant of these 3 vectors

$$= r + \sqrt{2}r = r(1 + \sqrt{2})$$

29. (a) Initial velocity, $\mathbf{v}_i = 10\sqrt{2}\ \hat{\mathbf{j}}$

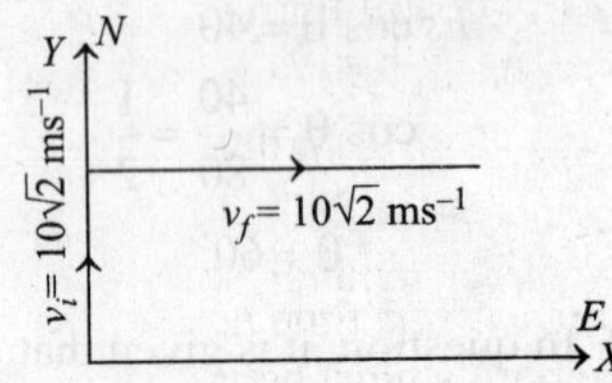

Final velocity, $\mathbf{v}_f = 10\sqrt{2}\ \hat{\mathbf{i}}$

$\therefore$ Change in velocity,

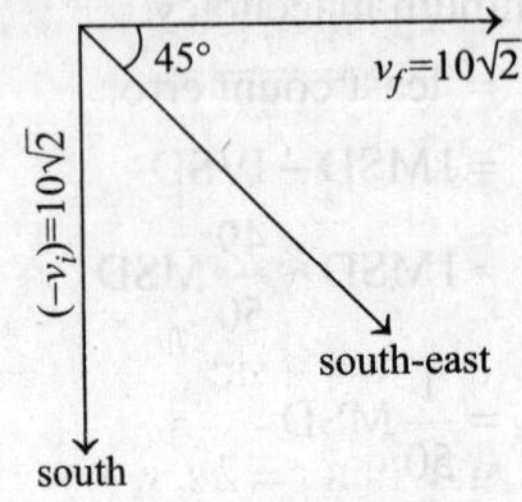

$$\Delta\mathbf{v} = \mathbf{v}_f - \mathbf{v}_i = 10\sqrt{2}\hat{\mathbf{i}} - 10\sqrt{2}\hat{\mathbf{j}}$$

$$= 10\sqrt{2}\ (\hat{\mathbf{i}} - \hat{\mathbf{j}})$$

$$\therefore\ |\Delta v| = 10\sqrt{2}\ \sqrt{1 + 1} = 20 \text{ m/s}$$

in south-east direction.

30. (d) Given, $A = 1.0 \text{ m} \pm 0.2 \text{ m}$, $B = 2.0 \text{ m} \pm 0.2 \text{ m}$

Let, $Y = \sqrt{AB} = \sqrt{(1.0)(2.0)} = 1.414$ m

Rounding off to two significant digits

$Y = 1.4$ m

$$\frac{\Delta Y}{Y} = \frac{1}{2}\left[\frac{\Delta A}{A} + \frac{\Delta B}{B}\right]$$

$$= \frac{1}{2}\left[\frac{0.2}{1.0} + \frac{0.2}{2.0}\right] = \frac{0.6}{2 \times 2.0}$$

$$\Rightarrow \quad \Delta Y = \frac{0.6Y}{2 \times 2.0}$$

$$= \frac{0.6 \times 1.4}{2 \times 2.0} = 0.212$$

Rounding off to one significant digit, $\Delta Y = 0.2$ m

Thus, correct value for $\sqrt{AB}$

$$= Y + \Delta Yr = 1.4 \text{ m} \pm 0.2 \text{ m}$$

31. (c) $\because\ \mathbf{v}_{AB} = \mathbf{v}_A - \mathbf{v}_B \quad \ldots(i)$

and $\mathbf{v}_{BC} = \mathbf{v}_B \quad \mathbf{v}_C \quad \ldots(ii)$

$\therefore\ \mathbf{v}_{CA} = \mathbf{v}_C - \mathbf{v}_A \quad \ldots(iii)$

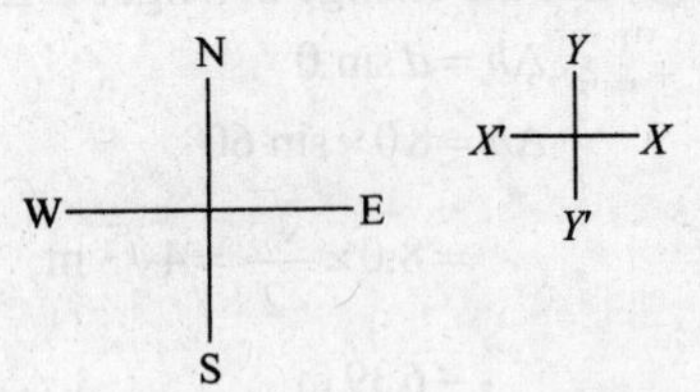

Adding Eqs. (i) and (ii), we get

$$\mathbf{v}_{AB} + \mathbf{v}_{BC} = \mathbf{v}_A - \mathbf{v}_C = \mathbf{v}_{AC}$$

$$\therefore \mathbf{v}_{CA} = -\mathbf{v}_{AC} = -(\mathbf{v}_{AB} + \mathbf{v}_{BC})$$

$$= (1\cos 45°\ \hat{\mathbf{i}} + 1\sin 45°\ \hat{\mathbf{j}})$$

$$+ (-1\cos 45°\ \hat{\mathbf{i}} + 1\sin 45°\ \hat{\mathbf{j}})$$

$$= -(2\sin 45°\ \hat{\mathbf{j}}) = -\sqrt{2}\ \hat{\mathbf{j}} \text{ ms}^{-1}$$

Therefore, the direction of velocity of boy C seen by boy A is $\sqrt{2}$ m/s towards south direction.

32. (c) Suppose $\mathbf{a} = a_1\hat{\mathbf{i}} + a_2\hat{\mathbf{j}} + a_3\hat{\mathbf{k}}$

Now, $(\hat{\mathbf{i}} \times \mathbf{a}) = a_2\hat{\mathbf{k}} - a_3\hat{\mathbf{j}}$

Now, $\hat{\mathbf{i}} \times (\hat{\mathbf{i}} \times \mathbf{a}) = -a_2\hat{\mathbf{j}} - a_3\hat{\mathbf{k}}$

Similarly, $\hat{\mathbf{j}} \times (\hat{\mathbf{j}} \times \mathbf{a}) = -a_1\hat{\mathbf{i}} - a_3\hat{\mathbf{k}}$

and $\hat{\mathbf{k}} \times (\hat{\mathbf{k}} \times \mathbf{a}) = -a_1\hat{\mathbf{i}} - a_2\hat{\mathbf{j}}$

$$\therefore \hat{\mathbf{i}}\ (\hat{\mathbf{i}} \times \mathbf{a}) + \hat{\mathbf{j}}\ (\hat{\mathbf{j}} \times \mathbf{a}) + \hat{\mathbf{k}}\ (\hat{\mathbf{k}} \times \mathbf{a})$$

$$= -2\,\mathbf{a}$$

33. (d) Linear acceleration due to $mg \sin\theta$ is downward. Hence, for pure rolling to continue, force of friction should act upwards, so that angular acceleration is anti-clockwise.

34. (d) By conservation of energy,

Initial total energy = Final total energy

$$(\text{TE})_i = (\text{TE})_f$$

$$\frac{1}{2}I\omega^2 = mgh$$

$\frac{1}{2} \times \frac{1}{3} ml^2 \omega^2 = mgh$

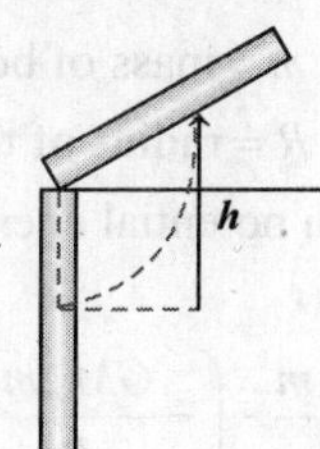

$\Rightarrow \quad h = \frac{1}{6} \frac{l^2 \omega^2}{g}$

35. (b) A.

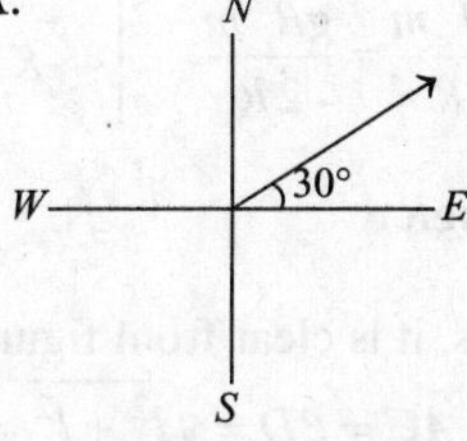

It represents a vector which is 30° north of east.

B.

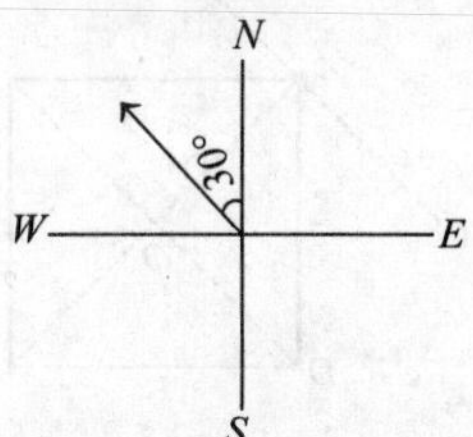

It represents a vector which is 30° west of north.

C.

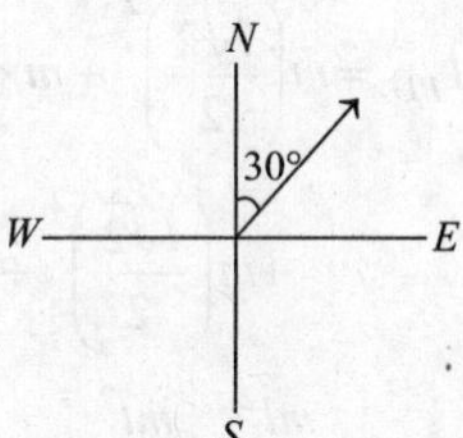

It represents a vector which is 30° east of north.

D.

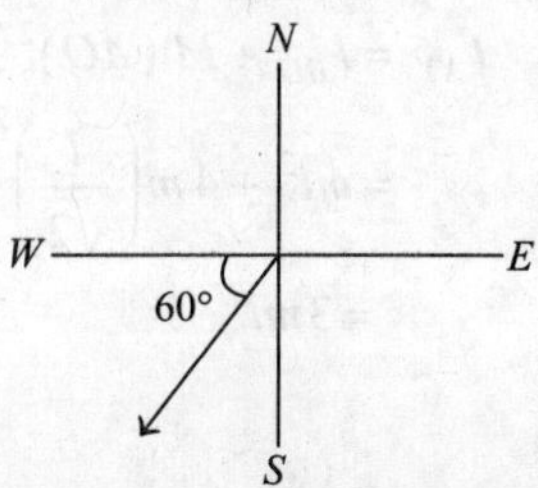

It represents a vector which is 60° south of west.

36. (c) The given situation is shown in the following figure

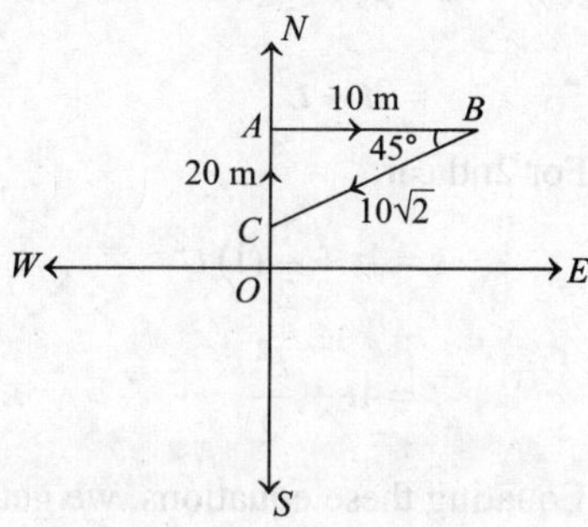

Here, **OA** represents 20 m north, **AB** represents 10 m east and **BC** represents $10\sqrt{2}$ m south-west.

Let $\hat{\mathbf{i}}$ and $\hat{\mathbf{j}}$ be the unit vectors along east and north directions respectively, then

$\mathbf{OA} = 20\hat{\mathbf{j}}$ m and $\mathbf{AB} = 10\hat{\mathbf{i}}$ m

$\mathbf{BC} = 10\sqrt{2} \sin 45° (-\hat{\mathbf{i}}) + 10\sqrt{2} \cos 45° (-\hat{\mathbf{j}})$

$\therefore \mathbf{OC} = 20\hat{\mathbf{j}} + 10\hat{\mathbf{i}} + 10(-\hat{\mathbf{i}}) + 10(-\hat{\mathbf{j}})$

$= 10\hat{\mathbf{j}}$

$|\mathbf{OC}| = 10$ m towards north.

37. (d) The resulting gravitational potential,

$V = -2G\left[\frac{1}{1} + \frac{1}{2} + \frac{1}{4} + \frac{1}{8} + \dots\right]$

$\Rightarrow V = -2G\left[1 + \frac{1}{2} + \frac{1}{2^2} + \frac{1}{2^3} \dots\right]$

$\Rightarrow V = -2G\left(1 - \frac{1}{2}\right)^{-1}$

$\Rightarrow \quad V = -\frac{2G}{1 - \frac{1}{2}}$

$= \frac{-2G}{\frac{1}{2}} = -4G$

$\therefore \quad x = 4$

38. (c) As 1 cal $= 4.2$ kg m^{2}s^{-2}

SI new system

$n_1 = 4.2 \qquad n_2 = ?$

$M_1 = 1\text{kg} \qquad M_2 = \alpha$ kg

$L_1 = 1\text{m} \qquad L_2 = \beta$ metre

$T_1 = 1\text{s} \qquad T_2 = \gamma$ second

Dimensional formula of energy is $[ML^2T^{-2}]$.

Comparing with $[M^a L^b T^c]$, we find out that $a = 1, b = 2, c = -2$

Now, $n_2 = n_1 \left[\frac{M_1}{M_2}\right]^a \left[\frac{L_1}{L_2}\right]^b \left[\frac{T_1}{T_2}\right]^c$

$= 4.2\left[\frac{1\text{ kg}}{\alpha\text{ kg}}\right]^1 \left[\frac{1\text{ m}}{\beta\text{ m}}\right]^2 \left[\frac{1\text{ s}}{\gamma\text{ s}}\right]^{-2}$

$= 4.2[\alpha^{-1} \beta^{-2} \gamma^2]$

$= \frac{42}{10}[\alpha^{-1} \beta^{-2} \gamma^2]$

$= \frac{p}{10}[\alpha^{-1} \beta^{-2} \gamma^q]$ (given)

$\therefore p = 42, q = 2$

$\therefore pq = 42 \times 2 = 84$

39. (c) Impulse = Area under F-t curve

$=$ Area of ΔABC

$= \frac{1}{2} \times OP \times AC$

$= \frac{1}{2} \times 18000 \times (2.5 - 1)$

$= 1.35 \times 10^4$ kg ms^{-1}

Average force $= \frac{\text{Impulse}}{\text{Time}}$

$= \frac{1.35 \times 10^4}{(2.5 - 1)} = 9000\text{ N}$

$= 9\text{ kN}$

40. (c) Let the height of the tower is h metre and ball takes t second to reach the ground when it falls freely.

$\therefore \quad h = \frac{1}{2} gt^2 \quad \dots(i)$

In last second, i.e. in t th second, ball travels $= 0.36\, h$

It means, in rest of time $(t - 1)$ s, ball travels a height

$= h - 0.36\, h = 0.64\, h$

Now, $0.64\, h = \frac{1}{2} g\, (t - 1)^2 \quad \dots(ii)$

Solving Eqs. (i) and (ii), we get $t = 5$ s and $h = 125$ m

41. (c) The free body diagram of 5 kg block is shown below.

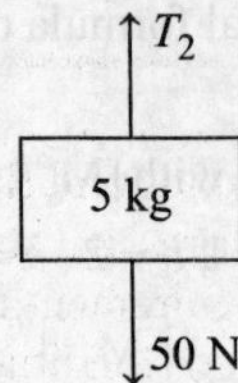

In equilibrium,

$$T_2 = 5\,g$$
$$= 5 \times 10 = 50\,N$$

⇒ Statement II is correct.

The free body diagram of the point P is shown as

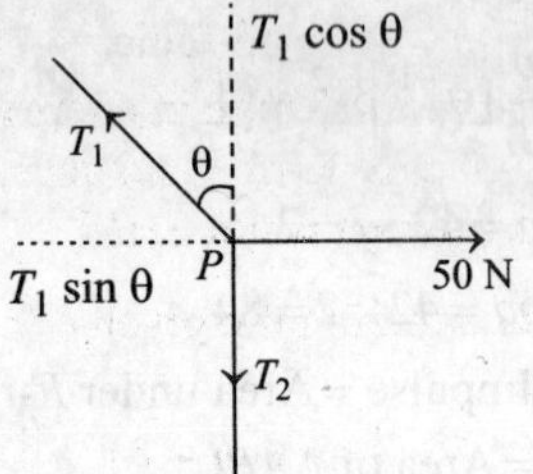

In equilibrium,

$$T_1 \sin\theta = 50\text{N} \quad \ldots\text{(i)}$$
$$\text{and } T_1 \cos\theta = T_2 = 50\,\text{N} \quad \ldots\text{(ii)}$$

Dividing Eq. (i) by Eq. (ii), we get

$$\tan\theta = 1$$
$$\Rightarrow \quad \theta = 45°$$

⇒ Statement IV is correct.

Now, from Eqn. (i),

$$T_1 \sin 45° = 50\text{N}$$
$$\Rightarrow T_1 \times \frac{1}{\sqrt{2}} = 50\text{N}$$
$$\Rightarrow \quad T_1 = 50\sqrt{2}\,\text{N}$$

Statement I is correct.

Hence, option (c) is correct.

42. (b) Both the cars reached at same position in time t.

Using 2nd equation of motion, i.e.

$$s = ut + \frac{1}{2}at^2$$

For 1st car,

$$s = 2t + \frac{1}{2}(2)t^2$$
$$= 2t + t^2 \quad \ldots\text{(i)}$$

For 2nd car,

$$s = 4t + \frac{1}{2}(1)t^2$$
$$= 4t + \frac{t^2}{2} \quad \ldots\text{(ii)}$$

Equating these equations, we get

$$4t + \frac{t^2}{2} = 2t + t^2$$
$$\Rightarrow \quad 2t = \frac{t^2}{2}$$
$$\Rightarrow \quad t = 4\text{ s}$$

Substituting value of t in Eq. (i), we get

$$s = 2(4) + (4)^2 = 24\text{ m}$$

43. (b) Given, $L = 100\,\text{m}$ and $s = 50\,\text{m}$

Work done by man,

$$mgL = mg\,(L - s) + mgs$$

Here, $mg\,(L - s)$ is the increase in potential energy of the man and mgs is the increase in potential energy of the balloon because the balloon would have been lifted up but for the climbing of the man.

$$\therefore \frac{\text{Increase in PE of man}}{\text{Increase in PE of balloon}} = \frac{mg\,(L - s)}{mgs} = \frac{L - s}{s}$$
$$= \frac{100 - 50}{50} = 2$$

44. (b) Gravitational potential energy of body on the earth's surface is

$$U = -\frac{GM_e m}{R}$$

At a height h from the earth's surface, its value is

$$U_h = -\frac{GM_e m}{(R + h)} = -\frac{GM_e m}{2R} \quad [\text{as } h = R]$$

where, M_e = mass of the earth,
m = mass of body
and R = radius of the earth.

∴ Gain in potential energy

$$= U_h - U$$
$$= -\frac{GM_e m}{2R} - \left(-\frac{GM_e m}{R}\right)$$
$$= -\frac{GM_e m}{2R} + \frac{GM_e m}{R}$$
$$= \frac{GM_e m}{2R} = \frac{gR^2 m}{2R} \quad \left[\text{as, } g = \frac{GM_e}{R^2}\right]$$
$$= \frac{1}{2}mgR$$

45. (b) As, it is clear from figure,

$$AC = BD = \sqrt{l^2 + l^2} = l\sqrt{2}$$

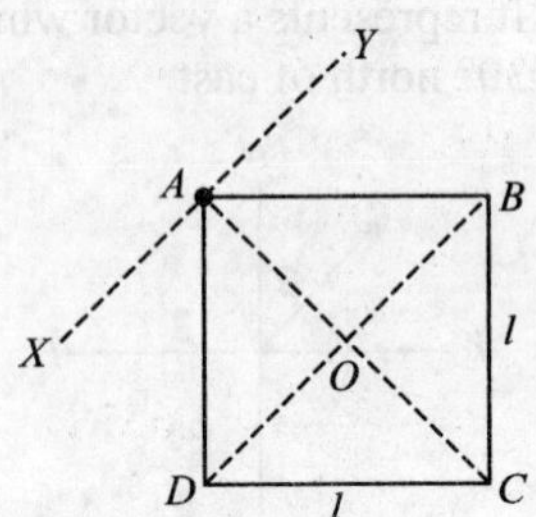

Moment of inertia of four point masses about BD,

$$I_{BD} = m\left(\frac{l\sqrt{2}}{2}\right)^2 + m \times 0 + m\left(\frac{l\sqrt{2}}{2}\right)^2 + m \times 0$$
$$= \frac{ml^2}{2} + \frac{ml^2}{2} = ml^2$$

Applying the theorem of parallel axes,

$$I_{XY} = I_{BD} + M\,(AO)^2$$
$$= ml^2 + 4\,m\left(\frac{l}{\sqrt{2}}\right)^2$$
$$= 3\,ml^2$$

SPT2 Syllabus Part Thru 2

1. (b) Fast processes are adiabatic.
Hence, $p_1V_1^\gamma = p_2V_2^\gamma$

$$\therefore\ p_2 = p_1\left(\frac{V_1}{V_2}\right)^\gamma = p\left(\frac{640}{80}\right)^{5/3}$$

$$= p(8)^{5/3} = 32p$$

2. (a) If $T_A > T_B$, i.e. body A is hotter than body B, then heat flows from A to B, i.e. from body at a higher temperature to body at a lower temperature till the temperature of both the bodies becomes same.
So, statements I and II are correct but III is incorrect.

3. (b) Using Boyle's law for constant temperature,

$$p_1V_1 = p_2V_2$$

$$\therefore\ V_2 = \frac{p_1V_1}{p_2}$$

$$= \frac{100\times 4}{150} = 2.667\ \text{L}$$

$\therefore$ Change in volume $= V_2 - V_1$
$= 2.667 - 4 = -1.333$ L

4. (b) The thermal stress in the rod $= Y\alpha\Delta\theta$
Thus, for same rise of temperature $(\Delta\theta)$, the thermal stress will be equal, if $Y_1\alpha_1 = Y_2\alpha_2$

or $\quad Y_1 : Y_2 = \alpha_2 : \alpha_1$

$\therefore\quad Y_1 : Y_2 = 3 : 2$

5. (c) According to Hooke's law, Modulus of elasticity,

$$E = \frac{F}{\pi r^2}\times\frac{l}{\Delta l}$$

$$\Rightarrow\ \Delta l = \frac{Fl}{\pi r^2 E}$$

$$\Rightarrow\ \Delta l \propto \frac{Fl}{r^2}$$

[$\because$ E is same for two wires]

$$\therefore\ \frac{\Delta l_1}{\Delta l_2} = \frac{F_1}{F_2}\times\frac{l_1}{l_2}\times\frac{r_2^2}{r_1^2}$$

$$= \frac{1}{4}\times\frac{2}{1}\times\left(\frac{3}{1}\right)^2 = \frac{9}{2}$$

6. (c) Slope, $\tan\theta = Y$
According to graph,

$$\theta_A > \theta_B > \theta_C$$

$$\Rightarrow\ \tan\theta_A > \tan\theta_B > \tan\theta_C$$

$$\Rightarrow Y_A > Y_B > Y_C$$

$\therefore$ A, B and C graphs are for steel, brass and rubber, respectively.

7. (c) When the pebble is falling through the viscous oil the viscous force is $\quad F = 6\pi\eta rv$
where r is radius of the pebble, v is instantaneous speed, η is coefficient of viscosity.
As the force is variable, hence acceleration is also variable, so v-t graph will not be straight line. First velocity increases and then becomes constant known as terminal velocity.

8. (c) Drag force,

$$F = \eta A\frac{dv}{dy} = \eta A\frac{v}{y}$$

$$= 15\times 2\times 10^4\times\frac{10}{0.25}$$

$$= 1.2\times 10^7\ \text{dyne}$$

9. (c) Let F be the weight on the original block. As, density is same for same object.
$\therefore$ New pressure $= \rho g\ (2H)$
$= 2(\rho gH) = 2p$

10. (c) Given, $r_1 = 4$ cm and $r_2 = 12$ cm
$F_1 = F$ and $F_2 = mg = 1400\times 10$N
According to Pascal's law,

$$F_1 = F_2\times\frac{r_1^2}{r_2^2}$$

$$= 14\times 10^3\times\left(\frac{4}{12}\right)^2$$

$$= 14\times 10^3\times\frac{1}{9} \simeq 1600\ \text{N}$$

11. (a) Since, solids and fluids can sustain compressive stress, which is the basic requirement for the propagation of longitudinal waves. Thus, these waves can be propagated through solids and fluids both.
So, both Statement I and Statement II are correct.

12. (b) Body collides elastically with walls of room. So, there will be no loss in its energy and it will remain colliding with walls of room, so its motion will be periodic.
There is no change in energy of the body, hence there is no acceleration, so its motion is not SHM.

13. (a) Comparing the given equation with

$$x = A\sin(\omega t + \delta)$$

$$A = 1.5\ \text{m},\ \omega = \frac{\pi}{4}\ \text{s}^{-1},$$

$$m = 2\ \text{kg} \qquad \text{(given)}$$

$\therefore$ Total energy is

$$E_r = \frac{1}{2}m\omega^2A^2$$

$$= \frac{1}{2}(2)\left(\frac{\pi}{4}\right)^2(1.5)^2$$

$$= 1.39\ \text{J}$$

14. (b) Velocity of transverse wave in the string, $v \propto \sqrt{T}$

$$\therefore\ \frac{v_1}{v_2} = \sqrt{\frac{T_1}{T_2}} = \sqrt{\frac{T_1}{3T_1}} \qquad [T_2 = 3T_1]$$

$$= \frac{1}{\sqrt{3}}$$

$$v_1 : v_2 = 1 : \sqrt{3}$$

15. (a) Node will occur, where

$$\frac{\pi x}{25} = \frac{\pi}{2}, \frac{3\pi}{2}, \frac{5\pi}{2}, \text{etc.}$$

or $x = 12.5$ cm, 37.5 cm, 62.5 cm, etc.

16. (d) For, 2 moles of Oxygen and 4 moles of Argon

$$\Delta U = 2C_{V_O}T + 4C_{V_{Ar}}T$$

$$= 2T\,(C_{V_O} + 2C_{V_{Ar}})$$

$$= 2T\left[\frac{R}{2/5} + 2\times\frac{R}{2/3}\right]$$

$$= 2TR\left[\frac{5+6}{2}\right] = 11\,RT$$

17. (c) A is true but R is false.
When a spring balance is used for a long time, it develops an elastic fatigue, the spring of such a balance takes longer time to recover its original configuration and therefore, it does not give correct measurement.

18. (d) Heat added to system is given by

$$\Delta Q = \Delta U + \Delta W$$

Here, $\Delta Q = 20\text{ cal} \simeq 84\text{ J}$

and $\Delta W = 50\text{ J}$

$\Rightarrow \Delta U = 84 - 50 = 34\text{ J}$

19. (c) The particle velocity is maximum at B and is given by

$$\frac{dy}{dt} = (v_p)_{max} = \omega A$$

Also wave velocity is $\frac{dx}{dt} = v = \frac{\omega}{k}$

So, slope $\frac{dy}{dx} = \frac{(v_p)_{max}}{v} = kA$

20. (b) Increase in internal energy,

$$\Delta U = \mu C_V\,\Delta T = \mu\left(\frac{R}{\gamma - 1}\right)\Delta T$$

$$\Rightarrow \Delta U = \frac{p\Delta V}{\gamma - 1} = \frac{p\,(2V - V)}{\gamma - 1} = \frac{pV}{\gamma - 1}$$

As, $pV = nRT = 2RT \quad [\because n = 2]$

$$\therefore\ \Delta U = \frac{2RT}{\gamma - 1}$$

21. (c) The stress-strain curves vary from material to material. These curves help us to understand how a given material deforms with increasing loads. Rubber is an elastomer.
It shows a permanent increase in its length after pulling several times of its length. Thus, it does not regain its original shape completely.

22. (b) According to Hooke's law, stress is found proportional to strain in the given curve upto point A, which is known as point of proportional limit.
Material in this region OA shows the elastic behaviour (material regains its original dimension only when load applied is less than or equal to certain elastic limit).

23. (a) The height of water in the tank becomes maximum when the volume of water flowing into the tank per second becomes equal to the volume flowing out per second.
Volume of water flowing out per second

$$= Av = A\sqrt{2gh} \qquad [\because v = 2gh]$$

Given that,
volume of water flowing per second

$$= 70\text{ cm}^3\text{ s}^{-1}$$

$$\Rightarrow \quad A\sqrt{2gh} = 70$$

$$\Rightarrow 1\times\sqrt{2\times 980\times h} = 70$$

$$\Rightarrow \quad 2\times 980\times h = 4900$$

$$\Rightarrow h = \frac{4900}{1960} \Rightarrow h = 2.5\text{ cm}$$

24. (a) Comparing the given equation with the standard equation of wave motion $y = A\sin\left(2\pi ft - \frac{2\pi}{\lambda}x\right)$ where A, f and λ are amplitude, frequency and wavelength, respectively.
Thus, amplitude $A = 5\text{ cm}$, $2\pi f = 4$

$\Rightarrow$ Frequency, $f = \frac{4}{2\pi} = 0.637\text{ Hz}$

Again, $\frac{2\pi}{\lambda} = 0.02$

or wavelength, $\lambda = \frac{2\pi}{0.02} = 100\,\pi\text{ cm}$

Velocity of the wave

$$v = f\lambda = \frac{4}{2\pi}\times\frac{2\pi}{0.02} = 200\text{ cms}^{-1}$$

25. (b) Given,
Number of degree of freedom, $f = 5$

As we know, $C_p = \left(1 + \frac{f}{2}\right)R$

$$C_p = \left(1 + \frac{5}{2}\right)8.31\text{ J mol}^{-1}\text{ K}^{-1}$$

Solving, we get

$$C_p = 29.08 \simeq 29\text{ J mol}^{-1}\text{ K}^{-1}$$

26. (a) When volume of the gas is kept constant and heat is required only for raising the temperature of one gram mole of the gas through 1°C or 1 K, no heat is spent in expansion of the gas. In case when pressure of the gas is kept constant, the gas would expand on heating. Therefore, some heat is spent in expansion of the gas against external pressure. This is in addition to the amount of heat energy required for raising the temperature of one gram mole of the gas through 1°C. Hence, specific heat at constant pressure is greater than the specific heat at constant volume.

27. (a) As, $p = \frac{a}{1 + \left(\frac{V}{b}\right)^2} = \frac{RT}{V}$

When $V = b$,

$$\frac{a}{1 + (1)^2} = \frac{RT}{b} \Rightarrow T = \frac{ab}{2R}$$

28. (b) V_{avg} at 27°C, 300 K for helium atom is 1.4 km-s^{-1}.
So, a significant fraction of He molecules have speeds greater than 11.2 km-s^{-1}.
So, Statement I and Statement II are correct.

29. (d) Ideal gas equation,

$$pV = \mu RT = \left(\frac{N}{N_A}\right)RT$$

where, N = Number of molecule,
N_A = Avogadro number

$$\therefore \quad \frac{N_1}{N_2} = \left(\frac{p_1}{p_2}\right)\left(\frac{V_1}{V_2}\right)\left(\frac{T_2}{T_1}\right)$$

$$= \left(\frac{p}{2p}\right)\left(\frac{V}{\frac{V}{4}}\right)\left(\frac{2T}{T}\right) = \frac{4}{1}$$

Thus, the ratio of number of molecules in jar A and B is 4 : 1.

30. (a) Strain = fractional change in length

$$= \frac{\Delta l}{l} = \frac{l\alpha t}{l}$$

$$= \alpha t = 12\times 10^{-6}\times 30$$

$$= 36\times 10^{-5}$$

31. (d) Given, $y = a\sin\omega t + b\cos\omega t$

Let $a = A\cos\theta$ and $b = A\sin\theta$

Then,

$y = A\cos\theta.\sin\omega t + A\sin\theta.\cos\omega t$

$y = A\sin(\omega t + \phi)$

which is in the form of SHM.

From Eq. (i)

$a^2 + b^2 = A^2\cos^2\theta + A^2\sin^2\theta$

$\Rightarrow \quad A = \sqrt{a^2 + b^2}$

32. (b) From Bernoulli's principle

$$p_1 + \frac{1}{2}\rho v_1^2 = p_2 + \frac{1}{2}\rho v_2^2$$

$$p_1 - p_2 = \frac{1}{2}\rho(v_2^2 - v_1^2) \quad \ldots(i)$$

$$mg = (p_1 - p_2)2A$$

$$= \frac{1}{2}\rho(2A)(v_2^2 - v_1^2) \text{ [from Eq. (i)]}$$

$$= \frac{1}{2}\times 1\times 2\times 10\times(80^2 - 70^2)$$

$mg = 10\times 1500$

$\therefore m = 1500\,\text{kg}$

33. (a) Using formula for C_V of a mixture of two gases, we have

$\Rightarrow (C_V)_{\text{mix}}$

$$= \frac{n_A(C_V)_A + n_B(C_V)_B}{n_A + n_B}$$

$$\Rightarrow \frac{13}{6}R = \frac{1\times\frac{3}{2}R + n_B\times\frac{5}{2}R}{1 + n_B}$$

$\Rightarrow 13 + 13n_B = 9 + 15n_B$

$\Rightarrow n_B = 2\,\text{g-mol}$

34. (d) Here, $A = 0.06$ m

Also, $\frac{5\lambda}{2} = 0.025\text{ m} \Rightarrow \lambda = 0.01$ m

Now, standard equation of wave

$$Y = A\sin\frac{2\pi}{\lambda}(vt - x)$$

$$= 0.06\sin 2\pi(33000t - 100x)$$

35. (a) Here, $a = 1\text{ cm} = 0.01$ m. The mass will remain in contact with surface, if $mg = m\omega^2 a$

or $\quad \omega = \sqrt{g/a}$

or $\quad 2\pi v = \sqrt{g/a}$

or $\quad v = \frac{1}{2\pi}\sqrt{\frac{g}{a}} = \frac{7}{2\times 22}\sqrt{\frac{980}{1}}$

$= 4.9\text{ Hz} \approx 5\text{ Hz}$

36. (b) We know that,

$$h = \frac{2T}{r\rho g} = \frac{2\times 75\times 10^{-3}}{0.25\times 10^{-3}\times 10^3\times 10}$$

$= 6\times 10^{-2}$ m

$= 60\times 10^{-3}$ m

$= 60$ mm

Since, $h_1 r_1 = h_2 r_2$

$$\Rightarrow \quad r_2 = \frac{h_1 r_1}{h_2} \quad [\because h_1 = h = 60\text{mm}]$$

$$= \frac{60\times 0.25}{25} = 0.6\text{ mm}$$

37. (c) Given, $m = 4$ kg

$x = 10\text{ cm} = 0.1$ m

$F = 25$ N

As we know, the magnitude of spring force

$F = kx$

$25\text{ N} = k(0.1\text{ m})$

$\Rightarrow \quad k = 250$ N/m

Now, time period of the oscillation,

$$T = 2\pi\sqrt{\frac{m}{k}}$$

$$\Rightarrow \quad T = 2\pi\sqrt{\frac{4}{250}} = 0.8$$

Time period, $T = 0.8$ s

38. (a) Cycle is clockwise. Hence, heat will be given to the gas, as work done will be positive.

$Q = W =$ Area of triangle

$= \frac{1}{2}\times 2\times 1 = 1$ J

39. (c) Outside pressure = 1 atm

Pressure inside first bubble

= 1.01 atm

Pressure inside second bubble

= 1.02 atm

Excess pressure,

$\Delta p_1 = 1.01 - 1 = 0.01$ atm

Excess pressure,

$\Delta p_2 = 1.02 - 1 = 0.02$ atm

$$\Delta p \propto \frac{1}{r}$$

$$\Rightarrow \quad r \propto \frac{1}{\Delta p}$$

$$\Rightarrow \quad \frac{r_1}{r_2} = \frac{\Delta p_2}{\Delta p_1} = \frac{0.02}{0.01} = \frac{2}{1}$$

Since, $V = \frac{4}{3}\pi r^3$

$$\therefore \quad \frac{V_1}{V_2} = \left(\frac{r_1}{r_2}\right)^3 = \left(\frac{2}{1}\right)^3 = \frac{8}{1}$$

40. (d) A diatomic molecule has 5 degrees of freedom due to translational and rotational motion. It will have 2 more degrees of freedom due to vibrational motion at a very high temperature i.e., beyond 5000 K.

So, total degrees of freedom $f = 7$

Internal energy of 1 mole of this gas

$$U = \frac{7}{2}RT$$

Molar specific heat at constant volume,

$$C_V = \frac{dU}{dT} = \frac{7}{2}R$$

Molar specific heat at constant pressure,

$$C_p = C_V + R = \frac{9}{2}R$$

Diatomic gas constant,

$$\gamma = \frac{C_p}{C_V} = \frac{9}{7}$$

41. (d) $R_A = \frac{10}{3KA} \quad \left(\because R = \frac{l}{KA}\right)$

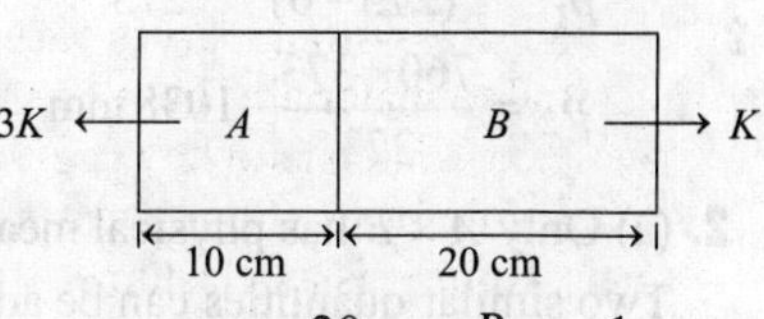

$$R_B = \frac{20}{KA} \Rightarrow \frac{R_A}{R_B} = \frac{1}{6}$$

So, let $R_A = R$, then $R_B = 6R$

Heat current,

$$H = \frac{\text{Temperature difference}}{\text{Total resistance}}$$

$$= \frac{35}{7R} = \frac{5}{R}$$

Now, temperature difference across A

$$= H \times R_A = \frac{5}{R} \times R = 5°C$$

42. (b) In steady state, the amount of heat flowing from one face to the other face in time t is given by

$Q = \dfrac{kA(\theta_1 - \theta_2)t}{l}$, where k is coefficient of thermal conductivity of material of rod

$$\Rightarrow \quad Q \propto \frac{A}{l} \propto \frac{r^2}{l} \quad \ldots(i)$$

As the metallic rod is melted and the material is formed into a rod of half the radius

$$V_1 = V_2$$

$$\Rightarrow \quad \pi r_1^2 l_1 = \pi r_2^2 l_2$$

$$\Rightarrow \quad l_1 = \frac{l_2}{4} \quad \ldots(ii)$$

Now, from Eqs. (i) and (ii), we get

$$\frac{Q_1}{Q_2} = \frac{r_1^2}{l_1} \times \frac{l_2}{r_2^2}$$

$$= \frac{r_1^2}{l_1} \times \frac{4 l_1}{(r_1/2)^2}$$

$$\Rightarrow \quad Q_1 = 16 Q_2 \Rightarrow Q_2 = \frac{Q}{16}$$

43. (d) Let initial temperature in Fahrenheit and Celsius scales be F_1 and C_1, respectively and the final temperature be F_2 and C_2, respectively.

From relation,

$$\frac{F - 32}{180} = \frac{C}{100}$$

$$\text{or} \quad \frac{F_1 - 32}{180} = \frac{C_1}{100} \quad \ldots(i)$$

$$\text{or} \quad \frac{F_2 - 32}{180} = \frac{C_2}{100} \quad \ldots(ii)$$

Subtracting Eq. (i) from Eq. (ii), we get

$$\frac{F_2 - 32 - F_1 + 32}{180} = \frac{C_2 - C_1}{100}$$

$$\frac{F_2 - F_1}{180} = \frac{C_2 - C_1}{100}$$

Given, $C_2 - C_1 = 30°C$

$$\Rightarrow F_2 - F_1 = \frac{180}{100} \times 30° \text{ C} = 54° \text{F}$$

$\therefore$ The increase in temperature on Fahrenheit scale is 54°.

44. (d) As, $\dfrac{C - 0}{200 - 0} = \dfrac{N - 200}{800 - 200} \quad \ldots(i)$

If $C = N = x$, then substituting value in Eq. (i), we get

$$\frac{x}{200} = \frac{x - 200}{600}$$

$$x = \frac{x - 200}{3}$$

$$3x = x - 200$$

$$2x = -200$$

$$x = -100°C$$

45. (b) Two springs, each of spring constant k_1 in parallel, give equivalent spring constant of $2k_1$ and this is in series with another spring of spring constant k_2, so equivalent spring constant

$$k = \left(\frac{1}{k_2} + \frac{1}{2k_1}\right)^{-1}$$

NSS1 NEET Stepping Stones 1

1. (d) We know that, $pV = nRT$

$$\Rightarrow \quad p \propto T \Rightarrow \frac{p_2}{p_1} = \frac{T_2}{T_1}$$

$$\frac{p_2}{p_1} = \frac{(273 + 100)}{(273 + 0)} = \frac{373}{273}$$

$$p_2 = \frac{760 \times 373}{273} \simeq 1038 \text{ mm}$$

2. (a) Only $A \times B$ has physical meaning. Two similar quantities can be added or subtracted.

3. (c) Substituting $C_p - C_V = R$ and checking, we have

$$\frac{C_p - R}{C_V + R} = \frac{\frac{\gamma R}{\gamma - 1} - R}{\frac{R}{\gamma - 1} + R}$$

$$= \frac{R\left(\frac{\gamma}{\gamma - 1} - 1\right)}{R\left(\frac{1}{\gamma - 1} + 1\right)} = \frac{\gamma - (\gamma - 1)}{1 + (\gamma - 1)}$$

$$= \frac{\gamma - \gamma + 1}{\gamma}$$

$$\frac{C_p - R}{C_V + R} = \frac{1}{\gamma}$$

So, option (c) is incorrect and options (a), (b) and (d) are correct.

4. (c) $pT^2 = \text{constant } (C)$

$$\Rightarrow \quad \frac{nRT}{V} \cdot T^2 = C \Rightarrow T^3 \cdot V^{-1} = C'$$

Differentiating, we get

$$\Rightarrow \quad \frac{3T^2}{V} \cdot dT - \frac{T^3}{V^2} \cdot dV = 0$$

$$\Rightarrow \quad 3dT = \frac{T}{V} dV$$

$$\text{or} \quad dV = \frac{3}{T} \cdot V \cdot dT$$

Comparing with $dV = V \cdot \gamma \, dT$, we get coefficient of volumetric expansion,

$$\gamma = \frac{3}{T}$$

5. (b) When temperature of the material is increased, then due to the weakening of inter-molecular forces, the elastic properties in general decrease, it means elastic constant decreases.

6. (c) Horizontal distance travelled by frog will be maximum, if it makes a jump at angle, $\theta = 45°$. For maximum range,

$$R_{max} = \frac{u^2}{g} \quad \dots \text{(i)}$$

∴ From Eq. (i),

$$0.3 = \frac{u^2}{10}$$

or $u = \sqrt{3}$ m/s

Horizontal component of velocity of frog, $u_x = u\cos\theta$

$$= \sqrt{3}\cos 45^\circ = \sqrt{\frac{3}{2}} \text{ m/s}$$

Total distance covered by it in 10 s,

$$x = u_x t = \sqrt{\frac{3}{2}} \times 10$$

$$= 1.224 \times 10$$

$$= 12.24 \text{ m}$$

7. (c) Statement I is correct and Statement II is incorrect.
There is no zero graviational potential point between the moon and the earth as gravitational potentials of moon and earth always have negative signs.

8. (d) Tangential acceleration is the rate of change of magnitude of velocity,

i.e. $a_t = \dfrac{d|\mathbf{v}|}{dt}$

Now, $\mathbf{v} = 4t\hat{\mathbf{i}} + t^2\hat{\mathbf{j}}$

$$|\mathbf{v}| = \sqrt{(4t)^2 + (t^2)^2}$$

$$= \sqrt{16t^2 + t^4}$$

$$a_t = \frac{d}{dt}(\sqrt{16t^2 + t^4})$$

$$\Rightarrow \quad a_t = \frac{1}{2\sqrt{16t^2 + t^4}}(32t + 4t^3)$$

At $t = 2$s,

$$a_t = \frac{32(2) + 4(2)^3}{2\sqrt{16(2)^2 + (2)^4}} = \frac{12}{\sqrt{5}} \text{ m/s}^2$$

9. (b) As two solid spheres are equal in masses, so

$$m_A = m_B$$

$$\Rightarrow \frac{4}{3}\pi R_A^3 \rho_A = \frac{4}{3}\pi R_B^3 \rho_B$$

$$\Rightarrow \quad \frac{R_A}{R_B} = \left(\frac{\rho_B}{\rho_A}\right)^{1/3}$$

The moment of inertia of a solid sphere about diameter,

$$I = \frac{2}{5}mR^2$$

$$\Rightarrow \frac{I_A}{I_B} = \left(\frac{R_A}{R_B}\right)^2 \quad (\text{as } m_A = m_B)$$

$$\therefore \quad \frac{I_A}{I_B} = \left(\frac{\rho_B}{\rho_A}\right)^{2/3}$$

$$\Rightarrow \quad \frac{I_B}{I_A} = \left(\frac{\rho_A}{\rho_B}\right)^{2/3}$$

10. (a) Graph (I) represents the one-dimensional motion because total distance covered by a particle always increases with time.
Graphs (II) and (III) do not represent the one-dimensional motion, because at a particular time, there cannot be two values of position or velocity.
Graph (IV) is not possible, because speed can never be negative.
In graphs III and IV, velocity and speed are ploted for negative time, which is not possible.

11. (a) Given, $\omega = 0$, $\omega_0 = 100 \text{ rev min}^{-1}$
and $t = 15$ s
From equation of angular motion,

$$0 = \omega_0 - \alpha t$$

$$\Rightarrow \quad \alpha = \frac{\omega_0}{t}$$

$$= \frac{(100 \times 2\pi)/60}{15}$$

$$= 0.69 \text{ rad s}^{-2}$$

$$\simeq 0.7 \text{ rad s}^{-2}$$

Now, angle rotated before coming to rest is given by

$$\theta = \frac{\omega_0^2}{2\alpha} = \frac{\left(\frac{100 \times 2\pi}{60}\right)^2}{2 \times 0.7}$$

$$(\because \omega^2 = \omega_0^2 - 2\alpha\theta)$$

$$= 78.25 \text{ rad}$$

∴ Number of revolutions $= \dfrac{\theta}{2\pi} = 12.5$

12. (a) Pressure at the bottom of tank,

$$p = h\rho g = 3 \times 10^5 \text{ N/m}^2$$

Pressure due to liquid column,

$$p_1 = p - p_0$$

$$= 3 \times 10^5 - 1 \times 10 = 2 \times 10^5$$

and velocity of water, $v = \sqrt{2gh}$

$$v = \sqrt{\frac{2p_1}{\rho}} = \sqrt{\frac{2 \times 2 \times 10^5}{10^3}}$$

$$v = \sqrt{400} \text{ m/s}$$

13. (d) A gas molecule escapes atmosphere of a planet when its rms speed exceeds escape speed.
In critical condition, $v_{rms} = v_{escape}$

or $\sqrt{\dfrac{3kT}{m}} = \sqrt{2gR_e}$

$$\Rightarrow \quad T = \frac{2gR_e m}{3k}$$

$$\Rightarrow \quad T = \frac{2 \times 9.8 \times 6.4 \times 10^6 \times 0.34 \times 10^{-26}}{3(1.38 \times 10^{-23})}$$

$$= 10.30 \times 10^3 \simeq 10^4 \text{ K}$$

Therefore, 10^4 K is the temperature at which hydrogen molecules will escape from the earth's surface.

14. (c) $C_V = \dfrac{f}{2}R$, $C_p = \left(\dfrac{f}{2} + 1\right)R$

For mono-atomic, $f = 3$

$$C_V = \frac{3}{2}R, C_p = \left(\frac{3}{2} + 1\right)R = \frac{5}{2}R$$

From, $C_p - C_V = R$

$$\frac{5}{2}R - \frac{3}{2}R = R$$

$$r = \frac{C_p}{C_V} = \frac{\frac{5}{2}}{\frac{3}{2}} = \frac{5}{3}$$

15. (c) Work done = Change in KE

$$= \frac{1}{2}m(v^2 - u^2)$$

$$= \frac{1}{2} \times 0.5 \times 25 \times 8$$

$$= 50 \text{ J}$$

16. (b) Translational degree of freedom of a diatomic gas (O_2) is three and rotational kinetic energy is two.
Therefore, according to law of equipartition of energy, $\dfrac{K_T}{K_R} = \dfrac{3}{2}$
Further, intermolecular force between ideal gas molecules is zero. Hence, potential energy is zero.

17. (c) Here, work done by a car,

i.e. $W_g = mgh$

$$= 1400 \times 10 \times 10$$

$$= 140000 \text{ J}$$

Speed of car = 54 kmph

$$= 54 \times \frac{5}{18}$$
$$= 15\, ms^{-1}$$

Work done = Total KE − Total PE

$$= \frac{1}{2}mv^2 - mgh$$
$$= \frac{1}{2} \times 1400 \times (15)^2 - 1400 \times 10 \times 10$$
$$= 157500 - 140000$$
$$= 17500 = 17.5\, kJ$$

18. (c) $B = \dfrac{dp}{\left(\dfrac{dV}{V}\right)}$

$\therefore \quad B = \dfrac{\dfrac{mg}{A}}{\dfrac{dV}{V}}$

$\Rightarrow \quad \dfrac{dV}{V} = \dfrac{mg}{AB}$ ... (i)

For a sphere, $V = \dfrac{4\pi R^3}{3}$

$\Rightarrow \quad dV = \dfrac{4\pi}{3}(3R^2 dR)$

$\Rightarrow \quad \dfrac{dV}{V} = \dfrac{3dR}{R}$ ... (ii)

From Eqs. (i) and (ii),

$$\frac{dR}{R} = \frac{mg}{3AB}$$

19 (c) Time period, $T = 2\pi\sqrt{\dfrac{l}{g}}$

$\therefore \quad \dfrac{\Delta T}{T} = \dfrac{1}{2}\dfrac{\Delta l}{l}$

Error in time period in one day

$\Rightarrow \quad \Delta T = \dfrac{1}{2} \times \dfrac{0.1}{100} \times 24 \times 3600$

$= \dfrac{1}{2} \times \dfrac{0.1}{100} \times 86400$

$\Rightarrow \Delta T = 43.2\, s$

20. (d) Magnitude of velocity of particle when it is at displacement x from mean position,

$$v = \omega\sqrt{(A^2 - x^2)}$$

Also, magnitude of acceleration of particle in SHM,

$$a = \omega^2 x$$

Given, when $x = 2\,cm$

$$v = a$$
$$\omega\sqrt{A^2 - x^2} = \omega^2 x$$
$$\omega = \frac{\sqrt{A^2 - x^2}}{x}$$

[$\because$ Given, $A = 4\,cm$]

$$\omega = \frac{\sqrt{16-4}}{2} = \sqrt{3}$$

$\therefore$ Time period of motion,

$$T = \frac{2\pi}{\omega} = \frac{2\pi}{\sqrt{3}}$$
$$T = \frac{2\pi}{\sqrt{3}}$$

21. (a) The dimension of LHS of each relation is [L].

(i) Dimension of RHS

$= [L] \sin [LT^{-1}][T]$

$= [L] \sin [L]$

As angle is not dimensionless here. Therefore, this formula is wrong.

(ii) Dimension of

$\text{RHS} = \dfrac{[L]}{[T]} \sin \dfrac{[T]}{[L]}$

$= [LT^{-1}] \sin [TL^{-1}]$

As angle is not dimensionless here, therefore this formula is wrong.

(iii) Dimension of

$\text{RHS} = [L]\left[\sin \dfrac{[T]}{[T]} + \cos \dfrac{[T]}{[T]}\right] = [L]$

As angle is dimensionless and dimension of RHS is equal to the dimension of LHS, therefore this formula is correct.

(iv) Dimension of RHS

$= [L] \sin \dfrac{[T]}{[T]} = [L]$

Its angle is dimensionless and dimension of RHS is equal to dimension of LHS.

22. (a) Let the final temperature of mixture be T°C.

Heat lost by water,

$$H_1 = 19 \times 1(30 - T)$$
$$= 570 - 19T$$

Heat taken by ice,

$$H_2 = ms_i \Delta T + ms_w T$$
$$H_2 = 5 \times 0.5 \times 20 + 5 \times 80 + 5T$$

Using principle of calorimetry

$$H_1 = H_2$$

$\Rightarrow 5 \times (0.5)\, 20 + 5 \times 80 + 5T = 570 - 19T$

$\Rightarrow \quad 24T = 570 - 450 = 120$

$\Rightarrow \quad T = 5°C$

23. (b) As, root mean square speed of gas molecule is

$$v_{rms} = \sqrt{\frac{3k_b T}{m}}$$

or $\quad v_{rms} \propto \sqrt{T}$

v_{rms} is to reduce two times, i.e. the temperature of the gas will have to reduce four times or

$$\frac{T'}{T} = \left(\frac{v'_{rms}}{v_{rms}}\right)^2 = \frac{1}{4}$$

During adiabatic process,

$$TV^{\gamma-1} = T'V'^{\gamma-1}$$
$$\frac{V'}{V} = 4^{\frac{1}{1.5-1}}$$
$$\frac{V'}{V} = 4^2$$
$$V' = 16V$$

24. (c) Let initial velocity of bullet $= u$

Final velocity of bullet $= \dfrac{u}{3}$

Distance travelled by bullet, $s = 4\,cm$

Using $v^2 - u^2 = 2as$

$$\left(\frac{u}{3}\right)^2 = u^2 - 2a(4)$$

$\Rightarrow \quad a = \dfrac{8u^2}{9(8)} = \dfrac{u^2}{9}$

By equation of motion,

$v^2 - u^2 = 2as$ [put $s = 4 + x$, $a = \dfrac{u^2}{9}$]

$\Rightarrow \quad u^2 = 2\left[\dfrac{u^2}{9}\right](4 + x) \quad [\because v = 0]$

$\Rightarrow \quad x = 0.5\, m$

25. (d) Let the angle made by the instantaneous velocity with the horizontal be α. Then,

$$\tan \alpha = \frac{v_y}{v_x} = \frac{u \sin \theta - g}{u \cos \theta}$$

Given, $\alpha = 45°$ when $t = 1\,s$

$$\tan 45° = \frac{u \sin \theta - gt}{u \cos \theta}$$

$\Rightarrow u\cos\theta = u\sin\theta - g$ ... (i)

$\alpha = 0°$ when $t = 2$ s

$$\tan 0° = \frac{u\sin\theta - gt}{u\cos\theta}$$

$\Rightarrow u\sin\theta - 2g = 0$ ... (ii)

On solving Eqs. (i) and (ii), we have

$u\sin\theta = 2g$

$\Rightarrow u\cos\theta = g$

Squaring and adding

$\Rightarrow u = \sqrt{5}g = 10\sqrt{5}\ \text{ms}^{-1}$

26. (b) Given, condition, $h_1 = h_2$

For projectile maximum height attained,

$$h = \frac{u^2\sin^2\theta}{2g}$$

$$u_1^2\sin^2 45° = u_2^2\sin^2\theta$$

$$\sin^2\theta = \frac{u_1^2}{u_2^2}\sin^2 45°$$

$$\sin^2\theta = \frac{1}{2}\cdot\frac{1}{2} = \frac{1}{4} \quad \left[\because \text{Given}, \frac{u_1}{u_2} = \frac{1}{\sqrt{2}}\right]$$

$$\sin\theta = \frac{1}{2}$$

$$\theta = 30°$$

So, angle of projection of B will be 30°.

27. (a) The solution of this question can be understood by plotting a p-V graph for the compression of a gas isothermally and adiabatically simultaneously to half of its initial volume, i.e.

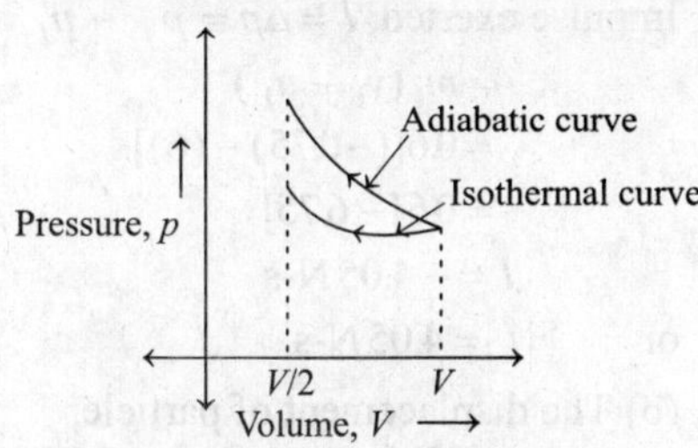

Since, the isothermal curve is less steeper than the adiabatic curve. So, area under the (p-V) curve for adiabatic process has more magnitude than isothermal curve. Hence, work done in adiabatic process will be more than in isothermal process.

28. (a) Least KE is at maximum height.

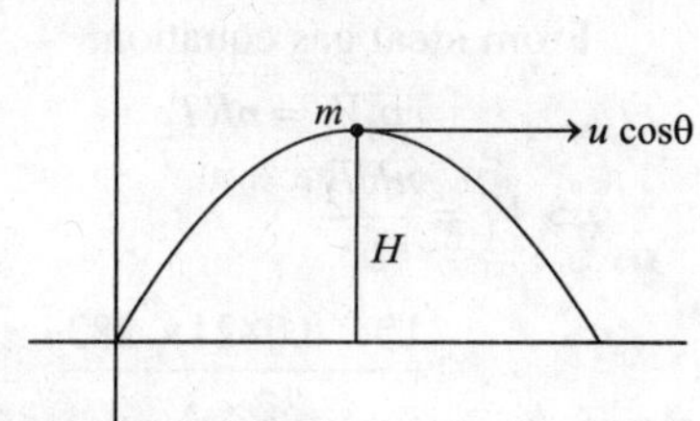

$\therefore$ Angular momentum is

$$\mathbf{L} = \mathbf{r}\times\mathbf{p}$$

$$= m(u\cos\theta)H$$

$$= mu\cos\theta\cdot\frac{u^2\sin^2\theta}{2g}$$

$$= 0.865\times10^{-3}$$

$$\simeq 0.9\times10^{-3}\ \text{kg m}^2\text{s}^{-1}$$

29. (b) Speed of conveyor belt, $u = 2$ m/s

$\mu = 0.4$

Acceleration of bag due to slipping motion, $a = \mu g = 0.4\times10 = 4\ \text{m/s}^2$

$(\because g = 10\ \text{m/s}^2)$

If s be the distance travelled by the bag on the belt during slipping motion, then $v^2 = u^2 - 2as$

$\Rightarrow 0 = u^2 - 2as$

$$\Rightarrow s = \frac{u^2}{2a} = \frac{2^2}{2\times4} = 0.5\ \text{m}$$

30. (b) Let, thickness of layer be x.

So, volume, V = Area × x

$V = A\times x$ $\quad(\because x = 2r)$

$$\Rightarrow 2r = \frac{V}{A}$$

$$\Rightarrow r = \frac{V}{2A} \quad \text{... (i)}$$

And $\Delta p = \dfrac{T}{r}$

We know that,

$$F = \Delta p\times A = \frac{T}{r}\times A$$

$$F = \frac{T}{\left(\frac{V}{2A}\right)}\times A \quad \text{[from Eq. (i)]}$$

$$T = \frac{F\times V}{2A^2}$$

where, $F = 16\times10^5$ dyne,

$V = 0.04\ \text{cm}^3$,

$A = 20\ \text{cm}^2$

$$\Rightarrow T = \frac{16\times10^5\times0.04}{2\times20^2}$$

$$= 80\ \text{dyne/cm}$$

31. (d) Statement I is valid only when increase in KE is small. Statement II is correct.

32. (c) Given, $F = 125$ N

$$F = \frac{dp}{dt}$$

$p = nmv$

(n = number of bullets fired)

$$F = \frac{d}{dt}(nmv) = mv\frac{dn}{dt}$$

$$125 = \frac{10}{1000}\times250\times\frac{dn}{dt}$$

$$\frac{dn}{dt} = \frac{125\times100}{250}$$

$$\Rightarrow \frac{dn}{dt} = 50$$

33. (a) Given, radius of wire $A = 2\times$ radius of wire B,

i.e. $r_A = 2r_B$

Also, tension $T_B = T_A$

Mass of string A, M_A

= Volume × Density

$= (\pi r_A^2)\times l_A\times\rho_A$ ... (i)

and $M_B = (\pi r_B^2)\times l_B\times\rho_B$ ... (ii)

Dividing Eq. (i) by Eq. (ii), we get

$$\frac{M_A}{M_B} = \frac{r_A^2}{r_B^2}\cdot\frac{l_A}{l_B} \quad (\because \rho_A = \rho_B)$$

$$\frac{\frac{M_A}{l_A}}{\frac{M_B}{l_B}} = \frac{r_A^2}{r_B^2} \quad \text{... (iii)}$$

Since, linear mass density, $\mu = \dfrac{m}{l}$

$$\therefore \frac{\mu_A}{\mu_B} = \frac{\frac{m_A}{l_A}}{\frac{m_B}{l_B}} = \left(\frac{r_A}{r_B}\right)^2$$

[using Eqs. (iii)]

We know, speed of transverse wave,

$$v=\sqrt{\frac{T}{\mu}}$$

$$\frac{v_A}{v_B}=\sqrt{\frac{\mu_B}{\mu_A}}=\frac{r_B}{r_A}=\frac{1}{2}\quad(\because r_A=2r_B)$$

34. (d) $F\propto\frac{1}{R^n}$

$$\frac{mv^2}{R}\propto\frac{1}{R^n}$$

or $v\propto\frac{1}{R^{\frac{n-1}{2}}}$

$$T=\frac{2\pi R}{v}$$

$$\Rightarrow T\propto\frac{R}{v}$$

$$\Rightarrow T\propto R^{1+\frac{n-1}{2}}$$

or $T\propto R^{\frac{n+1}{2}}$

35. (c) I. The instantaneous speed is always positive as it is the magnitude of the velocity at an instant.

II. For $t=0\text{s}$ to $t=5\text{s}$, the motion is uniform. So, the average velocity and the instantaneous velocity are equal.

III. During $t=0\text{s}$ to $t=5\text{s}$. The slope of the graph is positive, hence the average velocity and the velocity both are positive. During $t=5\text{s}$ to $t=10\text{s}$. The slope of the graph is negative, hence the velocity is negative. Since, there is change in sign of velocity at $t=5\text{s}$ the car changes its direction at that instant.

IV. In figure, instantaneous velocity during $t=0\text{s}$ to $t=5\text{s}$ is positive. Also, the speed is always a positive value.

36. (c) Initial condition,

Given, $m=10\text{g}$

$\Rightarrow$ Number of moles, $n=\frac{M}{M_0}=\frac{10}{32}$

$\Rightarrow$ $p_1=3\text{ atm}$

$T_1=10^\circ\text{C}=10+273=283\text{ K}$

A. Let volume of the gas before expansion $=V_1$

From ideal gas equation,

$$p_1V_1=nRT_1$$

$$\Rightarrow V_1=\frac{nRT_1}{p_1}$$

$$=\frac{10\times0.0821\times283}{32\times3}$$

$$=2.42\text{ L}$$

B. At constant pressure, applying Charles' law,

$$\frac{V_1}{T_1}=\frac{V_2}{T_2}\qquad\text{...(i)}$$

Given, $V_2=10\text{ L}, T_2=?$

Using Eq. (i), we get

$$T_2=\left(\frac{V_2}{V_1}\right)\times T_1$$

$$=\left(\frac{10}{2.42}\right)\times283\text{ K}$$

$$=1169.4\text{ K}$$

C. Density before expansion,

$$d_1=\frac{\text{Mass}}{V_1}=\frac{10}{2.42}=4.13\text{ gL}^{-1}$$

D. Density after expansion,

$$d_2=\frac{\text{Mass}}{V_2}=\frac{10}{10}=1\text{ gL}^{-1}$$

Hence, A $\rightarrow$ 3, B $\rightarrow$ 4, C $\rightarrow$ 1 and D $\rightarrow$ 2.

37. (d) $\Delta l=\frac{Fl}{\pi r^2Y}$

$l_A=2\text{ m}, l_B=1.5\text{ m},$

$\frac{Y_A}{Y_B}=\frac{7}{4}, r_B=2\text{ mm}=2\times10^{-3}\text{ m}$

and $\frac{F_A}{F_B}=1$

As, it is given that $\Delta l_A=\Delta l_B$

$$\Rightarrow\frac{F_Al_A}{\pi r_A^2Y_A}=\frac{F_Bl_B}{\pi r_B^2Y_B}$$

$$\Rightarrow r_A^2=\frac{F_A}{F_B}\cdot\frac{l_A}{l_B}\cdot\frac{Y_B}{Y_A}\cdot r_B^2$$

$$=1\times\frac{2}{1.5}\times\frac{4}{7}\times4\times10^{-6}\text{ m}$$

$$=3.04\times10^{-6}\text{ m}$$

or $r_A=1.7\times10^{-3}\text{ m}\Rightarrow r_A=1.7\text{ mm}$

38. (a) The situation given in the question is shown below

6 m/s 3 m/s (1) (2)

Before collision

(1) v_1 (2) v_2

After collision

Using conservation of linear momentum,

$$\mathbf{p}_i=\mathbf{p}_f$$

$$m_1\mathbf{u}_1+m_2\mathbf{u}_2=m_1\mathbf{v}_1+m_2\mathbf{v}_2$$

Here, $m_1=0.6\text{ kg}, m_2=0.6\text{ kg},$

$\mathbf{u}_1=6\hat{\mathbf{i}}\text{ m/s}, \mathbf{u}_2=-3\hat{\mathbf{i}}\text{ m/s}$

$$0.6\times6\hat{\mathbf{i}}+0.6\times(-3\hat{\mathbf{i}})=0.6\times\mathbf{v}_1+0.6\,\mathbf{v}_2$$

$$0.6\,\mathbf{v}_1+0.6\,\mathbf{v}_2=1.8\,\hat{\mathbf{i}}$$

$$\mathbf{v}_1+\mathbf{v}_2=3\hat{\mathbf{i}}$$

or $v_1+v_2=3$ ...(i)

From the formula of coefficient of restitution,

$$e=\frac{\mathbf{v}_2-\mathbf{v}_1}{u_1-u_2}$$

$$\frac{1}{2}=\frac{v_2-v_1}{6-(-3)}$$

$$\frac{1}{2}=\frac{v_2-v_1}{9}$$

$$v_2-v_1=\frac{9}{2}=4.5\qquad\text{... (ii)}$$

On solving Eqs. (i) and (ii), we get

$v_1=-0.75\text{ m/s}, v_2=3.75\text{ m/s}$

Impulse exerted, $I=\Delta p=p_f-p_i$

$$=m_1(v_1-u_1)$$

$$=0.6[(-0.75)-(6)]$$

$$=0.6[-6.75]$$

$$I=-4.05\text{ N-s}$$

or $|I|=4.05\text{ N-s}$

39. (b) The displacement of particle, executing SHM,

$$y=5\sin\left(4t+\frac{\pi}{3}\right)\qquad\text{... (i)}$$

Velocity of particle,

$$\left(\frac{dy}{dt}\right)=\frac{5d}{dt}\sin\left(4t+\frac{\pi}{3}\right)$$

$$=5\cos\left(4t+\frac{\pi}{3}\right)\cdot4$$

$$=20\cos\left(4t+\frac{\pi}{3}\right)$$

Velocity at $t = \left(\frac{T}{4}\right)$

$$\left(\frac{dy}{dt}\right)_{t=\frac{T}{4}} = 20\cos\left(4 \times \frac{T}{4} + \frac{\pi}{3}\right)$$

or $$v = 20\cos\left(T + \frac{\pi}{3}\right) \quad \ldots \text{(ii)}$$

Comparing the given equation with standard equation of SHM,

$y = a\sin(\omega t + \phi)$

As, $\omega = \frac{2\pi}{T}$ or $T = \frac{2\pi}{\omega}$

$T = \frac{2\pi}{4}$ or $T = \left(\frac{\pi}{2}\right)$

Now, putting value of T in Eq. (ii), we get

$$v = 20\cos\left(\frac{\pi}{2} + \frac{\pi}{3}\right) = -20\sin\frac{\pi}{3}$$

$$= -20 \times \frac{\sqrt{3}}{2} = -10 \times \sqrt{3}$$

The kinetic energy of particle,

$$\text{KE} = \frac{1}{2}mv^2 = \frac{1}{2} \times 2 \times 10^{-3} \times (-10\sqrt{3})^2 = 0.3\,\text{J}$$

40. (a) $h = \frac{2T\cos\theta}{\rho rg}$

$\Rightarrow h \propto \frac{1}{r}$

So, when radius is doubled, height becomes half.

$\therefore \quad h' = h/2$

$\Rightarrow \quad M = \rho\pi r^2 h$

$\therefore \quad M' = \rho\pi r'^2 h'$

$\therefore \quad \frac{M'}{M} = \frac{r'^2 h'}{r^2 h}$

$$= \frac{(2r)^2 (h/2)}{r^2 h} = 2$$

$\Rightarrow \quad M' = 2M$

41. (d) From the relation between velocity v and displacement x,

$$v = \omega\sqrt{(A^2 - x^2)}$$

Squaring on both sides, we get

$$v^2 = \omega^2 (A^2 - x^2) \quad \ldots \text{(i)}$$

and we know that, $a = -\omega^2 x$

or $a^2 = (-\omega^2 x)^2$

$$= \omega^4 x^2 \quad \ldots \text{(ii)}$$

From the Eqs. (i) and (ii), we get

$$v^2 = -\frac{a^2}{\omega^2} + \omega^2 A^2$$

The above equation is similar to a straight line equation,

$$y = mx + C$$

The line has positive slope and negative intercept on Y-axis.

The graph between v^2 and a^2 can be drawn as

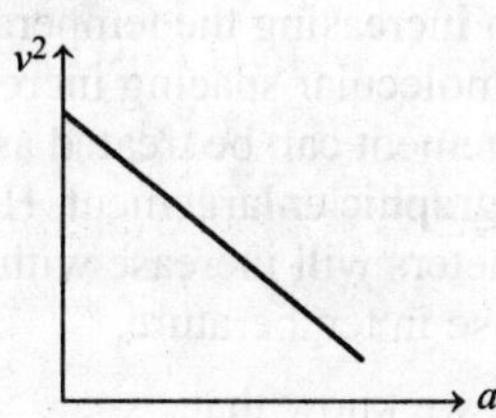

42. (d) Given, $m = \frac{M}{2}$

As $\quad p_i = p_f$

So, $\quad mv_0 = \frac{m}{2} v_0'$

$\Rightarrow \quad v_0 = \frac{v_0'}{2}$

$\Rightarrow \quad v_0' = 2v_0$

$\Rightarrow \quad \omega' A' = 2\omega A \quad [\because v_0 = \omega A]$

$\Rightarrow \left(\frac{\omega'}{\omega}\right)\left(\frac{A'}{A}\right) = 2$

$\Rightarrow \sqrt{\frac{m}{m'}} f = 2 \quad \left(\because \omega \propto \frac{1}{\sqrt{m}}\right)$

$\Rightarrow \quad \sqrt{2} f = 2$

$\Rightarrow \quad f = \sqrt{2}$

43. (b) $\frac{3\lambda}{2} = 2$ or $\lambda = \frac{4}{3}$ m

Velocity, $v = f\lambda$

$$= 240 \times \frac{4}{3} = 320\,\text{m/s}$$

Also $\quad f_1 = \frac{240}{3} = 80\,\text{Hz}$

44. (b) According to question, we know that $\Delta V = V_0\, \gamma \Delta T$

$\Rightarrow \Delta V = a^3 \cdot (3\alpha)\, \Delta T$

According to question,

$6a^2 = 24$

[$\because$ Total surface area of cube $= 6a^2$]

$\Rightarrow \quad a^2 = 4$

$\Rightarrow \quad a = 2$

$\Rightarrow \quad \Delta V = 2^3 (3 \times 5 \times 10^{-4}) \times 10$

$$= 1200 \times 10^{-4}\ \text{m}^3$$

$$= 1200 \times 10^2 = 1.2 \times 10^5\ \text{cm}^3$$

45. (c) $v_{\text{rms}} = \sqrt{\frac{3RT}{M}}$

$v_{\text{rms}} \propto \frac{T}{\sqrt{M}}$. As T and M are same for both gas. So, v_{rms} will be same and statement (A) is correct.

As, $\quad pV = NkT$

as, V and T is constant

$\Rightarrow \quad p \propto N$

$\Rightarrow \quad \frac{p_1}{p_2} = \frac{N_1}{N_2} \Rightarrow \frac{p_1}{p_2} = \frac{1}{4}$

So, statement (B) is correct.

As statements (A) and (B) are correct. So, (C) and (D) must be wrong.

NSS2 NEET Stepping Stones 2

1. (d) Given, elongation of spring = 1 cm

According to question,

$$\frac{kx_1}{kx_2} = \frac{F_1}{F_2} = \left(\frac{r_2}{r_1}\right)^2$$

$$\Rightarrow \frac{x_1}{x_2} = \left(\frac{800+6400}{6400}\right)^2$$

$$\Rightarrow x_2 = \frac{64}{81}x_1 = \frac{64}{81} = 0.79 \text{ cm}$$

2. (c) Dimensions of $\frac{a}{V^2}$ = Dimensions of pressure

$\Rightarrow$ Dimensions of $a = [pV^2]$
$= [ML^{-1}T^{-2}][L^3]^2 = [ML^5T^{-2}]$

Dimensions of $b = [V] = [L^3]$

Dimensions of $ab = [ML^8T^{-2}]$

3. (b) Change in momentum of wire = – Change in momentum of bead

Change in momentum of bead
$= mv - (-mv) = 2mv$

Time taken by bead to turn
$= \frac{\pi(d/2)}{v} = \frac{\pi d}{2v}$

Force exterted by bead on wire
= Rate of momentum change
$= \frac{4mv^2}{\pi d}$

4. (d) At $t = 4.5$ s, wave is reflected from a rigid end, so a crest is reflected as a trough.

5. (a) $W_{CA} = nR\Delta T = -nRT_0$

For the work done from B to C,
$W_{BC} = 2nRT_0 \ln 2$

$$W_{AB} = nRT \cdot \ln\left(\frac{2V_0}{V}\right) = nRT_0 \ln 2$$

Heat absorbed $Q_{AB} = W_{AB}$, because it is an isothermal process.

Heat supplied,

$$\Delta Q_{AB} = nC_V\Delta T = \frac{n\gamma RT_0}{\gamma - 1}$$

$$\text{Cyclic efficiency, } \eta = \frac{W_{net}}{Q_{in}}$$

$$\text{Cycle efficiency} = \frac{2\ln 2 - 1}{\left[\frac{\gamma}{(\gamma-1)}\right]}$$

6. (b) The significant figures in 12.0 is 3 and in 0.038 is 3.
The addition of these two numbers with correct significant figures will be 12.0, i.e. 3 significant figures instead of 12.038. Thus, statement I is incorrect.
Also, for a physical quantity, the product of numerical value (n) and its unit (u) is always constant.
i.e. $n \times u$ = constant
or $\quad n \propto \frac{1}{u}$
Thus, given statement II is incorrect.

7. (a) On increasing the temperature, inter-molecular spacing increases and arrangement can be treated as photographic enlargement. Hence, all parameters will increase with increase in temperature.

8. (a) As we know that,

$$\text{Horizontal range, } R = \frac{2u^2 \sin\theta\cos\theta}{g}$$

where, u is projection speed and θ is angle of projection.

$$\text{Time of flight, } T = \frac{2u\sin\theta}{g}$$

$$\text{Given,} \quad R = \frac{10\sqrt{3}}{2}T^2$$

Putting the values of R and T, we get

$$\frac{2u^2\sin\theta\cos\theta}{g} = \frac{10\sqrt{3}}{2}\left(\frac{2u\sin\theta}{g}\right)^2$$

we get $\quad \cot\theta = \sqrt{3}$

$\Rightarrow \quad \theta = 30°$

9. (b) Kinetic energy in SHM is given as,

$$K = \frac{1}{2}k(A^2 - y^2)$$

$$\text{Total energy, } E = \frac{1}{2}kA^2$$

$$\text{Thus, } \frac{K}{E} = \frac{A^2 - y^2}{A^2} = 1 - \left(\frac{y}{A}\right)^2$$

At $\quad t = T/4, y = 2$

$$\frac{K}{E} = 1 - \left(\frac{2}{4}\right)^2 = \frac{3}{4}$$

10. (b) The kinetic energy of an ideal gas molecules at T temperature is given as $E_K = \frac{3}{2}k_BT$, where k_B is Boltzmann's constant.

If $T = 0$ K, then $E_K = \frac{3}{2}k_B \times 0$

$$E_K = 0$$

The potential energy of gas molecules will depend on its configuration. It is completely independent of temperature.
The vibrational energy are significant at higher temperature. At very low temperatures, the value of vibrational kinetic energy is almost zero and at 0 K temperature, it is equal to zero.

11. (c) Given, $R = 9.5$ mm
$= 9.5 \times 10^{-3}$ m
$L = 81\text{ cm} = 81 \times 10^{-2}$ m,
and $\quad F = 6.2 \times 10^4$ N

The stress in the bar,

$$\frac{F}{\pi R^2} = \frac{6.2 \times 10^4}{3.14 \times (9.5 \times 10^{-3})^2}$$
$$= 0.022 \times 10^{10} \text{ N/m}^2$$
$$= 2.2 \times 10^8 \text{ N/m}^2$$

12. (a) A ball which is spinning drags the fluid along with it. The given figure shows the streamlines of fluid and spinning at the same line.
The ball is moving forward and relative to it, the fluid is moving backwards.
Therefore, the velocity of the fluid above to the ball is larger and below is smaller. This difference in the velocity of fluid result in pressure difference between the lower and upper faces and there is a net upward force on the ball. This is called magnus efect.

13. (a) Number of seconds lost in a day,

$$\Delta t = \frac{1}{2}\alpha\,\Delta\theta \times 86400$$

The coefficient of linear expansion of metal pendulum,

$$\alpha = \frac{2\Delta t}{\Delta\theta \times 86400} = \frac{2 \times 14.5}{25 \times 86400}$$

$$\alpha = 1.34 \times 10^{-5} /{}^\circ\text{C}$$

14. (a) Given, kinetic energy, $K = 20t^2$

$$\therefore \quad K = \frac{1}{2}mv^2 \Rightarrow \frac{1}{2}mv^2 = 20t^2$$

or $v^2 = \frac{40}{m}t^2$ or $v = \sqrt{\frac{40}{m}}\, t$

Acceleration, $a = \frac{dv}{dt} = \frac{d}{dt}\left(\sqrt{\frac{40}{m}}\, t\right)$

$$a = \sqrt{\frac{40}{m}}$$

Force, $F = ma = m\sqrt{\frac{40}{m}}$

$$\Rightarrow \quad F = \sqrt{40m}$$

which is constant.

15. (b) Maximum height reached by the projectile,

$$H_{\max} = \left.\frac{u^2 \sin^2\theta}{2g}\right|_{\theta = 90^\circ} = \frac{u^2}{2g}$$

$$\therefore \frac{(H_{\max})_1}{(H_{\max})_2} = \left(\frac{u_1}{u_2}\right)^2 = \left(\frac{u}{u/2}\right)^2 = 4$$

$$\therefore (H_{\max})_2 = \frac{(H_{\max})_1}{4} = \frac{64}{4} = 16\,\text{m}$$

16. (c) Parachute bails out at height H from ground, velocity at A,

$$v = \sqrt{2gh}$$

$$= \sqrt{2 \times 9.8 \times 50} = \sqrt{980}\ \text{ms}^{-1}$$

Velocity at ground, $v_1 = 3\ \text{ms}^{-1}$

Acceleration $= -2\ \text{ms}^{-2}$

$h = 50$ m, H, A, $v = \sqrt{2gh}$, $v_1 = 3$ m/s, Ground

$$\therefore \; H - h = \frac{v^2 - v_1^2}{2 \times 2} = \frac{980 - 9}{4}$$

$$= \frac{971}{4} = 242.75$$

$$\Rightarrow H = 242.75 + h$$

$$= 242.75 + 50 \approx 293\ \text{m}$$

17. (d) $Y = \frac{FL}{A \cdot \Delta L}$

or $F = \frac{YA \cdot \Delta L}{L}$

So, $F \propto \Delta L$

$$\therefore \quad \frac{F_1}{F_2} = \frac{\Delta L_1}{\Delta L_2}$$

Here, $F_1 = T_1, F_2 = T'$

$$\Delta L_1 = l - L$$

and $\Delta L_2 = l' - L$

So, $\frac{T}{T'} = \frac{l - L}{l' - L}$

or $Tl' - TL = T'l - T'L$

$$L(T' - T) = T'l - Tl'$$

$$L = \frac{T'l - Tl'}{T' - T}$$

18. (b) Given,

m, F

From second law of motion,

$$F = ma$$

$$a = \frac{F}{m}$$

Force applied is linearly dependent on time

$$F \propto t \Rightarrow F = kt$$

$$(k = \text{constant})$$

$$a = \frac{kt}{m} \text{ or } a \propto t$$

We plot *a versus t* graph and it will be linear from origin.

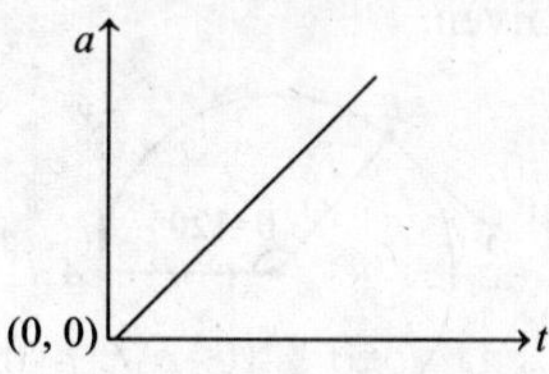

19. (a) Height of water in the capillary tube,

$$h = \frac{2T\cos\theta}{r\rho g}$$

$$\Rightarrow \quad h \propto \frac{1}{r}$$

$$\therefore \quad \frac{h_2}{h_1} = \frac{r_1}{r_2} = \frac{3r_1}{r_1} = 3$$

$$h_2 = 3h_1$$

$$= 3 \times 2.0 = 6\,\text{cm}$$

20. (d) Limiting force of static friction and kinetic friction does not depend on the area of contact but they depend on materials.

21. (b) If x_1 and x_2 are the positions of masses m_1 and m_2, the position of the centre of mass is given by

$$x_{CM} = \frac{m_1x_1 + m_2x_2}{m_1 + m_2}$$

If x_1 change by Δx_1 and x_2 change by Δx_2, then change in x_{CM} will be

$$\Delta x_{CM} = \frac{m_1\Delta x_1 + m_2\Delta x_2}{m_1 + m_2} \quad \text{...(i)}$$

Given, $\Delta x_{CM} = 0$ and $\Delta x_1 = d = 2$ cm

Using these values in Eq. (i), we get

$$m_1 d + m_2\Delta x_2 = 0$$

$$\Rightarrow \quad \Delta x_2 = -\frac{m_1}{m_2} \cdot d$$

$\therefore$ Distance moved by second mass m_2,

$$\Delta x_2 = \frac{m_1 d}{m_2}$$

Here, $m_1 = 3$ kg, $m_2 = 2$ kg, $d = 2$ cm

$$\Delta x_2 = \frac{3}{2} \times 2 = 3\ \text{cm}$$

22. (b) The time period of an oscillating spring is given by

$$T = 2\pi\sqrt{\frac{m}{k}}, \text{ i.e. } T \propto \frac{1}{\sqrt{k}}$$

Since, the spring constant is large for hard spring, therefore hard spring has a less periodic time as compared to soft spring.

23. (b) Energy per mole of a gas is

$$\frac{f}{2}RT = \frac{f}{2}pV$$

where, f = degree of freedom.

For a monoatomic and a diatomic gas, degree of freedom for translational motion are same, $f = 3$

$\therefore$ Translational energy for a diatomic gas

$$= \frac{3}{2}RT = \frac{3}{2}pV$$

and total energy for a diatomic gas

$$= \frac{5}{2}RT = \frac{5}{2}pV$$

Hence, ratio $= \dfrac{\frac{3}{2}pV}{\frac{5}{2}pV} = \dfrac{3}{5}$

24. (d)

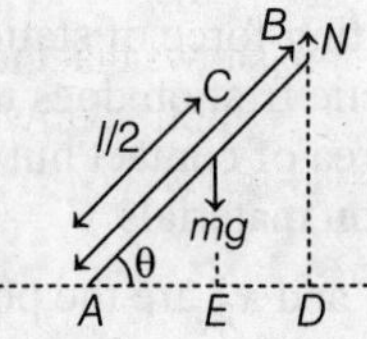

Taking torque around point A.
Using principle of moments of force.
$$N(AD) - W(AE) = 0$$
$$AD = l\cos\theta$$
$$AE = \frac{l}{2}\cos\theta$$
$$mg \times \frac{l}{2}\cos\theta = N \times l\cos\theta$$
$$\Rightarrow \quad N = \frac{mg}{2} = \frac{w}{2}$$

25. (c) Linear momentum is conserved,
$$p_i = p_f$$
$$m_1 v_1 = m_2 v_2$$
$$1000 \times 6 = 1200 \times v_2$$
$$v_2 = 5\,\text{m/s}$$

26. (b) As we know that, SI unit of following terms are

A. R_H (Rydberg constant) = m^{-1}

B. h (Planck's constant)
$$= \text{Js} = \text{kg m}^2\text{s}^{-1}$$

C. Magnetic field energy density
$$(\mu_B) = \frac{\text{Energy}}{\text{Volume}} = \frac{\text{kg m}^2\text{s}^{-2}}{\text{m}^3}$$
$$= \text{kgm}^{-1}\text{s}^{-2}$$

D. η (coefficient of viscosity)
$$\because \quad F = \eta A\frac{dv}{dx}$$
$$\therefore \quad \eta = \frac{Fdx}{A\,dv} = \frac{\text{kg ms}^{-2}\cdot\text{m}}{\text{m}^2.\text{ms}^{-1}}$$
$$= \text{kgm}^{-1}\text{s}^{-1}$$

So, the correct match is A-3, B-2, C-4 and D-1.

27. (b) Given, instantaneous velocity,
$$v = \alpha t + \beta t^2$$

Here, $t_1 = 1\text{s}$ and $t_2 = 2\text{s}$

As, $\quad v = \frac{ds}{dt}$
$$\Rightarrow \quad ds = vdt \Rightarrow ds = (\alpha t + \beta t^2)dt$$

Integrating both sides, we get
$$s = \left(\alpha\frac{t^2}{2} + \frac{\beta t^3}{3}\right)\Bigg|_1^2$$
$$= \frac{\alpha}{2}[2^2 - 1^2] + \frac{\beta}{3}[2^3 - 1^3]$$
$$= \frac{\alpha}{2}[4-1] + \frac{\beta}{3}[8-1]$$
$$= \frac{3\alpha}{2} + \frac{7\beta}{3}$$

28. (c) Using Bernoulli's theorem,
$$p_1 + \frac{1}{2}\rho v_1^2 + \rho g h_1$$
$$= p_2 + \frac{1}{2}\rho v_2^2 + \rho g h_2$$

For the horizontal motion of the plane
$$h_1 = h_2$$

Then, $\quad p_1 + \frac{1}{2}\rho v_1^2 = p_2 + \frac{1}{2}\rho v_2^2$

or $\quad p_2 - p_1 = \frac{1}{2}\rho\,(v_1^2 - v_2^2)$
$$= \frac{1}{2} \times 1.3\,[120^2 - 90^2]$$
$$= 4095\,\text{N/m}^2$$

29. (c) p-V diagram of the gas is a straight line passing through origin. Hence, $p \propto V$ or pV^{-1} = constant.

Molar heat capacity in the process pV^x = constant is
$$C = \frac{R}{\gamma - 1} + \frac{R}{1-x}; \text{ here } \gamma = 1.4$$
(for diatomic gas)
$$\Rightarrow \quad C = \frac{R}{1.4-1} + \frac{R}{1+1} \qquad (\because x = -1)$$
$$\Rightarrow \quad C = 3R$$

30. (c) Given,

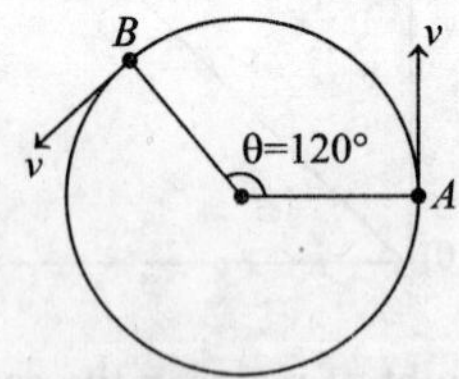

Given, $v = \pi$ m/s or $R\omega = \pi$
$$\omega = \frac{\pi}{R}\text{ rad/s}$$

Angular displacement,
$$\theta = 120° = \frac{2\pi}{3}$$

Using $\theta = \omega t$
$$t = \frac{\theta}{\omega} = \frac{2\pi/3}{\pi/R} = \frac{2R}{3}$$

linear displacement,
$$d = 2R\sin(\theta/2)$$
$$d = 2R\sin\left(\frac{120°}{2}\right)$$
$$= 2R\sin 60° = 2R\frac{\sqrt{3}}{2} = R\sqrt{3}$$

Average velocity $= \frac{d}{t} = \frac{R\sqrt{3}}{2R/3} = \frac{3\sqrt{3}}{2}$
$$= 1.5\sqrt{3}\text{ m/s}$$

31. (d) $\omega = \frac{2\pi}{T} = \frac{\pi}{4}$ s. Therefore,

$y = A\sin\frac{\pi}{4}t$. Now, put $t = 1$s and then $t = 2$s, we get
$$y_1 = 8\sin\frac{\pi}{4} = \frac{8}{\sqrt{2}},\ y_2 = 8\sin\frac{\pi}{\sqrt{2}} = 8$$
$$\therefore \quad \frac{y_1}{y_2 - y_1} = \frac{\frac{8}{\sqrt{2}}}{8 - \frac{8}{\sqrt{2}}}$$
$$= \frac{1}{\sqrt{2}-1} = \sqrt{2}+1$$

32. (c) Given,
Kinetic energies of A, B and C are equal.
$$\Rightarrow \quad K_A = K_B = K_C$$
$$\Rightarrow \quad \frac{1}{2}m_A v_A^2 = \frac{1}{2}m_B v_B^2 = \frac{1}{2}m_C v_C^2$$
$$\Rightarrow \quad \frac{m_A^2 v_A^2}{m_A} = \frac{m_B^2 v_B^2}{m_B} = \frac{m_C^2 v_C^2}{m_C}$$
$$\Rightarrow \quad \frac{p_A^2}{m_A} = \frac{p_B^2}{m_B} = \frac{p_C^2}{m_C}$$
$$\Rightarrow \quad \frac{p_A}{\sqrt{m_A}} = \frac{p_B}{\sqrt{m_B}} = \frac{p_C}{\sqrt{m_C}}$$
$$\Rightarrow p_A : p_B : p_C$$
$$= \sqrt{m_A} : \sqrt{m_B} : \sqrt{m_C}$$
$$= \sqrt{400} : \sqrt{1200} : \sqrt{1600}$$
$$= 2 : 2\sqrt{3} : 4 = 1 : \sqrt{3} : 2$$

33. (d) Temperature of mixture,
$$\theta = \frac{m_1 c_1 \theta_1 + m_2 c_2 \theta_2}{m_1 c_1 + m_2 c_2}$$
$$\Rightarrow 40 = \frac{m_1 \times 0.2 \times 48 + 100 \times 0.5 \times 20}{m_1 \times 0.2 + 100 \times 0.5}$$
$$\Rightarrow 40 = \frac{9.6m_1 + 1000}{0.2m_1 + 50}$$
$$\Rightarrow \quad 8m_1 + 2000 = 9.6m_1 + 1000$$
$$\Rightarrow 9.6m_1 - 8m_1 = 1000$$
$$\Rightarrow \quad 1.6m_1 = 1000$$
$$\Rightarrow m_1 = 625\,\text{g}$$

34. (d) $TV^{\gamma-1}$ = constant

for $\gamma = \frac{3}{2}$

$$T_i V^{\frac{3}{2}-1} = T_f (2V)^{\frac{3}{2}-1}$$

$$T_i V^{\frac{1}{2}} = T_f 2^{\frac{1}{2}} \cdot V^{\frac{1}{2}}$$

$$T_f = \frac{T_i}{\sqrt{2}}$$

Now, $W = \frac{nR\Delta T}{1-\gamma}$

$$= \frac{1R\left(\frac{T}{\sqrt{2}} - T\right)}{1-\frac{3}{2}}$$

$$= 2RT\left(1-\frac{1}{\sqrt{2}}\right)$$

$$W = RT(2-\sqrt{2})$$

35. (a) For the planet,

$$T_1 = 200 \text{ days}$$

$$R_1 = R \Rightarrow R_2 = \frac{R}{4}$$

$\therefore$ $T_2 = ?$

According to Kepler's law,

$$T^2 \propto R^3$$

$$\therefore \quad \frac{T_2}{T_1} = \left(\frac{R_2}{R_1}\right)^{3/2}$$

$$= \left(\frac{R/4}{R}\right)^{3/2}$$

$$= \left(\frac{1}{4}\right)^{3/2} = \frac{1}{8}$$

$$\therefore \quad T_2 = \frac{T_1}{8} = \frac{200}{8}$$

$$= 25 \text{ days}$$

36. (b) At height h, acceleration due to gravity,

$$g_h = g \cdot \frac{R^2}{(R+h)^2}$$

At $h = 2R$,

$$g_h = g\frac{R^2}{(R+2R)^2}$$

$$\Rightarrow \quad g_h = \frac{g}{9}$$

For second pendulum, time period is 2 s.

$$\Rightarrow \quad T = 2\pi\sqrt{\frac{l}{g_h}}$$

$$\Rightarrow \quad \frac{T^2 \cdot g_h}{4\pi^2} = l$$

$$\text{or} \quad l = \frac{T^2 \cdot g}{4\pi^2 \times 9} \quad \left[\because g_h = \frac{g}{9}\right]$$

$$= \frac{4 \times \pi^2}{4\pi^2 \times 9}$$

$$\Rightarrow \quad l = \frac{1}{9} \text{ m}$$

37. (b) Acceleration = Constant, (the acceleration-time graph is parallel to the time axis and acceleration is positive)

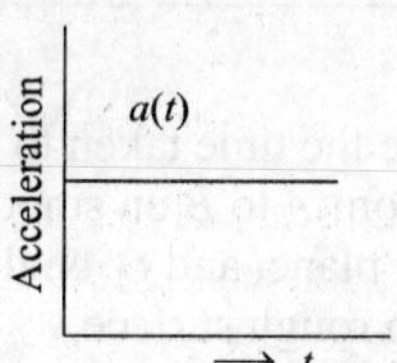

$$a = \frac{dv}{dt}$$

As we know,

$$\frac{dv}{dt} = C$$

$$\Rightarrow \quad \int dv = C\int dt$$

$$\Rightarrow \quad v = Ct + C_0$$

The velocity-time graph is straight line with positive slope

$$v = dx/dt$$

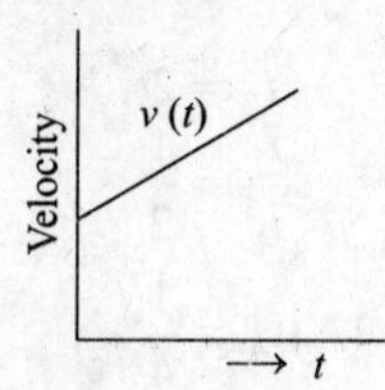

As we know,

$$\frac{dx}{dt} = Ct + C_0$$

$$\Rightarrow \quad \int dx = \int (Ct + C_0)\, dt$$

$$\Rightarrow \quad x = \frac{Ct^2}{2} + C_0 t + C_1$$

This equation shows that the distance-time graph is upward concave parabola.

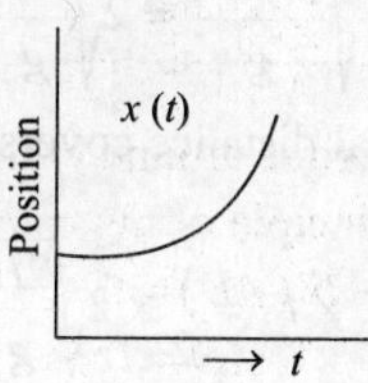

38. (d) Given, $x = t^3 - 6t^2 + 9t$

Velocity, $v = 3t^2 - 12t + 9$

or $\quad v = 3(t-1)(t-3)$

So, velocity changes sign at $t = 1$ s to $t = 3$ s

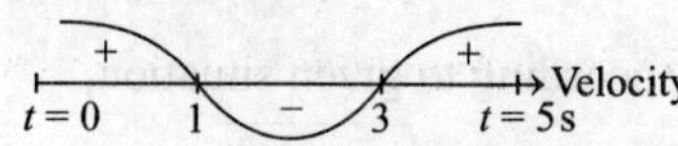

Hence, movement of particle is as follows,

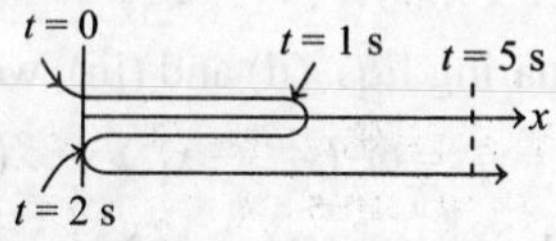

Position at $t = 0$ s, $x = 0$ m

Position at $t = 1$ s, $x = 4$ m

Position at $t = 3$ s, $x = 0$ m

Position at $t = 5$ s, $x = 20$ m

So, distance of particle at $t = 5$ s

$$d = 4 + 4 + 20 = 28 \text{ m}$$

Displacement of particle at $t = 5$ s is $x = 20$ m.

$$\text{Ratio} = \frac{d}{x} = \frac{28}{20} = \frac{7}{5}$$

39. (c) For ball of mass M, time to reach ground,

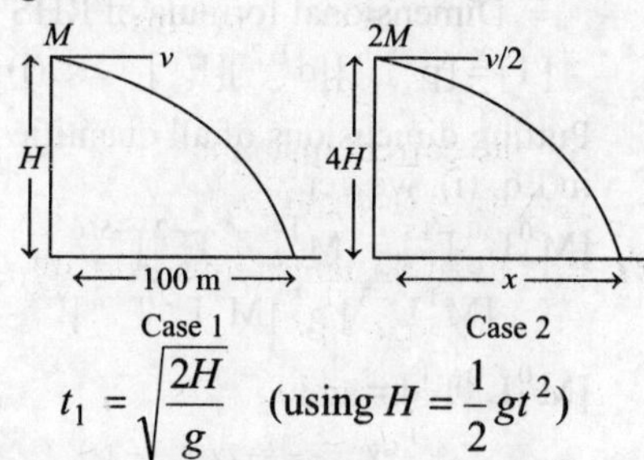

$$t_1 = \sqrt{\frac{2H}{g}} \quad \left(\text{using } H = \frac{1}{2}gt^2\right)$$

So, horizontal distance covered

$$= 100 = v_x \times t_1$$

$$\Rightarrow \quad 100 = v \times \sqrt{\frac{2H}{g}} \quad \ldots\text{(i)}$$

For ball of mass $2M$, time to reach ground

$$t_2 = \sqrt{\frac{2(4H)}{g}} = 2\sqrt{\frac{2H}{g}}$$

Horizontal distance covers by 2nd ball

$$= v_x \times t_2 = \frac{v}{2} \times 2\sqrt{\frac{2H}{g}}$$

$$= v\sqrt{\frac{2H}{g}} = 100\text{ m} \quad \text{[from Eq. (i)]}$$

40. (d) Velocity of a particle performing simple harmonic motion is given by

$$v = \pm\,\omega\sqrt{A^2 - x^2} \quad \text{...(i)}$$

According to given situation,

$$v_1 = \omega\sqrt{A^2 - x_1^2} \quad \text{...(ii)}$$

and $v_2 = \omega\sqrt{A^2 - x_2^2}$ ...(iii)

Squaring Eqs. (ii) and (iii), we get

$$v_1^2 = \omega^2 (A^2 - x_1^2) \quad \text{...(iv)}$$

and $v_2^2 = \omega^2 (A^2 - x_2^2)$ ...(v)

From Eqs. (iv) and (v), we get

$$v_1^2 - v_2^2 = \omega^2 (x_2^2 - x_1^2)$$

$$= \left(\frac{2\pi}{T}\right)^2 (x_2^2 - x_1^2)$$

$$T = 2\pi\sqrt{\frac{(x_2^2 - x_1^2)}{(v_1^2 - v_2^2)}}$$

41. (a) According to the question,

$$T \propto p^{-5/6}\, d^{1/2} E^{\gamma}$$

Dimensional formula of LHS

= Dimensional formula of RHS

$$[\text{T}] = [\text{p}^{-5/6}][\text{d}^{1/2}][\text{E}^{\gamma}] \quad \text{...(i)}$$

Putting dimensions of all quantities in Eq. (i), we get

$$[\text{M}^0\text{L}^0\text{T}^1] = [\text{M}^1\text{L}^{-1}\text{T}^{-2}]^{-5/6} [\text{M}^1\text{L}^{-3}]^{1/2} [\text{M}^1\text{L}^2\text{T}^{-2}]^{\gamma}$$

$$[\text{M}^0\text{L}^0\text{T}^1] = [\text{M}^{\frac{-5}{6}+\frac{1}{2}+\gamma}\ \text{L}^{\frac{5}{6}-\frac{3}{2}+2\gamma}\ \text{T}^{\frac{5}{3}-2\gamma}]$$

On comparing both sides, we get

$$-\frac{5}{6} + \frac{1}{2} + \gamma = 0$$

or $\gamma = \frac{5}{6} - \frac{1}{2} = \frac{1}{3}$

42. (c) The acceleration produced in the block on the smooth surface,

$$a_1 = g \sin 45° = \frac{g}{\sqrt{2}} \quad \text{... (i)}$$

For rough surface,

$$a_2 = \frac{g}{\sqrt{2}}(1 - \mu_k) \quad \text{...(ii)}$$

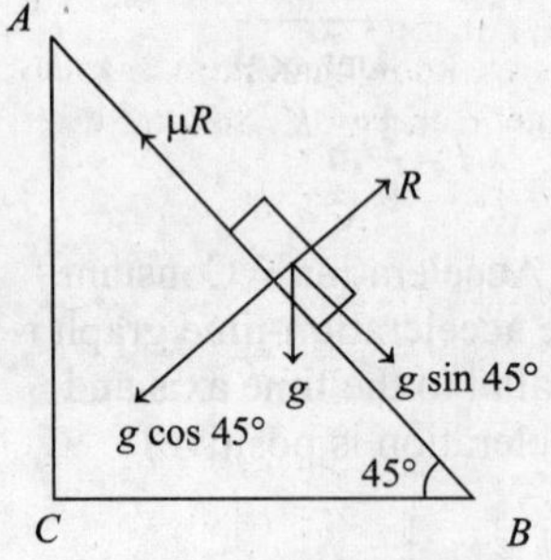

Let t_1 be the time taken to reach the block from A to B on smooth inclined plane, and t_2 be the time taken on rough surface.

$$AB = 0 + \frac{1}{2}a_1 t_1^2 = \frac{1}{2}a_2 t_2^2$$

$\therefore \quad a_1 t_1^2 = a_2 t_2^2$

or $\quad \frac{t_1}{t_2} = \sqrt{\frac{a_2}{a_1}}$

Substituting the values from Eqs. (i) and (ii), we get

$$\frac{t_1}{t_2} = \sqrt{\frac{\frac{g}{\sqrt{2}}(1-\mu_k)}{\frac{g}{\sqrt{2}}}} = \sqrt{1-\mu_k}$$

Since, $\quad t_2 = 2t_1$

$\Rightarrow \quad \frac{t_1}{t_2} = \frac{1}{2}$

$\therefore \quad 1 - \mu_k = \frac{1}{4}$

or $\quad \mu_k = 1 - \frac{1}{4}$

$$= 0.75$$

43. (b) $a = \frac{\text{Net pulling force}}{\text{Total force}}$

$$= \frac{5g - 3g}{8} = \frac{g}{4}$$

Equation of motion of 5 kg block gives

$$5g - T = 5a = \frac{5g}{4}$$

$\therefore \quad T = \frac{15g}{4}$

$$= 36.75 \text{ N}$$

44. (b) $d\rho = \frac{\rho}{B} \cdot dp$

or $\quad \frac{d\rho}{\rho} = \frac{dp}{B}$

$$\frac{0.1}{100} = \frac{dp}{2.1 \times 10^9}$$

$\therefore dp = 2.1 \times 10^6 \text{ N/m}^2$

45. (d) The moment of inertia of the wheel about its axis, $I_1 = mr^2$

The moment of inertia of every spoke,

$$I_2 = \frac{mr^2}{3}$$

[considering as a rod and axis of the rod passing through one end]

So, total moment of inertia of wheel about its axis (i.e. passing through centre and perpendicular to its plane),

$$I_C = I_1 + 6I_2 = mr^2 + 6 \times \frac{1}{3}mr^2$$

$I_C = 3\,mr^2$ [$\because$ Number of spokes = 6]

If moment of inertia of wheel passing through point P and perpendicular to the plane is I_P, then using parallel axes theorem,

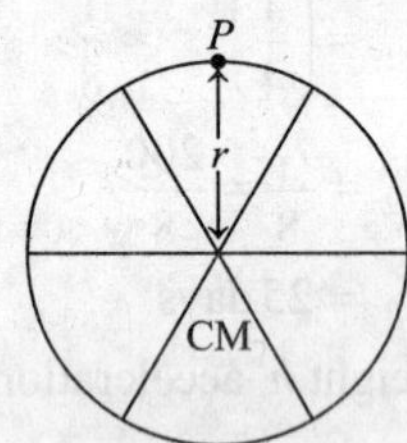

we can write

$$I = I_{\text{CM}} + Md^2$$

$$M = 6m + m = 7\,m,\ d = r$$

$$I_P = I_C + (7m)r^2$$

$$= 3mr^2 + 7mr^2$$

$$I_P = 10mr^2$$

NSS3 NEET Stepping Stones 3

1. (b) When a body is thrown upwards, its velocity starts decreasing and air resistance becomes smaller. Moreover when body falls down, then velocity starts increasing and air resistance becomes larger.

2. (c) During propagation of a plane progressive mechanical wave, all the particles are vibrating with different phases.

3. (c) A non-inertial frame has a non-zero acceleration, so equation in a non-inertial frame is

$$F_{\text{applied}} + F_{\text{pseudo}} = ma$$

Hence, Newton's laws are not valid.

4. (d) Mechanical energy at striking point = Mechanical energy at distance r from the centre

$$-\frac{GMm}{R} + \frac{1}{2}mv^2 = -\frac{GMm}{r} + 0$$

or $$\frac{v^2}{2} = \frac{GM}{R} - \frac{GM}{r}$$

$$\frac{v^2}{2} = GM\left(\frac{1}{R} - \frac{1}{r}\right)$$

$$\frac{v^2}{2} = gR^2\left(\frac{r-R}{Rr}\right)\left(\because g = \frac{GM}{R^2}\right)$$

$$v = \sqrt{\frac{2gR(r-R)}{r}}$$

5. (d) Force on block = Force of friction

$$\mu mg = ma$$

or $$a = \mu g$$

Time taken by block to come to rest,

$$t = \frac{v}{\mu g} \quad [\text{from } v = u + at]$$

6. (c) Maximum load that can be supported by cable is 320 kg, so for either part, it is also 320 kg.

7. (c) Angular momentum of planet remains constant, so

$$mv_1d_1 = mv_2d_2$$

or $$v_2 = v_1 d_1 / d_2$$

8. (b) By using, $\Delta Q = nC_p\Delta T$

and $$\Delta U = nC_V\Delta T$$

$\therefore$ Fraction of heat used in work done

$$= \frac{\Delta W}{\Delta Q} = \frac{\Delta Q - \Delta U}{\Delta Q}$$

$$= 1 - \frac{C_V}{C_p} = 1 - \frac{1}{\gamma}$$

9. (b) For hollow sphere, $\dfrac{K^2}{R^2} = \dfrac{2}{3}$

As we know that, ratio of rotational kinetic energy K_R to total kinetic energy K_T

$$\Rightarrow \frac{K_R}{K_T} = \frac{\frac{K^2}{R^2}}{1 + \frac{K^2}{R^2}}$$

or $$K_R = \left(\frac{\frac{K^2}{R^2}}{1 + \frac{K^2}{R^2}}\right) \times K_T$$

As $K_T = mgh = 3 \times 10 \times 20 = 600$ J

$$\therefore \quad K_R = \frac{\frac{2}{3}}{1 + \frac{2}{3}} \times 600 = 240 \text{ J}$$

10. (c) From the work-energy theorem,

$$W_{\text{conservative}} + W_{\text{non-conservative}} = \Delta\text{KE}$$

$$-\Delta U + W_{\text{non-conservative}} = \Delta\text{KE}$$

$$W_{\text{non-conservative}} = \Delta\text{KE} + \Delta U$$

or $$W_{\text{non-conservative}} = \Delta\text{ME}$$

If total work done by all non-conservative forces is zero,

i.e. $W_{\text{non-conservative}} = 0$

Then, $\Delta\text{ME} = 0$

Mechanical energy of the system remains constant, then mechanical energy conservation principle holds true.

11. (c) Given, $T = 4$ s

$$\Rightarrow \frac{2u\sin\theta}{g} = 4 \Rightarrow u\sin\theta = 20 \quad (g = 10 \text{ m/s}^2)$$

Also, for maximum range, $\theta = 45°$

$$\Rightarrow u\sin 45° = 20$$

$$\Rightarrow u = 20\sqrt{2} \text{ m/s}$$

Now, $$R_{\max} = \frac{u^2}{g}$$

$$\Rightarrow R_{\max} = \frac{(20\sqrt{2})^2}{10} = 80 \text{ m}$$

12. (b) Let initial amplitude and time period be A and T and final be A' and T', respectively.

Given, $T' = 2T$

As, maximum velocity,

$$v_{\max} = A\omega = \text{constant}$$

$$A'\omega' = A\omega \quad \ldots\text{(i)}$$

or $$A' \times \frac{2\pi}{T'} = A \times \frac{2\pi}{T}$$

or $$A' \times \frac{2\pi}{2T} = A \times \frac{2\pi}{T} \text{ or } A' = 2A \quad \ldots\text{(ii)}$$

It means, amplitude becomes double.

Maximum acceleration, $a_{\max} = \omega^2 A$

$$a'_{\max} = \omega'^2 A'$$

$$= \omega^2 2A = 2\omega^2 A = 2a_{\max}$$

[using Eqs. (i) and (ii)]

It means, maximum acceleration becomes double.

13. (d) From, $d_f = \dfrac{d_1}{(1 + \gamma\Delta T)}$

Fractional change $= \dfrac{d_1 - d_f}{d_1}$

$$= 1 - \frac{d_f}{d_1}$$

$$= 1 - (1 + \gamma\Delta T)^{-1} = 1 - (1 - \gamma\Delta T)$$

$$[\because (1+x)^n \approx 1 + nx = n/2]$$

$$= 5 \times 10^{-4} \times 50 = 0.025$$

14. (c) Unit of $\dfrac{h \times \sqrt{\varepsilon\mu}}{R}$

$$= \left(\frac{\text{J} \cdot \text{s} \times \frac{1}{\text{ms}^{-1}}}{\text{m}^{-1}}\right)$$

$$= \text{J} \cdot \text{s}^2$$

Now, $[\text{J}]\,[\text{s}^2] = [\text{ML}^2\text{T}^{-2}\text{T}^2]$

$$= [\text{ML}^2]$$

These are dimensions of moment of inertia.

15. (a) Let speed of sound be v.

Also L and r be the length and radius of the pipe respectively, fundamental frequency of a pipe (say closed organ pipe),

$$f = \frac{v}{4(L+e)}$$

where, $e = 0.6r$ is the end correction.

$$f = \frac{v}{4(l+0.6r)} \text{ or } \frac{v}{2(2l+1.2r)}$$

Therefore, if r is less, f will be more.

Both Statement I and Statement II are correct.

16. (b) When two springs of spring constant k_1 and k_2 are connected in series. The effective value of the composite spring k is given by

$$\frac{1}{k} = \frac{1}{k_1} + \frac{1}{k_2}, k = \frac{k_1 k_2}{k_1 + k_2}$$

Given, $t_1 = 2\pi\sqrt{\frac{m}{k_1}}, t_2 = 2\pi\sqrt{\frac{m}{k_2}}$ ... (i)

$$T = 2\pi\sqrt{\frac{m(k_1+k_2)}{k_1 k_2}}$$

$$= 2\pi\sqrt{\frac{m}{k_1} + \frac{m}{k_2}}$$

$$T^2 = 4\pi^2\left(\frac{m}{k_1} + \frac{m}{k_2}\right)$$

$$= 4\pi^2\frac{m}{k_1} + 4\pi^2\frac{m}{k_2}$$

From Eq. (i), $T^2 = t_1^2 + t_2^2$

17. (b) The frequency of the air column is given by $f = \frac{v}{\lambda}$, where v is the velocity of sound in air and λ is the wavelength.

But $v = \sqrt{\frac{\gamma RT}{M}}$, thus it is dependent of temperature.

or $f \propto \sqrt{T}$

Let the frequency of the tuning fork be f, thus the frequency of the air column at 15° C = $f + 4$

and the frequency of the air column at 10° C = $f + 3$

As, the frequency decreases with decrease temperature

$$\Rightarrow \frac{f+4}{f+3} = \sqrt{\frac{288}{283}}$$

$$\Rightarrow \frac{f+4}{f+3} = 1.00879$$

$$\Rightarrow f + 4 = 1.00879 f + 3.02638$$

$$\Rightarrow 8.79 \times 10^{-3} f = 0.97362$$

$$f = 110.76 \text{ Hz}$$

18. (a) $mg \sin\theta - f = ma$ ... (i)

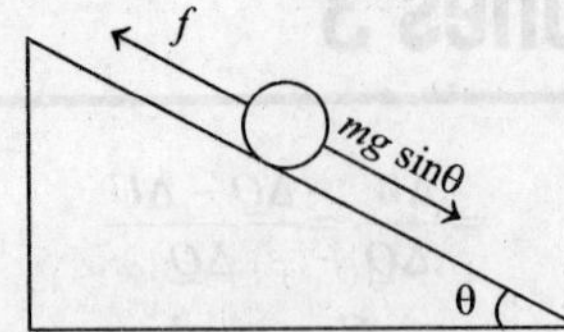

Also, $rF = \tau = I\alpha = \frac{MR^2}{2} \times \frac{a}{R}$

$$a = \frac{g \sin\theta}{1 + \frac{K^2}{R^2}} = \frac{2}{3} g \sin\theta$$

From Eq. (i), $mg \sin\theta - \frac{2}{3} mg \sin\theta = f$

$$\Rightarrow f = \frac{1}{3} mg \sin\theta \quad \text{... (ii)}$$

$$f = \mu mg \cos\theta = \frac{1}{3} mg \sin\theta$$

$$\Rightarrow \mu = \frac{1}{3} \tan\theta$$

19. (b) In case of adiabatic process,

$$TV^{\gamma-1} = \text{constant}$$

$$T_1 V_1^{\gamma-1} = T_2 V_2^{\gamma-1}$$

$$\therefore 300 V^{\frac{2}{3}} = T(2V)^{\frac{2}{3}} \quad \left(\because \gamma = \frac{5}{3}\right)$$

$$T = \frac{300}{2^{\frac{2}{3}}} = 189 \text{ K}$$

Now, the change in internal energy is given by

$$\Delta U = \frac{-nR(\Delta T)}{\gamma - 1}$$

$$\Delta U = \frac{-2 \times 8.31 \times (300 - 189)}{\frac{5}{3} - 1}$$

$$= -2767.23 \text{ J}$$

20. (d) Total energy on the Earth's surface = Total energy at the maximum height

$$\frac{1}{2} mv^2 + \left(-\frac{GMm}{R}\right) = -\frac{GMm}{R+h}$$

$$v^2 = \frac{2GM}{R}\left(1 - \frac{R}{R+h}\right) = 2gR\left(\frac{h}{R+h}\right)$$

$$(\because GM = gR^2)$$

Now for A, $v_A^2 = 2gR\left(\frac{h_A}{R+h_A}\right) = \frac{4gR}{3}$

or $\frac{h_A}{R+h_A} = \frac{2}{3}$

$$\Rightarrow h_A = 2R$$

and for B,

$$v_B^2 = 2gR\left(\frac{h_B}{R+h_B}\right) = \frac{2gR}{3}$$

or $\frac{h_B}{R+h_B} = \frac{1}{3} \Rightarrow h_B = \frac{R}{2}$

$$\therefore \frac{h_A}{h_B} = 4$$

21. (b) Heat release to convert steam at 200°C into 100°C steam,

$$Q_1 = 1 \times \frac{1}{2} \times 100 = 50 \text{ kcal}$$

Heat release to convert steam at 100°C into water at 100°C

$$Q_2 = 540 \times 1 = 540 \text{ kcal}$$

Heat release to convert water at 100° C into 0°C water,

$$Q_3 = 1 \times 1 \times 100 = 100 \text{ kcal}$$

Heat release to convert water into 0°C into ice at 0°C,

$$Q_4 = 1 \times 80 = 80 \text{ kcal}$$

Heat release 0°C ice into – 20° C ice.

$$Q_5 = 1 \times \frac{1}{2} \times 20 = 10 \text{ kcal}$$

Now, $Q_1 + Q_2 = 50 + 540 = 590$ kcal

$Q_1 + Q_3 = 50 + 100 = 150$ kcal

$Q_2 + Q_5 = 540 + 10 = 550$ kcal

$Q_3 + Q_4 = 100 + 80 + 180$ kcal

Hence, A → 3, B → 2, C → 4, D → 1.

22. (b) Let x be the compressed length.

Initial KE = PE of spring + work done against friction

$$\frac{1}{2} mv^2 = \frac{1}{2} kx^2 + fx$$

$$\frac{1}{2} \times 2 \times (4)^2 = \left(\frac{1}{2} \times 10000 \times x^2\right) + 15x$$

$$16 = 5000x^2 + 15x$$

$$5000x^2 + 15x - 16 = 0$$

$$x_2 = \frac{-15 \pm \sqrt{(15)^2 - 4 \times 5000 \times (-16)}}{2 \times 5000}$$

$$x_2 = \frac{-15 \pm 565.88}{10000}$$

(neglecting negative value)

$$x = 0.055 \text{ m} = 5.5 \text{ cm}$$

23. (d) Time taken to reach the bag in the ground, $t = \sqrt{\frac{2h}{g}} = \sqrt{\frac{2 \times 490}{9.8}} = 10\text{s}$

The distance can be calculated using $R = ut = 150 \times 10 = 1500 \text{m}$

24. (c) As, joule is the SI unit of energy and dimensional formula of energy is $[ML^2T^{-2}]$.

Now, $n_1 [M_1L_1^2T_1^{-2}] = n_2[M_2L_2^2T_2^{-2}]$

$$n_2 = n_1\left[\frac{M_1}{M_2}\right]^1\left[\frac{L_1}{L_2}\right]^2\left[\frac{T_1}{T_2}\right]^{-2}$$

$$= 1\times\left[\frac{1\text{kg}}{10\text{kg}}\right]^1\left[\frac{1\text{m}}{1\text{km}}\right]^2\left[\frac{1\text{s}}{1\text{min}}\right]^{-2}$$

$$= 1\times\left[\frac{1\text{kg}}{10\text{kg}}\right]^1\left[\frac{1\text{m}}{10^3\text{m}}\right]^2\left[\frac{1\text{s}}{60\text{s}}\right]^{-2}$$

$$= 1\times 10^{-1}\times 10^{-6}\times 36\times 10^{+2}$$

$$n_2 = 36\times 10^{-5}$$

25. (b) Given, equation of displacement of the particle,

$$y = \sin^3 \omega t = \frac{3\sin\omega t - \sin 3\omega t}{4}$$

$$\left(\sin^3\theta = \frac{3\sin\theta - \sin 3\theta}{4}\right)$$

$$\Rightarrow \frac{dy}{dt} = \left[\frac{\frac{d}{dt}(3\sin\omega t) - \frac{d}{dt}(\sin 3\omega t)}{4}\right]$$

$$\Rightarrow 4\frac{dy}{dt} = 3\omega\cos\omega t - [3\omega\cos 3\omega t]$$

$$4\frac{d^2y}{dt^2} = -3\omega^2\sin\omega t + 9\omega^2\sin 3\omega t$$

$$\Rightarrow \frac{d^2y}{dt^2} = -\frac{3\omega^2(\sin\omega t - 3\sin 3\omega t)}{4}$$

$\Rightarrow \frac{d^2y}{dt^2}$ is not proportional to y.

Hence, motion is not SHM.

As, the expression is involving sine functions, hence it will be periodic.

26. (a) For a real gas, internal energy,

$$dU = CdT - \left[p - T\left(\frac{dp}{dT}\right)_V\right]dV$$

So, internal energy depends on both temperature and volume.

The first term in the equation is for kinetic energy and the second term is for potential energy.

27. (a) Before entering the water, the velocity of ball is $\sqrt{2gh}$. If after entering the water, this velocity does not change, then this value should be equal to the terminal velocity. Therefore,

$$\sqrt{2gh} = \frac{2}{9}\frac{r^2(\rho-\sigma)g}{\eta}$$

$$\therefore \quad h = \frac{\left\{\frac{2}{9}\frac{r^2(\rho-\sigma)g}{\eta}\right\}^2}{2g}$$

$$= \frac{2}{81}\times\frac{r^4(\rho-\sigma)^2 g}{\eta^2}$$

$$= \frac{2}{81}\times\frac{(3\times10^{-4})^4(10^4-10^3)^2\times 9.8}{(9.8\times10^{-6})^2}$$

$$= 1.65\times 10^3 \text{ m}$$

28. (a) Strain $= \frac{\Delta L}{L} = \frac{\text{Stress}}{Y} = \frac{5\times10^7}{2\times10^{11}}$

$$= 2.5\times 10^{-4}$$

Given, $\frac{\Delta V}{V} = 0.02\% = \frac{0.02}{100} = 2\times10^{-4}$

And $\quad V = \pi r^2 L$

On differentiating it by taking V_1, r_1 and L as independent variables, we get

$$\Delta V = 2\pi rL\,\Delta r + \pi r^2\Delta L$$

$$\frac{\Delta V}{V} = \frac{2\pi rL\Delta r + \pi r^2\Delta L}{\pi r^2 L}$$

$$\frac{\Delta V}{V} = 2\frac{\Delta r}{r} + \frac{\Delta L}{L}$$

$$2\times10^{-4} = 2\frac{\Delta r}{r} + 2.5\times10^{-4}$$

$$\frac{\Delta r}{r} = -\frac{0.5\times10^{-4}}{2} = -0.25\times10^{-4}$$

Hence, the fractional decrease in radius of the wire $= +\,0.25\times10^{-4}$

29. (d) Heat released by steam in conversion to water a 100°C, $Q_1 = mL = 8\times 540 = 4320$ cal

Heat required to raise temperature of water from 50°C to 100°C,

$Q_2 = mS\,\Delta\theta = 40\times1\times50 = 2000$ J

$$Q_1 > Q_2$$

Hence, all steam is not converted to water.

Steam converted into water is

$$m = \frac{Q_2}{L} = \frac{2000}{540} = 3.7\text{ g}$$

$\therefore$ Final mass of water

$= 40 + 3.7 = 43.7$ g

30. (b) Since, the block moves with constant speed, no net force act on the block. Therefore, force of friction f_r, must balance the horizontal component is applied force $F\cos 30°$.

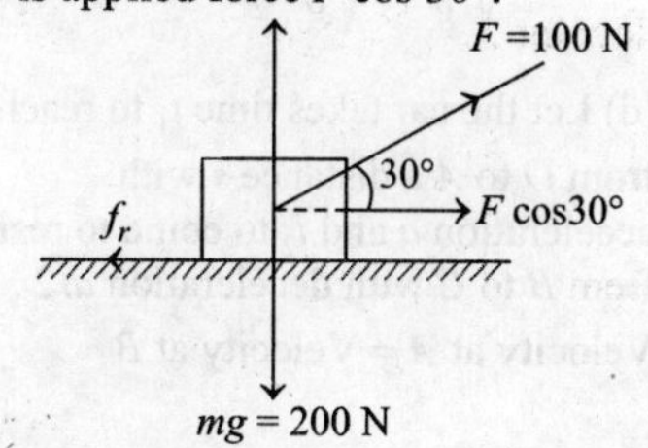

$$f_r = f\cos 30°$$

But $f_r = \mu Mg - \mu F\sin 30°$

$$= \mu\times 200 - \mu\times 100\times\frac{1}{2} = 150\mu$$

$$\therefore 150\mu = F\cos 30° = 100\cos 30°$$

$$\mu = \frac{100\times\sqrt{3}}{150\times 2} = 0.58$$

31. (a) The equation of trajecting of the ball,

$$y = x\tan\theta - \frac{1}{2}\frac{g}{u^2\cos^2\theta}x^2$$

At the ground level point $+\,Q$,

$y = 1.2$ m

$x = 110$ m, $\theta = 45°$

$$1.2 = 110\tan 45° - \frac{10}{2u^2\cos^2 45°}\times(110)^2$$

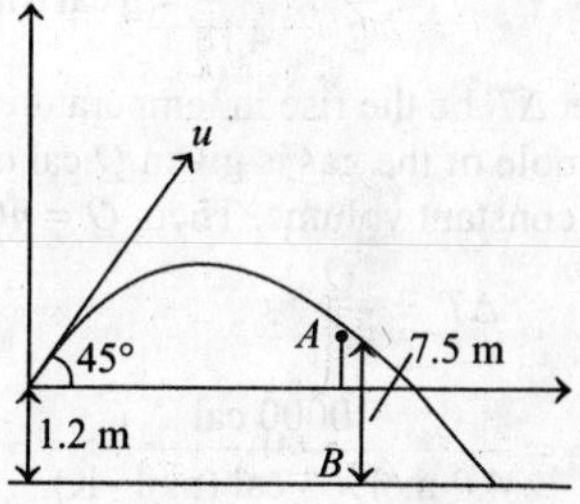

$$u^2 = \left(\frac{10\times(110)^2}{2\times 108.8\times\frac{1}{2}}\right) = \frac{(110)^2}{10.88}$$

$$u = \frac{110}{\sqrt{10.88}}$$

32. (b) Let s be the total distance.

$$t_1 = \frac{\frac{s}{3}}{v_1} = \frac{s}{3v_1}$$

Further, t_2 is the time for each remaining part of the journey, then the remaining distance is $s - \frac{s}{3} = \frac{2s}{3}$

$$\frac{2s}{3} = v_2t_2 + v_3t_2 = (v_2+v_3)t_2$$

$$t_2 = \frac{2s}{3(v_2+v_3)}$$

Now average velocity,

$$v = \frac{\text{Total displacement}}{\text{Total time}}$$

$$= \frac{s}{t_1 + 2t_2} = \frac{s}{\frac{s}{3v_1} + \frac{4s}{3(v_2+v_3)}}$$

$$v = \frac{3v_1(v_2+v_3)}{v_2+v_3+4v_1}$$

33. (b) As, $F = \frac{dp}{dt} \Rightarrow F = \frac{d}{dt}(3t^2 + 4) = 6t$

$ma = 6t,\ 2a = 6t$

$\Rightarrow \quad a = (3t)\ \text{m/s}^2$

So, $\quad a \propto t$

So, the sphere moving with a variable acceleration.

34. (b) Given, $P = 10^6\ \text{N/m}^2$,

$V = 10\text{L} = 10^{-2} M^3$

$T = 27 + 273 = 300K$

$\therefore n = \frac{pV}{RT} = \frac{10^6 \times 10^{-2}}{8.31 \times 300} = 4.0$

For monoatomic gas, $C_V = \frac{3}{2}R$

Thus, $C_V = \frac{3}{2} \times 8.31\ \text{J/mol-K}$

$= \frac{3}{2} \times \frac{8.31}{4.18} \approx 3\ \text{cal /(mol-K)}$

Let ΔT be the rise in temperature, when n mole of the gas is given Q cal of heat at constant volume. Then, $Q = nC_V\Delta T$

or $\quad \Delta T = \frac{Q}{nC_V}$

$= \frac{10000\ \text{cal}}{4.0\ \text{mol} \times 3\ \text{cal (mol - K)}} = 833\ \text{K}$

$\Delta T = T_f - T_i$

$T_f = \Delta T + T_i = 833 + 300 = 1133\ \text{K}$

35. (b) Given, radius of steel cable,

$r = 1.5\ \text{cm} = 1.5 \times 10^{-2}\ \text{m}$

Maximum stress $= 10^8\ \text{N/m}^2$

$\therefore$ Area of cross-section of cable,

$A = \pi r^2 = \pi(1.5 \times 10^{-2})^2$

Maximum stress

$= \frac{\text{Maximum force}}{\text{Area of cross - section}}$

or Maximum force = Maximum stress × Area of cross-section

$= 10^8 \times \pi \times (1.5 \times 10^{-2})^2$

$= 7.1 \times 10^4\ \text{N}$

36. (d) Given, ratio of radius of two wires,

$r_1 : r_2 = 2 : 1 \Rightarrow \frac{r_1}{r_2} = \frac{2}{1}$

and ratio in their lengths,

$l_1 : l_2 = 1 : 2 \Rightarrow \frac{l_1}{l_2} = \frac{1}{4}$

As, $\quad Y = \frac{Fl}{A\Delta l} \Rightarrow \Delta l = \frac{Fl}{AY}$

$\Delta l \propto \frac{l}{A}$

$\therefore \quad \frac{\Delta l_1}{\Delta l_2} = \frac{l_1 A_2}{l_2 A_1} \Rightarrow \frac{\Delta l_1}{\Delta l_2} = \frac{l_1}{l_2} \cdot \frac{r_2^2}{r_1^2}$

$= \frac{1}{4} \cdot \left(\frac{1}{2}\right)^2 = \frac{1}{16}$

37. (a) Let the truck accelerates for time t_1 and decelerates for time t_2, where t is the total time.

Velocity of the truck after t_1,

$v = 0 + at_1 = at_1$

Since, the car finally stops after time t,

$\therefore \quad v = u + at$

$0 = at_1 - b(t - t_1)$

$(a + b)t_1 = bt$

$t_1 = \left(\frac{b}{a + b}\right)t$

Now, the maximum velocity of the car after time t_1, $v_{\max} = 0 + at_1 = \left(\frac{ab}{a + b}\right)t$

38. (d) When the ball is projected from the top of the building vertically upward with speed u, it reaches the ground in time t_1.

Let n be the height of the building, then

$h = ut + \frac{1}{2}gt^2$

$h = -ut_1 + \frac{1}{2}gt_1^2 \quad \text{... (i)}$

For second situation,

$h = ut_2 + \frac{1}{2}gt_2^2 \quad \text{... (ii)}$

From Eqs. (i) and (ii),

$-u(t_2 + t_1) + \frac{1}{2}g(t_1^2 - t_2^2) = 0$

or $\quad u = \frac{1}{2}g(t_1 - t_2)$

Substituting the value in Eq. (ii), we get

$h = \frac{1}{2}gt_2(t_1 - t_2) + \frac{1}{2}gt_2^2$

$= \frac{1}{2}gt_2[t_1 - t_2 + t_2] = \frac{1}{2}gt_1t_2$

when the ball falls freely from height h, it takes time t, then $h = 0 + \frac{1}{2}gt^2$

$t = \sqrt{\frac{2h}{g}} = \sqrt{\frac{2}{g} \cdot \frac{1}{2}gt_1t_2} = \sqrt{t_1t_2}$

39. (d) Let the car takes time t_1 to reach from O to A a distance s with acceleration a and t_2 to come to rest from B to C with deceleration $a/2$.

Velocity at A = Velocity at B

$at_1 = \frac{a}{2}t_2 \Rightarrow t_2 = 2t_1$

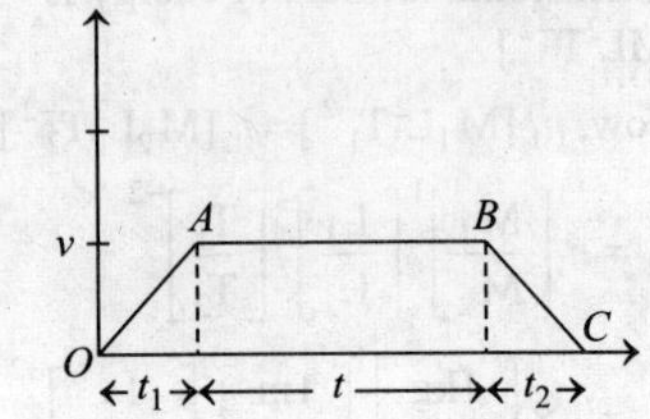

Now, $s_1 = 0 + \frac{1}{2}at_1^2 = \frac{1}{2}at_1^2 = s$ (given)

$s_2 = (at_1)t \quad (\because v = 0 + a)$

$s_3 = (at_1)t_2 - \frac{1}{2} \cdot \frac{a}{2}t_2^2$

$= at_1 2t_1 - \frac{a}{4}(2t_1)^2$

$= 2at_1^2 - at_1^2 = at_1^2$

But, $s_1 + s_2 + s_3 = 15s$

$\therefore \frac{1}{2}at_1^2 + at_1t + at_1^2 = 15s$

$\frac{3}{2}at_1^2 + at_1t = 15s$

$3s + at_1t = 15s$

$at_1\ t = 12S = 12\frac{1}{2}at_1^2$

$t_1 = \frac{t}{6} \quad \therefore s = \frac{at^2}{72}$

40. (c) At height h above the surface of earth,

$g_h = \left(\frac{R}{R + h}\right)^2 g = \left(1 - \frac{2h}{R}\right)g \quad \text{... (i)}$

and at a depth h from the surface of earth, $g_h' = \left(1 - \frac{h}{R}\right)g \quad \text{... (ii)}$

From Eq. (i), $\frac{g_h}{g} = 1 - \frac{2h}{R}$

or $\quad 1 - \frac{g_h}{g} = \frac{2h}{R}$

$\frac{g - g_h}{g} = \frac{2h}{R} = 1\% \quad \text{... (iii)}$

Similarly for Eq (ii), we get

$\frac{g - g_h'}{g} = \frac{h}{R}$

$= \frac{1}{2}\%$ or 0.5% decreases

41. (c) Maximum kinetic energy = Energy of oscillation in SHM

$\therefore \quad 8 = \frac{1}{2}kA^2 \Rightarrow kA^2 = 16 \quad \text{...(i)}$

Further, $2\pi\sqrt{\frac{m}{k}} = 4 \quad (\because T = 4\text{s})$

$\therefore \quad \frac{1}{k}=\frac{4}{\pi^2}$ or $k=\frac{\pi^2}{4}$ ...(ii)

From Eqs. (i) and (ii), we get

$k \approx 2.5\ \text{Nm}^{-1}$ and $A \approx 2.53\ \text{m}$

Maximum acceleration of the particle will be $a_{max}=\omega^2 A=\frac{k}{m}A$

$$=\left(\frac{2.5}{1}\right)(2.53) \approx 6.3\ \text{ms}^{-2}$$

42. (a) Root mean square speed of a gas molecule is given by

$$v_{rms}=\sqrt{\frac{3RT}{M}}$$

and $v_{av}=\sqrt{\frac{8RT}{\pi M}}$

We have, $v_{rms}=1260$ m/s

So, $\frac{v_{av}}{v_{rms}}=\frac{\sqrt{\frac{8RT}{\pi M}}}{\sqrt{\frac{3RT}{M}}} \Rightarrow \frac{v_{av}}{1260}=\sqrt{\frac{8}{3\pi}}$

$$\Rightarrow v_{av}=1260\times\sqrt{\frac{8}{3\pi}} \Rightarrow v_{av}=1161\ \text{m/s}$$

43. (b) Let the length and area of cross-section of rods be l and A, respectively.

Thermal resistance of rod A,

$$R_A=\frac{l}{K_A A}$$

Thermal resistance of rod B,

$$R_B=\frac{l}{K_B A}$$

Thermal resistance of rod C,

$$R_C=\frac{l}{K_C A}$$

Like electrical equivalent circuit, thermal resistance in series are added. In question, rods are joined end-to-end i.e. arrangement in series,

$$R_s=R_A+R_B+R_C$$

$$\frac{3l}{K_{eff}A}=\frac{l}{K_A A}+\frac{l}{K_B A}+\frac{l}{K_C A}$$

or $\frac{3}{K_{eff}}=\frac{1}{K_A}+\frac{1}{K_B}+\frac{1}{K_C}$

Here, $K_A=2K_B$ and $K_C=\frac{K_B}{2}$

$$\therefore \quad \frac{3}{K_{eff}}=\frac{1}{2K_B}+\frac{1}{K_B}+\frac{2}{K_B}$$

$$=\frac{1+2+4}{2K_B}=\frac{7}{2K_B}$$

or $K_{eff}=\frac{6}{7}K_B$

44. (a) For isothermal process,

$T=$ constant, $\Delta E_{int}=0$

$\Rightarrow \quad \Delta Q=\Delta W$

For adiabatic process,

$\Delta Q=0$

$\Rightarrow \quad \Delta E_{int}=-\Delta W$

For free expansion,

$\Delta Q=\Delta W=\Delta E_{int}=0$

Hence, A $\rightarrow$ 3, B $\rightarrow$ 2, C $\rightarrow$ 4 and D $\rightarrow$ 1.

45. (b) Angular displacement in $\frac{3\pi}{10}$ s,

$$\omega=\frac{v}{r}=\frac{10}{2}=5\ \text{rad/s}$$

$$\theta=\omega t=5\times\frac{3\pi}{10}$$

$$=\frac{3\pi}{2}\ \text{rad}$$

After travelling $\frac{3\pi}{2}$ rad angular displacement, the position of particle will be at point Q, as shown in the figure.

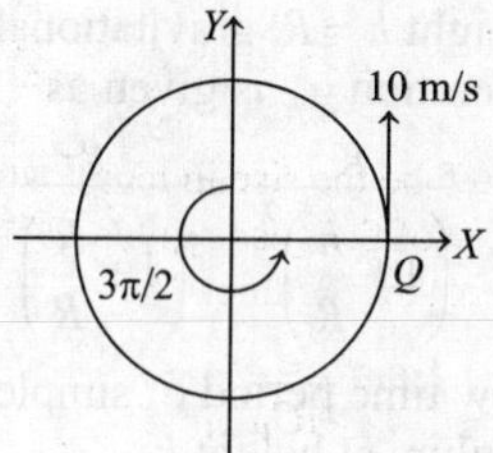

While revolving in circular path, particle have centripetal acceleration only (when speed is constant) which acts towards the centre of circular path. Thus, $t=\frac{3\pi}{5}$ s, the direction of particle is along negative X-axis.

NSS4 NEET Stepping Stones 4

1. (a) There is no external torque is working, therefore the ball will move continue with the same angular velocity along the original orbit of the spacecraft.

2. (c) Given, $v=25$ m/s, $u=15$ m/s, $s=150$ m

$\therefore \quad v^2-u^2=2as$

$$a=\frac{v^2-u^2}{2s}=\frac{(25)^2-(15)^2}{2\times150}$$

$$=\frac{625-225}{300}=\frac{400}{300}$$

$$=\frac{4}{3}\ \text{m/s}^2$$

Now, $v=u+at$

$$t=\frac{v-u}{a}=\frac{25-15}{4/3}$$

$$=\frac{10\times3}{4}=7.5$$

3. (b) Work done during adiabatic process is given by

$$W=\frac{\mu R}{\gamma-1}[T_i-T_f]$$

$$=\frac{5\times8.3}{\frac{7}{5}-1}[0+273)(400+273)]$$

$$=-\frac{5\times8.3\times5}{2}[400]$$

$$=-41.5\times10^3\ \text{J}=-41.5\ \text{kJ}$$

The negative sign indicates that this work is done on the gas during compression.

Now using the first law of thermodynamics,

$$\Delta U=\Delta Q-\Delta W$$

$$=0-(-41.5)$$

[In adiabatic process, $\Delta Q=0$]

$$=41.5\ \text{kJ}$$

4. (a) Here, $A_1=16\text{cm}^2$

$A_2=40\text{cm}^2$

$\therefore \quad \Delta A=(40-16)=24\ \text{cm}^2$

$= 24 \times 10^{-4}\ m^2$

$W = 5 \times 10^{-4}$ J

Now, workdone = surface tension × change in area × number of film surfaces

$$W = T \times \Delta A \times n$$

$$T = \frac{W}{\Delta A \times n} = \frac{5 \times 10^{-4}}{24 \times 10^{-4} \times 2}$$

$$= \frac{5}{48} = 0.1\ \text{N/m}$$

5. (a) Time period of simple pendulum on the earth's surface,

$$T = 2\pi\sqrt{\frac{l}{g}} \quad \ldots\text{(i)}$$

Where, l is length of pendulum.

At height $h = R$, gravitational acceleration g_h is given as

$$g_h = \frac{g}{\left(1+\frac{h}{R}\right)^2} = \frac{g}{\left(1+\frac{R}{R}\right)^2} = \frac{g}{4}$$

∴ New time period of simple pendulum at height h.

$$T' = 2\pi\sqrt{\frac{l}{g_h}} = 2\pi\sqrt{\frac{l}{g/4}}$$

$$= 2 \times 2\pi\sqrt{\frac{l}{g}} = 2T \quad \text{[From Eq. (i)]}$$

$$= xT \quad \text{[Given]}$$

$\therefore \quad x = 2$

6. (d) None of the given relations in (a), (b) and (c) can be derived using dimensional analysis. Method of dimensions cannot be used to derive exponential, logarithmic, trigonometric or product of power functions.

7. (b) Given, $A = 5$ cm, $x = 3$ cm

The velocity of a particle in SHM,

$$v = \omega\sqrt{A^2 - x^2}$$

and acceleration, $a = \omega^2 x$

$\because \quad |v| = |a|$

$$\omega\sqrt{A^2 - x^2} = \omega^2 x$$

$$\sqrt{A^2 - x^2} = \omega x$$

$$\Rightarrow \quad A^2 - x^2 = \omega^2 x^2$$

$$\omega = \sqrt{\frac{A^2 - x^2}{x^2}}$$

$$\sqrt{\frac{25-9}{9}} = \frac{4}{3}$$

$$\therefore \text{Time period, } T = \frac{2\pi}{\omega} = \frac{2\pi \times 3}{4} = 4.7\ \text{s}$$

8. (b) Ideal gas expands isothermally from volume V_1 to V_2 (shown by the curve ab) and then compressed to the original volume V_1 adiabatically (shown by the curve bc).

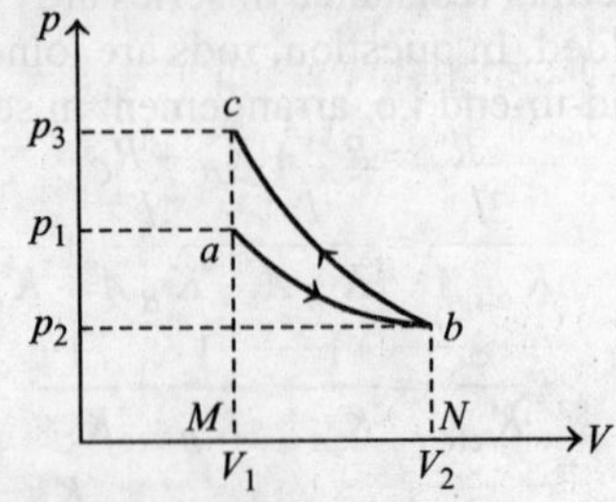

For isothermal expansion $(a \rightarrow b)$,

$$p_1V_1 = p_2V_2$$

or $$p_1 = p_2\left(\frac{V_2}{V_1}\right)$$

For adiabatic compression $(b \rightarrow c)$,

$$p_3V_1^{\gamma} = p_2V_2^{\gamma}$$

or $$p_3 = p_2\left(\frac{V_2}{V_1}\right)^{\gamma}$$

$\because \gamma > 1$ and $V_2 > V_1$

Hence, $p_3 > p_1$

Further, the slope of the adiabatic curve is γ times the slope of the isothermal curve and since $\gamma > 1$, therefore adiabatic curve will lie above the isothermal curve as shown in the graph.

Work done = Area $abNMa$ – Area $cbNMc$

Work done = – [Area $cabc$], i.e. negative

$\therefore \quad W < 0$

9. (c) Given, period of revolution of planet A, $T_A = 27T_B$

From Kepler's 3rd law of planetary motion,

$$T^2 = R^3$$

$$\therefore \quad \left(\frac{R_A}{R_B}\right)^3 = \left(\frac{T_A}{T_B}\right)^2$$

$$\left(\frac{R_A}{R_B}\right)^3 = (27)^2$$

$$\frac{R_A}{R_B} = 3^2 = 9$$

$$\Rightarrow \quad R_A = 9R_B$$

10. (d) As ball drops in water, its velocity increases till it reaches terminal velocity. So, KE first increases and then it becomes constant.

11. (c) Statement I is correct but Statement II is incorrect.

Statement I direct refers to law of inertia and according to it an object will remain at rest or in uniform motion in a straight line unless acted upon by an external force.

In an accelerating frame, we also have a pseudo force.

Hence in an accelerating frame,

$F_{\text{applied}} + F_{\text{pseudo}} = m \times a_{\text{body}}$.

12. (b)

During the upward motion, the component of mg parallel to the plane is $mg \sin \theta$, which is in the direction opposite to motion that decreases the velocity of centre of mass.

Also, for pure rolling, the relation $v_{CM} = \omega R$ must be obeyed.

Therefore, ω must decrease. Here, only friction can provide a torque about the centre. Torque due to friction must be opposite to ω. Therefore, friction force will act up the plane during upward journey.

13. (b) The given situation is as shown in the figure below.

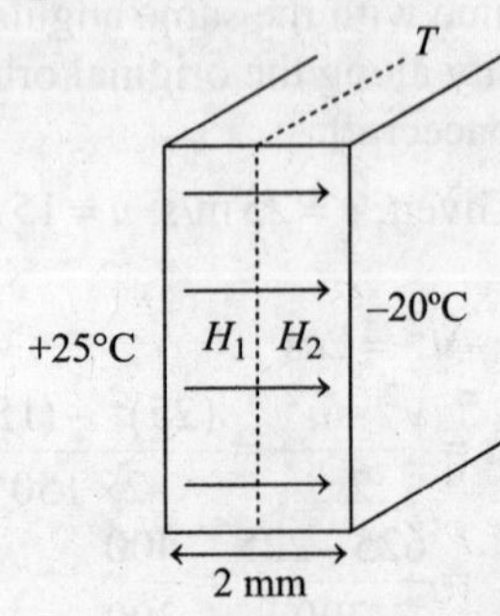

Let the temperature of mid-point be $T°$ C.

At steady state, rate of heat transfer from inside to outside will be same.

$$H_1 = H_2$$

$$\frac{K_1 A_1 \Delta T_1}{l_1} = \frac{K_2 A_2 \Delta T_2}{l_2} \quad ...(i)$$

Here, $K_1 = K_2$, $A_1 = A_2$

and $l_1 = l_2 = 1\,\text{mm}$

So, from Eq. (i),

$$\Delta T_1 = \Delta T_2$$

$$25 - T = T - (-20)$$

$$2T = 25 - 20$$

or $T = \frac{5}{2} = 2.5\,°\text{C}$

14. (d) Specific heat capacity, $s = \frac{\Delta Q}{m \Delta T}$,

where m is mass of substance. Its SI unit is $\text{Jkg}^{-1}\text{K}^{-1}$.

Molar specific heat capacity

$C = \frac{\Delta Q}{\mu \Delta T}$, where μ is number of moles. Its SI unit is $\text{Jmol}^{-1}\text{K}^{-1}$.

Both of these are constants characteristics of a substance and are independent of its mass.

Therefore, A is false but R is true.

15. (a) Heat evolved in a resistance is given by

$$H = I^2 RT$$

Maximum percentage error in H is

$$\left(\frac{\Delta H}{H} \times 100\right)_{\max} = \left(2\frac{\Delta I}{I} + \frac{\Delta R}{R} + \frac{\Delta T}{T}\right)\%$$

$$= (2 \times 1 + 2 + 2)$$

$$= 6\%$$

16. (d) Area of cross-section of metal rod,

$$A = \sqrt{\pi r_1^2 \times \pi r_2^2}$$

$$= \pi r_1 r_2$$

$$Y = \frac{F}{A} \times \frac{l}{\Delta l}$$

$$\Delta l = \frac{F}{Y} \cdot \frac{l}{A} = \frac{Fl}{\pi r_1 r_2 Y}$$

17. (b) From A to B,

$$W_{AB} = p(V_B - V_A) = 10(2-1)$$

$$= 10\,\text{J}$$

From B to C, volume is constant, hence $W_{BC} = 0$

Given $Q = 5\,\text{J}$ for the closed cycle $ABCA$, thus, work done during the closed cycle is also 5J.

Now, $W_{\text{total}} = W_{AB} + W_{BC} + W_{CA} = 5\,\text{J}$

$$10 + 0 + W_{CA} = 5\,\text{J}$$

$$W_{CA} = -5\,\text{J}$$

18. (b) Temperature gradient

$$= \frac{\theta_1 - \theta_2}{l} = \frac{100 - 0}{1} = 100°\text{C/m}$$

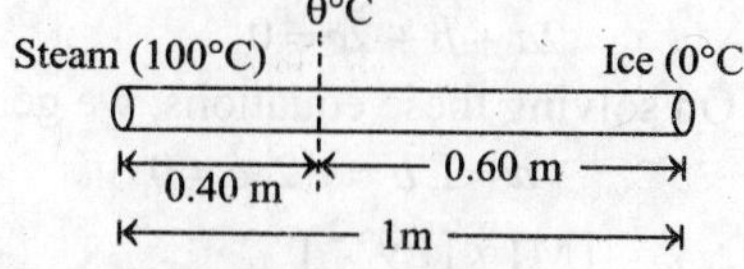

Also, $\frac{100 - \theta}{0.40} = \frac{\theta - 0}{0.60}$

$$100 - \theta = \frac{2}{3}\theta \Rightarrow \frac{5}{3}\theta = 100$$

or $\theta = 60°\text{C}$

19. (b) Remember that octave is twice of the fundamental. If f is the frequency of first tuning fork, then the frequency of last tuning fork must be $2f$. Since, any two successive forks produce 4 beats/s,

Frequency of 2nd fork is

$$f + 4 = f + 1 \times 4$$

that of 3rd fork is $f + 8 = f + 2 \times 4$

that of 4th fork is $f + 12 = f + 3 \times 4$

and finally that of Nth fork is

$$f + (N-1)4$$

where, N is the total number of forks.

Given,

$$f + (N-1)4 = 2f$$

$$(N-1)4 = f = 256$$

$$N - 1 = 64$$

$\therefore$ $N = 65$

20. (d) Given, $v = at + \frac{b}{t + c}$

From principle of homogeneity,

$$[at] = [v]$$

$$[aT] = [\text{LT}^{-1}]$$

$$[a] = [\text{LT}^{-2}]$$

Also, $\frac{[b]}{[t + c]} = [v] = [\text{LT}^{-1}]$

$$b = [\text{LT}^{-1}][\text{T}] = [\text{L}]$$

and $[t + c] = [\text{T}]$

$$c = [\text{T}]$$

21. (a) Resultant wave, $y = y_1 + y_2$

$$y = 20\cos\frac{x}{2}\sin 5t$$

On comparing with the standard equation,

$$y = 2A\cos\left(\frac{2\pi x}{\lambda}\right)\sin\left(\frac{2\pi vt}{\lambda}\right)$$

$$= 2A\cos kx \sin \omega t$$

we get, $\frac{2\pi}{\lambda} = \frac{1}{2}$

or $\lambda = 4\pi$

Now minimum distance between node and anti-node is

$$\frac{\lambda}{4} = \pi = 3.14\,\text{cm}$$

22. (a) $V_t = V_0(1 + \gamma t)$

$$L_t^3 = L_0(1 + \alpha_1 t)L_0^2(1 + \alpha_2 t)^2$$

$$= L_0^3(1 + \alpha_1 t)(1 + \alpha_2 t)^2 \quad ...(i)$$

$$V_t = V_0(1 + \gamma t)$$

or $L_t^3 = L_0^3(1 + \gamma t)$

$$= L_0^3(1 + \alpha_1 t)(1 + \alpha_2 t)^2$$

[from Eq. (i)]

or $1 + \gamma t = (1 + \alpha_1 t)(1 + \alpha_2 t)^2$

$$\approx (1 + \alpha_1 t)(1 + 2\alpha_2 t)$$

$\because$ α_1 and α_2 are very small.

$$= 1 + (\alpha_1 + 2\alpha_2)t + 2\alpha_1\alpha_2 t^2$$

The product $2\alpha_1\alpha_2 t^2$ is negligibly small.

$\therefore$ $1 + \gamma t = 1 + (\alpha_1 + 2\alpha_2)t$

or $\gamma = \alpha_1 + 2\alpha_2$

23. (b) C is the centre of mass of the triangular structure shown in the figure.

$$AR = \sqrt{l^2 - \left(\frac{l}{2}\right)^2} = \frac{\sqrt{3}}{2} \cdot l$$

$$\therefore CR = \frac{AR}{3} = \frac{l}{2\sqrt{3}} = CP = CQ$$

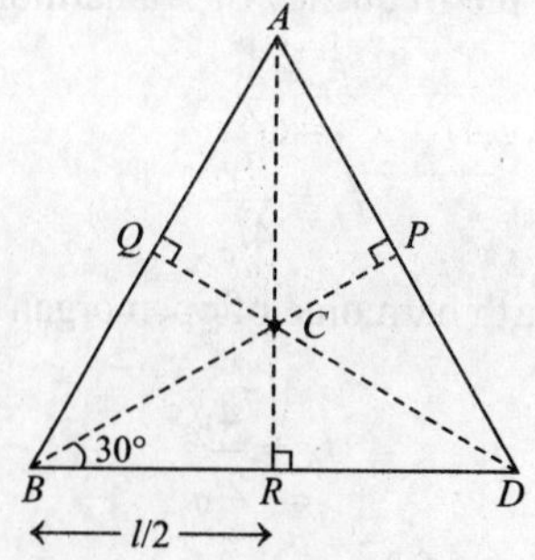

Now moment of inertia of either rod about an axis passing through its middle point (centre) and perpendicular to its length,

$$I_{CM} = \frac{ml^2}{12}$$

Using the theorem of parallel axes, the moment of inertia of either rod about an axis passing through C and perpendicular to the plane of the structure,

$$I = I_{CM} + m(CP)^2$$

$$= \frac{ml^2}{12} + m\left(\frac{l}{2\sqrt{3}}\right)^2$$

$$= \frac{ml^2}{12} + \frac{ml^2}{12} = \frac{ml^2}{6}$$

24. (c) The range of a projectile on level ground for which air resistance is negligible.

$R = \frac{v_0^2 \sin 2\theta_0}{g}$, where v_0 is the initial speed and θ_0 is the initial angle relative to the horizontal. Solving for initial angle gives

$\theta_0 = \frac{1}{2}\sin^{-1}\left(\frac{gR}{v_0^2}\right)$, where

Given, $R = 7.0\,\text{m}, v_0 = 12.0\,\text{m/s}$ and $g = 9.8\,\text{m/s}^2$

Therefore,

$$\theta_0 = \frac{1}{2}\sin^{-1}\left(\frac{(9.80\,\text{m/s}^2)(7.0\,\text{m})}{(12.0\,\text{m/s})^2}\right)$$

$$= 14.2^\circ$$

25. (a) Third overtone of closed organ pipe means its seventh harmonic. The length of closed organ pipe is therefore

$$l_c = \frac{7\lambda}{4} \Rightarrow \lambda = \frac{4l_c}{7}$$

and the frequency of 7th harmonic is

$$f_7 = \frac{v}{\lambda}$$

$$f_7 = \frac{7v}{4l_c}$$

Fourth harmonic of open organ pipe is

$$f_4 = \frac{4v}{2l_0}$$

Given $(f_7)_{\text{closed}} = (f_4)_{\text{open}}$

$$\frac{7v}{4l_c} = \frac{4v}{2l_0}$$

$$\therefore \quad \frac{l_c}{l_0} = \frac{14}{16} = \frac{7}{8}$$

26. (a) Let $M \propto E^a v^b F^c$

or $M = k[\text{ML}^2\text{T}^{-2}]^a[\text{LT}^{-1}]^b[\text{MLT}^{-2}]^c$

$$M = k[\text{M}]^{a+c}[\text{L}]^{2a+b+c}[\text{T}]^{2a+b+2c}$$

$a + c = 1$; $2a + b + c = 0$,

$$2a + b + 2c = 0$$

On solving these equations, we get

$$a = 1, b = -2, c = 0$$

$$\therefore \quad [\text{M}] \propto [\text{Ev}^{-2}]$$

27. (d) For adiabatic change, $\Delta Q = 0$

$$\therefore \quad \Delta U = \Delta Q - \Delta W = -\Delta W$$

$$\mu C_V \Delta T = -\Delta W = +146 \times 10^3\ \text{J}$$

(Work is performed on the system, hence negative)

$$C_V = \frac{146 \times 10^3}{\mu \cdot \Delta T}$$

$$= \frac{146 \times 10^3}{10^3 \times 7} = \frac{146}{7}\ \text{J/mole-K}$$

But $C_V = \frac{f}{2}R$

$$\therefore \quad \frac{f}{2}R = \frac{146}{7}$$

$$f = \frac{146}{7} \times \frac{2}{R} = \frac{146}{7} \times \frac{2}{8.3}$$

$$f \approx 5$$

Hence, the gas is diatomic.

28. (d) Given, heat supplied at constant volume is Q.

$$\therefore \quad Q = nC_V\Delta T$$

For same change in temperature, if heat supplied at constant pressure is Q', then

$$Q' = nC_p\Delta T$$

So, we have

$$\frac{Q'}{Q} = \frac{nC_p\Delta T}{nC_V\Delta T}$$

$$\Rightarrow \quad \frac{Q'}{Q} = \frac{C_p}{C_V}$$

$$\Rightarrow \quad Q' = Q\gamma \qquad \left[\because \gamma = \frac{C_p}{C_V}\right]$$

As given gas is diatomic, so $\gamma = 7/5$

$$\therefore \quad Q' = \frac{7}{5}Q$$

29. (a) $\eta = 0.001\,\text{Nm}^{-2}\text{s}$

Rate of flow = 1000 litres per minute

$= 1\,\text{m}^3$ per second

Volume of water conveyed per second

$$v = \frac{1}{60}\,\text{m}^3$$

$$\eta = \frac{\pi p r^4}{8lv}$$

$$p = \frac{\eta 8 l v}{\pi r^4}$$

$$p = \frac{0.001 \times 8 \times 5000}{\frac{22}{7} \times (0.05)^4} \times \frac{1}{60}$$

$$= 33953\,\text{Nm}^{-2}$$

$$= 3.4 \times 10^4\ \text{Nm}^{-2}$$

30. (b) In x-direction,

Given $v_{0,x} = 3\,\text{m/s}$

$a_x = 0\,\text{m/s}^2$

$v_x = v_{0,x}$ = constant = 3.00 m/s

In y-direction (vertical),

Given, $v_{0,y} = 0.00\,\text{m/s}$,

$a_y = -g = -9.80\,\text{m/s}^2$,

$$\Delta y = (y - y_0) = -5.00\,\text{m}$$

$$v_y^2 = v_{0,y}^2 - 2g(y - y_0)$$

$$v_y = \sqrt{(0\,\text{m/s})^2 - 2(9.80\,\text{m/s}^2)(-5.00\,\text{m})}$$

$$= 9.90\,\text{m/s}$$

Now we can calculate the final velocity,

$$v = \sqrt{v_x^2 + v_y^2}$$

$$= \sqrt{(3.00\,\text{m/s})^2 + (9.90\,\text{m/s})^2}$$

$$= 10.3\,\text{m/s}$$

31. (d) Consider the motion of ball in frame of balloon, so various parameters of ball in frame of balloon are as follows

$(u+v)$

g

Initial velocity, $\mathbf{u} = \mathbf{u}_{\text{ball}} - \mathbf{u}_{\text{balloon}}$

$= u-(-v)$
$= u+v$

Acceleration of ball,

$$\mathbf{a} = \mathbf{a}_{ball} - \mathbf{a}_{balloon}$$
$$= -g-(0)$$
$$\mathbf{a} = -g$$

Let t be the time, when ball passes by the balloon.

From 2nd equation of motion,

$$s = ut + \frac{1}{2}at^2$$
$$0 = (u+v)\times t + \frac{1}{2}(-g)t^2$$

or $t = \dfrac{2(u+v)}{g}$

32. (b) If a rigid body is moved in such a way that all the particles constituting it undergo circular motion about a common axis, then that type of motion is called rotational motion.

Motion of a pendulum represents to and fro movement about its equilibrium. This represents oscillatory motion.

Motion of car on a straight road represents rectilinear motion.

Motion of a ball thrown by a boy at an angle with horizontal represents projectile motion.

Hence, A $\rightarrow$ 4, B $\rightarrow$ 3, C $\rightarrow$ 2 and D $\rightarrow$ 1.

33. (c) Force acting on particle,

$$F = -\frac{dU}{dx} = -\frac{d}{dx}2(1-\cos 5x)$$
$$F = -2[0+5\sin 5x]$$

or $F = -10\sin 5x$ N

For small oscillations means small values of x,

$$\sin 5x \simeq 5x$$
$$F = -10\times 5x$$
$$F = -50x \quad \ldots \text{(i)}$$

Force on spring mass system,

$$F = -kx \quad \ldots \text{(ii)}$$

On comparing Eqs. (i) and (ii), we get

$$k = 50$$

As time period,

$$T = 2\pi\sqrt{\frac{m}{k}} = 2\pi\sqrt{\frac{0.5}{50}}$$
$$T = \frac{\pi}{5}\text{ s}$$

34. (c) After applying tangential force, let top face make angle θ (angular displacement) as shown in the figure below.

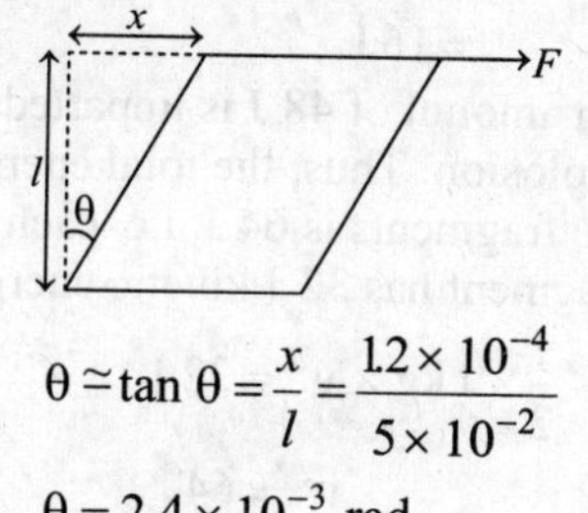

$$\theta \simeq \tan\theta = \frac{x}{l} = \frac{1.2\times 10^{-4}}{5\times 10^{-2}}$$
$$\theta = 2.4\times 10^{-3} \text{ rad}$$

Rigidity modulus, $\eta = \dfrac{F/A}{\theta} = \dfrac{F}{A\theta}$

$$\eta = \frac{10^5}{(5\times 10^{-2})^2\times 2.4\times 10^{-3}}$$
$$\eta = 1.67\times 10^{10} \text{ Nm}^{-2}$$

35. (d) Using conservation of angular momentum,

Initial angular momentum of the system = Final angular momentum of the system

$$L_i = L_f$$
$$I_i\omega_i = I_f\omega_f$$

Since earth is nearly spherical in nature, so its moment of inertia,

$$I = \frac{2}{5}MR^2$$

$\Rightarrow \quad \dfrac{2}{5}MR^2\omega_i = \dfrac{2}{5}M\left(\dfrac{R}{n}\right)^2\omega_f$

or $\quad \omega_f = n^2\omega_i$

or $\quad \dfrac{2\pi}{T_f} = n^2\dfrac{2\pi}{T_i}$

$\Rightarrow \quad \dfrac{1}{T_f} = \dfrac{n^2}{T_i} \Rightarrow T_f = \dfrac{T_i}{n^2}$

$\Rightarrow \quad T_f = \dfrac{T}{n^2}$ (here, $T_i = T$)

36. (c) Consider two bodies A and B having moment of inertia I and $2I$.

Kinetic energy of rotation for the body A, $K_A = (1/2)I\omega_A^2$

where, ω_A is angular speed of the body A.

Kinetic energy of rotation for the body B,

$$K_B = \frac{1}{2}(2I)\omega_B^2$$

According to the question, $K_A = K_B$

$\Rightarrow \quad \dfrac{1}{2}I\omega_A^2 = \dfrac{1}{2}(2I)\omega_B^2$

$\Rightarrow \quad \omega_A^2 = 2\omega_B^2 \Rightarrow \left(\dfrac{\omega_A}{\omega_B}\right)^2 = 2$

$\Rightarrow \quad \dfrac{\omega_A}{\omega_B} = \sqrt{2}$

$\Rightarrow \quad \omega_A : \omega_B = \sqrt{2}:1$

37. (d) $m_1v_1\hat{\mathbf{i}} + m_2v_2\hat{\mathbf{i}} = m_1v_3\hat{\mathbf{i}} + m_2v_4\hat{\mathbf{i}}$

$$2mv_1\hat{\mathbf{i}} + mv_2\hat{\mathbf{i}} = 2m\left(\frac{v_1}{2}\right)\hat{\mathbf{i}} + mv_4\hat{\mathbf{i}}$$

$\Rightarrow \quad v_4 = v_1 + v_2$

or $\quad v_1 = v_4 - v_2$

38. (c) Statement I is correct but Statement II is incorrect.

The propeller of a motor boat cuts the water surface laterally and also pushes it in backward direction. Hence, it will result in both longitudinal and transverse waves.

39. (a) $v_{rms} \propto \sqrt{T}$

$\therefore$ When v_{rms} is doubled, temperature is 4 times

i.e. $T \rightarrow 4T$

$$Q = nC_v\Delta T$$
$$= \frac{15}{28}\times\frac{5}{2}\times R\times[4T-T]$$
$$= \frac{15}{28}\times\frac{5}{2}\times 8.3\times 3\times 300$$
$$\approx 10000 \text{ J} = 10 \text{ kJ}$$

40. (b) For an adiabatic process,

$$pV^\gamma = \text{constant}$$

Differentiating above expression,

$$\gamma pV^{\gamma-1}dV + V^\gamma dp = 0$$

$\Rightarrow \quad V^\gamma dp = -\gamma pV^{\gamma-1}dV$

$\Rightarrow \quad \dfrac{dp}{dV} = -\dfrac{\gamma pV^{\gamma-1}}{V^\gamma} = -\gamma\left(\dfrac{p}{V}\right)$

$\therefore$ Slope of adiabatic curve,

$$\left[\frac{dp}{dV}\right]_{adiabatic} = -\frac{\gamma p}{V}$$

So, slope of p-V graph is more for gas which has higher value of γ.

As, we know that,

$$\gamma_{monoatomic} > \gamma_{diatomic} > \gamma_{polyatomic}$$

So,
$(\text{slope})_{\text{monoatomic}} > (\text{slope})_{\text{diatomic}} > (\text{slope})_{\text{polyatomic}}$

From the graph, it is clear that
$(\text{slope})_C > (\text{slope})_B > (\text{slope})_A$
Hence, $A \rightarrow$ Polyatomic, $B \rightarrow$ Diatomic, $C \rightarrow$ Monoatomic

Note For linear arrangement of triatomic gas, $\gamma = \frac{9}{7}$ and for non-linear arrangement, it is $\frac{4}{3}$.

41. (c) Let, m = mass of ball
Velocity of ball just before collision

$$v^2 = u^2 + 2gh$$
$$v_1 = \sqrt{2gh} \quad (u = 0) \text{...(i)}$$

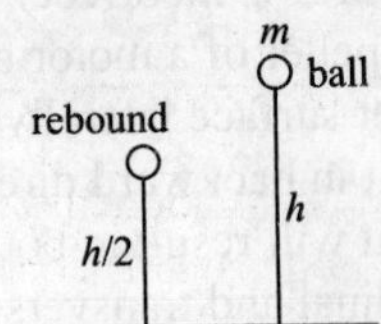

Velocity just after collision,

$$v_2 = \sqrt{2g\frac{h}{2}} \quad \text{...(ii)}$$

Change in kinetic energy,

$$\Delta KE = \frac{1}{2}m(2gh) - \frac{1}{2}mgh \quad \text{...(iii)}$$

Percentage loss in kinetic energy

$$= \frac{1}{2}mgh$$

$$\frac{\Delta KE}{KE_i} \times 100 = \frac{\frac{1}{2}mgh}{\frac{1}{2}mg2h} \times 100 = 50\%$$

42. (d) Initial horizontal momentum = Final horizontal momentum

$$2\,\text{kg} \times 4\,\text{m/s} = 1\,\text{kg} \times v\cos\theta\,\text{m/s} + 1\,\text{kg} \times v\cos\theta\,\text{m/s}$$

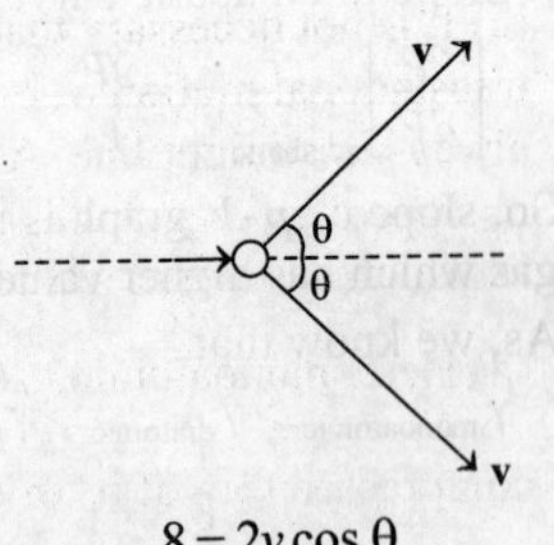

$$8 = 2v\cos\theta$$
$$v\cos\theta = 4\,\text{m/s} \quad \text{... (i)}$$

The initial kinetic energy of the shell

$$= \frac{1}{2} \times 2\,\text{kg} \times (4\,\text{m/s})^2$$
$$= 16\,\text{J}$$

An amount of 48 J is imparted by explosion. Thus, the total energy of the fragments is 64 J, i.e. each fragment has 32 J kinetic energy.

$$\frac{1}{2} \times 1\,\text{kg} \times v^2 = 32\,\text{J}$$
$$v^2 = 64$$
$$v = 8\,\text{m/s} \text{ and } v\cos\theta = 4$$
$$\cos\theta = \frac{1}{2} \Rightarrow \theta = 60°$$

43. (a) Given, length of string, L
radius of circle, $r = \frac{L}{\sqrt{2}}$

From figure,

$$\sin\theta = \frac{r}{L} = \frac{L}{L\sqrt{2}} = \frac{1}{\sqrt{2}}$$
$$\Rightarrow \quad \theta = 45°$$

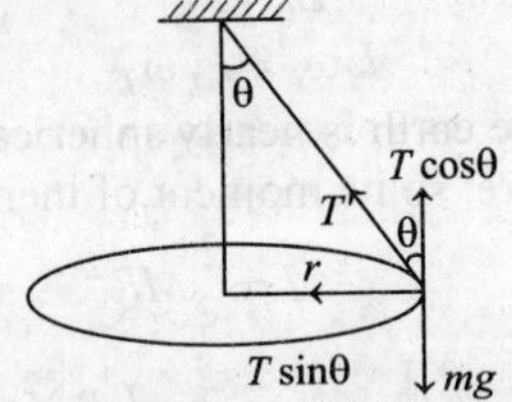

$$T\sin\theta = \frac{mv^2}{r} \quad \text{... (i)}$$
$$T\cos\theta = mg \quad \text{... (ii)}$$

Divide Eqs. (i) by (ii)

$$\Rightarrow \frac{T\sin\theta}{T\cos\theta} = \frac{\frac{mv^2}{r}}{mg} \Rightarrow \tan\theta = \frac{v^2}{rg}$$

$$\Rightarrow \quad 1 = \frac{v^2}{rg} \quad (\because \tan 45° = 1)$$

$$\Rightarrow \quad v = \sqrt{rg}$$

44. (a) The mass of the liquid that rises in the capillary tube is concentrated at a height $\frac{h}{2}$, which is the centre of mass of the liquid in the capillary. If M is the mass of the liquid in the capillary, then its potential energy U is given by

$$U = Mg\frac{h}{2}$$
$$M = \pi r^2 h\rho$$
$$h = \frac{2T}{\rho rg} \quad \text{... (i)}$$

Thus, the potential energy,

$$U = \frac{Mgh}{2} = \frac{\pi r^2 h^2 \rho g}{2}$$

Substituting the value of h from Eq. (i), we get

$$U = \frac{\pi r^2 \rho g}{2}\left[\frac{4T^2}{\rho^2 r^2 g^2}\right] = \frac{2\pi T^2}{\rho g}$$

45. (b) As, position vector,

$$\mathbf{r} = x\hat{\mathbf{i}} + y\hat{\mathbf{j}}$$
$$= 3t\hat{\mathbf{i}} + 3t(1-4t)\hat{\mathbf{j}}$$
$$\mathbf{r} = 3t\hat{\mathbf{i}} + (3t - 12t^2)\hat{\mathbf{j}}$$

Velocity vector,

$$\mathbf{v} = \frac{d\mathbf{r}}{dt} = \frac{d}{dt}[3t\hat{\mathbf{i}} + (3t - 12t^2)\hat{\mathbf{j}}]$$
$$= 3\hat{\mathbf{i}} + (3 - 24t)\hat{\mathbf{j}}$$

Acceleration vector,

$$\mathbf{a} = \frac{d\mathbf{v}}{dt} = \frac{d}{dt}[3\hat{\mathbf{i}} + (3-24t)\hat{\mathbf{j}}]$$
$$= -24\hat{\mathbf{j}}\,\text{m/s}^2$$

Let the time, when $\mathbf{v}$ makes angle 45° with $\mathbf{a}$ be t.

As, we know, $\cos\theta = \frac{\mathbf{v}\cdot\mathbf{a}}{va}$, where θ is the angle between $\mathbf{a}$ and $\mathbf{v}$.

$$\Rightarrow \cos 45° = \frac{[3\hat{\mathbf{i}} + (3-24t)\hat{\mathbf{j}}]\cdot[-24\hat{\mathbf{j}}]}{\sqrt{3^2 + (3-24t)^2}\cdot 24}$$

$$\frac{1}{\sqrt{2}} = -\frac{(3-24t)}{\sqrt{9 + (3-24t)^2}}$$

or $\quad \frac{1}{2} = \frac{(3-24t)^2}{9 + (3-24t)^2}$

or $\quad 9 + (3-24t)^2 = 2(3-24t)^2$

or $\quad 9 = (3-24t)^2$

or $\quad (3-24t) = \pm 3$

Taking positive sign,

$$3 - 24t = +3$$

or $\quad t = 0$ (not possible)

Taking negative sign,

$$3 - 24t = -3$$

or $\quad t = \frac{6}{24} = \frac{1}{4}\,\text{s}$

NSS5 NEET Stepping Stones 5

1. (b) Given, $x = a + bt^2$

Differentiating both sides w.r.t t

$$v = \frac{d}{dt}(a + bt^2)$$

$$\Rightarrow \quad v = 2bt$$

Instantaneous velocity, $v = 2 \times 3 \times 3$

$$= 18 \text{ cm/s}$$

2. (c) Internal energy of a gas at T kelvin,

$$U = n\frac{f}{2}RT$$

$\therefore$ Internal energy of O_2 molecules,

$$U_1 = 3 \times \frac{5}{2} R \times 300$$

or $\quad U_1 = 2250R$

and internal energy of Ar molecules,

$$U_2 = 1 \times \frac{3}{2} \times R \times 300$$

$$= 450R$$

Total internal energy

$$= U_1 + U_2 = 2700R$$

3. (c) The stress at the base of the mountain $= h\rho g$

The stress must be less than the elastic limits, otherwise the rock begins to fall down.

Stress $\leq$ Elastic limit

$h\rho g \leq$ Elastic limit

$$h \leq \frac{\text{Elastic Limit}}{\rho g}$$

For maximum value of h,

$$h_{max} = \frac{\text{Elastic limit}}{\rho g} = \frac{3.43 \times 10^8}{3 \times 10^3 \times 9.8}$$

$$h_{max} = 1.1667 \times 10^4 \text{ m}$$

$$h_{max} = 11.667 \text{ km}$$

4. (b) The average kinetic energy per molecules of a gas is given as

$$K_{avg} = \frac{1}{2} k_B T$$

$\therefore$It is independent of degree of freedom.

As we know that, $\gamma = \frac{C_p}{C_V}$ and value of γ decreases as atomicity of gas increases. Hence, $\frac{C_p}{C_V}$ decreases as atomicity increases.

5. (d) Gyromagnetic ratio is the ratio of magnetic moment and angular momentum.

Gyromagnetic ratio

$$= \frac{m}{L} = \frac{e}{2m_e} \text{ (for electron)}$$

So, dimensions of gyromagnetic ratio

$$= \frac{[e]}{[m]} = \frac{[It]}{[m]} = [M^{-1}L^0TA]$$

6. (c) As car starts from rest, then initial velocity is zero and let uniform acceleration be a.

Using third equation of motion,

$$v^2 = u^2 + 2as$$

$$v^2 = 0^2 + 2as$$

or $\quad v^2 = 2as \quad \quad \ldots(i)$

From the graph, when $s = 4$ m, then $v = 20$ m/s

Putting these values in Eq. (i), we get

$$(20)^2 = 2 \times a \times (4)$$

$$20 \times 20 = 8a$$

$$a = \frac{400}{8}$$

$$a = 50 \text{ m/s}^2$$

7. (a) Beat frequency $= f_1 - f_2$

$$= \frac{v}{2L} - \frac{v}{2(L + l)}$$

$$= \frac{v}{2L}\left[1 - \frac{L}{L + l}\right]$$

$$= \frac{v}{2L}\left[\frac{l}{L + l}\right]$$

$$= \frac{v}{2L} \cdot \frac{l}{L} \quad \left[\begin{array}{l} \because l << L \\ \text{So, } L + l = L \end{array}\right]$$

$$= \frac{vl}{2L^2}$$

8. (c) A is true but R is false.

Wood absorbs more heat but as iron is more conductive, it appears hot due to large rate of heat conduction.

9. (a) As normal force of surface acts in perpendicular direction, so it changes only perpendicular component of momentum.

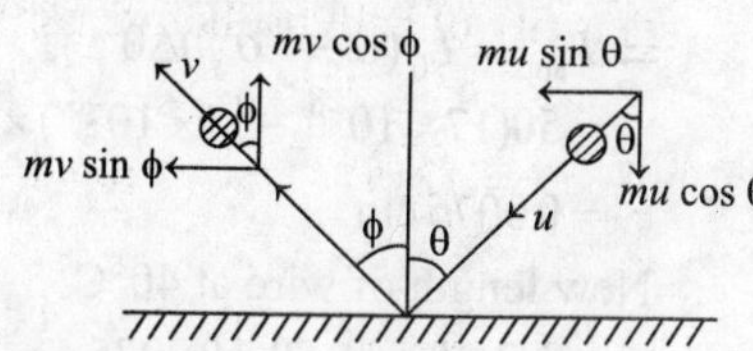

Horizontal component of momentum remains constant, so force

$$= \frac{\Delta p}{\Delta t} = \frac{p_f - p_i}{\Delta t}$$

$$= \frac{m(v\cos\phi - u\cos\theta)}{\Delta t}$$

10. (c) As, $U = -x$, $K = \frac{x}{2}$

$\therefore$Total energy of satellite $= U + K$

$$= -x + \frac{x}{2} = \frac{-x}{2}$$

$\therefore$ Energy needed to escape $= \frac{x}{2}$

If escape speed is v_e, then

$$\frac{1}{2}mv_e^2 = \frac{x}{2}$$

or $\quad v_e = \sqrt{\frac{x}{m}}$

11. (c) It is not necessary that translational motion of body is always in straight line. A parabolic motion of an object without rotation is also translational motion.

12. (d) Here, monoatomic gas $(\gamma = 5/3)$ compressed to $\frac{1}{8}$ of its original volume

$$pV^{\gamma} = \text{constant}$$

$$\Rightarrow \quad \frac{p_2}{p_1} = \left(\frac{V_1}{V_2}\right)^{\gamma}$$

$$p_2 = (8)^{5/3} p_1 = 32 p_1$$

13. (d) With temperature rise (same 25°C for both), steel scale and copper wire both expand. Hence, length of copper wire w.r.t. steel scale or apparent length of copper wire after rise in temperature

$$L_{\text{app}} = L'_c - L'_s$$

$$= [L_0(1 + \alpha_c \Delta\theta) - L_0(1 + \alpha_s \Delta\theta]$$

$$\Rightarrow L_{\text{app}} = L_0(\alpha_c - \alpha_s)\Delta\theta$$

$$= 50(17 \times 10^{-6} - 11 \times 10^{-6}) \times 25$$

$$= 0.0075 \text{ cm}$$

New length of wire at 40°C

$$= L_0 + L_{\text{app}} = 50 + 0.0075$$

$$= 50.0075 \text{ cm}$$

14. (a) Equating dimensions, we can write

$$K = \frac{\tau}{L} = \frac{[\text{ML}^2\text{T}^{-2}]}{[\text{ML}^2\text{T}^{-1}]} = [\text{T}^{-1}]$$

$$M = \frac{\tau\omega}{I} = \frac{[\text{ML}^2\text{T}^{-2}]\,[\text{T}^{-1}]}{[\text{ML}^2]}$$

$$\therefore \quad KM = [\text{T}^{-1}]\,[\text{T}^{-3}] = [\text{T}^{-4}]$$

15. (b) $A_1 = 10, A_2 = 20, \delta = \frac{\pi}{3}$

The amplitude of resultant wave,

$$A = \sqrt{A_1^2 + A_2^2 + 2A_1A_2\cos\delta}$$

$$= \sqrt{10^2 + 20^2 + 2(10)(20)\left(\frac{1}{2}\right)}$$

$$= 10\sqrt{7} \text{ units}$$

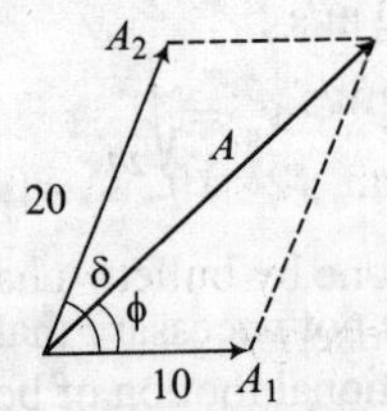

$$\phi = \tan^{-1}\left[\frac{A_2\sin\delta}{A_1 + A_2\cos\delta}\right]$$

$$= \tan^{-1}\left[\frac{20\left(\frac{\sqrt{3}}{2}\right)}{10 + 20\left(\frac{1}{2}\right)}\right]$$

$$= \tan^{-1}\left(\frac{\sqrt{3}}{2}\right)$$

So, the resultant wave,

$$y = 10\sqrt{7}\cos\left[5x + 25t + \tan^{-1}\left(\frac{\sqrt{3}}{2}\right)\right]$$

16. (a) Force on the side walls,

F_1 = Average pressure × Curved surface area

$$\text{or} \quad F_1 = \left(\frac{\rho gh}{2}\right)(2\pi Rh)$$

$$= \pi R\rho gh^2$$

(ρ = density of liquid)

Force on the bottom, F_2 = Pressure at the bottom × Area of the bottom

$$= (\rho gh)(\pi R^2) = \pi\rho ghR^2$$

Given, $\quad F_1 = F_2$

$$\therefore \quad \pi R\rho gh^2 = \pi\rho ghR^2$$

$$\Rightarrow \quad h = R$$

17. (a) When no retardation, then

$$T_0 = \frac{2u\sin\alpha}{g}$$

When air retardation of $\frac{g}{10}$ exist, then

$$T = \frac{u\sin\alpha}{g + \frac{g}{10}} + \frac{u\sin\alpha}{g - \frac{g}{10}}$$

$$T = \frac{2u\sin\alpha}{g}\cdot\left(\frac{5}{11} + \frac{5}{9}\right)$$

$$T = T_0 \times 5 \times \frac{20}{99} = \frac{100}{99}T_0$$

So, percentage increases

$$= \left(\frac{100}{99} - 1\right) \times 100$$

Percentage increases by 1%

18. (a) Here, $mc_{\text{iron}}\Delta T = \frac{1}{4}mgh$

$$\Delta T = \frac{gh}{4 \times c_{\text{iron}}} = \frac{10 \times 10}{4 \times 470}$$

$$= \frac{100}{1880} = 5.3 \times 10^{-2}\,°\text{C}$$

19. (b) $g_h = g\left(1 - \frac{2h}{R}\right)$

$$w = mg \Rightarrow \frac{dw_h}{dh} = m\frac{dg_h}{dh}$$

$$\therefore \quad \left|\frac{dw_h}{dh}\right| = m\left|\frac{d}{dh}\left(g - \frac{2\cdot g\cdot h}{R}\right)\right|$$

$$= m\frac{2g}{R} = \frac{2mg}{R}$$

$$\Rightarrow \quad \left|\frac{dw_h}{dh}\right| = \frac{2mg}{R}h^0$$

$$\Rightarrow \quad \frac{dw_h}{dh} \propto h^0$$

20. (c) $y(x, t) = \frac{1}{1000}\sin(40x - 4t)$

We know that,

$$y(x, t) = A\sin\left(\frac{2\pi x}{\lambda} - \frac{2\pi t}{T}\right)$$

$$A = \frac{1}{1000} \text{ m}$$

$$\frac{2\pi}{\lambda} = 40$$

$$\Rightarrow \quad \lambda = \frac{2\pi}{40} = \frac{\pi}{20} \text{ m}$$

$$\frac{2\pi}{T} = 4$$

$$\Rightarrow \quad \nu = \frac{4}{2\pi} = \frac{2}{\pi}$$

$\therefore$ Wave velocity,

$$v = \nu\lambda = \frac{2}{\pi} \times \frac{\pi}{20} = \frac{1}{10} \text{ m/s}$$

$$= 10 \text{ cm/s}$$

21. (a) Terminal speed of a sphere falling in a viscous fluid is

$$V_T = \frac{2}{9}\frac{r^2}{\eta}(\rho_0 - \rho_f)g$$

where, η = coefficient of viscosity of fluid,

ρ_0 = density of falling sphere and ρ_f = density of fluid.

i.e. $\quad v_T \propto r^2 \quad$ ...(i)

Equating the volumes

$$\Rightarrow \quad \frac{4}{3}\pi R^3 = 27 \times \frac{4}{3}\pi r^3 \Rightarrow r = \frac{R}{3}$$

So, from Eq. (i), we have

$$\frac{v_1}{v_2} = \frac{R^2}{\left(\frac{R}{3}\right)^2} = 9$$

22. (c) Heat rejected by steam on complete condensation

$= mL = 10\text{ g} \times 540\text{ cal g}^{-1}$

$= 5400\text{ cal}$

Heat rejected by water at 100°C to cool down upto 0°C

$= ms\Delta t$

$= 10\text{ g} \times \dfrac{1\text{ cal}}{\text{g}°\text{C}} \times (100-0)°\text{C}$

$= 1000\text{ cal}$

So, maximum heat supplied to ice $= 6400\text{ cal}$

If m = mass of ice melted, then mL = heat from steam

$m = \dfrac{6400\text{ cal}}{80\text{ calg}^{-1}} = 80\text{ g}$

Ice remains in mixture

$= 100 - 80 = 20\text{ g}$

Water in mixture = 80 g + 10 g = 90 g

23. (c) At displacement x,

$U_1 = \dfrac{1}{2}m\omega^2x^2 \Rightarrow x = \sqrt{\dfrac{2U_1}{m\omega^2}}$

Similarly, $y = \sqrt{\dfrac{2U_2}{m\omega^2}}$

When displacement is $(x+y)$, potential energy,

$U = \dfrac{1}{2}m\omega^2(x+y)^2$

$= \dfrac{1}{2}m\omega^2(x^2+y^2+2xy)$

$= \dfrac{1}{2}m\omega^2x^2 + \dfrac{1}{2}m\omega^2y^2 + m\omega^2xy$

$= U_1 + U_2 + m\omega^2\sqrt{\dfrac{2U_1}{m\omega^2}\cdot\dfrac{2U_2}{m\omega^2}}$

$= U_1 + U_2 + 2\sqrt{U_1U_2}$

24. (b) Time taken by the bullet to move a horizontal distance R is

$t = \dfrac{R}{u\cos\theta}$

The vertical height covered during this time,

Vertical components of velocity,

$u_y = u\sin\theta$

$h = u_yt - \dfrac{1}{2}gt^2$

$= u\sin\theta \times \dfrac{R}{u\cos\theta} - \dfrac{g}{2}\left(\dfrac{R}{u\cos\theta}\right)^2$

$= R\tan\theta - \dfrac{gR^2}{2u^2\cos^2\theta}$

25. (c) The escape velocity from surface of any planet is given as

$v = \sqrt{\dfrac{2GM}{R}}$ ...(i)

For given planet, $M = \dfrac{M_e}{9}, R = \dfrac{R_e}{2}$

From Eq. (i),

$v = \sqrt{\dfrac{2G\left(\dfrac{M_e}{9}\right)}{\dfrac{R_e}{2}}}$

$= \sqrt{\dfrac{2}{9}}\sqrt{\dfrac{2GM_e}{R_e}}$

$= \sqrt{\dfrac{2}{9}}v_e = \dfrac{\sqrt{2}}{3}v_e$

$\Rightarrow \quad x = 2$

26. (c) Let v be the velocity of platform in downward direction just after the man jumps up with velocity u. From momentum conservation,

$Mu - (M+2m)v = 0$

$\Rightarrow \quad v = \dfrac{Mu}{M+2m}$

$= \dfrac{3m}{3m+2m}(10) \quad (\because M = 3m)$

$= 6\text{ ms}^{-1}$

After the man leaves, $T - mg = ma$

and $(M+m)g - T = (M+m)a$

$\therefore \quad a = \dfrac{Mg}{M+2m}$

$= \dfrac{3m}{3m+2m}(10) = 6\text{ ms}^{-2}$

$v^2 = 2ad$

$\Rightarrow d = \dfrac{(6)^2}{2(6)} = 3\text{ m}$

27. (c) $\mathbf{r} = (3\hat{\mathbf{i}} + 4\hat{\mathbf{j}})$ m and

$\mathbf{v} = (4\hat{\mathbf{i}} - 3\hat{\mathbf{j}})$ m/s

$\mathbf{v} = \omega \times \mathbf{r}$

As $\mathbf{r}$ and $\mathbf{v}$ are on XY-plane, ω should be along Z-axis.

Let $\omega = z\hat{\mathbf{k}}$

Then, $\omega \times \mathbf{r} = 3z\hat{\mathbf{j}} - 4z\hat{\mathbf{i}}$

$\mathbf{v} = 4\hat{\mathbf{i}} - 3\hat{\mathbf{j}}$

On comparing these two equations, we have

$z = -1$

$\therefore \quad \omega = -\hat{\mathbf{k}}$

28. (a) Length of the wire is $l = 20\text{ m}$

Radius of the wire is $r = 2\times10^{-3}$ m

Increase in length is

$\Delta l = 0.031\times10^{-3}$ m

$g = (3.1\times\pi)\text{ ms}^{-2}$

Young's modulus,

$Y = \dfrac{Fl}{A\,\Delta l} = \dfrac{(mg)l}{\pi r^2(\Delta l)}$

$\therefore \; Y = \dfrac{4\times3.1\times\pi\times20}{\pi(2\times10^{-3})^2\times0.031\times10^{-3}}$

$= 2\times10^{12}\text{ Nm}^{-2}$

29. (b) $3\left(\dfrac{v}{4L_c}\right) = 2\left(\dfrac{v}{2L_o}\right)$ (given)

$\therefore \quad \dfrac{L_c}{L_o} = \dfrac{3}{4}$

Also, $n\left(\dfrac{v}{4L_c}\right) = m\left(\dfrac{v}{2L_o}\right)$ (given)

$\dfrac{n}{m} = 2\left(\dfrac{L_c}{L_o}\right) = \dfrac{6}{4} = \dfrac{3}{2}$

$\dfrac{n}{m} = \dfrac{3}{2} = \dfrac{9}{6}$

$\therefore \quad n = 9$ and $m = 6$

30. (c) $m = 15\text{g} = 15\times10^{-3}$ kg

$u = 540$ m/s

$v = 360$ m/s

$s = 20\text{ cm} = 2\times10^{-2}\text{ m} = 0.2\text{ m}$

Workdone by bullet = change in its kinetic energy

$W = \dfrac{1}{2}mu^2 - \dfrac{1}{2}mv^2$

$= \dfrac{1}{2}m(u^2 - v^2)$

$= \dfrac{1}{2}\times15\times10^{-3}[(540)^2 - (360)^2]$

$= 1215\text{ J}$

31. (a) We know that, the kinetic energy, $K = \frac{1}{2}mv^2 = \frac{1}{2}I\omega^2$

where, $m = 27$ kg (mass of the body),

$\omega = 3$ rads^{-1} (angular velocity)

and $I = 3$ kg-m^2 (moment of inertia).

$v = ?$ or $mv^2 = I\omega^2$

$\Rightarrow \quad v^2 = \frac{I\omega^2}{m}$

$\Rightarrow \quad v^2 = \frac{3\times 3^2}{27}$

$\Rightarrow \quad v^2 = \frac{27}{27} = 1$

$\Rightarrow$ Velocity of body,

$v = \sqrt{1} = 1$ ms^{-1}

32. (b) Volume of wire, $V = L\times \pi r^2$

$= 1\times \pi(10^{-3})^2 = \pi\times 10^{-6}$ m^3

Area of square cross-section

$= (2\times 10^{-3})^2 = 4\times 10^{-6}$ m^2

Length of new wire

$= \frac{\text{Volume}}{\text{Area}} = \frac{\pi\times 10^{-6}}{4\times 10^{-6}} = \frac{\pi}{4}$ m

Initial extension,

$x = \frac{FL}{AY} = \frac{F}{Y}\left(\frac{1}{\pi\times 10^{-6}}\right)$

$\therefore \quad \frac{F}{Y} = (\pi\times 10^{-6})x$

Final extension,

$x' = \frac{FL'}{A'Y} = \frac{F}{Y}\cdot\frac{L'}{A'}$

or $x' = (\pi\times 10^{-6})x\cdot\frac{\pi/4}{4\times 10^{-6}} = \frac{\pi^2}{16}x$

33. (a) $pV^{3/2}$ = constant,

$pV = nRT$

Combining $pV^{3/2} = k_1$

$\Rightarrow \quad pV\cdot\sqrt{V} = k_1$

$\Rightarrow \quad nRT\cdot\sqrt{V} = k_1$

$\Rightarrow \quad T\sqrt{V}$ = constant

$\Rightarrow \quad T_1V_1^{1/2} = T_2V_2^{1/2}$

When $V_2 = \left(\frac{V_1}{2}\right)$,

$T_2 = T_1\left(\frac{V_1}{V_2}\right)^{1/2} = T_1(2^{1/2})$

So, final temperature of gas is $T_2 = \sqrt{2}\,T$.

34. (d) Given, $A = 1.0$ m $\pm$ 0.2 m

$B = 2.0$ m $\pm$ 0.2 m

Let $x = \sqrt{AB} = \sqrt{1.0\times 2.0}$

$= 1.414$ m

Rounding off to two significant digits,

$x = \sqrt{AB} = 1.4$ m

Now, $\frac{\Delta x}{x} = \frac{1}{2}\left[\frac{\Delta A}{A} + \frac{\Delta B}{B}\right]$

$= \frac{1}{2}\left[\frac{0.2}{1.0} + \frac{0.2}{2.0}\right] = \frac{0.6}{2\times 2.0}$

$\Delta x = \frac{0.6\times x}{2\times 2.0} = 0.15\times 1.414$

$= 0.2121$

Rounding off to one significant digit,

$\Delta x = 0.2$ m

Thus, $\sqrt{AB} = 1.4$ m $\pm$ 0.2 m

35. (d) $v_{\max} = A\omega = 0.04$ ms^{-1}

$x = A\sin\omega t$

$\Rightarrow \quad a = -A\omega^2\sin\omega t$

$\therefore \quad a = -\omega^2 x$

At $\quad x = 0.02$ m,

$|a| = 0.06$ ms^{-2} (given)

$\therefore \quad \omega^2(0.02) = 0.06$

$\Rightarrow \quad \omega = \sqrt{3}$ rad s^{-1}

$\therefore \quad T = \frac{2\pi}{\omega} = \frac{2\pi}{\sqrt{3}} = 3.63$ s

$A = \frac{0.04}{\omega} = \frac{0.04}{\sqrt{3}} = 2.31\times 10^{-2}$ m

36. (a) Let m be the mass per unit length of the rope and M is the total mass, then $\quad M = ml$

The mass of the rope of length l_1 that can overhangs from the edge of the table without slipping is ml_1.

Now, weight of rope lying on the table

$= m(l - l_1)g$

Weight of overhanging part of rope

$= ml_1 g$

Static friction $= \mu N = \mu m(l - l_1)g$

For the rope to be in equilibrium

$ml_1 g \le \mu m(l - l_1)g$

$l_1 \le \mu(l - l_1)$

$l_1(1+\mu) \le l\mu$

$l_1 \le \frac{\mu}{1+\mu}l$

or $\quad (l_1)_{\max} = \frac{\mu}{1+\mu}l$

37. (a) Total acceleration,

$a = \sqrt{a_t^2 + a_r^2}$

$= \sqrt{\left(\frac{dv}{dt}\right)^2 + \left(\frac{v^2}{R}\right)^2}$

where, $\quad v = \alpha\sqrt{s}$

Differentiating $v = \alpha\sqrt{s}$ w. r. t. time, we get

$\frac{dv}{dt} = \alpha\frac{s^{-1/2}}{2}\frac{ds}{dt}$

Substituting $\frac{ds}{dt} = \alpha\sqrt{s}$, we have

$\frac{dv}{dt} = \frac{\alpha^2}{2}$

Now, substituting $\frac{dv}{dt}$ and v in the expression of a, we have

$a = \sqrt{\left(\frac{\alpha^2}{2}\right)^2 + \left[\frac{\alpha^2 s}{R}\right]^2}$

This gives $a = \alpha^2\sqrt{\frac{1}{4} + \frac{s^2}{R^2}}$

38. (b) $v_{CM} = \frac{mv_0 + M(0)}{m+M} = \frac{mv_0}{m+M}$ (this is constant)

$\therefore$ In centre of mass reference frame, relative velocity of mass m,

$u_m = v_0 - \frac{mv_0}{m+M} = \frac{Mv_0}{m+M}$

and of mass M, $u_M = -\frac{mv_0}{m+M}$

$K_i = \frac{1}{2}mu_m^2 + \frac{1}{2}Mu_M^2$

$$= \frac{1}{2} m\left(\frac{Mv_0}{m+M}\right)^2 + \frac{1}{2} M\left(\frac{mv_0}{m+M}\right)^2$$

or $\quad K_i = \frac{1}{2} \cdot \frac{mM v_0^2}{m+M}$

In centre of mass reference frame, at maximum compression, m and M are at rest.

$\therefore$ By conservation of energy,

$$K_f = 0$$

So, $\quad \frac{1}{2} k x_{max}^2 = \frac{1}{2} \cdot \frac{mM v_0^2}{m+M}$

$$x_{max} = \sqrt{\frac{mM}{k(m+M)}}\, v_0$$

39. (d) Force constant,

$$k = \frac{F}{y} = \frac{30}{0.3} = 100 \text{ N/m}$$

When 5 kg weight is placed,
force, $F' = mg = 5 \times 10 = 50\text{N}$

$\therefore$Displacement $= \frac{F'}{k} = \frac{50}{100} = 0.5 \text{ m}$

$= 50$ cm

Time period,

$$T = 2\pi\sqrt{\frac{m}{k}} = 2\pi\sqrt{\frac{5}{100}}$$

$$= \frac{\pi}{\sqrt{5}} \text{ s.}$$

Angular frequency,

$$\omega = \frac{2\pi}{T} = \frac{2\pi}{\frac{\pi}{\sqrt{5}}} = 2\sqrt{5} \text{ rad/s}$$

40. (a) In adiabatic process

$$pV^{\gamma} = \text{constant}$$

$$p^{1-\gamma} T^{\gamma} = \text{constant} \quad \text{... (i)}$$

$$p \propto T^3$$

$$pT^{-3} = \text{constant} \quad \text{... (ii)}$$

Using Eq. (i) can be rewritten as

$$pT^{\frac{\gamma}{1-\gamma}} = \text{constant} \quad \text{... (iii)}$$

From Eqs. (ii) and (iii), we get

$$\frac{\gamma}{1-\gamma} = -3$$

$$\gamma = -3 + 3\gamma$$

$$3 = 2\gamma$$

$$\gamma = \frac{3}{2}$$

41. (a) Let the displacement-time equation of simple harmonic motion is given as

$$x = A \sin(\omega t + \phi) \quad \text{...(i)}$$

From given figure, $A = 4$ m

$T = 6$ s

$\therefore \quad \omega = \frac{2\pi}{T} = \frac{2\pi}{6} = \frac{\pi}{3}$ rad/s

Initially (at $t = 0$), $x = 0$

From Eq. (i), $0 = A \sin(\omega \times 0 + \phi)$

$A \sin \phi = 0$

or $\quad \sin \phi = 0$

$\Rightarrow \quad \phi = 0, \pi, 2\pi.$

ϕ cannot be zero as particle is going away from mean position to the left extreme position.

$$\phi = \pi$$

Equation, $x = 4 \sin\left(\frac{\pi}{3} t + \pi\right)$ m

42. (a) Given, change in internal energy,

$$\Delta U = \frac{Q}{4}$$

From first law of thermodynamics,

$$\Delta Q = \Delta U + \Delta W$$

$$Q = \frac{Q}{4} + W$$

$$W = \frac{3Q}{4} = \frac{R}{1-n} \Delta T \quad \text{...(i)}$$

For a monoatomic gas,

$$\Delta U = \frac{3}{2} RT$$

$\Rightarrow \quad \Delta U = \frac{3}{2} R\Delta T = \frac{Q}{4} \quad$ ...(ii)

From Eqs. (i) and (ii), we get

$$\frac{9}{2} R = \frac{R}{1-n}$$

or $\quad 1 - n = \frac{2}{9}$

$\Rightarrow \quad n = \frac{7}{9}$

43. (d) The speed of the block is

$$v = \frac{2\pi\,(25\text{cm})}{2} = 0.78 \text{ m/s}$$

The acceleration of the block is

$$a = \frac{v^2}{r} = \frac{(0.785)^2}{0.25} = 2.46 \text{ m/s}^2$$

(towards the centre)

From Newton's second law

$$N = ma$$

$$N = 100 \times 2.46 \times 10^{-3}$$

$$N = 0.246 \text{ N}$$

44. (a) The given situation in question is as follows.

← 50 m →		
u=0		
5 kg	→ 30 N	5 kg

Let, the coefficient of kinetic friction be μ.

Acceleration,

$$a = \frac{F - f}{m} = \frac{F - \mu mg}{m}$$

$$a = \frac{30 - \mu \times 5 \times 10}{5}$$

$$= 6 - 10\mu$$

Using second equation of motion,

$$s = ut + \frac{1}{2} at^2$$

$\Rightarrow \quad 50 = 0 + \frac{1}{2}(6 - 10\mu) \times 10^2$

$\Rightarrow 6 - 10\mu = 1.0$

$\Rightarrow \quad \mu = 0.5$

45. (d) Let radius of sphere formed from second part is r, then mass of second part = volume × density

$$\frac{1}{8} M = \frac{4}{3}\pi r^3 \times \frac{M}{\frac{4}{3}\pi R^3}$$

$\therefore \quad r = R/2$

$$I_1 = \frac{\frac{7}{8} M \times (2R)^2}{2} = \frac{7}{4} MR^2$$

$$I_2 = \frac{2}{5} \times \frac{1}{8} M \times \left(\frac{R}{2}\right)^2 = \frac{MR^2}{80}$$

$\therefore \quad \frac{I_1}{I_2} = 140$

PHYSICS VOLUME I

MIND MAP

- Units and Measurement
- Motion in a Straight Line
- Motion in a Plane
- Laws of Motion
- Work, Energy and Power
- Rotational Motion
- Gravitation
- Mechanical Properties of Solids
- Mechanical Properties of Fluids
- Thermal Properties of Matter
- Thermodynamics
- Kinetic Theory of Gases
- Oscillations
- Waves

MEDACE

Test 1

Syllabus

- Units of Measurements, System of Units
- SI Units, Fundamental and Derived Units
- Dimensions of Physical Quantities, Dimensional Analysis and Its Applications

NCERT Page 1 to 3, Page 7 to 9

For deeper insight **Scan the QR Code**

Physical Quantities : Their Magnitude and Units

All those quantities, which are used to describe the laws of physics, are called physical quantities, e.g. length, mass, volume, etc.

The standard amount of a physical quantity chosen to measure the physical quantity of same kind is called a physical unit.

The essential requirements of physical unit are given below.

(i) It should be of suitable size.
(ii) It should be easily accessible.
(iii) It should not vary with time.
(iv) It should be easily reproducible.
(v) It should not depend on physical conditions like pressure, volume, etc.

System of Units

A complete set of the fundamental units and derived units, is called as the system of units.

Three such systems of units are as follows:

- **CGS system** This system is also called Gaussian system. The base units for length, mass and time in this system are centimetre, gram and second, respectively.
- **FPS system** This system is a British system which uses foot, pound and second as base units of length, mass and time, respectively.
- **MKS system** This system is a French system which uses metre, kilogram and second as base units of length, mass and time, respectively.

Supplementary Units

- **Plane angle** It is the ratio of length of arc to the radius of circle. Its unit is radian with symbol rad.

  i.e., $d\theta = \dfrac{dS}{r}$

- **Solid angle** It is the ratio of the intercepted area dA of the spherical surface to the square of its radius. Its unit is steradian with symbol sr.

  i.e., $d\Omega = \dfrac{dA}{r^2}$

Fundamental Units

Those physical quantities which are independent of other physical quantities and not defined in terms of other physical quantities are called fundamental or base quantities.

Base Quantity	SI units	
	Name / Symbol	Definition
Length	Metre (m)	It is defined by taking the fixed numerical value of the speed of light in vacuum (c) to be 299792458 when expressed in the unit ms^{-1}.
Mass	Kilogram (kg)	It is defined by taking the fixed numerical value of the Planck constant h to be $6.62607015 \times 10^{-34}$ when expressed in the unit Js, which is equal to kg-m^2s^{-1}.
Time	Second (s)	It is defined by taking the fixed numerical value of the caesium frequency $\Delta\nu_{Cs}$, the unperturbed ground state hyperfine transition frequency of the caesium-133 atom, to be 9192631770 when expressed in the unit Hz, which is equal to s^{-1}.
Electric current	Ampere (A)	It is defined by taking the fixed numerical value of the elementary charge e to be $1.602176634 \times 10^{-19}$ when expressed in the unit C.
Thermo-dynamic temper-ature	Kelvin (K)	It is defined by taking the fixed numerical value of the Boltzmann constant k to be 1.380649×10^{-23} when expressed in the unit JK^{-1}, which is equal to kg-$m^2s^{-2}K^{-1}$.
Amount of Substance	Mole (mol)	One mole contains exactly $6.02214076 \times 10^{23}$ elementary entities. This number is the fixed numerical value of the Avogadro constant N_A, when expressed in the unit mol^{-1} and is called the Avogadro number. The amount of substance, symbol n, of a system is a measure of the number of specified elementary entities.
Luminous intensity	Candela (cd)	It is defined by taking the fixed numerical value of the luminous intensity of monochromatic radiation of frequency 540×10^{12} Hz, K_{cd}, to be 683 when expressed in the unit lm W^{-1}, which is equal to cd sr W^{-1} or cd sr $kg^{-1}m^{-2}s^3$.

Derived Units

The units of measurement of all other physical quantities which can be obtained from fundamental units are called derived units.

Common SI Prefixes and Symbols for Multiples and Sub-multiples

Multiple			Sub-multiple		
Factor	Prefix	Symbol	Factor	Prefix	Symbol
10^{18}	Exa	E	10^{-18}	atto	a
10^{15}	Peta	P	10^{-15}	femto	f
10^{12}	Tera	T	10^{-12}	pico	p
10^{9}	Giga	G	10^{-9}	nano	n
10^{6}	Mega	M	10^{-6}	micro	µ
10^{3}	Kilo	k	10^{-3}	milli	m
10^{2}	Hecto	h	10^{-2}	centi	c
10^{1}	Deca	da	10^{-1}	deci	d

Dimensional Formula

The expression which shows how and which of the fundamental quantities represent the dimension of physical quantity.

e.g. Acceleration = $[M^0LT^{-2}]$

Mass density = $[ML^{-3}T^0]$

Dimensions of a Physical Quantity

The dimensions of a physical quantity are the power to which the units of base quantities are raised to represent a derived unit of that quantity.

Uses of Dimensional Analysis

- **Conversion of units from one system to another**

  $$n_2 = n_1\left[\frac{M_1}{M_2}\right]^a \left[\frac{L_1}{L_2}\right]^b \left[\frac{T_1}{T_2}\right]^c$$

- **To check dimensional correctness of an equation.**

  A physical quantity equation will be dimensionally correct, if the dimensions of all terms occuring on the both sides of the equation are same.

- **Deducing relation among the physical quantities.**

  Say, $Q = f(X, Y, Z)$

  Let, $Q \propto X^a$, $Q \propto Y^b$, $Q \propto Z^c$

  Thus, $Q \propto X^a Y^b Z^c$

Dimensional Formulae of Some Physical Quantities

The table given below gives the dimensional formulae and SI units of some physical quantities frequently used in physics.

Physical quantity	SI units	Dimensional formula
Area	m^2	$[M^0L^2T^0]$
Volume	m^3	$[M^0L^3T^0]$
Density	kg/m^3	$[ML^{-3}T^0]$
Trigonometric ratio	No units	$[M^0L^0T^0]$
Efficiency	No units	$[M^0L^0T^0]$
Refractive index	No units	$[M^0L^0T^0]$
Quality factor	No units	$[M^0L^0T^0]$
Magnification	No units	$[M^0L^0T^0]$
Velocity	m/s	$[M^0LT^{-1}]$
Acceleration	m/s^2	$[M^0LT^{-2}]$
Force	kg-m/s^2	$[MLT^{-2}]$
Work	kg-m^2/s^2 = N-m = joule or J	$[ML^2T^{-2}]$
Energy	Joule	$[ML^2T^{-2}]$
Torque	N-m	$[ML^2T^{-2}]$
Power	J/s or W	$[ML^2T^{-3}]$
Momentum	kg-m/s	$[MLT^{-1}]$
Impulse	N-s	$[MLT^{-1}]$
Angle	radian or rad	$[M^0L^0T^0]$
Strain	No units	$[M^0L^0T^0]$
Stress	N/m^2	$[ML^{-1}T^{-2}]$
Pressure	N/m^2	$[ML^{-1}T^{-2}]$

Limitations

- It cannot establish the formulae containing trigonometrical exponential and logarithmic terms.
- If a physical quantity depends on three physical quantities out of which two quantitities have same dimensions, we cannot establish relation among them.

Test 2

Syllabus
- Accuracy and Precision
- Least Count
- Significant Figures
- Errors in Measurement

NCERT Page 3 to 6

For deeper insight **Scan the QR Code**

Chapter 01

Accuracy and Precision

The two terms accuracy and precision are often used interchangeably but they have specific meanings. Its better to understand these terms through following differentiation.

Accuracy
- It represents how close the measured value to the true value.
- Accuracy of measurement depends on the resolution of the measuring instrument.
- It represents the correctness of the measurement.

Precision
- It represents how close are multiple measurements.
- Precision is determined by the least count of the measuring instrument. Smaller the least count, greater is the precision.
- It represents the agreement between two or more measured values.

Significant Figures

- All the non-zero digits are significant.
- All the zeros in between two non-zero digits are significant no matter, where the decimal point is if at all.
- If the number is less than 1, the zero on the right of decimal point but to the left of first non-zero digit are not significant.
- Zeros after the last non-zero digit are significant.
- In a number without decimal point, say terminal zeros - such as 1500 have two significant figures.

Rules to Determine Significant Figures

For determining number of significant figures, we use the following rules.

Rule 1 All non-zero digits are significant, e.g. $x = 2567$ has four significant figures.

Rule 2 The zeros appearing between two non-zero digits are significant, no matter where the decimal point is, if at all, e.g. 6.028 has 4 significant figures.

Rule 3 If the number is less than 1, all zero(s) on the right of decimal point but to the left of first non-zero digit are not significant. e.g. 0.0042 has two significant figures.

Rule 4 The terminal or trailing zero(s) in a number without a decimal point are not significant. Thus, 426 m = 42600 cm = 426000 mm has three significant figures.

Rule 5 In a number with decimal, zeros to the right of last non-zero digit are significant. e.g. 4.600 or 0.002300 have four significant figures each.

Rule 6 The power of 10 is irrelevant to the determination of significant figures. e.g. In the measurements, 2.30 m $= 2.30 \times 10^2$ cm $= 2.30 \times 10^3$ mm. The significant figures are three in each measurement, because all zeros appearing in the base number in the scientific notation (in the power of 10) are not significant.

Rule 7 A choice of change of different units does not change the number of significant digits or figures in a measurement. e.g. The length 7.03 cm has three significant figures. But in different units, the same value can be written as 0.0703 m or 70.3 mm. All these measurements have the same number of significant figures (digits 7, 0 and 3) namely three.

Mathematical Operations of Significant Figures

The result of a mathematical operation involving measured values of quantities cannot be more accurate than the measured value themselves.

Addition or Subtraction

Suppose in the measured values to be added or subtracted, the least number of significant digits after the decimal is n. Then, in the sum or difference also, the number of significant digits after the decimal should be n.

e.g. $1.2 + 3.45 + 6.789 = 11.439 \approx 11.4$

Here, the least number of significant digits after the decimal is one.

Multiplication or Division

Suppose in the measured values to be multiplied or divided, the least number of significant digits be n, then in the product or quotient, the number of significant digits should also be n.

e.g. $1.2 \times 36.72 = 44.064 \approx 44$

The least number of significant digits in the measured values are two.

Rounding Off

In physics, calculation is a vital part and during that, we shall reduce the number to the required extent and that is why there is a need to round off numbers. The process of omitting the non-significant digits and retaining only the desired number of significant digits, incorporating the required modifications to the last significant digit is called rounding off the number. Like mathematical operations of significant figures, rounding off numbers also follow certain rules

Rules For Rounding off a Measurement

- If the digit to be dropped is less than 5, then the preceding digit is left unchanged.
  For example, $x = 7.82$ is rounded off to 7.8 and $x = 3.94$ is rounded off to 3.9.
- If the digit to be dropped is more than 5, then the preceding digit is raised by one.
  For example, $x = 6.87$ is rounded off to 6.9 and $x = 12.78$ is rounded off to 12.8.
- If the digit to be dropped is 5 followed by digits other than zero, then the preceding digit is raised by one.
  For example, $x = 16.351$ is rounded off to 16.4 and $x = 6.758$ is rounded off to 6.8.

Combination of Errors

While performing mathematical operations such as addition, subtraction, division, multiplication, etc, the error combination depends on the type of mathematical operation performed on physical quantities.

Gross Error

- These errors can be arise due to extreme carelessness of the observer.
- Recording the observations with an instrument without adjusting it properly.
- Reading an observation wrongly.

Errors in Measurement

- The difference between true and measured value of a quantity is called error of measurement.
  Error = True value − Measured value

Systematic Error

- **Instrumental error** They occur due to imperfect design or manufacture of calibration of the measuring instrument.
- **Imperfection in experimental technique** It occurs due to the experimental arrangement limitation.
- **Personal error** These errors arise due to inexperience of the observer, such as lack of proper setting of apparatus and taking observations without proper precaution.
- **Error due to external causes** Various parameters such as change in temperature, pressure, volume, etc.

Random Errors

- The random errors are those errors which occur irregularly in the measurement. Their sign and magnitude both are random.
- There is no exact cause of such errors. These errors arise due to random and unpredictable fluctuations in experimental condition. e.g. Fluctuation in voltage supply, mechanical vibration of experimental set ups.

Least Count Error

- This error is due to the limitation imposed by the least count of the measuring instrument.
- It is a uncertainty associated with the resolution of the measuring instrument.

Error in Case of Measured Quantity Raised to a Power

Assumed the nth power of A and B,

then $Z = \frac{A^n}{B^n}$

$$\pm\frac{\Delta Z}{Z} = \pm n\frac{\Delta A}{A} \pm n\frac{\Delta B}{B}$$

Power of A and B,

$$\frac{\Delta Z}{Z} = \pm\left(n\frac{\Delta A}{A} + \frac{n\Delta B}{B}\right)$$

Absolute Error

- The magnitude of the difference between the true value of a quantity and the individual measured value is called the absolute error.
- It is denoted by $|\Delta a|$.
- $|\Delta a|$ = Actual value − Measured value

Mean Absolute Error

The arithmetic mean of the magnitudes of absolute error in all the measurements.

$$\Delta a_{mean} = \sum_{i=1}^{n} \frac{|\Delta a_i|}{n}$$

Relative Error/Fractional Error

- The ratio of mean absolute error to the mean value of the quantity measured.
- Relative error $(\delta a) = \frac{\text{Mean absolute error}}{\text{Mean value}}$

$$\delta a = \frac{\Delta a_{mean}}{a_m}$$

Percentage Error

When fractional error or relative error is expressed in percentage, then Percentage error,

$$(\delta a) = \frac{\Delta a_{mean}}{a_m} \times 100\ \%$$

Error of a Sum or Difference

- The limiting errors in two physical quantities A and B are $\pm\Delta A$ and $\pm\Delta B$ respectively, then
- **For sum** $Z = A + B$, the maximum possible error, $\Delta Z = \Delta A + \Delta B$
- **For difference** $Z = A - B$, maximum possible error, $\Delta Z = \Delta A + \Delta B$

Error of a Product

Assumed $Z = AB$, measured value of A and B are $A \pm \Delta A$ and $B \pm \Delta B$, then relative error of product,

$$\left(\frac{\Delta Z}{Z}\right) = \pm\left[\frac{\Delta A}{A} + \frac{\Delta B}{B}\right]$$

Error of a Quotient

Assumed $Z = A/B$, then measured value

$$Z \pm \Delta Z = \frac{A \pm \Delta A}{B \pm \Delta B} = Z\left(1 \pm \frac{\Delta A}{A}\right)\left(1 \pm \frac{\Delta B}{B}\right)^{-1}$$

∴ The relative error of quotient

$$\pm\frac{\Delta Z}{Z} = \pm\frac{\Delta A}{A} \pm \frac{\Delta B}{B}$$

Test 1

Syllabus
- Position, Path Length and Displacement
- Uniform and Non-uniform Motion - Speed, Velocity & Acceleration
- Kinematic Equations of Uniformly Accelerated Motion
- Equations of Motion for Object Under Gravity

NCERT Page 15 to 21

For deeper insight **Scan the QR Code**

Chapter 02

Frame of Reference

- The frame of reference is a co-ordinate system with a clock w.r.t which, an observer can describe the position, displacement and acceleration of an object.
- **Inertial Frame of Reference**
  It is that frame of reference which is either at rest or in the state of uniform motion.
- **Non-Inertial Frame of Reference**
  It is that form of reference which performs accelerated motion with respect to an inertial frame of reference.

Classification of Motion

On the basis of the number of co-ordinates required to specify the position of an object, the motion of the object can be classified in three terms.

- **One Dimensional Motion**
  The motion of an object is considered as one dimensional, if only one co-ordinate is needed to specify the position of the object.

In one dimensional motion, the object moves along a straight line, e.g. A boy running on a straight line, motion of freely falling body, etc.

- **Two Dimensional Motion**
  The motion of an object is considered as two dimensional, if two co-ordinates are needed to specify the position of the object.
  In two dimensional motion, the object moves in a plane. e.g. Motion of billiard ball.
- **Three Dimensional Motion**
  The motion of an object is considered as three dimensional, if all the three co-ordinates are needed to specify the position of the object.

Velocity

- The rate of change of position of an object with time is called the velocity of that object.

$$\text{Velocity} = \frac{\text{Displacement}}{\text{Time}}$$

- **Average Velocity**
  The change in position or displacement divided by the time interval in which that displacement occur.

Position

- The point where an object is situated is called position.
- Position determined by the co-ordinate axis that is, marked in units of length and that has positive and negative direction.

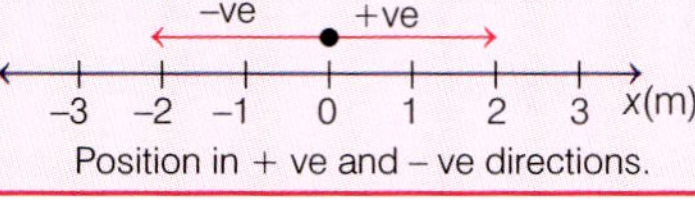

Position in + ve and – ve directions.

Distance

- Length of the path covered by an object in a given time-interval is known as its path length or distance travelled.
- Its SI unit is metre.

Displacement

- The change in position of an object in a particular direction.
- Displacement, $\Delta x = x_2 - x_1$
- **Case I** $x_2 > x_1$, Δx is positive
- **Case II** $x_1 > x_2$, Δx is negative
- **Case III** $x_1 = x_2$, Δx is zero

Speed

- The distance covered by an object divided by the time taken by it to cover that distance is called speed.

$$\text{Speed} = \frac{\text{Distance travelled}}{\text{Time taken}}$$

- Speed is a scalar quantity.
- **Average Speed**
- The total distance travelled by the object divided by the total time taken.

$$\text{Average speed} = \frac{\text{Total distance travelled}}{\text{Total time taken}}$$

$$v_{avg} = \frac{s_1 + s_2}{t_1 + t_2}$$

Acceleration

- The rate of change of velocity with time is called acceleration.
- It is a vector quantity.
- It's SI unit is metre per second square (m/s^2).
- The dimensional formula is $[M^0L^1T^{-2}]$.
- **Retardation**
  When the velocity of a body increases with time, then acceleration will be positive and when the velocity of a body decreases with time (i.e. $u > v$), then acceleration becomes negative. This negative acceleration is called deceleration or retardation. In other words, retardation opposes the motion of body.
- **Average Acceleration**
- The change in velocity divided by time interval.
- Average acceleration $= \frac{\Delta v}{\Delta t} = \frac{\mathbf{v_2} - \mathbf{v_1}}{t_2 - t_1}$

Uniform Motion

- An object travels equal distance in equal intervals along a straight line.
- **When object is stationary**
- Suppose that an object is at rest at a distance a from the origin.
- From the graph (ii) it is clear that, the position of the object remains same w.r.t. time.

Non-uniform Motion

- An object travels equal displacement in unequal interval of time.
- The speed of the body or its direction of motion or both change with time.
- **When Object is in Variable Motion**
- Object covers unequal distance in equal interval of time.
- The position-time graph of varying motion will not be a straight line.

Kinematic Equations

- **For uniformly accelerated motion,** the displacement, time, initial velocity, final velocity and acceleration are related by three simple equations are called kinematic equations of motion.
- **Velocity-Time Relation,** $v = u + at$
- **Position-Time Relation,** $x = ut + \frac{1}{2}at^2$
- **Position-Velocity Relation,** $v^2 = u^2 + 2ax$

Free Fall

- Free fall is defined as situation in which an object moves only under the influence of gravity.
- Free fall is just a downward movement with no initial force or velocity.
- The free fall of any object is just a natural phenomenon on earth without support.

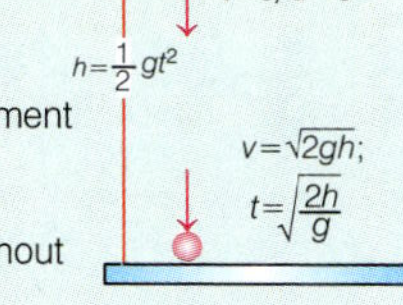

Motion of an Object Under Gravity

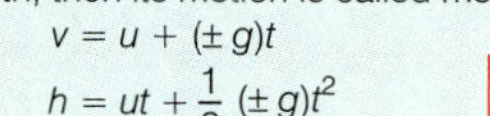

- When an object is thrown vertically upwards or fall towards the earth, then its motion is called motion under gravity.

$$v = u + (\pm g)t$$
$$h = ut + \frac{1}{2}(\pm g)t^2$$
$$v^2 = u^2 + 2(\pm g)h$$

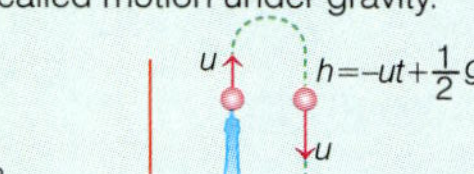

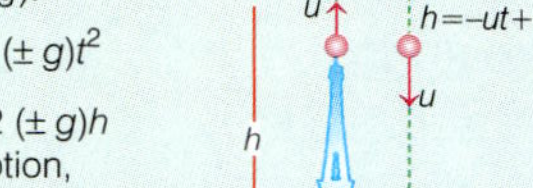

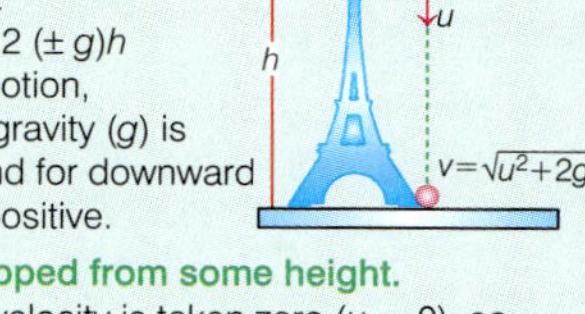

- In case of upward motion, acceleration due to gravity (g) is taken as negative and for downward motion, g taken as positive.
- **If a particle is dropped from some height.**
  In this case, initial velocity is taken zero ($u = 0$), so equations of motion are
  (i) $v = gt$
  (ii) $h = \frac{1}{2}gt^2$
  (iii) $v^2 = 2gh$
  (iv) $H_n = \frac{g}{2}(2n - 1)$
- **For fast calculation in objective problems, remember the following results**

(i) Maximum height attained by a particle, thrown upwards from ground, $h = \frac{u^2}{2g}$

(ii) Velocity of particle at the time of striking the ground when released ($u = 0$) from a height h is $v = \sqrt{2gh}$

(iii) In above point (ii), time for collision of particle with ground,

$$t = \sqrt{\frac{2h}{g}}$$

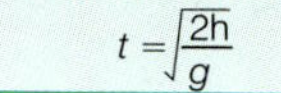

Test 2

Syllabus • Relative Velocity and Graphs

NCERT Page 16,17,20

For deeper insight **Scan the QR Code**

Different Cases of Relative Velocity

Case I When the two objects move with equal velocities, i.e. $\mathbf{v}_A = \mathbf{v}_B$ or $\mathbf{v}_B - \mathbf{v}_A = 0$. It means, the two objects stay at constant distance apart during the whole journey. In this case, the position-time graph of two objects are parallel straight lines.

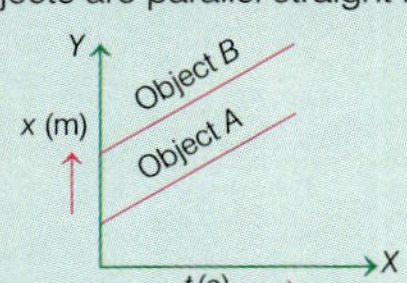

Case II If both objects *A* and *B* move along parallel straight lines in the opposite direction, then relative velocity of *B* w.r.t. *A* is given as

$$\mathbf{v}_{BA} = \mathbf{v}_B - (-\mathbf{v}_A) = \mathbf{v}_B + \mathbf{v}_A$$

and the relative velocity of *A* w.r.t. *B* is given by $\mathbf{v}_{AB} = \mathbf{v}_A - (-\mathbf{v}_B) = \mathbf{v}_A + \mathbf{v}_B$

Case III If $\mathbf{v}_A < \mathbf{v}_B$, $\mathbf{v}_A - \mathbf{v}_B$ is negative. Then,

$$\mathbf{x} - \mathbf{x}_0 < 0 \Rightarrow \mathbf{x} < \mathbf{x}_0$$

where, $\mathbf{x}_0$ = initial displacement of object *A* w.r.t. *B* and $\mathbf{x}$ = displacement of object *A* w.r.t. *B* at time *t*. i.e. $(\mathbf{x} - \mathbf{x}_0)$ is negative. It means the separation between the two objects will go on decreasing and two objects will meet and object *B* will overtake object *A* at this time. In this case, relative velocity of *A* w.r.t. *B*, i.e.

$$\mathbf{v}_{AB} = \mathbf{v}_A - \mathbf{v}_B = -\mathbf{v}_{BA}$$

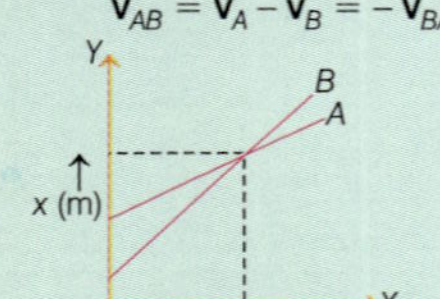

Case IV If $\mathbf{v}_A > \mathbf{v}_B$, $\mathbf{v}_A - \mathbf{v}_B$ is positive. Then, $\mathbf{x} - \mathbf{x}_0 > \mathbf{0}$, i.e. $(\mathbf{x} - \mathbf{x}_0)$ is positive. It means the separation between the two objects will go on increasing with time, i.e. the separation $(\mathbf{x} - \mathbf{x}_0)$ between them will increase by an amount $(\mathbf{v}_A - \mathbf{v}_B)$ after each unit of time. Therefore, their position-time graphs will open out gradually as shown below.

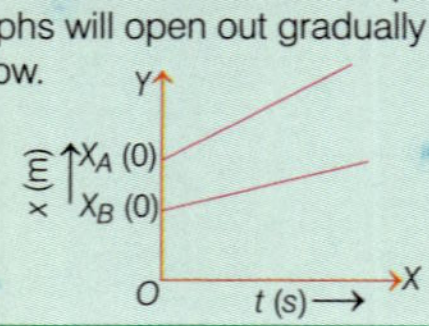

Relative Motion in One Dimension

- **Relative velocity**

The term relative is frequently used for comparison of displacement, velocity and acceleration of the two objects.

The time rate of change of relative position of one object with respect to another is called relative velocity.

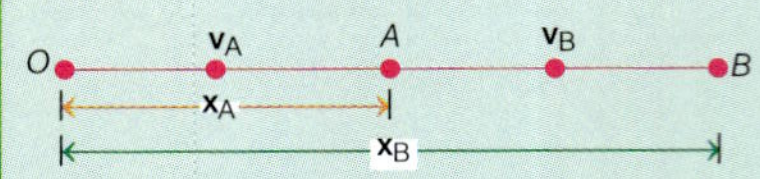

$\therefore$ Their velocities are $v_A = \dfrac{dx_A}{dt}$ and $v_B \dfrac{dx_B}{dt}$

The displacement of *B* relative to *A*,

$$\mathbf{x}_{BA} = \mathbf{x}_B - \mathbf{x}_A$$

The velocity of *B* relative to *A*

$$\mathbf{v}_{BA} = \mathbf{v}_B - \mathbf{v}_A$$

Relative acceleration of *A* with respect to *B* Is

$$\mathbf{a}_{AB} = \mathbf{a}_A - \mathbf{a}_B$$

Analysis of Graph of Straight Line

If the variation of a physical quantity *y* with other physical quantity *x* is linear, then it can be written as

$$y = mx + C$$

Here $m = \tan\theta$ is called slope of graph with positive *X*-axis and *C* is intercept on *Y*-axis. θ is the angle meas ured with positive *x*-direction

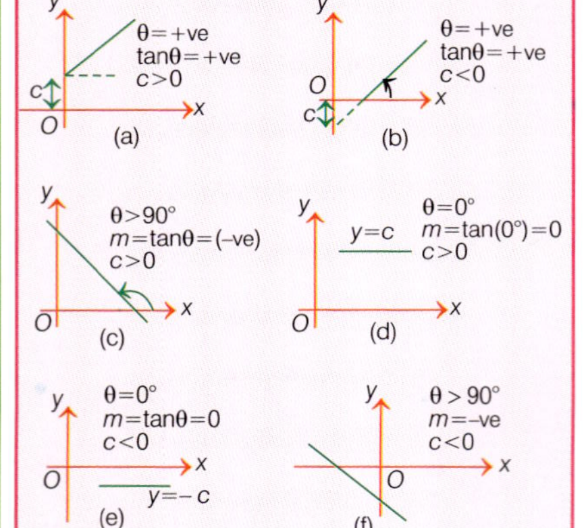

Position-Time Graph

- Position-time graph gives instantaneous value of position at any instant.
- The slope of tangent drawn to the graph at any instant of time gives the instantaneous velocity at that instant.
- The *s*-*t* graph cannot make sharp turns.

Different Cases of position-time graph

Different Cases	*s*-*t* graph	Main feature of graph
At rest	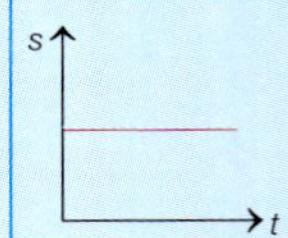	Slope $= \tan 0° = \dfrac{dy}{dx} = 0$, $v = 0$
Uniform motion	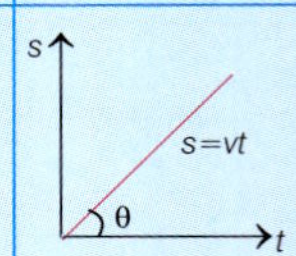 $s = vt$	Slope $= \tan\theta = \dfrac{dy}{dx}$ = constant, v=constant or $a = 0$
Uniform accelerated motion with $u=0$, $s=0$ at $t=0$	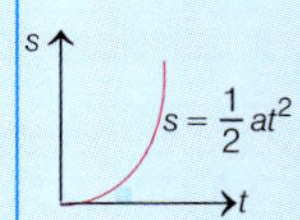 $s = \dfrac{1}{2}at^2$	$u=0$, i.e. slope of *s*-*t* graph at $t=0$ should be zero, at any point of curve, when slope $= \tan\theta = \dfrac{dy}{dx}$ Increasing, then velocity increase
Uniform accelerated motion with $u \neq 0$, $s=0$ at $t=0$	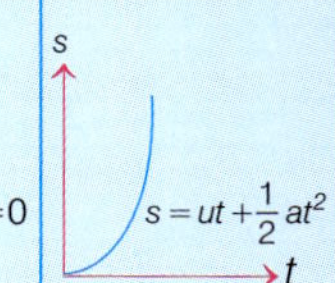 $s = ut + \dfrac{1}{2}at^2$	Slope of *s*-*t* graph gradually goes on increasing $\tan\theta = \dfrac{dy}{dx}$ increasing as we move from origin towards right.
Uniform retarded motion	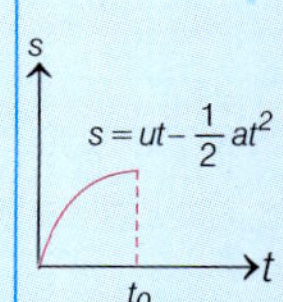 $s = ut - \dfrac{1}{2}at^2$	θ is decreasing so *v* is decreasing , *a* is negative. $\tan\theta = \dfrac{dy}{dx}$ decreases while moving from origin towards right.

Velocity-Time Graph

(i) Velocity-time graph gives the instantaneous value of velocity at any instant.

(ii) The slope of tangent drawn on graph gives instantaneous acceleration.

(iii) Area under *v*-*t* graph with time axis gives the value of displacement covered in given time.

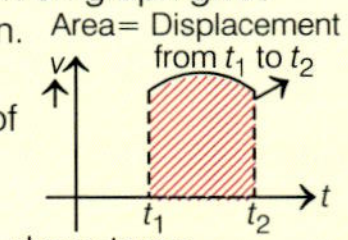

(iv) The *v*-*t* curve cannot take sharp turns.

Different Cases	*v*-*t* graph	Main feature of graph
Uniform motion	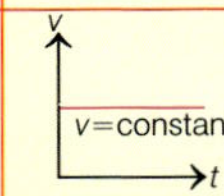 v=constant	(i) $\theta = 0°$ (ii) v = constant (iii) Slope of *v*-*t* graph $dv/dt = \tan\theta = a = 0$
Uniformaly motion with $u = 0$ and $s = 0$ at $t = 0$	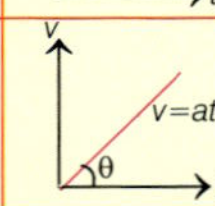 $v = at$	Slope of v-t graph $dv/dt = \tan\theta$ is constant, so $u=0$ a=constant, i.e. $v=0$ at $t=0$
Uniformaly accelerated motion with $u \neq 0$ but $s = 0$ at $t = 0$	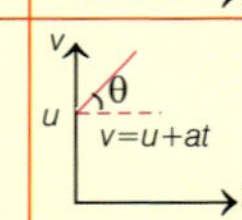 $v = u + at$	Positive constant acceleration because θ is constant and $< 90°$ but the initial velocity of the particle is positive.
Uniformly retarded motion	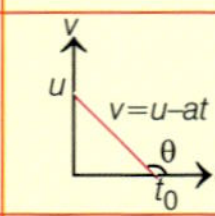 $v = u - at$	Slope of *v*-*t* graph $dv/dt = \tan\theta = -a$ (retardation)
Non-uniformly accelerated motion	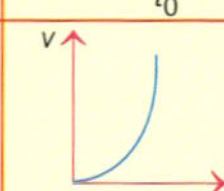	Slope of *v*-*t* graph $dv/dt = \tan\theta$ is increasing, so acceleration is increasing.
Non-uniformly decelerated motion	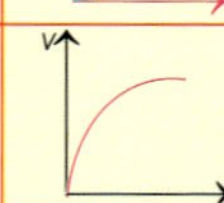	θ is decreasing, so acceleration is decreasing, but not retarding.

Acceleration-Time Graph

The area of the *a*-*t* graph between time t_1 to t_2 gives the change in velocity.

As, $a = \dfrac{dv}{dt} \Rightarrow dv = a\,dt$

$$\int_{v_1}^{v_2} dv = \int_{t_1}^{t_2} a\,dt \Rightarrow v_2 - v_1 = \int_{t_1}^{t_2} a\,dt$$

Change in velocity = Area of the *a*–*t* graph

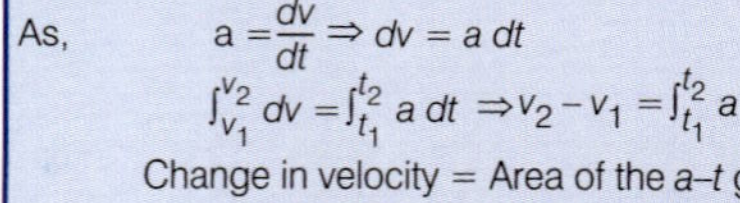

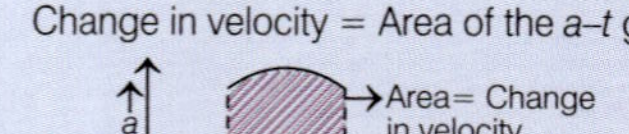

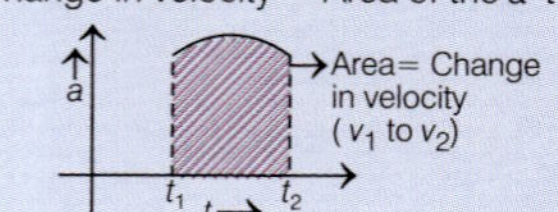

Test 1

Syllabus
- Scalars and Vectors
- Addition and Subtraction of Vectors
- Scalar and Vector Products
- Unit Vectors
- Resolution of Vectors
- Motion in a Plane and Projectile Motion

NCERT Page 28 to 38

For deeper insight **Scan the QR Code**

Chapter 03

Physical Quantities

It is a physical property of a material or system that can be quantified by measurement.

Scalar Quantities

- Those physical quantities which have only magnitude but no direction.
- It is specified completely by a single number along with proper unit. e.g. Time, mass, length, etc.

Vector Quantities

- Those physical quantities which have both magnitude and direction.
- These obey the triangular law or parallelogram law of addition and subtraction. e.g. Velocity, acceleration, momentum, etc.

Collinear Vector

- The two or more vectors are said to be collinear, when they act along the same line or parallel lines. e.g. Tug of war

A B (a) A B (b) A B (c)

Co-initial Vector

- The vector which has the same initial point are called co-initial vectors.
- Two vectors **A** and **B** have been drawn from the initial point *O*, therefore *A* and *B* are called co-initial vectors.

Equal Vectors

Two vectors are said to be equal, if they have equal magnitude and same direction.

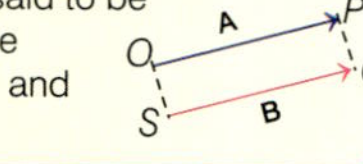

Unit Vector

A vector having magnitude equal to unity but having a specific direction is called a unit vector.

$$\hat{A} = \frac{\mathbf{A}}{|\mathbf{A}|} = \frac{\text{Vector}}{\text{Magnitude of the vector}}$$

Position Vector

- A vector that extends from a reference point to the point at which particle is located is called position vector.

Position vector, $r = x\hat{i} + y\hat{j}$

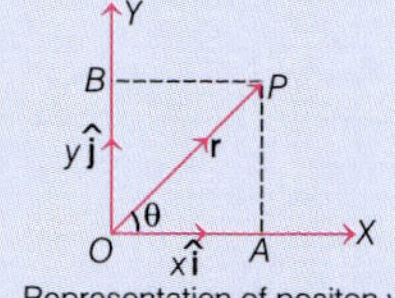

Representation of positon vector

Direction of this position vector **r** is given by the angle θ with *X*-axis, where

$$\Rightarrow \quad \theta = \tan^{-1}\left(\frac{y}{x}\right)$$

In three dimensions, the position vector is represented as

$$r = x\hat{i} + y\hat{j} + z\hat{k}$$

Displacement Vector

- Representation of displacement vector

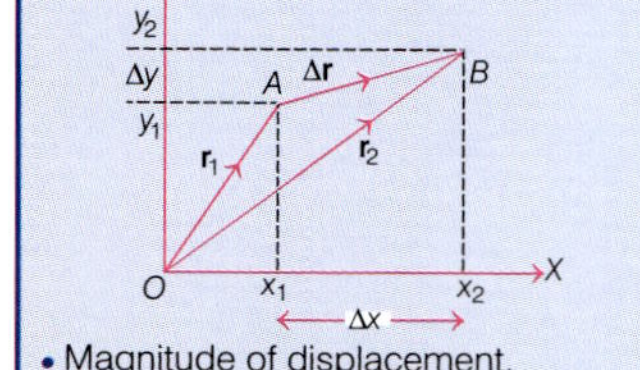

- Magnitude of displacement,

$$|\Delta \mathbf{r}| = \sqrt{(\Delta x)^2 + (\Delta y)^2}$$
$$= \sqrt{(x_2 - x_1)^2 + (y_2 - y_1)^2}$$

Direction of the displacement vector $\Delta\mathbf{r}$ is given by

$$\tan\theta = \left(\frac{\Delta y}{\Delta x}\right)$$
$$\theta = \tan^{-1}\left(\frac{\Delta y}{\Delta x}\right)$$

Average Velocity

The average velocity of an object is the ratio of the displacement and time interval.

i.e., $\mathbf{v} = \frac{\Delta \mathbf{r}}{\Delta t} = v_x\hat{\mathbf{i}} + v_y\hat{\mathbf{j}}$

Addition of Vectors

- Two vectors can be added, if both of them are of same nature.
- **Triangle law of vector addition**
  If two vectors can be represented both in magnitude and direction by the two sides of triangle taken in same order.

Resultant vector, $\mathbf{R} = \mathbf{A} + \mathbf{B}$

Properties of Addition of Vectors

(i) It follows commutative property, i.e. $\mathbf{A} + \mathbf{B} = \mathbf{B} + \mathbf{A}$

(ii) It follows associative property, i.e., $(\mathbf{A} + \mathbf{B}) + \mathbf{C} = \mathbf{A} + (\mathbf{B} + \mathbf{C})$

(iii) It obeys distributive property, i.e. $\lambda(\mathbf{A} + \mathbf{B}) = \mathbf{A}\lambda + \lambda\mathbf{B}$

(iv) It follows identity property i.e., $\mathbf{A} + \mathbf{0} = \mathbf{A}$

Subtraction of Vectors

It is expressed as

$\mathbf{R} = \mathbf{A} + (-\mathbf{B})$

$\mathbf{R} = \mathbf{A} - \mathbf{B}$

Properties of Subtraction of Vector

(i) It does not follow commutative properties, i.e., $\mathbf{A} - \mathbf{B} \neq \mathbf{B} - \mathbf{A}$

(ii) It does not follow associative property, i.e., $\mathbf{A} - (\mathbf{B} - \mathbf{C}) \neq (\mathbf{A} - \mathbf{B}) - \mathbf{C}$

(iii) It follows distributive property, i.e, $\lambda(\mathbf{A} - \mathbf{B}) = \lambda\mathbf{A} - \lambda\mathbf{B}$

(iv) It follows identity property, i.e., $\mathbf{A} - \mathbf{0} = \mathbf{A}$

Instantaneous Acceleration

The instantaneous acceleration of an object is given by

$$\mathbf{a} = \lim_{\Delta t \to 0} \frac{\Delta \mathbf{v}}{\Delta t} = \frac{d\mathbf{v}}{dt}$$

Average Acceleration

The average acceleration of an object is the ratio of change in velocity and time interval.

i.e. $\mathbf{a} = \frac{\Delta \mathbf{v}}{\Delta t} = a_x\hat{\mathbf{i}} + a_y\hat{\mathbf{j}}$

Instantaneous Velocity

The instantaneous velocity is given by

$$\mathbf{v} = \lim_{\Delta t \to 0} \frac{\Delta \mathbf{r}}{\Delta t} = \frac{d\mathbf{r}}{dt}$$

Vector Multiplied by a Real Number

If a vector multiplied by a real number, then the resultant vector is also a vector whose magnitude is changed but the direction remain same.

$$|\lambda\mathbf{A}| = \lambda|\mathbf{A}|, \text{ if } \lambda > 0$$

where, λ is a scalar number.

Resolution of Vectors

- Any vector can be resolved into components along two given vectors **a** and **b** lying in the same plane.

$$\mathbf{A} = \lambda_1\mathbf{a} + \lambda_2\mathbf{b}$$

where, λ_1 and λ_2 real numbers.

Parallelogram Law

- If two vectors acting on a particle at the same time are represented in magnitude and direction by the adjacent side of a parallelogram drawn from same point, then their resultant vector is along the diagonal of parallelogram.

Projectile Projected Horizontally from a Tower

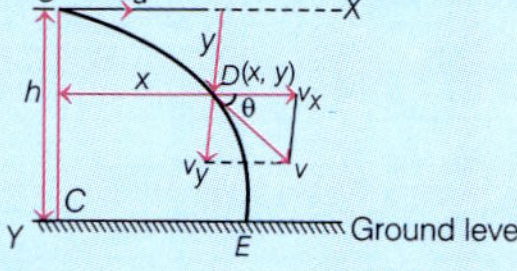

Horizontal Components	Vertical Components
$u_x = u$	$u_y = 0$
$a_x = 0\ (F_x = 0)$	$a_y = -g$

- **Different terms related to this type of projectile motion are**

(i) Equation of trajectory, $y = -\frac{1}{2}\left(\frac{g}{u^2}\right)x^2$

(ii) Time of flight, $T = \sqrt{\frac{2h}{g}}$

(iii) Horizontal range, $R = u\sqrt{\frac{2h}{g}}$

(iv) Velocity of projectile at any instant, $v = \sqrt{u^2 + g^2t^2}$

at an angle θ with horizontal, where $\theta = \tan^{-1}\left(\frac{v_y}{v_x}\right) = \frac{gt}{u}$

Projectile Motion

Projectile motion is a form of motion in which an object is thrown with some initial velocity near the earth's surface and it moves along a curved path under the action of gravity alone.

Horizontal Range

The horizontal range is distance covered by the projectile during its time of flight.

Horizontal range, $R = \frac{u^2 \sin 2\theta}{g}$

Here, maximum horizontal range,

$$R_{max} = \frac{u^2}{g} \quad [\because \theta = 45°]$$

Time of Flight

Total time for which projectile is in flight, i.e. time during the motion of projectile.

Total time of flight, $T = \frac{2u\sin\theta}{g}$

Maximum Height

The maximum vertical height attained by an object above the point of projectile during its flight.

Maximum height, $H = \frac{u^2 \sin^2\theta}{2g}$

Equation of Projectile

- **Motion along horizontal direction (*OX*)**

Time, $t = \frac{x}{u\cos\theta}$

- **Motion along vertical direction (*OY*)**

Total vertical distance,

$$y = x\tan\theta - \left(\frac{1}{2}\frac{g}{u^2\cos^2\theta}\right)x^2$$

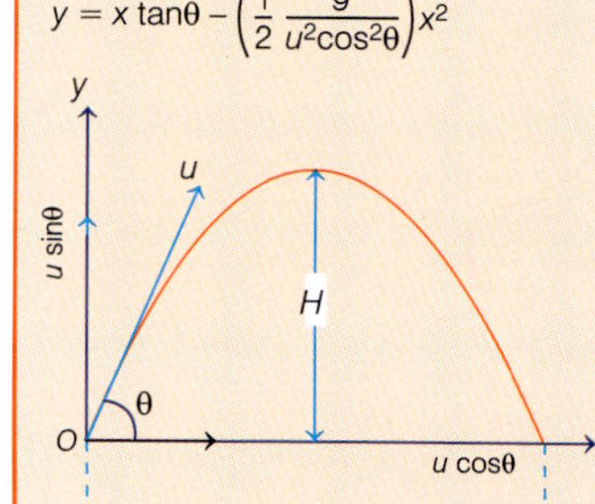

Test 2

Syllabus
- Relative Velocity in 2D
- Rain-man Problem
- River-boat (or man) Problem

NCERT Page 28 to 38

For deeper insight **Scan the QR Code**

Chapter 03

Relative Velocity

Motion of one object wrt to another object is called relative motion. The relative velocity of an object A w.r.t. object B,

$$\mathbf{v_{AB} = v_A - v_B}$$

Relative velocity of object B w.r.t. A,

$$\mathbf{v_{BA} = v_B - v_A}$$

Clearly, $\mathbf{v_{AB} = -v_{BA}}$

Relative Motion in One Dimension (Overtaking and Chasing)

- **Relative motion for different phases**

(i) When two bodies moving towards each other

$$t = \frac{d + L_1 + L_2}{v_1 + v_2}$$

(ii) When two bodies moving in the same direction

(a) $$t = \frac{d + L_1 + L_2}{v_1 - v_2}$$

(b) $d + L_1 + L_2 = (u_1 - u_2)t + \frac{1}{2}(a_1 - a_2)t^2$

Minimum Separation to Avoid Collision

$u_{rel} = u_1 - u_2$, $a_{net} = -a_1$

$0 = u_{rel}^2 + 2a_{rel}s_{rel}$

$0 = (u_1 - u_2)^2 - 2a_1 s$

$$s = \frac{(u_1 - u_2)^2}{2a_1}$$

To avoid collision,

$$s \le d$$

$$\Rightarrow d \ge \frac{(u_1 - u_2)^2}{2a_1}$$

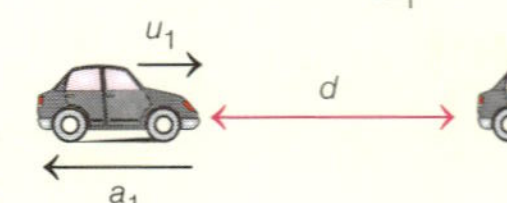

Man-river Problem

For a man swimming relative to river water

1. v_{MR} or $v_{M/Still\ water}$ = velocity due to effort of man, or velocity of man in still water
2. v_R = Velocity of river
3. v_M = Resultant velocity of man with respect to ground

(i) Up Stream

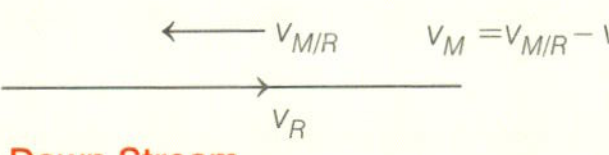

(ii) Down Stream

$v_{M/R}$ $\quad v_M = v_{M/R} + v_R$

v_R

(iii) Swimming across the river

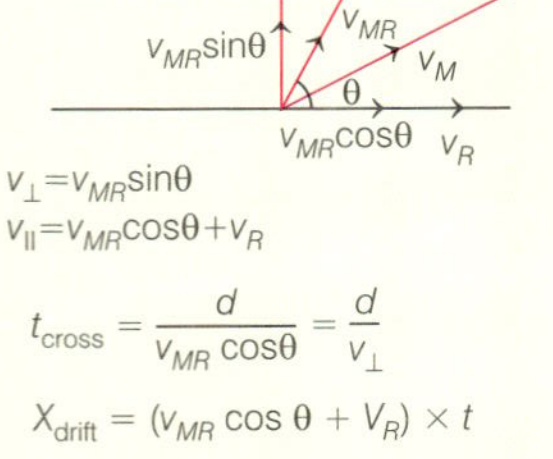

1. $v_\perp = v_{MR}\sin\theta$
2. $v_\parallel = v_{MR}\cos\theta + v_R$

$$t_{cross} = \frac{d}{v_{MR}\cos\theta} = \frac{d}{v_\perp}$$

$$X_{drift} = (v_{MR}\cos\theta + v_R) \times t$$

$$= v_{MR}\cos\theta \times t + v_R t$$

Due to effort of man (first term); Additional due to push of river (second term)

Shortest time	Shortest Path
$\theta = 90$, $\sin\theta = 1$	Horizontal component of v_m becomes 0
$t = \dfrac{d}{v_{MR}\sin\theta}$	$\Rightarrow v_{MR}\sin\theta = v_R$
$t_{min} = \dfrac{d}{v_{MR}}$	$v_{MR}\cos\theta = v_m$
$x_{drift} = v_R \times t$	Condition for no drifting
$v_m = \sqrt{(v_{MR})^2 + (v_R)^2}$	$\Rightarrow \sin\theta = \dfrac{v_R}{v_{MR}}$
	$\Rightarrow t_{cross} = \dfrac{d}{v_m}$
	$\Rightarrow v_m = \sqrt{v_{MR}^2 - v_R^2}$
	$\Rightarrow$ Drift = 0

Drift

It is defined as the displacement of man in the direction of river flow as shown below.

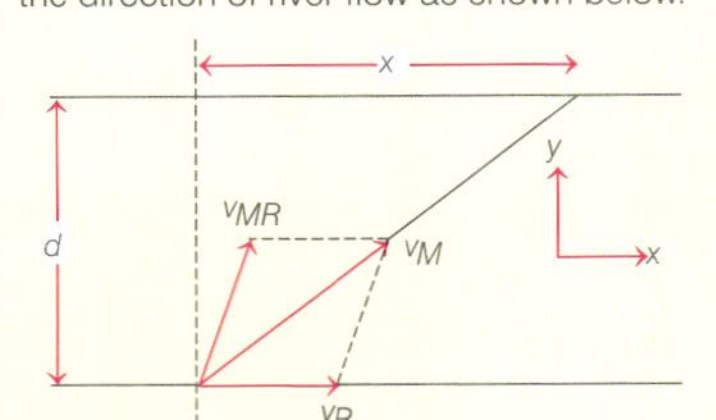

It is simply the displacement along X-axis. During the period, the man crosses the river. $(v_{MR}\cos\theta + v_R)$ is the components of velocity of man in the direction of river flow and this component of velocity is responsible for drift along the river flow. If drift is x, then

$$x = (v_{MR}\cos\theta + v_R) \times \frac{d}{v_{MR}\sin\theta}$$

- If a man travels downstream in a river, then the time taken by the man to cover a distance d is

$$t_1 = \frac{d}{v_1 + v_2}$$

If a man swims upstream in a river, then the time taken by him to cover a distance d is

$$t_2 = \frac{d}{v_1 - v_2}$$

So, $$\frac{t_1}{t_2} = \frac{v_1 - v_2}{v_1 + v_2}$$

Note

If $v_R > v_{MR}$, then it is not possible to have zero drift. In this case, the minimum drift corresponding to shortest possible path is non-zero and the condition for minimum drift can be proved to be

$\cos\theta = -\dfrac{v_{MR}}{v_R}$ or $\sin\phi = \dfrac{v_{MR}}{v_R}$ for minimum but non-zero drift.

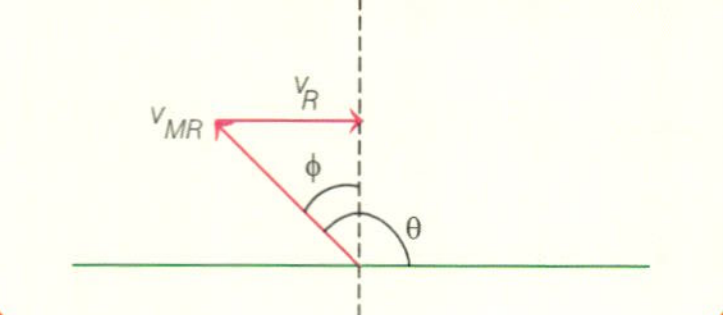

Man - rain Problem

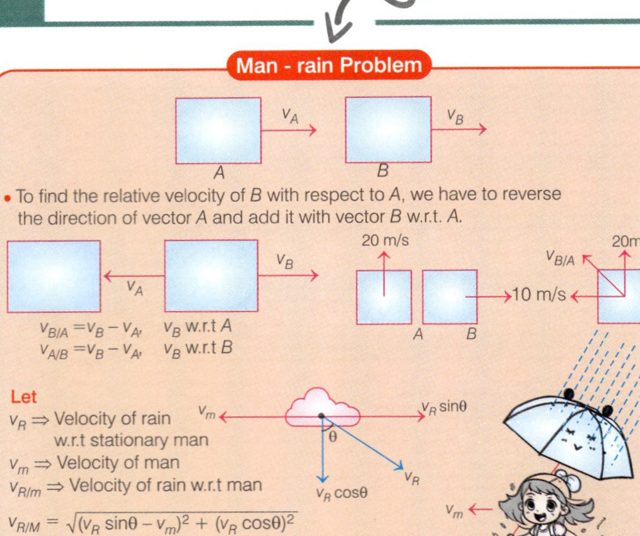

- To find the relative velocity of B with respect to A, we have to reverse the direction of vector A and add it with vector B w.r.t. A.

$v_{B/A} = v_B - v_A$, v_B w.r.t A

$v_{A/B} = v_B - v_A$, v_B w.r.t B

20 m/s, 10 m/s, 20m/s, $v_{B/A}$

Let

$v_R \Rightarrow$ Velocity of rain w.r.t stationary man

$v_m \Rightarrow$ Velocity of man

$v_{R/m} \Rightarrow$ Velocity of rain w.r.t man

$$v_{R/M} = \sqrt{(v_R\sin\theta - v_m)^2 + (v_R\cos\theta)^2}$$

- **Case 1** Rain is falling vertically downward

$v_R\sin\theta > v_m$

$$v_{R/M} = \sqrt{(v_R\cos\theta)^2 + (v_R\sin\theta - v_m)^2}$$

$$\tan\theta = \frac{v_R\sin\theta - v_m}{v_R\cos\theta}$$

$$\theta = \tan^{-1}\left(\frac{v_R\sin\theta - v_m}{v_R\cos\theta}\right)$$

- **Case 2** When rain is falling at angle θ

$v_m > v_R\sin\theta$

$$v_{R/M} = \sqrt{(v_R\cos\theta)^2 + (v_R\sin\theta - v_m)^2}$$

$$\theta = \tan^{-1}\left(\frac{v_m - v_R\sin\theta}{v_R\cos\theta}\right)$$

- **Case 3** When rain is falling in the opposite direction with respect to man

$v_m = v_R\sin\theta$

$v_{R/M} = v_R\sin\theta$

$\theta = 0$

- **minimum distance**

$$d_{min} = \frac{d \times v}{\sqrt{v^2 + u^2}}$$

Time taken to reach minimum distance $= \dfrac{d \times v}{v^2 + u^2}$

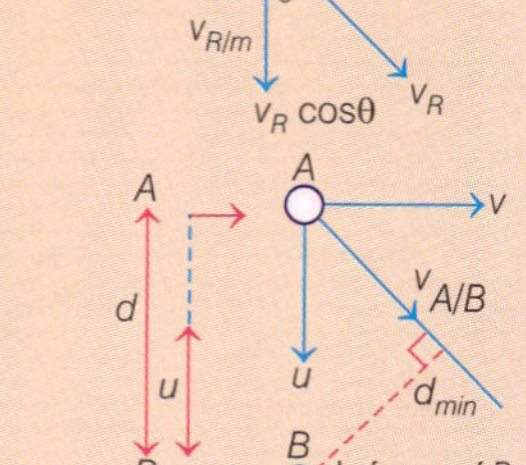

Test 3

Syllabus
- Uniform Circular Motion
- Centripetal Acceleration
- Acceleration of Particle in Non-uniform Circular Motion

NCERT Page 28 to 38

For deeper insight **Scan the QR Code**

Chapter 03

Radius Vector

When a particle moves on a circular path, its distance from the centre is fixed and it is equal to radius of the circle. If the centre of the circle is taken as origin, then the vector joining centre to the particle is called radius vector. It is directed from centre to the particle and its magnitude is same as radius.

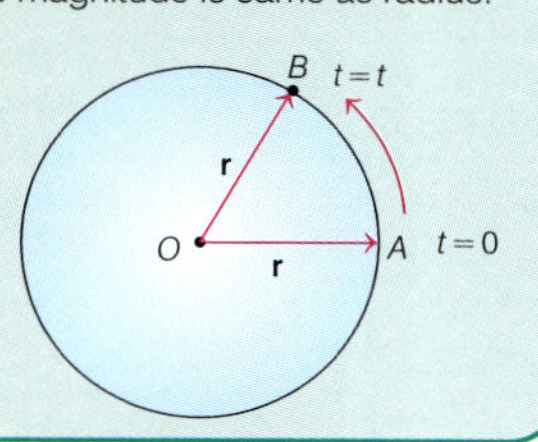

Angular Position

Suppose, a particle P is moving on a circular path of radius r and centre O, as shown in figure. The position of the particle P at a given instant may be described by the angle θ between OP and OX. This angle θ is called the angular position of the particle. As the particle moves on the circle, its angular position θ changes. Angular position is a scalar quantity with SI unit as **'radian'**.

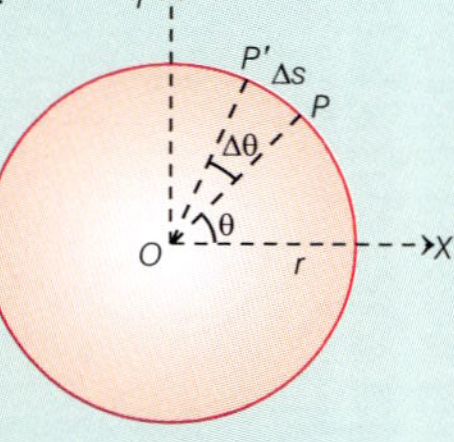

- **In uniform circular motion**
  - magnitude of velocity does not change
  - direction of velocity changes
  - velocity changes
  - angular velocity is constant
  - centripetal acceleration changes (only in direction)
  - linear momentum changes
  - angular momentum w.r.t. centre does not change.

Angular Displacement

The angle traced out by the radius vector at the centre of the circular path in the given time is called angular displacement.
It is denoted by $\Delta\theta$ and expressed in radians. In the figure OP_1 is the initial and OP_2 is the final position vectors of the particle.

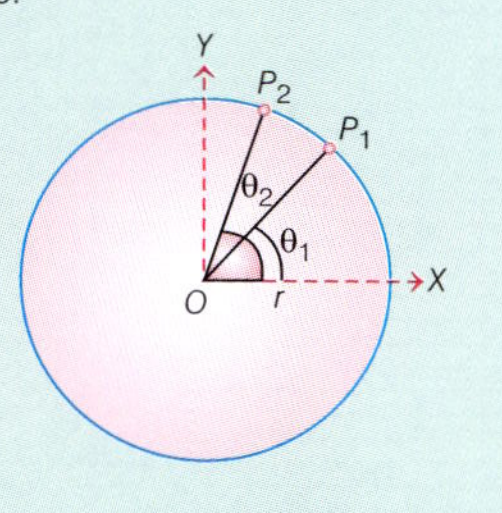

$$\Delta\theta = \theta_2 - \theta_1$$

Angular displacement is a scalar quantity with SI unit as **'radian'**.
Infinitesimally, small angular displacement is an axial vector, which means that its direction is always along the axis of rotation and the direction may be found using right hand thumb rule.

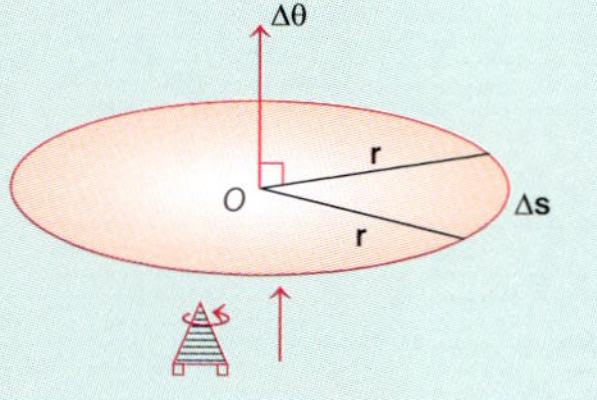

Non-uniform Circular Motion

- Speed not constant
- Velocity changes in direction and magnitude
- a_c = Centripetal acceleration
- a_t = tangential acceleration

$$\frac{d\omega}{dt} \times \mathbf{r} = \alpha \times \mathbf{r}$$

- ω = Changes $\rightarrow \alpha$ angular acceleration

Horizontal circular motion

$$T = \frac{mv^2}{r} = mr\omega^2 = ml\omega^2$$

Angular Velocity

Rate of change of angular displacement of a particle performing circular motion is called angular velocity.

Angular velocity, $\omega = \dfrac{\Delta\theta}{\Delta t}$

$$\omega_{av} = \frac{\theta_2 - \theta_1}{t_2 - t_1} = \frac{\Delta\theta}{\Delta t}$$

$$\omega_{instantaneous} = \frac{d\theta}{dt}$$

(for uniform circular motion, $\omega_{av} = \omega$)

Instantaneous angular velocities is an axial vector with dimensions $[M^0L^0T^{-1}]$ and unit is rad/s. It is directed along a line passing through centre (O) and perpendicular to the plane of circular motion, containing **r** and **Δs**. If a particle makes N revolutions, its angular displacement is $\theta = 0$

Direction of Angular Velocity

Direction of angular velocity is given in the same way as that of angular displacement.

Observer | Observer
Screw advancement | Screw advancement
(a) Anti-clockwise motion (b) Clockwise motion

When the particle rotates in anti-clockwise direction as seen by observer, angular velocity is along a line passing through the centre and perpendicular to the plane of the circle and towards the observer. This is along a direction, where screw advances as shown in figure.

Angular Acceleration

The rate of change of angular velocity of a particle performing circular motion is called angular acceleration.
Angular acceleration, $\alpha = \dfrac{\Delta\omega}{\Delta t}$

$$\alpha_{av} = \frac{\omega_2 - \omega_1}{t_2 - t_1} = \frac{\Delta\omega}{\Delta t}$$

Instantaneous angular acceleration,

$$\alpha_{ins} = \lim_{\Delta t \to 0} \frac{\Delta\omega}{\Delta t} = \frac{d\omega}{dt} = \frac{d^2\theta}{dt^2} = \frac{\omega d\omega}{d\theta}$$

The SI unit of angular acceleration is rads^{-2} and its dimensional formula is $[M^0L^0T^{-2}]$. If $\alpha = 0$, circular motion is said to uniform.

Relation between Linear and Angular Parameters

- **Linear and Angular Displacement**
  The length of path travelled by the body along the circumference of the circle is known as arc length. Here,
  l = Arc length

$$l = \frac{\theta}{2\pi} = r\theta$$

$$\theta = 2\pi r \times \frac{\text{arc length}}{\text{radius}} = \frac{l}{r}$$

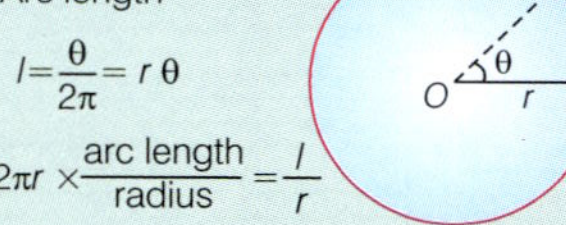

Arc length of a travelled body

- **Linear and Angular Velocity**
  Linear velocity (v) and angular velocity (ω) of a particle performing uniform circular motion of radius r is given by

$$v = \omega \times r$$

In vector form, $\mathbf{v} = \omega \times \mathbf{r}$

Centripetal Acceleration

When a particle is in uniform circular motion, its speed remains constant but velocity changes continuously because of change in direction of motion. Therefore, motion of the particle is accelerated. This acceleration is called centripetal acceleration and it is directed along radial direction towards centre of the circle. It is given by

$$a_r = a_c = \frac{v^2}{r}$$

It is also called **radial acceleration.**
If we put, $v = r\omega$
where, ω is angular velocity, then centripetal acceleration, $a_r = a_c = r\omega^2$

Equation of Angular Motion

- Constant angular velocity :
  ω = constant
- Constant angular acceleration

$\Rightarrow \quad \omega = \omega_0 + \alpha t$

$\Rightarrow \quad \theta = \omega_0 t + 1/2\,\alpha t^2$

$\Rightarrow \quad \omega^2 = \omega_0^2 + 2\alpha(\theta)$

Centripetal acceleration directed towards centre a_c is due to change in the direction of velocity

$$a_c = \frac{v^2}{R} = a_c = r\omega^2$$

$\mathbf{a}_c \perp \mathbf{v} \quad \mathbf{F}_c \perp \mathbf{S}$

Tangential Acceleration

In direction of tangent

$$a_1 = \frac{dv}{dt} = r\alpha, \quad \alpha = \frac{d\omega}{dt}$$

Tangential force, $F_t = ma_t$ is due to change in magnitude of velocity.
Resultant acceleration,

$$a_r = \sqrt{a_c^2 + a_t^2}$$

Velocity is tangent to the circle

Uniform Circular Motion

- Speed Constant
- Direction of velocity changes
- ω = constant
- $a_c = \dfrac{v^2}{r} = r\omega^2$
- $a_t = 0$

Test 1

Syllabus

- Force, Inertia and Newton's First Law of Motion
- Momentum and Newton's Second Law of Motion
- Impulse and Newton's Third Law of Motion
- Law of Conservation of Linear Momentum and Its Applications

NCERT Page 51 to 57

For deeper insight **Scan the QR Code**

Chapter 04

Linear Momentum

The linear momentum of a particle is defined as product of its mass and velocity.

$\mathbf{p} = m\mathbf{v}$

- Its SI unit is kilogram-metre/second.
- It is a vector quantity.
- Its dimensional formula is $[MLT^{-1}]$.
- If p = constant, then $v \propto \frac{1}{m}$.

Heavier is the body, smaller will be its velocity.

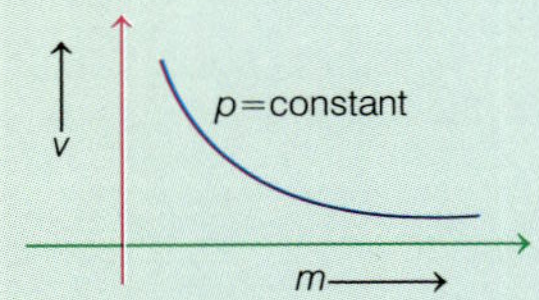

- If v = constant, then $p \propto m$.

The heaviest body will have largest momentum.

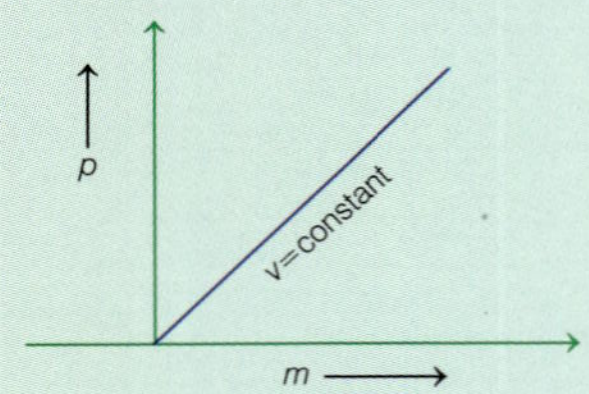

Law of Conservation of Linear Momentum

The total momentum of an isolated system (a system having no external force acting on it) of constant mass remains constant or conserved and does not change with time.

$F_{ext} = 0 \Rightarrow \Delta p = 0$ or $p_i = p_f$

Initial momentum = Final momentum

This principle is a consequence of Newton's second and third law of motion.

- Total momentum,

$$\mathbf{p} = \mathbf{p}_1 + \mathbf{p}_2 + \dots + \mathbf{p}_n = \sum_{i=1}^{n} \mathbf{p}_i$$

- If resultant external force acting on a system is zero, then linear momentum of system remains conserved.

i.e. $p_i = p_f$

Newton's First Law of Motion

- Every body continues in its state of rest or of uniform motion in a straight line unless it is compelled by some external force to change that state.
- If the net external force on a body is zero, then its acceleration will be zero.
- Acceleration will be non-zero, if there is net external force.

Example

If a body at rest, continues in its state of rest, a book on the table will continue to remain there unless we displace it.

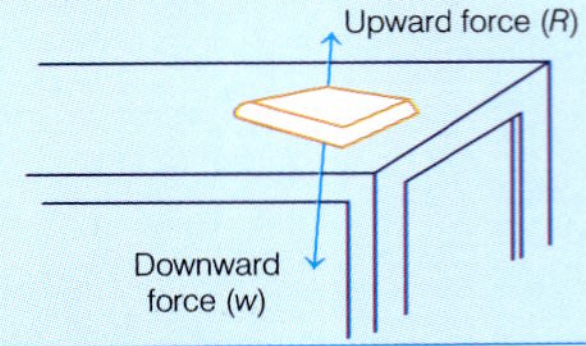

Newton's Second Law of Motion

- Rate of change in linear momentum of a body is directly proportional to applied force and takes place in the direction in which the force acts.
- $\mathbf{F} = \frac{\Delta \mathbf{p}}{\Delta t}$ (on the basis of experiment.)
- For constant mass, $\mathbf{F} = m\mathbf{a}$
- Instantaneous Force $\mathbf{F} = \frac{d\mathbf{p}}{dt}$; Average Force $\mathbf{F}_{av} = \frac{\Delta \mathbf{p}}{\Delta t} = \frac{\mathbf{p}_f - \mathbf{p}_i}{\Delta t}$
- A bullet fired on a window passes through it making a clean hole while a stone breaks the whole window.

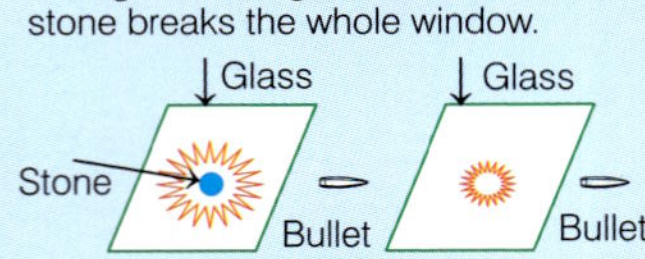

Newton's Third Law of Motion

- When a body exerts a force on second body, the second body also exert force on first body. The two forces are equal in magnitude and opposite in direction.

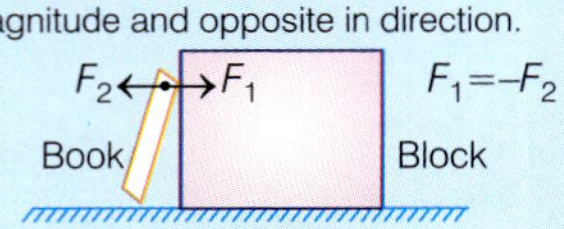

F_1 = Force applied by book on block
F_2 = Force applied by block on book

Important Features of Newton's Third Law of Motion

(i) Newton's third law of motion is applicable irrespective of the nature of the forces

The forces of action and reaction may be mechanical, gravitational, electrical or of any other nature.

(ii) Action reaction forces always act on two different bodies

If they act on the same body, the resultant force would be zero and there could never be accelerated motion.

(iii) The force of action and reaction may not cancel each other

This is because action and reaction, though equal and opposite forces but act on different bodies and so cannot cancel each other.

(iv) No action can occur in the absence of a reaction

In a tug of war, one team can pull the rope only if the other team is pulling the other end of the rope. No force can be exerted, if the other end is free. One team exerts the force of action and the other team provides the force of reaction.

Inertia

- A body cannot change its state of rest or uniform motion along a straight line unless acted by an external force. This property is called inertia. Inertia has no unit and dimension.

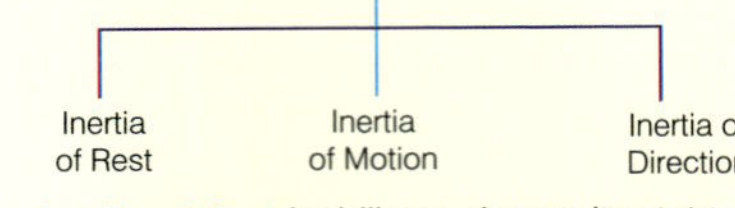
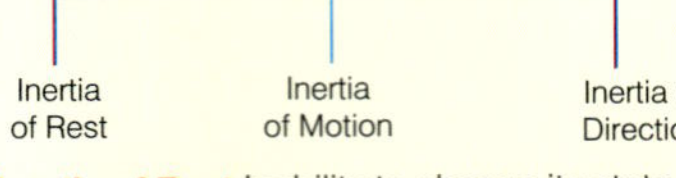

- **Inertia of Rest** Inability to change its state of rest by itself.
- **Inertia of Motion** Inability of a body to change its state of uniform motion by itself.
- **Inertia of Direction** Inability of a body to change direction of motion by itself.

Impulse

- A large force acting for a short time to produce a finite change in momentum.

Impulse $= F \cdot \Delta t = \Delta p$

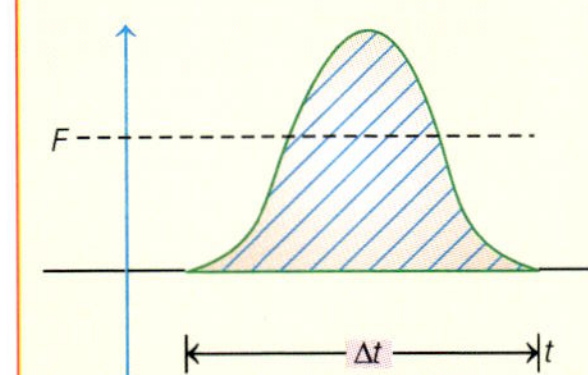

Some Common Forces

- **Normal Reaction**
  - Occurs when two surfaces are in contact with each other.
  - Always perpendicular to the surface.

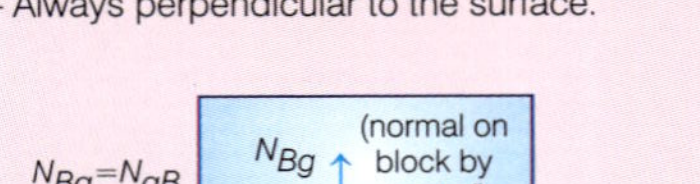
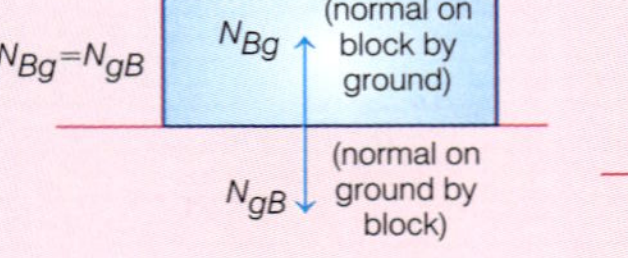

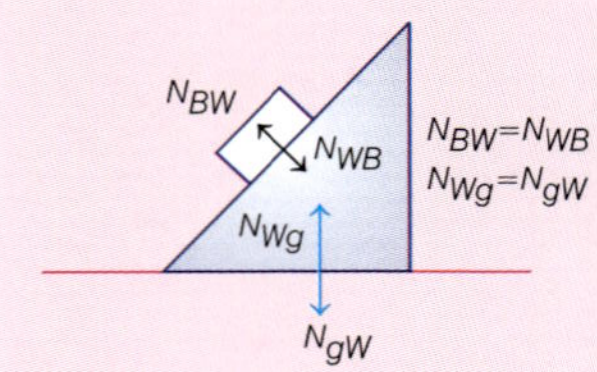

- **Tension**

  It is a restoring force developed when a longitudinal force is applied on a body.

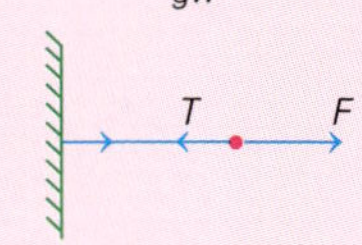

- **Properties of ideal rope**
  - Massless in nature
  - Tension is same everywhere
  - Opposes only elongation
  - On compression it becomes slack
  - Tension always acts away from the object
  - Can support both elongation and compression

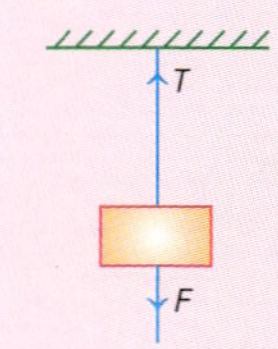

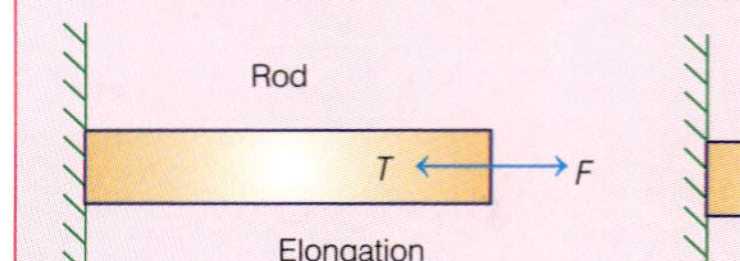

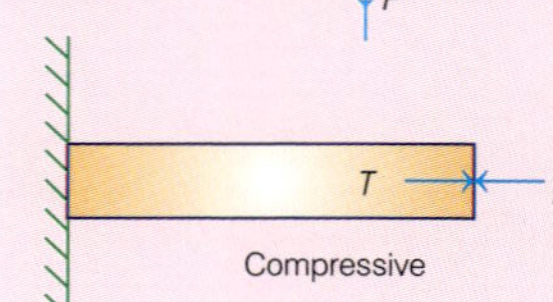

Test 2

Syllabus
- Equilibrium of Concurrent Forces
- Motion of Objects in Contact
- Tension in Strings

NCERT Page 57 to 60

For deeper insight **Scan the QR Code**

Motion of Connected Bodies

Force and acceleration of some connected bodies is given below.

$F_1 > F_2$, $F_1 - F_2 = Ma$

$a = \frac{F_1 - F_2}{M}$

$F_2 \leftarrow$ M $\rightarrow F_1$ (a)

Condition	Free body diagram	Equation	Force and acceleration
F → A (m_1), B (m_2) on ground	F → m_1 ← f (a →)	$F - f = m_1a$	$a = \frac{F}{m_1 + m_2}$
	f → m_2 (a →)	$f = m_2a$	$f = \frac{m_2F}{m_1 + m_2}$
A (m_1), B (m_2) ← F on ground	m_1 ← f (a ←)	$f = m_1a$	$a = \frac{F}{m_1 + m_2}$
	f → m_2 ← F (a ←)	$F - f = m_2a$	$f = \frac{m_1F}{m_1 + m_2}$
F → A (m_1), B (m_2), C (m_3) on ground	F → m_1 ← f_1 (a →)	$F - f_1 = m_1a$	$a = \frac{F}{m_1 + m_2 + m_3}$
	f_1 → m_2 ← f_2 (a →)	$f_1 - f_2 = m_2a$	$f_1 = \frac{(m_1 + m_2)F}{m_1 + m_2 + m_3}$
Here, f, f_1 and f_2 are normal reactions between blocks	f_2 → m_3 (a →)	$f_2 = m_3a$	$f_2 = \frac{m_3F}{m_1 + m_2 + m_3}$

Tension in a Rope

Tension will be different at different points on a rope.

Mass per unit length $= \frac{M}{L}$

Mass of x length of rope $= \frac{M}{L}x$

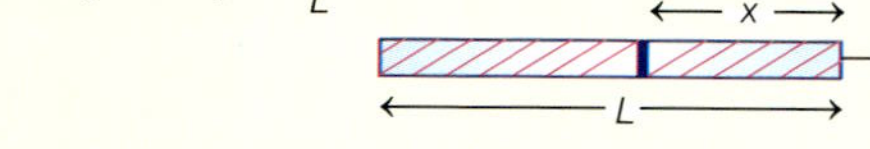

Mass of given length $= \frac{\text{Total mass}}{\text{Total length}} \times$ given length

$a_{rope} = \frac{\mathbf{F}}{M}$

For $(L-x)$ rope length, $\mathbf{F} = m\mathbf{a} \Rightarrow \mathbf{T} = m_2 \frac{\mathbf{F}}{M}$

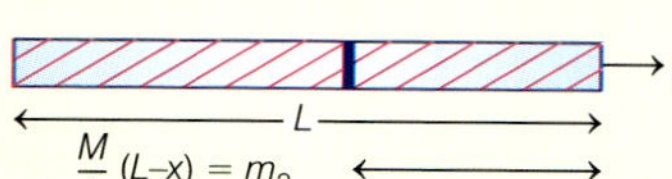

$\frac{M}{L}(L-x) = m_2$ $\qquad \frac{M}{L}x = m_1$

Static Equilibrium

The physical state in which all components of a system are at rest and the net force is equal to zero throughout the system.

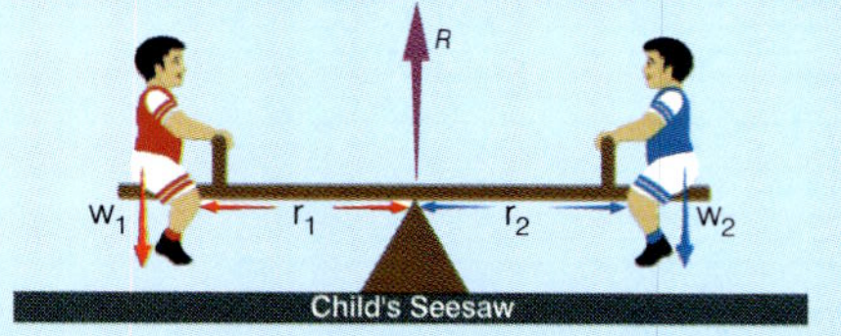

r is the distance from the pivot point to the point, where the force is applied, F is magnitude of the force and w is weight.

$w_1 r_1 = w_2 r_2$

Equilibrium of a particle

- The body under the action of concurrent forces will be in equilibrium only when the vector sum of forces is zero.
- Mathematically, $\Sigma \mathbf{F}_{net} = 0$

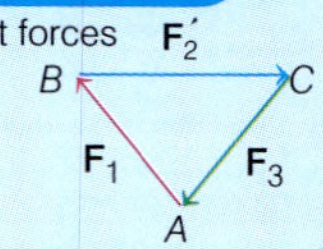

Lami's Theorem

It states that, "if three forces acting on a particle are in equilibrium, then each force is proportional to the sine of the angle between the other two forces."

If an object O is in equilibrium under three concurrent coplanar forces $\mathbf{F}_1$, $\mathbf{F}_2$ and $\mathbf{F}_2$ as shown in figure.

$$\frac{\mathbf{F}_1}{\sin\alpha} = \frac{\mathbf{F}_2}{\sin\beta} = \frac{\mathbf{F}_3}{\sin\gamma}$$

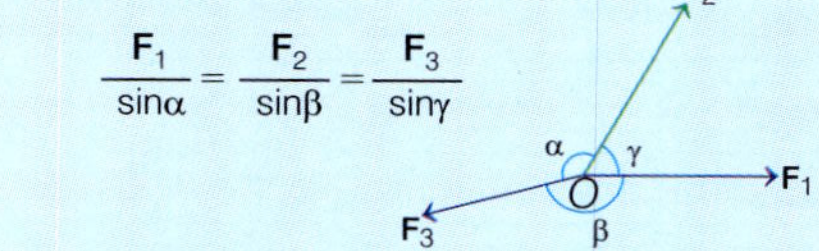

Pulley-Block System

- **Ideal Pulley System**

$M_1 > M_2$

$a = \frac{F}{M} = \frac{M_1 - M_2}{M_1 + M_2} g$, $T = \frac{2M_1M_2}{M_1 + M_2} g$

$a = \frac{M_1 g}{M_1 + M_2}$

$T = \frac{M_1 M_2}{M_1 + M_2} g$

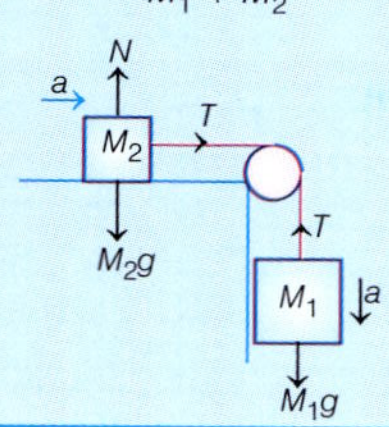

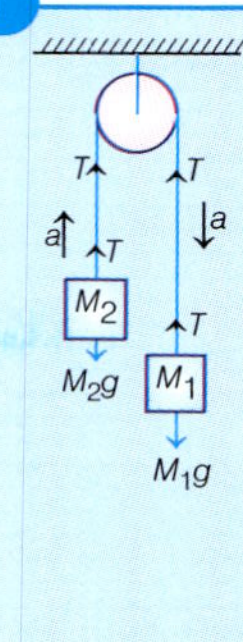

Lift Problems

Apparent weight of body in a lift

Reading of weighing machine = Reaction force exerted by weighing machine divided by (g)

Apparent weight, $(w_{apparent})$ = Reaction force (R)

Case 1 : Lift is at rest, $R = mg$, $w_{apparent} = w_{actual} = mg$

Case 2 : Lift moving up or down with constant velocity

$R = mg$, $w_{apparent} = w_{actual} = mg$

Case 3 : Accelerated upward at rate of 'a'

$R - mg = ma \Rightarrow R = m(g + a) = w_{app}$

$w_{apparent} > w_{actual} \rightarrow$ Feels over weight

If lift is accelerated upward at a rate of 'g'

$R - mg = mg$, $R = 2mg$, $w_{app} = 2 \times w_{act}$

Case 4 : Accelerated downward at a rate of 'a'

$mg - R = ma$, $R = m(g - a) = w_{app} < w_{act}$

Accelerated downward at a rate of g [Free-fall]

$mg - R = mg$, $R = mg - mg = 0$, $w_{app} = 0$

Graph for lift moving from ground floor to first floor

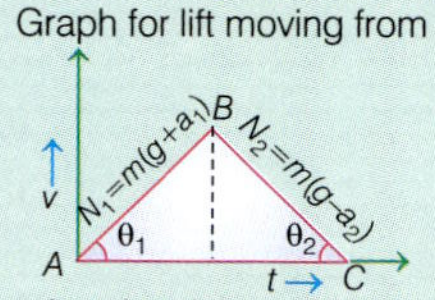

Acceleration, $a_1 = \tan\theta_1$

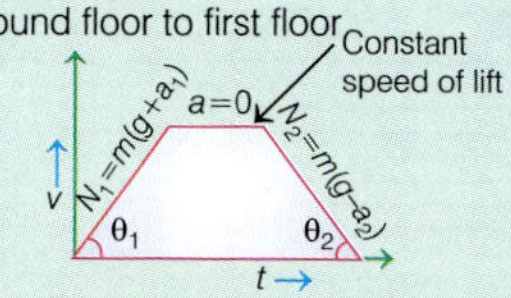

Retardation, $a_2 = \tan\theta_2$

Motion of Blocks Connected by Massless String

Condition	Free body diagram	Equation	Tension and acceleration
A (m_1) –T– B (m_2) → F on ground	m_1 → T (a →)	$T = m_1a$	$a = \frac{F}{m_1 + m_2}$
	T ← m_2 → F (a →)	$F - T = m_2a$	$T = \frac{m_1F}{m_1 + m_2}$
F ← A (m_1) –T– B (m_2) on ground	F ← m_1 → T (a ←)	$F - T = m_1a$	$a = \frac{F}{m_1 + m_2}$
	T ← m_2 (a ←)	$T = m_2a$	$T = \frac{m_2F}{m_1 + m_2}$
A (m_1) –T_1– B (m_2) –T_2– C (m_3) → F on ground	m_1 → T_1	$T_1 = m_1a$	$a = \frac{F}{m_1 + m_2 + m_3}$
	T_1 ← m_2 → T_2 (a →)	$T_2 - T_1 = m_2a$	$T_1 = \frac{m_1F}{m_1 + m_2 + m_3}$
	T_2 ← m_3 → F (a →)	$F - T_2 = m_3a$	$T_2 = \frac{(m_1 + m_2)F}{m_1 + m_2 + m_3}$

Test 3

Syllabus

- Static and Kinetic Friction, Laws of Friction and Rolling Friction
- Dynamics of Uniform Circular motion
- Centripetal Force and Its Applications
- Vehicle on a Level Circular Road, Vehicle on a Banked Road.

NCERT Page 60 to 66

For deeper insight **Scan the QR Code**

Chapter 04

Angle of Friction

- Angle (θ) made by resultant of normal (N) and frictional force (f_s) with normal.

$R = \sqrt{N^2 + f_s^2}$, where R is resultant

$\tan\theta = \frac{f_s}{N}$

When $f_s = (f_s)_{max}$, $R = N\sqrt{1+\mu_s^2}$

$\tan\theta = \mu_s$, μ_s is coefficient of static friction

(i) $f = 0$
$\tan\theta = 0$
$\therefore\ \theta = 0$

(ii) $0 < f_s < (f_s)_{max}$

$0 \le \tan\theta \le \mu_s$

$N < R < N\sqrt{1+\mu_s^2}$

(iii) $f_s = (f_s)_{max}$, $R_{max} = N\sqrt{1+\mu_s^2}$

$(f_s)_{max} = \mu_s N$

Friction Varies with Applied Force as Follow

As the F increases, F_s increases accordingly to balance it. This shows static friction is self adjusting force. Also, F_k is less than F_s max.

Friction

- When a body slips or tends to slip over the surface of another body, then a force develops parallel to surface in contact, in opposite direction. This is friction force.
- It is non-conservative force, i.e. work done by this forces depends on the path.

Static Friction

- If a body tends to slip over the surface of another body, then it is frictional force acting between their surfaces.
- When applied force is less than limiting friction, then block does not move.

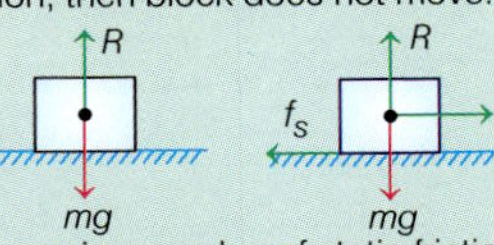

- The maximum value of static friction between two surfaces in contact is called **limiting friction**.

Kinetic Friction

- If the object is sliding, then friction forces between their surfaces is called **kinetic friction** or **sliding friction**.
- If applied force exceeds the limiting value of friction force, i.e. $F > (f_s)_{max}$, then block starts slipping over the inclined plane.

So, $f_K < f_L$ (slightly)
$f_K < (f_s)_{max}$

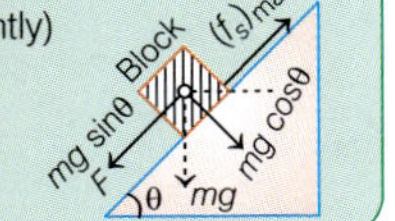

Laws of Kinetic Friction

(i) The force of kinetic friction is proportional to the normal force, which presses the two surfaces together. Mathematically, $f_k = \mu_k N$ where μ_k is the coefficient of kinetic friction.

(ii) It is independent of the surface area of contact.

(iii) It is independent of the speed of sliding, provided that the resulting heat does not alter the condition of the surface.

Rolling Friction

- When an object rolls on a surface without slipping, then the friction force between the surface, is called rolling friction.

Example

- Ball bearings are used to reduce the friction between the rolling part.

Laws of Static Friction

(i) The force of static friction is proportional to the normal force exerted by other surface normally on the former.

(ii) The static frictional force is given by $f_s \le \mu_s N$, where μ_s is the coefficient of static friction.

(iii) The less than or equal to sign in the equation represents the adjusting nature of the force of static friction.

(iv) The equality sign in the equation holds only when the static frictional force has its maximum value.

(v) It is independent of the area of contact between the two surfaces.

Motion of a Rough Inclined Plane

(i) When body is moving downward with acceleration a and the force of friction between inclined plane and the body is F.

$a = (\sin\theta - \mu\cos\theta)g$, $R = mg\cos\theta$

(ii) When body is moving upward due to a force F applied on it as shown in the figure.

Motion of a Car on a Banked Road

- The large amount of friction between the tyres and the road produces considerable wear and tear of tyres. To avoid this, the curved road is given an inclined sloping upwards towards outer circumference.
- The system of raising outer edge of curved road above its inner edge called banking of the curved road. Maximum velocity of vehicle on banked road,

$$v_{max} = \sqrt{\frac{rg(\mu_s + \tan\theta)}{(1 - \mu_s\tan\theta)}}$$

- **Special case** When $\mu_s = 0$, then $v_{max} = \sqrt{rg\tan\theta}$

i.e. Banking angle $\theta = \tan^{-1}\left(\frac{v^2}{rg}\right)$

Circular Motion of a Car on a Level Road

- When a vehicle goes round a curved road, it requires some centripetal force. While rounding the curve, the wheels of the vehicle have a tendency to leave the curved path and regain the straight line path.

- For the car to stay on the road, the maximum force of friction must be equal to or greater than the centripetal force.

$\frac{mv^2}{r} \le \mu_s mg \Rightarrow v \le \sqrt{\mu_s rg}$

$v_{max} = \sqrt{\mu_s rg}$

- Maximum velocity with which a vehicle can go round on level curve without skidding,

$v = \sqrt{\mu_s rg}$

Angle of Repose

- Value of angle of inclination at which the force of static friction equal to limiting friction.
- If angle of friction be α(block tend to slip),then

$\tan\alpha = \mu_s \Rightarrow \theta = \alpha$

Dynamics of Circular Motion

- When an object moves on a circular path, a force acts on it, whose direction is towards the centre of the path, this force is called centripetal force.
- It is given as

$F = \frac{mv^2}{r}$

Example

- Condition for v_A to be minimum, for which the body just completes the circular path

$v_A = \sqrt{5gR}$, $T_A = 6\,mg$
$v_B = \sqrt{gR}$, $T_B = 0$
$v_C = \sqrt{3gR}$, $T_C = 3\,mg$
$v_P = \sqrt{gR(3+2\cos\theta)}$
$T_P = 3mg(1+\cos\theta)$

Bending of a Cyclist

- When a cyclist takes turn along a circular path on a level road, he requires necessary centripetal force towards the centre of path.
- Bending of cyclist turning for safe going, $N\sin\theta = mv^2/r$
and $N\cos\theta = mg$
Maximum speed without slipping,
$v = \sqrt{rg\tan\theta}$

Test 1

Syllabus

- Work Done by Constant Force
- Work Done by Variable Force
- Conservative and Non-Conservative Force
- Kinetic Energy, Potential Energy

NCERT
Page 71 to 72
Page 73 to 76
Page 77 to 78

For deeper insight **Scan the QR Code**

Chapter 05

Scalar Product

- The product of the magnitude of vectors **A** and **B** and the cosine of the angle θ between them. Then,

  $\mathbf{A}\cdot\mathbf{B} = AB\cos\theta$

- It is a scalar quantity.
- It is also called dot product.

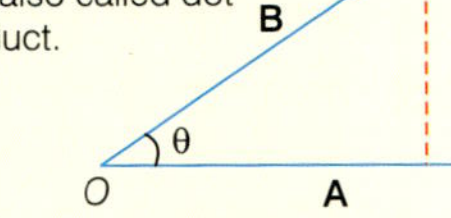

Work

We define the work done by a constant force on a body as the product of the force F and the displacement s through which the body is displaced in the direction of force.

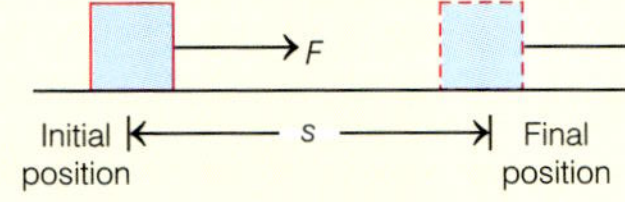

Work done, when force and displacement are in the same direction

The work done W is given by $W = F.s$

Work done by Constant Force

- The product of component of force in the direction of the displacement and the magnitude of the displacement.
- The work done by a constant force is given by, $W = \mathbf{F}\cdot\mathbf{s} \Rightarrow Fs\cos\theta$

(i) If $\theta = 0°$, $W = Fs\cos 0° = Fs$
(ii) If $\theta = 90°$; $W = Fs\cos 90° = 0$
(iii) If $\theta = 180°$; $W = Fs\cos 180 = -F\cdot s$

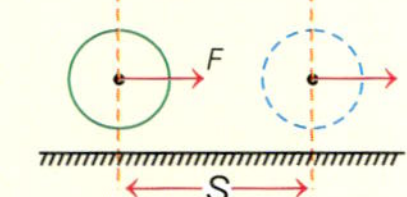

Conservative Force

Work done by the force in displacing an object depends only on the initial and final positions of an object.

Non-Conservative Force

If the work done by a force in displacing an object from one position to another, depends upon the path between the two positions.

Nature of Positive Work Done

- When applied force and displacement has same direction, then the work is said to be positive work.
- When θ is acute, then cosθ is positive $0 \le \theta < 90°$.
- Work done $(W) = Fs\cos\theta =$ Positive

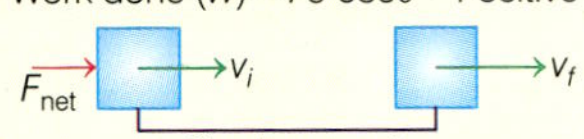

Nature of Negative Work Done

- When force applied and displacement has opposite direction, then it is said to be negative work.
- When θ is obtuse, then cos θ is negative $90° < \theta \le 180$.

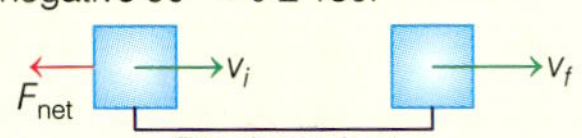

Zero Work

If a body gets displaced in the direction perpendicular to the direction of the applied force. Work done $(W) = Fs\cos 90° =$ zero

Work Done by Spring Force

Magnitude of spring force, $F_s = -kx$

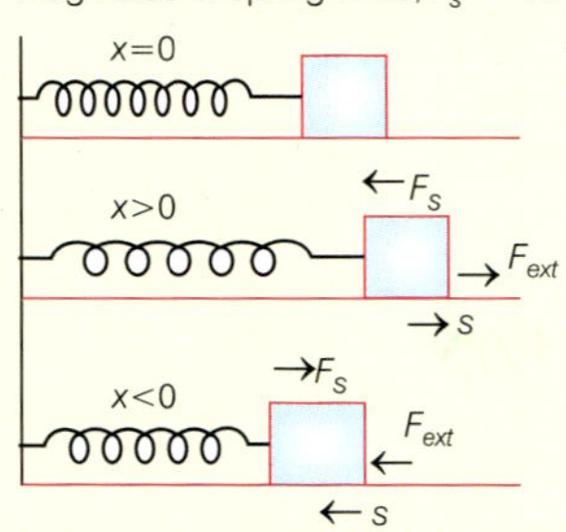

$$W_s = \int \mathbf{F}_s \cdot d\mathbf{x} = -\int kx\,dx$$
$$= -\frac{1}{2}k\left(x_f^2 - x_i^2\right)$$

Energy

- The energy of a body is defined as its capacity for doing work.
- It is a scalar quantity.
- Its dimensional formula is $[ML^2T^{-2}]$.
- It is measured in the same units as work. i.e. Joule in SI and erg in CGS system.

Kinetic Energy

- The energy possessed by a body by virtue of its motion is called kinetic energy.

  i.e. $KE = \frac{1}{2}mv^2$

- **Relation between kinetic energy and linear momentum**
- Linear momentum, $p = \sqrt{2mKE}$

Cases

(i) If p = constant, this is shown in graph

$KE \propto \frac{1}{m}$

(ii) If KE = constant, $p^2 \propto m$ or $p \propto \sqrt{m}$

(iii) If mass = constant, $p^2 \propto KE$

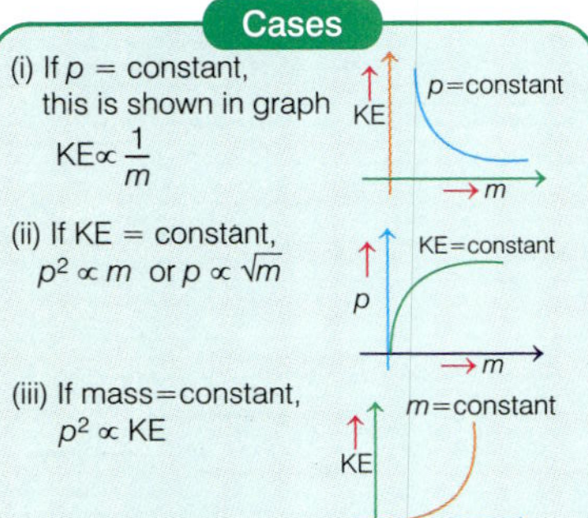

Work Done by a Variable Force

Let a variable force F acts on a body along the fixed direction, say X-axis.

The magnitude of force F depends on x.

$dW = \mathbf{F}.d\mathbf{s}$

$W = \int \mathbf{F}.d\mathbf{s} = \int \mathbf{F}ds\cos\theta$

in terms of rectangular components

$$\mathbf{F} = \mathbf{F}_x\hat{\mathbf{i}} + \mathbf{F}_y\hat{\mathbf{j}} + \mathbf{F}_z\hat{\mathbf{k}}$$
$$W = \int \mathbf{F}_x d_x\hat{\mathbf{i}} + \int \mathbf{F}_y d_y\hat{\mathbf{j}} + \int \mathbf{F}_z d_z\hat{\mathbf{k}}$$
$$W = \mathbf{F}_x s_x + \mathbf{F}_y s_y + \mathbf{F}_z s_z$$

Graphical representation of work done

$dW = \mathbf{F}.d$

$W = \int_{x_i}^{x_f} dW = \int_{x_i}^{x_f} f.dx$

W = Area under F-x graph

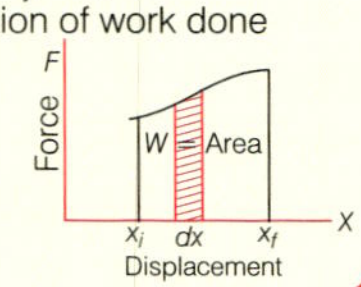

Potential Energy

- The energy possessed by the body by virtue of its position or configuration in same field.
- Can either be positive, negative or zero according to point of reference
- Force always acts from higher potential to lower potential
- Dimensional formula of potential energy is $[ML^2T^{-2}]$.
- The SI unit of potential energy is joule (J).

Identifying forces with the help of potential energy.

(i) Force opposing the motion

On increasing x, if U increase

$\frac{dU}{dx} =$ positive (*BC* portion of graph)

(ii) Force supporting the motion

On increasing x, if U decrease

$\frac{dU}{dx} =$ negative (*CD* portion of graph)

(iii) Zero force

On increasing x, if U does not change.

$\frac{dU}{dx} = 0$ (*B, C* points on the graph)

Types of potential energy

- Elastic potential energy
- Electric potential energy
- Gravitational potential energy

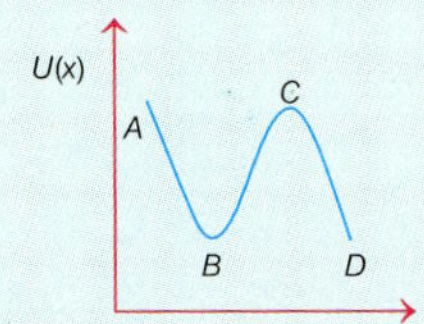

Elastic Potential Energy of a Spring

Potential energy of a spring is the energy associated with the state of compression or expansion of an elastic spring. When the spring is stretched or compressed by an amount x from its unstretched position, then elastic potential energy of spring, $U = 1/2\,kx^2$

(where, k = spring constant)

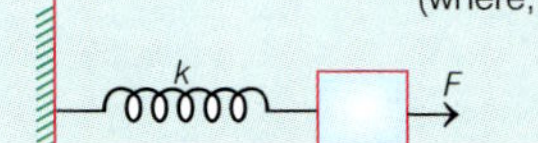

The work done in stretching the spring by external applied force,

$$W = \int_0^x F\,dx = \int_0^x kx\,dx = \frac{1}{2}kx^2$$

The work done by stretching or compressing force is positive. But the work done by the spring is negative because the force exerted by the spring is always opposite to elongation or contraction.

Work done by the spring, $W = -\frac{1}{2}kx^2$

When length of spring changes from $x = x_i$ to $x = x_f$

$$W = \int_{x_i}^{x_f} F\,dx = \int_{x_i}^{x_f} kx\,dx = \frac{1}{2}k(x_i^2 - x_f^2)$$

Test 2

Syllabus
- Work-Energy Theorem
- Conservation of Energy

NCERT
Page 73
Page 76 to 77
Page 78 to 83

For deeper insight **Scan the QR Code**

Chapter 05

Work-Energy Theorem

- **For constant force**

We use the equation of motion,

$v^2 - u^2 = 2as$

or $\frac{1}{2}mv^2 - \frac{1}{2}mu^2 = mas$

or $\frac{1}{2}mv^2 - \frac{1}{2}mu^2 = W$ or $K_f - K_i = W$

- **For variable force**

Variable force acts on a body of mass m and produce displacement in its own direction ($\theta = 0°$), then small work done,

$dW = \mathbf{F} \cdot d\mathbf{s} = Fds \cos 0° = Fds$

Change in kinetic energy, $K_f - K_i = \int_{x_i}^{x_f} Fds$

Potential Energy Curve for Equilibrium

At , kinetic energy, K = $E_{mech} - U(x)$

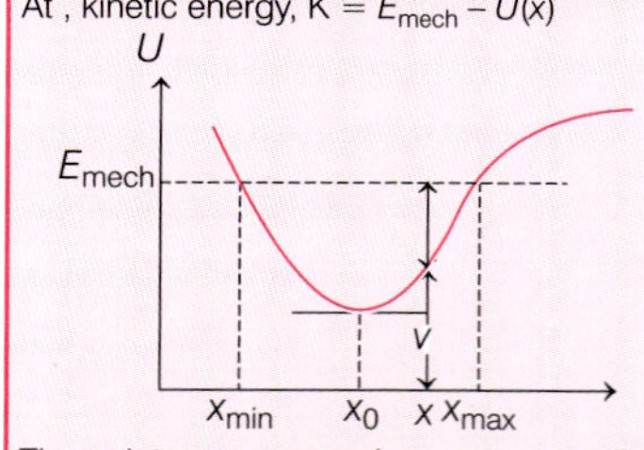

The points x= x_{max} and x= x_{min} are called turning points. At these points, velocity of the particle decreases to zero and reverses.

From x_{min} to x_0, slope of is negative,

$$F = -\frac{dU}{dx}$$

F is positive and acts towards x_0 .

At x_0, F=0. So, x_0 is known as **stable equilibrium point.**

Beyond x_0, slope is positive, indicating a negative force, towards x_0.

Relation between Potential Energy and Force

Potential energy is defined for a conservative force only. For non-conservative forces, it has no meaning. The change in potential energy (dU) of a system corresponding to a conservative internal force is given by

$$U = \int_{\infty}^{r} \mathbf{F} . d\mathbf{r} = -W$$

- **For three dimensional motion of the particle**

$$\mathbf{F} = -\left(\frac{\partial U}{\partial x}\hat{\mathbf{i}} + \frac{\partial U}{\partial y}\hat{\mathbf{j}} + \frac{\partial U}{\partial z}\hat{\mathbf{k}}\right)$$

Equilibrium

If a large number of forces act on a system or on an object simultaneously in such a way that the resultant force on it is zero, then it is said to be in translational equilibrium. If the forces acting on the object are conservative and it is in equilibrium, then

$$\mathbf{F}_{net} = 0 \Rightarrow -\frac{dU}{dr} = 0$$

Types of Equilibrium

- **Stable equilibrium** An object is said to be in stable equilibrium, if on slight displacement from equilibrium position, it has tendency to come back. Here, potential energy in equilibrium position is minimum as compared to its neighbouring points or $\frac{d^2U}{dx^2}$=positive.

- **Unstable equilibrium** An object is said to be in unstable equilibrium, if on slight displacement from equilibrium position, it moves in the direction of displacement.
In unstable equilibrium, potential energy is maximum or $\frac{d^2U}{dx^2}$=negative.

- **Neutral equilibrium**
An object is said to be in neutral equilibrium, if on displacement from its equilibrium position, it has neither the tendency to move in direction of displacement nor to come back to equilibrium position. In neutral equilibrium, potential energy of the object is constant or $\frac{d^2U}{dx^2}=0$

Work done in Case of a Chain

Case I The work done by the pulling force to bring the hanging part on to the table.

Weight of hanging part $= \frac{m}{n} g$

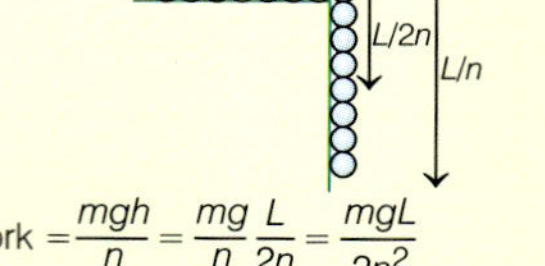

$$\text{Work} = \frac{mgh}{n} = \frac{mg}{n}\frac{L}{2n} = \frac{mgL}{2n^2}$$

Case II Work done in pulling the chain partially, such that $\frac{1}{n_2}$ part is hanging from the edge of the table is given by $W = \frac{mgl}{2}\left[\frac{1}{n_1^2} - \frac{1}{n_2^2}\right]$

Geometrical Interpretation of Work Done

Work done = Area under force *versus* displacement curve.

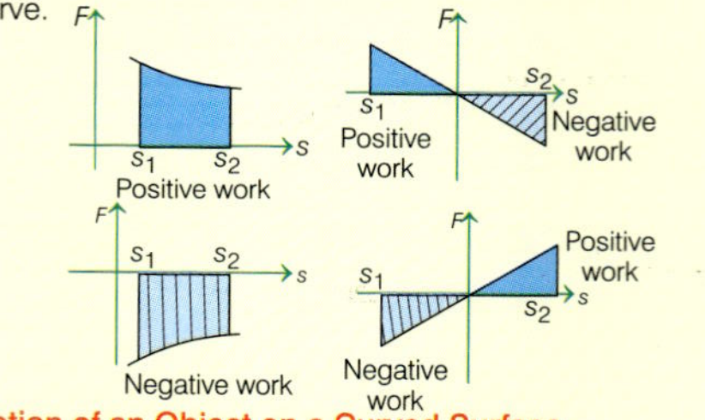

Motion of an Object on a Curved Surface

When a car moves on a convex bridge of radius r,

Centripetal force $= mg \cos\theta - N = \frac{mv^2}{r}$

and reaction force, $N = mg \cos \theta - \frac{mv^2}{r}$

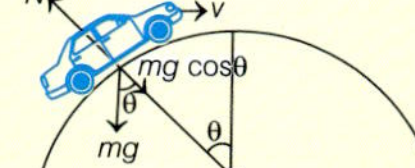

When a car moves on a concave bridge of radius r,

Centripetal force $= N - mg \cos\theta = \frac{mv^2}{r}$

and reaction force, $N = mg \cos \theta + \frac{mv^2}{r}$

Concave bridge

Law of Conservation of Energy

Energy can neither be created nor be destroyed, it can only be transformed from one form to another form.

- **Conservation of mechanical energy**

The total mechanical energy (sum of kinetic energy and potential energy) of a system is conserved, if the forces acting on it are conservative.

$$\frac{1}{2}mv^2 + mgh = \text{constant}$$

Graphical Representation

The kinetic energy is converted to potential energy and *vice-versa*. However, the total mechanical energy remains constant.

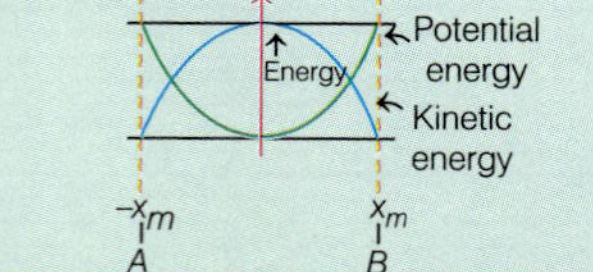

Mechanical Energy of a Stretched Spring

If the block of mass m is extended to position, x_m and released from rest, then total mechanical energy at any arbitary point x,

$$\frac{1}{2}kx_m^2 = \frac{1}{2}kx^2 + \frac{1}{2}mv^2$$

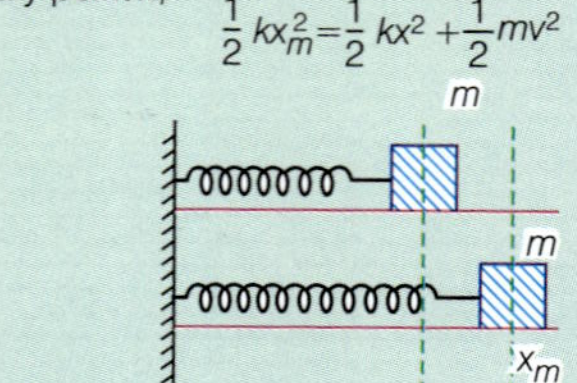

Freely Falling Body

The mechanical energy of a freely falling body remains constant at all position.

$E_A = E_B = E_C$ =Constant

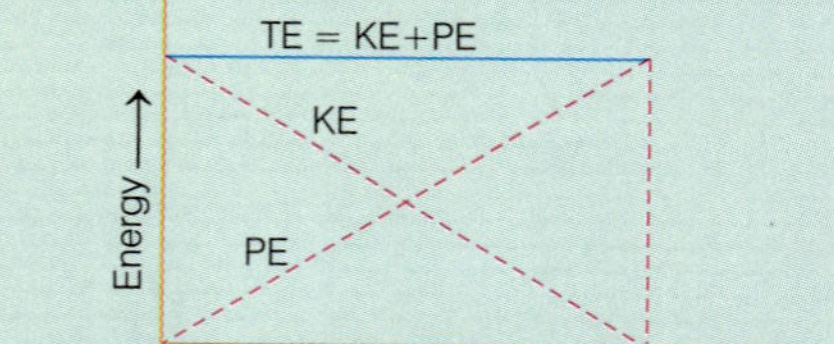

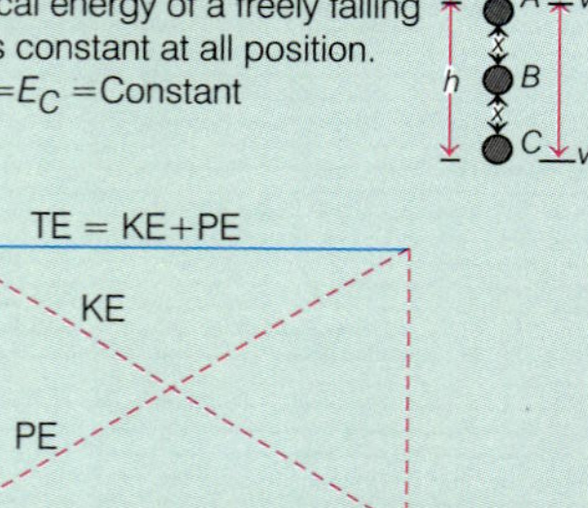

Test 3

Syllabus
- Power, Motion of Vertical Circle
- Elastic and Inelastic Collisions in One and Two Dimensions

NCERT Page 83 to 86

For deeper insight **Scan the QR Code**

Chapter 05

Power

The rate of doing work is called the power.
Average power (P_{av}) = Rate of doing work.

$$P_{av} = \frac{W}{t}$$

- Instantaneous power

$$P_{av} = \frac{dW}{dt} = \mathbf{F} \cdot \frac{d\mathbf{s}}{dt} = \mathbf{F} \cdot \mathbf{v}$$

- Power is a scalar quantity.
- The dimensional formula of power is $[ML^2T^{-3}]$.
- SI unit of power is watt (W).

- Relation between units:
- 1 watt = 1 joule/s = 10^7 erg/s
- 1 HP = 746 watt, 1MW = 10^6 watt
- 1kW = 10^3 watt
- If work done by two bodies is same, then Power $\propto$ 1/Time
- Power multiplied by time always gives work, 1 kWh = 3.6×10^6 Joule.
- Slope of work-time curve gives Instantaneous power

Graphical Representation

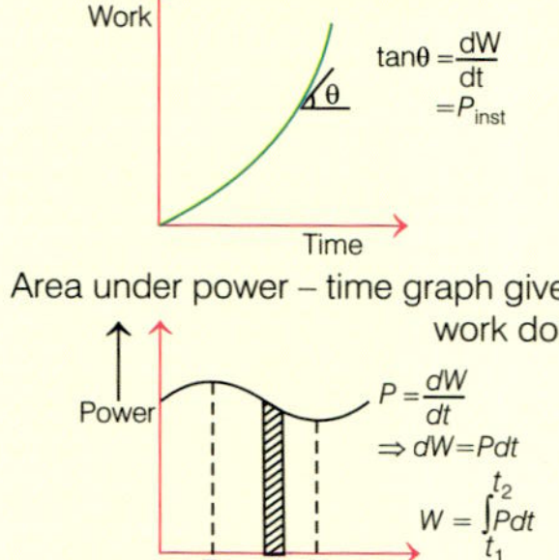

Instantaneous Power

The instantaneous power of an agent is defined as the limiting value of the average power of the agent in a small time interval, i.e. when the time interval approaches to zero. When work done by a force **F** for a small displacement dr is $dW = \mathbf{F} \cdot dr$, then instantaneous power can be given as

$$P = \lim_{\Delta t \to 0} \frac{\Delta W}{\Delta t} = \frac{dW}{dt}, \quad dW = \mathbf{F} . d\mathbf{r}$$

$$P = F . \frac{dr}{dt}$$

Position and Velocity

Position and velocity in terms of power (P=constant)

(i) Velocity, $v = \left[\frac{2Pt}{m}\right]^{1/2}$

(ii) Position, $s = \left[\frac{8P}{9m}\right]^{1/2} t^{3/2}$

Power delivered by an elevator

$a = 0$, $T = (M+m)g$
$P = \mathbf{T.v}$
Power, $P = (M+m)gV$

Power of a water drawing pump

- Power, $P = \frac{dW}{dt} = \frac{dm}{dt}\left[gh + \frac{v^2}{2}\right]$
- h = height of water level
  $\frac{dm}{dt} \Rightarrow$ mass flow rate of pump
  v $\longrightarrow$ Velocity of water outlet
- Power required to just lift water, $v = 0$
  $$P = gh\frac{dm}{dt}$$
- Efficiency of pump,
  $$\mu = \frac{\text{Output power}}{\text{Input power}}$$

Elastic Collision in two Dimensions

Consider two bodies A and B of masses M_1 and M_2 moving along the same straight line with velocities u_1 and u_2, respectively. After the collision, two bodies move with velocities v_1 and v_2 along the direction of making angle θ and ϕ.
Here,

$$M_1u_1 + M_2u_2 = M_1v_1 \cos\theta + M_2v_2 \cos\phi$$
$$0 = M_1v_1 \sin\theta + (-M_2v_2 \sin\phi)$$
$$\Rightarrow M_1v_1 \sin\theta - M_2v_2 \sin\phi = 0$$

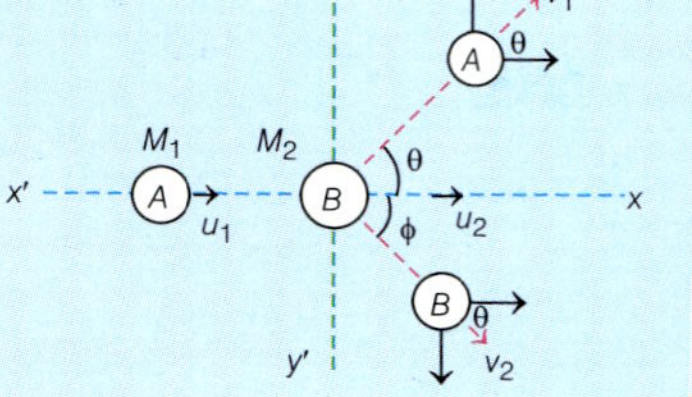

Motion of a Particle Tied to a String in Vertical Circle

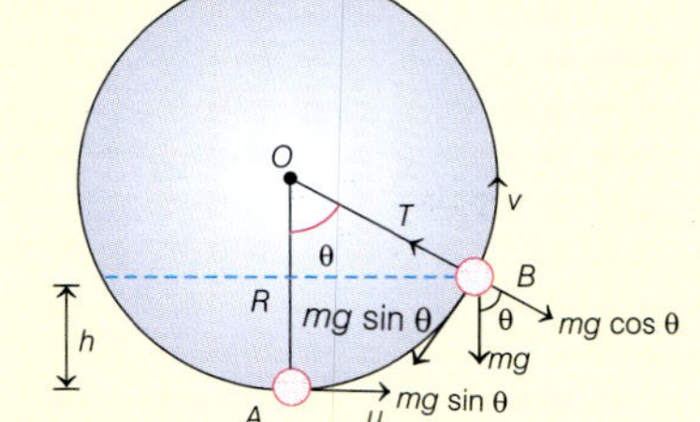

Here, we have, $h = R(1 - \cos\theta)$
Now, from conservation of mechanical energy, we have

$$\frac{1}{2}m(u^2 - v^2) = mgh$$

The necessary centripetal force is provided by the resultant of tension T and $mg \cos\theta$.

$$\therefore \quad T - mg\cos\theta = \frac{mv^2}{R}$$

As speed of the particle decreases with height, tension in the string is maximum at the bottom. The particle will complete the circle, if the string does not slack even at the highest point.
Now, following conclusions can be made using above

(i) Minimum velocity at highest point, so that particle complete the circle $v_{min} = \sqrt{gR}$, at this velocity, tension in the string is zero.

(ii) Minimum velocity at lowest point, so that particle complete the circle $v_{min} = \sqrt{5gR}$, at this velocity, tension in the string is 6 mg.

(iii) When string is horizontal, then minimum velocity is $\sqrt{3gR}$ and tension in this condition in string is $3mg$.

Perfectly Inelastic Collision

Those collisions, in which the colliding bodies stick together after the collision and then move with a common velocity, are called perfectly inelastic collision.

Inelastic Collision in one Dimension

- The collision, in which momentum is conserved with some loss of kinetic energy and the colliding bodies continue to move along the same straight line after collision.
- For a perfectly inelastic collision, $v_2 - v_1 = 0$ and therefore, $e = 0$.

Collision

Collision between two bodies is defined as mutual interaction of the bodies for a short interval of time as a result of which the energy and momentum of the interacting bodies change.

Perfectly Inelastic Collision in two Dimensions

Consider two bodies A and B of masses M_1 and M_2 moving with velocities u_1 and u_2 along oblique direction.
After collision, two bodies stick together and move along a direction, so as to conserve momentum.
Conservation along X-axis,
$M_1u_1 \cos\theta + M_2u_2 = (M_1 + M_2) v \cos\phi$
Along Y-axis $M_1u_1 \sin\theta = (M_1 + M_2) v \sin\phi$

Elastic Collision in one Dimension

- Consider two perfectly elastic bodies A and B of masses M_1 and M_2 moving along the same straight line with velocities u_1 and u_2 respectively.
- If velocity of A is greater than B
  i.e., $u_1 > u_2$, then two bodies collides.

$$\frac{1}{2}M_1u_1^2 + \frac{1}{2}M_2u_2^2 = \frac{1}{2}M_1v_1^2 + \frac{1}{2}M_2v_2^2$$

In this type of collision, both momentum and kinetic energy are conserved and the colliding bodies continue to move along the same straight line after collision.

$$v_1 = \frac{(M_1 - M_2)u_1 + 2M_2u_2}{M_1 + M_2},$$

$$v_2 = \frac{(M_2 - M_1)u_2 + 2M_1u_1}{M_1 + M_2}$$

Elastic Collision

Those collisions, in which both momentum and kinetic energy of the system are conserved, are called elastic collisions.

Inelastic Collision

Those collisions, in which the momentum of the system is conserved but the kinetic energy is not conserved are called inelastic collisions.

Test 1

Syllabus
- Centre of Mass
- Linear Momentum of a System of Particles
- Moment of Inertia and Related Theorems

NCERT Page 95 to 103, Page 114 to 116

For deeper insight **Scan the QR Code**

Chapter 06

Vector Product of Two Vectors

The vector product of two vectors is given by

$\mathbf{R} = \mathbf{A} \times \mathbf{B}$

$|\mathbf{R}| = AB \sin\theta \, \hat{n}$

Properties of Vector Products

(i) $\mathbf{A} \times \mathbf{B} = -\mathbf{B} \times \mathbf{A}$

(ii) $\mathbf{A} \times (\mathbf{B} + \mathbf{C}) = (\mathbf{A} \times \mathbf{B}) + (\mathbf{A} \times \mathbf{C})$

(iii) $\mathbf{A} = a_x \hat{i} + a_y \hat{j} + a_z \hat{k}$ and $\mathbf{B} = b_x \hat{i} + b_y \hat{j} + b_z \hat{k}$

Then, $\mathbf{A} \times \mathbf{B} = \begin{vmatrix} \hat{i} & \hat{j} & \hat{k} \\ a_x & a_y & a_z \\ b_x & b_y & b_z \end{vmatrix}$

Centre of Mass

The point in the system, where the whole mass of the system can be supposed to be concentrated.

For a System of Two Particles

- For two particles,

$$X_{cm} = \frac{m_1 x_1 + m_2 x_2}{m_1 + m_2}$$

- The distance of the centre of mass of a system of two particle from the origin is equal to the mass weighted mean of their distances from the origin.

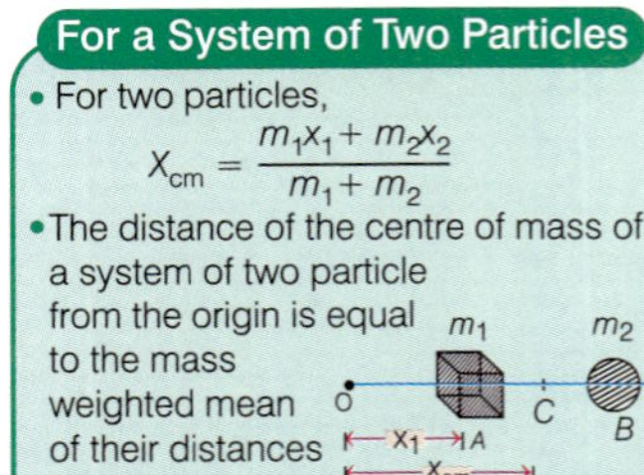
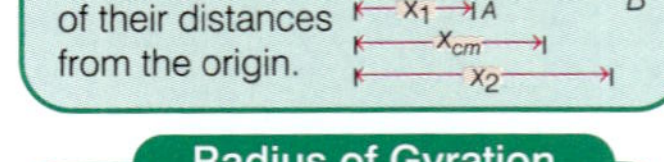

Radius of Gyration

The distance from the axis of rotation at which, if the whole mass of the body were concentrated, its moment of inertia about the given axis would be the same as with the actual distribution od mass

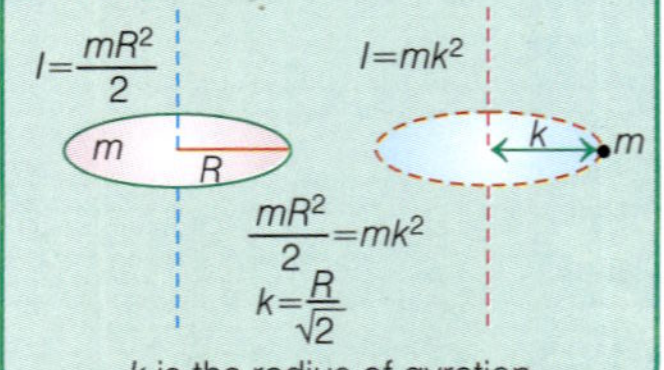

k is the radius of gyration

Centre of Mass for Various Shapes

Uniformly distributed mass	Centre of mass
(i) Rod	$\left(\frac{L}{2}, 0\right)$
(ii) Square Lamina	$\left(\frac{L}{2}, \frac{L}{2}\right)$
(iii) Semicircular Ring	$\left(0, \frac{2R}{\pi}\right)$
(iv) Hemispherical shell	$\left(0, \frac{R}{2}\right)$
(v) Solid Circular cone	$\left(0, \frac{h}{4}\right)$
(vi) Solid Hemisphere	$\left(0, \frac{3R}{8}\right)$

Centre of Mass for Continuous Body

$$r_{cm} = \frac{\int dm.r}{\int dm}$$

λ = mass per unit length
σ = mass per unit area
ρ = mass per unit volume

(i) Mass distributed over length $\Rightarrow dm = \lambda \, dl$

(ii) Mass distributed over area $\Rightarrow dm = \sigma \, dA$

(iii) Mass distributed over volume $\Rightarrow dm = \rho dV$

Centre of Mass for System of *n* Particles

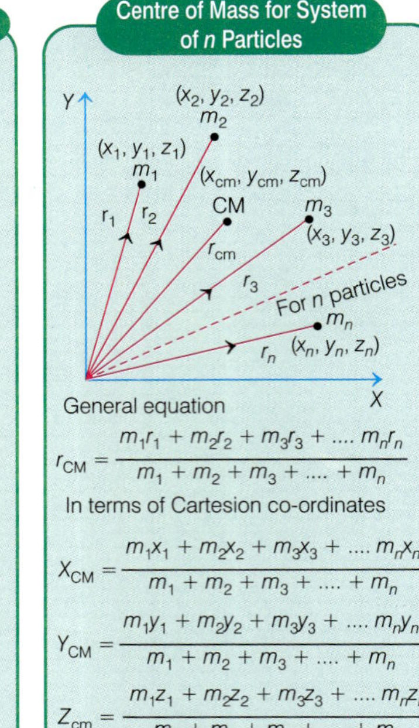

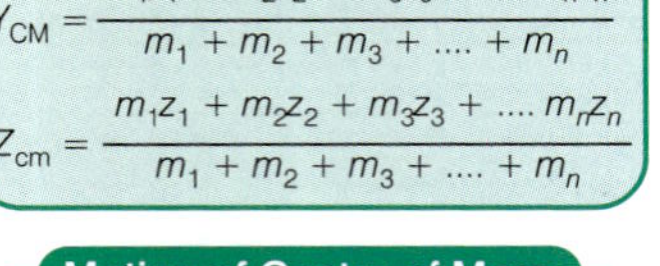

General equation

$$r_{CM} = \frac{m_1 r_1 + m_2 r_2 + m_3 r_3 + \dots m_n r_n}{m_1 + m_2 + m_3 + \dots + m_n}$$

In terms of Cartesion co-ordinates

$$X_{CM} = \frac{m_1 x_1 + m_2 x_2 + m_3 x_3 + \dots m_n x_n}{m_1 + m_2 + m_3 + \dots + m_n}$$

$$Y_{CM} = \frac{m_1 y_1 + m_2 y_2 + m_3 y_3 + \dots m_n y_n}{m_1 + m_2 + m_3 + \dots + m_n}$$

$$Z_{cm} = \frac{m_1 z_1 + m_2 z_2 + m_3 z_3 + \dots m_n z_n}{m_1 + m_2 + m_3 + \dots + m_n}$$

Motion of Centre of Mass

The moment of inertia of a single particle about an axis is given by

$$I = mr^2$$

Here, m is the mass of the particle and r is distance from the axis under consideration.

MI of Two Point Masses

$$I_{CM} = m_1 r_1^2 + m_2 r_2^2$$

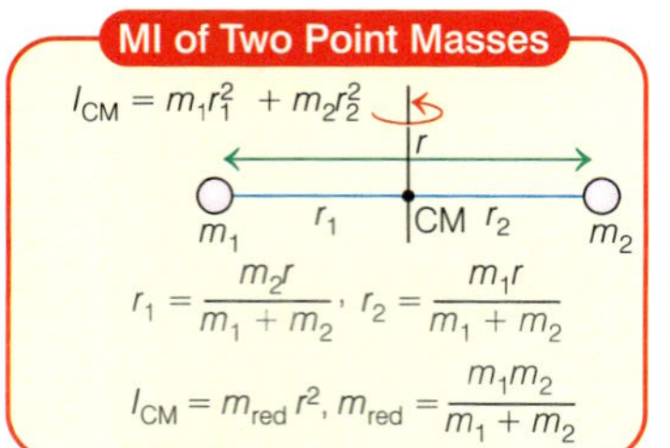

$$r_1 = \frac{m_2 r}{m_1 + m_2}, \; r_2 = \frac{m_1 r}{m_1 + m_2}$$

$$I_{CM} = m_{red} r^2, \; m_{red} = \frac{m_1 m_2}{m_1 + m_2}$$

Moment of Inertia

- The property of a body by virtue of which it opposes the torque tending to change its state of rest or of uniform rotation about axis.
- The moment of inertia is given by

$$I = \sum_{i=1}^{n} m_i r_i^2$$

- Radius of Gyration, $K = \sqrt{\frac{I}{m}}$

Theorem of Parallel Axis

- The MI of a body about an axis is equal to the sum of moment of inertia of body about parallel axis passing through its centre of mass and product of its mass and square of perpendicular distance between the two parallel axis.
- $I = I_{CM} + mr^2$
- Here, I_{CM} is moment of inertia about centre of mass, m is mass of lamina, r is distance between two parallel axis.

Theorem of parallel axes is applicable for any type of rigid body whether it is a two dimensional or three dimensional.

Theorem of Perpendicular Axis

- The MI of a planar body about an axis perpendicular to its plane is equal to the sum of moment of inertia about two perpendicular axis.
- $I_z = I_x + I_y$

Here, I_x, I_y and I_z are the moments of inertia of the plane body.

In theorem of perpendicular axes, the point of intersection of the three axes (X, Y and Z) may be any point on the plane of body (it may even lie outside the body). This point may or may not be the centre of mass of the body.

Moment of Inertia of Regular Shapes

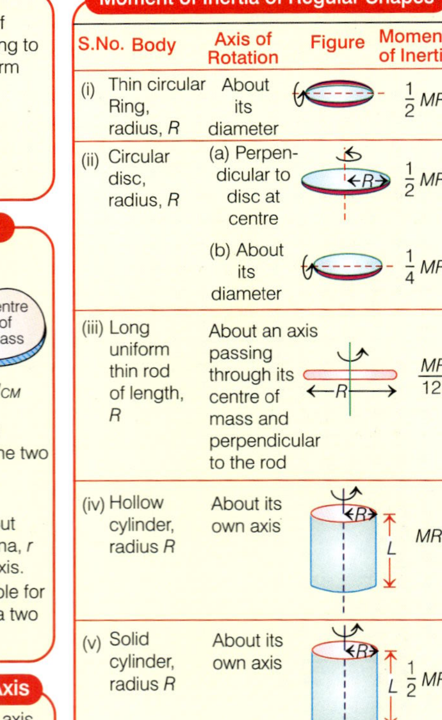
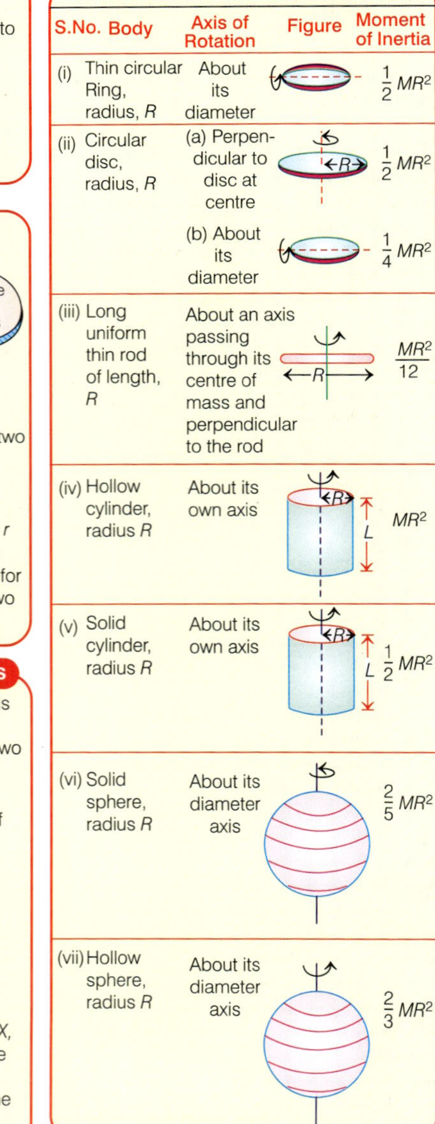

S.No.	Body	Axis of Rotation	Moment of Inertia
(i)	Thin circular Ring, radius, R	About its diameter	$\frac{1}{2}MR^2$
(ii)	Circular disc, radius, R	(a) Perpendicular to disc at centre	$\frac{1}{2}MR^2$
		(b) About its diameter	$\frac{1}{4}MR^2$
(iii)	Long uniform thin rod of length, R	About an axis passing through its centre of mass and perpendicular to the rod	$\frac{MR^2}{12}$
(iv)	Hollow cylinder, radius R	About its own axis	MR^2
(v)	Solid cylinder, radius R	About its own axis	$\frac{1}{2}MR^2$
(vi)	Solid sphere, radius R	About its diameter axis	$\frac{2}{5}MR^2$
(vii)	Hollow sphere, radius R	About its diameter axis	$\frac{2}{3}MR^2$

Test 2

Syllabus
- Moment of Force and Torque
- Angular Momentum and Angular Momentum Conservation
- Equilibrium of Rigid Body

NCERT Page 105 to 114

For deeper insight **Scan the QR Code**

Torque or Moment of Force

Torque is a quantity which measures the capability of a force to rotate a body. Torque due to a force is also known as the moment of a force. Torque is the rotational analogue of force of linear motion.

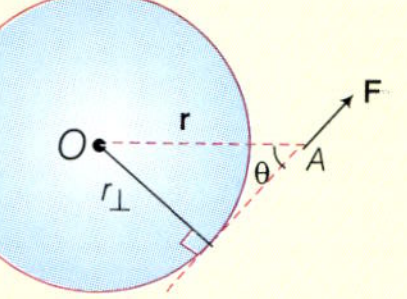

It is defined as the product of the force and the perpendicular distance between the line of action of the force and the axis of rotation. This perpendicular distance is known as the force arm.

$$\text{Torque}, \tau = \text{Force arm} \times \text{Force}$$
$$\tau = rF \sin\theta$$

where, θ is the angle between **r** and **F**.

The SI unit of torque is N-m and its dimensions are $[ML^2T^{-2}]$.

Torque is an axial vector, i.e. its direction is always perpendicular to the plane containing vectors **r** and **F** in accordance with right-hand screw rule.

There is a mathematical relation between torque (τ), angular acceleration (α) and moment of inertia (I) and that can be given as $\tau = I\alpha$

The above expression is similar to the expression of Newton's second law for translational motion with constant mass.

Some important results of torque are as follows

(i) If $\theta = 0°$ or $180°$, the torque of force is zero.

(ii) $\tau = \mathbf{r} \times \mathbf{F}$ is a vector product, so on reversing the direction of **F**, the direction of torque is reversed. If directions of both **r** and **F** are reversed, then direction of τ remains the same.

(iii) If the total torque acting on the rigid body vanishes, i.e. the vector sum of the torques on the rigid body is zero.

$$\tau_1 + \tau_2 + \tau_3 + \dots + \tau_n = \sum_{i=1}^{n} \tau = 0$$

Then, the body is said to be in **rotational equilibrium.**

Centre of Gravity

If a body is supposed on a point such that total gravitational torque about this point is zero.

Work Done by Torque

Consider a rigid body acted upon by a force F at a perpendicular distance r from the axis of rotation. Let under the action of this force, the body rotates through an angle $d\theta$.

Work done = Torque × Displacement = $\tau d\theta$

The power associated with the work done by a torque acting on a rotating body is given by

$$\text{Power}(P) = \frac{dW}{dt} = \tau\frac{d\theta}{dt} = \tau\omega$$

where, $\tau\omega$ is also known as **instantaneous rotational power.**

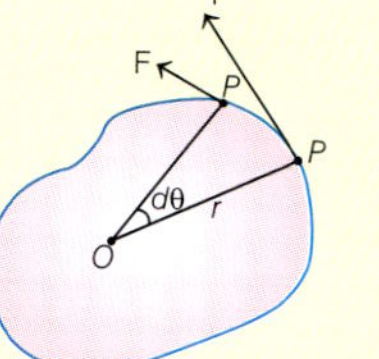

Force acting on a rigid body at perpendicular distance

Equilibrium of a Rigid Body

Two necessary conditions for equilibrium of a rigid body are

(i) resultant external force acting on the body must be zero.

$$\Sigma \mathbf{F} = 0$$

This is condition of **translational equilibrium.**

(ii) The resultant external torque about any axis must be zero.

$$\Sigma\tau = 0$$

This is the condition for **rotational equilibrium.**

From these two conditions we can conclude that,

(i) An object in translational equilibrium may not be in rotational equilibrium.

(ii) An object in rotational equilibrium may not be in translational equilibrium.

Relation between Angular and Linear Velocities

The linear velocity of a particle rotating about a fixed axis is given by

$$v = \omega r$$

where, ω is angular velocity of particle.

Angular Momentum

- It represents the rotational motion of an object around a fixed point or axis.
- A net external torque is required to change the angular momentum of an object
- Angular momentum, $\mathbf{L} = (\mathbf{r} \times \mathbf{v})m$
- SI unit of angular momentum is kg m^2s^{-1}
- It is a vector quantity.

Angular Momentum of a Point Mass

Angular momentum about origin

$$\mathbf{L}_0 = \mathbf{r} \times \mathbf{p} = m(\mathbf{r} \times \mathbf{v})$$
$$\mathbf{p} = m\mathbf{v}$$

- **When $\theta = 0°$ or $180°$**

$$L_0 = mvr \sin 180° = 0$$

or

$$mvr \sin 0° = 0$$

Angular momentum is minimum

- **When $\theta = 90°$**

$$|\mathbf{L}| = rp \sin\theta = rp \sin 90° = L_{max}$$

Conservation of Angular Momentum

If there is no external torque, angular momentum is conserved

$$\tau = \frac{dL}{dt}$$

$$\text{If } \tau = 0 \Rightarrow \frac{dL}{dt} = 0$$

$$L = \text{Constant}$$
$$I\omega = \text{Constant}$$
$$I_1\omega_1 = I_2\omega_2$$

If moment of inertia increases angular velocity decreases and if moment of inertia decreases angular velocity increases.

Angular Momentum of a Particle about Some Point

Angular momentum of a particle (of mass m) about a point is defined as the moment of its linear momentum (p) about the point.

$$\mathbf{L} = \mathbf{r} \times p = \mathbf{r} \times (m\mathbf{v}) = m(\mathbf{r} \times \mathbf{v})$$

Here, **r** is the radius vector of particle A about O at that instant of time.

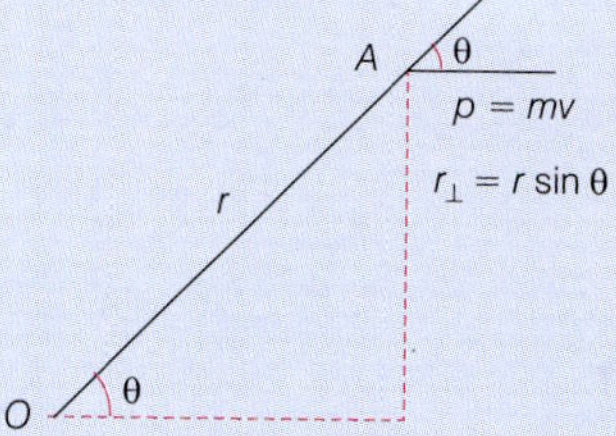

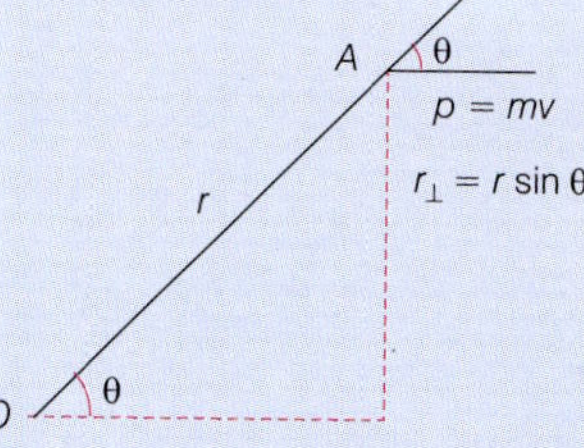

The magnitude of L is

$$L = mvr \sin\theta = mvr_\perp$$

Here, $r_\perp = r\sin\theta$ is the perpendicular distance of line of action of velocity v from point O. The direction of L is same as that of r × v. The SI unit of angular momentum is kg-m^2s^{-1} and its dimensions are $[ML^2T^{-1}]$.

- Angular momentum is given by $\mathbf{L} = \mathbf{r} \times \mathbf{p}$

We can obtain the three rectangular components of angular momentum, i.e. L_x, L_y and L_z

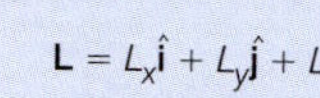

$$\mathbf{L} = L_x\hat{\mathbf{i}} + L_y\hat{\mathbf{j}} + L_z\hat{\mathbf{k}}$$
$$\mathbf{r} = x\hat{\mathbf{i}} + y\hat{\mathbf{j}} + z\hat{\mathbf{k}}$$
$$p = p_x\hat{\mathbf{i}} + p_y\hat{\mathbf{j}} + p_x\hat{\mathbf{k}}$$
$$\mathbf{L}_x = (yp_z - zp_y)$$
$$\mathbf{L}_y = (zp_x - xp_z)$$
$$\mathbf{L}_z = (xp_y - yp_x)$$

- If the particle is moving in yz-plane, it has the angular momentum component only in x-direction,

i.e. $\mathbf{L}_y = \mathbf{L}_z = 0$ and $\mathbf{L}_x \neq 0$.

Similarly, if the particle is moving in xz-plane, $\mathbf{L}_y \neq 0$, $\mathbf{L}_x = \mathbf{L}_y = 0$ and if the particle is moving in xy-plane only, $\mathbf{L}_z \neq 0$, $\mathbf{L}_x = \mathbf{L}_y = 0$.

Syllabus

- Rigid Body Rotation and Equation of Rotational Motion
- Comparison of Linear and Rotational Motion
- Rolling Motion

NCERT Page 116 to 123

For deeper insight **Scan the QR Code**

Motion

Pure Translational Motion
All the particles of the body have same velocity and move along parallel paths at any instant of time.

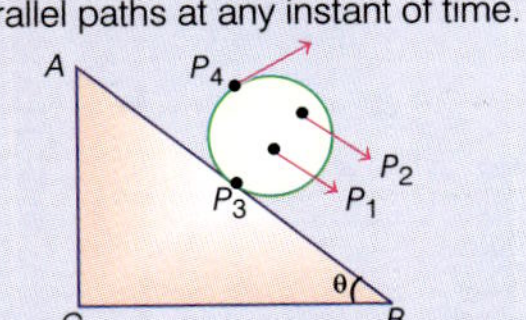

Pure Rotational Motion Every particle of the body moves in a circle, which lies in a plane perpendicular to the axis of rotation and has its centre on the axis. The line or fixed axis about which the body is rotating is known as **axis of rotation.**

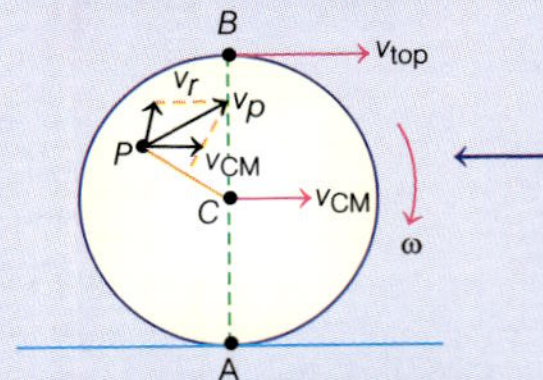

Rolling Motion The combination of pure rotational motion and pure translational motion is called rolling motion.

Rigid Body Rotation

Let a rigid body with rotational inertia I is acted upon by a torque τ and this produces an angular acceleration α. Then, we have

- Torque, $\tau = I\alpha$
- Angular speed of rigid body after t seconds,

  $\omega = \omega_0 + \alpha t$

  ω_0 = Initial angular speed.
- Angular displacement is

  $$\theta = \omega_0 t + \frac{1}{2}\alpha t^2$$
- Angular displacement θ is also given by

  $$\omega^2 - \omega_0^2 = 2\alpha\theta$$

Rotational Kinetic Energy of Particles

The energy due to rotational motion of a body is known as rotational kinetic energy.

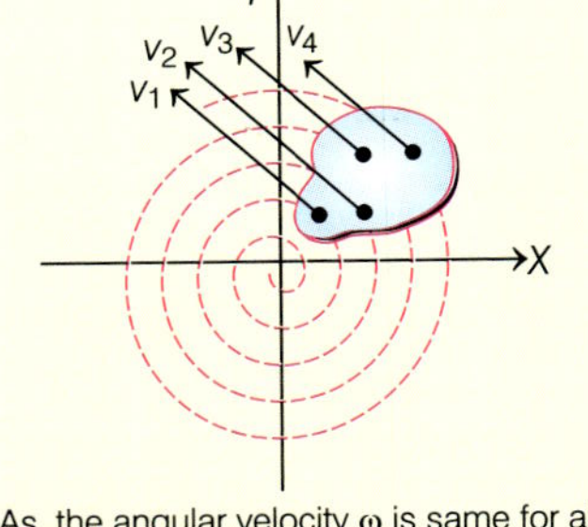

As, the angular velocity ω is same for all the particles of rigid body.

So, $$K = \frac{1}{2}\omega^2\left(\sum_{i=1}^{n} m_i r_i^2\right)$$

The quantity $\Sigma(m_i r_i^2)$ depends on distribution of mass around axis of rotation. This quantity is called moment of inertia.

Kinetic energy, $K = \frac{1}{2}I\omega^2$

When $\omega = 1$, rotational kinetic energy $= \frac{1}{2}I$

or Moment of inertia, $I = 2 \times$ Rotational kinetic energy

Hence, the moment of inertia of a rigid body about an axis of rotation is numerically equal to twice the rotational kinetic energy of the body when it is rotating with unit angular velocity about that axis. Rotational kinetic energy depends upon axis of rotation.

Comparison of Linear and Rotational Motions

Linear Motion	Rotational Motion
• If linear acceleration is zero, u = constant, $s = ut$	• If angular acceleration is zero, ω = constant, $\theta = \omega t$
• If linear acceleration is constant, $v = u + at$; $s = ut + \frac{1}{2}at^2$; $v^2 - u^2 = 2as$	• If angular acceleration is constant, $\omega = \omega_0 + \alpha t$; $\theta = \omega_0 t + \frac{1}{2}\alpha t^2$; $\omega^2 - \omega_0^2 = 2\alpha\theta$
• If linear acceleration is not constant, $v = \frac{dx}{dt}$; $a = \frac{dv}{dt}$; $vdv = adx$	• If angular acceleration is not constant, $\omega = \frac{d\theta}{dt}$; $\alpha = \frac{d\omega}{dt}$; $\omega d\omega = \alpha d\theta$
• Mass, m	• Moment of Inertia, $I = \Sigma Mr^2$
• Linear momentum, $p = mv$	• Angular momentum, $L = I\omega$
• Force $F = ma = \frac{dp}{dt}$	• Torque, $\tau = I\alpha = dL/dt$
• Kinetic energy, $K = \frac{1}{2}mv^2$	• Rotational kinetic energy, $K_{rot} = \frac{1}{2}I\omega^2$
• Work-Kinetic energy theorem, $W = \Delta K = \frac{1}{2}m(v^2 - u^2)$	• Work-Kinetic energy theorem, $W = \Delta K = \frac{1}{2}I(\omega^2 - \omega_0^2)$
• Power, $P = \mathbf{F} \times \mathbf{v}$	• Power, $P = \tau\omega$

Rolling Down on a Rough Inclined Plane

A body of mass m and radius R rolling down a plane inclined at an angle θ with the horizontal. If the body rolls without slipping, then the centre of mass of the body moves in a straight line.

Different forces acting on the body are

(i) Frictional force (f) acting upwards at the point of contact with inclined plane and parallel to the inclined plane.

(ii) Normal reaction of inclined plane (N).

(iii) Weight of the body (mg) acting vertically downwards through the centre of mass of body.

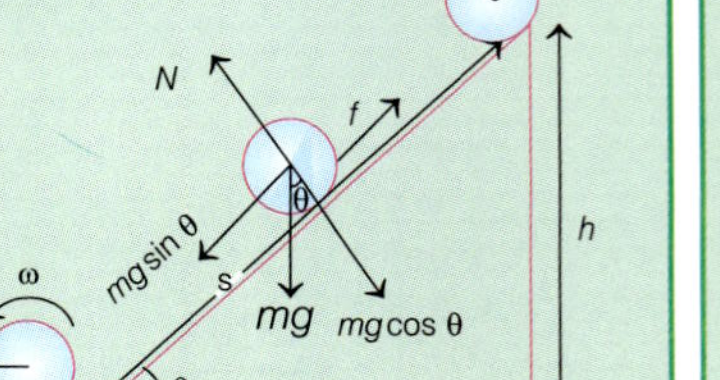

Rolling Motion

When a body performs translatory motion as well as rotational motion, then this type of motion is known as rolling motion. e.g. Motion of football rolling on a surface. In rolling motion, the velocity of centre of mass represents linear motion while angular velocity represents rotational motion.

(a) (b)

The kinetic energy of a rolling body is equal to the sum of kinetic energies of translational and rotational motion.

$\therefore$ Total kinetic energy of a rolling body = Rotational kinetic energy + Translational kinetic energy

$$= \frac{1}{2}I\omega^2 + \frac{1}{2}mv_{CM}^2$$

Pure Rolling Motion

If the velocity of point of contact with respect to the surface is zero, then it is known as pure rolling.

(a) (b)

For pure rotational motion, velocity of centre of mass is zero given by the relation, $v = R\omega$

In the above figure, when we observe the motion of contact point P on the disc, we find that it has two simultaneous motions

(i) Linear forward velocity v because whole body is moving forward.

(ii) Linear backward velocity ωR due to rotation of the disc as a whole in clockwise direction. In case of pure rolling, these two velocities become equal.

Test 1

Syllabus
- The Universal law of Gravitation
- Acceleration due to Gravity and Its Variation with Altitude and Depth

NCERT Page 131 to 134

For deeper insight **Scan the QR Code**

Chapter 07

Newton's Universal Law

- Every material particle in the universe exerts an attractive force on another particle which is called gravitational force.
- The gravitational force acting between two bodies is directly proportional to the product of their masses and inversely proportional to the square of the distance between the bodies.
- $F = \frac{G\,m_1 m_2}{r^2}$
- Vector form, $\mathbf{F} = \frac{G\,m_1 m_2}{r^3}\hat{\mathbf{r}}$
- Gravitational force acting between two particles does not depend on the nature of the particle and medium.
- This force is always attractive.
- This force is conservative in nature.
- Here, $F \propto \frac{1}{r^2}$, then graph between F and r will be hyperbola.

Vector form of Universal Law

$\mathbf{F}_{21}$ = force on 2 due to 1

$$\mathbf{F}_{21} = -\frac{Gm_1m_2}{r_{21}^2}(-\hat{\mathbf{r}}_{21})$$

Similarly,

$\mathbf{F}_{12}$ = force on 1 due to 2

$$\mathbf{F}_{12} = -\frac{Gm_1m_2}{r_{12}^3}(\hat{\mathbf{r}}_{12}) \quad \text{or} \quad \mathbf{F}_{21} = \frac{Gm_1m_2}{r_{12}^3}\hat{\mathbf{r}}_{12}$$

Clearly, gravitational force follows Newton's third law $\mathbf{F}_{21} = -\mathbf{F}_{12}$.

Important Points about Gravitational Force

- Gravitational force is
  - always attractive in nature
  - independent of the nature of medium between masses.
  - independent of pressure or absence of other bodies.
  - a central force act along the line joining centre of gravity of two bodies.
- Conservative force
- Value of universal gravitational constant is $G = 6.67 \times 10^{-11}$ Nm^{2}kg^{-2}

Force on a Particle due to Number of Point Masses

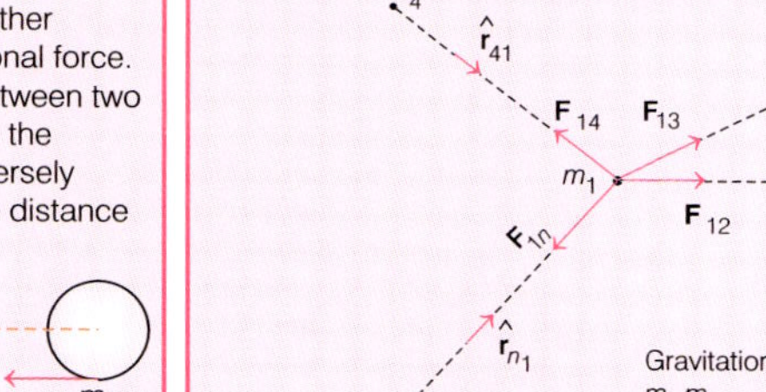

$$F = F_{12} + F_{13} + F_{14} + \ldots + F_{1n}$$

It states that, the resultant gravitational force F acting on a particle due to number of point masses is equal to the vector sum of forces exerted by the individual masses on the given particle.

Acceleration due to Gravity of the Earth

- The force of gravity acting on a body having unit mass is known as acceleration due to gravity.
- According to Newton's second law, the acceleration due to gravity,

$$g = \frac{F}{m} \text{ or } \frac{GM}{R^2} = g \quad \text{or} \quad g = \frac{4}{3}\pi GR\rho$$

- **Gravitation**
  - The acceleration due to gravity is directed towards the centre of the Earth.
  - It is a vector quantity.
  - Near the surface of the earth, the standard value for acceleration due to gravity is approximately 9.81 m/s^2.

Variation in g due to Shape of the Earth

- Earth is not in perfect shape. It is flat at the poles and bulged at the equator.
- Equatorial radius is about 21 km greater than the polar radius.
- On the earth's surface,

$$g = \frac{GM_e}{R_e^2} \text{ or } g \propto \frac{1}{R_e^2}$$

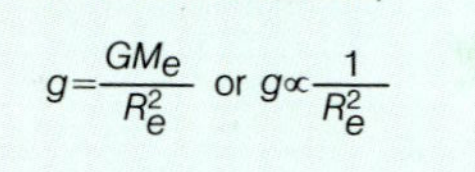

Acceleration of Moon's Surface due to Gravity

Acceleration due to Moon's gravity on Moon surface is $\frac{g_e}{6}$.

$$\frac{M_m}{R_m^2} = \frac{1}{6}\frac{M_e}{R_e^2}\left(g = \frac{GM}{R^2}\right)$$

Acceleration due to Earth's gravity on Moon surface is $\simeq \frac{g_e}{(60)^2}$ or $\frac{g_e}{3600}$

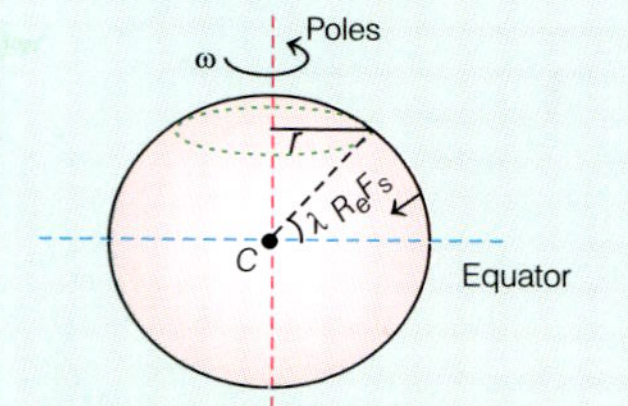

$$g_1 = \frac{g_e}{(60)^2}, \text{ while } g_2 = \frac{g_e}{6}$$

Variation in g due to Axial Rotation of Earth

The change in g is caused by the centrifugal force acting on the Earth's rotation.

The earth spins at a constant angular velocity, while the mass travels in a circular path of radius r at an angular velocity.

The radius of the circular path followed is $r = R\cos\theta$

Force on $m = m\omega^2 r = m\omega^2 R\cos\theta$

If the observed value of g at the latitude λ is represented by g_λ, then

$g_\lambda = g_e - R_e\omega^2\cos^2\lambda$

At equator, $\lambda = 0$, $\cos\lambda = 1$

$\therefore g_\lambda = g_e - R_e\omega^2$

At poles, $\lambda = 90°$, $\cos\lambda = 0$

$\therefore g_\lambda = g_e$, i.e, $g_p > g_e$

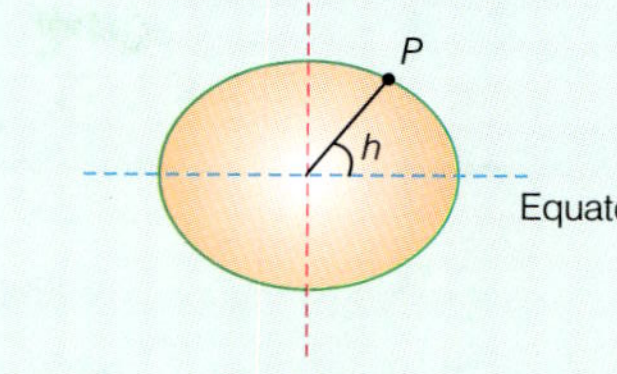

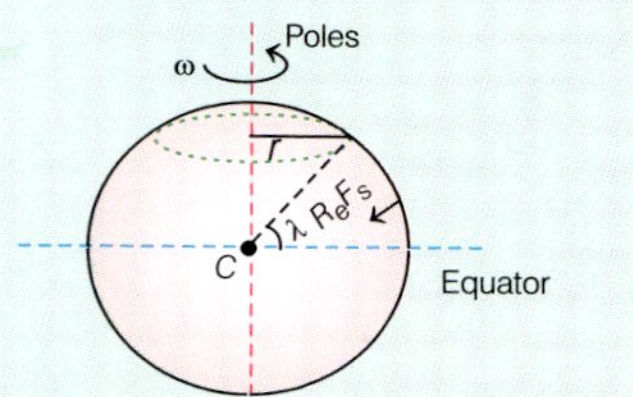

Variation in the Value of Acceleration due to Gravity

Variation due to height 'h'

$$g' = \frac{GM}{(R+h)^2}$$

$$g' = \frac{gR^2}{(R+h)^2}$$

General Equation

Approximate equation $h << R$ ($h < 100$ km)

Use, $g' = g\left(1 - \frac{2h}{R}\right)$

Note

If $h << R$, then decrease in the value of g with height

Absolute decrease $= \Delta g = g - g' = \frac{2hg}{R}$

Fractional decrease $= \frac{\Delta g}{g} = \frac{g-g'}{g} = \frac{2h}{R}$

Percentage decrease $= \frac{\Delta g}{g} = \frac{g-g'}{g} \times 100 = \frac{2h}{R} \times 100$

- **Variation due to depth d**

$g' = g\left[1 - \frac{d}{R}\right] = \frac{gr}{R}$

Absolute decrease $= \frac{\Delta g}{g} = g - g' = \frac{dg}{R}$

Fractional decrease $= \frac{\Delta g}{g} = \frac{g-g'}{g} = \frac{d}{R}$

Percentage decrease $= \frac{\Delta g}{g} \times 100 = \frac{d}{R} \times 100$

- **Important graph**

The graphical representation of change in the value of g' with height and depth

For $r \le R$, $g' = \frac{gr}{R}$ and for $r \ge R$, $g' = \frac{gR^2}{r^2}$

Test 2

Syllabus
- Gravitational Potential
- Gravitational Potential Energy
- Escape velocity

NCERT Page 134 to 136

For deeper insight **Scan the QR Code**

Chapter 07

Gravitational Potential

- Gravitational potential at a point is the potential energy associated with a unit mass due to its position in the gravitational field of another body.
- At infinity, gravitational potential is zero as gravitational force is zero there.
- Here, $V = \frac{W}{m}$

Gravitational Potential For Point Mass

The work done in bringing a unit mass slowly from reference point (infinity) to a given point in the gravitational field, is called the gravitational potential at that point. This work is done by the external agent in bringing the mass. The gravitational potential is denoted by V.

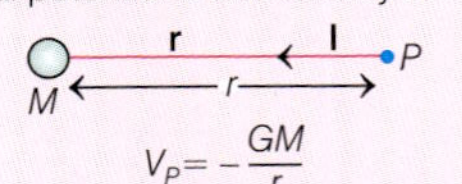

$$V_P = -\frac{GM}{r}$$

At $r=\infty$, value of V_p = maximum, equal to zero

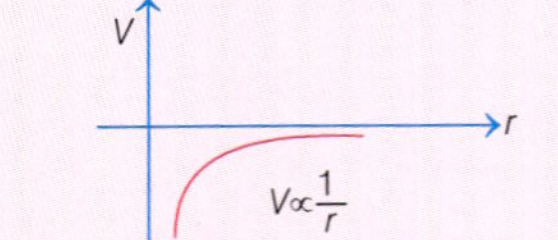

Field due to a Uniform Spherical Shell

For an external point (P), the shell may be treated as a single particle of same mass placed at its centre (O).

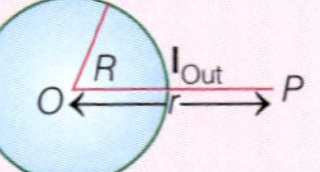

Thus, at an external point, the gravitational field is given by

$$E(r) = \frac{GM}{r^2} \text{ (for } r \ge R)$$

At $r = R$ (the surface of shell),

$$E = \frac{GM}{r^2}$$

and otherwise, $E \propto \frac{1}{r^2}$

At an internal point, the field inside a uniform spherical shell is zero. Thus, E versus r graph is as shown below

Field due to a uniform Solid Sphere

Field at an external point A uniform solid sphere may be treated as a single particle of same mass placed at its centre (O) for calculating the gravitational field at an external point (P).

$$E(r) = \frac{GM}{r^2}$$

$r \ge R$ or $E \propto \frac{1}{r^2}$

Here, r is the distance of the point from the centre of the sphere and R is the radius of sphere.

Field at an internal point The gravitational field due to a uniform sphere at an internal point (P) is proportional to the distance (r) of the point from the centre of the sphere.

The gravitational field at the centre is zero and at surface is $\frac{GM}{R^2}$, where R is the radius of the sphere.

$$E(r) = \frac{GM}{R^3} \cdot r$$

$r \le R$ or $E(r) \propto r$

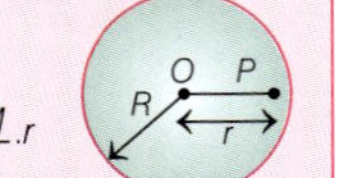

Gravitational Field Intensity

The intensity of gravitational field at any point in the gravitational field due to a given mass is defined as the force experienced by a unit mass placed at that point provided the presence of that unit mass does not alter the original gravitational field. Usually, it is denoted by E or I.

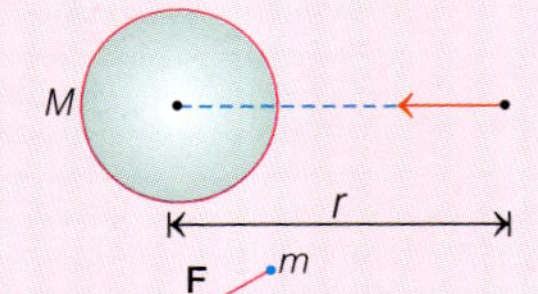

$$\mathbf{I} = \frac{\mathbf{F}}{m}$$

It is a vector quantity and its direction is same as that of gravitational force.

SI unit is N/kg and dimensional formula is $[M^0LT^{-2}]$.

Due to point mass

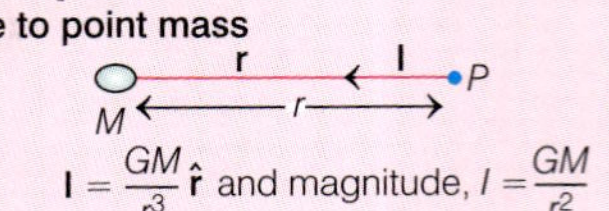

$\mathbf{I} = \frac{GM}{r^3}\hat{\mathbf{r}}$ and magnitude, $I = \frac{GM}{r^2}$

Gravitational Potential Energy

The energy of a system of two masses is equal to negative of work done by the gravitational field of one mass in bringing other mass from infinity to its present position.

A Body Placed in Earth's Gravitational Field

- Potential energy,

$$U = -\frac{GM_e m}{r}$$

- $W_{BA} = GM_e m\left[\frac{1}{r_1} - \frac{1}{r}\right]$

Gravitational Potential Due to other Bodies

Solid Sphere

Case 1

$$V_{out} = \frac{-GM}{r}$$

Case 2

$r = R$

$$V_{surface} = \frac{-GM}{R}$$

Case 3

$$V_{in} = \frac{-GM}{2R^3}(3R^2 - r^2)$$

At centre, $V_{centre} = \frac{-3}{2}\frac{GM}{R} = \frac{-3}{2}V_{surface}$

Graph

Hollow Sphere

Case 1

$r > R$

$$V_{out} = \frac{-GM}{r}$$

Case 2

$r = R$

$$V_{surface} = \frac{-GM}{R}$$

Case 3

$V_{in} = V_{surface}$ = same everywhere

Graph

Relation Between Field And Potential

The relation between gravitational field and potential is given by

$$I = -\frac{dV}{dr} \text{ and } \Delta V = -\int \mathbf{I} \cdot d\mathbf{r} \quad \mathbf{I} = -\left(\frac{\partial V}{\partial X}\hat{\mathbf{i}} + \frac{\partial V}{\partial Y}\hat{\mathbf{j}} + \frac{\partial V}{\partial z}\hat{\mathbf{k}}\right)$$

Escape Speed

- That minimum speed with which a body has to be projected vertically upward from the surface of the earth, so that it just crosses the gravitational field of the earth and never return back to earth by itself.
- At infinity, $U_\infty = 0$ and $K_\infty = 0$

Then, $v_e = \sqrt{\frac{2GM_e}{R_e}}$

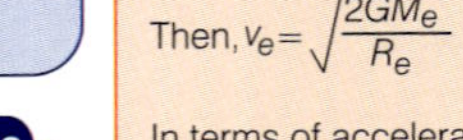

In terms of acceleration due to gravity, $v_e = \sqrt{2gR_e}$

Thus, $v_e = 11.2 \times 10^3$ m/s or 11.2 km / s

Escape Energy

- The minimum kinetic energy with which the body should be projected upward from earth surface, so that it may move to infinity, crossing gravitational field of earth.

$$U_e = \frac{1}{2}mv_e^2 = \frac{Gm_e m}{R_e} = mgR_e$$

Facts

- There is no atmosphere at the moon. Escape speed on the moon surface,

$$v_e = \sqrt{2g_m R_m} = \sqrt{2 \times 1.63 \times 1.74 \times 10^6} = 2.38 \text{ km/s}$$

which is less than the velocity of gas molecules on moon.

- **Black hole** In black hole, escape velocity is greater than the speed of light.

Then, $v_e = \sqrt{\frac{2GM}{R}} \ge c$

Here, $c = 3 \times 10^8$ m/s

Test 3

Syllabus

- Kepler's Law of Planetary Motion
- Motion of Satellite
- Time Period and Energy of Satellite
- Orbital Velocity

NCERT
Page 128 to 129
Page 137 to 139

For deeper insight **Scan the QR Code**

Chapter 07

Kepler's First Law : Law of Orbits

- All planets revolve around the sun in elliptical orbits and the sun lies at one of the foci of ellipse.
- Eccentricity of ellipse, $e = \sqrt{1 - \frac{b^2}{a^2}}$

Kepler's Second Law: Law of Areas

- The line joining a planet to the sun sweeps equal area in equal time interval, i.e. areal speed of the planet remains constant in its orbit.
- When a planet is at the farthest position from the sun, its velocity is minimum and when it is nearest to the sun, its velocity is maximum.

Here, $\frac{dA}{dt} = \frac{L}{2m}$ = constant

Kepler's Third law : Law of Periods

- Square of time period of revolution T of a planet about the sun is directly proportional to cube of the semi-major axis a of their elliptical orbit.
  i.e. $T^2 \propto a^3$
- For circular orbit, $a = b = r$ (radius)

$\therefore \quad T^2 \propto r^3$

Satellites

- Those bodies which revolve around a planet are called satellites.
- The path of these satellites are elliptical with the centre of planet at a focus .

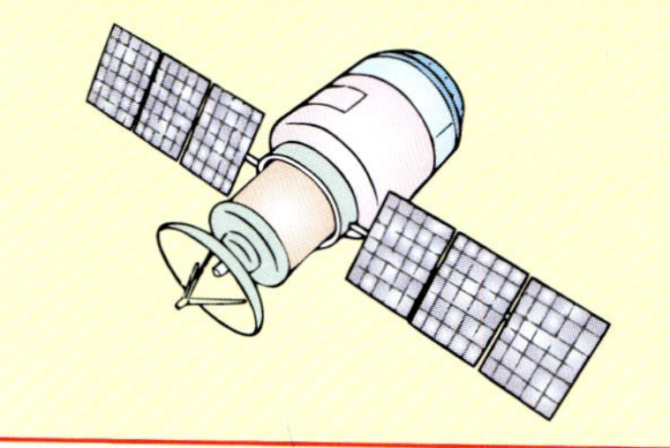

Orbital Velocity of a Satellite

Orbit at a height 'h' from the surface,

$$v_o = \sqrt{\frac{GM}{(R-h)}} = \sqrt{\frac{gR^2}{(R-h)}}$$

If orbit is closer to earth's surface (neglect h) (called first cosmic velocity)

$$v_e = \sqrt{\frac{GM}{R}} = \sqrt{gR}$$

Note For easy calculations,

$\sqrt{gR} = 8$ km/s or $\sqrt{\frac{GM}{R}} = 8$ km/s $= 8 \times 10^3$ m/s

or $\frac{GM}{R} = 64 \times 10^6$

- Orbital velocity of a satellite is independent of mass of the satellite.
- It decreases with increase in the radius of the orbit and with increase in the height of the satellite.
- It depends on the mass and radius of the planet about which the satellite revolves.
- The angular momentum of a satellite of mass m moving with velocity v_o in an orbit of radius r $(= R + h)$ is given by $L = \sqrt{GMm^2r}$.

Graph of Orbital Speed

- The variation of orbital speed is given by

$$v_o = \sqrt{\frac{GM}{r}}$$

Time Period

- Time taken by a satellite to complete one cycle around the earth is called its time period or period of revolution (T).

Here,

$$T = \frac{2\pi r^{3/2}}{\sqrt{GM_e}}$$

$$T = 2\pi \sqrt{\frac{(R_e + h)^3}{gR_e^2}}$$

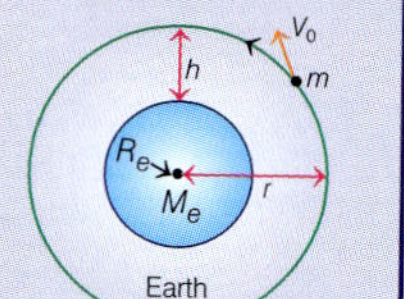

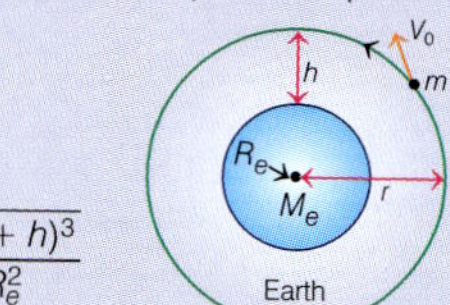

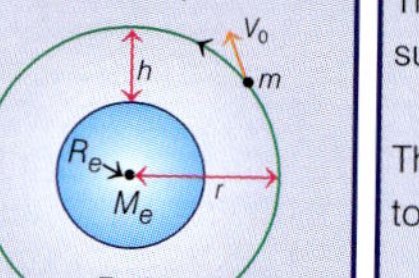

Graph of Time Period

- The variation of time period is $T^2 \propto r^3$
- Therefore, satellite obeys Kepler's third law of planetary motion.
- Greater is the distance of satellite from the earth's surface, greater will be its time period of revolution.

Energy

In a circular orbit of radius r around the earth (planet), gravitational potential energy of a satellite,

$$U = -\frac{GM_em}{r}$$

- Kinetic energy, $K = \frac{1}{2}mv_o^2 = \frac{1}{2}m\left(\sqrt{\frac{GM_e}{r}}\right)^2$

$$K = \frac{GM_em}{2r}$$

- Total energy, $E = -\frac{GM_em}{2r}$

Relation between KE, U and TE
$U = 2$ TE
KE = TE

Graph

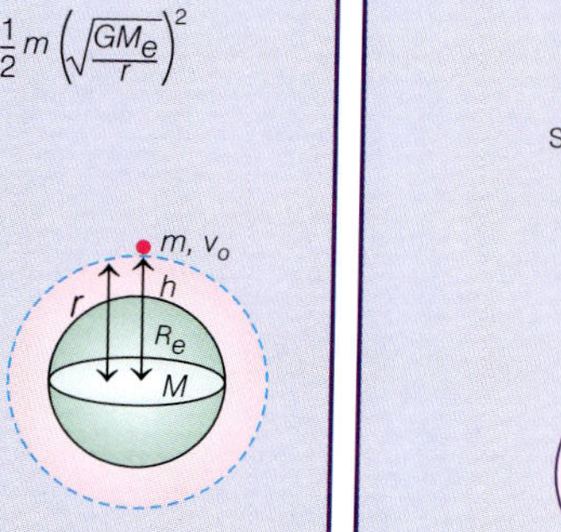

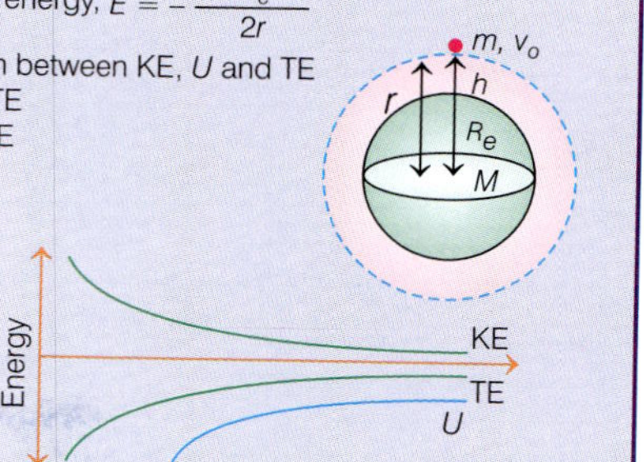

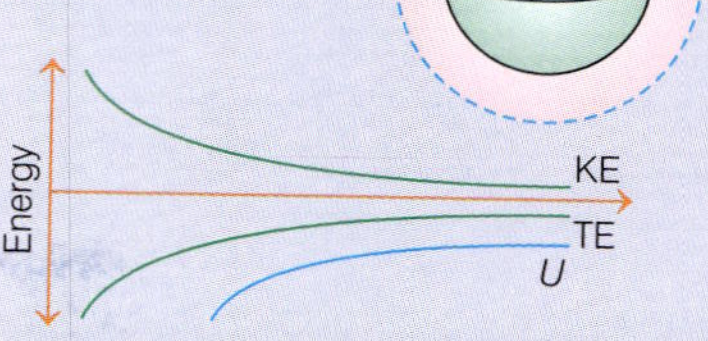

The total energy of the satellite is negative only when it is bound to the earth. It means that its orbit is an ellipse or circle. It is positive when satellite is not bound to any star or its equivalent. In this case, the path covered by satellite will be hyperbola.

Relation between Orbital Velocity and Escape Velocity

The escape velocity of a body from the earth's surface,

$$v_e = \sqrt{2gR}$$

The orbital velocity of a satellite revolving close to earth's surface,

$$v_o = \sqrt{gR}$$

$$\frac{v_e}{v_o} = \frac{\sqrt{2gR}}{\sqrt{gR}} = \sqrt{2}$$

$$v_e = \sqrt{2}v_o \quad \ldots(i)$$

So, Eq. (i) represents that the escape velocity of a body from the earth's surface is $\sqrt{2}$ times its orbital velocity in a circular orbit just above the earth's surface.

Height of satellite

The height of satellite is the distance between the satellite and the earth's surface or it's orbit height. It can be calculated as

$$h = \left(\frac{T^2gR^2}{4\pi^2}\right)^{1/3} - R$$

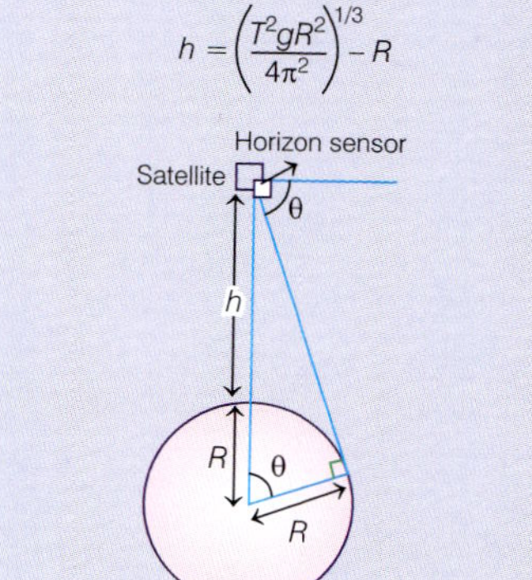

Binding Energy of satellite

The energy required by a satellite to leave its orbit around the earth and escape to infinity, is known as binding energy of satellite.

Binding energy of satellite $= \frac{GMm}{2r}$

Test 1

Syllabus
- Elastic Behaviour
- Stress and Strain
- Hooke's Law
- Young's Modulus, Bulk Modulus and Modulus of Rigidity

NCERT Page -167 to 175

For deeper insight **Scan the QR Code**

Chapter 08

Stress and Strain

- When a body is subjected to a deforming force, a restoring force is developed in the body. This restoring force per unit area is known as stress.
- This restoring force is equal in magnitude but opposite in direction to the applied force.

$$\text{Stress} = \frac{\text{Restoring force } (F)}{\text{Area of cross-section } (A)}$$

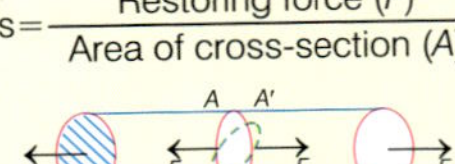

- SI unit is N/m^2 or pascal (Pa) and CGS system unit is $dyne/cm^2$.
- Strain is defined as the ratio of change in shape of an object to the original shape.
- Strain is a pure number, it has no unit.

$$\text{Strain} = \frac{\text{Change in configuration of the object}}{\text{Original configuration of the object}}$$

Normal Stress

- Restoring force acting normally on any surface inside a body per unit area is called normal stress.

$$\text{Normal stress} = \frac{F_N}{A}$$

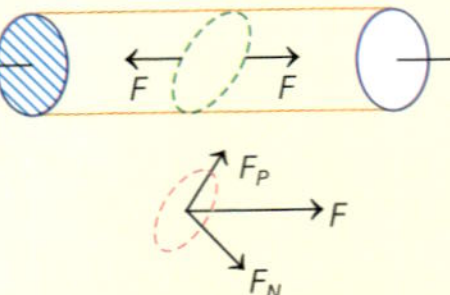

Longitudinal Stress and Strain

- When a deforming force is acting on the cross-sectional area along the length of a body, then it changes length of the body.
- Tensile stress $= \frac{F}{A}$
- **Longitudinal Strain**
  It is defined as the change in length per unit length of the object on the application of deforming force.

$$\text{Longitudinal strain} = \frac{\text{Change in length } (\Delta l)}{\text{Original length } (l)}$$

Elastic Moduli

- The ratio of stress and strain is called modulus of elasticity.
- It has great importance for structural and manufacturing engineering designs.

Young's Modulus of Elasticity

- The ratio of longitudinal stress to longitudinal strain produced in the body is called Young's modulus of elasticity of material of body.

$$Y = \frac{\text{Longitudinal stress}}{\text{Longitudinal strain}} = \frac{FL}{A\Delta L}$$

Volume Stress and Strain

When a deforming force acting on a body is uniformly acting on each point of the body normal to the surface, then volume of this body is changed.

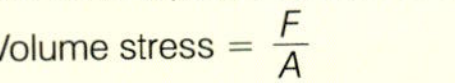

- Volume stress $= \frac{F}{A}$
  = Excess pressure on the body (Δp)
  It is also known as hydraulic stress.
- **Volumetric Strain**
  It is defined as the change in volume per unit volume of the object on application of deforming force.

$$\text{Volumetric strain} = \frac{\text{Change in volume } (\Delta V)}{\text{Original volume } (V)}$$

Tangential or Shear Stress and Strain

When a force acting tangentially on the surface of a body, then it changes shape of the body and the body is said to sheared.
If the cross-sectional area of the cylinder is A and tangential force F, then tangential stress $= \frac{F}{A}$

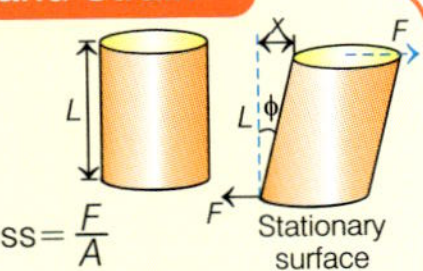

- **Tangential or Shearing strain**
  It is defined as the ratio of displacement (x) of the upper surface to the distance (L) between two faces on the application of deforming force.

$$\text{Shearing strain} = \frac{\text{Displacement } (x)}{\text{Distance } (L)}$$

Hooke's Law

- According to this law, for small values of strain, the stress produced in a body is directly proportional to strain.

$$\frac{\text{Stress}}{\text{Strain}} = E = \text{constant}$$

- Greater is the value of modulus of elasticity of the body, then it will be more elastic.
- Hooke's law is an empirical law and is found to be valid for most materials. However, there are some materials which do not exhibit this linear relationship.

Force Constant of Wire

Force required to produce unit elongation in a wire is called force constant of material of wire. It is denoted by k.

$$k = \frac{F}{\Delta l} = \frac{YA}{l} \qquad \left(\because \frac{F}{\Delta l} = \frac{YA}{l}\right)$$

Note:- A wire is just like a spring of force constant , so all formulae which we use in case of a spring can be applied to a wire also.

Compressibility

The reciprocal of the bulk modulus of the material of a body is called the compressibility of that material. Thus,

$$\text{Compressibility} = \frac{1}{|B|} = \frac{\Delta V}{pV} = k$$

The SI unit of compressibility is $m^2 N^{-1}$ and its dimensions are $[M^{-1} LT^2]$.
The bulk modulus is defined for all solids, liquids and gases. The value of B for solids are much larger than for liquids and that for liquids are much larger than for gases. Thus, solids are least compressible, while gases are most compressible.

Elastomers

- Materials which has very large elastic region but does not obey Hooke's law. There is no well defined plastic region.
  Example : Tissue of aorta, rubber, etc.

Bulk Modulus of Elasticity

- The ratio of volume stress to the volume strain produced in a substance is called bulk modulus of elasticity of that substance.

$$B = \frac{\text{Volume or Normal stress}}{\text{Volume strain}}$$

$$B = \frac{F/A}{\Delta V/V} = -\frac{pV}{\Delta V}$$

Modulus of Rigidity

- The ratio of produced tangential stress in an object to shear strain is called modulus of rigidity.
  It is denoted by G or η.
- Tangential stress (Shear stress) $= \frac{F}{A}$
- Modulus of rigidity is given by

$$\eta \text{ or } G = \frac{\text{Tangential stress}}{\text{Shear strain}}$$

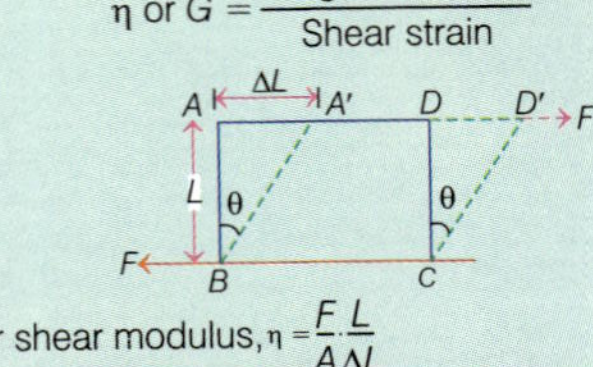

or shear modulus, $\eta = \frac{F}{A}\frac{L}{\Delta L}$

Elastic and Plastic Behaviour of Solids

- A body that returns to its original shape and size on the removal of deforming force is called **elastic body** and this property is called **elasticity**.
- If a body does not show any tendency to regain its original shape and size even after the removal of deforming force are called **plastic body** and this property is called **plasticity**.

Applications of Elastic Behaviour of Materials

- A mild steel has a yield strength (σ_y) and has a lifting capacity M kg, then area of cross-section of the rope should at least be
  $$A \geq \frac{Mg}{\sigma_y}$$
- A bar of length l, breadth b, and depth d, when loaded at the centre by a load w sags by $\delta = \frac{wl^3}{4bd^3Y}$

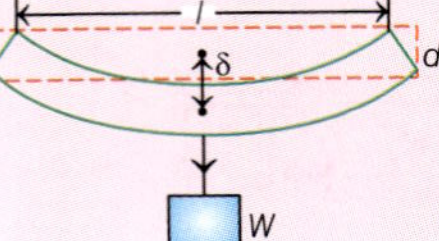

Test 2

Syllabus
- Stress - Strain Curve
- Thermal Stress & Strain
- Energy Stored in Deformed Body

NCERT Page -169 to 170

For deeper insight **Scan the QR Code**

Chapter 08

Stress-Strain Curve

- When a wire is stretched (breaking stress) by a load, it is seen that for small value of load, the extension produced in the wire is proportional to the load.
- If the weight is gradually increased, then length of the wire also increases gradually.

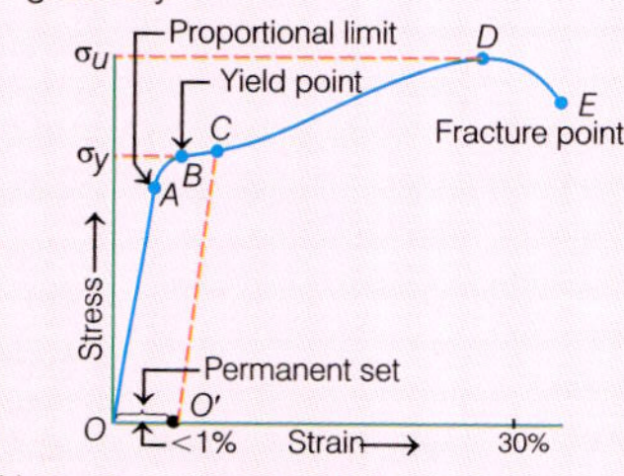

Here, σ_u = ultimate tensile strength and σ_y = yield strength
- If the ultimate strength and fracture points are closed, the material is said to be brittle.
- If they are far apart, the material is said to be ductile.

Nature of the Stress-Strain Curve

The stress-strain curve differ considerably for different materials. The steeper curve indicates a stiffer material, line parallel to the strain axis indicates a ductile material and in the absence of yield point or plastic behaviour refer to a brittle material.

- **Ductile and Brittle Materials**
  On the basis of elastic and plastic properties, materials can be classified in two ways; ductile materials and brittle materials.The materials which have large plastic range of extension are called ductile materials. As shown in the stress-strain curve, the fracture point is widely separated from the elastic limit.
  Such materials undergo an irreversible increase in length before snapping. So, they can be drawn into thin wires, e.g. copper, silver, iron, aluminium, etc.
  The materials which have very small range of plastic extension are called brittle materials. Such materials break as soon as the stress is increased beyond the elastic limit. Their breaking point lies just close to their elastic limit as shown in figure, e.g. cast iron, glass, ceramics, etc.

Malleability

When a solid is compressed, a stage is reached beyond which it cannot regains its original shape after the deforming force is removed. This is the elastic limit point (A') for compression. The solid then behaves like a plastic body. The yield point (B') obtained under compression is called crushing point. After this stage, metals are said to be malleable i.e. they can be hammered or rolled into thin sheets e.g. gold, silver, lead etc.

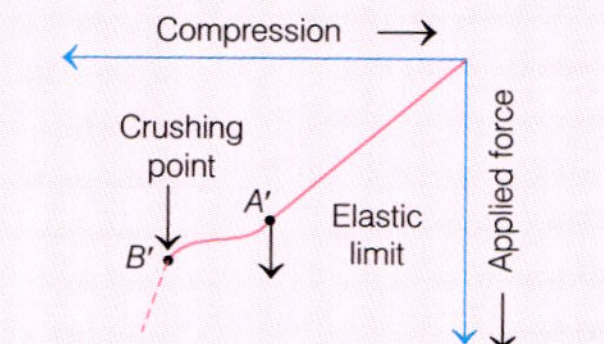

Factors Affecting Elasticity

(i) **Effect of temperature** Almost for all materials, the modulus of elasticity decreases with the rise in temperature but the elasticity of invar steel remains unchanged with the change in temperature.

(ii) **Effect of impurities** The addition of impurities affects the elastic properties depending on whether impurities are themselves more or less elastic. When carbon is added to iron and potassium to gold, their elasticities are strengthened.

(iii) **Effect of annealing** By annealing (i.e. heating and then cooling gradually) large crystal grains are formed and hence, the elasticity of the material decreases.

(iv) **Effect of hammering and rolling** By hammering and rolling, crystal grains break up into smaller units and hence, the elasticity of the material increases.

Elastic Hysteresis

As a natural consequence of the elasticity after effect, the strain in the body tends to lag behind the stress applied to the body, so that during a rapidly changing stress, the strain is greater for the same value of stress. This lag of strain behind the stress is called elastic hysteresis.

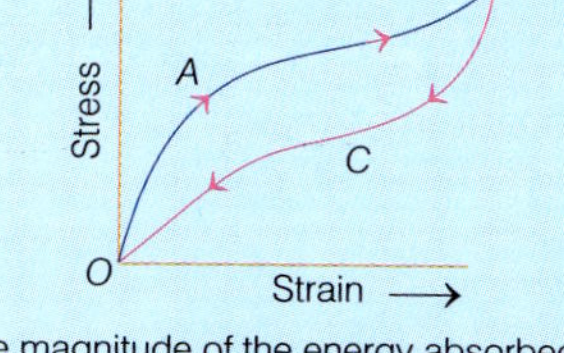

The magnitude of the energy absorbed is proportional to the area of the loop. The material having low elastic hysteresis have low elastic relaxation time.

Thermal Stresses and Strains

Whenever there is some increase or decrease in the temperature of the body, it causes the body to expand or contract. If the body is allowed to expand or contract freely, with the rise or fall in the temperature, no stresses are induced in the body. But, if the deformation of the body is prevented, some stresses are induced in the body. Such stresses are called thermal stresses or temperature stresses.
The corresponding strains are called thermal strains or temperature strains.

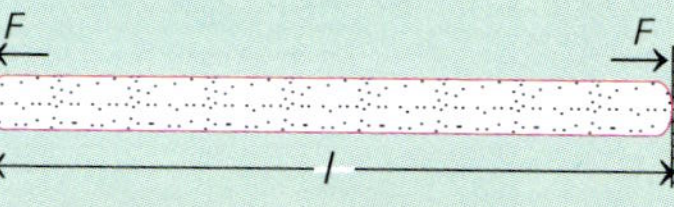

Stress-Strain Curve Features

When a graph between stress and strain is plotted, then

(i) The stress is found to be proportional to strain(% elongation) upto point A. Thus, Hooke's law is fully obeyed in this region, the point A is known as point of **proportional limit**.

(ii) When stress is increased beyond A, then for small stress, there is a large strain in the wire upto point B.

(iii) When the load is gradually removed between points O to B, the wire return to its original length. The wire regains its original dimension only when load applied is less than or equal to certain limit, this limit is called **elastic limit**. The point B on stress-strain curve is known as **elastic limit** or **yield point.** The material of the wire in the region OB shows the elastic behaviour, hence known as **elastic region**.

(iv) If the stress or load increases beyond point B, the strain further increases. This increase in strain represented by BC part of the curve. Now, if the load is removed, the wire does not regain its original length. But the increase in the length of the wire is permanent. In other words, there is permanent strain equal to OO' in the wire even when the stress is zero. This permanent strain in the wire is known as **permanent set**.

(v) Now, as the stress beyond C is increased, there is huge strain in the wire. This huge increase in the strain for small stress is represented by CD part of the curve. The wire breaks at point E which is also known as **fracture point**. The material of the wire from point C to point D shows the **plastic behaviour** or **plastic deformation**. The stress needed to cause the actual fracture of the material is known as **breaking stress.**

Stress-Strain curve of Elastic Tissue

In our body, the elastic tissue of aorta (the large blood vessel carrying blood from the heart) is an elastomer.
For which the stress-strain curve is shown in figure.

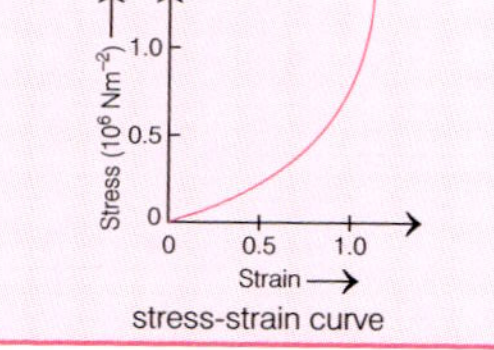

stress-strain curve

Breaking Stress of Some Materials

Material	Breaking stress (in Nm^{-2})
Aluminium	2.2×10^8
Iron	3.0×10^8
Brass	4.7×10^8
Phosphor bronze	5.6×10^8
Steel	5 to 20×10^8
Glass	10×10^8

Energy Stored in a Deformed Body

- When a wire is stretched, an external work is done against internal restoring force produced in the wire. This work is stored in the form of elastic potential energy in the wire.
- Potential energy, $U = W = \frac{1}{2} \times$ Weight $\times$ Extension in length
- Energy stored in the wire per unit volume
  Energy density is given by $U' = \frac{U}{V} = \frac{1}{2} \times$ Stress $\times$ Strain

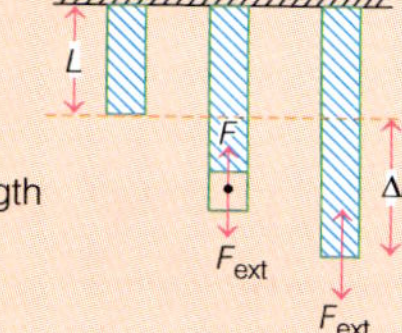

Test 1

Syllabus
- Thrust and Pressure
- Pascals Law and Its Applications
- Archimedes' Principle and Buoyant Force

NCERT Page 180 to 186

For deeper insight **Scan the QR Code**

Chapter 09

Absolute Pressure and Gauge Pressure

The excess pressure above atmospheric pressure is usually called gauge pressure and the total pressure is called absolute pressure. Thus,
Gauge pressure
= Absolute pressure – Atmospheric pressure

Absolute pressure is always greater than or equal to zero, while gauge pressure can be negative also.

Manometer

It consists of a *U*-tube containing a suitable liquid i.e., a low density liquid (such as oil) for measuring small pressure differences and a high density liquid (such as mercury) for large pressure differences. One end of the tube is open to the atmosphere and the other end is connected to the system whose pressure we want to measure, then

$$p_x = p_{atm} + h\rho_m g, \quad h\rho_m g = p_x - p_{atm}$$

Density of Liquid

Density (ρ) of a liquid or any substance is defined as the mass per unit volume.

$$\therefore \quad \text{Density, } \rho = \frac{\text{Mass}}{\text{Volume}} = \lim_{\Delta V \to 0} \frac{\Delta m}{\Delta V} = \frac{dm}{dV}$$

SI unit of density is kgm^{-3} and its dimensions are $[ML^{-3}T^0]$ and CGS unit is gcm^{-3}.

Relative Density (RD)

In case of a liquid (or a substance), sometimes an another term relative density (RD) or specific gravity is defined. It is the ratio of density of the liquid (or a substance) to the density of water at 4°C.

$$\text{Hence, RD} = \frac{\text{Density of liquid or substance}}{\text{Density of water at 4°C}}$$

Relative density is a pure ratio, so it has no units.

Atmospheric Pressure

The gaseous envelope surrounding the earth is called earth's atmosphere. The pressure exerted by the atmosphere is called atmospheric pressure.

Pressure

- The pressure of liquid at a point is the thrust exerted by the liquid at rest per unit area.
- The SI unit of pressure is Nm^{-2}. It has been named as pascal (Pa). Pressure, $p = F/A$
- CGS unit of pressure is $dyne/cm^2$.

Hydrostatic Paradox

The pressure exerted by a liquid depends only on the height of fluid column and is independent of the shape of the containing vessel.

Measurement of Pressure

- **Barometer**

It is a device used to measure atmospheric pressure. In principle, any liquid can be used to fill the barometer, but mercury is the substance of choice because its high density makes possible an instrument of reasonable size.
A barometer is an inverted evacuated tube, put over a mercury volume. Outside pressure pushes mercury into tube till the weight of liquid column equalises the force due to external pressure. In given diagram, in equilibrium,

$$p_1 = p_2$$

Here, p_1 = atmospheric pressure (p_0)
and $p_2 = 0 + \rho gh = \rho gh$

where, ρ = density of mercury

$$\therefore \quad p_0 = \rho gh$$

Thus, the mercury barometer read the atomospheric pressure (p_0) directly from the height of the mercury column.

Variation of Pressure with Depth

- Consider a fluid at rest having density ρ contained in a cylindrical vessel. So, pressure will be distributed all side but depend on height of the vessel.
- Pressure difference, $p_2 - p_1 = h\rho g$
- Pressure, $p = p_a + h\rho g$
- Gauge pressure $= p - p_0 = h\rho g$

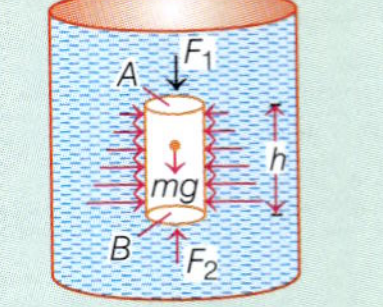

Pascal's Law

The pressure is applied on any part of the fluid placed in equilibrium inside a vessel, then this pressure is transmitted to each part of the fluid in all directions without decay in magnitude.

Applications of Pascal's Law

- **Hydraulic Lift**

It is used to lift the heavy loads. This is made by connecting two cylindrical vessels of different cross-sections. Each cylindrical vessel contains air tight frictionless pistons.
An incompressible liquid is filled inside the vessel.

$$p = \frac{F_1}{A_1}; F_2 = pA_2 = \frac{F_1}{A_1}A_2$$

$A_2 >> A_1$, therefore $F_2 >>> F_1$

Hydraulic lift

- **Hydraulic Brake**

The working of the hydraulic brakes is also based on the Pascal's law.

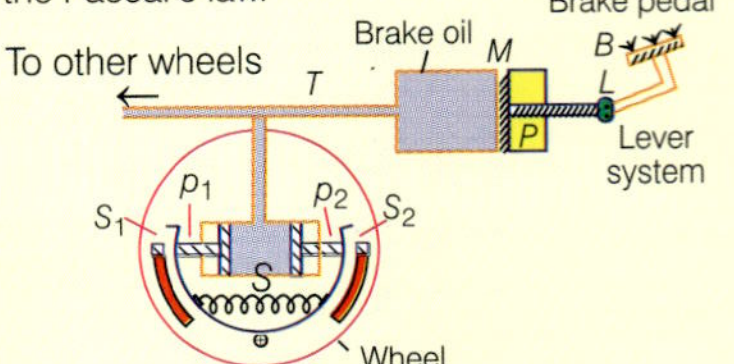

Important Points Related to Fluid Pressure

(i) At a point in the liquid column, the pressure applied on it is same in all directions.

(ii) In a liquid, pressure will be same at all points at the same level.

(iii) The pressure exerted by a liquid depends only on the height of fluid column and is independent of the shape of the containing vessel.

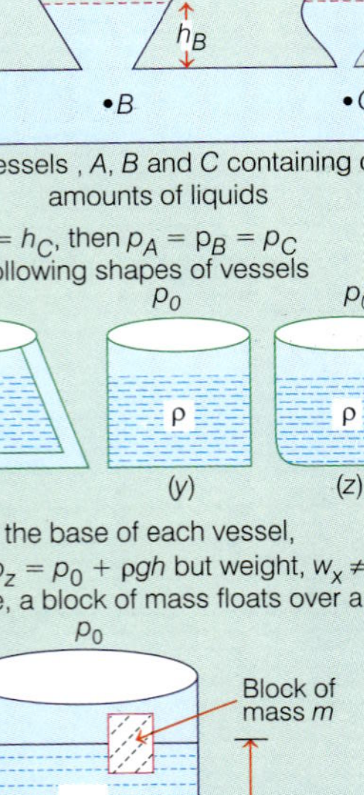

The three vessels, *A*, *B* and *C* containing different amounts of liquids

If $h_A = h_B = h_C$, then $p_A = p_B = p_C$

(iv) Consider following shapes of vessels

(x) (y) (z)

Pressure at the base of each vessel,

$p_x = p_y = p_z = p_0 + \rho gh$ but weight, $w_x \neq w_y \neq w_z$

(v) In the figure, a block of mass floats over a fluid surface

Block of mass *m*

Pressure at the base of the vessel is

$$p = p_0 + \rho gh + \frac{mg}{A}$$

Archimedes' Principle

If a heavy object is immersed in water, it seems to weight less than when it is in air. This is because the water exerts a net upward normal force called buoyant force. The Archimedes' principle gives the magnitude of buoyant force on a body. It states that, "a body wholly or partially submerged in a fluid experiences an upward force which is equal to the weight of the displaced fluid." Thus, the magnitude of buoyant force (*F*) which is also called upthrust is given by

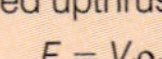

$$F = V_i \rho_L g$$

Test 2

Syllabus
- Flow of Liquids
- Bernoulli's Theorem
- Applications of Bernoulli's Theorem

NCERT Page 186 to 190

For deeper insight **Scan the QR Code**

Chapter 09

Laminar Flow

If the liquid flows over a horizontal surface in the form of layers of different velocities, then the flow of liquid is called laminar flow.

Turbulent Flow

When a liquid moves with a velocity greater than its critical velocity, the motion of the particles of fluid becomes disordered and irregular.

Few examples of turbulent flow are

(i) a jet of air striking a flat plate.
(ii) the smoke rising from a burning stock of wood.
(iii) when a fast flowing stream encounters rocks, foamy whirlpool like regions are formed.

Critical Velocity

The maximum velocity of fluid upto which its flow remains streamlined and beyond which its flow becomes turbulent is called critical velocity.

Equation of Continuity

During the streamline flow of the non-viscous and incompressible fluid through a pipe of varying cross-section, the product of area of cross-section and normal fluid velocity remains constant throughout the flow.

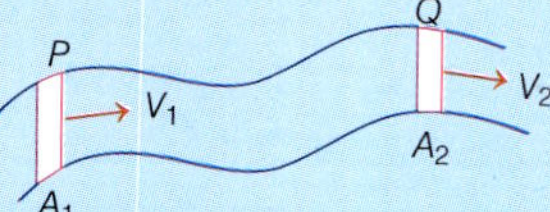

A liquid is flowing through a tube of non-uniform cross-section

Thus, $$A_1V_1 = A_2V_2$$

$$Av = \text{constant or } v \propto \frac{1}{A}$$

or $$\rho_1 A_1 V_1 = \rho_2 A_2 V_2$$

Note The product AV is the volume flow rate dV/dt, the rate at which volume crosses a section of the tube. Hence,

$$\frac{dV}{dt} = \text{volume flow rate} = Av$$

The mass flow rate is the mass flow per unit time through a cross-section.

$$\frac{dm}{dt} = \rho \cdot \frac{dV}{dt}$$

Streamline Flow

Steady flow of a fluid is the flow in which every particle of the fluid follows exactly the same path as its preceding particle and same velocity at every point. Properties of streamline are given below

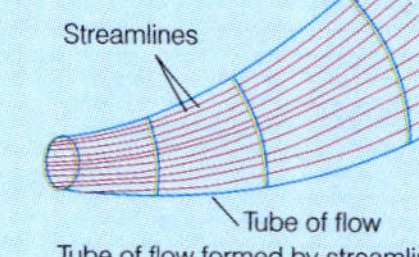

Tube of flow formed by streamlines

(i) In streamline flow, two streamlines cannot cross each other. If they do so, the particles of the liquid at the point of intersection will have two different directions for their flow, which will decrease the steady nature of the liquid flow.
(ii) The greater is the crowding of streamlines at a place greater is the velocity of the liquid particles at that place and *vice-versa*.
(iii) Streamline flow is possible only if the liquid velocity does not exceed a limiting value called critical velocity.
(iv) The bundle of streamlines forming a tubular region is called a tube of flow.

Dynamic Lift

- It is the force that acts on a body, by virtue of its motion through a fluid such as airplane wing, a hydrofoil or a spinning ball. The deviation of spinning ball from its parabolic trajectory can be explained on the basis of Bernoulli's principle.

(i) **When ball is moving without spin in air,** then speed of air above and below the ball is same, hence pressure difference is zero. Therefore, air exerts no upward or downward force on the ball.
(ii) **When ball is moving with spin in air,** then speed of air above and below to the ball is not same, hence, pressure difference is created due to which non-zero net force acts on the ball.

- **Magnus effect** When a ball is moving in air with spin, then due to difference in the velocities of air results in the pressure difference between the lower and upper faces and there is net upward force on the ball. This dynamic lift due to spinning is called **Magnus effect.**
- **Airofoil or lift on aircraft wing** An aircraft wing is designed, so that air moves faster over the top of the wings that it does under the wings, thus making the air pressure less on top than underneath. This difference in pressure results in a net upward lifting force on the wings.

Bernoulli's Theorem

Bernoulli's theorem is based on the law of conservation of energy and applied to ideal fluids. It states that the sum of pressure energy per unit volume, kinetic energy per unit volume and potential energy per unit volume of an incompressible, non-viscous fluid in a streamlined irrotational flow remains constant at every cross-section throughout the liquid flow. Mathematically, it can be expressed as

$$p + \frac{1}{2}\rho v^2 + \rho g h = \text{constant}$$

Bernoulli's Principle

- In streamlined flow of an incompressible and non-viscous fluid, the sum of pressure energy, kinetic energy and potential energy remain constant at each point of the flow,

$$p + \frac{1}{2}\rho v^2 + \rho g h = \text{Constant}$$

- In terms of pressure head, velocity head and gravitational head,

$$\frac{p}{\rho g} + \frac{v^2}{2g} + h = \text{Constant}$$

Speed of Efflux

- The outflow of a fluid is called efflux and the speed of the liquid coming out is called speed of efflux.

$$v = \sqrt{2gh}$$

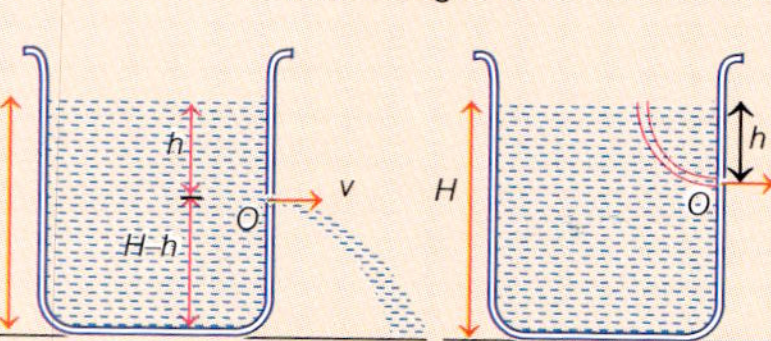

"The velocity of efflux of a liquid issuing out of an orifice is the same as it would attain, if allowed to fall freely through the vertical height between the liquid surface and orifice."

The above statement is also known as Torricelli's theorem.

- **Range** The range of liquid, i.e. the horizontal distance covered by liquid coming out of the hole is given by

$$R = 2\sqrt{h(H-h)}$$

Time taken to empty a tank is given by the formula when hole is at bottom

$$t = \frac{A}{a}\sqrt{\frac{2H}{g}}$$

Venturimeter

It is a device which is used to measure the flow speed of incompressible fluid. According to given figure, speed of fluid at wide neck is given as

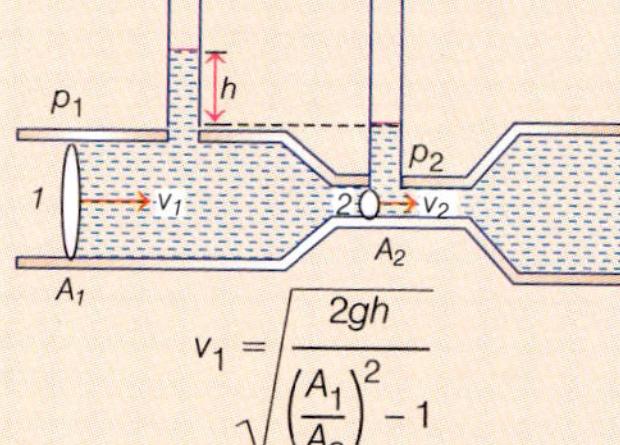

$$v_1 = \sqrt{\frac{2gh}{\left(\frac{A_1}{A_2}\right)^2 - 1}}$$

- The discharge or volume flow rate can be obtained as

$$\frac{dV}{dt} = A_1 v_1 = A_1\sqrt{\frac{2gh}{\left(\frac{A_1}{A_2}\right)^2 - 1}}$$

- The **venturi effect** can be used to give a qualitative understanding of the lift of an airplane wing and the path of a pitcher's curve ball. An airplane wing is designed, so that air moves faster over the top of the wing that it does under the wing, thus making the air pressure less on top than underneath. This difference in pressure results in a net upward lifting force on the wing.

Atomizer or Spryer

The working of an atomizer which is used to spray liquids is based on Bernoulli's principle. Figure shows that the essential parts of an atomizer. When the rubber balloon is pressed, the air rushes out of the horizontal tube B decreasing the pressure to p_2 which is less than the atmosphere pressure p_1 in the container. As a result, the liquid rises up in the vertical tube A. When it collides with the high speed air in tube B, it breaks up into a fine spray.

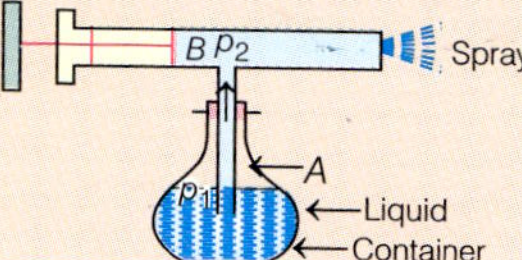

Test 3

Syllabus

- Viscosity, Stokes Law and Terminal Velocity
- Surface Tension and Energy
- Excess of Pressure in Bubbles

NCERT Page 190 to 197

For deeper insight **Scan the QR Code**

Chapter 09

Viscosity

The property of fluid by virtue of which it opposes the relative motion between its different layers.

- The SI unit of viscosity is Poiseuille (Pl). Its other units are Nsm^{-2} or Pa-s.
  According to Newton, the frictional force F (or viscous force) between two layers depends upon the following factors
  (i) Force F is directly proportional to the area of the layers in contact.
  (ii) Force F is directly proportional to the velocity gradient between the layers.
  Combining these two, we have

$$F \propto A \frac{dv}{dy}$$

$$F = \eta A \frac{dv}{dy}$$

Stoke's Law

When a small sphere of radius r is moving with v velocity inside a homogeneous fluid, then retarding viscous force acting on the sphere, $F = 6\pi\eta r v$

Terminal Velocity

The constant velocity attained by a freely falling body inside a viscous medium is called terminal velocity.

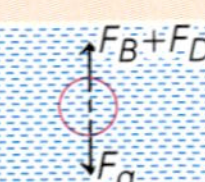

The forces acting on the sphere are
(i) weight w of the sphere acting vertically downwards.
(ii) upthrust buoyant force acting vertically upwards.
(iii) viscous force acting vertically upwards, i.e. in a direction opposite to velocity of the sphere.

$$v_t = \frac{2}{9}\frac{r^2(\rho - \sigma)g}{\eta}$$

Figure shows the variation of the velocity v of the sphere with time

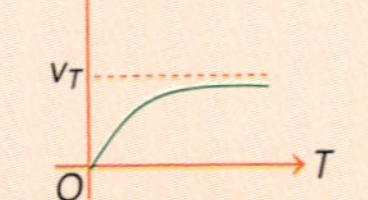

Variation of velocity of a sphere falling through a liquid, with time.

Coefficient of Viscosity

Newton found that the viscous force acts between two layers of fluid is

(i) $F \propto A$

(ii) $F \propto \frac{dv}{dz}$

Hence, $F = -\eta A \frac{dv}{dz}$; $\eta = \frac{F/A}{dv/dz}$

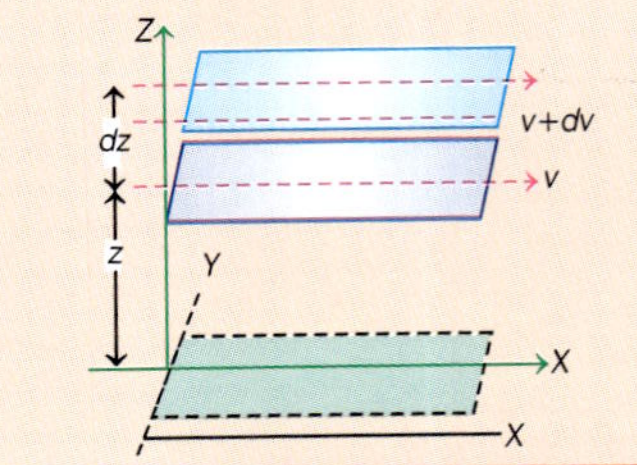

Surface Tension

It is the tending of liquid surfaces at rest to shrink into the minimum surface area possible and behaves as a streched membrane.

$$S = \frac{Fd}{2dl} = \frac{F}{2l}$$

- **Measurement of Surface Tension**
  Let an imaginary line PQ is drawn tangentially anywhere on the liquid surface. This lines divides into two parts. One side of line exert force of attraction on the other part. This is perpendicular to the line and plane of surface of liquid.
  - SI unit of surface tension is N/m and dimensional formula is $[MT^{-2}]$.
  - This is a scalar quantity (magnitude is constant and direction is not defined)
  - CGS unit of surface tension is dyne/cm.

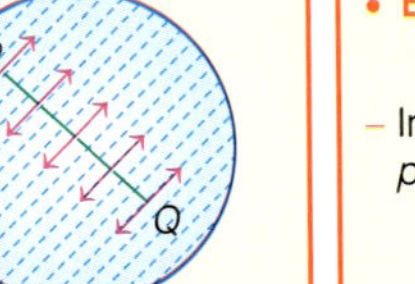

Surface Energy

At a constant temperature, the amount of work done in expanding of the area of the free surface of liquid by unity against the cohesive force called surface energy.

$$\text{Surface energy} = \frac{\text{Work done in increasing the surface area}}{\text{Increase in surface area}}$$

Factors Affecting of Surface Tension

- **Temperature**
  - Surface tension of liquids decrease with increase in temperature and attains zero value at particular temperature, called **critical temperature**
  - For small temperature differences, surface tension decreases almost linear by as $S_t = S_o(1 - \alpha t)$
- **Addition of impurities**
  Surface tension of liquid changes, with addition of impurities. Surface tension decreases in presence of contaminated substances such as dust particles on the surface of liquid.

Drops and Bubbles

- **Excess pressure**
  In equilibrium, the pressure inside a drop or bubble is more than pressure on its outer surface. Difference of these two pressures is called excess pressure.
- **Excess pressure inside a liquid drop**

$$\Delta p = \frac{2S}{R}$$

- In ordinary conditions, $p = p_0$ = Atmospheric pressure

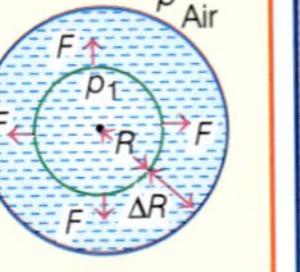

$$p_i = p + \frac{2S}{R} = p_0 + \frac{2S}{R}$$

- **Excess pressure inside a soap bubble**

$$\Delta p = \frac{4S}{R}$$

- In ordinary conditions, $p = p_0$ = Atmospheric pressure

$$p_i = p + \frac{4S}{R} = p_0 + \frac{4S}{R}$$

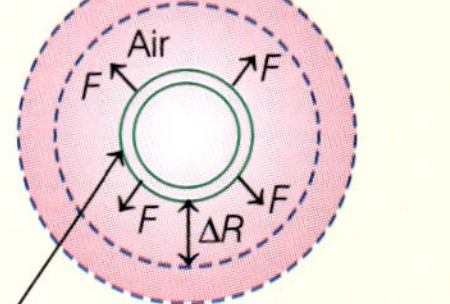

Surface Energy Density

The surface energy density of a liquid is numerically equal to the surface energy of unit surface area of a liquid.

$$T = \frac{E_S}{A} = \frac{\text{Surface energy}}{\text{Surface area}}$$

Example

Spraying of liquid results cooling, when a liquid is sprayed the large number of small drops are formed. As a result, surface area or surface energy increases. Thus, internal energy decreases, which depends on temperature.

Angle of Contact

The angle between tangent to liquid surface at the point of contact and the solid surface inside is called angle of contact (θ) of that liquid with that solid.

Liquid drop

θ

low contact angle, high surface energy

- **Value of angle of contact depend**
  - Nature of the solid and liquid in contact.
  - Cleanliness of the surface in contact.
  - Temperature of the liquid.

Liquid drop

θ

High contact angle, low surface energy

- Those liquids which wet the solid (water wets glass) have angle of contact θ < 90° (acute angle)
  - Ordinary water with glass, θ = 8°
  - Pure water with glass, θ = 0°
- Those liquid which do not wet the solid (glass and mercury) have angle of contact θ > 90° (obtuse angle).
  - Mercury with glass, θ = 135°

Glass, θ, Water

Glass, θ, Mercury

Capillarity

- The phenomena of fall or rise of liquid in a capillary narrow tube is known as capillarity.
  - When angle of contact of liquid with capillary tube is acute, then liquid rises in the capillary tube.
  - When angle of contact of liquid with capillary tube is obtuse (θ > 90°), then liquid falls in capillary tube.

Rise of liquid in a capilary tube, $h = \frac{2S\cos\theta}{r\rho g}$

Test 1

Syllabus
- Heat and Temperature
- Ideal Gas Equation and Absolute Temperature
- Thermal Expansion

NCERT Page -202 to 207

For deeper insight **Scan the QR Code**

Temperature

Temperature is the measure of degree of hotness or coldness of a body and it is the condition of body which determines the direction of heat flow.

- **Measurement of Temperature**
  - A measure of temperature is obtained using a thermometer on some specified scales. These scales commonly called unit of temperature.
  - It measure the temperature of body in Kelvin (K), degree centigrade (°C) and degree Fahrenheit (°F).
- **Graph**
  The graph of Fahrenheit temperature (T_f) *versus* celsius or centigrade temperature (T_C)
  (T_f; 212; 32; Straight Line; ΔT_c; 0; 100°C; T_c)
- **Conversion of Temperature**
  The ice and steam point of water are 32° F and 212° F, respectively on Fahrenheit scale and 0° and 100°C, respectively on Celsius scale. There are 100 equal interval between two reference points in celsius scale and 180 divisions in Fahrenheit scale.

  For Fahrenheit : $T_f = \frac{9}{5}T_c + 32$, **For Kelvin** : $T_K = T_C + 273.15$
- **Relation of Different Scales** $\frac{C}{100} = \frac{F-32}{180} = \frac{R}{80} = \frac{K-273.15}{100}$

Thermometers

The thermometers work on the thermometric property, *i.e.* the property which changes with temperature like any physical quantity such as length, volume, pressure, resistance, etc. which varies linearly with a certain range of temperature. Let X denotes the thermometric physical quantity and X_0, X_{100} and X_t be its values at 0°C, 100°C and t°C respectively. Then,

$$\text{Temperature, } t = \frac{X_t - X_0}{X_{100} - X_0} \times 100°\text{C}$$

Different types of Thermometers

Some different types of thermometers are given below

(i) Mercury thermometer In this thermometer, the length of a mercury column from some fixed point is taken as thermometric property.

$$t = \left(\frac{l_t - l_0}{l_{100} - l_0}\right) \times 100°\text{C}$$

(ii) Constant volume gas thermometer It works on the principle of change in pressure with temperature when the volume is kept constant.

$$t = \left(\frac{p_t - p_0}{p_{100} - p_0} \times 100\ °\text{C}\right)$$

Note For constant pressure gas thermometers, $t = \left(\frac{V_t - V_0}{V_{100} - V_0} \times 100°\text{C}\right)$

(iii) Platinum resistance thermometer It works on the principle of variation of resistance of metals with temperature.
In Kelvin scale, we can write $= \left(\frac{R_t}{R_{tr}} \times 273.16\ K\right)$

where, R_{tr} = resistance of wire at 273.16 K.
Here, temperature coefficient of resistance (α) is given by, $\alpha = \frac{R_{100} - R_0}{R_0 \times 100}$

Heat

Heat is the form of energy transferred between two (or more) systems or a system and its surrounding by virtue of temperature difference.

- **Transmission of Heat**
  When two bodies at different temperatures are brought in contact with each other, then heat flows from higher temperature to lower temperature. This flow of heat is called transmission of heat.
- **One Calorie**
  One calorie is equal to the amount of heat energy required to raise the temperature of one gram of water through 1°C (e.g. From 14.5°C to 15.5°C)

Ideal Gas Equation

- **Ideal Gas Equation**
  The ideal gas relationship as

  $pV = R \times (nT) \Rightarrow \frac{pV}{T} = nR$ (Constant)

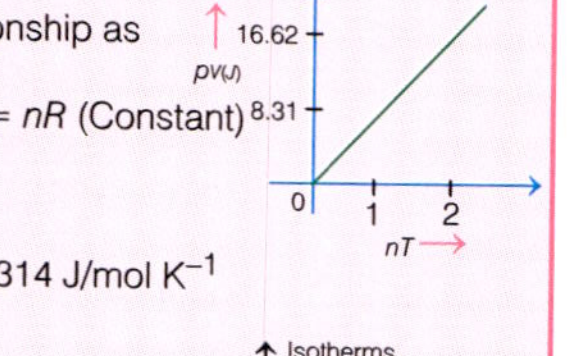

For two variables,

$\frac{p_f V_f}{T_f} = \frac{p_i V_i}{T_i}$ $\because R = 8.314$ J/mol K^{-1}

- **Boyle's Law**
  It is given by english chemist Robert Boyle.
  Here, pressure is inversely proportional to the volume at constant temperature.
  i.e., $p \propto \frac{1}{V}$

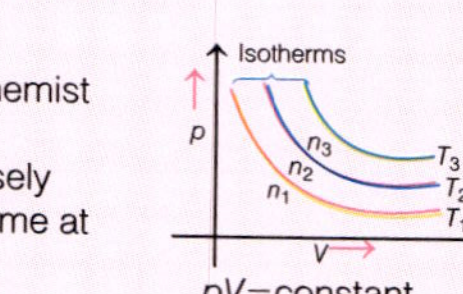

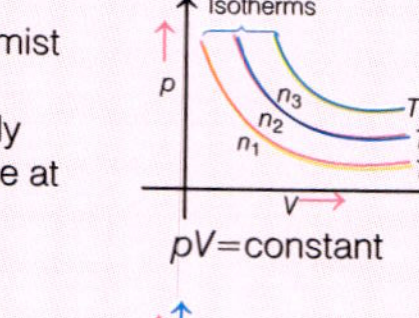

- **Charles' Law**
  It is given by French Scientist Jacques Charles. Here, volume of gas is directly proportional to the temperature at constant pressure.
  i.e., $V \propto T$

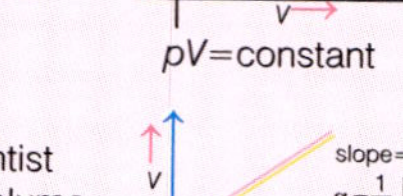

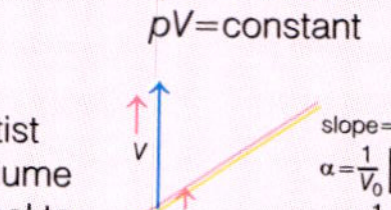

Absolute Temperature

- Theoretically, there is no limit for maximum temperature but there is a sharp point for minimum temperature called absolute temperature.
- The graph is extrapolated,– 273.15°C

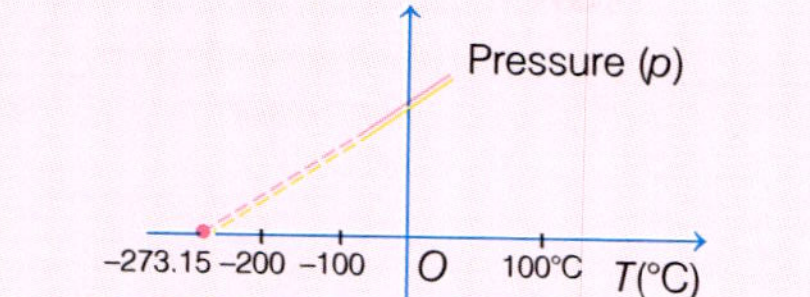

Thermal Expansion

The phenomenon of change in dimensions of an object due to heat or temperature supplied is known as thermal expansion.

Area Expansion

- The expansion in the area of surface due to increase in its temperature is called area expansion.
- Expansion in area, $A = A_0(1 + \alpha_A \Delta T)$

(A; ΔA)

Linear Expansion

- The expansion in length of a body due to increase in its temperature is called the linear expansion.
- Expansion in length, $L = L_0(1 + \alpha_l \Delta T)$

(l; Δl)

Volume Expansion

The expansion in the volume of an object due to increase in its temperature is known as volume expansion.
Expansion in volume, $V = V_0(1 + \alpha_V \Delta T)$

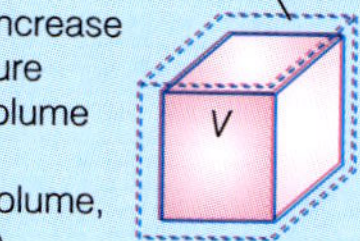

Relation among Coefficients of Expansion

- The coefficient of expansion can be given as
  $$\alpha_l = \frac{\Delta l}{l\Delta T},\ \alpha_A = \frac{\Delta A}{A\Delta T},\ \alpha_V = \frac{\Delta V}{V\Delta T}$$
- The relation among coefficient of expansion is given by
  $$\alpha_l : \alpha_A : \alpha_V = 1 : 2 : 3$$

Variation of Density with Temperature

Most of the substances expand when they are heated, *i.e.* volume of a given mass of a substance increases on heating, so the density should decrease as $\left(\text{as } \rho \propto \frac{1}{V}\right)$

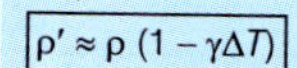

$\rho' \approx \rho\,(1 - \gamma\Delta T)$

Anomalous Expansion of Water

- Water contracts on heating between the temperature 0°C to 4°C. When water cooled below the room temperature, the volume of given amount of water decreases until its temperature reaches to 4°C and below 4°C the volume again increases.
- If temperature of the top layer of water decreases below 4°C it becomes less dense and remains at the surface.

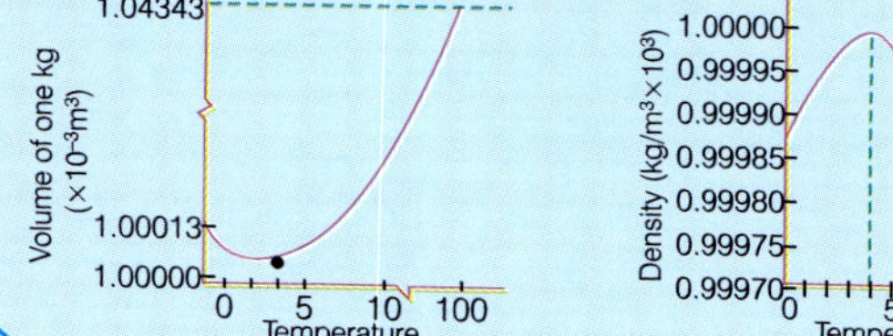

Test 2

Syllabus

- Specific Heat Capacity
- Calorimetry
- Change of State, Latent Heat
- Heat Transfer (Conduction, Convention and Radiation)

NCERT Page -208 to 218

For deeper insight **Scan the QR Code**

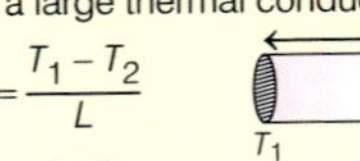

Chapter 10

Specific Heat Capacity

The amount of heat required to raise the temperature of unit mass of a substance by unity is known as specific heat capacity of the substance. It is denoted by c.

$$\text{Specific heat capicty, } c = \frac{1}{m}\frac{\Delta Q}{\Delta T}$$

$$\therefore \quad \text{Heat, } \Delta Q = mc\Delta T$$

The SI unit of specific heat capacity is $\text{Jkg}^{-1}\,\text{K}^{-1}$ and its dimensional formula is $[\text{M}^0\,\text{L}^2\,\text{T}^{-2}\,\text{K}^{-1}]$

Important points related to specific heat capacity are given below.

(i) The specific heat capacity of water is approximately 1 cal/g°C.

(ii) Specific heat capacity is the property of material and constant for a particular material.

Relation Between Heat Capacity and Specific Heat Capacity

As we know that, heat capacity, $S = \frac{\Delta Q}{\Delta T}$

As we know that, Specific heat capacity, $c = \frac{1}{m}\frac{\Delta Q}{\Delta T}$

$\therefore S = m \times c$

i.e. Heat capacity = Mass × Specific heat capacity

Change of State

The process of conversion of one state of a substance into another state is known as change of state.

- **Fusion and Melting Point** The process of change of state from solid to liquid is called **fusion**. The temperature at which solid states liquify is called melting point.
- **Freezing and Freezing Point** The process of change of state from liquid to solid is called **freezing**. The temperature at which liquid starts to freeze is known as the **freezing point**.
- **Vaporisation and Boiling Point** The process of change of state from liquid to vapour is called vaporisation. The temperature at which the liquid and the vapour states of the substance co-exist is called boiling point.
- **Sublimation** The process of change of state directly from solid to vapour is known as sublimation.
- The temperature and pressure at which all three phases of a substance co-exist simultaneously is known as the triple point.

Latent Heat

The amount of heat transferred per unit mass during the change of phase of a substance without any change in its temperature.

- $Q = mL \Rightarrow L = \frac{Q}{m}$
- Latent heat of fusion, $L_f = \frac{Q}{m}$
- Latent heat of vaporisation, $L_v = \frac{Q}{m}$
- SI unit is Jkg^{-1}
- $L_{\text{fusion of ice}} = 80$ cal/g
- $L_{\text{vapour of water}} = 540$ cal/g

Latent heat of fusion or melting It is the quantity of heat required to change the state of a substance from solid to liquid state at its melting point. It is denoted by L_f.

Latent heat of vaporisation It is the quantity of heat required to change the state of unit mass of a substance from liquid to vapour state at its boiling point. It is denoted by L_v.

Heat Capacity

The amount of heat needed to change the temperature by unity i.e., 1°C, it is denoted by S and SI unit JK^{-1}

$$\text{Heat capacity, } S = \frac{\Delta Q}{\Delta T}$$

Heating Curve

The graph between temperature and time is called heating curve. Suppose, the heat is supplied to the solid at constant rate P, then a graph is plotted between temperature and time as shown below.

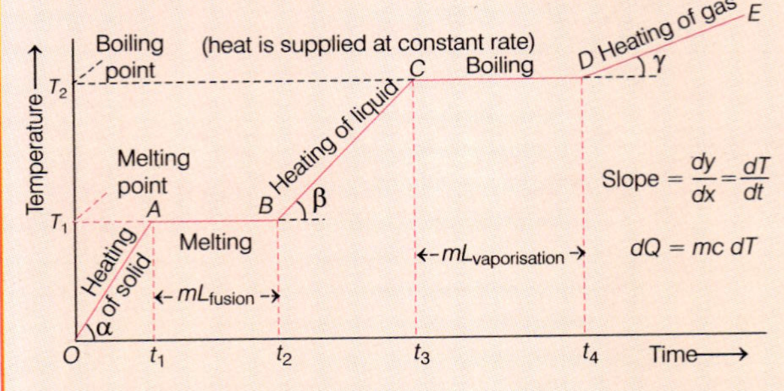

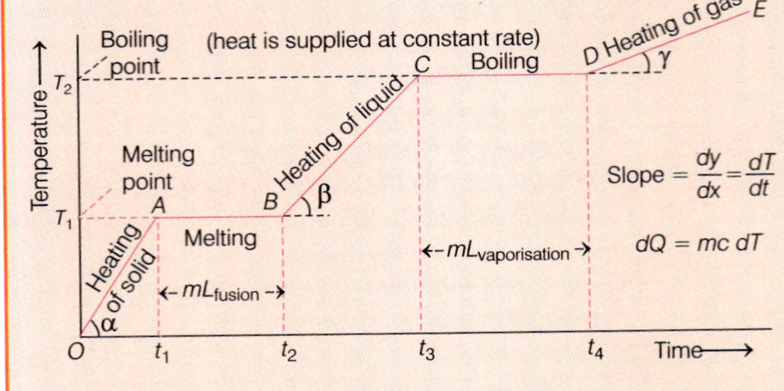

Calorimetry

The branch of physics that deals with the measurement of heat is called calorimetry.

- **Principle of Calorimetry** The principle of calorimetry states that total heat lost by the hotter body equals to the total heat gained by the colder body, provided there is no exchange of heat with the surroundings. i.e.

Heat lost by hotter body = Heat gained by colder body

The principle of calorimetry is based on the law of conservation of energy.

Heat lost by first body = Heat gained by second body

$$\Rightarrow \quad m_1c_1(T_1 - T) = m_2c_2(T - T_2)$$

$\therefore$ Common temperature of the mixture at equilibrium, $T = \frac{m_1c_1T_1 + m_2c_2T_2}{m_1c_1 + m_2c_2}$

Water Equivalent of a Substance

Water equivalent of an object is the amount of water that absorbs or gives out the same amount of heat as is done by the substance when heated or cooled through same temperature difference as that of object. To attain the same temperature as that of water, the calorimeter gains some heat.

Water equivalent of an object = Mass of the object × Specific heat of material of object

or $\quad W = mc$

Water equivalent is usually expressed in gram.

Heat Transfer

- **Conduction** The transfer of heat taking place due to molecular vibration (i.e., molecular collisions).
- **Thermal conductivity** The ability of material to conduct the heat through it is known as thermal conductivity.

$$\text{Heat transfer, } Q = KA\frac{\Delta T}{L}t$$

- **Convection** Convection is the process in which heat is transferred from one point to another by the actual motion of matter from a region of higher to lower temperature. e.g. Land breeze, sea breeze.
- **Radiation** A mode of transfer of heat from one place to another without heating the intervening medium. Heat transferred by thermal radiation.

Rate of Heat Transfer and Temperature Gradient

When a quantity of heat Q is transferred through the rod in a time t, the rate of heat flow is

$$H = \frac{Q}{t} = KA\frac{dT}{dx}$$

SI unit of temperature gradient is Km^{-1} or $°\text{Cm}^{-1}$.

Thermal conductivity The constant K (in the above expression) is called the thermal conductivity, which is a measure of the ability of a material to conduct heat. A substance with a large thermal conductivity K is a

$$\frac{dT}{dx} = \frac{T_1 - T_2}{L}$$

Therefore, the heat ΔQ transferred in time Δt is

$$\Delta Q = KA\left(\frac{T_1 - T_2}{L}\right)\Delta t$$

The SI unit of K is $\text{Js}^{-1}\,\text{m}^{-1}\text{K}^{-1}$ or $\text{Wm}^{-1}\,\text{K}^{-1}$ and its dimensions are $[\text{MLT}^{-3}\text{K}^{-1}]$.

Thermal Resistance

Heat flow rate is analogous to flow of electric current. Relation of electric current and potential difference is,

$$I = \frac{V_1 - V_2}{R} = \frac{V_1 - V_2}{l\rho}A = \frac{\sigma A}{l}(V_2 - V_1)$$

$$\text{Heat current, } H = \frac{Q}{t} = \frac{T_1 - T_2}{(l/KA)}$$

Thermal resistance $R_{th} = \frac{l}{KA}$

We can also use the analogy to find equivalent resistance to heat flow.

For series combination of slabs, $R_{eq} = R_1 + R_2 + \ldots = \frac{l_1}{K_1A} + \frac{l_2}{K_2A} + \ldots$

And for parallel combination, $\frac{1}{R_{eq}} = \frac{K_1A}{l_1} + \frac{K_2A}{l_2} + \ldots$

Test 1

Syllabus
- Thermal Equilibrium and Zeroth Law of Thermodynamics
- Concept of Temperature, Heat, Work and Internal Energy
- First Law of Thermodynamics

NCERT Page -226 to 230

For deeper insight **Scan the QR Code**

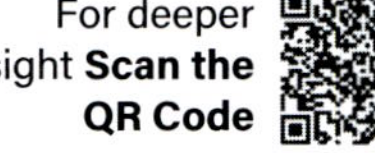

Chapter 11

Thermodynamic System

- Thermodynamic system is an assembly of an extremely large number of particles, so that the assembly has a certain value of pressure, volume and temperature.
- There are three types of thermodynamic systems, which are open system, closed system and isolated system.

(i) **Open System** It exchanges both heat (or energy) and matter with its surroundings.

Matter (in or out)
Container without lid and with conducting walls
Heat (in or out)

(ii) **Closed System** It exchanges only heat (or energy), but no matter with its surroundings.

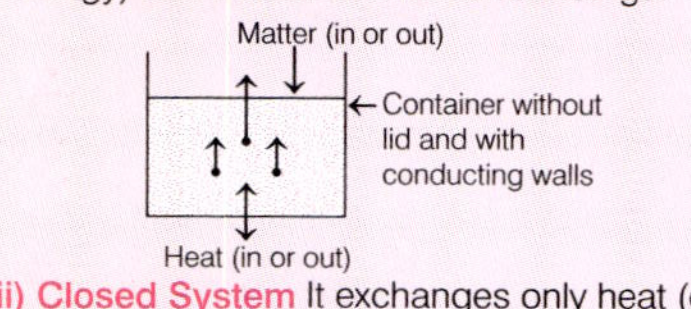

(iii) **Isolated System** It exchanges neither heat (or energy) nor matter with its surroundings.

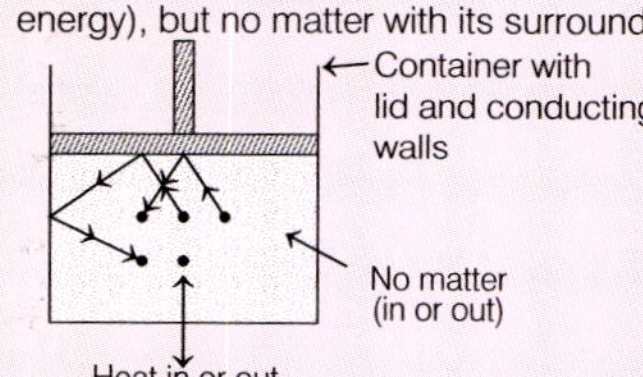

Thermodynamic or State Variables

- The quantities like pressure (p), volume (V) and temperature (T) which help us to completely specify state of thermodynamic system are called thermodynamic variables. Thermodynamic variables may be extensive or intensive in nature.
- **Extensive Variables** Extensive variables are those which depends on the size of the system. e.g. Internal energy U, volume V and total mass M are extensive variables
- **Intensive Variables** Intensive variables are those which do not depend on the size of the system. e.g. pressure p, temperature T and density ρ are intensive variables.

Equation of State

The equation which represents the relationship between the state variables of a system is called its equation of state. e.g. For an ideal gas, the equation of state is $pV = nRT$.

Thermodynamic Terms

- **Thermodynamic Process**
  When state of a system changes, then thermodynamic variables associated with the system like pressure p, volume V and temperature T also changes. This process is known as thermodynamic process.
- **Thermal Equilibrium**
  Two systems are said to be in thermal equilibrium, if there is no net flow of heat between them when they are brought into thermal contact.
- **Adiabatic and Diathermic Wall**
  Adiabatic wall is an insulating wall between two thermodynamic systems which does not allow flow of energy (or heat) from one system to another system. Diathermic wall is a conducting wall between two thermodynamic systems which allows energy flow (or heat) from one system to another system.

Concept of Temperature

Temperature is the measure of hotness or coldness expressed in terms of any arbitrary scale and indicating the spontaneous flow of heat energy.

Zeroth Law of Thermodynamics

The Zeroth law of thermodynamics states that, if two systems A and B are separately in thermal equilibrium with a third system C, then A and B are in thermal equilibrium with each other.

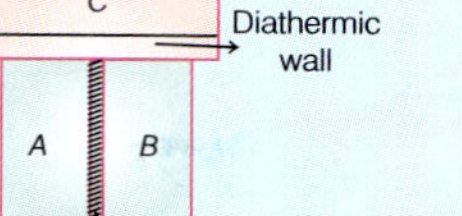

Hence, from Zeroth law, if systems A and B are separately in thermal equilibrium with C, then

$$T_A = T_C \text{ and } T_B = T_C \Rightarrow T_A = T_B$$

So, systems A and B will also be in thermal equilibrium with each other.

Thermodynamic Equilibrium

When macroscopic variables (like pressure, volume, temperature, mass, composition, etc.) that characterise the system do not change with time, then system is said to be in thermodynamic equilibrium.

Heat

- The energy that exchanged between a system and its surrounding because of the temperature difference between them.
- SI unit of heat is joule.

Internal Energy

- Energy due to the configuration and motion of the molecules of thermodynamical system is called internal energy.
- **Internal Kinetic Energy U_K** This is due to the motion of molecules.
- **Internal Potential Energy U_P** This is due to the configuration of molecules.

Thus, total internal energy, $U = U_K + U_P$

First Law of Thermodynamics

First law of thermodynamics is a statement of conservation of energy. It states that, if some quantity of heat is supplied to a system capable of doing external work, then the quantity of heat absorbed by the system is equal to the sum of the increase in the internal energy of the system and the external work done by the system.

i.e. Heat supplied, $\Delta Q = \Delta U + \Delta W$

Thermodynamics Sign Conventions

Process	Convention
Heat added to the system	$\Delta Q > 0$, i.e. positive
Heat removed from the system	$\Delta Q < 0$, i.e. negative
Work done by the system (volume increases)	$\Delta W > 0$, i.e. positive
Work done on the system (volume decreases)	$\Delta W < 0$, i.e. negative
When temperature of the system rises	$\Delta U > 0$, i.e. positive
When temperature of the system falls	$\Delta U < 0$, i.e. negative

Work

- By work, we mean work done by the system or on the system.
- Work done, $W = \int_{V_i}^{V_f} dW = \int_{V_i}^{V_f} p\,dV$
- If system expands, $V_f > V_i$ i.e., W = positive
- If system contracts, $V_f < V_i$ i.e., W = negative

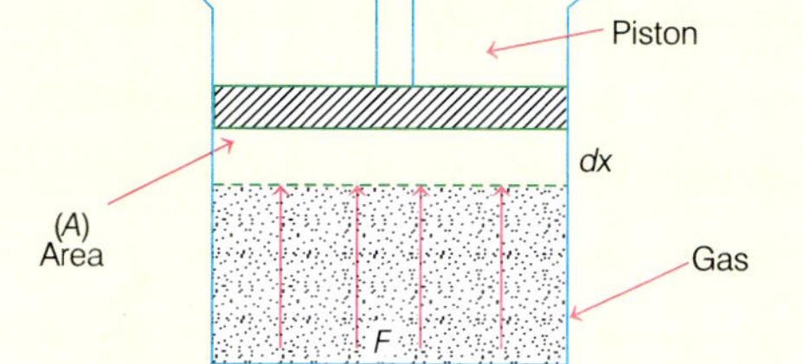
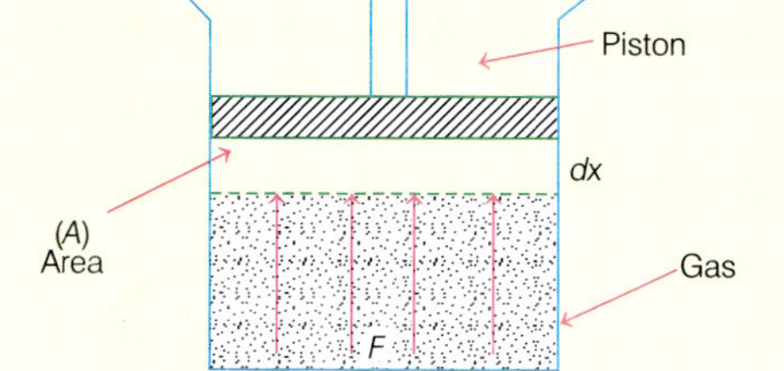

Internal Energy of an Ideal Gas

- There are no molecular forces of attraction, so that the intermolecular forces are zero and gas does not posseses intermolecular potential energy. Thus, $U = U_K + U_P$; $U_P = 0$, $U = U_K$

Internal Energy of Real Gases

- Intermolecular forces are not negligible.
- The molecules of real gas exert mutual force of attraction on one another, thus internal energy of real gas is less than the ideal gas under the same conditions.

Applications of First Law of Thermodynamics

Applications of first law of thermodynamics are given below

- **Melting Process** When a substance melts, the change in volume (dV) is very small and can be neglected. The temperature of the substance remains unchanged during melting process. Heat absorbed during melting process,
$$\Delta Q = mL = \Delta U$$
- **Boiling Point** When a liquid is heated, it changes into vapour at constant temperature (called boiling point) and pressure. U_L = Internal energy of liquid, U_V = Internal energy of vapour
$$mL = (U_v - U_l) + p(V_v - V_l)$$

Limitations of First Law of Thermodynamics

- First law does not indicate direction of heat transfer.
- It does not state conditions under which heat can be transformed into work (or *vice-versa*).
- It does not indicate that total heat cannot be converted completely into work.

Test 2

Syllabus
- Thermodynamic Processes : Isothermal and Adiabatic Processes
- Second Law of Thermodynamics : Reversible and Irreversible Process

NCERT Page -233 to 237

For deeper insight **Scan the QR Code**

Chapter 11

Specific Heat Capacity

The amount of heat required to change the temperature of unit mass of a substance by unity. $s = \frac{1}{m}\left(\frac{\Delta Q}{\Delta T}\right)$

Specific Heat Capacity of Water

- The amount of heat required to raise the temperature of one gram of water by one degree centigrade.
- The specific heat of water varies slightly with temperature.

Molar Specific Heat Capacity

- Heat capacity per mole is known as molar specific heat capacity.

$$c = \frac{s}{n} = \frac{1}{n}\left(\frac{\Delta Q}{\Delta T}\right)$$

- SI unit of molar specific heat capacity is J/mol-K

Relation Between C_p and C_V

- For an ideal gas, the relation between C_p and C_V is given as,

$$C_p - C_V = R$$

This is called **Mayer's formula**.

- The ratio of C_p and C_V is notified by γ.

i.e., $\gamma = C_p/C_V$

Here, $C_p = \left(\frac{\Delta Q}{\Delta T}\right)_p$ and $C_V = \left(\frac{\Delta Q}{\Delta T}\right)_V$

Quasi-Static Process

- A hypothetical process in which at every stage the system remains in equilibrium.
- Practically, a process that are sufficiently slow are consider as quasi-static process.

Isothermal Process

- That process in which temperature of a thermodynamical system remains constant.

Example Melting of ice (or any solid) at melting point.

- **p-V Diagram**
Follows Boyle's law, $p_iV_i = p_fV_f$
Thus, pV = constant

- **Work done**
– Work done = Area under p-V graph

$$W_{iso} = 2.303\, nRT \log\left(\frac{V_f}{V_i}\right)$$

– If $V_f > V_i$, then $W > 0$ (Isothermal expansion)
– If $V_f < V_i$, then $W < 0$ (Isothermal compression)

- **V-T graph** Temperature of the gas remains constant during isothermal process.

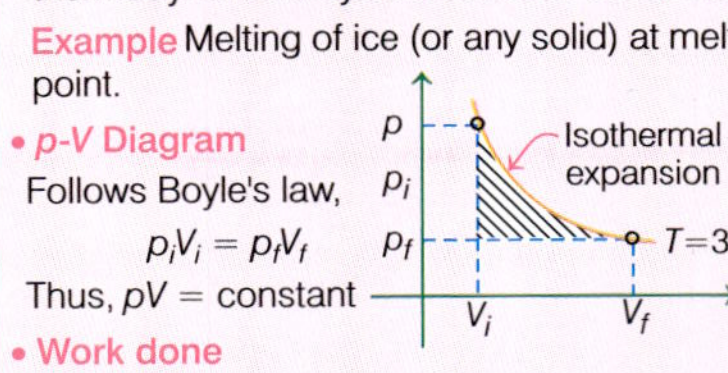

Slope $= \frac{dV}{dT} = \infty$

- **p-T graph** Similar to V-T graph, p-T graph is parallel to p-axis.

Slope $= \frac{dp}{dT} = \infty$

- **Slope of p-V graph** For isothermal process pV = constant

Slope of graph $= -\tan\phi$

$$= \frac{dp}{dV} = -\frac{p}{V}$$

- **Specific and Molar Heat Capacity** During isothermal process, $\Delta T = 0$

$\therefore$ Specific heat capacity, $s = \frac{\Delta Q}{m\Delta T} = \frac{\Delta Q}{m(0)} = \infty$

$\therefore$ Molar heat capacity, $C_{iso} = \frac{\Delta Q}{n\Delta T} = \infty$

Isochoric Process

- Volume of the system remains constant. If heat added to system, its pressure increase and if heat extracted, pressure will be reduced.
- Work done, $\Delta W = 0$
- Change in internal energy, $\Delta U = nC_V\Delta T$
- **p-T graph** For isochoric process, $\frac{p}{T}$ = constant.
- **V-T graph** In isochoric process, volume remains constant. So, pressure changes resulting in change of temperature as shown below.

Slope $= \frac{dV}{dT} = 0$

Work done as volume remains constant,
i.e. $V = \text{constant} \Rightarrow \Delta V = 0$
$\therefore$ Work done, $\Delta W = p\Delta V = 0$

First Law of Thermodynamics for Isochoric Process
For isochoric process, $\Delta Q = nC_V\Delta T$
From first law of thermodynamics, we get
$$\Delta Q = \Delta U + \Delta W$$
As (for isochoric process), $\Delta Q = nC_V\Delta T = 0$
For one mole of a gas,
$n = 1 \Rightarrow \Delta Q = C_V\Delta T = \Delta U$

Second Law of Thermodynamics

Second law of thermodynamics may be stated in various ways, but two statements are worth mentioning which are as follows

- **Kelvin-Planck Statement** No process is possible which can completely convert heat absorbed from a reservoir into work.
- **Clausius Statement** No process is possible which can transfer heat from a cold body to a hot body without doing any external work.
- According to IInd law the state of entropy of the entire universe, as an isolated system, will always increase over time. Mathematically, this law is represented as

$$\Delta S_{uni} > 0$$

where, ΔS_{uni} is the change in the entropy of the universe.

Adiabatic Process

- The process, in which there is no exchange of heat between system and surrounding take place.

- **p-V Diagram**
From first law of thermodyamics,
$$\Delta Q = \Delta U + \Delta W$$
– Adiabatic process, pV^γ = Constant
Thus, $p_iV_i^\gamma = p_fV_f^\gamma$

- **Work done**
– Work done in an adiabatic process,

$$W = \int_{V_i}^{V_f} p\,dV = \int_{V_i}^{V_f} \frac{K}{V^\gamma}\,dV$$

– Work done, $W = \frac{nR(T_i - T_f)}{\gamma - 1}$

- **V-T graph** In adiabatic process with increase in temperature, volume decreases exponentially as shown in figure.

$TV^{\gamma-1}$ = constant

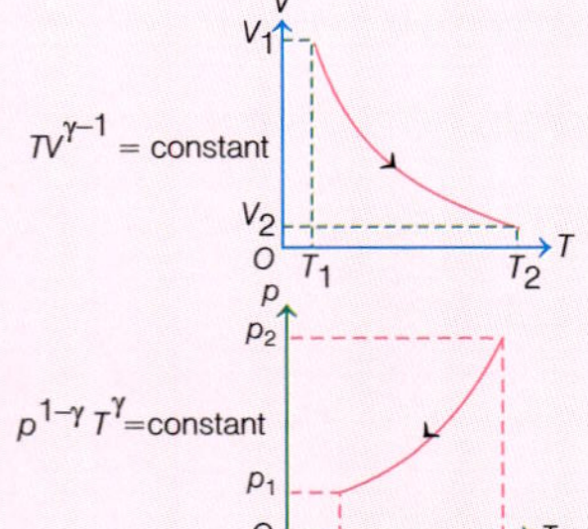

- **p-T graph** For adiabatic process with decrease in temperature, pressure decreases as shown in figure.

$p^{1-\gamma}T^\gamma$ = constant

Isobaric Process

- Pressure of the system remains constant.
- Work done, $W = nR(T_f - T_i)$
- As temperature of gas changes, so its internal energy also changes.

Graphs Graphs related to isobaric process are given in figure.

- **p-V graph** In an isobaric process, pressure of the gas remains constant. Therefore, p-V graph associated with this process is a straight line parallel to X-axis (having slope, $\frac{dp}{dV} = 0$) as shown below.

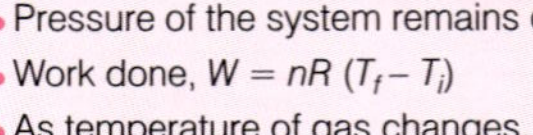
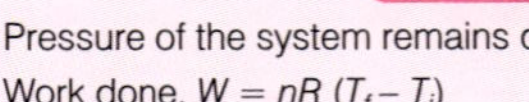
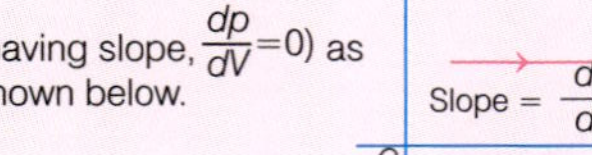

Slope $= \frac{dp}{dV} = 0$ — Isobaric expansion

Slope $= \frac{dp}{dV} = 0$ — Isobaric compression

- **V-T graph** In isobaric process, $\frac{V}{T}$ = constant

$\therefore$ $V \propto T$

i.e. V-T graph is a straight line passing through origin as shown in figure.

Slope of the V-T graph, $\tan\theta = \frac{V}{T} = \frac{nR}{p}$ = constant

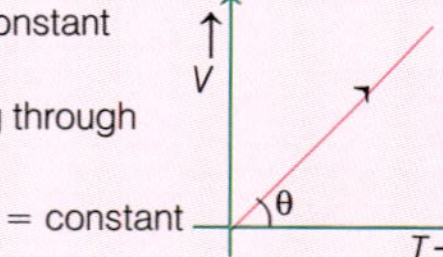

Test 1

Syllabus
- Equation of State of a Perfect Gas and Work Done on Compressing a Gas
- Kinetic Theory of Gases-Assumptions, Concept of Pressure
- Kinetic Interpretation of Temperature
- RMS Speed of Gas Molecules and Avagadro's Hypothesis

NCERT Page 246 to 251

For deeper insight **Scan the QR Code**

Chapter 12

Pressure of an Ideal Gas

- The force exerted by the gas molecules on unit area of the walls of container is called pressure of gas.
- Impulse = Change in momentum

$$F\Delta t = \Delta p_x = -2mv_x$$

- Average force exerted,

$$F = -\frac{2mv_x}{\Delta t} = \frac{(-2mv_x)}{\left(\frac{2l}{v_x}\right)}, F = -\frac{mv_x^2}{l}$$

- Pressure of an ideal gas, $p = \frac{1}{3}\frac{mn}{V}v_{rms}^2$

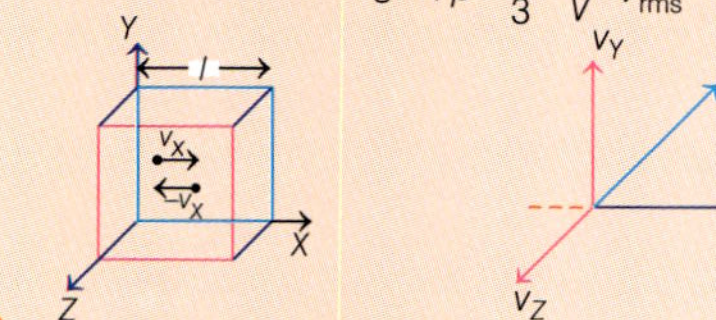

Behaviour of Real Gas and Ideal Gas

- A real gas behaves as an ideal gas most closely at low pressure and high temperature.

$$pV = \mu RT \Rightarrow \frac{pV}{\mu T} = R$$

- Behaviour of real gas approach ideal gas at low pressure

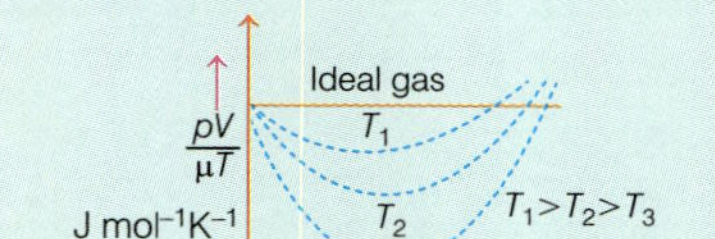

Avogadro's Hypothesis

- Equal volumes of all gases under identical conditions of pressure and temperature will contain equal number of molecules.
- Avogadro's number, $N_A = 6.023 \times 10^{23}$ mol^{-1}
- Density, $\rho = \frac{PM_0}{RT}$

Dalton's Law of Partial Pressure

- Total pressure of mixture of non-interacting ideal gases is equal to the sum of partial pressure exerted by individual gases in the mixture.

$$p = p_1 + p_2 + p_3 + \dots$$

Work done on Compressing a Gas

It is the amount of energy added to the system when its volume is reduced.

$$W = -p\Delta V$$

The negative sign in the formula ensures that the sign of the work is consistent with the convention that when a gas expands it does work on its environment and losses energy.

The work done on compressing a gas can also be referred as strain volume or pV. The work done on compressing a gas can be shown under three processes:

- **Isothermal Compression** When the gas cooled with a coolent stream while packed in a blower.
- **Adiabatic Compression** When there is no cooling, the gas temperature increases as the force increases.
- **Polytropic Compression** When temperature increases as heat is removed so specific heat is negative.

Behaviour of Gases

- In a gas, molecules are far from each other and their mutual interactions are negligible except when two molecules collide.
- Gases at low pressures and high temperatures, much above that at which they liquify satisfy $pV = Nk_BT$, observation tells that k_B is same for all gases.
- **For different gases**

$$\frac{p_1V_1}{N_1T_1} = \frac{p_2V_2}{N_2T_2} = \frac{p_3V_3}{N_3T_3} \dots = k_B = \text{constant.}$$

Boltzmann's constant,

$$k_B = 1.38 \times 10^{-23} \text{ J/K}$$

Boyle's Law

- According to this law, at constant temperature, volume of definite quantity of a gas is inversely proportional to its pressure (p).

Therefore, $V \propto \frac{1}{p}$ (constant temperature)

$$p_1V_1 = p_2V_2 = \text{Constant}$$

- p-V curve for temperatures T_1 and T_2 is as shown in figure.

T_1 T_2 $T_2>T_1$ p V→

Atomic Hypothesis

All things are made of atoms. The atoms are little particles that moves around in perpetual motion, attracting each other when they are a little distance apart, but repelling upon being squeezed into another.

Internal Energy of Gases

- **Monoatomic Gases**
  Total internal energy of one mole of monoatomic gas, $U = \frac{3}{2}RT$
- **Diatomic Gases**
  Total internal energy of one mole of diatomic gas, $U = \frac{5}{2}RT$
- **Triatomic Gases**
  Total internal energy of one triatomic linear gas is $\frac{7}{2}RT$
- **Solids**
  Total internal energy of one mole of solid, $U = 3RT$

Kinetic Theory of an Ideal Gas

A gas which obeys all gaseous laws under all conditions of pressure and temperature is called ideal gas.

Charles' Law

- According to this law, at constant pressure, volume of definite quantity of a gas is directly proportional to absolute temperature (T) of the gases. Therefore, $V \propto T$ (constant pressure)

$$\frac{V_1}{T_1} = \frac{V_2}{T_2} = \text{constant and } V_t = V_0\left(\frac{273 + t}{273}\right)$$

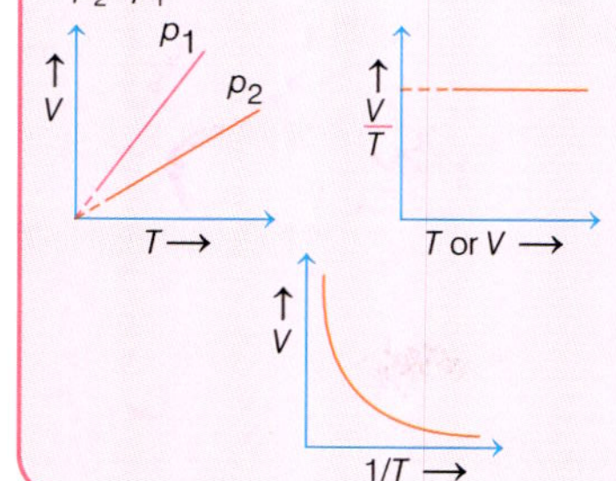

Kinetic Interpretation of Temperature

- In kinetic theory, the kinetic interpretation of temperature states that the average kinetic energy of the gas molecules of an ideal gas is directly proportional to absolute temperature of the molecules.
- Molecular arrangements in solids, liquids and gases.

Solid Liquid Gas

Average Speed

This is equal to average of the speed of molecules

i.e., $v_{av} = \frac{v_1 + v_2 + \dots + v_n}{n}$

- The relation among most probable speed, average speed and rms speed is given by

$$v_{mp} : v_{av} : v_{rms} = \sqrt{\frac{2RT}{M}} : \sqrt{\frac{8RT}{\pi M}} : \sqrt{\frac{3RT}{M}}$$

Assumption of Kinetic Theory of Gases

- The density and the distribution of molecules is uniform throughout the gas.
- There is no intermolecular forces between molecules of gas except during collision.
- Specific heat capacities C_p and C_V of an ideal gas do not depend on the temperature.

Root Mean Square Speed

This speed is equal to the square root of the mean value of square of the velocities.

$$v_{rms} = \sqrt{\left(\frac{v_1^2 + v_2^2 + v_3^2 + \dots v_n^2}{n}\right)}$$

Most Probable Speed

The speed with which most of the molecules move is called most probable speed.

$$v_{mp} = \sqrt{\frac{2RT}{M}} = \left(\sqrt{\frac{2}{3}}\right) v_{rms} = 0.816\, v_{rms}$$

Concept of Temperature

- **Relation between temperature and rms speed** $\frac{1}{3}Mv_{rms}^2 = RT \Rightarrow v_{rms} = \sqrt{\frac{3RT}{M}}$
- Temperature of gas is directly proportional to square root mean square velocity.
- **Relation between temperature and molecular kinetic energy**

$$E = \frac{3}{2}kT$$

Gay-Lussac's Law

- At constant volume, pressure of a definite quantity of gas is directly proportional to absolute temperature.
- Therefore, $p \propto T$ $\frac{p_1}{T_1} = \frac{p_2}{T_2}$ and $p_t = p_0 + p_0 \times \frac{t}{273}$

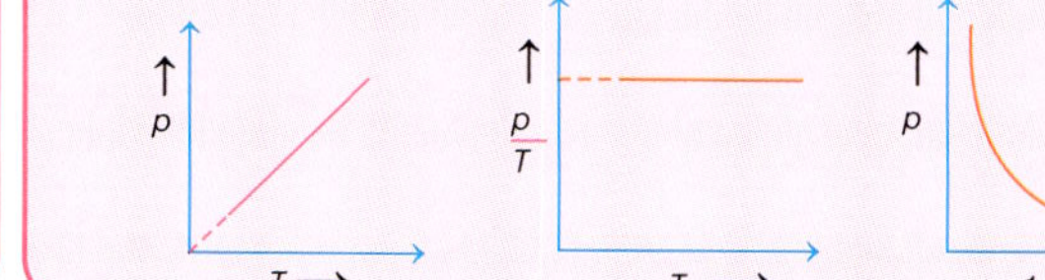
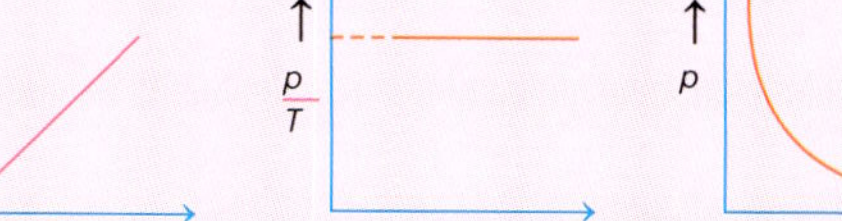

Test 2

Syllabus
- Degree of Freedom
- Law of Equipartition of Energy
- Applications of Specific Heat of Gases
- Mean Free Path

NCERT Page 252 to 255

For deeper insight **Scan the QR Code**

Chapter 12

Degree of Freedom

Total number of condition or coordinates or independent quantities required to completely describe the position and configuration of a dynamical system.

Degree of freedom, $f = 3N - k$

- **For monoatomic gas**, such as helium, neon, argon, have translational degree of freedom.
  If $N = 1$ and $k = 0$, then $f = 3 \times 1 - 0 = 3$
- **For diatomic gas**, such as oxygen, hydrogen, nitrogen etc.
  $\therefore \quad f = 5$
- **For triatomic gas**, such as H_2S, SO_2 have translational degree of freedom.
  $f = 5$(for linear), $f = 6$ (for non-linear)

At very high temperature (~ 5000 K), gas molecules have two additional degree of freedom due to vibration along bond. When two-bonded atoms vibrate, then their PE and KE changes, this accounts for two additional degree of freedom.

Degree of freedom of diatomic or triatomic linear gas molecule at high temperature = 7.

Note Degree of freedom for different gases can also be given by the formula, $f = 3N - k$

where, N = number of particles in the system

and K = number of independent relations between the particles

Degree of Freedom of different gases

Atomicity of gas	Transitional	Rotational	Total	Representation
Monoatomic, e.g. Ar, Ne, ideal gas, etc.	3	0	3	Y, X, Z
Diatomic, e.g. O_2, Cl_2, N_2, etc.	3	2	5	
Triatomic (linear), e.g. CO_2, C_2H_2, etc.	3	2	5	O=C=O
Triatomic (Non-linear) or Polyatomic, e.g. H_2O, NH_3, CH_4, etc.	3	3	6	

Specific Heat Capacity

The amount of heat required to change the temperature of unit mass of a substance by unity is known as specific heat capacity of the substance.

Specific heat capacity, $s = \frac{S}{m} = \frac{1}{m}\frac{\Delta Q}{\Delta T}$

It depends on the nature of substance and its temperature. Its unit J/kg-K.

Molar Specific Heat Capacity

- The amount of heat required to raise the temperature of one gram mole of a substance by unity is called molar specific heat capacity of the substance.
- Heat capacity per mole is known as molar specific heat capacity or molar heat capacity, $C = \frac{S}{n} = \frac{1}{n}\left(\frac{\Delta Q}{\Delta T}\right)$

(i) Molar heat capacity at constant pressure $C_p = \left(\frac{\Delta Q}{n\Delta T}\right)_{\text{constant pressure}}$

(i) Molar heat capacity at constant volume $C_V = \left(\frac{\Delta Q}{n\Delta T}\right)_{\text{constant volume}}$

Relation between C_p and C_V

For an ideal gas, the relation between C_p and C_V is

$$C_p - C_V = R$$

– This relation is known as **Mayer's formula.**
– The ratio of C_p and C_V is notified by γ. Therefore, $\gamma = \frac{C_p}{C_V}$
– It is known as heat capacity ratio.

From the above two relation between C_p and C_V, we get

$$C_V = \frac{R}{\gamma - 1} \text{ and } C_p = \frac{\gamma R}{\gamma - 1}$$

The ratio in terms of degrees of freedom is $\gamma = 1 + \frac{2}{f}$

Values of C_V, C_p and γ

Atomicity of gas	f	C_V	C_p	γ
Monoatomic	3	$\frac{3}{2}R$	$\frac{5}{2}R$	$\frac{5}{3} = 1.67$
Diatomic, and Triatomic linear (at normal temperature)	5	$\frac{5}{2}R$	$\frac{7}{2}R$	$\frac{7}{5} = 1.4$
Poly atomic and triangular (Non-linear)	6	$\frac{6}{2}R = 3R$	$\frac{8}{2}R = 4R$	$\frac{4}{3} = 1.33$

For n moles of a gas, internal energy at temperature T is

$$U = \frac{nfRT}{2} \text{ and } U = nC_VT$$

Change in internal energy is given by $\Delta U = nC_V\Delta T$

Law of Equipartition of Energy

- For a dynamic system in thermal equilibrium, the total energy is distributed equally amongst all the degree of freedom and the energy associated with each molecule per degree of freedom is (1/2) k_BT.
- Translational energy of monoatomic, $\langle E_t \rangle = (3/2)\, k_B T$.

  Internal energy, $U = \frac{n}{2} f_R T$.

Equipartition of Energy of gas

Types of gas	f	Translational energy of one molecule	Internal energy of one molecule
Monoatomic gas	3	$\frac{3}{2}k_BT$	$\frac{3}{2}RT$
Diatomic gas			
(a) excluding vibration	5	$\frac{5}{2}k_BT$	$\frac{5}{2}RT$
(b) including vibration	7	$\frac{7}{2}k_BT$	$\frac{7}{2}RT$
Polyatomic gas like CO_2H_2O	6	$\frac{6}{2}k_BT = 3k_BT$	$\frac{6}{2}RT = 3RT$

- **Different energies of a system of degree of freedom are as follows**

(i) Total energy associated with each molecule $= \frac{f}{2}k_BT$

(ii) Total energy associated with N-molecule $= \frac{f}{2}Nk_BT$

(iii) Total energy associated with 1 mole $= \frac{f}{2}RT$

(iv) Total energy associated with μ moles $= \frac{f}{2}\mu RT$

(v) Total energy associated with each gram $= \frac{f}{2}\frac{RT}{M}$

(vi) Total energy associated with m gram $= \frac{f}{2}\frac{mRT}{M}$
where, M is molecular mass.

Mean Free Path

- The average distance travelled by a molecule between two successive collisions is known as the mean free path of the molecule.
- Mean free path, $\lambda = \frac{1}{\sqrt{2}n\pi d^2}$

  Here,
  d = diameter of each molecule and
  n = number of molecules per unit volume.
- The mean free path in gases is of the order of thousands of angstroms.

Test 1

Syllabus
- Periodic and Oscillatory Motion
- Simple Harmonic Motion & Its Characteristics

NCERT Page 260 to 267

For deeper insight **Scan the QR Code**

Chapter 13

Amplitude and Phase

- **Amplitude** (A) The maximum displacement of particle from its mean position is defined as amplitude.
- **Phase** (ϕ) Time varying quantity, which can fully describe displacement and velocity of particle is called phase. Its unit is radian.

In the given graph, two SHM having same amplitude A and same angular frequency ω are shown.

Their phase angle ϕ are different. A phase difference of 2π radian corresponds to a path difference of 1 wavelength.

Angular frequency (ω)

The rate of change of phase angle of particles (executing SHM) with respect to time is called angular frequency. Its unit is radian/second.

Angular frequency,

$$\omega = \frac{2\pi}{\text{Time period } (T)} = 2\pi \times \text{Frequency } (n)$$

Restoring Force

- The force which tend to bring the particle to its equilibrium position when particle is displaced from its equilibrium position is called restoring force.
- In equilibrium position, value of restoring force is zero.

Period and Frequency

- The smallest interval of time after which a periodic motion is repeated is called its **period**.

Examples
- Period of revolution of the planet mercury is 88 earth days.
- Period of vibration of a quartz crystal is expressed in units of microsecond (10^{-6}), i.e. μs.
- The number of oscillations per unit is called **frequency**. The relation between frequency and period is given by $\text{Frequency} = \frac{1}{\text{Period}}$

Periodic Motion

- When a particle (or a body) moves, along a definite path such that it repeats its motion after a definite time interval, motion is called periodic motion.
- If $y(t)$ is the displacement of particle, then $y(t) = y(t + T) = y(t + 2T) = \ldots$

Examples
- Rotational motion of the earth about its own axis.
- Motion of the earth about the sun in an elliptical orbit.

Periodic Function

- The function which repeats its value in regular interval of time or period is called periodic function
  $f(t) = A \cos \omega t$ (cosine function)
  $f(t) = A \sin \omega t$ (sine function)
  Also, $f(t) = A \sin \omega t + B \cos \omega t$
- Any periodic function can be expressed as a superposition of sine and cosine function of different time period with suitable coefficient.

F-x and a-x Graphs

In SHM, $F = -kx$ or $a = -\omega^2 x$, i.e. F-x graph or a-x graph is a straight line passing through the origin with negative slope. The corresponding graphs are shown below.

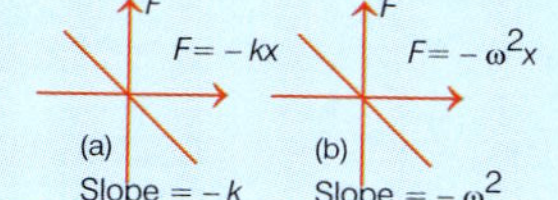

Displacement

- Change in position of a particle with respect to origin but in oscillation, we use term displacement as the change in position with respect to mean position or reference point.

Examples
- Consider a block is attached to a spring at one of its end, the other end of which is fixed to rigid wall. Genenally, it is convenient to measure the displacement variable as the block from mean position of the oscillation with time

(System of spring-block)

Oscillatory Motion

- In periodic motion in which a particle (or object) undergoes back and forth or to and fro motion about a definite point along the same path is called oscillatory or vibratory motion.

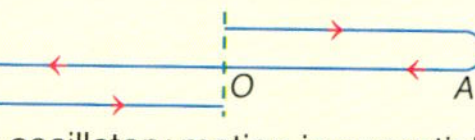

- Each oscillatory motion is essentially a periodic motion but each periodic motion is not essentially oscillatory.

Examples
- Motion of piston of an engine.
- Motion of molecules in solids.

Simple Harmonic Motion

- If a particle undergoes a motion to and fro about a fixed point (equilibrium position) such that
  - Motion remains along a straight line.
  - Force or acceleration acting on the particle must always be directed towards equilibrium position.
  - In SHM, if force acting on the particle is F and its displacement is y, then $F \propto -y$ or $F = -ky$

Equations of SHM

The motion of a particle executing SHM can be expressed by the following equations $x(t) = A \cos(\omega t + \phi)$ $y(t) = A \sin(\omega t + \phi)$

- **Equation of SHM** The particle executing simple harmonic motion oscillates such that its force is always directed towards the mean position and magnitude of force is proportional to the displacement of the particle from mean position.

This is the equation governing motion of the particle in SHM

Solution of equation $\frac{d^2x}{dt^2} + \omega^2 x = 0$ gives value of displacement x. The displacement of a particle executing SHM at any instant (t) is given by $x = A \sin(\omega t + \phi)$ or $x = A \cos(\omega t + \phi)$ Here, A = amplitude,

SHM and Uniform Circular Motion

When a particle is moving with uniform speed on the circumference of circle, then the motion of the foot of perpendicular dropped from the position of particle on any diameter along the diameter is simple hamonic motion.

Curves in S.H.M

- **Time-displacement equation**
  $y = A \sin \omega t$

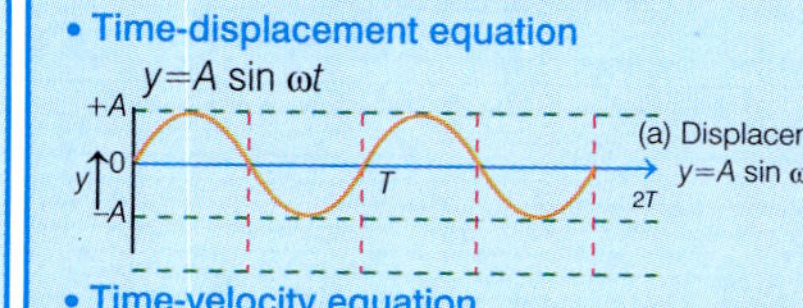

- **Time-velocity equation**
  $v = \frac{dy}{dt} = A\omega \cos \omega t$

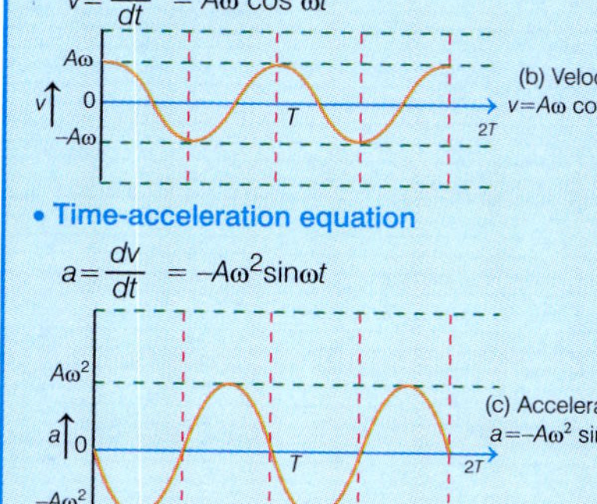

- **Time-acceleration equation**
  $a = \frac{dv}{dt} = -A\omega^2 \sin \omega t$

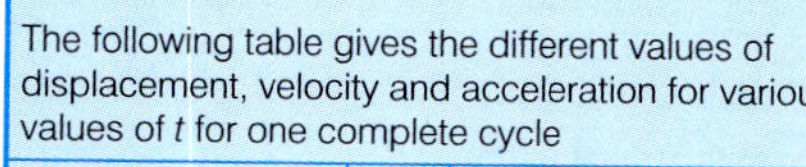

The following table gives the different values of displacement, velocity and acceleration for various values of t for one complete cycle

Time, (t)	0	$T/4$	$T/2$	$3T/2$	T
Phase angle, (ωt)	0	π	$\pi/2$	$3\pi/2$	2π
Displacement, $x(t)$	$+A$ (max)	0 (min)	$-A$ (max)	0 (min)	$+A$ (max)
Velocity $v(t)$	0 (min)	$-\omega A$ (max)	0 (min)	$+\omega A$ (max)	0 (min)
Acceleration $a(t)$	$-\omega^2 A$ (max)	0 (min)	$+\omega^2 A$ (max)	0 (min)	$-\omega^2 A$ (max)

Characteristics of SHM

- **Amplitude** The maximum displacement of particle executing SHM.
- **Phase** Phase of a oscillating particle is that quantity which refers to the position and direction of motion of the particle at that instant. $y = A \cos(\omega t + \phi)$, where ϕ is phase difference.
- **Velocity** At any instant, the rate of change of displacement with respect to time of particle executing SHM is known as its velocity.
  $$v = \omega \sqrt{A^2 - x^2}$$
  - At mean position, $x = 0$, $v = \omega A$
  - At extreme position, $x = A$, $v = 0$ (Minimum velocity), $v(t) = -\omega A \sin(\omega t + \phi)$
- **Acceleration** At any instant, the rate of change of velocity with respect to time of particle executing SHM is known as acceleration.
  $$a = -\omega^2 x$$
  - At mean position, $x = 0$, $a = 0$
  - At extreme position, $x = A$, $a = -\omega^2 A$, $a(t) = -\omega^2 A \cos(\omega t + \phi)$

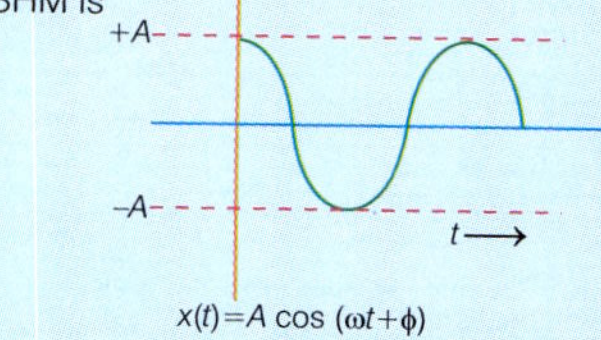

Test 2

Syllabus
- Force Law for Simple Harmonic Motion
- Energy in Simple Harmonic Motion

NCERT Page 267 to 269

For deeper insight **Scan the QR Code**

Chapter 13

Force Law for Simple Harmonic Motion

The force acting on a particle of mass in SHM is given as

$$F(t) = ma = -m\omega^2 x(t)$$

i.e. $F(t) = -kx(t)$

where, $k = m\omega^2$

$\Rightarrow$ $\omega = \sqrt{\frac{k}{m}}$

- Force is always directed towards the mean position, hence it is sometimes called the **restoring force in SHM.**
- When a particle oscillating under such a force which is linearly proportional to displacement then it is called linear harmonic oscillator.
- When a linear simple harmonic oscillator consisting of a block of mass attached to a spring is pulled or pushed and released it starts oscillating back and forth about its equilibrium position under the action of a restoring force.

$$F = -kx, \text{ where } k = \text{spring constant}$$

- Stiff springs have high value of k, while soft springs have low value of k.
- Kinetic energy *versus* time equation can also be written as

$$K = \frac{1}{2} mA^2\omega^2 [1 - \cos^2 (\omega t + \phi)]$$

This function is also periodic with angular frequency 2ω. Thus, kinetic energy in SHM is also periodic with double the frequency, then that of x, v and a. But these oscillations are not simple harmonic in nature, because d^2K/dt^2 is not proportional to $-K$.

Average Kinetic and Potential Energy

The average kinetic energy in one time period is equal to average potential energy in one time period for a body executing SHM and is given by

$$\langle KE\rangle = \langle PE\rangle = \frac{1}{4} m\omega^2 A^2$$

where m, ω and A are mass of the body, angular frequency and amplitude of SHM, respectively.

Energy in SHM

The particle executing SHM has both types of energy: **potential energy** and **kinetic energy**. When a body is displaced from its equilibrium position by doing work upon it, the body acquires potential energy. However, when the body is released, it begins to move back with a velocity, thus acquiring kinetic energy.

Kinetic Energy

The relation for kinetic energy of a particle executing SHM can be expressed in two forms, i.e. in terms of displacement and in terms of time.

(i) Kinetic energy in terms of displacement If mass of the particle executing SHM is m and its displacement at any instant is x, then

$$KE = \frac{1}{2} m\omega^2 (A^2 - x^2)$$

where, A = amplitude of SHM.

As, $\omega = \sqrt{\frac{k}{m}} \Rightarrow \omega^2 = k/m$

$\therefore$ $KE = \frac{1}{2} k(A^2 - x^2)$

Special Cases

- Kinetic energy is maximum at mean position, i.e. at $x = 0$, $KE_{max} = \frac{1}{2} m\omega^2 A^2$
- Kinetic energy is minimum or zero at extreme position, i.e. at $x = \pm A$, KE_{min} = zero

(ii) Kinetic energy in terms of time Kinetic energy of a particle executing SHM at any time t is given by

$$KE = \frac{1}{2} m\omega^2 A^2 \cos^2 \omega t$$

i.e. Kinetic energy of a particle executing SHM is a periodic function of time. Kinetic energy *versus* time graph is given below

Kinetic energy; KE_{max}; $KE_{max} = \frac{1}{2} m\omega^2 A^2$; 0; $\frac{T}{4}$; $\frac{T}{2}$; $\frac{3T}{4}$; T; Time $(t) \rightarrow$

From the above graph, it is clear that at $t = 0, T/2, T$, etc., kinetic energy has its maximum value.

For $x = \pm A$ or $t = \frac{T}{4}, \frac{3T}{4}$, the kinetic energy has its minimum value.

Clearly, twice in each cycle, kinetic energy acquire its peak values. It is a periodic function of time, where the time period equals to $T/2$.

Potential Energy

The relation for potential energy of a particle executing SHM in terms of displacement and in terms of time are as follows

(i) Potential energy in terms of displacement If the displacement of particle executing SHM at any instant is x, then

$$\text{Potential energy, } U = \frac{1}{2} m\omega^2 x^2 = \frac{1}{2} kx^2$$

- **Special cases**

Potential energy is maximum at extreme position, i.e. at $x = \pm A$

$$U_{max} = \frac{1}{2} m\omega^2 A^2$$

Potential energy is minimum (zero) at mean position, i.e. at $x = 0$,

$$U_{min} = 0$$

(ii) Potential energy in terms of time Potential energy of a particle executing SHM at any time t is given by $U = \frac{1}{2} m\omega^2 A^2 \sin^2 \omega t$

Potential energy *versus* time graph is given below

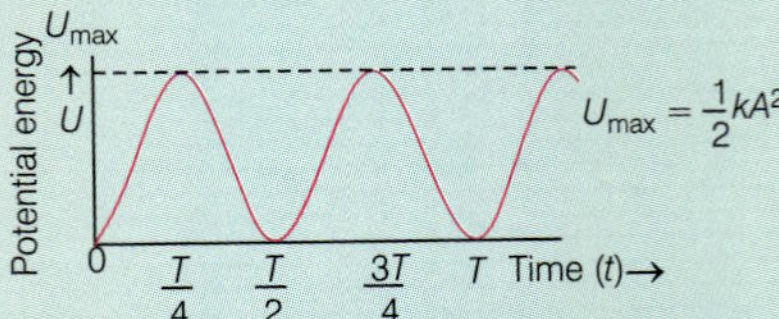

From the graph, it is clear that at mean position (i.e. $x = 0$ or $t = 0, T/2, T$), potential energy is minimum and at extreme position (i.e. $x = \pm A$ or $t = T/4, 3T/4$), its value is maximum. Clearly, twice in each cycle, potential energy acquires its peak values.

Hence, the potential energy is the periodic function of time with a period of $T/2$.

Note

- The frequency of oscillation of potential energy and kinetic energy is twice as that of displacement or velocity or acceleration
- The average value of kinetic energy and potential energy is

$$K_{av} = U_{av} = \frac{1}{2} E = \frac{1}{4} kA^2$$

Total Energy

Total energy can be obtained by adding potential and kinetic energies. Therefore,

$$E = K + U = \frac{1}{2} m\omega^2 (A^2 - x^2) + \frac{1}{2} m\omega^2 x^2$$

$$E = \frac{1}{2} m\omega^2 A^2 \text{ or } E = \frac{1}{2} kA^2$$

which is a constant quantity, i.e. it remains same at all instant and at all displacement.

Figure shows the variation of kinetic energy (K), potential energy (U) and total energy (E) as a function of time [shown in Fig. (a)] and displacement [shown in Fig. (b)] for a particle executing SHM.

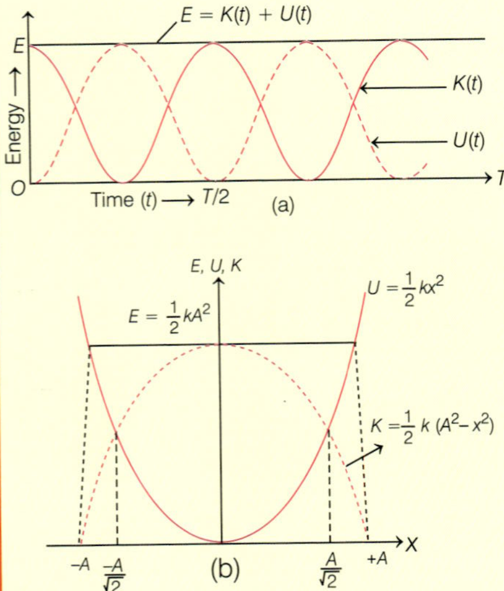

Result concluded from the graph

(i) The total energy remains constant at all t or x. So, it is shown by straight line parallel to time.

(ii) Also, $U = \frac{1}{2} kx^2$ and $K = \frac{1}{2} k(A^2 - x^2)$, so the graphs of U and K *versus* x are parabolic.

(iii) Both kinetic energy and potential energy reach maximum value twice, during each period of SHM.

(iv) In the course of motion, kinetic energy increases at the expense of potential energy or *vice-versa*. Therefore, we may say that during an oscillation, there is a continuous exchange of kinetic and potential energies.

Test 3

Syllabus
- Simple Pendulum
- Spring - Mass System
- Some Other Systems Executing Simple Harmonic Motion

NCERT Page 270 to 271

For deeper insight **Scan the QR Code**

Chapter 13

Simple Pendulum

- If a point mass is suspended with a massless, inextensible and perfectly flexible string from a rigid support, the arrangement is called simple pendulum.
- Restoring force acting on the bob, $F = -mg\sin\theta$
- If θ is very small, $F = -mg\dfrac{x}{L}$
- Acceleration of bob, $a = \dfrac{F}{m} = -\dfrac{gx}{L}$
- Time period, $T = 2\pi\sqrt{\dfrac{L}{g}}$
- **Effective Length**
  Time period of pendulum depend on its effective length $T \propto \sqrt{L}$ or $T^2 \propto L$

The time period of a simple pendulum of length l, when

(i) it is suspended from the roof of a vehicle, which moves without friction down an inclined plane of inclination θ, then time period is given by

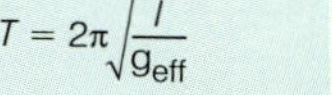

$$T = 2\pi\sqrt{\frac{l}{g_{eff}}}$$

where, $g_{eff} = g\cos\theta$

(ii) Its bob of density ρ is immersed in a liquid of density σ, then time period is given by

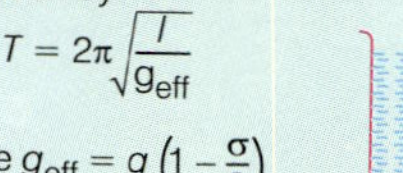

$$T = 2\pi\sqrt{\frac{l}{g_{eff}}}$$

where $g_{eff} = g\left(1 - \dfrac{\sigma}{\rho}\right)$

Density of liquid $= \sigma$

Density of bob $= \rho$

(iii) It is suspended from the roof of a lift, which moves vertically upward or downward with acceleration 'a', then time period is given by

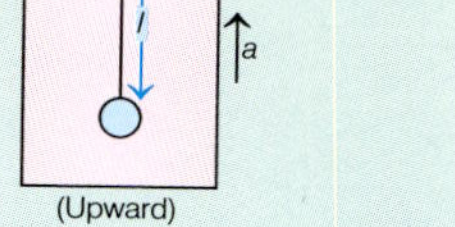

(Upward)

$$T = 2\pi\sqrt{\frac{l}{g_{eff}}}$$

where, $g_{eff} = (g + a)$

(Downward)

$$T = 2\pi\sqrt{\frac{l}{g_{eff}}}$$

where, $g_{eff} = (g - a)$

Time Period of Simple Pendulum in Different Situations

- Small angle approximation $\sin\theta = \theta$ is valid upto $\theta \le 14°$ or 0.24 radians.
  For small angular displacements, $\sin\theta \approx \theta$ and time period of oscillation is,
  $$T = 2\pi\sqrt{\frac{l}{g}}$$
- If a simple pendulum is in a lift which is accelerating upwards with acceleration a, then time period of simple pendulum,
  $$T = 2\pi\sqrt{\frac{l}{g+a}}$$
  time period will decrease.
- If a simple pendulum is in a lift which is accelerating downwards with acceleration a, then time period of simple pendulum,
  $$T = 2\pi\sqrt{\frac{l}{g-a}}$$
  i.e., time period will increase.
- If a simple pendulum is in a car which is accelerating horizontally with acceleration a, then time period of pendulum will be
  $$T = 2\pi\sqrt{\frac{l}{g_{eff}}}$$
  where, $g_{eff} = \sqrt{g^2 + a^2}$ i.e., time period will decrease.
  In this case, equilibrium position will not be vertical but will make an angle $\theta = -\tan^{-1}(a/g)$ to the vertical in a direction opposite to the acceleration.

Second Pendulum

If the time period of a simple pendulum is 2 second, it is called second pendulum.
Time period of second pendulum, T

$$T = 2s = 2\pi\sqrt{\frac{l}{g}}$$

As, on the earth's surface, $g = 9.8\ \text{ms}^{-2} \approx \pi^2\text{ms}^{-2}$

$\therefore$ The length of second pendulum on earth's surface is 1 m.

Cases of Equivalent Spring

If the length of spring of spring constant k is made n times, then its effective spring constant $k' = k/n$ and time period becomes, $T' = \sqrt{n}T$

If the spring of spring constant k into n equal parts, the spring constant of each part,

$$k' = nk$$

Time period of each spring $T' = \dfrac{T}{\sqrt{n}}$

Spring Block System

- Let a particle of mass m is executing SHM with angular frequency ω, then
- Acceleration of the body, $a = \dfrac{F}{m}$ or $a = -\omega^2 x$
- Time period, $T = 2\pi\sqrt{\dfrac{m}{k}}$

If two masses m_1 and m_2 are connected by a spring of spring constant k and made to oscillate on horizontal surface. Then, time period is given by

$$T = 2\pi\sqrt{\frac{\mu}{k}}$$

Two blocks connected by a spring

Here, μ = reduced mass $= \dfrac{m_1 m_2}{m_1 + m_2}$

In vertical Plane

- Net force acting on the body at a distance x,
  $F = F_2 + mg = -k(l + x) + kl$
- Acceleration of body, $a = \dfrac{F}{m} = -\dfrac{k}{m}x$

Time period, $T = 2\pi\sqrt{\dfrac{m}{k}}$

Oscillations of Spring Combination

- **Series Combination**
  Two springs of spring constants k_1 and k_2 are joined in series as shown in figure.

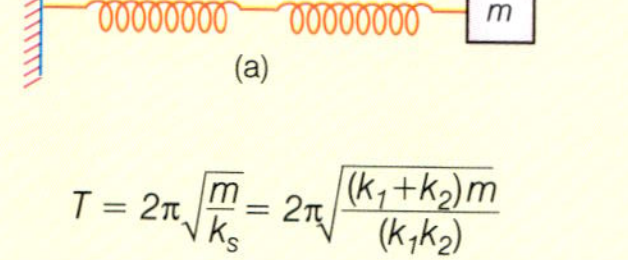

$$T = 2\pi\sqrt{\frac{m}{k_s}} = 2\pi\sqrt{\frac{(k_1+k_2)m}{(k_1k_2)}}$$

Series combination of springs

- **Parallel Combination**
  Two springs of spring constants k_1 and k_2 are joined in parallel as shown in figure.

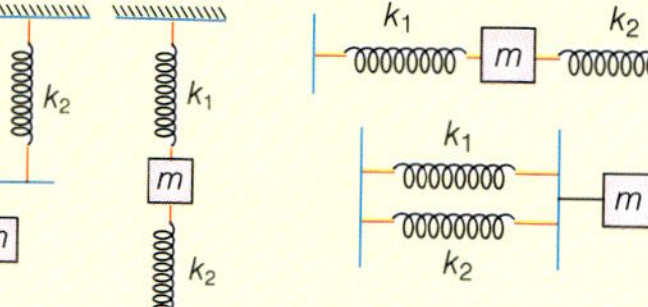

Parallel Combination of Springs

Then, spring constant, $k_p = (k_1 + k_2)$

Time period, $T = 2\pi\sqrt{\dfrac{m}{k_p}} = 2\pi\sqrt{\dfrac{m}{k_1+k_2}}$

(i) If the length of the spring is made n times, then the effective force constant becomes $1/n$ times and the time period becomes $\sqrt{n}$ times.

(ii) If a spring of spring constant k is divided into n equal parts, the spring constant of each part becomes nk and time period becomes $\dfrac{1}{\sqrt{n}}$ times.

(iii) The force constant of a stiffer spring is more than that of a soft spring.

(iv) Spring constant

$$\propto \frac{1}{\text{Extension}} \propto \frac{1}{\text{Length of spring}}$$

(v) If a spring is cut into two parts of lengths l_1 and l_2 such that $l_1 = nl_2$, then

$$\frac{k_1}{k_2} = \frac{1}{n}$$

Test 1

Syllabus
- Longitudinal and Transverse Waves
- Speed of Travelling Waves

NCERT Page 278 to 281

For deeper insight **Scan the QR Code**

Chapter 14

Definition of Waves

Wave is that disturbance produced in a medium (or vacuum) in which energy and momentum propagates without transport of the particles of medium.

Electromagnetic Waves

Those waves which do not require any medium for their propagation are called electromagnetic or inelastic waves.

Example : Visible light, ultraviolet, heat waves etc.

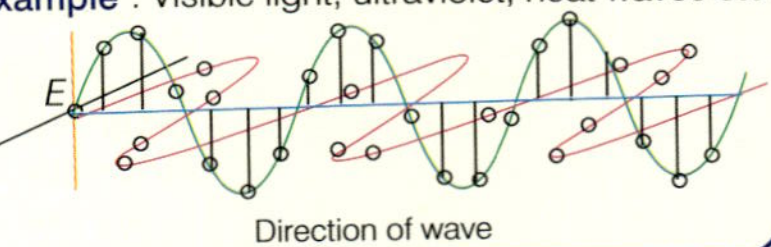

Mechanical Waves

- The waves which require medium for their propagation are called mechanical or elastic waves.
  Example : Sound waves, seismic waves, water waves, etc. Direction of wave
- A wave is a disturbance that transfers energy and momentum from one point to another in space or in a medium.
- Waves can be mechanical waves that requires a medium to travel or can be non-mechanical which does not require any medium for propagation.
- A travelling pulse or a wave that causes medium particles to oscillate perpendicular to the direction of propagation of wave is a transverse wave.

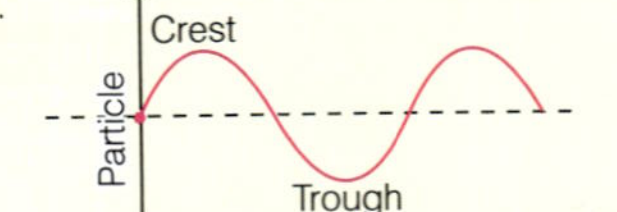

- A longitudinal wave causes compressions and rarefactions in layers of medium by oscillating particles along the direction of travel of wave.

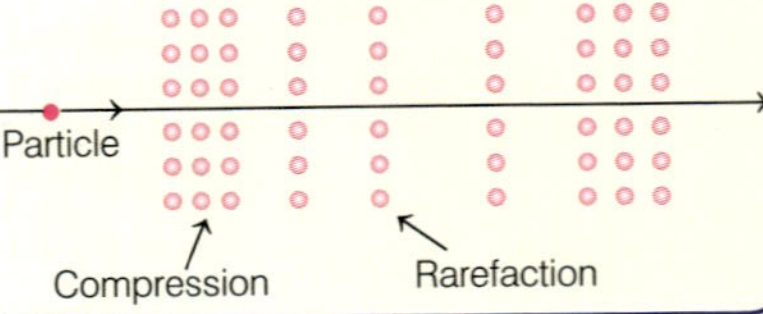

Displacement in Progressive Waves

- Displacement, $y(x, t) = a \sin(kx - \omega t + \phi)$
  $y(x, t) = A \sin(kx - \omega t) + B \cos(kx - \omega t)$
  where, $a = \sqrt{A^2 + B^2}$ and $\phi = \tan^{-1}(B/A)$
- The wave travelling in the negative direction of X-axis, $y(x, t) = a \sin(kx + \omega t + \phi)$

Amplitude

Maximum displacement of a particle from their equilibrium position, as a wave pass through them is known as amplitude.

Time Period

Time taken by a particle of medium to complete its one vibration during the propagation.

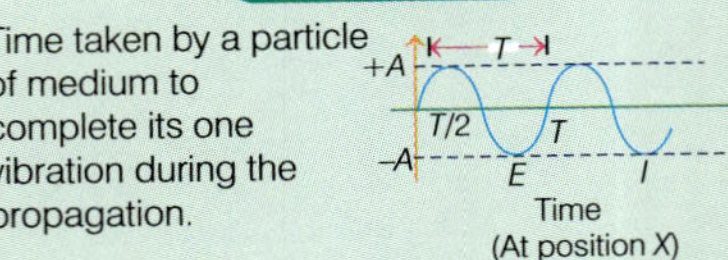

Frequency

Number of vibrations that a particle of medium completes in one second during the wave propagation.

$$f = \frac{1}{\text{Time period } (T)}$$

Phase

Physical quantity which refers to the position and direction of the motion of the particle at an instant during the propagation.

Wavelength

Distance travelled by a wave during one time period is called wavelength.

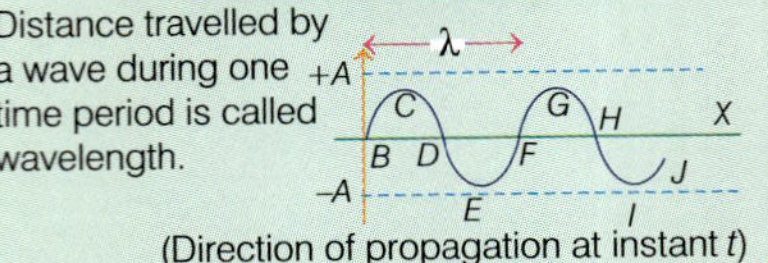

Matter Waves

- These types of waves are associated with microscopic particles i.e., electron, proton and other fundamental particles.
- These waves represent the wave like nature of a moving particle.

Transverse Waves

When particle of a medium vibrate perpendicular to the direction of propagation of wave, the wave is called transverse wave.

Examples : Waves produced in strings of musical instrument, visible light, etc.

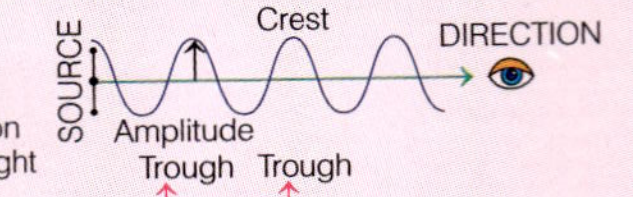

Speed of a Transverse Wave on a Stretched String Speed of transverse wave over a string is a function of (i) the linear mass density or mass per unit length (m) and (ii) tension (T).

It is given by $v = \sqrt{\frac{T}{\mu}}$

This speed is independent of frequency of wave.

Longitudinal Waves

When particles of medium vibrate in the direction of propagation of wave, the wave is called longitudinal wave.

Examples : Spring waves, sound waves, etc.

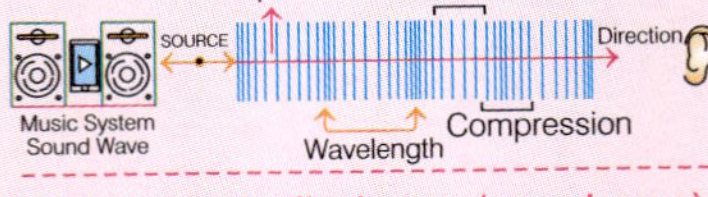

Speed of a longitudinal wave (sound wave) in a medium

Speed of longitudinal waves in a medium,

$$v = \sqrt{\frac{B}{\rho}}$$

where, bulk modulus of the medium, $B = \frac{\Delta p}{\Delta V/V}$

Sound Waves

Sound is a form of energy which produces a sensation of hearing in our ears.

Sound waves in air are of longitudinal nature.

(i) **Infrasonic waves** Longitudinal waves having frequencies below 20 Hz are called infrasonic waves. They cannot be heard by human beings.

(ii) **Audible waves** Longitudinal waves having frequencies lying between 20-20000 Hz are called audible waves.

(iii) **Ultrasonic waves** Longitudinal waves having frequencies above 20000 Hz are called ultrasonic waves. They are produced and heard by bats. They have a large energy content.

Media for Transverse Waves

- The particles motion is perpendicular to the direction of propagation of the wave. As the wave propagates, each element of the medium undergoes a shearing strain.
- Here, propagated only in those media which can sustain shearing stress, such as solids and surface of liquids but not gases and inside liquids.

Media for Longitudinal Waves

- In a medium like a steel bar, both transverse and longitudinal waves can propagate while air can sustain only longitudinal waves.
- Waves may be one-dimensional, two dimensional or three dimensional. Mode of dimension will be according to the propagation of energy in one, two and three dimensions.

Factors Affecting the Speed of Sound in Air

The following factors affect the speed of sound in air (or gas)

- **Effect of Temperature**
  Speed of sound in air is proportional to square root of absolute temperature.

$$\Rightarrow \quad v \propto \sqrt{T}$$

$$\text{or} \quad \frac{v_1}{v_2} = \sqrt{\frac{T_1}{T_2}}$$

- **Effect of Pressure**
  The speed of sound in a gas, $v = \sqrt{\frac{\gamma p}{\rho}}$

  From this formula, it appears that $v \propto \sqrt{p}$. But actually it is not so because

  $\frac{p}{\rho} = \frac{RT}{M}$ = constant at constant temperature.

Speed of sound, v vs Pressure, p (graph with origin O)

Hence, if the temperature of a gas remains constant, then there is no effect of pressure change on the speed of sound in the gas.

- **Effect of Humidity**
  The density of moist air (i.e. air mixed with water vapour) is less than the density of dry air. It is clear from the formula, $v = \sqrt{\gamma p/\rho}$ that the speed of sound in moist air is slightly greater than that in dry air.
  So, speed of sound increases with increase in humidity.
- **Effect of Frequency**
  The speed of sound in air is independent of its frequency. Sound waves of different frequencies travel with the same speed in air but their wavelengths in air are different.

Test 2

Syllabus
- Displacement Relation for Progressive Wave
- Beats
- Principal of Superposition of Waves
- Reflection of Waves- Standing Waves

NCERT Page 281 to 289 Page 293

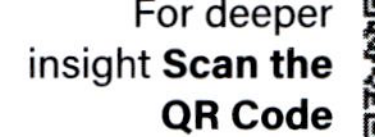

For deeper insight **Scan the QR Code**

Chapter 14

Progressive or Travelling Wave

- When a source of disturbance agitates a medium and energy as well as momentum is distributed or dissipated across the medium, a wave is produced.
- Wave carries energy and momentum from source to another point across medium. In propagation of a wave, medium particles are oscillating either transversely or longitudinally. Displacement of a particle is a function of its position and time. It can be represented as,
$$y(x, t) = f(x \pm vt)$$
- The function y is called wave function which depends only on position of particle x and time t.

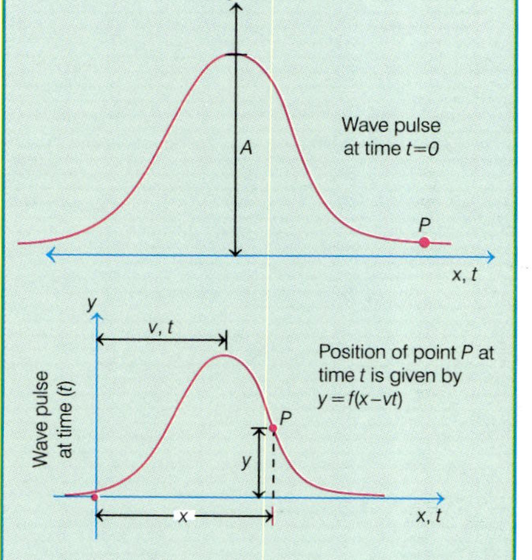

- Equation of the form $y = f(at \pm bx)$ represents progressive or travelling waves.

Particle Velocity in Plane Progressive Harmonic Wave

When a wave passes through a medium, medium particles oscillate in SHM.
particle displacement, $y = A \sin(\omega t - kx)$

Particle velocity, $v = \frac{dy}{dt} = A\omega \cos(\omega t - kx)$

Plane Progressive Harmonic Wave

For a travelling sinusoidal wave which is generally called progressive harmonic wave as shown,

Displacement of a particle at position x at time t is given by,

$$y = A \sin(kx + \omega t + \phi)$$

Amplitude; Oscillating term; Phase; Angular wave number; Position of particle; Instantaneous time; Angular frequency; Initial phase; Displacement of particle. Positive sign for a wave travelling in negative x-direction. Negative sign for a wave travelling in positive x-direction.

Principle of Superposition of Waves

Two or more waves can travel simultaneously in a medium without affecting the motion of one another. The resultant displacement of each particle of the medium at any instant is equal to the vector sum of the individual displacement produced by the two waves. This principle is called principle of superposition.

Equation of the two waves reaching at a point are,
$$y_1 = A_1 \sin(kx - \omega t)$$
and
$$y_2 = A_2 \sin(kx - \omega t + \phi)$$

The resultant displacement of the point, where the waves meet is given by

$$y = y_1 + y_2 = A_1 \sin(kx - \omega t) + A_2 \sin(kx - \omega t + \phi)$$

or $y = A \sin(kx - \omega t + \theta)$

or $A = \sqrt{A_1^2 + A_2^2 + 2A_1A_2 \cos\phi}$

$$\tan\theta = \frac{A_2 \sin\phi}{A_1 + A_2 \cos\phi} \Rightarrow \theta = \tan^{-1}\left[\frac{A_2 \sin\phi}{A_1 + A_2 \cos\phi}\right]$$

Reflection of waves

When a wave meets a surface, due to change of medium, a part of it is reflected and a part of it can be transmitted across the boundary into another medium.

(i) The frequency of incident, reflected and transmitted wave remains unchanged.
i.e. $f_{incident} = f_{reflected} = f_{transmitted}$

(ii) In reflection from a denser medium (or rigid support), phase changes by 180° and its direction is reversed.

Downward reaction causes pulse to invert upon reflection.

Hard boundary: Incident wave $y_1 = A_1 \sin(\omega t - kx)$; Transmitted wave $y_1 = A_1 \sin(\omega t - k_2x)$; Reflected wave $y_1 = A_1 \sin(\omega t + k_1x + \pi)$

Soft boundary: Incident wave $y_1 = A_1 \sin(\omega t - k_1x)$; Transmitted wave $y_1 = A_1 \sin(\omega t - k_2x)$; Reflected wave $y_1 = A_1 \sin(\omega t + k_1x)$

If incident wave is $y = A \sin(\omega t - kx)$, then wave reflected from hard boundary will be
$$y = A \sin(\omega t + kx + \pi)$$
or $y = -A \sin(\omega t + kx)$

$\therefore \sin(\pi + \theta) = -\sin\theta$

(iii) If wave is reflected from a soft boundary, then phase of reflected wave remains same but its direction is reversed.

(iv) If there is a loss of energy, then amplitude of reflected (or transmitted) wave will be less than that of incident wave.

Beats

- When two sound waves of nearly same frequency are produced simultaneously, then the intensity of resultant sound wave increases and decreases with time.
- This change in the intensity of sound is called as the phenomenon of beats.
- Number of beats produced in one second called beat frequency. Beat frequency $= f_1 - f_2$

Interference of Waves

Due to superposition of two (or more) waves at a point, energy is redistributed non-uniformly among oscillating particles. Non-uniform distribution of energy is called Interference. Interference is sustained when two coherent waves of same frequency propagate in same direction and superimpose on each other, then the intensity of resultant wave becomes maximum at some points and minimum at some other points.

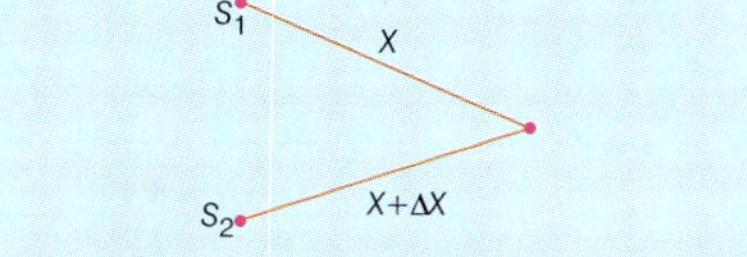

$$A^2 = A_1^2 + A_2^2 + 2A_1A_2 \cos\phi$$

If the resultant wave has maximum amplitude, then the interference is called **constructive interference.**

For maximum amplitude, $\cos\phi = +1$
or $\phi = 0, 2\pi, \ldots, 2n\pi$

Resultant amplitude, $A = A_{max} = A_1 + A_2$

If $A_1 = A_2 = a$

Graph for constructive interference

If the resultant wave has minimum amplitude, then the interference is called **destructive interference.**

For minimum amplitude, $\cos\phi = -1$
or $\phi = \pi, 3\pi, 2(n+1)\pi$

Resultant amplitude, $A = A_{min} = A_1 - A_2$

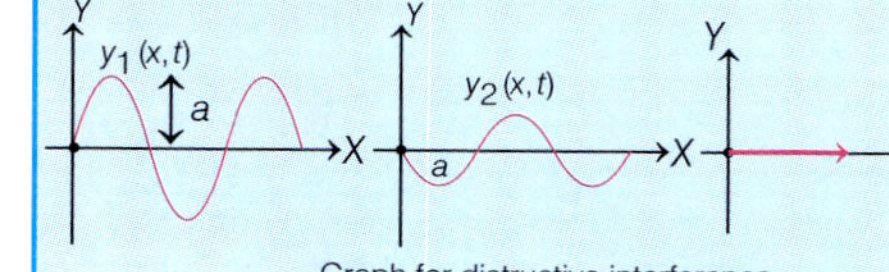

Graph for distructive interference

Essential Condition for Hearing Beats

For beats to be audible, the difference in the frequency of the two sound waves should not exceed 10. If the difference is more than 10, we shall hear more than 10 beats per second. But due to persistence of hearing, our ear is not able to distinguish between two sounds as separate, if the time interval between them is less than (1/10)th of a second. Hence, beats heard will not be distinct, if the number of beats produced per second is more than 10.

Test 3

Syllabus
- Standing Waves in Strings and Organ Pipe
- Fundamental Mode and Harmonics

NCERT Page 289 to 293

For deeper insight **Scan the QR Code**

Chapter 14

Standing/Stationary Waves

When two harmonic waves of equal frequency and amplitude travelling through a medium (say, string) in opposite directions superimpose each other, we get stationary waves.

$y = 2A \sin(kx)\cos(\omega t), y = 2A \sin\left(\frac{2\pi x}{\lambda}\right)\cos\left(\frac{2\pi t}{T}\right)$

The points at which the amplitude is zero are called nodes. At nodes, there is no motion. The points at which the amplitude is maximum are called anti-nodes. Also, the distance between successive nodes or anti-nodes is $\lambda/2$ whereas distance between adjacent node and anti-node is $\lambda/4$.

Position of nodes/anti-nodes

Position of nodes Nodes are the points on the string, where the amplitude of oscillation of constituents is zero.

i.e. $\sin kx = 0$

$kx = n\pi$ (where, $n = 0, 1, \ldots$)

$\frac{2\pi}{\lambda}x = n\pi \Rightarrow x = \frac{n\lambda}{2}$

Position of anti-nodes Anti-nodes are the points on the string, where the amplitude of oscillation of the constituents is maximum.

For maximum amplitude,

$\sin kx = \pm 1$

$\Rightarrow \quad kx = (2n+1)\frac{\pi}{2}$

where, $n = 0, 1, 2 \ldots$ or $x = (2n+1)\frac{\lambda}{4}$

Comparison Between Travelling & Stationary waves

Travelling waves	Stationary waves
• These waves advance in a medium with definite velocity.	• These waves remain stationary between two boundaries in the medium.
• In these waves, all particles of the medium oscillate with same frequency and amplitude.	• In these waves, all particles except nodes oscillate with same frequency but different amplitude.
• In these waves, all the particles of the medium do not pass through their mean positions simultaneously at any instant.	• In these waves, all particles of the medium pass through their mean positions simultaneously twice in each time period.

Vibrations of Air Columns in Organ Pipes

Organ pipes are musical instruments which are used to produce musical sound by blowing air into the pipe. This pipe is a cylindrical tube which may be open at one end called closed organ pipe or open at both end called open organ pipe.

(a) closed organ pipe (a) Open organ pipe

Closed Organ Pipe

- Frequency, $f = (2n+1)\frac{v}{4L}$

$n = 0, 1, 2, 3 \ldots$

- **Fundamental tone** If we blow at open mouth of organ pipe gently, then the lowest frequency is produced.

$L = \frac{\lambda}{4}$ or $\lambda = 4L$ or $f \propto \frac{1}{L}$

- **First over tone**

$L = \frac{3\lambda}{4}$ or $\lambda = \frac{4L}{3}$

$\therefore$ Frequency of the node produced

$f = \frac{3v}{4L}$

- It is also called **third harmonics**

(iii) Second overtone

$L = \frac{5\lambda}{4}, f_5 = \frac{5v}{4L} \Rightarrow f_3 = 5f_1$

This mode is called **5th harmonic** or **2nd overtone.**

Note - In organ pipe, the anti-node is not formed exactly at the open end. The reflection takes place little above the open end. If length of organ pipe is L and end-correction is e then length of air column in open pipe will be $(L+2e)$ and in closed pipe, $(L+e)$

For open organ pipe, $f = \frac{nv}{2(L+2e)}$

where n = 1, 2, 3, ...

For Closed organ pipe, $f = (2n+1)\frac{v}{4(L+e)}$

where n = 0, 1, 2, 3 ...

Open Organ Pipe

- For a pipe opened at both ends, each end is an anti-node.
- Frequency, $f = n.\frac{v}{2L}$
- **Fundamental tone**

If we blow air on one end of an organ pipe gently, then an anti-node is formed on both ends in between them.

$L = \frac{\lambda}{2}$ or $\lambda = 2L$

$f_1 = \frac{v}{\lambda} = \frac{v}{2L}$

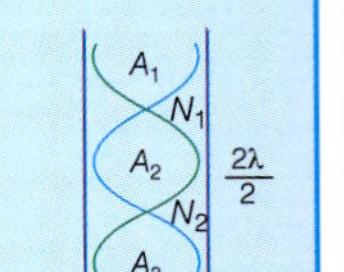

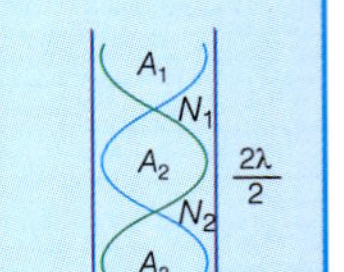

- **First overtone**

$L = 2\frac{\lambda}{2}$ or $\lambda = L$

$f_2 = \frac{v}{\lambda} = \frac{v}{L}$

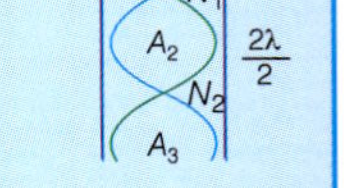

(ii) Second overtone

$\lambda = \frac{2L}{3} \Rightarrow L = \frac{3\lambda}{2}$

$\Rightarrow f_3 = \frac{3v}{2L}$ or $f_3 = 3f_1$

This mode is called **3rd harmonic** or **2nd overtone.**

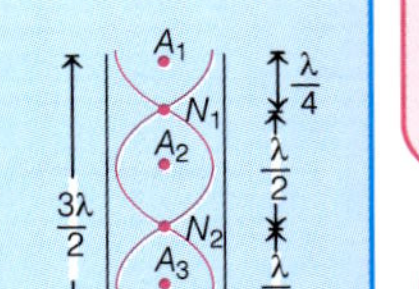

Some Important Points Related with Stationary Waves

Some important points related with stationary waves are given below.

(i) Standing wave is an example of interference. Node means destructive interference and anti-node means constructive interference.

(ii) At anti-node position, displacement is maximum and hence velocity is maximum but strain is minimum. Strain = Slope of stationary wave pattern, i.e. dy/dx

At nodal position, displacement and velocity are minimum but strain is maximum.

(iii) When a wave is reflected off a real surface, a part of energy is absorbed by the surface. As a result, energy, intensity and amplitude of reflected wave is always less than that of incident wave. Two waves differ in their amplitudes having same frequency and wavelength and propagate in reverse or opposite direction always give stationary wave pattern by their superposition.

Vibration of Stretched String

- **Laws of Transverse Vibration of a Stretched String**

(i) Law of length For a given string under a tension (T), the frequency of the vibrating string is inversely proportional to the vibrating length (L) of the string.

i.e. $f \propto \frac{1}{L} \Rightarrow fL = \text{constant}$

$\Rightarrow \quad f_1L_1 = f_2L_2$

(ii) Law of tension The frequency of the uniform string of given length is proportional to square root of the tension (T) in the string.

$f \propto \sqrt{T} \Rightarrow \frac{f}{\sqrt{T}} = \text{constant}$

$\Rightarrow \quad \frac{f_1}{f_2} = \sqrt{\frac{T_1}{T_2}}$

(iii) Law of mass For a given vibrating length and tension of the string, the frequency of the vibrating string is inversely proportional to the square root of the mass per unit length of the string.

$f \propto \frac{1}{\sqrt{\mu}}$

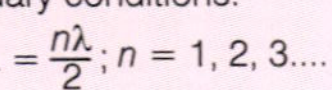

Vibration of String Fixed at Both Ends

- A stretched string having length L fixed at both ends, then boundary conditions.

$L = \frac{n\lambda}{2}; n = 1, 2, 3....$

- Possible wavelength,

$\lambda = \frac{2L}{n}; n = 1, 2, 3....$

- Frequencies, $f = \frac{nv}{2L}; n = 1, 2, 3....$

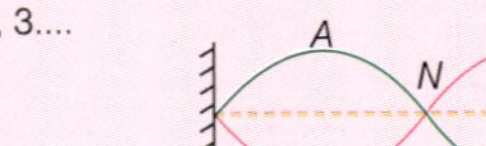

Modes of Vibration

The manner in which the string vibrates and give rise to a standing wave is known as mode of vibration of the string.

$L = \frac{n\lambda}{2}, f = \frac{nv}{2L}$

- **First mode of vibration** The mode of vibration in which string will vibrate in one segment or the lowest possible natural frequency (fundamental mode),

$L = \frac{\lambda}{2}$ and $f = \frac{v}{2L}$

- **Second mode of vibration** The mode of vibration in which string will vibrate in two segments called second harmonic.

$L = \lambda$ and $f = \frac{v}{L}$

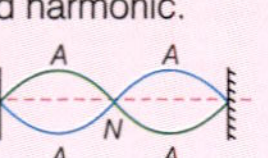

MEDACE

OMR SHEET

ROLL No.

1	1	1	1	1	1	1	1	1	1
2	2	2	2	2	2	2	2	2	2
3	3	3	3	3	3	3	3	3	3
4	4	4	4	4	4	4	4	4	4
5	5	5	5	5	5	5	5	5	5
6	6	6	6	6	6	6	6	6	6
7	7	7	7	7	7	7	7	7	7
8	8	8	8	8	8	8	8	8	8
9	9	9	9	9	9	9	9	9	9
0	0	0	0	0	0	0	0	0	0

TEST BOOKLET No.

1	1	1	1	1	1	1
2	2	2	2	2	2	2
3	3	3	3	3	3	3
4	4	4	4	4	4	4
5	5	5	5	5	5	5
6	6	6	6	6	6	6
7	7	7	7	7	7	7
8	8	8	8	8	8	8
9	9	9	9	9	9	9
0	0	0	0	0	0	0

TEST BOOKLET Code

Q No.	Response				Q No.	Response			
001	a	b	c	d	051	a	b	c	d
002	a	b	c	d	052	a	b	c	d
003	a	b	c	d	053	a	b	c	d
004	a	b	c	d	054	a	b	c	d
005	a	b	c	d	055	a	b	c	d
006	a	b	c	d	056	a	b	c	d
007	a	b	c	d	057	a	b	c	d
008	a	b	c	d	058	a	b	c	d
009	a	b	c	d	059	a	b	c	d
010	a	b	c	d	060	a	b	c	d
011	a	b	c	d	061	a	b	c	d
012	a	b	c	d	062	a	b	c	d
013	a	b	c	d	063	a	b	c	d
014	a	b	c	d	064	a	b	c	d
015	a	b	c	d	065	a	b	c	d
016	a	b	c	d	066	a	b	c	d
017	a	b	c	d	067	a	b	c	d
018	a	b	c	d	068	a	b	c	d
019	a	b	c	d	069	a	b	c	d
020	a	b	c	d	070	a	b	c	d
021	a	b	c	d	071	a	b	c	d
022	a	b	c	d	072	a	b	c	d
023	a	b	c	d	073	a	b	c	d
024	a	b	c	d	074	a	b	c	d
025	a	b	c	d	075	a	b	c	d
026	a	b	c	d	076	a	b	c	d
027	a	b	c	d	077	a	b	c	d
028	a	b	c	d	078	a	b	c	d
029	a	b	c	d	079	a	b	c	d
030	a	b	c	d	080	a	b	c	d
031	a	b	c	d	081	a	b	c	d
032	a	b	c	d	082	a	b	c	d
033	a	b	c	d	083	a	b	c	d
034	a	b	c	d	084	a	b	c	d
035	a	b	c	d	085	a	b	c	d
036	a	b	c	d	086	a	b	c	d
037	a	b	c	d	087	a	b	c	d
038	a	b	c	d	088	a	b	c	d
039	a	b	c	d	089	a	b	c	d
040	a	b	c	d	090	a	b	c	d
041	a	b	c	d	091	a	b	c	d
042	a	b	c	d	092	a	b	c	d
043	a	b	c	d	093	a	b	c	d
044	a	b	c	d	094	a	b	c	d
045	a	b	c	d	095	a	b	c	d
046	a	b	c	d	096	a	b	c	d
047	a	b	c	d	097	a	b	c	d
048	a	b	c	d	098	a	b	c	d
049	a	b	c	d	099	a	b	c	d
050	a	b	c	d	100	a	b	c	d

DECLARATION BY THE CANDIDATE

I declare that particulars and signature on this OMR Answer sheet are mine and are Name as in Attendance Sheet. I fruther declare that particulars filled in and Signature as well as the circles darkened on this ORIGINALCOPY is same as in OFFICE COPY.

Signature with time (in running handwriting)

CANDIDATE's NAME (in running handwriting)

MOTHER's NAME (in running handwriting)

FATHER's NAME (in running handwriting)

CANDIDATE LEFT HAND IMPRESSION

SIGNATURE OF INVIGILATOR'S WITH TIME

1

2

OMR SHEET

ROLL No.

1	1	1	1	1	1	1	1	1	1
2	2	2	2	2	2	2	2	2	2
3	3	3	3	3	3	3	3	3	3
4	4	4	4	4	4	4	4	4	4
5	5	5	5	5	5	5	5	5	5
6	6	6	6	6	6	6	6	6	6
7	7	7	7	7	7	7	7	7	7
8	8	8	8	8	8	8	8	8	8
9	9	9	9	9	9	9	9	9	9
0	0	0	0	0	0	0	0	0	0

TEST BOOKLET No.

1	1	1	1	1	1	1
2	2	2	2	2	2	2
3	3	3	3	3	3	3
4	4	4	4	4	4	4
5	5	5	5	5	5	5
6	6	6	6	6	6	6
7	7	7	7	7	7	7
8	8	8	8	8	8	8
9	9	9	9	9	9	9
0	0	0	0	0	0	0

TEST BOOKLET Code

Q No.	Response				Q No.	Response			
001	a	b	c	d	051	a	b	c	d
002	a	b	c	d	052	a	b	c	d
003	a	b	c	d	053	a	b	c	d
004	a	b	c	d	054	a	b	c	d
005	a	b	c	d	055	a	b	c	d
006	a	b	c	d	056	a	b	c	d
007	a	b	c	d	057	a	b	c	d
008	a	b	c	d	058	a	b	c	d
009	a	b	c	d	059	a	b	c	d
010	a	b	c	d	060	a	b	c	d
011	a	b	c	d	061	a	b	c	d
012	a	b	c	d	062	a	b	c	d
013	a	b	c	d	063	a	b	c	d
014	a	b	c	d	064	a	b	c	d
015	a	b	c	d	065	a	b	c	d
016	a	b	c	d	066	a	b	c	d
017	a	b	c	d	067	a	b	c	d
018	a	b	c	d	068	a	b	c	d
019	a	b	c	d	069	a	b	c	d
020	a	b	c	d	070	a	b	c	d
021	a	b	c	d	071	a	b	c	d
022	a	b	c	d	072	a	b	c	d
023	a	b	c	d	073	a	b	c	d
024	a	b	c	d	074	a	b	c	d
025	a	b	c	d	075	a	b	c	d
026	a	b	c	d	076	a	b	c	d
027	a	b	c	d	077	a	b	c	d
028	a	b	c	d	078	a	b	c	d
029	a	b	c	d	079	a	b	c	d
030	a	b	c	d	080	a	b	c	d
031	a	b	c	d	081	a	b	c	d
032	a	b	c	d	082	a	b	c	d
033	a	b	c	d	083	a	b	c	d
034	a	b	c	d	084	a	b	c	d
035	a	b	c	d	085	a	b	c	d
036	a	b	c	d	086	a	b	c	d
037	a	b	c	d	087	a	b	c	d
038	a	b	c	d	088	a	b	c	d
039	a	b	c	d	089	a	b	c	d
040	a	b	c	d	090	a	b	c	d
041	a	b	c	d	091	a	b	c	d
042	a	b	c	d	092	a	b	c	d
043	a	b	c	d	093	a	b	c	d
044	a	b	c	d	094	a	b	c	d
045	a	b	c	d	095	a	b	c	d
046	a	b	c	d	096	a	b	c	d
047	a	b	c	d	097	a	b	c	d
048	a	b	c	d	098	a	b	c	d
049	a	b	c	d	099	a	b	c	d
050	a	b	c	d	100	a	b	c	d

DECLARATION BY THE CANDIDATE

I declare that particulars and signature on this OMR Answer sheet are mine and are Name as in Attendance Sheet. I futher declare that particulars filled in and Signature as well as the circles darkened on this ORIGINALCOPY is same as in OFFICE COPY.

Signature with time (in running handwriting)

CANDIDATE's NAME (in running handwriting)

MOTHER's NAME (in running handwriting)

FATHER's NAME (in running handwriting)

CANDIDATE LEFT HAND IMPRESSION

SIGNATURE OF INVIGILATOR'S WITH TIME

1

2

MEDACE

OMR SHEET

ROLL No.

1	1	1	1	1	1	1	1	1	1
2	2	2	2	2	2	2	2	2	2
3	3	3	3	3	3	3	3	3	3
4	4	4	4	4	4	4	4	4	4
5	5	5	5	5	5	5	5	5	5
6	6	6	6	6	6	6	6	6	6
7	7	7	7	7	7	7	7	7	7
8	8	8	8	8	8	8	8	8	8
9	9	9	9	9	9	9	9	9	9
0	0	0	0	0	0	0	0	0	0

TEST BOOKLET No.

1	1	1	1	1	1	1
2	2	2	2	2	2	2
3	3	3	3	3	3	3
4	4	4	4	4	4	4
5	5	5	5	5	5	5
6	6	6	6	6	6	6
7	7	7	7	7	7	7
8	8	8	8	8	8	8
9	9	9	9	9	9	9
0	0	0	0	0	0	0

TEST BOOKLET Code

Q No.	Response			
001	a	b	c	d
002	a	b	c	d
003	a	b	c	d
004	a	b	c	d
005	a	b	c	d
006	a	b	c	d
007	a	b	c	d
008	a	b	c	d
009	a	b	c	d
010	a	b	c	d
011	a	b	c	d
012	a	b	c	d
013	a	b	c	d
014	a	b	c	d
015	a	b	c	d
016	a	b	c	d
017	a	b	c	d
018	a	b	c	d
019	a	b	c	d
020	a	b	c	d
021	a	b	c	d
022	a	b	c	d
023	a	b	c	d
024	a	b	c	d
025	a	b	c	d
026	a	b	c	d
027	a	b	c	d
028	a	b	c	d
029	a	b	c	d
030	a	b	c	d
031	a	b	c	d
032	a	b	c	d
033	a	b	c	d
034	a	b	c	d
035	a	b	c	d
036	a	b	c	d
037	a	b	c	d
038	a	b	c	d
039	a	b	c	d
040	a	b	c	d
041	a	b	c	d
042	a	b	c	d
043	a	b	c	d
044	a	b	c	d
045	a	b	c	d
046	a	b	c	d
047	a	b	c	d
048	a	b	c	d
049	a	b	c	d
050	a	b	c	d

Q No.	Response			
051	a	b	c	d
052	a	b	c	d
053	a	b	c	d
054	a	b	c	d
055	a	b	c	d
056	a	b	c	d
057	a	b	c	d
058	a	b	c	d
059	a	b	c	d
060	a	b	c	d
061	a	b	c	d
062	a	b	c	d
063	a	b	c	d
064	a	b	c	d
065	a	b	c	d
066	a	b	c	d
067	a	b	c	d
068	a	b	c	d
069	a	b	c	d
070	a	b	c	d
071	a	b	c	d
072	a	b	c	d
073	a	b	c	d
074	a	b	c	d
075	a	b	c	d
076	a	b	c	d
077	a	b	c	d
078	a	b	c	d
079	a	b	c	d
080	a	b	c	d
081	a	b	c	d
082	a	b	c	d
083	a	b	c	d
084	a	b	c	d
085	a	b	c	d
086	a	b	c	d
087	a	b	c	d
088	a	b	c	d
089	a	b	c	d
090	a	b	c	d
091	a	b	c	d
092	a	b	c	d
093	a	b	c	d
094	a	b	c	d
095	a	b	c	d
096	a	b	c	d
097	a	b	c	d
098	a	b	c	d
099	a	b	c	d
100	a	b	c	d

DECLARATION BY THE CANDIDATE

I declare that particulars and signature on this OMR Answer sheet are mine and are Name as in Attendance Sheet. I fruther declare that particulars filled in and Signature as well as the circles darkened on this ORIGINALCOPY is same as in OFFICE COPY.

Signature with time (in running handwriting)

CANDIDATE's NAME (in running handwriting)

MOTHER's NAME (in running handwriting)

FATHER's NAME (in running handwriting)

CANDIDATE LEFT HAND IMPRESSION

SIGNATURE OF INVIGILATOR'S WITH TIME

1

2

OMR SHEET

ROLL No.

1	1	1	1	1	1	1	1	1	1
2	2	2	2	2	2	2	2	2	2
3	3	3	3	3	3	3	3	3	3
4	4	4	4	4	4	4	4	4	4
5	5	5	5	5	5	5	5	5	5
6	6	6	6	6	6	6	6	6	6
7	7	7	7	7	7	7	7	7	7
8	8	8	8	8	8	8	8	8	8
9	9	9	9	9	9	9	9	9	9
0	0	0	0	0	0	0	0	0	0

TEST BOOKLET No.

1	1	1	1	1	1	1
2	2	2	2	2	2	2
3	3	3	3	3	3	3
4	4	4	4	4	4	4
5	5	5	5	5	5	5
6	6	6	6	6	6	6
7	7	7	7	7	7	7
8	8	8	8	8	8	8
9	9	9	9	9	9	9
0	0	0	0	0	0	0

TEST BOOKLET Code

Q No.	Response				Q No.	Response			
001	a	b	c	d	051	a	b	c	d
002	a	b	c	d	052	a	b	c	d
003	a	b	c	d	053	a	b	c	d
004	a	b	c	d	054	a	b	c	d
005	a	b	c	d	055	a	b	c	d
006	a	b	c	d	056	a	b	c	d
007	a	b	c	d	057	a	b	c	d
008	a	b	c	d	058	a	b	c	d
009	a	b	c	d	059	a	b	c	d
010	a	b	c	d	060	a	b	c	d
011	a	b	c	d	061	a	b	c	d
012	a	b	c	d	062	a	b	c	d
013	a	b	c	d	063	a	b	c	d
014	a	b	c	d	064	a	b	c	d
015	a	b	c	d	065	a	b	c	d
016	a	b	c	d	066	a	b	c	d
017	a	b	c	d	067	a	b	c	d
018	a	b	c	d	068	a	b	c	d
019	a	b	c	d	069	a	b	c	d
020	a	b	c	d	070	a	b	c	d
021	a	b	c	d	071	a	b	c	d
022	a	b	c	d	072	a	b	c	d
023	a	b	c	d	073	a	b	c	d
024	a	b	c	d	074	a	b	c	d
025	a	b	c	d	075	a	b	c	d
026	a	b	c	d	076	a	b	c	d
027	a	b	c	d	077	a	b	c	d
028	a	b	c	d	078	a	b	c	d
029	a	b	c	d	079	a	b	c	d
030	a	b	c	d	080	a	b	c	d
031	a	b	c	d	081	a	b	c	d
032	a	b	c	d	082	a	b	c	d
033	a	b	c	d	083	a	b	c	d
034	a	b	c	d	084	a	b	c	d
035	a	b	c	d	085	a	b	c	d
036	a	b	c	d	086	a	b	c	d
037	a	b	c	d	087	a	b	c	d
038	a	b	c	d	088	a	b	c	d
039	a	b	c	d	089	a	b	c	d
040	a	b	c	d	090	a	b	c	d
041	a	b	c	d	091	a	b	c	d
042	a	b	c	d	092	a	b	c	d
043	a	b	c	d	093	a	b	c	d
044	a	b	c	d	094	a	b	c	d
045	a	b	c	d	095	a	b	c	d
046	a	b	c	d	096	a	b	c	d
047	a	b	c	d	097	a	b	c	d
048	a	b	c	d	098	a	b	c	d
049	a	b	c	d	099	a	b	c	d
050	a	b	c	d	100	a	b	c	d

DECLARATION BY THE CANDIDATE

I declare that particulars and signature on this OMR Answer sheet are mine and are Name as in Attendance Sheet. I fruther declare that particulars filled in and Signature as well as the circles darkened on this ORIGINALCOPY is same as in OFFICE COPY.

Signature with time (in running handwriting)

CANDIDATE's NAME (in running handwriting)

MOTHER's NAME (in running handwriting)

FATHER's NAME (in running handwriting)

CANDIDATE LEFT HAND IMPRESSION

SIGNATURE OF INVIGILATOR'S WITH TIME

1

2

MED ACE

OMR SHEET

ROLL No.

TEST BOOKLET No.

TEST BOOKLET Code

Q No.	Response			
001	a	b	c	d
002	a	b	c	d
003	a	b	c	d
004	a	b	c	d
005	a	b	c	d
006	a	b	c	d
007	a	b	c	d
008	a	b	c	d
009	a	b	c	d
010	a	b	c	d
011	a	b	c	d
012	a	b	c	d
013	a	b	c	d
014	a	b	c	d
015	a	b	c	d
016	a	b	c	d
017	a	b	c	d
018	a	b	c	d
019	a	b	c	d
020	a	b	c	d
021	a	b	c	d
022	a	b	c	d
023	a	b	c	d
024	a	b	c	d
025	a	b	c	d
026	a	b	c	d
027	a	b	c	d
028	a	b	c	d
029	a	b	c	d
030	a	b	c	d
031	a	b	c	d
032	a	b	c	d
033	a	b	c	d
034	a	b	c	d
035	a	b	c	d
036	a	b	c	d
037	a	b	c	d
038	a	b	c	d
039	a	b	c	d
040	a	b	c	d
041	a	b	c	d
042	a	b	c	d
043	a	b	c	d
044	a	b	c	d
045	a	b	c	d
046	a	b	c	d
047	a	b	c	d
048	a	b	c	d
049	a	b	c	d
050	a	b	c	d

Q No.	Response			
051	a	b	c	d
052	a	b	c	d
053	a	b	c	d
054	a	b	c	d
055	a	b	c	d
056	a	b	c	d
057	a	b	c	d
058	a	b	c	d
059	a	b	c	d
060	a	b	c	d
061	a	b	c	d
062	a	b	c	d
063	a	b	c	d
064	a	b	c	d
065	a	b	c	d
066	a	b	c	d
067	a	b	c	d
068	a	b	c	d
069	a	b	c	d
070	a	b	c	d
071	a	b	c	d
072	a	b	c	d
073	a	b	c	d
074	a	b	c	d
075	a	b	c	d
076	a	b	c	d
077	a	b	c	d
078	a	b	c	d
079	a	b	c	d
080	a	b	c	d
081	a	b	c	d
082	a	b	c	d
083	a	b	c	d
084	a	b	c	d
085	a	b	c	d
086	a	b	c	d
087	a	b	c	d
088	a	b	c	d
089	a	b	c	d
090	a	b	c	d
091	a	b	c	d
092	a	b	c	d
093	a	b	c	d
094	a	b	c	d
095	a	b	c	d
096	a	b	c	d
097	a	b	c	d
098	a	b	c	d
099	a	b	c	d
100	a	b	c	d

DECLARATION BY THE CANDIDATE

I declare that particulars and signature on this OMR Answer sheet are mine and are Name as in Attendance Sheet. I fruther declare that particulars filled in and Signature as well as the circles darkened on this ORIGINALCOPY is same as in OFFICE COPY.

Signature with time (in running handwriting)

CANDIDATE's NAME (in running handwriting)

MOTHER's NAME (in running handwriting)

FATHER's NAME (in running handwriting)

CANDIDATE LEFT HAND IMPRESSION

SIGNATURE OF INVIGILATOR'S WITH TIME

1

2

MEDACE

OMR SHEET

ROLL No.

1	1	1	1	1	1	1	1	1	1
2	2	2	2	2	2	2	2	2	2
3	3	3	3	3	3	3	3	3	3
4	4	4	4	4	4	4	4	4	4
5	5	5	5	5	5	5	5	5	5
6	6	6	6	6	6	6	6	6	6
7	7	7	7	7	7	7	7	7	7
8	8	8	8	8	8	8	8	8	8
9	9	9	9	9	9	9	9	9	9
0	0	0	0	0	0	0	0	0	0

TEST BOOKLET No.

1	1	1	1	1	1	1
2	2	2	2	2	2	2
3	3	3	3	3	3	3
4	4	4	4	4	4	4
5	5	5	5	5	5	5
6	6	6	6	6	6	6
7	7	7	7	7	7	7
8	8	8	8	8	8	8
9	9	9	9	9	9	9
0	0	0	0	0	0	0

TEST BOOKLET Code

Q No.	Response				Q No.	Response			
001	a	b	c	d	051	a	b	c	d
002	a	b	c	d	052	a	b	c	d
003	a	b	c	d	053	a	b	c	d
004	a	b	c	d	054	a	b	c	d
005	a	b	c	d	055	a	b	c	d
006	a	b	c	d	056	a	b	c	d
007	a	b	c	d	057	a	b	c	d
008	a	b	c	d	058	a	b	c	d
009	a	b	c	d	059	a	b	c	d
010	a	b	c	d	060	a	b	c	d
011	a	b	c	d	061	a	b	c	d
012	a	b	c	d	062	a	b	c	d
013	a	b	c	d	063	a	b	c	d
014	a	b	c	d	064	a	b	c	d
015	a	b	c	d	065	a	b	c	d
016	a	b	c	d	066	a	b	c	d
017	a	b	c	d	067	a	b	c	d
018	a	b	c	d	068	a	b	c	d
019	a	b	c	d	069	a	b	c	d
020	a	b	c	d	070	a	b	c	d
021	a	b	c	d	071	a	b	c	d
022	a	b	c	d	072	a	b	c	d
023	a	b	c	d	073	a	b	c	d
024	a	b	c	d	074	a	b	c	d
025	a	b	c	d	075	a	b	c	d
026	a	b	c	d	076	a	b	c	d
027	a	b	c	d	077	a	b	c	d
028	a	b	c	d	078	a	b	c	d
029	a	b	c	d	079	a	b	c	d
030	a	b	c	d	080	a	b	c	d
031	a	b	c	d	081	a	b	c	d
032	a	b	c	d	082	a	b	c	d
033	a	b	c	d	083	a	b	c	d
034	a	b	c	d	084	a	b	c	d
035	a	b	c	d	085	a	b	c	d
036	a	b	c	d	086	a	b	c	d
037	a	b	c	d	087	a	b	c	d
038	a	b	c	d	088	a	b	c	d
039	a	b	c	d	089	a	b	c	d
040	a	b	c	d	090	a	b	c	d
041	a	b	c	d	091	a	b	c	d
042	a	b	c	d	092	a	b	c	d
043	a	b	c	d	093	a	b	c	d
044	a	b	c	d	094	a	b	c	d
045	a	b	c	d	095	a	b	c	d
046	a	b	c	d	096	a	b	c	d
047	a	b	c	d	097	a	b	c	d
048	a	b	c	d	098	a	b	c	d
049	a	b	c	d	099	a	b	c	d
050	a	b	c	d	100	a	b	c	d

DECLARATION BY THE CANDIDATE

I declare that particulars and signature on this OMR Answer sheet are mine and are Name as in Attendance Sheet. I fruther declare that particulars filled in and Signature as well as the circles darkened on this ORIGINALCOPY is same as in OFFICE COPY.

Signature with time (in running handwriting)

CANDIDATE's NAME (in running handwriting)

MOTHER's NAME (in running handwriting)

FATHER's NAME (in running handwriting)

CANDIDATE LEFT HAND IMPRESSION

SIGNATURE OF INVIGILATOR'S WITH TIME

1

2

MED ACE

OMR SHEET

ROLL No.

TEST BOOKLET No.

TEST BOOKLET Code

Q No.	Response				Q No.	Response			
001	a	b	c	d	051	a	b	c	d
002	a	b	c	d	052	a	b	c	d
003	a	b	c	d	053	a	b	c	d
004	a	b	c	d	054	a	b	c	d
005	a	b	c	d	055	a	b	c	d
006	a	b	c	d	056	a	b	c	d
007	a	b	c	d	057	a	b	c	d
008	a	b	c	d	058	a	b	c	d
009	a	b	c	d	059	a	b	c	d
010	a	b	c	d	060	a	b	c	d
011	a	b	c	d	061	a	b	c	d
012	a	b	c	d	062	a	b	c	d
013	a	b	c	d	063	a	b	c	d
014	a	b	c	d	064	a	b	c	d
015	a	b	c	d	065	a	b	c	d
016	a	b	c	d	066	a	b	c	d
017	a	b	c	d	067	a	b	c	d
018	a	b	c	d	068	a	b	c	d
019	a	b	c	d	069	a	b	c	d
020	a	b	c	d	070	a	b	c	d
021	a	b	c	d	071	a	b	c	d
022	a	b	c	d	072	a	b	c	d
023	a	b	c	d	073	a	b	c	d
024	a	b	c	d	074	a	b	c	d
025	a	b	c	d	075	a	b	c	d
026	a	b	c	d	076	a	b	c	d
027	a	b	c	d	077	a	b	c	d
028	a	b	c	d	078	a	b	c	d
029	a	b	c	d	079	a	b	c	d
030	a	b	c	d	080	a	b	c	d
031	a	b	c	d	081	a	b	c	d
032	a	b	c	d	082	a	b	c	d
033	a	b	c	d	083	a	b	c	d
034	a	b	c	d	084	a	b	c	d
035	a	b	c	d	085	a	b	c	d
036	a	b	c	d	086	a	b	c	d
037	a	b	c	d	087	a	b	c	d
038	a	b	c	d	088	a	b	c	d
039	a	b	c	d	089	a	b	c	d
040	a	b	c	d	090	a	b	c	d
041	a	b	c	d	091	a	b	c	d
042	a	b	c	d	092	a	b	c	d
043	a	b	c	d	093	a	b	c	d
044	a	b	c	d	094	a	b	c	d
045	a	b	c	d	095	a	b	c	d
046	a	b	c	d	096	a	b	c	d
047	a	b	c	d	097	a	b	c	d
048	a	b	c	d	098	a	b	c	d
049	a	b	c	d	099	a	b	c	d
050	a	b	c	d	100	a	b	c	d

DECLARATION BY THE CANDIDATE

I declare that particulars and signature on this OMR Answer sheet are mine and are Name as in Attendance Sheet. I fruther declare that particulars filled in and Signature as well as the circles darkened on this ORIGINALCOPY is same as in OFFICE COPY.

Signature with time (in running handwriting)

CANDIDATE's NAME (in running handwriting)

MOTHER's NAME (in running handwriting)

FATHER's NAME (in running handwriting)

CANDIDATE LEFT HAND IMPRESSION

SIGNATURE OF INVIGILATOR'S WITH TIME

1

2

OMR SHEET

ROLL No.

1	1	1	1	1	1	1	1	1	1
2	2	2	2	2	2	2	2	2	2
3	3	3	3	3	3	3	3	3	3
4	4	4	4	4	4	4	4	4	4
5	5	5	5	5	5	5	5	5	5
6	6	6	6	6	6	6	6	6	6
7	7	7	7	7	7	7	7	7	7
8	8	8	8	8	8	8	8	8	8
9	9	9	9	9	9	9	9	9	9
0	0	0	0	0	0	0	0	0	0

TEST BOOKLET No.

1	1	1	1	1	1	1
2	2	2	2	2	2	2
3	3	3	3	3	3	3
4	4	4	4	4	4	4
5	5	5	5	5	5	5
6	6	6	6	6	6	6
7	7	7	7	7	7	7
8	8	8	8	8	8	8
9	9	9	9	9	9	9
0	0	0	0	0	0	0

TEST BOOKLET Code

Q No.	Response			
001	a	b	c	d
002	a	b	c	d
003	a	b	c	d
004	a	b	c	d
005	a	b	c	d
006	a	b	c	d
007	a	b	c	d
008	a	b	c	d
009	a	b	c	d
010	a	b	c	d
011	a	b	c	d
012	a	b	c	d
013	a	b	c	d
014	a	b	c	d
015	a	b	c	d
016	a	b	c	d
017	a	b	c	d
018	a	b	c	d
019	a	b	c	d
020	a	b	c	d
021	a	b	c	d
022	a	b	c	d
023	a	b	c	d
024	a	b	c	d
025	a	b	c	d
026	a	b	c	d
027	a	b	c	d
028	a	b	c	d
029	a	b	c	d
030	a	b	c	d
031	a	b	c	d
032	a	b	c	d
033	a	b	c	d
034	a	b	c	d
035	a	b	c	d
036	a	b	c	d
037	a	b	c	d
038	a	b	c	d
039	a	b	c	d
040	a	b	c	d
041	a	b	c	d
042	a	b	c	d
043	a	b	c	d
044	a	b	c	d
045	a	b	c	d
046	a	b	c	d
047	a	b	c	d
048	a	b	c	d
049	a	b	c	d
050	a	b	c	d

Q No.	Response			
051	a	b	c	d
052	a	b	c	d
053	a	b	c	d
054	a	b	c	d
055	a	b	c	d
056	a	b	c	d
057	a	b	c	d
058	a	b	c	d
059	a	b	c	d
060	a	b	c	d
061	a	b	c	d
062	a	b	c	d
063	a	b	c	d
064	a	b	c	d
065	a	b	c	d
066	a	b	c	d
067	a	b	c	d
068	a	b	c	d
069	a	b	c	d
070	a	b	c	d
071	a	b	c	d
072	a	b	c	d
073	a	b	c	d
074	a	b	c	d
075	a	b	c	d
076	a	b	c	d
077	a	b	c	d
078	a	b	c	d
079	a	b	c	d
080	a	b	c	d
081	a	b	c	d
082	a	b	c	d
083	a	b	c	d
084	a	b	c	d
085	a	b	c	d
086	a	b	c	d
087	a	b	c	d
088	a	b	c	d
089	a	b	c	d
090	a	b	c	d
091	a	b	c	d
092	a	b	c	d
093	a	b	c	d
094	a	b	c	d
095	a	b	c	d
096	a	b	c	d
097	a	b	c	d
098	a	b	c	d
099	a	b	c	d
100	a	b	c	d

DECLARATION BY THE CANDIDATE

I declare that particulars and signature on this OMR Answer sheet are mine and are Name as in Attendance Sheet. I fruther declare that particulars filled in and Signature as well as the circles darkened on this ORIGINALCOPY is same as in OFFICE COPY.

Signature with time (in running handwriting)

CANDIDATE's NAME (in running handwriting)

MOTHER's NAME (in running handwriting)

FATHER's NAME (in running handwriting)

CANDIDATE LEFT HAND IMPRESSION

SIGNATURE OF INVIGILATOR'S WITH TIME

1

2

MEDACE

OMR SHEET

ROLL No.

1	1	1	1	1	1	1	1	1	1
2	2	2	2	2	2	2	2	2	2
3	3	3	3	3	3	3	3	3	3
4	4	4	4	4	4	4	4	4	4
5	5	5	5	5	5	5	5	5	5
6	6	6	6	6	6	6	6	6	6
7	7	7	7	7	7	7	7	7	7
8	8	8	8	8	8	8	8	8	8
9	9	9	9	9	9	9	9	9	9
0	0	0	0	0	0	0	0	0	0

TEST BOOKLET No.

1	1	1	1	1	1	1
2	2	2	2	2	2	2
3	3	3	3	3	3	3
4	4	4	4	4	4	4
5	5	5	5	5	5	5
6	6	6	6	6	6	6
7	7	7	7	7	7	7
8	8	8	8	8	8	8
9	9	9	9	9	9	9
0	0	0	0	0	0	0

TEST BOOKLET Code

Q No.	Response				Q No.	Response			
001	a	b	c	d	051	a	b	c	d
002	a	b	c	d	052	a	b	c	d
003	a	b	c	d	053	a	b	c	d
004	a	b	c	d	054	a	b	c	d
005	a	b	c	d	055	a	b	c	d
006	a	b	c	d	056	a	b	c	d
007	a	b	c	d	057	a	b	c	d
008	a	b	c	d	058	a	b	c	d
009	a	b	c	d	059	a	b	c	d
010	a	b	c	d	060	a	b	c	d
011	a	b	c	d	061	a	b	c	d
012	a	b	c	d	062	a	b	c	d
013	a	b	c	d	063	a	b	c	d
014	a	b	c	d	064	a	b	c	d
015	a	b	c	d	065	a	b	c	d
016	a	b	c	d	066	a	b	c	d
017	a	b	c	d	067	a	b	c	d
018	a	b	c	d	068	a	b	c	d
019	a	b	c	d	069	a	b	c	d
020	a	b	c	d	070	a	b	c	d
021	a	b	c	d	071	a	b	c	d
022	a	b	c	d	072	a	b	c	d
023	a	b	c	d	073	a	b	c	d
024	a	b	c	d	074	a	b	c	d
025	a	b	c	d	075	a	b	c	d
026	a	b	c	d	076	a	b	c	d
027	a	b	c	d	077	a	b	c	d
028	a	b	c	d	078	a	b	c	d
029	a	b	c	d	079	a	b	c	d
030	a	b	c	d	080	a	b	c	d
031	a	b	c	d	081	a	b	c	d
032	a	b	c	d	082	a	b	c	d
033	a	b	c	d	083	a	b	c	d
034	a	b	c	d	084	a	b	c	d
035	a	b	c	d	085	a	b	c	d
036	a	b	c	d	086	a	b	c	d
037	a	b	c	d	087	a	b	c	d
038	a	b	c	d	088	a	b	c	d
039	a	b	c	d	089	a	b	c	d
040	a	b	c	d	090	a	b	c	d
041	a	b	c	d	091	a	b	c	d
042	a	b	c	d	092	a	b	c	d
043	a	b	c	d	093	a	b	c	d
044	a	b	c	d	094	a	b	c	d
045	a	b	c	d	095	a	b	c	d
046	a	b	c	d	096	a	b	c	d
047	a	b	c	d	097	a	b	c	d
048	a	b	c	d	098	a	b	c	d
049	a	b	c	d	099	a	b	c	d
050	a	b	c	d	100	a	b	c	d

DECLARATION BY THE CANDIDATE

I declare that particulars and signature on this OMR Answer sheet are mine and are Name as in Attendance Sheet. I futher declare that particulars filled in and Signature as well as the circles darkened on this ORIGINALCOPY is same as in OFFICE COPY.

Signature with time (in running handwriting)

CANDIDATE's NAME (in running handwriting)

MOTHER's NAME (in running handwriting)

FATHER's NAME (in running handwriting)

CANDIDATE LEFT HAND IMPRESSION

SIGNATURE OF INVIGILATOR'S WITH TIME

1

2

MEDACE

OMR SHEET

ROLL No.

1	1	1	1	1	1	1	1	1	1
2	2	2	2	2	2	2	2	2	2
3	3	3	3	3	3	3	3	3	3
4	4	4	4	4	4	4	4	4	4
5	5	5	5	5	5	5	5	5	5
6	6	6	6	6	6	6	6	6	6
7	7	7	7	7	7	7	7	7	7
8	8	8	8	8	8	8	8	8	8
9	9	9	9	9	9	9	9	9	9
0	0	0	0	0	0	0	0	0	0

TEST BOOKLET No.

1	1	1	1	1	1	1
2	2	2	2	2	2	2
3	3	3	3	3	3	3
4	4	4	4	4	4	4
5	5	5	5	5	5	5
6	6	6	6	6	6	6
7	7	7	7	7	7	7
8	8	8	8	8	8	8
9	9	9	9	9	9	9
0	0	0	0	0	0	0

TEST BOOKLET Code

Q No.	Response	Q No.	Response
001	(a) (b) (c) (d)	051	(a) (b) (c) (d)
002	(a) (b) (c) (d)	052	(a) (b) (c) (d)
003	(a) (b) (c) (d)	053	(a) (b) (c) (d)
004	(a) (b) (c) (d)	054	(a) (b) (c) (d)
005	(a) (b) (c) (d)	055	(a) (b) (c) (d)
006	(a) (b) (c) (d)	056	(a) (b) (c) (d)
007	(a) (b) (c) (d)	057	(a) (b) (c) (d)
008	(a) (b) (c) (d)	058	(a) (b) (c) (d)
009	(a) (b) (c) (d)	059	(a) (b) (c) (d)
010	(a) (b) (c) (d)	060	(a) (b) (c) (d)
011	(a) (b) (c) (d)	061	(a) (b) (c) (d)
012	(a) (b) (c) (d)	062	(a) (b) (c) (d)
013	(a) (b) (c) (d)	063	(a) (b) (c) (d)
014	(a) (b) (c) (d)	064	(a) (b) (c) (d)
015	(a) (b) (c) (d)	065	(a) (b) (c) (d)
016	(a) (b) (c) (d)	066	(a) (b) (c) (d)
017	(a) (b) (c) (d)	067	(a) (b) (c) (d)
018	(a) (b) (c) (d)	068	(a) (b) (c) (d)
019	(a) (b) (c) (d)	069	(a) (b) (c) (d)
020	(a) (b) (c) (d)	070	(a) (b) (c) (d)
021	(a) (b) (c) (d)	071	(a) (b) (c) (d)
022	(a) (b) (c) (d)	072	(a) (b) (c) (d)
023	(a) (b) (c) (d)	073	(a) (b) (c) (d)
024	(a) (b) (c) (d)	074	(a) (b) (c) (d)
025	(a) (b) (c) (d)	075	(a) (b) (c) (d)
026	(a) (b) (c) (d)	076	(a) (b) (c) (d)
027	(a) (b) (c) (d)	077	(a) (b) (c) (d)
028	(a) (b) (c) (d)	078	(a) (b) (c) (d)
029	(a) (b) (c) (d)	079	(a) (b) (c) (d)
030	(a) (b) (c) (d)	080	(a) (b) (c) (d)
031	(a) (b) (c) (d)	081	(a) (b) (c) (d)
032	(a) (b) (c) (d)	082	(a) (b) (c) (d)
033	(a) (b) (c) (d)	083	(a) (b) (c) (d)
034	(a) (b) (c) (d)	084	(a) (b) (c) (d)
035	(a) (b) (c) (d)	085	(a) (b) (c) (d)
036	(a) (b) (c) (d)	086	(a) (b) (c) (d)
037	(a) (b) (c) (d)	087	(a) (b) (c) (d)
038	(a) (b) (c) (d)	088	(a) (b) (c) (d)
039	(a) (b) (c) (d)	089	(a) (b) (c) (d)
040	(a) (b) (c) (d)	090	(a) (b) (c) (d)
041	(a) (b) (c) (d)	091	(a) (b) (c) (d)
042	(a) (b) (c) (d)	092	(a) (b) (c) (d)
043	(a) (b) (c) (d)	093	(a) (b) (c) (d)
044	(a) (b) (c) (d)	094	(a) (b) (c) (d)
045	(a) (b) (c) (d)	095	(a) (b) (c) (d)
046	(a) (b) (c) (d)	096	(a) (b) (c) (d)
047	(a) (b) (c) (d)	097	(a) (b) (c) (d)
048	(a) (b) (c) (d)	098	(a) (b) (c) (d)
049	(a) (b) (c) (d)	099	(a) (b) (c) (d)
050	(a) (b) (c) (d)	100	(a) (b) (c) (d)

DECLARATION BY THE CANDIDATE

I declare that particulars and signature on this OMR Answer sheet are mine and are Name as in Attendance Sheet. I futher declare that particulars filled in and Signature as well as the circles darkened on this ORIGINALCOPY is same as in OFFICE COPY.

Signature with time (in running handwriting)

CANDIDATE's NAME (in running handwriting)

MOTHER's NAME (in running handwriting)

FATHER's NAME (in running handwriting)

CANDIDATE LEFT HAND IMPRESSION

SIGNATURE OF INVIGILATOR'S WITH TIME

1

2

OMR SHEET

ROLL No.

1	1	1	1	1	1	1	1	1	1
2	2	2	2	2	2	2	2	2	2
3	3	3	3	3	3	3	3	3	3
4	4	4	4	4	4	4	4	4	4
5	5	5	5	5	5	5	5	5	5
6	6	6	6	6	6	6	6	6	6
7	7	7	7	7	7	7	7	7	7
8	8	8	8	8	8	8	8	8	8
9	9	9	9	9	9	9	9	9	9
0	0	0	0	0	0	0	0	0	0

TEST BOOKLET No.

1	1	1	1	1	1	1
2	2	2	2	2	2	2
3	3	3	3	3	3	3
4	4	4	4	4	4	4
5	5	5	5	5	5	5
6	6	6	6	6	6	6
7	7	7	7	7	7	7
8	8	8	8	8	8	8
9	9	9	9	9	9	9
0	0	0	0	0	0	0

TEST BOOKLET Code

Q No.	Response				Q No.	Response			
001	a	b	c	d	051	a	b	c	d
002	a	b	c	d	052	a	b	c	d
003	a	b	c	d	053	a	b	c	d
004	a	b	c	d	054	a	b	c	d
005	a	b	c	d	055	a	b	c	d
006	a	b	c	d	056	a	b	c	d
007	a	b	c	d	057	a	b	c	d
008	a	b	c	d	058	a	b	c	d
009	a	b	c	d	059	a	b	c	d
010	a	b	c	d	060	a	b	c	d
011	a	b	c	d	061	a	b	c	d
012	a	b	c	d	062	a	b	c	d
013	a	b	c	d	063	a	b	c	d
014	a	b	c	d	064	a	b	c	d
015	a	b	c	d	065	a	b	c	d
016	a	b	c	d	066	a	b	c	d
017	a	b	c	d	067	a	b	c	d
018	a	b	c	d	068	a	b	c	d
019	a	b	c	d	069	a	b	c	d
020	a	b	c	d	070	a	b	c	d
021	a	b	c	d	071	a	b	c	d
022	a	b	c	d	072	a	b	c	d
023	a	b	c	d	073	a	b	c	d
024	a	b	c	d	074	a	b	c	d
025	a	b	c	d	075	a	b	c	d
026	a	b	c	d	076	a	b	c	d
027	a	b	c	d	077	a	b	c	d
028	a	b	c	d	078	a	b	c	d
029	a	b	c	d	079	a	b	c	d
030	a	b	c	d	080	a	b	c	d
031	a	b	c	d	081	a	b	c	d
032	a	b	c	d	082	a	b	c	d
033	a	b	c	d	083	a	b	c	d
034	a	b	c	d	084	a	b	c	d
035	a	b	c	d	085	a	b	c	d
036	a	b	c	d	086	a	b	c	d
037	a	b	c	d	087	a	b	c	d
038	a	b	c	d	088	a	b	c	d
039	a	b	c	d	089	a	b	c	d
040	a	b	c	d	090	a	b	c	d
041	a	b	c	d	091	a	b	c	d
042	a	b	c	d	092	a	b	c	d
043	a	b	c	d	093	a	b	c	d
044	a	b	c	d	094	a	b	c	d
045	a	b	c	d	095	a	b	c	d
046	a	b	c	d	096	a	b	c	d
047	a	b	c	d	097	a	b	c	d
048	a	b	c	d	098	a	b	c	d
049	a	b	c	d	099	a	b	c	d
050	a	b	c	d	100	a	b	c	d

DECLARATION BY THE CANDIDATE

I declare that particulars and signature on this OMR Answer sheet are mine and are Name as in Attendance Sheet. I futher declare that particulars filled in and Signature as well as the circles darkened on this ORIGINALCOPY is same as in OFFICE COPY.

Signature with time (in running handwriting)

CANDIDATE's NAME (in running handwriting)

MOTHER's NAME (in running handwriting)

FATHER's NAME (in running handwriting)

CANDIDATE LEFT HAND IMPRESSION

SIGNATURE OF INVIGILATOR'S WITH TIME

1

2

MEDACE

OMR SHEET

ROLL No.

1	1	1	1	1	1	1	1	1	1
2	2	2	2	2	2	2	2	2	2
3	3	3	3	3	3	3	3	3	3
4	4	4	4	4	4	4	4	4	4
5	5	5	5	5	5	5	5	5	5
6	6	6	6	6	6	6	6	6	6
7	7	7	7	7	7	7	7	7	7
8	8	8	8	8	8	8	8	8	8
9	9	9	9	9	9	9	9	9	9
0	0	0	0	0	0	0	0	0	0

TEST BOOKLET No.

1	1	1	1	1	1	1
2	2	2	2	2	2	2
3	3	3	3	3	3	3
4	4	4	4	4	4	4
5	5	5	5	5	5	5
6	6	6	6	6	6	6
7	7	7	7	7	7	7
8	8	8	8	8	8	8
9	9	9	9	9	9	9
0	0	0	0	0	0	0

TEST BOOKLET Code

Q No.	Response	Q No.	Response
001	(a) (b) (c) (d)	051	(a) (b) (c) (d)
002	(a) (b) (c) (d)	052	(a) (b) (c) (d)
003	(a) (b) (c) (d)	053	(a) (b) (c) (d)
004	(a) (b) (c) (d)	054	(a) (b) (c) (d)
005	(a) (b) (c) (d)	055	(a) (b) (c) (d)
006	(a) (b) (c) (d)	056	(a) (b) (c) (d)
007	(a) (b) (c) (d)	057	(a) (b) (c) (d)
008	(a) (b) (c) (d)	058	(a) (b) (c) (d)
009	(a) (b) (c) (d)	059	(a) (b) (c) (d)
010	(a) (b) (c) (d)	060	(a) (b) (c) (d)
011	(a) (b) (c) (d)	061	(a) (b) (c) (d)
012	(a) (b) (c) (d)	062	(a) (b) (c) (d)
013	(a) (b) (c) (d)	063	(a) (b) (c) (d)
014	(a) (b) (c) (d)	064	(a) (b) (c) (d)
015	(a) (b) (c) (d)	065	(a) (b) (c) (d)
016	(a) (b) (c) (d)	066	(a) (b) (c) (d)
017	(a) (b) (c) (d)	067	(a) (b) (c) (d)
018	(a) (b) (c) (d)	068	(a) (b) (c) (d)
019	(a) (b) (c) (d)	069	(a) (b) (c) (d)
020	(a) (b) (c) (d)	070	(a) (b) (c) (d)
021	(a) (b) (c) (d)	071	(a) (b) (c) (d)
022	(a) (b) (c) (d)	072	(a) (b) (c) (d)
023	(a) (b) (c) (d)	073	(a) (b) (c) (d)
024	(a) (b) (c) (d)	074	(a) (b) (c) (d)
025	(a) (b) (c) (d)	075	(a) (b) (c) (d)
026	(a) (b) (c) (d)	076	(a) (b) (c) (d)
027	(a) (b) (c) (d)	077	(a) (b) (c) (d)
028	(a) (b) (c) (d)	078	(a) (b) (c) (d)
029	(a) (b) (c) (d)	079	(a) (b) (c) (d)
030	(a) (b) (c) (d)	080	(a) (b) (c) (d)
031	(a) (b) (c) (d)	081	(a) (b) (c) (d)
032	(a) (b) (c) (d)	082	(a) (b) (c) (d)
033	(a) (b) (c) (d)	083	(a) (b) (c) (d)
034	(a) (b) (c) (d)	084	(a) (b) (c) (d)
035	(a) (b) (c) (d)	085	(a) (b) (c) (d)
036	(a) (b) (c) (d)	086	(a) (b) (c) (d)
037	(a) (b) (c) (d)	087	(a) (b) (c) (d)
038	(a) (b) (c) (d)	088	(a) (b) (c) (d)
039	(a) (b) (c) (d)	089	(a) (b) (c) (d)
040	(a) (b) (c) (d)	090	(a) (b) (c) (d)
041	(a) (b) (c) (d)	091	(a) (b) (c) (d)
042	(a) (b) (c) (d)	092	(a) (b) (c) (d)
043	(a) (b) (c) (d)	093	(a) (b) (c) (d)
044	(a) (b) (c) (d)	094	(a) (b) (c) (d)
045	(a) (b) (c) (d)	095	(a) (b) (c) (d)
046	(a) (b) (c) (d)	096	(a) (b) (c) (d)
047	(a) (b) (c) (d)	097	(a) (b) (c) (d)
048	(a) (b) (c) (d)	098	(a) (b) (c) (d)
049	(a) (b) (c) (d)	099	(a) (b) (c) (d)
050	(a) (b) (c) (d)	100	(a) (b) (c) (d)

DECLARATION BY THE CANDIDATE

I declare that particulars and signature on this OMR Answer sheet are mine and are Name as in Attendance Sheet. I futher declare that particulars filled in and Signature as well as the circles darkened on this ORIGINALCOPY is same as in OFFICE COPY.

Signature with time (in running handwriting)

CANDIDATE's NAME (in running handwriting)

MOTHER's NAME (in running handwriting)

FATHER's NAME (in running handwriting)

CANDIDATE LEFT HAND IMPRESSION

SIGNATURE OF INVIGILATOR'S WITH TIME

1

2

MEDACE

OMR SHEET

ROLL No.

1	1	1	1	1	1	1	1	1	1
2	2	2	2	2	2	2	2	2	2
3	3	3	3	3	3	3	3	3	3
4	4	4	4	4	4	4	4	4	4
5	5	5	5	5	5	5	5	5	5
6	6	6	6	6	6	6	6	6	6
7	7	7	7	7	7	7	7	7	7
8	8	8	8	8	8	8	8	8	8
9	9	9	9	9	9	9	9	9	9
0	0	0	0	0	0	0	0	0	0

TEST BOOKLET No.

1	1	1	1	1	1	1
2	2	2	2	2	2	2
3	3	3	3	3	3	3
4	4	4	4	4	4	4
5	5	5	5	5	5	5
6	6	6	6	6	6	6
7	7	7	7	7	7	7
8	8	8	8	8	8	8
9	9	9	9	9	9	9
0	0	0	0	0	0	0

TEST BOOKLET Code

Q No.	Response				Q No.	Response			
001	a	b	c	d	051	a	b	c	d
002	a	b	c	d	052	a	b	c	d
003	a	b	c	d	053	a	b	c	d
004	a	b	c	d	054	a	b	c	d
005	a	b	c	d	055	a	b	c	d
006	a	b	c	d	056	a	b	c	d
007	a	b	c	d	057	a	b	c	d
008	a	b	c	d	058	a	b	c	d
009	a	b	c	d	059	a	b	c	d
010	a	b	c	d	060	a	b	c	d
011	a	b	c	d	061	a	b	c	d
012	a	b	c	d	062	a	b	c	d
013	a	b	c	d	063	a	b	c	d
014	a	b	c	d	064	a	b	c	d
015	a	b	c	d	065	a	b	c	d
016	a	b	c	d	066	a	b	c	d
017	a	b	c	d	067	a	b	c	d
018	a	b	c	d	068	a	b	c	d
019	a	b	c	d	069	a	b	c	d
020	a	b	c	d	070	a	b	c	d
021	a	b	c	d	071	a	b	c	d
022	a	b	c	d	072	a	b	c	d
023	a	b	c	d	073	a	b	c	d
024	a	b	c	d	074	a	b	c	d
025	a	b	c	d	075	a	b	c	d
026	a	b	c	d	076	a	b	c	d
027	a	b	c	d	077	a	b	c	d
028	a	b	c	d	078	a	b	c	d
029	a	b	c	d	079	a	b	c	d
030	a	b	c	d	080	a	b	c	d
031	a	b	c	d	081	a	b	c	d
032	a	b	c	d	082	a	b	c	d
033	a	b	c	d	083	a	b	c	d
034	a	b	c	d	084	a	b	c	d
035	a	b	c	d	085	a	b	c	d
036	a	b	c	d	086	a	b	c	d
037	a	b	c	d	087	a	b	c	d
038	a	b	c	d	088	a	b	c	d
039	a	b	c	d	089	a	b	c	d
040	a	b	c	d	090	a	b	c	d
041	a	b	c	d	091	a	b	c	d
042	a	b	c	d	092	a	b	c	d
043	a	b	c	d	093	a	b	c	d
044	a	b	c	d	094	a	b	c	d
045	a	b	c	d	095	a	b	c	d
046	a	b	c	d	096	a	b	c	d
047	a	b	c	d	097	a	b	c	d
048	a	b	c	d	098	a	b	c	d
049	a	b	c	d	099	a	b	c	d
050	a	b	c	d	100	a	b	c	d

DECLARATION BY THE CANDIDATE

I declare that particulars and signature on this OMR Answer sheet are mine and are Name as in Attendance Sheet. I futher declare that particulars filled in and Signature as well as the circles darkened on this ORIGINALCOPY is same as in OFFICE COPY.

Signature with time (in running handwriting)

CANDIDATE's NAME (in running handwriting)

MOTHER's NAME (in running handwriting)

FATHER's NAME (in running handwriting)

CANDIDATE LEFT HAND IMPRESSION

SIGNATURE OF INVIGILATOR'S WITH TIME

1

2

MEDACE

OMR SHEET

ROLL No.

1	1	1	1	1	1	1	1	1	1
2	2	2	2	2	2	2	2	2	2
3	3	3	3	3	3	3	3	3	3
4	4	4	4	4	4	4	4	4	4
5	5	5	5	5	5	5	5	5	5
6	6	6	6	6	6	6	6	6	6
7	7	7	7	7	7	7	7	7	7
8	8	8	8	8	8	8	8	8	8
9	9	9	9	9	9	9	9	9	9
0	0	0	0	0	0	0	0	0	0

TEST BOOKLET No.

1	1	1	1	1	1	1
2	2	2	2	2	2	2
3	3	3	3	3	3	3
4	4	4	4	4	4	4
5	5	5	5	5	5	5
6	6	6	6	6	6	6
7	7	7	7	7	7	7
8	8	8	8	8	8	8
9	9	9	9	9	9	9
0	0	0	0	0	0	0

TEST BOOKLET Code

Q No.	Response				Q No.	Response			
001	a	b	c	d	051	a	b	c	d
002	a	b	c	d	052	a	b	c	d
003	a	b	c	d	053	a	b	c	d
004	a	b	c	d	054	a	b	c	d
005	a	b	c	d	055	a	b	c	d
006	a	b	c	d	056	a	b	c	d
007	a	b	c	d	057	a	b	c	d
008	a	b	c	d	058	a	b	c	d
009	a	b	c	d	059	a	b	c	d
010	a	b	c	d	060	a	b	c	d
011	a	b	c	d	061	a	b	c	d
012	a	b	c	d	062	a	b	c	d
013	a	b	c	d	063	a	b	c	d
014	a	b	c	d	064	a	b	c	d
015	a	b	c	d	065	a	b	c	d
016	a	b	c	d	066	a	b	c	d
017	a	b	c	d	067	a	b	c	d
018	a	b	c	d	068	a	b	c	d
019	a	b	c	d	069	a	b	c	d
020	a	b	c	d	070	a	b	c	d
021	a	b	c	d	071	a	b	c	d
022	a	b	c	d	072	a	b	c	d
023	a	b	c	d	073	a	b	c	d
024	a	b	c	d	074	a	b	c	d
025	a	b	c	d	075	a	b	c	d
026	a	b	c	d	076	a	b	c	d
027	a	b	c	d	077	a	b	c	d
028	a	b	c	d	078	a	b	c	d
029	a	b	c	d	079	a	b	c	d
030	a	b	c	d	080	a	b	c	d
031	a	b	c	d	081	a	b	c	d
032	a	b	c	d	082	a	b	c	d
033	a	b	c	d	083	a	b	c	d
034	a	b	c	d	084	a	b	c	d
035	a	b	c	d	085	a	b	c	d
036	a	b	c	d	086	a	b	c	d
037	a	b	c	d	087	a	b	c	d
038	a	b	c	d	088	a	b	c	d
039	a	b	c	d	089	a	b	c	d
040	a	b	c	d	090	a	b	c	d
041	a	b	c	d	091	a	b	c	d
042	a	b	c	d	092	a	b	c	d
043	a	b	c	d	093	a	b	c	d
044	a	b	c	d	094	a	b	c	d
045	a	b	c	d	095	a	b	c	d
046	a	b	c	d	096	a	b	c	d
047	a	b	c	d	097	a	b	c	d
048	a	b	c	d	098	a	b	c	d
049	a	b	c	d	099	a	b	c	d
050	a	b	c	d	100	a	b	c	d

DECLARATION BY THE CANDIDATE

I declare that particulars and signature on this OMR Answer sheet are mine and are Name as in Attendance Sheet. I fruther declare that particulars filled in and Signature as well as the circles darkened on this ORIGINALCOPY is same as in OFFICE COPY.

Signature with time (in running handwriting)

CANDIDATE's NAME (in running handwriting)

MOTHER's NAME (in running handwriting)

FATHER's NAME (in running handwriting)

CANDIDATE LEFT HAND IMPRESSION

SIGNATURE OF INVIGILATOR'S WITH TIME

1

2

MEDACE

OMR SHEET

ROLL No.

1	1	1	1	1	1	1	1	1	1
2	2	2	2	2	2	2	2	2	2
3	3	3	3	3	3	3	3	3	3
4	4	4	4	4	4	4	4	4	4
5	5	5	5	5	5	5	5	5	5
6	6	6	6	6	6	6	6	6	6
7	7	7	7	7	7	7	7	7	7
8	8	8	8	8	8	8	8	8	8
9	9	9	9	9	9	9	9	9	9
0	0	0	0	0	0	0	0	0	0

TEST BOOKLET No.

1	1	1	1	1	1	1
2	2	2	2	2	2	2
3	3	3	3	3	3	3
4	4	4	4	4	4	4
5	5	5	5	5	5	5
6	6	6	6	6	6	6
7	7	7	7	7	7	7
8	8	8	8	8	8	8
9	9	9	9	9	9	9
0	0	0	0	0	0	0

TEST BOOKLET Code

Q No.	Response				Q No.	Response			
001	a	b	c	d	051	a	b	c	d
002	a	b	c	d	052	a	b	c	d
003	a	b	c	d	053	a	b	c	d
004	a	b	c	d	054	a	b	c	d
005	a	b	c	d	055	a	b	c	d
006	a	b	c	d	056	a	b	c	d
007	a	b	c	d	057	a	b	c	d
008	a	b	c	d	058	a	b	c	d
009	a	b	c	d	059	a	b	c	d
010	a	b	c	d	060	a	b	c	d
011	a	b	c	d	061	a	b	c	d
012	a	b	c	d	062	a	b	c	d
013	a	b	c	d	063	a	b	c	d
014	a	b	c	d	064	a	b	c	d
015	a	b	c	d	065	a	b	c	d
016	a	b	c	d	066	a	b	c	d
017	a	b	c	d	067	a	b	c	d
018	a	b	c	d	068	a	b	c	d
019	a	b	c	d	069	a	b	c	d
020	a	b	c	d	070	a	b	c	d
021	a	b	c	d	071	a	b	c	d
022	a	b	c	d	072	a	b	c	d
023	a	b	c	d	073	a	b	c	d
024	a	b	c	d	074	a	b	c	d
025	a	b	c	d	075	a	b	c	d
026	a	b	c	d	076	a	b	c	d
027	a	b	c	d	077	a	b	c	d
028	a	b	c	d	078	a	b	c	d
029	a	b	c	d	079	a	b	c	d
030	a	b	c	d	080	a	b	c	d
031	a	b	c	d	081	a	b	c	d
032	a	b	c	d	082	a	b	c	d
033	a	b	c	d	083	a	b	c	d
034	a	b	c	d	084	a	b	c	d
035	a	b	c	d	085	a	b	c	d
036	a	b	c	d	086	a	b	c	d
037	a	b	c	d	087	a	b	c	d
038	a	b	c	d	088	a	b	c	d
039	a	b	c	d	089	a	b	c	d
040	a	b	c	d	090	a	b	c	d
041	a	b	c	d	091	a	b	c	d
042	a	b	c	d	092	a	b	c	d
043	a	b	c	d	093	a	b	c	d
044	a	b	c	d	094	a	b	c	d
045	a	b	c	d	095	a	b	c	d
046	a	b	c	d	096	a	b	c	d
047	a	b	c	d	097	a	b	c	d
048	a	b	c	d	098	a	b	c	d
049	a	b	c	d	099	a	b	c	d
050	a	b	c	d	100	a	b	c	d

DECLARATION BY THE CANDIDATE

I declare that particulars and signature on this OMR Answer sheet are mine and are Name as in Attendance Sheet. I futher declare that particulars filled in and Signature as well as the circles darkened on this ORIGINALCOPY is same as in OFFICE COPY.

Signature with time (in running handwriting)

CANDIDATE's NAME (in running handwriting)

MOTHER's NAME (in running handwriting)

FATHER's NAME (in running handwriting)

CANDIDATE LEFT HAND IMPRESSION

SIGNATURE OF INVIGILATOR'S WITH TIME

1

2

MEDACE

OMR SHEET

ROLL No.

1	1	1	1	1	1	1	1	1	1
2	2	2	2	2	2	2	2	2	2
3	3	3	3	3	3	3	3	3	3
4	4	4	4	4	4	4	4	4	4
5	5	5	5	5	5	5	5	5	5
6	6	6	6	6	6	6	6	6	6
7	7	7	7	7	7	7	7	7	7
8	8	8	8	8	8	8	8	8	8
9	9	9	9	9	9	9	9	9	9
0	0	0	0	0	0	0	0	0	0

TEST BOOKLET No.

1	1	1	1	1	1	1
2	2	2	2	2	2	2
3	3	3	3	3	3	3
4	4	4	4	4	4	4
5	5	5	5	5	5	5
6	6	6	6	6	6	6
7	7	7	7	7	7	7
8	8	8	8	8	8	8
9	9	9	9	9	9	9
0	0	0	0	0	0	0

TEST BOOKLET Code

Q No.	Response				Q No.	Response			
001	a	b	c	d	051	a	b	c	d
002	a	b	c	d	052	a	b	c	d
003	a	b	c	d	053	a	b	c	d
004	a	b	c	d	054	a	b	c	d
005	a	b	c	d	055	a	b	c	d
006	a	b	c	d	056	a	b	c	d
007	a	b	c	d	057	a	b	c	d
008	a	b	c	d	058	a	b	c	d
009	a	b	c	d	059	a	b	c	d
010	a	b	c	d	060	a	b	c	d
011	a	b	c	d	061	a	b	c	d
012	a	b	c	d	062	a	b	c	d
013	a	b	c	d	063	a	b	c	d
014	a	b	c	d	064	a	b	c	d
015	a	b	c	d	065	a	b	c	d
016	a	b	c	d	066	a	b	c	d
017	a	b	c	d	067	a	b	c	d
018	a	b	c	d	068	a	b	c	d
019	a	b	c	d	069	a	b	c	d
020	a	b	c	d	070	a	b	c	d
021	a	b	c	d	071	a	b	c	d
022	a	b	c	d	072	a	b	c	d
023	a	b	c	d	073	a	b	c	d
024	a	b	c	d	074	a	b	c	d
025	a	b	c	d	075	a	b	c	d
026	a	b	c	d	076	a	b	c	d
027	a	b	c	d	077	a	b	c	d
028	a	b	c	d	078	a	b	c	d
029	a	b	c	d	079	a	b	c	d
030	a	b	c	d	080	a	b	c	d
031	a	b	c	d	081	a	b	c	d
032	a	b	c	d	082	a	b	c	d
033	a	b	c	d	083	a	b	c	d
034	a	b	c	d	084	a	b	c	d
035	a	b	c	d	085	a	b	c	d
036	a	b	c	d	086	a	b	c	d
037	a	b	c	d	087	a	b	c	d
038	a	b	c	d	088	a	b	c	d
039	a	b	c	d	089	a	b	c	d
040	a	b	c	d	090	a	b	c	d
041	a	b	c	d	091	a	b	c	d
042	a	b	c	d	092	a	b	c	d
043	a	b	c	d	093	a	b	c	d
044	a	b	c	d	094	a	b	c	d
045	a	b	c	d	095	a	b	c	d
046	a	b	c	d	096	a	b	c	d
047	a	b	c	d	097	a	b	c	d
048	a	b	c	d	098	a	b	c	d
049	a	b	c	d	099	a	b	c	d
050	a	b	c	d	100	a	b	c	d

DECLARATION BY THE CANDIDATE

I declare that particulars and signature on this OMR Answer sheet are mine and are Name as in Attendance Sheet. I fruther declare that particulars filled in and Signature as well as the circles darkened on this ORIGINALCOPY is same as in OFFICE COPY.

Signature with time (in running handwriting)

CANDIDATE's NAME (in running handwriting)

MOTHER's NAME (in running handwriting)

FATHER's NAME (in running handwriting)

CANDIDATE LEFT HAND IMPRESSION

SIGNATURE OF INVIGILATOR'S WITH TIME

1

2

MEDACE

OMR SHEET

ROLL No.

1	1	1	1	1	1	1	1	1	1
2	2	2	2	2	2	2	2	2	2
3	3	3	3	3	3	3	3	3	3
4	4	4	4	4	4	4	4	4	4
5	5	5	5	5	5	5	5	5	5
6	6	6	6	6	6	6	6	6	6
7	7	7	7	7	7	7	7	7	7
8	8	8	8	8	8	8	8	8	8
9	9	9	9	9	9	9	9	9	9
0	0	0	0	0	0	0	0	0	0

TEST BOOKLET No.

1	1	1	1	1	1	1
2	2	2	2	2	2	2
3	3	3	3	3	3	3
4	4	4	4	4	4	4
5	5	5	5	5	5	5
6	6	6	6	6	6	6
7	7	7	7	7	7	7
8	8	8	8	8	8	8
9	9	9	9	9	9	9
0	0	0	0	0	0	0

TEST BOOKLET Code

Q No.	Response			
001	a	b	c	d
002	a	b	c	d
003	a	b	c	d
004	a	b	c	d
005	a	b	c	d
006	a	b	c	d
007	a	b	c	d
008	a	b	c	d
009	a	b	c	d
010	a	b	c	d
011	a	b	c	d
012	a	b	c	d
013	a	b	c	d
014	a	b	c	d
015	a	b	c	d
016	a	b	c	d
017	a	b	c	d
018	a	b	c	d
019	a	b	c	d
020	a	b	c	d
021	a	b	c	d
022	a	b	c	d
023	a	b	c	d
024	a	b	c	d
025	a	b	c	d
026	a	b	c	d
027	a	b	c	d
028	a	b	c	d
029	a	b	c	d
030	a	b	c	d
031	a	b	c	d
032	a	b	c	d
033	a	b	c	d
034	a	b	c	d
035	a	b	c	d
036	a	b	c	d
037	a	b	c	d
038	a	b	c	d
039	a	b	c	d
040	a	b	c	d
041	a	b	c	d
042	a	b	c	d
043	a	b	c	d
044	a	b	c	d
045	a	b	c	d
046	a	b	c	d
047	a	b	c	d
048	a	b	c	d
049	a	b	c	d
050	a	b	c	d

Q No.	Response			
051	a	b	c	d
052	a	b	c	d
053	a	b	c	d
054	a	b	c	d
055	a	b	c	d
056	a	b	c	d
057	a	b	c	d
058	a	b	c	d
059	a	b	c	d
060	a	b	c	d
061	a	b	c	d
062	a	b	c	d
063	a	b	c	d
064	a	b	c	d
065	a	b	c	d
066	a	b	c	d
067	a	b	c	d
068	a	b	c	d
069	a	b	c	d
070	a	b	c	d
071	a	b	c	d
072	a	b	c	d
073	a	b	c	d
074	a	b	c	d
075	a	b	c	d
076	a	b	c	d
077	a	b	c	d
078	a	b	c	d
079	a	b	c	d
080	a	b	c	d
081	a	b	c	d
082	a	b	c	d
083	a	b	c	d
084	a	b	c	d
085	a	b	c	d
086	a	b	c	d
087	a	b	c	d
088	a	b	c	d
089	a	b	c	d
090	a	b	c	d
091	a	b	c	d
092	a	b	c	d
093	a	b	c	d
094	a	b	c	d
095	a	b	c	d
096	a	b	c	d
097	a	b	c	d
098	a	b	c	d
099	a	b	c	d
100	a	b	c	d

DECLARATION BY THE CANDIDATE

I declare that particulars and signature on this OMR Answer sheet are mine and are Name as in Attendance Sheet. I futher declare that particulars filled in and Signature as well as the circles darkened on this ORIGINALCOPY is same as in OFFICE COPY.

Signature with time (in running handwriting)

CANDIDATE's NAME (in running handwriting)

MOTHER's NAME (in running handwriting)

FATHER's NAME (in running handwriting)

CANDIDATE LEFT HAND IMPRESSION

SIGNATURE OF INVIGILATOR'S WITH TIME

1

2

MEDACE

OMR SHEET

ROLL No.

1	1	1	1	1	1	1	1	1	1
2	2	2	2	2	2	2	2	2	2
3	3	3	3	3	3	3	3	3	3
4	4	4	4	4	4	4	4	4	4
5	5	5	5	5	5	5	5	5	5
6	6	6	6	6	6	6	6	6	6
7	7	7	7	7	7	7	7	7	7
8	8	8	8	8	8	8	8	8	8
9	9	9	9	9	9	9	9	9	9
0	0	0	0	0	0	0	0	0	0

TEST BOOKLET No.

1	1	1	1	1	1	1
2	2	2	2	2	2	2
3	3	3	3	3	3	3
4	4	4	4	4	4	4
5	5	5	5	5	5	5
6	6	6	6	6	6	6
7	7	7	7	7	7	7
8	8	8	8	8	8	8
9	9	9	9	9	9	9
0	0	0	0	0	0	0

TEST BOOKLET Code

Q No.	Response				Q No.	Response			
001	a	b	c	d	051	a	b	c	d
002	a	b	c	d	052	a	b	c	d
003	a	b	c	d	053	a	b	c	d
004	a	b	c	d	054	a	b	c	d
005	a	b	c	d	055	a	b	c	d
006	a	b	c	d	056	a	b	c	d
007	a	b	c	d	057	a	b	c	d
008	a	b	c	d	058	a	b	c	d
009	a	b	c	d	059	a	b	c	d
010	a	b	c	d	060	a	b	c	d
011	a	b	c	d	061	a	b	c	d
012	a	b	c	d	062	a	b	c	d
013	a	b	c	d	063	a	b	c	d
014	a	b	c	d	064	a	b	c	d
015	a	b	c	d	065	a	b	c	d
016	a	b	c	d	066	a	b	c	d
017	a	b	c	d	067	a	b	c	d
018	a	b	c	d	068	a	b	c	d
019	a	b	c	d	069	a	b	c	d
020	a	b	c	d	070	a	b	c	d
021	a	b	c	d	071	a	b	c	d
022	a	b	c	d	072	a	b	c	d
023	a	b	c	d	073	a	b	c	d
024	a	b	c	d	074	a	b	c	d
025	a	b	c	d	075	a	b	c	d
026	a	b	c	d	076	a	b	c	d
027	a	b	c	d	077	a	b	c	d
028	a	b	c	d	078	a	b	c	d
029	a	b	c	d	079	a	b	c	d
030	a	b	c	d	080	a	b	c	d
031	a	b	c	d	081	a	b	c	d
032	a	b	c	d	082	a	b	c	d
033	a	b	c	d	083	a	b	c	d
034	a	b	c	d	084	a	b	c	d
035	a	b	c	d	085	a	b	c	d
036	a	b	c	d	086	a	b	c	d
037	a	b	c	d	087	a	b	c	d
038	a	b	c	d	088	a	b	c	d
039	a	b	c	d	089	a	b	c	d
040	a	b	c	d	090	a	b	c	d
041	a	b	c	d	091	a	b	c	d
042	a	b	c	d	092	a	b	c	d
043	a	b	c	d	093	a	b	c	d
044	a	b	c	d	094	a	b	c	d
045	a	b	c	d	095	a	b	c	d
046	a	b	c	d	096	a	b	c	d
047	a	b	c	d	097	a	b	c	d
048	a	b	c	d	098	a	b	c	d
049	a	b	c	d	099	a	b	c	d
050	a	b	c	d	100	a	b	c	d

DECLARATION BY THE CANDIDATE

I declare that particulars and signature on this OMR Answer sheet are mine and are Name as in Attendance Sheet. I futher declare that particulars filled in and Signature as well as the circles darkened on this ORIGINALCOPY is same as in OFFICE COPY.

Signature with time (in running handwriting)

CANDIDATE's NAME (in running handwriting)

MOTHER's NAME (in running handwriting)

FATHER's NAME (in running handwriting)

CANDIDATE LEFT HAND IMPRESSION

SIGNATURE OF INVIGILATOR'S WITH TIME

1

2

MEDACE

OMR SHEET

ROLL No.

1	1	1	1	1	1	1	1	1	1
2	2	2	2	2	2	2	2	2	2
3	3	3	3	3	3	3	3	3	3
4	4	4	4	4	4	4	4	4	4
5	5	5	5	5	5	5	5	5	5
6	6	6	6	6	6	6	6	6	6
7	7	7	7	7	7	7	7	7	7
8	8	8	8	8	8	8	8	8	8
9	9	9	9	9	9	9	9	9	9
0	0	0	0	0	0	0	0	0	0

TEST BOOKLET No.

1	1	1	1	1	1	1
2	2	2	2	2	2	2
3	3	3	3	3	3	3
4	4	4	4	4	4	4
5	5	5	5	5	5	5
6	6	6	6	6	6	6
7	7	7	7	7	7	7
8	8	8	8	8	8	8
9	9	9	9	9	9	9
0	0	0	0	0	0	0

TEST BOOKLET Code

Q No.	Response				Q No.	Response			
001	a	b	c	d	051	a	b	c	d
002	a	b	c	d	052	a	b	c	d
003	a	b	c	d	053	a	b	c	d
004	a	b	c	d	054	a	b	c	d
005	a	b	c	d	055	a	b	c	d
006	a	b	c	d	056	a	b	c	d
007	a	b	c	d	057	a	b	c	d
008	a	b	c	d	058	a	b	c	d
009	a	b	c	d	059	a	b	c	d
010	a	b	c	d	060	a	b	c	d
011	a	b	c	d	061	a	b	c	d
012	a	b	c	d	062	a	b	c	d
013	a	b	c	d	063	a	b	c	d
014	a	b	c	d	064	a	b	c	d
015	a	b	c	d	065	a	b	c	d
016	a	b	c	d	066	a	b	c	d
017	a	b	c	d	067	a	b	c	d
018	a	b	c	d	068	a	b	c	d
019	a	b	c	d	069	a	b	c	d
020	a	b	c	d	070	a	b	c	d
021	a	b	c	d	071	a	b	c	d
022	a	b	c	d	072	a	b	c	d
023	a	b	c	d	073	a	b	c	d
024	a	b	c	d	074	a	b	c	d
025	a	b	c	d	075	a	b	c	d
026	a	b	c	d	076	a	b	c	d
027	a	b	c	d	077	a	b	c	d
028	a	b	c	d	078	a	b	c	d
029	a	b	c	d	079	a	b	c	d
030	a	b	c	d	080	a	b	c	d
031	a	b	c	d	081	a	b	c	d
032	a	b	c	d	082	a	b	c	d
033	a	b	c	d	083	a	b	c	d
034	a	b	c	d	084	a	b	c	d
035	a	b	c	d	085	a	b	c	d
036	a	b	c	d	086	a	b	c	d
037	a	b	c	d	087	a	b	c	d
038	a	b	c	d	088	a	b	c	d
039	a	b	c	d	089	a	b	c	d
040	a	b	c	d	090	a	b	c	d
041	a	b	c	d	091	a	b	c	d
042	a	b	c	d	092	a	b	c	d
043	a	b	c	d	093	a	b	c	d
044	a	b	c	d	094	a	b	c	d
045	a	b	c	d	095	a	b	c	d
046	a	b	c	d	096	a	b	c	d
047	a	b	c	d	097	a	b	c	d
048	a	b	c	d	098	a	b	c	d
049	a	b	c	d	099	a	b	c	d
050	a	b	c	d	100	a	b	c	d

DECLARATION BY THE CANDIDATE

I declare that particulars and signature on this OMR Answer sheet are mine and are Name as in Attendance Sheet. I fruther declare that particulars filled in and Signature as well as the circles darkened on this ORIGINALCOPY is same as in OFFICE COPY.

Signature with time (in running handwriting)

CANDIDATE's NAME (in running handwriting)

MOTHER's NAME (in running handwriting)

FATHER's NAME (in running handwriting)

CANDIDATE LEFT HAND IMPRESSION

SIGNATURE OF INVIGILATOR'S WITH TIME

1

2

MEDACE

OMR SHEET

ROLL No.

1	1	1	1	1	1	1	1	1	1
2	2	2	2	2	2	2	2	2	2
3	3	3	3	3	3	3	3	3	3
4	4	4	4	4	4	4	4	4	4
5	5	5	5	5	5	5	5	5	5
6	6	6	6	6	6	6	6	6	6
7	7	7	7	7	7	7	7	7	7
8	8	8	8	8	8	8	8	8	8
9	9	9	9	9	9	9	9	9	9
0	0	0	0	0	0	0	0	0	0

TEST BOOKLET No.

1	1	1	1	1	1	1
2	2	2	2	2	2	2
3	3	3	3	3	3	3
4	4	4	4	4	4	4
5	5	5	5	5	5	5
6	6	6	6	6	6	6
7	7	7	7	7	7	7
8	8	8	8	8	8	8
9	9	9	9	9	9	9
0	0	0	0	0	0	0

TEST BOOKLET Code

Q No.	Response				Q No.	Response			
001	a	b	c	d	051	a	b	c	d
002	a	b	c	d	052	a	b	c	d
003	a	b	c	d	053	a	b	c	d
004	a	b	c	d	054	a	b	c	d
005	a	b	c	d	055	a	b	c	d
006	a	b	c	d	056	a	b	c	d
007	a	b	c	d	057	a	b	c	d
008	a	b	c	d	058	a	b	c	d
009	a	b	c	d	059	a	b	c	d
010	a	b	c	d	060	a	b	c	d
011	a	b	c	d	061	a	b	c	d
012	a	b	c	d	062	a	b	c	d
013	a	b	c	d	063	a	b	c	d
014	a	b	c	d	064	a	b	c	d
015	a	b	c	d	065	a	b	c	d
016	a	b	c	d	066	a	b	c	d
017	a	b	c	d	067	a	b	c	d
018	a	b	c	d	068	a	b	c	d
019	a	b	c	d	069	a	b	c	d
020	a	b	c	d	070	a	b	c	d
021	a	b	c	d	071	a	b	c	d
022	a	b	c	d	072	a	b	c	d
023	a	b	c	d	073	a	b	c	d
024	a	b	c	d	074	a	b	c	d
025	a	b	c	d	075	a	b	c	d
026	a	b	c	d	076	a	b	c	d
027	a	b	c	d	077	a	b	c	d
028	a	b	c	d	078	a	b	c	d
029	a	b	c	d	079	a	b	c	d
030	a	b	c	d	080	a	b	c	d
031	a	b	c	d	081	a	b	c	d
032	a	b	c	d	082	a	b	c	d
033	a	b	c	d	083	a	b	c	d
034	a	b	c	d	084	a	b	c	d
035	a	b	c	d	085	a	b	c	d
036	a	b	c	d	086	a	b	c	d
037	a	b	c	d	087	a	b	c	d
038	a	b	c	d	088	a	b	c	d
039	a	b	c	d	089	a	b	c	d
040	a	b	c	d	090	a	b	c	d
041	a	b	c	d	091	a	b	c	d
042	a	b	c	d	092	a	b	c	d
043	a	b	c	d	093	a	b	c	d
044	a	b	c	d	094	a	b	c	d
045	a	b	c	d	095	a	b	c	d
046	a	b	c	d	096	a	b	c	d
047	a	b	c	d	097	a	b	c	d
048	a	b	c	d	098	a	b	c	d
049	a	b	c	d	099	a	b	c	d
050	a	b	c	d	100	a	b	c	d

DECLARATION BY THE CANDIDATE

I declare that particulars and signature on this OMR Answer sheet are mine and are Name as in Attendance Sheet. I futher declare that particulars filled in and Signature as well as the circles darkened on this ORIGINALCOPY is same as in OFFICE COPY.

Signature with time (in running handwriting)

CANDIDATE's NAME (in running handwriting)

MOTHER's NAME (in running handwriting)

FATHER's NAME (in running handwriting)

CANDIDATE LEFT HAND IMPRESSION

SIGNATURE OF INVIGILATOR'S WITH TIME

1

2